Explication

- The Use of Conventional Metaphors for Death in John Donne's "Death Be Not Proud"
  Ch. 31, p. 920

- A Reading of Emily Dickinson's "There's a certain Slant of light"
  Ch. 31, p. 924

Paper-in-Progress

- *Explication:* The Use of Conventional Metaphors for Death in John Donne's "Death Be Not Proud" (draft, outline, and final paper)
  Ch. 31, p. 917

Research Paper

- How William Faulkner's Narrator Cultivates a Rose for Emily
  Ch. 33, p. 948

WELCOME TO THE BOOK COMPANION SITE FOR LITERATURE TO GO

At **bedfordstmartins.com/meyerlit** you'll find:

- *VirtuaLit* tutorials for close reading
- *AuthorLinks* for research
- *LitQuizzes* for self-testing
- *LitGloss* for literary terms
- Sample Papers modeling MLA style

E-PAGES FOR LITERATURE TO GO

bedfordstmartins.com/meyerlit/ epages

The e-Pages for *Literature to Go* feature recordings of celebrated writers and actors reading stories, poems, and drama scenes from the anthology — with questions that students can complete online. For a complete list of e-Pages, please see the book's last page.

Literature to Go

Literature to Go

SECOND EDITION

MICHAEL MEYER

University of Connecticut

BEDFORD/ST. MARTIN'S   BOSTON • NEW YORK

For Bedford/St. Martin's

Developmental Editor: Christina Gerogiannis
Executive Editor: Ellen Thibault
Senior Production Editor: Karen S. Baart
Assistant Production Manager: Joe Ford
Marketing Manager: Stacey Propps
Editorial Assistant: Amanda Legee
Copyeditor: Melissa Cook
Senior Art Director: Anna Palchik
Text Design: Claire Seng-Niemoeller
Cover Design: Billy Boardman
Cover Art: Candy Kitchen by Joseph Craig English. Used with permission of the artist.
Composition: Jouve
Printing and Binding: RR Donnelley and Sons

President, Bedford/St. Martin's: Denise B. Wydra
Editor in Chief: Karen S. Henry
Director of Marketing: Karen R. Soeltz
Production Director: Susan W. Brown
Director of Rights and Permissions: Hilary Newman

Acknowledgments

FICTION

Raymond Carver. "Popular Mechanics" from *What We Talk about When We Talk about Love* by Raymond Carver. Copyright © 1974, 1976, 1978, 1980, 1981 by Raymond Carver. Used by permission of Alfred A. Knopf, a division of Random House, Inc. Any third party use of this material, outside of this publication, is prohibited. Interested parties must apply directly to Random House, Inc., for permission.

May-lee Chai. "Saving Sourdi," *ZYZZYVA*, no. 3 (Winter 2001), pp. 139–58. Copyright © 2001 by May-lee Chai. Used by permission of the author.

Junot Díaz. "How to Date a Browngirl, Blackgirl, Whitegirl, or Halfie" from *Drown* by Junot Díaz. Copyright © 1996 by Junot Díaz. Used by permission of Riverhead Books, an imprint of Penguin Group (USA) Inc. First appeared in *The New Yorker.*

Andre Dubus. "Killings" from *Finding a Girl in America* by Andre Dubus. Copyright © 1980 by Andre Dubus. Reprinted by permission of David R. Godine, Publisher, Inc.

Acknowledgments and copyrights are continued at the back of the book on pages 975–80, which constitute an extension of the copyright page. It is a violation of the law to reproduce these selections by any means whatsoever without the written permission of the copyright holder.

For My Wife
Regina Barreca

About Michael Meyer

Michael Meyer, Emeritus Professor of English, has taught writing and literature courses for more than thirty years — since 1981 at the University of Connecticut and before that at the University of North Carolina at Charlotte and the College of William and Mary. In addition to being an experienced teacher, Meyer is a highly regarded literary scholar. His scholarly articles have appeared in distinguished journals such as *American Literature, Studies in the American Renaissance,* and *Virginia Quarterly Review.* An internationally recognized authority on Henry David Thoreau, Meyer is a former president of the Thoreau Society and coauthor (with Walter Harding) of *The New Thoreau Handbook,* a standard reference source. His first book, *Several More Lives to Live: Thoreau's Political Reputation in America,* was awarded the Ralph Henry Gabriel Prize by the American Studies Association. He is also the editor of *Frederick Douglass: The Narrative and Selected Writings.* He has lectured on a variety of American literary topics from Cambridge University to Peking University. His other books for Bedford/St. Martin's include *The Bedford Introduction to Literature,* Tenth Edition; *The Compact Bedford Introduction to Literature,* Ninth Edition; *Poetry: An Introduction,* Seventh Edition; and *Thinking and Writing about Literature,* Second Edition.

Preface for Instructors

Literature to Go, Second Edition, is the long-trusted anthology *The Bedford Introduction to Literature*, sized and priced to go. Created in response to instructors' requests for an essential version of the full-length book — with a selection of literature that reflects the classic canon and the new — *Literature to Go* is a brief and inexpensive collection of stories, poems, and plays, accompanied by class-tested, reliable pedagogy and unique features that bring literature to life for students. The hope is that the engaging selections and accessible instruction in *Literature to Go* will inspire students to become lifelong readers of imaginative literature, as well as more thoughtful and skillful writers.

As before, the text is flexibly organized into four parts focusing on fiction, poetry, drama, and critical thinking and writing. The first three parts explain the literary elements of each genre and how to write about them. These three parts also explore several additional approaches to reading literature and conclude with an anthology of literary works. The fourth part provides detailed instruction on thinking, reading, and writing about literature that can be assigned selectively throughout the course. Sample student papers and hundreds of assignments appear in the text, offering students the support they need to read and write about literature.

Literature to Go accommodates many different teaching styles. The second edition features a new in-depth chapter created with fiction writer Dagoberto Gilb; a new case study on the world of work; advice from contemporary authors directed to students, written especially for the anthology; and e-Pages featuring writers and actors reading selections from the book.

FEATURES OF *LITERATURE TO GO,* SECOND EDITION

A wide and well-balanced selection of literature — sized and priced to go

35 stories, 219 poems, and 13 plays represent a variety of periods, nationalities, cultures, styles, and voices — from the serious to the humorous, and from the traditional to the contemporary. Each selection has been

chosen for its appeal to students and for its effectiveness in demonstrating the elements, significance, and pleasures of literature. As in the previous edition, canonical works by Ernest Hemingway, John Keats, Susan Glaspell, and many others are generously represented. In addition, there are many contemporary selections from writers such as Junot Diaz, Natasha Trethewey, and David Henry Hwang, as well as a rich sampling of works by writers from other cultures. Recent and international selections appear throughout the anthology.

Many options for teaching and learning about literature

In an effort to make literature come to life for students, and the course a pleasure to teach for instructors, *Literature to Go* offers these innovative features:

Perspectives on literature Intriguing documents — including critical essays, interviews, and contextual images — appear throughout the book to stimulate class discussion and writing.

Connections between "popular" and "literary" culture The poetry and drama introductions incorporate examples from popular culture, effectively introducing students to the literary elements of a given genre through what they already know. For example, students are introduced to the elements of poetry through greeting card verse and song lyrics by Bruce Springsteen and to elements of drama through a television script from *Seinfeld.* Lively visuals throughout the anthology present images that demonstrate how literature is woven into the fabric of popular culture and art. These images help students recognize the imprint of literature on their everyday lives.

From Chapter 9: "A Study of Flannery O'Connor."

Case studies that treat authors in depth Each genre section includes one or more chapters that focus closely on a major literary figure. Chapters on Flannery O'Connor, Dagoberto Gilb, Billy Collins, and William Shakespeare are complemented by biographical introductions (with author photographs), critical perspectives, cultural documents (such as letters and draft manuscript pages), and images that serve to contextualize the works. A variety of critical thinking and writing questions follow the selections to stimulate student responses. All these supplementary materials engage students more fully with the writers and their works.

Plenty of help with reading, writing, and research

Critical reading* Advice on how to read literature appears at the beginning of each genre section. Sample Close Readings of selections, including Kate Chopin's "The Story of an Hour" (Fiction), William Hathaway's "Oh, Oh" (Poetry), and Susan Glaspell's *Trifles* (Drama), provide analyses of the language, images, and other literary elements at work in these selections. Interpretive annotations clearly show students the process of close reading and provide examples of the kind of critical thinking that leads to strong academic writing.

A Sample Close Reading

Later in the book, Chapter 29, "Reading and the Writing Process," provides more instruction on how to read a work closely, annotate a text, take notes, keep a reading journal, and develop a topic into a thesis, with a section on arguing persuasively about literature. An Index of Terms appears at the back of the book, and a glossary provides thorough explanations of more than two hundred terms central to the study of literature.

The writing and research process Five chapters (29–33) cover every step of the writing process — from generating topics to documenting sources — while sample student papers model the results.

Of these chapters, three — "Writing about Fiction" (30), "Writing about Poetry" (31), and "Writing about Drama" (32) — focus on genre-specific writing assignments.

Five sample student papers — all with MLA-style documentation — model how to analyze and argue about literature and how to support ideas by citing examples. The papers are integrated throughout the book, as are "Questions for Writing" units that guide students through particular writing tasks: reading and writing responsively, developing a topic into a revised thesis, and writing about multiple works by an author.

Chapter 33, "The Literary Research Paper," offers detailed advice for finding,

A sample student explication on Emily Dickinson's "There's a certain Slant of light" includes parenthetical citations and a Works Cited page.

*A reference chart on the book's inside front cover outlines all of the book's help for reading and writing about literature.

evaluating, and incorporating sources in a paper and includes current, detailed MLA documentation guidelines.

Questions for critical reading and writing   Hundreds of questions and assignments — "Considerations for Critical Thinking and Writing," "Connections to Other Selections," "First Response" prompts, and "Creative Response" assignments — spark students' interest, sharpen their thinking, and improve their reading, discussion, and writing skills.

NEW TO THIS EDITION

68 fresh selections

Rick Moody, author of "Boys."

14 stories, 51 poems, and 3 plays representing canonical, multicultural, contemporary, and popular literature are new to this edition. Complementing the addition of several classic literary works that have long made classroom discussion come alive are numerous stories, poems, and plays that are new to an introduction to literature anthology. These new works include stories by Maggie Mitchell, Tobias Wolff, and Rick Moody; poems by Sherman Alexie, Natasha Trethewey, and Jill McDonough; and plays by Andrew Biss and David Ives.

Natasha Trethewey, author of "On Captivity."

An in-depth chapter on esteemed fiction writer Dagoberto Gilb, created with Dagoberto Gilb

Gilb presents three of his stories in Chapter 10 alongside his own insights — written specifically for the anthology — into each work, and shares a collection of rare photographs and manuscript pages. Like its parallel chapter created with Billy

From Chapter 10: "A Study of Dagoberto Gilb: The Author Reflects on Three Stories."

Collins (Ch. 21), this new collection continues the book's emphasis on literature as a living, changing art form. Once again, students will enjoy the opportunity to have a major writer speak directly to them, this time as only Dagoberto Gilb can, about how he writes and why he writes—and what it has been like along the way.

A thematic case study titled "The World of Work"

A thematic case study on our working lives offers poems that are as varied, rich, and often personal as the subject itself—with works such as Michael Chitwood's "Men Throwing Bricks" (on the day-to-day of manual labor) and Marge Piercy's "To be of use" (an empowering ode to a strong work ethic).

Reading and writing advice from contemporary authors

Brief selections throughout the book titled "When I Read" and "When I Write" were written by contemporary authors especially for the anthology. This advice and insight written directly to students gives them a unique opportunity to hear from many notable writers like Martín Espada, Tony Hoagland, and Marilyn Nelson. Students will learn about how these authors work, about their reading habits, and perhaps most important, about what drives them to be writers.

e-Pages for Literature to Go

The e-Pages for *Literature to Go* feature recordings of celebrated writers and actors reading contemporary and classic stories, poems, and scenes from the anthology—with questions that students can complete online. They will hear John Updike reading "A & P," Jamaica Kincaid reading "Girl," and more—giving them new insights into the authors on the page and a new understanding and enjoyment of what they have read. For a complete list of e-Pages, please see the book's last page. To access e-Pages for *Literature to Go*, visit **bedfordstmartins.com/meyerlit/epages**.

ACKNOWLEDGMENTS

This book has benefited from the ideas, suggestions, and corrections of scores of careful readers who helped transform various stages of an evolving manuscript into a finished book and into subsequent editions. I remain grateful to those I have thanked in previous prefaces, particularly the late Robert Wallace of Case Western Reserve University. In addition, many instructors who used the first edition of *Literature to Go* responded to a questionnaire for the book. For their valuable comments and advice, I am grateful to Althea Allard, Community College of Rhode Island; Jessica Barksdale, Diablo Valley College; Debbie Borchers, Pueblo Community College; Robert Brown, Tunxis Community College; Becky DiBiasio, Assumption College; Kelsey Ford, Middlesex Community College; Robert Galin, University of New Mexico–Gallup Branch; Sondra Guttman, Loyola University Maryland; Grace Haddox, El Paso Community College; Kimberly Hall, Harrisburg Area Community College; Jonathan Hartmann, University of New Haven; Schahara Hudelson, South Plains College; Elizabeth Juckett, West Virginia University; Victoria Kingsley, University of Massachusetts, Boston; Terry Kirts, Indiana University–Purdue University Indianapolis; Tamara Kuzmenkov, Tacoma Community College; Mary Libertin, Shippensburg University of Pennsylvania; Susan Lipscomb, Houghton College; Debra Matier, College of Southern Idaho; David Merchant, Louisiana Technical University; Gail Miller, Berkeley College; Marlene Posner Falken, Broward College; Shannon Rauwerda, Broward College; James Read, Allan Hancock College; Bonnie Spears, Chaffey College; Karen Stewart, Norwich University; Kathryn Swanson, Augsburg College; Karen Toloui, Diablo Valley College; Michael Tomanek, Minnesota State University Moorhead; Marilynn Turner, Asnuntuck; and Margaret Walton, Berkeley College.

I would also like to give special thanks to the following instructors who contributed teaching tips to *Resources for Teaching Literature to Go*: Sandra Adickes, Helen J. Aling, Sr. Anne Denise Brenann, Robin Calitri, James H. Clemmer, Robert Croft, Thomas Edwards, Elizabeth Kleinfeld, Olga Lyles, Timothy Peters, Catherine Rusco, Robert M. St. John, Richard Stoner, Nancy Veiga, Karla Walters, and Joseph Zeppetello.

I am also indebted to those who cheerfully answered questions and generously provided miscellaneous bits of information. What might have seemed to them like inconsequential conversations turned out to be important leads. Among these friends and colleagues are Raymond Anselment, Barbara Campbell, Ann Charters, Karen Chow, John Christie, Eleni Coundouriotis, Irving Cummings, William Curtin, Patrick Hogan, Lee Jacobus, Thomas Jambeck, Bonnie Januszewski-Ytuarte, Greta Little, George Monteiro, Brenda Murphy, Joel Myerson, Rose Quiello, Thomas Recchio, William Sheidley, Stephanie Smith, Milton Stern, Kenneth Wilson, and the dedicated reference librarians at the Homer Babbidge Library, University of Connecticut. I am particularly happy to acknowledge the tactful help of Roxanne Cody, owner of R. J. Julia Booksellers in Madison, Connecticut, whose passion for books authorizes her as the consummate matchmaker for writers, readers, and titles. It's a wonder that somebody doesn't call the cops.

I continue to be grateful for what I have learned from teaching my students and for the many student papers I have received over the years that I have used in various forms to serve as good and accessible models of student writing. I am also indebted to Stefanie Wortman and Valerie

Duff-Strautmann for their extensive work on the second edition of *Resources for Teaching Literature To Go*.

At Bedford/St. Martin's, my debts once again require more time to acknowledge than the deadline allows. Charles H. Christensen and Joan E. Feinberg initiated this project and launched it with their intelligence, energy, and sound advice. This book has also benefited from the savvy insights of Denise Wydra and Steve Scipione. Earlier editions of *The Bedford Introduction to Literature*, from which this book is adapted, were shaped by editors Karen Henry, Kathy Retan, Alanya Harter, Aron Keesbury, and Ellen Thibault; their work was as first rate as it was essential. As development editor for the second edition, Christina Gerogiannis expertly kept the book on track and made the journey a pleasure to the end; her valuable contributions richly remind me of how fortunate I am to be a Bedford/St. Martin's author. Amanda Legee, editorial assistant, gracefully handled a variety of editorial tasks. Permissions were deftly arranged by Kalina Ingham, Arthur Johnson, Martha Friedman, and Susan Doheny. The difficult tasks of production were skillfully managed by Karen Baart, whose attention to details and deadlines was essential to the completion of this project. Melissa Cook provided careful copyediting, and Anne True and Barbara Price did meticulous proofreading. I thank all of the people at Bedford/St. Martin's—including Billy Boardman, who designed the cover, and Stacey Propps, the marketing manager—who helped to make this formidable project a manageable one.

Finally, I am grateful to my sons Timothy and Matthew for all kinds of help, but mostly I'm just grateful they're my sons. And for making all the difference, I thank my wife, Regina Barreca.

—Michael Meyer

YOU GET MORE DIGITAL CHOICES FOR *LITERATURE TO GO*

Literature to Go doesn't stop with a book. Online, you'll find both free and affordable premium resources to help students get even more out of the book and your course. You'll also find convenient instructor resources, and even a nationwide community of teachers. To learn more about or order any of the products below, contact your Bedford/St. Martin's sales representative, e-mail sales support (sales_support@bfwpub.com), or visit the Web site at **bedfordstmartins.com/meyertogo/catalog**.

You have access to e-Pages for Literature to Go

The e-Pages for *Literature to Go* allow your students to hear great literature out loud. A rich library of audio recordings features thirty celebrated authors, including Gwendolyn Brooks and Robert Pinsky, and actors reading works from the anthology—with questions students can complete online. You and your students can access the e-Pages at **bedfordstmartins.com/meyerlit/epages**. Students receive access automatically with the purchase of a new book. If the activation code printed on the inside back cover of the student edition doesn't work, it might be expired. Students can purchase access at the e-Pages site. Instructors don't need an access code; you can access the e-Pages if you already have instructor access, or you can request instructor access at the e-Pages site. You can also use the free tools accompanying the e-Pages to upload a syllabus, readings, and assignments to share with the class.

Literature to Go *is also an e-book*

Literature to Go is available in a variety of e-book formats. For details, visit **bedfordstmartins.com/meyertogo/formats**.

Literature to Go *comes with free videos*

Bring today's best writers into your classroom with *VideoCentral: Literature*, our growing library of more than fifty videos with today's writers. Biographical notes and questions make each video an assignable module. See **bedfordstmartins.com/videolit/catalog**.

This resource can be packaged for free with new student editions of this book. An activation code is required. To order *VideoCentral: Literature* with this print text, use ISBN 978-1-4576-6743-5.

Visit the book companion site for Literature to Go *bedfordstmartins.com/meyerlit*

Supplement your print text with our free and open resources for literature (no codes required) and flexible premium content.

Get free online help for your students   The book companion site for *Literature to Go* provides close reading help, reference materials, and support for working with sources.

- *VirtuaLit* tutorials for close reading (fiction, poetry, and drama)
- *AuthorLinks* and biographies for 800 authors
- *LitQuizzes* on poetic elements and hundreds of literary works
- Glossary of literary terms
- MLA-style student papers
- A sampler of author videos and additional literature
- Help for finding and citing sources

Access your instructor resources and get teaching ideas you can use today

Are you looking for professional resources for teaching literature and writing? How about some help with planning classroom activities?

Download your instructor's manual   This comprehensive manual offers teaching support for every selection, useful for new and experienced instructors alike. Resources include commentaries, biographical information, and writing assignments, as well as teaching tips from instructors who have taught with the book, additional suggestions for connections among the selections, and thematic groupings with questions for discussion and writing. The manual is available in print and online at **bedfordstmartins.com/meyertogo/catalog**.

Teaching Central   We've gathered all of our print and online professional resources in one place. You'll find landmark reference works, sourcebooks on pedagogical issues, award-winning collections, and practical advice for the classroom — all free for instructors and available at **bedfordstmartins.com/teachingcentral**.

LitBits: **Ideas for Teaching Literature and Creative Writing**   Our new *LitBits* blog — hosted by a growing team of instructors, poets, novelists, and scholars — offers a fresh, regularly updated collection of ideas and assignments. You'll find simple ways to teach with new media, excite your students with activities, and join an ongoing conversation about teaching. Go to **bedfordstmartins.com/litbits/catalog** and **bedfordstmartins.com/litbits**.

Order content for your course management system   Content cartridges for the most common course management systems — Blackboard, Canvas, Angel, Moodle, Sakai, and Desire2Learn — allow you to easily download Bedford/St. Martin's digital materials for your course. For more information, visit **bedfordstmartins.com/coursepacks**.

Package one of our best-selling brief handbooks at a discount   Do you need a pocket-sized handbook for your course? Package *Easy Writer* by Andrea Lunsford or *A Pocket Style Manual* by Diana Hacker and Nancy Sommers with this text at a 20% discount. For more information, go to **bedfordstmartins.com/easywriter/catalog** or **bedfordstmartins.com/pocket/catalog**.

Teach longer works at a nice price   Volumes from our literary reprint series — the Case Studies in Contemporary Criticism series, Bedford

Cultural Edition series, the Bedford Shakespeare series, and the Bedford College Editions — can be shrink-wrapped with *Literature to Go* at a discount. For a complete list of available titles, visit **bedfordstmartins .com/literaryreprints/catalog**.

Package works from our video and DVD library   Qualified adopters can choose from selected videos and DVDs of plays and stories included in *Literature to Go*. To learn more, contact your Bedford/St. Martin's sales representative or e-mail sales support (**sales_support@bfwpub.com**).

TradeUp and save 50%

TradeUp

Get 50% off all trade titles when packaged with your textbook!

Add more value and choice to your students' learning experiences by packaging their Bedford/St. Martin's textbook with one of a thousand titles from our sister publishers such as Farrar, Straus and Giroux and St. Martin's Press — at a discount of 50% off the regular price.

Brief Contents

Contents

xix

Fiction in Depth   243

POETRY   333

The Elements of Poetry   335

e   bedfordstmartins.com/meyerlit/epages

16. Symbol, Allegory, and Irony 430

Symbol 430

Allegory 432

Irony 435

17. Sounds 450

Listening to Poetry 450

Rhyme 456

Poems for Further Study 461

xxviii   CONTENTS

Poetry in Depth   525

21. A Study of Billy Collins: The Author Reflects on Five Poems 527

22. A Thematic Case Study: The World of Work 552

A Collection of Poems 561

23. Poems for Further Reading 563

DRAMA

The Study of Drama

24. Reading Drama

 bedfordstmartins.com/meyerlit/epages

bedfordstmartins.com/meyerlit/epages

CRITICAL THINKING AND WRITING 889

Literature to Go

INTRODUCTION

Reading
Imaginative Literature

To seek the source, the impulse of a
story is like tearing a flower to pieces for
wantonness.

— KATE CHOPIN

THE NATURE OF LITERATURE

Literature does not lend itself to a single tidy definition because the making of it over the centuries has been as complex, unwieldy, and natural as life itself. Is literature everything that has been written, from ancient prayers to graffiti? Does it include songs and stories that were not written down until many years after they were recited? Does literature include the television scripts from *Seinfeld* as well as Shakespeare's *King Lear*? Is literature only writing that has permanent value and continues to move people? Must literature be true or beautiful or moral? Should it be socially useful?

Although these kinds of questions are not conclusively answered in this book, they are implicitly raised by the stories, poems, and plays included here. No definition of literature, particularly a brief one, is likely to satisfy everyone because definitions tend to weaken and require qualification when confronted by the uniqueness of individual works. In this context it is worth recalling Herman Melville's humorous use of a definition of a whale in *Moby-Dick* (1851). In the course of the novel, Melville presents his imaginative and symbolic whale as inscrutable, but he begins with a quotation from Georges Cuvier, a French naturalist who defines a whale in his nineteenth-century study *The Animal Kingdom* this way: "The whale is a mammiferous animal without hind feet." Cuvier's description is technically correct, of course, but there is little wisdom in it. Melville understood that the reality of the whale (which he describes as the "ungraspable phantom of life") cannot be caught by isolated facts. If the full meaning of the whale is to be understood, it must be sought on the open sea of experience, where the whale itself is, rather than in exclusionary definitions. Facts and definitions are helpful; however, they do not always reveal the whole truth.

Despite Melville's reminder that a definition can be too limiting and even comical, it is useful for our purposes to describe literature as a fiction consisting of carefully arranged words designed to stir the imagination. Stories, poems, and plays are fictional. They are made up—imagined—even when based on actual historic events. Such imaginative writing differs from other kinds of writing because its purpose is not primarily to transmit facts or ideas. Imaginative literature is a source more of pleasure than of information, and we read it for basically the same reasons we listen to music or view a dance: enjoyment, delight, and satisfaction. Like other art forms, imaginative literature offers pleasure and usually attempts to convey a perspective, mood, feeling, or experience. Writers transform the facts the world provides—people, places, and objects—into experiences that suggest meanings.

Consider, for example, the difference between the following factual description of a snake and a poem on the same subject. Here is *Webster's Eleventh New Collegiate Dictionary*'s definition:

> any of numerous limbless scaled reptiles (suborder Serpentes syn. Ophidia) with a long tapering body and with salivary glands often modified to produce venom which is injected through grooved or tubular fangs.

Contrast this matter-of-fact definition with Emily Dickinson's poetic evocation of a snake in "A narrow Fellow in the Grass":

A narrow Fellow in the Grass
Occasionally rides —
You may have met Him—did you not
His notice sudden is —

The Grass divides as with a Comb —   5
A spotted shaft is seen —
And then it closes at your feet
And opens further on —

He likes a Boggy Acre
A floor too cool for Corn—   10
Yet when a Boy, and Barefoot —
I more than once at Noon

Have passed, I thought, a Whip lash
Unbraiding in the Sun

When stooping to secure it   15
It wrinkled, and was gone —

Several of Nature's People
I know, and they know me —
I feel for them a transport
Of cordiality —   20

But never met this Fellow
Attended, or alone
Without a tighter breathing
And Zero at the Bone —

The dictionary provides a succinct, anatomical description of what a snake is, while Dickinson's poem suggests what a snake can mean. The definition offers facts; the poem offers an experience. The dictionary would probably allow someone who had never seen a snake to sketch one with reasonable accuracy. The poem also provides some vivid subjective descriptions — for example, the snake dividing the grass "as with a Comb" — yet it offers more than a picture of serpentine movements. The poem conveys the ambivalence many people have about snakes — the kind of feeling, for example, so evident on the faces of visitors viewing the snakes at a zoo. In the poem there is both a fascination with and a horror of what might be called snakehood; this combination of feelings has been coiled in most of us since Adam and Eve.

A good deal more could be said about the numbing fear that undercuts the affection for nature at the beginning of this poem, but the point here is that imaginative literature gives us not so much the full, factual proportions of the world as some of its experiences and meanings. Instead of defining the world, literature encourages us to try it out in our imaginations.

THE VALUE OF LITERATURE

Mark Twain once shrewdly observed that a person who chooses not to read has no advantage over a person who is unable to read. In industrialized societies today, however, the question is not who reads, because nearly everyone can and does, but what is read. Why should anyone spend precious time with literature when there is so much reading material available that provides useful information about everything from the daily news to personal computers? Why should a literary artist's imagination compete for attention that could be spent on the firm realities that constitute everyday life? In fact, national best-seller lists much less often include collections of stories, poems, or plays than they do cookbooks and, not surprisingly, diet books. Although such fare may be filling, it doesn't stay with you. Most people have other appetites too.

Certainly one of the most important values of literature is that it nourishes our emotional lives. An effective literary work may seem to speak directly to us, especially if we are ripe for it. The inner life that good writers reveal in their characters often gives us glimpses of some portion of ourselves. We can be moved to laugh, cry, tremble, dream, ponder, shriek, or rage with a character by simply turning a page instead of turning our lives upside down. Although the experience itself is imagined, the emotion is real. That's why the final chapters of a good adventure novel can make a reader's heart race as much as a 100-yard dash or why the repressed love of Hester Prynne in *The Scarlet Letter* by Nathaniel Hawthorne is painful to a sympathetic reader. Human emotions speak a universal language regardless of when or where a work was written.

In addition to appealing to our emotions, literature broadens our perspectives on the world. Most of the people we meet are pretty much like ourselves, and what we can see of the world even in a lifetime is astonishingly limited. Literature allows us to move beyond the inevitable boundaries of our own lives and culture because it introduces us to people different from ourselves, places remote from our neighborhoods, and times other than our own. Reading makes us more aware of life's possibilities as well as its subtleties and ambiguities. Put simply, people who read literature experience more life and have a keener sense of a common human identity than those who do not. It is true, of course, that many people go through life without reading imaginative literature, but that is a loss rather than a gain. They may find themselves troubled by the same kinds of questions that reveal Daisy Buchanan's restless, vague discontentment in F. Scott Fitzgerald's *The Great Gatsby:* "What'll we do with ourselves this afternoon?" cried Daisy, "and the day after that, and the next thirty years?"

Sometimes students mistakenly associate literature more with school than with life. Accustomed to reading it in order to write a paper or pass an examination, students may perceive such reading as a chore instead of a pleasurable opportunity, something considerably less important than studying for the "practical" courses that prepare them for a career. The study of literature, however, is also practical because it engages you in the kinds of problem solving important in a variety of fields, from philosophy to science and technology. The interpretation of literary texts requires you to deal with uncertainties, value judgments, and emotions; these are unavoidable aspects of life.

People who make the most significant contributions to their professions—whether in business, engineering, teaching, or some other area—tend to be challenged rather than threatened by multiple possibilities. Instead of retreating to the way things have always been done, they bring freshness and creativity to their work. F. Scott Fitzgerald once astutely described the "test of a first-rate intelligence" as "the ability to hold two opposed ideas in the mind at the same time, and still retain the ability to function." People with such intelligence know how to read situations, shape questions, interpret details, and evaluate competing points of view. Equipped with a healthy respect for facts, they also understand the value of pursuing hunches and exercising their imaginations. Reading literature encourages a suppleness of mind that is helpful in any discipline or work.

Once the requirements for your degree are completed, what ultimately matters are not the courses listed on your transcript but the sensibilities and habits of mind that you bring to your work, friends, family, and, indeed, the rest of your life. A healthy economy changes and grows with the times; people do too if they are prepared for more than simply filling a job description. The range and variety of life that literature affords can help you to interpret your own experiences and the world in which you live.

To discover the insights that literature reveals requires careful reading and sensitivity. One of the purposes of a college Introduction to Literature class is to cultivate the analytic skills necessary for reading well. Class discussions often help establish a dialogue with a work that perhaps otherwise would not speak to you. Analytic skills can also be developed by writing about what you read. Writing is an effective means of clarifying your responses and ideas because it requires you to account for the author's use of language as well as your own. This book is based on two premises: that reading literature is pleasurable and that reading and understanding a work sensitively by thinking, talking, or writing about it increases the pleasure of the experience of it.

Understanding its basic elements — such as point of view, symbol, theme, tone, irony, and so on — is a prerequisite to an informed appreciation of literature. This kind of understanding allows you to perceive more in a literary work in much the same way that a spectator at a tennis match sees more if he or she understands the rules and conventions of the game. But literature is not simply a spectator sport. The analytic skills that open up literature also have their uses when you watch a television program or film and, more important, when you attempt to sort out the significance of the people, places, and events that constitute your own life. Literature enhances and sharpens your perceptions. What could be more lastingly practical as well as satisfying?

THE CHANGING LITERARY CANON

Perhaps the best reading creates some kind of change in us: We see more clearly; we're alert to nuances; we ask questions that previously didn't occur to us. Henry David Thoreau had that sort of reading in mind when he remarked in *Walden* that the books he valued most were those that caused him to date "a new era in his life from the reading." Readers are sometimes changed by literature, but it is also worth noting that the life of a literary work can also be affected by its readers. Melville's *Moby-Dick*, for example, was not valued as a classic until the 1920s, when critics rescued the novel from the obscurity of being cataloged in many libraries (including Yale's) not under fiction but under cetology, the study of whales. Indeed, many writers contemporary to Melville who were important and popular in the nineteenth century — William Cullen Bryant, Henry Wadsworth Longfellow, and James Russell Lowell, to name a few — are now mostly unread; their names appear more often inscribed on elementary schools built early in this century than in anthologies. Clearly, literary reputations and what is valued as great literature change over time and in the eyes of readers.

Such changes have steadily accelerated as the literary *canon* — those works considered by scholars, critics, and teachers to be the most important to read and study — has undergone a significant series of shifts. Some writers who previously were overlooked, undervalued, neglected, or studiously ignored have been brought into focus in an effort to create a more diverse literary canon, one that recognizes the contributions of the many cultures that make up American society. Since the 1960s, for example, some critics have reassessed writings by women who had been left out of the standard literary traditions dominated by male writers. Many more female writers are now read alongside the male writers who traditionally populated literary history. Hence, a reader of Mark Twain and Stephen Crane is now just as likely to encounter Kate Chopin in a literary anthology. Until fairly recently, Chopin was mostly regarded as a minor local colorist of Louisiana life. In the 1960s, however, the feminist movement helped to establish her present reputation as a significant voice in American literature owing to the feminist concerns so compellingly articulated by her female characters. This kind of enlargement of the canon also resulted from another reform movement of the 1960s. The civil rights movement sensitized literary critics to the political, moral, and aesthetic necessity of rediscovering African American literature, and more recently Asian and Hispanic writers have been making their way into the canon. Moreover, on a broader scale the canon is being revised and enlarged to include the works of writers from parts of the world other than the West, a development that reflects the changing values, concerns, and complexities of recent decades, when literary landscapes have shifted as dramatically as the political boundaries of much of the world.

No semester's reading list — or anthology — can adequately or accurately echo all the new voices competing to be heard as part of the mainstream literary canon, but recent efforts to open up the canon attempt to sensitize readers to the voices of women, minorities, and writers from all over the world. This development has not occurred without its urgent advocates or passionate dissenters. It's no surprise that issues about race, gender, and class often get people off the fence and on their feet. Although what we regard as literature — whether it's called great, classic, or canonical — continues to generate debate, there is no question that such controversy will continue to reflect readers' values as well as the writers they admire.

FICTION

The Elements
of Fiction

1

Reading Fiction

What we do might be done in solitude and with great desperation, but it tends to produce exactly the opposite. It tends to produce community and in many people hope and joy.

— JUNOT DÍAZ

READING FICTION RESPONSIVELY

Reading a literary work responsively can be an intensely demanding activity. Henry David Thoreau — about as intense and demanding a reader and writer as they come — insists that "books must be read as deliberately and reservedly as they were written." Thoreau is right about the necessity for a conscious, sustained involvement with a literary work. Imaginative literature does demand more from us than, say, browsing through *People* magazine in a dentist's waiting room, but Thoreau makes the process sound a little more daunting than it really is. For when we respond to the demands of responsive reading, our efforts are usually rewarded with pleasure as well as understanding. Careful, deliberate reading — the kind that engages a reader's imagination as it calls forth the writer's — is a means of exploration that can take a reader outside whatever circumstance or experience previously defined his or her world. Just as we respond moment by moment to people and situations in our lives, we also respond to literary works as we read them, though we may not be fully aware of how we are affected at each point along the way. The more conscious we are of how and why we respond to works in particular ways, the more likely we are to be imaginatively engaged in our reading.

In a very real sense both the reader and the author create the literary work. How a reader responds to a story, poem, or play will help to determine its meaning. The author arranges the various elements that constitute his or her craft—elements such as plot, character, setting, point of view, symbolism, theme, and style, which you will be examining in subsequent chapters—but the author cannot completely control the reader's response any more than a person can absolutely predict how a remark or action will be received by a stranger, a friend, or even a family member. Few authors *tell* readers how to respond. Our sympathy, anger, confusion, laughter, sadness, or whatever the feeling might be is left up to us to experience. Writers may have the talent to evoke such feelings, but they don't have the power and authority to enforce them. Because of the range of possible responses produced by imaginative literature, there is no single, correct, definitive response or interpretation. There can be readings that are wrongheaded or foolish, and some readings are better than others—that is, more responsive to a work's details and more persuasive—but that doesn't mean there is only one possible reading of a work.

Experience tells us that different people respond differently to the same work. Consider, for example, how often you've heard Melville's *Moby-Dick* described as one of the greatest American novels. This, however, is how a reviewer in *New Monthly Magazine* described the book when it was published in 1851: It is "a huge dose of hyperbolical slang, maudlin sentimentalism and tragic-comic bubble and squeak." Melville surely did not intend or desire this response; but there it is, and it was not a singular, isolated reaction. This reading—like any reading—was influenced by the values, assumptions, and expectations that the readers brought to the novel from both previous readings and life experiences. The reviewer's refusal to take the book seriously may have caused him to miss the boat from the perspective of many other readers of *Moby-Dick*, but it indicates that even "classics" (perhaps especially those kinds of works) can generate disparate readings.

Consider the following brief story by Kate Chopin, a writer whose fiction (like Melville's) sometimes met with indifference or hostility in her own time. As you read, keep track of your responses to the central character, Mrs. Mallard. Write down your feelings about her in a substantial paragraph when you finish the story. Think, for example, about how you respond to the emotions she expresses concerning news of her husband's death. What do you think of her feelings about marriage? Do you think you would react the way she does under similar circumstances?

Explore contexts
for Kate Chopin
and approaches
to this story at
bedfordstmartins.com/
meyerlit.

KATE CHOPIN (1851–1904)

The Story of an Hour   1894

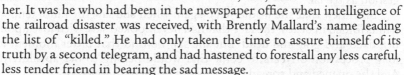

Knowing that Mrs. Mallard was afflicted with a heart
trouble, great care was taken to break to her as gently
as possible the news of her husband's death.

It was her sister Josephine who told her, in broken
sentences; veiled hints that revealed in half concealing.
Her husband's friend Richards was there, too, near
her. It was he who had been in the newspaper office when intelligence of
the railroad disaster was received, with Brently Mallard's name leading
the list of "killed." He had only taken the time to assure himself of its
truth by a second telegram, and had hastened to forestall any less careful,
less tender friend in bearing the sad message.

She did not hear the story as many women have heard the same,
with a paralyzed inability to accept its significance. She wept at once,
with sudden, wild abandonment, in her sister's arms. When the storm of
grief had spent itself she went away to her room alone. She would have
no one follow her.

There stood, facing the open window, a comfortable, roomy armchair. Into this she sank, pressed down by a physical exhaustion that
haunted her body and seemed to reach into her soul.

She could see in the open square before her house the tops of trees   5
that were all aquiver with the new spring life. The delicious breath of
rain was in the air. In the street below a peddler was crying his wares. The
notes of a distant song which some one was singing reached her faintly,
and countless sparrows were twittering in the eaves.

There were patches of blue sky showing here and there through the
clouds that had met and piled one above the other in the west facing her
window.

She sat with her head thrown back upon the cushion of the chair,
quite motionless, except when a sob came up into her throat and
shook her, as a child who has cried itself to sleep continues to sob in its
dreams.

She was young, with a fair, calm face, whose lines bespoke repression
and even a certain strength. But now there was a dull stare in her eyes,
whose gaze was fixed away off yonder on one of those patches of blue
sky. It was not a glance of reflection, but rather indicated a suspension of
intelligent thought.

There was something coming to her and she was waiting for it,
fearfully. What was it? She did not know; it was too subtle and elusive
to name. But she felt it, creeping out of the sky, reaching toward her
through the sounds, the scents, the color that filled the air.

Now her bosom rose and fell tumultuously. She was beginning to   10
recognize this thing that was approaching to possess her, and she was

striving to beat it back with her will — as powerless as her two white slender hands would have been.

When she abandoned herself a little whispered word escaped her slightly parted lips. She said it over and over under her breath: "free, free, free!" The vacant stare and the look of terror that had followed it went from her eyes. They stayed keen and bright. Her pulses beat fast, and the coursing blood warmed and relaxed every inch of her body.

She did not stop to ask if it were or were not a monstrous joy that held her. A clear and exalted perception enabled her to dismiss the suggestion as trivial.

She knew that she would weep again when she saw the kind, tender hands folded in death; the face that had never looked save with love upon her, fixed and gray and dead. But she saw beyond that bitter moment a long procession of years to come that would belong to her absolutely. And she opened and spread her arms out to them in welcome.

There would be no one to live for her during those coming years; she would live for herself. There would be no powerful will bending hers in that blind persistence with which men and women believe they have a right to impose a private will upon a fellow-creature. A kind intention or a cruel intention made the act seem no less a crime as she looked upon it in that brief moment of illumination.

And yet she had loved him — sometimes. Often she had not. What 15 did it matter! What could love, the unsolved mystery, count for in face of this possession of self-assertion which she suddenly recognized as the strongest impulse of her being!

"Free! Body and soul free!" she kept whispering.

Josephine was kneeling before the closed door with her lips to the keyhole, imploring for admission. "Louise, open the door! I beg; open the door — you will make yourself ill. What are you doing, Louise? For heaven's sake open the door."

"Go away. I am not making myself ill." No; she was drinking in a very elixir of life through that open window.

Her fancy was running riot along those days ahead of her. Spring days, and summer days, and all sorts of days that would be her own. She breathed a quick prayer that life might be long. It was only yesterday she had thought with a shudder that life might be long.

She arose at length and opened the door to her sister's importuni- 20 ties. There was a feverish triumph in her eyes, and she carried herself unwittingly like a goddess of Victory. She clasped her sister's waist, and together they descended the stairs. Richards stood waiting for them at the bottom.

Some one was opening the front door with a latchkey. It was Brently Mallard who entered, a little travel-stained, composedly carrying his gripsack and umbrella. He had been far from the scene of accident, and did not even know there had been one. He stood amazed at Josephine's piercing cry; at Richards' quick motion to screen him from the view of his wife.

But Richards was too late.

When the doctors came they said she had died of heart disease — of joy that kills.

A SAMPLE CLOSE READING

An Annotated Section of "The Story of an Hour"

Even as you read a story for the first time, you can highlight passages, circle or underline words, and write responses in the margins. Subsequent readings will yield more insights once you begin to understand how various elements such as plot, characterization, and wording build toward the conclusion and what you perceive to be the story's central ideas. The following annotations for the first eleven paragraphs of "The Story of an Hour" provide a perspective written by someone who had read the work several times. Your own approach might, of course, be quite different — as the sample paper that follows the annotated passage amply demonstrates.

The title could point to the brevity of the story — only 23 short paragraphs — or to the decisive nature of what happens in a very short period of time. Or both.

KATE CHOPIN (1851–1904)

The Story of an Hour

Mrs. Mallard's first name (Louise) is not given until paragraph 17, yet her sister Josephine is named immediately. This emphasizes Mrs. Mallard's married identity.

Knowing that Mrs. Mallard was afflicted with a heart trouble, great care was taken to break to her as gently as possible the news of her husband's death.

It was her sister Josephine who told her, in broken sentences; veiled hints that revealed in half concealing. Her husband's friend Richards was there, too, near her. It was he who had been in the newspaper office when intelligence of the railroad disaster was received, with Brently Mallard's name leading the list of "killed." He had only taken the time to assure himself of its truth by a second telegram, and had hastened to forestall any less careful, less tender friend in bearing the sad message.

Given the nature of the cause of Mrs. Mallard's death at the story's end, it's worth noting the ambiguous description that she "was afflicted with a heart trouble." Is this one of Chopin's (rather than Josephine's) "veiled hints"?

She did not hear the story as many women have heard the same, with a paralyzed inability to accept its significance. She wept at once, with sudden, wild abandonment, in her sister's arms. When the storm of grief

When Mrs. Mallard weeps with "wild abandonment," the reader is again confronted with an ambiguous phrase: she grieves in an overwhelming manner yet seems to express relief at being abandoned by Brently's death.

These 3 paragraphs create an increasingly "open" atmosphere that leads to the "delicious" outside where there are inviting sounds and "patches of blue sky." There's a definite tension between the inside and outside worlds.

Though still stunned by grief, Mrs. Mallard begins to feel a change come over her owing to her growing awareness of a world outside her room.

What that change is remains "too subtle and elusive to name."

Mrs. Mallard's conflicted struggle is described in passionate, physical terms as if she is "possess[ed]" by a lover she is "powerless" to resist.

Once Mrs. Mallard has "abandoned" herself (see the "abandonment" in paragraph 3), the reader realizes that her love is to be "free, free, free." Her recognition is evident in the "coursing blood [that] warmed and relaxed every inch of her body."

had spent itself she went away to her room alone. She would have no one follow her.

There stood, facing the open window, a comfortable, roomy armchair. Into this she sank, pressed down by a physical exhaustion that haunted her body and seemed to reach into her soul.

She could see in the open square before her house 5 the tops of trees that were all aquiver with the new spring life. The delicious breath of rain was in the air. In the street below a peddler was crying his wares. The notes of a distant song which some one was singing reached her faintly, and countless sparrows were twittering in the eaves.

There were patches of blue sky showing here and there through the clouds that had met and piled one above the other in the west facing her window.

She sat with her head thrown back upon the cushion of the chair, quite motionless, except when a sob came up into her throat and shook her, as a child who has cried itself to sleep continues to sob in its dreams.

She was young, with a fair, calm face, whose lines bespoke repression and even a certain strength. But now there was a dull stare in her eyes, whose gaze was fixed away off yonder on one of those patches of blue sky. It was not a glance of reflection, but rather indicated a suspension of intelligent thought.

There was something coming to her and she was waiting for it, fearfully. What was it? She did not know; it was too subtle and elusive to name. But she felt it, creeping out of the sky, reaching toward her through the sounds, the scents, the color that filled the air.

Now her bosom rose and fell tumultuously. She was 10 beginning to recognize this thing that was approaching to possess her, and she was striving to beat it back with her will—as powerless as her two white slender hands would have been.

When she abandoned herself a little whispered word escaped her slightly parted lips. She said it over and over under her breath: "free, free, free!" The vacant stare and the look of terror that had followed it went from her eyes. They stayed keen and bright. Her pulses beat fast, and the coursing blood warmed and relaxed every inch of her body. . . .

Do you find Mrs. Mallard a sympathetic character? Some readers think that she is callous, selfish, and unnatural — even monstrous — because she ecstatically revels in her newly discovered sense of freedom so soon after learning of her husband's presumed death. Others read her as a victim of her inability to control her own life in a repressive, male-dominated society. Is it possible to hold both views simultaneously, or are they mutually exclusive? Are your views in any way influenced by your being male or female? Does your age affect your perception? What about your social and economic background? Does your nationality, race, or religion in any way shape your attitudes? Do you have particular views about the institution of marriage that inform your assessment of Mrs. Mallard's character? Have other reading experiences — perhaps a familiarity with some of Chopin's other stories — predisposed you one way or another to Mrs. Mallard?

Understanding potential influences might be useful in determining whether a particular response to Mrs. Mallard is based primarily on the story's details and their arrangement or on an overt or a subtle bias that is brought to the story. If you unconsciously project your beliefs and assumptions onto a literary work, you run the risk of distorting it to accommodate your prejudice. Your feelings can be a reliable guide to interpretation, but you should be aware of what those feelings are based on.

Often specific questions about literary works cannot be answered definitively. For example, Chopin does not explain why Mrs. Mallard suffers a heart attack at the end of this story. Is the shock of seeing her "dead" husband simply too much for this woman "afflicted with a heart trouble"? Does she die of what the doctors call a "joy that kills" because she is so glad to see her husband? Is she so profoundly guilty about feeling "free" at her husband's expense that she has a heart attack? Is her death a kind of willed suicide in reaction to her loss of freedom? Your answers to these questions will depend on which details you emphasize in your interpretation of the story and the kinds of perspectives and values you bring to it. If, for example, you read the story from a feminist perspective, you would be likely to pay close attention to Chopin's comments about marriage in paragraph 14. Or if you read the story as an oblique attack on the insensitivity of physicians of the period, you might want to find out whether Chopin wrote elsewhere about doctors (she did) and compare her comments with historic sources.

Reading responsively makes you an active participant in the process of creating meaning in a literary work. The experience that you and the author create will most likely not be identical to another reader's encounter with the same work, but then that's true of nearly any experience you'll have, and it is part of the pleasure of reading. Indeed, talking and writing about literature is a way of sharing responses so that they can be enriched and deepened.

A SAMPLE STUDENT PAPER

Differences in Responses to Kate Chopin's "The Story of an Hour"

The paper below was written in response to an assignment that called for a three- to four-page discussion of how different readers might interpret Mrs. Mallard's character.

Villa 1

Wally Villa

Professor Brian

English 210

12 March 2013

Differences in Responses to
Kate Chopin's "The Story of an Hour"

Kate Chopin's "The Story of an Hour" appears merely to explore a woman's unpredictable reaction to her husband's assumed death and reappearance, but actually Chopin offers Mrs. Mallard's bizarre story to reveal problems that are

[margin note: Thesis providing writer's interpretation of story's purpose.]

inherent in the institution of marriage. By offering this depiction of a marriage that stifles the woman to the point that she celebrates the death of her kind and loving husband, Chopin challenges her readers to examine their own views of marriage and relationships between men and women. Each reader's judgment of Mrs. Mallard and her behavior inevitably stems from his or her own personal feelings about marriage

[margin note: Introduction setting up other reader responses discussed later in paper.]

and the influences of societal expectations. Readers of differing genders, ages, and marital experiences are, therefore, likely to react differently to Chopin's startling portrayal of the Mallards' marriage, and that certainly is true of my response to the story compared to my father's and grandmother's responses.

Marriage often establishes boundaries between people that make them unable to communicate with each other. The Mallards' marriage was evidently crippled by both their inability to talk to one another and Mrs. Mallard's

[margin note: Analysis of story's portrayal of marriage, with textual evidence.]

conviction that her marriage was defined by a "powerful will bending hers in that blind persistence with which men and women believe they have a right to impose a private will upon a fellow-creature" (14). Yet she does not recognize that it is not just men who impose their will upon women and that the problems inherent in marriage affect men and women equally. To me, Mrs. Mallard is a somewhat sympathetic character, and I appreciate her longing to live out the "years to

Villa 2

come that would belong to her absolutely" (14). However, I also believe that she could have tried to improve her own situation somehow, either by reaching out to her husband or by abandoning the marriage altogether. Chopin uses Mrs. Mallard's tragedy to illuminate aspects of marriage that are harmful and, in this case, even deadly. Perhaps the Mallards' relationship should be taken as a warning to others: sacrificing one's own happiness in order to satisfy societal expectations can poison one's life and even destroy entire families.

Analysis of character and plot, connecting with story's purpose.

When my father read "The Story of an Hour," his reaction to Mrs. Mallard was more antagonistic than my own. He sees Chopin's story as a timeless "battle of the sexes," serving as further proof that men will never really be able to understand what it is that women want. Mrs. Mallard endures an obviously unsatisfying marriage without ever explaining to her husband that she feels trapped and unfulfilled. Mrs. Mallard dismisses the question of whether or not she is experiencing a "monstrous joy" (14) as trivial, but my father does not think that this is a trivial question. He believes Mrs. Mallard is guilty of a monstrous joy because she selfishly celebrates the death of her husband without ever having allowed him the opportunity to understand her feelings. He believes that, above all, Brently Mallard should be seen as the most victimized character in the story. Mr. Mallard is a good, kind man, with friends who care about him and a marriage that he thinks he can depend on. He "never looked save with love" (14) upon his wife, his only "crime" (14) was his presence in the house, and yet he is the one who is bereaved at the end of the story, for reasons he will never understand. Mrs. Mallard's passion for her newly discovered freedom is perhaps understandable, but according to my father, Mr. Mallard is the character most deserving of sympathy.

Contrasting summary and analysis of another reader's response.

Maybe not surprisingly, my grandmother's interpretation of "The Story of an Hour" was radically different from both mine and my father's. My grandmother was married in 1936 and widowed in 1959 and therefore can identify with Chopin's characters, who live at the turn of the century. Her first reaction, aside from her unwavering support for Mrs. Mallard and her predicament, was that this story demonstrates the differences between the ways men and women related to each other a century ago and the way they relate today. Unlike my father, who thinks Mrs. Mallard is too passive, my grandmother believes that Mrs. Mallard doesn't even know that she is feeling repressed until after she is told that Brently is dead. In 1894, divorce was so scandalous and

Contrasting summary and analysis of another reader's response.

Cultural and historical background providing context for response and story itself.

Villa 3

stigmatized that it simply wouldn't have been an option for Mrs. Mallard, and so her only way out of the marriage would have been one of their deaths. Being relatively young, Mrs. Mallard probably considered herself doomed to a long life in an unhappy marriage. My grandmother also feels that, in spite of all we know of Mrs. Mallard's feelings about her husband and her marriage, she still manages to live up to everyone's expectations of her as a woman both in life and in death. She is a dutiful wife to Brently, as she is expected to be. She weeps "with sudden, wild abandonment" when she hears the news of his death; she locks herself in her room to cope with her new situation; and she has a fatal heart attack upon seeing her husband arrive home. Naturally the male doctors would think that she died of the "joy that kills" (15) — nobody could have guessed that she was unhappy with her life, and she would never have wanted them to know.

> **Analysis supported with textual evidence.**

Interpretations of "The Story of an Hour" seem to vary according to the gender, age, and experience of the reader. While both male and female readers can certainly sympathize with Mrs. Mallard's plight, female readers — as was evident in our class discussions — seem to relate more easily to her predicament and are quicker to exonerate her of any responsibility for her unhappy situation. Conversely, male readers are more likely to feel compassion for Mr. Mallard, who loses his wife for reasons that will always remain entirely unknown to him. Older readers probably understand more readily the strength of social forces and the difficulty of trying to deny societal expectations concerning gender roles in general and marriage in particular. Younger readers seem to feel that Mrs. Mallard is too passive and that she could have improved her domestic life immeasurably if she had taken the initiative to either improve or end her relationship with her husband. Ultimately, how each individual reader responds to Mrs. Mallard's story reveals his or her own ideas about marriage, society, and how men and women communicate with each other.

> **Conclusion summarizing reader responses explored in the paper.**

Villa 4

Work Cited

Chopin, Kate. "The Story of an Hour." *Literature to Go*. Ed. Michael Meyer. 2nd ed. Boston: Bedford/St. Martin's, 2014. 13–15. Print.

Before beginning your own writing assignment on fiction, you should review Chapter 30, "Writing about Fiction," as well as Chapter 29, "Reading and the Writing Process," which provides a step-by-step explanation of how to choose a topic, develop a thesis, and organize various types of writing assignments. If you use outside sources, you should also be familiar with the conventional documentation procedures described in Chapter 33, "The Literary Research Paper."

EXPLORATIONS AND FORMULAS

Each time we pick up a work of fiction, go to the theater, or turn on the television, we have a trace of the same magical expectation that can be heard in the voice of a child who begs, "Tell me a story." Human beings have enjoyed stories ever since they learned to speak. Whatever the motive for creating stories—even if simply to delight or instruct—the basic human impulse to tell and hear stories existed long before the development of written language. Myths about the origins of the world and legends about the heroic exploits of demigods were among the earliest forms of storytelling to develop into oral traditions, which were eventually written down. These narratives are the ancestors of the stories we read on the printed page today.

The stories that appear in anthologies for college students are generally chosen for their high literary quality. Such stories can affect us at the deepest emotional level, reveal new insights into ourselves or the world, and stretch us by exercising our imaginations. The following chapters on plot, character, setting, and the other elements of literature are designed to provide the terms and concepts that can help you understand how a work of fiction achieves its effects and meanings. It is worth acknowledging, however, that many people buy and read fiction that is quite different from the stories usually anthologized in college texts. What about all those paperbacks with exciting, colorful covers near the cash registers in shopping malls and airports?

These books, known as *formula fiction*, are the adventure, western, detective, science fiction, and romance novels that entertain millions of readers annually. What makes them so popular? What do their characters, plots, and themes offer readers that accounts for the tremendous sales of stories with titles like *Caves of Doom, Silent Scream, Colt .45,* and *Forbidden Ecstasy*? Many of the writers included in this anthology have enjoyed wide popularity and written best-sellers, but there are more readers of formula fiction than there are readers of Ernest Hemingway, William Faulkner, or Joyce Carol Oates, to name only a few. Formula novels do provide entertainment, of course, but that makes them no different from serious stories, if entertainment means pleasure. Any of the stories in this or any other anthology can be read for pleasure.

Formula fiction, though, is usually characterized as escape literature. There are sensible reasons for this description. Adventure stories about soldiers of fortune are eagerly read by men who live pretty average lives doing ordinary jobs. Romance novels about attractive young women falling in love with tall, dark, handsome men are read mostly by women who dream themselves out of their familiar existences. The excitement, violence, and passion that such stories trade on are a kind of reprieve from everyday experience.

And yet readers of serious fiction may also use it as a refuge, a liberation from monotony and boredom. Mark Twain's humorous stories have, for example, given countless hours of pleasurable relief to readers who would rather spend time in Twain's light and funny world than in their own. Others might prefer the terror of Edgar Allan Poe's fiction or the painful predicament of two lovers in a Joyce Carol Oates story.

Although the specific elements of formula fiction differ depending on the type of story, some basic ingredients go into all westerns, mysteries, adventures, science fiction, and romances. From the very start, a reader can anticipate a happy ending for the central character, with whom he or she will identify. There may be suspense, but no matter what or how many the obstacles, complications, or near defeats, the hero or heroine succeeds and reaffirms the values and attitudes the reader brings to the story. Virtue triumphs, love conquers all, honesty is the best policy, and hard work guarantees success. Hence, the villains are corralled, the wedding vows are exchanged, the butler confesses, and gold is discovered at the last moment. The visual equivalents of such formula stories are readily available at movie theaters and in television series. Some are better than others, but all are relatively limited by the writer's goal of giving an audience what will sell.

Although formula fiction may not offer many surprises, it provides pleasure to a wide variety of readers. College professors, for example, are just as likely to be charmed by formula stories as anyone else. Readers of serious fiction who revel in exploring more challenging imaginative worlds can also enjoy formulaic stories, which offer little more than an image of the world as a simple place in which our assumptions and desires are confirmed. The familiarity of a given formula is emotionally satisfying because we are secure in our expectations of it. We know at the start of a Sherlock Holmes story that the mystery will be solved by that famous detective's relentless scientific analysis of the clues, but we take pleasure in seeing how Holmes unravels the mystery before us. Similarly, we know that James Bond's wit, grace, charm, courage, and skill will ultimately prevail over the diabolic schemes of eccentric villains, but we volunteer for the mission anyway.

Perhaps that happens for the same reason that we climb aboard a roller coaster: No matter how steep and sharp the curves, we stay on a track that is both exciting and safe. Although excitement, adventure, mystery, and romance are major routes to escape in formula fiction, most of us make that trip only temporarily, for a little relaxation and fun. Momentary relief from our everyday concerns is as healthy and desirable as an occasional daydream or fantasy. Such reading is a form of play because we — like spectators of or participants in a game — experience a formula of excitement, tension, and then release that can fascinate us regardless of how many times the game is played.

Many publishers of formula fiction — such as romance, adventure, or detective stories — issue a set number of new novels each month. Readers can buy them in stores or subscribe to them through the mail. These same publishers send "tip sheets" on request to authors who want to write for a particular series. The details of the formula differ from one series to another, but each tip sheet covers the basic elements that go into a story.

The following composite tip sheet summarizes the typical advice offered to authors by publishers of romance novels — among the most popular titles published in the United States; it has been estimated that four out of every ten paperbacks sold are romance novels. The categories and the tone of the language in this composite tip sheet are derived from a number of publishers and provide a glimpse of how formula fiction is written and what the readers of romance novels are looking for in their escape literature.

A Composite of a Romance Tip Sheet

Plot

The story focuses on the growing relationship between the heroine and hero. After a number of complications, they discover lasting love and make a permanent commitment to each other in marriage. The plot should move quickly. Background information about the heroine should be kept to a minimum. The hero should appear as early as possible (preferably in the first chapter and no later than the second), so that the hero's and heroine's feelings about each other are in the foreground as they cope with misperceptions that keep them apart until the final pages of the story. The more tension created by their uncertainty about each other's love, the greater the excitement and anticipation for the reader.

Love is the major interest. Do not inject murder, extortion, international intrigue, hijacking, horror, or supernatural elements into the plot. Controversial social issues and politics, if mentioned at all, should never be allowed a significant role. Once the heroine and hero meet, they should clearly be interested in each other, but that interest should be complicated by some kind of misunderstanding. He, for example, might find her too ambitious, an opportunist, cold, or flirtatious; or he might assume that she is attached to someone else. She might think he is haughty, snobbish, power hungry, indifferent, or contemptuous of her. The reader knows what they do not: that eventually these obstacles will be overcome. Interest is sustained by keeping the lovers apart until very near the end so that the reader will stay with the plot to see how they get together.

Heroine

The heroine is a modern American woman between the ages of nineteen and twenty-eight who reflects today's concerns. The story is told in the third person from her point of view. She is attractive and nicely dressed but not glamorous; glitter and sophistication should be reserved for the other woman (the heroine's rival for the hero), whose flashiness will compare unfavorably with the heroine's modesty. When the heroine does dress up, however, her beauty should be stunningly apparent. Her trim figure is appealing but not abundant; a petite healthy appearance is desirable. Both her looks and her clothes should be generously detailed.

Her personality is spirited and independent without being pushy or stubborn because she knows when to give in. Although sensitive, she doesn't cry every time she is confronted with a problem (though she might cry in private moments). A sense of humor is helpful. Because she is on her own, away from parents (usually deceased) or other protective relationships, she is self-reliant as well as vulnerable. The story may begin with her on the verge of an important decision about her life. She is clearly competent but not entirely certain of her own qualities. She does not take her attractiveness for granted or realize how much the hero is drawn to her.

Common careers for the heroine include executive secretary, nurse, 5 teacher, interior designer, assistant manager, department store buyer, travel agent, or struggling photographer (no menial work). She can also be a doctor, lawyer, or other professional. Her job can be described in some detail and made exciting, but it must not dominate her life. Although she is smart, she is not extremely intellectual or defined by her work. Often she meets the hero through work, but her major concerns center on love, marriage, home, and family. White wine is okay, but she never drinks alone—or uses drugs. She may be troubled, frustrated, threatened, and momentarily thwarted in the course of the story, but she never totally gives in to despair or desperation. She has strengths that the hero recognizes and admires.

Hero

The hero should be about ten years older than the heroine and can be foreign or American. He needn't be handsome in a traditional sense, but he must be strongly masculine. Always tall and well built (not brawny or thick) and usually dark, he looks as terrific in a three-piece suit as he does in sports clothes. His clothes reflect good taste and an affluent lifestyle. Very successful professionally and financially, he is a man in charge of whatever work he's engaged in (financier, doctor, publisher, architect, business executive, airline pilot, artist, etc.). His wealth is manifested in his sophistication and experience.

His past may be slightly mysterious or shrouded by some painful moment (perhaps with a woman) that he doesn't want to discuss. Whatever the circumstance — his wife's death or divorce are common — it was not his fault. Avoid chronic problems such as alcoholism, drug addiction, or sexual dysfunctions. To others he may appear moody, angry, unpredictable, and explosively passionate, but the heroine eventually comes to realize his warm, tender side. He should be attractive not only as a lover but also as a potential husband and father.

Secondary Characters

Because the major interest is in how the heroine will eventually get together with the hero, the other characters are used to advance the action. There are three major types:

(1) *The Other Woman:* Her vices serve to accent the virtues of the heroine; immediately beneath her glamorous sophistication is a deceptive, selfish, mean-spirited, rapacious predator. She may seem to have the hero in her clutches, but she never wins him in the end.

(2) *The Other Man:* He usually falls into two types: (a) the decent sort who is there when the hero isn't around and (b) the selfish sort who schemes rather than loves. Neither is a match for the hero.

(3) *Other Characters:* Like furniture, they fill in the background and are useful for positioning the hero and heroine. These characters are familiar types such as the hero's snobbish aunt, the heroine's troubled younger siblings, the loyal friend, or the office gossip. They should be realistic, but they must not be allowed to obscure the emphasis on the lovers. The hero may have children from a previous marriage, but they should rarely be seen or heard. It's usually simpler and better not to include them.

Setting

The setting is usually contemporary. Romantic, exciting places are best: New York City, London, Paris, Rio, the mountains, the ocean — wherever it is exotic and love's possibilities are the greatest. Marriage may take the heroine and hero to a pretty suburb or small town.

Love Scenes

The hero and heroine may make love before marriage. The choice will depend largely on the heroine's sensibilities and circumstances. She should reflect modern attitudes. If the lovers do engage in premarital sex, it should be made clear that neither is promiscuous, especially the heroine. Even if their relationship is consummated before marriage, their lovemaking should not occur until late in the story. There should be at least several passionate scenes, but complications, misunderstandings, and interruptions should keep the couple from actually making love until they have made a firm commitment to each other. Descriptions should appeal to the senses; however, detailed, graphic close-ups are unacceptable. Passion can be presented sensually but not clinically; the lovemaking should be seen through a soft romantic lens. Violence and any out-of-the-way sexual acts should not even be hinted at. No coarse language.

Writing

Avoid extremely complex sentences, very long paragraphs, and lengthy descriptions. Use concise, vivid details to create the heroine's world. Be sure to include full descriptions of the hero's and heroine's physical features and clothes. Allow the reader to experience the romantic mood surrounding the lovers. Show how the heroine feels; do not simply report her feelings. Dialogue should sound like ordinary conversation, and the overall writing should be contemporary English without slang, difficult foreign expressions, strange dialects, racial epithets, or obscenities (*hell, damn,* and a few other mild swears are all right).

Length

55,000 to 65,000 words in ten to twelve chapters.   15

Considerations for Critical Thinking and Writing

1. **First response.** Given the expectations implied by the tip sheet, what generalizations can you make about those likely to write formula fiction? Does the tip sheet change the way you think about romantic fiction or other kinds of formula fiction?

2. Who is the intended audience for this type of novel? Try to describe the audience in detail: How does a romance novel provide escape for these readers?

3. Why should the hero be "about ten years older than the heroine"? If he is divorced, why is it significant that "it was not his fault"?

4. Why do you think the hero and heroine are kept apart by complications until the end of the story? Does the outline of the plot sound familiar to you or remind you of any other stories?

5. Why do you think restrictions are placed on the love scenes?

6. Why are "extremely complex sentences, very long paragraphs, and lengthy descriptions" discouraged?

7. Explain how the tip sheet confirms traditional views of male and female roles in society. Does it accommodate any broken traditions?

8. **Creative response.** Try writing a scene for a formula romance, or read the excerpt from Edgar Rice Burroughs's *Tarzan of the Apes* (p. 45) and try an adventure scene.

A COMPARISON OF TWO STORIES

Each of the following contemporary pieces of fiction is about a woman who experiences deep sorrow. The first, from *A Secret Sorrow* by Karen van der Zee, is an excerpt from a romance by Harlequin Books, a major publisher of formula fiction that has sold well over a billion copies of its romance titles — enough to supply about 20 percent of the world's population. The second piece, Gail Godwin's "A Sorrowful Woman," is a complete short story that originally appeared in *Esquire;* it is not a formula story.

Read each selection carefully and look for evidence of formulaic writing in the chapters from *A Secret Sorrow.* Pay particular attention to the advice on plotting and characterization offered in the composite tip sheet. As you read Godwin's short story, think about how it is different from van der Zee's excerpt; note also any similarities. The questions that follow the stories should help you consider how the experiences of reading the two are different.

KAREN VAN DER ZEE (B. 1947)

Born and raised in Holland, Karen van der Zee lives in the United States, where she has become a successful romance writer, contributing more than thirty novels to the popular Harlequin series. This excerpt consists of the final two chapters of *A Secret Sorrow.* This is what has happened so far: The central character, Faye, is recuperating from the psychological effects of a serious car accident in which she received a permanent internal injury. After the accident, she quits her job and breaks her engagement to Greg. She moves into her brother Chuck's house and falls in love with Kai, a visit-

By permission of the author.

ing Texan and good friend of her brother. At the end of Chapter 10, Kai insists on knowing why she will not marry him and asks, "Who is Doctor Jaworski?"

From *A Secret Sorrow*   1981

Chapter Eleven

Faye could feel the blood drain from her face and for one horrifying moment she thought she was going to faint right in Kai's arms. The room tilted and everything swirled around in a wild madman's dance. She clutched at him for support, fighting for control, trying to focus at some point beyond his shoulder. Slowly, everything steadied.

"I . . . I don't know him," she murmured at last. "I . . . "

He reached in the breast pocket of his shirt, took out a slip of paper, and held it out for her to see. One glance and Faye recognized it as the note from Doctor Martin with Doctor Jaworski's name scrawled on it, thickly underlined.

"How did you get that?" Her voice was a terrified whisper. She was still holding on, afraid she would fall if she let go.

"I found it on the floor in my bedroom. It must have fallen out of 5 your wallet along with everything else on Saturday morning."

Yes—oh God! Her legs were shaking so badly, she knew it was only his arms that kept her from falling.

"Who is Doctor Jaworski, Faye?" His voice was patiently persistent.

"I . . . he . . . " Her voice broke. "Let me go, please let me go." She felt as if she were suffocating in his embrace and she struggled against him, feebly, but it was no use.

"He's a psychiatrist, isn't he?" His voice was gentle, very gentle, and she looked up at him in stunned surprise.

He knew, oh God, he knew. She closed her eyes, a helpless sense of 10 inevitability engulfing her.

"You know," she whispered. "How do you know?"

"Simple. Two minutes on the phone to Chicago." He paused. "Doctor Martin—was he one of the doctors who treated you at the hospital?"

"Yes."

"Why did he give you Doctor Jaworski's name? Did he want you to make an appointment with him?"

"Yes." Despondency overtook her. There was no going back now. No 15 escape from the truth. No escape from his arms. Resistance faded and she felt numbed and lifeless. It didn't matter any more. Nothing mattered.

"Did you?" Kai repeated.

"Did I what?"

"See him—Doctor Jaworski."

"No."

"Why did Doctor Martin want you to see a psychiatrist?" 20

"I . . . " Faye swallowed miserably. "It's . . . it's therapy for grieving . . . mourning." She made a helpless gesture with her hand. "When people lose a . . . a wife, or husband for instance, they go through a more or less predictable pattern of emotions . . . " She gave him a quick glance, then looked away. "Like denial, anger. . . . "

" . . . depression, mourning, acceptance," Kai finished for her, and she looked back at him in surprise.

"Yes."

His mouth twisted in a little smile. "I'm not totally ignorant about subjects other than agronomy." There was a momentary pause as he scrutinized her face. "Why did you need that kind of therapy, Faye?"

And then it was back again, the resistance, the revolt against his 25 probing questions. She stiffened in defense—her whole body growing rigid with instinctive rebellion.

"It's none of your business!"

"Oh, yes, it is. We're talking about our life together. Your life and mine."

She strained against him, hands pushing against his chest. "Let me go! Please let me go!" Panic changed into tears. She couldn't take his nearness any more, the feel of his hard body touching hers, the strength of him.

"No, Faye, no. You're going to tell me. Now. I'm not letting you go until you've told me everything. Everything, you hear?"

"I can't!" she sobbed. "I can't!"

"Faye," he said slowly, "you'll *have* to. You told me you love me, but you don't want to marry me. You have given me no satisfactory reasons, and I'll be damned if I'm going to accept your lack of explanations."

"You have no right to demand an explanation!"

"Oh, yes, I have. You're part of me, Faye. Part of my life."

"You talk as if you own me!" She was trembling, struggling to get away from him. She couldn't stand there, so close to him with all the pent-up despair inside her, the anger, the fear of what she knew not how to tell him.

His hands were warm and strong on her back, holding her steady. Then, with one hand, he tilted back her head and made her look at him. "You gave me your love — I own that," he said softly. "True loving involves commitment, vulnerability, trust. Don't you trust me, Faye?"

New tears ran silently down her cheeks. "If I told you," she blurted out, "you wouldn't . . . you wouldn't . . . "

"I wouldn't *what?*"

"You wouldn't want me any more!" The words were wrenched from her in blind, agonizing grief. "You wouldn't *want* me any more!"

He shook his head incredulously. "What makes you think you can make that decision for me? Do you have so little trust in my love for you?"

Faye didn't answer, couldn't answer. Through a mist of tears he was nothing but a blur in front of her eyes.

"What is so terrible that you can't tell me?"

She shrank inwardly, as if shriveling away in pain. "Let me go," she whispered. "Please let me go and I'll tell you."

After a moment's hesitation Kai released her. Faye backed away from him, feeling like a terrified animal. She stood with her back against the wall, glad for the support, her whole body shaking. She took a deep breath and wiped her face dry with her hand.

"I'm afraid . . . afraid to marry you."

"Afraid?" He looked perplexed. "Afraid of what? Of me? Of marriage?"

Faye closed her eyes, taking another deep breath. "I can't be what you want me to be. We can't have the kind of life you want." She looked at him, standing only a few feet away, anguish tearing through her. "I'm so afraid . . . you'll be disappointed," she whispered.

"Oh God, Faye," he groaned, "I love you." He came toward her and panic surged through her as he held her against the wall, his hands reaching up to catch her face between them.

30

35

40

45

"Don't," she whispered. "Please, don't touch me." But it was no use. His mouth came down on hers and he kissed her with a hard, desperate passion.

"I love you," he said huskily. "I love you."

Faye wrenched her face free from his hands. "Don't touch me! Please   50
don't touch me!" She was sobbing now, her words barely audible. Her knees gave way and her back slid down along the wall until she crumpled on to the floor, face in her hands.

Kai took a step backward and pulled her up. "Stand up, Faye. For God's sake stand up!" He held her against the wall and she looked at him, seeing every line in his dark face, the intense blue of his eyes, and knew that this was the moment, that there was no more waiting.

And Kai knew it too. His eyes held hers locked in unrelenting demand. "Why should I be disappointed, Faye? *Why?*"

Her heart was thundering in her ears and it seemed as if she couldn't breathe, as if she were going to drown.

"Because . . . because I can't give you children! Because I can't get pregnant! I can't have babies! That's why!" Her voice was an agonized cry, torn from the depths of her misery. She yanked down his arms that held her locked against the wall and moved away from him. And then she saw his face.

It was ashen, gray under his tan. He stared at her as if he had never   55
seen her before.

"Oh my God, Faye . . . " His voice was low and hoarse. "Why didn't you tell me, why . . . "

Faye heard no more. She ran out the door, snatching her bag off the chair as she went by. The only thought in her mind was to get away — away from Kai and what was in his eyes.

She reached for Kai's spare set of car keys in her bag, doing it instinctively, knowing she couldn't walk home alone in the dark. How she managed to get the keys in the door lock and in the ignition she never knew. Somehow, she made it home.

The phone rang as Faye opened the front door and she heard Chuck answer it in the kitchen.

"She's just got in," he said into the mouthpiece, smiling at Faye   60
as she came into view. He listened for a moment, nodded. "Okay, fine with me."

Faye turned and walked up the stairs, taking deep breaths to calm her shattered nerves. Kai hadn't wasted any time checking up on her. She didn't care what he was telling Chuck, but she wasn't going to stand there listening to a one-sided conversation. But only a second later Chuck was behind her on the stairs.

"Kai wanted to know whether you'd arrived safely."

"I did, thank you," she said levelly, her voice surprisingly steady.

"I take it you ran out and took off with his car?"

"Did he say that?"   65

"No. He was *worried* about you. He wanted to make sure you went home." He sounded impatient, and she couldn't blame him. She was making life unbearable for everyone around her. Everybody worried about her. Everybody loved her. Everything should be right. Only it wasn't.

"Well, I'm home now, and I'm going to bed. Good night."

"Good night, Faye."

Faye lay in bed without any hope of sleep. Mechanically she started to sort through her thoughts and emotions, preparing mentally for the next confrontation. There would be one, she didn't doubt it for a moment. But she needed time — time to clear her head, time to look at everything in a reasonable, unemotional way.

It was a temptation to run — get in the car and keep driving, but it 70 would be a stupid thing to do. There was no place for her to go, and Kai would find her, no matter what. If there was one thing she knew about Kai it was his stubbornness and his persistence. She had to stick it out, right here, get it over with, deal with it. Only she didn't know how.

She lay listening to the stillness, just a few sounds here and there — the house creaking, a car somewhere in the distance, a dog barking. She had to think, but her mind refused to cooperate. She *had* to think, decide what to say to Kai the next time she saw him, but she couldn't think, she *couldn't think.*

And then, as she heard the door open in the silence, the quiet footsteps coming up the stairs, she knew it was too late, that time had run out.

Without even knocking he came into her room and walked over to the bed. She could feel the mattress sag as his weight came down on it. Her heart was pounding like a sledgehammer, and then his arms came around her and he drew her against him.

"Faye," he said quietly, "please marry me."

"No," she said thickly. "No." She could feel him stiffen against her 75 and she released herself from his arms and slid off the bed. She switched on the light and stood near the window, far from the bed, far from Kai. "I don't expect you to play the gentleman, I don't expect you to throw out a life of dreams just for the sake of chivalry. You don't have to marry me, Kai." She barely recognized her own voice. It was like the cool calm sound of a stranger, unemotional, cold. "You don't have to marry me," she repeated levelly, giving him a steady look.

Her words were underlined by the silence that followed, a silence loaded with a strange, vibrating energy, a force in itself, filling the room.

Kai rose to his feet, slowly, and the face that looked at her was like that of a stranger, a dangerous, angry stranger. Never before had she seen him so angry, so full of hot, fuming fury.

"Shut up," he said in a low, tight voice. "Shut up and stop playing the martyr!"

The sound of his voice and the words he said shocked Faye into silence. She stared at him open-mouthed, and then a slow, burning anger arose inside her.

"How dare you! How . . ."   80

He strode toward her and took her upper arms and shook her. "Shut up and listen to me! What the hell are you thinking? What the hell did you expect me to do when you told me? You throw me a bomb and then walk out on me! What did you expect my reaction to be? Was I supposed to stay cool and calm and tell you it didn't matter? Would you have married me then? Well, let me tell you something! It matters! It matters to me! I am not apologizing for my reaction!" He paused, breathing hard. "You know I always wanted children, but what in God's name makes you think you're the only one who has the right to feel bad about it? I have that right too, you hear! I love you, dammit, and I want to marry you, and if we can't have children I have all the right in the world to feel bad about it!"

He stopped talking. He was still breathing hard and he looked at her with stormy blue eyes. Faye felt paralyzed by his tirade and she stared at him, incapable of speech. She couldn't move, she couldn't think.

"Why do you think I want you for my wife?" he continued on a calmer note. "Because you're some kind of baby factory? What kind of man do you think I am? I love *you*, not your procreating ability. So we have a problem. Well, we'll learn to deal with it, one way or another."

There was another silence, and still Faye didn't speak, and she realized she was crying, soundlessly, tears slowly dripping down her cheeks. She was staring at his chest, blindly, not knowing what to think, not thinking at all.

He lifted her chin, gently. "Look at me, Faye."   85

She did, but his face was only a blur.

"Faye, we're in this together — you and I. Don't you see that? It's not just *your* problem, it's *ours*."

"No," she whispered. "No!" She shook her head wildly. "You have a choice, don't you see that? You don't have to marry me. You could marry someone else and have children of your own."

"Oh, God, Faye," he groaned, "you're wrong. Don't you know? Don't you see? I *don't* have a choice. I never did have a choice, or a chance. Not since I met you and fell in love with you. I don't *want* anybody else, don't you understand that? I want you, only you."

She wanted to believe it, give in to him. Never before had she wanted 90
anything more desperately than she wanted to give in to him now. But she couldn't, she couldn't. . . . She closed her eyes, briefly, fighting for reason, common sense.

"Kai, I . . . I can't live all my life with your regret and your disappointment. Every time we see some pregnant woman, every time we're with somebody else's children I'll feel I've failed you! I . . . " Her voice broke and new sobs came unchecked.

He held her very tightly until she calmed down and then he put her from him a little and gave her a dark, compelling look.

"It's not *my* regret, or *my* disappointment," he said with quiet emphasis. "It's *ours*. We're not talking about *you* or *me*. We're talking about *us*. I love you, and you love me, and that's the starting point, that comes first. From then on we're in it together."

Faye moved out of his arms, away from him, but her legs wouldn't carry her and she sank into a chair. She covered her face with her hands and tried desperately to stop the crying, to stop the tears from coming and coming as if they would never end.

"How . . . how can I ever believe it?"   95

"Because I'm asking you to," he said quietly. He knelt in front of her, took her hands away from her wet face. "Look at me, Faye. No other woman can give me what you can—yourself, your love, your warmth, your sense of humor. All the facets of your personality that make up the final you. I've known other women, Faye, but none of them have ever stirred in me any feelings that come close to what I feel for you. You're an original, remember? There's no replacement for an original. There are only copies, and I don't want a copy. To me you're special, and you'll have to believe it, take it on faith. That's what love is all about."

He was holding her hands in his, strong brown hands, and she was looking down on them, fighting with herself, fighting with everything inside her to believe what he was saying, to accept it, to give in to it.

Leaning forward, Kai kissed her gently on the mouth and smiled. "It's all been too much too soon for you, hasn't it? You never really got a chance to get over the shock, and when I fell in love with you it only made things worse." He smiled ruefully and Faye was surprised at his insight.

"Yes," she said. "It all happened too fast."

"Bad timing. If only we could have met later, after you'd sorted it all   100 out in your mind, then it would never have been such a crisis."

She looked at him doubtfully. "It wouldn't have changed the facts."

"No, but it might have changed your perspective."

Would it have? she wondered. Could she ever feel confident and secure in her worth as a woman? Or was she at this moment too emotionally bruised to accept that possibility?

"I don't understand," he said, "why I never guessed what was wrong. Now that I know, it all seems so obvious." He looked at her thoughtfully. "Faye," he said gently, "I want you to tell me exactly what happened to you, what Doctor Martin told you."

She stared at him, surprised a little. A thought stirred in the back of   105 her mind. Greg. He had never even asked. The why and the what had not interested him. But Kai, he wanted to know. She swallowed nervously and began the story, slowly, word for word, everything Doctor Martin had said. And he listened, quietly, not interrupting. "So you see," she said at last, "we don't have to hope for any miracles either."

"We'll make our own miracles," he said, and smiled. "Come here," he said then, "kiss me."

She did, shyly almost, until he took over and lifted her up and carried her to the bed. He looked down on her, eyes thoughtful. "I won't pretend I understand your feelings about this, the feelings you have about yourself as a woman, but I'll try." He paused for a moment. "Faye," he said then, speaking with slow emphasis, "don't *ever*, not for a single moment, think that you're not good enough for me. You're the best there is, Faye, the very best."

His mouth sought hers and he kissed her with gentle reassurance at first, then with rising ardor. His hands moved over her body, touching her with sensual, intimate caresses.

"You're my woman, Faye, you're mine . . . "

Her senses reeled. She could never love anyone like she loved him.   110 No one had ever evoked in her this depth of emotion. This was real, this was forever. Kai wanted her as much as ever. No chivalry, this, no game of pretense, she was very sure of that. And when he lifted his face and looked at her, it was all there in his eyes and the wonder of it filled her with joy.

"Do you believe me now?" he whispered huskily. "Do you believe I love you and want you and need you?"

She nodded wordlessly, incapable of uttering a sound.

"And do you love me?"

Again she nodded, her eyes in his.

"Okay, then." In one smooth flowing movement he got to his feet.   115 He crossed to the closet, opened it, and took out her suitcases. He put one on the end of the bed and began to pile her clothes in it, taking armfuls out of the closet.

Faye watched incredulously. "What are you doing?" she managed at last.

Kai kept on moving around, opening drawers, taking out her things, filling the suitcase until it could hold no more. "Get dressed. We're going home."

"Home . . . ?"

For a moment he stopped and he looked at her with a deep blue glitter in his eyes. "Yes, *home* — where you belong. With me, in my house, in my bed, in my arms."

"Oh, Kai," she said tremulously, smiling suddenly. "It's midnight!"   120

His eyes were very dark. "I've waited long enough, I'm not waiting any more. You're coming with me, now. And I'm not letting you out of my sight until we're safely married. I don't want you getting any crazy ideas about running off to save me from myself, or some such notion."

Her throat was dry. "Please, let's not rush into it! Let's think about it first!"

Calmly he zipped up the full suitcase, swung it off the bed, and put it near the door. "I'm not rushing into anything," he said levelly. "I've wanted to marry you for quite a while, remember?"

He crossed to the bed, sat down next to her, and put his arm around her. "Faye, I wish you wouldn't worry so. I'm not going to change my mind. And I haven't shelved my hopes for a family, either." There was a brief silence. "When we're ready to have kids, we'll have them. We'll adopt them. There are orphanages the world over, full of children in need of love and care. We'll do whatever it takes. We'll get them, one way or another."

Faye searched his face, faint hope flickering deep inside her.   125

"Would you want that?"

"Why not?"

"I don't know, really. I thought you . . . it isn't the same."

"No," he said levelly, "it isn't. Adoption is a different process from pregnancy and birth, but the kids will be ours just the same and we'll love them no less."

"Yes," she said, "yes." And suddenly it seemed as if a light had been   130 turned on inside her, as if suddenly she could see again, a future with Kai, a future with children.

A bronzed hand lifted her face. "Look, Faye, I'll always be sorry. I'll always be sorry not to see you pregnant, not to see you with a big stomach knowing you're carrying my child, but I'll live."

Faye lowered her eyes and tears threatened again. With both his hands he cupped her face.

"Look at me, Faye. I want you to stop thinking of yourself as a machine with a defect. You're not a damaged piece of merchandise, you hear? You're a living, breathing human being, a warm-blooded female, and I love you."

Through a haze of tears she looked at him, giving a weak smile. "I love you too." She put her arms around him and he heaved an unsteady breath.

"Faye," he said huskily, "you're my first and only choice."   135

Chapter Twelve

Kai and Faye had their family, two girls and a boy. They came to them one at a time, from faraway places, with small faces and large dark eyes full of fear. In their faces Faye could read the tragedies of war and death and poverty. They were hungry for love, hungry for nourishment and care. At night they woke in terror, screaming, their memories alive in sleep.

Time passed, and in the low white ranch house under the blue skies of Texas they flourished like the crops in the fields. They grew tall and straight and healthy and the fear in their dark eyes faded. Like their father they wore jeans and boots and large-brimmed hats, and they rode horses and played the guitar. They learned to speak English with a Southern twang.

One day Kai and Faye watched them as they played in the garden, and joy and gratitude overflowed in Faye's heart. Life was good and filled with love.

"They're all ours," she said. Even now after all these years she sometimes still couldn't believe it was really so.

Kai smiled at her. His eyes, still very blue, crinkled at the corners.   140 "Yes, and you're all mine."

"They don't even look like us," she said. "Not even a tiny little bit." No blondes, no redheads.

Taking her in his arms, Kai kissed her. "They're true originals, like their mother. I wouldn't want it any other way."

There was love in his embrace and love in his words and in her heart there was no room now for doubt, no room for sorrow.

Sometimes in the night he would reach for her and she would wake to his touch, his hands on her breast, her stomach, searching. In the warm darkness of their bed she would come to him and they would hold each other close and she knew he had been dreaming.

She knew the dream. She was walking away from him, calling out   145 that she couldn't marry him, the words echoing all around. *"I can't marry you! I can't marry you!"* And Kai was standing there watching her go, terrified, unable to move, his legs frozen to the ground. He wanted to follow her, keep her from leaving, but his legs wouldn't move.

Kai had told her of the dream, of the panic that clutched at him as he watched her walk out of his life. And always he would wake and search for her in the big bed, and she knew of only one way to reassure him. And in the warm afterglow of lovemaking, their bodies close together, she knew that to him she was everything, to him she was the only woman, beautiful, complete, whole.

GAIL GODWIN (B. 1937)

Born in Birmingham, Alabama, Gail Godwin was educated at the University of North Carolina and the University of Iowa, where she earned a Ph.D. in English in 1971. She is a full-time writer who has won grants from the National Endowment for the Arts, the Guggenheim Foundation, and the American Institute for the Arts and Letters. Among her novels are *Glass People* (1971), *A Mother and Two Daughters* (1981), *The Finishing School* (1985), *Evensong* (1999), and *Queen of the Underworld* (2006). Her short stories have been collected in several volumes including *Dream Children* (1976) and *Mr. Bedford and the Muses* (1983).

Alan Carey / The Image Works.

A Sorrowful Woman   1971

Once upon a time there was a wife and mother one too many times

One winter evening she looked at them: the husband durable, receptive, gentle; the child a tender golden three. The sight of them made her so sad and sick she did not want to see them ever again.

She told the husband these thoughts. He was attuned to her; he understood such things. He said he understood. What would she like him to do? "If you could put the boy to bed and read him the story about the monkey who ate too many bananas, I would be grateful." "Of course," he said. "Why, that's a pleasure." And he sent her off to bed.

The next night it happened again. Putting the warm dishes away in the cupboard, she turned and saw the child's gray eyes approving her movements. In the next room was the man, his chin sunk in the open collar of his favorite wool shirt. He was dozing after her good supper. The shirt was the gray of the child's trusting gaze. She began yelping without tears, retching in between. The man woke in alarm and carried her in his arms to bed. The boy followed them up the stairs, saying, "It's all right, Mommy," but this made her scream. "Mommy is sick," the father said, "go wait for me in your room."

The husband undressed her, abandoning her only long enough to root beneath the eiderdown for her flannel gown. She stood naked except for her bra, which hung by one strap down the side of her body; she had not the impetus to shrug it off. She looked down at the right nipple, shriveled with chill, and thought, How absurd, a vertical bra. "If only there were instant sleep," she said, hiccuping, and the husband bundled her into the gown and went out and came back with a sleeping draught guaranteed swift. She was to drink a little glass of cognac followed by a big glass of dark liquid and afterwards there was just time to say Thank you and could you get him a clean pair of pajamas out of the laundry, it came back today.

The next day was Sunday and the husband brought her breakfast 5 in bed and let her sleep until it grew dark again. He took the child for a walk, and when they returned, red-cheeked and boisterous, the father made supper. She heard them laughing in the kitchen. He brought her up a tray of buttered toast, celery sticks, and black bean soup. "I am the luckiest woman," she said, crying real tears. "Nonsense," he said. "You need a rest from us," and went to prepare the sleeping draught, find the child's pajamas, select the story for the night.

She got up on Monday and moved about the house till noon. The boy, delighted to have her back, pretended he was a vicious tiger and followed her from room to room, growling and scratching. Whenever she came close, he would growl and scratch at her. One of his sharp little claws ripped her flesh, just above the wrist, and together they paused to watch a thin red line materialize on the inside of her pale arm and spill over in little beads. "Go away," she said. She got herself upstairs and locked the door. She called the husband's office and said, "I've locked myself away from him. I'm afraid." The husband told her in his richest voice to lie down, take it easy, and he was already on the phone to call one of the baby-sitters they often employed. Shortly after, she heard the girl let herself in, heard the girl coaxing the frightened child to come and play.

After supper several nights later, she hit the child. She had known she was going to do it when the father would see. "I'm sorry," she said, collapsing on the floor. The weeping child had run to hide. "What has happened to me, I'm not myself anymore." The man picked her tenderly from the floor and looked at her with much concern. "Would it help if we got, you know, a girl in? We could fix the room downstairs. I want you to feel freer," he said, understanding these things. "We have the money for a girl. I want you to think about it."

And now the sleeping draught was a nightly thing, she did not have to ask. He went down to the kitchen to mix it, he set it nightly beside her bed. The little glass and the big one, amber and deep rich brown, the flannel gown and the eiderdown.

The man put out the word and found the perfect girl. She was young, dynamic, and not pretty. "Don't bother with the room, I'll fix it up myself." Laughing, she employed her thousand energies. She painted the room white, fed the child lunch, read edifying books, raced the boy to the mailbox, hung her own watercolors on the fresh-painted walls, made spinach soufflé, cleaned a spot from the mother's coat, made them all laugh, danced in stocking feet to music in the white room after reading the child to sleep. She knitted dresses for herself and played chess with the husband. She washed and set the mother's soft ash-blonde hair and gave her neck rubs, offered to.

The woman now spent her winter afternoons in the big bedroom. 10 She made a fire in the hearth and put on slacks and an old sweater she had loved at school, and sat in the big chair and stared out the window at snow-ridden branches, or went away into long novels about other people moving through other winters.

The girl brought the child in twice a day, once in the later afternoon when he would tell of his day, all of it tumbling out quickly because there was not much time, and before he went to bed. Often now, the man took his wife to dinner. He made a courtship ceremony of it, inviting her beforehand so she could get used to the idea. They dressed and were beautiful together again and went out into the frosty night. Over candlelight he would say, "I think you are better, you know." "Perhaps I am," she would murmur. "You look . . . like a cloistered queen," he said once, his voice breaking curiously.

One afternoon the girl brought the child into the bedroom. "We've been out playing in the park. He found something he wants to give you, a surprise." The little boy approached her, smiling mysteriously. He placed his cupped hands in hers and left a live dry thing that spat brown juice in her palm and leapt away. She screamed and wrung her hands to be rid of the brown juice. "Oh, it was only a grasshopper," said the girl. Nimbly she crept to the edge of the curtain, did a quick knee bend, and reclaimed the creature, led the boy competently from the room.

"The girl upsets me," said the woman to her husband. He sat frowning on the side of the bed he had not entered for so long. "I'm sorry, but there it is." The husband stroked his creased brow and said he was sorry too. He really did not know what they would do without that treasure of a girl. "Why don't you stay here with me in bed," the woman said.

Next morning she fired the girl who cried and said, "I loved the little boy, what will become of him now?" But the mother turned away her face and the girl took down the watercolors from the walls, sheathed the records she had danced to, and went away.

"I don't know what we'll do. It's all my fault, I know. I'm such a bur- 15
den, I know that."

"Let me think. I'll think of something." (Still understanding these things.)

"I know you will. You always do," she said.

With great care he rearranged his life. He got up hours early, did the shopping, cooked the breakfast, took the boy to nursery school. "We will manage," he said, "until you're better, however long that is." He did his work, collected the boy from the school, came home and made the supper, washed the dishes, got the child to bed. He managed everything. One evening, just as she was on the verge of swallowing her draught, there was a timid knock on her door. The little boy came in wearing his pajamas. "Daddy has fallen asleep on my bed and I can't get in. There's not room."

Very sedately she left her bed and went to the child's room. Things were much changed. Books were rearranged, toys. He'd done some new drawings. She came as a visitor to her son's room, wakened the father and helped him to bed. "Ah, he shouldn't have bothered you," said the man, leaning on his wife. "I've told him not to." He dropped into his own bed and fell asleep with a moan. Meticulously she undressed him. She folded and hung his clothes. She covered his body with the bedclothes. She flicked off the light that shone in his face.

The next day she moved her things into the girl's white room. She 20
put her hairbrush on the dresser; she put a note pad and pen beside the bed. She stocked the little room with cigarettes, books, bread, and cheese. She didn't need much.

At first the husband was dismayed. But he was receptive to her needs. He understood these things. "Perhaps the best thing is for you to follow it through," he said. "I want to be big enough to contain whatever you must do."

All day long she stayed in the white room. She was a young queen, a virgin in a tower; she was the previous inhabitant, the girl with all the energies. She tried these personalities on like costumes, then discarded them. The room had a new view of streets she'd never seen that way before. The sun hit the room in late afternoon and she took to brushing her hair in the sun. One day she decided to write a poem. "Perhaps a sonnet." She took up her pen and pad and began working from words that had lately lain in her mind. She had choices for the sonnet, ABAB or

ABBA for a start. She pondered these possibilities until she tottered into a larger choice: she did not have to write a sonnet. Her poem could be six, eight, ten, thirteen lines, it could be any number of lines, and it did not even have to rhyme.

She put down the pen on top of the pad.

In the evenings, very briefly, she saw the two of them. They knocked on her door, a big knock and a little, and she would call Come in, and the husband would smile though he looked a bit tired, yet somehow this tiredness suited him. He would put her sleeping draught on the bedside table and say, "The boy and I have done all right today," and the child would kiss her. One night she tasted for the first time the power of his baby spit.

"I don't think I can see him anymore," she whispered sadly to the   25 man. And the husband turned away, but recovered admirably and said, "Of course, I see."

So the husband came alone. "I have explained to the boy," he said. "And we are doing fine. We are managing." He squeezed his wife's pale arm and put the two glasses on her table. After he had gone, she sat look-ing at the arm.

"I'm afraid it's come to that," she said. "Just push the notes under the door; I'll read them. And don't forget to leave the draught outside."

The man sat for a long time with his head in his hands. Then he rose and went away from her. She heard him in the kitchen where he mixed the draught in batches now to last a week at a time, storing it in a corner of the cupboard. She heard him come back, leave the big glass and the little one outside on the floor.

Outside her window the snow was melting from the branches, there were more people on the streets. She brushed her hair a lot and seldom read anymore. She sat in her window and brushed her hair for hours, and saw a boy fall off his new bicycle again and again, a dog chasing a squir-rel, an old woman peek slyly over her shoulder and then extract a parcel from a garbage can.

In the evening she read the notes they slipped under her door. The   30 child could not write, so he drew and sometimes painted his. The notes were painstaking at first; the man and boy offering the final strength of their day to her. But sometimes, when they seemed to have had a bad day, there were only hurried scrawls.

One night, when the husband's note had been extremely short, lov-ing but short, and there had been nothing from the boy, she stole out of her room as she often did to get more supplies, but crept upstairs instead and stood outside their doors, listening to the regular breathing of the man and boy asleep. She hurried back to her room and drank the draught.

She woke earlier now. It was spring, there were birds. She listened for sounds of the man and the boy eating breakfast; she listened for the roar of the motor when they drove away. One beautiful noon, she went out to look at her kitchen in the daylight. Things were changed. He had bought some new dish towels. Had the old ones worn out? The canisters seemed closer to the sink. She got out flour, baking powder, salt, milk (he bought a different brand of butter), and baked a loaf of bread and left it cooling on the table.

The force of the two joyful notes slipped under her door that evening pressed her into the corner of the little room; she had hardly space to breathe. As soon as possible, she drank the draught.

Now the days were too short. She was always busy. She woke with the first bird. Worked till the sun set. No time for hair brushing. Her fingers raced the hours.

Finally, in the nick of time, it was finished one late afternoon. Her ³⁵ veins pumped and her forehead sparkled. She went to the cupboard, took what was hers, closed herself into the little white room and brushed her hair for a while.

The man and boy came home and found: five loaves of warm bread, a roast stuffed turkey, a glazed ham, three pies of different fillings, eight molds of the boy's favorite custard, two weeks' supply of fresh-laundered sheets and shirts and towels, two hand-knitted sweaters (both of the same gray color), a sheath of marvelous watercolor beasts accompanied by mad and fanciful stories nobody could ever make up again, and a tablet full of love sonnets addressed to the man. The house smelled redolently of renewal and spring. The man ran to the little room, could not contain himself to knock, flung back the door.

"Look, Mommy is sleeping," said the boy. "She's tired from doing all our things again." He dawdled in a stream of the last sun for that day and watched his father roll tenderly back her eyelids, lay his ear softly to her breast, test the delicate bones of her wrist. The father put down his face into her fresh-washed hair.

"Can we eat the turkey for supper?" the boy asked.

CONSIDERATIONS FOR CRITICAL THINKING AND WRITING

1. **FIRST RESPONSE.** How did you respond to the excerpt from *A Secret Sorrow* and to "A Sorrowful Woman"? Do you like one more than the other? Is one of the women — Faye or Godwin's unnamed wife — more likable than the other?

2. Describe what you found appealing in each story. Can you point to passages in both that strike you as especially well written or interesting? Was there anything in either story that did not appeal to you? Why?

3. How do the two women's attitudes toward family life differ? How does that difference constitute the problem in each story?

4. How would you describe the theme — the central point and meaning — in each story?

5. To what extent might "A Sorrowful Woman" be regarded as an unromantic sequel to *A Secret Sorrow*?
6. Can both stories be read a second or third time and still be interesting? Why or why not?
7. Explain how you think a romance formula writer would end "A Sorrowful Woman," or write the ending yourself.
8. Contrast what marriage means in the two stories.

2

Plot

Never mistake motion for action.
— ERNEST HEMINGWAY

Created by a writer's imagination, a work of fiction need not be factual or historically accurate. Although actual people, places, and events may be included in fiction, facts are not as important as is the writer's use of them. We can learn much about Russian life in the early part of the nineteenth century from Leo Tolstoy's *War and Peace*, but that historical information is incidental to Tolstoy's exploration of human nature. Tolstoy, like most successful writers, makes us accept as real the world in his novel no matter how foreign it may be to our own reality. One of the ways a writer achieves this acceptance and engagement—and one of a writer's few obligations—is to interest us in what is happening in the story. We are carried into the writer's fictional world by the plot.

🏠 Explore the literary element in this chapter at bedfordstmartins.com/meyerlit.

 Plot is the author's arrangement of incidents in a story. It is the organizing principle that controls the order of events. This structure is, in a sense, what remains after a writer edits out what is irrelevant to the story being told. What is told takes on meaning as it is brought into focus by a skillful writer who selects and orders the events that constitute the story's plot. Events can be presented in a variety of orders. A chronological arrangement begins with what happens first, then second, and so on, until the last incident is related. The events in William Faulkner's "A Rose for Emily," however, are not arranged in chronological order because that would give away the story's surprise ending; instead, Faulkner moves back and forth between the past and present to provide information that leads up to the final startling moment (which won't be given away here either; the story begins on p. 52).

Some stories begin at the end and then lead up to why or how events worked out as they did. If you read the first paragraph of Ralph Ellison's "Battle Royal" (p. 180), you'll find an example of this arrangement that will make it difficult for you to stop reading. Stories can also begin in the middle of things (the Latin term for this common plot strategy is *in medias res*). In this kind of plot we enter the story on the verge of some important moment. John Updike's "A & P" (p. 157) begins with the narrator, a teenager working at a checkout counter in a supermarket, telling us: "In walks these three girls in nothing but bathing suits." Right away we are brought into the middle of a situation that will ultimately create the conflict in the story.

Another common strategy is the *flashback*, a device that informs us about events that happened before the opening scene of a work. Nearly all of Ellison's "Battle Royal" takes the form of a flashback as the narrator recounts how his identity as a black man was shaped by the circumstances that attended a high-school graduation speech he delivered twenty years earlier in a hotel ballroom before a gathering of the town's leading white citizens, most of whom were "quite tipsy." Whatever the plot arrangement, you should be aware of how the writer's conscious ordering of events affects your responses to the action.

EDGAR RICE BURROUGHS (1875–1950)

A great many stories share a standard plot pattern. The following excerpt from Edgar Rice Burroughs's novel *Tarzan of the Apes* provides a conventional plot pattern in which the *character*, an imagined person in the story, is confronted with a problem leading to a climactic struggle that is followed by a resolution of the problem. The elements of a conventional plot are easily recognizable to readers familiar with fast-paced, action-packed mysteries, spy thrillers, westerns, or adventure stories. These page-turners are carefully plotted so that the reader is swept up by the action.

Burroughs's novel, published in 1914 and the first of a series of enormously popular Tarzan books and films, charts the growth to manhood of a child raised in the African jungle by great apes. Tarzan struggles to survive his primitive beginnings and to reconcile what he has learned in the jungle with his equally powerful instincts to be a civilized human being. One of the more exciting moments in Tarzan's development is

his final confrontation with his old enemy,
Terkoz, a huge tyrannical ape that has kid-
napped Jane, a pretty nineteen-year-old
from Baltimore, Maryland, who has accompanied her father on an expedition to the
jungle.

In the chapter preceding this excerpt,
Tarzan falls in love with Jane and writes
this pointed, if not eloquent, note to her:
"I am Tarzan of the Apes. I want you. I am
yours. You are mine." Just as he finishes the
note, he hears "the agonized screams of a
woman" and rushes to their source to find
Esmeralda, Jane's maid, hysterical with fear
and grief. She reports that Jane, the fair and
gentle embodiment of civilization in the

Special Collection, Rare Books, Burroughs
Memorial Collection, University of Louisville.

story, has been carried off by a gorilla. Here is the first half of the next
chapter, which illustrates how Burroughs plots the sequence of events so
that the emphasis is on physical action.

From *Tarzan of the Apes*   *1914*

From the time Tarzan left the tribe of great anthropoids in which he had
been raised, it was torn by continual strife and discord. Terkoz proved
a cruel and capricious king, so that, one by one, many of the older and
weaker apes, upon whom he was particularly prone to vent his brutish
nature, took their families and sought the quiet and safety of the far
interior.

But at last those who remained were driven to desperation by the
continued truculence of Terkoz, and it so happened that one of them
recalled the parting admonition of Tarzan:

"If you have a chief who is cruel, do not do as the other apes do, and
attempt, any one of you, to pit yourself against him alone. But, instead,
let two or three or four of you attack him together. Then, if you will do
this, no chief will dare to be other than he should be, for four of you can
kill any chief who may ever be over you."

And the ape who recalled this wise counsel repeated it to several of
his fellows, so that when Terkoz returned to the tribe that day he found a
warm reception awaiting him.

There were no formalities. As Terkoz reached the group, five huge,   5
hairy beasts sprang upon him.

At heart he was an arrant coward, which is the way with bullies
among apes as well as among men; so he did not remain to fight and die,
but tore himself away from them as quickly as he could and fled into the
sheltering boughs of the forest.

Two more attempts he made to rejoin the tribe, but on each occasion he was set upon and driven away. At last he gave it up, and turned, foaming with rage and hatred, into the jungle.

For several days he wandered aimlessly, nursing his spite and looking for some weak thing on which to vent his pent anger.

It was in this state of mind that the horrible, manlike beast, swinging from tree to tree, came suddenly upon two women in the jungle.

He was right above them when he discovered them. The first inti- 10 mation Jane Porter had of his presence was when the great hairy body dropped to the earth beside her, and she saw the awful face and the snarling, hideous mouth thrust within a foot of her.

One piercing scream escaped her lips as the brute hand clutched her arm. Then she was dragged toward those awful fangs which yawned at her throat. But ere they touched that fair skin another mood claimed the anthropoid.

The tribe had kept his women. He must find others to replace them. This hairless white ape would be the first of his new household, and so he threw her roughly across his broad, hairy shoulders and leaped back into the trees, bearing Jane away.

Esmeralda's scream of terror had mingled once with that of Jane, and then, as was Esmeralda's manner under stress of emergency which required presence of mind, she swooned.

But Jane did not once lose consciousness. It is true that that awful face, pressing close to hers, and the stench of the foul breath beating upon her nostrils, paralyzed her with terror; but her brain was clear, and she comprehended all that transpired.

With what seemed to her marvelous rapidity the brute bore her 15 through the forest, but still she did not cry out or struggle. The sudden advent of the ape had confused her to such an extent that she thought now that he was bearing her toward the beach.

For this reason she conserved her energies and her voice until she could see that they had approached near enough to the camp to attract the succor she craved.

She could not have known it, but she was being borne farther and farther into the impenetrable jungle.

The scream that had brought Clayton and the two older men stumbling through the undergrowth had led Tarzan of the Apes straight to where Esmeralda lay, but it was not Esmeralda in whom his interest centered, though pausing over her he saw that she was unhurt.

For a moment he scrutinized the ground below and the trees above, until the ape that was in him by virtue of training and environment, combined with the intelligence that was his by right of birth, told his wondrous woodcraft the whole story as plainly as though he had seen the thing happen with his own eyes.

And then he was gone again into the swaying trees, following the 20 high-flung spoor which no other human eye could have detected, much less translated.

At boughs' ends, where the anthropoid swings from one tree to another, there is most to mark the trail, but least to point the direction of the quarry; for there the pressure is downward always, toward the small end of the branch, whether the ape be leaving or entering a tree. Nearer the center of the tree, where the signs of passage are fainter, the direction is plainly marked.

Here, on this branch, a caterpillar has been crushed by the fugitive's great foot, and Tarzan knows instinctively where that same foot would touch in the next stride. Here he looks to find a tiny particle of the demolished larva, ofttimes not more than a speck of moisture.

Again, a minute bit of bark has been upturned by the scraping hand, and the direction of the break indicates the direction of the passage. Or some great limb, or the stem of the tree itself has been brushed by the hairy body, and a tiny shred of hair tells him by the direction from which it is wedged beneath the bark that he is on the right trail.

Nor does he need to check his speed to catch these seemingly faint records of the fleeing beast.

To Tarzan they stand out boldly against all the myriad other scars 25 and bruises and signs upon the leafy way. But strongest of all is the scent, for Tarzan is pursuing up the wind, and his trained nostrils are as sensitive as a hound's.

There are those who believe that the lower orders are specially endowed by nature with better olfactory nerves than man, but it is merely a matter of development.

Man's survival does not hinge so greatly upon the perfection of his senses. His power to reason has relieved them of many of their duties, and so they have, to some extent, atrophied, as have the muscles which move the ears and scalp, merely from disuse.

The muscles are there, about the ears and beneath the scalp, and so are the nerves which transmit sensations to the brain, but they are underdeveloped because they are not needed.

Not so with Tarzan of the Apes. From early infancy his survival had depended upon acuteness of eyesight, hearing, smell, touch, and taste far more than upon the more slowly developed organ of reason.

The least developed of all in Tarzan was the sense of taste, for he could 30 eat luscious fruits, or raw flesh, long buried, with almost equal appreciation; but in that he differed but slightly from more civilized epicures.

Almost silently the ape-man sped on in the track of Terkoz and his prey, but the sound of his approach reached the ears of the fleeing beast and spurred it on to greater speed.

Three miles were covered before Tarzan overtook them, and then Terkoz, seeing that further flight was futile, dropped to the ground in a small open glade, that he might turn and fight for his prize or be free to escape unhampered if he saw that the pursuer was more than a match for him.

He still grasped Jane in one great arm as Tarzan bounded like a leopard into the arena which nature had provided for this primeval-like battle.

When Terkoz saw that it was Tarzan who pursued him, he jumped to the conclusion that this was Tarzan's woman, since they were of the same kind — white and hairless — and so he rejoiced at this opportunity for double revenge upon his hated enemy.

To Jane the strange apparition of this godlike man was as wine to   35
sick nerves.

From the description which Clayton and her father and Mr. Philander had given her, she knew that it must be the same wonderful creature who had saved them, and she saw in him only a protector and a friend.

But as Terkoz pushed her roughly aside to meet Tarzan's charge, and she saw the great proportions of the ape and the mighty muscles and the fierce fangs, her heart quailed. How could any vanquish such a mighty antagonist?

Like two charging bulls they came together, and like two wolves sought each other's throat. Against the long canines of the ape was pitted the thin blade of the man's knife.

Jane — her lithe, young form flattened against the trunk of a great tree, her hands tight pressed against her rising and falling bosom, and her eyes wide with mingled horror, fascination, fear, and admiration — watched the primordial ape battle with the primeval man for possession of a woman — for her.

As the great muscles of the man's back and shoulders knotted   40
beneath the tension of his efforts, and the huge biceps and forearm held at bay those mighty tusks, the veil of centuries of civilization and culture were swept from the blurred vision of the Baltimore girl.

When the long knife drank deep a dozen times of Terkoz's heart's blood, and the great carcass rolled lifeless upon the ground, it was a primeval woman who sprang forward with outstretched arms toward the primeval man who had fought for her and won.

And Tarzan?

He did what no red-blooded man needs lessons in doing. He took his woman in his arms and smothered her upturned, panting lips with kisses.

For a moment Jane lay there with half-closed eyes. For a moment — the first in her young life — she knew the meaning of love.

But as suddenly as the veil had been withdrawn it dropped again,   45
and an outraged conscience suffused her face with its scarlet mantle, and a mortified woman thrust Tarzan of the Apes from her and buried her face in her hands.

Tarzan had been surprised when he had found the girl he had learned to love after a vague and abstract manner a willing prisoner in his arms. Now he was surprised that she repulsed him.

He came close to her once more and took hold of her arm. She turned upon him like a tigress, striking his great breast with her tiny hands.

Tarzan could not understand it.

A moment ago, and it had been his intention to hasten Jane back to her people, but that little moment was lost now in the dim and distant past of things which were but can never be again, and with it the good intention had gone to join the impossible.

Since then Tarzan of the Apes had felt a warm, lithe form close 50 pressed to his. Hot, sweet breath against his cheek and mouth had fanned a new flame to life within his breast, and perfect lips had clung to his in burning kisses that had seared a deep brand into his soul — a brand which marked a new Tarzan.

Again he laid his hand upon her arm. Again she repulsed him. And then Tarzan of the Apes did just what his first ancestor would have done.

He took his woman in his arms and carried her into the jungle.

This episode begins with *exposition*, the background information the reader needs to make sense of the situation in which the characters are placed. The first eight paragraphs let us know that Terkoz has been overthrown as leader of the ape tribe and that he is roaming the jungle "looking for some weak thing on which to vent his pent anger." This exposition is in the form of a flashback. (Recall that the previous chapter ended with Esmeralda's report of the kidnapping; now we will see what happened.)

Once this information supplies a context for the characters, the plot gains momentum with the *rising action*, a complication that intensifies the situation: Terkoz, looking for a victim, discovers the vulnerable Esmeralda and Jane. His first impulse is to kill Jane, but his "mood" changes when he remembers that he has no woman of his own after having been forced to leave the tribe (more exposition). Hence, there is a further complication in the rising action when he decides to carry her off. Just when it seems that the situation could not get any worse, it does. The reader is invited to shudder even more than if Terkoz had made a meal of Jane because she may have to endure the "awful face," "foul breath," and lust of this beast.

When Tarzan finally catches up to Terkoz, the *conflict* of this episode fully emerges. Tarzan must save the woman he loves by defeating his long-standing enemy. Terkoz seeks to achieve a "double revenge" by killing Tarzan and taking his woman. Terkoz's assumption that Jane is Tarzan's woman is a *foreshadowing*, a suggestion of what is yet to come. In this conflict Tarzan is the *protagonist* or *hero*, the central character who engages our interest and empathy. *Protagonist* is often a more useful term than *hero* or *heroine*, however, because the central character of a story can be despicable as well as heroic. Terkoz is the *antagonist*, the force that opposes the protagonist.

The battle between Tarzan and Terkoz creates *suspense* because the reader is made anxious about what is going to happen. Burroughs makes certain that the reader will worry about the outcome by having Jane wonder, "How could any vanquish such a mighty antagonist?" If we are caught up in the moment, we watch the battle, as Jane does, with "mingled horror, fascination, fear, and admiration" to see what will happen next. The moment of greatest emotional tension, the *climax*, occurs when Tarzan kills Terkoz. Tarzan's victory is the **resolution** of the conflict, also known as the *dénouement* (a French word meaning the "untying of the knot"). This could have been the conclusion to the episode except that Jane and Tarzan simultaneously discover their "primeval" selves sexually drawn to each other. Burroughs resolves one conflict — the battle with Terkoz — but then immediately creates another by raising the question of what a respectable professor's daughter from Baltimore is doing in the sweaty arms of a panting, half-naked man.

For a brief moment the cycle of conflict, suspense, and resolution begins again as Jane passionately kisses Tarzan; then her "outraged conscience" causes her to regain her sense of propriety and she pushes him away. Although Tarzan succeeds in the encounter with Terkoz, he is not successful with Jane. However, Burroughs creates suspense for a third time at the very end of the episode, when the "new Tarzan," having been transformed by this sexual awakening, "took his woman in his arms and carried her into the jungle." What will he do next? Despite the novel's implausibility (beginning with the premise that apes could raise a human child) and its heavy use of coincidences (not the least of which is Tarzan's donning a loincloth for the first time only four pages before he meets Jane), the story is difficult to put down. The plot swings us swiftly and smoothly from incident to incident, even if there is an occasional interruption, such as Burroughs's discussion of evolution, in the flow of the action.

The primary conflict that Tarzan experiences in his battle with Terkoz is external. External conflict is popular in adventure stories because the protagonist's physical struggles with a formidable foe or the ever-present dangers of a dense jungle echoing wild screams provide plenty of excitement. External conflicts may place the protagonist in opposition to another individual, nature, or society. Tarzan's battle with societal values begins the moment he instinctively takes Jane in his arms to carry her off into the jungle. He will learn that an individual's conflict with society can be as frustrating as it is complex, which is why so many plots in serious fiction focus on this conflict. It can be seen, to cite only two examples, in a mysterious stranger's alienation from a materialistic culture in Herman Melville's "Bartleby, the Scrivener" (p. 101) and in a young black man's struggle with racism in Ralph Ellison's "Battle Royal" (p. 180).

Conflict may also be internal; in such a case some moral or psychological issue must be resolved within the protagonist. Inner conflicts frequently accompany external ones, as in Godwin's "A Sorrowful Woman" (p. 36). Godwin's story is quiet and almost uneventful compared with *Tarzan of the Apes*. The conflict, though puzzling, is more significant in "A Sorrowful Woman" because that story subtly explores some troubling issues that cannot be resolved simply by "huge biceps" or a "lithe, young form." The protagonist struggles with both internal and external forces. We are not told why she withdraws from her considerate husband and beautiful son. There is no exposition to explain why she is hopelessly "sad and sick" of them. There is no readily identifiable antagonist in her way, but there are several possibilities. Her antagonist is some part of herself that cannot find satisfaction in playing the roles of wife and mother, yet her husband and child also seem to bear some of the responsibility, as does the domestic environment that defines her.

Although Burroughs makes enormous demands on Tarzan to survive the perils of the jungle, the author makes few demands on the reader. In part, that's why *Tarzan of the Apes* is so much fun: We sit back while Tarzan does all the work, struggling heroically through all the conflicts Burroughs has planted along his jungle paths. Godwin's story, in contrast, illustrates that there are other kinds of plots, less dependent on action but equally full of conflict. This kind of reading is more demanding, but ultimately often more satisfying, because as we confront conflicts in serious fiction we read not only absorbing stories but also ourselves. We are invited not to escape life but to look long and hard at it. Although serious fiction can be as diverting and pleasurable as most standard action-packed plots, serious fiction offers an additional important element: a perspective on experience that reflects rather than deflects life.

The two stories that follow — William Faulkner's "A Rose for Emily" and Andre Dubus's "Killings" — are remarkable for the different kinds of tension produced in each by a subtle use of plot.

WILLIAM FAULKNER (1897–1962)

Born into an old Mississippi family that had lost its influence and wealth during the Civil War, William Faulkner lived nearly all his life in the South writing about Yoknapatawpha County, an imagined Mississippi county similar to his home in Oxford. Among his novels based on this fictional location are *The Sound and the Fury* (1929), *As I Lay Dying* (1930), *Light in August* (1932), and *Absalom, Absalom!* (1936). Although his writings are regional in their emphasis on local social history, his concerns are broader. In his 1950 acceptance speech for the Nobel Prize for Literature, he insisted that the "problems of the human heart in conflict with itself . . . alone can make good writing because only that is worth writing about,

Courtesy of the Colfield Collection, Southern Media Archive, University of Mississippi. Special Collections.

worth the agony and the sweat." This commitment is evident in his novels and in *The Collected Stories of William Faulkner* (1950).

A Rose for Emily   1931

I

When Miss Emily Grierson died, our whole town went to her funeral: the men through a sort of respectful affection for a fallen monument, the women mostly out of curiosity to see the inside of her house, which no one save an old manservant—a combined gardener and cook—had seen in at least ten years.

It was a big, squarish frame house that had once been white, decorated with cupolas and spires and scrolled balconies in the heavily lightsome style of the seventies, set on what had once been our most select street. But garages and cotton gins had encroached and obliterated even the august names of that neighborhood; only Miss Emily's house was left, lifting its stubborn and coquettish decay above the cotton wagons and the gasoline pumps—an eyesore among eyesores. And now Miss Emily had gone to join the representatives of those august names where they lay in the cedar-bemused cemetery among the ranked and anonymous graves of Union and Confederate soldiers who fell at the battle of Jefferson.

Alive, Miss Emily had been a tradition, a duty, and a care; a sort of hereditary obligation upon the town, dating from that day in 1894 when Colonel Sartoris, the mayor—he who fathered the edict that no Negro woman should appear on the streets without an apron—remitted her taxes, the dispensation dating from the death of her father on into perpetuity. Not that Miss Emily would have accepted charity. Colonel Sartoris invented an involved tale to the effect that Miss Emily's father had loaned money to the town, which the town, as a matter of business, preferred this way of repaying. Only a man of Colonel Sartoris' generation and thought could have invented it, and only a woman could have believed it.

When the next generation, with its more modern ideas, became mayors and aldermen, this arrangement created some little dissatisfaction. On the first of the year they mailed her a tax notice. February came, and there was no reply. They wrote her a formal letter, asking her to call at the sheriff's office at her convenience. A week later the mayor wrote her himself, offering to call or to send his car for her, and received in reply a note on paper of an archaic shape, in a thin, flowing calligraphy in faded ink, to the effect that she no longer went out at all. The tax notice was also enclosed, without comment.

They called a special meeting of the Board of Aldermen. A deputation waited upon her, knocked at the door through which no visitor had passed since she ceased giving china-painting lessons eight or ten years earlier. They were admitted by the old Negro into a dim hall from which a stairway mounted into still more shadow. It smelled of dust and 5

disuse—a close, dank smell. The Negro led them into the parlor. It was
furnished in heavy, leather-covered furniture. When the Negro opened
the blinds of one window, they could see that the leather was cracked;
and when they sat down, a faint dust rose sluggishly about their thighs,
spinning with slow motes in the single sun-ray. On a tarnished gilt easel
before the fireplace stood a crayon portrait of Miss Emily's father.

They rose when she entered—a small, fat woman in black, with a
thin gold chain descending to her waist and vanishing into her belt, leaning on an ebony cane with a tarnished gold head. Her skeleton was small
and spare; perhaps that was why what would have been merely plump-
ness in another was obesity in her. She looked bloated, like a body long
submerged in motionless water, and of that pallid hue. Her eyes, lost in
the fatty ridges of her face, looked like two small pieces of coal pressed
into a lump of dough as they moved from one face to another while the
visitors stated their errand.

She did not ask them to sit. She just stood in the door and listened
quietly until the spokesman came to a stumbling halt. Then they could
hear the invisible watch ticking at the end of the gold chain.

Her voice was dry and cold. "I have no taxes in Jefferson. Colonel
Sartoris explained it to me. Perhaps one of you can gain access to the city
records and satisfy yourselves."

"But we have. We are the city authorities, Miss Emily. Didn't you get
a notice from the sheriff, signed by him?"

"I received a paper, yes," Miss Emily said. "Perhaps he considers him- 10
self the sheriff . . . I have no taxes in Jefferson."

"But there is nothing on the books to show that, you see. We must
go by the—"

"See Colonel Sartoris. I have no taxes in Jefferson."

"But, Miss Emily—"

"See Colonel Sartoris." (Colonel Sartoris had been dead almost ten
years.) "I have no taxes in Jefferson. Tobe!" The Negro appeared. "Show
these gentlemen out."

II

So she vanquished them, horse and foot, just as she had vanquished their 15
fathers thirty years before about the smell. That was two years after her
father's death and a short time after her sweetheart—the one we believed
would marry her—had deserted her. After her father's death she went
out very little; after her sweetheart went away, people hardly saw her at
all. A few of the ladies had the temerity to call, but were not received, and
the only sign of life about the place was the Negro man—a young man
then—going in and out with a market basket.

"Just as if a man—any man—could keep a kitchen properly," the
ladies said; so they were not surprised when the smell developed. It was
another link between the gross, teeming world and the high and mighty
Griersons.

A neighbor, a woman, complained to the mayor, Judge Stevens, eighty years old.

"But what will you have me do about it, madam?" he said.

"Why, send her word to stop it," the woman said. "Isn't there a law?"

"I'm sure that won't be necessary," Judge Stevens said. "It's probably 20 just a snake or a rat that nigger of hers killed in the yard. I'll speak to him about it."

The next day he received two more complaints, one from a man who came in diffident deprecation. "We really must do something about it, Judge. I'd be the last one in the world to bother Miss Emily, but we've got to do something." That night the Board of Aldermen met—three graybeards and one younger man, a member of the rising generation.

"It's simple enough," he said. "Send her word to have her place cleaned up. Give her a certain time to do it in, and if she don't . . . "

"Dammit, sir," Judge Stevens said, "will you accuse a lady to her face of smelling bad?"

So the next night, after midnight, four men crossed Miss Emily's lawn and slunk about the house like burglars, sniffing along the base of the brickwork and at the cellar openings while one of them performed a regular sowing motion with his hand out of a sack slung from his shoulder. They broke open the cellar door and sprinkled lime there, and in all the outbuildings. As they recrossed the lawn, a window that had been dark was lighted and Miss Emily sat in it, the light behind her, and her upright torso motionless as that of an idol. They crept quietly across the lawn and into the shadow of the locusts that lined the street. After a week or two the smell went away.

That was when people had begun to feel really sorry for her. People 25 in our town, remembering how old lady Wyatt, her great-aunt, had gone completely crazy at last, believed that the Griersons held themselves a little too high for what they really were. None of the young men were quite good enough for Miss Emily and such. We had long thought of them as a tableau, Miss Emily a slender figure in white in the background, her father a spraddled silhouette in the foreground, his back to her and clutching a horsewhip, the two of them framed by the back-flung front door. So when she got to be thirty and was still single, we were not pleased exactly, but vindicated; even with insanity in the family she wouldn't have turned down all of her chances if they had really materialized.

When her father died, it got about that the house was all that was left to her; and in a way, people were glad. At last they could pity Miss Emily. Being left alone, and a pauper, she had become humanized. Now she too would know the old thrill and the old despair of a penny more or less.

The day after his death all the ladies prepared to call at the house and offer condolence and aid, as is our custom. Miss Emily met them at the door, dressed as usual and with no trace of grief on her face. She told them that her father was not dead. She did that for three days, with the ministers calling on her, and the doctors, trying to persuade her to let them dispose of the body. Just as they were about to resort to law and force, she broke down, and they buried her father quickly.

We did not say she was crazy then. We believed she had to do that. We remembered all the young men her father had driven away, and we knew that with nothing left, she would have to cling to that which had robbed her, as people will.

III

She was sick for a long time. When we saw her again, her hair was cut short, making her look like a girl, with a vague resemblance to those angels in colored church windows — sort of tragic and serene.

The town had just let the contracts for paving the sidewalks, and in the summer after her father's death they began the work. The construction company came with niggers and mules and machinery, and a foreman named Homer Barron, a Yankee — a big, dark, ready man, with a big voice and eyes lighter than his face. The little boys would follow in groups to hear him cuss the niggers, and the niggers singing in time to the rise and fall of picks. Pretty soon he knew everybody in town. Whenever you heard a lot of laughing anywhere about the square, Homer Barron would be in the center of the group. Presently we began to see him and Miss Emily on Sunday afternoons driving in the yellow-wheeled buggy and the matched team of bays from the livery stable.

At first we were glad that Miss Emily would have an interest, because the ladies all said, "Of course a Grierson would not think seriously of a Northerner, a day laborer." But there were still others, older people, who said that even grief could not cause a real lady to forget *noblesse oblige*° — without calling it *noblesse oblige*. They just said, "Poor Emily. Her kinsfolk should come to her." She had some kin in Alabama; but years ago her father had fallen out with them over the estate of old lady Wyatt, the crazy woman, and there was no communication between the two families. They had not even been represented at the funeral.

And as soon as the old people said, "Poor Emily," the whispering began. "Do you suppose it's really so?" they said to one another. "Of course it is. What else could . . . " This behind their hands; rustling of craned silk and satin behind jalousies closed upon the sun of Sunday afternoon as the thin, swift clop-clop-clop of the matched team passed: "Poor Emily."

She carried her head high enough — even when we believed that she was fallen. It was as if she demanded more than ever the recognition of her dignity as the last Grierson; as if it had wanted that touch

noblesse oblige: The obligation of people of high social position.

of earthiness to reaffirm her imperviousness. Like when she bought the rat poison, the arsenic. That was over a year after they had begun to say "Poor Emily," and while the two female cousins were visiting her.

"I want some poison," she said to the druggist. She was over thirty then, still a slight woman, though thinner than usual, with cold, haughty black eyes in a face the flesh of which was strained across the temples and about the eye-sockets as you imagine a lighthouse-keeper's face ought to look. "I want some poison," she said.

"Yes, Miss Emily. What kind? For rats and such? I'd recom—"   35

"I want the best you have. I don't care what kind."

The druggist named several. "They'll kill anything up to an elephant. But what you want is—"

"Arsenic," Miss Emily said. "Is that a good one?"

"Is . . . arsenic? Yes, ma'am. But what you want—"

"I want arsenic."   40

The druggist looked down at her. She looked back at him, erect, her face like a strained flag. "Why, of course," the druggist said. "If that's what you want. But the law requires you to tell what you are going to use it for."

Miss Emily just stared at him, her head tilted back in order to look him eye for eye, until he looked away and went and got the arsenic and wrapped it up. The Negro delivery boy brought her the package; the druggist didn't come back. When she opened the package at home there was written on the box, under the skull and bones: "For rats."

IV

So the next day we all said, "She will kill herself"; and we said it would be the best thing. When she had first begun to be seen with Homer Barron, we had said, "She will marry him." Then we said, "She will persuade him yet," because Homer himself had remarked—he liked men, and it was known that he drank with the younger men in the Elks' Club—that he was not a marrying man. Later we said, "Poor Emily" behind the jalousies as they passed on Sunday afternoon in the glittering buggy, Miss Emily with her head high and Homer Barron with his hat cocked and a cigar in his teeth, reins and whip in a yellow glove.

Then some of the ladies began to say that it was a disgrace to the town and a bad example to the young people. The men did not want to interfere, but at last the ladies forced the Baptist minister—Miss Emily's people were Episcopal—to call upon her. He would never divulge what happened during that interview, but he refused to go back again. The next Sunday they again drove about the streets, and the following day the minister's wife wrote to Miss Emily's relations in Alabama.

So she had blood-kin under her roof again and we sat back to watch   45
developments. At first nothing happened. Then we were sure that they were to be married. We learned that Miss Emily had been to the jeweler's

and ordered a man's toilet set in silver, with the letters H. B. on each piece. Two days later we learned that she had bought a complete outfit of men's clothing, including a nightshirt, and we said, "They are married." We were really glad. We were glad because the two female cousins were even more Grierson than Miss Emily had ever been.

So we were not surprised when Homer Barron — the streets had been finished some time since — was gone. We were a little disappointed that there was not a public blowing-off, but we believed that he had gone on to prepare for Miss Emily's coming, or to give her a chance to get rid of the cousins. (By that time it was a cabal, and we were all Miss Emily's allies to help circumvent the cousins.) Sure enough, after another week they departed. And, as we had expected all along, within three days Homer Barron was back in town. A neighbor saw the Negro man admit him at the kitchen door at dusk one evening.

And that was the last we saw of Homer Barron. And of Miss Emily for some time. The Negro man went in and out with the market basket, but the front door remained closed. Now and then we would see her at a window for a moment, as the men did that night when they sprinkled the lime, but for almost six months she did not appear on the streets. Then we knew that this was to be expected too; as if that quality of her father which had thwarted her woman's life so many times had been too virulent and too furious to die.

When we next saw Miss Emily, she had grown fat and her hair was turning gray. During the next few years it grew grayer and grayer until it attained an even pepper-and-salt iron-gray, when it ceased turning. Up to the day of her death at seventy-four it was still that vigorous iron-gray, like the hair of an active man.

From that time on her front door remained closed, save for a period of six or seven years, when she was about forty, during which she gave lessons in china-painting. She fitted up a studio in one of the downstairs rooms, where the daughters and granddaughters of Colonel Sartoris' contemporaries were sent to her with the same regularity and in the same spirit that they were sent to church on Sundays with a twenty-five-cent piece for the collection plate. Meanwhile her taxes had been remitted.

Then the newer generation became the backbone and the spirit of 50 the town, and the painting pupils grew up and fell away and did not send their children to her with boxes of color and tedious brushes and pictures cut from the ladies' magazines. The front door closed upon the last one and remained closed for good. When the town got free postal delivery, Miss Emily alone refused to let them fasten the metal numbers above her door and attach a mailbox to it. She would not listen to them.

Daily, monthly, yearly we watched the Negro grow grayer and more stooped, going in and out with the market basket. Each December we sent her a tax notice, which would be returned by the post office a week later, unclaimed. Now and then we would see her in one of the downstairs windows — she had evidently shut up the top floor of the house — like the carven torso of an idol in a niche, looking or not looking at us, we could never tell which. Thus she passed from generation to generation — dear, inescapable, impervious, tranquil, and perverse.

And so she died. Fell ill in the house filled with dust and shadows, with only a doddering Negro man to wait on her. We did not even know she was sick; we had long since given up trying to get information from the Negro. He talked to no one, probably not even to her, for his voice had grown harsh and rusty, as if from disuse.

She died in one of the downstairs rooms, in a heavy walnut bed with a curtain, her gray head propped on a pillow yellow and moldy with age and lack of sunlight.

V

The Negro met the first of the ladies at the front door and let them in, with their hushed, sibilant voices and their quick, curious glances, and then he disappeared. He walked right through the house and out the back and was not seen again.

The two female cousins came at once. They held the funeral on the second day, with the town coming to look at Miss Emily beneath a mass of bought flowers, with the crayon face of her father musing profoundly above the bier and the ladies sibilant and macabre; and the very old men — some in their brushed Confederate uniforms — on the porch and the lawn, talking of Miss Emily as if she had been a contemporary of theirs, believing that they had danced with her and courted her perhaps, confusing time with its mathematical progression, as the old do, to whom all the past is not a diminishing road but, instead, a huge meadow which no winter ever quite touches, divided from them now by the narrow bottle-neck of the most recent decade of years. 55

Already we knew that there was one room in that region above stairs which no one had seen in forty years, and which would have to be forced. They waited until Miss Emily was decently in the ground before they opened it.

The violence of breaking down the door seemed to fill this room with pervading dust. A thin, acrid pall as of the tomb seemed to lie everywhere upon this room decked and furnished as for a bridal: upon the valance curtains of faded rose color, upon the rose-shaded lights, upon the dressing table, upon the delicate array of crystal and the man's toilet things backed with tarnished silver, silver so tarnished that the monogram was obscured. Among them lay a collar and tie, as if they had just been removed, which, lifted, left upon the surface a pale crescent in the dust. Upon a chair hung the suit, carefully folded; beneath it the two mute shoes and the discarded socks.

The man himself lay in the bed.

For a long while we just stood there, looking down at the profound and fleshless grin. The body had apparently once lain in the attitude of an embrace, but now the long sleep that outlasts love, that conquers even the grimace of love, had cuckolded him. What was left of him, rotted beneath what was left of the nightshirt, had become inextricable from the bed in which he lay; and upon him and upon the pillow beside him lay that even coating of the patient and biding dust.

Then we noticed that in the second pillow was the indentation of a head. One of us lifted something from it, and leaning forward, that faint and invisible dust dry and acrid in the nostrils, we saw a long strand of iron-gray hair.

60

Considerations for Critical Thinking and Writing

1. **FIRST RESPONSE.** How might this story be rewritten as a piece of formula fiction? You could write it as a romance, detective, or horror story — whatever strikes your fancy. Does Faulkner's version have elements of formulaic fiction?

2. What is the effect of the final paragraph of the story? How does it contribute to your understanding of Emily? Why is it important that we get this information last rather than at the beginning of the story?

3. Contrast the order of events as they happen in the story with the order in which they are told. How does this plotting create interest and suspense?

4. Faulkner uses a number of gothic elements in this plot: the imposing decrepit house, the decayed corpse, and the mysterious secret horrors connected with Emily's life. How do these elements forward the plot and establish the atmosphere?

5. In what sense does the narrator's telling of the story serve as "A Rose for Emily"? Why do you think the narrator uses *we* rather than *I*?

6. Explain how Emily's reasons for murdering Homer are related to her personal history and to the ways she handled previous conflicts.

7. Discuss how Faulkner's treatment of the North and South contributes to the meaning of the story.

8. **CONNECTION TO ANOTHER SELECTION.** Contrast Faulkner's ordering of events with Peter Meinke's "The Cranes" (p. 192). How does each author's arrangement of incidents create different effects on the reader?

Andre Dubus (1936–1999)

Though a native of Louisiana, where he attended the Christian Brothers School and McNeese State College, Andre Dubus lived much of his life in Massachusetts; many of his stories are set in the Merrimack Valley north of Boston. After college Dubus served as an officer for five years in the Marine Corps. He then took an M.F.A. at the University of Iowa in 1966 and began

teaching at Bradford College in Massachusetts. His fiction earned him numerous
awards, and he was both a Guggenheim
and a MacArthur Fellow. Among his collections of fiction are *Separate Flights* (1975);
Adultery and Other Choices (1977); *Finding a
Girl in America* (1980), from which "Killings" is taken; *The Last Worthless Evening*
(1986); *Collected Stories* (1988); and *Dancing
after Hours* (1996). In 1991 he published *Broken Vessels,* a collection of autobiographical essays. His stories are often tense with
violence, anger, tenderness, and guilt; they
are populated by characters who struggle
to understand and survive their experiences, painful with failure and the weight

© Marion Ettlinger.

of imperfect relationships. In "Killings," the basis for a 2001 film titled *In
the Bedroom,* Dubus offers a powerful blend of intimate domestic life and
shocking violence.

Killings   *1979*

On the August morning when Matt Fowler buried his youngest son,
Frank, who had lived for twenty-one years, eight months, and four
days, Matt's older son, Steve, turned to him as the family left the
grave and walked between their friends, and said: "I should kill him."
He was twenty-eight, his brown hair starting to thin in front where he
used to have a cowlick. He bit his lower lip, wiped his eyes, then said
it again. Ruth's arm, linked with Matt's, tightened; he looked at her.
Beneath her eyes there was swelling from the three days she had suffered. At the limousine Matt stopped and looked back at the grave,
the casket, and the Congregationalist minister who he thought had
probably had a difficult job with the eulogy though he hadn't seemed
to, and the old funeral director who was saying something to the six
young pallbearers. The grave was on a hill and overlooked the Merrimack, which he could not see from where he stood; he looked at the
opposite bank, at the apple orchard with its symmetrically planted
trees going up a hill.

Next day Steve drove with his wife back to Baltimore where he managed the branch office of a bank, and Cathleen, the middle child, drove
with her husband back to Syracuse. They had left the grandchildren with
friends. A month after the funeral Matt played poker at Willis Trottier's
because Ruth, who knew this was the second time he had been invited,
told him to go, he couldn't sit home with her for the rest of her life, she

was all right. After the game Willis went outside to tell everyone good night and, when the others had driven away, he walked with Matt to his car. Willis was a short, silver-haired man who had opened a diner after World War II, his trade then mostly very early breakfast, which he cooked, and then lunch for the men who worked at the leather and shoe factories. He now owned a large restaurant.

"He walks the Goddamn streets," Matt said.

"I know. He was in my place last night, at the bar. With a girl."

"I don't see him. I'm in the store all the time. Ruth sees him. She 5 sees him too much. She was at Sunnyhurst today getting cigarettes and aspirin, and there he was. She can't even go out for cigarettes and aspirin. It's killing her."

"Come back in for a drink."

Matt looked at his watch. Ruth would be asleep. He walked with Willis back into the house, pausing at the steps to look at the starlit sky. It was a cool summer night; he thought vaguely of the Red Sox, did not even know if they were at home tonight; since it happened he had not been able to think about any of the small pleasures he believed he had earned, as he had earned also what was shattered now forever: the quietly harried and quietly pleasurable days of fatherhood. They went inside. Willis's wife, Martha, had gone to bed hours ago, in the rear of the large house which was rigged with burglar and fire alarms. They went downstairs to the game room: the television set suspended from the ceiling, the pool table, the poker table with beer cans, cards, chips, filled ashtrays, and the six chairs where Matt and his friends had sat, the friends picking up the old banter as though he had only been away on vacation; but he could see the affection and courtesy in their eyes. Willis went behind the bar and mixed them each a Scotch and soda; he stayed behind the bar and looked at Matt sitting on the stool.

"How often have you thought about it?" Willis said.

"Every day since he got out. I didn't think about bail. I thought I wouldn't have to worry about him for years. She sees him all the time. It makes her cry."

"He was in my place a long time last night. He'll be back." 10

"Maybe he won't."

"The band. He likes the band."

"What's he doing now?"

"He's tending bar up to Hampton Beach. For a friend. Ever notice even the worst bastard always has friends? He couldn't get work in town. It's just tourists and kids up to Hampton. Nobody knows him. If they do, they don't care. They drink what he mixes."

"Nobody tells me about him." 15

"I hate him, Matt. My boys went to school with him. He was the same then. Know what he'll do? Five at the most. Remember that woman about seven years ago? Shot her husband and dropped him off the bridge in the Merrimack with a hundred-pound sack of cement and said all the way through it that nobody helped her. Know where she is

now? She's in Lawrence now, a secretary. And whoever helped her, where
the hell is he?"

"I've got a .38 I've had for years, I take it to the store now. I tell Ruth
it's for the night deposits. I tell her things have changed: we got junkies
here now too. Lots of people without jobs. She knows though."

"What does she know?"

"She knows I started carrying it after the first time she saw him
in town. She knows it's in case I see him, and there's some kind of a
situation—"

He stopped, looked at Willis, and finished his drink. Willis mixed   20
him another.

"What kind of situation?"

"Where he did something to me. Where I could get away with it."

"How does Ruth feel about that?"

"She doesn't know."

"You said she does, she's got it figured out."   25

He thought of her that afternoon: when she went into Sunnyhurst, Strout was waiting at the counter while the clerk bagged the
things he had bought; she turned down an aisle and looked at soup
cans until he left.

"Ruth would shoot him herself, if she thought she could hit him."

"You got a permit?"

"No."

"I do. You could get a year for that."   30

"Maybe I'll get one. Or maybe I won't. Maybe I'll just stop bringing
it to the store."

Richard Strout was twenty-six years old, a high school athlete, football
scholarship to the University of Massachusetts where he lasted for
almost two semesters before quitting in advance of the final grades that
would have forced him not to return. People then said: Dickie can do the
work; he just doesn't want to. He came home and did construction work
for his father but refused his father's offer to learn the business; his two
older brothers had learned it, so that Strout and Sons trucks going about
town, and signs on construction sites, now slashed wounds into Matt
Fowler's life. Then Richard married a young girl and became a bartender,
his salary and tips augmented and perhaps sometimes matched by his
father, who also posted his bond. So his friends, his enemies (he had
those: fist fights or, more often, boys and then young men who had not
fought him when they thought they should have), and those who simply
knew him by face and name, had a series of images of him which they
recalled when they heard of the killing: the high school running back,
the young drunk in bars, the oblivious hard-hatted young man eating
lunch at a counter, the bartender who could perhaps be called courteous
but not more than that: as he tended bar, his dark eyes and dark, wide-
jawed face appeared less sullen, near blank.

One night he beat Frank. Frank was living at home and waiting for September, for graduate school in economics, and working as a lifeguard at Salisbury Beach, where he met Mary Ann Strout, in her first month of separation. She spent most days at the beach with her two sons. Before ten o'clock one night Frank came home; he had driven to the hospital first, and he walked into the living room with stitches over his right eye and both lips bright and swollen.

"I'm all right," he said, when Matt and Ruth stood up, and Matt turned off the television, letting Ruth get to him first: the tall, muscled but slender suntanned boy. Frank tried to smile at them but couldn't because of his lips.

"It was her husband, wasn't it?" Ruth said.   35

"Ex," Frank said. "He dropped in."

Matt gently held Frank's jaw and turned his face to the light, looked at the stitches, the blood under the white of the eye, the bruised flesh.

"Press charges," Matt said.

"No."

"What's to stop him from doing it again? Did you hit him at all?   40 Enough so he won't want to next time?"

"I don't think I touched him."

"So what are you going to do?"

"Take karate," Frank said, and tried again to smile.

"That's not the problem," Ruth said.

"You know you like her," Frank said.   45

"I like a lot of people. What about the boys? Did they see it?"

"They were asleep."

"Did you leave her alone with him?"

"He left first. She was yelling at him. I believe she had a skillet in her hand."

"Oh for God's sake," Ruth said.   50

Matt had been dealing with that too: at the dinner table on evenings when Frank wasn't home, was eating with Mary Ann; or, on the other nights—and Frank was with her every night—he talked with Ruth while they watched television, or lay in bed with the windows open and he smelled the night air and imagined, with both pride and muted sorrow, Frank in Mary Ann's arms. Ruth didn't like it because Mary Ann was in the process of divorce, because she had two children, because she was four years older than Frank, and finally—she told this in bed, where she had during all of their marriage told him of her deepest feelings: of love, of passion, of fears about one of the children, of pain Matt had caused her or she had caused him—she was against it because of what she had heard: that the marriage had gone bad early, and for most of it Richard and Mary Ann had both played around.

"That can't be true," Matt said. "Strout wouldn't have stood for it."

"Maybe he loves her."

"He's too hot-tempered. He couldn't have taken that."

But Matt knew Strout had taken it, for he had heard the stories too. 55
He wondered who had told them to Ruth; and he felt vaguely annoyed
and isolated: living with her for thirty-one years and still not knowing
what she talked about with her friends. On these summer nights he did
not so much argue with her as try to comfort her, but finally there was no
difference between the two: she had concrete objections, which he tried
to overcome. And in his attempt to do this, he neglected his own objections, which were the same as hers, so that as he spoke to her he felt as
disembodied as he sometimes did in the store when he helped a man
choose a blouse or dress or piece of costume jewelry for his wife.

"The divorce doesn't mean anything," he said. "She was young and
maybe she liked his looks and then after a while she realized she was living with a bastard. I see it as a positive thing."

"She's not divorced yet."

"It's the same thing. Massachusetts has crazy laws, that's all. Her age is
no problem. What's it matter when she was born? And that other business:
even if it's true, which it probably isn't, it's got nothing to do with Frank,
and it's in the past. And the kids are no problem. She's been married six
years; she ought to have kids. Frank likes them. He plays with them. And
he's not going to marry her anyway, so it's not a problem of money."

"Then what's he doing with her?"

"She probably loves him, Ruth. Girls always have. Why can't we just 60
leave it at that?"

"He got home at six o'clock Tuesday morning."

"I didn't know you knew. I've already talked to him about it."

Which he had: since he believed almost nothing he told Ruth, he
went to Frank with what he believed. The night before, he had followed
Frank to the car after dinner.

"You wouldn't make much of a burglar," he said.

"How's that?" 65

Matt was looking up at him; Frank was six feet tall, an inch and a
half taller than Matt, who had been proud when Frank at seventeen out-
grew him; he had only felt uncomfortable when he had to reprimand
or caution him. He touched Frank's bicep, thought of the young taut
passionate body, believed he could sense the desire, and again he felt the
pride and sorrow and envy too, not knowing whether he was envious of
Frank or Mary Ann.

"When you came in yesterday morning, I woke up. One of these
mornings your mother will. And I'm the one who'll have to talk to her.
She won't interfere with you. Okay? I know it means—" But he stopped,
thinking: I know it means getting up and leaving that suntanned girl
and going sleepy to the car, I know—

"Okay," Frank said, and touched Matt's shoulder and got into the car.

There had been other talks, but the only long one was their first one:
a night driving to Fenway Park, Matt having ordered the tickets so they
could talk, and knowing when Frank said yes, he would go, that he knew

the talk was coming too. It took them forty minutes to get to Boston, and they talked about Mary Ann until they joined the city traffic along the Charles River, blue in the late sun. Frank told him all the things that Matt would later pretend to believe when he told them to Ruth.

"It seems like a lot for a young guy to take on," Matt finally said.   70
"Sometimes it is. But she's worth it."
"Are you thinking about getting married?"
"We haven't talked about it. She can't for over a year. I've got school."
"I *do* like her," Matt said.

He did. Some evenings, when the long summer sun was still low in   75
the sky, Frank brought her home; they came into the house smelling of suntan lotion and the sea, and Matt gave them gin and tonics and started the charcoal in the backyard, and looked at Mary Ann in the lawn chair: long and very light brown hair (Matt thinking that twenty years ago she would have dyed it blonde), and the long brown legs he loved to look at; her face was pretty; she had probably never in her adult life gone unnoticed into a public place. It was in her wide brown eyes that she looked older than Frank; after a few drinks Matt thought what he saw in her eyes was something erotic, testament to the rumors about her; but he knew it wasn't that, or all that: she had, very young, been through a sort of pain that his children, and he and Ruth, had been spared. In the moments of his recognizing that pain, he wanted to tenderly touch her hair, wanted with some gesture to give her solace and hope. And he would glance at Frank, and hope they would love each other, hope Frank would soothe that pain in her heart, take it from her eyes; and her divorce, her age, and her children did not matter at all. On the first two evenings she did not bring her boys, and then Ruth asked her to bring them the next time. In bed that night Ruth said, "She hasn't brought them because she's embarrassed. She shouldn't feel embarrassed."

Richard Strout shot Frank in front of the boys. They were sitting on the living room floor watching television, Frank sitting on the couch, and Mary Ann just returning from the kitchen with a tray of sandwiches. Strout came in the front door and shot Frank twice in the chest and once in the face with a 9 mm automatic. Then he looked at the boys and Mary Ann, and went home to wait for the police.

It seemed to Matt that from the time Mary Ann called weeping to tell him until now, a Saturday night in September, sitting in the car with Willis, parked beside Strout's car, waiting for the bar to close, that he had not so much moved through his life as wandered through it, his spirit like a dazed body bumping into furniture and corners. He had always been a fearful father: when his children were young, at the start of each summer he thought of them drowning in a pond or the sea, and he was relieved when he came home in the evenings and they were there; usually that relief was his only acknowledgment of his fear, which he never spoke of, and which he controlled within his heart. As he had when they were very young and all of them in turn, Cathleen too, were drawn to the high oak in the backyard, and had to climb it. Smiling, he watched them, imagining the fall: and he was poised to catch the small body before it hit the earth. Or his legs were poised; his hands were in his pockets or his arms were folded and, for the child looking down, he appeared relaxed and confident while his heart beat with the two words he wanted to call out but did not: *Don't fall.* In winter he was less afraid: he made sure the ice would hold him before they skated, and he brought or sent them to places where they could sled without ending in the street. So he and his children had survived their childhood, and he only worried about them when he knew they were driving a long distance, and then he lost Frank in a way no father expected to lose his son, and he felt that all the fears he had borne while they were growing up, and all the grief he had been afraid of, had backed up like a huge wave and struck him on the beach and swept him out to sea. Each day he felt the same and when he was able to forget how he felt, when he was able to force himself not to feel that way, the eyes of his clerks and customers defeated him. He wished those eyes were oblivious, even cold; he felt he was withering in their tenderness. And beneath his listless wandering, every day in his soul he shot Richard Strout in the face; while Ruth, going about town on errands, kept seeing him. And at nights in bed she would hold Matt and cry, or sometimes she was silent and Matt would touch her tightening arm, her clenched fist.

As his own right fist was now, squeezing the butt of the revolver, the last of the drinkers having left the bar, talking to each other, going to their separate cars which were in the lot in front of the bar, out of Matt's vision. He heard their voices, their cars, and then the ocean again, across the street. The tide was in and sometimes it smacked the sea wall. Through the windshield he looked at the dark red side wall of the bar, and then to his left, past Willis, at Strout's car, and through its windows he could see the now-emptied parking lot, the road, the sea wall. He could smell the sea.

The front door of the bar opened and closed again and Willis looked at Matt then at the corner of the building; when Strout came around it alone Matt got out of the car, giving up the hope he had kept all night (and for the past week) that Strout would come out with friends, and Willis would simply drive away; thinking: *All right then. All right;* and he went around the front of Willis's car, and at Strout's he stopped and aimed over the hood at Strout's blue shirt ten feet away. Willis was aiming too, crouched on Matt's left, his elbow resting on the hood.

"Mr. Fowler," Strout said. He looked at each of them, and at the   80
guns. "Mr. Trottier."

Then Matt, watching the parking lot and the road, walked quickly between the car and the building and stood behind Strout. He took one leather glove from his pocket and put it on his left hand.

"Don't talk. Unlock the front and back and get in."

Strout unlocked the front door, reached in and unlocked the back, then got in, and Matt slid into the back seat, closed the door with his gloved hand, and touched Strout's head once with the muzzle.

"It's cocked. Drive to your house."

When Strout looked over his shoulder to back the car, Matt aimed at his temple and did not look at his eyes.

"Drive slowly," he said. "Don't try to get stopped."

They drove across the empty front lot and onto the road, Willis's headlights shining into the car; then back through town, the sea wall on the left hiding the beach, though far out Matt could see the ocean; he uncocked the revolver; on the right were the places, most with their neon signs off, that did so much business in summer: the lounges and cafés and pizza houses, the street itself empty of traffic, the way he and Willis had known it would be when they decided to take Strout at the bar rather than knock on his door at two o'clock one morning and risk that one insomniac neighbor. Matt had not told Willis he was afraid he could not be alone with Strout for very long, smell his smells, feel the presence of his flesh, hear his voice, and then shoot him. They left the beach town and then were on the high bridge over the channel: to the left the smacking curling white at the breakwater and beyond that the dark sea and the full moon, and down to his right the small fishing boats bobbing at anchor in the cove. When they left the bridge, the sea was blocked by abandoned beach cottages, and Matt's left hand was sweating in the glove. Out here in the dark in the car he believed Ruth knew. Willis had come to his house at eleven and asked if he wanted a nightcap; Matt went to the bedroom for his wallet, put the gloves in one trouser pocket and the .38 in the other and went back to the living room, his hand in his pocket covering the bulge of the cool cylinder pressed against his fingers, the butt against his palm. When Ruth said good night she looked at his face, and he felt she could see in his eyes the gun, and the night he was going to. But he knew he couldn't trust what he saw. Willis's wife had taken her sleeping pill, which gave her eight hours—the reason, Willis had told Matt, he had the alarms installed, for nights when he was late at the restaurant—and when it was all done and Willis got home he would leave ice and a trace of Scotch and soda in two glasses in the game room and tell Martha in the morning that he had left the restaurant early and brought Matt home for a drink.

"He was making it with my wife." Strout's voice was careful, not pleading.

Matt pressed the muzzle against Strout's head, pressed it harder than he wanted to, feeling through the gun Strout's head flinching and moving forward; then he lowered the gun to his lap.

"Don't talk," he said.

Strout did not speak again. They turned west, drove past the Dairy Queen closed until spring, and the two lobster restaurants that faced each other and were crowded all summer and were now also closed, onto the short bridge crossing the tidal stream, and over the engine Matt could hear through his open window the water rushing inland under the bridge; looking to his left he saw its swift moonlit current going back into the marsh which, leaving the bridge, they entered: the salt marsh stretching out on both sides, the grass tall in patches but mostly low and leaning earthward as though windblown, a large dark rock sitting as though it rested on nothing but itself, and shallow pools reflecting the bright moon.

Beyond the marsh they drove through woods, Matt thinking now of the hole he and Willis had dug last Sunday afternoon after telling their wives they were going to Fenway Park. They listened to the game on a transistor radio, but heard none of it as they dug into the soft earth on the knoll they had chosen because elms and maples sheltered it. Already some leaves had fallen. When the hole was deep enough they covered it and the piled earth with dead branches, then cleaned their shoes and pants and went to a restaurant farther up in New Hampshire where they ate sandwiches and drank beer and watched the rest of the game on television. Looking at the back of Strout's head he thought of Frank's grave; he had not been back to it; but he would go before winter, and its second burial of snow.

He thought of Frank sitting on the couch and perhaps talking to the children as they watched television, imagined him feeling young and strong, still warmed from the sun at the beach, and feeling loved, hearing Mary Ann moving about in the kitchen, hearing her walking into the living room; maybe he looked up at her and maybe she said something, looking at him over the tray of sandwiches, smiling at him, saying something the way women do when they offer food as a gift, then the front door opening and this son of a bitch coming in and Frank seeing that he meant the gun in his hand, this son of a bitch and his gun the last person and thing Frank saw on earth.

When they drove into town the streets were nearly empty: a few slow cars, a policeman walking his beat past the darkened fronts of stores. Strout and Matt both glanced at him as they drove by. They were on the main street, and all the stoplights were blinking yellow. Willis and Matt had talked about that too: the lights changed at midnight, so there would be no place Strout had to stop and where he might try to run. Strout turned down the block where he lived and Willis's headlights were no longer with Matt in the back seat. They had planned that too, had decided it was best for just the one car to go to the house, and again Matt had said nothing about his fear of being alone with Strout, especially in his house: a duplex, dark as all the houses on the street were, the street itself lit at the corner of each block. As Strout turned into the driveway Matt thought of the one insomniac neighbor, thought of some man or woman sitting alone in the dark living room, watching the all-night channel from Boston. When Strout stopped the car near the front of the house, Matt said: "Drive it to the back."

He touched Strout's head with the muzzle.   95

"You wouldn't have it cocked, would you? For when I put on the brakes."

Matt cocked it, and said: "It is now."

Strout waited a moment; then he eased the car forward, the engine doing little more than idling, and as they approached the garage he gently braked. Matt opened the door, then took off the glove and put it in his pocket. He stepped out and shut the door with his hip and said: "All right."

Strout looked at the gun, then got out, and Matt followed him across the grass, and as Strout unlocked the door Matt looked quickly at the row of small backyards on either side, and scattered tall trees, some evergreens, others not, and he thought of the red and yellow leaves on the trees over the hole, saw them falling soon, probably in two weeks, dropping slowly, covering. Strout stepped into the kitchen.

"Turn on the light."   100

Strout reached to the wall switch, and in the light Matt looked at his wide back, the dark blue shirt, the white belt, the red plaid pants.

"Where's your suitcase?"

"My suitcase?"

"Where is it?"

"In the bedroom closet."   105

"That's where we're going then. When we get to a door you stop and turn on the light."

They crossed the kitchen, Matt glancing at the sink and stove and refrigerator: no dishes in the sink or even the dish rack beside it, no grease splashings on the stove, the refrigerator door clean and white. He did not want to look at any more but he looked quickly at all he could see: in the living room magazines and newspapers in a wicker basket, clean ashtrays, a record player, the records shelved next to it, then down the hall where, near the bedroom door, hung a color photograph of Mary Ann and the two boys sitting on a lawn — there was no house in the picture — Mary Ann smiling at the camera or Strout or whoever held the camera, smiling as she had on Matt's lawn this summer while he waited for the charcoal and they all talked and he looked at her brown legs and at Frank touching her arm, her shoulder, her hair; he moved down the hall with her smile in his mind, wondering: was that when they were both playing around and she was smiling like that at him and they were happy, even sometimes, making it worth it? He recalled her eyes, the pain in them, and he was conscious of the circles of love he was touching with the hand that held the revolver so tightly now as Strout stopped at the door at the end of the hall.

"There's no wall switch."

"Where's the light?"

"By the bed."   110

"Let's go."

Matt stayed a pace behind, then Strout leaned over and the room was lighted: the bed, a double one, was neatly made; the ashtray on the bedside table clean, the bureau top dustless, and no photographs; probably so the girl—who *was* she?—would not have to see Mary Ann in the bedroom she believed was theirs. But because Matt was a father and a husband, though never an ex-husband, he knew (and did not want to know) that this bedroom had never been theirs alone. Strout turned around; Matt looked at his lips, his wide jaw, and thought of Frank's doomed and fearful eyes looking up from the couch.

"Where's Mr. Trottier?"

"He's waiting. Pack clothes for warm weather."

"What's going on?"   115

"You're jumping bail."

"Mr. Fowler—"

He pointed the cocked revolver at Strout's face. The barrel trembled but not much, not as much as he had expected. Strout went to the closet and got the suitcase from the floor and opened it on the bed. As he went to the bureau, he said: "He was making it with my wife. I'd go pick up my kids and he'd be there. Sometimes he spent the night. My boys told me."

He did not look at Matt as he spoke. He opened the top drawer and Matt stepped closer so he could see Strout's hands: underwear and socks, the socks rolled, the underwear folded and stacked. He took them back to the bed, arranged them neatly in the suitcase, then from the closet he was taking shirts and trousers and a jacket; he laid them on the bed and Matt followed him to the bathroom and watched from the door while he packed those things a person accumulated and that became part of him so that at times in the store Matt felt he was selling more than clothes.

"I wanted to try to get together with her again." He was bent over the   120 suitcase. "I couldn't even talk to her. He was always with her. I'm going to jail for it; if I ever get out I'll be an old man. Isn't that enough?"

"You're not going to jail."

Strout closed the suitcase and faced Matt, looking at the gun. Matt went to his rear, so Strout was between him and the lighted hall; then using his handkerchief he turned off the lamp and said: "Let's go."

They went down the hall, Matt looking again at the photograph, and through the living room and kitchen, Matt turning off the lights and talking, frightened that he was talking, that he was telling this lie he had not planned: "It's the trial. We can't go through that, my wife and me. So you're leaving. We've got you a ticket, and a job. A friend of Mr. Trottier's. Out west. My wife keeps seeing you. We can't have that anymore."

Matt turned out the kitchen light and put the handkerchief in his pocket, and they went down the two brick steps and across the lawn. Strout put the suitcase on the floor of the back seat, then got into the front seat and Matt got in the back and put on his glove and shut the door.

"They'll catch me. They'll check passenger lists."   125

"We didn't use your name."

"They'll figure that out too. You think I wouldn't have done it myself if it was that easy?"

He backed into the street, Matt looking down the gun barrel but not at the profiled face beyond it.

"You were alone," Matt said. "We've got it worked out."

"There's no planes this time of night, Mr. Fowler."   130

"Go back through town. Then north on 125."

They came to the corner and turned, and now Willis's headlights were in the car with Matt.

"Why north, Mr. Fowler?"

"Somebody's going to keep you for a while. They'll take you to the airport." He uncocked the hammer and lowered the revolver to his lap and said wearily: "No more talking."

As they drove back through town, Matt's body sagged, going limp   135
with his spirit and its new and false bond with Strout, the hope his lie had given Strout. He had grown up in this town whose streets had become places of apprehension and pain for Ruth as she drove and walked, doing what she had to do; and for him too, if only in his mind as he worked and chatted six days a week in his store; he wondered now if his lie would have worked, if sending Strout away would have been enough; but then he knew that just thinking of Strout in Montana or whatever place lay at the end of the lie he had told, thinking of him walking the streets there, loving a girl there (who *was* she?) would be enough to slowly rot the rest of his days. And Ruth's. Again he was certain that she knew, that she was waiting for him.

They were in New Hampshire now, on the narrow highway, passing the shopping center at the state line, and then houses and small stores and sandwich shops. There were few cars on the road. After ten minutes he raised his trembling hand, touched Strout's neck with the gun, and said: "Turn in up here. At the dirt road."

Strout flicked on the indicator and slowed.

"Mr. Fowler?"

"They're waiting here."

Strout turned very slowly, easing his neck away from the gun. In   140
the moonlight the road was light brown, lighter and yellowed where the headlights shone; weeds and a few trees grew on either side of it, and ahead of them were the woods.

"There's nothing back here, Mr. Fowler."

"It's for your car. You don't think we'd leave it at the airport, do you?"

He watched Strout's large, big-knuckled hands tighten on the wheel, saw Frank's face that night: not the stitches and bruised eye and swollen lips, but his own hand gently touching Frank's jaw, turning his wounds to the light. They rounded a bend in the road and were out of sight of the highway: tall trees all around them now, hiding the moon. When they reached the abandoned gravel pit on the left, the bare flat earth and steep pale embankment behind it, and the black crowns of trees at its top, Matt said: "Stop here."

Strout stopped but did not turn off the engine. Matt pressed the gun hard against his neck, and he straightened in the seat and looked in the rearview mirror, Matt's eyes meeting his in the glass for an instant before looking at the hair at the end of the gun barrel.

"Turn it off."   145

Strout did, then held the wheel with two hands, and looked in the mirror.

"I'll do twenty years, Mr. Fowler; at least. I'll be forty-six years old."

"That's nine years younger than I am," Matt said, and got out and took offthe glove and kicked the door shut. He aimed at Strout's ear and pulled back the hammer. Willis's headlights were off and Matt heard him walking on the soft thin layer of dust, the hard earth beneath it. Strout opened the door, sat for a moment in the interior light, then stepped out onto the road. Now his face was pleading. Matt did not look at his eyes, but he could see it in the lips.

"Just get the suitcase. They're right up the road."

Willis was beside him now, to his left. Strout looked at both guns.   150
Then he opened the back door, leaned in, and with a jerk brought the suitcase out. He was turning to face them when Matt said: "Just walk up the road. Just ahead."

Strout turned to walk, the suitcase in his right hand, and Matt and Willis followed; as Strout cleared the front of his car he dropped the suitcase and, ducking, took one step that was the beginning of a sprint to his right. The gun kicked in Matt's hand, and the explosion of the shot surrounded him, isolated him in a nimbus of sound that cut him off from all his time, all his history, isolated him standing absolutely still on the dirt road with the gun in his hand, looking down at Richard Strout squirming on his belly, kicking one leg behind him, pushing himself forward, toward the woods. Then Matt went to him and shot him once in the back of the head.

───────────

Driving south to Boston, wearing both gloves now, staying in the middle lane and looking often in the rearview mirror at Willis's headlights, he relived the suitcase dropping, the quick dip and turn of Strout's back, and the kick of the gun, the sound of the shot. When he walked to Strout, he still existed within the first shot, still trembled and breathed with it. The second shot and the burial seemed to be happening to someone else, someone he was watching. He and Willis each held an arm and pulled Strout face-down off the road and into the woods, his bouncing sliding belt white under the trees where it was so dark that when they stopped at the top of the knoll, panting and sweating, Matt could not see where Strout's blue shirt ended and the earth began.

They pulled off the branches then dragged Strout to the edge of the hole and went behind him and lifted his legs and pushed him in. They stood still for a moment. The woods were quiet save for their breathing, and Matt remembered hearing the movements of birds and small animals after the first shot. Or maybe he had not heard them. Willis went down to the road. Matt could see him clearly out on the tan dirt, could see the glint of Strout's car and, beyond the road, the gravel pit. Willis came back up the knoll with the suitcase. He dropped it in the hole and took off his gloves and they went down to his car for the spades. They worked quietly. Sometimes they paused to listen to the woods. When they were finished Willis turned on his flashlight and they covered the earth with leaves and branches and then went down to the spot in front of the car, and while Matt held the light Willis crouched and sprinkled dust on the blood, backing up till he reached the grass and leaves, then he used leaves until they had worked up to the grave again. They did not stop. They walked around the grave and through the woods, using the light on the ground, looking up through the trees to where they ended at the lake. Neither of them spoke above the sounds of their heavy and clumsy strides through low brush and over fallen branches. Then they reached it: wide and dark, lapping softly at the bank, pine needles smooth under Matt's feet, moonlight on the lake, a small island near its middle, with black, tall evergreens. He took out the gun and threw for the island: taking two steps back on the pine needles, striding with the throw and going to one knee as he followed through, looking up to see the dark shapeless object arcing downward, splashing.

They left Strout's car in Boston, in front of an apartment building on Commonwealth Avenue. When they got back to town Willis drove slowly over the bridge and Matt threw the keys into the Merrimack. The sky was turning light. Willis let him out a block from his house, and walking home he listened for sounds from the houses he passed. They were quiet. A light was on in his living room. He turned it off and undressed in there, and went softly toward the bedroom; in the hall he smelled the smoke, and he stood in the bedroom doorway and looked at the orange of her cigarette in the dark. The curtains were closed. He went to the closet and put his shoes on the floor and felt for a hanger.

"Did you do it?" she said.

He went down the hall to the bathroom and in the dark he washed his hands and face. Then he went to her, lay on his back, and pulled the sheet up to his throat.

"Are you all right?" she said.

"I think so."

Now she touched him, lying on her side, her hand on his belly, his thigh.

"Tell me," she said.

155

He started from the beginning, in the parking lot at the bar; but   160
soon with his eyes closed and Ruth petting him, he spoke of Strout's
house: the order, the woman presence, the picture on the wall.

"The way she was smiling," he said.

"What about it?"

"I don't know. Did you ever see Strout's girl? When you saw him in
town?"

"No."

"I wonder who she was."   165

Then he thought: *not was: is. Sleeping now she is his girl.* He opened his
eyes, then closed them again. There was more light beyond the curtains.
With Ruth now he left Strout's house and told again his lie to Strout,
gave him again that hope that Strout must have for a while believed, else
he would have to believe only the gun pointed at him for the last two
hours of his life. And with Ruth he saw again the dropping suitcase, the
darting move to the right: and he told of the first shot, feeling her hand
on him but his heart isolated still, beating on the road still in that explosion like thunder. He told her the rest, but the words had no images for
him, he did not see himself doing what the words said he had done; he
only saw himself on that road.

"We can't tell the other kids," she said. "It'll hurt them, thinking he
got away. But we mustn't."

"No."

She was holding him, wanting him, and he wished he could make
love with her but he could not. He saw Frank and Mary Ann making love
in her bed, their eyes closed, their bodies brown and smelling of the sea;
the other girl was faceless, bodiless, but he felt her sleeping now; and he
saw Frank and Strout, their faces alive; he saw red and yellow leaves falling on the earth, then snow: falling and freezing and falling; and holding
Ruth, his cheek touching her breast, he shuddered with a sob that he
kept silent in his heart.

Considerations for Critical Thinking and Writing

1. **FIRST RESPONSE.** How do you feel about Matt's act of revenge? Trace
   the emotions his character produces in you as the plot unfolds.

2. Discuss the significance of the title. Why is "Killings" a more appropriate title than "Killers"?

3. What are the effects of Dubus's ordering of events in the story?
   How would the effects be different if the story were told in a chronological order?

4. Describe the Fowler family before Frank's murder. How does the
   murder affect Matt?

5. What is learned about Richard from the flashback in paragraphs
   32 through 75? How does this information affect your attitude
   toward him?

6. What is the effect of the description of Richard shooting Frank in paragraph 76?

7. How well planned is Matt's revenge? Why does he lie to Richard about sending him out west?

8. Describe Matt at the end of the story when he tells his wife about the killing. How do you think this revenge killing will affect the Fowler family?

9. How might "Killings" be considered a love story as well as a murder story?

10. **CONNECTION TO ANOTHER SELECTION.** Compare and contrast Matt's motivation for murder with Emily's in "A Rose for Emily" (p. 52). Which character made you feel more empathy and sympathy for his or her actions? Why?

3

Character

When I find a well-drawn character in fiction or biography, I generally take a warm personal interest in him, for the reason that I have known him before — met him on the river.

— MARK TWAIN

Character is essential to plot. Without characters Burroughs's *Tarzan of the Apes* would be a travelogue through the jungle and Faulkner's "A Rose for Emily" little more than a faded history of a sleepy town in the South. If stories were depopulated, the plots would disappear because characters and plots are interrelated. A dangerous jungle is important only because we care what effect it has on a character. Characters are influenced by events just as events are shaped by characters. Tarzan's physical strength is the result of his growing up in the jungle, and his strength, along with his inherited intelligence, allows him to be master there.

The methods by which a writer creates people in a story so that they seem actually to exist are called ***characterization***. Huck Finn never lived, yet those who have read Mark Twain's novel about his adventures along the Mississippi River feel as if they know him. A good writer gives us the illusion that a character is real, but we should also remember that a character is not an actual person but instead has been created by the author. Though we might walk out of a room in which Huck Finn's Pap talks racist nonsense, we would not throw away the book in a similar fit of anger. This illusion of reality is the magic that allows us to move beyond the circumstances of our own lives into a writer's fictional world, where we can

Explore the literary element in this chapter at bedfordstmartins.com/meyerlit.

encounter everyone from royalty to paupers, murderers, lovers, cheaters, martyrs, artists, destroyers, and, nearly always, some part of ourselves. To understand our response to a story, we should be able to recognize the methods of characterization the author uses.

CHARLES DICKENS (1812–1870)

Charles Dickens is well known for creating characters who have stepped off the pages of his fictions into the imaginations and memories of his readers. His characters are successful not because readers might have encountered such people in their own lives, but because his characterizations are vivid and convincing. He manages to make strange and eccentric people appear familiar. The following excerpt from *Hard Times* is the novel's entire first chapter. In it Dickens introduces and characterizes a school principal addressing a classroom full of children.

© National Portrait Gallery, London.

From *Hard Times*   1854

"Now, what I want is, Facts. Teach these boys and girls nothing but Facts. Facts alone are wanted in life. Plant nothing else, and root out everything else. You can only form the minds of reasoning animals upon Facts: nothing else will ever be of any service to them. This is the principle on which I bring up my own children, and this is the principle on which I bring up these children. Stick to Facts, sir!"

The scene was a plain, bare, monotonous vault of a schoolroom, and the speaker's square forefinger emphasized his observations by underscoring every sentence with a line on the schoolmaster's sleeve. The emphasis was helped by the speaker's square wall of a forehead, which had his eyebrows for its base, while his eyes found commodious cellarage in two dark caves, overshadowed by the wall. The emphasis was helped by the speaker's mouth, which was wide, thin, and hard set. The emphasis was helped by the speaker's voice, which was inflexible, dry, and dictatorial. The emphasis was helped by the speaker's hair, which bristled on the skirts of his bald head, a plantation of firs to keep the wind from its shining surface, all covered with knobs, like the crust of a plum pie, as if the head had scarcely warehouse-room for the hard facts stored inside. The speaker's obstinate carriage, square coat, square legs, square shoulders—nay, his very neckcloth, trained to take him by the throat with an unaccommodating grasp, like a stubborn fact, as it was—all helped the emphasis.

"In this life, we want nothing but Facts, sir; nothing but Facts!"

The speaker, and the schoolmaster, and the third grown person present, all backed a little, and swept with their eyes the inclined plane of little vessels then and there arranged in order, ready to have imperial gallons of facts poured into them until they were full to the brim.

Dickens withholds his character's name until the beginning of the second chapter; he calls this fact-bound educator Mr. Gradgrind. Authors sometimes put as much time and effort into naming their characters as parents invest in naming their children. Names can be used to indicate qualities that the writer associates with the characters. Mr. Gradgrind is precisely what his name suggests. The "schoolmaster" employed by Gradgrind is Mr. M'Choakumchild. Pronounce this name aloud and you have the essence of this teacher's educational philosophy. In Nathaniel Hawthorne's *The Scarlet Letter,* Chillingworth is cold and relentless in his single-minded quest for revenge. The innocent and youthful protagonist in Herman Melville's *Billy Budd* is nipped in the bud by the evil Claggart, whose name simply sounds unpleasant. Of course, not every name is suggestive of the qualities a character may embody, but it is frequently worth determining what is in a name.

The only way to tell whether a name reveals character is to look at the other information the author supplies about the character. We evaluate fictional characters in much the same way we understand people in our own lives. By piecing together bits of information, we create a context that allows us to interpret their behavior. We can predict, for instance, that an acquaintance who is a chronic complainer is not likely to have anything good to say about a roommate. We interpret words and actions in the light of what we already know about someone, and that is why keeping track of what characters say (and how they say it) along with what they do (and don't do) is important.

Authors reveal characters by other means too. Physical descriptions can indicate important inner qualities; disheveled clothing, a crafty smile, or a blush might communicate as much as or more than what a character says. Characters can also be revealed by the words and actions of others who respond to them. In literature, moreover, we have one great advantage that life cannot offer; a work of fiction can give us access to a person's thoughts. Although in Herman Melville's "Bartleby, the Scrivener" (p. 101) we learn about Bartleby primarily through descriptive details, words, actions, and his relationships with the other characters, Melville allows us to enter the lawyer's consciousness.

Authors have two major methods of presenting characters: **showing** and **telling**. Characters shown in dramatic situations reveal themselves indirectly by what they say and do. In the first paragraph of the excerpt

from *Hard Times,* Dickens shows us some of Gradgrind's utilitarian educational principles by having him speak. We can infer the kind of person
he is from his reference to boys and girls as "reasoning animals," but we
are not told what to think of him until the second paragraph. It would
be impossible to admire Gradgrind after reading the physical description
of him and the school that he oversees. The adjectives in the second paragraph make the author's evaluation of Gradgrind's values and personality clear: Everything about him is rigidly "square"; his mouth is "thin,
and hard set"; his voice is "inflexible, dry, and dictatorial"; and he pre-
sides over a "plain, bare, monotonous vault of a schoolroom." Dickens
directly lets us know how to feel about Gradgrind, but he does so artistically. Instead of simply being presented with a statement that Gradgrind
is destructively practical, we get a detailed and amusing description.

We can contrast Dickens's direct presentation in this paragraph with
the indirect showing that Gail Godwin uses in "A Sorrowful Woman."
Godwin avoids telling us how we should think about the characters. Their
story includes little description and no evaluations or interpretations by
the author. To determine the significance of the events, the reader must
pay close attention to what the characters say and do. Like Godwin, many
twentieth-century authors favor showing over telling because showing
allows readers to discover the meanings, which modern authors are often
reluctant to impose on an audience for whom fixed meanings and values
are not as strong as they once were. However, most writers continue to
reveal characters by telling as well as showing when the technique suits
their purposes — when, for example, a minor character must be sketched
economically or when a long time has elapsed, causing changes in a major
character. Telling and showing complement each other.

Characters can be convincing whether they are presented by telling
or showing, provided their actions are *motivated.* There must be reasons
for how they behave and what they say. If adequate motivation is offered,
we can understand and find *plausible* their actions no matter how bizarre.
In "A Rose for Emily" (p. 52), Faulkner makes Emily Grierson's intimacy
with a corpse credible by preparing us with information about her father's
death along with her inability to leave the past and live in the present.
Emily turns out to be *consistent.* Although we are surprised by the ending
of the story, the behavior it reveals is compatible with her temperament.

Some kinds of fiction consciously break away from our expectations
of traditional realistic stories. Consistency, plausibility, and motivation
are not very useful concepts for understanding and evaluating characterizations in modern *absurdist literature*, for instance, in which characters
are often alienated from themselves and their environment in an irrational world. In this world there is no possibility for traditional heroic
action; instead we find an antihero who has little control over events.
Yossarian from Joseph Heller's *Catch-22* is an example of a protagonist
who is thwarted by the absurd terms on which life offers itself to many
twentieth-century characters.

In most stories we expect characters to act plausibly and in ways consistent with their personalities, but that does not mean that characters cannot develop and change. A *dynamic* character undergoes some kind of change because of the action of the plot. Huck Finn's view of Jim, the runaway slave in Mark Twain's novel, develops during their experiences on the raft. Huck discovers Jim's humanity and therefore cannot betray him, because Huck no longer sees his companion as merely the property of a white owner. On the other hand, Huck's friend, Tom Sawyer, is a *static* character because he does not change. He remains interested only in high adventure, even at the risk of Jim's life. As static characters often do, Tom serves as a foil to Huck; his frivolous concerns are contrasted with Huck's serious development. A *foil* helps to reveal by contrast the distinctive qualities of another character.

The extent to which a character is developed is another means by which character can be analyzed. The novelist E. M. Forster coined the terms *flat* and *round* to distinguish degrees of character development. A *flat character* embodies one or two qualities, ideas, or traits that can be readily described in a brief summary. For instance, Mr. M'Choakumchild in Dickens's *Hard Times* stifles students instead of encouraging them to grow. Flat characters tend to be one-dimensional. They are readily accessible because their characteristics are few and simple; they are not created to be psychologically complex.

Some flat characters are immediately recognizable as *stock characters*. These stereotypes are particularly popular in formula fiction, television programs, and action movies. Stock characters are types rather than individuals. The poor but dedicated writer falls in love with a hard-working understudy, who gets nowhere because the corrupt producer favors his boozy, pampered mistress for the leading role. Characters such as these — the loyal servant, the mean stepfather, the henpecked husband, the dumb blonde, the sadistic army officer, the dotty grandmother — are prepackaged; they lack individuality because their authors have, in a sense, not imaginatively created them but simply summoned them from a warehouse of clichés and social prejudices. Stock characters can become fresh if a good writer makes them vivid, interesting, or memorable, but too often a writer's use of these stereotypes is simply weak characterization.

Round characters are more complex than flat or stock characters. Round characters have more depth and require more attention. They may surprise us or puzzle us. Although they are more fully developed, round characters are also more difficult to summarize because we are aware of competing ideas, values, and possibilities in their lives. As a flat character, Huck Finn's alcoholic, bigoted father is clear to us; we know that Pap is the embodiment of racism and irrationality. But Huck is considerably less predictable because he struggles with what Twain calls a "sound heart and a deformed conscience."

In making distinctions between flat and round characters, you must understand that an author's use of a flat character—even as a protagonist—does not necessarily represent an artistic flaw. Moreover, both flat and round characters can be either dynamic or static. Each plot can be made most effective by its own special kind of characterization. Terms such as *round* and *flat* are helpful tools to use to determine what we know about a character, but they are not an infallible measurement of the quality of a story.

The next three stories—May-lee Chai's "Saving Sourdi," Junot Díaz's "How to Date a Browngirl, Blackgirl, Whitegirl, or Halfie," and Herman Melville's "Bartleby, the Scrivener"—offer character studies worthy of close analysis. As you read them, notice the methods of characterization used to bring each to life.

MAY-LEE CHAI

Courtesy of Jason Doiy.

May-lee Chai, the first of her family to be born in the United States, is a San Francisco author and graduate of Yale University. Chai has worked as a reporter for the Associated Press and taught creative writing at San Francisco State University, the University of Wyoming, and Amherst College. She is the author of seven books, including *My Lucky Face* (2001), *Glamorous Asians: Short Stories and Essays* (2004), and *Hapa Girl: A Memoir* (2007); and coauthor, with her father, Winberg Chai, of *The Girl from Purple Mountain* (2002). Her novels *Dragon Chica* (2010) and *Tiger Girl* (2013) are about the characters in "Saving Sourdi."

> WHEN I WRITE "When I was a teenager, I lived on a farm. I'd get up early in the morning while it was still dark and write bad sci-fi stories for 20 minutes before I had to go out for chores. That was my escape. The stories were terrible, but the act of writing was my salvation." —MAY-LEE CHAI

Saving Sourdi   *2001*

Once, when my older sister, Sourdi, and I were working alone in our family's restaurant, just the two of us and the elderly cook, some men got drunk and I stabbed one of them. I was eleven.

I don't remember where Ma had gone that night. But I remember we were tired and it was late. We were one of the only restaurants that stayed open past nine in those days. The men had been growing louder, until they were our only customers, and, finally, one of them staggered up and put his arm across Sourdi's shoulders. He called her his "China doll," and his friends hooted at this.

Sourdi looked distressed and tried to remove his arm, but he held her tighter. She said, "Please," in her incense-sweet voice, and he smiled and said, "Say it again nice and I might just have to give you a kiss."

That summer we'd just moved to South Dakota. After all the crummy jobs Ma had had to take in Texas, where we'd first come to the U.S., where our sponsors lived, we were so proud to be working in our own restaurant. When we moved to South Dakota, I thought we'd find the real America, the one where we were supposed to be, not the hot sweaty America where we lived packed together in an apartment with bars on the windows on a street where angry boys in cars played loud music and shot guns at each other in the night. The summer we moved to join my uncle's family to run the Silver Palace, I was certain we would at last find the life we deserved.

Now I was panicked. I wanted Ma to be there. Ma would know what   5 to do. She always did. I stood there, chewing my nails, wishing I could make them go away. The men's voices were so loud in my ears, I was drowning in the sound.

I ran into the kitchen. I had this idea to get the cook and the cleaver, but the first thing that caught my eye was this little paring knife on the counter next to a bowl of oranges. I grabbed the knife and ran back out to Sourdi.

"Get away from my sister!" I shouted, waving the paring knife.

The men were silent for about three seconds, then they burst into laughter.

I charged and stabbed the man in the sleeve.

In a movie or a television show this kind of scene always unfolds in   10 slow motion, but everything happened so fast. I stabbed the man, Sourdi jumped free, Ma came rushing in the front door waving her arms. "Omi-god! What happen?"

"Jesus Christ!" The man shook his arm as though it were on fire, but the paring knife was stuck in the fabric of his jeans jacket.

I thought Ma would take care of everything now. And I was right, she did, but not the way I had imagined. She started apologizing to the man, and she helped him take off his jacket. She made Sourdi get the first-aid kit from the bathroom, "Quick! Quick!" Ma even tried to put some ointment on his cut, but he just shrugged her off.

I couldn't believe it. I wanted to take the knife back and stab myself. That's how I felt when I heard her say, "No charge, on the house," for their dinner, despite the $50-worth of pitchers they'd had.

Ma grabbed me by the shoulders. "Say you sorry. Say it." I pressed my lips firmly together and hung my head. Then she slapped me.

I didn't start crying until after the men had left. "But, Ma," I said,   15 "he was hurting Sourdi!"

"Then why Sourdi not do something?" Ma twisted my ear. "You not thinking. That your problem. You always not think!"

Afterwards, Sourdi said I was lucky. The knife had only grazed the man's skin. They could have sued us. They could have pressed charges.

"I don't care!" I hissed then. "I shoulda killed him! I shoulda killed that sucker!"

Sourdi's face changed. I'd never seen my sister look like that. Not ever. Especially not at me. I was her favorite. But she looked then the way I felt inside. Like a big bomb was ticking behind her eyes.

We were sitting together in the bathroom. It was late at night, and everyone else was asleep. Sometimes we locked ourselves in the bathroom then, just the two of us, so we could talk about things like boys at school or who was the cutest actor on television shows we liked or how we felt when our family fought, when Uncle and Auntie yelled at each other, or when Ma grew depressed and smoked too much and looked at us as though she wished we'd never been born.

This night, however, Sourdi looked at me grimly. "Oh, no, Nea. Don't ever say that. Don't ever talk like that."

I was going to smile and shrug and say something like "I was just kidding," but something inside me couldn't lie tonight. I crossed my arms over my flat chest, and I stuck out my lower lip, like I'd seen the tough girls at school do. "Anyone mess like that with me, I'm gonna kill him!"

Sourdi took me by the shoulders then and shook me so hard I thought she was going to shake my head right off my body. She wouldn't stop even after I started to cry.

"Stop, stop!" I begged. "I'll be good! I promise, I'll be good!"

Finally, she pushed me away from her and sat on the toilet, with her head in her hands. Although she'd been the one hurting me, she looked as though she'd been beaten up, the way she sat like that, her shoulders hunched over her lap, as though she were trying to make herself disappear.

"I was trying to protect you," I said through my tears. "I was trying to save you. You're so stupid! I should just let that man diss you!"

Sourdi's head shot up and I could see that she had no patience left. Her eyes were red and her nostrils flared. She stood up and I took a step back quickly. I thought she was going to grab me and shake me again, but this time she just put her hand on my arm. "They could take you away. The police, they could put you in a foster home. All of us."

A chill ran through my whole body, like a live current. We all knew about foster homes. Rudy Gutierrez in third grade was taken away from his parents after the teacher noticed some bruises on his back. He'd tried to shoplift some PayDays from the 7-Eleven and got caught. When his dad got home that weekend, he let him have it. But after the school nurse took a look at him, Rudy was taken away from his parents and sent to live in a foster home. His parents couldn't speak English so good and didn't know what was happening until too late. Anyway, what kind of lawyer could they afford? We heard later from his cousin in Mrs. Chang's homeroom that Rudy's foster-dad had molested him. The cousin said

20

25

Rudy ran away from that home, but he got caught. At any rate, none of us ever saw him again.

"You want to go to a foster home?" Sourdi asked me.

"No," I whispered.   30

"Then don't be so stupid!"

I started crying again, because I realized Sourdi was right. She kissed me on the top of my head and hugged me to her. I leaned my head against her soft breasts that had only recently emerged from her chest and pretended that I was a good girl and that I would always obey her. What I didn't tell Sourdi was that I was still a wicked girl. I was glad I'd stabbed that man. I was crying only because life was so unfair.

We used to say that we'd run away, Sourdi and me. When we were older. After she graduated. She'd be my legal guardian. We'd go to California to see the stars. Paris. London. Cambodia even, to light incense for the bones of our father. We'd earn money working in Chinese restaurants in every country we visited. We had enough experience; it had to be worth something.

We'd lie awake all night whispering back and forth. I'd climb into Sourdi's bed, claiming that I couldn't sleep, curling into a ball beside my older sister, the smell of her like salt and garlic and a sweet scent that emanated directly from her skin. Sometimes I'd stroke Sourdi's slick hair, which she plaited into a thick wet braid so that it would be wavy in the morning. I would stay awake all night, pinching the inside of Sourdi's arm, the soft flesh of her thigh, to keep my sister from falling asleep and leaving me alone.

When she first started seeing Duke, I used to think of him as some-   35
thing like a bookmark, just holding a certain space in her life until it was time for her to move on. I never thought of him as a fork in the road, dividing my life with Sourdi from Sourdi's life with men.

In those days, I didn't understand anything.

Ma had hired Duke to wash dishes at the Palace that first summer. At first, we paid him no mind. He was just this funny-looking white kid, hair that stuck up straight from his head when he wasn't wearing his silly baseball cap backwards, skinny as a stalk of bamboo, long legs and long arms that seemed to move in opposition to each other. Chopstick-boy I called him, just to be mean. He took it as a compliment.

I could see why he fell in love with Sourdi. My sister was beautiful. Really beautiful, not like the girls in magazines with their pale, pinched faces, pink and powdery, brittle girls. Sourdi looked like a statue that had been rescued from the sea. She was smooth where I had angles and soft where I was bone. Sourdi's face was round, her nose low and wide, her eyes crescent-shaped like the quarter moon, her hair sleek as seaweed. Her skin was a burnished cinnamon color. Looking at Sourdi, I could pretend I was beautiful, too. She had so much to spare.

At first, Duke and Sourdi only talked behind the Palace, pretending to take a break from the heat of the kitchen. I caught them looking at the stars together.

The first time they kissed, I was there, too. Duke was giving us a ride 40 after school in his pickup. He had the music on loud and the windows were open. It was a hot day for October, and the wind felt like a warm ocean that we could swim in forever. He was going to drop us off at the Palace, but then Duke said he had something to show us, and we circled around the outskirts of town, taking the gravel road that led to the open fields, beyond the highway where the cattle ranches lay. Finally, he pulled off the gravel road and parked.

"You want us to look at cows?" I asked impatiently, crossing my arms.

He laughed at me then and took Sourdi by the hand. We hiked through a ditch to the edge of an empty cornfield long since harvested, the stubble of cornstalks poking up from the black soil, pale and bone-like. The field was laced with a barbed-wire fence to keep the cattle in, though I couldn't see any cows at all. The whole place gave me the creeps.

Duke held the strands of barbed wire apart for Sourdi and me and told us to crawl under the fence.

"Just trust me," he said.

We followed him to a spot in the middle of the field. "It's the center 45 of the world," Duke said. "Look." And he pointed back to where we'd come from, and suddenly I realized the rest of the world had disappeared. The ground had appeared level, but we must have walked into a tiny hollow in the plains, because from where we stood there was only sky and field for as far as our eyes could see. We could no longer see the road or Duke's pickup, our town, or even the green smudge of cottonwoods that grew along the Yankton River or the distant hills of Nebraska. There was nothing overhead, either; the sky was unbroken by clouds, smooth as an empty rice bowl. "It's just us here," Duke said. "We're alone in the whole universe."

All at once, Sourdi began to breathe funny. Her face grew pinched, and she wiped at her eyes with the back of her hand.

"What's wrong?" Duke asked stupidly.

Then Sourdi was running wildly. She took off like an animal startled by a gunshot. She was trying to head back to the road, but she tripped over the cornstalks and fell onto her knees. She started crying for real.

I caught up to her first — I've always been a fast runner. As Duke approached, I put my arms around Sourdi.

"I thought you'd like it," Duke said.   50

"We're city girls," I said, glaring at him. "Why would we like this hick stuff?"

"I'm sorry," Sourdi whispered. "I'm so sorry."

"What are you sorry for? It's his fault!" I pointed out.

Now Duke was kneeling next to Sourdi. He tried to put his arm over her shoulder, too. I was going to push him away, when Sourdi did something very surprising. She put both her arms around his neck and leaned against him, while Duke said soft, dumb-sounding things that I couldn't quite hear. Then they were kissing.

I was so surprised, I stared at them before I forced myself to look away. Then I was the one who felt like running, screaming, for the road. 55

On the way back to the Palace, Duke and Sourdi didn't talk, but they held hands. The worst part was I was sitting between them.

Ma didn't seem to notice anything for a while, but then with Ma it was always hard to know what she was thinking, what she knew and what she didn't. Sometimes she seemed to go through her days like she was made of stone. Sometimes she erupted like a volcano.

Uncle fired Duke a few weeks later. He said it was because Duke had dropped a tray of dishes. It was during the Saturday lunch rush when Sourdi and I weren't working and couldn't witness what had happened.

"He's a clumsy boy," Ma agreed after work that night, when we all sat around in the back booths and ate our dinner.

Sourdi didn't say anything. She knew Ma knew. 60

She kept seeing Duke, of course. They were both juniors, and there was only one high school in town. Now when I crept into Sourdi's bed at night, when she talked about running away, she meant Duke and her. I was the one who had to pipe up that I was coming with them, too. What we didn't know was that Ma was making plans as well.

Uncle first introduced his friend Mr. Chhay in the winter. I'd had a strange dream the night before. I hadn't remembered it at all until Mr. Chhay walked into the Palace, with his hangdog face and his suit like a salesman's. He sat in a corner booth with Uncle and, while they talked, he shredded a napkin, then took the scraps of paper and rolled them between his thumb and index finger into a hundred tiny red balls. He left them in the ashtray, like a mountain of fish eggs. Seeing them, I remembered my dream.

I was swimming in the ocean. I was just a small child, but I wasn't afraid at all. The sea was liquid turquoise, the sunlight yellow as gold against my skin. Fish were swimming alongside me. I could see through the clear water to the bottom of the sea. The fish were schooling around me and below me, and they brushed against my feet when I kicked the water. Their scales felt like bones scraping my toes. I tried to push them away, but the schools grew more dense, until I was swimming amongst them under the waves.

The fish began to spawn around me and soon the water was cloudy with eggs. I tried to break through the film, but the eggs clung to my skin. The water darkened as we entered a sea of kelp. I pushed against the dark slippery strands like Sourdi's hair. I realized I was pushing against my sister, wrapped in the kelp, suspended just below the surface of the water. Then I woke up.

I thought about that dream seeing that old guy Mr. Chhay with 65
Uncle and I knew they were up to no good. I wanted to warn Sourdi, but
she seemed to understand without my having to tell her anything.

Uncle called over to her and introduced her to his friend. But Sourdi
wouldn't even look at Mr. Chhay. She kept her eyes lowered, though he tried
to smile and talk to her. She whispered so low in reply that no one could
understand a word she said. I could tell the man was disappointed when he
left. His shoulders seemed barely able to support the weight of his jacket.

Mr. Chhay wrote letters to Uncle, to Ma. He thanked them for their
hospitality and enclosed pictures of his business and his house, plus a
formal portrait of himself looking ridiculous in another suit, standing
in front of some potted plants, his hair combed over the bald spot in the
middle of his head.

The next time he came to visit the Palace, he brought gifts. A giant
Chinese vase for Ma, Barbie dolls for my younger sisters and cousin, a
Christian music cassette tape for me, and a bright red leather purse for
Sourdi.

Ma made Sourdi tell him thank you.

And that was all she said to him. 70

But this old guy was persistent. He took us all out to eat at a steak-
house once. He said he wanted to pay back Uncle for some good deed
he'd done a long time ago when they both first came to America. I could
have told him, Sourdi hated this kind of food. She preferred Mexican,
tacos, not this Midwest cowboy stuff. But Ma made us all thank him.

"Thank you, Mr. Chhay," we said dutifully. He'd smiled so all his
yellow teeth showed at once. "Oh, please, call me Older Brother," he said.

It was the beginning of the end. I should have fought harder then. I
should have stabbed this man, too.

I saw Duke at Sourdi's wedding. She invited him for the ceremony proper,
the reception, too, but he didn't show up until the end. I almost didn't
see him at all. He was slouching through the parking lot of St. Agnes,
wearing his best hightops and the navy-blue suit that his mother had
insisted upon buying for graduation. I wasn't used to him looking like
a teenage undertaker, but I recognized his loping gait immediately. That
afternoon of Sourdi's wedding, he was holding a brown bag awkwardly
behind his back, as if trying to conceal the fact that he was drinking as
conspicuously as possible.

I was standing inside the bingo hall, before the row of squat windows, 75
my back turned to the festivities, the exploding flash capturing the tipsy
toasts, the in-laws singing off-key to the rented karaoke machine.

Then it really became too much to bear, and I had to escape the terrible heat, the flickering fluorescent lights. I slipped from the church
into the ferocious March wind and gave it my best shot, running across
the hard lawn, but the too-tight heels pinched my toes and the stiff
taffeta bodice of the cotton-candy-pink bridesmaid's dress might as

well have been a vise around my rib cage. I had intended to make it off church property, run to the empty field that stretched low and dark all the way to the horizon, but I only made it to the end of the walk near the rectory before vomiting into Sister Kevin's over-tended tulip patch.

Duke came over and sat on his haunches beside me, while I puked. I let him hold back my hair, while the wedding cake and wine cooler that I'd tried poured from my mouth.

Finally, I spat a few times to clear my mouth, then sat back on my rear end.

After a few minutes, I could take a sip from Duke's beer.

We didn't talk.   80

I took out the pack of cigarettes I'd stolen from Ma's purse and lit one. It took five puffs before I could mask the taste of bile and sugar.

The wind was blowing fiercely from the northwest, whipping my hair about my face like a widow's veil, throwing dust from the parking lot around us like wedding rice.

After a long while, Duke stood up and walked back down the side-walk lined with yellow daffodils. He walked bow-legged, like all the boys in our town, farmers' sons, no matter how cool Duke tried to be. I bur-ied my head in my arms and watched him from under one polyester-covered armpit as he climbed back into his pickup and pulled away with a screech. As he left the parking lot, he tossed the brown bag with the empty bottle of Bud out the window. It fell into the street, where it rolled and rolled until it disappeared into a ditch.

Ma liked Sourdi's husband. He had a steady job, a house. She didn't mind he was so old and Sourdi just eighteen when they married. In her eyes, eighteen was a good age to start a family. "I was younger than Sourdi when I get married," Ma liked to say.

When Sourdi sent pictures home for the holidays, Ma ooohed and   85
aaahed as though they were winning lottery tickets. My sister and her old husband in front of a listing Christmas tree, a pile of presents at their feet. Then, the red-faced baby sprawled on a pink blanket on the living room carpet, drooling in its shiny high chair, slumped in its Snugli like a rock around Sourdi's neck.

"Look. Sony," Ma pointed at the big-screen television in the back-ground of the New Year's pictures. "Sourdi say they got all new washer/ dryer, too. Maytag."

When I looked at my sister's pictures, I could see that she looked tired.

Sourdi always said that Ma used to be a very brave woman. She also said that Ma used to be a beautiful woman who liked to have her hair fixed in salons, who wore pretty dresses and knew how to dance in all the fashionable styles. I don't remember this mother. I remember the mother who worked two jobs for us.

I might never have seen Duke again if it were not for Sourdi's strange phone call one Saturday evening nearly two years after her wedding. I was fourteen and a half.

At first, I hadn't recognized my older sister's voice.   90

"Who is this?" I demanded, thinking: heavy breathing, prank caller.

"Who d'you think?" Sourdi was crying, a tiny crimped sound that barely crept out of the receiver. Then her voice steadied with anger and grew familiar. "Is Ma there?"

"What's the matter? What happened?"

"Just let me speak to Ma, O.K.?" There was a pause, as Sourdi blew her nose. "Tell her it's important."

I lured Ma from the TV room without alerting my younger sisters.   95
Ma paced back and forth in the kitchen between the refrigerator and the stove, nodding and muttering, "Mmm, mmm, uh-hmm." I could just hear the tinny squeak of Sourdi's panicked voice.

I sat on the floor, hugging my knees, in the doorway to the hall, just out of Ma's line of sight.

Finally, Ma said, in the tone normally reserved for refusing service to the unruly or arguing with a customer who had a complaint, "It's always like this. Every marriage is hard. Sometimes there is nothing you can do—"

Then Ma stopped pacing. "Just minute," she said and she took the phone with her into the bathroom, shutting the door firmly behind her.

When she came out again, twenty-two minutes later, she ignored me completely. She set the phone back on the counter without saying a word.

"So?" I prompted.   100

"I'm tired." Ma rubbed her neck with one hand. "Just let me rest. You girls, it's always something. Don't let your old mother rest."

She yawned extravagantly. She claimed she was too tired to watch any more TV. She had to go to bed, her eyes just wouldn't stay open.

I tried calling Sourdi, but the phone only rang and rang.

The next morning, Sunday, I called first thing, but then *he* picked up, my sister's husband.

"Oh, is this Nea?" he said, so cheerfully it was obvious he was hiding   105
something.

"Yes, I'd like to speak to my sister."

"I'm sorry, Little Sister." I just hated when he called me that. "My wife is out right now. But I'll tell her you called. She'll be sorry she missed you."

It was eight o'clock in the morning, for Chrissake.

"Oh, thank you," I said, sweet as pie. "How's the baby?"

"So well!" Then he launched into a long explanation about his   110
daughter's eating habits, her rather average attempts to crawl, the simple words she was trying to say. For all I knew, Sourdi could have been right there, fixing his breakfast, washing his clothes, cleaning up his messes. I thought of my sister's voice in my ear, the tiny sound like something breaking.

It was all I could do to disguise the disdain in my voice. "Be sure to tell Sourdi to call back. Ma found that recipe she wanted. That special delicious recipe she was looking for. I can't tell you what it is, Ma's secret recipe, but you'll really be surprised."

"Oh, boy," the jerk said. "I didn't know about any secret recipe."

"That's why it's a secret." I hung up. I couldn't breathe. My chest hurt. I could feel my swollen heart pressing against my ribs.

The next afternoon, I tried calling back three more times, but no one answered.

At work that evening, Ma was irritable. She wouldn't look me in the eyes when I tried to get her attention. Some little kid spilled his Coke into a perfectly good plate of House Special Prawns and his parents insisted they be given a new order—and a new Coke—on the house. There was a minor grease fire around quarter to nine—the smoke alarms all went off at the same time—and then the customers started complaining about the cold, too, once we had opened all the doors and windows to clear the air. Fairly average as far as disasters went, but they put Ma in a sour mood.

Ma was taking a cigarette break out back by the dumpsters, smoke curling from her nostrils, before I could corner her. She wasn't in the mood to talk, but after the nicotine fix took hold, she didn't tell me to get back to work, either.

I asked Ma if I could have a smoke. She didn't get angry. She smiled in her tired way, the edges of her mouth twitching upwards just a little, and said, "Smoking will kill you." Then she handed me her pack.

"Maybe Sourdi should come back home for a while," I suggested.

"She's a married woman. She has her own family now."

"She's still part of our family."

Ma didn't say anything, just tilted her head back and blew smoke at the stars, so I continued, "Well, don't you think she might be in trouble? She was crying, you know. It's not like Sourdi." My voice must have slipped a tad, just enough to sound disrespectful, because Ma jerked upright, took the cigarette out of her mouth and glared at me.

"What you think? You so smart? You gonna tell me what's what?" Ma threw her cigarette onto the asphalt. "You not like your sister. Your sister know how to bear things!"

She stormed back into the kitchen, and Ma ignored me for the rest of the evening.

I called Sourdi one more time, after Ma and my sisters had gone to bed and I finally had the kitchen to myself, the moon spilling from the window onto the floor in a big, blue puddle. I didn't dare turn on the lights.

This time, my sister answered. "Mmm. . . . Hello?"

"Sourdi?"

"What time is it?"

"Sssh." My heart beat so loudly, I couldn't hear my own voice. "How are you doing?"

"Oh, we're fine. The baby, she's doing real good. She's starting to talk—"

"No, no, no. I mean, what happened the other night?"

"What?"

Another voice now, low, a man's voice, just beneath the snow on the line. Then suddenly a shriek.

"Uh-oh. I just woke her up." Sourdi's voice grew fainter as she spoke to him: "Honey, can you check the baby's diaper?" Then she said to me, "I have to go. The baby, she's hungry, you know."

"Let him handle it. I have to talk to you a minute, O.K.? Just don't go, Sourdi. What's going on? What did you say to Ma?"

Sourdi sighed, like a balloon losing its air. "Oh . . . nothing. Look, I really have to go. Talk to you later, Nea." She hung up. 135

I called back in twenty minutes, surely long enough to change a diaper, but the phone only rang forlornly, ignored.

I considered taking Ma's car, but then Ma wouldn't be able to get to work and I wasn't sure how long I needed to be gone. Then I thought of Duke.

Even though it was far too late in the night, I called Duke. He was still in town, two years after graduation. I'd heard he was working as a mechanic at the Standard station. I found his number in the phone book.

"It's Nea. Pick up your phone, Duke," I hissed into his machine. "It's an emergency!"

"Nea?!" He was yawning. "My God. What time is it?" 140

"Duke! It's important! It's Sourdi, she's in trouble."

There was a pause while I let him absorb all this.

"You have to drive me to Des Moines. We have to get her."

"What happened?"

"Look, I don't have time to explain. We have to go tonight. It's an 145 emergency. A matter of life and death."

"Did you call the police?"

"Don't be stupid. Sourdi would never call the cops. She loves that jerk."

"What?" Duke whispered, "Her husband, he beat her up?"

"Duke, I told you, I can't say anything right now. But you have to help me."

He agreed to meet me at the corner, where there'd be no chance Ma 150 could hear his truck. I'd be waiting.

It was freezing. The wind stung my cheeks, which wasn't a good sign. Could be rain coming, or worse, snow. Even when the roads were clear, it was a good six-hour drive. I didn't want to think how long it would take if we ran into a late-season blizzard.

There was the roar of a souped-up engine and then a spray of gravel. Snoop Doggy Dogg growled over the wind.

"Duke! What took you?"

He put his hand over the door, barring me from climbing up. "You want me to help or not?"

"Don't joke." 155

I pulled myself inside and then made Duke back up rather than run in front of the house. Just in case Ma woke up.

"How come your Ma didn't want to come?"

"She doesn't know."

"Sourdi didn't want to worry her?"

"Mmm." There was no point trying to shout above Snoop Dogg.   160

He was obviously tired. When Duke was tired, he turned his music up even louder than normal. I'd forgotten that. Now the bass underneath the rap was vibrating in my bones. But at least he did as I asked and took off toward the highway.

Soon the squat buildings of town, the used-car lots on the route in from the interstate with their flapping colored flags, and the metal storage units of the Sav-U-Lot passed from view, and there was nothing before us but the black sky and the highway and the patches of snow on the shoulders glowing briefly in the wake of the headlights.

I must have fallen asleep, though I don't remember feeling tired. I was standing on the deck of a boat in an inky ocean, trying to read the stars, but every time I found one constellation, the stars began to blink and fade. I squinted at them, but the stars would not stay in place. Then my head snapped forward as the pickup careened off the shoulder.

The pickup landed in a ditch. Metal glittered in the headlights; the fields on this side of the highway were strung with barbed wire.

We got out by sacrificing our jackets, stuffing them under the back   165 tires until we had enough traction to slide back onto the pavement.

I insisted upon driving. "I got my license," I lied. "And I'm not tired at all."

Duke settled into the passenger seat, his arms folded across his chest, his head tilted back, preparing to go to sleep again.

"D'ya think she'll be happy to see me?" he said out of the blue. "Sourdi sent me a Christmas card with a picture of the baby. Looks just like. . . . But I didn't write back or nothing. She probably thought I was angry. She mad at me, you think?"

"Sourdi's never mad at anybody."

"She must be mad at her husband if she wants you to come get her."   170

"She doesn't know we're coming."

"What!"

"I didn't have time to explain to her."

"You're not running away from home, are you?" Duke's eyes narrowed and his voice grew slow as if he thought he was suddenly being clever.

"Yeah, I'm running away to Des Moines."   175

Once upon a time, in another world, a place almost unimaginable to me sitting in the pickup with Madonna singing "Lucky Star" on the radio, Sourdi had walked across a minefield, carrying me on her back. She was nine and I was four. Because she'd told me, I could see it all clearly, better than if I actually remembered: the startled faces of people who'd tripped a mine, their limbs in new arrangements, the bones peeking through the earth. Sourdi had said it was safest to step on the bodies; that way you knew a mine was no longer there.

This was nothing I would ever tell Duke. It was our own personal story, just for Sourdi and me to share. Nobody's business but ours.

I would walk on bones for my sister, I vowed. I would put my bare feet on rotting flesh. I would save Sourdi.

We found the house in West Des Moines after circling for nearly an hour through the identical streets with their neat lawns and boxy houses and chain link fences. I refused to allow Duke to ask for directions from any of the joggers or the van that sputtered by, delivering the *Register*. He figured people in the neighborhood would know, just ask where the Oriental family lived. I told him to go to hell. Then we didn't talk for a while.

But as soon as we found Locust Street, I recognized the house. I 180
knew it was Sourdi's even though it had been painted a different color since the last set of pictures. The lace undercurtains before the cheerful flowered draperies, the flourishing plants in the windows, next to little trinkets, figurines in glass that caught the light. Every space crammed with something sweet.

The heater in Duke's truck began to make a high-pitched, sick-cat whine as we waited, parked across the street, staring at Sourdi's house.

"So, are we going to just sit here?"

"Shh," I said irritably. "Just wait a minute." Somehow I had imagined that Sourdi would sense our presence, the curtains would stir, and I'd only have to wait a moment for my sister to come running out the front door. But we sat patiently, shivering, staring at Sourdi's house. Nothing moved.

"Her husband's home," I said stupidly. "He hasn't gone to work yet."

"He wouldn't dare try anything. Not with the both of us here. We 185
should just go and knock."

"They're probably still asleep."

"Nea, what's the matter with you? What are you afraid of all of a sudden?"

I'd had it with Duke. He just didn't understand anything. I hopped out of the truck and ran through the icy air, my arms wrapped around my body. The sidewalk was slick beneath my sneakers, still damp from the ditch, and I slid onto my knees on the driveway. My right hand broke the fall. A sharp jagged pain shot up to my elbow and stayed there, throbbing. I picked myself up and ran limping to the door and rang.

No one answered for a minute, and then it was him.

"What on earth? Nea!" Sourdi's husband was dressed for work, but he hadn't shaved yet. He looked even older than I remembered, his thinning hair flat across his skull, his bloodshot eyes and swollen lids still heavy from sleep. He might have been handsome once, decades ago, but I saw no evidence of it now. He held the door open and I slipped into the warmth without even removing my shoes first. "How did you get here? Is your mother coming, too?" 190

My eyes started to water, the transition from cold to heat. Slowly the room came into focus. It was a mess. Baby toys on the carpet, shoes in a pile by the door, old newspapers scattered on an end table anchored by a bowl of peanut shells. The TV was blaring somewhere, and a baby was crying.

Sourdi emerged from the kitchen, dressed in a bright pink sweatsuit emblazoned with the head of Minnie Mouse, pink slippers over her feet, the baby on her hip. She had a bruise across her cheekbone and the purple remains of a black eye. Sourdi didn't say anything for a few seconds as she stared at me, blinking, her mouth falling open. "Where's Ma?"

"Home."

"Oh, no." Sourdi's face crumpled. "Is everything all right?"

I couldn't believe how dense my sister had become. We used to be able to communicate without words. "Everything's fine . . . at home. Of course." I tried to give her a look so that she'd understand that I had come to rescue her, but Sourdi stood rigidly in place in the doorway to the kitchen, her mouth twitching, puzzled. 195

"Please, Little Sister, sit down," her husband said. "Let me make you some tea."

Someone banged on the front door, three times. Before I could begin to feel annoyed that Duke couldn't even wait five minutes, that he just had to ruin everything, my sister's husband opened the door again. I didn't bother to turn, instead I watched Sourdi's eyes widen and her wide mouth pucker into an O as she gasped, "Duke!"

"What's goin' on?" Duke said.

Then everyone stared at me with such identical expressions of non-comprehension that I had to laugh. Then I couldn't stop, because I hadn't slept and it was so cold and my nose was running and I didn't have any Kleenex.

"I said, what the hell is going on?" Duke repeated. 200

Sourdi's husband approached Duke. He smiled. "You must be Nea's—"

But by now, Duke had seen Sourdi's bruises. His mouth twisted into a sneer. "You bastard! I oughtta—" He punched Sourdi's husband in the nose. Sourdi screamed, her husband bent over double. Duke drew back his fist again, but Sourdi ran forward and grabbed him. She was punching him on the chest, "Out! Out! You! I'll call the police!" She tried to claw him with her nails, but Duke threw his arms up around his head.

Sourdi's husband stood up. Blood gushed from his nose all over his white shirt and tie.

"Come on!" I said stupidly. "Come on, Sourdi, let's go!"

But it was pretty obvious that she didn't want to leave.   205

The baby began shrieking.

I started crying, too.

After everyone had calmed down, Duke went down the street to the 7-Eleven to get a bag of ice for Mr. Chhay, who kept saying "I'm fine, don't worry," even though his nose had turned a deep scarlet and was starting to swell.

It turned out Sourdi's husband hadn't beaten her up. An economy-size box of baby wipes had fallen off the closet shelf and struck her full in the eye.

While Mr. Chhay went into the bedroom to change his clothes, I sat   210
with Sourdi in the kitchen as she tried to get the squawling baby to eat its breakfast.

"Nea, what's wrong with you?"

"What's wrong with me? Don't you get it? I was trying to help you!"

Sourdi sighed as the baby spat a spoonful of the glop onto the table. "I'm a married woman. I'm not just some girl anymore. I have my own family. You understand that?"

"You were crying." I squinted at my sister. "I heard you."

"I'm gonna have another baby, you know. That's a big step. That's a   215
big thing." She said this as though it explained everything.

"You sound like an old lady. You're only twenty, for Chrissake. You don't have to live like this. Ma is wrong. You can be anything, Sourdi."

Sourdi pinched her nose between two fingers. "Everything's gonna be fine. We just had a little argument, but it's O.K. We had a good talk. He understands now. I'm still gonna go to school. I haven't changed my mind. After the baby gets a little bigger, I mean, both babies. Maybe when they start preschool."

Just then her husband came back into the kitchen. He had to use the phone to call work. His face looked like a gargoyle's.

Sourdi looked at me then, so disappointed. I knew what she was thinking. She had grown up, and I had merely grown unworthy of her love.

After Duke got back with the ice, he and Sourdi's husband shook   220
hands. Duke kept saying, "Gosh, I'm so sorry," and Mr. Chhay kept repeating, "No problem, don't worry."

Then Sourdi's husband had to go. We followed him to the driveway. My sister kissed him before he climbed into his Buick. He rolled down the window, and she leaned in and kissed him again.

I turned away. I watched Duke standing in the doorway, holding the baby in his arms, cooing at its face. In his tough wannabe clothes, the super-wide jeans and his fancy sneakers and the chain from his wallet to his belt loops, he looked surprisingly young.

Sourdi lent us some blankets and matching his-and-hers Donald and Daisy Duck sweatshirts for the trip back, since our coats were still wet and worthless.

"Don't tell Ma I was here, O.K.?" I begged Sourdi. "We'll be home by afternoon. She'll just think I'm with friends or something. She doesn't have to know, O.K.?"

Sourdi pressed her full lips together into a thin line and nodded in a way that seemed as though she were answering a different question. And I knew that I couldn't trust my sister to take my side anymore.   225

As we pulled away from Sourdi's house, the first icy snowflakes began to fall across the windshield.

Sourdi stood in the driveway with the baby on her hip. She waved to us as the snow swirled around her like ashes.

She had made her choice, and she hadn't chosen me.

Sourdi told me a story once about a magic serpent, the Naga, with a mouth so large, it could swallow people whole. Our ancestors carved Naga into the stones of Angkor Wat to scare away demons. Sourdi said people used to believe they could come alive in times of great evil and protect the temples. They could eat armies.

I wished I was a Naga. I would have swallowed the whole world in one gulp.   230

But I have no magic powers. None whatsoever.

CONSIDERATIONS FOR CRITICAL THINKING AND WRITING

1. FIRST RESPONSE. How does your response to Nea develop over the course of the story? Is she a dynamic or a static character?

2. Explain how Nea and Sourdi serve as character foils to one another.

3. Discuss whether you think Duke is a flat or a round character.

4. What is the effect of the story's being told from Nea's perspective? How might the story be different if it were told from the mother's point of view?

5. Do you think Mr. Chhay is a good or bad husband?

6. How does the information about Nea and Sourdi's trip through the minefield affect your understanding of Nea's relationship with her sister?

7. Comment on the title. Why wouldn't an alternative like "Nea the Troublemaker" be appropriate?

8. CONNECTION TO ANOTHER SELECTION. Compare the characterization of Nea in "Saving Sourdi" and of Sammy in John Updike's "A & P" (p. 157). In what sense do both characters see themselves as rescuers?

JUNOT DÍAZ (b. 1968)

Born in Santo Domingo, Dominican Republic, Junot Díaz moved with his family to the
United States when he was seven years old.
He grew up in New Jersey and graduated from
Rutgers University and then earned an M.F.A.
from Cornell University. His first short story
collection *Drown* (1996) centers on a teenage
narrator from the Dominican Republic who
makes his way as an impoverished immigrant
in New Jersey. The story that follows is drawn
from that collection. Díaz's novel *The Brief
Wondrous Life of Oscar Wao* (2007) was awarded
a number of prizes, including the Pulitzer. He
teaches creative writing at the Massachusetts
Institute of Technology.

© Scott Lituchy/Star Ledger/CORBIS.

How to Date a Browngirl, Blackgirl, Whitegirl, or Halfie   1996

Wait for your brother and your mother to leave the apartment. You've
already told them that you're feeling too sick to go to Union City to visit
that tía° who likes to squeeze your nuts. (He's gotten big, she'll say.) And
even though your moms knows you ain't sick you stuck to your story
until finally she said, Go ahead and stay, malcriado.°

Clear the government cheese from the refrigerator. If the girl's
from the Terrace stack the boxes behind the milk. If she's from the
Park or Society Hill hide the cheese in the cabinet above the oven, way
up where she'll never see. Leave yourself a reminder to get it out before
morning or your moms will kick your ass. Take down any embarrassing
photos of your family in the campo,° especially the one with the half-
naked kids dragging a goat on a rope leash. The kids are your cousins
and by now they're old enough to understand why you're doing what
you're doing. Hide the pictures of yourself with an Afro. Make sure the
bathroom is presentable. Put the basket with all the crapped-on toilet paper under the sink. Spray the bucket with Lysol, then close the
cabinet.

Shower, comb, dress. Sit on the couch and watch TV. If she's an outsider her father will be bringing her, maybe her mother. Neither of them

tía: Aunt.
malcriado: Spoiled, pampered.
campo: Countryside.

want her seeing any boys from the Terrace — people get stabbed in the Terrace — but she's strong-headed and this time will get her way. If she's a whitegirl you know you'll at least get a hand job.

The directions were in your best handwriting, so her parents won't think you're an idiot. Get up from the couch and check the parking lot. Nothing. If the girl's local, don't sweat it. She'll flow over when she's good and ready. Sometimes she'll run into her other friends and a whole crowd will show up at your apartment and even though that means you ain't getting shit it will be fun anyway and you'll wish these people would come over more often. Sometimes the girl won't flow over at all and the next day in school she'll say sorry, smile and you'll be stupid enough to believe her and ask her out again.

Wait and after an hour go out to your corner. The neighborhood is full of traffic. Give one of your boys a shout and when he says, Are you still waiting on that bitch? say, Hell yeah.   5

Get back inside. Call her house and when her father picks up ask if she's there. He'll ask, Who is this? Hang up. He sounds like a principal or a police chief, the sort of dude with a big neck, who never has to watch his back. Sit and wait. By the time your stomach's ready to give out on you, a Honda or maybe a Jeep pulls in and out she comes.

Hey, you'll say.

Look, she'll say. My mom wants to meet you. She's got herself all worried about nothing.

Don't panic. Say, Hey, no problem. Run a hand through your hair like the whiteboys do even though the only thing that runs easily through your hair is Africa. She will look good. The white ones are the ones you want the most, aren't they, but usually the out-of-towners are black, blackgirls who grew up with ballet and Girl Scouts, who have three cars in their driveways. If she's a halfie don't be surprised that her mother is white. Say, Hi. Her moms will say hi and you'll see that you don't scare her, not really. She will say that she needs easier directions to get out and even though she has the best directions in her lap give her new ones. Make her happy.

You have choices. If the girl's from around the way, take her to El Cibao° for dinner. Order everything in your busted-up Spanish. Let her correct you if she's Latina and amaze her if she's black. If she's not from around the way, Wendy's will do. As you walk to the restaurant talk about school. A local girl won't need stories about the neighborhood but the other ones might. Supply the story about the loco who'd been storing canisters of tear gas in his basement for years, how one day the canisters cracked and the whole neighborhood got a dose of the military strength stuff. Don't tell her that your moms knew right away what it was, that she recognized its smell from the year the United States invaded your island.   10

El Cibao: Named after a region in the Dominican Republic.

Hope that you don't run into your nemesis, Howie, the Puerto Rican kid with the two killer mutts. He walks them all over the neighborhood and every now and then the mutts corner themselves a cat and tear it to shreds, Howie laughing as the cat flips up in the air, its neck twisted around like an owl, red meat showing through the soft fur. If his dogs haven't cornered a cat, he will walk behind you and ask, Hey, Yunior, is that your new fuckbuddy?

Let him talk. Howie weighs about two hundred pounds and could eat you if he wanted. At the field he will turn away. He has new sneakers, and doesn't want them muddy. If the girl's an outsider she will hiss now and say, What a fucking asshole. A homegirl would have been yelling back at him the whole time, unless she was shy. Either way don't feel bad that you didn't do anything. Never lose a fight on a first date or that will be the end of it.

Dinner will be tense. You are not good at talking to people you don't know. A halfie will tell you that her parents met in the Movement, will say, Back then people thought it a radical thing to do. It will sound like something her parents made her memorize. Your brother once heard that one and said, Man, that sounds like a whole lot of Uncle Tomming to me. Don't repeat this.

Put down your hamburger and say, It must have been hard.

She will appreciate your interest. She will tell you more. Black 15 people, she will say, treat me real bad. That's why I don't like them. You'll wonder how she feels about Dominicans. Don't ask. Let her speak on it and when you're both finished eating walk back into the neighborhood. The skies will be magnificent. Pollutants have made Jersey sunsets one of the wonders of the world. Point it out. Touch her shoulder and say, That's nice, right?

Get serious. Watch TV but stay alert. Sip some of the Bermúdez° your father left in the cabinet, which nobody touches. A local girl may have hips and a thick ass but she won't be quick about letting you touch. She has to live in the same neighborhood you do, has to deal with you being all up in her business. She might just chill with you and then go home. She might kiss you and then go, or she might, if she's reckless, give it up, but that's rare. Kissing will suffice. A whitegirl might just give it up right then. Don't stop her. She'll take her gum out of her mouth, stick it to the plastic sofa covers and then will move close to you. You have nice eyes, she might say.

Tell her that you love her hair, that you love her skin, her lips, because, in truth, you love them more than you love your own.

She'll say, I like Spanish guys, and even though you've never been to Spain, say, I like you. You'll sound smooth.

You'll be with her until about eight-thirty and then she will want to wash up. In the bathroom she will hum a song from the radio and her

---

Bermúdez: A type of rum.

waist will keep the beat against the lip of the sink. Imagine her old lady coming to get her, what she would say if she knew her daughter had just lain under you and blown your name, pronounced with her eighth-grade Spanish, into your ear. While she's in the bathroom call one of your boys and say, Lo hice, loco.° Or just sit back on the couch and smile.

But usually it won't work this way. Be prepared. She will not want to   20 kiss you. Just cool it, she'll say. The halfie might lean back, breaking away from you. She will cross her arms, say, I hate my tits. Stroke her hair but she will pull away. I don't like anybody touching my hair, she will say. She will act like somebody you don't know. In school she is known for her attention-grabbing laugh, as high and far-ranging as a gull, but here she will worry you. You will not know what to say.

You're the only kind of guy who asks me out, she will say. Your neighbors will start their hyena calls, now that the alcohol is in them. You and the blackboys.

Say nothing. Let her button her shirt, let her comb her hair, the sound of it stretching like a sheet of fire between you. When her father pulls in and beeps, let her go without too much of a good-bye. She won't want it. During the next hour the phone will ring. You will be tempted to pick it up. Don't. Watch the shows you want to watch, without a family around to debate you. Don't go downstairs. Don't fall asleep. It won't help. Put the government cheese back in its place before your moms kills you.

Lo hice, loco: I did it, crazy.

CONSIDERATIONS FOR CRITICAL THINKING AND WRITING

1. **FIRST RESPONSE.** What expectations does the title create for you?
2. Describe the social and economic conditions in the Terrace neighborhood.
3. Point to five details about Yunior that characterize him particularly well for you.
4. Consider whether Yunior is a stock or round character.
5. Describe Yunior's perspective on females and sexuality. What is your response to these views?
6. To what extent does Yunior's potential date serve as a foil to him?
7. What do you think of the way in which race, class, and gender are presented in the story?
8. **CONNECTION TO ANOTHER SELECTION.** Discuss the teenage narrator's relationship to authority in Díaz's story and in John Updike's "A & P" (p. 157).
9. **CONNECTION TO ANOTHER SELECTION.** Compare and contrast attitudes toward love and romance in Díaz's story and in David Updike's "Summer" (p. 163).

HERMAN MELVILLE (1819–1891)

Hoping to improve his distressed financial situation, Herman Melville left New York and went to sea as a young common sailor. He returned to become an uncommon writer. His experiences at sea became the basis for his early novels: *Typee* (1846), *Omoo* (1847), *Mardi* (1849), *Redburn* (1849), and *White-Jacket* (1850). Ironically, with the publication of his masterpiece, *Moby-Dick* (1851), Melville lost the popular success he had enjoyed with his earlier books because his readers were not ready for its philosophical complexity. Although he wrote more, Melville's works were read less and slipped into obscurity. His final short novel, *Billy Budd,* was not published until the

Library of Congress, Prints and Photographs Division.

1920s, when critics rediscovered him. In "Bartleby, the Scrivener," Melville presents a quiet clerk in a law office whose baffling "passive resistance" disrupts the life of his employer, a man who attempts to make sense of Bartleby's refusal to behave reasonably.

Bartleby, the Scrivener   *1853*

A Story of Wall Street

I am a rather elderly man. The nature of my avocations, for the last thirty years, has brought me into more than ordinary contact with what would seem an interesting and somewhat singular set of men, of whom, as yet, nothing, that I know of, has ever been written—I mean, the law-copyists, or scriveners. I have known very many of them, professionally and privately, and, if I pleased, could relate diverse histories, at which good-natured gentlemen might smile, and sentimental souls might weep. But I waive the biographies of all other scriveners, for a few passages in the life of Bartleby, who was a scrivener, the strangest I ever saw, or heard of. While, of other law-copyists, I might write the complete life, of Bartleby nothing of that sort can be done. I believe that no materials exist, for a full and satisfactory biography of this man. It is an irreparable loss to literature. Bartleby was one of those beings of whom nothing is ascertainable, except from the original sources, and, in his case, those are very small. What my own astonished eyes saw of Bartleby, *that* is all I know of him, except, indeed, one vague report, which will appear in the sequel.

Ere introducing the scrivener, as he first appeared to me, it is fit I make some mention of myself, my *employés,* my business, my chambers, and general surroundings, because some such description is indispensable to an adequate understanding of the chief character about to be presented. Imprimis:° I am a man who, from his youth upwards, has been filled with a profound conviction that the easiest way of life is the best. Hence, though I belong to a profession proverbially energetic and nervous, even to turbulence, at times, yet nothing of that sort have I ever suffered to invade my peace. I am one of those unambitious lawyers who never address a jury, or in any way draw down public applause; but, in the cool tranquillity of a snug retreat, do a snug business among rich men's bonds, and mortgages, and title-deeds. All who know me, consider me an eminently *safe* man. The late John Jacob Astor,° a personage little given to poetic enthusiasm, had no hesitation in pronouncing my first grand point to be prudence; my next, method. I do not speak it in vanity, but simply record the fact, that I was not unemployed in my profession by the late John Jacob Astor; a name which, I admit, I love to repeat; for it hath a rounded and orbicular sound to it, and rings like unto bullion. I will freely add, that I was not insensible to the late John Jacob Astor's good opinion.

Some time prior to the period at which this little history begins, my avocations had been largely increased. The good old office, now extinct in the State of New York, of a Master in Chancery, had been conferred upon me. It was not a very arduous office, but very pleasantly remunerative. I seldom lose my temper; much more seldom indulge in dangerous indignation at wrongs and outrages; but I must be permitted to be rash here and declare, that I consider the sudden and violent abrogation of the office of Master in Chancery, by the new Constitution, as a — premature act; inasmuch as I had counted upon a life-lease of the profits, whereas I only received those of a few short years. But this is by the way.

My chambers were up stairs, at No. — Wall Street. At one end, they looked upon the white wall of the interior of a spacious skylight shaft, penetrating the building from top to bottom.

This view might have been considered rather tame than other- 5
wise, deficient in what landscape painters call "life." But, if so, the view from the other end of my chambers offered, at least, a contrast, if nothing more. In that direction, my windows commanded an unobstructed view of a lofty brick wall, black by age and everlasting shade; which wall required no spyglass to bring out its lurking beauties, but, for the benefit of all near-sighted spectators, was pushed up to within ten feet of my window-panes. Owing to the great height of the surrounding buildings, and my chambers being on the second floor, the interval between this wall and mine not a little resembled a huge square cistern.

At the period just preceding the advent of Bartleby, I had two persons as copyists in my employment, and a promising lad as an office-boy. First, Turkey; second, Nippers; third, Ginger Nut. These may seem names, the like of which are not usually found in the Directory. In truth, they were

Imprimis: In the first place.
John Jacob Astor (1763–1848): An enormously wealthy American capitalist.

nicknames, mutually conferred upon each other by my three clerks, and were deemed expressive of their respective persons or characters. Turkey was a short, pursy Englishman, of about my own age—that is, somewhere not far from sixty. In the morning, one might say, his face was of a fine florid hue, but after twelve o'clock, meridian—his dinner hour—it blazed like a grate full of Christmas coals; and continued blazing—but, as it were, with a gradual wane—till six o'clock, P.M., or thereabouts; after which, I saw no more of the proprietor of the face, which, gaining its meridian with the sun, seemed to set with it, to rise, culminate, and decline the following day, with the like regularity and undiminished glory. There are many singular coincidences I have known in the course of my life, not the least among which was the fact, that, exactly when Turkey displayed his fullest beams from his red and radiant countenance, just then, too, at that critical moment, began the daily period when I considered his business capacities as seriously disturbed for the remainder of the twenty-four hours. Not that he was absolutely idle, or averse to business then; far from it. The difficulty was, he was apt to be altogether too energetic. There was a strange, inflamed, flurried, flighty recklessness of activity about him. He would be incautious in dipping his pen into his inkstand. All his blots upon my documents were dropped there after twelve o'clock, meridian. Indeed, not only would he be reckless, and sadly given to making blots in the afternoon, but, some days, he went further, and was rather noisy. At such times, too, his face flamed with augmented blazonry, as if cannel coal had been heaped on anthracite. He made an unpleasant racket with his chair; spilled his sand-box; in mending his pens, impatiently split them all to pieces, and threw them on the floor in a sudden passion; stood up, and leaned over his table, boxing his papers about in a most indecorous manner, very sad to behold in an elderly man like him. Nevertheless, as he was in many ways a most valuable person to me, and all the time before twelve o'clock, meridian, was the quickest, steadiest creature, too, accomplishing a great deal of work in a style not easily to be matched—for these reasons, I was willing to overlook his eccentricities, though, indeed, occasionally, I remonstrated with him. I did this very gently, however, because, though the civilest, nay, the blandest and most reverential of men in the morning, yet, in the afternoon, he was disposed, upon provocation, to be slightly rash with his tongue—in fact, insolent. Now, valuing his morning services as I did, and resolved not to lose them—yet, at the same time, made uncomfortable by his inflamed ways after twelve o'clock—and being a man of peace, unwilling by my admonitions to call forth unseemly retorts from him, I took upon me, one Saturday noon (he was always worse on Saturdays) to hint to him, very kindly, that, perhaps, now that he was growing old, it might be well to abridge his labors; in short, he need not come to my chambers after twelve o'clock, but, dinner over, had best go home to his lodgings, and rest himself till tea-time. But no; he insisted upon his afternoon devotions. His countenance became intolerably fervid, as he oratorically assured me—gesticulating with a long ruler at the other end of the room—that if his services in the morning were useful, how indispensable, then, in the afternoon?

"With submission, sir," said Turkey, on this occasion, "I consider myself your right-hand man. In the morning I but marshal and deploy my columns; but in the afternoon I put myself at their head, and gallantly charge the foe, thus"—and he made a violent thrust with the ruler.

"But the blots, Turkey," intimated I.

"True; but, with submission, sir, behold these hairs! I am getting old. Surely, sir, a blot or two of a warm afternoon is not to be severely urged against gray hairs. Old age—even if it blot the page—is honorable. With submission, sir, we *both* are getting old."

This appeal to my fellow-feeling was hardly to be resisted. At all   10 events, I saw that go he would not. So, I made up my mind to let him stay, resolving, nevertheless, to see to it that, during the afternoon, he had to do with my less important papers.

Nippers, the second on my list, was a whiskered, sallow, and, upon the whole, rather piratical-looking young man, of about five-and-twenty. I always deemed him the victim of two evil powers—ambition and indigestion. The ambition was evinced by a certain impatience of the duties of a mere copyist, an unwarrantable usurpation of strictly professional affairs such as the original drawing up of legal documents. The indigestion seemed betokened in an occasional nervous testiness and grinning irritability, causing the teeth to audibly grind together over mistakes committed in copying; unnecessary maledictions, hissed, rather than spoken, in the heat of business; and especially by a continual discontent with the height of the table where he worked. Though of a very ingenious mechanical turn, Nippers could never get this table to suit him. He put chips under it, blocks of various sorts, bits of pasteboard, and at last went so far as to attempt an exquisite adjustment, by final pieces of folded blotting-paper. But no invention would answer. If, for the sake of easing his back, he brought the table-lid at a sharp angle well up towards his chin, and wrote there like a man using the steep roof of a Dutch house for his desk, then he declared that it stopped the circulation in his arms. If now he lowered the table to his waistbands, and stooped over it in writing, then there was a sore aching in his back. In short, the truth of the matter was, Nippers knew not what he wanted. Or, if he wanted anything, it was to be rid of a scrivener's table altogether. Among the manifestations of his diseased ambition was a fondness he had for receiving visits from certain ambiguous-looking fellows in seedy coats, whom he called his clients. Indeed, I was aware that not only was he, at times, considerable of a ward-politician, but he occasionally did a little business at the justices' courts, and was not unknown on the steps of the Tombs.°

the Tombs: A jail in New York City.

I have good reason to believe, however, that one individual who called upon him at my chambers, and who, with a grand air, he insisted was his client, was no other than a dun, and the alleged title-deed, a bill. But, with all his failings, and the annoyances he caused me, Nippers, like his compatriot Turkey, was a very useful man to me; wrote a neat, swift hand; and, when he chose, was not deficient in a gentlemanly sort of deport-ment. Added to this, he always dressed in a gentlemanly sort of way; and so, incidentally, reflected credit upon my chambers. Whereas, with respect to Turkey, I had much ado to keep him from being a reproach to me. His clothes were apt to look oily, and smell of eating-houses. He wore his pantaloons very loose and baggy in summer. His coats were execrable, his hat not to be handled. But while the hat was a thing of indifference to me, inasmuch as his natural civility and deference, as a dependent Englishman, always led him to doff it the moment he entered the room, yet his coat was another matter. Concerning his coats, I reasoned with him; but with no effect. The truth was, I suppose, that a man with so small an income could not afford to sport such a lustrous face and a lus-trous coat at one and the same time. As Nippers once observed, Turkey's money went chiefly for red ink. One winter day, I presented Turkey with a highly respectable-looking coat of my own—a padded gray coat, of a most comfortable warmth, and which buttoned straight up from the knee to the neck. I thought Turkey would appreciate the favor, and abate his rashness and obstreperousness of afternoons. But no; I verily believe that buttoning himself up in so downy and blanket-like a coat had a per-nicious effect upon him—upon the same principle that too much oats are bad for horses. In fact, precisely as a rash, restive horse is said to feel his oats, so Turkey felt his coat. It made him insolent. He was a man whom prosperity harmed.

Though, concerning the self-indulgent habits of Turkey, I had my own private surmises, yet, touching Nippers, I was well persuaded that, whatever might be his faults in other respects, he was, at least, a tem-perate young man. But indeed, nature herself seemed to have been his vintner, and, at his birth, charged him so thoroughly with an irritable, brandy-like disposition, that all subsequent potations were needless. When I consider how, amid the stillness of my chambers, Nippers would sometimes impatiently rise from his seat, and stooping over his table, spread his arms wide apart, seize the whole desk, and move it, and jerk it, with a grim, grinding motion on the floor, as if the table were a perverse voluntary agent, intent on thwarting and vexing him, I plainly perceive that, for Nippers, brandy-and-water were altogether superfluous.

It was fortunate for me that, owing to its peculiar cause— indigestion—the irritability and consequent nervousness of Nip-pers were mainly observable in the morning, while in the afternoon he was comparatively mild. So that, Turkey's paroxysms only coming on about twelve o'clock, I never had to do with their eccentricities at one time. Their fits relieved each other, like guards. When Nippers' was on,

Turkey's was off; and *vice versa*. This was a good natural arrangement, under the circumstances.

Ginger Nut, the third on my list, was a lad, some twelve years old. His father was a carman, ambitious of seeing his son on the bench instead of a cart, before he died. So he sent him to my office, as student at law, errand-boy, cleaner, and sweeper, at the rate of one dollar a week. He had a little desk to himself, but he did not use it much. Upon inspection, the drawer exhibited a great array of the shells of various sorts of nuts. Indeed, to this quick-witted youth, the whole noble science of the law was contained in a nutshell. Not the least among the employments of Ginger Nut, as well as one which he discharged with the most alacrity, was his duty as cake and apple purveyor for Turkey and Nippers. Copying lawpapers being proverbially a dry, husky sort of business, my two scriveners were fain to moisten their mouths very often with Spitzenbergs, to be had at the numerous stalls nigh the Custom House and Post Office. Also, they sent Ginger Nut very frequently for that peculiar cake — small, flat, round, and very spicy — after which he had been named by them. Of a cold morning, when business was but dull, Turkey would gobble up scores of these cakes, as if they were mere wafers — indeed, they sell them at the rate of six or eight for a penny — the scrape of his pen blending with the crunching of the crisp particles in his mouth. Of all the fiery afternoon blunders and flurried rashness of Turkey, was his once moistening a ginger-cake between his lips, and clapping it on to a mortgage, for a seal. I came within an ace of dismissing him then. But he mollified me by making an oriental bow, and saying —

"With submission, sir, it was generous of me to find you in stationery on my own account." [15]

Now my original business — that of a conveyancer and title hunter, and drawer-up of recondite documents of all sorts — was considerably increased by receiving the Master's office. There was now great work for scriveners. Not only must I push the clerks already with me, but I must have additional help.

In answer to my advertisement, a motionless young man one morning stood upon my office threshold, the door being open, for it was summer. I can see that figure now — pallidly neat, pitiably respectable, incurably forlorn! It was Bartleby.

After a few words touching his qualifications, I engaged him, glad to have among my corps of copyists a man of so singularly sedate an aspect, which I thought might operate beneficially upon the flighty temper of Turkey, and the fiery one of Nippers.

I should have stated before that ground-glass folding-doors divided my premises into two parts, one of which was occupied by my scriveners, the other by myself. According to my humor, I threw open these doors, or closed them. I resolved to assign Bartleby a corner by the folding-doors, but on my side of them, so as to have this quiet man within easy call, in case any trifling thing was to be done. I placed his desk close up to a small side-window in that part of the room, a window which originally had afforded a lateral view of certain grimy brickyards and bricks, but which, owing to subsequent erections, commanded at present no view at all, though it gave some light. Within three feet of the panes was a wall, and the light came down from far above, between two lofty buildings, as from a very small opening in a dome. Still further to a satisfactory arrangement, I procured a high green folding screen, which might entirely isolate Bartleby from my sight, though not remove him from my voice. And thus, in a manner, privacy and society were conjoined.

At first, Bartleby did an extraordinary quantity of writing. As if long 20 famishing for something to copy, he seemed to gorge himself on my documents. There was no pause for digestion. He ran a day and night line, copying by sunlight and by candle-light. I should have been quite delighted with his application, had he been cheerfully industrious. But he wrote on silently, palely, mechanically.

It is, of course, an indispensable part of a scrivener's business to verify the accuracy of his copy, word by word. Where there are two or more scriveners in an office, they assist each other in this examination, one reading from the copy, the other holding the original. It is a very dull, wearisome, and lethargic affair. I can readily imagine that, to some sanguine temperaments, it would be altogether intolerable. For example, I cannot credit that the mettlesome poet, Byron, would have contentedly sat down with Bartleby to examine a law document of, say five hundred pages, closely written in a crimpy hand.

Now and then, in the haste of business, it had been my habit to assist in comparing some brief document myself, calling Turkey or Nippers for this purpose. One object I had, in placing Bartleby so handy to me behind the screen, was, to avail myself of his services on such trivial occasions. It was on the third day, I think, of his being with me, and before any necessity had arisen for having his own writing examined, that, being much hurried to complete a small affair I had in hand, I abruptly called to Bartleby. In my haste and natural expectancy of instant compliance, I sat with my head bent over the original on my desk, and my right hand sideways, and somewhat nervously extended with the copy, so that, immediately upon emerging from his retreat, Bartleby might snatch it and proceed to business without the least delay.

In this very attitude did I sit when I called to him, rapidly stating what it was I wanted him to do—namely, to examine a small paper with me. Imagine my surprise, nay, my consternation, when, without moving from his privacy, Bartleby, in a singularly mild, firm voice, replied, "I would prefer not to."

I sat awhile in perfect silence, rallying my stunned faculties. Immediately it occurred to me that my ears had deceived me, or Bartleby had entirely misunderstood my meaning. I repeated my request in the clearest tone I could assume; but in quite as clear a one came the previous reply, "I would prefer not to."

"Prefer not to," echoed I, rising in high excitement, and crossing 25
the room with a stride. "What do you mean? Are you moonstruck? I
want you to help me compare this sheet here — take it," and I thrust it
towards him.

"I would prefer not to," said he.

I looked at him steadfastly. His face was leanly composed; his gray
eye dimly calm. Not a wrinkle of agitation rippled him. Had there been
the least uneasiness, anger, impatience, or impertinence in his manner;
in other words, had there been anything ordinarily human about him,
doubtless I should have violently dismissed him from the premises. But
as it was, I should have as soon thought of turning my pale plaster-of-
paris bust of Cicero out of doors. I stood gazing at him awhile, as he
went on with his own writing, and then reseated myself at my desk. This
is very strange, thought I. What had one best do? But my business hurried me. I concluded to forget the matter for the present, reserving it for
my future leisure. So, calling Nippers from the other room, the paper
was speedily examined.

A few days after this, Bartleby concluded four lengthy documents, being quadruplicates of a week's testimony taken before me in
my High Court of Chancery. It became necessary to examine them.
It was an important suit, and great accuracy was imperative. Having
all things arranged, I called Turkey, Nippers, and Ginger Nut, from
the next room, meaning to place the four copies in the hands of my
four clerks, while I should read from the original. Accordingly, Turkey,
Nippers, and Ginger Nut had taken their seats in a row, each with his
document in his hand, when I called to Bartleby to join this interesting group.

"Bartleby! quick, I am waiting."

I heard a slow scrape of his chair legs on the uncarpeted floor, and 30
soon he appeared standing at the entrance of his hermitage.

"What is wanted?" said he, mildly.

"The copies, the copies," said I, hurriedly. "We are going to examine
them. There" — and I held towards him the fourth quadruplicate.

"I would prefer not to," he said, and gently disappeared behind the
screen.

For a few moments I was turned into a pillar of salt, standing at
the head of my seated column of clerks. Recovering myself, I advanced
towards the screen, and demanded the reason for such extraordinary
conduct.

"*Why* do you refuse?"   35

"I would prefer not to."

With any other man I should have flown outright into a dreadful
passion, scorned all further words, and thrust him ignominiously from
my presence. But there was something about Bartleby that not only
strangely disarmed me, but, in a wonderful manner, touched and discon-
certed me. I began to reason with him.

"These are your own copies we are about to examine. It is labor saving to you, because one examination will answer for your four papers. It is common usage. Every copyist is bound to help examine his copy. Is it not so? Will you not speak? Answer!"

"I prefer not to," he replied in a flute-like tone. It seemed to me that, while I had been addressing him, he carefully revolved every statement that I made; fully comprehended the meaning; could not gainsay the irresistible conclusion; but, at the same time, some paramount consideration prevailed with him to reply as he did.

"You are decided, then, not to comply with my request — a request   40
made according to common usage and common sense?"

He briefly gave me to understand, that on that point my judgment was sound. Yes: his decision was irreversible.

It is not seldom the case that, when a man is browbeaten in some unprecedented and violently unreasonable way, he begins to stagger in his own plainest faith. He begins, as it were, vaguely to surmise that, wonderful as it may be, all the justice and all the reason is on the other side. Accordingly, if any disinterested persons are present, he turns to them for some reinforcement for his own faltering mind.

"Turkey," said I, "what do you think of this? Am I not right?"

"With submission, sir," said Turkey, in his blandest tone, "I think that you are."

"Nippers," said I, "what do *you* think of it?"   45

"I think I should kick him out of the office."

(The reader of nice perceptions will have perceived that, it being morning, Turkey's answer is couched in polite and tranquil terms, but Nippers replies in ill-tempered ones. Or, to repeat a previous sentence, Nippers' ugly mood was on duty, and Turkey's off.)

"Ginger Nut," said I, willing to enlist the smallest suffrage in my behalf, "what do *you* think of it?"

"I think, sir, he's a little *luny*," replied Ginger Nut, with a grin.

"You hear what they say," said I, turning towards the screen, "come   50
forth and do your duty."

But he vouchsafed no reply. I pondered a moment in sore perplexity. But once more business hurried me. I determined again to postpone the consideration of this dilemma to my future leisure. With a little trouble we made out to examine the papers without Bartleby, though at every page or two Turkey deferentially dropped his opinion, that this proceeding was quite out of the common; while Nippers, twitching in his chair with a dyspeptic nervousness, ground out, between his set teeth, occasional hissing maledictions against the stubborn oaf behind the screen. And for his (Nippers') part, this was the first and the last time he would do another man's business without pay.

Meanwhile Bartleby sat in his hermitage, oblivious to everything but his own peculiar business there.

Some days passed, the scrivener being employed upon another lengthy work. His late remarkable conduct led me to regard his ways narrowly. I observed that he never went to dinner; indeed, that he never went anywhere. As yet I had never, of my personal knowledge, known him to be outside of my office. He was a perpetual sentry in the corner. At about eleven o'clock though, in the morning, I noticed that Ginger Nut would advance toward the opening in Bartleby's screen, as if silently beckoned thither by a gesture invisible to me where I sat. The boy would then leave the office, jingling a few pence, and reappear with a handful of ginger-nuts, which he delivered in the hermitage, receiving two of the cakes for his trouble.

He lives, then, on ginger-nuts, thought I; never eats a dinner, properly speaking; he must be a vegetarian, then; but no; he never eats even vegetables, he eats nothing but ginger-nuts. My mind then ran on in reveries concerning the probable effects upon the human constitution of living entirely on ginger-nuts. Ginger-nuts are so called, because they contain ginger as one of their peculiar constituents, and the final flavoring one. Now, what was ginger? A hot, spicy thing. Was Bartleby hot and spicy? Not at all. Ginger, then, had no effect upon Bartleby. Probably he preferred it should have none.

Nothing so aggravates an earnest person as a passive resistance. If 55 the individual so resisted be of a not inhumane temper, and the resisting one perfectly harmless in his passivity, then, in the better moods of the former, he will endeavor charitably to construe to his imagination what proves impossible to be solved by his judgment. Even so, for the most part, I regarded Bartleby and his ways. Poor fellow! thought I, he means no mischief; it is plain he intends no insolence; his aspect sufficiently evinces that his eccentricities are involuntary. He is useful to me. I can get along with him. If I turn him away, the chances are he will fall in with some less indulgent employer, and then he will be rudely treated, and perhaps driven forth miserably to starve. Yes. Here I can cheaply purchase a delicious self-approval. To befriend Bartleby; to humor him in his strange wilfulness, will cost me little or nothing, while I lay up in my soul what will eventually prove a sweet morsel for my conscience. But this mood was not invariable with me. The passiveness of Bartleby sometimes irritated me. I felt strangely goaded on to encounter him in new opposition — to elicit some angry spark from him answerable to my own. But, indeed, I might as well have essayed to strike fire with my knuckles against a bit of Windsor soap. But one afternoon the evil impulse in me mastered me, and the following little scene ensued:

"Bartleby," said I, "when those papers are all copied, I will compare them with you."

"I would prefer not to."

"How? Surely you do not mean to persist in that mulish vagary?"

No answer.

I threw open the folding-doors nearby, and turning upon Turkey 60
and Nippers, exclaimed:

"Bartleby a second time says, he won't examine his papers. What do
you think of it, Turkey?"

It was afternoon, be it remembered. Turkey sat glowing like a brass
boiler; his bald head steaming; his hands reeling among his blotted
papers.

"Think of it?" roared Turkey. "I think I'll just step behind his screen,
and black his eyes for him!"

So saying, Turkey rose to his feet and threw his arms into a pugi-
listic position. He was hurrying away to make good his promise, when
I detained him, alarmed at the effect of incautiously rousing Turkey's
combativeness after dinner.

"Sit down, Turkey," said I, "and hear what Nippers has to say. What 65
do you think of it, Nippers? Would I not be justified in immediately dismissing Bartleby?"

"Excuse me, that is for you to decide, sir. I think his conduct quite
unusual, and, indeed, unjust, as regards Turkey and myself. But it may
only be a passing whim."

"Ah," exclaimed I, "you have strangely changed your mind,
then — you speak very gently of him now."

"All beer," cried Turkey; "gentleness is effects of beer — Nippers and
I dined together to-day. You see how gentle *I* am, sir. Shall I go and black
his eyes?"

"You refer to Bartleby, I suppose. No, not to-day, Turkey," I replied;
"pray, put up your fists."

I closed the doors, and again advanced towards Bartleby. I felt addi- 70
tional incentives tempting me to my fate. I burned to be rebelled against
again. I remembered that Bartleby never left the office.

"Bartleby," said I, "Ginger Nut is away; just step around to the Post
Office, won't you?" (it was but a three minutes' walk) "and see if there is
anything for me."

"I would prefer not to."

"You *will* not?"

"I *prefer* not."

I staggered to my desk, and sat there in a deep study. My blind 75
inveteracy returned. Was there any other thing in which I could procure
myself to be ignominiously repulsed by this lean, penniless wight? — my
hired clerk? What added thing is there, perfectly reasonable, that he will
be sure to refuse to do?

"Bartleby!"

No answer.

"Bartleby," in a louder tone.

No answer.

"Bartleby," I roared.   80

Like a very ghost, agreeably to the laws of magical invocation, at the third summons, he appeared at the entrance of his hermitage.

"Go to the next room, and tell Nippers to come to me."

"I prefer not to," he respectfully and slowly said, and mildly disappeared.

"Very good, Bartleby," said I, in a quiet sort of serenely-severe self-possessed tone, intimating the unalterable purpose of some terrible retribution very close at hand. At the moment I half intended something of the kind. But upon the whole, as it was drawing towards my dinner-hour, I thought it best to put on my hat and walk home for the day, suffering much from perplexity and distress of mind.

Shall I acknowledge it? The conclusion of this whole business was, that it soon became a fixed fact of my chambers, that a pale young scrivener, by the name of Bartleby, had a desk there; that he copied for me at the usual rate of four cents a folio (one hundred words); but he was permanently exempt from examining the work done by him, that duty being transferred to Turkey and Nippers, out of compliment, doubtless, to their superior acuteness; moreover, said Bartleby was never, on any account, to be dispatched on the most trivial errand of any sort; and that even if entreated to take upon him such a matter, it was generally understood that he would "prefer not to"—in other words, that he would refuse point-blank. 85

As days passed on, I became considerably reconciled to Bartleby. His steadiness, his freedom from all dissipation, his incessant industry (except when he chose to throw himself into a standing revery behind his screen), his great stillness, his unalterableness of demeanor under all circumstances, made him a valuable acquisition. One prime thing was this—*he was always there*—first in the morning, continually through the day, and the last at night. I had a singular confidence in his honesty. I felt my most precious papers perfectly safe in his hands. Sometimes, to be sure, I could not, for the very soul of me, avoid falling into sudden spasmodic passions with him. For it was exceeding difficult to bear in mind all the time those strange peculiarities, privileges, and unheard-of exemptions, forming the tacit stipulations on Bartleby's part under which he remained in my office. Now and then, in the eagerness of dispatching pressing business, I would inadvertently summon Bartleby, in a short, rapid tone, to put his finger, say, on the incipient tie of a bit of red tape with which I was about compressing some papers. Of course, from behind the screen the usual answer, "I prefer not to," was sure to come; and then, how could a human creature, with the common infirmities of our nature, refrain from bitterly exclaiming upon such perverseness—such unreasonableness? However, every added repulse of this sort which I received only tended to lessen the probability of my repeating the inadvertence.

Here it must be said, that, according to the custom of most legal gentlemen occupying chambers in densely populated law buildings, there were several keys to my door. One was kept by a woman residing in the attic, which person weekly scrubbed and daily swept and dusted my apartments. Another was kept by Turkey for convenience sake. The third I sometimes carried in my own pocket. The fourth I knew not who had.

Now, one Sunday morning I happened to go to Trinity Church, to hear a celebrated preacher, and finding myself rather early on the ground I thought I would walk round to my chambers for a while. Luckily I had my key with me; but upon applying it to the lock, I found it resisted by something inserted from the inside. Quite surprised, I called out; when to my consternation a key was turned from within; and thrusting his lean visage at me, and holding the door ajar, the apparition of Bartleby appeared, in his shirt-sleeves, and otherwise in a strangely tattered *deshabille,* saying quietly that he was sorry, but he was deeply engaged just then, and — preferred not admitting me at present. In a brief word or two, he moreover added, that perhaps I had better walk round the block two or three times, and by that time he would probably have concluded his affairs.

Now, the utterly unsurmised appearance of Bartleby, tenanting my law-chambers of a Sunday morning, with his cadaverously gentlemanly *nonchalance,* yet withal firm and self-possessed, had such a strange effect upon me, that incontinently I slunk away from my own door, and did as desired. But not without sundry twinges of impotent rebellion against the mild effrontery of this unaccountable scrivener. Indeed, it was his wonderful mildness chiefly, which not only disarmed me, but unmanned me, as it were. For I consider that one, for the time, is sort of unmanned when he tranquilly permits his hired clerk to dictate to him, and order him away from his own premises. Furthermore, I was full of uneasiness as to what Bartleby could possibly be doing in my office in his shirt-sleeves, and in an otherwise dismantled condition of a Sunday morning. Was anything amiss going on? Nay, that was out of the question. It was not to be thought of for a moment that Bartleby was an immoral person. But what could he be doing there? — copying? Nay again, whatever might be his eccentricities, Bartleby was an eminently decorous person. He would be the last man to sit down to his desk in any state approaching to nudity. Besides, it was Sunday; and there was something about Bartleby that forbade the supposition that he would by any secular occupation violate the proprieties of the day.

Nevertheless, my mind was not pacified; and full of a restless curios- 90 ity, at last I returned to the door. Without hindrance I inserted my key, opened it, and entered. Bartleby was not to be seen. I looked round anxiously, peeped behind his screen; but it was very plain that he was gone. Upon more closely examining the place, I surmised that for an indefinite period Bartleby must have ate, dressed, and slept in my office, and that too without plate, mirror, or bed. The cushioned seat of a rickety old sofa in one corner bore the faint impress of a lean, reclining form. Rolled away under his desk, I found a blanket; under the empty grate, a blacking box and brush; on a chair, a tin basin, with soap and a ragged towel; in a newspaper a few crumbs of ginger-nuts and a morsel of cheese. Yes, thought I, it is evident enough that Bartleby has been making his home here, keeping bachelor's hall all by himself. Immediately then the thought came sweeping across me, what miserable friendlessness and loneliness are here revealed! His poverty is great; but his solitude, how horrible! Think of it. Of a Sunday, Wall Street is deserted as Petra;° and every night of every day it is an emptiness. This building, too, which of week-days hums with industry and life, at nightfall echoes with sheer vacancy, and all through Sunday is forlorn. And here Bartleby makes his home; sole spectator of a solitude which he has seen all populous—a sort of innocent and transformed Marius brooding among the ruins of Carthage?°

For the first time in my life a feeling of overpowering stinging melancholy seized me. Before, I had never experienced aught but a not unpleasing sadness. The bond of a common humanity now drew me irresistibly to gloom. A fraternal melancholy! For both I and Bartleby were sons of Adam. I remembered the bright silks and sparkling faces I had seen that day, in gala trim, swan-like sailing down the Mississippi of Broadway; and I contrasted them with the pallid copyist, and thought to myself, Ah, happiness courts the light, so we deem the world is gay; but misery hides aloof, so we deem that misery there is none. These sad fancyings—chimeras, doubtless, of a sick and silly brain—led on to other and more special thoughts, concerning the eccentricities of Bartleby. Presentiments of strange discoveries hovered round me. The scrivener's pale form appeared to me laid out, among uncaring strangers, in its shivering winding-sheet.

Suddenly I was attracted by Bartleby's closed desk, the key in open sight left in the lock.

I mean no mischief, seek the gratification of no heartless curiosity, thought I; besides, the desk is mine, and its contents, too, so I will make bold to look within. Everything was methodically arranged, the papers smoothly placed. The pigeon-holes were deep, and removing the files of documents, I groped into their recesses. Presently I felt something there, and dragged it out. It was an old bandanna handkerchief, heavy and knotted. I opened it, and saw it was a saving's bank.

I now recalled all the quiet mysteries which I had noted in the man. I remembered that he never spoke but to answer; that, though at intervals he had considerable time to himself, yet I had never seen him reading—no, not even a newspaper; that for long periods he would stand looking out, at his pale window behind the screen, upon the dead brick

Petra: An ancient Arabian city whose ruins were discovered in 1812.
Marius . . . of Carthage: Gaius Marius (157–86 B.C.), an exiled Roman general, sought refuge in the African city-state of Carthage, which was destroyed by the Romans in the Third Punic War.

wall; I was quite sure he never visited any refectory or eating-house; while his pale face clearly indicated that he never drank beer like Turkey; or tea and coffee even, like other men; that he never went anywhere in particular that I could learn; never went out for a walk, unless, indeed, that was the case at present; that he had declined telling who he was, or whence he came, or whether he had any relatives in the world; that though so thin and pale, he never complained of ill-health. And more than all, I remembered a certain unconscious air of pallid — how shall I call it? — of pallid haughtiness, say, or rather an austere reserve about him, which had positively awed me into my tame compliance with his eccentricities, when I had feared to ask him to do the slightest incidental thing for me, even though I might know, from his long-continued motionlessness, that behind his screen he must be standing in one of those dead-wall reveries of his.

Revolving all these things, and coupling them with the recently 95
discovered fact, that he made my office his constant abiding place and home, and not forgetful of his morbid moodiness; revolving all these things, a prudential feeling began to steal over me. My first emotions had been those of pure melancholy and sincerest pity; but just in proportion as the forlornness of Bartleby grew and grew to my imagination, did that same melancholy merge into fear, that pity into repulsion. So true it is, and so terrible, too, that up to a certain point the thought or sight of misery enlists our best affections; but, in certain special cases, beyond that point it does not. They err who would assert that invariably this is owing to the inherent selfishness of the human heart. It rather proceeds from a certain hopelessness of remedying excessive and organic ill. To a sensitive being, pity is not seldom pain. And when at last it is perceived that such pity cannot lead to effectual succor, common sense bids the soul be rid of it. What I saw that morning persuaded me that the scrivener was the victim of innate and incurable disorder. I might give alms to his body; but his body did not pain him; it was his soul that suffered, and his soul I could not reach.

I did not accomplish the purpose of going to Trinity Church that morning. Somehow, the things I had seen disqualified me for the time from church-going. I walked homeward, thinking what I would do with Bartleby. Finally, I resolved upon this — I would put certain calm questions to him the next morning, touching his history, etc., and if he declined to answer them openly and unreservedly (and I supposed he would prefer not), then to give him a twenty dollar bill over and above whatever I might owe him, and tell him his services were no longer required; but that if in any other way I could assist him, I would be happy to do so, especially if he desired to return to his native place, wherever that might be, I would willingly help to defray the expenses. Moreover, if, after reaching home, he found himself at any time in want of aid, a letter from him would be sure of a reply.

The next morning came.

"Bartleby," said I, gently calling to him behind his screen.

No reply.

"Bartleby," said I, in a still gentler tone, "come here; I am not going to ask you to do anything you would prefer not to do—I simply wish to speak to you."

Upon this he noiselessly slid into view.

"Will you tell me, Bartleby, where you were born?"

"I would prefer not to."

"Will you tell me *anything* about yourself?"

"I would prefer not to."

"But what reasonable objection can you have to speak to me? I feel friendly towards you."

He did not look at me while I spoke, but kept his glance fixed upon my bust of Cicero, which, as I then sat, was directly behind me, some six inches above my head.

"What is your answer, Bartleby?" said I, after waiting a considerable time for a reply, during which his countenance remained immovable, only there was the faintest conceivable tremor of the white attenuated mouth.

"At present I prefer to give no answer," he said, and retired into his hermitage.

It was rather weak in me I confess, but his manner, on this occasion, nettled me. Not only did there seem to lurk in it a certain calm disdain, but his perverseness seemed ungrateful, considering the undeniable good usage and indulgence he had received from me.

Again I sat ruminating what I should do. Mortified as I was at his behavior, and resolved as I had been to dismiss him when I entered my office, nevertheless I strangely felt something superstitious knocking at my heart, and forbidding me to carry out my purpose, and denouncing me for a villain if I dared to breathe one bitter word against this forlornest of mankind. At last, familiarly drawing my chair behind his screen, I sat down and said: "Bartleby, never mind, then, about revealing your history; but let me entreat you, as a friend, to comply as far as may be with the usages of this office. Say now, you will help to examine papers tomorrow or next day: in short, say now, that in a day or two you will begin to be a little reasonable:—say so, Bartleby."

"At present I would prefer not to be a little reasonable," was his mildly cadaverous reply.

Just then the folding-doors opened, and Nippers approached. He seemed suffering from an unusually bad night's rest, induced by severer indigestion than common. He overheard those final words of Bartleby.

"*Prefer not,* eh?" gritted Nippers—"I'd *prefer* him, if I were you, sir," addressing me—"I'd *prefer* him; I'd give him preferences, the stubborn mule! What is it, sir, pray, that he *prefers* not to do now?"

Bartleby moved not a limb.

"Mr. Nippers," said I, "I'd prefer that you would withdraw for the present."

Somehow, of late, I had got into the way of involuntarily using this word "prefer" upon all sorts of not exactly suitable occasions. And I trembled to think that my contact with the scrivener had already and seriously affected me in a mental way. And what further and deeper aberration might it not yet produce? This apprehension had not been without efficacy in determining me to summary measures.

As Nippers, looking very sour and sulky, was departing, Turkey blandly and deferentially approached.

"With submission, sir," said he, "yesterday I was thinking about Bartleby here, and I think that if he would but prefer to take a quart of good ale every day, it would do much towards mending him, and enabling him to assist in examining his papers."

"So you have got the word, too," said I, slightly excited.   120

"With submission, what word, sir?" asked Turkey, respectfully crowding himself into the contracted space behind the screen, and by so doing, making me jostle the scrivener. "What word, sir?"

"I would prefer to be left alone here," said Bartleby, as if offended at being mobbed in his privacy.

"*That's* the word, Turkey," said I — "*that's* it."

"Oh, *prefer?* oh yes — queer word. I never use it myself. But, sir, as I was saying, if he would but prefer — "

"Turkey," interrupted I, "you will please withdraw."   125

"Oh certainly, sir, if you prefer that I should."

As he opened the folding-door to retire, Nippers at his desk caught a glimpse of me, and asked whether I would prefer to have a certain paper copied on blue paper or white. He did not in the least roguishly accent the word "prefer." It was plain that it involuntarily rolled from his tongue. I thought to myself, surely I must get rid of a demented man, who already has in some degree turned the tongues, if not the heads of myself and clerks. But I thought it prudent not to break the dismission at once.

The next day I noticed that Bartleby did nothing but stand at his window in his dead-wall revery. Upon asking him why he did not write, he said that he had decided upon doing no more writing.

"Why, how now? what next?" exclaimed I, "do no more writing?"

"No more."   130

"And what is the reason?"

"Do you not see the reason for yourself?" he indifferently replied.

I looked steadfastly at him, and perceived that his eyes looked dull and glazed. Instantly it occurred to me, that his unexampled diligence in copying by his dim window for the first few weeks of his stay with me might have temporarily impaired his vision.

I was touched. I said something in condolence with him. I hinted that of course he did wisely in abstaining from writing for a while; and urged him to embrace that opportunity of taking wholesome exercise in the open air. This, however, he did not do. A few days after this, my other clerks being absent, and being in a great hurry to dispatch certain letters by the mail, I thought that, having nothing else earthly to do, Bartleby would surely be less inflexible than usual, and carry these letters to the Post Office. But he blankly declined. So, much to my inconvenience, I went myself.

Still added days went by. Whether Bartleby's eyes improved or not, 135 I could not say. To all appearance, I thought they did. But when I asked him if they did, he vouchsafed no answer. At all events, he would do no copying. At last, in replying to my urgings, he informed me that he had permanently given up copying.

"What!" exclaimed I; "suppose your eyes should get entirely well — better than ever before — would you not copy then?"

"I have given up copying," he answered, and slid aside.

He remained as ever, a fixture in my chamber. Nay — if that were possible — he became still more of a fixture than before. What was to be done? He would do nothing in the office; why should he stay there? In plain fact, he had now become a millstone to me, not only useless as a necklace, but afflictive to bear. Yet I was sorry for him. I speak less than truth when I say that, on his own account, he occasioned me uneasiness. If he would but have named a single relative or friend, I would instantly have written, and urged their taking the poor fellow away to some convenient retreat. But he seemed alone, absolutely alone in the universe. A bit of wreck in the mid-Atlantic. At length, necessities connected with my business tyrannized over all other considerations. Decently as I could, I told Bartleby that in six days' time he must unconditionally leave the office. I warned him to take measures, in the interval, for procuring some other abode. I offered to assist him in this endeavor, if he himself would but take the first step towards a removal. "And when you finally quit me, Bartleby," added I, "I shall see that you go not away entirely unprovided. Six days from this hour, remember."

At the expiration of that period, I peeped behind the screen, and lo! Bartleby was there.

I buttoned up my coat, balanced myself; advanced slowly towards 140 him, touched his shoulder, and said, "The time has come; you must quit this place; I am sorry for you; here is money; but you must go."

"I would prefer not," he replied, with his back still towards me.

"You *must*."

He remained silent.

Now I had an unbounded confidence in this man's common honesty. He had frequently restored to me sixpences and shillings carelessly dropped upon the floor, for I am apt to be very reckless in such shirt-button affairs. The proceeding, then, which followed will not be deemed extraordinary.

"Bartleby," said I, "I owe you twelve dollars on account; here are   145
thirty-two, the odd twenty are yours—Will you take it?" and I handed
the bills towards him.

But he made no motion.

"I will leave them here, then," putting them under a weight on the
table. Then taking my hat and cane and going to the door, I tranquilly
turned and added—"After you have removed your things from these
offices, Bartleby, you will of course lock the door—since every one is now
gone for the day but you—and if you please, slip your key underneath
the mat, so that I may have it in the morning. I shall not see you again; so
good-bye to you. If, hereafter, in your new place of abode, I can be of any
service to you, do not fail to advise me by letter. Good-bye, Bartleby, and
fare you well."

But he answered not a word; like the last column of some ruined
temple, he remained standing mute and solitary in the middle of the
otherwise deserted room.

As I walked home in a pensive mood, my vanity got the better of my
pity. I could not but highly plume myself on my masterly management
in getting rid of Bartleby. Masterly I call it, and such it must appear to
any dispassionate thinker. The beauty of my procedure seemed to consist
in its perfect quietness. There was no vulgar bullying, no bravado of any
sort, no choleric hectoring, and striding to and fro across the apartment,
jerking out vehement commands for Bartleby to bundle himself off with
his beggarly traps. Nothing of the kind. Without loudly bidding Bartleby
depart—as an inferior genius might have done—I *assumed* the ground
that depart he must; and upon that assumption built all I had to say.
The more I thought over my procedure, the more I was charmed with it.
Nevertheless, next morning, upon awakening, I had my doubts—I had
somehow slept off the fumes of vanity. One of the coolest and wisest
hours a man has, is just after he awakes in the morning. My procedure
seemed as sagacious as ever—but only in theory. How it would prove
in practice—there was the rub. It was truly a beautiful thought to have
assumed Bartleby's departure; but, after all, that assumption was simply
my own, and none of Bartleby's. The great point was, not whether I had
assumed that he would quit me, but whether he would prefer to do so.
He was more a man of preferences than assumptions.

After breakfast, I walked down town, arguing the probabilities *pro*   150
and *con*. One moment I thought it would prove a miserable failure, and
Bartleby would be found all alive at my office as usual; the next moment
it seemed certain that I should find his chair empty. And so I kept veering
about. At the corner of Broadway and Canal Street, I saw quite an excited
group of people standing in earnest conversation.

"I'll take odds he doesn't," said a voice as I passed.

"Doesn't go?—done!" said I, "put up your money."

I was instinctively putting my hand in my pocket to produce my
own, when I remembered that this was an election day. The words I had

overheard bore no reference to Bartleby, but to the success or non-success of some candidate for the mayoralty. In my intent frame of mind, I had, as it were, imagined that all Broadway shared in my excitement, and were debating the same question with me. I passed on, very thankful that the uproar of the street screened my momentary absent-mindedness.

As I had intended, I was earlier than usual at my office door. I stood listening for a moment. All was still. He must be gone. I tried the knob. The door was locked. Yes, my procedure had worked to a charm; he indeed must be vanished. Yet a certain melancholy mixed with this: I was almost sorry for my brilliant success. I was fumbling under the door mat for the key, which Bartleby was to have left there for me, when accidentally my knee knocked against a panel, producing a summoning sound, and in response a voice came to me from within—"Not yet; I am occupied."

It was Bartleby.

I was thunderstruck. For an instant I stood like the man who, pipe in mouth, was killed one cloudless afternoon long ago in Virginia, by summer lightning; at his own warm open window he was killed, and remained leaning out there upon the dreamy afternoon, till some one touched him, when he fell.

"Not gone!" I murmured at last. But again obeying that wondrous ascendancy which the inscrutable scrivener had over me, and from which ascendancy, for all my chafing, I could not completely escape, I slowly went down stairs and out into the street, and while walking round the block, considered what I should next do in this unheard-of perplexity. Turn the man out by an actual thrusting I could not; to drive him away by calling him hard names would not do; calling in the police was an unpleasant idea; and yet, permit him to enjoy his cadaverous triumph over me—this, too, I could not think of. What was to be done? or, if nothing could be done, was there anything further that I could *assume* in the matter? Yes, as before I had prospectively assumed that Bartleby would depart, so now I might retrospectively assume that departed he was. In the legitimate carrying out of this assumption, I might enter my office in a great hurry, and pretending not to see Bartleby at all, walk straight against him as if he were air. Such a proceeding would in a singular degree have the appearance of a home-thrust. It was hardly possible that Bartleby could withstand such an application of the doctrine of assumption. But upon second thoughts the success of the plan seemed rather dubious. I resolved to argue the matter over with him again.

"Bartleby," said I, entering the office, with a quietly severe expression, "I am seriously displeased. I am pained, Bartleby. I had thought better of you. I had imagined you of such a gentlemanly organization, that in any delicate dilemma a slight hint would suffice—in short, an assumption. But it appears I am deceived. Why," I added, unaffectedly starting, "you have not even touched that money yet," pointing to it, just where I had left it the evening previous.

155

He answered nothing.

"Will you, or will you not, quit me?" I now demanded in a sudden 160 passion, advancing close to him.

"I would prefer *not* to quit you," he replied, gently emphasizing the *not*.

"What earthly right have you to stay here? Do you pay any rent? Do you pay my taxes? Or is this property yours?"

He answered nothing.

"Are you ready to go on and write now? Are your eyes recovered? Could you copy a small paper for me this morning? or help examine a few lines? or step round to the Post Office? In a word, will you do anything at all, to give a coloring to your refusal to depart the premises?"

He silently retired into his hermitage. 165

I was now in such a state of nervous resentment that I thought it but prudent to check myself at present from further demonstrations. Bartleby and I were alone. I remembered the tragedy of the unfortunate Adams and the still more unfortunate Colt° in the solitary office of the latter; and how poor Colt, being dreadfully incensed by Adams, and imprudently permitting himself to get wildly excited, was at unawares hurried into his fatal act—an act which certainly no man could possibly deplore more than the actor himself. Often it had occurred to me in my ponderings upon the subject that had that altercation taken place in the public street, or at a private residence, it would not have terminated as it did. It was the circumstance of being alone in a solitary office, up stairs, of a building entirely unhallowed by humanizing domestic associations—an uncarpeted office, doubtless, of a dusty, haggard sort of appearance—this it must have been, which greatly helped to enhance the irritable desperation of the hapless Colt.

But when this old Adam of resentment rose in me and tempted me concerning Bartleby, I grappled him and threw him. How? Why, simply by recalling the divine injunction: "A new commandment give I unto you, that ye love one another." Yes, this it was that saved me. Aside from higher considerations, charity often operates as a vastly wise and prudent principle—a great safeguard to its possessor. Men have committed murder for jealousy's sake, and anger's sake, and hatred's sake, and selfishness' sake, and spiritual pride's sake; but no man, that ever I heard of, ever committed a diabolical murder for sweet charity's sake. Mere self-interest, then, if no better motive can be enlisted, should, especially with high-tempered men, prompt all beings to charity and philanthropy. At any rate, upon the occasion in question, I strove to drown my exasperated feelings towards the scrivener by benevolently construing his conduct. Poor fellow, poor fellow! thought I, he don't

Adams . . . Colt: Samuel Adams was killed by John C. Colt, brother of the gun maker, during a quarrel in 1842. After a sensational court case, Colt committed suicide just before he was to be hanged.

mean anything; and besides, he has seen hard times, and ought to be indulged.

I endeavored, also, immediately to occupy myself, and at the same time to comfort my despondency. I tried to fancy, that in the course of the morning, at such time as might prove agreeable to him, Bartleby, of his own free accord, would emerge from his hermitage and take up some decided line of march in the direction of the door. But no. Half-past twelve o'clock came; Turkey began to glow in the face, overturn his inkstand, and become generally obstreperous; Nippers abated down into quietude and courtesy; Ginger Nut munched his noon apple; and Bartleby remained standing at his window in one of his profoundest dead-wall reveries. Will it be credited? Ought I to acknowledge it? That afternoon I left the office without saying one further word to him.

Some days now passed, during which, at leisure intervals I looked a little into "Edwards on the Will," and "Priestley on Necessity."° Under the circumstances, those books induced a salutary feeling. Gradually I slid into the persuasion that these troubles of mine, touching the scrivener, had been all predestined from eternity, and Bartleby was billeted upon me for some mysterious purpose of an all-wise Providence, which it was not for a mere mortal like me to fathom. Yes, Bartleby, stay there behind your screen, thought I; I shall persecute you no more; you are harmless and noiseless as any of these old chairs; in short, I never feel so private as when I know you are here. At last I see it, I feel it; I penetrate to the predestined purpose of my life. I am content. Others may have loftier parts to enact; but my mission in this world, Bartleby, is to furnish you with office-room for such period as you may see fit to remain.

I believe that this wise and blessed frame of mind would have continued with me, had it not been for the unsolicited and uncharitable remarks obtruded upon me by my professional friends who visited the rooms. But thus it often is, that the constant friction of illiberal minds wears out at last the best resolves of the more generous. Though to be sure, when I reflected upon it, it was not strange that people entering my office should be struck by the peculiar aspect of the unaccountable Bartleby, and so be tempted to throw out some sinister observations concerning him. Sometimes an attorney, having business with me, and calling at my office, and finding no one but the scrivener there, would undertake to obtain some sort of precise information from him touching my whereabouts; but without heeding his idle talk, Bartleby would remain standing immovable in the middle of the room. So after contemplating him in that position for a time, the attorney would depart, no wiser than he came.

170

"*Edwards . . . Necessity*": Jonathan Edwards, in *Freedom of the Will* (1754), and Joseph Priestley, in *Doctrine of Philosophical Necessity* (1777), both argued that human beings do not have free will.

Also, when a reference was going on, and the room full of lawyers and witnesses, and business driving fast, some deeply-occupied legal gentleman present, seeing Bartleby wholly unemployed, would request him to run round to his (the legal gentleman's) office and fetch some papers for him. Thereupon, Bartleby would tranquilly decline, and yet remain idle as before. Then the lawyer would give a great stare, and turn to me. And what could I say? At last I was made aware that all through the circle of my professional acquaintance, a whisper of wonder was running round, having reference to the strange creature I kept at my office. This worried me very much. And as the idea came upon me of his possibly turning out a long-lived man, and keeping occupying my chambers, and denying my authority; and perplexing my visitors; and scandalizing my professional reputation; and casting a general gloom over the premises; keeping soul and body together to the last upon his savings (for doubtless he spent but half a dime a day), and in the end perhaps outlive me, and claim possession of my office by right of his perpetual occupancy: as all these dark anticipations crowded upon me more and more, and my friends continually intruded their relentless remarks upon the apparition in my room; a great change was wrought in me. I resolved to gather all my faculties together, and forever rid me of this intolerable incubus.

Ere revolving any complicated project, however, adapted to this end, I first simply suggested to Bartleby the propriety of his permanent departure. In a calm and serious tone, I commended the idea to his careful and mature consideration. But, having taken three days to meditate upon it, he apprised me, that his original determination remained the same; in short, that he still preferred to abide with me.

What shall I do? I now said to myself, buttoning up my coat to the last button. What shall I do? what ought I to do? what does conscience say I *should* do with this man, or, rather, ghost. Rid myself of him, I must; go, he shall. But how? You will not thrust him, the poor, pale, passive mortal — you will not thrust such a helpless creature out of your door? you will not dishonor yourself by such cruelty? No, I will not, I cannot do that. Rather would I let him live and die here, and then mason up his remains in the wall. What, then, will you do? For all your coaxing, he will not budge. Bribes he leaves under your own paper-weight on your table; in short, it is quite plain that he prefers to cling to you.

Then something severe, something unusual must be done. What! surely you will not have him collared by a constable, and commit his innocent pallor to the common jail? And upon what ground could you procure such a thing to be done? — a vagrant, is he? What! he a vagrant, a wanderer, who refuses to budge? It is because he will *not* be a vagrant, then, that you seek to count him *as* a vagrant. That is too absurd. No visible means of support: there I have him. Wrong again: for indubitably he *does* support himself, and that is the only unanswerable proof that any man can show of his possessing the means so to do. No more, then. Since he will not quit me, I must quit him. I will change my offices; I will move

elsewhere, and give him fair notice, that if I find him on my new premises
I will then proceed against him as a common trespasser.

Acting accordingly, next day I thus addressed him: "I find these cham- 175
bers too far from the City Hall; the air is unwholesome. In a word, I propose to remove my offices next week, and shall no longer require your
services. I tell you this now, in order that you may seek another place."

He made no reply, and nothing more was said.

On the appointed day I engaged carts and men, proceeded to my
chambers, and having but little furniture, everything was removed in
a few hours. Throughout, the scrivener remained standing behind the
screen, which I directed to be removed the last thing. It was withdrawn;
and, being folded up like a huge folio, left him the motionless occupant
of a naked room. I stood in the entry watching him a moment, while
something from within me upbraided me.

I re-entered, with my hand in my pocket — and — and my heart in my
mouth.

"Good-bye, Bartleby; I am going — good-bye, and God some way
bless you; and take that," slipping something in his hand. But it dropped
upon the floor, and then — strange to say — I tore myself from him whom
I had so longed to be rid of.

Established in my new quarters, for a day or two I kept the door 180
locked, and started at every footfall in the passages. When I returned to
my rooms, after any little absence, I would pause at the threshold for an
instant, and attentively listen, ere applying my key. But these fears were
needless. Bartleby never came nigh me.

I thought all was going well, when a perturbed-looking stranger visited me, inquiring whether I was the person who had recently occupied
rooms at No. — Wall Street.

Full of forebodings, I replied that I was.

"Then, sir," said the stranger, who proved a lawyer, "you are responsible for the man you left there. He refuses to do any copying; he refuses to
do anything; he says he prefers not to; and he refuses to quit the premises."

"I am very sorry, sir," said I, with assumed tranquillity, but an inward
tremor, "but, really, the man you allude to is nothing to me — he is no
relation or apprentice of mine, that you should hold me responsible
for him."

"In mercy's name, who is he?"   185

"I certainly cannot inform you. I know nothing about him. Formerly
I employed him as a copyist; but he has done nothing for me now for
some time past."

"I shall settle him, then — good morning, sir."

Several days passed, and I heard nothing more; and, though I often
felt a charitable prompting to call at the place and see poor Bartleby, yet
a certain squeamishness, of I know not what, withheld me.

All is over with him, by this time, thought I, at last, when, through
another week, no further intelligence reached me. But, coming to my

room the day after, I found several persons waiting at my door in a high state of nervous excitement.

"That's the man — here he comes," cried the foremost one, whom I 190 recognized as the lawyer who had previously called upon me alone.

"You must take him away, sir, at once," cried a portly person among them, advancing upon me, and whom I knew to be the landlord of No. — Wall Street. "These gentlemen, my tenants, cannot stand it any longer; Mr. B —," pointing to the lawyer, "has turned him out of his room, and he now persists in haunting the building generally, sitting upon the banisters of the stairs by day, and sleeping in the entry by night. Everybody is concerned; clients are leaving the offices; some fears are entertained of a mob; something you must do, and that without delay."

Aghast at this torrent, I fell back before it, and would fain have locked myself in my new quarters. In vain I persisted that Bartleby was nothing to me — no more than to any one else. In vain — I was the last person known to have anything to do with him, and they held me to the terrible account. Fearful, then, of being exposed in the papers (as one person present obscurely threatened), I considered the matter, and, at length, said, that if the lawyer would give me a confidential interview with the scrivener, in his (the lawyer's) own room, I would, that afternoon, strive my best to rid them of the nuisance they complained of.

Going up stairs to my old haunt, there was Bartleby silently sitting upon the banister at the landing.

"What are you doing here, Bartleby?" said I.

"Sitting upon the banister," he mildly replied.   195

I motioned him into the lawyer's room, who then left us.

"Bartleby," said I, "are you aware that you are the cause of great tribulation to me, by persisting in occupying the entry after being dismissed from the office?"

No answer.

"Now one of two things must take place. Either you must do something, or something must be done to you. Now what sort of business would you like to engage in? Would you like to re-engage in copying for some one?"

"No; I would prefer not to make any change."   200

"Would you like a clerkship in a dry-goods store?"

"There is too much confinement about that. No, I would not like a clerkship; but I am not particular."

"Too much confinement," I cried, "why, you keep yourself confined all the time!"

"I would prefer not to take a clerkship," he rejoined, as if to settle that little item at once.

"How would a bar-tender's business suit you? There is no trying of 205 the eyesight in that."

"I would not like it at all; though, as I said before, I am not particular."

His unwonted wordiness inspirited me. I returned to the charge.

"Well, then, would you like to travel through the country collecting bills for the merchants? That would improve your health."

"No, I would prefer to be doing something else."

"How, then, would going as a companion to Europe, to entertain some   210 young gentleman with your conversation — how would that suit you?"

"Not at all. It does not strike me that there is anything definite about that. I like to be stationary. But I am not particular."

"Stationary you shall be, then," I cried, now losing all patience, and, for the first time in all my exasperating connection with him, fairly flying into a passion. "If you do not go away from these premises before night, I shall feel bound — indeed, I *am* bound — to — to quit the premises myself!" I rather absurdly concluded, knowing not with what possible threat to try to frighten his immobility into compliance. Despairing of all further efforts, I was precipitately leaving him, when a final thought occurred to me — one which had not been wholly unindulged before.

"Bartleby," said I, in the kindest tone I could assume under such exciting circumstances, "will you go home with me now — not to my office, but my dwelling — and remain there till we can conclude upon some convenient arrangement for you at our leisure? Come, let us start now, right away."

"No: at present I would prefer not to make any change at all."

I answered nothing; but, effectually dodging every one by the sud-   215 denness and rapidity of my flight, rushed from the building, ran up Wall Street towards Broadway, and, jumping into the first omnibus, was soon removed from pursuit. As soon as tranquillity returned, I distinctly perceived that I had now done all that I possibly could, both in respect to the demands of the landlord and his tenants, and with regard to my own desire and sense of duty, to benefit Bartleby, and shield him from rude persecution. I now strove to be entirely care-free and quiescent; and my conscience justified me in the attempt; though, indeed, it was not so successful as I could have wished. So fearful was I of being again hunted out by the incensed landlord and his exasperated tenants, that, surrendering my business to Nippers, for a few days, I drove about the upper part of the town and through the suburbs, in my rockaway; crossed over to Jersey City and Hoboken, and paid fugitive visits to Manhattanville and Astoria. In fact, I almost lived in my rockaway for the time.

When again I entered my office, lo, a note from the landlord lay upon the desk. I opened it with trembling hands. It informed me that the writer had sent to the police, and had Bartleby removed to the Tombs as a vagrant. Moreover, since I knew more about him than any one else, he wished me to appear at that place, and make a suitable statement of the facts. These tidings had a conflicting effect upon me. At first I was indignant; but, at last, almost approved. The landlord's energetic, summary disposition, had led him to adopt a procedure which I do not think I would have decided upon myself; and yet, as a last resort, under such peculiar circumstances, it seemed the only plan.

As I afterwards learned, the poor scrivener, when told that he must be conducted to the Tombs, offered not the slightest obstacle, but, in his pale, unmoving way, silently acquiesced.

Some of the compassionate and curious by-standers joined the party; and headed by one of the constables arm-in-arm with Bartleby, the silent procession filed its way through all the noise, and heat, and joy of the roaring thoroughfares at noon.

The same day I received the note, I went to the Tombs, or, to speak more properly, the Halls of Justice. Seeking the right officer, I stated the purpose of my call, and was informed that the individual I described was, indeed, within. I then assured the functionary that Bartleby was a perfectly honest man, and greatly to be compassionated, however unaccountably eccentric. I narrated all I knew, and closed by suggesting the idea of letting him remain in as indulgent confinement as possible, till something less harsh might be done — though, indeed, I hardly knew what. At all events, if nothing else could be decided upon, the almshouse must receive him. I then begged to have an interview.

Being under no disgraceful charge, and quite serene and harm-   220
less in all his ways, they had permitted him freely to wander about the prison, and, especially, in the inclosed grass-platted yards thereof. And so I found him there, standing all alone in the quietest of the yards, his face towards a high wall, while all around, from the narrow slits of the jail windows, I thought I saw peering out upon him the eyes of murderers and thieves.

"Bartleby!"

"I know you," he said, without looking round — "and I want nothing to say to you."

"It was not I that brought you here, Bartleby," said I, keenly pained at his implied suspicion. "And to you, this should not be so vile a place. Nothing reproachful attaches to you by being here. And see, it is not so sad a place as one might think. Look, there is the sky, and here is the grass."

"I know where I am," he replied, but would say nothing more, and so I left him.

As I entered the corridor again, a broad meat-like man, in an apron,   225
accosted me, and, jerking his thumb over his shoulder, said — "Is that your friend?"

"Yes."

"Does he want to starve? If he does, let him live on the prison fare, that's all."

"Who are you?" asked I, not knowing what to make of such an unofficially speaking person in such a place.

"I am the grub-man. Such gentlemen as have friends here, hire me to provide them with something good to eat."

"Is this so?" said I, turning the turnkey.   230

He said it was.

"Well, then," said I, slipping some silver into the grub-man's hands (for so they called him), "I want you to give particular attention to my friend there; let him have the best dinner you can get. And you must be as polite to him as possible."

"Introduce me, will you?" said the grub-man, looking at me with an expression which seemed to say he was all impatience for an opportunity to give a specimen of his breeding.

Thinking it would prove of benefit to the scrivener, I acquiesced; and, asking the grub-man his name, went up with him to Bartleby.

"Bartleby, this is a friend; you will find him very useful to you."   235

"Your sarvant, sir, your sarvant," said the grub-man, making a low salutation behind his apron. "Hope you find it pleasant here, sir; nice grounds — cool apartments — hope you'll stay with us some time — try to make it agreeable. What will you have for dinner to-day?"

"I prefer not to dine to-day," said Bartleby, turning away. "It would disagree with me; I am unused to dinners." So saying, he slowly moved to the other side of the inclosure, and took up a position fronting the deadwall.

"How's this?" said the grub-man, addressing me with a stare of astonishment. "He's odd, ain't he?"

"I think he is a little deranged," said I, sadly.

"Deranged? deranged is it? Well, now, upon my word, I thought that   240 friend of yourn was a gentleman forger; they are always pale and genteel-like, them forgers. I can't help pity 'em — can't help it, sir. Did you know Monroe Edwards?" he added, touchingly, and paused. Then, laying his hand piteously on my shoulder, sighed, "he died of consumption at Sing-Sing. So you weren't acquainted with Monroe?"

"No, I was never socially acquainted with any forgers. But I cannot stop longer. Look to my friend yonder. You will not lose by it. I will see you again."

Some few days after this, I again obtained admission to the Tombs, and went through the corridors in quest of Bartleby; but without finding him.

"I saw him coming from his cell not long ago," said a turnkey, "may be he's gone to loiter in the yards."

So I went in that direction.

"Are you looking for the silent man?" said another turnkey, passing   245 me. "Yonder he lies — sleeping in the yard there. 'Tis not twenty minutes since I saw him lie down."

The yard was entirely quiet. It was not accessible to the common prisoners. The surrounding walls, of amazing thickness, kept off all sounds behind them. The Egyptian character of the masonry weighed upon me with its gloom. But a soft imprisoned turf grew under foot. The heart of the eternal pyramids, it seemed, wherein, by some strange magic, through the clefts, grass-seed, dropped by birds, had sprung.

Strangely huddled at the base of the wall, his knees drawn up, and lying on his side, his head touching the cold stones, I saw the wasted Bartleby. But nothing stirred. I paused; then went close up to him; stooped over, and saw that his dim eyes were open; otherwise he seemed profoundly sleeping. Something prompted me to touch him. I felt his hand, when a tingling shiver ran up my arm and down my spine to my feet.

The round face of the grub-man peered upon me now. "His dinner is ready. Won't he dine to-day, either? Or does he live without dining?"

"Lives without dining," said I, and closed the eyes.

"Eh! — He's asleep, ain't he?"

"With kings and counselors,"° murmured I.   250

There would seem little need for proceeding further in this history. Imagination will readily supply the meagre recital of poor Bartleby's interment. But, ere parting with the reader, let me say, that if this little narrative has sufficiently interested him, to awaken curiosity as to who Bartleby was, and what manner of life he led prior to the present narrator's making his acquaintance, I can only reply, that in such curiosity I fully share, but am wholly unable to gratify it. Yet here I hardly know whether I should divulge one little item of rumor, which came to my ear a few months after the scrivener's decease. Upon what basis it rested, I could never ascertain; and hence, how true it is I cannot now tell. But, inasmuch as this vague report has not been without a certain suggestive interest to me, however sad, it may prove the same with some others; and so I will briefly mention it. The report was this: that Bartleby had been a subordinate clerk in the Dead Letter Office at Washington, from which he had been suddenly removed by a change in the administration. When I think over this rumor, hardly can I express the emotions which seize me. Dead letters! does it not sound like dead men? Conceive a man by nature and misfortune prone to a pallid hopelessness, can any business seem more fitted to heighten it than that of continually handling these dead letters, and assorting them for the flames? For by the cart-load they are annually burned. Sometimes from out the folded paper the pale clerk takes a ring — the finger it was meant for, perhaps, moulders in the grave; a bank-note sent in swiftest charity — he whom it would relieve, nor eats nor hungers any more; pardon for those who died despairing; hope for those who died unhoping; good tidings for those who died stifled by unrelieved calamities. On errands of life, these letters speed to death.

Ah, Bartleby! Ah, humanity!

"With kings and counselors": From Job 3:13-14: "then had I been at rest, / With kings and counselors of the earth, / which built desolate places for themselves."

CONSIDERATIONS FOR CRITICAL THINKING AND WRITING

1. **FIRST RESPONSE.** How does the lawyer's description of himself serve to characterize him? Why is it significant that he is a lawyer? Are his understandings and judgments about Bartleby and himself always sound?

2. Why do you think Turkey, Nippers, and Ginger Nut are introduced to the reader before Bartleby?

3. Describe Bartleby's physical characteristics. How is his physical description a foreshadowing of what happens to him?

4. How does Bartleby's "I would prefer not to" affect the routine of the lawyer and his employees?

5. What is the significance of the subtitle: "A Story of Wall Street"?

6. Who is the protagonist? Whose story is it?

7. Does the lawyer change during the story? Does Bartleby? Who is the antagonist?

8. What motivates Bartleby's behavior? Why do you think Melville withholds the information about the Dead Letter Office until the end of the story? Does this background adequately explain Bartleby?

9. Does Bartleby have any lasting impact on the lawyer?

10. Do you think Melville sympathizes more with Bartleby or with the lawyer?

11. Describe the lawyer's changing attitudes toward Bartleby.

12. Consider how this story could be regarded as a kind of protest with nonnegotiable demands.

13. Discuss the story's humor and how it affects your response to Bartleby.

14. Trace your emotional reaction to Bartleby as he is revealed in the story.

15. **CONNECTION TO ANOTHER SELECTION.** Compare Bartleby's withdrawal from life with that of the protagonist in Gail Godwin's "A Sorrowful Woman" (p. 36). Why does each character choose death?

4

Setting

My role is to look at the world, get a true, not an idealized vision of it and hand it over to you in fictional form.

— FAY WELDON

Steve Elison / CORBIS.

Setting is the context in which the action of a story occurs. The major elements of setting are time, place, and the social environment that frames the characters. These elements establish the world in which the characters act. In most stories they also serve as more than backgrounds and furnishings. If we are sensitive to the contexts provided by setting, we are better able to understand the behavior of the characters and the significance of their actions. It may be tempting to read quickly through a writer's descriptions and ignore the details of the setting once a geographic location and a historic period are established. But if you read a story so impatiently, the significance of the setting may slip by you. That kind of reading is similar to traveling on interstate highways: A lot of ground gets covered, but very little is seen along the way.

If we ask why a writer chooses to include certain details in a work, then we are likely to make connections that relate the details to some larger purpose, such as the story's meaning. The final scene in Godwin's "A Sorrowful Woman" (p. 36) occurs in the spring, an ironic time for the action to be set because instead of rebirth for the protagonist there is only death. There is usually a reason for placing a story in a particular time or location. Melville's "Bartleby, the Scrivener" (p. 101), for example, takes on meaning as Bartleby's "dead-wall reveries" begin to reflect his

Explore the literary element in this chapter at bedfordstmartins.com/ meyerlit.

shattered vision of life. He is surrounded by walls. A folding screen separates him from others in the office; he is isolated. The office window
faces walls; there is no view to relieve the deadening work. Bartleby faces
a wall at the prison where he dies; the final wall is death. As the subtitle
indicates, this is "A Story of Wall Street." Unless the geographic location
or the physical details of a story are used merely as necessary props, they
frequently shed light on character and action. All offices have walls, but
Melville transforms the walls into an antagonist that represents the limitations Bartleby sees and feels all around him but does not speak of.

Time, location, and the physical features of a setting can all be relevant to the overall purpose of a story. So too is the social environment
in which the characters are developed. In Faulkner's "A Rose for Emily"
(p. 52) the changes in her southern town serve as a foil for Emily's tena-
cious hold on a lost past. She is regarded as a "fallen monument," as old-
fashioned and peculiar as the "stubborn and coquettish decay" of her
house. Neither she nor her house fits into the modern changes that are
paving and transforming the town. Without the social context, this story
would be mostly an account of a bizarre murder rather than an exploration of the conflicts Faulkner associated with the changing South. Setting enlarges the meaning of Emily's actions.

Not every story uses setting as a means of revealing mood, idea,
meaning, or characters' actions. Some stories have no particularly significant setting. It is entirely possible to envision a story in which two characters speak to each other about a conflict between them and little or no
mention is made of the time or place they inhabit. If, however, a shift in
setting would make a serious difference to our understanding of a story,
then the setting is probably an important element in the work. Consider
how different "Bartleby, the Scrivener" would be if it were set in a relaxed,
pleasant, sunny town in the South rather than in the grinding, limiting
materialism of Wall Street. Bartleby's withdrawal from life would be less
comprehensible and meaningful in such a setting. The setting is integral
to that story.

The following three stories — Ernest Hemingway's "Soldier's Home,"
Fay Weldon's "IND AFF, or Out of Love in Sarajevo," and Muriel Spark's
"The First Year of My Life" — include settings that serve to shape their
meanings.

ERNEST HEMINGWAY (1899–1961)

In 1918, a year after graduating from high school in Oak Park, Illinois,
Ernest Hemingway volunteered as an ambulance driver in World War I.
At the Italian front, he was seriously wounded. This experience haunted
him and many of the characters in his short stories and novels. *In Our
Time* (1925) is a collection of short stories, including "Soldier's Home,"
that reflect some of Hemingway's own attempts to readjust to life back

home after the war. *The Sun Also Rises* (1926), *A Farewell to Arms* (1929), and *For Whom the Bell Tolls* (1940) are also about war and its impact on people's lives. Hemingway courted violence all his life—in war, the bullring, the boxing ring, and big-game hunting. When he was sixty-two years old and terminally ill with cancer, he committed suicide. "Soldier's Home" takes place in a small town in Oklahoma; the war, however, is never distant from the protagonist's mind as he struggles to come home again.

Courtesy of the Ernest Hemingway Photographic Collection, John Fitzgerald Kennedy Library, Boston.

Soldier's Home   1925

Krebs went to the war from a Methodist college in Kansas. There is a picture which shows him among his fraternity brothers, all of them wearing exactly the same height and style collar. He enlisted in the Marines in 1917 and did not return to the United States until the second division returned from the Rhine in the summer of 1919.

There is a picture which shows him on the Rhine with two German girls and another corporal. Krebs and the corporal look too big for their uniforms. The German girls are not beautiful. The Rhine does not show in the picture.

By the time Krebs returned to his home town in Oklahoma the greeting of heroes was over. He came back much too late. The men from the town who had been drafted had all been welcomed elaborately on their return. There had been a great deal of hysteria. Now the reaction had set in. People seemed to think it was rather ridiculous for Krebs to be getting back so late, years after the war was over.

At first Krebs, who had been at Belleau Wood, Soissons, the Champagne, St. Mihiel, and in the Argonne° did not want to talk about the war at all. Later he felt the need to talk but no one wanted to hear about it. His town had heard too many atrocity stories to be thrilled by actualities. Krebs found that to be listened to at all he had to lie, and after he had done this twice he, too, had a reaction against the war and against talking about it. A distaste for everything that had happened to him in the war set in because of the lies he had told. All of the times that had been able to make him feel cool and clear inside himself when he thought of them; the times so long back when he had done the one thing, the only

---

Belleau Wood . . . Argonne: Sites of battles in World War I in which American troops were instrumental in pushing back the Germans.

thing for a man to do, easily and naturally, when he might have done something else, now lost their cool, valuable quality and then were lost themselves.

His lies were quite unimportant lies and consisted in attributing to 5 himself things other men had seen, done, or heard of, and stating as facts certain apocryphal incidents familiar to all soldiers. Even his lies were not sensational at the pool room. His acquaintances, who had heard detailed accounts of German women found chained to machine guns in the Argonne forest and who could not comprehend, or were barred by their patriotism from interest in, any German machine gunners who were not chained, were not thrilled by his stories.

Krebs acquired the nausea in regard to experience that is the result of untruth or exaggeration, and when he occasionally met another man who had really been a soldier and they talked a few minutes in the dressing room at a dance he fell into the easy pose of the old soldier among other soldiers: that he had been badly, sickeningly frightened all the time. In this way he lost everything.

During this time, it was late summer, he was sleeping late in bed, getting up to walk down town to the library to get a book, eating lunch at home, reading on the front porch until he became bored, and then walking down through the town to spend the hottest hours of the day in the cool dark of the pool room. He loved to play pool.

In the evening he practiced on his clarinet, strolled down town, read, and went to bed. He was still a hero to his two young sisters. His mother would have given him breakfast in bed if he had wanted it. She often came in when he was in bed and asked him to tell her about the war, but her attention always wandered. His father was noncommittal.

Before Krebs went away to the war he had never been allowed to drive the family motor car. His father was in the real estate business and always wanted the car to be at his command when he required it to take clients out into the country to show them a piece of farm property. The car always stood outside the First National Bank building where his father had an office on the second floor. Now, after the war, it was still the same car.

Nothing was changed in the town except that the young girls had 10 grown up. But they lived in such a complicated world of already defined alliances and shifting feuds that Krebs did not feel the energy or the courage to break into it. He liked to look at them, though. There were so many good-looking young girls. Most of them had their hair cut short. When he went away only little girls wore their hair like that or girls that were fast. They all wore sweaters and shirt waists with round Dutch collars. It was a pattern. He liked to look at them from the front porch as they walked on the other side of the street. He liked to watch them walking under the shade of the trees. He liked the round Dutch collars above their sweaters. He liked their silk stockings and flat shoes. He liked their bobbed hair and the way they walked.

When he was in town their appeal to him was not very strong. He did not like them when he saw them in the Greek's ice cream parlor. He did not want them themselves really. They were too complicated. There was something else. Vaguely he wanted a girl but he did not want to have to work to get her. He would have liked to have a girl but he did not want to have to spend a long time getting her. He did not want to get into the intrigue and the politics. He did not want to have to do any courting. He did not want to tell any more lies. It wasn't worth it.

He did not want any consequences. He did not want any consequences ever again. He wanted to live alone without consequences. Besides he did not really need a girl. The army had taught him that. It was all right to pose as though you had to have a girl. Nearly everybody did that. But it wasn't true. You did not need a girl. That was the funny thing. First a fellow boasted how girls mean nothing to him, that he never thought of them, that they could not touch him. Then a fellow boasted that he could not get along without girls, that he had to have them all the time, that he could not go to sleep without them.

That was all a lie. It was all a lie both ways. You did not need a girl unless you thought about them. He learned that in the army. Then sooner or later you always got one. When you were really ripe for a girl you always got one. You did not have to think about it. Sooner or later it would come. He had learned that in the army.

Now he would have liked a girl if she had come to him and not wanted to talk. But here at home it was all too complicated. He knew he could never get through it all again. It was not worth the trouble. That was the thing about French girls and German girls. There was not all this talking. You couldn't talk much and you did not need to talk. It was simple and you were friends. He thought about France and then he began to think about Germany. On the whole he had liked Germany better. He did not want to leave Germany. He did not want to come home. Still, he had come home. He sat on the front porch.

He liked the girls that were walking along the other side of the street. He liked the look of them much better than the French girls or the German girls. But the world they were in was not the world he was in. He would like to have one of them. But it was not worth it. They were such a nice pattern. He liked the pattern. It was exciting. But he would not go through all the talking. He did not want one badly enough. He liked to look at them all, though. It was not worth it. Not now when things were getting good again.

He sat there on the porch reading a book on the war. It was a history and he was reading about all the engagements he had been in. It was the most interesting reading he had ever done. He wished there were more maps. He looked forward with a good feeling to reading all the really good histories when they would come out with good detail maps. Now he was really learning about the war. He had been a good soldier. That made a difference.

One morning after he had been home about a month his mother came into his bedroom and sat on the bed. She smoothed her apron.

"I had a talk with your father last night, Harold," she said, "and he is willing for you to take the car out in the evenings."

"Yeah?" said Krebs, who was not fully awake. "Take the car out? Yeah?"

"Yes. Your father has felt for some time that you should be able to   20 take the car out in the evenings whenever you wished but we only talked it over last night."

"I'll bet you made him," Krebs said.

"No. It was your father's suggestion that we talk the matter over."

"Yeah. I'll bet you made him," Krebs sat up in bed.

"Will you come down to breakfast, Harold?" his mother said.

"As soon as I get my clothes on," Krebs said.   25

His mother went out of the room and he could hear her frying something downstairs while he washed, shaved, and dressed to go down into the dining-room for breakfast. While he was eating breakfast his sister brought in the mail.

"Well, Hare," she said. "You old sleepyhead. What do you ever get up for?"

Krebs looked at her. He liked her. She was his best sister.

"Have you got the paper?" he asked.

She handed him the Kansas City *Star* and he shucked off its brown   30 wrapper and opened it to the sporting page. He folded the *Star* open and propped it against the water pitcher with his cereal dish to steady it, so he could read while he ate.

"Harold," his mother stood in the kitchen doorway, "Harold, please don't muss up the paper. Your father can't read his *Star* if it's been mussed."

"I won't muss it," Krebs said.

His sister sat down at the table and watched him while he read.

"We're playing indoor over at school this afternoon," she said. "I'm going to pitch."

"Good," said Krebs. "How's the old wing?"   35

"I can pitch better than lots of the boys. I tell them all you taught me. The other girls aren't much good."

"Yeah?" said Krebs.

"I tell them all you're my beau. Aren't you my beau, Hare?"

"You bet."

"Couldn't your brother really be your beau just because he's your   40 brother?"

"I don't know."

"Sure you know. Couldn't you be my beau, Hare, if I was old enough and if you wanted to?"

"Sure. You're my girl now."

"Am I really your girl?"

"Sure."   45

"Do you love me?"

"Uh, huh."

"Will you love me always?"

"Sure."

"Will you come over and watch me play indoor?"   50

"Maybe."

"Aw, Hare, you don't love me. If you loved me, you'd want to come over and watch me play indoor."

Krebs's mother came into the dining-room from the kitchen. She carried a plate with two fried eggs and some crisp bacon on it and a plate of buckwheat cakes.

"You run along, Helen," she said. "I want to talk to Harold."

She put the eggs and bacon down in front of him and brought in a   55 jug of maple syrup for the buckwheat cakes. Then she sat down across the table from Krebs.

"I wish you'd put down the paper a minute, Harold," she said.

Krebs took down the paper and folded it.

"Have you decided what you are going to do yet, Harold?" his mother said, taking off her glasses.

"No," said Krebs.

"Don't you think it's about time?" His mother did not say this in a   60 mean way. She seemed worried.

"I hadn't thought about it," Krebs said.

"God has some work for everyone to do," his mother said. "There can be no idle hands in His Kingdom."

"I'm not in His Kingdom," Krebs said.

"We are all of us in His Kingdom."

Krebs felt embarrassed and resentful as always.   65

"I've worried about you so much, Harold," his mother went on. "I know the temptations you must have been exposed to. I know how weak men are. I know what your own dear grandfather, my own father, told us about the Civil War and I have prayed for you. I pray for you all day long, Harold."

Krebs looked at the bacon fat hardening on his plate.

"Your father is worried, too," his mother went on. "He thinks you have lost your ambition, that you haven't got a definite aim in life. Charley Simmons, who is just your age, has a good job and is going to be married. The boys are all settling down; they're all determined to get somewhere; you can see that boys like Charley Simmons are on their way to being really a credit to the community."

Krebs said nothing.

"Don't look that way, Harold," his mother said. "You know we love   70 you and I want to tell you for your own good how matters stand. Your father does not want to hamper your freedom. He thinks you should be allowed to drive the car. If you want to take some of the nice girls out riding with you, we are only too pleased. We want you to enjoy yourself. But you are going to have to settle down to work, Harold. Your father doesn't care what you start in at. All work is honorable as he says. But you've got to make a start at something. He asked me to speak to you this morning and then you can stop in and see him at his office."

"Is that all?" Krebs said.

"Yes. Don't you love your mother, dear boy?"

"No," Krebs said.

His mother looked at him across the table. Her eyes were shiny. She started crying.

"I don't love anybody," Krebs said.   75

It wasn't any good. He couldn't tell her, he couldn't make her see it. It was silly to have said it. He had only hurt her. He went over and took hold of her arm. She was crying with her head in her hands.

"I didn't mean it," he said. "I was just angry at something. I didn't mean I didn't love you."

His mother went on crying. Krebs put his arm on her shoulder.

"Can't you believe me, mother?"

His mother shook her head.   80

"Please, please, mother. Please believe me."

"All right," his mother said chokily. She looked up at him. "I believe you, Harold."

Krebs kissed her hair. She put her face up to him.

"I'm your mother," she said. "I held you next to my heart when you were a tiny baby."

Krebs felt sick and vaguely nauseated.   85

"I know, Mummy," he said. "I'll try and be a good boy for you."

"Would you kneel and pray with me, Harold?" his mother asked.

They knelt down beside the dining-room table and Krebs's mother prayed.

"Now, you pray, Harold," she said.

"I can't," Krebs said.   90

"Try, Harold."

"I can't."

"Do you want me to pray for you?"

"Yes."

So his mother prayed for him and then they stood up and Krebs 95
kissed his mother and went out of the house. He had tried so to keep his life from being complicated. Still, none of it had touched him. He had felt sorry for his mother and she had made him lie. He would go to Kansas City and get a job and she would feel all right about it. There would be one more scene maybe before he got away. He would not go down to his father's office. He would miss that one. He wanted his life to go smoothly. It had just gotten going that way. Well, that was all over now, anyway. He would go over to the schoolyard and watch Helen play indoor baseball.

Considerations for Critical Thinking and Writing

1. **FIRST RESPONSE.** The title, "Soldier's Home," focuses on the setting. Do you have a clear picture of Krebs's home? Describe it, filling in missing details from your associations of home, Krebs's routine, or anything else you can use.

2. What does the photograph of Krebs, the corporal, and the German girls reveal?

3. Belleau Wood, Soissons, the Champagne, St. Mihiel, and the Argonne were the sites of fierce and bloody fighting. What effect have these battles had on Krebs? Why do you think he won't talk about them to the people at home?

4. Why does Krebs avoid complications and consequences? How has the war changed his attitudes toward work and women? How is his hometown different from Germany and France? What is the conflict in the story?

5. Why do you think Hemingway refers to the protagonist as Krebs rather than Harold? What is the significance of his sister calling him "Hare"?

6. How does Krebs's mother embody the community's values? What does Krebs think of those values?

7. What is the resolution to Krebs's conflict?

8. Comment on the appropriateness of the story's title.

9. Explain how Krebs's war experiences are present throughout the story even though we get no details about them.

10. **CONNECTION TO ANOTHER SELECTION.** Compare the attitudes toward domestic life implicit in this story with those in Gail Godwin's "A Sorrowful Woman" (p. 36).

Fay Weldon (b. 1933)

Born in England and raised in New Zealand, Fay Weldon graduated from St. Andrew's University in Scotland. She wrote advertising copy for various companies and was a propaganda writer for the British Foreign Office before turning to fiction. She has written novels, short stories, plays, and radio scripts. In 1971 her script for an episode of *Upstairs, Downstairs* won an award from the Society of Film and Television Arts. She has written more than a score of novels, including *The Fat Woman's Joke* (1967), *Down Among the Women* (1971), *Praxis* (1978), *The Life and Loves of a She-Devil* (1983), *Life Force* (1991), *The Bulgari Connection* (2001), *She May Not Leave* (2005), *The Stepmother's Diary* (2008), and *Habits of the House* (2012),

Steve Elison / CORBIS.

and an equal number of plays and scripts. Her collections of short stories include *Moon over Minneapolis* (1992), *Wicked Women* (American edition, 1997), *A Hard Time to Be a Father* (1998), and *Nothing to Wear and Nowhere to Hide* (2002). Weldon often uses ironic humor to portray carefully drawn female characters coming to terms with the facts of their lives.

IND AFF   *1988*
or Out of Love in Sarajevo

This is a sad story. It has to be. It rained in Sarajevo, and we had expected fine weather.

The rain filled up Sarajevo's pride, two footprints set into a pavement which mark the spot where the young assassin Princip stood to shoot the Archduke Franz Ferdinand and his wife. (Don't forget his wife: everyone forgets his wife, the archduchess.) That was in the summer of 1914. Sarajevo is a pretty town, Balkan style, mountain-rimmed. A broad, swift, shallow river runs through its center, carrying the mountain snow away, arched by many bridges. The one nearest the two footprints has been named the Princip Bridge. The young man is a hero in these parts. Not only does he bring in the tourists — look, look, the spot, the very spot! — but by his action, as everyone knows, he lit a spark which fired the timber which caused World War I which crumbled the Austro-Hungarian Empire, the crumbling of which made modern Yugoslavia possible. Forty million dead (or was it thirty?) but who cares? So long as he loved his country.

The river, they say, can run so shallow in the summer it's known derisively as "the wet road." Today, from what I could see through the sheets of falling rain, it seemed full enough. Yugoslavian streets are always busy — no one stays home if they can help it (thus can an indecent shortage of housing space create a sociable nation) and it seemed as if by common consent a shield of bobbing umbrellas had been erected two meters high to keep the rain off the streets. It just hadn't worked around Princip's corner.

"Come all this way," said Peter, who was a professor of classical history, "and you can't even see the footprints properly, just two undistinguished puddles." Ah, but I loved him. I shivered for his disappointment. He was supervising my thesis on varying concepts of morality and duty in the early Greek States as evidenced in their poetry and drama. I was dependent upon him for my academic future. He said I had a good mind but not a first-class mind and somehow I didn't take it as an insult. I had a feeling first-class minds weren't all that good in bed.

Sarajevo is in Bosnia, in the center of Yugoslavia, that grouping 5 of unlikely states, that distillation of languages into the phonetic reasonableness of Serbo-Croatian. We'd sheltered from the rain in an ancient mosque in Serbian Belgrade; done the same in a monastery in Croatia; now we spent a wet couple of days in Sarajevo beneath other people's umbrellas. We planned to go on to Montenegro, on the coast, where the fish and the artists come from, to swim and lie in the sun, and recover from the exhaustion caused by the sexual and moral torments of the last year. It couldn't possibly go on raining forever. Could it? Satellite pictures showed black clouds swishing gently all over Europe, over the Balkans, into Asia — practically all the way from Moscow to London, in fact. It wasn't that Peter and myself were being singled out. No. It was raining on his wife, too, back in Cambridge.

Peter was trying to decide, as he had been for the past year, between his wife and myself as his permanent life partner. To this end we had gone away, off the beaten track, for a holiday; if not with his wife's blessing, at least with her knowledge. Were we really, truly suited? We had to be sure, you see, that this was more than just any old professor-student romance; that it was the Real Thing, because the longer the indecision went on the longer Mrs. Piper would be left dangling in uncertainty and distress. They had been married for twenty-four years; they had stopped loving each other a long time ago, of course — but there would be a fearful personal and practical upheaval entailed if he decided to leave permanently and shack up, as he put it, with me. Which I certainly wanted him to do. I loved him. And so far I was winning hands down. It didn't seem much of a contest at all, in fact. I'd been cool and thin and informed on the seat next to him in a Zagreb theater (Mrs. Piper was sweaty and only liked telly); was now eager and anxious for social and political instruction in Sarajevo (Mrs. Piper spat in the face of knowledge, he'd once told me); and planned to be lissome (and I thought topless but I hadn't quite decided: this might be the area where the age difference showed) while I splashed and shrieked like a bathing belle in the shallows of the Montenegrin coast. (Mrs. Piper was a swimming coach: I imagined she smelt permanently of chlorine.)

In fact so far as I could see, it was no contest at all between his wife and myself. But Peter liked to luxuriate in guilt and indecision. And I loved him with an inordinate affection.

Princip's prints are a meter apart, placed as a modern cop on a training shoot-out would place his feet — the left in front at a slight outward angle, the right behind, facing forward. There seemed great energy focused here. Both hands on the gun, run, stop, plant the feet, aim, fire! I could see the footprints well enough, in spite of Peter's complaint. They were clear enough to me.

We went to a restaurant for lunch, since it was too wet to do what we loved to do: that is, buy bread, cheese, sausage, wine, and go off somewhere in our hired car, into the woods or the hills, and picnic and make love. It was a private restaurant — Yugoslavia went over to a mixed capitalist-communist economy years back, so you get either the best or worst of both systems, depending on your mood — that is to say, we knew we would pay more but be given a choice. We chose the wild boar.

"Probably ordinary pork soaked in red cabbage water to darken it," said Peter. He was not in a good mood.   10

Cucumber salad was served first.

"Everything in this country comes with cucumber salad," complained Peter. I noticed I had become used to his complaining. I supposed that when you had been married a little you simply wouldn't hear it. He was forty-six and I was twenty-five.

"They grow a lot of cucumber," I said.

"If they can grow cucumbers," Peter then asked, "why can't they grow *mange-tout*°?" It seemed a why-can't-they-eat-cake sort of argument to me, but not knowing enough about horticulture not to be outflanked if I debated the point, I moved the subject on to safer ground.

"I suppose Princip's action couldn't really have started World War I,"   15
I remarked. "Otherwise, what a thing to have on your conscience! One little shot and the deaths of thirty million."

"Forty," he corrected me. Though how they reckon these things and get them right I can't imagine. "Of course he didn't start the war. That's just a simple tale to keep the children quiet. It takes more than an assassination to start a war. What happened was that the buildup of political and economic tensions in the Balkans was such that it had to find some release."

"So it was merely the shot that lit the spark that fired the timber that started the war, et cetera?"

"Quite," he said. "World War I would have had to have started sooner or later."

"A bit later or a bit sooner," I said, "might have made the difference of a million or so; if it was you on the battlefield in the mud and the rain you'd notice; exactly when they fired the starting-pistol; exactly when they blew the final whistle. Is that what they do when a war ends; blow a whistle? So that everyone just comes in from the trenches."

But he wasn't listening. He was parting the flesh of the soft collapsed   20
orangey-red pepper which sat in the middle of his cucumber salad; he was carefully extracting the pips. His nan had once told him they could never be digested, would stick inside and do terrible damage. I loved him for his dexterity and patience with his knife and fork. I'd finished my salad yonks ago, pips and all. I was hungry. I wanted my wild boar.

Peter might be forty-six, but he was six foot two and grizzled and muscled with it, in a dark-eyed, intelligent, broad-jawed kind of way. I adored him. I loved to be seen with him. "Muscular academic, not weedy academic" as my younger sister Clare once said. "Muscular academic is just

mange-tout: A sugar pea or bean (French).

a generally superior human being: everything works well from the brain to the toes. Weedy academic is when there isn't enough vital energy in the person, and the brain drains all the strength from the other parts." Well, Clare should know. Clare is only twenty-three, but of the superior human variety kind herself, vividly pretty, bright and competent — somewhere behind a heavy curtain of vibrant red hair, which she only parts for effect. She had her first degree at twenty. Now she's married to a Harvard professor of economics seconded to the United Nations. She can even cook. I gave up competing yonks ago. Though she too is capable of self-deception. I would say her husband was definitely of the weedy academic rather than the muscular academic type. And they have to live in Brussels.

The archduke's chauffeur had lost his way, and was parked on the corner trying to recover his nerve when Princip came running out of a café, planted his feet, aimed, and fired. Princip was nineteen — too young to hang. But they sent him to prison for life and, since he had TB to begin with, he only lasted three years. He died in 1918, in an Austrian prison. Or perhaps it was more than TB: perhaps they gave him a hard time, not learning till later, when the Austro-Hungarian Empire collapsed, that he was a hero. Poor Princip, too young to die — like so many other millions. Dying for love of a country.

"I love you," I said to Peter, my living man, progenitor already of three children by his chlorinated, swimming-coach wife.

"How much do you love me?"

"Inordinately! I love you with inordinate affection." It was a joke   25 between us. Ind Aff!

"Inordinate affection is a sin," he'd told me. "According to the Wesley-ans. John Wesley° himself worried about it to such a degree he ended up abbreviating it in his diaries, Ind Aff. He maintained that what he felt for young Sophy, the eighteen-year-old in his congregation, was not Ind Aff, which bears the spirit away from God towards the flesh: he insisted that what he felt was a pure and spiritual, if passionate, concern for her soul."

Peter said now, as we waited for our wild boar, and he picked over his pepper, "Your Ind Aff is my wife's sorrow, that's the trouble." He wanted, I knew, one of the long half-wrangles, half soul-sharings that we could keep going for hours, and led to piercing pains in the heart which could only be made better in bed. But our bedroom at the Hotel Europa was small and dark and looked out into the well of the building — a punishment room if ever there was one. (Reception staff did sometimes take against us.) When Peter had tried to change it in his quasi-Serbo-Croatian, they'd shrugged their Bosnian shoulders and pretended not to understand, so we'd decided to put up with it. I did not fancy pushing hard single beds together — it seemed easier not to have the pain in the heart in the first place. "Look," I said, "this holiday is supposed to be just the two of us, not Mrs. Piper as well. Shall we talk about something else?"

John Wesley (1703–1791): English religious leader and founder of Methodism.

Do not think that the archduke's chauffeur was merely careless, an inefficient chauffeur, when he took the wrong turning. He was, I imagine, in a state of shock, fright, and confusion. There had been two previous attempts on the archduke's life since the cavalcade had entered town. The first was a bomb which got the car in front and killed its driver. The second was a shot fired by none other than young Princip, which had missed. Princip had vanished into the crowd and gone to sit down in a corner café and ordered coffee to calm his nerves. I expect his hand trembled at the best of times—he did have TB. (Not the best choice of assassin, but no doubt those who arrange these things have to make do with what they can get.) The archduke's chauffeur panicked, took the wrong road, realized what he'd done, and stopped to await rescue and instructions just outside the café where Princip sat drinking his coffee.

"What shall we talk about?" asked Peter, in even less of a good mood.

"The collapse of the Austro-Hungarian Empire?" I suggested. 30 "How does an empire collapse? Is there no money to pay the military or the police, so everyone goes home? Or what?" He liked to be asked questions.

"The Hungro-Austrarian Empire," said Peter to me, "didn't so much collapse as fail to exist any more. War destroys social organizations. The same thing happened after World War II. There being no organized bodies left between Moscow and London—and for London read Washington, then as now—it was left to these two to put in their own puppet governments. Yalta, 1944. It's taken the best part of forty-five years for nations of West and East Europe to remember who they are."

"Austro-Hungarian," I said, "not Hungro-Austrarian."

"I didn't say Hungro-Austrarian," he said.

"You did," I said.

"Didn't," he said. "What the hell are they doing about our wild boar? 35 Are they out in the hills shooting it?"

My sister Clare had been surprisingly understanding about Peter. When I worried about him being older, she pooh-poohed it; when I worried about him being married, she said, "Just go for it, sister. If you can unhinge a marriage, it's ripe for unhinging, it would happen sooner or later, it might as well be you. See a catch, go ahead and catch! Go for it!"

Princip saw the archduke's car parked outside, and went for it. Second chances are rare in life: they must be responded to. Except perhaps his second chance was missing in the first place? Should he have taken his cue from fate, and just sat and finished his coffee, and gone home to his mother? But what's a man to do when he loves his country? Fate delivered the archduke into his hands: how could he resist it? A parked car, a uniformed and medaled chest, the persecutor of his country—how could Princip not, believing God to be on his side, but see this as His intervention, push his coffee aside and leap to his feet?

Two waiters stood idly by and watched us waiting for our wild boar. One was young and handsome in a mountainous Bosnian way—flashing eyes, hooked nose, luxuriant black hair, sensuous mouth. He was about my age. He smiled. His teeth were even and white. I smiled back, and instead of the pain in the heart I'd become accustomed to as an erotic sensation, now felt, quite violently, an associated yet different pang which got my lower stomach. The true, the real pain of Ind Aff!

"Fancy him?" asked Peter.

"No," I said. "I just thought if I smiled the wild boar might come 40 quicker."

The other waiter was older and gentler: his eyes were soft and kind. I thought he looked at me reproachfully. I could see why. In a world which for once, after centuries of savagery, was finally full of young men, unslaughtered, what was I doing with this man with thinning hair?

"What are you thinking of?" Professor Piper asked me. He liked to be in my head.

"How much I love you," I said automatically, and was finally aware how much I lied. "And about the archduke's assassination," I went on, to cover the kind of tremble in my head as I came to my senses, "and let's not forget his wife, she died too—how can you say World War I would have happened anyway. If Princip hadn't shot the archduke, something else, some undisclosed, unsuspected variable, might have come along and defused the whole political/military situation, and neither World War I nor II ever happened. We'll just never know, will we?"

I had my passport and my travelers' checks with me. (Peter felt it was less confusing if we each paid our own way.) I stood up, and took my raincoat from the peg.

"Where are you going?" he asked, startled.   45

"Home," I said. I kissed the top of his head, where it was balding. It smelt gently of chlorine, which may have come from thinking about his wife so much, but might merely have been that he'd taken a shower that morning. ("The water all over Yugoslavia, though safe to drink, is unusually chlorinated": Guide Book.) As I left to catch a taxi to the airport the younger of the two waiters emerged from the kitchen with two piled plates of roasted wild boar, potatoes duchesse, and stewed peppers. ("Yugoslavian diet is unusually rich in proteins and fats": Guide Book.) I could tell from the glisten of oil that the food was no longer hot, and I was not tempted to stay, hungry though I was. Thus fate—or was it Bosnian willfulness?—confirmed the wisdom of my intent.

And that was how I fell out of love with my professor, in Sarajevo, a city to which I am grateful to this day, though I never got to see very much of it, because of the rain.

It was a silly sad thing to do, in the first place, to confuse mere passing academic ambition with love: to try and outdo my sister Clare. (Professor Piper was spiteful, as it happened, and did his best to have my thesis refused, but I went to appeal, which he never thought I'd dare, and won. I had a first-class mind after all.) A silly sad episode, which I regret.

As silly and sad as Princip, poor young man, with his feverish mind, his bright tubercular cheeks, and his inordinate affection for his country, pushing aside his cup of coffee, leaping to his feet, taking his gun in both hands, planting his feet, aiming, and firing — one, two, three shots — and starting World War I. The first one missed, the second got the wife (never forget the wife), and the third got the archduke and a whole generation, and their children, and their children's children, and on and on forever. If he'd just hung on a bit, there in Sarajevo, that June day, he might have come to his senses. People do, sometimes quite quickly.

CONSIDERATIONS FOR CRITICAL THINKING AND WRITING

1. **FIRST RESPONSE.** Do you agree with Weldon's first line, "This is a sad story"? Explain why or why not.

2. How does the rain establish the mood for the story in the first five paragraphs?

3. Characterize Peter. What details concerning him reveal his personality?

4. Describe the narrator's relationship with Peter. How do you think he regards her? Why is she attracted to him?

5. Why is Sarajevo important for the story's setting? What is the effect of having the story of Princip's assassination of the Archduke Franz Ferdinand and his wife woven through the plot?

6. Describe Mrs. Piper. Though she doesn't appear in the story, she does have an important role. What do you think her role is?

7. What is "Ind Aff"? Why is it an important element of this story?

8. What is the significance of the two waiters (paras. 38–41)? How do they affect the narrator?

9. Why does the narrator decide to go home (para. 46)? Do you think she makes a reasoned or an impulsive decision? Explain why you think so.

10. **CONNECTION TO ANOTHER SELECTION.** Compare and contrast "IND AFF" and David Updike's "Summer" (p. 163) as love stories. Do you think that the stories end happily, or the way you would want them to end? Are the endings problematic?

MURIEL SPARK (1918–2006)

Born in Edinburgh, Scotland, Muriel Spark was a highly regarded novelist, short story writer, poet, and essayist honored as a Dame Commander of the British Empire (DBE). Although she didn't begin writing novels until she was nearly forty and a struggling single mother, she had a prolific career. Among her more than twenty-five novels are *The Comforters* (1957), *Memento Mori* (1959), *The Prime of Miss Jean Brodie* (1961), *The Mandelbaum Gate* (1965), *The Driver's Seat* (1970), *Loitering with Intent* (1981),

Symposium (1990), and *The Finishing School* (2004). Her *Complete Short Stories* appeared in 2001 and *All the Poems* in 2004. Death and violence as well as eccentric behavior are often present in her fiction, but so are humor and irony. Spark characterized her own writing as having "a comic strain" that is also "serious." "The First Year of My Life" serves as a fine example of that self-description of her work.

The First Year of My Life   1975

I was born on the first day of the second month of the last year of the First World War, a Friday. Testimony abounds that during the first year of my life I never smiled. I was known as the baby whom nothing and no one could make smile. Everyone who knew me then has told me so. They tried very hard, singing and bouncing me up and down, jumping around, pulling faces. Many times I was told this later by my family and their friends; but, anyway, I knew it at the time.

You will shortly be hearing of that new school of psychology, or maybe you have heard of it already, which after long and far-adventuring research and experiment has established that all of the young of the human species are born omniscient. Babies, in their waking hours, know everything that is going on everywhere in the world; they can tune in to any conversation they choose, switch on to any scene. We have all experienced this power. It is only after the first year that it was brainwashed out of us; for it is demanded of us by our immediate environment that we grow to be of use to it in a practical way. Gradually, our know-all brain-cells are blacked out, although traces remain in some individuals in the form of E.S.P., and in the adults of some primitive tribes.

It is not a new theory. Poets and philosophers, as usual, have been there first. But scientific proof is now ready and to hand. Perhaps the final touches are being put to the new manifesto in some cell at Harvard University. Any day now it will be given to the world, and the world will be convinced.

Let me therefore get my word in first, because I feel pretty sure, now, about the authenticity of my remembrance of things past. My autobiography, as I very well perceived at the time, started in the very worst year that the world had ever seen so far. Apart from being born bedridden and toothless, unable to raise myself on the pillow or utter anything but farmyard squawks or police-siren wails, my bladder and my bowels totally out of control, I was further depressed by the curious behavior of the two-legged mammals around me. There were those black-dressed people, females of the species to which I appeared to belong, saying they had lost their sons. I slept a great deal. Let them go and find their sons. It was like the special pin for my nappies which my mother or some other hoverer dedicated to my care was always losing. These careless women in black lost their husbands and their brothers. Then they came

to visit my mother and clucked and crowed over my cradle. I was not
amused.

"Babies never really smile till they're three months old," said my   5
mother. "They're not *supposed* to smile till they're three months old."

My brother, aged six, marched up and down with a toy rifle over his
shoulder:

> *The grand old Duke of York*
> *He had ten thousand men;*
> *He marched them up to the top of the hill*
> *And he marched them down again.*
>
> *And when they were up, they were up.*
> *And when they were down, they were down.*
> *And when they were neither down nor up*
> *They were neither up nor down.*

"Just listen to him!"

"Look at him with his rifle!"

I was about ten days old when Russia stopped fighting. I tuned in to
the Czar, a prisoner, with the rest of his family, since evidently the country had put him off his throne and there had been a revolution not long
before I was born. Everyone was talking about it. I tuned in to the Czar.
"Nothing would ever induce me to sign the treaty of Brest-Litovsk," he
said to his wife. Anyway, nobody had asked him to.

At this point I was sleeping twenty hours a day to get my strength   10
up. And from what I discerned in the other four hours of the day I knew
I was going to need it. The Western Front on my frequency was sheer
blood, mud, dismembered bodies, blistered crashes, hectic flashes of
light in the night skies, explosions, total terror. Since it was plain I had
been born into a bad moment in the history of the world, the future
bothered me, unable as I was to raise my head from the pillow and as yet
only twenty inches long. "I truly wish I were a fox or a bird," D. H. Lawrence was writing to somebody. Dreary old creeping Jesus. I fell asleep.

Red sheets of flame shot across the sky. It was 21st March, the fiftieth day of my life, and the German Spring Offensive had started before
my morning feed. Infinite slaughter. I scowled at the scene, and made an
effort to kick out. But the attempt was feeble. Furious, and impatient for
some strength, I wailed for my feed. After which I stopped wailing but
continued to scowl.

> *The grand old Duke of York*
> *He had ten thousand men* . . .

They rocked the cradle. I never heard a sillier song. Over in Berlin and
Vienna the people were starving, freezing, striking, rioting and yelling in

the streets. In London everyone was bustling to work and muttering that it was time the whole damn business was over.

The big people around me bared their teeth; that meant a smile, it meant they were pleased or amused. They spoke of ration cards for meat and sugar and butter.

"Where will it all end?"

I went to sleep. I woke and tuned in to Bernard Shaw who was telling someone to shut up. I switched over to Joseph Conrad who, strangely enough, was saying precisely the same thing. I still didn't think it worth a smile, although it was expected of me any day now. I got on to Turkey. Women draped in black huddled and chattered in their harems; yak-yak-yak. This was boring, so I came back to home base.

In and out came and went the women in British black. My mother's brother, dressed in his uniform, came coughing. He had been poison-gassed in the trenches. "*Tout le monde à la bataille!*"° declaimed Marshal Foch the old swine. He was now Commander-in-Chief of the Allied Forces. My uncle coughed from deep within his lungs, never to recover but destined to return to the Front. His brass buttons gleamed in the firelight. I weighed twelve pounds by now; I stretched and kicked for exercise, seeing that I had a lifetime before me, coping with this crowd. I took six feeds a day and kept most of them down by the time the *Vindictive* was sunk in Ostend harbor, on which day I kicked with special vigor in my bath.

In France the conscripted soldiers leapfrogged over the dead on the advance and littered the fields with limbs and hands, or drowned in the mud. The strongest men on all fronts were dead before I was born. Now the sentries used bodies for barricades and the fighting men were unhealthy from the start. I checked my toes and fingers, knowing I was going to need them. *The Playboy of the Western World* was playing at the Court Theatre in London, but occasionally I beamed over to the House of Commons which made me drop off gently to sleep. Generally, I preferred the Western Front where one got the true state of affairs. It was essential to know the worst, blood and explosions and all, for one had to be prepared, as the boy scouts said. Virginia Woolf yawned and reached for her diary. Really, I preferred the Western Front.

In the fifth month of my life I could raise my head from my pillow and hold it up. I could grasp the objects that were held out to me. Some of these things rattled and squawked. I gnawed on them to get my teeth started. "She hasn't smiled yet?" said the dreary old aunties. My mother, on the defensive, said I was probably one of those late smilers. On my wavelength Pablo Picasso was getting married and early in that month of July the Silver Wedding of King George V and Queen Mary was celebrated in joyous pomp at St. Paul's Cathedral. They drove through the streets of London with their children. Twenty-five years of domestic happiness. A lot of fuss and ceremonial handing over of swords went on at

Tout le monde à la bataille!: Everyone to the battle!

the Guildhall where the King and Queen received a cheque for £53,000 to dispose of for charity as they thought fit. *Tout le monde à la bataille!* Income tax in England had reached six shillings in the pound. Everyone was talking about the Silver Wedding; yak-yak-yak, and ten days later the Czar and his family, now in Siberia, were invited to descend to a little room in the basement. Crack, crack, went the guns; screams and blood all over the place, and that was the end of the Romanoffs. I flexed my muscles. "A fine healthy baby," said the doctor; which gave me much satisfaction.

Tout le monde à la bataille! That included my gassed uncle. My health had improved to the point where I was able to crawl in my playpen. Bertrand Russell was still cheerily in prison for writing something seditious about pacifism. Tuning in as usual to the Front Lines it looked as if the Germans were winning all the battles yet losing the war. And so it was. The upper-income people were upset about the income tax at six shillings to the pound. But all women over thirty got the vote. "It seems a long time to wait," said one of my drab old aunts, aged twenty-two. The speeches in the House of Commons always sent me to sleep which was why I missed, at the actual time, a certain oration by Mr. Asquith following the armistice on 11th November. Mr. Asquith was a greatly esteemed former prime minister later to be an Earl, and had been ousted by Mr. Lloyd George. I clearly heard Asquith, in private, refer to Lloyd George as "that damned Welsh goat."

The armistice was signed and I was awake for that. I pulled myself on to my feet with the aid of the bars of my cot. My teeth were coming through very nicely in my opinion, and well worth all the trouble I was put to in bringing them forth. I weighed twenty pounds. On all the world's fighting fronts the men killed in action or dead of wounds numbered 8,538,315 and the warriors wounded and maimed were 21,219,452. With these figures in mind I sat up in my high chair and banged my spoon on the table. One of my mother's black-draped friends recited:

> *I have a rendezvous with Death*
> *At some disputed barricade,*
> *When spring comes back with rustling shade*
> *And apple blossoms fill the air —*
> *I have a rendezvous with Death.*

Most of the poets, they said, had been killed. The poetry made them 20 dab their eyes with clean white handkerchiefs.

Next February on my first birthday, there was a birthday-cake with one candle. Lots of children and their elders. The war had been over two months and twenty-one days. "Why doesn't she smile?" My brother was to blow out the candle. The elders were talking about the war and the political situation. Lloyd George and Asquith, Asquith and Lloyd George. I remembered recently having switched on to Mr. Asquith at a private party where he had been drinking a lot. He was playing cards and when he came to cut the cards he tried to cut a large box of matches by mistake. On another occasion I had seen him putting his arm around a lady's shoulder in a Daimler motor car, and generally behaving towards her in a very friendly fashion. Strangely enough she said, "If you don't stop this nonsense immediately I'll order the chauffeur to stop and I'll get out." Mr. Asquith replied, "And pray, what reason will you give?" Well anyway it was my feeding time.

The guests arrived for my birthday. It was so sad, said one of the black widows, so sad about Wilfred Owen who was killed so late in the war, and she quoted from a poem of his:

> *What passing-bells for these who die as cattle?*
> *Only the monstrous anger of the guns.*

The children were squealing and toddling around. One was sick and another wet the floor and stood with his legs apart gaping at the puddle. All was mopped up. I banged my spoon on the table of my high chair.

> *But I've a rendezvous with Death*
> *At midnight in some flaming town;*
> *When spring trips north again this year,*
> *And I to my pledged word am true,*
> *I shall not fail that rendezvous.*

More parents and children arrived. One stout man who was warming his behind at the fire, said, "I always think those words of Asquith's after the armistice were so apt ... "

They brought the cake close to my high chair for me to see, with the candle shining and flickering above the pink icing. "A pity she never smiles."

"She'll smile in time," my mother said, obviously upset.

"What Asquith told the House of Commons just after the war," said that stout gentleman with his backside to the fire, " — so apt, what Asquith said. He said that the war has cleansed and purged the world, by God! I recall his actual words: 'All things have become new. In this great cleansing and purging it has been the privilege of our country to play her part ...' "

That did it. I broke into a decided smile and everyone noticed it, convinced that it was provoked by the fact that my brother had blown out the candle on the cake. "She smiled!" my mother exclaimed. And everyone was clucking away about how I was smiling. For good measure I crowed like a demented raven. "My baby's smiling!" said my mother.

"It was the candle on her cake," they said.

The cake be damned. Since that time I have grown to smile quite naturally, like any other healthy and house-trained person, but when I really mean a smile, deeply felt from the core, then to all intents and purposes it comes in response to the words uttered in the House of Commons after the First World War by the distinguished, the immaculately dressed and the late Mr. Asquith.

Considerations for Critical Thinking and Writing

1. **FIRST RESPONSE.** Discuss the story's point of view and its effect on you.

2. What is the significance of the settings? Why are they crucial to the plot?

3. What finally causes the baby to smile?

4. How does the use of language serve to characterize the narrator? Choose a paragraph in which the style seems to represent the narrator's sensibilities, and analyze the way in which diction and phrasing reveal tone.

5. Research one of the historical allusions to actual events, writers, and politicians that you are unfamiliar with in the story and discuss how it contributes to your understanding of the themes.

6. Stories about the horrors of war are not infrequent in literature. How does Spark avoid being predictable, clichéd, or sentimental?

7. Characterize the humor in the story. What adjectives would you employ to describe it?

8. **CONNECTION TO ANOTHER SELECTION.** Use the historical context Spark provides in her story as a means of explaining Krebs's behavior in Ernest Hemingway's "Soldier's Home" (p. 133).

5

Point of View

Reprinted courtesy of the Library
of Congress.

I mean to live and die by my
own mind.

—ZORA NEALE HURSTON

Because one of the pleasures of reading fiction consists of seeing the
world through someone else's eyes, it is easy to overlook the eyes that
control our view of the plot, characters, and setting. *Point of view* refers to
who tells us the story and how it is told. What we know and how we feel
about the events in a story are shaped by the author's choice of a point
of view. The teller of a story, the *narrator*, inevitably affects our understanding of the characters' actions by filtering what is told through his
or her own perspective. The narrator should not be confused with the
author who has created the narrative voice because the two are usually
distinct (more on this point later).

If the narrative voice is changed, the story will change. Consider,
for example, how different "Bartleby, the Scrivener" (p. 101) would
be if Melville had chosen to tell the story from Bartleby's point of
view instead of the lawyer's. With Bartleby as narrator, much of the
mystery concerning his behavior would be lost. The peculiar force
of his saying "I would prefer not to" would be lessened amid all the
other things he would have to say as narrator. Moreover, the lawyer's reaction — puzzled, upset, outraged, and finally sympathetic to
Bartleby — would be lost too. It would be entirely possible, of course,
to write a story from Bartleby's point of view, but it would not be the
story Melville wrote.

The possible ways of telling a story are many, and more than one point of view can be worked into a single story. However, the various points of view that storytellers draw on can be conveniently grouped into two broad categories: (1) the third-person narrator and (2) the first-person narrator. The third-person narrator uses *he, she,* or *they* to tell the story and does not participate in the action. The first-person narrator uses *I* and is a major or minor participant in the action. A second-person narrator, *you,* is possible but rarely used because of the awkwardness in thrusting the reader into the story, as in "You are minding your own business on a park bench when a drunk steps out of the bushes and demands your lunch bag."

Explore the literary element in this chapter at bedfordstmartins.com/ meyerlit.

Let's look now at the most important and most often used variations within first- and third-person narrations.

THIRD-PERSON NARRATOR
(Nonparticipant)

1. Omniscient (the narrator takes us inside the character[s])
2. Limited omniscient (the narrator takes us inside one or two characters)
3. Objective (the narrator is outside the character[s])

No type of third-person narrator appears as a character in a story. The *omniscient narrator* is all-knowing. From this point of view, the narrator can move from place to place and pass back and forth through time, slipping into and out of characters as no human being possibly could in real life. This narrator can report the characters' thoughts and feelings as well as what they say and do. In the excerpt from *Tarzan of the Apes* (p. 45), Burroughs's narrator tells us about events concerning Terkoz in another part of the jungle that long preceded the battle between Terkoz and Tarzan. We also learn Tarzan's and Jane's inner thoughts and emotions during the episode. And Burroughs's narrator describes Terkoz as "an arrant coward" and a bully, thereby evaluating the character for the reader. This kind of intrusion is called *editorial omniscience*. In contrast, narration that allows characters' actions and thoughts to speak for themselves is known as *neutral omniscience*. Most modern writers use neutral omniscience so that readers can reach their own conclusions.

The *limited omniscient narrator* is much more confined than the omniscient narrator. With limited omniscience the author very often restricts the narrator to the single perspective of either a major or a minor character. Sometimes a narrator can see into more than one character, particularly in a longer work that focuses, for example, on two characters alternately from one chapter to the next. Short stories, however, frequently are restricted by length to a single character's point of view. The way people, places, and events appear to that character is the way they appear to the reader. The reader has access to the thoughts and feelings of the characters revealed by the narrator, but neither the reader nor the narrator has access to the inner lives of any of the other characters in the story. The events in James Joyce's "Eveline" (p. 322) are viewed entirely through the protagonist's eyes. She unifies the story by being present through all the action.

In Hemingway's "Soldier's Home" (p. 133), a limited omniscient narration is the predominant point of view. Krebs's thoughts and reaction to being home from the war are made available to the reader by the narrator, who tells us that Krebs "felt embarrassed and resentful" or "sick and vaguely nauseated" by the small-town life he has reentered. Occasionally, however, Hemingway uses an *objective point of view* when he dramatizes particularly tense moments in a detached impersonal manner between Krebs and his mother. In the following excerpt, Hemingway's narrator shows us Krebs's feelings instead of telling us what they are. Krebs's response to his mother's concerns is presented without comment. The external details of the scene reveal his inner feelings.

> "I've worried about you so much, Harold," his mother went on. "I know the temptations you must have been exposed to. I know how weak men are. I know what your own dear grandfather, my own father, told us about the Civil War and I have prayed for you. I pray for you all day long, Harold."
>
> Krebs looked at the bacon fat hardening on his plate.
>
> "Your father is worried, too," his mother went on. "He thinks you have lost your ambition, that you haven't got a definite aim in life. Charley Simmons, who is just your age, has a good job and is going to be married. The boys are all settling down; they're all determined to get somewhere; you can see that boys like Charley Simmons are on their way to being really a credit to the community."
>
> Krebs said nothing.
>
> "Don't look that way, Harold. . . ."

When Krebs looks at the bacon fat, we can see him cooling and hardening too. Hemingway does not describe the expression on Krebs's face, yet we know it is a look that disturbs his mother as she goes on about what she thinks she knows. Krebs and his mother are clearly tense and upset; the details, action, and dialogue reveal that without the narrator telling the reader how each character feels.

FIRST-PERSON NARRATOR (Participant)

1. Major character
2. Minor character

With a *first-person narrator*, the *I* presents the point of view of only one character's consciousness. The reader is restricted to the perceptions, thoughts, and feelings of that single character. This is Melville's technique with the lawyer in "Bartleby, the Scrivener" (p. 101). Everything learned about the characters, action, and plot comes from the unnamed lawyer. Bartleby remains a mystery because we are limited to what the lawyer knows and reports. The lawyer cannot explain what Bartleby means because he does not entirely know himself. Melville's use of the first person encourages us to identify with the lawyer's confused reaction to Bartleby so that we pay attention not only to the scrivener but to the lawyer's response to him. We are as perplexed as the lawyer and share his effort to make sense of Bartleby.

The lawyer is an *unreliable narrator*, whose interpretation of events is different from the author's. We cannot entirely accept the lawyer's assessment of Bartleby because we see that the lawyer's perceptions are not totally to be trusted. Melville does not expect us, for example, to agree with the lawyer's suggestion that the solution to Bartleby's situation might be to "entertain some young gentleman with your conversation" on a trip to Europe. Given Bartleby's awful silences, this absurd suggestion reveals the lawyer's superficial understanding. The lawyer's perceptions frequently do not coincide with those Melville expects his readers to share. Hence the lawyer's unreliability preserves Bartleby's mysterious nature while revealing the lawyer's sensibilities. The point of view is artistically appropriate for Melville's purposes because the eyes through which we perceive the plot, characters, and setting are also the subject of the story.

Narrators can be unreliable for a variety of reasons: They might lack self-knowledge, like Melville's lawyer, or they might be innocent and inexperienced, like Ralph Ellison's young narrator in "Battle Royal" (p. 180). Youthful innocence frequently characterizes a *naive narrator* such as Mark Twain's Huck Finn or Holden Caulfield, J. D. Salinger's twentieth-century version of Huck in *The Catcher in the Rye*. These narrators lack the sophistication to interpret accurately what they see; they are unreliable because the reader must go beyond their understanding of events to comprehend the situations described. Huck and Holden describe their respective social environments, but the reader, with more experience, supplies the critical perspective that each boy lacks. In "Battle Royal" that perspective is supplemented by Ellison's dividing the narration between the young man who experiences events and the mature man who reflects back on those events.

Few generalizations can be made about the advantages or disadvantages of using a specific point of view. What can be said with confidence, however, is that writers choose a point of view to achieve particular effects because point of view determines what we know about the characters and events in a story. We should, therefore, be aware of who is telling the story and whether the narrator sees things clearly and reliably.

The next three works warrant a careful examination of their points of view. In John Updike's "A & P," a teenager makes a significant decision about his future while at a supermarket checkout counter, and another young man in David Updike's "Summer" discovers an equally important truth about the present. In Maggie Mitchell's "It Would Be Different If," a woman ponders a failed romance from her past.

JOHN UPDIKE (1932–2009)

John Updike grew up in the small town of Shillington, Pennsylvania, and on a family farm nearby. Academic success in school earned him a scholarship to Harvard, where he studied English and graduated in 1954. He soon sold his first story and poem to *The New Yorker.* Also an artist, Updike studied drawing in Oxford, England, and returned to take a position on the staff at *The New Yorker.* His first book, a collection of poems titled *The Carpentered Hen and Other Tame Creatures,* appeared in 1958, and the following year he published a book of stories and a novel, *The Poorhouse Fair,* which received the Rosenthal Founda-

© Boston Globe / Getty Images.

tion Award in 1960. Updike produced his second novel, *Rabbit, Run,* in the same year. The prolific Updike lived in Massachusetts the rest of his life and continued to publish essays, poems, a novel, or a book of stories nearly every year since 1959, including *The Centaur* (1963), winner of the National Book Award; *Rabbit Is Rich* (1981) and *Rabbit at Rest* (1990), both Pulitzer Prize winners; and *The Witches of Eastwick* (1984), which was made into a major motion picture (Warner Bros., 1987). His last novel was *Terrorist* (2006), and his last short story collection was *My Father's Tears and Other Stories* (2009). Updike's fiction is noted for its exemplary use of storytelling conventions, its unique prose style, and its engaging picture of middle-class American life.

A & P   1961

To hear "A & P" read by John Updike, visit bedfordstmartins.com/meyerlit/epages.

In walks these three girls in nothing but bathing suits. I'm in the third checkout slot, with my back to the door, so I don't see them until they're over by the bread. The one that caught my eye first was the one in the plaid green two-piece. She was a chunky kid, with a good tan and a sweet broad soft-looking can with those two crescents of white just under it, where the sun never seems to hit, at the top of the backs of her legs. I stood there with my hand on a box of HiHo crackers trying to remember if I rang it up or not. I ring it up again and the customer starts giving me hell. She's one of these cash-register-watchers, a witch about fifty with rouge on her cheekbones and no eyebrows, and I know it made her day to trip me up. She'd been watching cash registers for fifty years and probably never seen a mistake before.

By the time I got her feathers smoothed and her goodies into a bag — she gives me a little snort in passing, if she'd been born at the right time they would have burned her over in Salem — by the time I get her on her way the girls had circled around the bread and were coming back, without a pushcart, back my way along the counters, in the aisle between the checkouts and the Special bins. They didn't even have shoes on. There was this chunky one, with the two-piece — it was bright green and the seams on the bra were still sharp and her belly was still pretty pale so I guessed she just got it (the suit) — there was this one, with one of those chubby berry-faces, the lips all bunched together under her nose, this one, and a tall one, with black hair that hadn't quite frizzed right, and one of these sunburns right across under the eyes, and a chin that was too long — you know, the kind of girl other girls think is very "striking" and "attractive" but never quite makes it, as they very well know, which is why they like her so much — and then the third one, that wasn't quite so tall. She was the queen. She kind of led them, the other two peeking around and making their shoulders round. She didn't look around, not this queen, she just walked straight on slowly, on these long white prima-donna legs. She came down a little hard on her heels, as if she didn't walk in her bare feet that much, putting down her heels and then letting the weight move along to her toes as if she was testing the floor with every step, putting a little deliberate extra action into it. You never know for sure how girls' minds work (do you really think it's a mind in there or just a little buzz like a bee in a glass jar?) but you got the idea she had talked the other two into coming in here with her, and now she was showing them how to do it, walk slow and hold yourself straight.

She had on a kind of dirty-pink — beige maybe, I don't know — bathing suit with a little nubble all over it and, what got me, the straps were down. They were off her shoulders looped loose around the cool tops of her arms, and I guess as a result the suit had slipped a little on her, so all around the top of the cloth there was this shining rim. If it hadn't been there you wouldn't have known there could have been anything whiter than those shoulders. With the straps pushed off, there was nothing between the top of the suit and the top of her head except just *her,* this clean bare plane of the top of her chest down from the shoulder bones like a dented sheet of metal tilted in the light. I mean, it was more than pretty.

She had sort of oaky hair that the sun and salt had bleached, done up in a bun that was unraveling, and a kind of prim face. Walking into the A & P with your straps down, I suppose it's the only kind of face you *can* have. She held her head so high her neck, coming up out of those white shoulders, looked kind of stretched, but I didn't mind. The longer her neck was, the more of her there was.

She must have felt in the corner of her eye me and over my shoulder 5 Stokesie in the second slot watching, but she didn't tip. Not this queen. She kept her eyes moving across the racks, and stopped, and turned so slow it made my stomach rub the inside of my apron, and buzzed to the other two, who kind of huddled against her for relief, and then they all three of them went up the cat-and-dogfood-breakfast-cereal-macaroni-rice-raisins-seasonings-spreads-spaghetti-soft-drinks-crackers-and-cookies aisle. From the third slot I look straight up this aisle to the meat counter, and I watched them all the way. The fat one with the tan sort of fumbled with the cookies, but on second thought she put the package back. The sheep pushing their carts down the aisle—the girls were walking against the usual traffic (not that we have one-way signs or anything)—were pretty hilarious. You could see them, when Queenie's white shoulders dawned on them, kind of jerk, or hop, or hiccup, but their eyes snapped back to their own baskets and on they pushed. I bet you could set off dynamite in an A & P and the people would by and large keep reaching and checking oatmeal off their lists and muttering "Let me see, there was a third thing, began with A, asparagus, no, ah, yes, applesauce!" or whatever it is they do mutter. But there was no doubt, this jiggled them. A few houseslaves in pin curlers even looked around after pushing their carts past to make sure what they had seen was correct.

You know, it's one thing to have a girl in a bathing suit down on the beach, where what with the glare nobody can look at each other much anyway, and another thing in the cool of the A & P, under the fluorescent lights, against all those stacked packages, with her feet paddling along naked over our checker-board green-and-cream rubber-tile floor.

"Oh Daddy," Stokesie said beside me. "I feel so faint."

"Darling," I said. "Hold me tight." Stokesie's married, with two babies chalked up on his fuselage already, but as far as I can tell that's the only difference. He's twenty-two, and I was nineteen this April.

"Is it done?" he asks, the responsible married man finding his voice. I forgot to say he thinks he's going to be manager some sunny day, maybe in 1990 when it's called the Great Alexandrov and Petrooshki Tea Company or something.

What he meant was, our town is five miles from a beach, with a 10 big summer colony out on the Point, but we're right in the middle of town, and the women generally put on a shirt or shorts or something before they get out of the car into the street. And anyway these are usually women with six children and varicose veins mapping their legs and nobody, including them, could care less. As I say, we're right in the middle of town, and if you stand at our front doors you can see two banks and the Congregational church and the newspaper store and three real-estate offices and about twenty-seven old freeloaders tearing up Central Street because the sewer broke again. It's not as if we're on the Cape, we're north of Boston and there's people in this town haven't seen the ocean for twenty years.

The girls had reached the meat counter and were asking McMahon something. He pointed, they pointed, and they shuffled out of sight behind a pyramid of Diet Delight peaches. All that was left for us to see was old McMahon patting his mouth and looking after them sizing up their joints. Poor kids, I began to feel sorry for them, they couldn't help it.

Now here comes the sad part of the story, at least my family says it's sad, but I don't think it's so sad myself. The store's pretty empty, it being Thursday afternoon, so there was nothing much to do except lean on the register and wait for the girls to show up again. The whole store was like a pinball machine and I didn't know which tunnel they'd come out of. After a while they come around out of the far aisle, around the light bulbs, records at discount of the Caribbean Six or Tony Martin Sings or some such gunk you wonder they waste the wax on, sixpacks of candy bars, and plastic toys done up in cellophane that fall apart when a kid looks at them anyway. Around they come, Queenie still leading the way, and holding a little gray jar in her hands. Slots Three through Seven are unmanned and I could see her wondering between Stokes and me, but Stokesie with his usual luck draws an old party in baggy gray pants who stumbles up with four giant cans of pineapple juice (what do these bums *do* with all that pineapple juice? I've often asked myself). So the girls come to me. Queenie puts down the jar and I take it into my fingers icy cold. Kingfish Fancy Herring Snacks in Pure Sour Cream: 49¢. Now her hands are empty, not a ring or a bracelet, bare as God made them, and I wonder where the money's coming from. Still with that prim look she lifts a folded dollar bill out of the hollow at the center of her nubbled pink top. The jar went heavy in my hand. Really, I thought that was so cute.

Then everybody's luck begins to run out. Lengel comes in from haggling with a truck full of cabbages on the lot and is about to scuttle into that door marked MANAGER behind which he hides all day when the girls touch his eye. Lengel's pretty dreary, teaches Sunday school and the rest, but he doesn't miss that much. He comes over and says, "Girls, this isn't the beach."

Queenie blushes, though maybe it's just a brush of sunburn I was noticing for the first time, now that she was so close. "My mother asked me to pick up a jar of herring snacks." Her voice kind of startled me, the way voices do when you see the people first, coming out so flat and dumb yet kind of tony, too, the way it ticked over "pick up" and "snacks." All of a sudden I slid right down her voice into the living room. Her father and the other men were standing around in ice-cream coats and bow ties and the women were in sandals picking up herring snacks on toothpicks off a big glass plate and they were all holding drinks the color of water with olives and sprigs of mint in them. When my parents have somebody over they get lemonade and if it's a real racy affair Schlitz in tall glasses with "They'll Do It Every Time" cartoons stenciled on.

"That's all right," Lengel said. "But this isn't the beach." His repeat-   15
ing this struck me as funny, as if it had just occurred to him, and he had
been thinking all these years the A & P was a great big dune and he was
the head lifeguard. He didn't like my smiling—as I say he doesn't miss
much—but he concentrates on giving the girls that sad Sunday-school-
superintendent stare.

Queenie's blush is no sunburn now, and the plump one in plaid,
that I liked better from the back—a really sweet can—pipes up, "We
weren't doing any shopping. We just came in for the one thing."

"That makes no difference," Lengel tells her, and I could see from
the way his eyes went that he hadn't noticed she was wearing a two-piece
before. "We want you decently dressed when you come in here."

"We *are* decent," Queenie says suddenly, her lower lip pushing, getting sore now that she remembers her place, a place from which the
crowd that runs the A & P must look pretty crummy. Fancy Herring
Snacks flashed in her very blue eyes.

"Girls, I don't want to argue with you. After this come in here with
your shoulders covered. It's our policy." He turns his back. That's policy
for you. Policy is what the kingpins want. What the others want is juve-
nile delinquency.

All this while, the customers had been showing up with their   20
carts but, you know, sheep, seeing a scene, they had all bunched up on
Stokesie, who shook open a paper bag as gently as peeling a peach, not
wanting to miss a word. I could feel in the silence everybody getting nervous, most of all Lengel, who asks me, "Sammy, have you rung up their
purchase?"

I thought and said "No" but it wasn't about that I was thinking. I
go through the punches, 4, 9, GROC. TOT—it's more complicated than you
think, and after you do it often enough, it begins to make a little song,
that you hear words to, in my case "Hello *(bing)* there, you *(gung)* hap-py
pee-pul *(splat)!*"—the *splat* being the drawer flying out. I uncrease the bill,
tenderly as you may imagine, it just having come from between the two
smoothest scoops of vanilla I had ever known were there, and pass a half
and a penny into her narrow pink palm, and nestle the herrings in a bag
and twist its neck and hand it over, all the time thinking.

The girls, and who'd blame them, are in a hurry to get out, so I say "I
quit" to Lengel quick enough for them to hear, hoping they'll stop and
watch me, their unsuspected hero. They keep right on going, into the
electric eye; the door flies open and they flicker across the lot to their car,
Queenie and Plaid and Big Tall Goony-Goony (not that as raw material
she was so bad), leaving me with Lengel and a kink in his eyebrow.

"Did you say something, Sammy?"

"I said I quit."

"I thought you did."

"You didn't have to embarrass them."   25

"It was they who were embarrassing us."

I started to say something that came out "Fiddle-de-doo." It's a saying of my grandmother's, and I know she would have been pleased.

"I don't think you know what you're saying," Lengel said.

"I know you don't," I said. "But I do." I pull the bow at the back of   30
my apron and start shrugging it off my shoulders. A couple customers
that had been heading for my slot begin to knock against each other, like
scared pigs in a chute.

Lengel sighs and begins to look very patient and old and gray. He's
been a friend of my parents for years. "Sammy, you don't want to do this
to your Mom and Dad," he tells me. It's true, I don't. But it seems to
me that once you begin a gesture it's fatal not to go through with it. I
fold the apron, "Sammy" stitched in red on the pocket, and put it on
the counter, and drop the bow tie on top of it. The bow tie is theirs, if
you've ever wondered. "You'll feel this for the rest of your life," Lengel
says, and I know that's true, too, but remembering how he made the
pretty girl blush makes me so scrunchy inside I punch the No Sale tab
and the machine whirs "pee-pul" and the drawer splats out. One advantage to this scene taking place in summer, I can follow this up with a
clean exit, there's no fumbling around getting your coat and galoshes, I
just saunter into the electric eye in my white shirt that my mother ironed
the night before, and the door heaves itself open, and outside the sunshine is skating around on the asphalt.

I look around for my girls, but they're gone, of course. There wasn't
anybody but some young married screaming with her children about
some candy they didn't get by the door of a powder-blue Falcon station
wagon. Looking back in the big windows, over the bags of peat moss and
aluminum lawn furniture stacked on the pavement, I could see Lengel in
my place in the slot, checking the sheep through. His face was dark gray
and his back stiff, as if he'd just had an injection of iron, and my stomach
kind of fell as I felt how hard the world was going to be to me hereafter.

CONSIDERATIONS FOR CRITICAL THINKING AND WRITING

1. **FIRST RESPONSE.** Describe the setting. How accurate do you think
   Updike's treatment of the A & P is?

2. What kind of person is Sammy? How do his actions and speech
   constitute his own individual style?

3. Analyze the style of the first paragraph. How does it set the tone for
   the rest of the story?

4. What is the story's central conflict? Does it seem to be a serious or
   trivial conflict to you?

5. With what kind of values is Lengel associated? Do you feel any sympathy for him?

6. What do you think is Stokesie's function in the story?

7. Consider Sammy's treatment of the three girls. Do you think his
   account of them is sexist? Explain why or why not.

8. Locate the climax of the story. How does the climax affect your attitude toward Sammy?

9. How do you think the story would be different if it were told from another character's point of view instead of Sammy's?

10. Discuss the thematic significance of the story's final paragraph. Would you read the story differently if this last paragraph were eliminated?

11. **CONNECTION TO ANOTHER SELECTION.** Compare the tone established by the point of view in this story and in Maggie Mitchell's "It Would Be Different If" (p. 169).

DAVID UPDIKE (B. 1957)

Born in Ipswich, Massachusetts, David Updike is the son of author John Updike. David received his B.A. in art history at Harvard and his M.A. from Teachers College, Columbia University. His acclaimed children's books include *An Autumn Tale* (1988), *A Spring Story* (1989), *Seven Times Eight* (1990), *The Sounds of Summer* (1993), and *A Helpful Alphabet of Friendly Objects* (1998), which he coauthored with his father. "Summer," a poignant tale for adults, is part of *Out on the Marsh: Stories* (1988), a collection of his short fiction; his short stories have also appeared in *The New Yorker*. Updike resides in Cambridge, Massachusetts.

© Jan Brown.

Summer   1985

It was the first week in August, the time when summer briefly pauses, shifting between its beginning and its end: the light had not yet begun to change, the leaves were still full and green on the trees, the nights were still warm. From the woods and fields came the hiss of crickets; the line of distant mountains was still dulled by the edge of summer haze, the echo of fireworks was replaced by the rumble of thunder and the hollow premonition of school, too far off to imagine though dimly, dully felt. His senses were consumed by the joy of their own fulfillment: the satisfying swat of a tennis ball, the dappled damp and light of the dirt road after rain, the alternating sensations of sand, mossy stone, and pine needles under bare feet. His days were spent in the adolescent pursuit of childhood pleasures: tennis, a haphazard round of golf, a variant of baseball adapted to the local geography: two pine trees as foul poles, a broomstick as the bat, the apex of the small, secluded house the dividing line between home runs and outs. On rainy days they swatted bottle tops across the living room floor, and at night vented budding cerebral energy with games of chess thoughtfully played over glasses of iced tea. After dinner they would paddle the canoe to the middle of the lake, and drift beneath the vast, blue-black dome of sky, looking at the stars and speaking softly in tones which, with the waning summer, became increasingly philosophical: the sky's blue vastness, the distance and magnitude of stars, an endless succession of numbers, gave way to a rising sensation of infinity, eternity, an imagined universe with no bounds. But the sound of the paddle hitting against the side of the canoe, the faint shadow of surrounding mountains, the cry of a nocturnal bird brought them back to the happy, cloistered finity of their world, and they paddled slowly home and went to bed.

Homer woke to the slant and shadow of a summer morning, dressed in their shared cabin, and went into the house where Mrs. Thyme sat alone, looking out across the flat blue stillness of the lake. She poured him a cup of coffee and they quietly talked, and it was then that his happiness seemed most tangible. In this summer month with the Thymes, freed from the complications of his own family, he had released himself to them and, as interim member — friend, brother, surrogate son — he lived in a blessed realm between two worlds.

From the cool darkness of the porch, smelling faintly of moldy books and kerosene and the tobacco of burning pipes, he sat looking through the screen to the lake, shimmering beneath the heat of a summer afternoon: a dog lay sleeping in the sun, a bird hopped along a swaying branch, sunlight came in through the trees and collapsed on the sandy soil beside a patch of moss, or mimicked the shade and cadence of stones as they stepped to the edge of a lake where small waves lapped a damp rock and washed onto a sandy shore. An inverted boat lay decaying under a tree, a drooping American flag hung from its gnarled pole, a haphazard dock started out across the cove toward distant islands through which the white triangle of a sail silently moved.

The yellowed pages of the book from which he occasionally read swam before him: " . . . Holmes clapped the hat upon his head. It came right over the forehead and settled on the bridge of his nose. 'It is a question of cubic capacity' said he . . ." Homer looked up. The texture of the smooth, unbroken air was cleanly divided by the sound of a slamming door, echoing up into the woods around him. Through the screen he watched Fred's sister Sandra as she came ambling down the path, stepping lightly between the stones in her bare feet. She held a towel in one hand, a book in the other, and wore a pair of pale blue shorts — faded relics of another era. At the end of the dock she stopped, raised her hands above her head, stretching, and then sat down. She rolled over onto her stomach and, using the book as a pillow, fell asleep.

Homer was amused by the fact, that although she did this every day, 5 she didn't get any tanner. When she first came in her face was faintly flushed, and there was a pinkish line around the snowy band where her bathing suit strap had been, but the back of her legs remained an endearing, pale white, the color of eggshells, and her back acquired only the softest, brownish blur. Sometimes she kept her shoes on, other times a shirt, or sweater, or just collapsed onto the seat of the boat, her pale eyelids turned upward toward the pale sun; and as silently as she arrived, she would leave, walking back through the stones with the same, casual sway of indifference. He would watch her, hear the distant door slam, the shower running in the far corner of the house. Other times he would just look up and she would be gone.

On the tennis court she was strangely indifferent to his heroics. When the crucial moment arrived — Homer serving in the final game of the final set — the match would pause while she left, walking across the court, stopping to call the dog, swaying out through the gate. Homer watched her as she went down the path, and, impetus suddenly lost, he double faulted, stroked a routine backhand over the back fence, and the match was over.

When he arrived back at the house she asked him who won, but didn't seem to hear his answer. "I wish I could go sailing," she said, looking distractedly out over the lake.

At night, when he went out to the cottage where he and Fred slept, he could see her through the window as she lay on her bed, reading, her arm folded beneath her head like a leaf. Her nightgown, pulled and buttoned to her chin, pierced him with a regret that had no source or resolution, and its imagined texture floated in the air above him as he lay in bed at night, suspended in the surrounding darkness, the scent of pine, the hypnotic cadence of his best friend's breathing.

Was it that he had known her all his life, and as such had grown up in the shadow of her subtle beauty? Was it the condensed world of the lake, the silent reverence of surrounding woods, mountains, which heightened his sense of her and brought the warm glow of her presence into soft, amorous focus? She had the hair of a baby, the freckles of a child, and the sway of motherhood. Like his love, her beauty rose up in the world which spawned and nurtured it, and found in the family the medium in which it thrived, and in Homer distilled to a pure distant longing for something he had never had.

One day they climbed a mountain, and as the components of family 10 and friends strung out along the path on their laborious upward hike, he found himself tromping along through the woods with her with nobody else in sight. Now and then they would stop by a stream, or sit on a stump, or stone, and he would speak to her, and then they would set off again, he following her. But in the end this day exhausted him, following her pale legs and tripping sneakers over the ruts and stones and a thousand roots, all the while trying to suppress a wordless, inarticulate passion, and the last mile or so he left her, sprinting down the path in a reckless, solitary release, howling into the woods around him. He was lying on the grass, staring up into the patterns of drifting clouds when she came ambling down. "Wher'd you go? I thought I'd lost you," she said, and sat heavily down in the seat of the car. On the ride home, his elbow hopelessly held in the warm crook of her arm, he resolved to release his love, give it up, on the grounds that it was too disruptive to his otherwise placid life. But in the days to follow he discovered that his resolution had done little to change her, and her life went on its oblivious, happy course without him.

His friendship with Fred, meanwhile, continued on its course of athletic and boyhood fulfillment. Alcohol seeped into their diet, and an occasional cigarette, and at night they would drive into town, buy two enormous cans of Australian beer and sit at a small cove by the lake, talking. One night on the ride home Fred accelerated over a small bridge, and as the family station wagon left the ground their heads floated up to the ceiling, touched, and then came crashing down as the car landed and Fred wrestled the car back onto course. Other times they would take the motorboat out onto the lake and make sudden racing turns around buoys, sending a plume of water into the air and everything in the boat crashing to one side. But always with these adventures Homer felt a pang of absence, and was always relieved when they headed back toward the familiar cove, and home.

As August ran its merciless succession of beautiful days, Sandra drifted in and out of his presence in rising oscillations of sorrow and desire. She worked at a bowling alley on the other side of the lake, and in the evening Homer and Fred would drive the boat over, bowl a couple of strings, and wait for her to get off work. Homer sat at the counter and watched her serve up sloshing cups of coffee, secretly loathing the leering gazes of whiskered truck drivers, and loving her oblivious, vacant stare in answer, hip cocked, hand on counter, gazing up into the neon air above their heads. When she was finished, they would pile into the boat and skim through darkness the four or five miles home, and it was then, bundled beneath sweaters and blankets, the white hem of her waitressing dress showing through the darkness, their hair swept in the wind and their voices swallowed by the engine's slow, steady growl, that he felt most powerless to her attraction. As the boat rounded corners he would close his eyes and release himself to gravity, his body's warmth swaying into hers, guising his attraction in the thin veil of centrifugal force. Now and then he would lean into the floating strands of her hair and speak into her fragrance, watching her smile swell in the pale half-light of the moon, the umber glow of the boat's rear light, her laughter spilling backward over the swirling "V" of wake.

Into the humid days of August a sudden rain fell, leaving the sky a hard, unbroken blue and the nights clear and cool. In the morning when he woke, leaving Fred a heap of sighing covers in his bed, he stepped out into the first rays of sunlight that came through the branches of the trees and sensed, in the cool vapor that rose from damp pine needles, the piercing cry of a blue jay, that something had changed. That night as they ate dinner — hamburgers and squash and corn-on-the-cob — everyone wore sweaters, and as the sun set behind the undulating line of distant mountains — burnt, like a filament of summer into his blinking eyes — it was with an autumnal tint, a reddish glow. Several days later the tree at the end of the point bloomed with a sprig of russet leaves, one or two of which occasionally fell, and their lives became filled with an unspoken urgency. Life of summer went on in the silent knowledge that, with the slow, inexorable seepage of an hourglass, it was turning into fall. Another mountain was climbed, annual tennis matches were arranged and played. Homer and Fred became unofficial champions of the lake by trouncing the elder Dewitt boys, unbeaten in several years. "Youth, youth," glum Billy Dewitt kept saying over iced tea afterward, in jest, though Homer could tell he was hiding some greater sense of loss.

And the moment, the conjunction of circumstance that, through the steady exertion of will, minor adjustments of time and place, he had often tried to induce, never happened. She received his veiled attentions with a kind of amused curiosity, as if smiling back on inno-cence. One night they had been the last ones up, and there was a fleet-ing, shuddering moment before he stepped through the woods to his cabin and she went to her bed that he recognized, in a distant sort of way, as the moment of truth. But to touch her, or kiss her, seemed suddenly incongruous, absurd, contrary to something he could not put his finger on. He looked down at the floor and softly said good-night. The screen door shut quietly behind him and he went out into the darkness and made his way through the unseen sticks and stones, and it was only then, tripping drunkenly on a fallen branch, that he realized he had never been able to imagine the moment he distantly longed for.

The Preacher gave a familiar sermon about another summer having 15 run its course, the harvest of friendship reaped, and a concluding prayer that, "God willing, we will all meet again in June." That afternoon Homer and Fred went sailing, and as they swept past a neighboring cove Homer saw in its sullen shadows a girl sitting alone in a canoe, and in an eternal, melancholy signal of parting, she waved to them as they passed. And there was something in the way that she raised her arm which, when added to the distant impression of her fullness, beauty, youth, filled him with longing as their boat moved inexorably past, slapping the waves, and she disappeared behind a crop of trees.

The night before they were to leave they were all sitting in the liv-ing room after dinner — Mrs. Thyme sewing, Fred folded up with the morning paper, Homer reading on the other end of the couch where

Sandra was lying—when the dog leapt up and things shifted in such a way that Sandra's bare foot was lightly touching Homer's back. Mrs. Thyme came over with a roll of newspaper, hit the dog on the head and he leapt off. But to Homer's surprise Sandra's foot remained, and he felt, in the faint sensation of exerted pressure, the passive emanation of its warmth, a distant signal of acquiescence. And as the family scene continued as before it was with the accompanying drama of Homer's hand, shielded from the family by a haphazard wall of pillows, migrating over the couch to where, in a moment of breathless abandon, settled softly on the cool hollow of her arch. She laughed at something her mother had said, her toe twitched, but her foot remained. It was only then, in the presence of the family, that he realized she was his accomplice, and that, though this was as far as it would ever go, his love had been returned.

CONSIDERATIONS FOR CRITICAL THINKING AND WRITING

1. **FIRST RESPONSE.** How do you respond to this love story? Would the story be more satisfying if Homer and Sandra openly acknowledged their feelings for each other and kissed at the end? Why or why not?

2. What details in the first paragraph evoke particular feelings about August? What sort of mood is created by these details?

3. How is Homer's attraction to Sandra made evident in paragraphs 5 through 9?

4. Why do you think August is described as a "merciless succession of beautiful days" (para. 12)?

5. Analyze the images in paragraph 13 that evoke the impending autumn. What does Billy Dewitt's lament about "youth, youth" add to this description?

6. Discuss the transition between paragraphs 14 and 15. How is the mood effectively changed between the night and the next day?

7. What effect does Homer's friendship with Fred and his relationship with the Thyme family have on your understanding of his reticent attraction to Sandra?

8. What, if any, significance can you attach to the names of Homer, Sandra, Thyme, and the Dewitt boys?

9. How successful do you think Updike is in evoking youthful feeling about summer in this story? Explain why you responded positively or negatively to this evocation of summer.

10. **CONNECTION TO ANOTHER SELECTION.** Compare David Updike's treatment of summer as the setting of his story with John Updike's use of summer as the setting in "A & P" (p. 157).

11. **CONNECTION TO ANOTHER SELECTION.** Discuss "Summer" and Dagoberto Gilb's "Love in L.A." (p. 275) as love stories. Explain why you might prefer one over the other.

MAGGIE MITCHELL (B. 1970)

Maggie Mitchell grew up in a small town in the northernmost part of New York State, on the Canadian border. She received an undergraduate degree in English from Cornell University and a Ph.D. from the University of Connecticut, and she now teaches English at the University of West Georgia. Mitchell's short fiction has appeared in a number of literary magazines, including *New Ohio Review, American Literary Review,* and *Green Mountains Review.* The stark landscape of her childhood often finds its way into her short stories, as it does in "It Would Be Different If," which originally appeared in *New South.*

© Josh Masters.

It Would Be Different If   *2011*

Here's what I remember. If I could hate you, this is what I would hate you for. It's a summer night, humid, starry. It's already pretty late but we're all heading over to Canada, to a bar called the Shipyard. She is there, which surprises me, because the Shipyard is the kind of place where people crack beer bottles over each other's heads, and I wouldn't have thought it was her scene. But she's been hanging out with your sister Megan all summer, working down at the restaurant, back when it was still the Riverside. She's always around. She annoys me, but I don't suspect anything yet. There are two boats; we're splitting into groups. I'm standing on the dock, a beer in my hand. I've had a little too much to drink already, probably, because everything seems very dark, slightly confused. I'm trying to figure out which boat you're in so I don't get stuck in the other one. Just then a car happens to go by on Water Street and its headlights flicker across us. You're already in the first boat, and you're reaching your hand up toward the dock, smiling. I move blindly in your direction, thinking you're reaching for me, when another flash of light shows me that she is grabbing for your hand, you're swinging her down, the smile is for her, it's not a mistake. I stand on the dock in a miniskirt and a very skimpy cropped top, my hair sprayed into a sort of stiff gold cloud because it is the 80s. I feel, for the first time in my life, completely ridiculous. There's no turning back, though. I can't just announce, like a little kid, that I'm going home, I don't want to play anymore, though that's exactly what I feel.

The first boat is full. The headlights veer away: everything is dark again. I tumble somehow into the second boat, wishing I had something to cover myself with: I feel naked, although back then I always dressed like that, we all did. At the Shipyard I mostly stay in the bathroom, drinking and crying. I don't remember the boat ride home. But that's it, that's the end of it. That much I remember.

I've heard variations on this story from everyone, over the years. I'm always the victim, the one people feel sorry for. Maybe there are other versions where I get what's coming to me, where I've always needed to be put in my place, something like that, but I doubt it. People have never liked Amber much; they tend to be on my side. Or at least they did: as the years go by, I notice, that's less true. It's so long ago that people can't get too worked up about it anymore. Now they talk as if it was somehow inevitable, and we just didn't know it yet—you know, isn't life funny, but look how it all works out in the end. Except when it doesn't.

It would be different if we lived in the kind of place where people can disappear, never see each other again. It would be different if I could pretend you didn't exist. But there you are: you are at the post office, peering into your mailbox, pulling out a stack of envelopes and catalogues while I drop my electric bill in the mail slot; I wait till you turn around, to make sure you see me. You would rather not see me. You're at the table on the other side of the restaurant, bending forward to speak to her, or wiping food off your kid's face. You're getting gas, staring off into the distance, forgetting what you are doing. You don't notice that I'm driving by. What are you thinking of ? You're everywhere. I think you have ruined my life.

And now she's the one they feel sorry for. Yes, of course I know what   5
you've been up to. Everyone knows. I see your truck in the parking lot at Jude's every night, and they say you don't tend to leave alone. I see her sometimes: Amber. She looks smaller, paler, less pretty. I could almost feel sorry for her myself, to tell you the truth. I don't blame you, of course. It's just because it's all wrong. I could have told you it would happen.

I wasn't supposed to be one of those people, the unmarryable ones. I never expected to be. I had you, and we had plans, ever since our junior year: Nikki and Jeff. Nikki Gilbert. It sounded right. We joked about getting old, how you would go bald and I'd go pure white, and we'd go fishing in the summer, cross-country skiing in the winter, with our dog. It was a beagle. I had a bit of a stoop; you had put on some weight. You can't cancel that out.

It wasn't fair. She had gone away—to college, the city, whatever. She was the kind of person who goes away, doesn't come back: that's what everyone expected. But she did come back and she chose you, of all people. Why you? You're not like her. You are like us.

Well. Here's what I imagine. It's the best I can do. I am working, finishing up someone's hair. It's late afternoon — that quiet time when the sun starts to come in sideways. Whose hair? Someone like Deb White, not much of a talker, but lots of hair, complicated hair, ever since Don got his job back and they gave up on that hippie phase. I'm finished with the cut and now I'm styling it, taking my time because I don't have any more appointments that day, blowing it out section by section, working through the layers. Her eyes are half closed, I hum a little. It's nice.

Then I hear the door clang as it swings shut behind someone. I glance over and it's you. I am calm; we say nothing. I just nod, and you pick up a magazine and sit down on the couch to wait. Like anyone else. I don't rush Deb. If anything I slow down, taking extra time with each wave, making it perfect. You're just sitting there but somehow you fill the air, you're everywhere and invisible. I breathe you, I walk on you, I curl you into Deb's frosted waves. But I don't shake, or sweat. I'm not nervous. You're like a birthday, a red X on the calendar. Sooner or later you'll happen, one way or the other: it doesn't matter what I do. Eventually Deb rises to her feet, admires herself in the mirror. She writes a check; I don't take credit cards. It seems to take her forever, like one of those women in line at the grocery store. In the meantime I sweep up the heap of doll-like hair around the chair, straighten up the station. She makes an appointment for the next month. Finally she drifts toward the door and I follow her, because she is chatting about something, telling me a story about one of her daughters; she always does this. I wave as she maneuvers herself into her car, careful not to disturb her hair.

When I return to the shop you have seated yourself in the chair that 10 is probably still warm from its contact with Deb White's bony behind. I think of this, for some reason. I see myself smile in the mirror and our eyes, for the first time, meet each other's reflections. I drape a hunter green smock across you, attach it behind your neck with velcro straps.

I cut your hair. I use four different kinds of scissors, a razor, two combs, a touch of mousse. I used to cut your hair in high school, for practice. Now I do it better. Mostly I keep my eyes focused on your head, like an artist putting the final touches on some life-sized sculpture, but every now and then I look up, and there you are in the mirror. We always look at the same moment. We know exactly how long to wait between looks; we know not to overdo it. Your eyes are still the same blue as always but there are crinkles, now, at the corners. I think you are better looking than ever. My work does you justice: this is the best haircut you will ever, ever get.

I remove the smock when it's over. You do not pay. You don't speak. You look at me one more time, and you touch my hand — so far, given the circumstances, I have been the one to do all the touching — and then you leave. I wait until your truck has pulled away to sweep up the short brown hairs. I can't throw them away, so I tilt the contents of the dust-pan into one of the nice creamy envelopes I use for gift certificates.

I don't know what happens after that. Probably you don't leave her right away. But sooner or later I know you'll come. I'll be waiting. For now I'll settle for the trimmings, glossy and shampoo-scented, and for the traces of your reflection that you seem to have left in the mirror. You flicker endlessly between the stiff curls of middle-aged ladies in pastel pantsuits, the long doomed locks of small terrified boys, the towering, glittery updos of girls on their way to the prom. You remind me to wait, promise that things will be different. I believe you.

CONSIDERATIONS FOR CRITICAL THINKING AND WRITING

1. **FIRST RESPONSE.** What actually happens in this story? What is the status of the present in relation to memory and imagination?

2. How does the narrator invite the reader's sympathy? Is it important that we sympathize with her?

3. How trustworthy is the narrator's version of events? What specific lines or passages reinforce or undermine her perspective?

4. What kind of resolution does this story offer? Would you say that the conflict has been resolved, in any sense?

5. What does the narrator's way of relating this story—not *what* she says, but the way she says it—reveal about her world or about her character?

6. What sense do you get of the town in which this story is set? How important is the setting to your understanding of the story and the characters?

7. What is the significance of the final line of the story?

8. **CREATIVE RESPONSE.** Use what you think you can infer about the narrator from this story to craft a paragraph from a third-person point of view in which Nikki is portrayed unsympathetically.

9. **CONNECTION TO ANOTHER SELECTION.** In a short essay, compare this narrator's representation of her past to that of the narrator in Muriel Spark's "The First Year of My Life" (p. 147). What is the relationship between the narrative present and the remembered past in each story? How does it shape the ending in each case?

6

Symbolism

Now mind, I recognize no dichotomy
between art and protest.
— RALPH ELLISON

A *symbol* is a person, object, or event that suggests more than its literal meaning. This basic definition is simple enough, but the use of symbol in literature makes some students slightly nervous because they tend to regard it as a booby trap, a hidden device that can go off during a seemingly harmless class discussion. "I didn't see that when I was reading the story" is a frequently heard comment. This sort of surprise and recognition is both natural and common. Most readers go through a story for the first time getting their bearings, figuring out what is happening to whom and so on. Patterns and significant details often require a second or third reading before they become evident — before a symbol sheds light on a story. Then the details of a work may suddenly fit together, and its meaning may be reinforced, clarified, or enlarged by the symbol. Symbolic meanings are usually embedded in the texture of a story, but they are not "hidden"; instead, they are carefully placed. Reading between the lines (where there is only space) is unnecessary. What is needed is a careful consideration of the elements of the story, a sensitivity to its language, and some common sense.

Common sense is a good place to begin. Symbols appear all around us; anything can be given symbolic significance. Without symbols our lives would be stark and vacant. Awareness of a writer's use of symbols is not all that different from the kinds of perceptions and interpretations that allow us to make sense of our daily lives. We know, for example, that a ring used in a wedding is more than just a piece of jewelry because it suggests the unity and intimacy of a closed circle. The bride's gown may be white because we tend to associate innocence and purity with that color. Or consider the meaning of a small polo pony sewn on a shirt or some other article of clothing. What started as a company trademark has gathered around it a range of meanings suggesting everything from quality and money to preppiness or even silliness. The ring, the white gown, and the polo pony trademark are symbolic because each has meanings that go beyond its specific qualities and functions.

Explore the literary element in this chapter at bedfordstmartins.com/ meyerlit.

Symbols such as these that are widely recognized by a society or culture are called *conventional symbols*. The Christian cross, the Star of David, a swastika, or a nation's flag all have meanings understood by large groups of people. Certain kinds of experiences also have traditional meanings in Western cultures. Winter, the setting sun, and the color black suggest death, while spring, the rising sun, and the color green evoke images of youth and new beginnings. (It is worth noting, however, that individual cultures sometimes have their own conventions; some Eastern cultures associate white rather than black with death and mourning. And obviously the polo pony trademark would mean nothing to anyone totally unfamiliar with American culture.) Broadly shared symbolic meanings are second nature to us.

Writers use conventional symbols to reinforce meanings. Kate Chopin, for example, emphasizes the spring setting in "The Story of an Hour" (p. 13) as a way of suggesting the renewed sense of life that Mrs. Mallard feels when she thinks herself free from her husband.

A *literary symbol* can include traditional, conventional, or public meanings, but it may also be established internally by the total context of the work in which it appears. In "Soldier's Home" (p. 133), Hemingway does not use Krebs's family home as a conventional symbol of safety, comfort, and refuge from the war. Instead, Krebs's home becomes symbolic of provincial, erroneous presuppositions compounded by blind innocence, sentimentality, and smug middle-class respectability. The symbolic meaning of his home reveals that Krebs no longer shares his family's and town's view of the world. Their notions of love, the value of a respectable job, and a belief in God seem to him petty, complicated, and meaningless. The significance of Krebs's home is determined by the events within the story, which reverse and subvert the traditional associations readers might bring to it. Krebs's interactions with his family and the people in town reveal what home has come to mean to him.

A literary symbol can be a setting, character, action, object, name, or anything else in a work that maintains its literal significance while suggesting other meanings. Symbols cannot be restricted to a single meaning; they are suggestive rather than definitive. Their evocation of multiple meanings allows a writer to say more with less. Symbols can serve as economical devices for evoking complex ideas without a writer having to resort to painstaking explanations that would make a story more like an essay than an experience. The many walls in Melville's

"Bartleby, the Scrivener" (p. 101) cannot be reduced to one idea. They have multiple meanings that unify the story. The walls are symbols of the deadening, dehumanizing, restrictive repetitiveness of the office routine, as well as of the confining, materialistic sensibilities of Wall Street. They suggest whatever limits and thwarts human aspirations, including death itself. We don't know precisely what shatters Bartleby's will to live, but the walls in the story, through their symbolic suggestiveness, indicate the nature of the limitations that cause the scrivener to slip into hopelessness and his "dead-wall reveries."

When a character, object, or incident indicates a single, fixed meaning, the writer is using *allegory* rather than symbol. Whereas symbols have literal functions as well as multiple meanings, the primary focus in allegory is on the abstract idea called forth by the concrete object. John Bunyan's *Pilgrim's Progress,* published during the seventeenth century, is a classic example of allegory because the characters, action, and setting have no existence beyond their abstract meanings. Bunyan's purpose is to teach his readers the exemplary way to salvation and heaven. The protagonist, named Christian, flees the City of Destruction in search of the Celestial City. Along the way he encounters characters who either help or hinder his spiritual journey. Among them are Mr. Worldly Wiseman, Faithful, Prudence, Piety, and a host of others named after the virtues or vices they display. These characters, places, and actions exist solely to illustrate religious doctrine. Allegory tends to be definitive rather than suggestive. It drives meaning into a corner and keeps it there. Most modern writers prefer the exploratory nature of symbol to the reductive nature of pure allegory.

Stories often include symbols that you may or may not perceive on a first reading. Their subtle use is a sign of a writer's skill in weaving symbols into the fabric of the characters' lives. Symbols may sometimes escape you, but that is probably better than finding symbols where only literal meanings are intended. Allow the text to help you determine whether a symbolic reading is appropriate.

By keeping track of the total context of the story, you should be able to decide whether your reading is reasonable and consistent with the other facts; plenty of lemons in literature yield no symbolic meaning even if they are squeezed. Be sensitive to the meanings that the author associates with people, places, objects, and actions. You may not associate home with provincial innocence as Hemingway does in "Soldier's Home," but a close reading of the story will permit you to see how and why he constructs that symbolic meaning. If you treat stories like people — with tact and care — they ordinarily are accessible and enjoyable.

The next three stories — Tobias Wolff's "That Room," Ralph Ellison's "Battle Royal," and Peter Meinke's "The Cranes" — rely on symbols to convey meanings that go far beyond the specific incidents described in their plots.

TOBIAS WOLFF (B. 1945)

Born in Birmingham, Alabama, Tobias Wolff grew up in the state of Washington. After quitting high school, he worked on a ship and for a carnival. In the army he served four years as a paratrooper, after which he studied to pass the entrance exams for Oxford University, from which he graduated with high honors. He has published two memoirs — *This Boy's Life* (1989) and *In Pharaoh's Army: Memories of the Lost War* (1994). In addition to his two novels, *The Barracks Thief* (1984) and *Old School* (2003), he has published four short story collections: *In the Garden of North American Martyrs* (1981), *Back in the World* (1985), *The Night in Question* (1996), and *Our Story Begins* (2008). Wolff has taught literature and creative writing courses at Stanford University since 1997.

> WHEN I WRITE "I revise until I can't see a way to make a story better. Only then do I show it to a few trusted readers. If they spot a real weakness, I'll go back to work. Knowing when it's finished is a matter of instinct — an instinct that grows sharper with time and experience." — TOBIAS WOLFF

That Room   2008

The summer after my first year of high school, I got a case of independence and started hitchhiking to farms up and down the valley for daywork picking berries and mucking out stalls. Then I found a place where the farmer paid me ten cents an hour over minimum wage, and his plump, childless wife fed me lunch and fussed over me while I ate, so I stayed on there until school started.

While shoveling shit or hacking weeds out of a drainage ditch, I'd sometimes stop to gaze out toward the far fields, where the hands, as the farmer called them, were bucking bales of hay into a wagon, stacking them to teetering heights. Now and then a bark of laughter reached me, a tag end of conversation. The farmer hadn't let me work in the hay because I was too small, but I beefed up over the winter, and the following summer he let me join the crew.

So I was a hand. A hand! I went a little crazy with that word, with the pleasure of applying it to myself. Having a job like this changed everything. It delivered you from the reach of your parents, from the caustic scrutiny of your friends. It set you free among strangers in the eventful world, where you could practice being someone else until you *were* someone else. It put money in your pocket and allowed you to believe that your other life — your inessential, parenthetical life at home and school — was just a sop to those deluded enough to imagine you still needed them.

There were three others working the fields with me: the farmer's shy, muscle-bound nephew, Clemson, who was in my class at school but to whom I condescended because he was just an inexperienced kid, and two

Mexican brothers, Miguel and Eduardo. Miguel, short and stolid and solitary, spoke very little English, but rakish Eduardo did the talking for both of them. While the rest of us did the heavy work, Eduardo provided advice about girls and told stories in which he featured as a trickster and deft, indefatigable swordsman. He played it for laughs, but in the very materials of his storytelling—the dance halls and bars, the bumbling border guards, the clod-brained farmers and their insatiable wives, the larcenous cops, the whores who loved him—I felt the actuality of a life I knew nothing about yet somehow contrived to want for myself: a real life in a real world.

While Eduardo talked, Miguel labored silently beside us, now and 5 then grunting with the weight of a bale, his acne-scarred face flushed with heat, narrow eyes narrowed even tighter against the sun. Clemson and I sprinted and flagged, sprinted and flagged, laughing at Eduardo's stories, goading him with questions. Miguel never flagged, and never laughed. He sometimes watched his brother with what appeared to be mild curiosity; that was all.

The farmer, who owned a big spread with a lot of hay to bring in, should have hired more hands. He had only the four of us, and there was always the danger of rain. He was a relaxed, amiable man, but as the season wore on he grew anxious and began to push us harder and keep us longer. During the last week or so I spent the nights with Clemson's family, just down the road, so I could get to the farm with the others at sunup and work until dusk. The bales were heavy with dew when we started bringing them in. The air in the loft turned steamy from fermentation, and Eduardo warned the farmer that the hay might combust, but he held us to his schedule. Limping, sunburned, covered with scratches, I could hardly get out of bed in the morning. But although I griped with Clemson and Eduardo, I was secretly glad to take my place beside them, to work as if I had no choice.

Eduardo's car broke down toward the end of the week, and Clemson started driving him and Miguel to and from the decrepit motel where they lived with other seasonal workers. Sometimes, pulling up to their door, we'd all just sit there, saying nothing. We were that tired. Then one night Eduardo asked us in for a drink. Clemson, being a good boy, tried to beg off, but I got out with Miguel and Eduardo, knowing he wouldn't leave me. "Come on, Clem," I said, "don't be a homo." He looked at me, then turned the engine off.

That room. Jesus. The brothers had done their best, making their beds, keeping their clothes neatly folded in open suitcases, but you got swamped by the smell of mildew the moment you stepped inside. The floor was mushy underfoot and shedding squares of drab linoleum, the ceiling bowed and stained. The overhead light didn't quite reach the corners. Behind the mildew was another, unsettling smell. Clemson was a fastidious guy and writhed in distress as I made a show of being right at home.

We poured rye into our empty stomachs and listened to Eduardo, and before long we were all drunk. Someone came to the door and spoke to him in Spanish, and Eduardo went outside and didn't come back. Miguel and I kept drinking. Clemson was half asleep, his chin declining slowly toward his chest and snapping up again. Then Miguel looked at me. He slitted his eyes and looked at me hard, without blinking, and began to protest an injustice done him by our boss, or maybe another boss. I could barely understand his English, and he kept breaking into Spanish, which I didn't understand at all. But he was angry— I understood that much.

At some point he went across the room and came back and put a 10 pistol on the table, right in front of him. A revolver, long barrel, most of the bluing worn off. Miguel stared at me over the pistol and resumed his complaint, entirely in Spanish. He was looking at me, but I knew he was seeing someone else. I had rarely heard him speak before. Now the words poured out in an aggrieved singsong, and I saw that his own voice was lashing him on somehow, the very sound of his indignation proving that he had been wronged, feeding his rage, making him hate whoever he thought I was. I was too afraid to speak. All I could do was smile.

That room—once you enter it, you never really leave. You can forget you're there, you can go on as if you hold the reins, that the course of your life, yea even its *length,* will reflect the force of your character and the wisdom of your judgments. And then you hit an icy patch on a turn one sunny March day and the wheel in your hands becomes a joke and you no more than a spectator to your own dreamy slide toward the verge, and then you remember where you are.

Or you board a bus with thirty other young men. It's early, just before dawn. That's when the buses always leave, their lights dimmed, to avoid the attention of the Quakers outside the gate, but it doesn't work and they're waiting, silently holding up their signs, looking at you not with reproach but with sadness and sympathy as the bus drives past them and on toward the airport and the plane that will take you where you would not go—and at this moment you know exactly what your desires count for, and your plans, and all your strength of body and will. Then you know where you are, as you will know where you are when those you love die before their time—the time you had planned for them, for yourself with them—and when your daily allowance of words and dreams is withheld from you, and when your daughter drives the car straight into a tree. And if she walks away without a scratch you still feel that dark ceiling close overhead, and know where you are. And what can you do but what you did back in this awful room, with Miguel hating you for nothing and a pistol ready to hand? Smile and hope for a change of subject.

It came, this time. Clemson bolted up from his chair, bent forward, and puked all over the table. Miguel stopped talking. He stared at Clemson as if he'd never seen him before, and when Clemson began retching again Miguel jumped up and grabbed him by the shirt and pushed him toward the door. I took over and helped Clemson outside while Miguel looked on, shrieking his disgust. Disgust! Now *he* was the fastidious one. Revulsion had trumped rage, had trumped even hatred. Oh, how sweetly I tended Clemson that night! I thought he'd saved my life. And maybe he had.

The farmer's barn burned to the ground that winter. When I heard about it, I said, "Didn't I tell him? I did, I told that stupid sumbitch not to put up wet hay."

Considerations for Critical Thinking and Writing

1. **FIRST RESPONSE.** Why does the narrator describe his "life at home and school" as "inessential, parenthetical" (para. 3) in comparison to "a real life in a real world" (para. 4)?

2. Why is the work the narrator does on the farm important to him?

3. How are Eduardo and Miguel foils to one another?

4. Why is Miguel so angry?

5. How does the motel room and what happens in it take on symbolic meaning in this plot?

6. Discuss the significance of paragraphs 11–12. Why do you think they appear where they do and are set off from the rest of the story?

7. How is the bus trip described in paragraph 12 relevant to the narrator's experience? What kind of perspective on life is expressed in this paragraph?

8. Discuss your reading of the story's final paragraph and how it relates to the rest of the narration.

9. **CONNECTION TO ANOTHER SELECTION.** Discuss the similarities and differences related to the nature of what the protagonist learns about life in "That Room" and in either Ralph Ellison's "Battle Royal" (p. 180) or John Updike's "A & P" (p. 157).

RALPH ELLISON (1914–1994)

Born in Oklahoma and educated at the Tuskegee Institute in Alabama, where he studied music, Ralph Ellison gained his reputation as a writer on the strength of his only published novel, *Invisible Man* (1952). He also published some scattered short stories and two collections of essays, *Shadow and Act* (1964) and *Going to the Territory* (1986). Although his writing was not extensive, it is important because Ellison

Library of Congress, Prints and Photographs Division.

wrote about race relations in the context of universal human concerns. *Invisible Man* is the story of a young black man who moves from the South to the North and discovers what it means to be black in America. "Battle Royal," published in 1947 as a short story, became the first chapter of *Invisible Man*. It concerns the beginning of the protagonist's long struggle for an adult identity in a world made corrupt by racial prejudice.

Battle Royal   1947

It goes a long way back, some twenty years. All my life I had been looking for something, and everywhere I turned someone tried to tell me what it was. I accepted their answers too, though they were often in contradiction and even self-contradictory. I was naive. I was looking for myself and asking everyone except myself questions which I, and only I, could answer. It took me a long time and much painful boomeranging of my expectations to achieve a realization everyone else appears to have been born with: That I am nobody but myself. But first I had to discover that I am an invisible man!

And yet I am no freak of nature, nor of history. I was in the cards, other things having been equal (or unequal) eighty-five years ago. I am not ashamed of my grandparents for having been slaves. I am only ashamed of myself for having at one time been ashamed. About eighty-five years ago they were told that they were free, united with others of our country in everything pertaining to the common good, and, in everything social, separate like the fingers of the hand. And they believed it. They exulted in it. They stayed in their place, worked hard, and brought up my father to do the same. But my grandfather is the one. He was an odd old guy, my grandfather, and I am told I take after him. It was he who caused the trouble. On his deathbed he called my father to him and said, "Son, after I'm gone I want you to keep up the good fight. I never told you, but our life is a war and I have been a traitor all my born days, a spy in the enemy's country ever since I gave up my gun back in the Reconstruction. Live with your head in the lion's mouth. I want you to overcome 'em with yeses, undermine 'em with grins, agree 'em to death and destruction, let 'em swoller you till they vomit or bust wide open." They thought the old man had gone out of his mind. He had been the meekest of men. The younger children were rushed from the room, the shades drawn and the flame of the lamp turned so low that it sputtered on the wick like the old man's breathing. "Learn it to the young-uns," he whispered fiercely; then he died.

But my folks were more alarmed over his last words than over his dying. It was as though he had not died at all, his words caused so much anxiety. I was warned emphatically to forget what he had said and, indeed, this is the first time it has been mentioned outside the family circle. It had a tremendous effect upon me, however. I could never be sure of what he meant. Grandfather had been a quiet old man who never made any trouble, yet on his deathbed he had called himself a traitor and a spy, and he had spoken of his meekness as a dangerous activity. It became a constant puzzle which lay unanswered in the back of my mind. And whenever things went well for me I remembered my grandfather and felt guilty and uncomfortable. It was as though I was carrying out his advice in spite of myself. And to make it worse, everyone loved me for it. I was praised by the most lily-white men of the town. I was considered an example of desirable conduct—just as my grandfather had been. And what puzzled me was that the old man had defined it as *treachery*. When I was praised for my conduct I felt a guilt that in some way I was doing something that was really against the wishes of the white folks, that if they had understood they would have desired me to act just the opposite, that I should have been sulky and mean, and that that really would have been what they wanted, even though they were fooled and thought they wanted me to act as I did. It made me afraid that some day they would look upon me as a traitor and I would be lost. Still I was more afraid to act any other way because they didn't like that at all. The old man's words were like a curse. On my graduation day I delivered an oration in which I showed that humility was the secret, indeed, the very essence of progress. (Not that I believed this—how could I, remembering my grandfather?—I only believed that it worked.) It was a great success. Everyone praised me and I was invited to give the speech at a gathering of the town's leading white citizens. It was a triumph for our whole community.

It was in the main ballroom of the leading hotel. When I got there I discovered that it was on the occasion of a smoker, and I was told that since I was to be there anyway I might as well take part in the battle royal to be fought by some of my schoolmates as part of the entertainment. The battle royal came first.

All of the town's big shots were there in their tuxedoes, wolfing   5 down the buffet foods, drinking beer and whiskey and smoking black cigars. It was a large room with a high ceiling. Chairs were arranged in neat rows around three sides of a portable boxing ring. The fourth side was clear, revealing a gleaming space of polished floor. I had some misgivings over the battle royal, by the way. Not from a distaste for fighting, but because I didn't care too much for the other fellows who were to take part. They were tough guys who seemed to have no grandfather's curse worrying their minds. No one could mistake their toughness. And besides, I suspected that fighting a battle royal might detract from the dignity of my speech. In those pre-invisible days I visualized myself as a potential Booker T. Washington. But the other fellows didn't care too much for me either, and there were nine of them. I felt superior to them in my way, and I didn't like the manner in which we were all crowded together into the servants' elevator. Nor did they like my being there. In fact, as the warmly lighted floors flashed past the elevator we had words over the fact that I, by taking part in the fight, had knocked one of their friends out of a night's work.

We were led out of the elevator through a rococo hall into an anteroom and told to get into our fighting togs. Each of us was issued a pair of boxing gloves and ushered out into the big mirrored hall, which we entered looking cautiously about us and whispering, lest we might accidentally be heard above the noise of the room. It was foggy with cigar smoke. And already the whiskey was taking effect. I was shocked to see some of the most important men of the town quite tipsy. They were all there — bankers, lawyers, judges, doctors, fire chiefs, teachers, merchants. Even one of the more fashionable pastors. Something we could not see was going on up front. A clarinet was vibrating sensuously and the men were standing up and moving eagerly forward. We were a small tight group, clustered together, our bare upper bodies touching and shining with anticipatory sweat; while up front the big shots were becoming increasingly excited over something we still could not see. Suddenly I heard the school superintendent, who had told me to come, yell, "Bring up the shines, gentlemen! Bring up the little shines!"

We were rushed up to the front of the ballroom, where it smelled even more strongly of tobacco and whiskey. Then we were pushed into place. I almost wet my pants. A sea of faces, some hostile, some amused, ringed around us, and in the center, facing us, stood a magnificent blonde — stark naked. There was dead silence. I felt a blast of cold air chill me. I tried to back away, but they were behind me and around me. Some of the boys stood with lowered heads, trembling. I felt a wave of irrational guilt and fear. My teeth chattered, my skin turned to goose flesh, my knees knocked. Yet I was strongly attracted and looked in spite of myself. Had the price of looking been blindness, I would have looked. The hair was yellow like that of a circus kewpie doll, the face heavily powdered and rouged, as though to form an abstract mask, the eyes hollow and smeared a cool blue, the color of a baboon's butt. I felt a desire to spit upon her as my eyes brushed slowly over her body. Her breasts were firm and round as the domes of East Indian temples, and I stood so close as to see the fine skin texture and beads of pearly perspiration glistening like dew around the pink and erected buds of her nipples. I wanted at one and the same time to run from the room, to sink through the floor, or go to her and cover her from my eyes and the eyes of the others with my body; to feel the soft thighs, to caress her and destroy her, to love her and murder her, to hide from her, and yet to stroke where below the small American flag tattooed upon her belly her thighs formed a capital V. I had a notion that of all in the room she saw only me with her impersonal eyes.

And then she began to dance, a slow sensuous movement; the smoke of a hundred cigars clinging to her like the thinnest of veils. She seemed like a fair bird-girl girdled in veils calling to me from the angry surface of some gray and threatening sea. I was transported. Then I became aware of the clarinet playing and the big shots yelling at us. Some threatened us if we looked and others if we did not. On my right I saw one boy faint. And now a man grabbed a silver pitcher from a table and stepped close as he dashed ice water upon him and stood him up and forced two of us to support him as his head hung and moans issued from his thick bluish lips. Another boy began to plead to go home. He was the largest of the group, wearing dark red fighting trunks much too small to conceal the erection which projected from him as though in answer to the insinuating low-registered moaning of the clarinet. He tried to hide himself with his boxing gloves.

And all the while the blonde continued dancing, smiling faintly at the big shots who watched her with fascination, and faintly smiling at our fear. I noticed a certain merchant who followed her hungrily, his lips loose and drooling. He was a large man who wore diamond studs in a shirtfront which swelled with the ample paunch underneath, and each time the blonde swayed her undulating hips he ran his hand through the thin hair of his bald head and, with his arms upheld, his posture clumsy like that of an intoxicated panda, wound his belly in a slow and obscene grind. This creature was completely hypnotized. The music had quickened. As the dancer flung herself about with a detached expression on her face, the men began reaching out to touch her. I could see their beefy fingers sink into the soft flesh. Some of the others tried to stop them as she began to move around the floor in graceful circles, as they gave chase, slipping and sliding over the polished floor. It was mad. Chairs went crashing, drinks were spilt, as they ran laughing and howling after her. They caught her just as she reached a door, raised her from the floor, and tossed her as college boys are tossed at a hazing, and above her red, fixed-smiling lips I saw the terror and disgust in her eyes, almost like my own terror and that which I saw in some of the other boys. As I watched, they tossed her twice and her soft breasts seemed to flatten against the air and her legs flung wildly as she spun. Some of the more sober ones helped her to escape. And I started off the floor, heading for the anteroom with the rest of the boys.

Some were still crying in hysteria. But as we tried to leave we were 10 stopped and ordered to get into the ring. There was nothing to do but what we were told. All ten of us climbed under the ropes and allowed ourselves to be blindfolded with broad bands of white cloth. One of the men seemed to feel a bit sympathetic and tried to cheer us up as we stood with our backs against the ropes. Some of us tried to grin. "See that boy over there?" one of the men said. "I want you to run across at the bell and give it to him right in the belly. If you don't get him, I'm going to get you. I don't like his looks." Each of us was told the same. The blindfolds were put on. Yet even then I had been going over my speech. In my mind each word was as bright as flame. I felt the cloth pressed into place, and frowned so that it would be loosened when I relaxed.

But now I felt a sudden fit of blind terror. I was unused to darkness. It was as though I had suddenly found myself in a dark room filled with poisonous cottonmouths. I could hear the bleary voices yelling insistently for the battle royal to begin.

"Get going in there!"

"Let me at that big nigger!"

I strained to pick up the school superintendent's voice, as though to squeeze some security out of that slightly more familiar sound.

"Let me at those black sonsabitches!" someone yelled.   15

"No, Jackson, no!" another voice yelled. "Here, somebody, help me hold Jack."

"I want to get at that ginger-colored nigger. Tear him limb from limb," the first voice yelled.

I stood against the ropes trembling. For in those days I was what they called ginger-colored, and he sounded as though he might crunch me between his teeth like a crisp ginger cookie.

Quite a struggle was going on. Chairs were being kicked about and I could hear voices grunting as with a terrific effort. I wanted to see, to see more desperately than ever before. But the blindfold was tight as a thick skin-puckering scab and when I raised my gloved hands to push the layers of white aside a voice yelled, "Oh, no you don't, black bastard! Leave that alone!"

"Ring the bell before Jackson kills him a coon!" someone boomed in   20
the sudden silence. And I heard the bell clang and the sound of the feet scuffling forward.

A glove smacked against my head. I pivoted, striking out stiffly as someone went past, and felt the jar ripple along the length of my arm to my shoulder. Then it seemed as though all nine of the boys had turned upon me at once. Blows pounded me from all sides while I struck out as best I could. So many blows landed upon me that I wondered if I were not the only blindfolded fighter in the ring, or if the man called Jackson hadn't succeeded in getting me after all.

Blindfolded, I could no longer control my motions. I had no dignity. I stumbled about like a baby or a drunken man. The smoke had become thicker and with each new blow it seemed to sear and further restrict my lungs. My saliva became like hot bitter glue. A glove connected with my head, filling my mouth with warm blood. It was everywhere. I could not tell if the moisture I felt upon my body was sweat or blood. A blow landed hard against the nape of my neck. I felt myself going over, my head hitting the floor. Streaks of blue light filled the black world behind the blindfold. I lay prone, pretending that I was knocked out, but felt myself seized by hands and yanked to my feet. "Get going, black boy! Mix it up!" My arms were like lead, my head smarting from blows. I managed to feel my way to the ropes and held on, trying to catch my breath. A glove landed in my mid-section and I went over again, feeling as though the smoke had become a knife jabbed into my guts. Pushed this way and that by the legs milling around me, I finally pulled erect and discovered that I could see the black, sweat-washed forms weaving in the smoky-blue atmosphere like drunken dancers weaving to the rapid drumlike thuds of blows.

Everyone fought hysterically. It was complete anarchy. Everybody fought everybody else. No group fought together for long. Two, three, four, fought one, then turned to fight each other, were themselves attacked. Blows landed below the belt and in the kidney, with the gloves open as well as closed, and with my eye partly opened now there was not so much terror. I moved carefully, avoiding blows, although not too many to attract attention, fighting from group to group. The boys groped about like blind, cautious crabs crouching to protect their mid-sections, their heads pulled in short against their shoulders, their arms stretched nervously before them, with their fists testing the smoke-filled air like the knobbed feelers of hypersensitive snails. In one corner I glimpsed a boy violently punching the air and heard him scream in pain as he smashed his hand against a ring post. For a second I saw him bent over holding his hand, then going down as a blow caught his unprotected head. I played one group against the other, slipping in and throwing a punch then stepping out of range while pushing the others into the melee to take the blows blindly aimed at me. The smoke was agonizing and there were no rounds, no bells at three minute intervals to relieve our exhaustion. The room spun round me, a swirl of lights, smoke, sweating bodies surrounded by tense white faces. I bled from both nose and mouth, the blood spattering upon my chest.

The men kept yelling, "Slug him, black boy! Knock his guts out!"

"Uppercut him! Kill him! Kill that big boy!"   25

Taking a fake fall, I saw a boy going down heavily beside me as though we were felled by a single blow, saw a sneaker-clad foot shoot into his groin as the two who had knocked him down stumbled upon him. I rolled out of range, feeling a twinge of nausea.

The harder we fought the more threatening the men became. And yet, I had begun to worry about my speech again. How would it go? Would they recognize my ability? What would they give me?

I was fighting automatically when suddenly I noticed that one after another of the boys was leaving the ring. I was surprised, filled with panic, as though I had been left alone with an unknown danger. Then I understood. The boys had arranged it among themselves. It was the custom for the two men left in the ring to slug it out for the winner's prize. I discovered this too late. When the bell sounded two men in tuxedoes leaped into the ring and removed the blindfold. I found myself facing Tatlock, the biggest of the gang. I felt sick at my stomach. Hardly had the bell stopped ringing in my ears than it clanged again and I saw him moving swiftly toward me. Thinking of nothing else to do I hit him smash on the nose. He kept coming, bringing the rank sharp violence of stale sweat. His face was a black blank of a face, only his eyes alive — with hate of me and aglow with a feverish terror from what had happened to us all. I became anxious. I wanted to deliver my speech and he came at me as though he meant to beat it out of me. I smashed him again and again, taking his blows as they came. Then on a sudden impulse I struck him lightly and as we clinched, I whispered, "Fake like I knocked you out, you can have the prize."

"I'll break your behind," he whispered hoarsely.

"For *them?*"

"For *me,* sonofabitch!"   30

They were yelling for us to break it up and Tatlock spun me half around with a blow, and as a joggled camera sweeps in a reeling scene, I saw the howling red faces crouching tense beneath the cloud of blue-gray smoke. For a moment the world wavered, unraveled, flowed, then my head cleared and Tatlock bounced before me. That fluttering shadow before my eyes was his jabbing left hand. Then falling forward, my head against his damp shoulder, I whispered,

"I'll make it five dollars more."

"Go to hell!"

But his muscles relaxed a trifle beneath my pressure and I breathed,   35
"Seven?"

"Give it to your ma," he said, ripping me beneath the heart.

And while I still held him I butted him and moved away. I felt myself bombarded with punches. I fought back with hopeless desperation. I wanted to deliver my speech more than anything else in the world, because I felt that only these men could judge truly my ability, and now this stupid clown was ruining my chances. I began fighting carefully now, moving in to punch him and out again with my greater speed. A lucky blow to his chin and I had him going too—until I heard a loud voice yell, "I got my money on the big boy."

Hearing this, I almost dropped my guard. I was confused: Should I try to win against the voice out there? Would not this go against my speech, and was not this a moment for humility, for nonresistance? A blow to my head as I danced about sent my right eye popping like a jack-in-the-box and settled my dilemma. The room went red as I fell. It was a dream fall, my body languid and fastidious as to where to land, until the floor became impatient and smashed up to meet me. A moment later I came to. An hypnotic voice said FIVE emphatically. And I lay there, hazily watching a dark red spot of my own blood shaping itself into a butterfly, glistening and soaking into the soiled gray world of the canvas.

When the voice drawled TEN I was lifted up and dragged to a chair. I sat dazed. My eye pained and swelled with each throb of my pounding heart and I wondered if now I would be allowed to speak. I was wringing wet, my mouth still bleeding. We were grouped along the wall now. The other boys ignored me as they congratulated Tatlock and speculated as to how much they would be paid. One boy whimpered over his smashed hand. Looking up front, I saw attendants in white jackets rolling the portable ring away and placing a small square rug in the vacant space surrounded by chairs. Perhaps, I thought, I will stand on the rug to deliver my speech.

Then the M.C. called to us, "Come on up here boys and get your   40
money." We ran forward to where the men laughed and talked in their chairs, waiting. Everyone seemed friendly now.

"There it is on the rug," the man said. I saw the rug covered with coins of all dimensions and a few crumpled bills. But what excited me, scattered here and there, were the gold pieces.

"Boys, it's all yours," the man said. "You get all you grab."

"That's right, Sambo," a blond man said, winking at me confidentially.

I trembled with excitement, forgetting my pain. I would get the gold and the bills, I thought. I would use both hands. I would throw my body against the boys nearest me to block them from the gold.

"Get down around the rug now," the man commanded, "and don't   45
anyone touch it until I give the signal."

"This ought to be good," I heard.

As told, we got around the square rug on our knees. Slowly the man raised his freckled hand as we followed it upward with our eyes.

I heard, "These niggers look like they're about to pray!"

Then, "Ready," the man said. "Go!"

I lunged for a yellow coin lying on the blue design of the carpet,   50
touching it and sending a surprised shriek to join those rising around me. I tried frantically to remove my hand but could not let go. A hot, violent force tore through my body, shaking me like a wet rat. The rug was electrified. The hair bristled up on my head as I shook myself free. My muscles jumped, my nerves jangled, writhed. But I saw that this was not stopping the other boys. Laughing in fear and embarrassment, some were holding back and scooping up the coins knocked off by the painful contortions of the others. The men roared above us as we struggled.

"Pick it up, goddamnit, pick it up!" someone called like a bass-voiced parrot. "Go on, get it!"

I crawled rapidly around the floor, picking up the coins, trying to avoid the coppers and to get greenbacks and the gold. Ignoring the shock by laughing, as I brushed the coins off quickly, I discovered that I could contain the electricity—a contradiction, but it works. Then the men began to push us onto the rug. Laughing embarrassedly, we struggled out of their hands and kept after the coins. We were all wet and slippery and hard to hold. Suddenly I saw a boy lifted into the air, glistening with sweat like a circus seal, and dropped, his wet back landing flush upon the charged rug, heard him yell and saw him literally dance upon his back, his elbows beating a frenzied tattoo upon the floor, his muscles twitching like the flesh of a horse stung by many flies. When he finally rolled off, his face was gray and no one stopped him when he ran from the floor amid booming laughter.

"Get the money," the M.C. called. "That's good hard American cash!"

And we snatched and grabbed, snatched and grabbed. I was careful not to come too close to the rug now, and when I felt the hot whiskey breath descend upon me like a cloud of foul air I reached out and grabbed the leg of a chair. It was occupied and I held on desperately.

"Leggo, nigger! Leggo!"   55

The huge face wavered down to mine as he tried to push me free. But my body was slippery and he was too drunk. It was Mr. Colcord, who owned a chain of movie houses and "entertainment palaces." Each time he grabbed me I slipped out of his hands. It became a real struggle. I feared the rug more than I did the drunk, so I held on, surprising myself for a moment by trying to topple *him* upon the rug. It was such an enormous idea that I found myself actually carrying it out. I tried not to be obvious, yet when I grabbed his leg, trying to tumble him out of the chair, he raised up roaring with laughter, and, looking at me with soberness dead in the eye, kicked me viciously in the chest. The chair leg flew out of my hand and I felt myself going and rolled. It was as though I had rolled through a bed of hot coals. It seemed a whole century would pass before I would roll free, a century in which I was seared through the deepest levels of my body to the fearful breath within me and the breath seared and heated to the point of explosion. It'll all be over in a flash, I thought as I rolled clear. It'll all be over in a flash.

But not yet, the men on the other side were waiting, red faces swollen as though from apoplexy as they bent forward in their chairs. Seeing their fingers coming toward me I rolled away as a fumbled football rolls off the receiver's fingertips, back into the coals. That time I luckily sent the rug sliding out of place and heard the coins ringing against the floor and the boys scuffling to pick them up and the M.C. calling, "All right, boys, that's all. Go get dressed and get your money."

I was limp as a dish rag. My back felt as though it had been beaten with wires.

When we had dressed the M.C. came in and gave us each five dollars, except Tatlock, who got ten for being last in the ring. Then he told us to leave. I was not to get a chance to deliver my speech, I thought. I was going out into the dim alley in despair when I was stopped and told to go back. I returned to the ballroom, where the men were pushing back their chairs and gathering in groups to talk.

The M.C. knocked on a table for quiet. "Gentlemen," he said, "we   60 almost forgot an important part of the program. A most serious part, gentlemen. This boy was brought here to deliver a speech which he made at his graduation yesterday ..."

"Bravo!"

"I'm told that he is the smartest boy we've got out there in Greenwood. I'm told that he knows more big words than a pocket-sized dictionary."

Much applause and laughter.

"So now, gentlemen, I want you to give him your attention."

There was still laughter as I faced them, my mouth dry, my eye 65 throbbing. I began slowly, but evidently my throat was tense, because they began shouting, "Louder! Louder!"

"We of the younger generation extol the wisdom of that great leader and educator," I shouted, "who first spoke these flaming words of wisdom: 'A ship lost at sea for many days suddenly sighted a friendly vessel. From the mast of the unfortunate vessel was seen a signal: "Water, water; we die of thirst!" The answer from the friendly vessel came back: "Cast down your bucket where you are." The captain of the distressed vessel, at last heeding the injunction, cast down his bucket, and it came up full of fresh sparkling water from the mouth of the Amazon River.' And like him I say, and in his words, 'To those of my race who depend upon bettering their condition in a foreign land, or who underestimate the importance of cultivating friendly relations with the Southern white man, who is his next-door neighbor, I would say: "Cast down your bucket where you are" — cast it down in making friends in every manly way of the people of all races by whom we are surrounded . . .'"

I spoke automatically and with such fervor that I did not realize that the men were still talking and laughing until my dry mouth, filling up with blood from the cut, almost strangled me. I coughed, wanting to stop and go to one of the tall brass, sand-filled spittoons to relieve myself, but a few of the men, especially the superintendent, were listening and I was afraid. So I gulped it down, blood, saliva, and all, and continued. (What powers of endurance I had during those days! What enthusiasm! What a belief in the rightness of things!) I spoke even louder in spite of the pain. But still they talked and still they laughed, as though deaf with cotton in dirty ears. So I spoke with greater emotional emphasis. I closed my ears and swallowed blood until I was nauseated. The speech seemed a hundred times as long as before, but I could not leave out a single word. All had to be said, each memorized nuance considered, rendered. Nor was that all. Whenever I uttered a word of three or more syllables a group of voices would yell for me to repeat it. I used the phrase "social responsibility" and they yelled:

"What's that word you say, boy?"

"Social responsibility," I said.

"What?" 70

"Social . . ."

"Louder."

". . . responsibility."

"More!"

"Respon—" 75

"Repeat!"

"—sibility."

The room filled with the uproar of laughter until, no doubt, distracted by having to gulp down my blood, I made a mistake and yelled a phrase I had often seen denounced in newspaper editorials, heard debated in private.

"Social ..."

"What?" they yelled.   80

" ... equality—"

The laughter hung smokelike in the sudden stillness. I opened my eyes, puzzled. Sounds of displeasure filled the room. The M.C. rushed forward. They shouted hostile phrases at me. But I did not understand.

A small dry mustached man in the front row blared out, "Say that slowly, son!"

"What, sir?"

"What you just said!"   85

"Social responsibility, sir," I said.

"You weren't being smart, were you, boy?" he said, not unkindly.

"No, sir!"

"You sure that about 'equality' was a mistake?"

"Oh, yes, sir," I said. "I was swallowing blood."   90

"Well, you had better speak more slowly so we can understand. We mean to do right by you, but you've got to know your place at all times. All right, now, go on with your speech."

I was afraid. I wanted to leave but I wanted also to speak and I was afraid they'd snatch me down.

"Thank you, sir," I said, beginning where I had left off, and having them ignore me as before.

Yet when I finished there was a thunderous applause. I was surprised to see the superintendent come forth with a package wrapped in white tissue paper, and, gesturing for quiet, address the men.

"Gentlemen, you see that I did not overpraise this boy. He makes a 95
good speech and some day he'll lead his people in the proper paths. And I don't have to tell you that that is important in these days and times. This is a good, smart boy, and so to encourage him in the right direction, in the name of the Board of Education I wish to present him a prize in the form of this ..."

He paused, removing the tissue paper and revealing a gleaming calf-skin brief case.

" ... in the form of this first-class article from Shad Whitmore's shop."

"Boy," he said, addressing me, "take this prize and keep it well. Consider it a badge of office. Prize it. Keep developing as you are and some day it will be filled with important papers that will help shape the destiny of your people."

I was so moved that I could hardly express my thanks. A rope of bloody saliva forming a shape like an undiscovered continent drooled upon the leather and I wiped it quickly away. I felt an importance that I had never dreamed.

"Open it and see what's inside," I was told.   100

My fingers a-tremble, I complied, smelling the fresh leather and finding an official-looking document inside. It was a scholarship to the state college for Negroes. My eyes filled with tears and I ran awkwardly off the floor.

I was overjoyed; I did not even mind when I discovered that the gold pieces I had scrambled for were brass pocket tokens advertising a certain make of automobile.

When I reached home everyone was excited. Next day the neighbors came to congratulate me. I even felt safe from grandfather, whose death-bed curse usually spoiled my triumphs. I stood beneath his photograph with my brief case in hand and smiled triumphantly into his stolid black peasant's face. It was a face that fascinated me. The eyes seemed to follow everywhere I went.

That night I dreamed I was at a circus with him and that he refused to laugh at the clowns no matter what they did. Then later he told me to open my brief case and read what was inside and I did, finding an official envelope stamped with the state seal; and inside the envelope I found another and another, endlessly, and I thought I would fall of weariness. "Them's years," he said. "Now open that one." And I did and in it I found an engraved document containing a short message in letters of gold. "Read it," my grandfather said. "Out loud!"

"To Whom It May Concern," I intoned. "Keep This Nigger-Boy   105
Running."

I awoke with the old man's laughter ringing in my ears.

(It was a dream I was to remember and dream again for many years after. But at that time I had no insight into its meaning. First I had to attend college.)

CONSIDERATIONS FOR CRITICAL THINKING AND WRITING

1. **FIRST RESPONSE.** Discuss how the protagonist's expectations are similar to what has come to be known as the American dream — the assumption that ambition, hard work, perseverance, intelligence, and virtue always lead to success.

2. How does the first paragraph of the story sum up the conflict that the narrator confronts? In what sense is he "invisible"?

3. What is the symbolic significance of the naked blonde? What details reveal that she represents more than a sexual tease in the story?

4. How does the battle in the boxing ring and the scramble for money afterward suggest the kind of control whites have over blacks in the story?

5. How can the dream at the end of the story be related to the major incidents that precede it?

6. Given the grandfather's advice, explain how "meekness" can be a "dangerous activity" and a weapon against oppression.

7. Imagine the story as told from a third-person point of view. How would this change the story? Do you think the story would be more

or less effective told from a third-person point of view? Explain your answer.

8. **CONNECTION TO ANOTHER SELECTION.** Compare and contrast Ellison's view of the South with William Faulkner's in "A Rose for Emily" (p. 52).

PETER MEINKE (B. 1932)

Born in Brooklyn, New York, Peter Meinke was educated at Hamilton College (B.A., 1955), the University of Michigan (M.A., 1961), and the University of Minnesota (Ph.D., 1965). He has taught literature and creative writing at a number of schools, including Hamline University, Eckerd College, and Old Dominion University. Though Meinke is primarily a poet, he has also published two collections of short stories: *Piano Tuner* (1986), which won the Flannery O'Connor Award, and *Unheard Music* (2007). In a 1990 interview in *Clockwatch Review,* Meinke discussed the similarities he sees between short stories and poetry: "I think that certainly poetry and short stories are more alike than short stories and novels, because that's the main decision—leaving out the boffo endings, leaving out conversations that are extraneous. There's a big empty spot around poems and short stories, certainly. That's the thing they have very strongly in common." "The Cranes" is a fine example of the kind of literary economy that Meinke believes poetry and short stories often share.

> **WHEN I READ** "It's important for poets to read fiction, and fiction writers to read poetry—this could add depth to the fiction and clarity to the poetry."   —PETER MEINKE

The Cranes   1987

"Oh!" she said, "what are those, the huge white ones?" Along the marshy shore two tall and stately birds, staring motionless toward the Gulf, towered above the bobbing egrets and scurrying plovers.

"Well, I can't believe it," he said. "I've been coming here for years and never saw one."

"But what are they? Don't make me guess or anything; it makes me feel dumb." They leaned forward in the car, and the shower curtain spread over the front seat crackled and hissed.

"They've got to be whooping cranes, nothing else so big." One of the birds turned gracefully, as if to acknowledge the old Dodge parked alone in the tall grasses. "See the black legs and black wingtips? Big! Why don't I have my binoculars?" He looked at his wife and smiled.

"Well," he continued after a while, "I've seen enough birds. But 5 whooping cranes, they're rare. Not many left."

"They're lovely. They make the little birds look like clowns."

"I could use a few clowns," he said. "A few laughs never hurt anybody."

"Are you all right?" She put a hand on his thin arm. "I feel I'm responsible. Maybe this is the wrong thing."

"God, no!" His voice changed. "No way. I can't smoke, can't drink martinis, no coffee, no candy. I not only can't leap buildings in a single bound, I can hardly get up the goddamn stairs."

She was smiling. "Do you remember the time you drank nine martinis and asked that young priest to step outside and see whose side God was on?"

"What a jerk I was! How have you put up with me all this time?"

"Oh no! I was proud of you. You were so funny, and that priest was a snot."

"Now you tell me." The cranes were moving slowly over a small hillock, wings opening and closing like bellows. "It's all right. It's enough," he said again. "How old am I anyway, 130?"

"Really," she said, "it's me. Ever since the accident it's been one thing after another. I'm just a lot of trouble to everybody."

"Let's talk about something else," he said. "Do you want to listen to the radio? How about turning on that preacher station so we can throw up?"

"No," she said, "I just want to watch the birds. And listen to you."

"You must be pretty tired of that."

She turned her head from the window and looked into his eyes. "I never got tired of listening to you. Never."

"Well, that's good," he said. "It's just that when my mouth opens, your eyes tend to close."

"They do not!" she said, and began to laugh, but the laugh turned into a cough and he had to pat her on the back until she stopped. They leaned back in silence and looked toward the Gulf stretching out beyond the horizon. In the distance, the water looked like metal, still and hard.

"I wish they'd court," he said. "I wish we could see them court, the cranes. They put on a show. He bows like Nijinksy and jumps straight up in the air."

"What does she do?"

"She lies down and he lands on top of her."

"No," she said, "I'm serious."

"Well, I forget. I've never seen it. But I do remember that they mate for life and live a long time. They're probably older than we are. Their feathers are falling out and their kids never write."

She was quiet again. He turned in his seat, picked up an object wrapped in a plaid towel, and placed it between them in the front. "Here's looking at *you*, kid," he said.

"Do they really mate for life? I'm glad—they're so beautiful."

"Yep. Audubon said that's why they're almost extinct: a failure of imagination."

"I don't believe that," she said. "I think there'll always be whooping cranes."

"Why not?" he said.

"I wish the children were more settled. I keep thinking it's my fault."

"You think everything's your fault. Nicaragua. Ozone depletion. Nothing is your fault. They'll be fine, and anyway, they're not children anymore. Kids are different today, that's all. You were terrific." He paused. "You were terrific in ways I couldn't tell the kids about."

"I should hope not." She laughed and began coughing again, but held his hand when he reached over. When the cough subsided they sat quietly, looking down at their hands as if they were objects in a museum. "I used to have pretty hands," she said.

"I remember."

"Do you? Really?"   35

"I remember everything," he said.

"You always forgot everything."

"Well, now I remember."

"Did you bring something for your ears?"

"No, I can hardly hear anything, anyway." But he turned his head at   40 a sudden squabble among the smaller birds. The cranes were stepping delicately away from the commotion.

"I'm tired," she said.

"Yes." He leaned over and kissed her, barely touching her lips. "Tell me," he said, "did I really drink nine martinis?"

But she had already closed her eyes and only smiled. Outside, the wind ruffled the bleached-out grasses, and the birds in the white glare seemed almost transparent. The hull of the car gleamed beetle-like — dull and somehow sinister in its metallic isolation.

Suddenly, the two cranes plunged upward, their great wings beating the air and their long slender necks pointed like arrows toward the sun.

CONSIDERATIONS FOR CRITICAL THINKING AND WRITING

1. **FIRST RESPONSE.** What happens at the end of "The Cranes"? What do you think this story is about?

2. Point to incidences of suspenseful foreshadowing and discuss how they affect your understanding of the plot. Were you aware of the foreshadowing elements on a first reading or only after subsequent readings?

3. How might the cranes be read as both conventional and literary symbols in this story?

4. **CONNECTION TO ANOTHER SELECTION.** Consider how symbols convey the central meanings of "The Cranes" and of either Kate Chopin's "The Story of an Hour" (p. 13) or Gail Godwin's "A Sorrowful Woman" (p. 36).

7

Theme

To produce a mighty book, you must
choose a mighty theme.
— HERMAN MELVILLE,
from *Moby-Dick*, 1851

Theme is the central idea or meaning of a story. It provides a unifying
point around which the plot, characters, setting, point of view, symbols,
and other elements of a story are organized. In some works the theme
is explicitly stated. Nathaniel Hawthorne's "Wakefield," for example,
begins with the author telling the reader that the point of his story is
"done up neatly, and condensed into the final sentence." Most modern
writers, however, present their themes implicitly (as Hawthorne does
in the majority of his stories), so determining the underlying meaning of a work often requires more effort than it does from the reader of
"Wakefield." One reason for the difficulty is that the theme is fused into
the elements of the story, and these must be carefully examined in relation to one another as well as to the work as a whole. But then that's
the value of determining the theme, for it requires a close analysis of
all the elements of a work. Such a close reading often results in sharper
insights into this overlooked character or that seemingly unrelated incident. Accounting for the details and seeing how they fit together result
in greater understanding of the story.

Themes are not always easy to express, but some principles can
aid you in articulating the central meaning of a work. First distinguish
between the theme of a story and its subject. They are not equivalents.
Many stories share identical subjects, such as fate, death, innocence,

youth, loneliness, racial prejudice, and disillusionment. Karen van der Zee's "A Secret Sorrow" (p. 27) and Gail Godwin's "A Sorrowful Woman" (p. 36) both focus on marriage. Yet each story usually makes its own statement about the subject and expresses a different view of life.

Explore the literary element in this chapter at bedfordstmartins.com/ meyerlit.

Although readers may differ in their interpretations of a story, that does not mean that *any* interpretation is valid. If we were to assert that Krebs's dissatisfactions in Hemingway's "Soldier's Home" (p. 133) could be readily eliminated by his settling down to marriage and a decent job (his mother's solution), we would have missed Hemingway's purposes in writing the story; we would have failed to see how Krebs's war experiences have caused him to reexamine the assumptions and beliefs that previously nurtured him but now seem unreal to him. We would have to ignore much in the story in order to arrive at such a reading. To be valid, the statement of the theme should be responsive to the details of the story. It must be based on evidence within the story rather than solely on experiences, attitudes, or values the reader brings to the work—such as personally knowing a war veteran who successfully adjusted to civilian life after getting a good job and marrying. Familiarity with the subject matter of a story can certainly be an aid to interpretation, but it should not get in the way of seeing the author's perspective.

Sometimes readers too hastily conclude that a story's theme always consists of a moral, some kind of lesson that is dramatized by the various elements of the work. There are stories that do this—Hawthorne's "Wakefield," for example. Here are the final sentences in his story about a middle-aged man who drops out of life for twenty years:

> He has left us much food for thought, a portion of which shall lend its wisdom to a moral, and be shaped into a figure. Amid the seeming confusion of our mysterious world, individuals are so nicely adjusted to a system, and systems to one another and to a whole, that, by stepping aside for a moment, a man exposes himself to a fearful risk of losing his place forever. Like Wakefield, he may become, as it were, the Outcast of the Universe.

Most stories, however, do not include such direct caveats about the conduct of life. A tendency to look for a lesson in a story can produce a reductive and inaccurate formulation of its theme. Consider the damage done to Godwin's "A Sorrowful Woman" (p. 36) if its theme is described as this: "The woman in the story is too selfish to cope with the responsibilities of marriage." Godwin's focus in this story is on the woman's desperate response to her domestic identity rather than on her inability to be a good wife. In fact, a good many stories go beyond traditional social values to explore human behavior instead of condemning or endorsing it.

There is no precise formula that can take you to the center of a story's meaning and help you to articulate it. However, several strategies are practical and useful once you have read the story. Apply these pointers during a second or third reading:

1. Pay attention to the title of the story. It often provides a lead to a major symbol (Hemingway's "Soldier's Home," p. 133) or to the subject around which the theme develops (Godwin's "A Sorrowful Woman," p. 36).

2. Look for details in the story that have potential for symbolic meanings. Careful consideration of names, places, objects, minor characters, and incidents can lead you to the central meaning—for example, think of the stripper in Ellison's "Battle Royal" (p. 180). Be especially attentive to elements you did not understand on the first reading.

3. Decide whether the protagonist changes or develops some important insight as a result of the action. Carefully examine any generalizations the protagonist or narrator makes about the events in the story.

4. When you formulate the theme of the story in your own words, write it down in one or two complete sentences that make some point about the subject matter. Revenge may be the subject of a story, but its theme should make a statement about revenge: "Instead of providing satisfaction, revenge defeats the best in one's self " is one possibility.

5. Be certain that your expression of the theme is a generalized statement rather than a specific description of particular people, places, and incidents in the story. Contrast the preceding statement of a theme on revenge with this too-specific one: "In Nathaniel Hawthorne's *The Scarlet Letter*, Roger Chillingworth loses his humanity owing to his single-minded attempts to punish Arthur Dimmesdale for fathering a child with Chillingworth's wife, Hester." Hawthorne's theme is not restricted to a single fictional character named Chillingworth but to anyone whose life is ruined by revenge.

6. Be wary of using clichés as a way of stating theme. They tend to short-circuit ideas instead of generating them. It may be tempting to resort to something like "an eye for an eye" as a statement of the theme of *The Scarlet Letter*; however, even the slightest second thought reveals how much more ambiguous and complicated that story is.

7. Be aware that some stories emphasize theme less than others. Stories that have as their major purpose adventure, humor, mystery, or terror may have little or no theme. In Edgar Allan Poe's "The Pit and the Pendulum," for example, the protagonist is not used to condemn torture; instead, he becomes a sensitive gauge to measure the pain and horror he endures at the hands of his captors.

What is most valuable about articulating the theme of a work is the process by which the theme is determined. Ultimately, the theme is expressed by the story itself and is inseparable from the experience of reading the story. Tim O'Brien's explanation of one of his short stories, "How to Tell a True War Story," is probably true of most kinds of stories: "In a true war story, if there's a moral [or theme] at all, it's like the thread that makes the cloth. You can't tease it out. You can't extract the meaning without unraveling the deeper meaning." Describing the theme should not be a way to consume a story, to be done with it. It is a means of clarifying our thinking about what we've read and probably felt intuitively.

Stephen Crane's "The Bride Comes to Yellow Sky," Edgar Allan Poe's "The Cask of Amontillado," Joyce Carol Oates's "Hi Howya Doin," and Dagoberto Gilb's "Romero's Shirt" are four stories whose themes emerge from the authors' skillful use of plot, character, setting, and symbol.

STEPHEN CRANE (1871–1900)

Born in Newark, New Jersey, Stephen Crane attended Lafayette College and Syracuse University and then worked as a freelance journalist in New York City. He wrote newspaper pieces, short stories, poems, and novels for his entire, brief adult life. His first book, *Maggie: A Girl of the Streets* (1893), is a story about New York slum life and prostitution. His most famous novel, *The Red Badge of Courage* (1895), gives readers a vivid, convincing re-creation of Civil War battles, even though Crane had never been to war. However, Crane was personally familiar with the American West, where he traveled as a reporter. "The Bride Comes to Yellow Sky" includes some of the ingredients of a typical popular western—a confrontation between a marshal and a drunk who shoots up the town.

© Bettmann / CORBIS.

The Bride Comes to Yellow Sky   *1898*

I

The great Pullman was whirling onward with such dignity of motion that a glance from the window seemed simply to prove that the plains of Texas were pouring eastward. Vast flats of green grass, dull-hued spaces of mesquit and cactus, little groups of frame houses, woods of light and tender trees, all were sweeping into the east, sweeping over the horizon, a precipice.

A newly married pair had boarded this coach at San Antonio. The man's face was reddened from many days in the wind and sun, and a direct result of his new black clothes was that his brick-colored hands were constantly performing in a most conscious fashion. From time to time he looked down respectfully at his attire. He sat with a hand on each knee, like a man waiting in a barber's shop. The glances he devoted to other passengers were furtive and shy.

The bride was not pretty, nor was she very young. She wore a dress of blue cashmere, with small reservations of velvet here and there, and with steel buttons abounding. She continually twisted her head to regard her puff sleeves, very stiff, straight, and high. They embarrassed her. It was quite apparent that she had cooked, and that she expected to cook, dutifully. The blushes caused by the careless scrutiny of some passengers as she had entered the car were strange to see upon this plain, under-class countenance, which was drawn in placid, almost emotionless lines.

They were evidently very happy. "Ever been in a parlor-car before?" he asked, smiling with delight.

"No," she answered; "I never was. It's fine, ain't it?"   5

"Great! And then after a while we'll go forward to the diner, and get a big lay-out. Finest meal in the world. Charge a dollar."

"Oh, do they?" cried the bride. "Charge a dollar? Why, that's too much — for us — ain't it, Jack?"

"Not this trip, anyhow," he answered bravely. "We're going to go the whole thing."

Later he explained to her about the trains. "You see, it's a thousand miles from one end of Texas to the other; and this train runs right across it, and never stops but four times." He had the pride of an owner. He pointed out to her the dazzling fittings of the coach; and in truth her eyes opened wider as she contemplated the sea-green figured velvet, the shining brass, silver, and glass, the wood that gleamed as darkly brilliant as the surface of a pool of oil. At one end a bronze figure sturdily held a support for a separated chamber, and at convenient places on the ceiling were frescoes in olive and silver.

To the minds of the pair, their surroundings reflected the glory of   10
their marriage that morning in San Antonio; this was the environment of their new estate; and the man's face in particular beamed with an elation that made him appear ridiculous to the negro porter. This individual at times surveyed them from afar with an amused and superior grin. On other occasions he bullied them with skill in ways that did not make it exactly plain to them that they were being bullied. He subtly used all the manners of the most unconquerable kind of snobbery. He oppressed them; but of this oppression they had small knowledge, and they speedily forgot that infrequently a number of travelers covered them with stares of derisive enjoyment. Historically there was supposed to be something infinitely humorous in their situation.

"We are due in Yellow Sky at 3:42," he said, looking tenderly into her eyes.

"Oh, are we?" she said, as if she had not been aware of it. To evince surprise at her husband's statement was part of her wifely amiability. She took from a pocket a little silver watch; and as she held it before her, and stared at it with a frown of attention, the new husband's face shone.

"I bought it in San Anton' from a friend of mine," he told her gleefully.

"It's seventeen minutes past twelve," she said, looking up at him with a kind of shy and clumsy coquetry. A passenger, noting this play, grew excessively sardonic, and winked at himself in one of the numerous mirrors.

At last they went to the dining-car. Two rows of negro waiters, in glowing white suits, surveyed their entrance with the interest, and also the equanimity, of men who had been forewarned. The pair fell to the lot of a waiter who happened to feel pleasure in steering them through their meal. He viewed them with the manner of a fatherly pilot, his countenance radiant with benevolence. The patronage, entwined with the ordinary deference, was not plain to them. And yet, as they returned to their coach, they showed in their faces a sense of escape.

To the left, miles down a long purple slope, was a little ribbon of mist where moved the keening Rio Grande. The train was approaching it at an angle, and the apex was Yellow Sky. Presently it was apparent that, as the distance from Yellow Sky grew shorter, the husband became commensurately restless. His brick-red hands were more insistent in their prominence. Occasionally he was even rather absent-minded and far-away when the bride leaned forward and addressed him.

As a matter of truth, Jack Potter was beginning to find the shadow of a deed weigh upon him like a leaden slab. He, the town marshal of Yellow Sky, a man known, liked, and feared in his corner, a prominent person, had gone to San Antonio to meet a girl he believed he loved, and there, after the usual prayers, had actually induced her to marry him, without consulting Yellow Sky for any part of the transaction. He was now bringing his bride before an innocent and unsuspecting community.

Of course people in Yellow Sky married as it pleased them in accordance with a general custom; but such was Potter's thought of his duty to his friends, or of their idea of his duty, or of an unspoken form which does not control men in these matters, that he felt he was heinous. He had committed an extraordinary crime. Face to face with this girl in San Antonio, and spurred by his sharp impulse, he had gone headlong over all the social hedges. At San Antonio he was like a man hidden in the dark. A knife to sever any friendly duty, any form, was easy to his hand in that remote city. But the hour of Yellow Sky — the hour of daylight — was approaching.

He knew full well that his marriage was an important thing to his town. It could only be exceeded by the burning of the new hotel. His friends could not forgive him. Frequently he had reflected on the advisability of telling them by telegraph, but a new cowardice had been upon

15

him. He feared to do it. And now the train was hurrying him toward a scene of amazement, glee, and reproach. He glanced out of the window at the line of haze swinging slowly in toward the train.

Yellow Sky had a kind of brass band, which played painfully, to the delight of the populace. He laughed without heart as he thought of it. If the citizens could dream of his prospective arrival with his bride, they would parade the band at the station and escort them, amid cheers and laughing congratulations, to his adobe home.

He resolved that he would use all the devices of speed and plains-craft in making the journey from the station to his house. Once within that safe citadel, he could issue some sort of vocal bulletin, and then not go among the citizens until they had time to wear off a little of their enthusiasm.

The bride looked anxiously at him. "What's worrying you, Jack?"

He laughed again. "I'm not worrying, girl; I'm only thinking of Yellow Sky."

She flushed in comprehension.

A sense of mutual guilt invaded their minds and developed a finer tenderness. They looked at each other with eyes softly aglow. But Potter often laughed the same nervous laugh; the flush upon the bride's face seemed quite permanent.

The traitor to the feelings of Yellow Sky narrowly watched the speeding landscape. "We're nearly there," he said.

Presently the porter came and announced the proximity of Potter's home. He held a brush in his hand, and, with all his airy superiority gone, he brushed Potter's new clothes as the latter slowly turned this way and that way. Potter fumbled out a coin and gave it to the porter, as he had seen others do. It was a heavy and muscle-bound business, as that of a man shoeing his first horse.

The porter took their bag, and as the train began to slow they moved forward to the hooded platform of the car. Presently the two engines and their long string of coaches rushed into the station of Yellow Sky.

"They have to take water here," said Potter, from a constricted throat and in mournful cadence, as one announcing death. Before the train stopped his eye had swept the length of the platform, and he was glad and astonished to see there was none upon it but the station-agent, who, with a slightly hurried and anxious air, was walking toward the water-tanks. When the train had halted, the porter alighted first, and placed in position a little temporary step.

"Come on, girl," said Potter, hoarsely. As he helped her down they each laughed on a false note. He took the bag from the negro, and bade his wife cling to his arm. As they slunk rapidly away, his hang-dog glance perceived that they were unloading the two trunks, and also that the station-agent, far ahead near the baggage-car, had turned and was running toward him, making gestures. He laughed, and groaned as he laughed, when he noted the first effect of his marital bliss upon Yellow

Sky. He gripped his wife's arm firmly to his side, and they fled. Behind them the porter stood, chuckling fatuously.

II

The California express on the Southern Railway was due at Yellow Sky in twenty-one minutes. There were six men at the bar of the Weary Gentleman saloon. One was a drummer° who talked a great deal and rapidly; three were Texans who did not care to talk at that time; and two were Mexican sheep-herders, who did not talk as a general practice in the Weary Gentleman saloon. The barkeeper's dog lay on the board walk that crossed in front of the door. His head was on his paws, and he glanced drowsily here and there with the constant vigilance of a dog that is kicked on occasion. Across the sandy street were some vivid green grass-plots, so wonderful in appearance, amid the sands that burned near them in a blazing sun, that they caused a doubt in the mind. They exactly resembled the grass mats used to represent lawns on the stage. At the cooler end of the railway station, a man without a coat sat in a tilted chair and smoked his pipe. The fresh-cut bank of the Rio Grande circled near the town, and there could be seen beyond it a great plum-colored plain of mesquit.

Save for the busy drummer and his companions in the saloon, Yellow Sky was dozing. The new-comer leaned gracefully upon the bar, and recited many tales with the confidence of a bard who has come upon a new field.

"—and at the moment that the old man fell downstairs with the bureau in his arms, the old woman was coming up with two scuttles of coal, and of course—"

The drummer's tale was interrupted by a young man who suddenly appeared in the open door. He cried: "Scratchy Wilson's drunk, and has turned loose with both hands." The two Mexicans at once set down their glasses and faded out of the rear entrance of the saloon.

The drummer, innocent and jocular, answered: "All right, old man. 35 S'pose he has? Come in and have a drink, anyhow."

But the information had made such an obvious cleft in every skull in the room that the drummer was obliged to see its importance. All had become instantly solemn. "Say," said he, mystified, "what is this?" His three companions made the introductory gesture of eloquent speech; but the young man at the door forestalled them.

"It means, my friend," he answered, as he came into the saloon, "that for the next two hours this town won't be a health resort."

The barkeeper went to the door, and locked and barred it; reaching out of the window, he pulled in heavy wooden shutters, and barred them. Immediately a solemn, chapel-like gloom was upon the place. The drummer was looking from one to another.

"But, say," he cried, "what is this, anyhow? You don't mean there is going to be a gun-fight?"

drummer: Traveling salesman.

"Don't know whether there'll be a fight or not," answered one man, grimly; "but there'll be some shootin'—some good shootin'." 40

The young man who had warned them waved his hand. "Oh, there'll be a fight fast enough, if any one wants it. Anybody can get a fight out there in the street. There's a fight just waiting."

The drummer seemed to be swayed between the interest of a foreigner and a perception of personal danger.

"What did you say his name was?" he asked.

"Scratchy Wilson," they answered in chorus.

"And will he kill anybody? What are you going to do? Does this happen often? Does he rampage around like this once a week or so? Can he break in that door?" 45

"No; he can't break down that door," replied the barkeeper. "He's tried it three times. But when he comes you'd better lay down on the floor, stranger. He's dead sure to shoot at it, and a bullet may come through."

Thereafter the drummer kept a strict eye upon the door. The time had not yet called for him to hug the floor, but, as a minor precaution, he sidled near the wall. "Will he kill anybody?" he said again.

The men laughed low and scornfully at the question.

"He's out to shoot, and he's out for trouble. Don't see any good in experimentin' with him."

"But what do you do in a case like this? What do you do?" 50

A man responded: "Why, he and Jack Potter—"

"But," in chorus the other men interrupted, "Jack Potter's in San Anton'."

"Well, who is he? What's he got to do with it?"

"Oh, he's the town marshal. He goes out and fights Scratchy when he gets on one of these tears."

"Wow!" said the drummer, mopping his brow. "Nice job he's got." 55

The voices had toned away to mere whisperings. The drummer wished to ask further questions, which were born of an increasing anxiety and bewilderment; but when he attempted them, the men merely looked at him in irritation and motioned him to remain silent. A tense waiting hush was upon them. In the deep shadows of the room their eyes shone as they listened for sounds from the street. One man made three gestures at the barkeeper; and the latter, moving like a ghost, handed him a glass and a bottle. The man poured a full glass of whisky, and set down the bottle noiselessly. He gulped the whisky in a swallow, and turned again toward the door in immovable silence. The drummer saw that the barkeeper, without a sound, had taken a Winchester from beneath the bar. Later he saw this individual beckoning to him, so he tiptoed across the room.

"You better come with me back of the bar."

"No thanks," said the drummer, perspiring; "I'd rather be where I can make a break for the back door."

Whereupon the man of bottles made a kindly but peremptory gesture. The drummer obeyed it, and, finding himself seated on a box with his head below the level of the bar, balm was laid upon his soul at sight of various zinc and copper fittings that bore a resemblance to armor-plate. The barkeeper took a seat comfortably upon an adjacent box.

"You see," he whispered, "this here Scratchy Wilson is a wonder with a gun—a perfect wonder; and when he goes on the war-trail, we hunt our holes—naturally. He's about the last one of the old gang that used to hang out along the river here. He's a terror when he's drunk. When he's sober he's all right—kind of simple—wouldn't hurt a fly—nicest fellow in town. But when he's drunk—whoo!" 60

There were periods of stillness. "I wish Jack Potter was back from San Anton'," said the barkeeper. "He shot Wilson up once—in the leg—and he would sail in and pull out the kinks in this thing."

Presently they heard from a distance the sound of a shot, followed by three wild yowls. It instantly removed a bond from the men in the darkened saloon. There was a shuffling of feet. They looked at each other. "Here he comes," they said.

III

A man in a maroon-colored flannel shirt, which had been purchased for purposes of decoration, and made principally by some Jewish women on the East Side of New York, rounded a corner and walked into the middle of the main street of Yellow Sky. In either hand the man held a long, heavy, blue-black revolver. Often he yelled, and these cries rang through a semblance of a deserted village, shrilly flying over the roofs in a volume that seemed to have no relation to the ordinary vocal strength of a man. It was as if the surrounding stillness formed the arch of a tomb over him. These cries of ferocious challenge rang against walls of silence. And his boots had red tops with gilded imprints, of the kind beloved in winter by little sledding boys on the hillsides of New England.

The man's face flamed in a rage begot of whisky. His eyes, rolling, and yet keen for ambush, hunted the still doorways and windows. He walked with the creeping movement of the midnight cat. As it occurred to him, he roared menacing information. The long revolvers in his hands were as easy as straws; they were removed with an electric swiftness. The little fingers of each hand played sometimes in a musician's way. Plain from the low collar of the shirt, the cords of his neck straightened and sank, straightened and sank, as passion moved him. The only sounds were his terrible invitations. The calm adobes preserved their demeanor at the passing of this small thing in the middle of the street.

There was no offer of fight—no offer of fight. The man called to the sky. There were no attractions. He bellowed and fumed and swayed his revolvers here and everywhere. 65

The dog of the barkeeper of the Weary Gentleman saloon had not appreciated the advance of events. He yet lay dozing in front of his master's door. At sight of the dog, the man paused and raised his revolver humorously. At sight of the man, the dog sprang up and walked diagonally away, with a sullen head, and growling. The man yelled, and the dog broke into a gallop. As it was about to enter the alley, there was a loud noise, a whistling, and something spat the ground directly before it. The dog screamed, and, wheeling in terror, galloped headlong in a new direction. Again there was a noise, a whistling, and sand was kicked viciously before it. Fear-stricken, the dog turned and flurried like an animal in a pen. The man stood laughing, his weapons at his hips.

Ultimately the man was attracted by the closed door of the Weary Gentleman saloon. He went to it and, hammering with a revolver, demanded drink.

The door remaining imperturbable, he picked a bit of paper from the walk, and nailed it to the framework with a knife. He then turned his back contemptuously upon this popular resort and, walking to the opposite side of the street and spinning there on his heel quickly and lithely, fired at the bit of paper. He missed it by a half inch. He swore at himself, and went away. Later he comfortably fusilladed the windows of his most intimate friend. The man was playing with this town; it was a toy for him.

But still there was no offer of fight. The name of Jack Potter, his ancient antagonist, entered his mind, and he concluded that it would be a glad thing if he should go to Potter's house, and by bombardment induce him to come out and fight. He moved in the direction of his desire, chanting Apache scalp-music.

When he arrived at it, Potter's house presented the same still front 70 as had the other adobes. Taking up a strategic position, the man howled a challenge. But this house regarded him as might a great stone god. It gave no sign. After a decent wait, the man howled further challenges, mingling with them wonderful epithets.

Presently there came the spectacle of a man churning himself into deepest rage over the immobility of a house. He fumed at it as the winter wind attacks a prairie cabin in the North. To the distance there should have gone the sound of a tumult like the fighting of two hundred Mexicans. As necessity bade him, he paused for breath or to reload his revolvers.

IV

Potter and his bride walked sheepishly and with speed. Sometimes they laughed together shamefacedly and low.

"Next corner, dear," he said finally.

They put forth the efforts of a pair walking bowed against a strong wind. Potter was about to raise a finger to point the first appearance of the new home when, as they circled the corner, they came face to face with a man in a maroon-colored shirt, who was feverishly pushing cartridges into a large revolver. Upon the instant the man dropped his revolver to the ground and, like lightning, whipped another from its holster. The second weapon was aimed at the bridegroom's chest.

There was a silence. Potter's mouth seemed to be merely a grave for 75 his tongue. He exhibited an instinct to at once loosen his arm from the woman's grip, and he dropped the bag to the sand. As for the bride, her face had gone as yellow as old cloth. She was a slave to hideous rites, gazing at the apparitional snake.

The two men faced each other at a distance of three paces. He of the revolver smiled with a new and quiet ferocity.

"Tried to sneak up on me," he said. "Tried to sneak up on me!" His eyes grew more baleful. As Potter made a slight movement, the man thrust his revolver venomously forward. "No, don't you do it, Jack Potter. Don't you move a finger toward a gun just yet. Don't you move an eyelash. The time has come for me to settle with you and I'm goin' to do it my own way, and loaf along with no interferin'. So if you don't want a gun bent on you, just mind what I tell you."

Potter looked at his enemy. "I ain't got a gun on me, Scratchy," he said. "Honest, I ain't." He was stiffening and steadying, but yet somewhere at the back of his mind a vision of the Pullman floated: the seagreen figured velvet, the shining brass, silver, and glass, the wood that gleamed as darkly brilliant as the surface of a pool of oil—all the glory of marriage, the environment of the new estate. "You know I fight when it comes to fighting, Scratchy Wilson; but I ain't got a gun on me. You'll have to do all the shootin' yourself."

His enemy's face went livid. He stepped forward, and lashed his weapon to and fro before Potter's chest. "Don't you tell me you ain't got no gun on you, you whelp. Don't tell me no lie like that. There ain't a man in Texas ever seen you without no gun. Don't take me for no kid." His eyes blazed with light, and his throat worked like a pump.

"I ain't takin' you for no kid," answered Potter. His heels had not   80 moved an inch backward. "I'm takin' you for a damn fool. I tell you I ain't got a gun, and I ain't. If you're goin' to shoot me up, you better begin now; you'll never get a chance like this again."

So much enforced reasoning had told on Wilson's rage; he was calmer. "If you ain't got a gun, why ain't you got a gun?" he sneered. "Been to Sunday-school?"

"I ain't got a gun because I've just come from San Anton' with my wife. I'm married," said Potter. "And if I'd thought there was going to be any galoots like you prowling around when I brought my wife home, I'd had a gun, and don't you forget it."

"Married!" said Scratchy, not at all comprehending.

"Yes, married. I'm married," said Potter, distinctly.

"Married?" said Scratchy. Seemingly for the first time, he saw the   85 drooping, drowning woman at the other man's side. "No!" he said. He was like a creature allowed a glimpse of another world. He moved a pace backward, and his arm, with the revolver, dropped to his side. "Is this the lady?" he asked.

"Yes; this is the lady," answered Potter.

There was another period of silence.

"Well," said Wilson at last, slowly, "I s'pose it's all off now."

"It's all off if you say so, Scratchy. You know I didn't make the trouble." Potter lifted his valise.

"Well, I 'low it's off, Jack," said Wilson. He was looking at the ground. "Married!" He was not a student of chivalry; it was merely that in the presence of this foreign condition he was a simple child of the earlier plains. He picked up his starboard revolver, and, placing both weapons in their holsters, he went away. His feet made funnel-shaped tracks in the heavy sand.

CONSIDERATIONS FOR CRITICAL THINKING AND WRITING

1. **FIRST RESPONSE.** Think of a western you've read or seen: any of Larry McMurtry's books would work, such as *Lonesome Dove* or *Evening Star*. Compare and contrast the setting, characters, action, and theme in Crane's story with your western.

2. What is the nature of the conflict Marshal Potter feels on the train in Part I? Why does he feel that he committed a "crime" in bringing home a bride to Yellow Sky?

3. What is the function of the "drummer," the traveling salesman, in Part II?

4. What is the significance of the setting?

5. Is Scratchy Wilson too drunk, comical, and ineffective to be a sympathetic character? What is the meaning of his conceding that "I s'pose it's all off now" at the end of Part IV? Is he a dynamic or a static character?

6. What details seem to support the story's theme? Consider, for example, the descriptions of the bride's clothes and Scratchy Wilson's shirt and boots.

7. Explain why the heroes in western stories are rarely married and why Crane's use of marriage is central to his theme.

8. **CONNECTION TO ANOTHER SELECTION.** Write an essay comparing Crane's use of suspense with William Faulkner's in "A Rose for Emily" (p. 52).

EDGAR ALLAN POE (1809–1849)

Edgar Allan Poe grew up in the home of John Allan, in Richmond, Virginia, after his mother died in 1811, and he was educated in Scotland and England for five years before completing his classical education in Richmond. After a short stint at the University of Virginia, Poe went to Boston, where he began publishing his poetry. His foster father sent him to West Point Military Academy, but Poe was expelled and moved on to New York, where he published a book of poems inspired by the Romantic movement. Moving among

Courtesy of the Library of Congress.

editorial jobs in Baltimore, Richmond, and New York, Poe married his thirteen-year-old cousin Virginia Clemm. Early in his story-writing career, Poe published his only novel-length piece, *The Narrative of Arthur Gordon Pym* (1838), and the following year, he began to work in the genre of the supernatural and horrible, with the stories "William Wilson" and "The Fall of the House of Usher." He gained publicity with the detective story "The Murders in the Rue Morgue," became nationally famous with the publication of his poem "The Raven" in 1845, and died four years later in Baltimore after a drinking binge. Poe theorized that the short story writer should plan every word toward the achievement of a certain effect, and that stories should be read in a single sitting. Morbidity and dreamlike flights of fancy, for which Poe is often recognized, do not detract from his lucid crafting of suspense and his erudite control of language and symbol.

The Cask of Amontillado   1846

The thousand injuries of Fortunato I had borne as I best could; but when he ventured upon insult, I vowed revenge. You, who so well know the nature of my soul, will not suppose, however, that I gave utterance to a threat. *At length* I would be avenged; this was a point definitely settled—but the very definitiveness with which it was resolved precluded the idea of risk. I must not only punish, but punish with impunity. A wrong is unredressed when retribution overtakes its redresser. It is equally unredressed when the avenger fails to make himself felt as such to him who has done the wrong.

It must be understood, that neither by word nor deed had I given Fortunato cause to doubt my good-will. I continued, as was my wont, to smile in his face, and he did not perceive that my smile *now* was at the thought of his immolation.

He had a weak point—this Fortunato—although in other regards he was a man to be respected and even feared. He prided himself on his connoisseurship in wine. Few Italians have the true virtuoso spirit. For the most part their enthusiasm is adopted to suit the time and opportunity—to practise imposture upon the British and Austrian *millionnaires*. In painting and gemmary Fortunato, like his countrymen, was a quack—but in the matter of old wines he was sincere. In this respect I did not differ from him materially: I was skilful in the Italian vintages myself, and bought largely whenever I could.

It was about dusk, one evening during the supreme madness of the carnival season, that I encountered my friend. He accosted me with excessive warmth, for he had been drinking much. The man wore motley. He had on a tight-fitting parti-striped dress, and his head was surmounted by the conical cap and bells. I was so pleased to see him, that I thought I should never have done wringing his hand.

I said to him: "My dear Fortunato, you are luckily met. How remark- 5
ably well you are looking to-day! But I have received a pipe° of what
passes for Amontillado, and I have my doubts."

"How?" said he. "Amontillado? A pipe? Impossible! And in the
middle of the carnival!"

"I have my doubts," I replied; "and I was silly enough to pay the full
Amontillado price without consulting you in the matter. You were not to
be found, and I was fearful of losing a bargain."

"Amontillado!"

"I have my doubts."

"Amontillado!"   10

"And I must satisfy them."

"Amontillado!"

"As you are engaged, I am on my way to Luchesi. If any one has a
critical turn, it is he. He will tell me——"

"Luchesi cannot tell Amontillado from Sherry."

"And yet some fools will have it that his taste is a match for your   15
own."

"Come, let us go."

"Whither?"

"To your vaults."

"My friend, no; I will not impose upon your good nature. I perceive
you have an engagement. Luchesi——"

"I have no engagement;—come."   20

"My friend, no. It is not the engagement, but the severe cold with
which I perceive you are afflicted. The vaults are insufferably damp. They
are encrusted with nitre."

"Let us go, nevertheless. The cold is merely nothing. Amontillado!
You have been imposed upon. And as for Luchesi, he cannot distinguish
Sherry from Amontillado."

Thus speaking, Fortunato possessed himself of my arm. Putting on
a mask of black silk, and drawing a *roquelaire*° closely about my person, I
suffered him to hurry me to my palazzo.

There were no attendants at home; they had absconded to make
merry in honor of the time. I had told them that I should not return
until the morning, and had given them explicit orders not to stir from
the house. These orders were sufficient, I well knew, to insure their
immediate disappearance, one and all, as soon as my back was turned.

I took from their sconces two flambeaux, and giving one to Fortu-   25
nato, bowed him through several suites of rooms to the archway that led
into the vaults. I passed down a long and winding staircase, requesting
him to be cautious as he followed. We came at length to the foot of the

pipe: A large keg.
roquelaire: A short cloak.

descent, and stood together on the damp ground of the catacombs of the Montresors.

The gait of my friend was unsteady, and the bells upon his cap jingled as he strode.

"The pipe?" said he.

"It is farther on," said I; "but observe the white web-work which gleams from these cavern walls."

He turned toward me, and looked into my eyes with two filmy orbs that distilled the rheum of intoxication.

"Nitre?" he asked, at length.   30

"Nitre," I replied. "How long have you had that cough?"

"Ugh! ugh! ugh! — ugh! ugh! ugh! — ugh! ugh! ugh! — ugh! ugh! ugh! — ugh! ugh! ugh!"

My poor friend found it impossible to reply for many minutes.

"It is nothing," he said, at last.

"Come," I said, with decision, "we will go back; your health is precious.   35
You are rich, respected, admired, beloved; you are happy, as once I was. You are a man to be missed. For me it is no matter. We will go back; you will be ill, and I cannot be responsible. Besides, there is Luchesi ——"

"Enough," he said; "the cough is a mere nothing; it will not kill me. I shall not die of a cough."

"True — true," I replied; "and, indeed, I had no intention of alarming you unnecessarily; but you should use all proper caution. A draught of this Medoc will defend us from the damps."

Here I knocked off the neck of a bottle which I drew from a long row of its fellows that lay upon the mould.

"Drink," I said, presenting him the wine.

He raised it to his lips with a leer. He paused and nodded to me   40
familiarly, while his bells jingled.

"I drink," he said, "to the buried that repose around us."

"And I to your long life."

He again took my arm, and we proceeded.

"These vaults," he said, "are extensive."

"The Montresors," I replied, "were a great and numerous family."   45

"I forget your arms."

"A huge human foot d'or,° in a field azure; the foot crushes a serpent rampant whose fangs are imbedded in the heel."

"And the motto?"

"*Nemo me impune lacessit.*"°

"Good!" he said.   50

The wine sparkled in his eyes and the bells jingled. My own fancy grew warm with the Medoc. We had passed through walls of piled bones, with casks and puncheons intermingling into the inmost recesses of the

---

d'or: Of gold.

Nemo . . . lacessit (Latin): No one wounds me with impunity.

catacombs. I paused again, and this time I made bold to seize Fortunato by an arm above the elbow.

"The nitre!" I said; "see, it increases. It hangs like moss upon the vaults. We are below the river's bed. The drops of moisture trickle among the bones. Come, we will go back ere it is too late. Your cough——"

"It is nothing," he said; "let us go on. But first, another draught of the Medoc."

I broke and reached him a flagon of De Grâve. He emptied it at a breath. His eyes flashed with a fierce light. He laughed and threw the bottle upward with a gesticulation I did not understand.

I looked at him in surprise. He repeated the movement—a grotesque 55 one.

"You do not comprehend?" he said.

"Not I," I replied.

"Then you are not of the brotherhood."

"How?"

"You are not of the masons." 60

"Yes, yes," I said; "yes, yes."

"You? Impossible! A mason?"

"A mason," I replied.

"A sign," he said.

"It is this," I answered, producing a trowel from beneath the folds of 65 my *roquelaire*.

"You jest," he exclaimed, recoiling a few paces. "But let us proceed to the Amontillado."

"Be it so," I said, replacing the tool beneath the cloak, and again offering him my arm. He leaned upon it heavily. We continued our route in search of the Amontillado. We passed through a range of low arches, descended, passed on, and descending again, arrived at a deep crypt, in which the foulness of the air caused our flambeaux rather to glow than flame.

At the most remote end of the crypt there appeared another less spacious. Its walls had been lined with human remains, piled to the vault overhead, in the fashion of the great catacombs of Paris. Three sides of this interior crypt were still ornamented in this manner. From the fourth the bones had been thrown down, and lay promiscuously upon the earth, forming at one point a mound of some size. Within the wall thus exposed by the displacing of the bones, we perceived a still interior recess, in depth about four feet, in width three, in height six or seven. It seemed to have been constructed for no especial use within itself, but formed merely the interval between two of the colossal supports of the roof of the catacombs, and was backed by one of their circumscribing walls of solid granite.

It was in vain that Fortunato, uplifting his dull torch, endeavored to pry into the depth of the recess. Its termination the feeble light did not enable us to see.

"Proceed," I said; "herein is the Amontillado. As for Luchesi——" 70

"He is an ignoramus," interrupted my friend, as he stepped unsteadily forward, while I followed immediately at his heels. In an instant he had reached the extremity of the niche, and finding his progress arrested by the rock, stood stupidly bewildered. A moment more and I had fettered him to the granite. In its surface were two iron staples, distant from each other about two feet, horizontally. From one of these depended a short chain, from the other a padlock. Throwing the links about his waist, it was but the work of a few seconds to secure it. He was too much astounded to resist. Withdrawing the key I stepped back from the recess.

"Pass your hand," I said, "over the wall; you cannot help feeling the nitre. Indeed it is *very* damp. Once more let me *implore* you to return. No? Then I must positively leave you. But I must first render you all the little attentions in my power."

"The Amontillado!" ejaculated my friend, not yet recovered from his astonishment.

"True," I replied; "the Amontillado."

As I said these words I busied myself among the pile of bones of which I have before spoken. Throwing them aside, I soon uncovered a quantity of building stone and mortar. With these materials and with the aid of my trowel, I began vigorously to wall up the entrance of the niche.

I had scarcely laid the first tier of the masonry when I discovered that the intoxication of Fortunato had in a great measure worn off. The earliest indication I had of this was a low moaning cry from the depth of the recess. It was *not* the cry of a drunken man. There was then a long and obstinate silence. I laid the second tier, and the third, and the fourth; and then I heard the furious vibrations of the chain. The noise lasted for several minutes, during which, that I might hearken to it with the more satisfaction, I ceased my labors and sat down upon the bones. When at last the clanking subsided, I resumed the trowel, and finished without interruption the fifth, the sixth, and the seventh tier. The wall was now nearly upon a level with my breast. I again paused, and holding the flambeaux over the masonwork, threw a few feeble rays upon the figure within.

A succession of loud and shrill screams, bursting suddenly from the throat of the chained form, seemed to thrust me violently back. For a brief moment I hesitated—I trembled. Unsheathing my rapier, I began to grope with it about the recess; but the thought of an instant reassured me. I placed my hand upon the solid fabric of the catacombs, and felt satisfied. I reapproached the wall. I replied to the yells of him who clamored. I reechoed—I aided—I surpassed them in volume and in strength. I did this, and the clamorer grew still.

It was now midnight, and my task was drawing to a close. I had completed the eighth, the ninth, and the tenth tier. I had finished a portion of the last and the eleventh; there remained but a single stone to be fitted and plastered in. I struggled with its weight; I placed it partially in its

75

destined position. But now there came from out the niche a low laugh that erected the hairs upon my head. It was succeeded by a sad voice, which I had difficulty in recognizing as that of the noble Fortunato. The voice said—

"Ha! ha! ha!—he! he!—a very good joke indeed—an excellent jest. We will have many a rich laugh about it at the palazzo—he! he! he!—over our wine—he! he! he!"

"The Amontillado!" I said.   80

"He! he! he!—he! he! he!—yes, the Amontillado. But is it not getting late? Will not they be awaiting us at the palazzo, the Lady Fortunato and the rest? Let us be gone."

"Yes," I said, "let us be gone."

"*For the love of God, Montresor!*"

"Yes," I said, "for the love of God!"

But to these words I hearkened in vain for a reply. I grew impatient. I   85 called aloud:

"Fortunato!"

No answer. I called again:

"Fortunato!"

No answer still, I thrust a torch through the remaining aperture and let it fall within. There came forth in return only a jingling of the bells. My heart grew sick—on account of the dampness of the catacombs. I hastened to make an end of my labor. I forced the last stone into its position; I plastered it up. Against the new masonry I re-erected the old rampart of bones. For the half of a century no mortal has disturbed them. *In pace requiescat!*°

In pace requiescat! (Latin): In peace may he rest!

CONSIDERATIONS FOR CRITICAL THINKING AND WRITING

1. FIRST RESPONSE. How does this narrative compare as a "horror story" with versions of that genre you might have seen or read?

2. Explain how Poe creates suspense in this plot.

3. Characterize the narrator. What motivates his behavior?

4. Why do you think Poe never reveals Fortunato's original insult to the narrator?

5. Discuss the moments of irony in the story. How do they affect its tone?

6. How do you account for the narrator's sick feeling in the final paragraph? What does this suggest about the story's possible themes?

7. CONNECTION TO ANOTHER SELECTION. Compare the treatment of revenge in "The Cask of Amontillado" and in one of the following: William Faulkner's "A Rose for Emily" (p. 52), Andre Dubus's "Killings" (p. 60), or Joyce Carol Oates's "Hi Howya Doin" (p. 214).

Joyce Carol Oates (b. 1938)

Raised in upstate New York, Joyce Carol
Oates earned degrees at Syracuse University and the University of Wisconsin. Both
the range and volume of her writing are
extensive. A writer of novels, plays, short
stories, poetry, and literary criticism, she
has published over eighty books. Oates
has described the subject matter of her fiction as "real people in a real society," but
her method of expression ranges from the
realistic to the experimental. Her novels
include *them* (1969), *Do with Me What You
Will* (1973), *Childwold* (1976), *Bellefleur* (1980),
A Bloodsmoor Romance (1982), *Marya: A Life*
(1986), *You Must Remember This* (1987), *Black*

Reprinted by permission of Beth Gwinn.

Water (1992), *I'll Take You There* (2003), *Missing Mom* (2005), and *Mudwoman*
(2012). Among her collections of short stories are *Marriages and Infidelities*
(1972), *Raven's Wing* (1986), *The Assignation* (1988), *Heat* (1991), *Haunted: Tales
of the Grotesque* (1994), *Will You Always Love Me? and Other Stories* (1996),
The Collector of Hearts (1998), *Small Avalanches and Other Stories* (2004), *High
Lonesome: New and Selected Stories 1966–2006* (2006), *Dear Husband* (2009),
and *The Corn Maiden and Other Stories* (2011). This story's style is a fascinating exercise in creating tension.

Hi Howya Doin   2007

Good-looking husky guy six-foot-four in late twenties or early thirties,
Caucasian male, as the initial police report will note, he's solid-built as a
fire hydrant, carries himself like an athlete, or an ex-athlete just percep-
tibly thickening at the waist, otherwise in terrific condition like a bronze
figure in motion, sinewy arms pumping as he runs, long muscled legs,
chiseled-muscled calves, he's hurtling along the moist woodchip path at
the western edge of the university arboretum at approximately six P.M.,
Thursday evening, and there comes, from the other direction, a woman
jogger on the path, female in her late thirties, flushed face, downturned
eyes, dark hair threaded with gray like cobwebs, an awkward runner,
fleshy lips parted, holds her arms stiff at her sides, in a shrunken pull-
over shirt with a faded tiger cat on its front, not-large but sizable breasts
shaking as she runs, mimicked in the slight shaking of her cheeks, and
her hips in carrot-colored sweatpants, this is Madeline Hersey frowning
at the woodchip path before her, Madeline's exasperating habit of staring at the ground when she runs, oblivious of the arboretum, though at
this time in May it's dazzling with white dogwood, pink dogwood, vivid

yellow forsythia, Madeline is a lab technician at Squibb, lost in a laby-
rinth of her own tangled thoughts (career, lover, lover's "learning
disabled" child), startled out of her reverie by the loud aggressive-
friendly greeting *Hi! Howya doin!* flung out at her like a playful slap on
the buttocks as the tall husky jogger passes Madeline with the most
fleeting of glances, big-toothed bemused smile, and Madeline loses her
stride, in a faltering voice *Fine — thank you —* but the other jogger is past,
unhearing and now on the gravel path behind the university hospital,
now on the grassy towpath beside the old canal, in the greenly lushness
of University Dells Park where, in the late afternoon, into dusk joggers
are running singly and in couples, in groups of three or more, track-
team runners from the local high school, college students, white-haired
older runners both male and female, to these the husky jogger in skin-
tight mustard-yellow T-shirt, short navy-blue shorts showing his chiseled thigh muscles, size-twelve Nikes calls out *Hi Howya doin* in a big
bland booming voice, *Hi Howya doin* and a flash of big horsy teeth, long
pumping legs, pumping arms, it's his practice to come up close behind
a solitary jogger, a woman maybe, a girl, or an older man, so many
"older" men (forties, fifties, sixties, and beyond) in the university community, sometimes a younger guy who's sweated through his clothes,
beginning to breathe through his mouth, size-twelve Nikes striking the
earth like mallets, *Hi! Howya doin!* jolting Kyle Lindeman out of dreamy-
sexy thoughts, jolting Michelle Rossley out of snarled anxious thoughts,
there's Diane Hendricks who'd been an athlete in high school now
twenty pounds overweight, divorced, no kid, replaying in her head a
quarrel she'd had with a woman friend, goddamn she's angry! goddamn she's not going to call Ginny back, this time! trying to calm her
rush of thoughts like churning roiling water, trying to measure her
breaths Zen-fashion, inhale, exhale, inhale and out of nowhere into this
reverie a tall husky hurtling figure bears down upon her, toward her,
veering into her line of vision, instinctively Diane bears to the right to
give him plenty of room to pass her, hopes this is no one she knows
from work, no one who knows her, trying not to look up at him, tall
guy, husky, must weigh two-twenty, works out, has got to be an athlete,
or ex-athlete, a pang of sexual excitement courses through her, or is it
sexual dread even as *Hi! Howya doin!* rings out loud and bemused like an
elbow in Diane's left breast as the stranger pounds past her, in his wake
an odor of male sweat, acrid-briny male sweat and an impression of big
glistening teeth bared in a brainless grin or is it a mock-grin, death's-
head grin? — thrown off stride, self-conscious and stumbling, Diane
manages to stammer *Fine — I'm fine* as if the stranger brushing past her
is interested in her, or in her well-being, in the slightest, what a fool
Diane is! — yet another day, moist bright morning in the university dells
along the path beside the seed-stippled lagoon where amorous-
combative male mallard ducks are pursuing female ducks with much
squawking, flapping of wings, and splashing water, there comes the tall

husky jogger, Caucasian male six-foot-four, two-twenty pounds, no ID
as the initial police report will note, on this occasion the jogger is wearing a skin-tight black Judas Priest T-shirt, very short white-nylon shorts
revealing every surge, ripple, sheen of chiseled thigh muscles, emerging
out of a shadowy pathway at the edge of the birch woods to approach
Dr. Rausch of the university's geology department, older man, just
slightly vain of being "fit," dark-tinted aviator glasses riding the bridge
of his perspiring nose, Dr. Rausch panting as he runs, not running so
fast as he'd like, rivulets of sweat like melting grease down his back,
sides, sweating through his shirt, in baggy khaki shorts to the knee,
Dr. Rausch grinding his jaws in thought (departmental budget cuts! his
youngest daughter's wrecked marriage! his wife's biopsy next morning
at seven A.M., he will drive her to the medical center and wait for her,
return her home and yet somehow get to the tenure committee meeting
he's chairing at eleven A.M.) when *Hi! Howya doin!* jolts Dr. Rausch as if
the husky jogger in the black Judas Priest T-shirt has extended a playful
size-twelve foot into Dr. Rausch's path to trip him, suddenly he's
thrown off-stride, poor old guy, hasn't always been sixty-four years old,
sunken-chested, skinny white legs sprouting individual hairs like wires,
hard little pot belly straining at the unbelted waistline of the khaki
shorts, Dr. Rausch looks up squinting, is this someone he knows?
should know? who knows *him*? across the vertiginous span of thirty
years in the geology department Dr. Rausch has had so many students,
but before he can see who this is, or make a panting effort to reply in the
quick-casual way of youthful joggers, the husky jogger has passed by
Dr. Rausch without a second glance, legs like pistons of muscle, shimmering sweat-film like a halo about his body, fair-brown, russet-brown
hair in curls like wood shavings lifting halo-like from his large uplifted
head, big toothy smile, large broad nose made for deep breathing, enormous dark nostrils that look as if thumbs have been shoved into them,
soon again this shimmering male figure appears on the far side of the
dells, another afternoon on the Institute grounds, hard-pounding feet,
muscled arms pumping, on this day a navy blue T-shirt faded from
numerous launderings, another time the very short navy-blue shorts, as
he runs he exudes a yeasty body odor, sighting a solitary male jogger
ahead he quickens his pace to overtake him, guy in his early twenties,
university student, no athlete, about five-eight, skinny guy, running
with some effort, breathing through his mouth, and in his head a swirl
of numerals, symbols, equations, quantum optics, quantum noise, into
this reverie *Hi! Howya doin* is like a firecracker tossed by a prankish kid,
snappishly the younger jogger replies *I'm okay* as his face flushes, how
like high school, junior high kids pushing him around, in that instant
he's remembering, almost now limping, lost the stride, now life seems
pointless, you know it's pointless, you live, you die, look how his grandfather died, what's the point, there is none, as next day, next week, late
Friday afternoon of the final week in May along the canal towpath past

Linden Road where there are fewer joggers looming up suddenly in your line of vision, approaching you, a tall husky male jogger running in the center of the path, instinctively you bear to the right, instinctively you turn your gaze downward, no eye contact on the towpath, you've been lost in thought, coils of thought like electric currents burning-hot, scalding-hot, the very pain, anguish, futility of your thoughts, for what is your soul but your thoughts, upright flame cupped between your hands silently pleading *Don't speak to me, respect my privacy please* even as the oncoming jogger continues to approach, in the center of the path, inexorably, unstoppably, curly hairs on his arms shimmering with a bronze-roseate glow, big teeth bared in a smile *Hi! Howya doing!* loud and bland and booming mock-friendly, and out of the pocket of your nylon jacket you fumble to remove the snub-nosed, twenty-two-caliber Smith & Wesson revolver you'd stolen from your stepfather's lodge in Jackson Hole, Wyoming, three years before, hateful of the old drunk asshole you'd waited for him to ask if you'd taken it, were you the one to take his gun that's unlicensed, and your stepfather never asked, and you never told, and you lift the toy-like gun in a hand trembling with excitement, with trepidation, with anticipation, aim at the face looming at you like a balloon-face up close and fire and the bullet leaps like magic from the toy-weapon with unexpected force and short-range accuracy and enters the face at the forehead directly above the big-nostriled nose, in an instant the husky jogger in the mustard-yellow T-shirt drops to his knees on the path, already the mustard-yellow T-shirt is splashed with blood, on his belly now and brawny arms outspread, face flattened against the path fallen silent and limp as a cloth puppet when the puppeteer has lost interest and dropped the puppet, he's dead, *That's how I'm doin.*

CONSIDERATIONS FOR CRITICAL THINKING AND WRITING

1. **FIRST RESPONSE.** How is the style of this story particularly suited to jogging?
2. What is the effect of the narrator mentioning the "initial police report" in the second line?
3. Explain how the male jogger is a character foil to Madeline Hersey. How do the other joggers' responses to him further define his character?
4. How might this story be regarded as a kind of sociology of jogging? Consider whether or not it seems like an accurate rendition of it to you.
5. How does Oates subtly convey the passage of time in the narrative?
6. The inevitable question: Is this story funny? Why or why not?
7. **CONNECTION TO ANOTHER SELECTION.** Comment on the ways in which style is related to content in "Hi Howya Doin" and in Rick Moody's "Boys" (p. 238).

DAGOBERTO GILB (B. 1950)

A brief biography and introduction to Dagoberto Gilb's work appear in Chapter 10, "A Study of Dagoberto Gilb: The Author Reflects on Three Stories" (p. 265). Chapter 10 features Gilb's commentaries on three additional stories, as well as nonfiction excerpts from his writing, photographs, manuscript drafts, and an interview.

Romero's Shirt   *1993*

Juan Romero, a man not unlike many in this country, has had jobs in factories, shops, and stores. He has painted houses, dug ditches, planted trees, hammered, sawed, bolted, snaked pipes, picked cotton and chile and pecans, each and all for wages. Along the way he has married and raised his children and several years ago he finally arranged it so that his money might pay for the house he and his family live in. He is still more than twenty years away from being the owner. It is a modest house even by El Paso standards. The building, in an adobe style, is made of stone which is painted white, though the paint is gradually chipping off or being absorbed by the rock. It has two bedrooms, a den which is used as another, a small dining area, a living room, a kitchen, one bathroom, and a garage which, someday, he plans to turn into another place to live. Although in a development facing a paved street and in a neighborhood, it has the appearance of being on almost half an acre. At the front is a garden of cactus — nopal, ocotillo, and agave — and there are weeds that grow tall with yellow flowers which seed into thorn-hard burrs. The rest is dirt and rocks of various sizes, some of which have been lined up to form a narrow path out of the graded dirt, a walkway to the front porch — where, under a tile and one-by tongue and groove overhang, are a wooden chair and a love seat, covered by an old bedspread, its legless frame on the red cement slab. Once the porch looked onto oak trees. Two of them are dried-out stumps; the remaining one has a limb or two which still can produce leaves, but with so many amputations, its future is irreversible. Romero seldom runs water through a garden hose, though in the back yard some patchy grass can almost seem suburban, at least to him, when he does. Near the corner of his land, in the front, next to the sidewalk, is a juniper shrub, his only bright green plant, and Romero does not want it to yellow and die, so he makes special efforts on its behalf, washing off dust, keeping its leaves neatly pruned and shaped.

These days Romero calls himself a handyman. He does odd jobs, which is exactly how he advertises — "no job too small" — in the throwaway paper. He hangs wallpaper and doors, he paints, lays carpet, does just about anything someone will call and ask him to do. It doesn't earn him much, and sometimes it's barely enough, but he's his own boss, and he's had so many bad jobs over those other years, ones no more dependable, he's learned that this suits him. At one time Romero did want more, and he'd believed that he could have it simply through work, but no matter what he did his children still had to be born at the county hospital. Even years later it was there that his oldest son went for serious medical treatment because Romero couldn't afford the private hospitals. He tried not to worry about how he earned his money. In Mexico, where his parents were born and he spent much of his youth, so many things weren't available, and any work which allowed for food, clothes, and housing was to be honored — by the standards there, Romero lived well. Except this wasn't Mexico, and even though there were those who did worse even here, there were many who did better and had more, and a young Romero too often felt ashamed by what he saw as his failure. But time passed, and he got older. As he saw it, he didn't live in poverty, and *here,* he finally came to realize, was where he was, where he and his family were going to stay. Life in El Paso was much like the land — hard, but one could make do with what was offered. Just as his parents had, Romero always thought it was a beautiful place for a home.

Yet people he knew left — to Houston, Dallas, Los Angeles, San Diego, Denver, Chicago — and came back for holidays with stories of high wages and acquisition. And more and more people crossed the river, in rags, taking work, his work, at any price. Romero constantly had to discipline himself by remembering the past, how his parents lived; he had to teach himself to appreciate what he did have. His car, for example, he'd kept up since his early twenties. He'd had it painted three times in that period and he worked on it so devotedly that even now it was in as good a condition as almost any car could be. For his children he tried to offer more — an assortment of clothes for his daughter, lots of toys for his sons. He denied his wife nothing, but she was a woman who asked for little. For himself, it was much less. He owned some work clothes and T-shirts necessary for his jobs as well as a set of good enough, he thought, shirts he'd had since before the car. He kept up a nice pair of custom boots, and in a closet hung a pair of slacks for a wedding or baptism or important mass. He owned two jackets, a leather one from Mexico and a warm nylon one for cold work days. And he owned a wool plaid Pendleton shirt, his favorite piece of clothing, which he'd bought right after the car and before his marriage because it really was good-looking besides being functional. He wore it anywhere and everywhere with confidence that its quality would always be both in style and appropriate.

The border was less than two miles below Romero's home, and he could see, down the dirt street which ran alongside his property, the desert and mountains of Mexico. The street was one of the few in the city which hadn't yet been paved. Romero liked it that way, despite the run-off problems when heavy rains passed by, as they had the day before this day. A night wind had blown hard behind the rains, and the air was so clean he could easily see buildings in Juárez. It was sunny, but a breeze told him to put on his favorite shirt before he pulled the car up alongside the house and dragged over the garden hose to wash it, which was something he still enjoyed doing as much as anything else. He was organized, had a special bucket, a special sponge, and he used warm water from the kitchen sink. When he started soaping the car he worried about getting his shirt sleeves wet, and once he was moving around he decided a T-shirt would keep him warm enough. So he took off the wool shirt and draped it, conspicuously, over the juniper near him, at the corner of his property. He thought that if he couldn't help but see it, he couldn't forget it, and forgetting something outside was losing it. He lived near a school, and teenagers passed by all the time, and also there was regular foot-traffic — many people walked the sidewalk in front of his house, many who had no work.

After the car was washed, Romero went inside and brought out the 5 car wax. Waxing his car was another thing he still liked to do, especially on a weekday like this one when he was by himself, when no one in his family was home. He could work faster, but he took his time, spreading with a damp cloth, waiting, then wiping off the crust with a dry cloth. The exterior done, he went inside the car and waxed the dash, picked up some trash on the floorboard, cleaned out the glove compartment. Then he went for some pliers he kept in a toolbox in the garage, returned and began to wire up the rear license plate which had lost a nut and bolt and was hanging awkwardly. As he did this, he thought of other things he might do when he finished, like prune the juniper. Except his old shears had broken, and he hadn't found another used pair, because he wouldn't buy them new.

An old man walked up to him carrying a garden rake, a hoe, and some shears. He asked Romero if there was some yard work needing to be done. After spring, tall weeds grew in many yards, but it seemed a dumb question this time of year, particularly since there was obviously so little ever to be done in Romero's yard. But Romero listened to the old man. There were still a few weeds over there, and he could rake the dirt so it'd be even and level, he could clip that shrub, and probably there was something in the back if he were to look. Romero was usually brusque with requests such as these, but he found the old man unique and like-able and he listened and finally asked how much he would want for all those tasks. The old man thought as quickly as he spoke and threw out a number. Ten. Romero repeated the number, questioningly, and the old man backed up, saying well, eight, seven. Romero asked if that was for everything. Yes sir, the old man said, excited that he'd seemed to catch a customer. Romero asked if he would cut the juniper for three dollars. The old man kept his eyes on the evergreen, disappointed for a second, then thought better of it. Okay, okay, he said, but, I've been walking all day, you'll give me lunch? The old man rubbed his striped cotton shirt at his stomach.

Romero liked the old man and agreed to it. He told him how he should follow the shape which was already there, to cut it evenly, to take a few inches off all of it just like a haircut. Then Romero went inside, scrambled enough eggs and chile and cheese for both of them and rolled it all in some tortillas. He brought out a beer.

The old man was clearly grateful, but since his gratitude was keeping the work from getting done—he might talk an hour about his little ranch in Mexico, about his little turkeys and his pig—Romero excused himself and went inside. The old man thanked Romero for the food, and, as soon as he was finished with the beer, went after the work sincerely. With dull shears—he sharpened them, so to speak, against a rock wall—the old man snipped garishly, hopping and jumping around the bush, around and around. It gave Romero such great pleasure to watch that this was all he did from his front window.

The work didn't take long, so, as the old man was raking up the clippings, Romero brought out a five-dollar bill. He felt that the old man's dancing around that bush, in those baggy old checkered pants, was more inspiring than religion, and a couple of extra dollars was a cheap price to see old eyes whiten like a boy's.

The old man was so pleased that he invited Romero to that little ranch   10 of his in Mexico where he was sure they could share some aguardiente, or maybe Romero could buy a turkey from him—they were skinny but they could be fattened—but in any case they could enjoy a bottle of tequila together, with some sweet lemons. The happy old man swore he would come back no matter what, for he could do many things for Romero at his beautiful home. He swore he would return, maybe in a week or two, for surely there was work that needed to be done in the back yard.

Romero wasn't used to feeling so virtuous. He so often was disappointed, so often dwelled on the difficulties of life, that he had become hard, guarding against compassion and generosity. So much so that he'd even become spare with his words, even with his family. His wife whispered to the children that this was because he was tired, and, since it wasn't untrue, he accepted it as the explanation too. It spared him that worry, and from having to discuss why he liked working weekends and taking a day off during the week, like this one. But now an old man had made Romero wish his family were there with him so he could give as much, *more,* to them too, so he could watch their spin around dances—he'd missed so many—and Romero swore he would take them all into Juárez that night for dinner. He might even convince them to take a day, maybe two, for a drive to his uncle's house in Chihuahua instead, because he'd promised that so many years ago—so long ago they probably thought about somewhere else by now, like San Diego, or Los Angeles. Then he'd take them there! They'd go for a week, spend whatever it took. No expense could be so great, and if happiness was as easy as some tacos and a five-dollar bill, then how stupid it had been of him not to have offered it all this time.

Romero felt so good, felt such relief, he napped on the couch. When he woke up he immediately remembered his shirt, that it was already gone before the old man had even arrived—he remembered they'd walked around the juniper before it was cut. Nevertheless, the possibility that the old man took it wouldn't leave Romero's mind. Since he'd never believed in letting down, giving into someone like that old man, the whole experience became suspect. Maybe it was part of some ruse which ended with the old man taking his shirt, some food, money. This was how Romero thought. Though he held a hope that he'd left it somewhere else, that it was a lapse of memory on his part—he went outside, inside, looked everywhere twice, then one more time after that—his cynicism had flowered, colorful and bitter.

Understand that it was his favorite shirt, that he'd never thought of replacing it and that its loss was all Romero could keep his mind on, though he knew very well it wasn't a son, or a daughter, or a wife, or a mother or father, not a disaster of any kind. It was a simple shirt, in the true value of things not very much to lose. But understand also that Romero was a good man who tried to do what was right and who would harm no one willfully. Understand that Romero was a man who had taught himself to not care, to not want, to not desire for so long that he'd lost many words, avoided many people, kept to himself, alone, almost always, even when his wife gave him his meals. Understand that it was his favorite shirt and though no more than that, for him it was no less. Then understand how he felt like a fool paying that old man who, he considered, might even have taken it, like a fool for feeling so friendly and generous, happy, when the shirt was already gone, like a fool for having all those and these thoughts for the love of a wool shirt, like a fool for not being able to stop thinking them all, but especially the one reminding him that this was what he had always believed in, that loss was what he was most prepared for. And so then you might understand why he began to stare out the window of his home, waiting for someone to walk by absently with it on, for the thief to pass by, careless. He kept a watch out the window as each of his children came in, then his wife. He told them only what had happened and, as always, they left him alone. He stared out that window onto the dirt street, past the ocotillos and nopales and agaves, the junipers and oaks and mulberries in front of other homes of brick or stone, painted or not, past them to the buildings in Juárez, and he watched the horizon darken and the sky light up with the moon and stars, and the land spread with shimmering lights, so bright in the dark blot of night. He heard dogs barking until another might bark farther away, and then another, back and forth like that, the small rectangles and squares of their fences plotted out distinctly in his mind's eye as his lids closed. Then he heard a gust of wind bend around his house, and then came the train, the metal rhythm getting closer until it was as close as it could be, the steel pounding the earth like a beating heart, until it diminished and then faded away and then left the air to silence, to its quiet and dark, so still it was like death, or rest, sleep, until he could hear a grackle, and then another gust of wind, and then finally a car.

He looked in on his daughter still so young, so beautiful, becoming a woman who would leave that bed for another, his sons still boys when they were asleep, who dreamed like men when they were awake, and his wife, still young in his eyes in the morning shadows of their bed.

Romero went outside. The juniper had been cut just as he'd wanted 15 it. He got cold and came back in and went to the bed and blankets his wife kept so clean, so neatly arranged as she slept under them without him, and he lay down beside her.

Considerations for Critical Thinking and Writing

1. **FIRST RESPONSE.** How do Romero's attitudes toward work reveal his character and values?

2. Which details about El Paso seem important to you as a means of establishing the setting and the context of Romero's life?

3. What do you think is the function of the old man in the story? How does he affect Romero?

4. Write a sentence that captures what you think is the story's theme. Explain whether the theme is explicitly stated or is implicitly embedded in, for example, character, action, plot, or some other element in the story.

5. How might the use of a first-person point of view, instead of the third person, affect your understanding of and response to Romero?

6. Choose a substantial paragraph from the story and analyze its style, considering such elements as diction, sentence structure, and tone. How is the style related to its content?

7. Why do you think the story is titled "Romero's Shirt"? What symbolic values are associated with it in the story?

8. **CONNECTION TO ANOTHER SELECTION.** Discuss the treatment of domestic life, and in particular the image of the fathers, in "Romero's Shirt" and in Gilb's "Shout" (p. 279).

9. **CONNECTION TO ANOTHER SELECTION.** Consider the ending and tone of "Romero's Shirt" keeping in mind the two following poems about work: Jan Beatty's "My Father Teaches Me to Dream" (p. 556) and Michael Chitwood's "Men Throwing Bricks" (p. 556). Which of the two poems do you think seems to describe Romero's sensibilities more completely?

8

Style, Tone, and Irony

I like it when there is some feeling of threat or sense of menace in short stories. I think a little menace is fine to have in a story.

— RAYMOND CARVER

STYLE

Style is a concept that everyone understands on some level because in its broadest sense it refers to the particular way in which anything is made or done. Style is everywhere around us. The world is saturated with styles in cars, clothing, buildings, teaching, dancing, music, politics — in anything that reflects a distinctive manner of expression or design. Consider, for example, how a tune sung by the Beatles differs from the same tune performed by a string orchestra. There's no mistaking the two styles.

Authors also have different characteristic styles. *Style* refers to the distinctive manner in which a writer arranges words to achieve particular effects. That arrangement includes individual word choices and matters such as the length of sentences, their structure and tone, and the use of irony.

Diction refers to a writer's choice of words. Because different words evoke different associations in a reader's mind, the writer's choice of words is crucial in controlling a reader's response. The diction must be appropriate for the characters and the situations in which the author places them. Consider how inappropriate it would have been if Melville had had Bartleby respond to the lawyer's requests with "Hell no!"

instead of "I would prefer not to." The word *prefer* and the tentativeness of *would* help reinforce the scrivener's mildness, his dignity, and even his seeming reasonableness — all of which frustrate the lawyer's efforts to get rid of him. Bartleby, despite his passivity, seems to be in control of the situation. If he were to shout "Hell no!" he would appear angry, aggressive, desperate, and too informal, none of which would fit with his solemn, conscious decision to die. Melville makes the lawyer the desperate party by carefully choosing Bartleby's words.

Explore the literary elements in this chapter at bedfordstmartins.com/meyerlit.

Sentence structure is another element of a writer's style. Hemingway's terse, economical sentences are frequently noted and readily perceived. Here are the concluding sentences of Hemingway's "Soldier's Home" (p. 133), in which Krebs decides to leave home:

> He had tried so to keep his life from being complicated. Still, none of it had touched him. He had felt sorry for his mother and she had made him lie. He would go to Kansas City and get a job and she would feel all right about it. There would be one more scene maybe before he got away. He would not go down to his father's office. He would miss that one. He wanted his life to go smoothly. It had just gotten going that way. Well, that was all over now, anyway. He would go over to the schoolyard and watch Helen play indoor baseball.

Hemingway expresses Krebs's thought the way Krebs thinks. The style avoids any "complicated" sentence structures. Seven of the eleven sentences begin with the word *He.* There are no abstractions or qualifications. We feel as if we are listening not only to *what* Krebs thinks but to *how* he thinks. The style reflects his firm determination to make, one step at a time, a clean, unobstructed break from his family and the entangling complications they would impose on him.

Contrast this straightforward style with Vladimir Nabokov's description of a woman in his short story "The Vane Sisters." The sophisticated narrator teaches French literature at a women's college and is as observant as he is icily critical of the woman he describes in this passage:

> Her fingernails were gaudily painted, but badly bitten and not clean. Her lovers were a silent young photographer with a sudden laugh and two older men, brothers, who owned a small printing establishment across the street. I wondered at their tastes whenever I glimpsed, with a secret shudder, the higgledy-piggledy striation of black hairs that showed all along her pale shins through the nylon of her stockings with the scientific distinctness of a preparation flattened under glass; or when I felt, at her every movement, the dullish, stalish, not particularly conspicuous but all-pervading and depressing emanation that her seldom bathed flesh spread from under weary perfumes and creams.

This portrait — etched with a razor blade — is restrained but devastating. Hemingway's and Nabokov's uses of language are very different, yet each style successfully fuses what is said with how it is said. We could write summaries of both passages, but our summaries, owing to their styles, would not have the same effect as the originals. And that makes all the difference.

TONE

Style reveals *tone*, the author's implicit attitude toward the people, places, and events in a story. When we speak, tone is conveyed by our voice inflections, our wink of an eye, or some other gesture. A professor who says "You're going to fail the next exam" may be indicating concern, frustration, sympathy, alarm, humor, or indifference, depending on the tone of voice. In a literary work that spoken voice is unavailable; instead we must rely on the context in which a statement appears to interpret it correctly.

In Chopin's "The Story of an Hour" (p. 13), for example, we can determine that the author sympathizes with Mrs. Mallard despite the fact that her grief over her husband's assumed death is mixed with joy. Though Mrs. Mallard thinks she's lost her husband, she experiences relief because she feels liberated from an oppressive male-dominated life. That's why she collapses when she sees her husband alive at the end of the story. Chopin makes clear by the tone of the final line ("When the doctors came they said she had died of heart disease — of joy that kills") that the men misinterpret both her grief and joy, for in the larger context of Mrs. Mallard's emotions we see, unlike the doctors, that her death may well have been caused not by a shock of joy but by an overwhelming recognition of her lost freedom. We discover that through the tone. This stylistic technique is frequently an important element for interpreting a story. An insensitivity to tone can lead a reader astray in determining the theme of a work. Regardless of who is speaking in a story, it is wise to listen for the author's voice too.

IRONY

One of the enduring themes in literature is that things are not always what they seem to be. What we see — or think we see — is not always what we get. The unexpected complexity that often surprises us in life — what Herman Melville in *Moby-Dick* called the "universal thump" — is fertile ground for writers of imaginative literature. They cultivate that ground through the use of *irony*, a device that reveals a reality different from what appears to be true.

Verbal irony consists of a person saying one thing but meaning the opposite. If a student driver smashes into a parked car and the angry instructor turns to say "You sure did well today," the statement is an example of verbal irony. What is meant is the opposite of what is said. Verbal irony that is calculated to hurt someone by false praise is commonly known as *sarcasm*. In literature, however, verbal irony is usually not openly aggressive; instead, it is more subtle and restrained though no less intense.

In Godwin's "A Sorrowful Woman" (p. 36), a woman retreats from her family because she cannot live in the traditional role that her husband and son expect of her. When the husband tries to be sympathetic about her withdrawal from family life, the narrator tells us three times that "he understood such things" and that in "understanding these things" he tried to be patient by "[s]till understanding these things." The narrator's repetition of these phrases constitutes verbal irony because they call attention to the fact that the husband doesn't understand his wife at all. His "understanding" is really only a form of condescension that represents part of her problem rather than a solution.

Situational irony exists when there is an incongruity between what is expected to happen and what actually happens. For instance, at the climactic showdown between Marshal Potter and Scratchy Wilson in Crane's "The Bride Comes to Yellow Sky" (p. 198), there are no gunshots, only talk—and what subdues Wilson is not Potter's strength and heroism but the fact that the marshal is now married. To take one more example, the protagonist in Godwin's "A Sorrowful Woman" seems, by traditional societal standards, to have all that a wife and mother could desire in a family, but, given her needs, that turns out not to be enough to sustain even her life, let alone her happiness. In each of these instances the ironic situation creates a distinction between appearances and realities and brings the reader closer to the central meaning of the story.

As you read Raymond Carver's "Popular Mechanics," Susan Minot's "Lust," and Rick Moody's "Boys," pay attention to the authors' artful use of style, tone, and irony to convey meanings.

RAYMOND CARVER (1938–1988)

Born in 1938 in Clatskanie, Oregon, to working-class parents, Carver grew up in Yakima, Washington, was educated at Humboldt State College in California, and did graduate work at the University of Iowa. He married at age nineteen and during his college years worked at a series of low-paying jobs to help support his family. These difficult years eventually ended in divorce. He taught at a number of universities, among them the University of California, Berkeley; the University of Iowa; the University of Texas, El Paso; and

© Marion Ettlinger.

Syracuse University. Carver's collections of stories include *Will You Please Be Quiet, Please?* (1976); *What We Talk about When We Talk about Love* (1981), from which "Popular Mechanics" is taken; *Cathedral* (1984); and *Where I'm Calling From: New and Selected Stories* (1988). Though extremely brief, "Popular Mechanics" describes a stark domestic situation with a startling conclusion.

Popular Mechanics   *1981*

Early that day the weather turned and the snow was melting into dirty water. Streaks of it ran down from the little shoulder-high window that faced the backyard. Cars slushed by on the street outside, where it was getting dark. But it was getting dark on the inside too.

He was in the bedroom pushing clothes into a suitcase when she came to the door.

I'm glad you're leaving! I'm glad you're leaving! she said. Do you hear?

He kept on putting his things into the suitcase.

Son of a bitch! I'm so glad you're leaving! She began to cry. You can't 5 even look me in the face, can you?

Then she noticed the baby's picture on the bed and picked it up.

He looked at her and she wiped her eyes and stared at him before turning and going back to the living room.

Bring that back, he said.

Just get your things and get out, she said.

He did not answer. He fastened the suitcase, put on his coat, looked 10 around the bedroom before turning off the light. Then he went out to the living room.

She stood in the doorway of the little kitchen, holding the baby.

I want the baby, he said.

Are you crazy?

No, but I want the baby. I'll get someone to come by for his things.

You're not touching this baby, she said.   15

The baby had begun to cry and she uncovered the blanket from around his head.

Oh, oh, she said, looking at the baby.

He moved toward her.

For God's sake! she said. She took a step back into the kitchen.

I want the baby.   20

Get out of here!

She turned and tried to hold the baby over in a corner behind the stove.

But he came up. He reached across the stove and tightened his hands on the baby.

Let go of him, he said.

Get away, get away! she cried.   25

The baby was red-faced and screaming. In the scuffle they knocked down a flowerpot that hung behind the stove.

He crowded her into the wall then, trying to break her grip. He held on to the baby and pushed with all his weight.

Let go of him, he said.

Don't, she said. You're hurting the baby, she said.

I'm not hurting the baby, he said.   30

The kitchen window gave no light. In the near-dark he worked on her fisted fingers with one hand and with the other hand he gripped the screaming baby up under an arm near the shoulder.

She felt her fingers being forced open. She felt the baby going from her.

No! she screamed just as her hands came loose.

She would have it, this baby. She grabbed for the baby's other arm. She caught the baby around the wrist and leaned back.

But he would not let go. He felt the baby slipping out of his hands   35 and he pulled back very hard.

In this manner, the issue was decided.

Considerations for Critical Thinking and Writing

1. **First response.** Discuss the story's final lines. What is the "issue" that is "decided"?

2. Though there is little description of the setting in this story, how do the few details that are provided help to establish the tone?

3. How do small actions take on larger significance in the story? Consider the woman picking up the baby's picture and the knocked-down flowerpot.

4. Why is this couple splitting up? Do we know? Does it matter? Explain your response.

5. Discuss the title of the story. The original title was "Mine." Which do you think is more effective?

6. Explain how Carver uses irony to convey theme.

7. **Connection to another selection.** Compare Carver's style with Ernest Hemingway's in "Soldier's Home" (p. 133).

Susan Minot (b. 1956)

Born and raised in Massachusetts, Susan Minot earned a B.A. at Brown University and an M.F.A. at Columbia University. Before devoting herself full-time to writing, Minot worked as an assistant editor at *Grand Street* magazine. Her stories have appeared in *The Atlantic, Harper's, The*

New Yorker, Mademoiselle, and *Paris Review.*
Her short stories have been collected in *Lust
and Other Stories* (1989), and she has published four novels — *Monkeys* (1986), *Folly*
(1992), *Evening* (1998), and *Rapture* (2002), as
well as one volume of poetry, *Poems 4 A.M.*
(2002).

Lust   1984

Leo was from a long time ago, the first one I
ever saw nude. In the spring before the Hell-
mans filled their pool, we'd go down there
in the deep end, with baby oil, and like that.
I met him the first month away at boarding school. He had a halo from the campus
light behind him. I flipped.

Courtesy of Dinah Minot Hubley.

Roger was fast. In his illegal car, we drove to the reservoir, the radio
blaring, talking fast, fast, fast. He was always going for my zipper. He got
kicked out sophomore year.

By the time the band got around to playing "Wild Horses," I had
tasted Bruce's tongue. We were clicking in the shadows on the other side
of the amplifier, out of Mrs. Donovan's line of vision. It tasted like salt,
with my neck bent back, because we had been dancing so hard before.

Tim's line: "I'd like to see you in a bathing suit." I knew it was his line
when he said the exact same thing to Annie Hines.

You'd go on walks to get off campus. It was raining like hell, my   5
sweater as sopped as a wet sheep. Tim pinned me to a tree, the woods
light brown and dark brown, a white house half hidden with the lights
already on. The water was as loud as a crowd hissing. He made certain
comments about my forehead, about my cheeks.

We started off sitting at one end of the couch and then our feet were
squished against the armrest and then he went over to turn off the TV
and came back after he had taken off his shirt and then we slid onto the
floor and he got up again to close the door, then came back to me, a body
waiting on the rug.

You'd try to wipe off the table or to do the dishes and Willie would
untuck your shirt and get his hands up under in front, standing behind
you, making puffy noises in your ear.

He likes it when I wash my hair. He covers his face with it and if I start to say something, he goes, "Shush."

For a long time, I had Philip on the brain. The less they noticed you, the more you got them on the brain.

My parents had no idea. Parents never really know what's going on, 10 especially when you're away at school most of the time. If she met them, my mother might say, "Oliver seems nice" or "I like that one" without much of an opinion. If she didn't like them, "He's a funny fellow, isn't he?" or "Johnny's perfectly nice but a drink of water." My father was too shy to talk to them at all unless they played sports and he'd ask them about that.

The sand was almost cold underneath because the sun was long gone. Eben piled a mound over my feet, patting around my ankles, the ghostly surf rumbling behind him in the dark. He was the first person I ever knew who died, later that summer, in a car crash. I thought about it for a long time.

"Come here," he says on the porch.
I go over to the hammock and he takes my wrist with two fingers.
"What?"
He kisses my palm then directs my hand to his fly. 15

Songs went with whichever boy it was. "Sugar Magnolia" was Tim, with the line "Rolling in the rushes/down by the riverside." With "Darkness Darkness," I'd picture Philip with his long hair. Hearing "Under My Thumb" there'd be the smell of Jamie's suede jacket.

We hid in the listening rooms during study hall. With a record cover over the door's window, the teacher on duty couldn't look in. I came out flushed and heady and back at the dorm was surprised how red my lips were in the mirror.

One weekend at Simon's brother's, we stayed inside all day with the shades down, in bed, then went out to Store 24 to get some ice cream. He stood at the magazine rack and read through *MAD* while I got butterscotch sauce, craving something sweet.

I could do some things well. Some things I was good at, like math or painting or even sports, but the second a boy put his arm around me, I forgot about wanting to do anything else, which felt like a relief at first until it became like sinking into a muck.

It was different for a girl. 20

When we were little, the brothers next door tied up our ankles. They held the door of the goat house and wouldn't let us out till we showed them our underpants. Then they'd forget about being after us and when we played whiffle ball, I'd be just as good as they were.

Then it got to be different. Just because you have on a short skirt, they yell from the cars, slowing down for a while, and if you don't look, they screech off and call you a bitch.

"What's the matter with me?" they say, point-blank.
Or else, "Why won't you go out with me? I'm not asking you to get married," about to get mad.

Or it'd be, trying to be reasonable, in a regular voice, "Listen, I just 25 want to have a good time."
So I'd go because I couldn't think of something to say back that wouldn't be obvious, and if you go out with them, you sort of have to do something.

I sat between Mack and Eddie in the front seat of the pickup. They were having a fight about something. I've a feeling about me.

Certain nights you'd feel a certain surrender, maybe if you'd had wine. The surrender would be forgetting yourself and you'd put your nose to his neck and feel like a squirrel, safe, at rest, in a restful dream. But then you'd start to slip from that and the dark would come in and there'd be a cave. You make out the dim shape of the windows and feel yourself become a cave, filled absolutely with air, or with a sadness that wouldn't stop.

Teenage years. You know just what you're doing and don't see the things that start to get in the way.

Lots of boys, but never two at the same time. One was plenty to keep 30 you in a state. You'd start to see a boy and something would rush over you like a fast storm cloud and you couldn't possibly think of anyone else. Boys took it differently. Their eyes perked up at any little number that walked by. You'd act like you weren't noticing.

The joke was that the school doctor gave out the pill like aspirin. He didn't ask you anything. I was fifteen. We had a picture of him in assembly, holding up an IUD shaped like a T. Most girls were on the pill, if anything, because they couldn't handle a diaphragm. I kept the dial in my top drawer like my mother and thought of her each time I tipped out the yellow tablets in the morning before chapel.

If they were too shy, I'd be more so. Andrew was nervous. We stayed up with his family album, sharing a pack of Old Golds. Before it got light, we turned on the TV. A man was explaining how to plant seedlings. His mouth jerked to the side in a tic. Andrew thought it was a riot and kept imitating him. I laughed to be polite. When we finally dozed off, he dared to put his arm around me, but that was it.

You wait till they come to you. With half fright, half swagger, they stand one step down. They dare to touch the button on your coat then lose their nerve and quickly drop their hand so you – you'd do anything for them. You touch their cheek.

The girls sit around in the common room and talk about boys, smoking their heads off.

"What are you complaining about?" says Jill to me when we talk   35
about problems.

"Yeah," says Giddy. "You always have a boyfriend."

I look at them and think, As if.

I thought the worst thing anyone could call you was a cock-teaser. So, if you flirted, you had to be prepared to go through with it. Sleeping with someone was perfectly normal once you had done it. You didn't really worry about it. But there were other problems. The problems had to do with something else entirely.

Mack was during the hottest summer ever recorded. We were renting a house on an island with all sorts of other people. No one slept during the heat wave, walking around the house with nothing on which we were used to because of the nude beach. In the living room, Eddie lay on top of a coffee table to cool off. Mack and I, with the bedroom door open for air, sweated and sweated all night.

"I can't take this," he said at three A.M. "I'm going for a swim." He and   40
some guys down the hall went to the beach. The heat put me on edge. I sat on a cracked chest by the open window and smoked and smoked till I felt even worse, waiting for something – I guess for him to get back.

One was on a camping trip in Colorado. We zipped our sleeping bags together, the coyotes' hysterical chatter far away. Other couples murmured in other tents. Paul was up before sunrise, starting a fire for breakfast. He wasn't much of a talker in the daytime. At night, his hand leafed about in the hair at my neck.

There'd be times when you overdid it. You'd get carried away. All the next day, you'd be in a total fog, delirious, absent-minded, crossing the street and nearly getting run over.

The more girls a boy has, the better. He has a bright look, having reaped fruits, blooming. He stalks around, sure-shouldered, and you have the feeling he's got more in him, a fatter heart, more stories to tell. For a girl, with each boy it's as though a petal gets plucked each time.

Then you start to get tired. You begin to feel diluted, like watered-down stew.

Oliver came skiing with us. We lolled by the fire after everyone had gone   45 to bed. Each creak you'd think was someone coming downstairs. The silver loop bracelet he gave me had been a present from his girlfriend before.

On vacations, we went skiing, or you'd go south if someone invited you. Some people had apartments in New York that their families hardly ever used. Or summer houses, or older sisters. We always managed to find someplace to go.

We made the plan at coffee hour. Simon snuck out and met me at Main Gate after lights-out. We crept to the chapel and spent the night in the balcony. He tasted like onions from a submarine sandwich.

The boys are one of two ways: either they can't sit still or they don't move. In front of the TV, they won't budge. On weekends they play touch football while we sit on the sidelines, picking blades of grass to chew on, and watch. We're always watching them run around. We shiver in the stands, knocking our boots together to keep our toes warm, and they whizz across the ice, chopping their sticks around the puck. When they're in the rink, they refuse to look at you, only eyeing each other beneath low helmets. You cheer for them but they don't look up, even if it's a face-off when nothing's happening, even if they're doing drills before any game has started at all.

Dancing under the pink tent, he bent down and whispered in my ear. We slipped away to the lawn on the other side of the hedge. Much later, as he was leaving the buffet with two plates of eggs and sausage, I saw the grass stains on the knees of his white pants.

Tim's was shaped like a banana, with a graceful curve to it. They're all   50 different. Willie's like a bunch of walnuts when nothing was happening, another's as thin as a thin hot dog. But it's like faces; you're never really surprised.

Still, you're not sure what to expect.

I look into his face and he looks back. I look into his eyes and they look back at mine. Then they look down at my mouth so I look at his

mouth, then back to his eyes then, backing up, at his whole face. I think,
Who? Who are you? His head tilts to one side.

I say, "Who are you?"

"What do you mean?"

"Nothing."   55

I look at his eyes again, deeper. Can't tell who he is, what he thinks.

"What?" he says. I look at his mouth.

"I'm just wondering," I say and go wandering across his face. Study
the chin line. It's shaped like a persimmon.

"Who are you? What are you thinking?"

He says, "What the hell are you talking about?"   60

Then they get mad after, when you say enough is enough. After,
when it's easier to explain that you don't want to. You wouldn't dream of
saying that maybe you weren't really ready to in the first place.

Gentle Eddie. We waded into the sea, the waves round and plowing in,
buffalo-headed, slapping our thighs. I put my arms around his freckled
shoulders and he held me up, buoyed by the water, and rocked me like a
sea shell.

I had no idea whose party it was, the apartment jam-packed, stepping
over people in the hallway. The room with the music was practically empty,
the bare floor, me in red shoes. This fellow slides onto one knee and takes
me around the waist and we rock to jazzy tunes, with my toes pointing
heavenward, and waltz and spin and dip to "Smoke Gets in Your Eyes" or
"I'll Love You Just for Now." He puts his head to my chest, runs a sweeping
hand down my inside thigh and we go loose-limbed and sultry and as
smooth as silk and I stamp my red heels and he takes me into a swoon. I
never saw him again after that but I thought, I could have loved that one.

You wonder how long you can keep it up. You begin to feel as if
you're showing through, like a bathroom window that only lets in grey
light, the kind you can't see out of.

They keep coming around. Johnny drives up at Easter vacation from   65
Baltimore and I let him in the kitchen with everyone sound asleep. He
has friends waiting in the car.

"What are you, crazy? It's pouring out there," I say.

"It's okay," he says. "They understand."

So he gets some long kisses from me, against the refrigerator, before
he goes because I hate those girls who push away a boy's face as if she
were made out of Ivory soap, as if she's that much greater than he is.

The note on my cubby told me to see the headmaster. I had no idea
for what. He had received complaints about my amorous displays on the
town green. It was Willie that spring. The headmaster told me he didn't

care what I did but that Casey Academy had a reputation to uphold in the town. He lowered his glasses on his nose. "We've got twenty acres of woods on this campus," he said. "If you want to smooch with your boyfriend, there are twenty acres for you to do it out of the public eye. You read me?"

Everybody'd get weekend permissions for different places, then we'd all go to someone's house whose parents were away. Usually there'd be more boys than girls. We raided the liquor closet and smoked pot at the kitchen table and you'd never know who would end up where, or with whom. There were always disasters. Ceci got bombed and cracked her head open on the banister and needed stitches. Then there was the time Wendel Blair walked through the picture window at the Lowes' and got slashed to ribbons.

He scared me. In bed, I didn't dare look at him. I lay back with my eyes closed, luxuriating because he knew all sorts of expert angles, his hands never fumbling, going over my whole body, pressing the hair up and off the back of my head, giving an extra hip shove, as if to say *There*. I parted my eyes slightly, keeping the screen of my lashes low because it was too much to look at him, his mouth loose and pink and parted, his eyes looking through my forehead, or kneeling up, looking through my throat. I was ashamed but couldn't look him in the eye.

You wonder about things feeling a little off-kilter. You begin to feel like a piece of pounded veal.

At boarding school, everyone gets depressed. We go in and see the housemother, Mrs. Gunther. She got married when she was eighteen. Mr. Gunther was her high school sweetheart, the only boyfriend she ever had.

"And you knew you wanted to marry him right off?" we ask her.

She smiles and says, "Yes."

"They always want something from you," says Jill, complaining about her boyfriend.

"Yeah," says Giddy. "You always feel like you have to deliver something."

"You do," says Mrs. Gunther. "Babies."

After sex, you curl up like a shrimp, something deep inside you ruined, slammed in a place that sickens at slamming, and slowly you fill up with an overwhelming sadness, an elusive gaping worry. You don't try to explain it, filled with the knowledge that it's nothing after all, everything filling up finally and absolutely with death. After the briskness of loving, loving stops. And you roll over with death stretched out alongside you like a feather boa, or a snake, light as air, and you . . . you don't even ask for anything or try to say something to

70

75

him because it's obviously your own damn fault. You haven't been able to — to what? To open your heart. You open your legs but can't, or don't dare anymore, to open your heart.

It starts this way: 80
You stare into their eyes. They flash like all the stars are out. They look at you seriously, their eyes at a low burn and their hands no matter what starting off shy and with such a gentle touch that the only thing you can do is take that tenderness and let yourself be swept away. When, with one attentive finger they tuck the hair behind your ear, you —
You do everything they want.
Then comes after. After when they don't look at you. They scratch their balls, stare at the ceiling. Or if they do turn, their gaze is altogether changed. They are surprised. They turn casually to look at you, distracted, and get a mild distracted surprise. You're gone. Their blank look tells you that the girl they were fucking is not there anymore. You seem to have disappeared.

CONSIDERATIONS FOR CRITICAL THINKING AND WRITING

1. **FIRST RESPONSE.** What do you think of the narrator? Why? Do you agree with the definition the story offers for *lust*?

2. How effective is the narrator's description of teenage sex? What do you think she means when she says "You know just what you're doing and don't see the things that start to get in the way" (para. 28)?

3. Discuss the story's tone. Is it what you expected from the title?

4. What do you think is the theme of "Lust"? Does its style carry its theme?

5. What is the primary setting for the story? What does it reveal about the nature of the narrator's economic and social class?

6. In a *Publishers Weekly* interview (November 6, 1992), Minot observed, "There's more fictional material in unhappiness and disappointment and frustration than there is in happiness. Who was it said, 'Happiness is like a blank page'?" What do you think of this observation?

7. **CONNECTION TO ANOTHER SELECTION.** Compare the treatments of youthful sexuality in "Lust" and in David Updike's "Summer" (p. 163). Do you prefer one story to another? Why?

RICK MOODY (B. 1961)

Born in New York City, Rick Moody grew up in Connecticut and earned his undergraduate degree at Brown University and his M.F.A. at Columbia University. His first of four novels, *Garden State* (1992), won the Pushcart Editor's Choice Award. *The Ice Storm* (1994) was made into a popular film directed by Ang Lee in 1997 and was followed by three more novels: *Purple*

© Colin McPherson / CORBIS.

America (1996), *The Diviners* (2005), and *The Four Fingers of Death* (2010). Moody has also published three collections of short stories and novellas: *The Ring of Brightest Angels Along Heaven* (1995); *Demonology* (2001), which collects "Boys"; and *Right Livelihoods* (2007). "Boys" was included in *The Best American Short Stories 2001,* in which Moody describes how this experimental story began. He had heard a fellow writer, Max Steele, use the phrase "Then the boys entered the house" at a reading and found himself "preoccupied" with what is "perhaps the most essential gesture in a boy's life." He then "started playing around with the sentence."

Boys   2000

Boys enter the house, boys enter the house. Boys, and with them the ideas of boys (ideas leaden, reductive, inflexible), enter the house. Boys, two of them, wound into hospital packaging, boys with infant-pattern baldness, slung in the arms of parents, boys dreaming of breasts, enter the house. Twin boys, kettles on the boil, boys in hideous vinyl knapsacks that young couples from Edison, N.J., wear on their shirt fronts, knapsacks coated with baby saliva and staphylococcus and milk vomit, enter the house. Two boys, one striking the other with a rubberized hot dog, enter the house. Two boys, one of them striking the other with a willow switch about the head and shoulders, the other crying, enter the house. Boys enter the house speaking nonsense. Boys enter the house calling for mother. On a Sunday, in May, a day one might nearly describe as perfect, an ice cream truck comes slowly down the lane, chimes inducing salivation, and children run after it, not long after which boys dig a hole in the back yard and bury their younger sister's dolls two feet down, so that she will never find these dolls and these dolls will rot in hell, after which boys enter the house. Boys, trailing after their father like he is the Second Goddamned Coming of Christ Goddamned Almighty, enter the house, repair to the basement to watch baseball. Boys enter the house, site of devastation, and repair immediately to the kitchen, where they mix lighter fluid, vanilla pudding, drain-opening lye, balsamic vinegar, blue food coloring, calamine lotion, cottage cheese, ants, a plastic lizard one of them received in his Christmas stocking, tacks, leftover mashed potatoes, Spam, frozen lima beans, and chocolate syrup in a medium-sized saucepan and heat over a low flame until thick, afterward transferring the contents of this saucepan into a Pyrex lasagna dish, baking the Pyrex lasagna dish in the oven for nineteen minutes before attempting to persuade their sister that she should eat the mixture; later they smash three family heirlooms (the last, a glass egg, intentionally) in a two-and-a-half-hour stretch, whereupon they are sent to their bedroom until freed, in each case thirteen minutes after. Boys enter the house, starchy in pressed shirts and flannel pants that itch so bad, fresh from Sunday school instruction, blond and brown locks (respectively) plastered down but even so with a number of cowlicks protruding at odd angles, discon-solate and humbled, uncertain if boyish things — such as shooting at the neighbor's dog with a pump-action BB gun and gagging the fat boy up the street with a bandanna and showing their shriveled boy-penises to their younger sister — are exempted from the commandment to *Love the Lord thy God with all thy heart and with all thy soul and with all thy mind, and thy neighbor as thyself.* Boys enter the house in baseball gear (only one of the boys can hit): in their spikes, in mismatched tube socks that smell like Stilton cheese. Boys enter the house in soccer gear. Boys enter the house carrying skates. Boys enter the house with lacrosse sticks, and soon after, tossing a lacrosse ball lightly in the living room, they destroy a lamp. One boy enters the house sporting basketball clothes, the other wearing jeans and a sweatshirt. One boy enters the house bleeding pro-fusely and is taken out to get stitches, the other watches. Boys enter the house at the end of term carrying report cards, sneak around the house like spies of foreign nationality, looking for a place to hide the report cards for the time being (under a toaster? in a medicine cabinet?). One boy with a black eye enters the house, one boy without. Boys with acne enter the house and squeeze and prod large skin blemishes in front of their sister. Boys with acne-treatment products hidden about their per-sons enter the house. Boys, standing just up the street, sneak cigarettes behind a willow in the Elys' yard, wave smoke away from their natural fibers, hack terribly, experience nausea, then enter the house. Boys call each other *Retard, Homo, Geek,* and, later, *Neckless Thug, Theater Fag,* and enter the house exchanging further epithets. Boys enter house with nose-hair clippers, chase sister around house threatening to depilate her eye-brows. She cries. Boys attempt to induce girls to whom they would not have spoken only six or eight months prior to enter the house with them. Boys enter the house with girls efflorescent and homely and attempt to induce girls to sneak into their bedroom, as they still share a single bed-room; girls refuse. Boys enter the house, go to separate bedrooms. Boys, with their father (an arm around each of them), enter the house, but of the monologue preceding and succeeding this entrance, not a syllable is preserved. Boys enter the house having masturbated in a variety of locales. Boys enter the house having masturbated in train-station bath-rooms, in forests, in beach houses, in football bleachers at night under the stars, in cars (under a blanket), in the shower, backstage, on a plane, the boys masturbate constantly, identically, three times a day in some cases, desire like a madness upon them, at the mere sound of certain words, words that sound like other words, *interrogative* reminding them of *intercourse, beast* reminding them of *breast, sects* reminding them of *sex,* and so forth, the boys are not very smart yet, and as they enter the house they feel, as always, immense shame at the scale of this self-abusive cogi-tation, seeing a classmate, seeing a billboard, seeing a fire hydrant, seeing things that should not induce thoughts of masturbation (their sister, e.g.) and then thinking of masturbation anyway. Boys enter the house, go to their rooms, remove sexually explicit magazines from hidden stashes, put on loud music, feel despair. Boys enter the house worried; they argue. The boys are ugly, they are failures, they will never be loved, they enter the house. Boys enter the house and kiss their mother, who feels differently now they have outgrown her. Boys enter the house, kiss their mother, she explains the seriousness of their sister's difficulty, her diagnosis. Boys enter the house, having attempted to locate the spot in their yard where the dolls were buried, eight or nine years prior, without success; they go to their sister's room, sit by her bed. Boys enter the house and tell their completely bald sister jokes about baldness. Boys hold either hand of their sister, laying aside differences, having trudged grimly into the house. Boys skip school, enter house, hold vigil. Boys enter the house after their parents have both gone off to work, sit with their sister and with their sister's nurse. Boys enter the house carrying cases of beer. Boys enter the house, very worried now, didn't know more worry was possible. Boys enter the house carrying controlled substances, neither having told the other that he is carrying a controlled substance, though an intoxicated posture seems appropriate under the circumstances. Boys enter the house weeping and hear weeping around them. Boys enter the house embarrassed, silent, anguished, keening, afflicted, angry, woeful, grief-stricken. Boys enter the house on vacation, each clasps the hand of the other with genuine warmth, the one wearing dark colors and having shaved a portion of his head, the other having grown his hair out longish and wearing, uncharacteristically, a tie-dyed shirt. Boys enter the house on vacation and argue bitterly about politics (other subjects are no longer discussed), one boy supporting the Maoist insurgency in a certain Southeast Asian country, one believing that to change the system you need to work inside it; one boy threatens to beat the living shit out of the other, refuses crème brûlée, though it is created by his mother in order to keep the peace. One boy writes home and thereby enters the house only through a mail slot: he argues that the other boy is crypto-fascist, believing that the market can seek its own level on questions of ethics and morals; boys enter the house on vacation and announce future professions; boys enter the house on vacation and change their minds about professions; boys enter the house on vacation, and one boy brings home a sweetheart but throws a tantrum when it is suggested that the sweetheart will have to retire on the folding bed in the basement; the other boy, having no sweetheart, is distant and withdrawn, preferring to talk late into the night about family members gone from this world. Boys enter the house several weeks apart. Boys enter the house on days of heavy rain. Boys enter the house, in different calendar years, and upon entering, the boys seem to do nothing but compose manifestos, for the benefit of parents; they follow their mother around the place, having fashioned these manifestos in celebration of brand-new independence: *Mom, I like to lie in bed late into the morning watching game shows,* or, *I'm never going to date anyone but artists from now on, mad girls, dreamers, practicers of black magic,* or, *A man should eat bologna, sliced meats are important,* or, *An American should bowl at least once a year,* but these manifestos apply only for brief spells, after which they are reversed or discarded. Boys don't enter the house at all, except as ghostly afterimages of younger selves, fleeting images of sneakers dashing up a staircase; soggy towels on the floor of the bathroom; blue jeans coiled like asps in the basin of the washing machine; boys as an absence of boys, blissful at first, you put a thing down on a spot, put this book down, come back later, it's still there; you buy a box of cookies, eat three, later three are missing. Nevertheless, when boys next enter the house, which they ultimately must do, it's a relief, even if it's only in preparation for weddings of acquaintances from boyhood, one boy has a beard, neatly trimmed, the other has rakish sideburns, one boy wears a hat, the other boy thinks hats are ridiculous, one boy wears khakis pleated at the waist, the other wears denim, but each changes into his suit (one suit fits well, one is a little tight), as though suits are the liminary marker of adulthood. Boys enter the house after the wedding and they are slapping each other on the back and yelling at anyone who will listen, *It's a party!* One boy enters the house, carried by friends, having been arrested (after the wedding) for driving while intoxicated, complexion ashen; the other boy tries to keep his mouth shut: the car is on its side in a ditch, the car has the top half of a tree broken over its bonnet, the car has struck another car, which has in turn struck a third, *Everyone will have seen.* One boy misses his brother horribly, misses the past, misses a time worth being nostalgic over, a time that never existed, back when they set their sister's playhouse on fire; the other boy avoids all mention of that time; each of them is once the boy who enters the house alone, missing the other, each is devoted and each callous, and each plays his part on the telephone, over the course of months. Boys enter the house with fishing gear, according to prearranged date and time, arguing about whether to use lures or live bait, in order to meet their father for the fishing adventure, after which boys enter the house again, almost immediately, with live bait, having settled the question; boys boast of having caught fish in the past, though no fish has ever been caught: *Remember when the blues were biting?* Boys enter the house carrying their father, slumped. Happens so fast. Boys rush into the house leading EMTs to the couch in the living room where the body lies, boys enter the house, boys enter the house, boys enter the house. Boys hold open the threshold, awesome threshold that has welcomed them when they haven't even been able to welcome themselves, that threshold which welcomed them when they had to be taken in, here is its tarnished knocker, here is its euphonious bell, here's where the boys had to sand the door down because it never would hang right in the frame, here are the scuff marks from when boys were on the wrong side of the door demanding, here's where there were once milk bottles for the milkman, here's where the newspaper always landed, here's the mail slot, here's the light on the front step, illuminated, here's where the boys are standing, as that beloved man is carried out. Boys, no longer boys, exit.

CONSIDERATIONS FOR CRITICAL THINKING AND WRITING

1. **FIRST RESPONSE.** Write a paragraph that describes in detail the style of this story. In what ways is it conventional as well as unconventional?

2. What is the story's basic plot? What actually happens? Does it have any kind of pattern to it?

3. Who are the major characters? Is there an antagonist who produces a conflict? Explain why or why not.

4. How well do you think Moody captures boys' lives?

5. How is the plot related to the story's style?

6. What do you think is the significance of the final sentence?

7. **CONNECTION TO ANOTHER SELECTION.** Discuss how time is conveyed stylistically in this narrative and in Muriel Spark's "The First Year of My Life" (p. 147).

8. **CONNECTION TO ANOTHER SELECTION.** Compare the literary styles and their effects in this story and in Susan Minot's "Lust" (p. 230).

Fiction in Depth

9

A Study of Flannery O'Connor

In most English classes the short story has become a kind of literary specimen to be dissected. Every time a story of mine appears in a Freshman anthology, I have a vision of it, with its little organs laid open, like a frog in a bottle.
— FLANNERY O'CONNOR

I am always having it pointed out to me that life in Georgia is not at all the way I picture it, that escaped criminals do not roam the roads exterminating families, nor Bible salesmen prowl about looking for girls with wooden legs.
— FLANNERY O'CONNOR

When Flannery O'Connor (1925–1964) died of lupus before her fortieth birthday, her work was cruelly cut short. Nevertheless, she had completed two novels, *Wise Blood* (1952) and *The Violent Bear It Away* (1960), as well as thirty-one short stories. Despite her brief life and relatively modest output, her work is regarded as among the most distinguished American fiction of the mid-twentieth century. Her two collections of short stories, *A Good Man Is Hard to Find* (1955) and *Everything That Rises Must Converge* (1965), were included in *The Complete Stories of Flannery O'Connor* (1971), which won the National Book Award. The story included in this chapter offers a glimpse into the work of this important twentieth-century writer.

Cheers,
Flannery

A BRIEF BIOGRAPHY AND INTRODUCTION

O'Connor's fiction grapples with living a spiritual life in a secular world. Although this major concern is worked into each of her stories, she takes a broad approach to spiritual issues by providing moral, social, and psychological contexts that offer a wealth of insights and passion that her readers have found both startling and absorbing. Her stories are challenging because her characters, who initially seem radically different from people we know, turn out to be, by the end of each story, somehow familiar — somehow connected to us.

O'Connor inhabited simultaneously two radically different worlds. The world she created in her stories is populated with bratty children, malcontents, incompetents, pious frauds, bewildered intellectuals, deformed cynics, rednecks, hucksters, racists, perverts, and murderers who experience dramatically intense moments that surprise and shock readers. Her personal life, however, was largely uneventful. She humorously acknowledged

Flannery O'Connor and a Self-Portrait. The author poses in front of an accurate, if rather fierce self-portrait with one of her beloved ring-necked pheasants. As a child, O'Connor enjoyed raising birds, a passion that was sparked when one of her chickens, "a buff Cochin Bantam [that] had the distinction of being able to walk either forward or backward," was reported on in the press. "I had to have more and more chickens. . . . I wanted one with three legs or three wings but nothing in that line turned up. . . . My quest, whatever it was for, ended with peacocks," she wrote.
Reprinted by permission of Bettmann/CORBIS.

its quiet nature in 1958 when she claimed that "there won't be any biographies of me because, for only one reason, lives spent between the house and the chicken yard do not make exciting copy."

A broad outline of O'Connor's life may not offer very much "exciting copy," but it does provide clues about why she wrote such powerful fiction. The only child of Catholic parents, O'Connor was born in Savannah, Georgia, where she attended a parochial grammar school and high school. When she was thirteen, her father became ill with disseminated lupus, a rare, incurable blood disease, and had to abandon his real-estate business. The family moved to Milledgeville in central Georgia, where her mother's family had lived for generations. Because there were no Catholic schools in Milledgeville, O'Connor attended a public high school. In 1942, the year after her father died of lupus, O'Connor graduated from high school and enrolled in Georgia State College for Women. There she wrote for the literary magazine until receiving her diploma in 1945. Her stories earned her a fellowship to the Writers' Workshop at the University of Iowa, and for two years she learned to write steadily and seriously. She sold her first story to *Accent* in 1946 and earned her master of fine arts degree in 1947. She wrote stories about life in the rural South, and this subject matter, along with her devout Catholic perspective, became central to her fiction.

With her formal education behind her, O'Connor was ready to begin her professional career at the age of twenty-two. Equipped with determination ("No one can convince me that I shouldn't rewrite as much as I do") and offered the opportunity to be around other practicing writers, she moved to New York, where she worked on her first novel, *Wise Blood*. In 1950, however, she was diagnosed as having lupus, and, returning to Georgia for treatment, she took up permanent residence on her mother's farm in Milledgeville. There she lived a severely restricted but productive life, writing stories and raising peacocks.

With the exception of O'Connor's early years in Iowa and New York and some short lecture trips to other states, she traveled little. Although she made a pilgrimage to Lourdes (apparently more for her mother's sake than for her own) and then to Rome for an audience with the pope, her life was centered in the South. Like those of William Faulkner and many other southern writers, O'Connor's stories evoke the rhythms of rural southern speech and manners in insulated settings where widely diverse characters mingle. Also like Faulkner, she created works whose meanings go beyond their settings. She did not want her fiction to be seen in the context of narrowly defined regionalism: she complained that "in almost every hamlet you'll find at least one old lady writing epics in Negro dialect and probably two or three old gentlemen who have impossible historical novels on the way." Refusing to be caricatured, she knew that "the woods are full of regional writers, and it is the great horror of every serious Southern writer that he will become one of them." O'Connor's stories are rooted in rural southern culture, but in a larger sense they are set within the psychological and spiritual landscapes of the human soul.

O'Connor's deep spiritual convictions coincide with the traditional emphasis on religion in the South, where, she said, there is still the belief "that man has fallen and that he is only perfectible by God's grace, not by his own unaided efforts." Although O'Connor's Catholicism differs from the prevailing Protestant fundamentalism of the South, the religious ethos so pervasive even in rural southern areas provided fertile ground for the spiritual crises her characters experience. In a posthumous collection of her articles, essays, and reviews aptly titled *Mystery and Manners* (1969), she summarized her basic religious convictions:

> I am no disbeliever in spiritual purpose and no vague believer. I see from the standpoint of Christian orthodoxy. This means that for me the meaning of life is centered in our Redemption by Christ and what I see in the world I see in its relation to that. I don't think that this is a position that can be taken halfway or one that is particularly easy in these times to make transparent in fiction.

O'Connor realized that she was writing against the grain of the readers who discovered her stories in the *Partisan Review, Sewanee Review, Mademoiselle,* or *Harper's Bazaar.* Many readers thought that Christian dogma would make her writing doctrinaire, but she insisted that the perspective of Christianity allowed her to interpret the details of life and guaranteed her "respect for [life's] mystery." O'Connor's stories contain no prepackaged prescriptions for living, no catechisms that lay out all the answers. Instead, her characters struggle with spiritual questions in bizarre, incongruous situations. Their lives are grotesque — even comic — precisely because they do not understand their own spiritual natures. Their actions are extreme and abnormal. O'Connor explains the reasons for this in *Mystery and Manners;* she says she sought to expose the "distortions" of "modern life" that appear "normal" to her audience. Hence, she used "violent means" to convey her vision to a "hostile audience." "When you can assume that your audience holds the same beliefs you do, you can relax a little and use more normal means of talking to it." But when the audience holds different values, "you have to make your vision apparent by shock — to the hard of hearing you shout, and for the almost-blind you draw large and startling figures." O'Connor's characters lose or find their soul-saving grace in painful, chaotic circumstances that bear little or no resemblance to the slow but sure progress to the Celestial City of repentant pilgrims in traditional religious stories.

Because her characters are powerful creations who live convincing, even if ugly, lives, O'Connor's religious beliefs never supersede her storytelling. One need not be either Christian or Catholic to appreciate her concerns about human failure and degradation and her artistic ability to render fictional lives that are alternately absurdly comic and tragic. The ironies that abound in her work leave plenty of room for readers of all persuasions. O'Connor's work is narrow in the sense that her concerns are emphatically spiritual, but her compassion and her belief in human possibilities—even among the most unlikely characters—afford her fictions a capacity for wonder that is exhilarating. Her precise, deft use of language always reveals more than it seems to tell.

O'Connor's stories present complex experiences that cannot be tidily summarized; it takes the entire story to suggest the meanings. Read "A Good Man Is Hard to Find" for the pleasure of entering the remarkable world O'Connor creates. You're in for some surprises.

A Good Man Is Hard to Find   *1953*

The grandmother didn't want to go to Florida. She wanted to visit some of her connections in east Tennessee and she was seizing at every chance to change Bailey's mind. Bailey was the son she lived with, her only boy. He was sitting on the edge of his chair at the table, bent over the orange sports section of the *Journal.* "Now look here, Bailey," she said, "see here, read this," and she stood with one hand on her thin hip and the other rattling the newspaper at his bald head. "Here this fellow that calls himself The Misfit is aloose from the Federal Pen and headed toward Florida and you read here what it says he did to these people. Just you read it. I wouldn't take my children in any direction with a criminal like that aloose in it. I couldn't answer to my conscience if I did."

Bailey didn't look up from his reading so she wheeled around then and faced the children's mother, a young woman in slacks, whose face was as broad and innocent as a cabbage and was tied around with a green headkerchief that had two points on the top like a rabbit's ears. She was sitting on the sofa, feeding the baby his apricots out of a jar. "The children have been to Florida before," the old lady said. "You all ought to take them somewhere else for a change so they would see different parts of the world and be broad. They never have been to east Tennessee."

The children's mother didn't seem to hear her but the eight-year-old boy, John Wesley, a stocky child with glasses, said, "If you don't want to go to Florida, why dontcha stay at home?" He and the little girl, June Star, were reading the funny papers on the floor.

"She wouldn't stay at home to be queen for a day," June Star said without raising her yellow head.

"Yes and what would you do if this fellow, The Misfit, caught you?"   5 the grandmother asked.

"I'd smack his face," John Wesley said.

"She wouldn't stay at home for a million bucks," June Star said. "Afraid she'd miss something. She has to go everywhere we go."

"All right, Miss," the grandmother said. "Just remember that the next time you want me to curl your hair."

June Star said her hair was naturally curly.

The next morning the grandmother was the first one in the car,   10
ready to go. She had her big black valise that looked like the head of a
hippopotamus in one corner, and underneath it she was hiding a basket
with Pitty Sing, the cat, in it. She didn't intend for the cat to be left alone
in the house for three days because he would miss her too much and she
was afraid he might brush against one of the gas burners and accidentally asphyxiate himself. Her son, Bailey, didn't like to arrive at a motel
with a cat.

She sat in the middle of the back seat with John Wesley and June
Star on either side of her. Bailey and the children's mother and the baby
sat in front and they left Atlanta at eight forty-five with the mileage on
the car at 55890. The grandmother wrote this down because she thought
it would be interesting to say how many miles they had been when they
got back. It took them twenty minutes to reach the outskirts of the city.

The old lady settled herself comfortably, removing her white cotton
gloves and putting them up with her purse on the shelf in front of the
back window. The children's mother still had on slacks and still had her
head tied up in a green kerchief, but the grandmother had on a navy blue
straw sailor hat with a bunch of white violets on the brim and a navy
blue dress with a small white dot in the print. Her collars and cuffs were
white organdy trimmed with lace and at her neckline she had pinned a
purple spray of cloth violets containing a sachet. In case of an accident,
anyone seeing her dead on the highway would know at once that she was
a lady.

She said she thought it was going to be a good day for driving, neither
too hot nor too cold, and she cautioned Bailey that the speed limit was
fifty-five miles an hour and that the patrolmen hid themselves behind
billboards and small clumps of trees and sped out after you before you
had a chance to slow down. She pointed out interesting details of the
scenery: Stone Mountain; the blue granite that in some places came up
to both sides of the highway; the brilliant red clay banks slightly streaked
with purple; and the various crops that made rows of green lace-work on
the ground. The trees were full of silver-white sunlight and the meanest
of them sparkled. The children were reading comic magazines and their
mother had gone back to sleep.

"Let's go through Georgia fast so we won't have to look at it much,"
John Wesley said.

"If I were a little boy," said the grandmother, "I wouldn't talk about   15
my native state that way. Tennessee has the mountains and Georgia has
the hills."

"Tennessee is just a hillbilly dumping ground," John Wesley said,
"and Georgia is a lousy state too."

"You said it," June Star said.

"In my time," said the grandmother, folding her thin veined fingers,
"children were more respectful of their native states and their parents
and everything else. People did right then. Oh look at the cute little

pickaninny!" she said and pointed to a Negro child standing in the door of a shack. "Wouldn't that make a picture, now?" she asked and they all turned and looked at the little Negro out of the back window. He waved.

"He didn't have any britches on," June Star said.

"He probably didn't have any," the grandmother explained. "Little 20 niggers in the country don't have things like we do. If I could paint, I'd paint that picture," she said.

The children exchanged comic books.

The grandmother offered to hold the baby and the children's mother passed him over the front seat to her. She set him on her knee and bounced him and told him about the things they were passing. She rolled her eyes and screwed up her mouth and stuck her leathery thin face into his smooth bland one. Occasionally he gave her a faraway smile. They passed a large cotton field with five or six graves fenced in the middle of it, like a small island. "Look at the graveyard!" the grandmother said, pointing it out. "That was the old family burying ground. That belonged to the plantation."

"Where's the plantation?" John Wesley asked.

"Gone With the Wind," said the grandmother. "Ha. Ha."

When the children finished all the comic books they had brought, 25 they opened the lunch and ate it. The grandmother ate a peanut butter sandwich and an olive and would not let the children throw the box and the paper napkins out the window. When there was nothing else to do they played a game by choosing a cloud and making the other two guess what shape it suggested. John Wesley took one the shape of a cow and June Star guessed a cow and John Wesley said, no, an automobile, and June Star said he didn't play fair, and they began to slap each other over the grandmother.

The grandmother said she would tell them a story if they would keep quiet. When she told a story, she rolled her eyes and waved her head and was very dramatic. She said once when she was a maiden lady she had been courted by a Mr. Edgar Atkins Teagarden from Jasper, Georgia. She said he was a very good-looking man and a gentleman and that he brought her a watermelon every Saturday afternoon with his initials cut in it, E.A.T. Well, one Saturday, she said, Mr. Teagarden brought the watermelon and there was nobody at home and he left it on the front porch and returned in his buggy to Jasper, but she never got the watermelon, she said, because a nigger boy ate it when he saw the initials, E.A.T.! This story tickled John Wesley's funny bone and he giggled and giggled but June Star didn't think it was any good. She said she wouldn't marry a man that just brought her a watermelon on Saturday. The grandmother said she would have done well to marry Mr. Teagarden because he was a gentleman and had bought Coca-Cola stock when it first came out and that he had died only a few years ago, a very wealthy man.

They stopped at The Tower for barbecued sandwiches. The Tower was a part stucco and part wood filling station and dance hall set in a clearing outside of Timothy. A fat man named Red Sammy Butts ran it and there were signs stuck here and there on the building and for miles up and down the highway saying, TRY RED SAMMY'S FAMOUS BARBECUE. NONE LIKE FAMOUS RED SAMMY'S! RED SAM! THE FAT BOY WITH THE HAPPY LAUGH. A VETERAN! RED SAMMY'S YOUR MAN!

Red Sammy was lying on the bare ground outside The Tower with his head under a truck while a gray monkey about a foot high, chained to a small chinaberry tree, chattered nearby. The monkey sprang back into the tree and got on the highest limb as soon as he saw the children jump out of the car and run toward him.

Inside, The Tower was a long dark room with a counter at one end and tables at the other and dancing space in the middle. They all sat down at a board table next to the nickelodeon and Red Sam's wife, a tall burnt-brown woman with hair and eyes lighter than her skin, came and took their order. The children's mother put a dime in the machine and played "The Tennessee Waltz," and the grandmother said that tune always made her want to dance. She asked Bailey if he would like to dance but he only glared at her. He didn't have a naturally sunny disposition like she did and trips made him nervous. The grandmother's brown eyes were very bright. She swayed her head from side to side and pretended she was dancing in her chair. June Star said play something she could tap to so the children's mother put in another dime and played a fast number and June Star stepped out onto the dance floor and did her tap routine.

"Ain't she cute?" Red Sam's wife said, leaning over the counter.   30
"Would you like to come be my little girl?"

"No I certainly wouldn't," June Star said. "I wouldn't live in a broken-down place like this for a million bucks!" and she ran back to the table.

"Ain't she cute?" the woman repeated, stretching her mouth politely.

"Aren't you ashamed?" hissed the grandmother.

Red Sam came in and told his wife to quit lounging on the counter and hurry up with these people's order. His khaki trousers reached just to his hip bones and his stomach hung over them like a sack of meal swaying under his shirt. He came over and sat down at a table nearby and let out a combination sigh and yodel. "You can't win," he said. "You can't win," and he wiped his sweating red face off with a gray handkerchief. "These days you don't know who to trust," he said. "Ain't that the truth?"

"People are certainly not nice like they used to be," said the grandmother.   35

"Two fellers come in here last week," Red Sammy said, "driving a Chrysler. It was a old beat-up car but it was a good one and these boys looked all right to me. Said they worked at the mill and you know I let them fellers charge the gas they bought? Now why did I do that?"

"Because you're a good man!" the grandmother said at once.

"Yes'm, I suppose so," Red Sam said as if he were struck with this answer.

His wife brought the orders, carrying the five plates all at once without a tray, two in each hand and one balanced on her arm. "It isn't a soul in this green world of God's that you can trust," she said. "And I don't count nobody out of that, not nobody," she repeated, looking at Red Sammy.

"Did you read about that criminal, The Misfit, that's escaped?" 40 asked the grandmother.

"I wouldn't be a bit surprised if he didn't attack this place right here," said the woman. "If he hears about it being here, I wouldn't be none surprised to see him. If he hears it's two cent in the cash register, I wouldn't be a tall surprised if he. . . ."

"That'll do," Red Sam said. "Go bring these people their Co'-Colas," and the woman went off to get the rest of the order.

"A good man is hard to find," Red Sammy said. "Everything is getting terrible. I remember the day you could go off and leave your screen door unlatched. Not no more."

He and the grandmother discussed better times. The old lady said that in her opinion Europe was entirely to blame for the way things were now. She said the way Europe acted you would think we were made of money and Red Sam said it was no use talking about it, she was exactly right. The children ran outside into the white sunlight and looked at the monkey in the lacy chinaberry tree. He was busy catching fleas on himself and biting each one carefully between his teeth as if it were a delicacy.

They drove off again into the hot afternoon. The grandmother took 45 cat naps and woke up every few minutes with her own snoring. Outside of Toombsboro she woke up and recalled an old plantation that she had visited in this neighborhood once when she was a young lady. She said the house had six white columns across the front and that there was an avenue of oaks leading up to it and two little wooden trellis arbors on either side in front where you sat down with your suitor after a stroll in the garden. She recalled exactly which road to turn off to get to it. She knew that Bailey would not be willing to lose any time looking at an old house, but the more she talked about it, the more she wanted to see it once again and find out if the little twin arbors were still standing. "There was a secret panel in this house," she said craftily, not telling the truth but wishing that she were, "and the story went that all the family silver was hidden in it when Sherman° came through but it was never found. . . ."

"Hey!" John Wesley said. "Let's go see it! We'll find it! We'll poke all the woodwork and find it! Who lives there? Where do you turn off at? Hey Pop, can't we turn off there?"

"We never have seen a house with a secret panel!" June Star shrieked. "Let's go to the house with the secret panel! Hey Pop, can't we go see the house with the secret panel!"

Sherman: William Tecumseh Sherman (1820–1891), Union Army commander who led infamous marches through the South during the Civil War.

"It's not far from here, I know," the grandmother said. "It won't take over twenty minutes."

Bailey was looking straight ahead. His jaw was as rigid as a horseshoe. "No," he said.

The children began to yell and scream that they wanted to see the 50 house with the secret panel. John Wesley kicked the back of the front seat and June Star hung over her mother's shoulder and whined desperately into her ear that they never had any fun even on their vacation, that they could never do what THEY wanted to do. The baby began to scream and John Wesley kicked the back of the seat so hard that his father could feel the blows in his kidney.

"All right!" he shouted and drew the car to a stop at the side of the road. "Will you all shut up? Will you all just shut up for one second? If you don't shut up, we won't go anywhere."

"It would be very educational for them," the grandmother murmured.

"All right," Bailey said, "but get this: this is the only time we're going to stop for anything like this. This is the one and only time."

"The dirt road that you have to turn down is about a mile back," the grandmother directed. "I marked it when we passed."

"A dirt road," Bailey groaned.   55

After they had turned around and were headed toward the dirt road, the grandmother recalled other points about the house, the beautiful glass over the front doorway and the candle-lamp in the hall. John Wesley said that the secret panel was probably in the fireplace.

"You can't go inside this house," Bailey said. "You don't know who lives there."

"While you all talk to the people in front, I'll run around behind and get in a window," John Wesley suggested.

"We'll all stay in the car," his mother said.

They turned onto the dirt road and the car raced roughly along in a 60 swirl of pink dust. The grandmother recalled the times when there were no paved roads and thirty miles was a day's journey. The dirt road was hilly and there were sudden washes in it and sharp curves on dangerous embankments. All at once they would be on a hill, looking down over the blue tops of trees for miles around, then the next minute, they would be in a red depression with the dust-coated trees looking down on them.

"This place had better turn up in a minute," Bailey said, "or I'm going to turn around."

The road looked as if no one had traveled on it for months.

"It's not much farther," the grandmother said and just as she said it, a horrible thought came to her. The thought was so embarrassing that she turned red in the face and her eyes dilated and her feet jumped up, upsetting her valise in the corner. The instant the valise moved, the newspaper top she had over the basket under it rose with a snarl and Pitty Sing, the cat, sprang onto Bailey's shoulder.

The children were thrown to the floor and their mother, clutching the baby, was thrown out the door onto the ground; the old lady was thrown into the front seat. The car turned over once and landed right-side-up in a gulch off the side of the road. Bailey remained in the driver's seat with the cat—gray-striped with a broad white face and an orange nose—clinging to his neck like a caterpillar.

As soon as the children saw they could move their arms and legs, they scrambled out of the car, shouting, "We've had an ACCIDENT!" The grandmother was curled up under the dashboard, hoping she was injured so that Bailey's wrath would not come down on her all at once. The horrible thought she had before the accident was that the house she had remembered so vividly was not in Georgia but in Tennessee.

Bailey removed the cat from his neck with both hands and flung it out the window against the side of a pine tree. Then he got out of the car and started looking for the children's mother. She was sitting against the side of the red gutted ditch, holding the screaming baby, but she only had a cut down her face and a broken shoulder. "We've had an ACCIDENT!" the children screamed in a frenzy of delight.

"But nobody's killed," June Star said with disappointment as the grandmother limped out of the car, her hat still pinned to her head but the broken front brim standing up at a jaunty angle and the violet spray hanging off the side. They all sat down in the ditch, except the children, to recover from the shock. They were all shaking.

"Maybe a car will come along," said the children's mother hoarsely.

"I believe I have injured an organ," said the grandmother, pressing her side, but no one answered her. Bailey's teeth were clattering. He had on a yellow sport shirt with bright blue parrots designed in it and his face was as yellow as the shirt. The grandmother decided that she would not mention that the house was in Tennessee.

The road was about ten feet above and they could see only the tops of the trees on the other side of it. Behind the ditch they were sitting in there were more woods, tall and dark and deep. In a few minutes they saw a car some distance away on top of a hill, coming slowly as if the occupants were watching them. The grandmother stood up and waved both arms dramatically to attract their attention. The car continued to come on slowly, disappeared around a bend and appeared again, moving even slower, on top of the hill they had gone over. It was a big black battered hearse-like automobile. There were three men in it.

It came to a stop just over them and for some minutes, the driver looked down with a steady expressionless gaze to where they were sitting, and didn't speak. Then he turned his head and muttered something to the other two and they got out. One was a fat boy in black trousers and a red sweat shirt with a silver stallion embossed on the front of it. He moved around on the right side of them and stood staring, his mouth partly open in a kind of loose grin. The other had on khaki pants and a blue striped coat and a gray hat pulled down very low, hiding most of his face. He came around slowly on the left side. Neither spoke.

The driver got out of the car and stood by the side of it, looking down at them. He was an older man than the other two. His hair was just beginning to gray and he wore silver-rimmed spectacles that gave him a scholarly look. He had a long creased face and didn't have on any shirt or undershirt. He had on blue jeans that were too tight for him and was holding a black hat and a gun. The two boys also had guns.

"We've had an ACCIDENT!" the children screamed.

The grandmother had the peculiar feeling that the bespectacled man was someone she knew. His face was as familiar to her as if she had known him all her life but she could not recall who he was. He moved away from the car and began to come down the embankment, placing his feet carefully so that he wouldn't slip. He had on tan and white shoes and no socks, and his ankles were red and thin. "Good afternoon," he said. "I see you all had you a little spill."

"We turned over twice!" said the grandmother.   75

"Oncet," he corrected. "We seen it happen. Try their car and see will it run, Hiram," he said quietly to the boy with the gray hat.

"What you got that gun for?" John Wesley asked. "Whatcha gonna do with that gun?"

"Lady," the man said to the children's mother, "would you mind calling them children to sit down by you? Children make me nervous. I want all you all to sit down right together there where you're at."

"What are you telling US what to do for?" June Star asked.

Behind them the line of woods gaped like a dark open mouth.   80 "Come here," said their mother.

"Look here now," Bailey said suddenly, "we're in a predicament! We're in. . . ."

The grandmother shrieked. She scrambled to her feet and stood staring. "You're The Misfit!" she said. "I recognized you at once!"

"Yes'm," the man said, smiling slightly as if he were pleased in spite of himself to be known, "but it would have been better for all of you, lady, if you hadn't of reckernized me."

Bailey turned his head sharply and said something to his mother that shocked even the children. The old lady began to cry and The Misfit reddened.

"Lady," he said, "don't you get upset. Sometimes a man says things   85 he don't mean. I don't reckon he meant to talk to you thataway."

"You wouldn't shoot a lady, would you?" the grandmother said and removed a clean handkerchief from her cuff and began to slap at her eyes with it.

The Misfit pointed the toe of his shoe into the ground and made a little hole and then covered it up again. "I would hate to have to," he said.

"Listen," the grandmother almost screamed, "I know you're a good man. You don't look a bit like you have common blood. I know you must come from nice people!"

"Yes mam," he said, "finest people in the world." When he smiled he showed a row of strong white teeth. "God never made a finer woman than my mother and my daddy's heart was pure gold," he said. The boy with the red sweat shirt had come around behind them and was standing with his gun at his hip. The Misfit squatted down on the ground. "Watch them children, Bobby Lee," he said. "You know they make me nervous." He looked at the six of them huddled together in front of him and he seemed to be embarrassed as if he couldn't think of anything to say. "Ain't a cloud in the sky," he remarked, looking up at it. "Don't see no sun but don't see no cloud neither."

"Yes, it's a beautiful day," said the grandmother. "Listen," she said, 90 "you shouldn't call yourself The Misfit because I know you're a good man at heart. I can just look at you and tell."

"Hush!" Bailey yelled. "Hush! Everybody shut up and let me handle this!" He was squatting in the position of a runner about to sprint forward but he didn't move.

"I pre-chate that, lady," The Misfit said and drew a little circle in the ground with the butt of his gun.

"It'll take a half a hour to fix this here car," Hiram called, looking over the raised hood of it.

"Well, first you and Bobby Lee get him and that little boy to step over yonder with you," The Misfit said, pointing to Bailey and John Wesley. "The boys want to ast you something," he said to Bailey. "Would you mind stepping back in them woods there with them?"

"Listen," Bailey began, "we're in a terrible predicament! Nobody 95 realizes what this is," and his voice cracked. His eyes were as blue and intense as the parrots in his shirt and he remained perfectly still.

The grandmother reached up to adjust her hat brim as if she were going to the woods with him but it came off in her hand. She stood staring at it and after a second she let it fall to the ground. Hiram pulled Bailey up by the arm as if he were assisting an old man. John Wesley caught hold of his father's hand and Bobby Lee followed. They went off toward the woods and just as they reached the dark edge, Bailey turned and supporting himself against a gray naked pine trunk, he shouted, "I'll be back in a minute, Mamma, wait on me!"

"Come back this instant!" his mother shrilled but they all disappeared into the woods.

"Bailey Boy!" the grandmother called in a tragic voice but she found she was looking at The Misfit squatting on the ground in front of her. "I just know you're a good man," she said desperately. "You're not a bit common!"

"Nome, I ain't a good man," The Misfit said after a second as if he had considered her statement carefully, "but I ain't the worst in the world neither. My daddy said I was a different breed of dog from my brothers and sisters. 'You know,' Daddy said, 'it's some that can live their whole life out without asking about it and it's others has to know why it is, and this boy is one of the latters. He's going to be into everything!'" He put on his black hat and looked up suddenly and then away deep into the woods as if he were embarrassed again. "I'm sorry I don't have on a shirt before you ladies," he said, hunching his shoulders slightly. "We buried our clothes that we had on when we escaped and we're just making do until we can get better. We borrowed these from some folks we met," he explained.

"That's perfectly all right," the grandmother said. "Maybe Bailey has   100 an extra shirt in his suitcase."

"I'll look and see terrectly," The Misfit said.

"Where are they taking him?" the children's mother screamed.

"Daddy was a card himself," The Misfit said. "You couldn't put anything over on him. He never got in trouble with the Authorities though. Just had the knack of handling them."

"You could be honest too if you'd only try," said the grandmother. "Think how wonderful it would be to settle down and live a comfortable life and not have to think about somebody chasing you all the time."

The Misfit kept scratching in the ground with the butt of his gun as   105 if he were thinking about it. "Yes'm, somebody is always after you," he murmured.

The grandmother noticed how thin his shoulder blades were just behind his hat because she was standing up looking down on him. "Do you ever pray?" she asked.

He shook his head. All she saw was the black hat wiggle between his shoulder blades. "Nome," he said.

There was a pistol shot from the woods, followed closely by another. Then silence. The old lady's head jerked around. She could hear the wind move through the tree tops like a long satisfied insuck of breath. "Bailey Boy!" she called.

"I was a gospel singer for a while," The Misfit said. "I been most everything. Been in the arm service, both land and sea, at home and abroad, been twict married, been an undertaker, been with the railroads, plowed Mother Earth, been in a tornado, seen a man burnt alive oncet," and he looked up at the children's mother and the little girl who were sitting close together, their faces white and their eyes glassy; "I even seen a woman flogged," he said.

"Pray, pray," the grandmother began, "pray, pray...."   110

"I never was a bad boy that I remember of," The Misfit said in an almost dreamy voice, "but somewheres along the line I done something wrong and got sent to the penitentiary. I was buried alive," and he looked up and held her attention to him by a steady stare.

"That's when you should have started to pray," she said. "What did you do to get sent to the penitentiary that first time?"

"Turn to the right, it was a wall," The Misfit said, looking up again at the cloudless sky. "Turn to the left, it was a wall. Look up it was a ceiling, look down it was a floor. I forget what I done, lady. I set there and set there, trying to remember what it was I done and I ain't recalled it to this day. Oncet in a while, I would think it was coming to me, but it never come."

"Maybe they put you in by mistake," the old lady said vaguely.

"Nome," he said. "It wasn't no mistake. They had the papers on me."   115

"You must have stolen something," she said.

The Misfit sneered slightly. "Nobody had nothing I wanted," he said. "It was a head-doctor at the penitentiary said what I had done was kill my daddy but I known that for a lie. My daddy died in nineteen ought nineteen of the epidemic flu and I never had a thing to do with it. He was buried in the Mount Hopewell Baptist churchyard and you can see for yourself."

"If you would pray," the old lady said, "Jesus would help you."

"That's right," The Misfit said.

"Well then, why don't you pray?" she asked trembling with delight   120 suddenly.

"I don't want no hep," he said. "I'm doing all right by myself."

Bobby Lee and Hiram came ambling back from the woods. Bobby Lee was dragging a yellow shirt with bright blue parrots in it.

"Throw me that shirt, Bobby Lee," The Misfit said. The shirt came flying at him and landed on his shoulder and he put it on. The grandmother couldn't name what the shirt reminded her of. "No, lady," The Misfit said while he was buttoning it up, "I found out the crime don't matter. You can do one thing or you can do another, kill a man or take a tire off his car, because sooner or later you're going to forget what it was you done and just be punished for it."

The children's mother had begun to make heaving noises as if she couldn't get her breath. "Lady," he asked, "would you and that little girl like to step off yonder with Bobby Lee and Hiram and join your husband?"

"Yes, thank you," the mother said faintly. Her left arm dangled help-   125 lessly and she was holding the baby, who had gone to sleep, in the other. "Hep that lady up, Hiram," The Misfit said as she struggled to climb out of the ditch, "and Bobby Lee, you hold onto that little girl's hand."

"I don't want to hold hands with him," June Star said. "He reminds me of a pig."

The fat boy blushed and laughed and caught her by the arm and pulled her off into the woods after Hiram and her mother.

Alone with The Misfit, the grandmother found that she had lost her voice. There was not a cloud in the sky nor any sun. There was nothing around her but woods. She wanted to tell him that he must pray. She opened and closed her mouth several times before anything came out. Finally she found herself saying, "Jesus, Jesus," meaning Jesus will help you, but the way she was saying it, it sounded as if she might be cursing.

"Yes'm," The Misfit said as if he agreed. "Jesus thown everything off balance. It was the same case with Him as with me except He hadn't committed any crime and they could prove I had committed one because they had the papers on me. Of course," he said, "they never shown me my papers. That's why I sign myself now. I said long ago, you get your signature and sign everything you do and keep a copy of it. Then you'll know what you done and you can hold up the crime to the punishment and see do they match and in the end you'll have something to prove you ain't been treated right. I call myself The Misfit," he said, "because I can't make what all I done wrong fit what all I gone through in punishment."

There was a piercing scream from the woods, followed closely by a pistol report. "Does it seem right to you, lady, that one is punished a heap and another ain't punished at all?"   130

"Jesus!" the old lady cried. "You've got good blood! I know you wouldn't shoot a lady! I know you come from nice people! Pray! Jesus, you ought not to shoot a lady. I'll give you all the money I've got!"

"Lady," The Misfit said, looking beyond her far into the woods, "there never was a body that give the undertaker a tip."

There were two more pistol reports and the grandmother raised her head like a parched old turkey hen crying for water and called, "Bailey Boy, Bailey Boy!" as if her heart would break.

"Jesus was the only One that ever raised the dead," The Misfit continued, "and He shouldn't have done it. He thown everything off balance. If He did what He said, then it's nothing for you to do but thow away everything and follow Him, and if He didn't, then it's nothing for you to do but enjoy the few minutes you got left the best way you can — by killing somebody or burning down his house or doing some other meanness to him. No pleasure but meanness," he said and his voice had become almost a snarl.

"Maybe He didn't raise the dead," the old lady mumbled, not knowing what she was saying and feeling so dizzy that she sank down in the ditch with her legs twisted under her.   135

"I wasn't there so I can't say He didn't," The Misfit said. "I wisht I had of been there," he said, hitting the ground with his fist. "It ain't right I wasn't there because if I had of been there I would of known. Listen lady," he said in a high voice, "if I had of been there I would of known and I wouldn't be like I am now." His voice seemed about to crack and the grandmother's head cleared for an instant. She saw the man's face twisted close to her own as if he were going to cry and she murmured, "Why you're one of my babies. You're one of my own children!" She reached out and touched him on the shoulder. The Misfit sprang back as if a snake had bitten him and shot her three times through the chest. Then he put his gun down on the ground and took off his glasses and began to clean them.

Hiram and Bobby Lee returned from the woods and stood over the ditch, looking down at the grandmother who half sat and half lay in a puddle of blood with her legs crossed under her like a child's and her face smiling up at the cloudless sky.

Without his glasses, The Misfit's eyes were red-rimmed and pale and defenseless-looking. "Take her off and thow her where you thown the others," he said, picking up the cat that was rubbing itself against his leg.

"She was a talker, wasn't she?" Bobby Lee said, sliding down the ditch with a yodel.

"She would of been a good woman," The Misfit said, "if it had been 140 somebody there to shoot her every minute of her life."

"Some fun!" Bobby Lee said.

"Shut up, Bobby Lee," The Misfit said. "It's no real pleasure in life."

CONSIDERATIONS FOR CRITICAL THINKING AND WRITING

1. **FIRST RESPONSE.** How does O'Connor portray the family? What is comic about them? What qualities about them are we meant to take seriously? Are you shocked by what happens to them? Does your attitude toward them remain constant during the course of the story?

2. How do the grandmother's concerns about the trip to Florida foreshadow events in the story?

3. Describe the grandmother. How does O'Connor make her the central character?

4. Characterize The Misfit. What makes him so? Can he be written off as simply insane? How does the grandmother respond to him?

5. Why does The Misfit say that "Jesus thown everything off balance" (para. 129)? What does religion have to do with the brutal action of this story?

6. What does The Misfit mean at the end when he says about the grandmother, "She would of been a good woman . . . if it had been somebody there to shoot her every minute of her life"?

7. Describe the story's tone. Is it consistent? What is the effect of O'Connor's use of tone?

8. How is coincidence used to advance the plot? How do coincidences lead to ironies in the story?

9. Explain how the title points to the story's theme.

10. **CONNECTION TO ANOTHER SELECTION.** What makes "A Good Man Is Hard to Find" so difficult to interpret in contrast, say, to Hawthorne's "The Birthmark" (p. 304)?

Perspectives on O'Connor

FLANNERY O'CONNOR

On the Use of Exaggeration and Distortion   1969

When I write a novel in which the central action is a baptism, I am very well aware that for a majority of my readers, baptism is a meaningless rite, and so in my novel I have to see that this baptism carries enough awe and mystery to jar the reader into some kind of emotional recognition of its significance. To this end I have to bend the whole novel — its language, its structure, its action. I have to make the reader feel, in his bones if nowhere else, that something is going on here that counts. Distortion in this case is an instrument; exaggeration has a purpose, and the whole structure of the story or novel has been made what it is because of belief. This is not the kind of distortion that destroys; it is the kind that reveals, or should reveal.

From "Novelist and Believer" in *Mystery and Manners*

CONSIDERATIONS FOR CRITICAL THINKING AND WRITING

1. O'Connor says that exaggeration and distortion reveal something in her stories. What is the effect of such exaggeration and distortion in "A Good Man Is Hard to Find?" What is revealed by it?
2. Do you think that O'Connor's story has anything to offer a reader who has no religious faith? Explain why or why not.

JOSEPHINE HENDIN (B. 1946)

On O'Connor's Refusal to "Do Pretty"   1970

There is, in the memory of one Milledgeville matron, the image of O'Connor at nineteen or twenty who, when invited to a wedding shower for an old family friend, remained standing, her back pressed against the wall, scowling at the group of women who had sat down to lunch. Neither the devil nor her mother could make her say yes to this fiercely gracious female society, but Flannery O'Connor could not say no even in a whisper. She could not refuse the invitation but she would not accept it either. She did not exactly "fuss" but neither did she "do pretty."

From *The World of Flannery O'Connor*

CONSIDERATIONS FOR CRITICAL THINKING AND WRITING

1. How is O'Connor's personality revealed in this anecdote about her ambivalent response to society? Allow the description to be suggestive for you, and flesh out a brief portrait of her.

2. Consider how this personality makes itself apparent in "A Good Man Is Hard to Find." How does the anecdote help to characterize the narrator's voice in the story?

3. To what extent do you think biographical details such as this — assuming the Milledgeville matron's memory to be accurate — can shed light on a writer's works?

CLAIRE KATZ (B. 1935)

The Function of Violence in O'Connor's Fiction   1974

From the moment the reader enters O'Connor's backwoods, he is poised on the edge of a pervasive violence. Characters barely contain their rage; images reflect a hostile nature; and even the Christ to whom the characters are ultimately driven is a threatening figure . . . full of the apocalyptic wrath of the Old Testament.

O'Connor's conscious purpose is evident enough . . . : to reveal the need for grace in a world grotesque without a transcendent context. "I have found that my subject in fiction is the action of grace in territory largely held by the devil," she wrote [in *Mystery and Manners*], and she was not vague about what the devil is: "an evil intelligence determined on its own supremacy." It would seem that for O'Connor, given the fact of original Sin, any intelligence determined on its own supremacy was intrinsically evil. For in each work, it is the impulse toward secular autonomy, the smug confidence that human nature is perfectible by its own efforts, that she sets out to destroy, through an act of violence so intense that the character is rendered helpless, a passive victim of a superior power. Again and again she creates a fiction in which a character attempts to live autonomously, to define himself and his values, only to be jarred back to what she calls "reality" — the recognition of helplessness in the face of contingency, and the need for absolute submission to the power of Christ.

From "Flannery O'Connor's Rage of Vision"
in *American Literature*

CONSIDERATIONS FOR CRITICAL THINKING AND WRITING

1. Which O'Connor characters can be accurately described as having an "evil intelligence determined on its own supremacy" (para. 2)? Choose one character, and write an essay explaining how this description is central to the conflict of the story.

2. To what extent might "A Good Man Is Hard to Find" be accurately described as a story "in which a character attempts to live autonomously, to define . . . values, only to be jarred back to . . . 'reality' — the recognition of helplessness in the face of contingency . . ." (para. 2)?

Time Magazine, On *A Good Man Is Hard to Find*   1962

Highly unladylike . . . a brutal irony, a slam-bang humor, and a style of writing as balefully direct as a death sentence.

> From a *Time* magazine blurb quoted on the cover
> of the second American edition of *A Good Man Is Hard to Find*

Considerations for Critical Thinking and Writing

1. How adequate do you think this blurb is in characterizing the story?
2. **CREATIVE RESPONSE.** Write your own blurb for the story and be prepared to justify your pithy description.

A Study of Dagoberto Gilb:
The Author Reflects
on Three Stories

For me, fiction is life transformed
and fueled by imagination.
—DAGOBERTO GILB

Courtesy of Dagoberto Gilb.

INTRODUCTION

Dagoberto Gilb chose the three short stories in this chapter (as well as a
fourth story, "Romero's Shirt," in Chapter 7, p. 218) and provided commentary on each of them. Along with his personal observations on the
stories are relevant images and documents that offer perspectives for
interpreting and appreciating his fiction. Gilb's candid comments on
the stories are written specifically for readers who are interested in why
and how the stories were composed. He reveals some of the biographical

contexts and circumstances that led him to become an avid reader and then a successful writer (despite the dismal grade he received for his first college English paper) and how he managed to build a fictional world while working full time on construction sites.

In addition to the stories and commentaries, this chapter also offers contexts for the stories, including photographs of Gilb's family and his life as a construction carpenter in Los Angeles, California, and El Paso, Texas. Also included are a draft manuscript page from an essay collection, an edited galley from the short story "Uncle Rock" originally published in *The New Yorker,* Gilb's comments on physical labor and popular perceptions of Mexican American culture, and an interview with Michael Meyer that ranges from issues of political correctness to how "advocacy" is embedded in Gilb's literary art. You'll find this ex-carpenter to be a straightforward storyteller who makes a point of being on the level.

A BRIEF BIOGRAPHY

Born in Los Angeles in 1950, Dagoberto Gilb worked as a construction worker and a journeyman high-rise carpenter with the United Brotherhood of Carpenters for some sixteen years as he began hammering out his fiction. Though born and raised in California, he considered both Los Angeles and El Paso to be home. His Anglo father was a laconic, hardened World War II Marine Corps veteran who worked for nearly fifty years in a Los Angeles industrial laundry, and his mother was an undocumented Mexican immigrant, and their marriage ended early. Gilb's life, like his fiction, is grounded by working-class circumstances in which laborers sweat to pay bills and put food on the table. He does not list any unpaid internships in his résumé.

As Gilb acknowledges in *Gritos,* a collection of essays, he was not in his youth "precocious in matters of literature, even to the end of my teenage years when I still thought of 'book' more as a verb." He did, however, read on the job and make his way to junior college and then to the University of California, Santa Barbara, where he earned a B.A. and an M.A. studying philosophy and religious studies. In college, he devoured canonical American and European writers and then discovered Chicano literature, works that ultimately inspired him to write about his own experiences. After graduate school, he followed construction jobs between Los Angeles and El Paso, making a living and finding the material for framing much of his writing.

(*Top*) Dagoberto Gilb's mother. Los Angeles, California, late 1940s.
Courtesy of Dagoberto Gilb.

(*Right*) Dagoberto Gilb with his older son, Antonio. El Paso, Texas, 1978.
Courtesy of Dagoberto Gilb.

The author with his son, Antonio. Los Angeles, California, 1981. The
'62 Chevy pictured here is the very one mentioned on page 278.
Courtesy of Dagoberto Gilb.

Following some success in publishing a number of short stories in literary journals, a chapbook-size collection of stories, *Winners
on the Pass Line,* appeared in 1985. His first full collection, the critically
acclaimed book *The Magic of Blood* (1993), won the PEN/Ernest Hemingway Award as well as the Jesse Jones Award from the Texas Institute of
Letters and was a finalist for the PEN/Faulkner Award. On the heels of a
National Endowment for the Arts Fellowship, he published a novel, *The
Last Known Residence of Mickey Acuna* (1994), which was followed by a Guggenheim Foundation Fellowship. *Gritos* (2003), consisting of previously
published essays in such venues as *The New Yorker,* the *New York Times,*
the *Los Angeles Times,* and *The Nation,* along with commentaries written
for National Public Radio's "Fresh Air," offers a perspective on how a

Dagoberto Gilb at work. Los Angeles, California, 1986.
Courtesy of Dagoberto Gilb.

Mexican American working man became a nationally recognized working writer. Another novel, *The Flowers* (2008), and two more collections of stories, *Woodcuts of Women* (2001) and *Before the End, After the Beginning* (2011), have solidified his reputation as a highly regarded fiction writer. His works have been translated into Spanish, French, German, Italian, Japanese, Chinese, and Turkish, and he has been invited to be a visiting writer at a number of schools including the University of Texas at Austin, the University of Wyoming, the University of Arizona, and Vassar College.

Previously a tenured professor in the Creative Writing Program at Texas State University in San Marcos, Gilb is currently writer-in-residence and executive director of Centro Victoria, a center for Mexican American literature and culture at the University of Houston in Victoria, Texas, where the undergraduate student body is primarily Latino, a school he describes as "the smallest, most just barely at its beginning university in the country." Located equidistant from Houston, Austin, San Antonio, and Corpus Christi, in a state that in several years will be 50 percent Latino, Centro Victoria was founded, in part, to educate Texans of all ethnicities and educational levels—and others outside the state—about the history and culture of Mexican Americans, who make up two-thirds of the Latino population in the United States. The purpose of the center is to foster an understanding and appreciation of Mexican American literature and art in Texas and beyond.

(*Left*) The author in 2002, on the Brownsville, Texas–Matamoros, Mexico, borderline.
Courtesy of Dagoberto Gilb.

(*Below*) Dagoberto Gilb with his younger son, Ricardo. Uruapan, Mexico, 2005.
Courtesy of Dagoberto Gilb.

(*Top*) The author at the Pirámedes del Sol y
Luna, Mexico, 2008.
Courtesy of Dagoberto Gilb.

(*Right*) Dagoberto Gilb at the PEN/Faulkner
Reading at the Folger Shakespeare Library,
Washington, D.C., 2012.
Courtesy of Dagoberto Gilb.

One of Centro Victoria's major projects is to provide Texas students and teachers with lesson plans based on *Hecho en Tejas: An Anthology of Texas Mexican Literature* (2006), edited by Gilb, which ranges from sixteenth-century exploration narratives to twenty-first-century poetry and prose. By integrating Mexican American arts into the curriculum, the program elevates the vicissitudes of Latinos' lives—satisfactions as well as challenges—to an art and helps to validate the very existence and presence of Latinos in the United States who never before had the opportunity to read about their own unique experiences. Gilb makes clear in his introduction to *Hecho en Tejas* that the predominant popular attitude toward people of Mexican descent in the United States, whether toward legitimate citizens or the undocumented, what some in the media call "illegals," is shaped by cultural distortions:

> The kindest attitude portrays the culture as an homage in a children's museum, or as in a folklorico dance show, and the prevailing images, framed and shelved in the state's unconscious, are of men in sombreros and serapes walking burros, women patting tortillas or stuffing tamales in color-frilled white housedresses, while the stories of Mexican adventures are of border whorehouses and tequila drunks—not meant as harmful, only fascinating, and wild.

Gilb insists on moving beyond such patronizing images and passionately announces as the anthology's major theme: "We have been here, we are still here." (For a brief provocative comparison of Mexican American and African American cultural experiences in the West and South, see Gilb's "On Distortions of Mexican American Culture," p. 292.)

Furthering his goal of making Mexican Americans apparent in American culture, in 2011 Gilb founded *Huizache: The Magazine of Latino Literature*, published by Centro Victoria at the University of Houston–Victoria. Featuring literary works from mostly Latino writers who are largely neglected or ignored, the magazine also opens its pages to all fiction, poetry, and essays that challenge ethnic, gender, or social stereotyping. "A huizache," as explained on the title page, "is an acacia tree that is native to Mexico but also grows wild in South and East Texas. It irritates the regional farmers because, no matter what they do, it keeps growing and populating." The editor, Diana López, asks readers to "think of this journal as the nursery that fosters this tree and any species considered 'invasive.'" *Huizache* is founded on the energy, ambition, and neglected talent of Latino and Latina writers in Texas and the Southwest.

Gilb's own writing offers a broad landscape of Mexican American experience in a direct, straightforward style that is energized by his unapologetically hearty and robust take on ordinary life. His characters work pretty hard in the face of ugly inequities, make money but not enough of it, get fired, find work, fall in love, desire marriage, settle on divorce, suffer loss, maintain dignity, strive to succeed, frequently fail, raise kids, embody fear, and stubbornly persevere—all of them serially engaged in the disorderly conduct of being human.

Dagoberto Gilb

How Books Bounce   2012

Many have asked me, how did you become a writer? This is one of those ordinary questions that comes at Q&A's, but at mine I sometimes catch a snarky or world-weary, all-caps emphasis on the *you*. I could snap off a couple of words in defense, but the truth is that I, too, find me a curious representative of literature. Real writers are bred like champion racehorses, the offspring of Seabiscuit and Secretariat. When real writers discuss their careers, they refer back (modestly, of course) to what they published before their double-digit birthdays. They had books at home (that's all I need to say there). The very classiest universities begged them to be undergrads, and while there they briefly thought they might become a molecular chemist or an avant-garde sculptor. Now, modestly, these real writers will say they were probably better at one of those. Whereas, in contrast, I read my first book when I was seventeen because, in a less than advanced English class for we special few (I worked a full-time, graveyard shift job as a janitor), one day the teacher mentioned a novel hippies were reading. I wanted to know what hippies read because they seemed to have all kinds of easy goings-on that weren't like mine. And nothing in mine included any books. My pre-janitor years I can't say were busy with any poetic forms other than chrome spokes on wheels and girls who didn't read poetry either. Where I came up, balls were as close to books as I got. I bounced them, hit them, threw them, caught them, guarded them, blocked them, kicked them, jump-shot them. They weren't books. Nobody expected me to read them. I didn't. Neither was it suggested that maybe I try an actual volume with unrounded corners, though if anyone had, I would have made it bounce too.

I was not, in other words, born a writer. And then I went to a junior college. Much of that incentive was not so much improving my brains as not losing them, or my legs, walking point° in Vietnam (older friends, drafted, came back not doing great). My first freshman comp paper I got a D. The teacher told me she was being generous. When I failed the class, I was smart enough to know who took night classes — on the curve with the most tired day job students (mine was full-time too, a department store stock boy), this time, at a lesser community college, I got a B. I did not consider a major in chemistry. The only sculpture I knew of came from Mexico, which, cool-looking and deep, I couldn't say I understood any better than what was taught in art history (nothing Mexican, indigenous, colonial, or modern). I tried a business law class. I liked math but too much homework. Sociology, political science, geography, history, philosophy — each offered original news to me. I was learning. Excited, I began eating it all up. Though I still feared English. That second

---

walking point: Leading a patrol.

semester requirement, when you study literature, I remember having to look up a word in virtually every sentence of Melville's *Billy Budd*. Supposedly American, I thought it had to be from a foreign language, and I wasn't sure if I understood what exactly happened to Mr. Budd. I took the teacher at his word for the explanation of it. Great story!

Oh, how I then fell in love. In the beginning it was any books I called on or which called on me. Books stacked and piled and neatly lined up in rows, new or used or checked out (I even stole them, yes, I here confess!). There were the small ones forgotten in quirky, cramped bottom corners, and ones that took tall ladders to touch, and ones that saw so little light their covers seemed to have recast inward — I loved them the most, these difficult ones, hard to get to know, to understand, odd, too quiet and bashful, secret. When suddenly I became furtive: though I would never take a lit class again, I was reading novels and poetry.

How did I become a writer? Something happened, that's pretty clear. Did lightning strike and skip the ears hearing, override the memory but alter the brain? Am I the product of some secret government experiment that maybe went wrong? How did a boy who cared only about sports — what little reading I would do young was from a newspaper sports page — become a man who would idealize books like classic teams and then become one of its professional "athletes"?

I've always been obsessed with story. Whether it's nature or nurture, or what I like to call my family mess, I cannot recall a time when I wasn't listening to a story being told. Maybe because I have only a single blurry memory of my father leaving my childhood home, it opens with ones about him and my mother. Of German descent, he was born in Kentucky but came to Los Angeles young. She was baptized in Mexico City at the Basilica de Guadalupe. He joined the Marines to fight the Japanese after Pearl Harbor. She kept the rising sun flag he'd captured as an advanced scout. Older, he watched her growing up next door to the industrial laundry where he started working when he was thirteen, where she eventually did too as a teenager (not for long). She grew up in that house next door with her mother, who was my grandmother, who was the mistress of the owner of the laundry who owned the house (what in Spanish is known as *la casa chica*). My grandmother came to the United States after her husband, my grandfather, was killed. By knife, went the story, and in the back. My grandmother came to the United States following her sister, my great-aunt, whose mother — this story! — had been married at fourteen to a man in his sixties and she had . . . not sure how many but a number of children by him. When my great-aunt turned eighteen, her mother traveled from Xalapa and in the capital rented the finest limousine for a visit to the presidential palace. And thus, my great-aunt represented Mexico on a tour to Europe and the United States as an opera singer. She wound up in Hollywood, married to a minor French director. My grandmother died young, making my mother closer to my great-aunt. By the time I am old enough to first see her — old, a widow for years, hard for a young person to imagine any glamorous youth attaching to her—she is nothing but a seamstress who needed money, a job, one of fifty at the industrial laundry where my father had become the floor supervisor. She repaired the elastic on bras, my father, bitter by divorce and who knows, enjoyed pointing out. He gave me a job there when I too turned thirteen. And this was when I begin to have stories.

When I think about being a writer now, I can't help but think of the improbable travel that my genes have made to get here. This journey. And to think we *each* have one, no matter to what breeding or privilege we were born. Why we perk up to listen, why we are driven to, I have no idea. It's so fun to bounce books on your ride—it's a necessary skill. But go, get out there, and what I know is you'll meet people, you'll see places, you'll hear stories that only you will be able to tell.

—D. G.

Dagoberto Gilb
Love in L.A.   *1993*

Jake slouched in a clot of near motionless traffic, in the peculiar gray of concrete, smog, and early morning beneath the overpass of the Holly-wood Freeway on Alvarado Street. He didn't really mind because he knew how much worse it could be trying to make a left onto the onramp. He certainly didn't do that every day of his life, and he'd assure anyone who'd ask that he never would either. A steady occupation had its advantages and he couldn't deny thinking about that too. He needed an FM radio in something better than this '58 Buick he drove. It would have crushed vel-vet interior with electric controls for the L.A. summer, a nice warm heater and defroster for the winter drives at the beach, a cruise control for those longer trips, mellow speakers front and rear of course, windows that hum closed, snuffing out that nasty exterior noise of freeways. The fact was that he'd probably have to change his whole style. Exotic colognes, plush, dark nightclubs, maitais and daiquiris, necklaced ladies in satin gowns, misty and sexy like in a tequila ad. Jake could imagine lots of possibili-ties when he let himself, but none that ended up with him pressed onto a stalled freeway.

Jake was thinking about this freedom of his so much that when he glimpsed its green light he just went ahead and stared bye bye to the steadily employed. When he turned his head the same direction his wind-shield faced, it was maybe one second too late. He pounced the brake pedal and steered the front wheels away from the tiny brakelights but the smack was unavoidable. Just one second sooner and it would only have been close. One second more and he'd be crawling up the Toyota's trunk. As it was, it seemed like only a harmless smack, much less solid than the one against his back bumper.

Jake considered driving past the Toyota but was afraid the traffic ahead would make it too difficult. As he pulled up against the curb a few carlengths ahead, it occurred to him that the traffic might have helped him get away too. He slammed the car door twice to make sure it was closed fully and to give himself another second more, then toured front and rear of his Buick for damage on or near the bumpers. Not an impressionable scratch even in the chrome. He perked up. Though the car's beauty was secondary to its ability to start and move, the body and paint were clean except for a few minor dings. This stood out as one of his few clearcut accomplishments over the years.

Before he spoke to the driver of the Toyota, whose looks he could see might present him with an added complication, he signaled to the driver of the car that hit him, still in his car and stopped behind the Toyota, and waved his hands and shook his head to let the man know there was no problem as far as he was concerned. The driver waved back and started his engine.

"It didn't even scratch my paint," Jake told her in that way of his. 5 "So how you doin? Any damage to the car? I'm kinda hoping so, just so it takes a little more time and we can talk some. Or else you can give me your phone number now and I won't have to lay my regular b.s. on you to get it later."

He took her smile as a good sign and relaxed. He inhaled her scent like it was clean air and straightened out his less than new but not unhip clothes.

"You've got Florida plates. You look like you must be Cuban."

"My parents are from Venezuela."

"My name's Jake." He held out his hand.

"Mariana."   10

They shook hands like she'd never done it before in her life.

"I really am sorry about hitting you like that." He sounded genuine. He fondled the wide dimple near the cracked taillight. "It's amazing how easy it is to put a dent in these new cars. They're so soft they might replace waterbeds soon." Jake was confused about how to proceed with this. So much seemed so unlikely, but there was always possibility. "So maybe we should go out to breakfast somewhere and talk it over."

"I don't eat breakfast."

"Some coffee then."

"Thanks, but I really can't."   15

"You're not married, are you? Not that that would matter that much to me. I'm an openminded kinda guy."

She was smiling. "I have to get to work."

"That sounds boring."

"I better get your driver's license," she said.

Jake nodded, disappointed. "One little problem," he said. "I didn't 20 bring it. I just forgot it this morning. I'm a musician," he exaggerated greatly, "and, well, I dunno, I left my wallet in the pants I was wearing last night. If you have some paper and a pen I'll give you my address and all that."

He followed her to the glove compartment side of her car.

"What if we don't report it to the insurance companies? I'll just get it fixed for you."

"I don't think my dad would let me do that."

"Your dad? It's not your car?"

"He bought it for me. And I live at home."   25

"Right." She was slipping away from him. He went back around to the back of her new Toyota and looked over the damage again. There was the trunk lid, the bumper, a rear panel, a taillight.

"You do have insurance?" she asked, suspicious, as she came around the back of the car.

"Oh yeah," he lied.

"I guess you better write the name of that down too."

He made up a last name and address and wrote down the name of   30
an insurance company an old girlfriend once belonged to. He considered giving a real phone number but went against that idea and made one up.

"I act too," he lied to enhance the effect more. "Been in a couple of movies."

She smiled like a fan.

"So how about your phone number?" He was rebounding maturely.

She gave it to him.

"Mariana, you are beautiful," he said in his most sincere voice.   35

"Call me," she said timidly.

Jake beamed. "We'll see you, Mariana," he said holding out his hand. Her hand felt so warm and soft he felt like he'd been kissed.

Back in his car he took a moment or two to feel both proud and sad about his performance. Then he watched the rear view mirror as Mariana pulled up behind him. She was writing down the license plate numbers on his Buick, ones that he'd taken off a junk because the ones that belonged to his had expired so long ago. He turned the ignition key and revved the big engine and clicked into drive. His sense of freedom swelled as he drove into the now moving street traffic, though he couldn't stop the thought about that FM stereo radio and crushed velvet interior and the new car smell that would even make it better.

Dagoberto Gilb

On Writing "Love in L.A."   2012

I was unemployed when I wrote "Love in L.A." I wasn't happy about that. I had two young sons and a wife and a landlord and utility companies I supported and I drove an older car that needed, at the very least, springs and shocks and often gas. When I'd come back to L.A. in the early '80s after many years here and there but mostly El Paso, I did so with dreams of good money as a construction worker with high-rise skills. I'd joined the carpenter's union, and I was a journeyman, and there were cranes in the skyline everywhere. I was good at it. And work was great when I was working, but a job ended, and it always ended too fast . . . . As I was saying, I drove an old car, a 1962 Chevy II wagon. I used to joke around that it was a vintage classic. It came with a red vinyl interior its previous owner had done pretty in Juárez, and I kept the rest up. It roared with a rebuilt six-cylinder, and I did the tune-ups myself. I'd gotten it super cheap and the best you could say about it, years later, was that it still ran. I had no money for anything else. And I was, again, unemployed, close to broke.

I'd been going like this for years by then, surviving. Only surviving. Should I be trying to find some better line of work? Not to say that I hadn't tried before. Physically able, I could do this if there were regular paychecks. The last time there were no checks for too long, we lost our apartment. Could be this is nothing but the way life is. Lots of my friends didn't do much better. But with me there was also this: was it really that I was trying to be a writer? If I stopped wanting that, maybe even construction work would get easier for me to find because I would give in to it only. They were parallel dream worlds, one where I made a good living as a carpenter, another where I made a living as a writer. Most thought the writer one was fantasy. I didn't, but then I didn't know any better. I did know that I was having a hard time.

Were mine dreams that you have to push forward to reach, or were they fantasies that you get over?

Writing is like having a fever: your brain can't shy away, won't stop. It's a few lines of a lyric or melody that you can't shut down, a word or lover's name that follows you, whether you're talking to who you know or overhearing strangers, an image that has superimposed itself so equally on the familiar and not, that it can't be "out there," only in you. It won't quit you until you write it.

Her: I do not remember where I was driving from one day when I was inching along in some ridiculous street traffic caused by a minor accident. Except nothing in this part of Los Angeles, on Melrose Avenue, is minor, right? And it wasn't really so minor, as car-only damage goes. It was an elderly man, nondescript, whose little car had been rear-ended. He was standing there. A tall, leggy, too curvy woman in the bigger car (her hood wouldn't shut) was pacing and going on, upset as though it weren't her fault. She wore the highest heels and the slinkiest dress. It wasn't three in the morning, it was three in the afternoon. Like everyone else crawling by, it didn't seem like the man knew how to respond other than to stare at her.

Him: many years earlier, I knew a creepy guy who pretended his occupation was connected to Hollywood movies and that he had money. Since he was dark, he saw himself in an ethnic category of an Anthony Quinn or even a Charles Bronson, though more leading man — he would say that people thought he looked like Omar Sharif. Really only he saw Dr. Zhivago in his mirror. He combed his hair with a quality mousse once he began to share an apartment with an older dude who had done some TV show westerns, who knows what else, and drove a red Corvette convertible. Only slightly dangerous (low-level Tony Montana), he scored his women with props — he might lay out a black book to a certain page, incidentally, where no one could miss the famous names he had fake numbers for.

I worried I was as messed up as him, worse in a way, because I had a family. No I wasn't. Yes I was. No. Yes. Was I a construction worker pretending to be a writer? Writing was this full of it dude who was getting me. Or was I this man looking in a mirror, not seeing the screws tightening or falling out under my hardhat? Was I doing the right thing? Did I know what the right thing was? I worried that writing was that woman in the accident — excessive, spoiled, flashy, gaudy, not responsible for the wreck. Writing was beautiful, and sexy, and dramatic. Writing was fun even when there was a minor accident. Writing was L.A., cruising Melrose, a neighborhood where rich people lived lives unlike mine, drove Mercedes.

Then I wrote this story. I'd lived alone for a bit over by 3rd and Alvarado, an older *mexicano* part of town. I made her Venezuelan because I wanted her to be the fairy tale Latina beauty. I wanted her to be driving an economical Toyota. I wanted her to smile. I wanted her to have a family and be getting an education. I didn't want her to be a fool. Him, surviving, I wanted in an old luxury car with dreams, or fantasies, of a better one without dings, a little lost, a little scared, not in the system. I wanted them both in a brief moment together. The writer, I didn't know which of the two characters I was. The carpenter, I got another job out of the union hall soon after.

DAGOBERTO GILB

Shout   2001

He beat on the screen door. "Will somebody open this?!" Unlike most men, he didn't leave his hard hat in his truck, he took it inside his home, and he had it in his hand. His body was dry now, at least wasn't like it was two hours ago at work, when he wrung his T-shirt of sweat, made it drool between the fingers of his fist, he and his partner making as much of a joke out of it as they could. That's how hot it was, how humid, and it'd been like this, in the nineties and hundreds, for two weeks, and it'd been hot enough before that. All he could think about was unlacing his dirty boots, then peeling off those stinky socks, then the rest. He'd take a cold one into the shower. The second one. He'd down the first one right at the refrigerator. "Come on!"

Three and four were to be appreciated, five was mellow, and six let him nap before bed.

"I didn't hear you," his wife said.

"Didn't *hear* me? How *couldn't* you hear me? And why's it locked anyways? When I get here I don't feel like waiting to come in. Why can't you leave the thing unlocked?"

"Why do you think?"

"Well don't let the baby open it. I want this door open when I get 5 home." He carried on in Spanish, *hijos de* and *putas* and *madres* and *chingadas*. This was the only Spanish he used at home. He tossed the hard hat near the door, relieved to be inside, even though it was probably hotter than outside, even though she was acting mad. He took it that she'd been that way all day already.

Their children, three boys, were seven, four, and almost two, and they were, as should be expected, battling over something.

"Everybody shut up and be quiet!" he yelled. Of course that worsened the situation, because when he got mad he scared the baby, who immediately started crying.

"I'm so tired," he muttered.

She glared at him, the baby in her arms.

"You know sometimes I wish you were a man cuz I wouldn't let you 10 get away with looks like that. I wouldn't take half the shit I take from you." He fell back into the wooden chair nobody sat in except him when he laced the high-top boots on, or off, as he already had. "You know how hot it was today? A hundred and five. It's unbelievable." He looked at her closely, deeply, which he didn't often do, especially this month. She was trying to settle down the baby and turned the TV on to distract the other two.

"It's too hard to breathe," he said to her. He walked bare-footed for the beer and took out two. They were in the door tray of the freezer and almost frozen.

"So nothing happened today?" she asked. Already she wasn't mad at him. It was how she was, why they could get along.

"Nothing else was said. Maybe nothing's gonna happen. God knows this heat's making everybody act unnatural. But tomorrow's check day. If he's gonna get me most likely it'll be tomorrow." He finished a beer leaning against the tile near the kitchen sink, enjoying a peace that had settled into the apartment. The baby was content, the TV was on, the Armenians living an arm's reach away were chattering steadily, there was a radio on from an apartment in a building across from them, Mexican TV upstairs, pigeons, a dog, traffic noise, the huge city out there groaning its sound — all this silence in the apartment.

"There's other jobs," he said. "All of 'em end no matter what anyways."

It was a job neither of them wanted to end too soon. This year 15 he'd been laid up for months after he fell and messed up his shoulder and back. He'd been drunk — a happy one that started after work — but he did it right there at his own front door, playing around. At the same time the duplex apartment they'd been living in for years had been sold and they had to move here. It was all they could get, all they were offered, since so few landlords wanted three children, boys no less, at a monthly rent they could afford. They were lucky to find it and it wasn't bad as places went, but they didn't like it much. They felt like they were starting out again, and that did not seem right. They'd talked this over since they'd moved in until it degenerated into talk about separation. And otherwise, in other details, it also wasn't the best year of their lives.

He showered in warm water, gradually turning the hot water down until it came out as cold as the summer allowed, letting the iced beer do the rest.

She was struggling getting dinner together, the boys were loud and complaining about being hungry, and well into the fifth beer, as he sat near the bright color and ever-happy tingle of the TV set, his back stiffening up, he snapped.

"Everybody has to shut up! I can't stand this today! I gotta relax some!"

She came back at him screaming too. "I can't stand *you*!"

He leaped. "You don't talk to me like that!"   20

She came right up to him. "You gonna hit me?!"she dared him.

The seven-year-old ran to his bed but the other two froze up, waiting for the tension to ease enough before their tears squeezed out.

"Get away from me," he said trying to contain himself. "You better get away from me right now. You know, just go home, go to your mother's, just go."

"*You* go! *You* get out! We're gonna stay!"

He looked through her, then slapped a wall, rocking what seemed   25
like the whole building. "You don't know how close you are."

He wouldn't leave. He walked into the bedroom, then walked out, sweating. He went into the empty kitchen — they were all in the children's room, where there was much crying — and he took a plate and filled it with what she'd made and went in front of the tube and he clicked on a ball game, told himself to calm himself and let it all pass at least tonight, at least while the weather was like it was and while these other things were still bothering both of them, and then he popped the sixth beer. He wasn't going to fall asleep on the couch tonight.

Eventually his family came out, one by one peeking around a corner to see what he looked like. Then they ate in a whisper, even cutting loose here and there with a little giggle or gripe. Eventually the sun did set, though that did nothing to wash off the glue of heat.

And eventually the older boys felt comfortable enough to complain about bedtime. Only the baby cried — he was tired and wanted to sleep but couldn't because a cold had clogged his nose. Still, they were all trying to maintain the truce when from outside, a new voice came in: SHUT

THAT FUCKING KID UP YOU FUCKING PEOPLE! HEY! SHUT THAT FUCKING KID UP OVER THERE!

It was like an explosion except that he flew toward it. He shook the window screen with his voice. "You fuck yourself, asshole! You stupid asshole, you shut your mouth!" He ran out the other way, out the screen door and around and under the heated stars. "Come on out here, mouth! Come out and say that to my face!" He squinted at all the windows around him, no idea where it came from. "So come on! Say it right now!" There was no taker, and he turned away, his blood still bright red.

When he came back inside, the children had gone to bed and she was 30 lying down with the baby, who'd fallen asleep. He went back to the chair. The game ended, she came out, half-closing the door behind her, and went straight to their bed. He followed.

"I dunno," he said after some time. He'd been wearing shorts and nothing else since his shower, and it shouldn't have taken him so long, yet he just sat there on the bed. Finally he turned on the fan and it whirred, ticking as it pivoted left and right. "It doesn't do any good, but it's worse without it." He looked at her like he did earlier. "I'm kinda glad nobody came out. Afterwards I imagined some nut just shooting me, or a few guys coming. I'm getting too old for that shit."

She wasn't talking.

"So what did they say?" he asked her. "At the clinic?"

"Yes."

"Yes what?"   35

"That I am."

They both listened to the fan and to the mix of music from the Armenians and that TV upstairs.

"I would've never thought it could happen," he said. "That one time, and it wasn't even good."

"Maybe for you. I knew it then."

"You did?"   40

She rolled on her side.

"I'm sorry about all the yelling," he said.

"I was happy you went after that man. I always wanna do stuff like that."

He rolled to her.

"I'm too sticky. It's too hot."   45

"I have to. We do. It's been too long, and now it doesn't matter."

"It does matter," she said. "I love you."

"I'm sorry," he said, reaching over to touch her breast. "You know I'm sorry."

He took another shower afterward. A cold shower. His breath sputtered and noises hopped from his throat. He crawled into the bed naked, onto the sheet that seemed as hot as ever, and listened to outside, to that mournful Armenian music mixing with Spanish, and to the fan, and it had stilled him. It was joy, and it was so strange. She'd fallen asleep and so he resisted kissing her, telling her. He thought he should hold on to this as long as he could, until he heard the pitch of the freeway climb, telling him that dawn was near and it was almost time to go back to work.

Dagoberto Gilb

On Writing "Shout"   2012

I suspect that younger readers — though older ones too — believe that a writer would enjoy going back and reading his earlier work. Probably a few do. I do not. It's like going back and looking at old photographs. I see a younger me, which is to say this not lots older me now, and I think of all the decisions I made, or didn't, because I didn't know what I didn't know. Worse, I read these stories and see what I would cut over there and add right here. And who am I to do that now to these full-grown stories? I think about where I was in my head when I wrote them . . . but let me give you this easier where: when I wrote "Shout," we were living in an East Hollywood apartment building beneath an elderly Armenian couple who grew parsley in the cracks of the cement pathways, who were miserable whenever my two baby boys rode their noisy Big Wheels. If the horrible thing about construction work was those times I didn't have a job, one of the great things was those times when I didn't have a job — not banging nails meant, instead, me getting to stay home at my wooden desk. (I still had the one I bought used in college. Beside me then was a Mexican calavera who oversaw whatever was on it, which it does to this day, on a newer wood desk.) That was when I allowed myself to write "officially" these pages I wanted published, the ones crafted, the ones you read. Not to say I was not always writing. Even working eleven hours, six days a week for as many months as a job would hold me, I wrote every day, but it would be in a notebook, recording conversations, incidents, descriptions, deep philosophical insights, and dear diary type boo-hoos or longings. Thousands of pages accumulated. My best writing hours were when my sons were asleep, and there was quiet, though once I got onto something, I could work anytime, in any noise.

   It's surely obvious that much of my fiction comes from my own life and experiences. "Shout," for instance, could be said to have come out of the same period of my life as "Love in L.A." Hard to avoid what lasted over a decade. It used to be that most writers wrote out of their lived experience. Herman Melville, of *Moby Dick* (and *Billy Budd*), was a whaler. Nowadays people expect fiction to be nothing but mental creation and research, drawn on the page. Art is the imagination, goes this view, is the writer's desk alone, and the discipline there. That's not untrue, and it alone works well for very many. Gustave Flaubert, imagining a life as a woman, is said to have written one of the greatest novels of a woman, *Madame Bovary*. For me, fiction is life transformed and fueled by imagination. Experience often teaches by surprise — what cannot be predicted by the best reader in the library. My own favorite writers are out there, feeling the wind, on an adventure. Fiction I admire the most captures what, like life, smacks you when and where you're not looking, and the blow can seem so small, and it's so big.

Which brings up the subject of the small and the big, the short story and the novel. In many respects, a novel is simply a short story that is made larger, fuller, with more characters, more involved situations, a longer and more casual read. Thus, many short stories can be expanded into novels, or become segments of one. But I want to say that the best short fiction has more kinship with poetry: the goal is to reduce words and condense, and it is driven more by image than plot, both contrary to the novel. War can be described in a hundred pages of a battle scene, but might be more lastingly understood in an image of a tear falling, red itself or what is seen through it. There are never enough pages for love, but isn't it only the neighbor's *gallo* waking you up angry until you see, sound asleep next to you . . . .

The small. If novels are often about epic sweeps of history and issues, the big ideas of big egos, characters who are larger than whole nations and journeys that are bold, short fiction goes for what's left off-screen, following characters who would be minor against the headliners in those novels, but whose conclusions, The Ends, if less grandiose and more subtle, are anything shy of large.

And so, my own stories are about the small things and the people who aren't seen much in literature. There was a time when characters like those who populate my fiction were written about more, just not very much in recent decades. By that I mean common Americans, what many call working people, be they employed or looking to be. There are not a lot of stories about men like the main character in "Shout." I have found over the years that many know them as fathers and uncles, brothers and husbands, but they are not in the books they read. What you see in "Shout" as well is this man in a Mexican American family, yet another huge segment of American culture seldom read about. What I hoped to offer was not a simple portrayal of a construction worker coming home from work exhausted from a long day in the heat, not just a domestic squabble he causes with a patient wife, the mother of their three children. Left there, it would be a working-class cliché, the macho stereotype not only of that kind of man but also of a Mexican male. What I wanted seen was the same bullish rage he had in his home being used to defend his family when a stranger screams at them. And then the intimacy, what is hidden in the broad, usual expectation, what is forgotten when you don't know characters as living people, that the man and woman are lovers.

DAGOBERTO GILB
Uncle Rock   2011

In the morning, at his favorite restaurant, Erick got to order his favorite
American food, sausage and eggs and hash-brown *papitas*° fried crunchy
on top. He'd be sitting there, eating with his mother, not bothering anybody, and life was good, when a man started changing it all. Lots of times
it was just a man staring too much—but then one would come over.
Friendly, he'd put his thick hands on the table as if he were touching
water, and squat low, so that he was at sitting level, as though he were so
polite, and he'd smile, with coffee-and-tobacco-stained teeth. He might
wear a bolo tie and speak in a drawl. Or he might have on a tan uniform,
a company logo on the back, an oval name patch on the front. Or he'd be
in a nothing-special work shirt, white or striped, with a couple of pens
clipped onto the left side pocket, tucked into a pair of jeans or chinos
that were morning-clean still, with a pair of scuffed work boots that laced
up higher than regular shoes. He'd say something about her earrings, or
her bracelet, or her hair, or her eyes, and if she had on her white uniform
how nice it looked on her. Or he'd come right out with it and tell her how
pretty she was, how he couldn't keep himself from walking up, speaking
to her directly, and could they talk again? Then he'd wink at Erick. Such a
fine-looking boy! How old is he, eight or nine? Erick wasn't even small for
an eleven-year-old. He tightened his jaw then, slanted his eyes up from his
plate at his mom and not the man, definitely not this man he did not care
for. Erick drove a fork into a goopy American egg yolk and bled it into his
American potatoes. She wouldn't offer the man Erick's correct age either,
saying only that he was growing too fast.

She almost always gave the man her number if he was wearing a suit.
Not a sports coat but a buttoned suit with a starched white shirt and a
pinned tie meant something to her. Once in a while, Erick saw one of
these men again at the front door of the apartment in Silverlake. The
man winked at Erick as if they were buddies. Grabbed his shoulder or
arm, squeezed the muscle against the bone. What did Erick want to be
when he grew up? A cop, a jet-airplane mechanic, a travel agent, a court
reporter? A dog groomer? Erick stood there, because his mom said that
he shouldn't be impolite. His mom's date said he wanted to take Erick
along with them sometime. The three of them. What kind of places did
Erick think were fun? Erick said nothing. He never said anything when
the men were around, and not because of his English, even if that was
what his mother implied to explain his silence. He didn't talk to any of
the men and he didn't talk much to his mom either. Finally they took
off, and Erick's night was his alone. He raced to the grocery store and
bought half a gallon of chocolate ice cream. When he got back, he turned

papitas: Potatoes.

on the TV, scooted up real close, as close as he could, and ate his dinner with a soup spoon. He was away from all the men. Even though a man had given the TV to them. He was a salesman in an appliance store who'd bragged that a rich customer had given it to him and so why shouldn't he give it to Erick's mom, who couldn't afford such a good TV otherwise?

When his mom was working as a restaurant hostess, and was going to marry the owner, Erick ate hot-fudge sundaes and drank chocolate shakes. When she worked at a trucking company, the owner of all the trucks told her he was getting a divorce. Erick climbed into the rigs, with their rooms full of dials and levers in the sky. Then she started working in an engineer's office. There was no food or fun there, but even he could see the money. He was not supposed to touch anything, but what was there to touch — the tubes full of paper? He and his mom were invited to the engineer's house, where he had two horses and a stable, a swimming pool, and two convertible sports cars. The engineer's family was there: his grown children, his gray-haired parents. They all sat down for dinner in a dining room that seemed bigger than Erick's apartment, with three candelabras on the table, and a tablecloth and cloth napkins. Erick's mom took him aside to tell him to be well mannered at the table and polite to everyone. Erick hadn't said anything. He never spoke anyway, so how could he have said anything wrong? She leaned into his ear and said that she wanted them to know that he spoke English. That whole dinner he was silent, chewing quietly, taking the smallest bites, because he didn't want them to think he liked their food.

When she got upset about days like that, she told Erick that she wished they could just go back home. She was tired of worrying. "Back," for Erick, meant mostly the stories he'd heard from her, which never sounded so good to him: she'd had to share a room with her brothers and sisters. They didn't have toilets. They didn't have electricity. Sometimes they didn't have enough food. He saw this Mexico as if it were the backdrop of a movie on afternoon TV, where children walked around barefoot in the dirt or on broken sidewalks and small men wore wide-brimmed straw hats and baggy white shirts and pants. The women went to church all the time and prayed to alcoved saints and, heads down, fearful, counted rosary beads. There were rocks everywhere, and scorpions and tarantulas and rattlesnakes, and vultures and no trees and not much water, and skinny dogs and donkeys, and ugly bad guys with guns and bullet vests who rode laughing into town to drink and shoot off their pistols and rifles, driving their horses all over like dirt bikes on desert dunes. When they spoke English, they had stupid accents — his mom didn't have an accent like theirs. It didn't make sense to him that Mexico would only be like that, but what if it was close? He lived on paved, lighted city streets, and a bicycle ride away were the Asian drugstore and the Armenian grocery store and the corner where black Cubans drank coffee and talked Dodgers baseball.

When he was in bed, where he sometimes prayed, he thanked God ⁵ for his mom, who he loved, and he apologized for not talking to her, or to anyone, really, except his friend Albert, and he apologized for her never going to church and for his never taking Holy Communion, as Albert did—though only to God would he admit that he wanted to only because Albert did. He prayed for good to come, for his mom and for him, since God was like magic, and happiness might come the way of early morning, in the trees and bushes full of sparrows next to his open window, louder and louder when he listened hard, eyes closed.

The engineer wouldn't have mattered if Erick hadn't told Albert that he was his dad. Albert had just moved into the apartment next door and lived with both his mother and his father, and since Albert's mother already didn't like Erick's mom, Erick told him that his new dad was an engineer. Erick actually believed it, too, and thought that he might even get his own horse. When that didn't happen, and his mom was lying on her bed in the middle of the day, blowing her nose, because she didn't have the job anymore, that was when Roque came around again. Roque was nobody—or he was anybody. He wasn't special, he wasn't not. He tried to speak English to Erick, thinking that was the reason Erick didn't say anything when he was there. And Erick had to tell Albert that Roque was his uncle, because the engineer was supposed to be his new dad any minute. Uncle Rock, Erick said. His mom's brother, he told Albert. Roque worked at night and was around during the day, and one day he offered Erick and Albert a ride. When his mom got in the car, she scooted all the way over to Roque on the bench seat. Who was supposed to be her brother, Erick's Uncle Rock. Albert didn't say anything, but he saw what had happened, and that was it for Erick. Albert had parents, grandparents, and a brother and a sister, and he'd hang out only when one of his cousins wasn't coming by. Erick didn't need a friend like him.

What if she married Roque, his mom asked him one day soon afterward. She told Erick that they would move away from the apartment in Silverlake to a better neighborhood. He did want to move, but he wished that it weren't because of Uncle Rock. It wasn't just because Roque didn't have a swimming pool or horses or a big ranch house. There wasn't much to criticize except that he was always too willing and nice, too considerate, too generous. He wore nothing flashy or expensive, just ordinary clothes that were clean and ironed, and shoes he kept shined. He combed and parted his hair neatly. He didn't have a buzzcut like the men who didn't like kids. He moved slow, he talked slow, as quiet as night. He only ever said yes to Erick's mom. How could she not like him for that? He loved her so much—anybody could see his pride when he was with her. He signed checks and gave her cash. He knocked on their door carrying cans and fruit and meat. He was there when she asked, gone when she asked, back whenever, grateful. He took her out to restaurants on Sunset, to the movies in Hollywood, or on drives to the beach in rich Santa Monica.

Roque knew that Erick loved baseball. Did Roque like baseball? It was doubtful that he cared even a little bit — he didn't listen to games on the radio or TV, and he never looked at a newspaper. He loved boxing though. He knew the names of all the Mexican fighters as if they lived here, as if they were Dodgers players like Steve Yeager, Dusty Baker, Kenny Landreaux or Mike Marshall, or Pedro Guerrero. Roque did know about Fernando Valenzuela, everyone did, even his mom, which is why she agreed to let Roque take them to a game. What Mexican didn't love Fernando? Dodger Stadium was close to their apartment. He'd been there once with Albert and his family — well, outside it, on a nearby hill, to see the fireworks for Fourth of July. His mom decided that all three of them would go on a Saturday afternoon, since Saturday night, Erick thought, she might want to go somewhere else, even with somebody else.

Roque, of course, didn't know who the Phillies were. He knew nothing about the strikeouts by Steve Carlton or the homeruns by Mike Schmidt. He'd never heard of Pete Rose. It wasn't that Erick knew very much either, but there was nothing that Roque could talk to him about, if they were to talk.

If Erick showed his excitement when they drove up to Dodger Stadium and parked, his mom and Roque didn't really notice it. They sat in the bleachers, and for him the green of the field was a magic light; the stadium decks surrounding them seemed as far away as Rome. His body was somewhere it had never been before. The fifth inning? That's how late they were. Or were they right on time, because they weren't even sure they were sitting in the right seats yet when he heard the crack of the bat, saw the crowd around them rising as it came at them. Erick saw the ball. He had to stand and move and stretch his arms and want that ball until it hit his bare hands and stayed there. Everybody saw him catch it with no bobble. He felt all the eyes and voices around him as if they were every set of eyes and every voice in the stadium. His mom was saying something, and Roque, too, and then, finally, it was just him and that ball and his stinging hands. He wasn't even sure if it had been hit by Pete Guerrero. He thought for sure it had been, but he didn't ask. He didn't watch the game then — he couldn't. He didn't care who won. He stared at his official National League ball, reimagining what had happened. He ate a hot dog and drank a soda and he sucked the salted peanuts and the wooden spoon from his chocolate-malt ice cream. He rubbed the bumpy seams of his homerun ball.

Game over, they were the last to leave. People were hanging around, not going straight to their cars. Roque didn't want to leave. He didn't want to end it so quickly, Erick thought, while he still had her with him. Then one of the Phillies came out of the stadium door and people swarmed — boys mostly, but also men and some women and girls — and they got autographs before the player climbed onto the team's bus. Joe Morgan, they said. Then Garry Maddox appeared. Erick clutched the ball but he didn't have a pen. He just watched, his back to the gray bus the Phillies were getting into.

Then a window slid open. *Hey, big man,* a voice said. Erick really wasn't sure. *Gimme the ball, la pelota,*° the face in the bus said. *I'll have it signed, comprendes?*° *Échalo,*° *just toss it to me.* Erick obeyed. He tossed it up to the hand that was reaching out. The window closed. The ball was gone a while, so long that his mom came up to him, worried that he'd lost it. The window slid open again and the voice spoke to her. *We got the ball, Mom. It's not lost, just a few more.* When the window opened once more, this time the ball was there. *Catch.* There were all kinds of signatures on it, though none that he could really recognize except for Joe Morgan and Pete Rose.

Then the voice offered more, and the hand threw something at him. *For your mom, okay? Comprendes?* Erick stared at the asphalt lot where the object lay, as if he'd never seen a folded-up piece of paper before. *Para tu mamá, bueno?* He picked it up, and he started to walk over to his mom and Roque, who were so busy talking they hadn't noticed anything. Then he stopped. He opened the note himself. No one had said he couldn't read it. It said, *I'd like to get to know you. You are muy linda. Very beautiful and sexy. I don't speak Spanish very good, may be you speak better English, pero No Importa.*° *Would you come by tonite and let me buy you a drink?* There was a phone number and a hotel room number. A name, too. A name that came at him the way that the homerun had.

Erick couldn't hear. He could see only his mom ahead of him. She was talking to Roque, Roque was talking to her. Roque was the proudest man, full of joy because he was with her. It wasn't his fault he wasn't an engineer. Now Erick could hear again. Like sparrows hunting seed, boys gathered round the bus, calling out, while the voice in the bus was yelling at him, *Hey, big guy! Give it to her!* Erick had the ball in one hand and the note in the other. By the time he reached his mom and Roque, the note was already somewhere on the asphalt parking lot. *Look,* he said in a full voice. *They all signed my ball.*

la pelota: The ball.
comprendes?: Understand?
Échalo: Throw it.
pero No Importa: It doesn't matter.

Dagoberto Gilb
On Writing "Uncle Rock"   2012

Mostly I don't like talking about my work. What can I say without implying a boast that it is fine writing you will want to know at least as well as me, if not better? (Of course it is!) Not only tasteless, it's a little questionable. Because, of course, this is somebody else's occupation, not my mirror's. Do you go to a restaurant telling you that it has "The Best Mexican Food in

Texas!" (Of course it does, right?) All this aside, "Uncle Rock" might be one of my easiest stories to disassemble to see how it was put together.

As a craft, what I do isn't that much different than what a tile setter does. My fictional tiles, however, are broken, chipped, cracked, and come in different sizes and proportions and colors, and what I do is make a mosaic. There are sentences based on experience of my own years ago, and there are graphs which are what I remember doing with my sons when they were children; there are objects much like I owned, and a character who is memories of two people on the body of a third I worked with. Even within a single sentence, the imaginary is beside the Googled. The drama is invention. "Uncle Rock" appears to be a story of an eleven-year-old boy's life in the '80s, when really it is a set of disconnected images from several decades flipped through so quickly that it gives the illusion of movement (yes, like a "movie"), a story of a single experience. People read this story and assume it must be autobiographical. A compliment to my craft. You now know it was written willfully, by design.

Where the shards of tiles come from is what distinguishes what's mine from another writer's. And no doubt there are all sorts of piles to go through. I studied religion in college. That wasn't because I made a mistake and picked a degree plan that I thought I would cash in on. It's that I learned we live on a circling planet and noticed that I am alive and conscious. My curiosity about this has driven me to where I am. What I write is called literary fiction. The purpose of commercial fiction is, besides making money, to pass the time pleasantly, to get some relief from the grind—to entertain. Though this used to be more the function of reading in the past, now that is primarily handled by television and film. Literary fiction intends to entertain as well (and I say it does, more and especially so when it's great), and wishes to make money, but its goal—as is mine—is to reach out from the ordinary to realize the extraordinary. To point to the mystery that is being alive, in a strange place, in a time—a reader's, a writer's—that is not only in time. Is Erick's story about the '60s, '80s, these teens? Is his mom or Roque only a product of a class or culture? Is this story about males and single women, about the boundaries of love between a fatherless boy and a mother?

Don't think I'm denying that my fiction has autobiography in it. But this is true of most works of art, no more mine than many. Still, "Uncle Rock" could be used to do a clinical, psychological take on me through my work, digging out the root troubles haunting me. Most likely not wrong. It could be pointed out that, for instance, how the too wild single mother theme and character comes up here as it does in other pieces by me. That I have a *mami* issue. Probably true. But in my defense, my mom really did create some stories. Say you were the littlest broke, or even felt like splurging, treating yourself, or just felt like making life easy for yourself, and you knew where there was a chest of gold coins. Wouldn't you go there and grab one? It's only one here, and another couple in the past, not like I got greedy and grabbed the whole suitcase.

It's easiest for me to talk about my work when it has to do with advocacy. I would argue that all art advocates, like it or not, and that a writer represents a group of people and their interests. My fiction is very much about the common people in America, those who work and support families with their hands and bodies for hourly wages, who go about their lives hidden from media and celebrity links. Characters with "careers" like Erick's mother or Roque are not read about. Which brings up the American West—it is still unusual to read literary work set in and written by those who live west of the Mississippi. But it is more than rare to read stories set in the American Southwest, and more so still when they are about Mexican American people in their historical homeland—why the mountains and rivers and cities have names in Spanish. And I do that. My stories represent the Chicano story. It could be said that this is unavoidable for me, and that's not wrong, but my advocacy began only vaguely when I was young. In college I was lucky enough to see Luis Valdez's plays performed by his Teatro Campesino. I went to events supporting, and featuring, Cesar Chavez. Both were synonymous with the farm workers' movement. Broccoli, to me, only came from a Safeway grocery store, and other people ate that kind of food. But the urban Mexican American was, obviously, always there too. There was simply little to no publicly documented evidence of it. Many call this an "invisibility" of the culture and history in the United States. I don't see it that way, not when what's loved about the Mexican American West, from cowboys to adobes, from margaritas to enchiladas, tacos, and burritos, are now as American as an iPod and a hamburger. I say Mexican Americans are being ignored willfully, an ignorance that has gotten worse in the past decade as a seismic demographic shift is altering the region's, and nation's, political landscape.

Which finally brings me back to "Uncle Rock." Take it apart, and you find a description of the Mexican American situation: Roque, a working man who struggles with English, an anybody, nobody special, who only works hard and is steady, is the only one who treats Erick's mother well. He adores her. But, despite the humiliation she endures, she wants more than what he is able to offer. She is beautiful and attracts all kinds of attention, so how can she not want more than what everyone else accepts? Her American dream. Erick is as embarrassed by his mom as he is attached to her. He is bothered so much that he has gone mute—he does not want to talk to anyone but God and his friend Albert. From the outside, it would appear that his is a struggle with the English language. One day he realizes a dream. In the days of Fernandomania, Roque takes him and his mom to a Dodgers game. Not only does he get to go to his first professional baseball game, not only does he catch a homerun ball, but a famous baseball player wants to meet his mother. At first thrilled, as young as he is Erick knows the offer is disrespectful and crude. And when he walks back to the two of them, who are unaware of what happened, he speaks to them. I want Erick's voice to get louder, smarter, and more confident.

Perspectives

DAGOBERTO GILB

On Physical Labor   2003

From "Work Union," Gritos

Not everybody wants to sit at a desk for a living. So many of us come from cultures where it is expected that we will move our bodies in the wind and sun, at dawn and into dusk. Many of us have been taught by family that physical work feels good and is good — when the day is over, we know what we did because we see it, we feel the efforts in our feet and hands and bones, and when we go home, when the wife puts food on the table and the family sits down and eats, there is unmistakable pride that all of it is because we have done our job.

It is human to work, to bend and grip, to lift and pull. It's never about getting tired or dirty. There is nothing wrong with sweat and toil. It is only about conditions and decent wages that there can come complaint. This is what so many people don't understand, especially those who sit in chairs in offices. They see us tired, they see us worried. They say, Well, if you don't like your situation, why don't you get a better job? Because it isn't the job, the kind of work. The job is good. Being a carpenter, an electrician, a plumber, an ironworker, a laborer, those are all good. What isn't good is to be earning a living that can't bring in enough money to raise a healthy family, buy a home, go to a dentist and doctor, and be around comfortably for grandchildren.

A writer from Detroit who worked years for the Fisher Body Plant in Flint, Michigan, has recently been profiled in the newspapers because he won a prize for his writing. In the exultation of winning, he has been quoted often about those years he worked on the assembly line, saying, "I can't stress to you enough how much I hated it." This writer, he is certainly a good man, but like so many, he simply forgot what a joy employment is, what a job means to people and their families. There is only good in work, and the very best people are those who work hard.

DAGOBERTO GILB

On Distortions of Mexican American Culture   2011

From "La Próxima Parada Is Next," American Book Review

When Americans think of the South, some might think of its white society, Antebellum and post, its white literature, its wealth, yet the black culture is undeniably ever there, present. Others might discuss the history of the South in terms of black people, their history of slavery, their struggle with poverty, as the homeland of African Americans. This binary is a permanent overlay on the topography of the Southeast region, that quadrangle of the U.S. It is a black-white that has come to define much of America's internal history. Now consider a comparable Southwest quadrangle, one whose historical binary could be called — should be called — brown and white. We are all taught passionately about the American expansion into the West, cattle drives, cowboys and Indians, John Wayne movies, but if someone were to say it is the homeland of Mexican Americans, would anyone associate that with populations in Los Angeles, the state of New Mexico, El Paso, San Antonio, the Rio Grande Valley? Visitors thrill at oversized enchilada plates and the bountiful bowls of tortilla chips (Americanisms, both), visits to seventeenth- and early eighteenth-century missions, and they see and hear the vast numbers of "Mexican" people who speak to them in homegrown English at shops, stores, and stations — and yet somehow, relaxing in adobe-themed motels or new Spanish Villa homes, the binary here is not brown and white but *blank* and white, the dominant Mexican culture as if from an uninhabited ghost town. Meanwhile, what brown people they encounter — what articles appear in the media — are recent immigrants, invaders from the border. Part of American history? Curiously, if we were to assert that we are part of Mexico's history — which nobody here or there ever has or does — that would be far more of an outrage than lament that, unless photographed in folklorico costume, we have no images in our nation's history other than as foreigners.

Michael Meyer Interviews Dagoberto Gilb   2012

Meyer: Here is a potentially annoying but sincere usage question concerning a simple matter of terms that has caused me and my students to sometimes stumble: Do we (do you) use Chicano or Latino, Hispanic or Mexican American or Tex Mex to describe your writings? Should I even bring up feminine endings and hyphens as well? Do the terms define important distinctions? Is there a single umbrella term? Can you help sort this out for us?

Gilb: Aww, the rage of the nomenclature. All these words are better than the ones when I was young — "beaner" and "wetback" are the hit oldies, but just the word "Mexican," with but a soft decibel of racist tone, could clear the bench. The Chicano period was the beginning of the alternative. The problem with that became the masculine "o" at the end. Since the linguistic rules of Spanish reflected a macho boys' club mentality that did rule beyond usage, Chicanas rightfully fought for the equal status of the feminine "a," which has since created the slash usage, Chicana/o. It was the Nixon administration which came in with the word "Hispanic" as a "non-political" term (Chicanos and Chicanas, college-educated, did not vote Republican). It is a word now predominantly used in Republican circles. Latino, Latina, and Latina/o are the alternative to that. For me the problem with this is its application in the West. While Mexican Americans are close to 70 percent of the national demographic, Latinas and Latinos in the West are 95 percent Mexican American. One may note that neither do I love the hyphen that can be used in "Mexican American" (as in, the diminutive, hyphenated American). Me being me, I don't love the exhausting bureaucracy of slash world, and me being as American as the rest of us, I want nicknames of one or at most two syllables, so I've been going with the gender-neutral "MexAm" when it fits in easily. Sorry for the extra cap. And so it goes.

Meyer: It's not likely that any of your characters subscribe to the *American Book Review,* because they are mostly working-class, hardworking individuals struggling to earn a living. Do you think your work reaches an audience that includes the kind of characters that you write about? Do you worry about making the connection?

Gilb: Sadly, yes, improbable that an under-educated community would read or receive suggestions to read any of my writing, fiction or nonfiction. Is that because reading has become a luxury item? Is education a luxury item? Historically this has been true in most countries, in Europe, in Mexico, in Latin America. It was just less true in ours. At least as ideals went. Today, it would seem that's our direction. But putting that aside, my writing does reach a segment of the population that does care. And it touches enough even in my own community of people who recognize family members in the stories, who recognize their own voices through hearing mine. And I was invited into a literary world that has rewarded me. Not only have my books been published by Grove Press (the house whose books I was most infatuated with as a young reader), but my work has been in the most honored pages of the literary establishment — *The New Yorker* and *Harper's* magazines — and has been granted their finer awards. That doesn't mean that the mainstream public cares about what I do enough to make me a rich author, but it does mean that there is a respect in our country's literary marketplace for the ideas that pass through me and the people those ideas intend to honor. I am proud that this is true.

Meyer: In your comments about "Uncle Rock" you write that "It's easiest for me to talk about my work when it has to do with advocacy." Which of the four stories that you've chosen to include in this anthology do you think most fully seems to be an "advocacy story"?

Gilb: All art advocates. The one who says his doesn't, he's someone who's advocating for the way things are, someone who's comfortable.

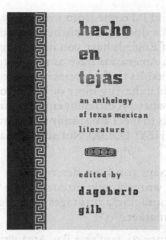

**hecho
en
tejas**

an anthology
of texas mexican
literature

edited by
**dagoberto
gilb**

*Hecho en Tejas: An Anthology
of Texas Mexican Literature*
was edited by Gilb and
published in 2006 by the
University of New Mexico
Press.

An event celebrating the anthology at the historic Cine El Rey Theatre. McAllen, Texas, 2007.
Courtesy of Dagoberto Gilb.

I'm not saying that's right or wrong (though I'm sure I would pick
a better or worse), only that it is a stance. For those who are less than
comfortable, that status of ghosts, in situations that are less romantic
or sitcom popular. I myself have gone through stages of understanding
about the role of advocacy. I used to think that, like Dostoevsky, it — the
politics, the spirituality — was contained in the art of the fiction alone,
not in tracts or marches. A writer writes quietly alone, no option. It's in
the finished work, and readers who are ready to find it, will. But I have
changed. Maybe because I became a parent. Maybe because, as a journeyman, I worked with an apprentice often. Maybe because I was a coach
for nine years and both yelled at and encouraged boys and girls who
needed the coaching and got better. Once I became a teacher, a professor even, I found that, being in front of a class, students knowing that

it was real and could be earned and I'd come from where they did, their learning altered their views, broke down their clichés and stereotypes. How many Chicano professors of English have you had? Why should it be surprising, even, that Mexican Americans have as many professional and personal complexities as others? As to the stories in this anthology, I don't really think of any one of them having more or less advocacy than another. Choose any of mine anywhere. A different emphasis in that one as opposed to this one, that's it. As to me, I am simply more aware of saying aloud, maybe saying louder, HEY! LOOK! Not sure if that's me, or survival in noisy times.

Meyer: In interviews and essays you have described the disadvantages of not being a northeastern writer snugly situated in the New York literary scene. Are there any encouraging advantages to being a southwestern writer in today's literary market?

Gilb: If you're from San Francisco, you're a Bay Area writer. From Oregon or Washington, a writer from the Pacific Northwest. Colorado, Utah, Wyoming, Montana, a western writer. If you're from the Southeast, a southern writer. If you live in New York, even Boston, you're a national writer. Hard to argue with the economic demographics and the number of readers who live in those cities and the history of colleges and universities there, as well as magazines and publishers. Traditions groove permanent paths. Hard for anyone to not follow the money, and that's where the money is, too. Also hard not to be born where you're born. The Southwest has always had an exoticized legacy. D. H. Lawrence and Georgia O'Keeffe are New Mexico. Meanwhile, the MexAm Southwest has barely registered on an art stat, but no doubt that too has to change. The Apaches came to learn the force of America's westward expansion onto their land. Mexican Americans — though probably less, are no more immigrant than those from European descent, despite the demagoguery — will be 50 percent of the American Southwest soon, and its beautiful culture and epic history is unavoidably blending into the American mainstream.

Meyer: You suffered a debilitating stroke in 2009 from which you have since remarkably recovered, but if you were to write a short story about that experience, the fact that it is your writing hand that remains impaired seems to conjure all kinds of symbolic meanings. What has that stroke meant to you as a writer?

Gilb: A story titled "please, thank you," first published in *Harper's* and then collected in *Before the End, After the Beginning,* does deal with a character, Mr. Sanchez, who suffered a stroke similar to the one I did. He and I have had to learn how to type only, first one-handed, then slowly with one finger on the other hand, instead of using a pen to write. I can't say I like it a lot, so I do not recommend anyone use the technique

Dagoberto Gilb's desk—and the Mexican calavera that oversees it,
mentioned in his essay "On Writing 'Shout'" (p. 283).
Courtesy of Dagoberto Gilb.

to gain insights or to seek material. Yes, it's hard not to consider the
metaphor: a writer losing the use of his writing hand. Add to that it
happening the night he is celebrating the beginning of a new future as a
full-time writer. But that metaphor is only one. Another is the obstacle
it is for many of us to be writers. To be artists. To do what we dream, not
what is expected, not what we accept. What we have to work hard for.
That has always been me, and so adding this new element is not really
new. When I wrote the stories for my last collection (mentioned above),
for me it was an act of calm defiance—no, I am not done yet—but also
gratitude for the generous gifts still given. I'm lucky I can do what I
always wanted to do, that I am a writer, and I only need a keyboard.
That's not so bad.

gilb / story
8

~~I don't want that, but then again, yes, that'd probaby be better, because, then again, I don't believe~~ *[au: not quite clear: what "that" refers to]*

~~that's the explanation.~~ *a third Mexican American* This is a campus where my work can be taught in a Chicano lit course only. I

[and I don't grasp this wholly; either re "me alone" I think, but can you clarify] wonder when, if ever, we ~~would~~ *will* be considered gourmet enough, talented enough, important enough.

I am guilty too because I don't think I'm smart enough. Flawed in a couple of personal areas,

I wish I could claim to be better here, I wish instead of wanting to collapse and watch HBO (even, I

admit, those cheap ~~TV~~ judge shows), I ~~read~~ *could* another book. I know those kind of writers. My God, *[ok overus]*

they are so brilliant and articulate. I ~~even~~ know a couple who are geniuses. But what I ~~can only~~ hope

might be seen is what gets undervalued: Not only has writing saved my life, projected it into New
and Washington, D.C.,

York and European fantasylands I'd never know otherwise, ~~but~~ *it* has offered me joy and fun. ~~In this,~~

there are limits to how much that might be seen in these essays. I assure you, everyone of them has

given me such pleasure and satisfaction, the same kind I ~~have~~ had when I used to cut wood with my
huge,
skilsaw and drive nails and build, watch a building rise ~~high~~ a fun of the kind that trowels the back
a
of a tile with adhesive and sets it in, ~~the~~ pattern mounting. Each word is rock I've placed personally *[yes]*
then   it's
into a wall—five go in and I pick through a pile and find another, shift them around until I like it. *[visible]*

I've chipped and knicked at most so ~~that~~ they look to me like good sentences, good paragraphs. If I
of
don't think of myself as the smartest, I do feel a strength in my working the craft, so that everytime I
maybe too
finish something I'm ~~impressed~~ proud of myself, can hardly believe I did it, that I could. ~~Because it's~~
the words   The words are   *[or]*
~~almost as though it came from another consciousness,~~ beyond my own physical self or nature,
of not
because ~~I don't think~~ I was born to be a writer, I've just done it anyway. Often this work is outright

fun, almost as fun as ~~it would be at~~ a good construction job where we were all muscles sweating and

laughing and building shit and getting paid ~~all~~ at the same time—living and working—except writing

work is alone, only an imaginary crew. Sometimes you see that laughter in these essays, but even

4G

A draft manuscript page for the introduction to Gilb's essay collection, *Gritos,* published in 2003 by Grove Press.
Courtesy of Dagoberto Gilb.

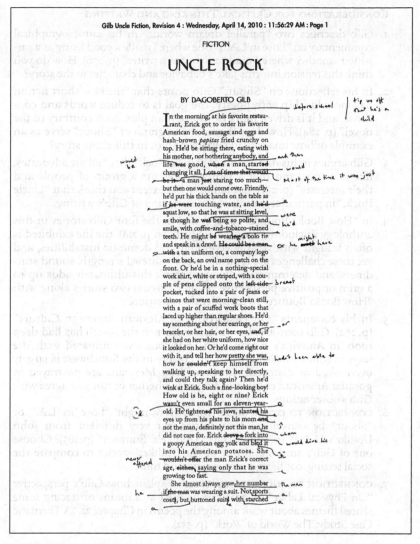

Gilb Uncle Fiction, Revision 4 : Wednesday, April 14, 2010 : 11:56:29 AM : Page 1

FICTION

UNCLE ROCK

BY DAGOBERTO GILB

In the morning, at his favorite restaurant, Erick got to order his favorite American food, sausage and eggs and hash-brown *papitas* fried crunchy on top. He'd be sitting there, eating with his mother, not bothering anybody, and life was good, when a man started changing it all. Lots of times that would be it—a man just staring too much—but then one would come over. Friendly, he'd put his thick hands on the table as if he were touching water, and he'd squat low, so that he was at sitting level, as though he was being so polite, and smile, with coffee-and-tobacco-stained teeth. He might be wearing a bolo tie and speak in a drawl. He could be a man with a tan uniform on, a company logo on the back, an oval name patch on the front. Or he'd be in a nothing-special work shirt, white or striped, with a couple of pens clipped onto the left-side pocket, tucked into a pair of jeans or chinos that were morning-clean still, with a pair of scuffed work boots that laced up higher than regular shoes. He'd say something about her earrings, or her bracelet, or her hair, or her eyes, and, if she had on her white uniform, how nice it looked on her. Or he'd come right out with it, and tell her how pretty she was, how he couldn't keep himself from walking up, speaking to her directly, and could they talk again? Then he'd wink at Erick. Such a fine-looking boy! How old is he, eight or nine? Erick wasn't even small for an eleven-year-old. He tightened his jaws, slanted his eyes up from his plate to his mom and not the man, definitely not this man he did not care for. Erick drove a fork into a goopy American egg yolk and bled it into his American potatoes. She wouldn't offer the man Erick's correct age, either, saying only that he was growing too fast.

She almost always gave her number if the man was wearing a suit. Not sports coat, but buttoned suit with starched

CONSIDERATIONS FOR CRITICAL THINKING AND WRITING

1. Gilb describes two "parallel dream worlds" in his autobiographical commentary on "Love in L.A.": "one where I made a good living as a carpenter, another where I made a living as a writer" (p. 278). How do you think this tension informs Jake's behavior and character in the story?

2. In his reflections on "Shout," Gilb posits that "the best short fiction has more kinship with poetry: the goal is to reduce words and condense, and it is driven more by image than plot, both contrary to the novel" (p. 284). How does the final paragraph of "Shout" serve as an example of how images can supersede plot in this short story?

3. Gilb argues in his discussion of "Uncle Rock" that "all art advocates, like it or not, and that a writer represents a group of people and their interests" (p. 291). Explain to what extent you think that "Uncle Rock," in particular, fulfills this description of Gilb's writing.

4. In "How Books Bounce" (p. 273) and in the four Gilb stories in this anthology (including "Romero's Shirt" on p. 218), the life exhibited is often fraught with volatile economic and domestic instabilities, and yet these challenges are typically met by shrewd strength, sound sturdiness, and determination. Do you think this ultimately adds up to a grim or positive perspective on life? Discuss two stories along with "How Books Bounce" to consider this question.

5. In his comments "On Distortions of Mexican American Culture" (p. 292), Gilb contrasts how black culture in the South has had deep roots in America's history and consciousness compared with the ways in which Mexican American culture in the Southwest is largely overlooked or distorted. Consider how Mexicans are portrayed in popular American culture and discuss whether or not you agree with Gilb's observations.

6. CONNECTION TO OTHER SELECTIONS. How might "Love in L.A." or "Shout" be considered love stories but very different from John Updike's "A & P" (p. 157) or David Updike's "Summer" (p. 163)? Choose one of Gilb's stories and one of the Updikes' stories to compare the social setting, conflicts, protagonists, and tone.

7. CONNECTION TO ANOTHER SELECTION. Explain how Gilb's perspective "On Physical Labor" (p. 292) can be used as a means of tracing some shared themes about work among the poems in Chapter 22, "A Thematic Case Study: The World of Work" (p. 552).

SUGGESTED TOPICS FOR LONGER PAPERS

1. "My own stories are about the small things and the people who aren't seen much in literature" ("On Writing 'Shout,'" p. 283). How do the four stories in this collection portray the details of working people's lives? What common themes emerge from those portrayals?

2. As executive director of Centro Victoria, Gilb has worked diligently to advance Mexican American literature and culture. Discuss the ways in which you think Gilb's four stories challenge social stereotyping.

A Collection
of Stories

Stories for Further Reading

A ratio of failures is built into the process of writing. The wastebasket has evolved for a reason.

—MARGARET ATWOOD

© Kathy deWitt/Alamy.

NATHANIEL HAWTHORNE (1804–1864)

Born in Salem, Massachusetts, Nathaniel Hawthorne came from a family that traced its roots back to the Puritans. After graduating from Bowdoin College in 1825, he returned home to Salem, where for the next twelve years he read and taught himself how to write. He published his first collection of stories, *Twice-Told Tales*, in 1837, followed by a second edition in 1842, and *Mosses from an Old Manse* in 1846. In 1849 he lost his job at the Salem Custom House and focused on his writing. In addition to *The Scarlet Letter* (1850), he wrote *The House*

By permission of the Peabody Essex Museum.

of Seven Gables (1851); *The Blithedale Romance* (1852); *The Snow-Image, and Other Twice-Told Tales* (1852); a campaign biography of his Bowdoin classmate, *The Life of Franklin Pierce* (1852); and two collections of stories for children, *A Wonder Book* (1852) and *Tanglewood Tales* (1853).

The Birthmark   1843

In the latter part of the last century there lived a man of science, an eminent proficient in every branch of natural philosophy, who not long before
our story opens had made experience of a spiritual affinity more attractive than any chemical one. He had left his laboratory to the care of an
assistant, cleared his fine countenance from the furnace smoke, washed
the stain of acids from his fingers, and persuaded a beautiful woman to
become his wife. In those days when the comparatively recent discovery
of electricity and other kindred mysteries of Nature seemed to open paths
into the region of miracle, it was not unusual for the love of science to rival
the love of woman in its depth and absorbing energy. The higher intellect,
the imagination, the spirit, and even the heart might all find their conge-
nial aliment in pursuits which, as some of their ardent votaries believed,
would ascend from one step of powerful intelligence to another, until the
philosopher should lay his hand on the secret of creative force and perhaps
make new worlds for himself. We know not whether Aylmer possessed this
degree of faith in man's ultimate control over Nature. He had devoted
himself, however, too unreservedly to scientific studies ever to be weaned
from them by any second passion. His love for his young wife might prove
the stronger of the two; but it could only be by intertwining itself with his
love of science, and uniting the strength of the latter to his own.

Such a union accordingly took place, and was attended with truly
remarkable consequences and a deeply impressive moral. One day, very
soon after their marriage, Aylmer sat gazing at his wife with a trouble in
his countenance that grew stronger until he spoke.

"Georgiana," said he, "has it never occurred to you that the mark
upon your cheek might be removed?"

"No, indeed," said she, smiling; but perceiving the seriousness of his
manner, she blushed deeply. "To tell you the truth it has been so often
called a charm that I was simple enough to imagine it might be so."

"Ah, upon another face perhaps it might," replied her husband; "but 5
never on yours. No, dearest Georgiana, you came so nearly perfect from
the hand of Nature that this slightest possible defect, which we hesitate
whether to term a defect or a beauty, shocks me, as being the visible mark
of earthly imperfection."

"Shocks you, my husband!" cried Georgiana, deeply hurt; at first
reddening with momentary anger, but then bursting into tears. "Then
why did you take me from my mother's side? You cannot love what
shocks you!"

To explain this conversation it must be mentioned that in the
center of Georgiana's left cheek there was a singular mark, deeply inter-
woven, as it were, with the texture and substance of her face. In the usual
state of her complexion—a healthy though delicate bloom—the mark
wore a tint of deeper crimson, which imperfectly defined its shape amid
the surrounding rosiness. When she blushed it gradually became more

indistinct, and finally vanished amid the triumphant rush of blood that bathed the whole cheek with its brilliant glow. But if any shifting motion caused her to turn pale, there was the mark again, a crimson stain upon the snow, in what Aylmer sometimes deemed an almost fearful distinctness. Its shape bore not a little similarity to the human hand, though of the smallest pygmy size. Georgiana's lovers were wont to say that some fairy at her birth hour had laid her tiny hand upon the infant's cheek, and left this impress there in token of the magic endowments that were to give her such sway over all hearts. Many a desperate swain would have risked life for the privilege of pressing his lips to the mysterious hand. It must not be concealed, however, that the impression wrought by this fairy sign manual varied exceedingly, according to the difference of temperament in the beholders. Some fastidious persons—but they were exclusively of her own sex—affirmed that the bloody hand, as they chose to call it, quite destroyed the effect of Georgiana's beauty, and rendered her countenance even hideous. But it would be as reasonable to say that one of those small blue stains which sometimes occur in the purest statuary marble would convert the Eve of Powers to a monster. Masculine observers, if the birthmark did not heighten their admiration, contented themselves with wishing it away, that the world might possess one living specimen of ideal loveliness without the semblance of a flaw. After his marriage,—for he thought little or nothing of the matter before,—Aylmer discovered that this was the case with himself.

Had she been less beautiful,—if Envy's self could have found aught else to sneer at,—he might have felt his affection heightened by the prettiness of this mimic hand, now vaguely portrayed, now lost, now stealing forth again and glimmering to and fro with every pulse of emotion that throbbed within her heart; but seeing her otherwise so perfect, he found this one defect grow more and more intolerable with every moment of their united lives. It was the fatal flaw of humanity which Nature, in one shape or another, stamps ineffaceably on all her productions, either to imply that they are temporary and finite, or that their perfection must be wrought by toil and pain. The crimson hand expressed the ineludible gripe° in which mortality clutches the highest and purest of earthly mold, degrading them into kindred with the lowest, and even with the very brutes, like whom their visible frames return to dust. In this manner, selecting it as the symbol of his wife's liability to sin, sorrow, decay, and death, Aylmer's somber imagination was not long in rendering the birthmark a frightful object, causing him more trouble and horror than ever Georgiana's beauty, whether of soul or sense, had given him delight.

At all the seasons which should have been their happiest, he invariably and without intending it, nay, in spite of a purpose to the contrary, reverted to this one disastrous topic. Trifling as it at first appeared, it so connected itself with innumerable trains of thought and modes of feeling

gripe: Grip.

that it became the central point of all. With the morning twilight Aylmer opened his eyes upon his wife's face and recognized the symbol of imperfection; and when they sat together at the evening hearth his eyes wandered stealthily to her cheek, and beheld, flickering with the blaze of the wood fire, the spectral hand that wrote mortality where he would fain have worshiped. Georgiana soon learned to shudder at his gaze. It needed but a glance with the peculiar expression that his face often wore to change the roses of her cheek into a deathlike paleness, amid which the crimson hand was brought strongly out, like a bas-relief of ruby on the whitest marble.

Late one night when the lights were growing dim, so as hardly to 10 betray the stain on the poor wife's cheek, she herself, for the first time, voluntarily took up the subject.

"Do you remember, my dear Aylmer," said she, with a feeble attempt at a smile, "have you any recollection of a dream last night about this odious hand?"

"None! none whatever!" replied Aylmer, starting; but then he added, in a dry, cold tone, affected for the sake of concealing the real depth of his emotion, "I might well dream of it; for before I fell asleep it had taken a pretty firm hold of my fancy."

"And you did dream of it?" continued Georgiana hastily; for she dreaded lest a gush of tears should interrupt what she had to say. "A terrible dream! I wonder that you can forget it. Is it possible to forget this one expression? — 'It is in her heart now; we must have it out!' Reflect, my husband; for by all means I would have you recall that dream."

The mind is in a sad state when Sleep, the all-involving, cannot confine her specters within the dim region of her sway, but suffers them to break forth, affrighting this actual life with secrets that perchance belong to a deeper one. Aylmer now remembered his dream. He had fancied himself with his servant Aminadab, attempting an operation for the removal of the birthmark; but the deeper went the knife, the deeper sank the hand, until at length its tiny grasp appeared to have caught hold of Georgiana's heart; whence, however, her husband was inexorably resolved to cut or wrench it away.

When the dream had shaped itself perfectly in his memory, Aylmer 15 sat in his wife's presence with a guilty feeling. Truth often finds its way to the mind close muffled in robes of sleep, and then speaks with uncompromising directness of matters in regard to which we practice an unconscious self-deception during our waking moments. Until now he had not been aware of the tyrannizing influence acquired by one idea over his mind, and of the lengths which he might find in his heart to go for the sake of giving himself peace.

"Aylmer," resumed Georgiana solemnly, "I know not what may be the cost to both of us to rid me of this fatal birthmark. Perhaps its removal may cause cureless deformity; or it may be the stain goes as deep as life itself. Again: do we know that there is a possibility, on any terms, of unclasping the firm grip of this little hand which was laid upon me before I came into the world?"

"Dearest Georgiana, I have spent much thought upon the subject," hastily interrupted Aylmer. "I am convinced of the perfect practicability of its removal."

"If there be the remotest possibility of it," continued Georgiana, "let the attempt be made at whatever risk. Danger is nothing to me; for life, while this hateful mark makes me the object of your horror and disgust,—life is a burden which I would fling down with joy. Either remove this dreadful hand, or take my wretched life! You have deep science. All the world bears witness of it. You have achieved great wonders. Cannot you remove this little, little mark, which I cover with the tips of two small fingers? Is this beyond your power, for the sake of your own peace, and to save your poor wife from madness?"

"Noblest, dearest, tenderest wife," cried Aylmer rapturously, "doubt not my power. I have already given this matter the deepest thought—thought which might almost have enlightened me to create a being less perfect than yourself. Georgiana, you have led me deeper than ever into the heart of science. I feel myself fully competent to render this dear cheek as faultless as its fellow; and then, most beloved, what will be my triumph when I shall have corrected what Nature left imperfect in her fairest work! Even Pygmalion, when his sculptured woman assumed life, felt not greater ecstasy than mine will be."

"It is resolved, then," said Georgiana, faintly smiling. "And, Aylmer, 20 spare me not, though you should find the birthmark take refuge in my heart at last."

Her husband tenderly kissed her cheek—her right cheek—not that which bore the impress of the crimson hand.

The next day Aylmer apprised his wife of a plan that he had formed whereby he might have opportunity for the intense thought and constant watchfulness which the proposed operation would require; while Georgiana, likewise, would enjoy the perfect repose essential to its success. They were to seclude themselves in the extensive apartments occupied by Aylmer as a laboratory, and where, during his toilsome youth, he had made discoveries in the elemental powers of Nature that had roused the admiration of all the learned societies in Europe. Seated calmly in this laboratory, the pale philosopher had investigated the secrets of the highest cloud region and of the profoundest mines; he had satisfied himself of the causes that kindled and kept alive the fires of the volcano; and had explained the mystery of fountains, and how it is that they gush forth, some so bright and pure, and others with such rich medicinal virtues, from the dark bosom of the earth. Here, too, at an earlier period, he had studied the wonders of the human frame, and attempted to fathom the very process by which Nature assimilates all her precious influences from earth and air, and from the spiritual world, to create and foster man, her masterpiece. The latter pursuit, however, Aylmer had long laid aside in unwilling recognition of the truth—against which all seekers sooner or later stumble—that our great creative Mother, while she amuses us with apparently working in the broadest sunshine, is yet severely careful to keep her own secrets, and, in spite of her pretended openness, shows us nothing but results. She permits us, indeed, to mar, but seldom to mend, and, like a jealous patentee, on no account to make. Now, however, Aylmer resumed these half-forgotten investigations, — not, of course, with such hopes or wishes as first suggested them, but because they involved much physiological truth and lay in the path of his proposed scheme for the treatment of Georgiana.

As he led her over the threshold of the laboratory, Georgiana was cold and tremulous. Aylmer looked cheerfully into her face, with intent to reassure her, but was so startled with the intense glow of the birth-mark upon the whiteness of her cheek that he could not restrain a strong convulsive shudder. His wife fainted.

"Aminadab! Aminadab!" shouted Aylmer, stamping violently on the floor.

Forthwith there issued from an inner apartment a man of low stat- 25 ure, but bulky frame, with shaggy hair hanging about his visage, which was grimed with the vapors of the furnace. This personage had been Aylmer's underworker during his whole scientific career, and was admirably fitted for that office by his great mechanical readiness, and the skill with which, while incapable of comprehending a single principle, he executed all the details of his master's experiments. With his vast strength, his shaggy hair, his smoky aspect, and the indescribable earthiness that encrusted him, he seemed to represent man's physical nature; while Aylmer's slender figure, and pale, intellectual face, were no less apt a type of the spiritual element.

"Throw open the door of the boudoir, Aminadab," said Aylmer, "and burn a pastille."

"Yes, master," answered Aminadab, looking intently at the lifeless form of Georgiana; and then he muttered to himself, "If she were my wife, I'd never part with that birthmark."

When Georgiana recovered consciousness she found herself breathing an atmosphere of penetrating fragrance, the gentle potency of which had recalled her from her deathlike faintness. The scene around her looked like enchantment. Aylmer had converted those smoky, dingy, somber rooms, where he had spent his brightest years in recondite pursuits, into a series of beautiful apartments not unfit to be the secluded abode of a lovely woman. The walls were hung with gorgeous curtains, which imparted the combination of grandeur and grace that no other species of adornment can achieve; and as they fell from the ceiling to the floor, their rich and ponderous folds, concealing all angles and straight lines, appeared to shut in the scene from infinite space. For aught Georgiana knew, it might be a pavilion among the clouds. And Aylmer, excluding the sunshine, which would have interfered with his chemical processes, had supplied its place with perfumed lamps, emitting flames of various hue, but all uniting in a soft, empurpled radiance. He now knelt by his wife's side, watching her earnestly, but without alarm; for he was confident in his science, and felt that he could draw a magic circle round her within which no evil might intrude.

"Where am I? Ah, I remember," said Georgiana faintly; and she placed her hand over her cheek to hide the terrible mark from her husband's eyes.

"Fear not, dearest!" exclaimed he. "Do not shrink from me! Believe 30 me, Georgiana, I even rejoice in this single imperfection, since it will be such a rapture to remove it."

"Oh, spare me!" sadly replied his wife. "Pray do not look at it again. I never can forget that convulsive shudder."

In order to soothe Georgiana, and, as it were, to release her mind from the burden of actual things, Aylmer now put in practice some of the light and playful secrets which science had taught him among its profounder lore. Airy figures, absolutely bodiless ideas, and forms of unsubstantial beauty came and danced before her, imprinting their momentary footsteps on beams of light. Though she had some indistinct idea of the method of these optical phenomena, still the illusion was almost perfect enough to warrant the belief that her husband possessed sway over the spiritual world. Then again, when she felt a wish to look forth from her seclusion, immediately, as if her thoughts were answered, the procession of external existence flitted across a screen. The scenery and the figures of actual life were perfectly represented, but with that bewitching, yet indescribable difference which always makes a picture, an image, or a shadow so much more attractive than the original. When wearied of this, Aylmer bade her cast her eyes upon a vessel containing a quantity of earth. She did so, with little interest at first; but was soon startled to perceive the germ of a plant shooting upward from the soil. Then came the slender stalk; the leaves gradually unfolded themselves; and amid them was a perfect and lovely flower.

"It is magical!" cried Georgiana. "I dare not touch it."

"Nay, pluck it," answered Aylmer: "pluck it, and inhale its brief perfume while you may. The flower will wither in a few moments and leave nothing save its brown seed vessels; but thence may be perpetuated a race as ephemeral as itself."

But Georgiana had no sooner touched the flower than the whole 35 plant suffered a blight, its leaves turning coal-black as if by the agency of fire.

"There was too powerful a stimulus," said Aylmer thoughtfully.

To make up for this abortive experiment, he proposed to take her portrait by a scientific process of his own invention. It was to be effected by rays of light striking upon a polished plate of metal. Georgiana assented; but, on looking at the result, was affrighted to find the features of the portrait blurred and indefinable; while the minute figure of a hand appeared where the cheek should have been. Aylmer snatched the metallic plate and threw it into a jar of corrosive acid.

Soon, however, he forgot these mortifying failures. In the intervals of study and chemical experiment he came to her flushed and exhausted, but seemed invigorated by her presence, and spoke in glowing language of the resources of his art. He gave a history of the long dynasty of the alchemists, who spent so many ages in quest of the universal solvent by which the golden principle might be elicited from all things vile and base. Aylmer appeared to believe that, by the plainest scientific logic, it was altogether within the limits of possibility to discover this long-sought medium; "but," he added, "a philosopher who should go deep enough to acquire the power would attain too lofty a wisdom to stoop to the exercise of it." Not less singular were his opinions in regard to the elixir vitae. He more than intimated that it was at his option to concoct a liquid that should prolong life for years, perhaps interminably; but that it would produce a discord in Nature which all the world, and chiefly the quaffer of the immortal nostrum, would find cause to curse.

"Aylmer, are you in earnest?" asked Georgiana, looking at him with amazement and fear. "It is terrible to possess such power, or even to dream of possessing it."

"Oh, do not tremble, my love," said her husband. "I would not 40 wrong either you or myself by working such inharmonious effects upon our lives; but I would have you consider how trifling, in comparison, is the skill requisite to remove this little hand."

At the mention of the birthmark, Georgiana, as usual, shrank as if a red-hot iron had touched her cheek.

Again Aylmer applied himself to his labors. She could hear his voice in the distant furnace-room giving directions to Aminadab, whose harsh, uncouth, misshapen tones were audible in response, more like the grunt or growl of a brute than human speech. After hours of absence, Aylmer reappeared and proposed that she should now examine his cabinet of chemical products and natural treasures of the earth. Among the former he showed her a small vial, in which, he remarked, was contained a gentle yet most powerful fragrance, capable of impregnating all the breezes that blow across a kingdom. They were of inestimable value, the contents of that little vial; and, as he said so, he threw some of the perfume into the air and filled the room with piercing and invigorating delight.

"And what is this?" asked Georgiana, pointing to a small crystal globe containing a gold-colored liquid. "It is so beautiful to the eye that I could imagine it the elixir of life."

"In one sense it is," replied Aylmer; "or rather, the elixir of immortality. It is the most precious poison that ever was concocted in this world. By its aid I could apportion the lifetime of any mortal at whom you might point your finger. The strength of the dose would determine whether he were to linger out years, or drop dead in the midst of a breath. No king on his guarded throne could keep his life if I, in my private station, should deem that the welfare of millions justified me in depriving him of it."

"Why do you keep such a terrific drug?" inquired Georgiana in 45 horror.

"Do not mistrust me, dearest," said her husband, smiling; "its virtuous potency is yet greater than its harmful one. But see! here is a powerful cosmetic. With a few drops of this in a vase of water, freckles may be washed away as easily as the hands are cleansed. A stronger infusion would take the blood out of the cheek, and leave the rosiest beauty a pale ghost."

"Is it with this lotion that you intend to bathe my cheek?" asked Georgiana, anxiously.

"Oh, no," hastily replied her husband; "this is merely superficial. Your case demands a remedy that shall go deeper."

In his interviews with Georgiana, Aylmer generally made minute inquiries as to her sensations and whether the confinement of the rooms and the temperature of the atmosphere agreed with her. These questions had such a particular drift that Georgiana began to conjecture that she was already subjected to certain physical influences, either breathed in with the fragrant air or taken with her food. She fancied likewise, but it might be altogether fancy, that there was a stirring up of her system — a strange, indefinite sensation creeping through her veins, and tingling, half painfully, half pleasurably, at her heart. Still, whenever she dared to look into the mirror, there she beheld herself pale as a white rose and with the crimson birthmark stamped upon her cheek. Not even Aylmer now hated it so much as she.

To dispel the tedium of the hours which her husband found it 50 necessary to devote to the processes of combination and analysis, Georgiana turned over the volumes of his scientific library. In many dark old tomes she met with chapters full of romance and poetry. They were the works of the philosophers of the middle ages, such as Albertus Magnus, Cornelius Agrippa, Paracelsus, and the famous friar who created the prophetic Brazen Head. All these antique naturalists stood in advance of their centuries, yet were imbued with some of their credulity, and therefore were believed, and perhaps imagined themselves to have acquired from the investigation of Nature a power above Nature, and from physics a sway over the spiritual world. Hardly less curious and imaginative were the early volumes of the Transactions of the Royal Society, in which the members, knowing little of the limits of natural possibility, were continually recording wonders or proposing methods whereby wonders might be wrought.

But to Georgiana the most engrossing volume was a large folio from her husband's own hand, in which he had recorded every experiment of his scientific career, its original aim, the methods adopted for its development, and its final success or failure, with the circumstances to which either event was attributable. The book, in truth, was both the history and emblem of his ardent, ambitious, imaginative, yet practical and laborious life. He handled physical details as if there were nothing beyond them; yet spiritualized them all, and redeemed himself from materialism by his strong and eager aspiration towards the infinite. In his grasp the veriest clod of earth assumed a soul. Georgiana, as she read, reverenced Aylmer and loved him more profoundly than ever, but with a less entire dependence on his judgment than heretofore. Much as he had accomplished, she could not but observe that his most splendid successes were almost invariably failures, if compared with the ideal at which he aimed. His brightest diamonds were the merest pebbles, and felt to be so by himself, in comparison with the inestimable gems which lay hidden beyond his reach. The volume, rich with achievements that had won renown for its author, was yet as melancholy a record as ever mortal hand had penned. It was the sad confession and continual exemplification of the shortcomings of the composite man, the spirit burdened with clay and working in matter, and of the despair that assails the higher nature at finding itself so miserably thwarted by the earthly part. Perhaps every man of genius in whatever sphere might recognize the image of his own experience in Aylmer's journal.

So deeply did these reflections affect Georgiana that she laid her face upon the open volume and burst into tears. In this situation she was found by her husband.

"It is dangerous to read in a sorcerer's books," said he with a smile, though his countenance was uneasy and displeased. "Georgiana, there are pages in that volume which I can scarcely glance over and keep my senses. Take heed lest it prove as detrimental to you."

"It has made me worship you more than ever," said she.

"Ah, wait for this one success," rejoined he, "then worship me if you will. I shall deem myself hardly unworthy of it. But come, I have sought you for the luxury of your voice. Sing to me, dearest." 55

So she poured out the liquid music of her voice to quench the thirst of his spirit. He then took his leave with a boyish exuberance of gaiety, assuring her that her seclusion would endure but a little longer, and that the result was already certain. Scarcely had he departed when Georgiana felt irresistibly impelled to follow him. She had forgotten to inform Aylmer of a symptom which for two or three hours past had begun to excite her attention. It was a sensation in the fatal birthmark, not painful, but which induced a restlessness throughout her system. Hastening after her husband, she intruded for the first time into the laboratory.

The first thing that struck her eye was the furnace, that hot and feverish worker, with the intense glow of its fire, which by the quantities of soot clustered above it seemed to have been burning for ages. There was a distilling apparatus in full operation. Around the room were retorts, tubes, cylinders, crucibles, and other apparatus of chemical research. An electrical machine stood ready for immediate use. The atmosphere felt oppressively close, and was tainted with gaseous odors which had been tormented forth by the processes of science. The severe and homely simplicity of the apartment, with its naked walls and brick pavement, looked strange, accustomed as Georgiana had become to the fantastic elegance of her boudoir. But what chiefly, indeed almost solely, drew her attention, was the aspect of Aylmer himself.

He was pale as death, anxious and absorbed, and hung over the furnace as if it depended upon his utmost watchfulness whether the liquid which it was distilling should be the draught of immortal happiness or misery. How different from the sanguine and joyous mien that he had assumed for Georgiana's encouragement!

"Carefully now, Aminadab; carefully, thou human machine; carefully, thou man of clay!" muttered Aylmer, more to himself than his assistant. "Now, if there be a thought too much or too little, it is all over."

"Ho! ho!" mumbled Aminadab. "Look, master! look!"   60

Aylmer raised his eyes hastily, and at first reddened, then grew paler than ever, on beholding Georgiana. He rushed towards her and seized her arm with a gripe that left the print of his fingers upon it.

"Why do you come hither? Have you no trust in your husband?" cried he impetuously. "Would you throw the blight of that fatal birthmark over my labors? It is not well done. Go, prying woman, go!"

"Nay, Aylmer," said Georgiana with the firmness of which she possessed no stinted endowment, "it is not you that have a right to complain. You mistrust your wife; you have concealed the anxiety with which you watch the development of this experiment. Think not so unworthily of me, my husband. Tell me all the risk we run, and fear not that I shall shrink; for my share in it is far less than your own."

"No, no, Georgiana!" said Aylmer impatiently; "it must not be."

"I submit," replied she calmly. "And, Aylmer, I shall quaff whatever 65 draught you bring me; but it will be on the same principle that would induce me to take a dose of poison if offered by your hand."

"My noble wife," said Aylmer, deeply moved, "I knew not the height and depth of your nature until now. Nothing shall be concealed. Know, then, that this crimson hand, superficial as it seems, has clutched its grasp into your being with a strength of which I had no previous conception. I have already administered agents powerful enough to do aught except to change your entire physical system. Only one thing remains to be tried. If that fails us we are ruined."

"Why did you hesitate to tell me this?" asked she.

"Because, Georgiana," said Aylmer in a low voice, "there is danger."

"Danger? There is but one danger—that this horrible stigma shall be left upon my cheek!" cried Georgiana. "Remove it, remove it, whatever be the cost, or we shall both go mad!"

"Heaven knows your words are too true," said Aylmer sadly. "And 70 now, dearest, return to your boudoir. In a little while all will be tested."

He conducted her back and took leave of her with a solemn tenderness which spoke far more than his words how much was now at stake. After his departure Georgiana became rapt in musings. She considered the character of Aylmer, and did it completer justice than at any previous moment. Her heart exulted, while it trembled, at his honorable love — so pure and lofty that it would accept nothing less than perfection nor miserably make itself contented with an earthlier nature than he had dreamed of. She felt how much more precious was such a sentiment than that meaner kind which would have borne with the imperfection for her sake, and have been guilty of treason to holy love by degrading its perfect idea to the level of the actual; and with her whole spirit she prayed that, for a single moment, she might satisfy his highest and deepest conception. Longer than one moment she well knew it could not be; for his spirit was ever on the march, ever ascending, and each instant required something that was beyond the scope of the instant before.

The sound of her husband's footsteps aroused her. He bore a crystal goblet containing a liquor colorless as water, but bright enough to be the draught of immortality. Aylmer was pale; but it seemed rather the consequence of a highly wrought state of mind and tension of spirit than of fear or doubt.

"The concoction of the draught has been perfect," said he, in answer to Georgiana's look. "Unless all my science have deceived me, it cannot fail."

"Save on your account, my dearest Aylmer," observed his wife, "I might wish to put off this birthmark of mortality by relinquishing mortality itself in preference to any other mode. Life is but a sad possession to those who have attained precisely the degree of moral advancement at which I stand. Were I weaker and blinder it might be happiness. Were I stronger, it might be endured hopefully. But, being what I find myself, methinks I am of all mortals the most fit to die."

"You are fit for heaven without tasting death!" replied her husband. 75 "But why do we speak of dying? The draught cannot fail. Behold its effect upon this plant."

On the window seat there stood a geranium diseased with yellow blotches, which had overspread all its leaves. Aylmer poured a small quantity of the liquid upon the soil in which it grew. In a little time, when the roots of the plant had taken up the moisture, the unsightly blotches began to be extinguished in a living verdure.

"There needed no proof," said Georgiana quietly. "Give me the goblet. I joyfully stake all upon your word."

"Drink, then, thou lofty creature!" exclaimed Aylmer, with fervid admiration. "There is no taint of imperfection on thy spirit. Thy sensible frame, too, shall soon be all perfect."

She quaffed the liquid and returned the goblet to his hand.

"It is grateful," said she, with a placid smile. "Methinks it is like 80 water from a heavenly fountain; for it contains I know not what of unobtrusive fragrance and deliciousness. It allays a feverish thirst that had parched me for many days. Now, dearest, let me sleep. My earthly senses are closing over my spirit like the leaves around the heart of a rose at sunset."

She spoke the last words with a gentle reluctance, as if it required almost more energy than she could command to pronounce the faint and lingering syllables. Scarcely had they loitered through her lips ere she was lost in slumber. Aylmer sat by her side, watching her aspect with the emotions proper to a man the whole value of whose existence was involved in the process now to be tested. Mingled with this mood, however, was the philosophic investigation characteristic of the man of science. Not the minutest symptom escaped him. A heightened flush of the cheek, a slight irregularity of breath, a quiver of the eyelid, a hardly perceptible tremor through the frame — such were the details which, as the moments passed, he wrote down in his folio volume. Intense thought had set its stamp upon every previous page of that volume, but the thoughts of years were all concentrated upon the last.

While thus employed, he failed not to gaze often at the fatal hand, and not without a shudder. Yet once, by a strange and unaccountable impulse, he pressed it with his lips. His spirit recoiled, however, in the very act; and Georgiana, out of the midst of her deep sleep, moved uneasily and murmured as if in remonstrance. Again Aylmer resumed his watch. Nor was it without avail. The crimson hand, which at first had been strongly visible upon the marble paleness of Georgiana's cheek, now grew more faintly outlined. She remained not less pale than ever; but the birthmark, with every breath that came and went, lost somewhat of its former distinctness. Its presence had been awful; its departure was more awful still. Watch the stain of the rainbow fading out of the sky, and you will know how that mysterious symbol passed away.

"By Heaven! it is well-nigh gone!" said Aylmer to himself, in almost irrepressible ecstasy. "I can scarcely trace it now. Success! success! And now it is like the faintest rose color. The lightest flush of blood across her cheek would overcome it. But she is so pale!"

He drew aside the window curtain and suffered the light of natural day to fall into the room and rest upon her cheek. At the same time he heard a gross, hoarse chuckle, which he had long known as his servant Aminadab's expression of delight.

"Ah, clod! ah, earthly mass!" cried Aylmer, laughing in a sort of frenzy, "you have served me well! Matter and spirit — earth and heaven — have both done their part in this! Laugh, thing of the senses! You have earned the right to laugh." 85

These exclamations broke Georgiana's sleep. She slowly unclosed her eyes and gazed into the mirror which her husband had arranged for that purpose. A faint smile flitted over her lips when she recognized how barely perceptible was now that crimson hand which had once blazed forth with such disastrous brilliancy as to scare away all their happiness. But then her eyes sought Aylmer's face with a trouble and anxiety that he could by no means account for.

"My poor Aylmer!" murmured she.

"Poor? Nay, richest, happiest, most favored!" exclaimed he. "My peerless bride, it is successful! You are perfect!"

"My poor Aylmer," she repeated, with a more than human tenderness, "you have aimed loftily; you have done nobly. Do not repent that with so high and pure a feeling, you have rejected the best the earth could offer. Aylmer, dearest Aylmer, I am dying!"

Alas! it was too true! The fatal hand had grappled with the mystery   90 of life, and was the bond by which an angelic spirit kept itself in union with a mortal frame. As the last crimson tint of the birthmark — that sole token of human imperfection — faded from her cheek, the parting breath of the now perfect woman passed into the atmosphere, and her soul, lingering a moment near her husband, took its heavenward flight. Then a hoarse, chuckling laugh was heard again! Thus ever does the gross fatality of earth exult in its invariable triumph over the immortal essence which, in this dim sphere of half development, demands the completeness of a higher state. Yet, had Aylmer reached a profounder wisdom, he need not thus have flung away the happiness which would have woven his mortal life of the selfsame texture with the celestial. The momentary circumstance was too strong for him; he failed to look beyond the shadowy scope of time, and, living once for all in eternity, to find the perfect future in the present.

ZORA NEALE HURSTON (1901–1960)

Raised in Eatonville, Florida, the first black incorporated township established in the United States, Zora Neale Hurston attended Howard University and graduated from Barnard College with an emphasis on anthropology. This abiding interest is reflected in her use of African American folklore in her fiction. An important figure writing stories and plays during the Harlem Renaissance in the 1920s and 1930s, she insisted on making known the humanity of black people and depicted their cultural heritage with respect and affection in an effort to overcome the crude stereotyping of

Reprinted courtesy of the Library of Congress.

the period. The author of four novels, *Jonah's Gourd Vine* (1934), *Their Eyes Were Watching God* (1937), *Moses, Man of the Mountain* (1939), and *Seraph of the Sewanee* (1948), Hurston's short stories are collected in *The Complete Stories* (1948). Her work, though largely neglected late in her life, was rediscovered in the 1970s through the conscientious inclusiveness of the women's movement.

Spunk   *1925*

A giant of a brown-skinned man sauntered up the one street of the village and out into the palmetto thickets with a small pretty woman clinging lovingly to his arm.

"Looka theah, folkses!" cried Elijah Mosley, slapping his leg gleefully. "Theah they go, big as life an' brassy, as tacks."

All the loungers in the store tried to walk to the door with an air of nonchalance but with small success.

"Now pee-eople!" Walter Thomas gasped. "Will you look at 'em!"

"But that's one thing Ah likes about Spunk Banks—he ain't skeered   5
of nothin' on God's green footstool—*nothin'!* He rides that log down at sawmill jus' like he struts 'round wid another man's wife—jus' don't give a kitty. When Tes' Miller got cut to giblets on that circle-saw, Spunk steps right up and starts ridin'. The rest of us was skeered to go near it."

A round-shouldered figure in overalls much too large came nervously in the door and the talking ceased. The men looked at each other and winked.

"Gimme some soda-water. Sass'prilla Ah reckon," the newcomer ordered, and stood far down the counter near the open pickled pig-feet tub to drink it.

Elijah nudged Walter and turned with mock gravity to the newcomer.

"Say, Joe, how's everything up yo' way? How's yo' wife?"

Joe started and all but dropped the bottle he was holding. He swal-   10
lowed several times painfully and his lips trembled.

"Aw 'Lige, you oughtn't to do nothin' like that," Walter grumbled. Elijah ignored him.

"She jus' passed heah a few minutes ago goin' thata way," with a wave of his hand in the direction of the woods.

Now Joe knew his wife had passed that way. He knew that the men lounging in the general store had seen her, moreover, he knew that the men knew *he* knew. He stood there silent for a long moment staring blankly, with his Adam's apple twitching nervously up and down his throat. One could actually *see* the pain he was suffering, his eyes, his face, his hands, and even the dejected slump of his shoulders. He set the bottle down upon the counter. He didn't bang it, just eased it out of his hand silently and fiddled with his suspender buckle.

"Well, Ah'm goin' after her to-day. Ah'm goin' an' fetch her back. Spunk's done gone too fur."

He reached deep down into his trouser pocket and drew out a hol-   15
low ground razor, large and shiny, and passed his moistened thumb back and forth over the edge.

"Talkin' like a man, Joe. 'Course that's *yo'* fambly affairs, but Ah like to see grit in anybody."

Joe Kanty laid down a nickel and stumbled out into the street.

Dusk crept in from the woods. Ike Clarke lit the swinging oil lamp that was almost immediately surrounded by candle-flies. The men laughed boisterously behind Joe's back as they watched him shamble woodward.

"You oughtn't to said whut you said to him, 'Lige—look how it worked him up," Walter chided.

"And Ah hope it did work him up. Tain't even decent for a man to   20 take and take like he do."

"Spunk will sho' kill him."

"Aw, Ah doan know. You never kin tell. He might turn him up an' spank him fur gettin' in the way, but Spunk wouldn't shoot no unarmed man. Dat razor he carried outa heah ain't gonna run Spunk down an' cut him, an' Joe ain't got the nerve to go to Spunk with it knowing he totes that Army .45. He makes that break outa heah to bluff us. He's gonna hide that razor behind the first palmetto root an' sneak back home to bed. Don't tell me nothin' 'bout that rabbit-foot colored man. Didn't he meet Spunk an' Lena face to face one day las' week an' mumble sumthin' to Spunk 'bout lettin' his wife alone?"

"What did Spunk say?" Walter broke in. "Ah like him fine but tain't right the way he carries on wid Lena Kanty, jus' 'cause Joe's timid 'bout fightin'."

"You wrong theah, Walter. Tain't 'cause Joe's timid at all, it's 'cause Spunk wants Lena. If Joe was a passle of wile cats Spunk would tackle the job just the same. He'd go after *anything* he wanted the same way. As Ah wuz sayin' a minute ago, he tole Joe right to his face that Lena was his. 'Call her and see if she'll come. A woman knows her boss an' she answers when he calls.' 'Lena, ain't I yo' husband?' Joe sorter whines out. Lena looked at him real disgusted but she don't answer and she don't move outa her tracks. Then Spunk reaches out an' takes hold of her arm an' says: 'Lena, youse mine. From now on Ah works for you an' fights for you an' Ah never wants you to look to nobody for a crumb of bread, a stitch of close or a shingle to go over yo' head, but *me* long as Ah live. Ah'll git the lumber foh owah house to-morrow. Go home an' git yo' things together!'

"'Thass mah house,' Lena speaks up. 'Papa gimme that.'   25

"'Well,' says Spunk, 'doan give up what's yours, but when youse inside doan forgit youse mine, an' let no other man git outa his place wid you!'

"Lena looked up at him with her eyes so full of love that they wuz runnin' over, an' Spunk seen it an' Joe seen it too, and his lip started to tremblin' and his Adam's apple was galloping up and down his neck like a race horse. Ah bet he's wore out half a dozen Adam's apples since Spunk's been on the job with Lena. That's all he'll do. He'll be back heah after while swallowin' an' workin' his lips like he wants to say somethin' an' can't."

"But didn't he do *nothin'* to stop 'em?"

"Nope, not a frazzlin' thing—jus' stood there. Spunk took Lena's arm and walked off jus' like nothin' ain't happened and he stood there gazin' after them till they was outa sight. Now you know a woman don't want no man like that. I'm jus' waitin' to see whut he's goin' to say when he gits back."

But Joe Kanty never came back, never. The men in the store heard the 30
sharp report of a pistol somewhere distant in the palmetto thicket and soon Spunk came walking leisurely, with his big black Stetson set at the same rakish angle and Lena clinging to his arm, came walking right into the general store. Lena wept in a frightened manner.

"Well," Spunk announced calmly, "Joe came out there wid a meat axe an' made me kill him."

He sent Lena home and led the men back to Joe—crumpled and limp with his right hand still clutching his razor.

"See mah back? Mah close cut clear through. He sneaked up an' tried to kill me from the back, but Ah got him, an' got him good, first shot," Spunk said.

The men glared at Elijah, accusingly.

"Take him up an' plant him in Stony Lonesome," Spunk said in a 35
careless voice. "Ah didn't wanna shoot him but he made me do it. He's a dirty coward, jumpin' on a man from behind."

Spunk turned on his heel and sauntered away to where he knew his love wept in fear for him and no man stopped him. At the general store later on, they all talked of locking him up until the sheriff should come from Orlando, but no one did anything but talk.

A clear case of self-defense, the trial was a short one, and Spunk walked out of the court house to freedom again. He could work again, ride the dangerous log-carriage that fed the singing, snarling, biting circle-saw; he could stroll the soft dark lanes with his guitar. He was free to roam the woods again; he was free to return to Lena. He did all these things.

"Whut you reckon, Walt?" Elijah asked one night later. "Spunk's gittin' ready to marry Lena!"

"Naw! Why, Joe ain't had time to git cold yit. Nohow Ah didn't figger Spunk was the marryin' kind."

"Well, he is," rejoined Elijah. "He done moved most of Lena's 40
things—and her along wid 'em—over to the Bradley house. He's buying it. Jus' like Ah told yo' all right in heah the night Joe was kilt. Spunk's crazy 'bout Lena. He don't want folks to keep on talkin' 'bout her—thass reason he's rushin' so. Funny thing 'bout that bob-cat, wan't it?"

"What bob-cat, 'Lige? Ah ain't heered 'bout none."

"Ain't cher? Well, night befo' las' as they was goin' to bed, a big black bob-cat, black all over, you hear me, *black,* walked round and round that house and howled like forty, an' when Spunk got his gun an' went to the winder to shoot it, he says it stood right still an' looked him in the eye, an' howled right at him. The thing got Spunk so nervoused up he" couldn't shoot. But Spunk says twan't no bob-cat nohow. He says it was Joe done sneaked back from Hell!"

"Humph!" sniffed Walter, "he oughter be nervous after what he done. Ah reckon Joe come back to dare him to marry Lena, or to come out an' fight. Ah bet he'll be back time and again, too. Know what Ah think? Joe wuz a braver man than Spunk."

There was a general shout of derision from the group.

"Thass a fact," went on Walter. "Lookit whut he done; took a razor 45 an' went out to fight a man he knowed toted a gun an' wuz a crack shot, too; 'nother thing Joe wuz skeered of Spunk, skeered plumb stiff! But he went jes' the same. It took him a long time to get his nerve up. Tain't nothin' for Spunk to fight when he ain't skeered of nothin'. Now, Joe's done come back to have it out wid the man that's got all he ever had. Y'all know Joe ain't never had nothin' nor wanted nothin' besides Lena. It musta been a h'ant cause ain't nobody never seen no black bob-cat."

" 'Nother thing," cut in one of the men, "Spunk was cussin' a blue streak to-day 'cause he 'lowed dat saw wuz wobblin'—almos' got 'im once. The machinist come, looked it over an' said it wuz alright. Spunk musta been leanin' t'wards it some. Den he claimed somebody pushed 'im but twan't nobody close to 'im. Ah wuz glad when knockin' off time came. I'm skeered of dat man when he gits hot. He'd beat you full of button holes as quick as he'd look atcher."

The men gathered the next evening in a different mood, no laughter. No badinage this time.

"Look, 'Lige, you goin' to set up wid Spunk?"

"Naw, Ah reckon not, Walter. Tell yuh the truth, Ah'm a li'l bit skittish. Spunk died too wicket—died cussin' he did. You know he thought he was done outa life."

"Good Lawd, who'd he think done it?"   50

"Joe."

"Joe Kanty? How come?"

"Walter, Ah b'leeve Ah will walk up thata way an' set. Lena would like it Ah reckon."

"But whut did he say, 'Lige?"

Elijah did not answer until they had left the lighted store and were 55 strolling down the dark street.

"Ah wuz loadin' a wagon wid scantlin' right near the saw when Spunk fell on the carriage but 'fore Ah could git to him the saw got him in the body—awful sight. Me an' Skint Miller got him off but it was too late. Anybody could see that. The fust thing he said wuz: 'He pushed me, 'Lige—the dirty hound pushed me in the back!'—he was spittin' blood at ev'ry breath. We laid him on the sawdust pile with his face to the East so's he could die easy. He helt mah han' till the last, Walter, and said: 'It was Joe, 'Lige . . . the dirty sneak shoved me . . . he didn't dare come to mah face . . . but Ah'll git the son-of-a-wood louse soon's Ah get there an' make hell too hot for him . . . Ah felt him shove me . . . !' Thass how he died."

"If spirits kin fight, there's a powerful tussle goin' on somewhere ovah Jordan 'cause Ah b'leeve Joe's ready for Spunk an' ain't skeered any more — yas, Ah b'leeve Joe pushed 'im mahself."

They had arrived at the house. Lena's lamentations were deep and loud. She had filled the room with magnolia blossoms that gave off a heavy sweet odor. The keepers of the wake tipped about whispering in frightened tones. Everyone in the village was there, even old Jeff Kanty, Joe's father, who a few hours before would have been afraid to come within ten feet of him, stood leering triumphantly down upon the fallen giant as if his fingers had been the teeth of steel that laid him low.

The cooling board consisted of three sixteen-inch boards on saw horses, a dingy sheet was his shroud.

The women ate heartily of the funeral baked meats and wondered 60 who would be Lena's next. The men whispered coarse conjectures between guzzles of whiskey.

JAMES JOYCE (1882–1941)

James Joyce was born in Dublin, Ireland, in 1882 and, in an imaginative sense, he never left that city. He received a strict Jesuit education, but once he began to doubt his faith during his final year at Belvedere College, Dublin, he felt his calling as a writer more and more strongly. Joyce studied modern languages at University College, Dublin, and taught himself Norwegian so he could read the plays of Henrik Ibsen in their original language. Ibsen's depiction of individual rebellion against community values resonated deeply for Joyce and contributed to his resolution to leave Ireland for Paris after he received his B.A. degree in 1902.

Courtesy of the Poetry/Rare Books Collection, UB Libraries, State University of New York at Buffalo.

Joyce returned to Dublin when his mother contracted a fatal illness, and he stayed on for a brief time, working as a schoolteacher. He departed for Switzerland, leaving Ireland for good, in 1904. Nora Barnacle, an uneducated young woman with little interest in literature, went with him. The couple lived in Trieste and Zurich, where Joyce taught school and wrote. He published *Dubliners* in 1914; "Eveline" is taken from this collection of short stories. *A Portrait of the Artist as a Young Man* followed in 1916. He and Nora moved to Paris in 1920 and remained there until World War II forced them back to Switzerland. He published *Ulysses* in Paris in 1922, but the book was banned in America and Britain until 1933. *Finnegan's Wake*, which Joyce considered his crowning achievement, took fourteen years to write and was published in 1939.

Eveline   *1914*

To hear "Eveline" read by Gabriel Byrne, visit bedfordstmartins.com/ meyerlit/epages.

She sat at the window watching the evening invade the avenue. Her head was leaned against the window curtains and in her nostrils was the odor of dusty cretonne. She was tired.

Few people passed. The man out of the last house passed on his way home; she heard his footsteps clacking along the concrete pavement and afterwards crunching on the cinder path before the new red houses. One time there used to be a field there in which they used to play every evening with other people's children. Then a man from Belfast bought the field and built houses in it — not like their little brown houses but bright brick houses with shining roofs. The children of the avenue used to play together in that field — the Devines, the Waters, the Dunns, little Keogh the cripple, she and her brothers and sisters. Ernest, however, never played: he was too grown up. Her father used often to hunt them in out of the field with his blackthorn stick; but usually little Keogh used to keep *nix* and call out when he saw her father coming. Still they seemed to have been rather happy then. Her father was not so bad then; and besides, her mother was alive. That was a long time ago; she and her brothers and sisters were all grown up; her mother was dead. Tizzie Dunn was dead, too, and the Waters had gone back to England. Everything changes. Now she was going to go away like the others, to leave her home.

Home! She looked round the room, reviewing all its familiar objects which she had dusted once a week for so many years, wondering where on earth all the dust came from. Perhaps she would never see again those familiar objects from which she had never dreamed of being divided. And yet during all those years she had never found out the name of the priest whose yellowing photograph hung on the wall above the broken harmonium beside the colored print of the promises made to Blessed Margaret Mary Alacoque. He had been a school friend of her father. Whenever he showed the photograph to a visitor her father used to pass it with a casual word:

—He is in Melbourne now.

She had consented to go away, to leave her home. Was that wise? She tried to weigh each side of the question. In her home anyway she had shelter and food; she had those whom she had known all her life about her. Of course she had to work hard both in the house and at business. What would they say of her in the Stores when they found out that she had run away with a fellow? Say she was a fool, perhaps; and her place would be filled up by advertisement. Miss Gavan would be glad. She had always had an edge on her, especially whenever there were people listening. 5

—Miss Hill, don't you see these ladies are waiting?

—Look lively, Miss Hill, please.

She would not cry many tears at leaving the Stores.

But in her new home, in a distant unknown country, it would not be like that. Then she would be married — she, Eveline. People would treat her with respect then. She would not be treated as her mother had been. Even now, though she was over nineteen, she sometimes felt herself in danger of her father's violence. She knew it was that that had given her the palpitations. When they were growing up he had never gone for her, like he used to go for Harry and Ernest, because she was a girl; but latterly he had begun to threaten her and say what he would do to her only for her dead mother's sake. And now she had nobody to protect her. Ernest was dead and Harry, who was in the church decorating business, was nearly always down somewhere in the country. Besides, the invariable squabble for money on Saturday nights had begun to weary her unspeakably. She always gave her entire wages — seven shillings — and Harry always sent up what he could but the trouble was to get any money from her father. He said she used to squander the money, that she had no head, that he wasn't going to give her his hard-earned money to throw about the streets, and much more, for he was usually fairly bad of a Saturday night. In the end he would give her the money and ask her had she any intention of buying Sunday's dinner. Then she had to rush out as quickly as she could and do her marketing, holding her black leather purse tightly in her hand as she elbowed her way through the crowds and returning home late under her load of provisions. She had hard work to keep the house together and to see that the two young children who had been left to her charge went to school regularly and got their meals regularly. It was hard work — a hard life — but now that she was about to leave it she did not find it a wholly undesirable life.

She was about to explore another life with Frank. Frank was very 10 kind, manly, open-hearted. She was to go away with him by the night-boat to be his wife and to live with him in Buenos Aires where he had a home waiting for her. How well she remembered the first time she had seen him; he was lodging in a house on the main road where she used to visit. It seemed a few weeks ago. He was standing at the gate, his peaked cap pushed back on his head and his hair tumbled forward over a face of bronze. Then they had come to know each other. He used to meet her outside the Stores every evening and see her home. He took her to see *The Bohemian Girl* and she felt elated as she sat in an unaccustomed part of the theater with him. He was awfully fond of music and sang a little. People knew that they were courting and, when he sang about the lass that loves a sailor, she always felt pleasantly confused. He used to call her Poppens out of fun. First of all it had been an excitement for her to have a fellow and then she had begun to like him. He had tales of distant countries. He had started as a deck boy at a pound a month on a ship of the Allan Line going out to Canada. He told her the names of the ships he had been on and the names of the different services. He had sailed through the Straits of Magellan and he told her stories of the terrible Patagonians. He had fallen on his feet in Buenos Aires, he said, and had come over to the old country just for a holiday. Of course, her father had found out the affair and had forbidden her to have anything to say to him.

—I know these sailor chaps, he said.

One day he had quarreled with Frank and after that she had to meet her lover secretly.

The evening deepened in the avenue. The white of two letters in her lap grew indistinct. One was to Harry; the other was to her father. Ernest had been her favorite but she liked Harry too. Her father was becoming old lately, she noticed; he would miss her. Sometimes he could be very nice. Not long before, when she had been laid up for a day, he had read her out a ghost story and made toast for her at the fire. Another day, when their mother was alive, they had all gone for a picnic to the Hill of Howth. She remembered her father putting on her mother's bonnet to make the children laugh.

Her time was running out but she continued to sit by the window, leaning her head against the window curtain, inhaling the odor of dusty cretonne. Down far in the avenue she could hear a street organ playing. She knew the air. Strange that it should come that very night to remind her of the promise to her mother, her promise to keep the home together as long as she could. She remembered the last night of her mother's illness; she was again in the close dark room at the other side of the hall and outside she heard a melancholy air of Italy. The organ-player had been ordered to go away and given sixpence. She remembered her father strutting back into the sickroom saying:

—Damned Italians! coming over here!   15

As she mused the pitiful vision of her mother's life laid its spell on the very quick of her being—that life of commonplace sacrifices closing in final craziness. She trembled as she heard again her mother's voice saying constantly with foolish insistence:

—Derevaun Seraun! Derevaun Seraun!°

She stood up in a sudden impulse of terror. Escape! She must escape! Frank would save her. He would give her life, perhaps love, too. But she wanted to live. Why should she be unhappy? She had a right to happiness. Frank would take her in his arms, fold her in his arms. He would save her.

She stood among the swaying crowd in the station at the North Wall. He held her hand and she knew that he was speaking to her, saying something about the passage over and over again. The station was full of soldiers with brown baggages. Through the wide doors of the sheds she caught a glimpse of the black mass of the boat, lying in beside the quay wall, with illumined portholes. She answered nothing. She felt her cheek pale and cold and, out of a maze of distress, she prayed to God to direct her, to show her what was her duty. The boat blew a long

Derevaun Seraun!: "The end of pleasure is pain!" (Gaelic).

mournful whistle into the mist. If she went, tomorrow she would be on the sea with Frank, steaming toward Buenos Aires. Their passage had been booked. Could she still draw back after all he had done for her? Her distress awoke a nausea in her body and she kept moving her lips in silent fervent prayer.

A bell clanged upon her heart. She felt him seize her hand: 20
—Come!

All the seas of the world tumbled about her heart. He was drawing her into them: he would drown her. She gripped with both hands at the iron railing.
—Come!

No! No! No! It was impossible. Her hands clutched the iron in frenzy. Amid the seas she sent a cry of anguish!
—Eveline! Evvy!   25

He rushed beyond the barrier and called to her to follow. He was shouted at to go on but he still called to her. She set her white face to him, passive, like a helpless animal. Her eyes gave him no sign of love or farewell or recognition.

JAMAICA KINCAID (B. 1949)

By permission of Trix Rosen.

Jamaica Kincaid was born Elaine Potter Richardson on the Caribbean island of Antigua. She moved to New York in 1965 to work as an au pair, studied photography at both the New School for Social Research and Franconia College, and changed her name to Jamaica Kincaid in 1973 with her first publication, "When I Was 17," a series of interviews. Over the next few years, she wrote for *The New Yorker* magazine, first as a freelancer and then as a staff writer. In 1978, Kincaid wrote her first piece of fiction, "Girl," published in *The New Yorker* and included in her debut short story collection, *At the Bottom of the River* (1983), which won an award from the Academy and Institute of Arts and Letters and was nominated for the PEN/Faulkner Award. Her other work includes *Annie John* (1985), *Lucy* (1990), *Autobiography of My Mother* (1994), and three nonfiction books, *A Small Place* (1988), *My Brother* (1997), and *Mr. Potter* (2002). Whether autobiographical fiction or nonfiction, her work usually focuses on the perils of postcolonial society, paralleled by an examination of rifts in mother-daughter relationships.

Explore contexts for Jamaica Kincaid and approaches to "Girl" at bedfordstmartins.com/meyerlit.

Girl   *1978*

Wash the white clothes on Monday and put them on the stone heap; wash the color clothes on Tuesday and put them on the clothesline to dry; don't walk barehead in the hot sun; cook pumpkin fritters in very hot sweet oil; soak your little cloths right after you take them off; when buying cotton to make yourself a nice blouse, be sure that it doesn't have gum on it, because that way it won't hold up well after a wash; soak salt fish overnight before you cook it; is it true that you sing benna° in Sunday school?; always eat your food in such a way that it won't turn someone else's stomach; on Sundays try to walk like a lady and not like the slut you are so bent on becoming; don't sing benna in Sunday school; you mustn't speak to wharf-rat boys, not even to give directions; don't eat fruits on the street — flies will follow you; *but I don't sing benna on Sundays at all and never in Sunday school;* this is how to sew on a button; this is how to make a buttonhole for the button you have just sewed on; this is how to hem a dress when you see the hem coming down and so to prevent yourself from looking like the slut I know you are so bent on becoming; this is how you iron your father's khaki shirt so that it doesn't have a crease; this is how you iron your father's khaki pants so that they don't have a crease; this is how you grow okra — far from the house, because okra tree harbors red ants; when you are growing dasheen,° make sure it gets plenty of water or else it makes your throat itch when you are eating it; this is how you sweep a corner; this is how you sweep a whole house; this is how you sweep a yard; this is how you smile to someone you don't like too much; this is how you smile to someone you don't like at all; this is how you smile to someone you like completely; this is how you set a table for tea; this is how you set a table for dinner; this is how you set a table for dinner with an important guest; this is how you set a table for lunch; this is how you set a table for breakfast; this is how to behave in the presence of men who don't know you very well, and this way they won't recognize immediately the slut I have warned you against becoming; be sure to wash every day, even if it is with your own spit; don't squat down to play marbles — you are not a boy, you know; don't pick people's flowers — you might catch something; don't throw stones at blackbirds, because it might not be a blackbird at all; this is how to make a bread pudding; this is how to make doukona;° this is how to make pepper pot;° this is how to make a good medicine for a cold; this is how to make a good medicine to throw away a child before it even becomes a child; this is how to catch a fish; this is how to throw back a fish you don't like, and that way something bad won't fall on you; this is how

To hear "Girl" read by Jamaica Kincaid, visit bedfordstmartins.com/ meyerlit/epages.

benna: Calypso music.
dasheen: The edible rootstock of taro, a tropical plant.
doukona: A spicy plantain pudding.
pepper pot: A stew.

to bully a man; this is how a man bullies you; this is how to love a man, and if this doesn't work there are other ways, and if they don't work don't feel too bad about giving up; this is how to spit up in the air if you feel like it, and this is how to move quick so that it doesn't fall on you; this is how to make ends meet; always squeeze bread to make sure it's fresh; *but what if the baker won't let me feel the bread?;* you mean to say that after all you are really going to be the kind of woman who the baker won't let near the bread?

ANNIE PROULX (B. 1935)

Annie Proulx was born in 1935 and did not finish her first book until 1988. She received a B.A. from the University of Vermont in 1969 and a master's degree from Sir George Williams University, both in history, and later became a freelance writer of articles for magazines in the United States. She published short stories occasionally until she had enough to make her first collection, *Heart Songs and Other Stories* (1988), which she followed with the novel *Postcards* in 1992. Her breakthrough novel was *The Shipping News* (1993), which won both the Pulitzer Prize and the National Book Award, and she has since produced two novels, *Accordion Crimes* (1996) and *The Old Ace in the Hole* (2003), and three books of short stories, *Close Range: Wyoming Stories* (1999), *Bad Dirt: Wyoming Stories 2* (2004), and *Fine Just the Way It Is: Wyoming Stories 3* (2008). Setting her works in places as distant as Newfoundland and Wyoming, Proulx conveys her dark, comic stories by creating a strong sense of place, using her talent for keen detail and for reproducing the peculiarities of local speech. *The Shipping News* and the short story "Brokeback Mountain" from *Close Range* were made into popular films.

Marc McAndrews/Getty Images.

55 Miles to the Gas Pump   1999

Rancher Croom in handmade boots and filthy hat, that walleyed cattleman, stray hairs like curling fiddle string ends, that warm-handed, quick-foot dancer on splintery boards or down the cellar stairs to a rack of bottles of his own strange beer, yeasty, cloudy, bursting out in garlands of foam, Rancher Croom at night galloping drunk over the dark plain, turning off at a place he knows to arrive at a canyon brink where he dismounts

To hear "55 Miles to the Gas Pump" read by Campbell Scott and Frances Fisher, visit bedfordstmartins.com/meyerlit/epages.

and looks down on tumbled rock, waits, then steps out, parting the air with his last roar, sleeves surging up windmill arms, jeans riding over boot tops, but before he hits he rises again to the top of the cliff like a cork in a bucket of milk.

Mrs. Croom on the roof with a saw cutting a hole into the attic where she has not been for twelve years thanks to old Croom's padlocks and warnings, whets to her desire, and the sweat flies as she exchanges the saw for a chisel and hammer until a ragged slab of peak is free and she can see inside: just as she thought: the corpses of Mr. Croom's paramours — she recognizes them from their photographs in the paper: MISSING WOMAN — some desiccated as jerky and much the same color, some moldy from lying beneath roof leaks, and all of them used hard, covered with tarry handprints, the marks of boot heels, some bright blue with the remnants of paint used on the shutters years ago, one wrapped in newspaper nipple to knee.

When you live a long way out you make your own fun.

MARK TWAIN (1835–1910)

© Bettmann/CORBIS.

Mark Twain is the pen name of Samuel Clemens, born in Missouri in 1835. Twain spent most of his childhood in Hannibal, Missouri, on the Mississippi River, and after the death of his father when he was eleven, he worked at a series of jobs to help support his family. A newspaper job prepared him to wander east working for papers and exploring St. Louis, New York, and Philadelphia. Later he trained as a steamboat pilot on the Mississippi and piloted boats professionally until the onset of the Civil War. Clemens had used a couple of different pseudonyms for minor publications before this point, but in 1863 he signed a travel narrative "Mark Twain," from a boating term that means "two fathoms deep," and the name for the great American humorist was created. Twain gained fame in 1865 with his story "The Celebrated Jumping Frog of Calaveras County," which appeared in the New York–based *Saturday Press.* He then became a traveling correspondent, writing pieces on his travels to Europe and the Middle East, and returned to the United States in 1870, when he married and moved to Connecticut. Twain produced *Roughing It* (1872) and *The Gilded Age* (1873) while he toured the country lecturing, and in 1876 published *The Adventures of Tom Sawyer,* an instant hit. His subsequent publications include *A Tramp Abroad* (1880), *The Prince and the Pauper* (1881), and the masterpiece *Adventures of Huckleberry Finn* (1884).

Often traveling and lecturing, Twain wrote several more books, including story collections, *The Tragedy of Pudd'nhead Wilson* (1894), and *Tom Sawyer, Detective* (1896), before he died in Italy in 1910. His work is noted for the combination of rough humor and vernacular language it often uses to convey keen social insights. In "The Story of the Good Little Boy" Twain offers his version of a Sunday-school lesson.

The Story of the Good Little Boy   *1870*

Once there was a good little boy by the name of Jacob Blivens. He always obeyed his parents, no matter how absurd and unreasonable their demands were; and he always learned his book, and never was late at Sabbath-school. He would not play hookey, even when his sober judgment told him it was the most profitable thing he could do. None of the other boys could ever make that boy out, he acted so strangely. He wouldn't lie, no matter how convenient it was. He just said it was wrong to lie, and that was sufficient for him. And he was so honest that he was simply ridiculous. The curious ways that that Jacob had, surpassed everything. He wouldn't play marbles on Sunday, he wouldn't rob birds' nests, he wouldn't give hot pennies to organ-grinders' monkeys; he didn't seem to take any interest in any kind of rational amusement. So the other boys used to try to reason it out and come to an understanding of him, but they couldn't arrive at any satisfactory conclusion. As I said before, they could only figure out a sort of vague idea that he was "afflicted," and so they took him under their protection, and never allowed any harm to come to him.

This good little boy read all the Sunday-school books; they were his greatest delight. This was the whole secret of it. He believed in the good little boys they put in the Sunday-school books; he had every confidence in them. He longed to come across one of them alive once; but he never did. They all died before his time, maybe. Whenever he read about a particularly good one he turned over quickly to the end to see what became of him, because he wanted to travel thousands of miles and gaze on him; but it wasn't any use; that good little boy always died in the last chapter, and there was a picture of the funeral, with all his relations and the Sunday-school children standing around the grave in pantaloons that were too short, and bonnets that were too large, and everybody crying into handkerchiefs that had as much as a yard and a half of stuff in them. He was always headed off in this way. He never could see one of those good little boys on account of his always dying in the last chapter.

Jacob had a noble ambition to be put in a Sunday-school book. He wanted to be put in, with pictures representing him gloriously declining to lie to his mother, and her weeping for joy about it; and pictures representing him standing on the doorstep giving a penny to a poor beggar-woman with six children, and telling her to spend it freely, but not to be extravagant, because extravagance is a sin; and pictures of him magnanimously refusing to tell on the bad boy who always lay in wait for him around the corner as he came from school, and welted him over the head with a lath, and then chased him home, saying, "Hi! hi!" as he proceeded. That was the ambition of young Jacob Blivens. He wished to be put in a Sunday-school book. It made him feel a little uncomfortable sometimes when he reflected that the good little boys always died. He loved to live, you know, and this was the most unpleasant feature about being a Sunday-school-book boy. He knew it was not healthy to be good. He knew it was more fatal than consumption to be so supernaturally good as the boys in the books were; he knew that none of them had ever been able to stand it long, and it pained him to think that if they put him in a book he wouldn't ever see it, or even if they did get the book out before he died it wouldn't be popular without any picture of his funeral in the back part of it. It couldn't be much of a Sunday-school book that couldn't tell about the advice he gave to the community when he was dying. So at last, of course, he had to make up his mind to do the best he could under the circumstances—to live right, and, hang on as long as he could, and have his dying speech all ready when his time came.

But somehow nothing ever went right with this good little boy; nothing ever turned out with him the way it turned out with the good little boys in the books. They always had a good time, and the bad boys had the broken legs; but in his case there was a screw loose somewhere, and it all happened just the other way. When he found Jim Blake stealing apples, and went under the tree to read to him about the bad little boy who fell out of a neighbor's apple tree and broke his arm, Jim fell out of the tree, too, but he fell on *him* and broke *his* arm, and Jim wasn't hurt at all. Jacob couldn't understand that. There wasn't anything in the books like it.

And once, when some bad boys pushed a blind man over in the mud, 5 and Jacob ran to help him up and receive his blessing, the blind man did not give him any blessing at all, but whacked him over the head with his stick and said he would like to catch him shoving *him* again, and then pretending to help him up. This was not in accordance with any of the books. Jacob looked them all over to see.

One thing that Jacob wanted to do was to find a lame dog that hadn't any place to stay, and was hungry and persecuted, and bring him home and pet him and have that dog's imperishable gratitude. And at last he found one and was happy; and he brought him home and fed him, but when he was going to pet him the dog flew at him and tore all the clothes off him except those that were in front, and made a spectacle of him that was astonishing. He examined authorities, but he could not understand the matter. It was of the same breed of dogs that was in the books, but it acted very differently. Whatever this boy did he got into trouble. The very things the boys in the books got rewarded for turned out to be about the most unprofitable things he could invest in.

Once, when he was on his way to Sunday-school, he saw some bad boys starting off pleasuring in a sailboat. He was filled with consternation, because he knew from his reading that boys who went sailing on Sunday invariably got drowned. So he ran out on a raft to warn them, but a log turned with him and slid him into the river. A man got him out pretty soon, and the doctor pumped the water out of him, and gave him a fresh start with his bellows, but he caught cold and lay sick abed nine weeks. But the most unaccountable thing about it was that the bad boys in the boat had a good time all day, and then reached home alive and well in the most surprising manner. Jacob Blivens said there was nothing like these things in the books. He was perfectly dumbfounded.

When he got well he was a little discouraged, but he resolved to keep on trying anyhow. He knew that so far his experiences wouldn't do to go in a book, but he hadn't yet reached the allotted term of life for good little boys, and he hoped to be able to make a record yet if he could hold on till his time was fully up. If everything else failed he had his dying speech to fall back on.

He examined his authorities, and found that it was now time for him to go to sea as a cabin-boy. He called on a ship-captain and made his application, and when the captain asked for his recommendations he proudly drew out a tract and pointed to the word, "To Jacob Blivens, from his affectionate teacher." But the captain was a coarse, vulgar man, and he said, "Oh, that be blowed! *that* wasn't any proof that he knew how to wash dishes or handle a slush-bucket, and he guessed he didn't want him." This was altogether the most extraordinary thing that ever happened to Jacob in all his life. A compliment from a teacher, on a tract, had never failed to move the tenderest emotions of ship-captains, and open the way to all offices of honor and profit in their gift — it never had in any book that ever *he* had read. He could hardly believe his senses.

This boy always had a hard time of it. Nothing ever came out according to the authorities with him. At last, one day, when he was around hunting up bad little boys to admonish, he found a lot of them in the old iron-foundry fixing up a little joke on fourteen or fifteen dogs, which they had tied together in long procession, and were going to ornament with empty nitroglycerin cans made fast to their tails. Jacob's heart was touched. He sat down on one of those cans (for he never minded grease when duty was before him), and he took hold of the foremost dog by the collar, and turned his reproving eye upon wicked Tom Jones. But just at that moment Alderman McWelter, full of wrath, stepped in. All the bad boys ran away, but Jacob Blivens rose in conscious innocence and began one of those stately little Sunday-school-book speeches which always commence with "Oh, sir!" in dead opposition to the fact that no boy, good or bad, ever starts a remark with "Oh, sir." But the alderman never waited to hear the rest. He took Jacob Blivens by the ear and turned him around, and hit him a whack in the rear with the flat of his hand; and in an instant that good little boy shot out through the roof and soared

332 STORIES FOR FURTHER READING

away toward the sun, with the fragments of those fifteen dogs stringing after him like the tail of a kite. And there wasn't a sign of that alderman or that old iron-foundry left on the face of the earth; and, as for young Jacob Blivens, he never got a chance to make his last dying speech after all his trouble fixing it up, unless he made it to the birds; because, although the bulk of him came down all right in a tree-top in an adjoining county, the rest of him was apportioned around among four townships, and so they had to hold five inquests on him to find out whether he was dead or not, and how it occurred. You never saw a boy scattered so.[1]

Thus perished the good little boy who did the best he could, but didn't come out according to the books. Every boy who ever did as he did prospered except him. His case is truly remarkable. It will probably never be accounted for.

---

[1] This glycerin catastrophe is borrowed from a floating newspaper item, whose author's name I would give if I knew it. M.T.

POETRY

The Elements
of Poetry

12

Reading Poetry

I think everyone has in his or her self the urge to express, and people do it with what they love, I suppose. Cooks do it with food; there are people who do it with hair, with clothing, fabric. I loved words, always, the sound of words, the feeling of words in my mouth, and so I did it that way.

LUCILLE CLIFTON

© Christopher Felver.

READING POETRY RESPONSIVELY

Perhaps the best way to begin reading poetry responsively is not to allow yourself to be intimidated by it. Come to it, initially at least, the way you might listen to a song on the radio. You probably listen to a song several times before you hear it all, before you have a sense of how it works, where it's going, and how it gets there. You don't worry about analyzing a song when you listen to it, even though after repeated experiences with it you know and anticipate a favorite part and know, on some level, why it works for you. Give yourself a chance to respond to poetry. The hardest work has already been done by the poet, so all you need to do at the start is listen for the pleasure produced by the poet's arrangement of words.

Try reading the following poem aloud. Read it aloud before you read it silently. You may stumble once or twice, but you'll make sense of it if you pay attention to its punctuation and don't stop at the end of every line where there is no punctuation. When you finish reading it, think about why it's titled "Snapping Beans."

LISA PARKER (B. 1972)

Snapping Beans   *1998*

For Fay Whitt

I snapped beans into the silver bowl
that sat on the splintering slats
of the porchswing between my grandma and me.
I was home for the weekend,
from school, from the North,   5
Grandma hummed "What A Friend We Have In Jesus"
as the sun rose, pushing its pink spikes
through the slant of cornstalks,
through the fly-eyed mesh of the screen.
We didn't speak until the sun overcame   10
the feathered tips of the cornfield
and Grandma stopped humming. I could feel
the soft gray of her stare
against the side of my face
when she asked, *How's school a-goin'?*   15
I wanted to tell her about my classes,
the revelations by book and lecture,
as real as any shout of faith
and potent as a swig of strychnine.
She reached the leather of her hand   20
over the bowl and cupped
my quivering chin; the slick smooth of her palm
held my face the way she held tomatoes
under the spigot, careful not to drop them,
and I wanted to tell her   25
about the nights I cried into the familiar
heartsick panels of the quilt she made me,
wishing myself home on the evening star.
I wanted to tell her
the evening star was a planet,   30
that my friends wore noserings and wrote poetry
about sex, about alcoholism, about Buddha.
I wanted to tell her how my stomach burned
acidic holes at the thought of speaking in class,
speaking in an accent, speaking out of turn,   35
how I was tearing, splitting myself apart
with the slow-simmering guilt of being happy
despite it all.
I said, *School's fine.*
We snapped beans into the silver bowl between us   40

and when a hickory leaf, still summer green,
skidded onto the porchfront,
Grandma said,
It's funny how things blow loose like that.

CONSIDERATIONS FOR CRITICAL THINKING AND WRITING

1. FIRST RESPONSE. Describe the speaker's feelings about starting a life at college. How do those feelings compare with your own experiences?

2. How does the grandmother's world differ from the speaker's at school? What details especially reveal those differences?

3. Discuss the significance of the grandmother's response to the hickory leaf in line 44. How do you read the last line?

The next poem creates a different kind of mood. Think about the title, "Those Winter Sundays," before you begin reading the poem. What associations do you have with winter Sundays? What emotions does the phrase evoke in you?

ROBERT HAYDEN (1913–1980)

Those Winter Sundays   1962

Sundays too my father got up early
and put his clothes on in the blueblack cold,
then with cracked hands that ached
from labor in the weekday weather made
banked fires blaze. No one ever thanked him.   5

I'd wake and hear the cold splintering, breaking.
When the rooms were warm, he'd call,
and slowly I would rise and dress,
fearing the chronic angers of that house,

Speaking indifferently to him,   10
who had driven out the cold
and polished my good shoes as well.
What did I know, what did I know
of love's austere and lonely offices?

Does the poem match the feelings you have about winter Sundays? Either way, your response can be useful in reading the poem. For most of us, Sundays are days at home; they might be cozy and pleasant experiences or they might be dull and depressing. Whatever they are, Sundays are more evocative than, say, Tuesdays. Hayden uses that response to call forth a sense of missed opportunity in the poem. The person who reflects on those winter Sundays didn't know until much later how much he had to thank his father for "love's austere and lonely offices." This is a poem about a cold past and a present reverence for his father—elements brought together by the phrase "Winter Sundays." *His* father? You may have noticed that the poem doesn't use a masculine pronoun; hence the voice could be a woman's. Does the gender of the voice make any difference to your reading? Would it make any difference about which details are included or what language is used?

What is most important about your initial readings of a poem is that you ask questions. If you read responsively, you'll find yourself asking all kinds of questions about the words, descriptions, sounds, and structure of a poem. The specifics of those questions will be generated by the particular poem. We don't, for example, ask how humor is achieved in "Those Winter Sundays" because there is none, but it is worth asking what kind of tone is established by the description of "the chronic angers of that house." The remaining chapters in this part of the book will help you to formulate and answer questions about a variety of specific elements in poetry, such as speaker, image, metaphor, symbol, rhyme, and rhythm. For the moment, however, read the following poem several times and note your response at different points in the poem. Then write down a half-dozen or so questions about what produces your response to the poem. To answer questions, it's best to know first what the questions are, and that's what the rest of this chapter is about.

JOHN UPDIKE (1932–2009)
Dog's Death   1969

She must have been kicked unseen or brushed by a car.
Too young to know much, she was beginning to learn
To use the newspapers spread on the kitchen floor
And to win, wetting there, the words, "Good dog! Good dog!"

We thought her shy malaise was a shot reaction.   5
The autopsy disclosed a rupture in her liver.
As we teased her with play, blood was filling her skin
And her heart was learning to lie down forever.

Monday morning, as the children were noisily fed
And sent to school, she crawled beneath the youngest's bed.   10
We found her twisted and limp but still alive.
In the car to the vet's, on my lap, she tried

To bite my hand and died. I stroked her warm fur
And my wife called in a voice imperious with tears.
Though surrounded by love that would have upheld her,   15
Nevertheless she sank and, stiffening, disappeared.

Back home, we found that in the night her frame,
Drawing near to dissolution, had endured the shame

Of diarrhoea and had dragged across the floor
To a newspaper carelessly left there. *Good dog.*   20

Here's a simple question to get started with your own questions: What would the poem's effect have been if Updike had titled it "Good Dog" instead of "Dog's Death"?

THE PLEASURE OF WORDS

The impulse to create and appreciate poetry is as basic to human experience as language itself. Although no one can point to the precise origins of poetry, it is one of the most ancient of the arts, because it has existed ever since human beings discovered pleasure in language. The tribal ceremonies of peoples without written languages suggest that the earliest primitive cultures incorporated rhythmic patterns of words into their rituals. These chants, very likely accompanied by the music of a simple beat and the dance of a measured step, expressed what people regarded as significant and memorable in their lives. They echoed the concerns of the chanters and the listeners by chronicling acts of bravery, fearsome foes, natural disasters, mysterious events, births, deaths, and whatever else brought people pain or pleasure, bewilderment or revelation. Later cultures, such as the ancient Greeks, made poetry an integral part of religion.

Thus, from its very beginnings, poetry has been associated with what has mattered most to people. These concerns — whether natural or supernatural — can, of course, be expressed without vivid images, rhythmic patterns, and pleasing sounds, but human beings have always sensed a magic in words that goes beyond rational, logical understanding. Poetry is not simply a method of communication; it is a unique experience in itself.

What is special about poetry? What makes it valuable? Why should we read it? How is reading it different from reading prose? To begin with, poetry pervades our world in a variety of forms, ranging from advertising jingles to song lyrics. These may seem to be a long way from the chants heard around a primitive campfire, but they serve some of the same purposes. Like poems printed in a magazine or book, primitive chants, catchy jingles, and popular songs attempt to stir the imagination through the carefully measured use of words.

Although reading poetry usually makes more demands than does the kind of reading we use to skim a magazine or newspaper, the appreciation of poetry comes naturally enough to anyone who enjoys playing with words. Play is an important element of poetry. Consider, for example, how the following words appeal to the children who gleefully chant them in playgrounds:

> I scream, you scream
> We all scream
> For ice cream.

These lines are an exuberant evocation of the joy of ice cream. Indeed, chanting the words turns out to be as pleasurable as eating ice cream. In poetry, the expression of the idea is as important as the idea expressed.

But is "I scream . . ." poetry? Some poets and literary critics would say that it certainly is one kind of poem because the children who chant it experience some of the pleasures of poetry in its measured beat and repeated sounds. However, other poets and critics would define poetry more narrowly and insist, for a variety of reasons, that this isn't true poetry but merely *doggerel*, a term used for lines whose subject matter is trite and whose rhythm and sounds are monotonously heavy-handed.

Although probably no one would argue that "I scream . . ." is a great poem, it does contain some poetic elements that appeal, at the very least, to children. Does that make it poetry? The answer depends on one's definition, but poetry has a way of breaking loose from definitions. Because there are nearly as many definitions of poetry as there are poets, Edwin Arlington Robinson's succinct observations are useful: "Poetry has two outstanding characteristics. One is that it is undefinable. The other is that it is eventually unmistakable."

This comment places more emphasis on how a poem affects a reader than on how a poem is defined. By characterizing poetry as "undefinable," Robinson acknowledges that it can include many different purposes, subjects, emotions, styles, and forms. What effect does the following poem have on you?

WILLIAM HATHAWAY (B. 1944)

Oh, Oh   *1982*

My girl and I amble a country lane,
moo cows chomping daisies, our own
sweet saliva green with grass stems.
"Look, look," she says at the crossing,
"the choo-choo's light is on." And sure
enough, right smack dab in the middle
of maple dappled summer sunlight
is the lit headlight — so funny.
An arm waves to us from the black window.
We wave gaily to the arm. "When I hear
trains at night I dream of being president,"
I say dreamily. "And me first lady," she
says loyally. So when the last boxcars,
named after wonderful, faraway places,

© William Hathaway.

and the caboose chuckle by we look   15
eagerly to the road ahead. And there,
poised and growling, are fifty Hell's Angels.

A SAMPLE CLOSE READING

An Annotated Version of "Oh, Oh"

After you've read a poem two or three times, a deeper, closer reading — line by line, word by word, syllable by syllable — will help you discover even more about it. Ask yourself: What happens (or does not happen) in the poem? What are the poem's central ideas? How do the poem's words, images, and sounds, for example, contribute to its meaning? What is the poem's overall tone? How is the poem put together?

You can flesh out your close reading by writing your responses in the margins of the page. The following interpretive notes offer but one way to read Hathaway's poem.

WILLIAM HATHAWAY (B. 1944)

Oh, Oh   1982

The title offers an interjection expressing strong emotion and foreboding.

The informal language conjures up an idyllic picture of a walk in the country, where the sights, sounds, and tastes are full of pleasure.

The carefully orchestrated *d*s, *m*s, *p*s, *ss* of lines 6–8 create sounds that are meant to be savored.

Filled with confidence and hope, the couple imagines a successful future together in exotic locations. Even the train is happy for them as it "chuckle[s]" in approval of their dreams.

> My girl and I amble a country lane,
> moo cows chomping daisies, our own
> sweet saliva green with grass stems.
> "Look, look," she says at the crossing,
> "the choo-choo's light is on." And sure   5
> enough, right smack dab in the middle
> of maple dappled summer sunlight
> is the lit headlight — so funny.
> An arm waves to us from the black window.
> We wave gaily to the arm. "When I hear   10
> trains at night I dream of being president,"
> I say dreamily. "And me first lady," she
> says loyally. So when the last boxcars,
> named after wonderful, faraway places,
> and the caboose chuckle by we look   15
> eagerly to the road ahead. And there,
> poised and growling, are fifty Hell's Angels.

The visual effect of the many *o*s in lines 1–5 (and 15) suggests an innocent, wide-eyed openness to experience while the repetitive *oo* sounds echo a kind of reassuring, satisfied cooing.

"Right smack dab in the middle" of the poem, the "black window" hints that all is not well.

Not until the very last line does "the road ahead" yield a terrifying surprise. The strategically "poised" final line derails the leisurely movement of the couple and brings their happy story to a dead stop. The emotional reversal parked in the last few words awaits the reader as much as it does the couple. The sight and sound of the motorcycle gang signal that what seemed like heaven is, in reality, hell: Oh, oh.

Hathaway's poem serves as a convenient reminder that poetry can be full of surprises. Full of confidence, this couple, like the reader, is unprepared for the shock to come. When we see those "fifty Hell's Angels," we are confronted with something like a bucket of cold water in the face.

But even though our expectations are abruptly and powerfully reversed, we are finally invited to view the entire episode from a safe distance — the distance provided by the delightful humor in this poem. After all, how seriously can we take a poem that is titled "Oh, Oh"? The poet has his way with us, but we are brought in on the joke, too. The terror takes on comic proportions as the innocent couple is confronted by no fewer than *fifty* Hell's Angels. This is the kind of raucous overkill that informs a short animated film produced some years ago titled *Bambi Meets Godzilla:* You might not have seen it, but you know how it ends. The poem's good humor comes through when we realize how pathetically inadequate the response of "Oh, Oh" is to the circumstances.

As you can see, reading a description of what happens in a poem is not the same as experiencing a poem. The exuberance of "I scream . . ." and the surprise of Hathaway's "Oh, Oh" are in the hearing or reading rather than in the retelling. A *paraphrase* is a prose restatement of the central ideas of a poem in your own language. Consider the difference between the following poem and the paraphrase that follows it. What is missing from the paraphrase?

ROBERT FRANCIS (1901–1987)

Catch   *1950*

Two boys uncoached are tossing a poem together,
Overhand, underhand, backhand, sleight of hand, every hand,
Teasing with attitudes, latitudes, interludes, altitudes,
High, make him fly off the ground for it, low, make him stoop,
Make him scoop it up, make him as-almost-as-possible miss it,   5
Fast, let him sting from it, now, now fool him slowly,
Anything, everything tricky, risky, nonchalant,
Anything under the sun to outwit the prosy,
Over the tree and the long sweet cadence down,
Over his head, make him scramble to pick up the meaning,   10
And now, like a posy, a pretty one plump in his hands.

Paraphrase: A poet's relationship to a reader is similar to a game of catch. The poem, like a ball, should be pitched in a variety of ways to challenge and create interest. Boredom and predictability must be avoided if the game is to be engaging and satisfying.

A paraphrase can help us achieve a clearer understanding of a poem, but, unlike a poem, it misses all of the sport and fun. It is the poem that "outwit[s] the prosy " because the poem serves as an example of what it suggests poetry should be. Moreover, the two players—the poet and the reader—are "uncoached." They know how the game is played, but their expectations do not preclude spontaneity and creativity or their ability to surprise and be surprised. The solid pleasure of the workout—of reading poetry—is the satisfaction derived from exercising your imagination and intellect. Perhaps the best way to approach a poem is similar to what Francis's "Catch" implies: Expect to be surprised, stay on your toes, and concentrate on the delivery.

A SAMPLE STUDENT ANALYSIS

Tossing Metaphors Together in Robert Francis's "Catch"

The following sample paper on Robert Francis's "Catch" was written in response to an assignment that asked students to discuss the use of metaphor in the poem. Notice that Chris Leggett's paper is clearly focused and well organized. His discussion of the use of metaphor in the poem stays on track from beginning to end without any detours concerning unrelated topics (for a discussion of *metaphors*, see pp. 415-17). His title draws on the central metaphor of the poem, and he organizes the paper around four key words used in the poem: "attitudes, latitudes, interludes, altitudes." These constitute the heart of the paper's four substantive paragraphs, and they are effectively framed by introductory and concluding paragraphs. Moreover, the transitions between paragraphs clearly indicate that the author was not merely tossing a paper together.

Chris Leggett

Professor Lyles

English 203-1

9 November 2012

        Tossing Metaphors Together in Robert Francis's "Catch"

     The word "catch" is an attention getter. It usually means something is about to be hurled at someone and that he or she is expected to catch it. "Catch" can also signal a challenge to another player if the toss is purposefully difficult. Robert Francis, in his poem "Catch," uses the extended

> Exploration of the meaning of the word *catch*.

Thesis statement identifying purpose of poem's metaphors.

Reference to specific language in poem, around which the paper is organized.

Introductory analysis of the poem's purpose.

Analysis of the meaning of *attitude* in the poem.

Discussion of how the attitude metaphor contributes to poem's tone.

Analysis of the meaning of *latitude* in the poem.

Discussion of how the latitude metaphor contributes to the poem's scope and message.

metaphor of two boys playing catch to explore the considerations a poet makes when "tossing a poem together" (line 1). Line 3 of "Catch" enumerates these considerations metaphorically as "attitudes, latitudes, interludes, [and] altitudes." While regular prose is typically straightforward and easily understood, poetry usually takes great effort to understand and appreciate. To exemplify this, Francis presents the reader not with a normal game of catch with the ball flying back and forth in a repetitive and predictable fashion, but with a physically challenging game in which one must concentrate, scramble, and exert oneself to catch the ball, as one must stretch the intellect to truly grasp a poem.

The first consideration mentioned by Francis is attitude. Attitude, when applied to the game of catch, indicates the ball's pitch in flight — upward, downward, or straight. It could also describe the players' attitudes toward each other or toward the game in general. Below this literal level lies *attitude*'s meaning in relation to poetry. Attitude in this case represents a poem's tone. A poet may "teas[e] with attitude" (3) by experimenting with different tones to achieve the desired mood. The underlying tone of "Catch" is a playful one, set and reinforced by the use of a game. This playfulness is further reinforced by such words and phrases as "teasing" (3), "outwit" (8), and "fool him" (6).

Considered also in the metaphorical game of catch is latitude, which, when applied to the game, suggests the range the object may be thrown— how high, how low, or how far. Poetic latitude, along similar lines, concerns a poem's breadth, or the scope of topic. Taken one level further, latitude suggests freedom from normal restraints or limitations, indicating the ability to go outside the norm to find originality of expression. The entire game of catch described in Francis's poem reaches outside the normal expectations of something being merely tossed back and forth in a predictable manner. The ball is thrown in almost every conceivable fashion, "overhand, underhand . . . every hand" (2). Other terms describing the throws — such as "tricky," "risky," "fast," "slowly," and "Anything under the sun"(6-8) — express endless latitude for avoiding predictability in Francis's game of catch and metaphorically in writing poetry.

During a game of catch the ball may be thrown at different intervals, establishing a steady rhythm or a broken, irregular one. Other intervening features, such as the field being played on or the weather, could also affect the

Leggett 3

game. These features of the game are alluded to in the poem by the use of the word "interludes." "Interlude" in the poetic sense represents the poem's form, which can similarly establish or diminish rhythm or enhance meaning. Lines 6 and 9, respectively, show a broken and a flowing rhythm. Line 6 begins rapidly as a hard toss that stings the catcher's hand is described. The rhythm of the line is immediately slowed, however, by the word "now" followed by a comma, followed by the rest of the line. In contrast, line 9 flows smoothly as the reader visualizes the ball flying over the tree and sailing downward. The words chosen for this line function perfectly. The phrase "the long sweet cadence down" establishes a sweet rhythm that reads smoothly and rolls off the tongue easily. The choice of diction not only affects the poem's rhythmic flow but also establishes through connotative language the various levels at which the poem can be understood, represented in "Catch" as altitude.

Analysis of the meaning of interlude *in the poem.*

Discussion of how the interlude metaphor contributes to the poem's form and rhythm.

While "altitudes" when referring to the game of catch means how high an object is thrown, in poetry it could refer to the level of diction, lofty or down-to-earth, formal or informal. It suggests also the levels at which a poem can be comprehended, the literal as well as the interpretive. In Francis's game of catch, the ball is thrown high to make the player reach, low to "make him stoop" (4), or "over his head [to] make him scramble" (10), implying that the player should have to exert himself to catch it. So too, then, should the reader of poetry put great effort into understanding the full meaning of a poem. Francis exemplifies this consideration in writing poetry by giving "Catch" not only an enjoyable literal meaning concerning the game of catch, but also a rich metaphorical meaning — reflecting the process of writing poetry. Francis uses several phrases and words with multiple meanings. The phrase "tossing a poem together" (1) can be understood as tossing something back and forth or the process of constructing a poem. While "prosy" (8) suggests prose itself, it also means the mundane or the ordinary. In the poem's final line the word "posy" of course represents a flower, while it is also a variant of the word "poesy," meaning poetry, or the practice of composing poetry.

Analysis of the meaning of altitudes *in the poem.*

Discussion of how the altitude metaphor contributes to the poem's literal and symbolic meanings, with references to specific language.

Francis effectively describes several considerations to be taken in writing poetry in order to "outwit the prosy" (8). His use of the extended metaphor in "Catch" shows that a poem must be unique, able to be comprehended on multiple levels, and a challenge to the reader. The various rhythms in the lines of "Catch" exemplify the ideas they express. While achieving an enjoyable poem on the literal level, Francis has also achieved a

Conclusion summarizing ideas explored in paper.

rich metaphorical meaning. The poem offers a good workout both physically and intellectually.

Work Cited

Francis, Robert. "Catch." *Literature to Go*. 2nd ed. Ed. Michael Meyer. Boston: Bedford/St. Martin's, 2014. 344. Print.

Before beginning your own writing assignment on poetry, you should review Chapter 31, "Writing about Poetry," and Chapter 29, "Reading and the Writing Process," which provides a step-by-step overview of how to choose a topic, develop a thesis, and organize various types of writing assignments. If you are using outside sources in your paper, you should make sure that you are familiar with the conventional documentation procedures described in Chapter 33, "The Literary Research Paper."

How does the speaker's description in Francis's "Catch" of what a reader might expect from reading poetry compare with the speaker's expectations concerning fiction in the next poem by Philip Larkin?

PHILIP LARKIN (1922–1985)

A Study of Reading Habits   *1964*

When getting my nose in a book
Cured most things short of school,
It was worth ruining my eyes
To know I could still keep cool,
And deal out the old right hook   5
To dirty dogs twice my size.

Later, with inch-thick specs,
Evil was just my lark:
Me and my cloak and fangs
Had ripping times in the dark.   10

The women I clubbed with sex!
I broke them up like meringues.

Don't read much now: the dude
Who lets the girl down before
The hero arrives, the chap   15
Who's yellow and keeps the store,
Seem far too familiar. Get stewed:
Books are a load of crap.

In "A Study of Reading Habits," Larkin distances himself from a speaker whose sensibilities he does not wholly share. The poet — and many readers — might identify with the reading habits described by the speaker in the first twelve lines, but Larkin uses the last six lines to criticize the speaker's attitude toward life as well as reading. The speaker recalls in lines 1–6 how as a schoolboy he identified with the hero, whose virtuous strength always triumphed over "dirty dogs," and in lines 7–12 he recounts how his schoolboy fantasies were transformed by adolescence into a fascination with violence and sex. This description of early reading habits is pleasantly amusing, because many readers of popular fiction will probably recall having moved through similar stages, but at the end of the poem the speaker provides more information about himself than he intends to.

As an adult the speaker has lost interest in reading because it is no longer an escape from his own disappointed life. Instead of identifying with heroes or villains, he finds himself identifying with minor characters who are irresponsible and cowardly. Reading is now a reminder of his failures, so he turns to alcohol. His solution, to "Get stewed" because "Books are a load of crap," is obviously self-destructive. The speaker is ultimately exposed by Larkin as someone who never grew beyond fantasies. Getting drunk is consistent with the speaker's immature reading habits. Unlike the speaker, the poet understands that life is often distorted by escapist fantasies, whether through a steady diet of popular fiction or through alcohol. The speaker in this poem, then, is not Larkin but a created identity whose voice is filled with disillusionment and delusion.

The problem with Larkin's speaker is that he misreads books as well as his own life. Reading means nothing to him unless it serves as an escape from himself. It is not surprising that Larkin has him read fiction rather than poetry because poetry places an especially heavy emphasis on language. Fiction, indeed any kind of writing, including essays and drama, relies on carefully chosen and arranged words, but poetry does so to an even greater extent. Notice, for example, how Larkin's deft use of trite expressions and slang characterizes the speaker so that his language reveals nearly as much about his dreary life as what he says. Larkin's speaker would have no use for poetry.

Here is a poem that looks quite different from most *verse*, a term used for lines composed in a measured rhythmical pattern, which are often, but not necessarily, rhymed.

ROBERT MORGAN (B. 1944)

Mountain Graveyard   1979

for the author of "Slow Owls"

Spore Prose

stone	notes
slate	tales
sacred	cedars
heart	earth
asleep	please
hated	death

Though unconventional in its appearance, this is unmistakably poetry because of its concentrated use of language. The poem demonstrates how serious play with words can lead to some remarkable discoveries. At first glance "Mountain Graveyard" may seem intimidating. What, after all, does this list of words add up to? How is it in any sense a poetic use of language? But if the words are examined closely, it is not difficult to see how they work. The wordplay here is literally in the form of a game. Morgan uses a series of *anagrams* (words made from the letters of other words, such as *read* and *dare*) to evoke feelings about death. "Mountain Graveyard" is one of several poems that Morgan has called "Spore Prose" (another anagram) because he finds in individual words the seeds of poetry. He wrote the poem in honor of the fiftieth birthday of another poet, Jonathan Williams, the author of "Slow Owls," whose title is also an anagram.

The title, "Mountain Graveyard," indicates the poem's setting, which is also the context in which the individual words in the poem interact to provide a larger meaning. Morgan's discovery of the words on the stones of a graveyard is more than just clever. The observations he makes among the silent graves go beyond the curious pleasure a reader experiences in finding that the words *sacred cedars*, referring to evergreens common in cemeteries, consist of the same letters. The surprise and delight of realizing the connection between *heart* and *earth* are tempered by the more sober recognition that everyone's story ultimately ends in the ground. The hope that the dead are merely asleep is expressed with a plea that is answered grimly by a hatred of death's finality.

The following poem also involves a startling discovery about words. With the peculiar title "l(a," the poem cannot be read aloud, so there

is no sound, but is there sense, a *theme* — a central idea or meaning —
in the poem?

E. E. CUMMINGS (1894–1962)

l(a   *1958*

l(a

le
af
fa

ll

s)
one
l

iness

© Bettmann/CORBIS.

CONSIDERATIONS FOR CRITICAL THINKING AND WRITING

1. **FIRST RESPONSE.** Discuss the connection between what appears
   inside and outside the parentheses in this poem.

2. What does Cummings draw attention to by breaking up the words? How
   do this strategy and the poem's overall shape contribute to its theme?

3. Which seems more important in this poem — what is expressed or
   the way it is expressed?

Although "Mountain Graveyard" and "l(a" do not resemble the kind
of verse that readers might recognize immediately as poetry on a page,
both are actually a very common type of poem, called the *lyric,* usually a
brief poem that expresses the personal emotions and thoughts of a single
speaker. Lyrics are often written in the first person, but sometimes — as
in "Mountain Graveyard" and "l(a" — no speaker is specified. Lyrics present a subjective mood, emotion, or idea. Very often they are about love
or death, but almost any subject or experience that evokes some intense
emotional response can be found in lyrics. In addition to brevity and
emotional intensity, lyrics are also frequently characterized by their musical qualities. The word *lyric* derives from the Greek word *lyre,* meaning
a musical instrument that originally accompanied the singing of a lyric.
Lyric poems can be organized in a variety of ways, such as the sonnet,
elegy, and ode (see Chapter 19), but it is enough to point out here that lyrics are an extremely popular kind of poetry with writers and readers.

The following anonymous lyric was found in a sixteenth-century
manuscript.

Anonymous

Western Wind

c. 1500

Western wind, when wilt thou blow,
The small rain down can rain?
Christ, if my love were in my arms,
And I in my bed again!

This speaker's intense longing for his lover is characteristic of lyric
poetry. He impatiently addresses the western wind that brings spring
to England and could make it possible for him to be reunited with the
woman he loves. We do not know the details of these lovers' lives because
this poem focuses on the speaker's emotion. We do not learn why the
lovers are apart or if they will be together again. We don't even know
if the speaker is a man. But those issues are not really important. The
poem gives us a feeling rather than a story.

Alfred, Lord Tennyson (1809–1892)

Crossing the Bar

1889

Sunset and evening star,
　　And one clear call for me!
And may there be no moaning of the bar,°   sandbar
　　When I put out to sea,

But such a tide as moving seems asleep,   5
　　Too full for sound and foam,
When that which drew from out the boundless deep
　　Turns again home.

Twilight and evening bell,
　　And after that the dark!   10
And may there be no sadness of farewell,
　　When I embark;

For tho' from out our bourne of Time and Place
　　The flood may bear me far,
I hope to see my Pilot face to face   15
　　When I have crost the bar.

Considerations for Critical Thinking and Writing

1. **FIRST RESPONSE.** How does Tennyson make clear that this poem is
   about more than a sea journey?
2. Why do you think Tennyson directed to his publishers to place
   "Crossing the Bar" as the last poem in all collections of his poetry?

3. Discuss the purpose of the punctuation (or its absence) at the end of each line.

4. **CONNECTION TO ANOTHER SELECTION.** Compare the speaker's mood in "Crossing the Bar" with that in Dylan Thomas's "Do Not Go Gentle into That Good Night" (p. 496).

A poem that tells a story is called a ***narrative poem***. Narrative poetry may be short or very long. An ***epic***, for example, is a long narrative poem on a serious subject chronicling heroic deeds and important events. Among the most famous epics are Homer's *Iliad* and *Odyssey*, the Old English *Beowulf*, Dante's *Divine Comedy*, and John Milton's *Paradise Lost*. More typically, however, narrative poems are considerably shorter, as is the case with the following poem, which tells the story of a child's memory of her father.

> **WHEN I WRITE** "There are lots of things that are going on in the world, in your room, or in that book you didn't read for class that could set you on fire if you gave them a chance. Poetry isn't only about what you feel, it's about what you think, and about capturing the way the world exists in one particular moment."   —REGINA BARRECA

REGINA BARRECA (B. 1957)

Nighttime Fires   1986

Courtesy of Robert Benson, © 2004.

When I was five in Louisville
we drove to see nighttime fires. Piled
    seven of us,
all pajamas and running noses, into the
    Olds,
drove fast toward smoke. It was after my
    father
lost his job, so not getting up in the
    morning
gave him time: awake past midnight, he read old newspapers
with no news, tried crosswords until he split the pencil
between his teeth, mad. When he heard
the wolf whine of the siren, he woke my mother,
and she pushed and shoved   10
us all into waking. Once roused we longed for burnt wood
and a smell of flames high into the pines. My old man liked
driving to rich neighborhoods best, swearing in a good mood
as he followed fire engines that snaked like dragons
and split the silent streets. It was festival, carnival.   15

If there were a Cadillac or any car
in a curved driveway, my father smiled a smile
from a secret, brittle heart.

His face lit up in the heat given off by destruction
like something was being made, or was being set right.   20
I bent my head back to see where sparks
ate up the sky. My father who never held us
would take my hand and point to falling cinders that
covered the ground like snow, or, excited, show us
the swollen collapse of a staircase. My mother   25
watched my father, not the house. She was happy
only when we were ready to go, when it was finally over
and nothing else could burn.
Driving home, she would sleep in the front seat
as we huddled behind. I could see his quiet face in the   30
rearview mirror, eyes like hallways filled with smoke.

This narrative poem could have been a short story
if the poet had wanted to say more about the "brittle
heart" of this unemployed man whose daughter so
vividly remembers the desperate pleasure he took in
watching fire consume other people's property. Indeed,

To hear
"Nighttime Fires" read
by Regina Barreca, visit
bedfordstmartins.com/
meyerlit/epages.

a reading of William Faulkner's famous short story "Barn Burning" suggests how such a character can be further developed and how his child
responds to him. The similarities between Faulkner's angry character and
the poem's father, whose "eyes [are] like hallways filled with smoke," are
coincidental, but the characters' sense of "something . . . being set right"
by flames is worth comparing. Although we do not know everything
about this man and his family, we have a much firmer sense of their story
than we do of the story of the couple in "Western Wind."

Although narrative poetry is still written, short stories and novels
have largely replaced the long narrative poem. Lyric poems tend to be
the predominant type of poetry today. Regardless of whether a poem
is a narrative or a lyric, however, the strategies for reading it are somewhat different from those for reading prose. Try these suggestions for
approaching poetry.

Suggestions for Approaching Poetry

1. Assume that it will be necessary to read a poem more than
   once. Give yourself a chance to become familiar with what the
   poem has to offer. Like a piece of music, a poem becomes more
   pleasurable with each encounter.

2. Pay attention to the title; it will often provide a helpful context
   for the poem and serve as an introduction to it. Larkin's "A
   Study of Reading Habits" is precisely what its title describes.

3. As you read a poem for the first time, avoid becoming entangled
   in words or lines that you don't understand. Instead, give yourself

a chance to take in the entire poem before attempting to resolve problems encountered along the way.

4. On a second reading, identify any words or passages that you don't understand. Look up words you don't know; these might include names, places, historical and mythical references, or anything else that is unfamiliar to you.

5. Read the poem aloud (or perhaps have a friend read it to you). You'll probably discover that some puzzling passages suddenly fall into place when you hear them. You'll find that nothing helps, though, if the poem is read in an artificial, exaggerated manner. Read in as natural a voice as possible, with slight pauses at line breaks. Silent reading is preferable to imposing a te-tumpty-te-tum reading on a good poem.

6. Read the punctuation. Poems use punctuation marks—in addition to the space on the page—as signals for readers. Be especially careful not to assume that the end of a line marks the end of a sentence, unless it is concluded by punctuation. Consider, for example, the opening lines of Hathaway's "Oh, Oh":

> My girl and I amble a country lane,
> moo cows chomping daisies, our own
> sweet saliva green with grass stems.

Line 2 above makes little or no sense if a reader stops after "own." Keeping track of the subjects and verbs will help you find your way among the sentences.

7. Paraphrase the poem to determine whether you understand what happens in it. As you work through each line of the poem, a paraphrase will help you to see which words or passages need further attention.

8. Try to get a sense of who is speaking and what the setting or situation is. Don't assume that the speaker is the author; often it is a created character.

9. Assume that each element in the poem has a purpose. Try to explain how the elements of the poem work together.

10. Be generous. Be willing to entertain perspectives, values, experiences, and subjects that you might not agree with or approve of. Even if baseball bores you, you should be able to comprehend its imaginative use in Francis's "Catch."

11. Don't expect to produce a definitive reading. Many poems do not resolve all of the ideas, issues, or tensions in them, and so it is not always possible to drive their meaning into an absolute corner. Your reading will explore rather than define the poem. Poems are not trophies to be stuffed and mounted. They're usually more elusive. And don't be afraid that a close reading will damage the poem. Poems aren't hurt when we analyze them; instead, they come alive as we experience them and put into words what we discover through them.

These strategies should be a useful means for getting inside poems to understand how they work. Furthermore, because reading poetry inevitably increases sensitivity to language, you're likely to find yourself a better reader of words in any form — whether in a novel, a newspaper editorial, an advertisement, a political speech, or a conversation — after having studied poetry. In short, many of the reading skills that make poetry accessible also open up the world you inhabit.

BILLY COLLINS (B. 1941)

Introduction to Poetry   *1988*

I ask them to take a poem
and hold it up to the light
like a color slide

or press an ear against its hive.

I say drop a mouse into a poem   5
and watch him probe his way out,

or walk inside the poem's room
and feel the walls for a light switch.

I want them to water-ski
across the surface of a poem   10
waving at the author's name on the shore.

But all they want to do
is tie the poem to a chair with rope
and torture a confession out of it.

They begin beating it with a hose   15
to find out what it really means.

CONSIDERATIONS FOR CRITICAL THINKING AND WRITING

1. **FIRST RESPONSE.** In what sense does this poem offer suggestions for approaching poetry? What kinds of advice does the speaker provide in lines 1–11?

2. How does the mood of the poem change beginning in line 12? What do you make of the shift from "them" to "they"?

3. Paraphrase the poem. How is your paraphrase different from what is included in the poem?

POETRY IN POPULAR FORMS

Before you try out these strategies for reading on a few more poems, it is worth acknowledging that the verse that enjoys the widest readership appears not in collections, magazines, or even anthologies for students, but in greeting cards. A significant amount of the personal daily mail delivered in the United States consists of greeting cards. That represents millions of lines of verse going by us on the street and in planes over our heads. These verses share some similarities with the poetry included in this anthology, but there are also important differences that indicate the need for reading serious poetry closely rather than casually.

The popularity of greeting cards is easy to explain: Just as many of us have neither the time nor the talent to make gifts for birthdays, weddings, anniversaries, graduations, Valentine's Day, Mother's Day, and other holidays, we are unlikely to write personal messages when cards conveniently say them for us. Although impersonal, cards are efficient and convey an important message no matter what the occasion for them: I care. These greetings are rarely serious poetry; they are not written to be. Nevertheless, they demonstrate the impulse in our culture to generate and receive poetry.

In a handbook for greeting-card freelancers, a writer and past editor of such verse began with this advice:

> Once you determine what you want to say — and in this regard it is best to stick to one basic idea — you must choose your words to do several things at the same time:
>
> 1. Your idea must be expressed as a complete idea; it must have a beginning, a middle, and an end.
>
> 2. There must be coherence in your verse. Every line must be linked logically and smoothly with its neighbors.
>
> 3. Your expressions . . . must be conversational. High-flown language rarely comes off successfully in greeting-card writing.
>
> 4. You must write with emphasis — and something else: enthusiasm. It's necessary to create interest in that all-important first line. From that point on, writing your verse is a matter of developing your idea and bringing it to a peak of emphasis in the last line. Occasionally you will find that you have shot your wad too early in the verse, and whatever you say after that point sounds like an afterthought.
>
> 5. You must do all of the above and at the same time make everything come out right in the meter-and-rhyme department.[1]

This advice is followed by a list of approximately fifty of the most frequently used rhyme sounds accompanied by rhyming words, such as *love, of, above* for the sound *uv*. The point of these prescriptions is that the

---

[1] Chris Fitzgerald, "Conventional Verse: The Sentimental Favorite," *The Greeting Card Writer's Handbook*, ed. H. Joseph Chadwick (Cincinnati: Writer's Digest, 1975), 13, 17.

verse must be written so that it is immediately accessible — consumable — by both the buyer and the recipient. Writers of these cards are expected to avoid any complexity.

Compare the following greeting-card verse with the poem that comes after it. "Magic of Love," by Helen Farries, has been a long-time favorite in a major greeting-card company's "wedding line"; with different endings it has been used also in valentines and friendship cards.

HELEN FARRIES (1918–2008)

Magic of Love   *date unknown*

There's a wonderful gift that can give you a lift,
It's a blessing from heaven above!
It can comfort and bless, it can bring happiness —
It's the wonderful MAGIC OF LOVE!

Like a star in the night, it can keep your faith bright,   5
Like the sun, it can warm your hearts, too —
It's a gift you can give every day that you live,
And when given, it comes back to you!

When love lights the way, there is joy in the day
And all troubles are lighter to bear,   10
Love is gentle and kind, and through love you will find
There's an answer to your every prayer!

May it never depart from your two loving hearts,
May you treasure this gift from above —
You will find if you do, all your dreams will come true,   15
In the wonderful MAGIC OF LOVE!

JOHN FREDERICK NIMS (1913–1999)

Love Poem   *1947*

My clumsiest dear, whose hands shipwreck vases,
At whose quick touch all glasses chip and ring,
Whose palms are bulls in china, burs in linen,
And have no cunning with any soft thing

Except all ill-at-ease fidgeting people: 5
The refugee uncertain at the door
You make at home; deftly you steady
The drunk clambering on his undulant floor.

Unpredictable dear, the taxi drivers' terror,
Shrinking from far headlights pale as a dime   10
Yet leaping before red apoplectic streetcars —
Misfit in any space. And never on time.

A wrench in clocks and the solar system. Only
With words and people and love you move at ease.
In traffic of wit expertly maneuver   15
And keep us, all devotion, at your knees.

Forgetting your coffee spreading on our flannel,
Your lipstick grinning on our coat,
So gaily in love's unbreakable heaven
Our souls on glory of spilt bourbon float.   20

Be with me, darling, early and late. Smash glasses —
I will study wry music for your sake.
For should your hands drop white and empty
All the toys of the world would break.

CONSIDERATIONS FOR CRITICAL THINKING AND WRITING

1. **FIRST RESPONSE.** Read these two works aloud. How are they different? How the same?

2. To what extent does the advice to would-be greeting-card writers apply to each work?

3. Compare the two speakers. Which do you find more appealing? Why?

4. How does Nims's description of love differ from Farries's?

In contrast to poetry, which transfigures and expresses an emotion or experience through an original use of language, the verse in "Magic of Love" relies on *clichés* — ideas or expressions that have become tired and trite from overuse, such as describing love as "a blessing from heaven above." Clichés anesthetize readers instead of alerting them to the possibility of fresh perceptions. They are used to draw out *stock responses* — predictable, conventional reactions to language, characters, symbols, or situations; God, heaven, the flag, motherhood, hearts, puppies, and peace are some often-used objects of stock responses. Advertisers manufacture careers from this sort of business.

Clichés and stock responses are two of the major ingredients of sentimentality in literature. **Sentimentality** exploits the reader by inducing responses that exceed what the situation warrants. This pejorative term should not be confused with *sentiment,* which is synonymous with *emotion* or *feeling.* Sentimentality cons readers into falling for the mass murderer who is devoted to stray cats, and it requires that we not think twice about what we're feeling because those tears shed for the little old lady, the rage aimed at the vicious enemy soldier, and the longing for the simple virtues of poverty might disappear under the slightest scrutiny. The experience of sentimentality is not unlike biting into a swirl of cotton candy; it's momentarily sweet but wholly insubstantial.

Clichés, stock responses, and sentimentality are generally the hallmarks of weak writing. Poetry — the kind that is unmistakable — achieves freshness, vitality, and genuine emotion that sharpen our perceptions of life.

Although the most widely read verse is found in greeting cards, the most widely *heard* poetry appears in song lyrics. Not all songs are poetic, but a good many share the same effects and qualities as poems. Consider these lyrics by Bruce Springsteen.

BRUCE SPRINGSTEEN (B. 1949)

Devils & Dust   2005

I got my finger on the trigger
But I don't know who to trust
When I look into your eyes
There's just devils and dust
We're a long, long way from home, Bobbie   5
Home's a long, long way from us
I feel a dirty wind blowing
Devils and dust

I got God on my side
I'm just trying to survive   10
What if what you do to survive
Kills the things you love
Fear's a powerful thing
It can turn your heart black you can trust
It'll take your God filled soul   15
And fill it with devils and dust

Well I dreamed of you last night
In a field of blood and stone
The blood began to dry
The smell began to rise   20
Well I dreamed of you last night, Bobbie
In a field of mud and bone
Your blood began to dry
The smell began to rise

We've got God on our side   25
We're just trying to survive
What if what you do to survive
Kills the things you love
Fear's a powerful thing, baby

It'll turn your heart black you can trust   30
It'll take your God filled soul
Fill it with devils and dust

Now every woman and every man
They want to take a righteous stand
Find the love that God wills   35
And the faith that He commands
I've got my finger on the trigger
And tonight faith just ain't enough
When I look inside my heart
There's just devils and dust   40

Well I've got God on my side
And I'm just trying to survive
What if what you do to survive
Kills the things you love
Fear's a dangerous thing   45
It can turn your heart black you can trust
It'll take your God filled soul
Fill it with devils and dust

Yeah, it'll take your God filled soul

Fill it with devils and dust   50

CONSIDERATIONS FOR CRITICAL THINKING AND WRITING

1. **FIRST RESPONSE.** How do images of war and the phrases that are repeated evoke a particular mood in this song?

2. Do you think this song can accurately be called a narrative poem? Why or why not? How would you describe its theme?

3. How does your experience of reading "Devils & Dust" compare with listening to Springsteen singing the song (available on *Devils & Dust*)?

POEMS FOR FURTHER STUDY

CORNELIUS EADY (B. 1954)

The Supremes   *1991*

We were born to be gray. We went to school,
Sat in rows, ate white bread,
Looked at the floor a lot. In the back
Of our small heads

A long scream. We did what we could,   5
And all we could do was

Turn on each other. How the fat kids suffered!
Not even being jolly could save them.

And then there were the anal retentives,
The terrified brown-noses, the desperately   10
Athletic or popular. This, of course,
Was training. At home

Our parents shook their heads and waited.
We learned of the industrial revolution,
The sectioning of the clock into pie slices.   15
We drank cokes and twiddled our thumbs. In the
Back of our minds

A long scream. We snapped butts in the showers,
Froze out shy girls on the dance floor,
Pin-pointed flaws like radar.   20
Slowly we understood: this was to be the world.

We were born insurance salesmen and secretaries,
Housewives and short order cooks,
Stock room boys and repairmen,
And it wouldn't be a bad life, they promised,   25
In a tone of voice that would force some of us
To reach in self-defense for wigs,
Lipstick,

Sequins.

CONSIDERATIONS FOR CRITICAL THINKING AND WRITING

1. **FIRST RESPONSE.** Who were the Supremes? Why is the title so crucial
   for this poem?

2. Explain how the meanings and mood of this poem would change if it
   ended with line 25.

3. How does the speaker's recollection of school experiences compare
   with your own?

4. **CONNECTION TO ANOTHER SELECTION.** Discuss the speakers' memories of school in "The Supremes" and in Judy Page Heitzman's "The
   Schoolroom on the Second Floor of the Knitting Mill" (p. 423).

ALBERTO RÍOS (B. 1952)

Seniors   1985

William cut a hole in his Levi's pocket
so he could flop himself out in class
behind the girls so the other guys
could see and shit what guts we all said.

Courtesy of Alberto
Ríos.

All Konga wanted to do over and over   5
was the rubber band trick, but he showed
everyone how, so nobody wanted to see
anymore and one day he cried, just cried
until his parents took him away forever.
Maya had a Hotpoint refrigerator standing   10
in his living room, just for his family to show
anybody who came that they could afford it.

Me, I got a French kiss, finally, in the catholic
darkness, my tongue's farthest half vacationing
loudly in another mouth like a man in Bermudas,   15
and my body jumped against a flagstone wall,
I could feel it through her thin, almost
nonexistent body: I had, at that moment, that moment,
a hot girl on a summer night, the best of all
the things we tried to do. Well, she   20
let me kiss her, anyway, all over.

Or it was just a flagstone wall
with a flaw in the stone, an understanding cavity
for burning young men with smooth dreams —
the true circumstance is gone, the true   25
circumstances about us all then
are gone. But when I kissed her, all water,
she would close her eyes, and they into somewhere
would disappear. Whether she was there
or not, I remember her, clearly, and she moves   30
around the room, sometimes, until I sleep.

I have lain on the desert in watch
low in the back of a pick-up truck
for nothing in particular, for stars, for
the things behind stars, and nothing comes   35
more than the moment: always now, here in a truck,
the moment again to dream of making love and sweat,
this time to a woman, or even to all of them
in some allowable way, to those boys, then,
who couldn't cry, to the girls before they were   40
women, to friends, me on my back, the sky over me
pressing its simple weight into her body
on me, into the bodies of them all, on me.

CONSIDERATIONS FOR CRITICAL THINKING AND WRITING

1. **FIRST RESPONSE.** Comment on the use of slang in the poem. Does it
   surprise you? How does it characterize the speaker?

2. How does the language of the final stanza differ from that of the first stanza? To what purpose?

3. Write an essay that discusses the speaker's attitudes toward sex and life. How are they related?

4. **CONNECTION TO ANOTHER SELECTION.** Think about "Seniors" as a kind of love poem and compare the speaker's voice here with the one in T. S. Eliot's "The Love Song of J. Alfred Prufrock" (p. 570). How are these two voices used to evoke different cultures? Of what value is love in these cultures?

LI HO (791–817)

A Beautiful Girl Combs Her Hair   *date unknown*

TRANSLATED BY DAVID YOUNG

Awake at dawn
she's dreaming
by cool silk curtains

fragrance of spilling hair
half sandalwood, half aloes   5

windlass creaking at the well
singing jade

the lotus blossom wakes, refreshed

her mirror
two phoenixes   10
a pool of autumn light

standing on the ivory bed
loosening her hair
watching the mirror

one long coil, aromatic silk   15
a cloud down to the floor

drop the jade comb — no sound

delicate fingers
pushing the coils into place
color of raven feathers   20

shining blue-black stuff
the jewelled comb will hardly hold it

spring wind makes me restless
her slovenly beauty upsets me

eighteen and her hair's so thick   25
she wears herself out fixing it!

she's finished now
the whole arrangement in place

in a cloud-patterned skirt
she walks with even steps   30
a wild goose on the sand

turns away without a word
where is she off to?

down the steps to break a spray of
    cherry blossoms   35

CONSIDERATIONS FOR CRITICAL THINKING AND WRITING

1. **FIRST RESPONSE.** Try to paraphrase the poem. What is lost by rewording?

2. How does the speaker use sensuous language to create a vivid picture of the girl?

3. What are the speaker's feelings toward the girl? Do they remain the same throughout the poem?

4. **CONNECTION TO ANOTHER SELECTION.** Write an essay that explores the differing portraits in this poem and in Robert Herrick's "Upon Julia's Clothes" (p. 488). Which portrait is more interesting to you? Explain why.

ROBERT FROST (1874–1963)

Design   1936

I found a dimpled spider, fat and white,
On a white heal-all,° holding up a moth
Like a white piece of rigid satin cloth—
Assorted characters of death and blight
Mixed ready to begin the morning right,   5
Like the ingredients of a witches' broth—
A snow-drop spider, a flower like a froth,
And dead wings carried like a paper kite.

What had the flower to do with being white,
The wayside blue and innocent heal-all?   10
What brought the kindred spider to that height,
Then steered the white moth thither in the night?
What but design of darkness to appall?—
If design govern in a thing so small.

2 *heal-all:* A common flower, usually blue, once used for medicinal purposes.

CONSIDERATIONS FOR CRITICAL THINKING AND WRITING

1. **FIRST RESPONSE.** What kinds of speculations are raised in the poem's final two lines? Consider the meaning of the title. Is there more than one way to read it?

2. How does the division of the stanzas in this sonnet serve to organize the speaker's thoughts and feelings? What is the predominant rhyme? How does that rhyme relate to the poem's meaning?

3. Which words seem especially rich in connotative meanings? Explain how they function in the sonnet.

4. **CONNECTION TO ANOTHER SELECTION.** Compare the ironic tone of "Design" with the tone of William Hathaway's "Oh, Oh" (p. 342). What would you have to change in Hathaway's poem to make it more like Frost's?

EDGAR ALLAN POE (1809–1849)

The Raven   *1845*

Once upon a midnight dreary, while I pondered, weak and weary,
Over many a quaint and curious volume of forgotten lore,
While I nodded, nearly napping, suddenly there came a tapping,
As of some one gently rapping, rapping at my chamber door.
"'Tis some visiter," I muttered, "tapping at my chamber door —   5
                    Only this, and nothing more."

Ah, distinctly I remember it was in the bleak December,
And each separate dying ember wrought its ghost upon the floor.
Eagerly I wished the morrow; — vainly I had tried to borrow
From my books surcease of sorrow — sorrow for the lost Lenore —   10
For the rare and radiant maiden whom the angels name Lenore —
                    Nameless here for evermore.

And the silken sad uncertain rustling of each purple curtain
Thrilled me — filled me with fantastic terrors never felt before;
So that now, to still the beating of my heart, I stood repeating   15
"'Tis some visiter entreating entrance at my chamber door —
Some late visiter entreating entrance at my chamber door; —
                    This it is, and nothing more."

Presently my soul grew stronger; hesitating then no longer,
"Sir," said I, "or Madam, truly your forgiveness I implore;   20
But the fact is I was napping, and so gently you came rapping,
And so faintly you came tapping, tapping at my chamber door,
That I scarce was sure I heard you" — here I opened wide the door; —
                    Darkness there, and nothing more.

Deep into that darkness peering, long I stood there wondering, fearing   25
Doubting, dreaming dreams no mortal ever dared to dream before;
But the silence was unbroken, and the darkness gave no token,
And the only word there spoken was the whispered word, "Lenore!"
This *I* whispered, and an echo murmured back the word, "Lenore!"
                              Merely this, and nothing more.   30

Then into the chamber turning, all my soul within me burning,
Soon I heard again a tapping somewhat louder than before.
"Surely," said I, "surely that is something at my window lattice;
Let me see, then, what thereat is, and this mystery explore —
Let my heart be still a moment and this mystery explore; —   35
                  " 'Tis the wind, and nothing more!"

Open here I flung the shutter, when, with many a flirt and flutter,
In there stepped a stately raven of the saintly days of yore;
Not the least obeisance made he; not an instant stopped or stayed he;
But, with mien of lord or lady, perched above my chamber door —   40
Perched upon a bust of Pallas° just above my chamber door —
                    Perched, and sat, and nothing more.

Then this ebony bird beguiling my sad fancy into smiling,
By the grave and stern decorum of the countenance it wore,
"Though thy crest be shorn and shaven, thou," I said, "art sure no craven,   45
Ghastly grim and ancient raven wandering from the Nightly shore —
Tell me what thy lordly name is on the Night's Plutonian shore°!" —
                    Quoth the raven, "Nevermore."

Much I marveled this ungainly fowl to hear discourse so plainly,
Though its answer little meaning — little relevancy bore;   50
For we cannot help agreeing that no sublunary being
Ever yet was blessed with seeing bird above his chamber door —
Bird or beast upon the sculptured bust above his chamber door,
                      With such name as "Nevermore."

But the raven, sitting lonely on the placid bust, spoke only   55
That one word, as if his soul in that one word he did outpour.
Nothing farther then he uttered — not a feather then he fluttered —
Till I scarcely more than muttered, "Other friends have flown before —
On the morrow *he* will leave me, as my hopes have flown before."
                    Quoth the raven, "Nevermore."   60

Wondering at the stillness broken by reply so aptly spoken,
"Doubtless," said I, "what it utters is its only stock and store,
Caught from some unhappy master whom unmerciful Disaster

41 *Pallas:* Pallas Athena, the goddess of wisdom and the arts.   47 *Plutonian shore:* The
dark underworld ruled by Pluto in Greek mythology.

Followed fast and followed faster—so, when Hope he would adjure,
Stern Despair returned, instead of the sweet Hope he dared adjure—   65
That sad answer, "Nevermore!"

But the raven still beguiling all my sad soul into smiling,
Straight I wheeled a cushioned seat in front of bird, and bust, and door;
Then upon the velvet sinking, I betook myself to linking
Fancy unto fancy, thinking what this ominous bird of yore—   70
What this grim, ungainly, ghastly, gaunt, and ominous bird of yore
Meant in croaking "Nevermore."

This I sat engaged in guessing, but no syllable expressing
To the fowl whose fiery eyes now burned into my bosom's core;
This and more I sat divining, with my head at ease reclining   75
On the cushion's velvet lining that the lamplight gloated o'er,
But whose velvet violet lining with the lamplight gloating o'er,
She shall press, ah, nevermore!

Then, methought, the air grew denser, perfumed from an unseen censer
Swung by angels whose faint foot-falls tinkled on the tufted floor.   80
"Wretch," I cried, "thy God hath lent thee—by these angels he hath sent thee
Respite—respite and Nepenthe° from thy memories of Lenore!
Let me quaff this kind Nepenthe and forget this lost Lenore!"
Quoth the raven, "Nevermore."

"Prophet!" said I, "thing of evil!—prophet still, if bird or devil!—   85
Whether Tempter sent, or whether tempest tossed thee here ashore,
Desolate, yet all undaunted, on this desert land enchanted—
On this home by Horror haunted—tell me truly, I implore—
Is there—*is* there balm in Gilead?°—tell me—tell me, I implore!"
Quoth the raven, "Nevermore."   90

"Prophet!" said I, "thing of evil!—prophet still, if bird or devil!
By that Heaven that bends above us—by that God we both adore—
Tell this soul with sorrow laden if, within the distant Aidenn,°
It shall clasp a sainted maiden whom the angels name Lenore—
Clasp a rare and radiant maiden whom the angels name Lenore."   95
Quoth the raven, "Nevermore."

"Be that word our sign of parting, bird or fiend!" I shrieked, upstarting—
"Get thee back into the tempest and the Night's Plutonian shore!
Leave no black plume as a token of that lie thy soul hath spoken!
Leave my loneliness unbroken—quit the bust above my door!   100
Take thy beak from out my heart, and take thy form from off my door!"
Quoth the raven, "Nevermore."

---

82 *Nepenthe:* A numbing drug.   89 *Gilead:* An allusion to medicinal healing in
Jeremiah 8:22.   93 *Aidenn:* Eden.

And the raven, never flitting, still is sitting, still is sitting
On the pallid bust of Pallas just above my chamber door;
And his eyes have all the seeming of a demon that is dreaming,   105
And the lamp-light o'er him streaming throws his shadow on the floor;
And my soul from out that shadow that lies floating on the floor
                                    Shall be lifted — nevermore!

CONSIDERATIONS FOR CRITICAL THINKING AND WRITING

1. **FIRST RESPONSE.** How do the word sounds in "The Raven" create a particular mood? Which words seem especially evocative to you?

2. Characterize the speaker of the poem. What sort of personality does he reveal to you?

3. Explain how Poe's language produces suspense throughout the poem.

4. **CONNECTION TO ANOTHER SELECTION.** Compare Poe's treatment of pain and suffering with Mary Oliver's in "The Poet with His Face in His Hands" (below).

MARY OLIVER (B. 1935)

The Poet with His Face in His Hands   2005

You want to cry aloud for your
mistakes. But to tell the truth the world
doesn't need any more of that sound.

So if you're going to do it and can't
stop yourself, if your pretty mouth can't   5
hold it in, at least go by yourself across

the forty fields and the forty dark inclines
of rocks and water to the place where
the falls are flinging out their white sheets

like crazy, and there is a cave behind all that   10
jubilation and water fun and you can
stand there, under it, and roar all you

want and nothing will be disturbed; you can
drip with despair all afternoon and still,
on a green branch, its wings just lightly touched   15

by the passing foil of the water, the thrush,
puffing out its spotted breast, will sing
of the perfect, stone-hard beauty of everything.

CONSIDERATIONS FOR CRITICAL THINKING AND WRITING

1. **FIRST RESPONSE.** Describe the kind of poet the speaker characterizes. What is the speaker's attitude toward that sort of poet?
2. Explain which single phrase used by the speaker to describe the poet most reveals for you the speaker's attitude toward the poet.
3. How is nature contrasted with the poet?
4. **CONNECTION TO ANOTHER SELECTION.** Compare the thematic use of nature in Oliver's poem and in Robert Frost's "Design" (p. 365).

13

Word Choice, Word Order, and Tone

By permission of The Granger Collection, New York.

I still feel that a poet has a duty to words, and that words can do wonderful things. And it's too bad to just let them lie there without doing anything with and for them.

— GWENDOLYN BROOKS

WORD CHOICE

Diction

Like all good writers, poets are keenly aware of *diction*, their choice of words. Poets, however, choose words especially carefully because the words in poems call attention to themselves. Characters, actions, settings, and symbols may appear in a poem, but in the foreground, before all else, is the poem's language. Also, poems are usually briefer than other forms of writing. A few inappropriate words in a 200-page novel (which would have about 100,000 words) create fewer problems than they would in a 100-word poem. Functioning in a compressed atmosphere, the words in a poem must convey meanings gracefully and economically. Readers therefore have to be alert to the ways in which those meanings are released.

Explore the poetic elements in this chapter at bedfordstmartins.com/meyerlit.

Although poetic language is often more intensely charged than ordinary speech, the words used in poetry are not necessarily different from everyday speech. Inexperienced readers may sometimes assume that language must be high-flown and out of date to be included in a poem: Instead of reading about a boy "enjoying a swim," they expect

371

to read about a boy "disporting with pliant arm o'er a glassy wave." During the eighteenth century this kind of *poetic diction* — the use of elevated language rather than ordinary language — was highly valued in English poetry, but since the nineteenth century, poets have generally overridden the distinctions that were once made between words used in everyday speech and those used in poetry. Today all levels of diction can be found in poetry.

A poet, like any writer, has several levels of diction from which to choose; they range from formal to middle to informal. *Formal diction* consists of a dignified, impersonal, and elevated use of language. Notice, for example, the formality of Thomas Hardy's description of the sunken luxury liner *Titanic* in this stanza from "The Convergence of the Twain" (the entire poem appears on pp. 388–89):

> In a solitude of the sea
> Deep from human vanity,
> And the Pride of Life that planned her, stilly couches she.

There is nothing casual or relaxed about these lines. Hardy's use of "stilly," meaning "quietly" or "calmly," is purely literary; the word rarely, if ever, turns up in everyday English.

The language used in Sharon Olds's "Last Night" (p. 386) represents a less formal level of diction; the speaker uses a *middle diction* spoken by most educated people. Consider how Olds's speaker struggles the next day to comprehend her passion:

> Love? It was more like dragonflies
> in the sun, 100 degrees at noon,
> the ends of their abdomens stuck together, I
> close my eyes when I remember.

The words used to describe this encounter are common enough, yet it is precisely Olds's use of language that evokes the extraordinary nature of this couple's connection.

Informal diction is evident in Philip Larkin's "A Study of Reading Habits" (p. 348). The speaker's account of his early reading is presented *colloquially*, in a conversational manner that in this instance includes slang expressions not used by the culture at large:

> When getting my nose in a book
> Cured most things short of school,
> It was worth ruining my eyes
> To know I could still keep cool,
> And deal out the old right hook
> To dirty dogs twice my size.

This level of diction is clearly not that of Hardy's or Olds's speakers.

Poets may also draw on another form of informal diction, called *dialect*. Dialects are spoken by definable groups of people from a particular geographic region, economic group, or social class. New England dialects are often heard in Robert Frost's poems, for example. Gwendolyn Brooks uses a black dialect in "We Real Cool" (p. 393) to characterize a group of pool players. Another form of diction related to particular groups is *jargon*, a category of language defined by a trade or profession. Sociologists, photographers, carpenters, baseball players, and dentists, for example, all use words that are specific to their fields. Sally Croft offers an appetizing dish of cookbook jargon in "Home-Baked Bread" (p. 409).

Many levels of diction are available to poets. The variety of diction to be found in poetry is enormous, and that is how it should be. No language is foreign to poetry because it is possible to imagine any human voice as the speaker of a poem. When we say a poem is formal, informal, or somewhere in between, we are making a descriptive statement rather than an evaluative one. What matters in a poem is not only which words are used but how they are used.

Denotations and Connotations

One important way that the meaning of a word is communicated in a poem is through sound: snakes *hiss,* saws *buzz.* This and other matters related to sound are discussed in Chapter 17. Individual words also convey meanings through denotations and connotations. *Denotations* are the literal, dictionary meanings of a word. For example, *bird* denotes a feathered animal with wings (other denotations for the same word include a shuttlecock, an airplane, or an odd person), but in addition to its denotative meanings, *bird* also carries *connotations*—associations and implications that go beyond a word's literal meanings. Connotations derive from how the word has been used and the associations people make with it. Therefore, the connotations of *bird* might include fragility, vulnerability, altitude, the sky, or freedom, depending on the context in which the word is used. Consider also how different the connotations are for the following types of birds: hawk, dove, penguin, pigeon, chicken, peacock, duck, crow, turkey, gull, owl, goose, coot, and vulture. These words have long been used to refer to types of people as well as birds. They are rich in connotative meanings.

Connotations derive their resonance from a person's experiences with a word. Those experiences may not always be the same, especially when the people having them are in different times and places. *Theater,* for instance, was once associated with depravity, disease, and sin, whereas today the word usually evokes some sense of high culture and perhaps visions of elegant opulence. In several ethnic communities in the United States many people would find *squid* appetizing, but elsewhere the word is likely to produce negative connotations. Readers must recognize, then, that words written in other times and places may have unexpected connotations. Annotations usually help in these matters, which is why it makes sense to pay attention to them when they are available.

Ordinarily, though, the language of poetry is accessible, even when the circumstances of the reader and the poet are different. Although connotative language may be used subtly, it mostly draws on associations experienced by many people. Poets rely on widely shared associations rather than the idiosyncratic response that an individual might have to a word. Someone who has received a severe burn from a fireplace accident may associate the word *hearth* with intense pain instead of home and family life, but that reader must not allow a personal experience to undermine the response the poet intends to evoke. Connotative meanings are usually public meanings.

Perhaps this can be seen most clearly in advertising, where language is also used primarily to convey moods and feelings rather than information. For instance, three decades of increasing interest in nutrition and general fitness have created a collective consciousness that advertisers have capitalized on successfully. Knowing that we want to be slender or lean or slim (not *spare* or *scrawny* and certainly not *gaunt*), advertisers have created a new word to describe beers, wines, sodas, cheeses, canned fruits, and other products that tend to make us overweight. The word is *lite*. The assumed denotative meaning of *lite* is "low in calories," but as close readers of ingredient labels know, some *lites* are heavier than regularly prepared products. There can be no doubt about the connotative meaning of *lite*, however. Whatever is *lite* cannot hurt you; less is more. Even the word is lighter than *light;* there is no unnecessary, droopy *g* or plump *h*. *Lite* is a brilliantly manufactured use of connotation.

Connotative meanings are valuable because they allow poets to be economical and suggestive simultaneously. In this way emotions and attitudes are carefully woven into the texture of the poem's language. Read the following poem and pay close attention to the connotative meanings of its words.

RANDALL JARRELL (1914–1965)
The Death of the Ball Turret Gunner   1945

To hear "The Death of the Ball Turret Gunner" read by Randall Jarrell, visit bedfordstmartins.com/meyerlit/epages.

From my mother's sleep I fell into the State
And I hunched in its belly till my wet fur froze.
Six miles from earth, loosed from its dream of life,
I woke to black flak and the nightmare fighters.
When I died they washed me out of the turret with a hose.

The title of this poem establishes the setting and the speaker's situation. Like the setting of a short story, the setting of a poem is important when the time and place influence what happens. "The Death of the Ball Turret Gunner" is set in the midst of a war and, more specifically, in a ball turret — a Plexiglas sphere housing machine guns on the underside of a bomber. The speaker's situation obviously places him in extreme danger; indeed, his fate is announced in the title.

Although the poem is written in the first-person singular, its speaker is clearly not the poet. Jarrell uses a *persona*, a speaker created by the poet. In this poem the persona is a disembodied voice that makes the gunner's story all the more powerful. What is his story? A paraphrase might read something like this:

> After I was born, I grew up to find myself at war, cramped into the turret of a bomber's belly some 31,000 feet above the ground. Below me were exploding shells from antiaircraft guns and attacking fighter planes. I was killed, and when the bomber returned to base, my remains were cleaned out of the turret so the next man could take my place.

This paraphrase is accurate, but its language is much less suggestive than the poem's. The first line of the poem has the speaker emerge from his "mother's sleep," the anesthetized sleep of her giving birth. The phrase also suggests the comfort, warmth, and security he knew as a child. This safety was left behind when he "fell," a verb that evokes the danger and involuntary movement associated with his subsequent "State" (*fell* also echoes, perhaps, the fall from innocence to experience related in the Bible).

Several dictionary definitions appear for the noun *state;* it can denote a territorial unit, the power and authority of a government, a person's social status, or a person's emotional or physical condition. The context provided by the rest of the poem makes clear that "State" has several denotative meanings here: Because it is capitalized, it certainly refers to the violent world of a government at war, but it also refers to the gunner's vulnerable status as well as his physical and emotional condition. By having "State" carry more than one meaning, Jarrell has created an intentional ambiguity. *Ambiguity* allows for two or more simultaneous interpretations of a word, a phrase, an action, or a situation, all of which can be supported by the context of a work. Through his ambiguous use of "State," Jarrell connects the horrors of war not just to bombers and gunners but to the governments that control them.

Related to this ambiguity is the connotative meaning of "State" in the poem. The context demands that the word be read with a negative charge. The word is not used with patriotic pride but to suggest an anonymous, impersonal "State" that kills rather than nurtures the life in its "belly." The state's "belly" is a bomber, and the gunner is "hunched" like a fetus in the cramped turret, where, in contrast to the warmth of his mother's womb, everything is frozen, even the "wet fur" of his flight jacket (newborn infants have wet fur too). The gunner is not just 31,000 feet from the ground but "Six miles from earth." *Six miles* has roughly the same denotative meaning as 31,000 feet, but Jarrell knew that the connotative meaning of *six miles* makes the speaker's position seem even more remote and frightening.

When the gunner is born into the violent world of war, he finds himself waking up to a "nightmare" that is all too real. The poem's final line is grimly understated, but it hits the reader with the force of an exploding shell: What the State-bomber-turret gives birth to is a gruesome death that is merely one of an endless series. It may be tempting to reduce the theme of this poem to the idea that "war is hell," but Jarrell's target is more specific. He implicates the "State," which routinely executes such violence, and he does so without preaching or hysterical denunciations. Instead, his use of language conveys his theme subtly and powerfully.

WORD ORDER

Meanings in poems are conveyed not only by denotations and connotations but also by the poet's arrangement of words into phrases, clauses, and sentences to achieve particular effects. The ordering of words into meaningful verbal patterns is called *syntax*. A poet can manipulate the syntax of a line to place emphasis on a word; this is especially apparent when a poet varies normal word order. In Emily Dickinson's "A narrow Fellow in the Grass" (p. 2), for example, the speaker says about the snake that "His notice sudden is." Ordinarily, that would be expressed as "his notice is sudden." By placing the verb *is* unexpectedly at the end of the line, Dickinson creates the sense of surprise we feel when we suddenly come upon a snake. Dickinson's inversion of the standard word order also makes the final sound of the line a hissing *is*.

TONE

Tone is the writer's attitude toward the subject, the mood created by all of the elements in the poem. Writing, like speech, can be characterized as serious or light, sad or happy, private or public, angry or affectionate, bitter or nostalgic, or by any other attitudes and feelings that human beings experience. In Jarrell's "The Death of the Ball Turret Gunner," the tone is clearly serious; the voice in the poem even sounds dead. Listen again to the persona's final words: "When I died they washed me out of the turret with a hose." The brutal, restrained matter-of-factness of this line is effective because the reader is called on to supply the appropriate anger and despair — a strategy that makes those emotions all the more convincing.

Consider how tone is used to convey meaning in the next poem, inspired by the author's contemplation of mortality.

COLETTE INEZ (B. 1931)

Back When All Was Continuous Chuckles   2004

after a line by Anselm Hollo°

Doris and I were helpless on the Beeline Bus
laughing at what was it? "What did the moron
who killed his mother and father eat
at the orphan's picnic?" "Crow?" Har-har.

The bus was grinding towards Hempstead,   5
past the cemetery whose stones Doris
and I found hilarious. Freaky ghouls and skeletons.
"What did the dead man say to the ghost?"

"I like the movie better than the book."
Even "I don't get it" was funny.   10
The war was on, rationing, sirens.
Silly billies, we poked each other's arms

with balled fists, held hands and howled
at crabby ladies in funny hats, dusty feathers,
fake fruit. Doris' mom wore this headgear   15
before she got the big C which no one said out loud.

In a shadowy room her skin seemed gray
as moon dust on Smith Street, at Doris' house
where we tiptoed down the hall.
Sometimes we heard moans from the back room   20

and I helped wring out cloths while Doris
brought water in a glass held to her mother's lips.
But soon we were flipping through joke books
and writhing on the floor, war news shut off

back when we pretended all was continuous chuckles,   25
and we rode the bus past Greenfield's rise
where stones, trumpeting angels,
would bear names we later came to recognize.

Anselm Hollo: Finnish poet (b. 1934) who teaches creative writing in the United
States.

CONSIDERATIONS FOR CRITICAL THINKING AND WRITING

1. **FIRST RESPONSE.** Compare the difference between the title and its
   slightly revised version as it appears in line 25. How does that difference reveal the theme?

2. At what point does the tone of the poem shift from chuckles to
   something else?

3. What is the effect of the rhymes in lines 26 and 28? How do the rhymes serve to reinforce the poem's theme?

4. **CONNECTION TO ANOTHER SELECTION.** Discuss the tone of this poem and that of Gwendolyn Brooks's "We Real Cool" (p. 393).

WHEN I WRITE "Although I usually wind up showing my poems to my best friend, sometimes I ask other people to be first-readers because I don't want to ask too much of my friend! I recently joined a poetry group. Their suggestions are useful, mostly in helping me see what I'm really trying to get at." — MARILYN NELSON

MARILYN NELSON (B. 1946)

How I Discovered Poetry   1997

It was like soul-kissing, the way the words
filled my mouth as Mrs. Purdy read from her desk.
All the other kids zoned an hour ahead to 3:15,
but Mrs. Purdy and I wandered lonely as clouds borne
by a breeze off Mount Parnassus. She must have seen   5
the darkest eyes in the room brim: The next day
she gave me a poem she'd chosen especially for me
to read to the all except for me white class.
She smiled when she told me to read it, smiled harder,
said oh yes I could. She smiled harder and harder   10
until I stood and opened my mouth to banjo playing
darkies, pickaninnies, disses and dats. When I finished
my classmates stared at the floor. We walked silent
to the buses, awed by the power of words.

CONSIDERATIONS FOR CRITICAL THINKING AND WRITING

1. **FIRST RESPONSE.** Trace your response to Mrs. Purdy from the beginning to the end of the poem.

2. What do the references to William Wordsworth's poem "I Wandered Lonely as a Cloud" and Mount Parnassus (look them up) in lines 4 and 5 suggest to you about the speaker?

3. How do you interpret the tone of the final two lines?

The next work is a *dramatic monologue*, a type of poem in which a character — the speaker — addresses a silent audience in such a way as to reveal unintentionally some aspect of his or her temperament or personality. What tone is created by Machan's use of a persona?

Katharyn Howd Machan (b. 1952)

Hazel Tells LaVerne   1976

To hear "Hazel Tells LaVerne" read by Katharyn Howd Machan, visit bedfordstmartins.com/meyerlit/epages.

```
last night
im cleanin out my
howard johnsons ladies room
when all of a sudden
up pops this frog                                    5
musta come from the sewer
swimmin aroun an tryin ta
climb up the sida the bowl
so i goes ta flushm down
but sohelpmegod he starts talkin                    10
bout a golden ball
an how i can be a princess
me a princess
well my mouth drops
all the way to the floor                            15
an he says
kiss me just kiss me
once on the nose
well i screams
ya little green pervert                             20
an i hitsm with my mop
an has ta flush
the toilet down three times
me
a princess                                         25
```

Considerations for Critical Thinking and Writing

1. **First response.** What do you imagine the situation and setting are for this poem? Do you like this revision of the fairy tale "The Frog Prince"?

2. What creates the poem's humor? How does Hazel's use of language reveal her personality? Is her treatment of the frog consistent with her character?

3. What is the theme? Is it conveyed through denotative or connotative language?

4. **Creative response.** Write what you think might be LaVerne's reply to Hazel. First, write LaVerne's response as a series of ordinary sentences, and then try editing and organizing them into poetic lines.

5. **Connection to another selection.** Although Robert Browning's "My Last Duchess" (p. 446) is a more complex poem than Machan's, both use dramatic monologues to reveal character. How are the strategies in each poem similar?

Martín Espada (b. 1957)

Latin Night at the Pawnshop   1987

Chelsea, Massachusetts
Christmas, 1987

The apparition of a salsa band
gleaming in the Liberty Loan
pawnshop window:

Golden trumpet,
silver trombone,
congas, maracas, tambourine,

all with price tags dangling
like the city morgue ticket
on a dead man's toe.

WHEN I WRITE "As a poet and a reader, I am most interested in the theme of justice. I am interested in poems that address justice vividly, concretely, specifically. Poets are, as Shelley put it, the 'unacknowledged legislators of the world.' We shouldn't leave justice to the lawyers and the politicians."
— MARTÍN ESPADA

CONSIDERATIONS FOR CRITICAL THINKING AND WRITING

1. **FIRST RESPONSE.** What is "Latin" about this night at the pawnshop?
2. What kind of tone is created by the poet's word choice and by the poem's rhythm?
3. Does it matter that this apparition occurs on Christmas night? Why or why not?
4. What do you think is the central point of this poem?

How do the speaker's attitude and tone change during the course of this next poem?

Paul Laurence Dunbar (1872–1906)

To a Captious Critic   1903

Dear critic, who my lightness so deplores,
Would I might study to be prince of bores,
Right wisely would I rule that dull estate —
But, sir, I may not; till you abdicate.

CONSIDERATIONS FOR CRITICAL THINKING AND WRITING

1. **FIRST RESPONSE.** How do Dunbar's vocabulary and syntax signal the level of diction used in the poem?
2. Describe the speaker's tone. How does it characterize the speaker as well as the critic?
3. **CREATIVE RESPONSE.** Using "To a Captious Critic" as a model, try writing a four-line witty reply to someone in your own life — perhaps a roommate, coach, teacher, waiter, dentist, or anyone else who provokes a strong response in you.

DICTION AND TONE IN FOUR LOVE POEMS

The first three of these love poems share the same basic situation and theme: A male speaker addresses a female (in the first poem it is a type of female) urging that love should not be delayed because time is short. This theme is as familiar in poetry as it is in life. In Latin this tradition is known as *carpe diem*, "seize the day." Notice how the poets' diction helps create a distinctive tone in each poem, even though the subject matter and central ideas are similar (although not identical) in all three.

ROBERT HERRICK (1591–1674)

To the Virgins, to Make Much of Time   *1648*

Gather ye rose-buds while ye may,
   Old Time is still a-flying;
And this same flower that smiles today,
   Tomorrow will be dying.

The glorious lamp of heaven, the sun,
   The higher he's a-getting,
The sooner will his race be run,
   And nearer he's to setting.

That age is best which is the first,
   When youth and blood are warmer;
But being spent, the worse, and worst
   Times still succeed the former.

Then be not coy, but use your time,
   And while ye may, go marry;
For having lost but once your prime,
   You may for ever tarry.

15

Courtesy of the National Portrait Gallery, London.

CONSIDERATIONS FOR CRITICAL THINKING AND WRITING

1. **FIRST RESPONSE.** Would there be any change in meaning if the title of this poem were "To Young Women, to Make Much of Time"? Do you think the poem can apply to young men, too?

2. What do the virgins have in common with the flowers (lines 1–4) and the course of the day (5–8)?

3. How does the speaker develop his argument? What will happen to the virgins if they don't "marry"? Paraphrase the poem.

4. What is the tone of the speaker's advice?

The next poem was also written in the seventeenth century, but it includes some words that have changed in usage and meaning over the past three hundred years. The title of Andrew Marvell's "To His Coy Mistress" requires some explanation. "Mistress" does not refer to a married man's illicit lover but to a woman who is loved and courted — a sweetheart. Marvell uses "coy" to describe a woman who is reserved and shy rather than coquettish or flirtatious. Often such shifts in meanings over time are explained in the notes that accompany reprintings of poems. You should keep in mind, however, that it is helpful to have a reasonably thick dictionary available when you are reading poetry. The most thorough is the *Oxford English Dictionary* (*OED*), which provides histories of words. The *OED* is a multivolume leviathan, but there are also other useful unabridged dictionaries and desk dictionaries.

Explore contexts for Andrew Marvell and approaches to this poem at bedfordstmartins.com/meyerlit.

Knowing a word's original meaning can also enrich your understanding of why a contemporary poet chooses a particular word. In "Design" (p. 365), Robert Frost raises provocative questions about the nature of evil and the existence of God in his dark examination of a moth's death, all presented in unexpected images of whiteness. He ends the poem with a series of questions concerning what causes "death and blight," wondering if it is a "design of darkness to appall" or no design at all, a universe informed only by random meaninglessness. Frost's precise contemporary use of "appall" captures the sense of consternation and dismay that such a frightening contemplation of death might evoke, but a dictionary reveals some further relevant insights. The dictionary's additional information about the history of *appall* shows us why it is the perfect word to establish the overwhelming effect of the poem. The word comes from the Middle English *appallen*, meaning "to grow faint," and in Old French *apalir* means "to grow pale" or white. These meanings reinforce the powerful sense of death buried in the images of whiteness throughout the poem. Moreover, Frost's "appall" also echoes a funeral pall, or coffin, allowing the word to bear even more connotative weight. Knowing the origin of *appall* gives us the full heft of the poet's word choice.

Although some of the language in "To His Coy Mistress" requires annotations for the modern reader, this poem continues to serve as a powerful reminder that time is a formidable foe, even for lovers.

ANDREW MARVELL (1621–1678)

To His Coy Mistress   1681

Had we but world enough, and time,
This coyness, lady, were no crime.
We would sit down, and think which way
To walk, and pass our long love's day.

Courtesy of the National Portrait Gallery, London.

Thou by the Indian Ganges'° side   5
Shouldst rubies find; I by the tide
Of Humber° would complain.° I would   *write love songs*
Love you ten years before the Flood,
And you should, if you please, refuse
Till the conversion of the Jews.   10
My vegetable love should grow°
Vaster than empires, and more slow;
An hundred years should go to praise
Thine eyes and on thy forehead gaze,
Two hundred to adore each breast,   15
But thirty thousand to the rest:
An age at least to every part,
And the last age should show your heart.
For, lady, you deserve this state,
Nor would I love at lower rate.   20
    But at my back I always hear
Time's wingèd chariot hurrying near;
And yonder all before us lie
Deserts of vast eternity.
Thy beauty shall no more be found,   25
Nor in thy marble vault shall sound
My echoing song; then worms shall try
That long preserved virginity,
And your quaint honor turn to dust,
And into ashes all my lust.   30
The grave's a fine and private place,
But none, I think, do there embrace.
    Now, therefore, while the youthful hue
Sits on thy skin like morning dew,
And while thy willing soul transpires°   *breathes forth*   35
At every pore with instant fires,
Now let us sport us while we may,
And now, like amorous birds of prey,
Rather at once our time devour
Than languish in his slow-chapped° power.   *slow-jawed*   40
Let us roll all our strength and all
Our sweetness up into one ball,
And tear our pleasures with rough strife
Thorough° the iron gates of life.   *through*
Thus, though we cannot make our sun   45
Stand still, yet we will make him run.

---

5 *Ganges:* A river in India sacred to the Hindus.   7 *Humber:* A river that flows
through Marvell's native town, Hull.   11 *My vegetable love . . .   grow:* A slow, unconscious growth.

CONSIDERATIONS FOR CRITICAL THINKING AND WRITING

1. **FIRST RESPONSE.** Do you think this *carpe diem* poem is hopelessly dated, or does it speak to our contemporary concerns?

2. This poem is divided into a three-part argument. Briefly summarize each section: if (lines 1–20), but (21–32), therefore (33–46).

3. What is the speaker's tone in lines 1–20? How much time would he spend adoring his mistress? Is he sincere? How does he expect his mistress to respond to these lines?

4. How does the speaker's tone change beginning with line 21? What is his view of time in lines 21–32? What does this description do to the lush and leisurely sense of time in lines 1–20? How do you think his mistress would react to lines 21–32?

5. In the final lines of Herrick's "To the Virgins, to Make Much of Time" (p. 381), the speaker urges the virgins to "go marry." What does Marvell's speaker urge in lines 33–46? How is the pace of these lines (notice the verbs) different from that of the first twenty lines of the poem?

6. This poem is sometimes read as a vigorous but simple celebration of flesh. Is there more to the theme than that?

The third in this series of *carpe diem* poems is a twenty-first-century work. The language of Ann Lauinger's "Marvell Noir" is more immediately accessible than that of Marvell's "To His Coy Mistress"; an ordinary dictionary will quickly identify any words unfamiliar to a reader. But the title might require a dictionary of biography for the reference to Marvell, as well as a dictionary of allusions to provide a succinct description that explains the reference to film noir. An ***allusion*** is a brief cultural reference to a person, a place, a thing, an event, or an idea in history or literature. Allusive words, like connotative words, are both suggestive and economical; poets use allusions to conjure up biblical authority, scenes from Shakespeare's plays, historic figures, wars, great love stories, and anything else that might serve to deepen and enrich their own work. The title of "Marvell Noir" makes two allusions that an ordinary dictionary may not explain, because it alludes to Marvell's most famous poem, "To His Coy Mistress," and to dark crime films (*noir* is "black" in French) of the 1940s that were often filmed in black and white featuring tough-talking, cynical heroes played by Humphrey Bogart and hardened, cold women played by Joan Crawford. Lauinger assumes that her reader will understand the allusions.

Allusions imply reading and cultural experiences shared by the poet and reader. Literate audiences once had more in common than they do today because more people had similar economic, social, and educational backgrounds. But a judicious use of specialized dictionaries, encyclopedias, and other reference tools such as Google Search on the Internet can help you decipher allusions that grow out of this body of experience. As you read more, you'll be able to make connections based on your own experiences with literature. In a sense, allusions make available what other human beings have deemed worth remembering, and that is certainly an economical way of supplementing and enhancing your own experience.

Lauinger's version of the *carpe diem* theme follows. What strikes you as particularly modern about it?

Ann Lauinger (b. 1948)

Marvell Noir   2005

Sweetheart, if we had the time,
A week in bed would be no crime.
I'd light your Camels, pour your Jack;
You'd do shiatsu on my back.
When you got up to scramble eggs,   5
I'd write a sonnet to your legs,
And you could watch my stubble grow.
Yes, gorgeous, we'd take it slow.
I'd hear the whole sad tale again:
A roadhouse band; you can't trust men;   10
He set you up; you had to eat,
And bitter with the bittersweet
Was what they dished you; Ginger lied;
You weren't there when Sanchez died;
You didn't know the pearls were fake . . .   15
Aw, can it, sport! Make no mistake,
You're in it, doll, up to your eyeballs!
Tears? Please! You'll dilute our highballs,
And make that angel face a mess
For the nice Lieutenant. I confess   20
I'm nuts for you—but take the rap?
You must think I'm some other sap!
And, precious, I kind of wish I was.
Well, when they spring you, give a buzz;
Guess I'll get back to Archie's wife,   25
And you'll get twenty-five to life.
You'll have time then, more than enough,
To reminisce about the stuff
That dreams are made of, and the men
You suckered. Sadly, in the pen   30
Your kind of talent goes to waste.
But Irish bars are more my taste
Than iron ones: stripes ain't my style.
You're going down; I promise I'll
Come visit every other year.   35
Now kiss me, sweet—the squad car's here.

CONSIDERATIONS FOR CRITICAL THINKING AND WRITING

1. **FIRST RESPONSE.** How does Lauinger's poem evoke Marvell's *carpe diem* poem (p. 382) and the tough-guy tone of a "noir" narrative, a crime story or thriller that is especially dark?

2. Discuss the ways in which time is a central presence in the poem.

3. Explain the allusion to dreams in lines 28–29.

4. **CONNECTION TO ANOTHER SELECTION.** Compare the speaker's voice in this poem with that of the speaker in Marvell's "To His Coy Mistress" (p. 382). What significant similarities and differences do you find?

This fourth love poem is a twentieth-century work in which the speaker's voice is a woman's. How does it sound different from the way the men speak in the previous three poems?

SHARON OLDS (B. 1942)

Last Night   1996

The next day, I am almost afraid.
Love? It was more like dragonflies
in the sun, 100 degrees at noon,
the ends of their abdomens stuck together, I
close my eyes when I remember. I hardly   5
knew myself, like something twisting and
twisting out of a chrysalis,
enormous, without language, all
head, all shut eyes, and the humming
like madness, the way they writhe away,   10
and do not leave, back, back,
away, back. Did I know you? No kiss,
no tenderness — more like killing, death-grip
holding to life, genitals
like violent hands clasped tight   15
barely moving, more like being closed
in a great jaw and eaten, and the screaming
I groan to remember it, and when we started
to die, then I refuse to remember,
the way a drunkard forgets. After,   20
you held my hands extremely hard as my
body moved in shudders like the ferry when its
axle is loosed past engagement, you kept me
sealed exactly against you, our hairlines
wet as the arc of a gateway after   25

a cloudburst, you secured me in your arms till I slept —
that was love, and we woke in the morning
clasped, fragrant, buoyant, that was
the morning after love.

CONSIDERATIONS FOR CRITICAL THINKING AND WRITING

1. **FIRST RESPONSE.** How is your response to this poem affected by the fact that the speaker is female? Explain why this is or isn't a *carpe diem* poem.

2. Comment on the descriptive passages of "Last Night." Which images seem especially vivid to you? How do they contribute to the poem's meaning?

3. Explain how the poem's tone changes from beginning to end.

4. **CONNECTION TO ANOTHER SELECTION.** How does the speaker's description of intimacy compare with Herrick's (p. 381) or Marvell's (p. 382)?

Perspective on Allusion

GENE WEINGARTEN (B. 1951), DAN WEINGARTEN (B. 1984),
AND DAVID CLARK (B. 1960)

Barney & Clyde   2012

CONSIDERATIONS FOR CRITICAL THINKING AND WRITING

1. Did you get the joke? Probably not, but how does a Google search help you?

2. Additional strips of *Barney & Clyde* can be found on the Internet, which provides information about the comic's characters as well as its writers and illustrator. How does that information serve to characterize the type of humor in the strip?

3. Choose a poem from Chapter 23, "Poems for Further Reading," that is rich in allusions and use the Internet to explain their function in the poem.

POEMS FOR FURTHER STUDY

THOMAS HARDY (1840–1928)

The Convergence of the Twain   1912

Lines on the Loss of the "Titanic"°

I

In a solitude of the sea
Deep from human vanity,
And the Pride of Life that planned her, stilly couches she.

II

Steel chambers, late the pyres
Of her salamandrine fires,°   5
Cold currents thrid,° and turn to rhythmic tidal lyres.   *thread*

III

Over the mirrors meant
To glass the opulent
The sea-worm crawls — grotesque, slimed, dumb, indifferent.

IV

Jewels in joy designed
To ravish the sensuous mind   10
Lie lightless, all their sparkles bleared and black and blind.

V

Dim moon-eyed fishes near
Gaze at the gilded gear
And query: "What does this vaingloriousness down here?"   15

VI

Well: while was fashioning
This creature of cleaving wing,
The Immanent Will that stirs and urges everything

"*Titanic*": A luxurious ocean liner, reputed to be unsinkable, which sank after hitting an iceberg on its maiden voyage in 1912. Only a third of the 2,200 passengers survived. 5 *salamandrine fires:* Salamanders were, according to legend, able to survive fire; hence the ship's fires burned even though under water.

VII

Prepared a sinister mate
For her — so gaily great —   20
A Shape of Ice, for the time far and dissociate.

VIII

And as the smart ship grew
In stature, grace, and hue,
In shadowy silent distance grew the Iceberg too.

IX

Alien they seemed to be: 25
No mortal eye could see
The intimate welding of their later history,

X

Or sign that they were bent
By paths coincident
On being anon twin halves of one august event,   30

XI

Till the Spinner of the Years
Said "Now!" And each one hears,
And consummation comes, and jars two hemispheres.

CONSIDERATIONS FOR CRITICAL THINKING AND WRITING

1. **FIRST RESPONSE.** Describe a contemporary disaster comparable to the sinking of the *Titanic*. How was your response to it similar to or different from the speaker's response to the fate of the *Titanic*?

2. How do the words used to describe the ship in this poem reveal the speaker's attitude toward the *Titanic*?

3. The diction of the poem suggests that the *Titanic* and the iceberg participate in something like an arranged marriage. What specific words imply this?

4. Who or what causes the disaster? Does the speaker assign responsibility?

DAVID R. SLAVITT (B. 1935)

Titanic   1983

Who does not love the *Titanic*?
If they sold passage tomorrow for that same crossing,
who would not buy?

To go down . . . We all go down, mostly
alone. But with crowds of people, friends, servants,   5
well fed, with music, with lights! Ah!

And the world, shocked, mourns, as it ought to do
and almost never does. There will be the books and movies
to remind our grandchildren who we were
and how we died, and give them a good cry.   10

Not so bad, after all. The cold
water is anesthetic and very quick.
The cries on all sides must be a comfort.

We all go: only a few, first-class.

CONSIDERATIONS FOR CRITICAL THINKING AND WRITING

1. **FIRST RESPONSE.** What, according to the speaker in this poem, is so
   compelling about the *Titanic*? Do you agree?
2. Discuss the speaker's tone. Is "Titanic" merely a sarcastic poem?
3. What is the effect of the poem's final line? What emotions does it elicit?
4. **CONNECTION TO ANOTHER SELECTION.** How does "Titanic" differ in
   its attitude toward opulence from Hardy's "The Convergence of the
   Twain" (p. 388)?
5. **CONNECTION TO ANOTHER SELECTION.** Which poem, "Titanic" or "The
   Convergence of the Twain," is more emotionally satisfying to you?
   Explain why.
6. **CONNECTION TO ANOTHER SELECTION.** Compare the speakers' tones in
   "Titanic" and "The Convergence of the Twain."

JOANNE DIAZ (B. 1972)

On My Father's Loss of Hearing   2006

I'd like to see more poems treat the deaf as being abled differently,
not lost or missing something, weakened, deficient.
   — from a listserv for the deaf

Abled differently — so vague compared
with deaf, obtuse but true to history,

from deave: to deafen, stun, amaze with
    noise.
Perhaps that's what we've done — amazed
    him with
our sorrows and complaints, the stupid
    jabs,
the loneliness of boredom in the house,

our wants so foreign to his own. What else
is there but loss? He's lost the humor of
sarcastic jokes, the snarky dialogue
of British films eludes him, phone calls
cast him adrift in that cochlear maze
that thrums and bristles even now, when
it doesn't have to: an unnecessary kind
of elegance, the vestige of a sense

© Jason Reblando. Reprinted by
permission of the photographer.

no longer obligated to transmit   15
the crack of thawing ice that fills the yard's
wide dip in winter, or the scrape of his
dull rake in spring, its prongs' vibration thrilled
by grass and peat moss. Imagine his desires
released like saffron pistils in the wind;   20
mark their trace against the cords of wood

he spent the summer splitting. See his quiet
flicker like a film, a Super-8
projected on the wall, and all of us
there, laughing on the porch without a sound.   25
No noisome cruelty, no baffled rage,
no aging children sullen in their lack.
Love hurts much less in this serenity.

CONSIDERATIONS FOR CRITICAL THINKING AND WRITING

1. **FIRST RESPONSE.** Why does the speaker prefer the word *deaf* to the phrase "abled differently" as a means of describing her father? Which description do you prefer? Why?

2. Explain how sound and silence move through the poem from beginning to end.

3. Choose a single word from each stanza that strikes you as particularly effective, and explain why you think Diaz chose it over other possibilities.

4. What do you make of the poem's final line? How does it relate to the tone of the rest of the poem?

Mary Oliver (b. 1935)

Oxygen   2005

Everything needs it: bone, muscles, and even,
while it calls the earth its home, the soul.
So the merciful, noisy machine

stands in our house working away in its
lung-like voice. I hear it as I kneel   5
before the fire, stirring with a

stick of iron, letting the logs
lie more loosely. You, in the upstairs room,
are in your usual position, leaning on your

right shoulder which aches   10
all day. You are breathing
patiently; it is a

beautiful sound. It is
your life, which is so close
to my own that I would not know   15

where to drop the knife of
separation. And what does this have to do
with love, except

everything? Now the fire rises
and offers a dozen, singing, deep-red   20
roses of flame. Then it settles

to quietude, or maybe gratitude, as it feeds
as we all do, as we must, upon the invisible gift:
our purest, sweet necessity: the air.

Considerations for Critical Thinking and Writing

1. **FIRST RESPONSE.** Though this is a poem about someone who is seriously ill, its tone isn't sad. Why not?

2. What is the connection between the loved one's breathing and the
   fire? How does the speaker's choice of words to describe each connect them?

3. In what sense might this celebration of oxygen be considered a love
   poem?

GWENDOLYN BROOKS (1917–2000)

We Real Cool

1960

:e To hear "We
Real Cool" read by
Gwendolyn Brooks, visit
bedfordstmartins.com/
meyerlit/epages.

The Pool Players.
Seven at the Golden Shovel.

We real cool. We
Left school. We

Lurk late. We
Strike straight. We

Sing sin. We
Thin gin. We

Jazz June. We
Die soon.

CONSIDERATIONS FOR CRITICAL THINKING AND WRITING

1. **FIRST RESPONSE.** How does the speech of the pool players in this poem help to characterize them? What is the effect of the pronouns coming at the ends of the lines? How would the poem sound if the pronouns came at the beginnings of lines?

2. What is the author's attitude toward the players? Is there a change in tone in the last line?

3. How is the pool hall's name related to the rest of the poem and its theme?

JOAN MURRAY (B. 1945)

We Old Dudes

2006

We old dudes. We
White shoes. We

Golf ball. We
Eat mall. We

Soak teeth. We
Palm Beach; We

Vote red. We
Soon dead.

> **WHEN I READ** "Reading stretches your mind and imagination. It lets you discover what you like and admire. Sometimes after I read a poem, I want to write one. It's as if someone's speaking my language, and I want to converse." —JOAN MURRAY

CONSIDERATIONS FOR CRITICAL THINKING AND WRITING

1. **FIRST RESPONSE.** Consider the poem's humor. To what extent does it make a serious point?

2. What does the reference to Palm Beach tell you about these "old dudes"?

3. **CREATIVE RESPONSE.** Write a poem similar in style that characterizes your life as a student.

4. **CONNECTION TO ANOTHER SELECTION.** Compare the themes of "We Old Dudes" and Brooks's "We Real Cool." How do the two poems speak to each other?

LOUIS SIMPSON (1923–2012)

In the Suburbs   *1963*

There's no way out.
You were born to waste your life.
You were born to this middleclass life

As others before you
Were born to walk in procession
To the temple, singing.

CONSIDERATIONS FOR CRITICAL THINKING AND WRITING

1. **FIRST RESPONSE.** Is the title of this poem especially significant? What images does it conjure up for you?

2. What does the repetition in lines 2–3 suggest?

3. Discuss the possible connotative meanings of lines 5 and 6. Who are the "others before you"?

JOHN KEATS (1795–1821)

Ode on a Grecian Urn   *1819*

I

Thou still unravished bride of quietness,
   Thou foster-child of silence and slow time,
Sylvan° historian, who canst thus express
   A flowery tale more sweetly than our rhyme:
What leaf-fringed legend haunts about thy shape   5
   Of deities or mortals, or of both,
      In Tempe or the dales of Arcady?°
What men or gods are these? What maidens loath?
   What mad pursuit? What struggle to escape?
      What pipes and timbrels? What wild ecstasy?   10

---

3 *Sylvan:* Rustic. The urn is decorated with a forest scene.   7 *Tempe, Arcady:* Beautiful rural valleys in Greece.

II

Heard melodies are sweet, but those unheard
  Are sweeter; therefore, ye soft pipes, play on;
Not to the sensual ear, but, more endeared,
  Pipe to the spirit ditties of no tone:
Fair youth, beneath the trees, thou canst not leave   15
  Thy song, nor ever can those trees be bare;
    Bold Lover, never, never canst thou kiss,
Though winning near the goal — yet, do not grieve;
  She cannot fade, though thou hast not thy bliss,
    For ever wilt thou love, and she be fair!   20

III

Ah, happy, happy boughs! that cannot shed
  Your leaves, nor ever bid the Spring adieu;
And, happy melodist, unwearièd,
  For ever piping songs for ever new;
More happy love! more happy, happy love!   25
  For ever warm and still to be enjoyed,
    For ever panting, and for ever young;
All breathing human passion far above,
  That leaves a heart high-sorrowful and cloyed,
    A burning forehead, and a parching tongue.   30

IV

Who are these coming to the sacrifice?
  To what green altar, O mysterious priest,
Lead'st thou that heifer lowing at the skies,
  And all her silken flanks with garlands drest?
What little town by river or sea shore,   35
  Or mountain-built with peaceful citadel,
    Is emptied of this folk, this pious morn?
And, little town, thy streets for evermore
  Will silent be; and not a soul to tell
    Why thou art desolate, can e'er return.   40

V

O Attic° shape! Fair attitude! with brede°
  Of marble men and maidens overwrought,
With forest branches and the trodden weed;
    Thou, silent form, dost tease us out of thought

41 *Attic:* Possessing classic Athenian simplicity;   *brede:* Design.

396   WORD CHOICE, WORD ORDER, AND TONE

As doth eternity: Cold Pastoral!   45
    When old age shall this generation waste,
      Thou shalt remain, in midst of other woe
Than ours, a friend to man, to whom thou say'st,
    Beauty is truth, truth beauty — that is all
      Ye know on earth, and all ye need to know.   50

CONSIDERATIONS FOR CRITICAL THINKING AND WRITING

1. **FIRST RESPONSE.** What does the speaker's diction reveal about his attitude toward the urn in this ode? Does his view develop or change?

2. How is the happiness in stanza 3 related to the assertion in lines 11-12 that "Heard melodies are sweet, but those unheard / Are sweeter"?

3. What is the difference between the world depicted on the urn and the speaker's world?

4. What do lines 49 and 50 suggest about the relation of art to life? Why is the urn described as a "Cold Pastoral" (line 45)?

5. Which world does the speaker seem to prefer, the urn's or his own?

6. Describe the overall tone of the poem.

7. **CONNECTION TO ANOTHER SELECTION.** Write an essay comparing the view of time in this ode with that in Marvell's "To His Coy Mistress" (p. 382). Pay particular attention to the connotative language in each poem.

8. **CONNECTION TO ANOTHER SELECTION.** Compare the tone and attitude toward life in this ode with those in John Keats's "To Autumn" (p. 410).

14

Images

© Joel Benjamin.

I think poetry is always a kind of faith.
It is the kind that I have.

— NATASHA TRETHEWEY

POETRY'S APPEAL TO THE SENSES

A poet, to borrow a phrase from Henry James, is one on whom nothing is lost. Poets take in the world and give us impressions of what they experience through images. An *image* is language that addresses the senses. The most common images in poetry are visual; they provide verbal pictures of the poets' encounters — real or imagined — with the world. But poets also create images that appeal to our other senses. Li Ho arouses several senses in "A Beautiful Girl Combs Her Hair" (p. 364):

Awake at dawn
she's dreaming
by cool silk curtains

fragrance of spilling hair
half sandalwood, half aloes

windlass creaking at the well
singing jade

These vivid images deftly blend textures, fragrances, and sounds that tease out the sensuousness of the moment.

🏠 Explore the
poetic element
in this chapter at
bedfordstmartins.com/
meyerlit.

397

Images give us the physical world to experience in our imaginations. Some poems, like the following one, are written to do just that; they make no comment about what they describe.

WILLIAM CARLOS WILLIAMS (1883–1963)

Poem   *1934*

As the cat
climbed over
the top of

the jamcloset
first the right   5
forefoot

carefully
then the hind
stepped down

into the pit of   10
the empty
flowerpot

This poem defies paraphrase because it is all an image of agile movement. No statement is made about the movement; the title, "Poem" — really no title — signals Williams's refusal to comment on the movements. To impose a meaning on the poem, we'd probably have to knock over the flowerpot.

We experience the image in Williams's "Poem" more clearly because of how the sentence is organized into lines and groups of lines, or stanzas. Consider how differently the sentence reads if it is arranged as prose:

> As the cat climbed over the top of the jamcloset, first the right fore-foot carefully then the hind stepped down into the pit of the empty flowerpot.

The poem's line and stanza division transforms what is essentially an awkward prose sentence into a rhythmic verbal picture. Especially when the poem is read aloud, this line and stanza division allows us to feel the image we see. Even the lack of a period at the end suggests that the cat is only pausing.

Images frequently do more than offer only sensory impressions, however. They also convey emotions and moods.

What mood is established in this next poem's view of Civil War troops moving across a river?

WALT WHITMAN (1819–1892)
Cavalry Crossing a Ford   *1865*

A line in long array where they wind betwixt green islands,
They take a serpentine course, their arms flash in the sun — hark to the
    musical clank,
Behold the silvery river, in it the splashing horses loitering stop to drink,
Behold the brown-faced men, each group, each person, a picture, the
    negligent rest on the saddles,
Some emerge on the opposite bank, others are just entering the ford — while,
Scarlet and blue and snowy white,
The guidon flags flutter gaily in the wind.

CONSIDERATIONS FOR CRITICAL THINKING AND WRITING

1. **FIRST RESPONSE.** Do the colors and sounds establish the mood of this
   poem? What *is* the mood?
2. How would the poem's mood have been changed if Whitman had
   used "look" or "see" instead of "behold" (lines 3–4)?
3. Where is the speaker as he observes this troop movement?
4. Does "serpentine" in line 2 have an evil connotation in this poem?
   Explain your answer.

Whitman seems to capture momentarily all of the troop's actions,
and through carefully chosen, suggestive details — really very few — he
succeeds in making "each group, each person, a picture." Specific details,
even when few are provided, give us the impression that we see the entire
picture; it is as if those are the details we would remember if we had
viewed the scene ourselves. Notice, too, that the movement of the "line
in long array" is emphasized by the continuous winding syntax of the
poem's lengthy lines.

Movement is also central to the next poem, in which action and
motion are created through carefully chosen verbs.

DAVID SOLWAY (B. 1941)
Windsurfing   *1993*

> **WHEN I READ** "The good
> poet always generates a sense
> of lexical surprise, an openness
> toward the unexpected, a feeling
> of novelty and delight."
> — DAVID SOLWAY

It rides upon the wrinkled hide
of water, like the upturned hull
of a small canoe or kayak
waiting to be righted — yet its law
is opposite to that of boats,   5
it floats upon its breastbone and
brings whatever spine there is to light.

A thin shaft is slotted into place.
Then a puffed right-angle of wind
pushes it forward, out into the bay,   10
where suddenly it glitters into speed,
tilts, knifes up, and for the moment's
nothing but a slim projectile
of cambered fiberglass,
peeling the crests.   15

                    The man's
clamped to the mast, taut as a guywire.
Part of the sleek apparatus
he controls, immaculate nerve
of balance, plunge and curvet,   20
he clinches all component movements
into single motion.
It bucks, stalls, shudders, yaws, and dips
its hissing sides beneath the surface
that sustains it, tensing   25
into muscle that nude ellipse
of lunging appetite and power.

And now the mechanism's wholly
dolphin, springing toward its prey
of spume and beaded sunlight,   30
tossing spray, and hits the vertex
of the wide, salt glare of distance,
and reverses.

                    Back it comes through
a screen of particles,   35
scalloped out of water, shimmer
and reflection, the wind snapping
and lashing it homeward,
shearing the curve of the wave,
breaking the spell of the caught breath   40
and articulate play of sinew, to enter
the haven of the breakwater
and settle in a rush of silence.

Now the crossing drifts
in the husk of its wake   45
and nothing's the same again
as, gliding elegantly on a film of water,
the man guides
his brash, obedient legend
into shore.   50

CONSIDERATIONS FOR CRITICAL THINKING AND WRITING

1. **FIRST RESPONSE.** Draw a circle around the verbs that seem especially effective in conveying a strong sense of motion, and explain why they are effective.

2. How is the man made to seem to be one with his board and sail?

3. How does the rhythm of the poem change beginning with line 44?

4. **CONNECTION TO ANOTHER SELECTION.** Consider the effects of the images in "Windsurfing" and Li Ho's "A Beautiful Girl Combs Her Hair" (p. 364). In an essay, explain how these images elicit the emotional responses they do.

"Windsurfing" is awash with images of speed, fluidity, and power. Even the calming aftermath of the breakwater is described as a "rush of silence," adding to the sense of motion that is detailed and expanded throughout the poem. The tone of the images and mood of the speaker are consistent in Solway's "Windsurfing." In Matthew Arnold's "Dover Beach," however, they shift as the theme is developed.

MATTHEW ARNOLD (1822–1888)

Dover Beach   1867

The sea is calm tonight.
The tide is full, the moon lies fair
Upon the straits; — on the French coast the light
Gleams and is gone; the cliffs of England stand,
Glimmering and vast, out in the tranquil bay.   5
Come to the window, sweet is the night-air!
Only, from the long line of spray
Where the sea meets the moon-blanched land,
Listen! you hear the grating roar
Of pebbles which the waves draw back, and fling,   10
At their return, up the high strand,
Begin, and cease, and then again begin,
With tremulous cadence slow, and bring
The eternal note of sadness in.

Sophocles long ago   15
Heard it on the Aegean, and it brought
Into his mind the turbid ebb and flow
Of human misery;° we

15–18 *Sophocles . . . misery:* In *Antigone* (lines 656–77), Sophocles likens the disasters that beset the house of Oedipus to a "mounting tide."

Find also in the sound a thought,
Hearing it by this distant northern sea.   20

The Sea of Faith
Was once, too, at the full, and round earth's shore
Lay like the folds of a bright girdle furled.
But now I only hear
Its melancholy, long, withdrawing roar,   25
Retreating, to the breath
Of the night-wind, down the vast edges drear
And naked shingles° of the world.   *pebble beaches*

Ah, love, let us be true
To one another! for the world, which seems   30
To lie before us like a land of dreams,
So various, so beautiful, so new,
Hath really neither joy, nor love, nor light,
Nor certitude, nor peace, nor help for pain;
And we are here as on a darkling plain   35
Swept with confused alarms of struggle and flight,
Where ignorant armies clash by night.

CONSIDERATIONS FOR CRITICAL THINKING AND WRITING

1. **FIRST RESPONSE.** Discuss what you consider to be this poem's central point. How do the speaker's descriptions of the ocean work toward making that point?

2. Contrast the images in lines 4–8 and 9–13. How do they reveal the speaker's mood? To whom is he speaking?

3. What is the cause of the "sadness" in line 14? What is the speaker's response to the ebbing "Sea of Faith"? Is there anything to replace his sense of loss?

4. What details of the beach seem related to the ideas in the poem? How is the sea used differently in lines 1–14 and 21–28?

5. Describe the differences in tone between lines 1–8 and 35–37. What has caused the change?

6. **CONNECTION TO ANOTHER SELECTION.** Explain how the images in Wilfred Owen's "Dulce et Decorum Est" (p. 407) develop further the ideas and sentiments suggested by Arnold's final line concerning "ignorant armies clash[ing] by night."

Consider the appetite for images displayed in the celebration of poetry in the following poem.

RUTH FORMAN (B. 1968)
Poetry Should Ride the Bus   1993

poetry should hopscotch in a polka dot dress
wheel cartwheels
n hold your hand
when you walk past the yellow crackhouse

poetry should wear bright red lipstick
n practice kisses in the mirror
for all the fine young men with fades
shootin craps around the corner

poetry should dress in fine plum linen suits
n not be so educated that it don't stop in
every now n then to sit on the porch
and talk about the comins and goins of the
    world

Photograph by Christine Bennett,
www.cbimages.org.

poetry should ride the bus
in a fat woman's Safeway bag
between the greens n chicken wings   15
to be served with tuesday's dinner

poetry should drop by a sweet potato pie
ask about the grandchildren
n sit through a whole photo album
on a orange plastic covered lazy boy with no place to go   20

poetry should sing red revolution love songs
that massage your scalp
and bring hope to your blood
when you think you're too old to fight

yeah   25
poetry should whisper electric blue magic
all the years of your life
never forgettin to look you in the soul
every once in a while
n smile   30

CONSIDERATIONS FOR CRITICAL THINKING AND WRITING

1. **FIRST RESPONSE.** How do the images in each stanza reveal the speaker's attitude toward poetry? Do you agree with the poem's ideas about what poetry should do and be?

2. What does the poem's diction tell you about the speaker?

3. Discuss the tone of this poem and why you think it does or does not work.

4. **CONNECTION TO ANOTHER SELECTION.** How does Forman's speaker's view of poetry compare with that of the speaker in Billy Collins's "Introduction to Poetry" (p. 356)?

POEMS FOR FURTHER STUDY

AMY LOWELL (1874–1925)

The Pond   1919

Cold, wet leaves
Floating on moss-colored water,
And the croaking of frogs—
Cracked bell-notes in the twilight.

CONSIDERATIONS FOR CRITICAL THINKING AND WRITING

1. **FIRST RESPONSE.** This poem is not a complete sentence. What is missing? Does it matter in terms of understanding what is described by the images?

2. What senses are stimulated by the images? Which sense seems to be the most dominant in the poem? Why?

3. **CREATIVE RESPONSE.** Is the title of the poem necessary to convey its meaning? Choose an appropriate alternate title and explain how it subtly suggests something different from "The Pond."

WILLIAM BLAKE (1757–1827)

London   1794

I wander through each chartered° street,   *defined by law*
Near where the chartered Thames does flow,
And mark in every face I meet
Marks of weakness, marks of woe.

In every cry of every man,   5
In every Infant's cry of fear,
In every voice, in every ban,
The mind-forged manacles I hear.

How the Chimney-sweeper's cry
Every black'ning Church appalls;   10
And the hapless Soldier's sigh
Runs in blood down Palace walls.

But most through midnight streets I hear
How the youthful Harlot's curse

Blasts the new-born Infant's tear,   15
And blights with plagues the Marriage hearse.

CONSIDERATIONS FOR CRITICAL THINKING AND WRITING

1. FIRST RESPONSE. What feelings do the visual images in this poem suggest to you?

2. What is the predominant sound heard in the poem?

3. What is the meaning of line 8? What is the cause of the problems
   that the speaker sees and hears in London? Does the speaker suggest
   additional causes?

4. The image in lines 11 and 12 cannot be read literally. Comment on its
   effectiveness.

5. How does Blake's use of denotative and connotative language enrich
   this poem's meaning?

6. An earlier version of Blake's last stanza appeared this way:

   > But most the midnight harlot's curse
   > From every dismal street I hear,
   > Weaves around the marriage hearse
   > And blasts the new-born infant's tear.

   Examine carefully the differences between the two versions. How do
   Blake's revisions affect his picture of London life? Which version do
   you think is more effective? Why?

MARY ROBINSON (1758–1800)

London's Summer Morning   *1806*

Who has not wak'd to list° the busy sounds   *listen to*
Of summer's morning, in the sultry smoke
Of noisy London? On the pavement hot
The sooty chimney-boy, with dingy face
And tatter'd covering, shrilly bawls his trade,   5
Rousing the sleepy housemaid. At the door
The milk-pail rattles, and the tinkling bell
Proclaims the dustman's office; while the street
Is lost in clouds impervious. Now begins
The din of hackney-coaches, waggons, carts;   10
While tinmen's shops, and noisy trunk-makers,
Knife-grinders, coopers, squeaking cork-cutters,
Fruit-barrows, and the hunger-giving cries
Of vegetable venders, fill the air.
Now ev'ry shop displays its varied trade,   15
And the fresh-sprinkled pavement cools the feet
Of early walkers. At the private door
The ruddy housemaid twirls the busy mop,

Annoying the smart 'prentice, or neat girl,
Tripping with band-box° lightly. Now the sun   *hatbox*   20
Darts burning splendour on the glitt'ring pane,
Save where the canvas awning throws a shade
On the gay merchandize. Now, spruce and trim,
In shops (where beauty smiles with industry),
Sits the smart damsel; while the passenger   25
Peeps thro' the window, watching ev'ry charm.
Now pastry dainties catch the eye minute
Of humming insects, while the limy snare
Waits to enthral them. Now the lamp-lighter
Mounts the tall ladder, nimbly vent'rous,   30
To trim the half-fill'd lamp; while at his feet
The pot-boy° yells discordant! All along   *drink server*
The sultry pavement, the old-clothes-man cries
In tones monotonous, and side-long views
The area for his traffic: now the bag   35
Is slily open'd, and the half-worn suit
(Sometimes the pilfer'd treasure of the base
Domestic spoiler), for one half its worth,
Sinks in the green abyss. The porter now
Bears his huge load along the burning way;   40
And the poor poet wakes from busy dreams,
To paint the summer morning.

CONSIDERATIONS FOR CRITICAL THINKING AND WRITING

1. **FIRST RESPONSE.** How effective is this picture of a London summer
   morning in 1806? Which images do you find particularly effective?

2. How does the end of the poem bring us full circle to its beginning?
   What effect does this structure have on your understanding of the
   poem?

3. **CREATIVE RESPONSE.** Try writing about the start of your own day — in
   the dormitory, at home, at the start of a class — using a series of
   images that provide a vivid sense of what happens and how you experience it.

4. **CONNECTION TO ANOTHER SELECTION.** How does Robinson's description of London differ from William Blake's "London," the previous
   poem? What would you say is the essential difference in purpose
   between the two poems?

Emily Dickinson (1830–1886)
Wild Nights — Wild Nights!   *c. 1861*

Wild Nights — Wild Nights!
Were I with thee
Wild Nights should be
Our luxury!

Futile — the Winds —   5
To a Heart in port —
Done with the Compass —
Done with the Chart!

Rowing in Eden —
Ah, the Sea!   10
Might I but moor — Tonight —
In Thee!

Considerations for Critical Thinking and Writing

1. **FIRST RESPONSE.** Thomas Wentworth Higginson, Dickinson's mentor, once said he was afraid that some "malignant" readers might "read into [a poem like this] more than that virgin recluse ever dreamed of putting there." What do you think?

2. Look up the meaning of *luxury* in a dictionary. Why does this word work especially well here?

3. Given the imagery of the final stanza, do you think the speaker is a man or a woman? Explain why.

4. **CONNECTION TO ANOTHER SELECTION.** Write an essay that compares the voice, figures of speech, and theme of this poem with those of Margaret Atwood's "you fit into me" (p. 414).

Wilfred Owen (1893–1918)
Dulce et Decorum Est   *1920*

Bent double, like old beggars under sacks,
Knock-kneed, coughing like hags, we cursed through sludge,
Till on the haunting flares we turned our backs,
And towards our distant rest began to trudge.
Men marched asleep. Many had lost their boots,   5
But limped on, blood-shod. All went lame, all blind;
Drunk with fatigue; deaf even to the hoots
Of gas-shells dropping softly behind.

Gas! GAS! Quick, boys! — An ecstasy of fumbling,
Fitting the clumsy helmets just in time;   10

But someone still was yelling out and stumbling
And flound'ring like a man in fire or lime . . . .
Dim through the misty panes and thick green light,
As under a green sea, I saw him drowning.

In all my dreams before my helpless sight   15
He plunges at me, guttering, choking, drowning.

If in some smothering dreams, you too could pace
Behind the wagon that we flung him in,
And watch the white eyes writhing in his face,
His hanging face, like a devil's sick of sin;   20
If you could hear, at every jolt, the blood
Come gargling from the froth-corrupted lungs,
Obscene as cancer, bitter as the cud
Of vile, incurable sores on innocent tongues, —
My friend, you would not tell with such high zest   25
To children ardent for some desperate glory,
The old lie: *Dulce et decorum est*
Pro patria mori.

CONSIDERATIONS FOR CRITICAL THINKING AND WRITING

1. **FIRST RESPONSE.** The Latin quotation in lines 27 and 28 is from Horace: "It is sweet and fitting to die for one's country." Owen served as a British soldier during World War I and was killed. Is this poem unpatriotic? What is its purpose?

2. Which images in the poem are most vivid? To which senses do they speak?

3. Describe the speaker's tone. What is his relationship to his audience?

4. How are the images of the soldiers in this poem different from the images that typically appear in recruiting posters?

RUTH FAINLIGHT (B. 1931)

Crocuses   2006

Pale, bare, tender stems rising
from the muddy winter-faded grass,

shivering petals the almost luminous
blue and mauve of bruises on the naked

bodies of men, women, children
herded into a forest clearing

before the shouted order, crack of gunfire,
final screams and prayers and moans.

CONSIDERATIONS FOR CRITICAL THINKING AND WRITING

1. **FIRST RESPONSE.** Comment on Fainlight's choice of title. What effect does it have on your reading of the poem?

2. Trace your response to each image in the poem and describe the poem's tone as it moves from line to line.

3. **CREATIVE RESPONSE.** Try writing an eight-line poem in the style of Fainlight's based on images that gradually but radically shift in tone.

SALLY CROFT (B. 1935)

Home-Baked Bread   *1981*

*Nothing gives a household a greater sense of stability and common comfort than
the aroma of cooling bread. Begin, if you like, with a loaf of whole wheat, which
requires neither sifting nor kneading, and go on from there to more cunning
triumphs.*

                                    — *The Joy of Cooking*

What is it she is not saying?
Cunning triumphs. It rings
of insinuation. Step into my kitchen,
I have prepared a cunning triumph
for you. Spices and herbs   5
sealed in this porcelain jar,

a treasure of my great-aunt
who sat up past midnight
in her Massachusetts bedroom
when the moon was dark. Come,   10
rest your feet. I'll make
you tea with honey and slices

of warm bread spread with peach butter.
I picked the fruit this morning
still fresh with dew. The fragrance   15
is seductive? I hoped you would say that.
See how the heat rises
when the bread opens. Come,

we'll eat together, the small flakes
have scarcely any flavor. What cunning   20
triumphs we can discover in my upstairs room
where peach trees breathe their sweetness
beside the open window and
sun lies like honey on the floor.

CONSIDERATIONS FOR CRITICAL THINKING AND WRITING

1. **FIRST RESPONSE.** Why does the speaker in this poem seize on the phrase "cunning triumphs" from the *Joy of Cooking* excerpt?

2. Distinguish between the voice we hear in lines 1–3 and the second voice in lines 3–24. Who is the "you" in the poem?

3. Why is the word "insinuation" an especially appropriate choice in line 3?

4. How do the images in lines 20–24 bring together all of the senses evoked in the preceding lines?

5. **CREATIVE RESPONSE.** Write a paragraph—or stanza—that describes the sensuous (and perhaps sensual) qualities of a food you enjoy.

JOHN KEATS (1795–1821)

To Autumn   *1819*

I

Season of mists and mellow fruitfulness,
    Close bosom-friend of the maturing sun;
Conspiring with him how to load and bless
    With fruit the vines that round the thatch-eves run;
To bend with apples the mossed cottage-trees,   5
    And fill all fruit with ripeness to the core;
        To swell the gourd, and plump the hazel shells
    With a sweet kernel; to set budding more,
And still more, later flowers for the bees,
Until they think warm days will never cease,   10
        For summer has o'er-brimmed their clammy cells.

II

Who hath not seen thee oft amid thy store?
    Sometimes whoever seeks abroad may find
Thee sitting careless on a granary floor,
    Thy hair soft-lifted by the winnowing wind;   15
Or on a half-reaped furrow sound asleep,
    Drowsed with the fume of poppies, while thy hook°   *scythe*
        Spares the next swath and all its twinèd flowers:
And sometimes like a gleaner thou dost keep
    Steady thy laden head across a brook;   20
    Or by a cider-press, with patient look,
        Thou watchest the last oozings hours by hours.

III

Where are the songs of spring? Ay, where are they?
   Think not of them, thou hast thy music too —
While barred clouds bloom the soft-dying day,   25
   And touch the stubble-plains with rosy hue;
Then in a wailful choir the small gnats mourn
   Among the river swallows,° borne aloft   *willows*
     Or sinking as the light wind lives or dies;
And full-grown lambs loud bleat from hilly bourn;°   *territory* 30
   Hedge-crickets sing; and now with treble soft
   The redbreast whistles from a garden-croft,
     And gathering swallows twitter in the skies.

CONSIDERATIONS FOR CRITICAL THINKING AND WRITING

1. **FIRST RESPONSE.** How is autumn made to seem like a person in each stanza of this ode?
2. Which senses are most emphasized in each stanza?
3. How is the progression of time expressed in the ode?
4. How does the imagery convey tone? Which words have especially strong connotative values?
5. What is the speaker's view of death?

15

Figures of Speech

© Bettmann/CORBIS.

> Like a piece of ice on a hot stove the
> poem must ride on its own melting.
>
> — ROBERT FROST

Figures of speech are broadly defined as a way of saying one thing in terms of something else. An overeager funeral director might, for example, be described as a vulture. Although figures of speech are indirect, they are designed to clarify, not obscure, our understanding of what they describe. Poets frequently use them because, as Emily Dickinson said, the poet's work is to "tell all the Truth but tell it slant" to capture the reader's interest and imagination. But figures of speech are not limited to poetry. Hearing them, reading them, or using them is as natural as using language itself.

Suppose that in the middle of a class discussion concerning the economic causes of World War II your history instructor introduces a series of statistics by saying, "Let's get down to brass tacks." Would anyone be likely to expect a display of brass tacks for students to examine? Of course not. To interpret the statement literally would be to wholly misunderstand the instructor's point that the time has come for a close look at the economic circumstances leading to the war. A literal response transforms the statement into the sort of hilariously bizarre material often found in a sketch by Stephen Colbert.

The class does not look for brass tacks because, in a nutshell, they understand that the instructor is speaking figuratively. They would

412

understand, too, that in the preceding sentence "in a nutshell" refers to brevity and conciseness rather than to the covering of a kernel of a nut. Figurative language makes its way into our everyday speech and writing as well as into literature because it is a means of achieving color, vividness, and intensity.

Consider the difference, for example, between these two statements:

Literal: The diner strongly expressed anger at the waiter.
Figurative: The diner leaped from his table and roared at the waiter.

The second statement is more vivid because it creates a picture of ferocious anger by likening the diner to some kind of wild animal, such as a lion or tiger. By comparison, "strongly expressed anger" is neither especially strong nor especially expressive; it is flat. Not all figurative language avoids this kind of flatness, however. Figures of speech such as "getting down to brass tacks" and "in a nutshell" are clichés because they lack originality and freshness. Still, they suggest how these devices are commonly used to give language some color, even if that color is sometimes a bit faded.

There is nothing weak about William Shakespeare's use of figurative language in the following passage from *Macbeth*. Macbeth has just learned that his wife is dead, and he laments her loss as well as the course of his own life.

WILLIAM SHAKESPEARE (1564–1616)

From *Macbeth* (Act V, Scene v)   *1605–1606*

Tomorrow, and tomorrow, and tomorrow
Creeps in this petty pace from day to day
To the last syllable of recorded time;
And all our yesterdays have lighted fools
The way to dusty death. Out, out, brief candle!   5
Life's but a walking shadow, a poor player,
That struts and frets his hour upon the stage,
And then is heard no more. It is a tale
Told by an idiot, full of sound and fury,
Signifying nothing.   10

This passage might be summarized as "life has no meaning," but such a brief paraphrase does not take into account the figurative language that reveals the depth of Macbeth's despair and his view of the absolute meaninglessness of life. By comparing life to a "brief candle," Macbeth emphasizes the darkness and death that surround human beings. The light of life is too brief and unpredictable to be of any comfort. Indeed, life for Macbeth is a "walking shadow," futilely playing a role that is more farcical than dramatic, because life is, ultimately, a desperate story filled with pain and devoid of significance. What the figurative language provides, then, is the emotional force of Macbeth's assertion; his comparisons are disturbing because they are so apt.

The remainder of this chapter discusses some of the most important figures of speech used in poetry. A familiarity with them will help you to understand how poetry achieves its effects.

SIMILE AND METAPHOR

The two most common figures of speech are simile and metaphor. Both compare things that are ordinarily considered unlike each other. A *simile* makes an explicit comparison between two things by using words such as *like, as, than, appears,* or *seems:* "A sip of Mrs. Cook's coffee is like a punch in the stomach." The force of the simile is created by the differences between the two things compared. There would be no simile if the comparison were stated this way: "Mrs. Cook's coffee is as strong as the cafeteria's coffee." This is a literal comparison because Mrs. Cook's coffee is compared with something like it, another kind of coffee. Consider how simile is used in this poem.

> Explore the poetic elements in this chapter at bedfordstmartins.com/ meyerlit.

MARGARET ATWOOD (B. 1939)

you fit into me   1971

you fit into me
like a hook into an eye

a fish hook
an open eye

© Sophie Bassouls/CORBIS SYGMA.

If you blinked on a second reading, you got the point of this poem because you recognized that the simile "like a hook into an eye" gives way to a play on words in the final two lines. There the hook and eye, no longer a pleasant domestic image of a clothing fastener or door latch that fits closely together, become a literal, sharp fishhook and a human eye. The wordplay qualifies the simile and drastically alters the tone of this poem by creating a strong and unpleasant surprise.

A *metaphor*, like a simile, makes a comparison between two unlike things, but it does so implicitly, without words such as *like* or *as:* "Mrs. Cook's coffee is a punch in the stomach." Metaphor asserts the identity of dissimilar things. Macbeth tells us that life *is* a "brief candle," life *is* "a walking shadow," life *is* "a poor player," life *is* "a tale / Told by an idiot." Metaphor transforms people, places, objects, and ideas into whatever the poet imagines them to be, and if metaphors are effective, the reader's experience, understanding, and appreciation of what is described are enhanced. Metaphors are frequently more demanding than similes because they are not signaled by particular words. They are both subtle and powerful.

Here is a poem about presentiment, a foreboding that something terrible is about to happen.

EMILY DICKINSON (1830–1886)
Presentiment — is that long Shadow — on the lawn —

ca. 1863

Presentiment — is that long Shadow — on the lawn —
Indicative that Suns go down —

The notice to the startled Grass
That Darkness — is about to pass —

The metaphors in this poem define the abstraction "Presentiment." The sense of foreboding that Dickinson expresses is identified with a particular moment — the moment when darkness is just about to envelop an otherwise tranquil, ordinary scene. The speaker projects that fear onto the "startled Grass" so that it seems any life must be frightened by the approaching "Shadow" and "Darkness" — two richly connotative words associated with death. The metaphors obliquely tell us ("tell it slant" was Dickinson's motto, remember) that presentiment is related to a fear of death, and, more important, the metaphors convey the feelings that attend that idea.

Some metaphors are more subtle than others because their comparison of terms is less explicit. Notice the difference between the following two metaphors, both of which describe a shaggy derelict refusing to leave the warmth of a hotel lobby: "He was a mule standing his ground" is a quite explicit comparison. The man is a mule; X is Y. But this metaphor is much more covert: "He brayed his refusal to leave." This second version is an *implied metaphor* because it does not explicitly identify the man with a mule. Instead it hints at or alludes to the mule. Braying is associated with mules and is especially appropriate in this context because of the mule's reputation for stub-bornness. Implied metaphors can slip by readers, but they offer the alert reader the energy and resonance of carefully chosen, highly con-centrated language.

Some poets write extended comparisons in which part or all of the poem consists of a series of related metaphors or similes. Extended metaphors are more common than extended similes. In "Catch" (p. 344), Robert Francis creates an **extended metaphor** that compares poetry to a game of catch. The entire poem is organized around this comparison. Because these comparisons are at work throughout the entire poem, they are called *controlling metaphors*. Extended comparisons can serve as a poem's organizing principle; they are also a reminder that in good poems metaphor and simile are not merely decorative but inseparable from what is expressed.

Notice the controlling metaphor in this poem, published posthu-mously, by a woman whose contemporaries identified her more as a wife and mother than as a poet. Bradstreet's first volume of poetry, *The Tenth Muse*, was published by her brother-in-law in 1650 without her prior knowledge.

ANNE BRADSTREET (CA. 1612–1672)

The Author to Her Book   1678

Thou ill-formed offspring of my feeble brain,
Who after birth did'st by my side remain,
Till snatched from thence by friends, less wise than true,
Who thee abroad exposed to public view;
Made thee in rags, halting, to the press to trudge,   5
Where errors were not lessened, all may judge.
At thy return my blushing was not small,
My rambling brat (in print) should mother call;
I cast thee by as one unfit for light,
Thy visage was so irksome in my sight;   10
Yet being mine own, at length affection would
Thy blemishes amend, if so I could:
I washed thy face, but more defects I saw,
And rubbing off a spot, still made a flaw.
I stretched thy joints to make thee even feet,   15
Yet still thou run'st more hobbling than is meet;
In better dress to trim thee was my mind,
But nought save homespun cloth in the house I find.
In this array, 'mongst vulgars may'st thou roam;
In critics' hands beware thou dost not come;   20
And take thy way where yet thou are not known.
If for thy Father asked, say thou had'st none;

And for thy Mother, she alas is poor,
Which caused her thus to send thee out of door.

    The extended metaphor likening her book to a child came naturally to Bradstreet and allowed her to regard her work both critically and affectionately. Her conception of the book as her child creates just the right tone of amusement, self-deprecation, and concern.

OTHER FIGURES

Perhaps the humblest figure of speech — if not one of the most familiar — is the pun. A *pun* is a play on words that relies on a word having more than one meaning or sounding like another word. For example, "A fad is in one era and out the other" is the sort of pun that produces obligatory groans. But most of us find pleasant and interesting surprises in puns. Here's one that has a slight edge to its humor.

EDMUND CONTI (B. 1929)

Pragmatist   *1985*

Apocalypse soon
Coming our way
Ground zero at noon
Halve a nice day.

    Grimly practical under the circumstances, the pragmatist divides the familiar cheerful cliché by half. As simple as this poem is, its tone is mixed because it makes us laugh and wince at the same time.
    Puns can be used to achieve serious effects as well as humorous ones. Although we may have learned to underrate puns as figures of speech, it is a mistake to underestimate their power and the frequency with which they appear in poetry. A close examination, for example, of Robert Frost's "Design" (p. 365) or almost any lengthy passage from a Shakespeare play will confirm the value of puns.
    Synecdoche is a figure of speech in which part of something is used to signify the whole: A neighbor is a "wagging tongue" (a gossip); a criminal is placed "behind bars" (in prison). Less typically, synecdoche refers to the whole used to signify the part: "Germany invaded Poland"; "Princeton won the fencing match." Clearly, certain individuals participated in these activities, not all of Germany or Princeton. Another related figure of speech is *metonymy*, in which something closely associated with a subject is substituted for it: "She preferred the silver screen [motion

pictures] to reading." "At precisely ten o'clock the paper shufflers [office workers] stopped for coffee."

Synecdoche and metonymy may overlap and are therefore some-times difficult to distinguish. Consider this description of a disapprov-ing minister entering a noisy tavern: "As those pursed lips came through the swinging door, the atmosphere was suddenly soured." The pursed lips signal the presence of the minister and are therefore a synecdoche, but they additionally suggest an inhibiting sense of sin and guilt that makes the bar patrons feel uncomfortable. Hence the pursed lips are also a metonymy, as they are in this context so closely connected with reli-gion. Although the distinction between synecdoche and metonymy can be useful, a figure of speech is usually labeled a metonymy when it over-laps categories.

Knowing the precise term for a figure of speech is, finally, less impor-tant than responding to its use in a poem. Consider how metonymy and synecdoche convey the tone and meaning of the following poem.

DYLAN THOMAS (1914–1953)

The Hand That Signed the Paper   1936

© Hulton-Deutsch Collection/CORBIS.

The hand that signed the paper felled a city;
Five sovereign fingers taxed the breath,
Doubled the globe of dead and halved a
    country;
These five kings did a king to death.

The mighty hand leads to a sloping
    shoulder,
The finger joints are cramped with chalk;
A goose's quill has put an end to murder
That put an end to talk.

The hand that signed the treaty bred a fever,
And famine grew, and locusts came;   10
Great is the hand that holds dominion over
Man by a scribbled name.

The five kings count the dead but do not soften
The crusted wound nor stroke the brow;
A hand rules pity as a hand rules heaven;   15
Hands have no tears to flow.

The "hand" in this poem is a synecdoche for a powerful ruler because it is a part of someone used to signify the entire person. The "goose's quill" is a metonymy that also refers to the power associated with the ruler's hand. By using these figures of speech, Thomas depersonalizes and ultimately dehumanizes the ruler. The final synecdoche tells us that "Hands have no tears to flow." It makes us see the political power behind the hand as remote and inhuman. How is the meaning of the poem enlarged when the speaker says, "A hand rules pity as a hand rules heaven"?

One of the ways writers energize the abstractions, ideas, objects, and animals that constitute their created worlds is through *personification*, the attribution of human characteristics to nonhuman things: Temptation pursues the innocent; trees scream in the raging wind; mice conspire in the cupboard. We are not explicitly told that these things are people; instead, we are invited to see that they behave like people. Perhaps it is human vanity that makes personification a frequently used figure of speech. Whatever the reason, personification, a form of metaphor that connects the nonhuman with the human, makes the world understandable in human terms. Consider this concise example from William Blake's *The Marriage of Heaven and Hell,* a long poem that takes delight in attacking conventional morality: "Prudence is a rich ugly old maid courted by Incapacity." By personifying prudence, Blake transforms what is usually considered a virtue into a comic figure hardly worth emulating.

Often related to personification is another rhetorical figure called *apostrophe*, an address either to someone who is absent and therefore cannot hear the speaker or to something nonhuman that cannot comprehend. Apostrophe provides an opportunity for the speaker of a poem to think aloud, and often the thoughts expressed are in a formal tone. John Keats, for example, begins "Ode on a Grecian Urn" (p. 394) this way: "Thou still unravished bride of quietness." Apostrophe is frequently accompanied by intense emotion that is signaled by phrasing such as "O Life." In the right hands—such as Keats's—apostrophe can provide an intense and immediate voice in a poem, but when it is overdone or extravagant it can be ludicrous. Modern poets are more wary of apostrophe than their predecessors because apostrophizing strikes many self-conscious twenty-first-century sensibilities as too theatrical. Thus modern poets tend to avoid exaggerated situations in favor of less charged though equally meditative moments, as in this next poem, with its amusing, half-serious cosmic twist.

JANICE TOWNLEY MOORE (B. 1939)

To a Wasp   1984

You must have chortled
finding that tiny hole
in the kitchen screen. Right
into my cheese cake batter

WHEN I WRITE "I began writing poetry as a freshman in college. I wrote using poetic diction and sometimes rhyme. Then I discovered 'modern poetry.' Seeing what was published in literary magazines quickly changed my style."
—JANICE TOWNLEY MOORE

you dived,   5
no chance to swim ashore,
no saving spoon,
the mixer whirring
your legs, wings, stinger,
churning you into such   10
delicious death.
Never mind the bright April day.
Did you not see
rising out of cumulus clouds
That fist aimed at both of us?   15

Moore's apostrophe "To a Wasp" is based on the simplest of domestic circumstances; there is almost nothing theatrical or exaggerated in the poem's tone until "That fist" in the last line, when exaggeration takes center stage. As a figure of speech, exaggeration is known as **overstatement** or **hyperbole** and adds emphasis without intending to be literally true: "The teenage boy ate everything in the house." Notice how the speaker of Andrew Marvell's "To His Coy Mistress" (p. 382) exaggerates his devotion in the following overstatement:

> An hundred years should go to praise
> Thine eyes and on thy forehead gaze,
> Two hundred to adore each breast,
> But thirty thousand to the rest:

That comes to 30,500 years. What is expressed here is heightened emotion, not deception.

The speaker also uses the opposite figure of speech, **understatement**, which says less than is intended. In the next section he sums up why he cannot take 30,500 years to express his love:

> The grave's a fine and private place,
> But none, I think, do there embrace.

The speaker is correct, of course, but by deliberately understating — saying "I think" when he is actually certain — he makes his point, that death will overtake their love, all the more emphatic. Another powerful example of understatement appears in the final line of Randall Jarrell's "The Death of the Ball Turret Gunner" (p. 374), when the disembodied voice of the machine-gunner describes his death in a bomber: "When I died they washed me out of the turret with a hose."

Paradox is a statement that initially appears to be self-contradictory but that, on closer inspection, turns out to make sense: "The pen is mightier than the sword." In a fencing match, anyone would prefer the sword, but if the goal is to win the hearts and minds of people, the art of persuasion can be more compelling than swordplay. To resolve the paradox, it is necessary to discover the sense that underlies the statement. If we see that "pen" and "sword" are used as metonymies for writing and violence, then the paradox rings true. *Oxymoron* is a condensed form of paradox in which two contradictory words are used together. Combinations such as "sweet sorrow," "silent scream," "sad joy," and "cold fire" indicate the kinds of startling effects that oxymorons can produce. Paradox is useful in poetry because it arrests a reader's attention by its seemingly stubborn refusal to make sense, and once a reader has penetrated the paradox, it is difficult to resist a perception so well earned. Good paradoxes are knotty pleasures. Here is a simple but effective one.

J. PATRICK LEWIS (B. 1942)
The Unkindest Cut   1993

Knives can harm you, heaven forbid;
Axes may disarm you, kid;
Guillotines are painful, but
There's nothing like a paper cut!

> **WHEN I WRITE** "Good writers are always searching for the strongest personified action verbs they can find. Verbs are muscles; adjectives are fat. As Mark Twain said, 'If you catch an adjective, kill it.' "
> —J. PATRICK LEWIS

We all know how bloody paper cuts can be, but this quatrain is also a humorous version of "the pen is mightier than the sword." The wounds escalate to the paper cut, which paradoxically is more damaging than even the broad blade of a guillotine. "The unkindest cut " of all (an allusion to Shakespeare's *Julius Caesar,* III.ii.188) is produced by chilling words on a page rather than cold steel, but it is more painfully fatal nonetheless.

The following poems are rich in figurative language. As you read and study them, notice how their figures of speech vivify situations, clarify ideas, intensify emotions, and engage your imagination. Although the terms for the various figures discussed in this chapter are useful for labeling the particular devices used in poetry, they should not be allowed to get in the way of your response to a poem. Don't worry about rounding up examples of figurative language. First relax and let the figures work their effects on you. Use the terms as a means of taking you further into poetry, and they will serve your reading well.

POEMS FOR FURTHER STUDY

GARY SNYDER (B. 1930)
How Poetry Comes to Me   1992

It comes blundering over the
Boulders at night, it stays
Frightened outside the
Range of my campfire

I go to meet it at the
Edge of the light

CONSIDERATIONS FOR CRITICAL THINKING AND WRITING

1. **FIRST RESPONSE.** How does personification in this poem depict the creative process?

2. Why do you suppose Snyder makes each successive line shorter?

3. **CREATIVE RESPONSE.** How would eliminating the title change your understanding of the poem? Substitute another title that causes you to reinterpret it.

ERNEST SLYMAN (B. 1946)

Lightning Bugs   *1988*

In my backyard,
They burn peepholes in the night
And take snapshots of my house.

CONSIDERATIONS FOR CRITICAL THINKING AND WRITING

1. **FIRST RESPONSE.** Explain why the title is essential to this poem.

2. What makes the description of the lightning bugs effective? How do the second and third lines complement each other?

3. **CREATIVE RESPONSE.** As Slyman has done, take a simple, common fact of nature and make it vivid by using a figure of speech to describe it.

WILLIAM CARLOS WILLIAMS (1883–1963)

To Waken an Old Lady   *1921*

Old age is
a flight of small
cheeping birds
skimming
bare trees   5
above a snow glaze.
Gaining and failing
they are buffeted
by a dark wind —
But what?   10
On harsh weedstalks
the flock has rested,
the snow

is covered with broken
seedhusks
and the wind tempered   15
by a shrill
piping of plenty.

CONSIDERATIONS FOR CRITICAL THINKING AND WRITING

1. **FIRST RESPONSE.** Consider the images and figures of speech in this
   poem and explain why you think it is a positive or negative assessment of old age.

2. How does the title relate to the rest of the poem?

3. **CONNECTION TO ANOTHER SELECTION.** Discuss the shift in tone in "To
   Waken an Old Lady" and in Colette Inez's "Back When All Was Continuous Chuckles" (p. 377).

WHEN I WRITE "Only on very rare occasions is a poem complete in a first draft. The first draft of a poem can sit for a long time waiting for its other half, or its meaning. Save everything you write, no matter how unhappy you are with it. You often won't see the beauty until later." —JUDY PAGE HEITZMAN

JUDY PAGE HEITZMAN (B. 1952)

The Schoolroom on the Second Floor of the Knitting Mill   1991

To hear "The Schoolroom on the Second Floor of the Knitting Mill" read by Judy Page Heitzman, visit bedfordstmartins.com/meyerlit/epages.

While most of us copied letters out of books,
Mrs. Lawrence carved and cleaned her nails.
Now the red and buff cardinals at my back-room window
make me miss her, her room, her hallway,
even the chimney outside   5
that broke up the sky.

In my memory it is afternoon.
Sun streams in through the door
next to the fire escape where we are lined up
getting our coats on to go out to the playground,   10
the tether ball, its towering height, the swings.
She tells me to make sure the line
does not move up over the threshold.
That would be dangerous.
So I stand guard at the door.   15
Somehow it happens
the way things seem to happen when we're not really looking,

or we are looking, just not the right way.
Kids crush up like cattle, pushing me over the line.

Judy is not a good leader is all Mrs. Lawrence says.   20
She says it quietly. Still, everybody hears.
Her arms hang down like sausages.
I hear her every time I fail.

CONSIDERATIONS FOR CRITICAL THINKING AND WRITING

1. **FIRST RESPONSE.** Does your impression of Mrs. Lawrence change from the beginning to the end of the poem? How so?
2. How can line 2 be read as an implied metaphor?
3. Discuss the use of similes in the poem. How do they contribute to the poem's meaning?

WILLIAM WORDSWORTH (1770–1850)

London, 1802   *1802*

Milton!° thou should'st be living at this hour:
England hath need of thee: she is a fen
Of stagnant waters: altar, sword, and pen,
Fireside, the heroic wealth of hall and bower,
Have forfeited their ancient English dower   5
Of inward happiness. We are selfish men;
Oh! raise us up, return to us again;
And give us manners, virtue, freedom, power.
Thy soul was like a star, and dwelt apart:
Thou hadst a voice whose sound was like the sea: 10
Pure as the naked heavens, majestic, free,
So didst thou travel on life's common way,
In cheerful godliness; and yet thy heart
The lowliest duties on herself did lay.

1 *Milton:* John Milton (1608–1674), poet, famous especially for his religious epic *Paradise Lost* and his defense of political freedom.

CONSIDERATIONS FOR CRITICAL THINKING AND WRITING

1. **FIRST RESPONSE.** Describe the poem's tone. Is it nostalgic, angry, or something else?
2. Explain the metonymies in lines 3–6 of this poem. What is the speaker's assessment of England?

3. How would the effect of the poem be different if it were in the form of an address to Wordsworth's contemporaries rather than an apostrophe to Milton? What qualities does Wordsworth attribute to Milton by the use of figurative language?

ROBERT FROST (1874–1963)

Fire and Ice   *1923*

Some say the world will end in fire,
Some say in ice.
From what I've tasted of desire
I hold with those who favor fire.
But if it had to perish twice,
I think I know enough of hate
To say that for destruction ice
Is also great
And would suffice.

CONSIDERATIONS FOR CRITICAL THINKING AND WRITING

1. **FIRST RESPONSE.** What characteristics of human behavior does the speaker associate with fire and ice?
2. What theories about the end of the world are alluded to in lines 1 and 2?
3. How does the speaker's use of understatement and rhyme affect the tone of this poem?

JOHN DONNE (1572–1631)

A Valediction: Forbidding Mourning   *1611*

As virtuous men pass mildly away,
    And whisper to their souls to go,
While some of their sad friends do say,
    The breath goes now, and some say, no:

So let us melt, and make no noise,   5
    No tear-floods, nor sigh-tempests move;
'Twere profanation of our joys
    To tell the laity our love.

Moving of th' earth° brings harms and fears,   *earthquakes*
    Men reckon what it did and meant,   10

But trepidation of the spheres,°
   Though greater far, is innocent.

Dull sublunary° lovers' love
   (Whose soul is sense) cannot admit
Absence, because it doth remove   15
   Those things which elemented° it.   *composed*

But we by a love so much refined,
   That ourselves know not what it is,
Inter-assured of the mind,
   Care less, eyes, lips, and hands to miss.   20

Our two souls therefore, which are one,
   Though I must go, endure not yet
A breach, but an expansion,
   Like gold to airy thinness beat.

If they be two, they are two so   25
   As stiff twin compasses are two;
Thy soul the fixed foot, makes no show
   To move, but doth, if th' other do.

And though it in the center sit,
   Yet when the other far doth roam,   30
It leans, and hearkens after it,
   And grows erect, as that comes home.

Such wilt thou be to me, who must
   Like th' other foot, obliquely run;
Thy firmness makes my circle just,°   35
   And makes me end, where I begun.

---

11 *trepidation of the spheres:* According to Ptolemaic astronomy, the planets sometimes moved violently, like earthquakes, but these movements were not felt by
people on earth.   13 *sublunary:* Under the moon; hence, mortal and subject to
change.   35 *circle just:* The circle is a traditional symbol of perfection.

CONSIDERATIONS FOR CRITICAL THINKING AND WRITING

1. **FIRST RESPONSE.** A valediction is a farewell. Donne wrote this poem
for his wife before leaving on a trip to France. What kind of "mourning" is the speaker forbidding?
2. Explain how the simile in lines 1–4 is related to the couple in lines
5–8. Who is described as dying?
3. How does the speaker contrast the couple's love to "sublunary lovers'
love" (line 13)?
4. Explain the similes in lines 24 and 25–36.

JIM STEVENS (B. 1922)

Schizophrenia   1992

It was the house that suffered most.

It had begun with slamming doors, angry feet scuffing the carpets,
dishes slammed onto the table,
greasy stains spreading on the cloth.

Certain doors were locked at night,   5
feet stood for hours outside them,
dishes were left unwashed, the cloth
disappeared under a hardened crust.

The house came to miss the shouting voices,
the threats, the half-apologies, noisy   10
reconciliations, the sobbing that followed.

Then lines were drawn, borders established,
some rooms declared their loyalties,
keeping to themselves, keeping out the other.
The house divided against itself.   15

Seeing cracking paint, broken windows,
the front door banging in the wind,
the roof tiles flying off, one by one,
the neighbors said it was a madhouse.

It was the house that suffered most.   20

CONSIDERATIONS FOR CRITICAL THINKING AND WRITING

1. FIRST RESPONSE. What is the effect of personifying the house in this poem?
2. How are the people who live in the house characterized? What does their behavior reveal about them? How does the house respond to them?
3. Comment on the title. If the title were missing, what, if anything, would be missing from the poem? Explain your answer.

WALT WHITMAN (1819–1892)

A Noiseless Patient Spider   1868

A noiseless patient spider,
I mark'd where on a little promontory it stood isolated,
Mark'd how to explore the vacant vast surrounding,
It launch'd forth filament, filament, filament, out of itself,
Ever unreeling them, ever tirelessly speeding them.   5

And you O my soul where you stand,
Surrounded, detached, in measureless oceans of space,
Ceaselessly musing, venturing, throwing, seeking the spheres to
    connect them,
Till the bridge you will need be form'd, till the ductile anchor hold,
Till the gossamer thread you fling catch somewhere, O my soul.   10

CONSIDERATIONS FOR CRITICAL THINKING AND WRITING

1. **FIRST RESPONSE.** Spiders are not usually regarded as pleasant creatures. Why does the speaker in this poem liken his soul to one? What
   similarities are there in the poem between spider and soul? Are there
   any significant differences?
2. How do the images of space relate to the connections made between
   the speaker's soul and the spider?

ELAINE MAGARRELL (B. 1928)

The Joy of Cooking   *1988*

I have prepared my sister's tongue,
scrubbed and skinned it,
trimmed the roots, small bones, and gristle.
Carved through the hump it slices thin and neat.
Best with horseradish   5
and economical—it probably will grow back.
Next time perhaps a creole sauce
or mold of aspic?

I will have my brother's heart,
which is firm and rather dry,   10
slow cooked. It resembles muscle
more than organ meat
and needs an apple-onion stuffing
to make it interesting at all.
Although beef heart serves six   15
my brother's heart barely feeds two.
I could also have it braised
and served in sour sauce.

CONSIDERATIONS FOR CRITICAL THINKING AND WRITING

1. **FIRST RESPONSE.** Describe the poem's tone. Do you find it amusing,
   bitter, or something else?

2. How are the tongue and heart used to characterize the sister and brother in this poem?

3. How is the speaker's personality revealed in the poem's language?

4. **CONNECTION TO ANOTHER SELECTION.** Write an essay that explains how cooking becomes a way of talking about something else in this poem and in Sally Croft's "Home-Baked Bread" (p. 409).

16

Symbol, Allegory, and Irony

© Barbara Savage Cheresh.

Poetry is serious business; literature is the
apparatus through which the world tries to
keep intact its important ideas and feelings.
— MARY OLIVER

SYMBOL

A *symbol* is something that represents something else. An object, a person,
a place, an event, or an action can suggest more than its literal meaning.
A handshake between two world leaders might be simply a greeting, but
if it is done ceremoniously before cameras, it could be a symbolic gesture signifying unity, issues resolved, and joint policies that will be followed. We live surrounded by symbols. When a $100,000 Mercedes-Benz
comes roaring by in the fast lane, we get a quick glimpse
of not only an expensive car but an entire lifestyle that   Explore the
suggests opulence, broad lawns, executive offices, and   poetic elements in
power. One of the reasons some buyers are willing to   this chapter at
spend roughly the cost of five Chevrolets for a single   bedfordstmartins.com/
                                                              meyerlit.
Mercedes-Benz is that they are aware of the car's symbolic value. A symbol is a vehicle for two things at once: It functions as itself, and it implies
meanings beyond itself.

The meanings suggested by a symbol are determined by the context
in which it appears. The Mercedes could symbolize very different things
depending on where it was parked. Would an American political candidate be likely to appear in a Detroit blue-collar neighborhood with such a
car? Probably not. Although a candidate might be able to afford the car, it

would be an inappropriate symbol for someone seeking votes from all of the people. As a symbol, the German-built Mercedes would backfire if voters perceived it as representing an entity partially responsible for layoffs of automobile workers or, worse, as a sign of decadence and corruption. Similarly, a huge portrait of Mao Tse-tung conveys different meanings to residents of Beijing than it would to farmers in Prairie Center, Illinois. Because symbols depend on contexts for their meaning, literary artists provide those contexts so that the reader has enough information to determine the probable range of meanings suggested by a symbol.

In the following poem, the speaker describes walking at night. How is the night used symbolically?

ROBERT FROST (1874–1963)

Acquainted with the Night   1928

To hear "Acquainted with the Night" read by Robert Frost, visit bedfordstmartins.com/meyerlit/epages.

I have been one acquainted with the night.
I have walked out in rain — and back in rain.
I have outwalked the furthest city light.

I have looked down the saddest city lane.
I have passed by the watchman on his beat   5
And dropped my eyes, unwilling to explain.

I have stood still and stopped the sound of feet
When far away an interrupted cry
Came over houses from another street,

But not to call me back or say good-by;   10
And further still at an unearthly height
One luminary clock against the sky

Proclaimed the time was neither wrong nor right.
I have been one acquainted with the night.

In approaching this or any poem, you should read for literal meanings first and then allow the elements of the poem to invite you to symbolic readings, if they are appropriate. Here the somber tone suggests that the lines have symbolic meaning, too. The flat matter-of-factness created by the repetition of "I have" (lines 1–5, 7, 14) understates the symbolic subject matter of the poem, which is, finally, more about the "night" located in the speaker's mind or soul than it is about walking away from a city and back again. The speaker is "acquainted with the night." The importance of this phrase is emphasized by Frost's title and by the fact that he begins and ends the poem with it. Poets frequently use this kind of repetition to alert readers to details that carry more than literal meanings.

The speaker in this poem has personal knowledge of the night but does not indicate specifically what the night means. To arrive at the potential meanings of the night in this context, it is necessary to look closely at its connotations, along with the images provided in the poem. The connotative meanings of night suggest, for example, darkness, death, and grief. By drawing on these connotations, Frost uses a *conventional symbol*—something that is recognized by many people to represent certain ideas. Roses conventionally symbolize love or beauty; laurels, fame; spring, growth; the moon, romance. Poets often use conventional symbols to convey tone and meaning.

Frost uses the night as a conventional symbol, but he also develops it into a *literary* or *contextual symbol* that goes beyond traditional, public meanings. A literary symbol cannot be summarized in a word or two. It tends to be as elusive as experience itself. The night cannot be reduced to or equated with darkness or death or grief, but it evokes those associations and more. Frost took what perhaps initially appears to be an overworked, conventional symbol and prevented it from becoming a cliché by deepening and extending its meaning.

The images in "Acquainted with the Night" lead to the poem's symbolic meaning. Unwilling, and perhaps unable, to explain explicitly to the watchman (and to the reader) what the night means, the speaker nevertheless conveys feelings about it. The brief images of darkness, rain, sad city lanes, the necessity for guards, the eerie sound of a distressing cry coming over rooftops, and the "luminary clock against the sky" proclaiming "the time was neither wrong nor right" all help to create a sense of anxiety in this tight-lipped speaker. Although we cannot know what unnamed personal experiences have acquainted the speaker with the night, the images suggest that whatever the night means, it is somehow associated with insomnia, loneliness, isolation, coldness, darkness, death, fear, and a sense of alienation from humanity and even time. Daylight—ordinary daytime thoughts and life itself—seems remote and unavailable in this poem. The night is literally the period from sunset to sunrise, but, more important, it is an internal state being felt by the speaker and revealed through the images.

Frost used symbols rather than an expository essay that would explain the conditions that cause these feelings because most readers can provide their own list of sorrows and terrors that evoke similar emotions. Through symbol, the speaker's experience is compressed and simultaneously expanded by the personal darkness that each reader brings to the poem. The suggestive nature of symbols makes them valuable for poets and evocative for readers.

ALLEGORY

Unlike expansive, suggestive symbols, *allegory* is a narration or description usually restricted to a single meaning because its events, actions, characters, settings, and objects represent specific abstractions or ideas. Although the elements in an allegory may be interesting in themselves, the emphasis tends to be on what they ultimately mean. Characters may be given names such as Hope, Pride, Youth, and Charity; they have few, if any, personal qualities beyond their abstract meanings. These personifications are a form of extended metaphor, but their meanings are severely restricted. They are not symbols because, for instance, the meaning of a character named Charity is precisely that virtue.

There is little or no room for broad speculation and exploration in allegories. If Frost had written "Acquainted with the Night" as an allegory, he might have named his speaker Loneliness and had him leave the City of Despair to walk the Streets of Emptiness, where Crime, Poverty, Fear, and other characters would define the nature of city life. The literal elements in an allegory tend to be de-emphasized in favor of the message. Symbols, however, function both literally and symbolically, so that "Acquainted with the Night" is about both a walk and a sense that something is terribly wrong.

Allegory especially lends itself to *didactic poetry*, which is designed to teach an ethical, moral, or religious lesson. Many stories, poems, and plays are concerned with values, but didactic literature is specifically created to convey a message. "Acquainted with the Night" does not impart advice or offer guidance. If the poem argued that city life is self-destructive or sinful, it would be didactic; instead, it is a lyric poem that expresses the emotions and thoughts of a single speaker.

Although allegory is often enlisted in didactic causes because it can so readily communicate abstract ideas through physical representations, not all allegories teach a lesson. Here is a poem describing a haunted palace while also establishing a consistent pattern that reveals another meaning.

EDGAR ALLAN POE (1809–1849)

The Haunted Palace   *1839*

I

In the greenest of our valleys,
    By good angels tenanted,
Once a fair and stately palace —
    Radiant palace — reared its head.
In the monarch Thought's dominion —   5
    It stood there!
Never seraph spread a pinion
    Over fabric half so fair.

II

Banners yellow, glorious, golden,
    On its roof did float and flow;   10
(This — all this — was in the olden
    Time long ago)

And every gentle air that dallied,
   In that sweet day,
Along the ramparts plumed and pallid,   15
   A wingèd odor went away.

III

Wanderers in that happy valley
   Through two luminous windows saw
Spirits moving musically
   To a lute's well-tunèd law,   20
Round about a throne, where sitting
   (Porphyrogene!)°   *born to purple, royal*
In state his glory well befitting,
   The ruler of the realm was seen.

IV

And all with pearl and ruby glowing   25
   Was the fair palace door,
Through which came flowing, flowing, flowing
   And sparkling evermore,
A troop of Echoes whose sweet duty
   Was but to sing,   30
In voices of surpassing beauty,
   The wit and wisdom of their king.

V

But evil things, in robes of sorrow,
   Assailed the monarch's high estate;
(Ah, let us mourn, for never morrow   35
   Shall dawn upon him, desolate!)
And, round about his home, the glory
   That blushed and bloomed
Is but a dim-remembered story
   Of the old time entombed.   40

VI

And travelers now within that valley,
   Through the red-litten windows see
Vast forms that move fantastically
   To a discordant melody;
While, like a rapid ghastly river,   45
   Through the pale door,
A hideous throng rush out forever,
   And laugh — but smile no more.

On one level this poem describes how a once happy palace is desolated by "evil things" (line 33). If the reader pays close attention to the diction, however, an allegorical meaning becomes apparent on a second reading. A systematic pattern develops in the choice of words used to describe the palace, so that it comes to stand for a human mind. The palace, banners, windows, door, echoes, and throng are equated with a person's head, hair, eyes, mouth, voice, and laughter. That mind, once harmoniously ordered, is overthrown by evil, haunting thoughts that lead to the mad laughter in the poem's final lines. Once the general pattern is seen, the rest of the details fall neatly into place to strengthen the parallels between the surface description of a palace and the allegorical representation of a disordered mind.

Modern writers generally prefer symbol over allegory because they tend to be more interested in opening up the potential meanings of an experience instead of transforming it into a closed pattern of meaning. Perhaps the major difference is that while allegory may delight a reader's imagination, symbol challenges and enriches it.

IRONY

Another important resource writers use to take readers beyond literal meanings is *irony*, a technique that reveals a discrepancy between what appears to be and what is actually true. Here is a classic example in which appearances give way to the underlying reality.

Edwin Arlington Robinson (1869–1935)

Richard Cory   *1897*

Whenever Richard Cory went down town,
We people on the pavement looked at him:
He was a gentleman from sole to crown,
Clean favored, and imperially slim.

And he was always quietly arrayed,   5
And he was always human when he talked;
But still he fluttered pulses when he said,
"Good-morning," and he glittered when he walked.

And he was rich — yes, richer than a king —
And admirably schooled in every grace: 10
In fine, we thought that he was everything
To make us wish that we were in his place.

So on we worked, and waited for the light,
And went without the meat, and cursed the bread;
And Richard Cory, one calm summer night,   15
Went home and put a bullet through his head.

Richard Cory seems to have it all. Those less fortunate, the "people on the pavement," regard him as well-bred, handsome, tasteful, and richly endowed with both money and grace. Until the final line of the poem, the reader, like the speaker, is charmed by Cory's good fortune, so quietly expressed in his decent, easy manner. That final, shocking line, however, shatters the appearances of Cory's life and reveals him to have been a desperately unhappy man. While everyone else assumes that Cory represented "everything" to which they aspire, the reality is that he could escape his miserable life only as a suicide. This discrepancy between what appears to be true and what actually exists is known as *situational irony*: What happens is entirely different from what is expected. We are not told why Cory shoots himself; instead, the irony in the poem shocks us into the recognition that appearances do not always reflect realities.

Words are also sometimes intended to be taken at other than face value. *Verbal irony* is saying something different from what is meant. If after reading "Richard Cory," you said, "That rich gentleman sure was happy," your statement would be ironic. Your tone of voice would indicate that just the opposite was meant; hence verbal irony is usually easy to detect in spoken language. In literature, however, a reader can sometimes take literally what a writer intends ironically. The remedy for this kind of misreading is to pay close attention to the poem's context. There is no formula that can detect verbal irony, but contradictory actions and statements as well as the use of understatement and overstatement can often be signals that verbal irony is present.

Consider how verbal irony is used in this poem.

KENNETH FEARING (1902–1961)

AD   *1938*

Wanted: Men;
Millions of men are *wanted at once* in a big new field;
New, tremendous, thrilling, great.
If you've ever been a figure in the chamber of horrors,
If you've ever escaped from a psychiatric ward,   5
If you thrill at the thought of throwing poison into wells, have
      heavenly visions of people, by the thousands, dying in flames —

You are the very man we want
We mean business and our business is *you*
Wanted: A race of brand-new men.

Apply: Middle Europe;   10
No skill needed;
No ambition required; no brains wanted and no character allowed;

Take a permanent job in the coming profession
Wages: *Death.*

This poem was written as Nazi troops stormed across Europe at the start of World War II. The advertisement suggests on the surface that killing is just an ordinary job, but the speaker indicates through understatement that there is nothing ordinary about the "business" of this *"coming profession."* Fearing uses verbal irony to indicate how casually and mindlessly people are prepared to accept the horrors of war.

"AD" is a *satire*, an example of the literary art of ridiculing a folly or vice in an effort to expose or correct it. The object of satire is usually some human frailty; people, institutions, ideas, and things are all fair game for satirists. Fearing satirizes the insanity of a world mobilizing itself for war: His irony reveals the speaker's knowledge that there is nothing *"New, tremendous, thrilling,* [or] *great"* about going off to kill and be killed. The implication of the poem is that no one should respond to advertisements for war. The poem serves as a satiric corrective to those who would troop off armed with unrealistic expectations: Wage war, and the wages consist of death.

Dramatic irony is used when a writer allows a reader to know more about a situation than a character does. This creates a discrepancy between what a character says or thinks and what the reader knows to be true. Dramatic irony is often used to reveal character. In the following poem the speaker delivers a public address that ironically tells us more about him than it does about the patriotic holiday he is commemorating.

E. E. CUMMINGS (1894–1962)
next to of course god america i   1926

To hear "next to of course america i" read by E. E. Cummings, visit bedfordstmartins.com/meyerlit/epages.

"next to of course god america i
love you land of the pilgrims' and so forth oh
say can you see by the dawn's early my
country 'tis of centuries come and go
and are no more what of it we should worry   5
in every language even deafanddumb
thy sons acclaim your glorious name by gorry
by jingo by gee by gosh by gum
why talk of beauty what could be more beautiful than these heroic happy dead   10
who rushed like lions to the roaring slaughter
they did not stop to think they died instead
then shall the voice of liberty be mute?"

He spoke. And drank rapidly a glass of water

This verbal debauch of chauvinistic clichés (notice the run-on phrases and lines) reveals that the speaker's relationship to God and country is not, as he claims, one of love. His public address suggests a hearty mindlessness that leads to "roaring slaughter" rather than to

reverence or patriotism. Cummings allows the reader to see through the
speaker's words to their dangerous emptiness. What the speaker means
and what Cummings means are entirely different. Like Fearing's "AD,"
this poem is a satire that invites the reader's laughter and contempt in
order to deflate the benighted attitudes expressed in it.

When a writer uses God, destiny, or fate to dash the hopes and expectations of a character or humankind in general, it is called *cosmic irony*.
In "The Convergence of the Twain" (p. 388), for example, Thomas Hardy
describes how "The Immanent Will" brought together the *Titanic* and a
deadly iceberg. Technology and pride are no match for "the Spinner of
the Years." Here's a painfully terse version of cosmic irony.

STEPHEN CRANE (1871–1900)
A Man Said to the Universe   1899

A man said to the universe:
"Sir, I exist!"
"However," replied the universe,
"The fact has not created in me
A sense of obligation."

Unlike in "The Convergence of the Twain," there is the slightest bit
of humor in Crane's poem, but the joke is on us.

Irony is an important technique that allows a writer to distinguish
between appearances and realities. In situational irony a discrepancy exists
between what we expect to happen and what actually happens; in verbal
irony a discrepancy exists between what is said and what is meant; in dramatic irony a discrepancy exists between what a character believes and what
the reader knows to be true; and in cosmic irony a discrepancy exists between
what a character aspires to and what universal forces provide. With each form
of irony, we are invited to move beyond surface appearances and sentimental
assumptions to see the complexity of experience. Irony is often used in literature to reveal a writer's perspective on matters that previously seemed settled.

POEMS FOR FURTHER STUDY

BOB HICOK (B. 1960)
Making it in poetry   2004

The young teller
at the credit union
asked why so many
small checks

from universities?   5
Because I write
poems I said. Why
haven't I heard
of you? Because
I write poems   10
I said.

CONSIDERATIONS FOR CRITICAL THINKING AND WRITING

1. **FIRST RESPONSE.** Explain how the speaker's verbal irony is central to the poem's humor.

2. What sort of portrait of the poet-speaker emerges from this very brief poem?

KEVIN PIERCE (B. 1958)

Proof of Origin   *2005*

NEWSWIRE — A U.S. judge ordered a Georgia school district to remove from textbooks stickers challenging the theory of evolution.

Though close to their hearts is the version that starts
With Adam and Eve and no clothes,
What enables their grip as the stickers they strip
Is Darwinian thumbs that oppose.

CONSIDERATIONS FOR CRITICAL THINKING AND WRITING

1. **FIRST RESPONSE.** How do the rhymes contribute to the humorous tone?

2. Discuss the levels of irony in the poem.

3. How do you read the title? Can it be explained in more than one way?

CARL SANDBURG (1878–1967)

Buttons   *1905*

I have been watching the war map slammed up for advertising in front
        of the newspaper office.
Buttons — red and yellow buttons — blue and black buttons — are shoved
        back and forth across the map.

A laughing young man, sunny with freckles,
Climbs a ladder, yells a joke to somebody in the crowd,
And then fixes a yellow button one inch west
And follows the yellow button with a black button one inch west.

(Ten thousand men and boys twist on their bodies in a red soak along a
    river edge,
Gasping of wounds, calling for water, some rattling death in their throats.)
Who would guess what it cost to move two buttons one inch on the war
    map here in front of the newspaper office where the freckle-faced
    young man is laughing to us?

CONSIDERATIONS FOR CRITICAL THINKING AND WRITING

1. **FIRST RESPONSE.** Why is the date of this poem significant?
2. Discuss the symbolic meaning of the buttons and whether you think
   the symbolism is too spelled out or not.
3. What purpose does the "laughing young man, sunny with freckles"
   (line 3) serve in the poem?
4. **CONNECTION TO ANOTHER SELECTION.** Discuss the symbolic treatment of war in this poem and in Kenneth Fearing's "AD" (p. 436).

ALLEN BRADEN (B. 1968)

The Hemlock Tree   *2000*

Did I mention that last night an owl swept down
from her perch in the hemlock nearby
to devour a wild dove tamed by Safeway birdseed?
Of course I can reconstruct the scene for you
from knowing how this testimony   5
beyond the limits of your city implies the inevitable
circuit of hunger, from knowing how all life must
enter into a kind of covenant with nature
for the living shall consume
                    the flesh of the living   10
and from the delicate evidence at hand:
a wreath of down and drops of blood.
And right now you might be wondering
about the wisteria spiraling up that hemlock,
inching a bit higher with each passing year,   15
offering loveliness in powder-blue clusters
for a few weeks of May, and all the while killing
the tree with its gradual, constrictive, necessary beauty.

CONSIDERATIONS FOR CRITICAL THINKING AND WRITING

1. **FIRST RESPONSE.** Braden carefully chooses the flora and fauna for this
   poem. Explain why you think he makes these particular choices.
2. Describe the speaker's attitude toward nature.
3. Consider whether or not there is any humor in this poem. Is the tone
   consistent?

Jim Tilley (b. 1950)

Boys   2010

My friends and I couldn't buy cherry bombs
on our weekly allowances. We hoped
that plain firecrackers would be enough
to tear off arms and legs, a private's, not ours.
We were the generals — we ran the war,
decided where to plant soldiers in trenches
we sculpted in mounds left by bulldozers
on the construction site. After the flap
about the Curry boy losing an eye,
we imposed a ceasefire for a week.   10
Then came the all-out surge to do some
serious damage, the kind that requires you
to eat two bowls of cornflakes every day
to build your army from cereal-box toys.

Considerations for Critical Thinking and Writing

1. **FIRST RESPONSE.** How does the speaker's diction and tone influence your impressions about the boys' play?
2. Despite the seemingly casual qualities of these lines, what formal elements of a sonnet does this poem employ?
3. How might you read this poem differently if it were titled "War" rather than "Boys"?

Alden Nowlan (1933–1983)

The Bull Moose   1962

Down from the purple mist of trees on the mountain,
lurching through forests of white spruce and cedar,
stumbling through tamarack swamps,
came the bull moose
to be stopped at last by a pole-fenced pasture.   5

Too tired to turn or, perhaps, aware
there was no place left to go, he stood with the cattle.
They, scenting the musk of death, seeing his great head
like the ritual mask of a blood god, moved to the other end
of the field, and waited.   10

The neighbors heard of it, and by afternoon
cars lined the road. The children teased him
with alder switches and he gazed at them

like an old, tolerant collie. The women asked
if he could have escaped from a Fair.   15

The oldest man in the parish remembered seeing
a gelded moose yoked with an ox for plowing.
The young men snickered and tried to pour beer
down his throat, while their girl friends took their pictures.

The bull moose let them stroke his tick-ravaged flanks,   20
let them pry open his jaws with bottles, let a giggling girl
plant a little purple cap
of thistles on his head.

When the wardens came, everyone agreed it was a shame
to shoot anything so shaggy and cuddlesome.   25
He looked like the kind of pet
women put to bed with their sons.

So they held their fire. But just as the sun dropped in the river
the bull moose gathered his strength
like a scaffolded king, straightened and lifted his horns   30
so that even the wardens backed away as they raised their rifles.
When he roared, people ran to their cars. All the young men
leaned on their automobile horns as he toppled.

CONSIDERATIONS FOR CRITICAL THINKING AND WRITING

1. **FIRST RESPONSE.** How does the speaker present the moose and the
   townspeople? How are the moose and townspeople contrasted? Discuss specific lines to support your response.

2. Explain how the symbols in this poem point to a conflict between
   humanity and nature. What do you think the speaker's attitude
   toward this conflict is?

3. **CONNECTION TO ANOTHER SELECTION.** In an essay compare and contrast how the animals portrayed in "The Bull Moose" and in David
   Shumate's "Shooting the Horse" (p. 512) are used as symbols.

JULIO MARZÁN (B. 1946)

Ethnic Poetry   1994

The ethnic poet said: "The earth is maybe
a huge maraca / and the sun a trombone /
and life / is to move your ass / to slow beats."
The ethnic audience roasted a suckling pig.

The ethnic poet said: "Oh thank Goddy,
     Goddy /   5
I be me, my toenails curled downward /

> **WHEN I WRITE** "Words you are
> sure convey your truest feelings
> or thoughts may record only
> sentiment, not a line of poetry,
> while another arrangement,
> different words in another tone
> or rhythm, unlock and reveal
> what you really wanted to say."
> —JULIO MARZÁN

deep, deep, deep into Mama earth."
The ethnic audience shook strands of sea shells.

The ethnic poet said: "The sun was created black /
so we should imagine light / and also dream /   10
a walrus emerging from the broken ice."
The ethnic audience beat on sealskin drums.

The ethnic poet said: "Reproductive organs /
Eagles nesting California redwoods /
Shut up and listen to my ancestors."   15
The ethnic audience ate fried bread and honey.

The ethnic poet said: "Something there is that
doesn't love a wall / That sends
the frozen-ground-swell under it."
The ethnic audience deeply understood humanity.   20

CONSIDERATIONS FOR CRITICAL THINKING AND WRITING

1. **FIRST RESPONSE.** What is the implicit definition of ethnic poetry in this poem?

2. The final stanza quotes lines from Robert Frost's "Mending Wall" (p. 574). Read the entire poem. Why do you think Marzán chooses these lines and this particular poem as one kind of ethnic poetry?

3. What is the poem's central irony? Pay particular attention to the final line. What is being satirized here?

4. **CONNECTION TO ANOTHER SELECTION.** Write an essay that discusses the speakers' ideas about what poetry should be in "Ethnic Poetry" and in Mary Oliver's "The Poet with His Face in His Hands" (p. 369).

DENISE DUHAMEL (B. 1961)
How It Will End   2009

WHEN I WRITE "I don't really believe in writer's block as I believe in writing. I believe in free associating and free writing until I get to an original idea, a line or word that will inspire me for a poem." —DENISE DUHAMEL

We're walking on the boardwalk
but stop when we see a lifeguard and his
        girlfriend
fighting. We can't hear what they're saying,
but it is as good as a movie. We sit on a bench to find out
how it will end. I can tell by her body language   5
he's done something really bad. She stands at the bottom
of the ramp that leads to his hut. He tries to walk halfway down
to meet her, but she keeps signaling *Don't come closer.*
My husband says, "Boy, he's sure in for it,"
and I say, "He deserves whatever's coming to him."   10
My husband thinks the lifeguard's cheated, but I think

she's sick of him only working part-time
or maybe he forgot to put the rent in the mail.
The lifeguard tries to reach out
and she holds her hand like Diana Ross   15
when she performed "Stop in the Name of Love."
The red flag that slaps against his station means strong currents.
"She has to just get it out of her system,"
my husband laughs, but I'm not laughing.
I start to coach the girl to leave the no-good lifeguard,   20
but my husband predicts she'll never leave.
I'm angry at him for seeing glee in their situation
and say, "That's your problem — you think every fight
is funny. You never take her seriously," and he says,
"You never even give the guy a chance and you're always nagging,   25
so how can he tell the real issues from the nitpicking?"
and I say, "She doesn't nitpick!" and he says, "Oh really?
Maybe he should start recording her tirades," and I say
"Maybe he should help out more," and he says
"Maybe she should be more supportive," and I say   30
"Do you mean supportive or do you mean support him?"
and my husband says that he's doing the best he can,
that's he's a lifeguard for Christ's sake, and I say
that her job is much harder, that she's a waitress
who works nights carrying heavy trays and is hit on all the time   35
by creepy tourists and he just sits there most days napping
and listening to "Power 96" and then ooh
he gets to be the big hero blowing his whistle
and running into the water to save beach bunnies who flatter him
and my husband says it's not as though she's Miss Innocence   40
and what about the way she flirts, giving free refills
when her boss isn't looking or cutting extra large pieces of pie
to get bigger tips, oh no she wouldn't do that because she's
         a saint
and he's the devil, and I say, "I don't know why you can't
         just admit
he's a jerk," and my husband says, "I don't know why you
         can't admit   45
she's a killjoy," and then out of the blue the couple is making up.
The red flag flutters, then hangs limp.
She has her arms around his neck and is crying into his shoulder.
He whisks her up into his hut. We look around, but no one is
         watching us.

CONSIDERATIONS FOR CRITICAL THINKING AND WRITING

1. **FIRST RESPONSE.** Discuss how Duhamel creates the ironic situation
   in this boardwalk scene.

2. What is the significance of the red flag that appears in lines 17 and 47? Are there any other details that you think yield symbolic meanings?

3. Explain the embedded complexity of the end of the final line of the poem: "We look around, but no one is watching us."

4. **CONNECTION TO ANOTHER SELECTION.** Compare the tensions that are exposed in this poem and in Jill McDonough's "Accident, Mass. Ave." (p. 583).

Mark Halliday (b. 1949)

Graded Paper   *1991*

On the whole this is quite successful work:
your main argument about the poet's ambivalence —
how he loves the very things he attacks —
is mostly persuasive and always engaging.

At the same time,   5
                    there are spots
where your thinking becomes, for me,
alarmingly opaque, and your syntax seems to jump
backwards through unnecessary hoops,
as on p. 2 where you speak of "precognitive awareness   10
not yet disestablished by the shell that encrusts
each thing that a person actually says"
or at the top of p. 5 where your discussion of
"subverbal undertow miming the subversion of self-belief
woven counter to desire's outreach"   15
leaves me groping for firmer footholds.
(I'd have said it differently,
or rather, said something else.)
And when you say that women "could not fulfill themselves" (p. 6)
"in that era" (only forty years ago, after all!)   20
are you so sure that the situation is so different today?
Also, how does Whitman bluff his way into
your penultimate paragraph? He is the *last* poet
I would have quoted in this context!
What plausible way of behaving   25
does the passage you quote represent? Don't you think
literature should ultimately reveal possibilities for *action*?

Please notice how I've repaired your use of semicolons.

And yet, despite what may seem my cranky response,
I do admire the freshness of   30
your thinking and your style; there is

a vitality here; your sentences thrust themselves forward
with a confidence as impressive as it is cheeky. . . .
You are not
          me, finally,   35
and though this is an awkward problem, involving
the inescapable fact that you are so young, so young
it is also a delightful provocation.

CONSIDERATIONS FOR CRITICAL THINKING AND WRITING

1. **FIRST RESPONSE.** How do you characterize the grader of this paper based on the comments about the paper?

2. Is the speaker a man or a woman? What makes you think so? Does the gender of the speaker affect your reading of the poem? How?

3. Explain whether or not you think the teacher's comments on the paper are consistent with the grade awarded it. How do you account for the grade?

4. **CONNECTION TO ANOTHER SELECTION.** Compare the ways in which Halliday reveals the speaker's character in this poem with the strategies used by Robert Browning in "My Last Duchess" (below).

ROBERT BROWNING (1812–1889)

My Last Duchess   1842

Ferrara°

That's my last Duchess painted on the wall,
Looking as if she were alive. I call
That piece a wonder, now: Frà Pandolf's°
          hands
Worked busily a day, and there she stands.
Will't please you sit and look at her? I said
"Frà Pandolf" by design, for never read
Strangers like you that pictured
          countenance,
The depth and passion of its earnest glance,
But to myself they turned (since none puts by
The curtain I have drawn for you, but I)   10
And seemed as they would ask me, if they durst,
How such a glance came there; so, not the first
Are you to turn and ask thus. Sir, 'twas not

Courtesy of the National Portrait
Gallery, London.

Ferrara: In the sixteenth century, the duke of this Italian city arranged to marry a second time after the mysterious death of his very young first wife.   3 *Frà Pandolf:* A fictitious artist.

Her husband's presence only, called that spot
Of joy into the Duchess' cheek: perhaps   15
Frà Pandolf chanced to say "Her mantle laps
Over my lady's wrist too much," or "Paint
Must never hope to reproduce the faint
Half-flush that dies along her throat": such stuff
Was courtesy, she thought, and cause enough   20
For calling up that spot of joy. She had
A heart — how shall I say? — too soon made glad,
Too easily impressed; she liked whate'er
She looked on, and her looks went everywhere.
Sir, 'twas all one! My favor at her breast,   25
The dropping of the daylight in the West,
The bough of cherries some officious fool
Broke in the orchard for her, the white mule
She rode with round the terrace — all and each
Would draw from her alike the approving speech,   30
Or blush, at least. She thanked men, — good! but thanked
Somehow — I know not how — as if she ranked
My gift of a nine-hundred-years-old name
With anybody's gift. Who'd stoop to blame
This sort of trifling? Even had you skill   35
In speech — which I have not — to make your will
Quite clear to such an one, and say, "Just this
Or that in you disgusts me; here you miss,
Or there exceed the mark" — and if she let
Herself be lessoned so, nor plainly set
Her wits to yours, forsooth, and made excuse,
— E'en then would be some stooping; and I choose
Never to stoop. Oh sir, she smiled, no doubt,
Whene'er I passed her; but who passed without
Much the same smile? This grew; I gave commands;   45
Then all smiles stopped together. There she stands
As if alive. Will't please you rise? We'll meet
The company below, then. I repeat,
The Count your master's known munificence
Is ample warrant that no just pretense   50
Of mine for dowry will be disallowed;
Though his fair daughter's self, as I avowed
At starting, is my object. Nay, we'll go
Together down, sir. Notice Neptune, though,
Taming a sea-horse, thought a rarity,   55
Which Claus of Innsbruck° cast in bronze for me!

To hear "My Last Duchess" read by Richard Howard, visit bedfordstmartins.com/meyerlit/epages.

56 *Claus of Innsbruck:* Also a fictitious artist.

CONSIDERATIONS FOR CRITICAL THINKING AND WRITING

1. FIRST RESPONSE. What do you think happened to the duchess?

2. To whom is the duke addressing his remarks about the duchess in this poem? What is ironic about the situation?

3. Why was the duke unhappy with his first wife? What does this reveal about him? What does the poem's title suggest about his attitude toward women in general?

4. What seems to be the visitor's response (lines 53–54) to the duke's account of his first wife?

5. CONNECTION TO ANOTHER SELECTION. Write an essay describing the ways in which the speakers of "My Last Duchess" and Katharyn Howd Machan's "Hazel Tells LaVerne" (p. 379) inadvertently reveal themselves.

WILLIAM BLAKE (1757–1827)

The Chimney Sweeper   *1789*

When my mother died I was very young,
And my father sold me while yet my tongue
Could scarcely cry " 'weep! 'weep! 'weep! 'weep!"
So your chimneys I sweep, and in soot I sleep.

There's little Tom Dacre, who cried when his head,   5
That curled like a lamb's back, was shaved: so I said
"Hush, Tom! never mind it, for when your head's bare
You know that the soot cannot spoil your white hair."

And so he was quiet, and that very night,
As Tom was a-sleeping, he had such a sight!   10
That thousands of sweepers, Dick, Joe, Ned, and Jack,
Were all of them locked up in coffins of black.

And by came an Angel who had a bright key,
And he opened the coffins and set them all free;
Then down a green plain leaping, laughing, they run,   15
And wash in a river, and shine in the sun.

Then naked and white, all their bags left behind,
They rise upon clouds and sport in the wind;
And the Angel told Tom, if he'd be a good boy,
He'd have God for his father, and never want joy.   20

And so Tom awoke; and we rose in the dark,
And got with our bags and our brushes to work.
Though the morning was cold, Tom was happy and warm;
So if all do their duty they need not fear harm.

Considerations for Critical Thinking and Writing

1. **FIRST RESPONSE.** Discuss the validity of this statement: "'The Chimney Sweeper' is a sentimental poem about a shameful eighteenth-century social problem; such a treatment of child abuse cannot be taken seriously."

2. Characterize the speaker in this poem and describe his tone. Is his tone the same as the poet's? Consider especially lines 7, 8, and 24.

3. What is the symbolic value of the dream in lines 11 to 20?

4. Why is irony central to the meaning of this poem?

17

Sounds

Bettmann/CORBIS.

> In a poem the words should be as pleasing
> to the ear as the meaning is to the mind.
> — MARIANNE MOORE

LISTENING TO POETRY

Poems yearn to be read aloud. Much of their energy, charm, and beauty come to life only when they are heard. Poets choose and arrange words for their sounds as well as for their meanings. Most poetry is best read with your lips, teeth, and tongue because they serve to articulate the effects that sound may have in a poem. When a voice is breathed into a good poem, there is pleasure in the reading, the saying, and the hearing.

🏠 Explore the poetic element in this chapter at bedfordstmartins.com/ meyerlit.

The earliest poetry — before writing and painting — was chanted or sung. The rhythmic quality of such oral performances served two purposes: It helped the chanting bard remember the lines and it entertained audiences with patterned sounds of language, which were sometimes accompanied by musical instruments. Poetry has always been closely related to music. Indeed, as the word suggests, lyric poetry evolved from songs. "Western Wind" (p. 352), an anonymous Middle English lyric, survived as song long before it was written down. Had Robert Frost lived in a nonliterate society, he probably would have sung some version — a very different version to be sure—of "Acquainted with the Night" (p. 431) instead of writing it down. Even though Frost creates a speaking rather than a singing voice, the speaker's anxious tone is distinctly heard in any careful reading of the poem.

Like lyrics, early narrative poems were originally part of an anonymous oral folk tradition. A *ballad* told a story that was sung from one generation to the next until it was finally transcribed. Since the eighteenth century, this narrative form has sometimes been imitated by poets who write *literary ballads*. John Keats's "La Belle Dame sans Merci" (p. 581) is, for example, a more complex and sophisticated nineteenth-century reflection of the original ballad traditions that developed in the fifteenth century and earlier. In considering poetry as sound, we should not forget that poetry traces its beginnings to song.

Of course, reading a ballad is not the same as hearing it. Like the lyrics of a song, many poems must be heard—or at least read with listening eyes—before they can be fully understood and enjoyed. The sounds of words are a universal source of music for human beings. This has been so from ancient tribes to bards to the two-year-old child in a bakery gleefully chanting "Cuppitycake, cuppitycake!"

Listen to the sound of this poem as you read it aloud. How do the words provide, in a sense, their own musical accompaniment?

JOHN UPDIKE (1932–2009)

Player Piano   *1958*

My stick fingers click with a snicker
And, chuckling, they knuckle the keys;
Light-footed, my steel feelers flicker
And pluck from these keys melodies.

My paper can caper; abandon   5
Is broadcast by dint of my din,
And no man or band has a hand in
The tones I turn on from within.

At times I'm a jumble of rumbles,
At others I'm light like the moon,   10
But never my numb plunker fumbles,
Misstrums me, or tries a new tune.

The speaker in this poem is a piano that can play automatically by means of a mechanism that depresses keys in response to signals on a perforated roll. Notice how the speaker's voice approximates the sounds of a piano. In each stanza a predominant sound emerges from the carefully chosen words. How is the sound of each stanza tuned to its sense?

Like Updike's "Player Piano," this next poem is also primarily about sounds.

MAY SWENSON (1919–1989)

A Nosty Fright

1984

The roldengod and the soneyhuckle,
the sack eyed blusan and the wistle theed
are all tangled with the oison pivy,
the fallen nine peedles and the wumbleteed.

A mipchunk caught in a wobceb tried   5
to hip and skide in a dandy sune
but a stobler put up a EEP KOFF sign.
Then the unfucky lellow met a phytoon

and was sept out to swea. He difted for drays
till a hassgropper flying happened to spot   10
the boolish feast all debraggled and wet,
covered with snears and tot.

Loonmight shone through the winey poods
where rushmooms grew among risted twoots.
Back blats flew betreen the twees   15
and orned howls hounded their soots.

A kumkpin stood with tooked creeth
on the sindow will of a house
where a icked wold itch lived all alone
except for her stoombrick, a mitten and a kouse.   20

"Here we part," said hassgropper.
"Pere we hart," said mipchunk, too.
They purried away on opposite haths,
both scared of some "Bat!" or "Scoo!"

October was ending on a nosty fright   25
with scroans and greeches and chanking clains,
with oblins and gelfs, coaths and urses,
skinning grulls and stoodblains.

Will it ever be morning, Nofember virst,
skue bly and the sappy hun, our friend?   30
With light breaves of wall by the fayside?
I sope ho, so that this oem can pend.

At just the right moments Swenson transposes letters to create amusing sound effects and wild wordplays. Although there is a story lurking in

"A Nosty Fright," any serious attempt to interpret its meaning is confronted with "a EEP KOFF sign." Instead, we are invited to enjoy the delicious sounds the poet has cooked up.

Few poems revel in sound so completely. More typically, the sounds of a poem contribute to its meaning rather than become its meaning. Consider how sound is used in the next poem.

EMILY DICKINSON (1830–1886)

A Bird came down the Walk —   c. 1862

A Bird came down the Walk —
He did not know I saw —
He bit an Angleworm in halves
And ate the fellow, raw,

And then he drank a Dew   5
From a convenient Grass —
And then hopped sidewise to the Wall
To let a Beetle pass —

He glanced with rapid eyes
That hurried all around —   10
They looked like frightened Beads, I thought —
He stirred his Velvet Head

Like one in danger, Cautious,
I offered him a Crumb
And he unrolled his feathers   15
And rowed him softer home —

Than Oars divide the Ocean,
Too silver for a seam —
Or Butterflies, off Banks of Noon
Leap, plashless as they swim.   20

This description of a bird offers a close look at how differently a bird moves when it hops on the ground than when it flies in the air. On the ground the bird moves quickly, awkwardly, and irregularly as it plucks up a worm, washes it down with dew, and then hops aside to avoid a passing beetle. The speaker recounts the bird's rapid, abrupt actions from a somewhat superior, amused perspective. By describing the bird in human terms (as if, for example, it chose to eat the worm "raw"), the speaker is almost condescending. But when the attempt to offer a crumb fails and the frightened bird flies off, the speaker is left looking up instead of down at the bird.

With that shift in perspective the tone shifts from amusement to awe in response to the bird's graceful flight. The jerky movements of lines 1 to 13 give way to the smooth motion of lines 15 to 20. The pace of the first three stanzas is fast and discontinuous. We tend to pause at the end of each line, and this reinforces a sense of disconnected movements. In contrast, the final six lines are to be read as a single sentence in one flowing movement, lubricated by various sounds.

Read again the description of the bird flying away. Several *o*-sounds contribute to the image of the serene, expansive, confident flight, just as the *s*-sounds serve as smooth transitions from one line to the next. Notice how these sounds are grouped in the following vertical columns:

unr*o*lled	s*o*fter	T*oo*	hi*s*	Ocean	Banks
r*o*wed	*O*ars	N*oo*n	feather*s*	*s*ilver	plashle*ss*
h*o*me	*O*r	s*o*fter	*s*eam	a*s*
*O*cean	*o*ff	*O*ars	Butterflie*s*	*s*wim

This blending of sounds (notice how "Leap, plashless" brings together the *p*- and *l*-sounds without a ripple) helps convey the bird's smooth grace in the air. Like a feathered oar, the bird moves seamlessly in its element.

The repetition of sounds in poetry is similar to the function of the tones and melodies that are repeated, with variations, in music. Just as the patterned sounds in music unify a work, so do the words in poems, which have been carefully chosen for the combinations of sounds they create. These sounds are produced in a number of ways.

The most direct way in which the sound of a word suggests its meaning is through **onomatopoeia**, which is the use of a word that resembles the sound it denotes: *quack, buzz, rattle, bang, squeak, bowwow, burp, choo-choo, ding-a-ling, sizzle*. The sound and sense of these words are closely related, but such words represent a very small percentage of the words available to us. Poets usually employ more subtle means for echoing meanings.

Onomatopoeia can consist of more than just single words. In its broadest meaning the term refers to lines or passages in which sounds help to convey meanings, as in these lines from Updike's "Player Piano":

> My stick fingers click with a snicker
> And, chuckling, they knuckle the keys.

The sharp, crisp sounds of these two lines approximate the sounds of a piano; the syllables seem to "click" against one another. Contrast Updike's rendition with the following lines:

> My long fingers play with abandon
> And, laughing, they cover the keys.

The original version is more interesting and alive because the sounds of the words are pleasurable and reinforce the meaning through a careful blending of consonants and vowels.

Alliteration is the repetition of the same consonant sounds at the beginnings of nearby words: "*d*escending *d*ewdrops," "*l*uscious *l*emons." Sometimes the term is also used to describe the consonant sounds within words: "tres*p*asser's re*p*roach," "we*dd*ed la*d*y." Alliteration is based on sound rather than spelling. "*K*een" and "*c*ar" alliterate, but "*c*ar" does not alliterate with "*c*ite." Rarely is heavy-handed alliteration effective. Used too self-consciously, it can distract instead of strengthening meaning or emphasizing a relation between words. Consider the relentless *h*'s in this line: "Horrendous horrors haunted Helen's happiness." Those *h*'s certainly suggest that Helen is being pursued, but they have a more comic than serious effect because they are overdone.

Assonance is the repetition of the same vowel sound in nearby words: "asl*ee*p under a tr*ee*," "t*i*me and t*i*de," "h*au*nt" and "*aw*esome," "*ea*ch *eve*ning." Both alliteration and assonance help to establish relations among words in a line or a series of lines. Whether the effect is *euphony* (lines that are musically pleasant to the ear and smooth, like the final lines of Dickinson's "A Bird came down the Walk—") or *cacophony* (lines that are discordant and difficult to pronounce, like the claim that "never my numb plunker fumbles" in Updike's "Player Piano"), the sounds of words in poetry can be as significant as the words' denotative or connotative meanings.

This next poem provides a feast of sounds. Read the poem aloud and try to determine the effects of its sounds.

ANYA KRUGOVOY SILVER (B. 1968)

French Toast   2010

Pain perdu: lost bread. Thick slices sunk in milk,
fringed with crisp lace of browned egg and scattered sugar.
Like spongiest challah, dipped in foaming cream
and frothy egg, richness drenching every yeasted
crevice and bubble, that's how sodden with luck   5
I felt when we fell in love. Now, at forty,
I remember that "lost bread" means bread that's gone
stale, leftover heels and crusts, too dry for simple
jam and butter. Still, week-old bread makes the best
French toast, soaks up milk as greedily as I turn   10
toward you under goose down after ten years
of marriage, craving, still, that sweet white immersion.

CONSIDERATIONS FOR CRITICAL THINKING AND WRITING

1. **FIRST RESPONSE.** What types of sounds does Silver use throughout this poem? What categories can you place them in? What is the effect of these sounds?

2. Explain what you think the poem's theme is.
3. Write an essay that considers the speaker's love of French toast along with the speaker's appetite for words. How are the two blended in the poem?
4. CREATIVE RESPONSE. Try writing a poem that emphasizes sounds about a food you love.

RHYME

Like alliteration and assonance, *rhyme* is a way of creating sound patterns. Rhyme, broadly defined, consists of two or more words or phrases that repeat the same sounds: *happy* and *snappy*. Rhyme words often have similar spellings, but that is not a requirement of rhyme; what matters is that the words sound alike: *vain* rhymes with *reign* as well as *rain*. Moreover, words may look alike but not rhyme at all. In *eye rhyme* the spellings are similar, but the pronunciations are not, as with *bough* and *cough*, or *brow* and *blow*.

Not all poems use rhyme. Many great poems have no rhymes, and many weak verses use rhyme as a substitute for poetry. These are especially apparent in commercial messages and greeting-card lines. At its worst, rhyme is merely a distracting decoration that can lead to dullness and predictability. But used skillfully, rhyme creates lines that are memorable and musical.

Here is a poem using rhyme that you might remember the next time you are in a restaurant.

RICHARD ARMOUR (1906–1989)

Going to Extremes   *1954*

Shake and shake
  The catsup bottle
None'll come—
  And then a lot'll.

The experience recounted in Armour's poem is common enough, but the rhyme's humor is special. The final line clicks the poem shut—an effect that is often achieved by the use of rhyme. That click provides a sense of a satisfying and fulfilled form. Rhymes have a number of uses: They can emphasize words, direct a reader's attention to relations between words, and provide an overall structure for a poem.

Rhyme is used in the following poem to imitate the sound of cascading water.

ROBERT SOUTHEY (1774–1843)

From *The Cataract of Lodore*   *1820*

> "How does the water
> Come down at Lodore?"
> . . . .

From its sources which well
  In the tarn on the fell;
    From its fountains   5
    In the mountains,
  Its rills and its gills;
Through moss and through brake,
    It runs and it creeps
    For awhile, till it sleeps   10
    In its own little lake.
  And thence at departing,
  Awakening and starting,
  It runs through the reeds
  And away it proceeds,   15
  Through meadow and glade,
    In sun and in shade,
And through the wood-shelter,
  Among crags in its flurry,
    Helter-skelter,   20
    Hurry-scurry.
  Here it comes sparkling,
And there it lies darkling;
Now smoking and frothing
  Its tumult and wrath in,   25
    Till in this rapid race
      On which it is bent,
    It reaches the place
    Of its steep descent.

    The cataract strong   30
    Then plunges along,
  Striking and raging
  As if a war waging
Its caverns and rocks among:
    Rising and leaping,   35
  Sinking and creeping,
  Swelling and sweeping,
Showering and springing,
    Flying and flinging,
    Writhing and ringing,   40
Eddying and whisking,

Spouting and frisking,
Turning and twisting,
    Around and around
With endless rebound!   45
Smiting and fighting,
    A sight to delight in;
Confounding, astounding,
Dizzying and deafening the ear with its sound.

. . . .

Dividing and gliding and sliding,   50
And falling and brawling and sprawling,
And driving and riving and striving,
And sprinkling and twinkling and wrinkling,
And sounding and bounding and rounding,
And bubbling and troubling and doubling,   55
And grumbling and rumbling and tumbling,
And clattering and battering and shattering;
Retreating and beating and meeting and sheeting,
Delaying and straying and playing and spraying,
Advancing and prancing and glancing and dancing,   60
Recoiling, turmoiling and toiling and boiling,
And gleaming and streaming and steaming and beaming,
And rushing and flushing and brushing and gushing,
And flapping and rapping and clapping and slapping,
And curling and whirling and purling and twirling,   65
And thumping and plumping and bumping and jumping,
And dashing and flashing and splashing and clashing;
And so never ending, but always descending,
Sounds and motions forever and ever are blending,
All at once and all o'er, with a mighty uproar;   70
And this way the water comes down at Lodore.

This deluge of rhymes consists of "Sounds and motions forever and ever . . . blending" (line 69). The pace quickens as the water creeps from its mountain source and then descends in rushing cataracts. As the speed of the water increases, so do the number of rhymes, until they run in fours: "dashing and flashing and splashing and clashing" (line 67). Most rhymes meander through poems instead of flooding them; nevertheless, Southey's use of rhyme suggests how sounds can flow with meanings. "The Cataract of Lodore" has been criticized, however, for overusing onomatopoeia. Some readers find the poem silly; others regard it as a brilliant example of sound effects. What do you think?

A variety of types of rhyme is available to poets. The most common form, **end rhyme**, comes at the ends of lines (lines 14–17).

It runs through the reeds
And away it proceeds,
Through meadow and glade,
In sun and in shade.

Internal rhyme places at least one of the rhymed words within the line, as in "Dividing and gliding and sliding" (line 50) or, more subtly, in the fourth and final words of "In mist or cloud, on mast or shroud."

The rhyming of single-syllable words such as *glade* and *shade* is known as *masculine rhyme*, as we see in these lines from A. E. Housman:

Loveliest of trees, the cherry now
Is hung with bloom along the bough.

Rhymes using words of more than one syllable are also called masculine when the same sound occurs in a final stressed syllable, as in *defend, contend; betray, away*. A *feminine rhyme* consists of a rhymed stressed syllable followed by one or more rhymed unstressed syllables, as in *butter, clutter; gratitude, attitude; quivering, shivering*. This rhyme is evident in John Millington Synge's verse:

Lord confound this surly sister,
Blight her brow and blotch and blister.

All of the examples so far have been *exact rhymes* because they share the same stressed vowel sounds as well as any sounds that follow the vowel. In *near rhyme* (also called *off rhyme*, *slant rhyme*, and *approximate rhyme*), the sounds are almost but not exactly alike. There are several kinds of near rhyme. One of the most common is *consonance*, an identical consonant sound preceded by a different vowel sound: *home, same; worth, breath; trophy, daffy*. Near rhyme can also be achieved by using different vowel sounds with identical consonant sounds: *sound, sand; kind, conned; fellow, fallow*. The dissonance of *blade* and *blood* in the following lines from Wilfred Owen helps to reinforce their grim tone:

Let the boy try along this bayonet-blade
How cold steel is, and keen with hunger of blood.

Near rhymes greatly broaden the possibility for musical effects in English, a language that, compared with Spanish or Italian, contains few exact rhymes. Do not assume, however, that a near rhyme represents a failed attempt at exact rhyme. Near rhymes allow a musical subtlety and variety and can avoid the sometimes overpowering jingling effects that exact rhymes may create.

These basic terms hardly exhaust the ways in which the sounds in poems can be labeled and discussed, but the terms can help you to describe how poets manipulate sounds for effect. Read "The Cow" (p. 460) aloud and try to determine how the sounds of the lines contribute to their sense.

Andrew Hudgins (b. 1951)

The Cow   2006

I love the red cow
with all of my heart.
She's gentle when pulling
my cherry-red cart.

We take her rich milk   5
and swallow it down.
With nothing, it's white,
with chocolate brown.

When she grows too feeble
to give us fresh cream,   10
we'll slit her red throat,
hang her from a beam,

and pull out her insides
to throw to the dogs,
just as we do   15
when we slaughter the hogs.

We've now owned six cows
that I can remember.
We drain them and gut them,
skin and dismember,   20

package and label them,
and stock up the freezer.
We all love beefsteak —
from baby to geezer!

Tossed on the grill,   25
the bloody steaks sputter.
As a last, grateful tribute,
so humble we stutter,

we offer up thanks
with a reverent mutter —   30
then slather her chops
with her own creamy butter.

Considerations for Critical Thinking and Writing

1. **FIRST RESPONSE.** Describe the tone of each stanza. How do the rhymes
   serve to establish the tone?
2. Characterize the speaker. How do you reconcile what is said in the
   first stanza with the description in the final stanza?

3. This poem appeared in the July/August 2006 humor issue of *Poetry*. How does that context affect your reading of it?

4. **CREATIVE RESPONSE.** Bring something to the table yourself: add a four-line stanza in Hudgins's style that rhymes and concludes the meal.

POEMS FOR FURTHER STUDY

LEWIS CARROLL (CHARLES LUTWIDGE DODGSON/1832–1898)

Jabberwocky   1871

'Twas brillig, and the slithy toves
   Did gyre and gimble in the wabe:
All mimsy were the borogoves,
   And the mome raths outgrabe.

"Beware the Jabberwock, my son!   5
   The jaws that bite, the claws that catch!
Beware the Jubjub bird, and shun
   The frumious Bandersnatch!"

He took his vorpal sword in hand;
   Long time the manxome foe he sought—   10
So rested he by the Tumtum tree,
   And stood awhile in thought.

And, as in uffish thought he stood,
   The Jabberwock, with eyes of flame,
Came whiffling through the tulgey wood,   15
   And burbled as it came!

One, two! One, two! And through and through
   The vorpal blade went snicker-snack!
He left it dead, and with its head
   He went galumphing back.   20

"And hast thou slain the Jabberwock?
   Come to my arms, my beamish boy!
O frabjous day! Callooh, Callay!"
   He chortled in his joy.

'Twas brillig, and the slithy toves   25
   Did gyre and gimble in the wabe:
All mimsy were the borogoves,
   And the mome raths outgrabe.

CONSIDERATIONS FOR CRITICAL THINKING AND WRITING

1. **FIRST RESPONSE.** What happens in this poem? Does it have any meaning?

2. Not all of the words used in this poem appear in dictionaries. In *Through the Looking Glass,* Humpty Dumpty explains to Alice that "'slithy' means 'lithe and slimy.' 'Lithe' is the same as 'active.' You see it's like a portmanteau — there are two meanings packed up into one word." Are there any other portmanteau words in the poem?

3. Which words in the poem sound especially meaningful, even if they are devoid of any denotative meanings?

4. **CONNECTION TO ANOTHER SELECTION.** Compare Carroll's strategies for creating sound and meaning with those used by Swenson in "A Nosty Fright" (p. 452).

DIANE LOCKWARD (B. 1953)

Linguini   2006

It was always linguini between us.
Linguini with white sauce, or
red sauce, sauce with basil snatched from
the garden, oregano rubbed between
our palms, a single bay leaf adrift amidst
plum tomatoes. Linguini with meatballs,
sausage, a side of brascioli. Like lovers
trying positions, we enjoyed it every way
we could — artichokes, mushrooms, little
neck clams, mussels, and calamari — linguini   10
twining and braiding us each to each.
Linguini knew of the kisses, the smooches,
the *molti baci.*° It was never spaghetti   *many kisses*
between us, not cappellini, nor farfalle,
vermicelli, pappardelle, fettucini, perciatelli,   15
or even tagliarini. Linguini we stabbed, pitched,
and twirled on forks, spun round and round
on silver spoons. Long, smooth, and always
al dente. In dark trattorias, we broke crusty panera,
toasted each other — *La dolce vita!*° — and sipped   *the sweet life* 20
Amarone,° wrapped ourselves in linguini,   *Italian wine*
briskly boiled, lightly oiled, salted, and lavished
with sauce. *Bellissimo, paradisio, belle gente!*°   *beautiful, paradise, beautiful people*
Linguini witnessed our slurping, pulling, and
sucking, our unraveling and raveling, chins   25

> **WHEN I WRITE** "Consider each poem you like or that intrigues you. Learn from the poem. Notice its moves. Ask yourself how they are achieved. Then imitate. Yes, imitate. This will teach you craft and help you develop your personal style." —DIANE LOCKWARD

glistening, napkins tucked like bibs in collars,
linguini stuck to lips, hips, and bellies, cheeks
flecked with *formaggio*° — parmesan, romano,   *cheese*
and shaved pecorino — strands of linguini flung
around our necks like two fine silk scarves.   30

CONSIDERATIONS FOR CRITICAL THINKING AND WRITING

1. **FIRST RESPONSE.** Read this poem aloud. Which words and sounds
   do you think make this such an exuberant celebration of linguini?
2. Comment on the effect of the repetitions of sound in the poem.
3. Consider the poem's final image. What would be missing if the "two
   fine silk scarves" were omitted?
4. **CONNECTION TO ANOTHER SELECTION.** What similarities and differences do you find in the use of sound in "Linguini" and in Silver's
   "French Toast" (p. 455)?

EMILY DICKINSON (1830–1886)

I heard a Fly buzz — when I died —   *c. 1862*

To hear "I heard a Fly buzz — when I died —" read by Robert Pinsky, visit bedfordstmartins.com/meyerlit/epages.

I heard a Fly buzz — when I died —
The Stillness in the Room
Was like the Stillness in the Air —
Between the Heaves of Storm —

The Eyes around — had wrung them dry —   5
And Breaths were gathering firm
For that last Onset — when the King
Be witnessed — in the Room —

I willed my Keepsakes — Signed away
What portion of me be   10
Assignable — and then it was
There interposed a Fly —

With Blue — uncertain stumbling Buzz —
Between the light — and me —
And then the Windows failed — and then   15
I could not see to see —

CONSIDERATIONS FOR CRITICAL THINKING AND WRITING

1. **FIRST RESPONSE.** What was expected to happen "when the King" was
   "witnessed" (lines 7–8)? What happened instead?
2. Why do you think Dickinson chooses a fly rather than perhaps a bee
   or gnat?

3. What is the effect of the last line? Why not end the poem with "I could not see" instead of the additional "to see"?

4. Discuss the sounds in the poem. Are there any instances of ono-matopoeia?

ROBERT FROST (1874–1963)

Stopping by Woods on a Snowy Evening   1923

Whose woods these are I think I know.
His house is in the village, though;
He will not see me stopping here
To watch his woods fill up with snow.

My little horse must think it queer   5
To stop without a farmhouse near
Between the woods and frozen lake
The darkest evening of the year.

He gives his harness bells a shake
To ask if there is some mistake.   10
The only other sound's the sweep
Of easy wind and downy flake.

The woods are lovely, dark and deep,
But I have promises to keep,
And miles to go before I sleep,   15
And miles to go before I sleep.

CONSIDERATIONS FOR CRITICAL THINKING AND WRITING

1. **FIRST RESPONSE.** What is the significance of the setting in this poem? How is tone conveyed by the images?

2. Although the last two lines are identical, they are not read at the same speed. Why the difference? What is achieved by the repetition?

3. What is the poem's rhyme scheme? What is the effect of the rhyme in the final stanza?

WILLIAM HEYEN (B. 1940)

The Trains   1984

Signed by Franz Paul Stangl, Commandant,
there is in Berlin a document,
an order of transmittal from Treblinka:

248 freight cars of clothing,
400,000 gold watches,   5
25 freight cars of women's hair.

Some clothing was kept, some pulped for paper.
The finest watches were never melted down.
All the women's hair was used for mattresses, or dolls.

Would these words like to use some of that same paper?   10
One of those watches may pulse in your own wrist.
Does someone you know collect dolls, or sleep on human hair?

He is dead at last, Commandant Stangl of Treblinka,
but the camp's three syllables still sound like freight cars
straining around a curve, Treblinka,   15

Treblinka. Clothing, time in gold watches,
women's hair for mattresses and dolls' heads.
Treblinka. The trains from Treblinka.

CONSIDERATIONS FOR CRITICAL THINKING AND WRITING

1. **FIRST RESPONSE.** How does the sound of the word *Treblinka* inform
   your understanding of the poem?
2. Why does the place name of Treblinka continue to resonate over time?
   To learn more about Treblinka, search the Web, perhaps starting at
   ushmm.org, the site of the United States Holocaust Memorial Museum.
3. Why do you suppose Heyen uses the word *in* instead of *on* in line 11?
4. Why is sound so important for establishing the tone of this poem? In
   what sense do "the camp's three syllables still sound like freight cars"
   (line 14)?

JOHN DONNE (1572–1631)
Song   *1633*

Go and catch a falling star,
  Get with child a mandrake root,°
Tell me where all past years are,
  Or who cleft the Devil's foot,
Teach me to hear mermaids singing,   5
  Or to keep off envy's stinging,
        And find
        What wind
Serves to advance an honest mind.

---

2 *mandrake root:* This V-shaped root resembles the lower half of the human body.

If thou be'st borne to strange sights,   10
  Things invisible to see,
Ride ten thousand days and nights,
  Till age snow white hairs on thee,
Thou, when thou return'st, wilt tell me
  All strange wonders that befell thee,   15
        And swear
        Nowhere
Lives a woman true, and fair.

If thou findst one, let me know,
  Such a pilgrimage were sweet —   20
Yet do not, I would not go,
  Though at next door we might meet;
Though she were true, when you met her,
  And last, till you write your letter,
        Yet she   25
        Will be
False, ere I come, to two or three.

CONSIDERATIONS FOR CRITICAL THINKING AND WRITING

1. **FIRST RESPONSE.** What is the speaker's tone in this poem? What is his view of a woman's love? What does the speaker's use of hyperbole reveal about his emotional state?

2. Do you think Donne wants the speaker's argument to be taken seriously? Is there any humor in the poem?

3. Most of these lines end with masculine rhymes. What other kinds of rhymes are used for end rhymes?

PAUL HUMPHREY (B. 1915)

Blow   1983

Her skirt was lofted by the gale;
When I, with gesture deft,
Essayed to stay her frisky sail
She luffed, and laughed, and left.

CONSIDERATIONS FOR CRITICAL THINKING AND WRITING

1. **FIRST RESPONSE.** How do alliteration and assonance contribute to the euphonic effects in this poem?

2. What is the poem's controlling metaphor? Why is it especially appropriate?

3. Explain the ambiguity of the title.

ROBERT FRANCIS (1901–1987)

The Pitcher   1953

His art is eccentricity, his aim
How not to hit the mark he seems to aim at,

His passion how to avoid the obvious,
His technique how to vary the avoidance.

The others throw to be comprehended. He   5
Throws to be a moment misunderstood.

Yet not too much. Not errant, arrant, wild,
But every seeming aberration willed.

Not to, yet still, still to communicate
Making the batter understand too late.   10

CONSIDERATIONS FOR CRITICAL THINKING AND WRITING

1. **FIRST RESPONSE.** Explain how each pair of lines in this poem works
   together to describe the pitcher's art.
2. Consider how the poem itself works the way a good pitcher does.
   Which lines illustrate what they describe?
3. Comment on the effects of the poem's rhymes. How are the final
   two lines different in their rhyme from the previous lines? How does
   sound echo sense in lines 9–10?
4. Write an essay that examines "The Pitcher" as an extended metaphor
   for talking about poetry. How well does the poem characterize strategies for writing poetry as well as pitching?

HELEN CHASIN (B. 1938)

The Word Plum   1968

The word *plum* is delicious

pout and push, luxury of
self-love, and savoring murmur
full in the mouth and falling
like fruit   5

taut skin
pierced, bitten, provoked into
juice, and tart flesh

question
and reply, lip and tongue   10
of pleasure.

CONSIDERATIONS FOR CRITICAL THINKING AND WRITING

1. **FIRST RESPONSE.** What is the effect of the repetitions of the alliteration and assonance throughout the poem? How does it contribute to the poem's meaning?

2. Which sounds in the poem are like the sounds one makes while eating a plum?

3. Discuss the title. Explain whether you think this poem is more about the word *plum* or about the plum itself. Can the two be separated in the poem?

4. **CONNECTION TO ANOTHER SELECTION.** How is Anya Krugovoy Silver's "French Toast" (p. 455) similar in technique to Chasin's poem? Try writing such a poem yourself: Choose a food to describe that allows you to evoke its sensuousness in sounds.

RICHARD WAKEFIELD (B. 1952)

The Bell Rope   2005

WHEN I READ "I like poems that don't tell me how the writer feels; they tell me how the world looks to someone who feels that way. They make sense by engaging the senses, and so they become an experience. The reader is not merely an audience but a participant."
— RICHARD WAKEFIELD

In Sunday school the boy who learned a
    psalm
by heart would get to sound the steeple
    bell
and send its tolling through the sabbath
    calm
to call the saved and not-so-saved as well.
For lack of practice all the lines are lost—
something about how angels' hands would bear
me up to God—but on one Pentecost
they won me passage up the steeple stair.
I leapt and grabbed the rope up high to ride
it down, I touched the floor, the rope went slack,   10
the bell was silent. Then, beatified,
I rose, uplifted as the rope pulled back.
I leapt and fell again; again it took
me up, but still the bell withheld its word—
until at last the church foundation shook   15
in bass approval, felt as much as heard,
and after I let go the bell tolled long
and loud as if repaying me for each
unanswered pull with heaven-rending song
a year of Sunday school could never teach   20
and that these forty years can not obscure.
Some nights when sleep won't come I think of how
just once there came an answer, clear and sure.
If I could find that rope I'd grasp it now.

Considerations for Critical Thinking and Writing

1. **FIRST RESPONSE.** Describe the rhyme scheme and then read the poem aloud. How does Wakefield manage to avoid making this heavily rhymed poem sound clichéd or sing-songy?

2. Comment on the appropriateness of Wakefield's choice of diction and how it relates to the poem's images.

3. Explain how sound becomes, in a sense, the theme of the poem.

4. **CONNECTION TO ANOTHER SELECTION.** Compare the images and themes of "The Bell Rope" with those in Cornelius Eady's "The Supremes" (p. 361).

18

Patterns of Rhythm

I would define, in brief, the Poetry of words
as the Rhythmical Creation of Beauty. Its
sole arbiter is Taste.

— EDGAR ALLAN POE[1]

The rhythms of everyday life surround us in regularly recurring movements and sounds. As you read these words, your heart pulsates while somewhere else a clock

🏠 Explore the poetic element in this chapter at bedfordstmartins.com/ meyerlit.

ticks, a cradle rocks, a drum beats, a dancer sways, a foghorn blasts, a wave recedes, or a child skips. We may tend to overlook rhythm because it is so tightly woven into the fabric of our experience, but it is there nonetheless, one of the conditions of life. Rhythm is also one of the conditions of speech because the voice alternately rises and falls as words are stressed or unstressed and as the pace quickens or slackens. In poetry *rhythm* refers to the recurrence of stressed and unstressed sounds. Depending on how the sounds are arranged, this can result in a pace that is fast or slow, choppy or smooth.

SOME PRINCIPLES OF METER

Poets use rhythm to create pleasurable sound patterns and to reinforce meanings. "Rhythm," Edith Sitwell once observed, "might be described as, to the world of sound, what light is to the world of sight. It shapes

[1] Photograph by W. S. Hartshorn. 1848. Prints and Photographs Division, Library of Congress.

and gives new meaning." Prose can use rhythm effectively too, but prose that does so tends to be an exception. The following exceptional lines are from a speech by Winston Churchill to the House of Commons after Allied forces lost a great battle to German forces at Dunkirk during World War II:

> We shall not flag or fail. We shall go on to the end. We shall fight in France, we shall fight on the seas and oceans, we shall fight with growing confidence and growing strength in the air, we shall defend our island, whatever the cost may be, we shall fight on the beaches, we shall fight on the landing grounds, we shall fight in the fields and in the streets, we shall fight in the hills; we shall never surrender.

The stressed repetition of "we shall" bespeaks the resolute singleness of purpose that Churchill had to convey to the British people if they were to win the war. Repetition is also one of the devices used in poetry to create rhythmic effects. In the following excerpt from "Song of the Open Road," Walt Whitman urges the pleasures of limitless freedom on his reader:

> Allons!° the road is before us!   *Let's go!*
> It is safe—I have tried it—my own feet have tried it well—be not
>   detain'd!
> Let the paper remain on the desk unwritten, and the book on the
>   shelf unopen'd!
> Let the tools remain in the workshop! Let the money remain unearn'd!
> Let the school stand! mind not the cry of the teacher!

These rhythmic lines quickly move away from conventional values to the open road of shared experiences. Their recurring sounds are created not by rhyme or alliteration and assonance (see Chapter 17) but by the repetition of words and phrases.

Although the repetition of words and phrases can be an effective means of creating rhythm in poetry, the more typical method consists of patterns of accented or unaccented syllables. Words contain syllables that are either stressed or unstressed. A **stress** (or **accent**) places more emphasis on one syllable than on another. We say "*syl*lable" not "syl*la*ble," "*emp*hasis" not "em*pha*sis." We routinely stress syllables when we speak: "*Is* she con*tent* with the *con*tents of the *yel*low *pack*age?" To distinguish between two people we might say "Is *she* con*tent* . . . ?" In this way stress can be used to emphasize a particular word in a sentence. Poets often arrange words so that the desired meaning is suggested by the rhythm; hence emphasis is controlled by the poet rather than left entirely to the reader.

When a rhythmic pattern of stresses recurs in a poem, the result is **meter**. Taken together, all the metrical elements in a poem make up what is called the poem's **prosody**. **Scansion** consists of measuring the stresses in a line to determine its metrical pattern. Several methods can be used to mark lines. One widely used system uses ′ for a stressed syllable and ˘ for an unstressed syllable. In a sense, the stress mark represents the equivalent of tapping one's foot to a beat:

> Hĭckŏrў, dĭckŏrў, dóck,
> The mŏuse răn ŭp the clóck.
> The clóck strŭck one,
> And dŏwn hĕ rún,
> Hĭckŏrў, dĭckŏrў, dóck.

In the first two lines and the final line of this familiar nursery rhyme we hear three stressed syllables. In lines 3 and 4, where the meter changes for variety, we hear just two stressed syllables. The combination of stresses provides the pleasure of the rhythm we hear.

To hear the rhythms of "Hickory, dickory, dock" does not require a formal study of meter. Nevertheless, an awareness of the basic kinds of meter that appear in English poetry can enhance your understanding of how a poem achieves its effects. Understanding the sound effects of a poem and having a vocabulary with which to discuss those effects can intensify your pleasure in poetry. Although the study of meter can be extremely technical, the terms used to describe the basic meters of English poetry are relatively easy to comprehend.

The *foot* is the metrical unit by which a line of poetry is measured. A foot usually consists of one stressed and one or two unstressed syllables. A vertical line is used to separate the feet: "The clock | struck one" consists of two feet. A foot of poetry can be arranged in a variety of patterns; here are five of the chief types:

Foot	Pattern	Example
iamb	˘ ′	awáy
trochee	′ ˘	Lóvelў
anapest	˘ ˘ ′	ŭnderstánd
dactyl	′ ˘ ˘	déspĕrătĕ
spondee	′ ′	déad sét

The most common lines in English poetry contain meters based on *iambic* feet. However, even lines that are predominantly iambic will often include variations to create particular effects. Other important patterns include *trochaic*, *anapestic*, and *dactylic* feet. The spondee is not a sustained meter but occurs for variety or emphasis.

Iambic
> Whăt képt | hĭs eýes | frŏm gív | ĭng báck | thĕ gáze

Trochaic
> Hé wăs | loúdĕr | thán thĕ | préachĕr

Anapestic
Ĭ ăm cálled | tŏ thĕ frónt | ŏf thĕ roóm

Dactylic
Síng ĭt ăll | mérrĭlў

These meters have different rhythms and can create different effects. Iambic and anapestic are known as **rising meters** because they move from unstressed to stressed sounds, while trochaic and dactylic are known as **falling meters**. Anapests and dactyls tend to move more lightly and rapidly than iambs or trochees. Although no single kind of meter can be considered always better than another for a given subject, it is possible to determine whether the meter of a specific poem is appropriate for its subject. A serious poem about a tragic death would most likely not be well served by lilting rhythms. Keep in mind, too, that though one or another of these four basic meters might constitute the predominant rhythm of a poem, variations can occur within lines to change the pace or call attention to a particular word.

A **line** is measured by the number of feet it contains. Here, for example, is an iambic line with three feet: "Ĭf shé | shŏuld wríte | ă nóte." These are the names for line lengths:

monometer: one foot   pentameter: five feet

dimeter: two feet   hexameter: six feet

trimeter: three feet   heptameter: seven feet

tetrameter: four feet   octameter: eight feet

By combining the name of a line length with the name of a foot type, we can describe the metrical qualities of a line concisely. Consider, for example, the pattern of feet and length of this line:

I didn't want the boy to hit the dog.

The iambic rhythm of this line falls into five feet; hence it is called **iambic pentameter**. Iambic is the most common pattern in English poetry because its rhythm appears so naturally in English speech and writing. Unrhymed iambic pentameter is called **blank verse**; Shakespeare's plays are built on such lines.

Less common than the iamb, trochee, anapest, or dactyl is the **spondee**, a two-syllable foot in which both syllables are stressed (´´). Note the effect of the spondaic foot at the beginning of this line:

Déad sét | ăgaínst | thĕ plán | hĕ wént | ăwáy.

Spondees can slow a rhythm and provide variety and emphasis, particularly in iambic and trochaic lines. A line that ends with a stressed syllable is said to have a **masculine ending**, whereas a line that ends with an extra unstressed syllable is said to have a **feminine ending**. Consider, for example, these two lines from Timothy Steele's "Waiting for the Storm" (the entire poem appears on p. 476):

feminine: Thĕ sánd | ăt mў féet | grŏw cóld | er̆,
masculine: Thĕ damp | air̆ chíll | ănd spréad.

The effects of English meters are easily seen in the following lines by Samuel Taylor Coleridge, in which the rhythm of each line illustrates the meter described in it:

Trochee trips from long to short;
From long to long in solemn sort
Slow Spondee stalks; strong foot yet ill able
Ever to come up with Dactylic trisyllable.
Iambics march from short to long—
With a leap and a bound the swift Anapests throng.

The speed of a line is also affected by the number of pauses in it. A pause within a line is called a *caesura* and is indicated by a double vertical line (||). A caesura can occur anywhere within a line and need not be indicated by punctuation, as seen in these lines by Walt Whitman:

Camerado, || I give you my hand!
I give you my love || more precious than money.

A slight pause occurs within each of these lines and at its end. Both kinds of pauses contribute to the lines' rhythm.

When a line has a pause at its end, it is called an *end-stopped line*. Such pauses reflect normal speech patterns and are often marked by punctuation. A line that ends without a pause and continues into the next line for its meaning is called a *run-on line*. Running over from one line to another is also called *enjambment*. The first and eighth lines of the following poem are run-on lines; the rest are end-stopped.

WILLIAM WORDSWORTH (1770–1850)

My Heart Leaps Up   1807

My heart leaps up when I behold
    A rainbow in the sky:
So was it when my life began;
So is it now I am a man;
So be it when I shall grow old,
    Or let me die!
The child is father of the Man;
And I could wish my days to be
Bound each to each by natural piety.

Run-on lines have a different rhythm from end-stopped lines. Lines 3 and 4 and lines 8 and 9 are iambic, but the effect of their two rhythms is very different when we read these lines aloud. The enjambment of lines 8 and 9 reinforces their meaning; just as the "days" are bound together, so are the lines.

The rhythm of a poem can be affected by several devices: the kind and number of stresses within lines, the length of lines, and the kinds of pauses that appear within lines or at their ends. In addition, as we saw in Chapter 17, the sound of a poem is affected by alliteration, assonance, rhyme, and consonance. These sounds help to create rhythms by controlling our pronunciations, as in the following lines by Alexander Pope:

Soft is the strain when Zephyr gently blows,
And the smooth stream in smoother numbers flows;
But when loud surges lash the sounding shore,
The hoarse, rough verse should like the torrent roar.

These lines are effective because their rhythm and sound work with their meaning.

Suggestions for Scanning a Poem

These suggestions should help you in talking about a poem's meter.

1. After reading the poem through, read it aloud and mark the stressed syllables in each line. Then mark the unstressed syllables.

2. From your markings, identify what kind of foot is dominant (iambic, trochaic, dactylic, or anapestic) and divide the lines into feet, keeping in mind that the vertical line marking a foot may come in the middle of a word as well as at its beginning or end.

3. Determine the number of feet in each line. Remember that there may be variations; some lines may be shorter or longer than the predominant meter. What is important is the overall pattern. Do not assume that variations represent the poet's inability to fulfill the overall pattern. Notice the effects of variations and whether they emphasize words and phrases or disrupt your expectation for some other purpose.

4. Listen for pauses within lines and mark the caesuras; many times there will be no punctuation to indicate them.

5. Recognize that scansion does not always yield a definitive measurement of a line. Even experienced readers may differ over the scansion of a given line. What is important is not a precise description of the line but an awareness of how a poem's rhythms contribute to its effects.

The following poem demonstrates how you can use an understanding of meter and rhythm to gain a greater appreciation for what a poem is saying.

TIMOTHY STEELE (B. 1948)

Waiting for the Storm   1986

Bréeze sént | ă wrínk | lĭng dárk | nĕss
Ăcróss | thĕ báy. || Ĭ knélt
Bĕnéath | ăn úp | turnĕd bóat,
Ănd, mó | mĕnt bў mó | mĕnt, félt

Thĕ sánd | ăt mў féet | grŏw cóld | ĕr,
Thĕ dámp | ăir chíll | ănd spréad.
Thĕn thĕ | fírst ráin | drŏps sóund | ĕd
Ŏn thĕ húll | ăbóve | mў héad.

The predominant meter of this poem is iambic trimeter, but there is plenty of variation as the storm rapidly approaches and finally begins to pelt the sheltered speaker. The emphatic spondee ("Breeze sent") pushes the darkness quickly across the bay while the caesura at the end of the sentence in line 2 creates a pause that sets up a feeling of suspense and expectation that is measured in the ticking rhythm of line 4, a run-on line that brings us into the chilly sand and air of the second stanza. Perhaps the most impressive sound effect used in the poem appears in the second syllable of "sounded" in line 7. That "ed" precedes the sound of the poem's final word, "head," just as if it were the first drop of rain hitting the hull above the speaker. The visual, tactile, and auditory images make "Waiting for the Storm" an intense sensory experience.

This next poem also reinforces meanings through its use of meter and rhythm.

WILLIAM BUTLER YEATS (1865–1939)

That the Night Come   1912

Shĕ líved | ĭn stórm | ănd strífe,
Hĕr sóul | hăd súch | ă desíre
Fŏr whát | proŭd déath | măy bríng
Thăt ít | cŏuld nót | ĕndúre
Thĕ cóm | mŏn góod | ŏf lífe,   5
Bŭt líved | ăs 'twére | ă kíng
Thăt páckĕd | hĭs már | rĭăge dáy

Wĭth bán | nĕrét | aňd pén | nŏn,
Trúmpĕt | aňd két | tlĕdrŭm,
Aňd thĕ | oŭtrág | eoŭs cán | nŏn,
Tŏ bún | dlĕ tíme | ăwáy
Thăt thĕ | níght cóme.

🔊 To hear "That the
Night Come" read by
Samantha Eggar, visit
bedfordstmartins.com/
meyerlit/epages.

Scansion reveals that the predominant meter here is iambic trimeter: Each line contains three stressed and unstressed syllables that form a regular, predictable rhythm through line 7. That rhythm is disrupted, however, when the speaker compares the woman's longing for what death brings to a king's eager anticipation of his wedding night. The king packs the day with noisy fanfares and celebrations to fill up time and distract himself. Unable to accept "The common good of life," the woman fills her days with "storm and strife." In a determined effort "To bundle time away," she, like the king, impatiently awaits the night.

Lines 8–10 break the regular pattern established in the first seven lines. The extra unstressed syllable in lines 8 and 10 along with the trochaic feet in lines 9 ("trumpet") and 10 ("And the") interrupt the basic iambic trimeter and parallel the woman's and the king's frenetic activity. These lines thus echo the inability of the woman and king to "endure" regular or normal time. The last line is the most irregular in the poem. The final two accented syllables sound like the deep resonant beats of a kettledrum or a cannon firing. The words "night come" dramatically remind us that what the woman anticipates is not a lover but the mysterious finality of death. The meter serves, then, in both its regularity and variations to reinforce the poem's meaning and tone.

The following poems are especially rich in their rhythms and sounds. As you read and study them, notice how patterns of rhythm and the sounds of words reinforce meanings and contribute to the poems' effects. And, perhaps most important, read the poems aloud so that you can hear them.

POEMS FOR FURTHER STUDY

JOHN MALONEY (B. 1947)

Good!

1999

The ball goes up off glass and rebounded
down the court, outlet flung to the quick guard
like clicking seconds: he dribbles, hounded
by hands, calls the play, stops short, looking hard
for a slant opening, fakes it twice, passes   5
into the center — he lobs to the small
forward, top of the key, a pick: asses
crash (the pick-and-roll), he cuts, bumps, the ball
reaches him as he turns, dribbles, sends it

back to the baseline, forward back to him,   10
jump—and in midair, twisting, he bends it
over a tangle of arms—SHOOTS, the rim
rattles as it jerks against the back joints,
and into the net, trippingly drop two points.

CONSIDERATIONS FOR CRITICAL THINKING AND WRITING

1. **FIRST RESPONSE.** Comment on the effects of the lines' rhythms.

2. Notice the precise pattern of rhyme. How is that related to the action in the poem?

3. **CONNECTION TO ANOTHER SELECTION.** Compare the diction and tone in "Good!" and in Jim Tilley's "Boys" (p. 441).

WILLIAM TROWBRIDGE (B. 1941)

Drumming behind You in the High School Band   1989

Rehearsing in street clothes after school,
we measured off the football field
in the spice and chill of early fall.
Through roll-off, counterpoint, and turn,
by the grunt and pop of blocking drill,   5
I marked the cadence of switching hips
no martial air could ever hold.
How left was left, how right was right!
We had a rhythm all our own
and made them march to it, slowing "The Stars   10
and Stripes Forever" as the sun stretched
our shadows toward the rising moon
and my heart kept stepping on my heels.

CONSIDERATIONS FOR CRITICAL THINKING AND WRITING

1. **FIRST RESPONSE.** Describe the various "cadences" of this poem.

2. How are the rhythms of the lines related to their meaning?

3. Using the images from the poem to make your point, discuss whether the speaker is simply an ogling cad or something else.

ALICE JONES (B. 1949)

The Foot   1993

Our improbable support, erected
on the osseous architecture
of the calcaneus, talus, cuboid,
navicular, cuneiforms, metatarsals,
phalanges, a plethora of hinges,   5

all strung together by gliding
tendons, covered by the pearly
plantar fascia, then fat-padded
to form the sole, humble surface
of our contact with earth.   10

Here the body's broadest tendon
anchors the heel's fleshy base,
the finely wrinkled skin stretches
forward across the capillaried arch,
to the ball, a balance point.   15

A wide web of flexor tendons
and branched veins maps the dorsum,
fades into the stub-laden bone
splay, the stuffed sausage sacks
of toes, each with a tuft   20

of proximal hairs to introduce
the distal nail, whose useless
curve remembers an ancestor,
the vanished creature's wild
and necessary claw.   25

Considerations for Critical Thinking and Writing

1. **FIRST RESPONSE.** What is the effect of the diction? What sort of tone
   is established by the use of anatomical terms? How do the terms
   affect the rhythm?

2. Jones has described the form of "The Foot" as "five stubby stanzas."
   Explain why the lines of this poem may or may not warrant this
   description of the stanzas.

Robert Herrick (1591–1674)

Delight in Disorder   *1648*

A sweet disorder in the dress
Kindles in clothes a wantonness.
A lawn° about the shoulders thrown   *linen scarf*
Into a fine distraction;
An erring lace, which here and there   5
Enthralls the crimson stomacher,
A cuff neglectful, and thereby
Ribbons to flow confusedly;
A winning wave, deserving note,
In the tempestuous petticoat;   10

A careless shoestring, in whose tie
I see a wild civility;
Do more bewitch me than when art
Is too precise in every part.

CONSIDERATIONS FOR CRITICAL THINKING AND WRITING

1. **FIRST RESPONSE.** Why does the speaker in this poem value "disorder" so highly? How do the poem's organization and rhythmic order relate to its theme? Are they "precise in every part" (line 14)?

2. Which words in the poem indicate disorder? Which words indicate the speaker's response to that disorder? What are the connotative meanings of each set of words? Why are they appropriate? What do they suggest about the woman and the speaker?

3. Write a short essay in which you agree or disagree with the speaker's views on dress.

BEN JONSON (1573–1637)

Still to Be Neat   *1609*

Still° to be neat, still to be dressed,   *continually*
As you were going to a feast;
Still to be powdered, still perfumed;
Lady, it is to be presumed,
Though art's hid causes are not found,   5
All is not sweet, all is not sound.

Give me a look, give me a face
That makes simplicity a grace;
Robes loosely flowing, hair as free;
Such sweet neglect more taketh me   10
Then all th' adulteries of art.
They strike mine eyes, but not my heart.

CONSIDERATIONS FOR CRITICAL THINKING AND WRITING

1. **FIRST RESPONSE.** What are the speaker's reservations about the lady in the first stanza? What do you think "sweet" means in line 6?

2. What does the speaker want from the lady in the second stanza? How has the meaning of "sweet" shifted from line 6 to line 10? What other words in the poem are especially charged with connotative meanings?

3. How do the rhythms of Jonson's lines help to reinforce meanings? Pay particular attention to lines 6 and 12.

4. **CONNECTION TO ANOTHER SELECTION.** Write an essay comparing the themes of "Still to Be Neat" and Herrick's preceding poem, "Delight in Disorder." How do the speakers make similar points but from different perspectives?

5. **CONNECTION TO ANOTHER SELECTION.** How does the rhythm of "Still to Be Neat" compare with that of "Delight in Disorder"? Which do you find more effective? Explain why.

WILLIAM BLAKE (1757–1827)

The Lamb   *1789*

Courtesy of the National Portrait Gallery, London.

Little Lamb, who made thee?
Dost thou know who made thee?
Gave thee life, and bid thee feed
By the stream and o'er the mead;
Gave thee clothing of delight,
Softest clothing, wooly, bright;
Gave thee such a tender voice,
Making all the vales rejoice?
   Little Lamb, who made thee?
   Dost thou know who made thee?

Little Lamb, I'll tell thee,
Little Lamb, I'll tell thee:
He is callèd by thy name,
For he calls himself a Lamb.
He is meek, and he is mild;
He became a little child.
I a child, and thou a lamb,
We are callèd by his name.
   Little Lamb, God bless thee!
   Little Lamb, God bless thee!   20

.e To hear "The Lamb" read by Brian Murray, visit bedfordstmartins.com/meyerlit/epages.

CONSIDERATIONS FOR CRITICAL THINKING AND WRITING

1. **FIRST RESPONSE.** This poem is from Blake's *Songs of Innocence*. Describe its tone. How do the meter, rhyme, and repetition help to characterize the speaker's voice?

2. Why is it significant that the animal addressed by the speaker is a lamb? What symbolic value would be lost if the animal were, for example, a doe?

3. How does the second stanza answer the question raised in the first? What is the speaker's view of the creation?

WILLIAM BLAKE (1757–1827)

The Tyger   *1794*

Tyger! Tyger! burning bright
In the forests of the night,
What immortal hand or eye
Could frame thy fearful symmetry?

In what distant deeps or skies   5
Burnt the fire of thine eyes?
On what wings dare he aspire?
What the hand dare seize the fire?

And what shoulder, and what art,
Could twist the sinews of thy heart?   10
And when thy heart began to beat,
What dread hand? and what dread feet?

What the hammer? what the chain?
In what furnace was thy brain?
What the anvil? what dread grasp   15
Dare its deadly terrors clasp?

When the stars threw down their spears,
And watered heaven with their tears,
Did he smile his work to see?
Did he who made the Lamb make thee?   20

Tyger! Tyger! burning bright
In the forests of the night,
What immortal hand or eye
Dare frame thy fearful symmetry?

CONSIDERATIONS FOR CRITICAL THINKING AND WRITING

1. **FIRST RESPONSE.** This poem from Blake's *Songs of Experience* is often paired with "The Lamb." Describe the poem's tone. Is the speaker's voice the same here as in "The Lamb"? Which words are repeated, and how do they contribute to the tone?

2. What is revealed about the nature of the tiger by the words used to describe its creation? What do you think the tiger symbolizes?

3. Unlike in "The Lamb," more than one question is raised in "The Tyger." What are these questions? Are they answered?

4. **CONNECTION TO ANOTHER SELECTION.** Compare the rhythms in "The Lamb" and "The Tyger." Each basically uses a seven-syllable line, but the effects are very different. Why?

5. **CONNECTION TO ANOTHER SELECTION.** Using these two poems as the basis of your discussion, describe what distinguishes innocence from experience.

CARL SANDBURG (1878–1967)
Chicago   1916

Hog Butcher for the World,
Tool Maker, Stacker of Wheat,
Player with Railroads and the Nation's Freight Handler;
Stormy, husky, brawling,
City of the Big Shoulders: 5

They tell me you are wicked and I believe them, for I have seen your
     painted women under the gas lamps luring the farm boys.
And they tell me you are crooked and I answer: Yes, it is true I have seen
     the gunman kill and go free to kill again.
And they tell me you are brutal and my reply is: On the faces of women
     and children I have seen the marks of wanton hunger.
And having answered so I turn once more to those who sneer at this my
     city, and I give them back the sneer and say to them:
Come and show me another city with lifted head singing so proud to be
     alive and coarse and strong and cunning.   10
Flinging magnetic curses amid the toil of piling job on job, here is a tall
     bold slugger set vivid against the little soft cities;
Fierce as a dog with tongue lapping for action, cunning as a savage
     pitted against the wilderness,
    Bareheaded,
    Shoveling,
    Wrecking,   15
    Planning,
    Building, breaking, rebuilding,
Under the smoke, dust all over his mouth, laughing with white teeth,
Under the terrible burden of destiny laughing as a young man laughs,
Laughing even as an ignorant fighter laughs who has never
     lost a battle,   20
Bragging and laughing that under his wrist is the pulse, and under his
     ribs the heart of the people,
    Laughing!
Laughing the stormy, husky, brawling laughter of Youth, half-naked,
     sweating, proud to be Hog Butcher, Tool Maker, Stacker of
     Wheat, Player with Railroads and Freight Handler to the Nation.

CONSIDERATIONS FOR CRITICAL THINKING AND WRITING

1. **FIRST RESPONSE.** Sandburg's personification of Chicago creates a
   strong identity for the city. Explain why you find the city attractive
   or not.
2. How do the length and rhythm of lines 1 to 5 compare with those of
   the final lines?

3. **CREATIVE RESPONSE.** Using "Chicago" as a model for style, try writing a tribute or condemnation about a place that you know well. Make an effort to use vivid images and stylistic techniques that capture its rhythms.

4. **CONNECTION TO ANOTHER SELECTION.** Compare "Chicago" with William Blake's "London" (p. 404) in style and theme.

ROBERT FROST (1874–1963)

"Out, Out—"°   *1916*

The buzz-saw snarled and rattled in the yard
And made dust and dropped stove-length sticks of wood,
Sweet-scented stuff when the breeze drew across it.
And from there those that lifted eyes could count
Five mountain ranges one behind the other   5
Under the sunset far into Vermont.
And the saw snarled and rattled, snarled and rattled,
As it ran light, or had to bear a load.
And nothing happened: day was all but done.
Call it a day, I wish they might have said   10
To please the boy by giving him the half hour
That a boy counts so much when saved from work.
His sister stood beside them in her apron
To tell them "Supper." At the word, the saw,
As if to prove saws knew what supper meant,   15
Leaped out at the boy's hand, or seemed to leap—
He must have given the hand. However it was,
Neither refused the meeting. But the hand!
The boy's first outcry was a rueful laugh,
As he swung toward them holding up the hand   20
Half in appeal, but half as if to keep
The life from spilling. Then the boy saw all—
Since he was old enough to know, big boy
Doing a man's work, though a child at heart—
He saw all spoiled. "Don't let him cut my hand off—   25
The doctor, when he comes. Don't let him, sister!"
So. But the hand was gone already.
The doctor put him in the dark of ether.
He lay and puffed his lips out with his breath.
And then—the watcher at his pulse took fright.   30
No one believed. They listened at his heart.
Little—less—nothing!—and that ended it.
No more to build on there. And they, since they
Were not the one dead, turned to their affairs.

"Out, Out—": From Act V, Scene v, of Shakespeare's *Macbeth.* See page 413.

Considerations for Critical Thinking and Writing

1. **FIRST RESPONSE.** This narrative poem is about the accidental death of a Vermont boy. What is the purpose of the story? Some readers have argued that the final lines reveal the speaker's callousness and indifference. What do you think?

2. How does Frost's allusion to *Macbeth* contribute to the meaning of this poem? Does the speaker seem to agree with the view of life expressed in Macbeth's lines?

3. Explain how the rhythm of lines 30–31 is related to the action they describe.

4. **CONNECTION TO ANOTHER SELECTION.** Compare the tone and theme of " 'Out, Out—' " with those of Stephen Crane's "A Man Said to the Universe" (p. 438).

19
Poetic Forms

© William Hathaway.

Writing a poem is like repacking a small suitcase for a long trip over and over. The balance of want and need.

— WILLIAM HATHAWAY

Poems come in a variety of shapes. Although the best poems always have their own unique qualities, many of them also conform to traditional patterns. Frequently the *form* of a poem—its overall structure or shape—follows an already established design. A poem that can be categorized by the patterns of its lines, meter, rhymes, and stanzas is considered a *fixed form* because it follows a prescribed model such as a sonnet. However, poems written in a fixed form do not always fit models precisely; writers sometimes work variations on traditional forms to create innovative effects.

Not all poets are content with variations on traditional forms. Some prefer to create their own structures and shapes. Poems that do not conform to established patterns of meter, rhyme, and stanza are called *free verse* or *open form* poetry. (See Chapter 20 for further discussion of open forms.) This kind of poetry creates its own ordering principles through the careful arrangement of words and phrases in line lengths that embody rhythms appropriate to the meaning. Modern and contemporary poets in particular have learned to use the blank space on the page as a significant functional element (for a striking example, see Cummings's "l(a" (p. 351). Good poetry of this kind is structured in ways that can be as demanding, interesting, and satisfying as fixed forms. Open and fixed forms represent different poetic styles, but they are identical in the sense that both use language in concentrated ways to convey meanings, experiences, emotions, and effects.

SOME COMMON POETIC FORMS

A familiarity with some of the most frequently used fixed forms of poetry is useful because it allows for a better understanding of how a poem works. Classifying patterns allows us to talk about the effects of established rhythm and rhyme and to recognize how significant variations from them affect the pace and meaning of the lines. An awareness of form also allows us to anticipate how a poem is likely to proceed. As we shall see, a sonnet creates a different set of expectations in a reader from those of, say, a limerick. A reader isn't likely to find in limericks the kind of serious themes that often make their way into sonnets. The discussion that follows identifies some of the important poetic forms frequently encountered in English poetry.

The shape of a fixed-form poem is often determined by the way in which the lines are organized into stanzas. A *stanza* consists of a grouping of lines, set off by a space, that usually has a set pattern of meter and rhyme. This pattern is ordinarily repeated in other stanzas throughout the poem. What is usual is not obligatory, however; some poems may use a different pattern for each stanza, somewhat like paragraphs in prose.

Traditionally, though, stanzas do share a common *rhyme scheme*, the pattern of end rhymes. We can map out rhyme schemes by noting patterns of rhyme with lowercase letters: The first rhyme sound is designated *a*, the second becomes *b*, the third *c*, and so on. Using this system, we can describe the rhyme scheme in the following poem this way: *aabb, ccdd, eeff.*

A. E. HOUSMAN (1859–1936)

Loveliest of trees, the cherry now   *1896*

Loveliest of trees, the cherry now	*a*
Is hung with bloom along the bough,	*a*
And stands about the woodland ride	*b*
Wearing white for Eastertide.	*b*
Now, of my threescore years and ten,	*c*
Twenty will not come again,	*c*
And take from seventy springs a score,	*d*
It only leaves me fifty more.	*d*
And since to look at things in bloom	*e*
Fifty springs are little room,	*e*

5

10

About the woodlands I will go   *f*
To see the cherry hung with snow.   *f*

CONSIDERATIONS FOR CRITICAL THINKING AND WRITING

1. **FIRST RESPONSE.** What is the speaker's attitude in this poem toward time and life?

2. Why is spring an appropriate season for the setting rather than, say, winter?

3. Paraphrase each stanza. How do the images in each reinforce the poem's themes?

4. Lines 1 and 12 are not intended to rhyme, but they are close. What is the effect of the near rhyme of "now" and "snow"? How does the rhyme enhance the theme?

Poets often create their own stanzaic patterns; hence there is an infinite number of kinds of stanzas. One way of talking about stanzaic forms is to describe a given stanza by how many lines it contains.

A *couplet* consists of two lines that usually rhyme and have the same meter; couplets are frequently not separated from each other by space on the page. A *heroic couplet* consists of rhymed iambic pentameter. Here is an example from Alexander Pope's "Essay on Criticism":

One science only will one genius fit;   *a*
So vast is art, so narrow human wit: *a*
Not only bounded to peculiar arts,   *b*
But oft in those confined to single parts.   *b*

A *tercet* is a three-line stanza. When all three lines rhyme, they are called a *triplet*. Two triplets make up the following captivating poem.

ROBERT HERRICK (1591–1674)
Upon Julia's Clothes   1648

Whenas in silks my Julia goes,   *a*
Then, then, methinks, how sweetly flows   *a*
That liquefaction of her clothes.   *a*

Next, when I cast mine eyes, and see   *b*
That brave vibration, each way free,   *b*
O, how that glittering taketh me!   *b*

CONSIDERATIONS FOR CRITICAL THINKING AND WRITING

1. **FIRST RESPONSE.** What purpose does alliteration serve in this poem?

2. Comment on the effect of the meter. How is it related to the speaker's description of Julia's clothes?

3. Look up the word *brave* in the *Oxford English Dictionary*. Which of its meanings is appropriate to describe Julia's movement? Some readers interpret lines 4–6 to mean that Julia has no clothes on. What do you think?

4. **CONNECTION TO ANOTHER SELECTION.** Compare the tone of this poem with that of Paul Humphrey's "Blow" (p. 466). Are the situations and speakers similar? Is there any difference in tone between these two poems?

Terza rima consists of an interlocking three-line rhyme scheme: aba, bcb, cdc, ded, and so on. Dante's Divine Comedy uses this pattern, as does Robert Frost's "Acquainted with the Night" (p. 431) and Percy Bysshe Shelley's "Ode to the West Wind" (p. 504).

A **quatrain**, or four-line stanza, is the most common stanzaic form in the English language and can have various meters and rhyme schemes (if any). The most common rhyme schemes are aabb, abba, aaba, and abcb. This last pattern is especially characteristic of the popular **ballad stanza**, which consists of alternating eight- and six-syllable lines. Samuel Taylor Coleridge adopted this pattern in "The Rime of the Ancient Mariner"; here is one representative stanza:

> All in a hot and copper sky
> The bloody Sun, at noon,
> Right up above the mast did stand,
> No bigger than the Moon.

There are a number of longer stanzaic forms, and the list of types of stanzas could be extended considerably, but knowing these three most basic patterns should prove helpful to you in talking about the form of a great many poems. In addition to stanzaic forms, there are fixed forms that characterize entire poems. Lyric poems can be, for example, sonnets, villanelles, sestinas, or epigrams.

Sonnet

The **sonnet** has been a popular literary form in English since the sixteenth century, when it was adopted from the Italian *sonnetto*, meaning "little song." A sonnet consists of fourteen lines, usually written in iambic pentameter. Because the sonnet has been such a favorite form, writers have experimented with many variations on its essential structure. Nevertheless, there are two basic types of sonnets: the Italian and the English.

The **Italian sonnet** (also known as the **Petrarchan sonnet**, from the fourteenth-century Italian poet Petrarch) divides into two parts. The first eight lines (the **octave**) typically rhyme *abbaabba*. The final six lines (the **sestet**) may vary; common patterns are *cdecde*, *cdcdcd*, and *cdccdc*. Very often the octave presents a situation, an attitude, or a problem that the sestet comments upon or resolves, as in John Keats's "On First Looking into Chapman's Homer."

JOHN KEATS (1795–1821)

On First Looking into Chapman's Homer°   1816

Courtesy of the National Portrait Gallery, London.

Much have I traveled in the realms of gold,
   And many goodly states and
      kingdoms seen;
   Round many western islands have
      I been
Which bards in fealty to Apollo° hold.
Oft of one wide expanse had I been told
   That deep-browed Homer ruled as his
      demesne;
   Yet did I never breathe its pure serene°   *atmosphere*
Till I heard Chapman speak out loud and bold:
Then felt I like some watcher of the skies
   When a new planet swims into his ken;   10
Or like stout Cortez° when with eagle eyes
   He stared at the Pacific—and all his men
Looked at each other with a wild surmise—
   Silent, upon a peak in Darien.

Chapman's Homer: Before reading George Chapman's (ca. 1560–1634) poetic Elizabethan translations of Homer's *Iliad* and *Odyssey,* Keats had known only stilted and pedestrian eighteenth-century translations.   4 *Apollo:* Greek god of poetry.   11 *Cortez:* Vasco Núñez de Balboa, not Hernando Cortés, was the first European to sight the Pacific from Darien, a peak in Panama.

CONSIDERATIONS FOR CRITICAL THINKING AND WRITING

1. **FIRST RESPONSE.** How do the images shift from the octave to the sestet? How does the tone change? Does the meaning change as well?

2. What is the controlling metaphor of this poem?

3. What is it that the speaker discovers?

4. How does the rhythm of the lines change between the octave and the sestet? How does that change reflect the tones of both the octave and the sestet?

5. Does Keats's mistake concerning Cortés and Balboa affect your reading of the poem? Explain why or why not.

The Italian sonnet pattern is also used in the next sonnet, but notice that the thematic break between octave and sestet comes within line 9 rather than between lines 8 and 9. This unconventional break helps to reinforce the speaker's impatience with the conventional attitudes he describes.

WILLIAM WORDSWORTH (1770–1850)
The World Is Too Much with Us   *1807*

The world is too much with us; late and soon,
Getting and spending, we lay waste our powers;
Little we see in Nature that is ours;
We have given our hearts away, a sordid boon!
This Sea that bares her bosom to the moon;   5
The winds that will be howling at all hours,
And are up-gathered now like sleeping flowers;
For this, for everything, we are out of tune;
It moves us not. — Great God! I'd rather be
A Pagan suckled in a creed outworn;   10
So might I, standing on this pleasant lea,
Have glimpses that would make me less forlorn;
Have sight of Proteus rising from the sea;
Or hear old Triton blow his wreathèd horn.

CONSIDERATIONS FOR CRITICAL THINKING AND WRITING

1. **FIRST RESPONSE.** What is the speaker's complaint in this sonnet?
   How do the conditions described affect him?

2. Look up "Proteus" and "Triton." What do these mythological allusions contribute to the sonnet's tone?

3. What is the effect of the personification of the sea and wind in the octave?

4. **CONNECTION TO ANOTHER SELECTION.** Compare the theme of this sonnet with that of Sherman Alexie's "The Facebook Sonnet" (p. 495).

The **English sonnet**, more commonly known as the **Shakespearean sonnet**, is organized into three quatrains and a couplet, which typically rhyme *abab cdcd efef gg*. This rhyme scheme is more suited to English poetry because English has fewer rhyming words than Italian. English sonnets, because of their four-part organization, also have more flexibility about where thematic breaks can occur. Frequently, however, the most pronounced break or turn happens in the concluding couplet.

In the following Shakespearean sonnet, the three quatrains compare the speaker's loved one to a summer's day and explain why the loved one is even more lovely. The couplet bestows eternal beauty and love upon both the loved one and the sonnet.

WILLIAM SHAKESPEARE (1564–1616)

Shall I compare thee to a summer's day?   1609

Shall I compare thee to a summer's day?
Thou art more lovely and more temperate:
Rough winds do shake the darling buds of May,
And summer's lease hath all too short a date.
Sometime too hot the eye of heaven shines,
And often is his gold complexion dimmed;
And every fair from fair sometime declines,
By chance, or nature's changing course, untrimmed.
But thy eternal summer shall not fade,
Nor lose possession of that fair thou ow'st°   *possess* 10
Nor shall death brag thou wand'rest in his shade,
When in eternal lines to time thou grow'st.
        So long as men can breathe or eyes can see,
        So long lives this, and this gives life to thee.

To hear "Shall I compare thee to a summer's day?" read by Sir John Gielgud, visit bedfordstmartins.com/meyerlit/epages.

CONSIDERATIONS FOR CRITICAL THINKING AND WRITING

1. **FIRST RESPONSE.** Describe the shift in tone and subject matter that begins in line 9.

2. Why is the speaker's loved one more lovely than a summer's day? What qualities does he admire in the loved one?

3. What does the couplet say about the relation between art and love?

4. Which syllables are stressed in the final line? How do these syllables relate to the line's meaning?

Sonnets have been the vehicles for all kinds of subjects, including love, death, politics, and cosmic questions. Although most sonnets tend to treat their subjects seriously, this fixed form is not limited to a fixed expression; humor is also possible in it. Compare this next Shakespearean sonnet with "Shall I compare thee to a summer's day?" They are, finally, both love poems, but their tones are markedly different.

WILLIAM SHAKESPEARE (1564–1616)

My mistress' eyes are nothing like the sun   1609

My mistress' eyes are nothing like the sun;
Coral is far more red than her lips' red;
If snow be white, why then her breasts are dun;
If hairs be wires, black wires grow on her head.
I have seen roses damasked red and white,   5
But no such roses see I in her cheeks;

And in some perfumes is there more delight
Than in the breath that from my mistress reeks.
I love to hear her speak, yet well I know
That music hath a far more pleasing sound;
I grant I never saw a goddess go:
My mistress, when she walks, treads on the ground.
    And yet, by heaven, I think my love as rare
    As any she,° belied with false compare.   *lady*

To hear "My mistress' eyes are nothing like the sun" read by Sir John Gielgud, visit bedfordstmartins.com/meyerlit/epages.

CONSIDERATIONS FOR CRITICAL THINKING AND WRITING

1. **FIRST RESPONSE.** What does "mistress" mean in this sonnet? Write a description of this particular mistress based on the images used in the sonnet.

2. What sort of person is the speaker? Does he truly love the woman he describes?

3. In what sense are this sonnet and "Shall I compare thee to a summer's day?" about poetry as well as love?

R. S. GWYNN (B. 1948)

Shakespearean Sonnet   *2010*

With a first line taken from the tv listings

A man is haunted by his father's ghost.
Boy meets girl while feuding families fight.
A Scottish king is murdered by his host.
Two couples get lost on a summer night.
A hunchback murders all who block his way.   5
A ruler's rivals plot against his life.
A fat man and a prince make rebels pay.
A noble Moor has doubts about his wife.
An English king decides to conquer France.
A duke learns that his best friend is a she.   10
A forest sets the scene for this romance.
An old man and his daughters disagree.
A Roman leader makes a big mistake.
A sexy queen is bitten by a snake.

CONSIDERATIONS FOR CRITICAL THINKING AND WRITING

1. **FIRST RESPONSE.** How many Shakespearean plays can you identify from the fourteen encapsulated plots that make up this poem?

2. Discuss the significance of the title.

3. **CREATIVE RESPONSE.** Try your hand at creating a poem — a sonnet or another form — in whole or in part from the channel guide on your TV.

MOLLY PEACOCK (B. 1947)

Desire   *1984*

It doesn't speak and it isn't schooled,
like a small foetal animal with wettened fur.
It is the blind instinct for life unruled,
visceral frankincense and animal myrrh.
It is what babies bring to kings,   5
an eyes-shut, ears-shut medicine of the heart
that smells and touches endings and beginnings
without the details of time's experienced *part-*
fit-into-part-fit-into-part. Like a paw,
it is blunt; like a pet who knows you   10
and nudges your knee with its snout — but more raw
and blinder and younger and more divine, too,
than the tamed wild — it's the drive for what is real,
deeper than the brain's detail: the drive to feel.

CONSIDERATIONS FOR CRITICAL THINKING AND WRITING

1. FIRST RESPONSE. Taken together, what do all of the metaphors
   that appear in this poem reveal about the speaker's conception of
   desire?

2. What is the "it" being described in lines 1–5? How do the allusions
   to the three wise men relate to the other metaphors used to define
   desire?

3. How is this English sonnet structured? What is the effect of its irregular meter?

4. CONNECTION TO ANOTHER SELECTION. Compare the treatment of
   desire in this poem with that of Sharon Olds's "Last Night" (p. 386).
   In an essay, identify the theme of each poem and compare their con-
   ceptions of desire. How alike are these two poems?

MARK JARMAN (B. 1952)

Unholy Sonnet   *1993*

After the praying, after the hymn-singing,
After the sermon's trenchant commentary
On the world's ills, which make ours secondary,
After communion, after the hand-wringing,
And after peace descends upon us, bringing   5
Our eyes up to regard the sanctuary
And how the light swords through it, and how, scary
In their sheer numbers, motes of dust ride, clinging —

There is, as doctors say about some pain,
Discomfort knowing that despite your prayers,   10
Your listening and rejoicing, your small part
In this communal stab at coming clean,
There is one stubborn remnant of your cares
Intact. There is still murder in your heart.

CONSIDERATIONS FOR CRITICAL THINKING AND WRITING

1. **FIRST RESPONSE.** Describe the rhyme scheme and structure of this
   sonnet. Explain why it is an English or Italian sonnet.

2. What are the effects of the use of "after" in lines 1, 2, 4, and 5 and
   "there" in lines 9, 13, and 14?

3. In what sense might this poem be summed up as a "communal stab"
   (line 12)? Discuss the accuracy of this assessment.

4. **CREATIVE RESPONSE.** Try writing a reply to the theme of Jarman's
   poem using the same sonnet form that he uses.

SHERMAN ALEXIE (B. 1966)

The Facebook Sonnet   2011

Welcome to the endless high-school
Reunion. Welcome to past friends
And lovers, however kind or cruel.
Let's undervalue and unmend

The present. Why can't we pretend   5
Every stage of life is the same?
Let's exhume, resume, and extend
Childhood. Let's all play the games

That occupy the young. Let fame
And shame intertwine. Let one's search   10
For God become public domain.
Let church.com become our church.

Let's sign up, sign in, and confess
Here at the altar of loneliness.

CONSIDERATIONS FOR CRITICAL THINKING AND WRITING

1. **FIRST RESPONSE.** Why does a fixed form rather than an open form
   seem especially appropriate for the themes of this poem?

2. What type of sonnet is this?

3. How might Facebook be regarded as the "altar of loneliness"
   (line 14)? Explain why you agree or disagree with the speaker's
   assessment.

Villanelle

The *villanelle* is a fixed form consisting of nineteen lines of any length divided into six stanzas: five tercets and a concluding quatrain. The first and third lines of the initial tercet rhyme; these rhymes are repeated in each subsequent tercet (*aba*) and in the final two lines of the quatrain (*abaa*). Moreover, line 1 appears in its entirety as lines 6, 12, and 18, while line 3 appears as lines 9, 15, and 19. This form may seem to risk monotony, but in competent hands a villanelle can create haunting echoes, as in Dylan Thomas's "Do Not Go Gentle into That Good Night."

DYLAN THOMAS (1914–1953)

Do Not Go Gentle into That Good Night   1952

To hear "Do Not Go Gentle into That Good Night" read by Dylan Thomas, visit bedfordstmartins.com/meyerlit/epages.

Do not go gentle into that good night,
Old age should burn and rave at close of day;
Rage, rage against the dying of the light.

Though wise men at their end know dark is right,
Because their words had forked no lightning they   5
Do not go gentle into that good night.

Good men, the last wave by, crying how bright
Their frail deeds might have danced in a green bay,
Rage, rage against the dying of the light.

Wild men who caught and sang the sun in flight,   10
And learn, too late, they grieved it on its way,
Do not go gentle into that good night.

Grave men, near death, who see with blinding sight
Blind eyes could blaze like meteors and be gay,
Rage, rage against the dying of the light.   15

And you, my father, there on the sad height,
Curse, bless, me now with your fierce tears, I pray.
Do not go gentle into that good night.
Rage, rage against the dying of the light.

CONSIDERATIONS FOR CRITICAL THINKING AND WRITING

1. **FIRST RESPONSE.** How does Thomas vary the meanings of the poem's two refrains: "Do not go gentle into that good night" and "Rage, rage against the dying of the light"?

2. Thomas's father was close to death when this poem was written. How does the tone contribute to the poem's theme?

3. How is "good" used in line 1?

4. Characterize the men who are "wise" (line 4), "Good" (7), "Wild" (10), and "Grave" (13).
5. What do figures of speech contribute to this poem?
6. Discuss this villanelle's sound effects.

Sestina

Although the *sestina* usually does not rhyme, it is perhaps an even more demanding fixed form than the villanelle. A sestina consists of thirty-nine lines of any length divided into six six-line stanzas and a three-line concluding stanza called an *envoy*. The difficulty lies in repeating the six words at the ends of the first stanza's lines at the ends of the lines in the other five six-line stanzas as well. Those words must also appear in the final three lines, where they often resonate important themes. The sestina originated in the Middle Ages, but contemporary poets continue to find it a fascinating and challenging form.

FLORENCE CASSEN MAYERS (B. 1940)

All-American Sestina   1996

One nation, indivisible
two-car garage
three strikes you're out
four-minute mile
five-cent cigar   5
six-string guitar

six-pack Bud
one-day sale
five-year warranty
two-way street   10
fourscore and seven years ago
three cheers

three-star restaurant
sixty-
four-dollar question   15
one-night stand
two-pound lobster
five-star general

five-course meal
three sheets to the wind   20
two bits
six-shooter
one-armed bandit
four-poster

four-wheel drive   25
five-and-dime
hole in one
three-alarm fire
sweet sixteen
two-wheeler   30

two-tone Chevy
four rms, hi flr, w/vu
six-footer
high five
three-ring circus   35
one-room schoolhouse

two thumbs up, five-karat diamond
Fourth of July, three-piece suit
six feet under, one-horse town

CONSIDERATIONS FOR CRITICAL THINKING AND WRITING

1. FIRST RESPONSE. Discuss the significance of the title; what is "All-
   American" about this sestina?
2. How is the structure of this poem different from that of a conventional
   sestina? (What structural requirement does Mayers add for this sestina?)
3. Do you think important themes are raised by this poem, as is traditional for a sestina? If so, what are they? If not, what is being played
   with by using this convention?
4. CONNECTION TO ANOTHER SELECTION. Describe and compare the
   strategy used to create meaning in "All-American Sestina" with that
   used by E. E. Cummings in "next to of course god america i" (p. 437).

Epigram

An *epigram* is a brief, pointed, and witty poem. Although most rhyme
and often are written in couplets, epigrams take no prescribed form.
Instead, they are typically polished bits of compressed irony, satire, or
paradox. Here is an epigram that defines itself.

SAMUEL TAYLOR COLERIDGE (1772–1834)
What Is an Epigram?   1802

What is an epigram? A dwarfish whole;
Its body brevity, and wit its soul.

These additional examples by David McCord and Paul Laurence
Dunbar satisfy Coleridge's definition.

DAVID McCORD (1897–1997)

Epitaph on a Waiter   *1933*

By and by
God caught his eye.

PAUL LAURENCE DUNBAR (1872–1906)

Theology   *1896*

There is a heaven, for ever, day by day,
The upward longing of my soul doth tell
   me so.
There is a hell, I'm quite as sure; for pray,
If there were not, where would my
   neighbors go?

Courtesy of the Ohio Historical Society.

CONSIDERATIONS FOR CRITICAL THINKING AND WRITING

1. **FIRST RESPONSE.** In what sense is each of these epigrams, as Coleridge puts it, a "dwarfish whole"?

2. Explain which of these epigrams, in addition to being witty, makes a serious point.

3. **CREATIVE RESPONSE.** Try writing a few epigrams that say something memorable about whatever you choose to focus on.

Limerick

The *limerick* is always light and humorous. Its usual form consists of five predominantly anapestic lines rhyming *aabba;* lines 1, 2, and 5 contain three feet, while lines 3 and 4 contain two. Limericks have delighted everyone from schoolchildren to sophisticated adults, and they range in subject matter from the simply innocent and silly to the satiric or obscene. The sexual humor helps to explain why so many limericks are written anonymously. Here is one that is anonymous but more concerned with physics than physiology.

ARTHUR HENRY REGINALD BUTLER (1879–1944)

There was a young lady named Bright   1923

There was a young lady named Bright,
Whose speed was far faster than light,
    She started one day
    In a relative way,
And returned on the previous night.

This next one is a particularly clever definition of a limerick.

LAURENCE PERRINE (1915–1995)

The limerick's never averse   1982

The limerick's never averse
To expressing itself in a terse
    Economical style,
    And yet, all the while,
The limerick's *always* a verse.

CONSIDERATIONS FOR CRITICAL THINKING AND WRITING

1. **FIRST RESPONSE.** How does this limerick differ from others you know? How is it similar?
2. Scan Perrine's limerick. How do the lines measure up to the traditional fixed metrical pattern?
3. **CREATIVE RESPONSE.** Try writing a limerick. Use the following basic pattern.

      ˘ ˘ ´   ˘ ˘ ´   ˘ ˘ ´
      ˘ ˘ ´   ˘ ˘ ´   ˘ ˘ ´
         ˘ ˘ ´   ˘ ˘ ´
         ˘ ˘ ´   ˘ ˘ ´
      ˘ ˘ ´   ˘ ˘ ´   ˘ ˘ ´

   You might begin with a friend's name or the name of your school or town. Your instructor is, of course, fair game, too, provided your tact matches your wit.

Haiku

Another brief fixed poetic form, borrowed from the Japanese, is the *haiku*. A haiku is usually described as consisting of seventeen syllables organized into three unrhymed lines of five, seven, and five syllables. Owing to language difference, however, English translations of haiku are often only approximated, because a Japanese haiku exists in time (Japanese syllables have duration). The number of syllables in our sense is not as significant as their duration in Japanese. These poems typically present an intense emotion or a vivid image of nature, which, in the Japanese, are also designed to lead to a spiritual insight.

MATSUO BASHŌ (1644–1694)

Under cherry trees   *date unknown*

Under cherry trees
Soup, the salad, fish and all . . .
Seasoned with petals.

CAROLYN KIZER (B. 1925)

After Bashō   *1984*

Tentatively, you
slip onstage this evening,
pallid, famous moon.

SONIA SANCHEZ (B. 1935)

c'mon man hold me   *1998*

c'mon man hold me
touch me before time love me
from behind your eyes.

> ### CONSIDERATIONS FOR CRITICAL THINKING AND WRITING
>
> 1. **FIRST RESPONSE.** What different emotions do these three haiku evoke?
> 2. What differences and similarities are there between the effects of a haiku and those of an epigram?
> 3. **CREATIVE RESPONSE.** Compose a haiku. Try to make it as allusive and suggestive as possible.

Elegy

An elegy in classical Greek and Roman literature was written in alternating hexameter and pentameter lines. Since the seventeenth century, however, the term *elegy* has been used to describe a lyric poem written to commemorate someone who is dead. The word is also used to refer to a serious meditative poem produced to express the speaker's melancholy thoughts. Elegies no longer conform to a fixed pattern of lines and stanzas, but their characteristic subject is related to death and their tone is mournfully contemplative.

BEN JONSON (1573–1637)
On My First Son   1603

Farewell, thou child of my right hand,° and joy.
My sin was too much hope of thee, loved boy;
Seven years thou wert lent to me, and I thee pay,
Exacted by thy fate, on the just day.°   his birthday
Oh, could I lose all father° now. For why   fatherhood   5
Will man lament the state he should envỳ?—
To have so soon 'scaped world's and flesh's rage,
And, if no other misery, yet age.
Rest in soft peace, and asked, say, "Here doth lie
Ben Jonson his best piece of poetry,"   10
For whose sake henceforth all his vows be such
As what he loves may never like too much.

1 *child of my right hand:* This phrase translates the Hebrew name "Benjamin," Jonson's son.

CONSIDERATIONS FOR CRITICAL THINKING AND WRITING

1. **FIRST RESPONSE.** Describe the tone of this elegy. What makes it so emotionally convincing?

2. In what sense is Jonson's son "his best piece of poetry" (line 10)?

3. Interpret the final two lines. Do they seem consistent with the rest of the poem? Why or why not?

BRENDAN GALVIN (B. 1938)
An Evel Knievel° Elegy   2008

We have all felt our parachutes
malfunctioning at a job interview
or cocktail party, with bystanders
reading the freefall on our faces,
and some of us have imagined   5
how it must have felt for you
above the Snake River Canyon
or the fountains outside Caesar's
Palace, though a mental bungee
reversed our flops before we were   10
converted to sacks of poker chips and spent

Evel Knievel (1938–2007): American motorcycle stunt performer whose daredevil jumps over lines of vehicles, canyons, and rivers were nationally televised in the 1960s and 70s.

a month or more in a coma. You were
our star-spangled Icarus,° Evel,
while we dressed off the rack
for working lives among the common 15
asps and vipers, never jumping
the rattlers in what you and
the networks considered a sport.
Stunts, Evel. We loved their heights
and distances from our gray quotidian 20
so much we bought the kids three
hundred million dollars' worth
of your wheels and getups. You were
our airborne Elvis, and rode
your rocket-powered bike through fire. 25
Which we admired, though some,
annealing or annulled, knew that
they stand in fire all their lives,
and turned away, and didn't applaud,
and would not suffer the loss 30
of your departure.

13 *Icarus:* In Greek mythology, a character who fell to the earth and died after refusing to heed his father's advice about not flying too close to the sun on manufactured
wings of wax and feathers that melted from the heat.

CONSIDERATIONS FOR CRITICAL THINKING AND WRITING

1. **FIRST RESPONSE.** To what extent is this poem a meditation upon popular culture as well as an elegy for Evel Knievel?

2. Discuss Galvin's use of metaphor to characterize Knievel. Choose
three metaphors that seem especially vivid to you and explain why.

3. Discuss the thematic significance of lines 26 to 31. How would you
read the poem differently if it ended in the middle of line 26?

Ode

An *ode* is characterized by a serious topic and formal tone, but no prescribed formal pattern describes all odes. In some odes the pattern of
each stanza is repeated throughout, while in others each stanza introduces a new pattern. Odes are lengthy lyrics that often include lofty
emotions conveyed by a dignified style. Typical topics include truth,
art, freedom, justice, and the meaning of life. Frequently such lyrics tend to be more public than private, and their speakers often use
apostrophe.

Percy Bysshe Shelley (1792–1822)

Ode to the West Wind   *1820*

I

O wild West Wind, thou breath of Autumn's being,
Thou, from whose unseen presence the leaves dead
Are driven, like ghosts from an enchanter fleeing,

Yellow, and black, and pale, and hectic red,
Pestilence-stricken multitudes: O thou,   5
Who chariotest to their dark wintry bed

The wingèd seeds, where they lie cold and low,
Each like a corpse within its grave, until
Thine azure sister of the Spring shall blow

Her clarion o'er the dreaming earth, and fill   10
(Driving sweet buds like flocks to feed in air)
With living hues and odors plain and hill:

Wild Spirit, which art moving everywhere;
Destroyer and preserver; hear, oh, hear!

II

Thou on whose stream, mid the steep sky's commotion,   15
Loose clouds like earth's decaying leaves are shed,
Shook from the tangled boughs of Heaven and Ocean,

Angels° of rain and lightning: there are spread   *messengers*
On the blue surface of thine airy surge,
Like the bright hair uplifted from the head   20

Of some fierce Maenad,° even from the dim verge
Of the horizon to the zenith's height,
The locks of the approaching storm. Thou dirge

Of the dying year, to which this closing night
Will be the dome of a vast sepulcher,   25
Vaulted with all thy congregated might

Of vapors, from whose solid atmosphere
Black rain, and fire, and hail will burst: oh, hear!

---

21 *Maenad:* In Greek mythology, a frenzied worshipper of Dionysus, god of wine and
fertility.

III

Thou who didst waken from his summer dreams
The blue Mediterranean, where he lay,   30
Lulled by the coil of his crystálline streams,

Beside a pumice isle in Baiae's bay,°
And saw in sleep old palaces and towers
Quivering within the wave's intenser day,

All overgrown with azure moss and flowers   35
So sweet, the sense faints picturing them! Thou
For whose path the Atlantic's level powers

Cleave themselves into chasms, while far below
The sea-blooms and the oozy woods which wear
The sapless foliage of the ocean, know   40

Thy voice, and suddenly grow gray with fear,
And tremble and despoil themselves: oh, hear!

IV

If I were a dead leaf thou mightest bear;
If I were a swift cloud to fly with thee;
A wave to pant beneath thy power, and share   45

The impulse of thy strength, only less free
Than thou, O uncontrollable! If even
I were as in my boyhood, and could be

The comrade by thy wanderings over Heaven,
As then, when to outstrip thy skyey speed   50
Scarce seemed a vision; I would ne'er have striven

As thus with thee in prayer in my sore need.
Oh, lift me as a wave, a leaf, a cloud!
I fall upon the thorns of life! I bleed!

A heavy weight of hours has chained and bowed   55
One too like thee: tameless, and swift, and proud.

V

Make me thy lyre,° even as the forest is:
What if my leaves are falling like its own!
The tumult of thy mighty harmonies

32 *Baiae's bay:* A bay in the Mediterranean Sea.   57 *Make me thy lyre:* Sound is produced on an Aeolian lyre, or wind harp, by wind blowing across its strings.

Will take from both a deep, autumnal tone,   60
Sweet though in sadness. Be thou, Spirit fierce,
My spirit! Be thou me, impetuous one!

Drive my dead thoughts over the universe
Like withered leaves to quicken a new birth!
And, by the incantation of this verse,   65

Scatter, as from an unextinguished hearth
Ashes and sparks, my words among mankind!
Be through my lips to unawakened earth

The trumpet of a prophecy! O Wind,
If Winter comes, can Spring be far behind?   70

CONSIDERATIONS FOR CRITICAL THINKING AND WRITING

1. **FIRST RESPONSE.** Write a summary of each of this ode's five sections.
2. What is the speaker's situation? What is his "sore need" (line 52)? What does the speaker ask of the wind in lines 57–70?
3. What does the wind signify in this ode? How is it used symbolically?
4. Determine the meter and rhyme of the first five stanzas. How do these elements contribute to the ode's movement? Is this pattern continued in the other four sections?

Parody

A *parody* is a humorous imitation of another, usually serious, work. It can take any fixed or open form because parodists imitate the tone, language, and shape of the original. While a parody may be teasingly close to a work's style, it typically deflates the subject matter to make the original seem absurd. Parody can be used as a kind of literary criticism to expose the defects in a work, but it is also very often an affectionate acknowledgment that a well-known work has become both institutionalized in our culture and fair game for some fun. Read Robert Frost's "The Road Not Taken" (p. 575) and then study this parody.

BLANCHE FARLEY (B. 1937)

The Lover Not Taken   1984

Committed to one, she wanted both
And, mulling it over, long she stood,
Alone on the road, loath
To leave, wanting to hide in the
        undergrowth.
This new guy, smooth as a yellow wood

> **WHEN I WRITE** "Keep your work, even if it is unfinished or not to your liking. It can be revised or even rewritten in another form. Maybe the original idea is what will prove valuable. Most importantly, despite all else going on in your life, despite rejection or feelings of discouragement, keep writing."
> — BLANCHE FARLEY

Really turned her on. She liked his hair,
His smile. But the other, Jack, had a claim
On her already and she had to admit, he did wear
Well. In fact, to be perfectly fair,
He understood her. His long, lithe frame   10

Beside hers in the evening tenderly lay.
Still, if this blond guy dropped by someday,
Couldn't way just lead on to way?
No. For if way led on and Jack
Found out, she doubted if he would ever come back.   15

Oh, she turned with a sigh.
Somewhere ages and ages hence,
She might be telling this. "And I —"
She would say, "stood faithfully by."
But by then who would know the difference?   20

With that in mind, she took the fast way home,
The road by the pond, and phoned the blond.

CONSIDERATIONS FOR CRITICAL THINKING AND WRITING

1. **FIRST RESPONSE.** To what degree does this poem duplicate Frost's style? How does it differ?

2. Does this parody seem successful to you? Explain what you think makes a successful parody.

3. **CREATIVE RESPONSE.** Choose a poet whose work you know reasonably well or would like to know better and determine what is characteristic about his or her style. Then choose a poem to parody. It's probably best to attempt a short poem or a section of a long work. If you have difficulty selecting an author, you might consider Herrick, Blake, Keats, Dickinson, Whitman, or Frost, as a number of their works are included in this book.

Perspective

ELAINE MITCHELL (1924–2013)

Form   *1994*

Is it a corset
or primal wave?
Don't try to force it.

Even endorse it
to shape and deceive.   5
Ouch, too tight a corset.

Take it off. No remorse. It
's an ace up your sleeve.
No need to force it.

Can you make a horse knit?   10
Who would believe?
Consider. Of course, it

might be a resource. Wit,
your grateful slave.
Form. Sometimes you force it,   15

sometimes divorce it
to make it behave.
So don't try to force it.
Respect a good corset.

CONSIDERATIONS FOR CRITICAL THINKING AND WRITING

1. **FIRST RESPONSE.** What is the speaker's attitude toward form?

2. Explain why you think the form of this poem does or does not conform to the speaker's advice.

3. Why is the metaphor of a corset an especially apt image for this poem?

Picture Poem

By arranging lines into particular shapes, poets can sometimes organize typography into *picture poems* of what they describe. Words have been arranged into all kinds of shapes, from apples to light bulbs. Notice how the shape of this next poem embodies its meaning.

WHEN I WRITE "I've shared my poems with a friend, who's also a poet, for decades now. He marks them up and gives them back; I do the same for him. You need a sympathetic critic who is not you, to help make your poetry as strong and clear as possible to readers who are not you." — MICHAEL MCFEE

MICHAEL McFEE (B. 1954)

In Medias Res°   1985

His waist
like the plot
thickens, wedding
pants now breathtaking,
belt no longer the cinch   5
it once was, belly's cambium
expanding to match each birthday,
his body a wad of anonymous tissue
swung in the same centrifuge of years
that separates a house from its foundation,   10
undermining sidewalks grim with joggers
and loose-filled graves and families
and stars collapsing on themselves,
no preservation society capable
of plugging entropy's dike,   15
under his zipper's sneer
a belly hibernation-
soft, ready for
the kill.

In Medias Res: A Latin term for a story that begins "in the middle of things."

CONSIDERATIONS FOR CRITICAL THINKING AND WRITING

1. **FIRST RESPONSE.** Explain how the title is related to this poem's shape and meaning.
2. Identify the puns. How do they work in the poem?
3. What is "cambium" (line 6)? Why is the phrase "belly's cambium" especially appropriate?
4. What is the tone of this poem? Is it consistent throughout?

20

Open Form

I'm not very good at communicating verbally. I'm somebody who listens more than talks. I like to listen and absorb. But when I need to connect with people and I need to reach out, I write.

— RUTH FORMAN

Photograph by Christine Bennett, www.cbimages.org.

Many poems, especially those written in the past century, are composed of lines that cannot be scanned for a fixed or predominant meter. Moreover, very often these poems do not rhyme. Known as *free verse* (from the French, *vers libre*), such lines can derive their rhythmic qualities from the repetition of words, phrases, or grammatical structures; the arrangement of words on the printed page; or some other means. In recent years the term *open form* has been used in place of *free verse* to avoid the erroneous suggestion that this kind of poetry lacks all discipline and shape.

Although the following poem does not use measurable meters, it does have rhythm.

WALT WHITMAN (1819–1892)
From *I Sing the Body Electric*   1855

🅴 To hear this portion of "I Sing the Body Electric" read by Brian Murray, visit bedfordstmartins.com/meyerlit/epages.

O my body! I dare not desert the likes of you in other
    men and women, nor the likes of the parts of you,
I believe the likes of you are to stand or fall with the likes of the soul,
    (and that they are the soul,)
I believe the likes of you shall stand or fall with my poems, and that they
    are my poems.

Man's, woman's, child's, youth's, wife's,
    husband's, mother's, father's, young
    man's, young woman's poems.
Head, neck, hair, ears, drop and tympan of
    the ears.
Eyes, eye-fringes, iris of the eye, eyebrows,
    and the waking or sleeping of the
    lids,
Mouth, tongue, lips, teeth, roof of the
    mouth, jaws, and the jaw-hinges,
Nose, nostrils of the nose, and the
    partition,
Cheeks, temples, forehead, chin, throat,
    back of the neck, neck-slue,
Strong shoulders, manly beard, scapula,
    hind-shoulders, and the ample side-
    round of the chest,

Courtesy of the Bayley-Whitman
Collection of Ohio Wesleyan University
of Delaware, Ohio.

Upper-arm, armpit, elbow-socket, lower-arm, arm-sinews, arm-bones,
Wrist and wrist-joints, hand, palm, knuckles, thumb, forefinger, finger-
    joints, finger-nails,
Broad breast-front, curling hair of the breast, breast-bone, breast-side,
Ribs, belly, backbone, joints of the backbone,
Hips, hip-sockets, hip-strength, inward and outward round,
    man-balls, man-root,   15
Strong set of thighs, well carrying the trunk above,
Leg-fibers, knee, knee-pan, upper-leg, under-leg,
Ankles, instep, foot-ball, toes, toe-joints, the heel;
All attitudes, all the shapeliness, all the belongings of my or your
    body or of any one's body, male or female,
The lung-sponges, the stomach-sac, the bowels sweet and clean,   20
The brain in its folds inside the skull-frame,
Sympathies, heart-valves, palate-valves, sexuality, maternity,
Womanhood, and all that is a woman, and the man that comes from
    woman,
The womb, the teats, nipples, breast-milk, tears, laughter, weeping,
    love-looks, love-perturbations and risings,
The voice, articulation, language, whispering, shouting aloud,   25
Food, drink, pulse, digestion, sweat, sleep, walking, swimming,
Poise on the hips, leaping, reclining, embracing, arm-curving and tightening,
The continual changes of the flex of the mouth, and around the eyes,
The skin, the sunburnt shade, freckles, hair,
The curious sympathy one feels when feeling with the hand
    the naked meat of the body,   30
The circling rivers the breath, and breathing it in and out,
The beauty of the waist, and thence of the hips, and thence
    downward toward the knees,

The thin red jellies within you or within me, the bones and the marrow
    in the bones,
The exquisite realization of health;
O I say these are not the parts and poems of the body only,
    but of the soul,   35
O I say now these are the soul!

CONSIDERATIONS FOR CRITICAL THINKING AND WRITING

1. **FIRST RESPONSE.** What informs this speaker's attitude toward the
   human body?
2. Read the poem aloud. Is it simply a tedious enumeration of body
   parts, or do the lines achieve some kind of rhythmic cadence?

Open form poetry is sometimes regarded as formless because it is unlike
the strict fixed forms of a sonnet, villanelle, or sestina. But even though open
form poems may not employ traditional meters and rhymes, they still rely
on an intense use of language to establish rhythms and relations between
meaning and form. Open form poems use the arrangement of words and
phrases on the printed page, pauses, line lengths, and other means to create
unique forms that express their particular meaning and tone.

The excerpt from Whitman's "I Sing the Body Electric" demonstrates
how the white space on a page and rhythmic cadences can be aligned with
meaning, but there is one kind of open form poetry that doesn't even
look like poetry on a page. A *prose poem* is printed as prose and represents,
perhaps, the most clear opposite of fixed forms. Here is a brief example.

DAVID SHUMATE (B. 1950)

Shooting the Horse   2004

I unlatch the stall door, step inside, and stroke the silky neck of the old
mare like a lover about to leave. I take an ear in hand, fold it over, and run
my fingers across her muzzle. I coax her head up so I can blow into those
nostrils. All part of the routine we taught each other long ago. I turn
a half turn, pull a pistol from my coat, raise it to that long brow with
the white blaze and place it between her sleepy eyes. I clear my throat.
A sound much louder than it should be. I squeeze the trigger and the
horse's feet fly out from under her as gravity gives way to a force even
more austere, which we have named mercy.

CONSIDERATIONS FOR CRITICAL THINKING AND WRITING

1. **FIRST RESPONSE.** Describe the range of emotions that this poem produces for you.
2. Think of other words that could be substituted for *mercy* in the final
   line. How does your choice change the tone and theme of the poem?

3. Rearrange the poem so that its words, phrases, and sentences are set up to use the white space on the page to convey tone and meaning. Which version do you prefer? Why?

4. **CONNECTION TO ANOTHER SELECTION.** Compare the treatment of the death of the horse in this poem with that of the bovine in "The Cow" by Andrew Hudgins (p. 460).

RICHARD HAGUE (B. 1947)

Directions for Resisting the SAT

1996

Do not believe in October or May
or in any Saturday morning with pencils.
Do not observe the rules of gravity,
commas, history.
Lie about numbers.
Blame your successes,
every one of them,
on rotten luck.
Resign all clubs and committees.
Go down with the ship — any ship.   10
Speak nothing like English.
Desire to live whole,
like an oyster or snail,
and follow no directions.
Listen to no one.   15

Make your marks on everything.

> WHEN I READ "In an increasingly distracting and distracted world, poems are countercultural. They can pay attention — to public and private life, to the world of nature and rituals and things, in ways akin to prayer, or to precise and pointed cursing — like magic spells. They name what ails us."
> — RICHARD HAGUE

CONSIDERATIONS FOR CRITICAL THINKING AND WRITING

1. **FIRST RESPONSE.** What is the speaker's subversive message? What do you think of the advice offered?

2. What kinds of assumptions do you suppose Hague makes about readers' attitudes toward the SAT? To what extent do you share those attitudes?

3. Discuss Hague's use of spacing and line breaks. What is the effect of the space between lines 15 and 16?

WILLIAM CARLOS WILLIAMS (1883–1963)

The Red Wheelbarrow

1923

so much depends
upon

a red wheel
barrow

To hear "The Red Wheelbarrow" read by William Carlos Williams, visit bedfordstmartins.com/meyerlit/epages.

glazed with rain
water

beside the white
chickens.

CONSIDERATIONS FOR CRITICAL THINKING AND WRITING

1. **FIRST RESPONSE.** What "depends upon" the things mentioned in the poem? What is the effect of these images? Do they have a particular meaning?
2. Do these lines have any kind of rhythm?
3. How does this poem resemble a haiku? How is it different?

Much of the poetry published today is written in open form; however, many poets continue to take pleasure in the requirements imposed by fixed forms. Some write both fixed form and open form poetry. Each kind offers rewards to careful readers as well. Here are several more open form poems that establish their own unique patterns.

ELLEN BASS (B. 1947)

Gate C22   *2002*

At gate C22 in the Portland airport
a man in a broad-band leather hat kissed
a woman arriving from Orange County.
They kissed and kissed and kissed. Long
        after

> WHEN I WRITE "The hardest part of writing 'Gate C22' was the opening—locating the people in concise and natural syntax. I wrote the first three lines over and over. They were the foundation and until I could get them, I couldn't go on with the poem." —ELLEN BASS

the other passengers clicked the handles of their carry-ons   5
and wheeled briskly toward short-term parking,
the couple stood there, arms wrapped around each other
like he'd just staggered off the boat at Ellis Island,
like she'd been released at last from ICU, snapped
out of a coma, survived bone cancer, made it down   10
from Annapurna° in only the clothes she was wearing.

Neither of them was young. His beard was gray.
She carried a few extra pounds you could imagine
her saying she had to lose. But they kissed lavish
kisses like the ocean in the early morning,   15
the way it gathers and swells, sucking
each rock under, swallowing it
again and again. We were all watching—

---

11 *Annapurna:* A mountain in the Himalayas.

passengers waiting for the delayed flight
to San Jose, the stewardesses, the pilots,   20
the aproned woman icing Cinnabons, the man selling
sunglasses. We couldn't look away. We could
taste the kisses crushed in our mouths.

But the best part was his face. When he drew back
and looked at her, his smile soft with wonder, almost   25
as though he were a mother still open from giving birth,
as your mother must have looked at you, no matter
what happened after — if she beat you or left you or
you're lonely now — you once lay there, the vernix
not yet wiped off, and someone gazed at you   30
as if you were the first sunrise seen from the earth.
The whole wing of the airport hushed,
all of us trying to slip into that woman's middle-aged body,
her plaid Bermuda shorts, sleeveless blouse, glasses,
little gold hoop earrings, tilting our heads up.   35

CONSIDERATIONS FOR CRITICAL THINKING AND WRITING

1. **FIRST RESPONSE.** What is it that is so riveting about this kiss?
2. Explain how each stanza increases the sense of wonder in the speaker.
3. Discuss Bass's use of similes as a means of creating tone.
4. **CONNECTION TO ANOTHER SELECTION.** Compare the poets' use of setting to establish theme in "Gate C22" and in George Eliot's "In a London Drawingroom" (p. 570).

JULIO MARZÁN (B. 1946)

The Translator at the Reception
for Latin American Writers   *1997*

Air-conditioned introductions,
then breezy Spanish conversation
fan his curiosity to know
what country I come from.
"Puerto Rico and the Bronx."   5

Spectacled downward eyes
translate disappointment
like a poison mushroom
puffed in his thoughts as if,
after investing a sizable   10
intellectual budget, transporting
a huge cast and camera crew

to film on location
Mayan pyramid grandeur,
indigenes whose ancient gods   15
and comet-tail plumage
inspire a glorious epic
of revolution across a continent,
he received a lurid script
for a social documentary   20
rife with dreary streets
and pathetic human interest,
meager in the profits of high culture.

Understandably he turns,
catches up with the hostess,   25
praising the uncommon quality
of her offerings of cheese.

CONSIDERATIONS FOR CRITICAL THINKING AND WRITING

1. **FIRST RESPONSE.** What is the speaker's attitude toward the person
   he meets at the reception? What lines in particular lead you to that
   conclusion?

2. Why is that person so disappointed about the answer, "Puerto Rico
   and the Bronx" (line 5)?

3. Explain lines 6 to 23. How do they reveal both the speaker and the
   person encountered at the reception?

4. Why is the setting of this poem significant?

ANONYMOUS

The Frog   *date unknown*

What a wonderful bird the frog are!
When he stand he sit almost;
When he hop he fly almost.
He ain't got no sense hardly;
He ain't got no tail hardly either.
When he sit, he sit on what he ain't got almost.

CONSIDERATIONS FOR CRITICAL THINKING AND WRITING

1. **FIRST RESPONSE.** How is the poem a description of the speaker as well
   as of a frog?

2. Though this poem is ungrammatical, it does have a patterned structure. How does the pattern of sentences create a formal structure?

Natasha Trethewey (b. 1966)

On Captivity   2007

© Joel Benjamin.

Being all Stripped as Naked as We were Born,
and endeavoring to hide our Nakedness, these
Cannaballs took [our] Books, and tearing out
the Leaves would give each of us a Leaf to
cover us . . .

—*Jonathan Dickinson, 1699*

At the hands now
    of their captors, those
        they've named *savages*,
    do they say the word itself
savagely—hissing

that first letter,
    the serpent's image,
        releasing
    thought into speech?
For them now,   10

everything is flesh
    as if their thoughts, made
        suddenly corporeal,
    reveal even more
their nakedness—   15

the shame of it:
    their bodies rendered
        plain as the natives'—
    homely and pale,
their ordinary sex,   20

the secret illicit hairs
    that do not (cannot)
        cover enough.
    This is how they are brought,
naked as newborns,   25

to knowledge. Adam and Eve
    in the New World,
        they have only the Bible
    to cover them. Think of it:
a woman holding before her   30

the torn leaves of *Genesis,*
    and a man covering himself
        with the Good Book's
    frontispiece — his own name
inscribed on the page.   35

CONSIDERATIONS FOR CRITICAL THINKING AND WRITING

1. **FIRST RESPONSE.** Trethewey has written about the sources of her
   epigraph: "Because the conquerors made use of the written word
   to claim land [in North America] inhabited by native people,
   I found the detail of settlers forced to cover themselves with torn
   pages from books a compelling irony" (*The Best American Poetry
   2008,* p. 182). How does this comment contribute to the central
   irony in the poem?
2. Discuss Trethewey's use of alliteration in lines 1 to 9.
3. In what sense are the captors "brought, / naked as newborns, / to
   knowledge" (lines 24–26)?

CHRISTINA GEROGIANNIS (B. 1981)

Headland   2007

                          1

There is no sadness
but held in the bedroom of the
rented house from two years ago.

I should say no
definite sadness.   5

                          2

On the dresser:
a small sample of jasper.
Late summer, the house smelled of bleach.

In every corner we tried
to clean it of the day.   10

                          3

The telephone rang in the living day.
After that, the prepared slideshow, the
walking in and walking out.

The photos on corkboard.
The ordeal over.   15

4

The quilt stained white in places
from mopping bleach onto the ceiling
and not moving the quilt.

I could smell bleach underneath and
thought of the acres around the house.   20

5

Here, in the driveway,
is Celeste in her workout clothes.
This is ending everything.

Quarries, unfamiliar, not
just unfamiliar —   25

6

Home is over for us.
Here, in the kitchen,
we learn of a new death.

Celeste is polite and leaves. Acres surround
the house, protection from nothing, really.   30

7

In the living world I collected rocks
and minerals, and was interested in
telescopes, meridians. Hills, quarries —

the land at home, whatever it was.
At this hour, clean. Later, start again.   35

QUESTIONS FOR CRITICAL THINKING AND WRITING

1. **FIRST RESPONSE.** What is lost in "Headland"? How does "no definite sadness" characterize feelings about a place that has been lost?

2. What does Gerogiannis achieve by describing emotions, places, and objects in ambiguous terms? Are there parallel details to "no definite sadness" that characterize the absences referred to in the poem?

3. Is "Headland" a place, a geological formation, or a mental territory? How does this affect your sense of the title?

Tato Laviera (b. 1951)

AmeRícan   *1985*

we gave birth to a new generation,
AmeRícan, broader than lost gold
never touched, hidden inside the
puerto rican mountains.

we gave birth to a new generation,   5
AmeRícan, it includes everything
imaginable you-name-it-we-got-it
society.

we gave birth to a new generation,
AmeRícan salutes all folklores,   10
european, indian, black, spanish,
and anything else compatible:

AmeRícan,   singing to composer pedro flores'° palm
             trees high up in the universal sky!

AmeRícan,   sweet soft spanish danzas gypsies   15
             moving lyrics la *española*° cascabelling   *Spanish*
             presence always singing at our side!

AmeRícan,   beating jíbaro° modern troubadours
             crying guitars romantic continental
             bolero love songs!   20

AmeRícan,   across forth and across back
             back across and forth back
             forth across and back and forth
             our trips are walking bridges!

             it all dissolved into itself, the attempt   25
             was truly made, the attempt was truly
             absorbed, digested, we spit out
             the poison, we spit out the malice,
             we stand, affirmative in action,
             to reproduce a broader answer to the   30
             marginality that gobbled us up abruptly!

AmeRícan,   walking plena-rhythms° in new york,
             strutting beautifully alert, alive,
             many turning eyes wondering,
             admiring!   35

---

13 *pedro flores:* Puerto Rican composer of popular romantic songs. 18 *jíbaro:* A particular style of music played by Puerto Rican mountain farmers. 32 *plena-rhythms:* African–Puerto Rican folklore, music, and dance.

AmeRícan,   defining myself my own way any way many
             ways Am e Rícan, with the big R and the
             accent on the í!

AmeRícan,   like the soul gliding talk of gospel
             boogie music!   40

AmeRícan,   speaking new words in spanglish tenements,
             fast tongue moving street corner *"que
             corta"*° talk being invented at the insistence   *that cuts*
             of a smile!

AmeRícan,   abounding inside so many ethnic english   45
             people, and out of humanity, we blend
             and mix all that is good!

AmeRícan,   integrating in new york and defining our
             own *destino,*° our own way of life,   *destiny*

AmeRícan,   defining the new america, humane america,   50
             admired america, loved america, harmonious
             america, the world in peace, our energies
             collectively invested to find other civili-
             zations, to touch God, further and further,
             to dwell in the spirit of divinity!   55

AmeRícan,   yes, for now, for i love this, my second
             land, and i dream to take the accent from
             the altercation, and be proud to call
             myself american, in the u.s. sense of the
             word, AmeRícan, America!   60

CONSIDERATIONS FOR CRITICAL THINKING AND WRITING

1. **FIRST RESPONSE.** How does the arrangement of lines communicate a sense of energy and vitality?

2. How does the speaker portray Puerto Ricans living in the United States?

3. How does the poet describe the United States?

PETER MEINKE (B. 1932)

The ABC of Aerobics   *1983*

Air seeps through alleys and our diaphragms
balloon blackly with this mix of
carbon monoxide and the thousand corrosives a city
doles out free to its constituents;

everyone's jogging through Edgemont Park,   5
frightened by death and fatty tissue,
gasping at the maximal heart rate,
hoping to outlive all the others streaming
in the lanes like lemmings lurching toward their last
jump. I join in despair   10
knowing my arteries jammed with
lint and tobacco, lard and bourbon — my
medical history a noxious marsh:
newts and moles slink through the sodden veins,
owls hoot in the lungs' dark branches;   15
probably I shall keel off the john like
queer Uncle George and lie on the bathroom floor
raging about Shirley Clark, my true love in
seventh grade, God bless her wherever she lives
tied to that turkey who hugely   20
undervalues the beauty of her tiny earlobes, one
view of which (either one: they are both perfect)
would add years to my life and I could skip these
x-rays, turn in my insurance card, and trade
yoga and treadmills and jogging and zen and   25
zucchini for drinking and dreaming of her, breathing hard.

CONSIDERATIONS FOR CRITICAL THINKING AND WRITING

1. **FIRST RESPONSE.** How does the title help to establish a pattern throughout the poem? How does the pattern contribute to the poem's meaning?

2. How does the speaker feel about exercise? How do his descriptions of his physical condition serve to characterize him?

3. A primer is a book that teaches children to read or introduces them, in an elementary way, to the basics of a subject. The title "The ABC of Aerobics" indicates that this poem is meant to be a primer. What is it trying to teach us? Is its final lesson serious or ironic?

4. Discuss Meinke's use of humor. Is it effective?

5. **CONNECTION TO ANOTHER SELECTION.** Compare the speaker's treatment of the past in this poem with that in Billy Collins's "Nostalgia" (p. 536). Which speaker do you find more appealing? Why?

Found Poem

This next selection is a *found poem*, unintentional verse discovered in a nonpoetic context, such as a conversation, news story, or an advertisement. Found poems are playful reminders that the words in poems are very often the language we use every day. Whether such found language should be regarded as a poem is an issue left for you to consider.

DONALD JUSTICE (1925–2004)

Order in the Streets   1969

(From instructions printed on a child's toy, Christmas 1968, as reported in the New York Times*)*

I. 2. 3.
Switch on.

Jeep rushes
to the scene
of riot   5

Jeep goes
in all directions
by mystery action.

Jeep stops periodically
to turn hood over   10

machine gun appears
with realistic
shooting noise.

After putting down riot,
jeep goes   15
back to the headquarters.

CONSIDERATIONS FOR CRITICAL THINKING AND WRITING

1. **FIRST RESPONSE.** What is the effect of arranging these instructions in discrete lines? How are the language and meaning enhanced by this arrangement?

2. **CREATIVE RESPONSE.** Look for phrases or sentences in ads, textbooks, labels, or directions — in anything that might inadvertently contain provocative material that would be revealed by arranging the words in verse lines. You may even discover some patterns of rhyme and rhythm. After arranging the lines, explain why you organized them as you did.

Poetry in Depth

21

A Study of Billy Collins:
The Author Reflects
on Five Poems

More interesting to me than what a poem means is how it travels. In the classroom, I like to substitute for the question, "What is the meaning of the poem?" other questions: "How does this poem go?" or "How does this poem travel through itself in search of its own ending?"

—BILLY COLLINS

Billy Collins selected the five poems presented in this chapter and provided commentaries for each so that readers of this anthology might gain a sense of how he, a former poet laureate and teacher, writes and thinks about poetry. In his perspectives on the poems, Collins explores a variety of literary elements ranging from the poems' origins, allusions, images, metaphors, symbols, and tone to his strategies for maintaining his integrity and sensitivity to both language and the reader. Be advised, however, that these discussions do not constitute CliffsNotes to the poems; Collins does not interpret a single one of them for us. Instead of "beating it with a hose / to find out what it really means," as he writes in his poem "Introduction to Poetry" (p. 356), he "hold[s] it up to the light" so that we can see more clearly how each poem works. He explains that the purpose of his discussions is to have students "see how a poem gets written from the opening lines, through the shifts and maneuvers of the body to whatever closure the poem manages to achieve . . . to make the process of writing a poem less mysterious without taking away the mystery that is at the heart of every good poem."

Along with Collins's illuminating and friendly tutorial, the chapter also provides some additional contexts, such as photos from the poet's personal collection; a screen shot that offers a look at his unique — and dynamic — Web presence, which includes a collection of short animated films set to his work; a draft manuscript page; and an interview with Michael Meyer.

A BRIEF BIOGRAPHY AND AN INTRODUCTION TO HIS WORK

Born in New York City in 1941, Billy Collins grew up in Queens, the only child of a nurse and an electrician. His father had hoped that he might go to the Harvard Business School, but following his own lights, after graduating from College of the Holy Cross, he earned a Ph.D. at the University of California, Riverside, in Romantic poetry, and then began a career in the English department at Lehman College, City University of New York, where he taught writing and literature for more than thirty years. He has also tutored writers at the National University of Ireland at Galway, Sarah Lawrence College, Arizona State University, Columbia University, and Rollins College. Along the way, he wrote poems that eventually earned him a reputation among many people as the most popular living poet in America.

Among his ten collections of poetry are *Ballistics* (2008), *The Trouble with Poetry* (2005), *Nine Horses* (2002), *Sailing Alone Around the Room* (2001), *Picnic, Lightning* (1998), *The Art of Drowning* (1995), *Questions About Angels* (1991), and *The Apple That Astonished Paris* (1988). Collins also edited two anthologies of contemporary poetry designed to entice high school students: *Poetry 180: A Turning Back to Poetry* (2003) and *180 More: Extraordinary Poems for Every Day* (2005). His many honors include fellowships from the New York Foundation for the Arts, the National Endowment for the Arts, and the Guggenheim Foundation. *Poetry* magazine has awarded him the Oscar Blumenthal Prize, the Bess Hokin Prize, the Frederick Bock Prize, and the Levinson Prize.

Billy Collins on his first day as a student at St. Joan of Arc School, Jackson Heights, N.Y., 1948.
© Courtesy of Billy Collins.

" I climbed into the building where all the letters of the alphabet and all the numbers were waiting for me. "

Billy Collins on his first day at College of the Holy Cross, 1959.
© Courtesy of Billy Collins.

Collins characterizes himself as someone who was once a professor who wrote poems but who is now a poet who occasionally teaches. This transformation was hard earned because he didn't publish his first complete book of poems until he was in his early forties, with no expectation that twenty years later he would be named United States Poet Laureate

Billy Collins, senior photo, College of the Holy Cross, 1963.
© Courtesy of Billy Collins.

Of this photo, Collins remarks, "The striped pants must be blamed on the '70s. I might add that quitting smoking was about the coolest thing I have ever done."
Courtesy of Billy Collins.

(a gift of hope to writers everywhere). Just as writing poetry has been good for Billy Collins, he has been good for poetry. Both their reputations have risen simultaneously owing to his appeal to audiences that pack high school auditoriums, college halls, and public theaters all over the country. His many popular readings — including broadcasts on National Public Radio — have helped to make him a best-selling poet, a phrase that is ordinarily an oxymoron in America.

Unlike many poetry readings, Collins's are attended by readers and fans who come to whoop, holler, and cheer after nearly every poem, as well as to laugh out loud. His audiences are clearly relieved to be in the presence of a poet who speaks to them (not down) without a trace of pretension, superiority, or presumption. His work is welcoming and readable because he weaves observations about the commonplace materials of our lives — the notes we write in the margins of our books, the food we eat, the way we speak, even the way we think of death — into startling, evocative insights that open our eyes wider than they were before.

To understand Collins's attraction to audiences is to better understand his appeal on the page. He wins the affection of audiences with his warmth and genial charm, an affability that makes him appear unreserved and approachable but never intrusive or over the top. He is a quieter, suburban version of Walt Whitman — with a dash of Emily Dickinson's reserve. He gives just enough and lets the poems do the talking so that he remains as mysteriously appealing as his poems. His persona is well crafted and serves to engage readers in the world of his art rather than in his personal life. In a parallel manner, he has often described the openings of his poems as "hospitable" — an invitation to the reader to move further into the poem without having to worry about getting lost in the kind of self-referential obscurity and opacity that sometimes characterize modern poetry.

Perhaps not surprisingly, some critics and fellow poets have objected that Collins's poems may sometimes bear up to little more than the pleasures of one reading. Collins, however, believes immediate pleasure can be a primary motivation for reading poetry, and he argues that a poem using simple language should not be considered simpleminded. In his work, the ordinary, the everyday, and the familiar often become curious, unusual, and surprising the more closely the poems are read. In interviews, he has compared a first reading of his poems to a reading of the large E at the top of an eye chart in an optometrist's office. What starts out clear and unambiguous gradually becomes more complicated and demanding as we squint to make our way to the end. That big E — it might be read as "enter" — welcomes us in and gives us the confidence to enjoy the experience, but it doesn't mean that there aren't challenges ahead. The casual, "easy" read frequently becomes a thought-provoking compound of humor, irony, and unconventional wisdom. Humor is such an essential part of Collins's work that in 2004 he was the first recipient of the Poetry Foundation's Mark Twain Award for Humor in Poetry. Given this remarkable trifecta of humor, popularity, and book sales, it is hardly to be unexpected that Collins gives some of his colleagues — as Mark Twain might have put it — the "fantods," but his audiences and readers eagerly anticipate whatever poetic pleasures he will offer them next. In any case, Whitman made the point more than 150 years ago in his preface to *Leaves of Grass*: "The proof of a poet is that his country absorbs him as affectionately as he has absorbed it."

(*Above*) The poet with his dog, Luke. Scarsdale, N.Y., 1970s.
Courtesy of Billy Collins.

(*Right*) Billy Collins, in his office at Lehman College, 1984.
Courtesy of Billy Collins.

BILLY COLLINS

"How Do Poems Travel?"   2008

Asking a poet to examine his or her own work is a bit like trying to get a puppy interested in looking in a mirror. Parakeets take an interest in their own reflections but not puppies, who are too busy smelling everything and tumbling over themselves to have time for self-regard. Maybe the difficulty is that most imaginative poems issue largely from the intuitive right side of the brain, whereas literary criticism draws on the brain's more rational, analytic left side. So, writing about your own writing involves getting up, moving from one room of the brain to another, and taking all the furniture with you. When asked about the source of his work, one contemporary poet remarked that if he knew where his poems came from, he would go there and never come back. What he was implying is that much of what goes on in the creative moment takes place on a stealthy level beneath the writer's conscious awareness. If creative work did not offer access to this somewhat mysterious, less than rational region, we would all be writing annual reports or law briefs, not stories, plays, and poems.

Just because you don't know what you are doing doesn't mean you are not doing it; so let me say what I do know about the writing process. While writing a poem, I am also listening to it. As the poem gets underway, I am pushing it forward — after all, I am the one holding the pencil — but I am also ready to be pulled in the direction that the poem seems to want to go. I am willfully writing the poem, but I am also submitting to the poem's will. Emerson once compared writing poetry to ice-skating. I think he meant that both the skater on a frozen pond and the poet on the page might end up going places they didn't intend to go. And Mario Andretti, the Grand Prix driver, once remarked that "If you think everything is under control, you're just not driving fast enough."

Total control over any artistic material eliminates the possibility of surprise. I would not bother to start a poem if I already knew how it was going to end. I try to "maintain the benefits of my ignorance," as another poet put it, letting the poem work toward an understanding of itself (and of me) as I go along. In a student essay, the idea is to stick to the topic. In much imaginative poetry, the pleasure lies in finding a way to escape the initial topic, to transcend the subject and ride the poem into strange, unforeseen areas. As poet John Ashbery put it: "In the process of writing, all sorts of unexpected things happen that shift the poet away from his plan; these accidents are really what we mean whenever we talk about Poetry." Readers of poetry see only the finished product set confidently on the page; but the process of writing a poem involves uncertainty, ambiguity, improvisation, and surprise.

I think of poetry as the original travel literature in that a poem can take me to an imaginative place where I have never been. A good poem often progresses by a series of associative leaps, including sudden shifts in time and space, all of which results in a kind of mental journey. I never know the ending of the poem when I set out, but I am aware that I am moving the poem toward some destination, and when I find the ending, I recognize it right away. More interesting to me than what a poem means is how it travels. In the classroom, I like to substitute for the question, "What is the meaning of the poem?" other questions: "How does this poem go?" or "How does this poem travel through itself in search of its own ending?" Maybe a few of my poems that follow will serve as illustrations, and I hope what I have said so far will help you articulate how poems go and how they find their endings.

BILLY COLLINS

Osso Buco°   *1995*

I love the sound of the bone against the plate
and the fortress-like look of it
lying before me in a moat of risotto,
the meat soft as the leg of an angel
who has lived a purely airborne existence.   5
And best of all, the secret marrow,
the invaded privacy of the animal
prized out with a knife and swallowed down
with cold, exhilarating wine.

I am swaying now in the hour after dinner,   10
a citizen tilted back on his chair,
a creature with a full stomach —
something you don't hear much about in poetry,
that sanctuary of hunger and deprivation.
You know: the driving rain, the boots by the door,   15
small birds searching for berries in winter.

But tonight, the lion of contentment
has placed a warm, heavy paw on my chest,
and I can only close my eyes and listen
to the drums of woe throbbing in the distance   20
and the sound of my wife's laughter
on the telephone in the next room,
the woman who cooked the savory osso buco,
who pointed to show the butcher the ones she wanted.
She who talks to her faraway friend   25
while I linger here at the table
with a hot, companionable cup of tea,

Osso Buco: An Italian veal dish; translated as "hole [*buco*] bone [*osso*]."

feeling like one of the friendly natives,
a reliable guide, maybe even the chief's favorite son.

Somewhere, a man is crawling up a rocky hillside   30
on bleeding knees and palms, an Irish penitent
carrying the stone of the world in his stomach;
and elsewhere people of all nations stare
at one another across a long, empty table.

But here, the candles give off their warm glow,   35
the same light that Shakespeare and Izaak Walton wrote by,
the light that lit and shadowed the faces of history.
Only now it plays on the blue plates,
the crumpled napkins, the crossed knife and fork.

In a while, one of us will go up to bed   40
and the other one will follow.
Then we will slip below the surface of the night
into miles of water, drifting down and down
to the dark, soundless bottom
until the weight of dreams pulls us lower still,   45
below the shale and layered rock,
beneath the strata of hunger and pleasure,
into the broken bones of the earth itself,
into the marrow of the only place we know.

BILLY COLLINS
On Writing "Osso Buco"   2008

The critic Terry Eagleton pointed out that "writing is just language which can function perfectly well in the physical absence of its author." In other words, the author does not have to accompany his or her writing into the world to act as its interpreter or chaperone. One way for a poem to achieve that kind of independence is to exhibit a certain degree of clarity, at least in the opening lines. The ideal progression of a poem is from the clear to the mysterious. A poem that begins simply can engage the reader by establishing a common ground and then lead the reader into more challenging, less familiar territory. Robert Frost's poems are admirable models of this process of deepening. Of course, if the initial engagement is not made early, it's hard to see how the participation of a reader can be counted on.

"Osso Buco" opens with a gourmand's appreciation of a favorite dish, one commonly served up in Italian restaurants. The one thing I knew at the outset was that the poem was going to be a meditation on the subject of contentment. Misery, despondency, melancholy, and just plain human wretchedness are more likely to be the moods of poetry. Indeed, happiness in serious literature is often mistaken for a kind of cowlike stupidity. I thought I would address that imbalance by taking on the challenge of writing about the pleasures of a full stomach. Even the gloomiest of philosophers admits that there are occasional interruptions in the despondency that is the human lot; so why not pay those moments some poetic attention?

To me, the image of "the lion of contentment" suggested a larger set of metaphors connected to African exploration that might add glue to the poem. A metaphor can be deployed in one line of a poem and then dropped, but other times the poem develops an interest in its own language and a metaphor can be extended and explored. The result can bind together a number of disparate thoughts by giving them a common vocabulary. Thus, in this extended metaphor that begins with "the lion of contentment," "drums of woe" are heard "throbbing in the distance," and later the speaker feels like "one of the friendly natives" or "even the chief's favorite son."

In the fourth stanza, the camera pulls back from the domestic scene of the poem and its mood of contentment to survey examples of human suffering taking place elsewhere. The man with bleeding knees is a reference to the religious pilgrims who annually climb Croagh Patrick, a rocky mountain in the west of Ireland. The image of the "long, empty table" is meant to express the condition of world hunger and famine. But the poem offers those images only in contrast to its insistent theme: satisfaction. Back in the kitchen, there is the candle-lit scene of pleasures recently taken. The mention of Shakespeare and Izaak Walton, who wrote *The Compleat Angler,* a whimsical book on the pleasures of fly-fishing, adds some historic perspective and shows the speaker to be a person of some refinement, an appreciator of literature, history, and, of course, food.

The poem so far has made two noticeable maneuvers, shifting to a global then a historical perspective, but in the final stanza the poem takes its biggest turn when it hits upon the resolving metaphor of geology. The couple retires to bed — another pleasure — descends into sleep, then deeper into dreams, then deeper still through the layers of the earth and into its very center, a "marrow" which harkens back to the bone marrow of the eaten calf. Thus the poem travels from the domestic setting of a kitchen to the plains of Africa, a mountain in Ireland, then back to the kitchen before boring into the core of the earth itself — a fairly extensive journey for a poem of only fifty lines, but not untypical of the kind of ground a lyric poem can quickly cover.

BILLY COLLINS

Nostalgia   *1991*

Remember the 1340s? We were doing a dance called the Catapult.
You always wore brown, the color craze of the decade,
and I was draped in one of those capes that were popular,
the ones with unicorns and pomegranates in needlework.

Everyone would pause for beer and onions in the afternoon,   5
and at night we would play a game called "Find the Cow."
Everything was hand-lettered then, not like today.

Where has the summer of 1572 gone? Brocade and sonnet
marathons were the rage. We used to dress up in the flags
of rival baronies and conquer one another in cold rooms of stone.   10
Out on the dance floor we were all doing the Struggle
while your sister practiced the Daphne all alone in her room.
We borrowed the jargon of farriers for our slang.
These days language seems transparent, a badly broken code.

The 1790s will never come again. Childhood was big.   15
People would take walks to the very tops of hills
and write down what they saw in their journals without speaking.
Our collars were high and our hats were extremely soft.
We would surprise each other with alphabets made of twigs.
It was a wonderful time to be alive, or even dead.   20

I am very fond of the period between 1815 and 1821.
Europe trembled while we sat still for our portraits.
And I would love to return to 1901 if only for a moment,
time enough to wind up a music box and do a few dance steps,
or shoot me back to 1922 or 1941, or at least let me   25
recapture the serenity of last month when we picked
berries and glided through afternoons in a canoe.

Even this morning would be an improvement over the present.
I was in the garden then, surrounded by the hum of bees
and the Latin names of flowers, watching the early light   30
flash off the slanted windows of the greenhouse
and silver the limbs on the rows of dark hemlocks.

As usual, I was thinking about the moments of the past,
letting my memory rush over them like water
rushing over the stones on the bottom of a stream.   35
I was even thinking a little about the future, that place
where people are doing a dance we cannot imagine,
a dance whose name we can only guess.

BILLY COLLINS

On Writing "Nostalgia"   2008

"Nostalgia" offers me the opportunity to say something about poetic
form. Broadly speaking, *form* can mean any feature of a poem that keeps
it together and gives it unity. Form is the nails and glue that hold the
emotions and thoughts of a poem in place. Naturally, poets are in the

business of self-expression, but paradoxically they are always looking for limits. Form can be inherited — the sonnet is an enduring example — or the poet may make up his own rules as he goes along. He might even decide at some point to break the very rules he just imposed upon himself. In either case, formal rules give the poet an enclosed space in which to work, and they keep the poem from descending into chaos or tantrum. As poet Stephen Dunn put it, "form is the pressure that an artist puts on his material in order to see what it will bear."

The Irish poet W. B. Yeats felt that "all that is personal will rot unless it is packed in ice and salt." For a formalist poet like Yeats, "ice and salt," which were common food preservatives of his day, probably meant rhyme and meter. After Walt Whitman showed in *Leaves of Grass* (1855) that poems could be written without those two traditional supporting pillars, poets still had many other formal devices at their disposal. Just because poets could now write poems without a design of rhyme words at the ends of lines or a regular meter such as iambic pentameter did not mean they had abandoned form. Some of these alternative formal strategies would include line length, stanza choice, repetition, rhetorical development (beginning–middle–end), and thematic recurrence as well as patterns of sound and imagery. Focusing on form allows us to see that poetry can combine a high level of imaginative freedom with the imposition of boundaries and rules of procedure. For the reader, the coexistence of these two contrary elements — liberty and restriction — may be said to create a pleasurable tension found to a higher degree in poetry than in any other literary genre.

An apparent formal element in "Nostalgia," besides its use of stanza breaks, is the chronological sequence it obediently follows. After the absurd opening question (to which the only answer is no), the poem moves forward from the Middle Ages (the 1340s would place us smack in the middle of the Black Death) to the Renaissance, to the beginnings of English Romanticism, that being 1798, when the first edition of *Lyrical Ballads*, a poetic collaboration between Wordsworth and Coleridge, was published. The poem then continues to travel forward in time, but now more whimsically with dates that seem plucked out of the air — 1901, 1922, 1941 — before arriving rather abruptly at "last month" and then "this morning." If nothing else, the poem demonstrates poetry's freedom from normal time constraints as it manages to travel more than six hundred years from the Middle Ages to the present in only twenty-eight lines.

When the poem does arrive at the present, the speaker morphs from a kind of thousand-year-old man into an actual person, a sympathetic fellow who likes to garden and who appreciates the sounds and sights of the natural world. The imaginary historical journey of the poem ends amid the bees and flowers of the speaker's garden, where he continues to dwell nostalgically on the past until his attention turns to the future, really the only place left for him to go. Having relinquished his power as an eyewitness to centuries of human civilization, the speaker trails off in a dreamy speculation about the unknowable dance crazes of the future.

The poem takes a lot of imaginative liberties in the oddness of its premise and its free-ranging images, yet, formally speaking, it is held together by a strict chronological line drawn from the distant historical past right through the present moment and into the future.

I don't recall how a lot of my poems got started, but I do remember that this poem arose out of a kind of annoyance. Just as a grain of sand can irritate an oyster into producing a pearl by coating it with a smooth surface, so a poem may be irked into being. What was bugging me in this case was the popular twentieth-century habit of breaking the past into decades ("the fifties," "the sixties," and so forth), constructs which amounted to little more than a collage of stereotypes. What a gross simplification of this mysterious, invisible thing we call the past, I thought. Even worse, each decade was so sentimentalized as to make one feel that its passing was cause for feelings of melancholy and regret. "Nostalgia," then, is a poem with a motive, that is, to satirize that kind of enforced nostalgia.

Billy Collins

Questions About Angels   *1991*

Of all the questions you might want to ask
about angels, the only one you ever hear
is how many can dance on the head of a pin.

No curiosity about how they pass the eternal time
besides circling the Throne chanting in Latin   5
or delivering a crust of bread to a hermit on earth
or guiding a boy and girl across a rickety wooden bridge.

Do they fly through God's body and come out singing?
Do they swing like children from the hinges
of the spirit world saying their names backwards and forwards?   10
Do they sit alone in little gardens changing colors?

What about their sleeping habits, the fabric of their robes,
their diet of unfiltered divine light?
What goes on inside their luminous heads? Is there a wall
these tall presences can look over and see hell?   15

If an angel fell off a cloud, would he leave a hole
in a river and would the hole float along endlessly
filled with the silent letters of every angelic word?

If an angel delivered the mail, would he arrive
in a blinding rush of wings or would he just assume   20
the appearance of the regular mailman and
whistle up the driveway reading the postcards?

No, the medieval theologians control the court.
The only question you ever hear is about
the little dance floor on the head of a pin   25
where halos are meant to converge and drift invisibly.

It is designed to make us think in millions,
billions, to make us run out of numbers and collapse
into infinity, but perhaps the answer is simply one:
one female angel dancing alone in her stocking feet,   30
a small jazz combo working in the background.

She sways like a branch in the wind, her beautiful
eyes closed, and the tall thin bassist leans over
to glance at his watch because she has been dancing
forever, and now it is very late, even for musicians.   35

BILLY COLLINS
On Writing "Questions About Angels"   2008

I find that it doesn't take much to get a poem going. A poem can start
casually with something trivial and then develop significance along the
way. The first inkling may act as a keyhole that allows the poet to look
into an imaginary room. When I started to write "Questions About
Angels," I really had nothing on my mind except that odd, speculative
question: How many angels can dance on the head of a pin? Seemingly
unanswerable, the question originated as an attempt to mock certain
medieval philosophers (notably Thomas Aquinas) who sought to solve
arcane theological mysteries through the sheer application of reason. I
had first heard the question when I was studying theology at a Jesuit college, but well before that, the phrase had made its way into the mainstream of modern parlance. It was typical of me to want to begin a poem
with something everyone knows and then proceed from there. The poem
found a direction to go in when it occurred to me to open up the discussion to include other questions. At that point, it was "Game on."

My investigation really begins in the second stanza, which draws on
traditional images of angels in religious art, either worshipping God or
paying helpful visits to earth, assisting the poor and protecting the innocent. Then the questions become more fanciful — off-the-wall, really:
"Do they fly through God's body and come out singing?" No doubt you
could come up with questions of your own about angel behavior; clearly,
that has become the poem's game — an open inquiry into the spirit life of
these creatures.

After the poem's most bizarre question, which involves a hole that
a fallen angel has left in a river, the interrogation descends into the

everyday with the image of an angel delivering mail, not gloriously "in a blinding rush of wings" but just like "the regular mailman." After a reminder of the monopoly "the medieval theologians" seem to have on questions about angels, the poem makes a sudden turn (one I did not see coming) by offering a simple, irreducible answer to that unanswerable question. On the little word "but" (line 29), the poem drops down abruptly from "billions" to "one," and the scene shrinks from heaven to a jazz club located in eternity.

In the process of composing a poem, the poet is mentally juggling many concerns, one of the most dominant and persistent being how the poem is going to find a place to end, a point where the journey of the poem was meant to stop, a point where the poet does not want to say any more, and the reader has heard just enough. In this case, the moment she appeared — rather miraculously, as I remember — I knew that this beautiful angel "dancing alone in her stocking feet" was how the poem would close. She was the hidden destination the poem was moving toward all along without my knowing it. I had only to add the detail of the bored bassist and the odd observation that even musicians playing in eternity cannot be expected to stay awake forever.

Billy Collins

Litany   2002

You are the bread and the knife,
The crystal goblet and the wine.
—Jacques Crickillon

You are the bread and the knife,
the crystal goblet and the wine.
You are the dew on the morning grass,
and the burning wheel of the sun.
You are the white apron of the baker,   5
and the marsh birds suddenly in flight.

However, you are not the wind in the orchard,
the plums on the counter,
or the house of cards.
And you are certainly not the pine-scented air.   10
There is no way you are the pine-scented air.

It is possible that you are the fish under the bridge,
maybe even the pigeon on the general's head,
but you are not even close
to being the field of cornflowers at dusk.   15

And a quick look in the mirror will show
that you are neither the boots in the corner
nor the boat asleep in its boathouse.

It might interest you to know,
speaking of the plentiful imagery of the world,   20
that I am the sound of rain on the roof.

I also happen to be the shooting star,
the evening paper blowing down an alley,
and the basket of chestnuts on the kitchen table.

I am also the moon in the trees   25
and the blind woman's teacup.
But don't worry, I am not the bread and the knife.
You are still the bread and the knife.
You will always be the bread and the knife,
not to mention the crystal goblet and — somehow —   30
    the wine.

BILLY COLLINS

On Writing "Litany"   2008

As the epigraph to this poem indicates, "Litany" was written in reaction
to another poem, a love poem I came across in a literary magazine by a
poet I had not heard of. What struck me about his poem was its reliance
on a strategy that had its heyday in the love sonnets of the Elizabethan
age, namely, the convention of flattering the beloved by comparing her
to various aspects of nature. Typically, her eyes were like twin suns, her
lips red as coral or rubies, her skin pure as milk, and her breath as sweet
as flowers or perfume. Such exaggerations were part of the overall tendency to idealize women who featured in the courtly love poetry
of the time, each of whom was as unattainable as she was beautiful and
as cruel as she was fair. It took Shakespeare to point out the ridiculous-
ness of these hyperboles, questioning in one of his sonnets the very
legitimacy of comparisons ("Shall I compare thee to a summer's day?"
[p. 492]), then drenching the whole process with the cold water of realism
("My mistress' eyes are nothing like the sun" [p. 492]). You might think
that would have put an end to the practice, but the habit of appealing
to women's vanity through comparisons persists even in the poetry of
today. That poem in the magazine prompted me to respond.

    Starting with the same first two lines, "Litany" seeks to rewrite the
earlier poem by offering a corrective. It aims to point out the latent silliness in such comparisons and perhaps the potential absurdity at the
heart of metaphor itself. The poem even wants us to think about the
kind of romantic relationships that would permit such discourse.

The poem opens by adding some new metaphors (morning dew, baker's apron, marsh birds) to the pile, but in the second stanza, the poem reverses direction by trading in flattery for a mock-serious investigation of what this woman might be and what she is not. Instead of appealing to her sense of her own beauty, the speaker is perfectly willing to insult her by bringing up her metaphoric shortcomings. By the time he informs her that "There is no way you are the pine-scented air" and "you are not even close / to being the field of cornflowers at dusk," we know that this is a different kind of love poem altogether.

The second big turn comes in the fifth stanza when the speaker unexpectedly begins comparing himself to such things as "the sound of rain on the roof." Notice that the earlier comparisons were not all positive. The "pigeon on the general's head" should remind us of an equestrian statue in a park, and we all know what pigeons like to do to statues. But the speaker is not the least bit ashamed to flatter himself with a string of appealing images including a "shooting star," a "basket of chestnuts," and "the moon in the trees." Turning attention away from the "you" of the poem to the speaker is part of the poem's impertinence — the attentive lover turns into an egomaniac — but it echoes a strategy used by Shakespeare himself. Several of his sonnets begin by being about the beloved but end by being about the poet, specifically about his power to bestow immortality on the beloved through his art. Thus, what begins as a love poem ends as a self-love poem.

The last thing to notice is that "Litany" has a circular structure: It ends by swinging back to its beginning, to the imagery of the epigraph. True to the cheekiness of the speaker, his last words are devoted to tossing the woman a bit of false reassurance that she is still and will always be "the bread and the knife." For whatever that's worth.

BILLY COLLINS

Building with Its Face Blown Off   2005

How suddenly the private
is revealed in a bombed-out city,
how the blue and white striped wallpaper

of a second story bedroom is now
exposed to the lightly falling snow   5
as if the room had answered the explosion

wearing only its striped pajamas.
Some neighbors and soldiers
poke around in the rubble below

and stare up at the hanging staircase,   10
the portrait of a grandfather,
a door dangling from a single hinge.

And the bathroom looks almost embarrassed
by its uncovered ochre walls,
the twisted mess of its plumbing,   15

the sink sinking to its knees,
the ripped shower curtain,
the torn goldfish trailing bubbles.

It's like a dollhouse view
as if a child on its knees could reach in   20
and pick up the bureau, straighten a picture.

Or it might be a room on a stage
in a play with no characters,
no dialogue or audience,

no beginning, middle and end—   25
just the broken furniture in the street,
a shoe among the cinder blocks,

a light snow still falling
on a distant steeple, and people
crossing a bridge that still stands.   30

And beyond that—crows in a tree,
the statue of a leader on a horse,
and clouds that look like smoke,

and even farther on, in another country
on a blanket under a shade tree,   35
a man pouring wine into two glasses

and a woman sliding out
the wooden pegs of a wicker hamper
filled with bread, cheese, and several kinds of olives.

Perspective

On "Building with Its Face Blown Off": Michael Meyer Interviews Billy Collins   2009

Meyer: The subject matter of your poetry is well known for being typically about the patterns and rhythms of everyday life, along with its delights, humor, ironies, and inevitable pain. "Building with Its Face Blown Off," however, explicitly concerns war and is implicitly political. What prompted this minority report in your writing?

Collins: It's true that I usually steer away from big historical subjects in my poems. I don't want to assume a level of authority beyond what a reader might trust, nor do I want to appear ridiculous by taking a firm stand against some moral horror that any other humane person would naturally oppose. A few years back, I consciously avoided joining the movement called "Poets against the War" because I thought it was as self-obviating as "Generals for the War." A direct approach to subjects as enormous as war or slavery or genocide carries the risk that the poet will be smothered under the weight of the topic. Plus, readers are already morally wired to respond in a certain way to such things. As a writer, you want to *create* an emotion, not merely activate one that already exists in the reader. And who wants to preach to the choir? I have come across few readers of poetry who are all for war; and, besides, poets have enough work to do without trying to convert the lost. William Butler Yeats put it best in his "On Being Asked for a War Poem":

> I think it better that in times like these
> A poet's mouth be silent, for in truth
> We have no gift to set a statesman right;
> He has had enough of meddling who can please
> A young girl in the indolence of her youth,
> Or an old man upon a winter's night.

Before poetry can be political, it must be personal.

That's my dim view of poems that do little more than declare that the poet, walking the moral high road, is opposed to ethically reprehensible acts. But the world does press in on us, and I was stopped in my tracks one morning when I saw in a newspaper still another photograph of a bombed-out building, which echoed all the similar images I had seen for too many decades in too many conflicts around the world in Dresden, Sarajevo, or Baghdad, wherever shells happen to fall. That photograph revealed one personal aspect of the war: the apartment of a family blown wide open for all to see. "Building with Its Face Blown Off" was my response.

Meyer: The images in the poem have a photojournalistic quality, but they are snapped through the lens of personification rather than a camera. Isn't a picture better than a thousand words?

Collins: I wanted to avoid the moralistic antiwar rhetoric that the underlying subject invites, so I stuck to the visual. A photojournalist once observed that to capture the horrors of war, you don't have to go to the front lines and photograph actual armed conflict: just take a picture of a child's shoe lying on a road. That picture would be worth many words, but as a poet I must add, maybe not quite a thousand. In this poem, I wanted to downplay the horrible violence of the destruction by treating the event as a mere social embarrassment, an invasion of domestic privacy. As Chekhov put it, if you want to get the reader emotionally involved, write cold. For the same reason, I deployed nonviolent metaphors such as the dollhouse and the theater, where the fourth wall is absent. The poem finds a way to end by withdrawing from the scene like a camera pulling back to reveal a larger world. Finally, we are looking down as from a blimp on another country, one where the absence of war provides the tranquility that allows a man and a woman to have a picnic.

A reader once complimented me for ending this poem with olives, the olive branch being a traditional symbol of peace. Another reader heard an echo of Ernest Hemingway's short story "In Another Country," which concerns World War I. Just between you and me, neither of these references had ever occurred to me; but I am always glad to take credit for such happy accidents even if it is similar to drawing a target around a bullet hole. No writer can — or should want to — have absolute control over the reactions of his readers.

Meyer: In your essay on writing "Nostalgia," you point out that "formal rules give the poet an enclosed space in which to work, and they keep the poem from descending into chaos or tantrum" (p. 538). How does form in "Building with Its Face Blown Off" prevent its emotions and thoughts from being reduced to a prose bumper sticker such as "War is hell"?

Collins: I hope what keeps this poem from getting carried away with its traumatic subject is its concentration on the photograph so that the poem maintains a visual, even cinematic, focus throughout. You could think of the poem as a one-minute movie — a short subject about a big topic. Another sign of apparent form here is the division of the poem into three-line stanzas, or tercets, which slow down the reader's progress through the poem. Just as readers should pause slightly at the end of every poetic line (even an unpunctuated one — the equivalent of half a comma), they should also observe a little pause between stanzas. Poetry is famous for condensing large amounts of mental and emotional material into small packages, and it also encourages us to slow down from the speed at which we usually absorb information. The stanzas give the poem a look of regularity, and some of them make visible the grammatical structure of the poem's sentences. Regular stanzas suggest that the poem comes in sections, and they remind us that poetry is a spatial arrangement of words on the page. Think of such stanzas as stones in a stream; the reader steps from one to the next to get to other side.

Meyer: In a classroom discussion of the final two stanzas, one of my students read the couple's picnic scene as "offering an image of hope and peace in contrast to the reckless destruction that precedes it," while another student countered that the scene appeared to be a depiction of "smug indifference and apathy to suffering." Care to comment?

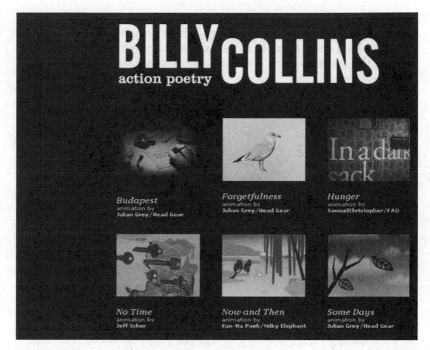

Billy Collins Action Poetry Web Site. In a 2003 interview with the American Booksellers Association, Billy Collins explained that his goal as United States Poet Laureate was for poetry "to pop up in unexpected places, like the daily announcement in high schools and on airplanes." At the Web site for the Billy Collins Action Poetry film project (www.bcactionpoet .org), you can view artful new interpretations of the poet's work and hear them read aloud by Collins himself, in what makes for an imaginative and elegant combination of poetry and technology.
Produced by the J. Walter Thompson ad agency and the Sundance Channel.

Collins: I find it fascinating that such contrary views of the poem's ending could exist. Probably the most vexing question in poetry studies concerns interpretation. One thing to keep in mind is that readers of poetry, students especially, are much more preoccupied with "meaning" than poets are. While I am writing, I am not thinking about the poem's meaning; I am only trying to write a good poem, which involves securing the form of the poem and getting the poem to hold together so as to stay true to itself. Thinking about what my poem means would only distract me from the real work of poetry. Neurologically speaking, I am trying to inhabit the intuitive side of the brain, not the analytical side where critical thought and "study questions" come from. "Meaning," if I think of it at all, usually comes as an afterthought.

But the question remains: How do poets react to interpretations of their work? Generally speaking, once a poem is completed and then published, it is out of the writer's hands. I'm disposed to welcome interpretations that I did not consciously intend—that doesn't mean my unconscious didn't play a role—as long as those readings do not twist the poem out of shape. In "Building with Its Face Blown Off," I added the picnicking couple simply as a sharp contrast to the scene of destruction in the war-torn city. The man and woman are free to enjoy the

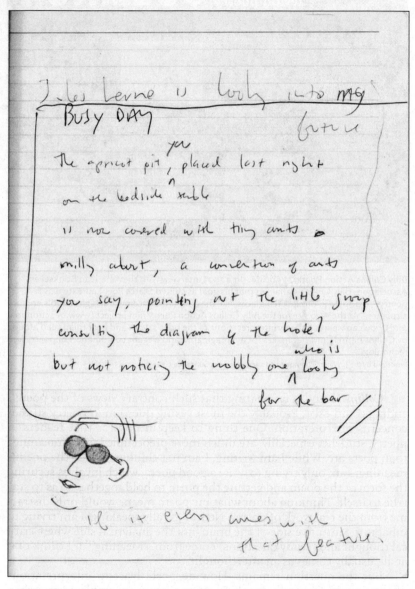

A draft of the unpublished poem "Busy Day" from an undated page of Collins's notebooks.
Courtesy of Billy Collins.

luxury of each other's company, the countryside, wine, cheese, and even a choice of olives. Are they a sign of hope? Well, yes, insofar as they show us that the whole world is not at war. Smugness? Not so much to my mind, even though that strikes me as a sensible reaction. But if a reader claimed that the couple represented Adam and Eve, or more absurdly, Antony and Cleopatra, or Donny and Marie Osmond, then I would question the person's common sense or sanity. I might even ring for Security. Mainly, the couple is there simply to show us what is no longer available to the inhabitants of the beleaguered city and to give me a place to end the poem.

CONSIDERATIONS FOR CRITICAL THINKING AND WRITING

1. In his commentary on "Osso Buco," Collins observes that "happiness in serious literature is often mistaken for a kind of cowlike stupidity" (pp. 535–36). How does the language of the poem maneuver around that kind of sentimental quicksand?

2. What other "formal strategies" can you find in "Nostalgia" (p. 536) in addition to the use of stanza breaks and the chronological sequence that Collins discusses? What other poetic elements serve to unify this satiric poem?

3. **CREATIVE RESPONSE.** Collins explains that he began "Questions About Angels" by setting out to mock the medieval speculative question of how many angels can dance on the head of a pin. He also describes his discovery of how to end the poem in line 29 after the word "but" (p. 540) with the image of the female angel dancing by herself in a jazz club. That was his solution. Try writing your own final six lines as you discover them from the preceding twenty-nine.

4. As Collins indicates, the speaker in "Litany" writes a parodic love poem that "ends as a self-love poem" (p. 543). Is the "cheekiness" in his language appealing to you? Explain why or why not.

5. In the final paragraph in "On 'Building with Its Face Blown Off'" (pp. 547–49), Collins offers some commonsense observations about literary interpretation and how to read a poem sensitively and sensibly. He also acknowledges that wild misreadings might cause him to "ring for Security." Write an essay on "How Not to Interpret a Poem" that articulates what you think are some of the most important problems to avoid.

SUGGESTED TOPICS FOR LONGER PAPERS

1. Analyze the humor in four of Collins's poems included in this anthology (see also "Introduction to Poetry" [p. 356]). What purpose does the humor serve? Does the humor appeal to you? Explain why or why not, giving examples.

2. View the poems available on the Billy Collins Action Poetry Web site (see page 547 and www.bcactionpoet.org), where you can find visual interpretations of individual poems and hear Collins read the poems aloud. Choose three of the poems and write an analysis of

how the visual and auditory representations affect your response to the poems' language. Explain why you think this approach enhances or diminishes — or is simply different from — reading the poem on a page.

As you read multiple works by the same author, you're likely to be struck by the similarities and differences in those selections. You'll begin to recognize situations, events, characters, issues, perspectives, styles, and strategies — even recurring words or phrases — that provide a kind of signature, making the poems in some way identifiable with that particular writer.

The following questions can help you to respond to multiple works by the same author. They should help you to listen to how a writer's works can speak to one another and to you.

1. What topics reappear in the writer's work? What seem to be the major concerns of the author?

2. Does the author have a definable worldview that can be discerned from work to work? Is, for example, the writer liberal, conservative, apolitical, or religious?

3. What social values come through in the author's work? Does he or she seem to identify with a particular group or social class?

4. Is there a consistent voice or point of view from work to work? Is it a persona or the author's actual self?

5. How much of the author's own life experiences and historical moments make their way into the works?

6. Does the author experiment with style from work to work, or are the works mostly consistent with one another?

7. Can the author's work be identified with a literary tradition, such as *carpe diem* poetry, that aligns his or her work with that of other writers?

8. What is distinctive about the author's writing? Is the language innovative? Are the themes challenging? Are the voices conventional? Is the tone characteristic?

9. Could you identify another work by the same author without a name being attached to it? What are the distinctive features that allow you to do so?

10. Do any of the writer's works seem *not* to be by that writer? Why?

11. What other writers are most like this author in style and content? Why?

12. Has the writer's work evolved over time? Are there significant changes or developments? Are there new ideas and styles, or do the works remain largely the same?

13. How would you characterize the author's writing habits? Is it possible to anticipate what goes on in different works, or are you surprised by their content or style?

14. Can difficult or ambiguous passages in a work be resolved by referring to a similar passage in another work?

15. What does the writer say about his or her own work? Do you trust the teller or the tale? Which do you think is more reliable?

22

A THEMATIC CASE STUDY
The World of Work

I'll tell you the best literary characters
are individualistic; they let out what
they have in them; they give themselves
full sweep and play. This is true,
especially in America, where thought is
untrammeled and men are free.
— WALT WHITMAN[1]

This chapter offers some contemporary poems that are thematically connected to business and labor. The vicissitudes associated with making a
living are not typically the subject matter chosen by poets, who have traditionally and historically preferred to write about less mundane matters,
such as love, nature, spirituality, grief, death, or almost any other side of
life that isn't set at a job site or in an office. However much this view of
poets may be a stereotype, by the time President Calvin Coolidge confidently declared in 1925 that "the business of America is business," there
was an impressive record of objections to such a narrow materialistic
assertion. Consider, for example, Henry David Thoreau's assessment
in this nineteenth-century journal entry: "In my experience nothing is
so opposed to poetry — not crime — as business. It is a negation of life"
(June 29, 1852).

Not many poems replicate the kind of exuberant optimism about
the business of work to be found in this excerpt from Walt Whitman's
"I Hear America Singing" (1867):

[1] Courtesy of the Bayley-Whitman Collection of Ohio Wesleyan University of Delaware, Ohio.

552

I hear America singing, the varied carols I hear,
Those of mechanics, each one singing his as it should be blithe and strong,
The carpenter singing his as he measures his plank or beam,
The mason singing his as he makes ready for work, or leaves off work,
The boatman singing what belongs to him in his boat, the deckhand
    singing on the steamboat deck,
The shoemaker singing as he sits on his bench, the hatter singing as he
    stands. . . .

Whitman's poem celebrates the energy he perceived in workers and business: "In modern times the new word *Business,* has been brought to the front & now dominates individuals and nations. . . . Business shall be, nay, is the word of the modern hero." In recent times in the face of economic turmoil, crushing debt, and widespread unemployment, however, Thoreau's negative critique seems to resonate more than does Whitman's cheerful expectations.

    The world of work — the business of earning a living — seems to be in sharper and more problematic focus these days because it is necessarily on most people's minds, including the imaginations of many poets. The chapter's focus is not just about earning money, though the first poem, "Money," by former business executive and now poet Dana Gioia, certainly acknowledges how obsessively central money can be. The following poems about earning a living are also about personal integrity, working conditions, and the meaning of life, topics that are explored from a variety of perspectives and that evoke the misery and joy, as well as the despair and satisfaction, that going to work can pay out.

DANA GIOIA (B. 1950)

Money   *1991*

Money is a kind of poetry.   — *Wallace Stevens*

Money, the long green,
cash, stash, rhino, jack
or just plain dough.

Chock it up, fork it over,
shell it out. Watch it   5
burn holes through pockets.

To be made of it! To have it
to burn! Greenbacks, double eagles,
megabucks and Ginnie Maes.

It greases the palm, feathers a nest,   10
holds heads above water,
makes both ends meet.

Money breeds money.
Gathering interest, compounding daily.
Always in circulation.   15

Money. You don't know where it's been,
but you put it where your mouth is.
And it talks.

CONSIDERATIONS FOR CRITICAL THINKING AND WRITING

1. FIRST RESPONSE. Explain whether the poem supports or challenges
   Stevens's epigraph.
2. How does money "talk" through Gioia's choice of diction?
3. Research Wallace Stevens's biography in terms of his relationship to
   business. Why is he an especially appropriate source for the quotation that begins the poem?

WHEN I READ "My advice is to read a lot of poetry, to begin with the contemporary and
get an ear for contemporary poetic speech; then read your way gradually into the past.
Form a strong attachment to a poet whose work you love, and immerse yourself in the
work. Then find another." — TONY HOAGLAND

TONY HOAGLAND (B. 1953)

America   2003

Then one of the students with blue hair and a tongue stud
Says that America is for him a maximum-security prison

Whose walls are made of RadioShacks and Burger Kings, and MTV
     episodes
Where you can't tell the show from the commercials,

And as I consider how to express how full of shit I think he is,   5
He says that even when he's driving to the mall in his Isuzu

Trooper with a gang of his friends, letting rap music pour over them
Like a boiling Jacuzzi full of ballpeen hammers, even then he feels

Buried alive, captured and suffocated in the folds
Of the thick satin quilt of America   10

And I wonder if this is a legitimate category of pain,
Or whether he is just spin doctoring a better grade,

And then I remember that when I stabbed my father in the dream
     last night,
It was not blood but money

That gushed out of him, bright green hundred-dollar bills   15
Spilling from his wounds, and — this is the weird part —,

He gasped, "Thank god — those Ben Franklins were
Clogging up my heart —

And so I perish happily,
Freed from that which kept me from my liberty" —   20

Which is when I knew it was a dream, since my dad
Would never speak in rhymed couplets,

And I look at the student with his acne and cell phone and phony
        ghetto clothes
And I think, "I am asleep in America too,

And I don't know how to wake myself either,"   25
And I remember what Marx said near the end of his life:

"I was listening to the cries of the past,
When I should have been listening to the cries of the future."

But how could he have imagined 100 channels of 24-hour
        cable
Or what kind of nightmare it might be   30

When each day you watch rivers of bright merchandise run
        past you
And you are floating in your pleasure boat upon this river

Even while others are drowning underneath you
And you see their faces twisting in the surface of the waters

And yet it seems to be your own hand   35
Which turns the volume higher?

CONSIDERATIONS FOR CRITICAL THINKING AND WRITING

1. **FIRST RESPONSE.** This poem consists of two sentences. How do they differ in tone and meaning?
2. Discuss the humor embedded in this serious poem.
3. To what extent does this poem reflect your own views about American life?
4. **CONNECTION TO ANOTHER SELECTION.** Compare the perspective offered in "America" with that in Tato Laviera's "AmeRícan" (p. 520).

Jan Beatty (b. 1952)

My Father Teaches Me to Dream   1996

You want to know what work is?
I'll tell you what work is:
Work is work.
You get up. You get on the bus.
You don't look from side to side.   5
You keep your eyes straight ahead.
That way nobody bothers you — see?
You get off the bus. You work all day.
You get back on the bus at night. Same thing.
You go to sleep. You get up.   10
You do the same thing again.
Nothing more. Nothing less.
There's no handouts in this life.
All this other stuff you're looking for —
it ain't there.   15
Work is work.

Considerations for Critical Thinking and Writing

1. **FIRST RESPONSE.** How likely is it that the son or daughter of this father actually asked for a definition of work? What do you imagine prompted the start of this explanation?

2. Discuss the effect of the use of repeated words and phrases. How are they related to the father's message?

3. Consider what the title reveals about the "you" of the poem.

Michael Chitwood (b. 1958)

Men Throwing Bricks   2007

© Derek Anderson.

The one on the ground lofts two at
      a time
with just the right lift for them to
      finish
their rise as the one on the scaffold
      turns
to accept them like a gift and place
      them
on the growing stack. They chime slightly
on the catch. You'd have to do this daily,
morning and afternoon, not to marvel.

1. **First response.** Explain the title's ironic surprise.

2. Discuss the sounds in the poem. How does it "chime"?

3. Why is "marvel" a better choice to describe the men throwing bricks than the phrase "be impressed"?

4. **Connection to another selection.** Compare Chitwood's treatment of these working men with Joyce Sutphen's perspective on the men and their work in "Guys Like That" (below).

David Ignatow (1914–1997)

The Jobholder   1998

I stand in the rain waiting for my bus
and in the bus I wait for my stop.
I get let off and go to work
where I wait for the day to end
and then go home, waiting for the bus,   5
of course, and my stop.

And at home I read and wait
for my hour to go to bed
and I wait for the day I can retire
and wait for my turn to die.   10

1. **First response.** How do the effects of repetition and brevity contribute to the theme of this poem?

2. Characterize the speaker's attitude toward work and life.

3. **Connection to another selection.** Compare Ignatow's representation of work with Jan Beatty's in "My Father Teaches Me to Dream" (p. 556).

Joyce Sutphen (b. 1949)

Guys Like That   2007

Drive very nice cars, and from
where you sit in your dented
last-century version of the
most ordinary car in America, they

look dark-suited and neat and fast.   5
Guys like that look as if they are thinking

about wine and marble floors, but
really they are thinking about TiVo

and ESPN. Women think that guys
like that are different from the guys   10
driving the trucks that bring cattle
to slaughter, but guys like that are

planning worse things than the death
of a cow. Guys who look like that—
so clean and cool—are quietly moving   15
money across the border, cooking books,

making deals that leave some people
rich and some people poorer
than they were before guys like that
robbed them at the pump and on   20

their electricity bills, and even
now, guys like that are planning how
to divide up that little farm they just
passed, the one you used to call home.

CONSIDERATIONS FOR CRITICAL THINKING AND WRITING

1. **FIRST RESPONSE.** How does the phrase "Guys Like That" take on different meanings as the poem progresses?

2. Discuss the poem as a critique of American business practices.

3. Why do you think Sutphen writes this poem specifically from a woman's point of view?

4. **CONNECTION TO ANOTHER SELECTION.** Consider the treatment of men's relationship to domestic life in "Guys Like That" and in Florence Cassen Mayers' "All American Sestina" (p. 497).

MARGE PIERCY (B. 1936)

To be of use   1973

The people I love the best
jump into work head first
without dallying in the shallows
and swim off with sure strokes almost out of sight.
They seem to become natives of that element,   5
the black sleek heads of seals
bouncing like half-submerged balls.

I love people who harness themselves, an ox to a heavy cart,
who pull like water buffalo, with massive patience,

who strain in the mud and the muck to move things forward,   10
who do what has to be done, again and again.

I want to be with people who submerge
in the task, who go into the fields to harvest
and work in a row and pass the bags along,
who are not parlor generals and field deserters   15
but move in a common rhythm
when the food must come in or the fire be put out.

The work of the world is common as mud.
Botched, it smears the hands, crumbles to dust.
But the thing worth doing well done   20
has a shape that satisfies, clean and evident.
Greek amphoras for wine or oil,
Hopi vases that held corn, are put in museums
but you know they were made to be used.
The pitcher cries for water to carry   25
and a person for work that is real.

Considerations for Critical Thinking and Writing

1. **FIRST RESPONSE.** How does the poem's figurative language suggest the sort of worker the speaker admires?
2. What do you consider to be "work that is real" (line 26)?
3. What is the significance of the title?
4. **CONNECTION TO ANOTHER SELECTION.** Compare the sense of what constitutes meaningful work in this poem with that in William Blake's "The Chimney Sweeper" (p. 448).

Suggested Topics for Longer Papers

1. There are many contemporary songs about work. Choose one of the poems in this chapter and in terms of poetic elements — such as diction, tone, imagery, figures of speech, sound, and rhythm — compare its themes with the lyrics of a song you admire.
2. Choose one of the writers represented in this chapter and read more poems in his or her collections. Choose five poems that you think make an interesting and coherent thematic grouping and write an analysis that reveals important elements of the poet's style and characteristic concerns.

A Collection
of Poems

23

Poems for
Further Reading

There is so much clutter that isn't you. You have
to develop a focus and ask: Is this what I see,
or is that what someone else told me she sees?
What do I see? What do I feel? Your true voice is
absolutely faithful to your perception.
— GAIL GODWIN

Alan Carey/ The Image Works.

ANONYMOUS (TRADITIONAL SCOTTISH BALLAD)

Bonny Barbara Allan   *date unknown*

It was in and about the Martinmas° time,
    When the green leaves were afalling,
That Sir John Graeme, in the West Country,
    Fell in love with Barbara Allan.

He sent him men down through the town,   5
    To the place where she was dwelling:
"Oh haste and come to my master dear,
    Gin° ye be Barbara Allan."   *if*

O hooly,° hooly rose she up,   *slowly*
    To the place where he was lying,   10

---

1 *Martinmas:* St. Martin's Day, November 11.

And when she drew the curtain by:
    "Young man, I think you're dying."

"O it's I'm sick, and very, very sick,
    And 'tis a' for Barbara Allan."—
"O the better for me ye's never be,   15
    Tho your heart's blood were aspilling."

"O dinna ye mind,° young man," she said,   *don't you remember*
    "When ye was in the tavern adrinking,
That ye made the health° gae round and round,   *toasts*
    And slighted Barbara Allan?"   20

He turned his face unto the wall,
    And death was with him dealing:
"Adieu, adieu, my dear friends all,
    And be kind to Barbara Allan."

And slowly, slowly raise her up,   25
    And slowly, slowly left him,
And sighing said she could not stay,
    Since death of life had reft him.

She had not gane a mile but twa,
    When she heard the dead-bell ringing,   30
And every jow° that the dead-bell geid,   *stroke*
    It cried, "Woe to Barbara Allan!"

"O mother, mother, make my bed!
    O make it saft and narrow!
Since my love died for me today,   35
    I'll die for him tomorrow."

WILLIAM BLAKE (1757–1827)

Infant Sorrow   *1794*

My mother groand! my father wept.
Into the dangerous world I leapt:
Helpless naked piping loud:
Like a fiend hid in a cloud.

Struggling in my father's hands:
Striving against my swadling bands
Bound and weary I thought best
To sulk upon my mother's breast.

Research the poets in this chapter at bedfordstmartins.com/meyerlit.

ELIZABETH BARRETT BROWNING (1806–1861)

When our two souls stand up erect and strong   *1850*

When our two souls stand up erect and strong,
Face to face, silent, drawing nigh and nigher,
Until the lengthening wings break into fire
At either curvèd point—what bitter wrong
Can the earth do to us, that we should not long   5
Be here contented? Think. In mounting higher,
The angels would press on us and aspire
To drop some golden orb of perfect song
Into our deep, dear silence. Let us stay
Rather on earth, Belovèd,—where the unfit   10
Contarious moods of men recoil away
And isolate pure spirits, and permit
A place to stand and love in for a day,
With darkness and the death-hour rounding it.

ROBERT BURNS (1759–1796)

A Red, Red Rose   *1799*

O my luve's like a red, red rose
That's newly sprung in June;
O my luve's like the melodie
That's sweetly played in tune.

As fair art thou, my bonny lass,   5
So deep in luve am I;
And I will luve thee still my dear,
Till a' the seas gang° dry—   *go*

Till a' the seas gang dry, my dear,
And the rocks melt wi' the sun: 10
O I will luve thee still, my dear,
While the sands o' life shall run.

And fare thee weel, my only luve,
And fare thee weel awhile!
And I will come again, my luve,   15
Though it were a thousand mile.

GEORGE GORDON, LORD BYRON (1788–1824)

She Walks in Beauty   1814

From Hebrew Melodies

I

She walks in Beauty, like the night
    Of cloudless climes and starry skies;
And all that's best of dark and bright
    Meet in her aspect and her eyes:
Thus mellowed to that tender light   5
    Which Heaven to gaudy day denies.

II

One shade the more, one ray the less,
    Had half impaired the nameless grace
Which waves in every raven tress,
    Or softly lightens o'er her face;   10
Where thoughts serenely sweet express,
    How pure, how dear their dwelling-place.

III

And on that cheek, and o'er that brow,
    So soft, so calm, yet eloquent,
The smiles that win, the tints that glow,   15
    But tell of days in goodness spent,
A mind at peace with all below,
    A heart whose love is innocent!

LUCILLE CLIFTON (1936–2010)

this morning (for the girls of eastern high school)   1987

this morning
this morning
            i met myself

coming in

a bright
jungle girl
shining
quick as a snake

© Christopher Felver.

a tall
tree girl a   10
me girl

        i met myself
this morning
coming in

and all day   15
i have been
a black bell
ringing
i survive

      survive   20

survive

SAMUEL TAYLOR COLERIDGE (1772–1834)

Kubla Khan: or, a Vision in a Dream°   *1798*

In Xanadu did Kubla Khan°
    A stately pleasure-dome decree:
Where Alph, the sacred river, ran
Through caverns measureless to man
    Down to a sunless sea.   5
So twice five miles of fertile ground
With walls and towers were girdled round:
And here were gardens bright with sinuous rills
Where blossomed many an incense-bearing tree;
And there were forests ancient as the hills,   10
Enfolding sunny spots of greenery.

But oh! that deep romantic chasm which slanted
Down the green hill athwart a cedarn cover!°
A savage place! as holy and enchanted
As e'er beneath a waning moon was haunted   15
By woman wailing for her demon-lover!
And from this chasm, with ceaseless turmoil seething,

Vision in a Dream: This poem came to Coleridge in an opium-induced dream, but he was interrupted by a visitor while writing it down. He was later unable to remember the rest of the poem.
1 *Kubla Khan:* The historical Kublai Khan (1216–1294, grandson of Genghis Khan) was the founder of the Mongol dynasty in China.
13 *athwart . . . cover:* Spanning a grove of cedar trees.

As if this earth in fast thick pants were breathing,
A mighty fountain momently was forced,
Amid whose swift half-intermitted burst   20
Huge fragments vaulted like rebounding hail,
Of chaffy grain beneath the thresher's flail:
And 'mid these dancing rocks at once and ever
It flung up momently the sacred river.
Five miles meandering with a mazy motion   25
Through wood and dale the sacred river ran,
Then reached the caverns measureless to man,
And sank in tumult to a lifeless ocean:
And 'mid this tumult Kubla heard from far
Ancestral voices prophesying war!   30
        The shadow of the dome of pleasure
        Floated midway on the waves;
        Where was heard the mingled measure
        From the fountain and the caves.
It was a miracle of rare device,   35
A sunny pleasure-dome with caves of ice!

        A damsel with a dulcimer
        In a vision once I saw:
        It was an Abyssinian maid,
        And on her dulcimer she played,   40
        Singing of Mount Abora.
        Could I revive within me
        Her symphony and song,
        To such a deep delight 'twould win me,
That with music loud and long,   45
I would build that dome in air,
That sunny dome! those caves of ice!
And all who heard should see them there,
And all should cry, Beware! Beware!
His flashing eyes, his floating hair!   50
Weave a circle round him thrice,
And close your eyes with holy dread,
For he on honey-dew hath fed,
And drunk the milk of Paradise.

EMILY DICKINSON (1830–1886)

Because I could not stop for Death —   *c. 1863*

Because I could not stop for Death —
He kindly stopped for me —
The Carriage held but just Ourselves —
And Immortality.

We slowly drove — He knew no haste   5
And I had put away
My labor and my leisure too,
For His Civility —

We passed the School, where Children strove
At Recess — in the Ring —   10
We passed the Fields of Gazing Grain —
We passed the Setting Sun —

Or rather — He passed Us —
The Dews drew quivering and chill —
For only Gossamer, my Gown —   15
My Tippet° — only Tulle —   shawl

We paused before a House that seemed
A Swelling of the Ground —
The Roof was scarcely visible —
The Cornice — in the Ground —   20

Since then — 'tis Centuries — and yet
Feels shorter than the Day
I first surmised the Horses' Heads
Were toward Eternity —

JOHN DONNE (1572–1631)

The Flea   1633

Mark but this flea, and mark in this°
How little that which thou deny'st me is;
It sucked me first, and now sucks thee,
And in this flea our two bloods mingled be;
Thou know'st that this cannot be said   5
A sin, nor shame, nor loss of maidenhead,
        Yet this enjoys before it woo,
        And pampered swells with one blood made of two,
        And this, alas, is more than we would do.°

Oh stay, three lives in one flea spare,   10
Where we almost, yea more than, married are.
This flea is you and I, and this
Our marriage bed, and marriage temple is;
Though parents grudge, and you, we're met
And cloistered in these living walls of jet.   15

To hear "The Flea"
read by Richard
Burton, visit
bedfordstmartins.com/
meyerlit/epages.

---

1 *mark in this:* Take note of the moral lesson in this object.   9 *more than we would do:*
That is, if we do not join our blood in conceiving a child.

Though use° make you apt to kill me,   *habit*
Let not to that, self-murder added be,
And sacrilege, three sins in killing three.

Cruel and sudden, hast thou since
Purpled thy nail in blood of innocence?   20
Wherein could this flea guilty be,
Except in that drop which it sucked from thee?
Yet thou triumph'st, and say'st that thou
Find'st not thyself, nor me, the weaker now;
    'Tis true; then learn how false, fears be;   25
    Just so much honor, when thou yield'st to me,
    Will waste, as this flea's death took life from thee.

GEORGE ELIOT (MARY ANN EVANS/1819–1880)

In a London Drawingroom   1865

The sky is cloudy, yellowed by the smoke,
For view there are the houses opposite,
Cutting the sky with one long line of wall
Like solid fog: far as the eye can stretch
Monotony of surface and of form   5
Without a break to hang a guess upon.
No bird can make a shadow as it flies,
For all its shadow, as in ways o'erhung
By thickest canvas, where the golden rays
Are clothed in hemp. No figure lingering   10
Pauses to feed the hunger of the eye
Or rest a little on the lap of life.
All hurry on and look upon the ground
Or glance unmarking at the passersby.
The wheels are hurrying, too, cabs, carriages   15
All closed, in multiplied identity.
The world seems one huge prison-house and court
Where men are punished at the slightest cost,
With lowest rate of color, warmth, and joy.

T. S. ELIOT (1888–1965)

The Love Song of J. Alfred Prufrock   1917

S'io credesse che mia risposta fosse
A persona che mai tornasse al mondo,
Questa fiamma staria senza più scosse.
Ma perciocchè giammai di questo fondo

Non tornò vivo alcun, s'i'odo il vero,
Senza tema d'infamia ti rispondo. °

Let us go then, you and I,
When the evening is spread out against the sky
Like a patient etherized upon a table;
Let us go, through certain half-deserted streets,
The muttering retreats   5
Of restless nights in one-night cheap hotels
And sawdust restaurants with oyster-shells:
Streets that follow like a tedious argument
Of insidious intent
To lead you to an overwhelming question . . .   10
Oh, do not ask, "What is it?"
Let us go and make our visit.

In the room the women come and go
Talking of Michelangelo.

The yellow fog that rubs its back upon the window panes,   15
The yellow smoke that rubs its muzzle on the window panes
Licked its tongue into the corners of the evening,
Lingered upon the pools that stand in drains,
Let fall upon its back the soot that falls from chimneys,
Slipped by the terrace, made a sudden leap,   20
And seeing that it was a soft October night,
Curled once about the house, and fell asleep.

And indeed there will be time°
For the yellow smoke that slides along the street,
Rubbing its back upon the window panes;   25
There will be time, there will be time
To prepare a face to meet the faces that you meet;
There will be time to murder and create,
And time for all the works and days° of hands
That lift and drop a question on your plate: 30
Time for you and time for me,

Epigraph: *S'io credesse . . . rispondo:* Dante's *Inferno,* 27:58–63. In the Eighth Chasm
of the Inferno, Dante and Virgil meet Guido da Montefeltro, one of the False Counselors, who is punished by being enveloped in an eternal flame. When Dante asks
Guido to tell his life story, the spirit replies: "If I thought that my answer were to one
who might ever return to the world, this flame would shake no more; but since from
this depth none ever returned alive, if what I hear is true, I answer you without fear
of infamy."
23 *there will be time:* An allusion to Ecclesiastes 3:1–8: "To everything there is a season,
and a time to every purpose under heaven. . . ."
29 *works and days:* Hesiod's eighth-century B.C. poem *Works and Days* gives practical
advice on how to conduct one's life in accordance with the seasons.

And time yet for a hundred indecisions,
And for a hundred visions and revisions,
Before the taking of a toast and tea.

In the room the women come and go   35
Talking of Michelangelo.

    And indeed there will be time
To wonder, "Do I dare?" and, "Do I dare?" —
Time to turn back and descend the stair,
With a bald spot in the middle of my hair —   40
(They will say: "How his hair is growing thin!")
My morning coat, my collar mounting firmly to the chin,
My necktie rich and modest, but asserted by a simple pin —
(They will say: "But how his arms and legs are thin!")
Do I dare   45
Disturb the universe?
In a minute there is time
For decisions and revisions which a minute will reverse.

    For I have known them all already, known them all:
Have known the evenings, mornings, afternoons,   50
I have measured out my life with coffee spoons;
I know the voices dying with a dying fall
Beneath the music from a farther room.
    So how should I presume?

    And I have known the eyes already, known them all —   55
The eyes that fix you in a formulated phrase.
And when I am formulated, sprawling on a pin,
When I am pinned and wriggling on the wall,
Then how should I begin
To spit out all the butt-ends of my days and ways?   60
    And how should I presume?

    And I have known the arms already, known them all —
Arms that are braceleted and white and bare
(But in the lamplight, downed with light brown hair!)
    Is it perfume from a dress   65
    That makes me so digress?
Arms that lie along a table, or wrap about a shawl.
    And should I then presume?
    And how should I begin?

    Shall I say, I have gone at dusk through narrow streets,   70
And watched the smoke that rises from the pipes
Of lonely men in shirtsleeves, leaning out of windows? . . .

I should have been a pair of ragged claws
Scuttling across the floors of silent seas.

And the afternoon, the evening, sleeps so peacefully!   75
Smoothed by long fingers,
Asleep . . . tired . . . or it malingers,
Stretched on the floor, here beside you and me.
Should I, after tea and cakes and ices,
Have the strength to force the moment to its crisis?   80
But though I have wept and fasted, wept and prayed,
Though I have seen my head (grown slightly bald) brought in upon
        a platter,°
I am no prophet — and here's no great matter;
I have seen the moment of my greatness flicker,
And I have seen the eternal Footman hold my coat, and snicker,   85
        And in short, I was afraid.

        And would it have been worth it, after all,
After the cups, the marmalade, the tea,
Among the porcelain, among some talk of you and me,
Would it have been worth while   90
To have bitten off the matter with a smile,
To have squeezed the universe into a ball°
To roll it toward some overwhelming question,
To say: "I am Lazarus,° come from the dead,
Come back to tell you all, I shall tell you all" —   95
If one, settling a pillow by her head,
        Should say: "That is not what I meant at all;
        That is not it, at all."

        And would it have been worth it, after all,
Would it have been worth while,   100
After the sunsets and the dooryards and the sprinkled streets,
After the novels, after the teacups, after the skirts that trail along
        the floor —
And this, and so much more? —
It is impossible to say just what I mean!
But as if a magic lantern threw the nerves in patterns on a screen: 105
Would it have been worth while
If one, settling a pillow or throwing off a shawl,
And turning toward the window, should say:
        "That is not it at all,
        That is not what I meant, at all."   110

---

82 *head . . . upon a platter:* At Salome's request, Herod had John the Baptist decapi-
tated and had the severed head delivered to her on a platter (see Matt. 14:1–12 and
Mark 6:17–29).
92 *squeezed the universe into a ball:* See Andrew Marvell's "To His Coy Mistress" (p. 382),
lines 41–42: "Let us roll all our strength and all / Our sweetness up into one ball."
94 *Lazarus:* The brother of Mary and Martha who was raised from the dead by Jesus
(John 11:1–44). In Luke 16:19–31, a rich man asks that another Lazarus return from the
dead to warn the living about their treatment of the poor.

No! I am not Prince Hamlet, nor was meant to be;
Am an attendant lord,° one that will do
To swell a progress,° start a scene or two,   *state procession*
Advise the prince: withal, an easy tool,
Deferential, glad to be of use,   115
Politic, cautious, and meticulous;
Full of high sentence, but a bit obtuse;
At times, indeed, almost ridiculous—
Almost, at times, the Fool.

I grow old . . . I grow old . . .   120
I shall wear the bottoms of my trousers rolled.
      Shall I part my hair behind? Do I dare to eat a peach?
I shall wear white flannel trousers, and walk upon
      the beach.
I have heard the mermaids singing, each to each.

I do not think that they will sing to me.   125

I have seen them riding seaward on the waves,
Combing the white hair of the waves blown back
When the wind blows the water white and black.

We have lingered in the chambers of the sea
By seagirls wreathed with seaweed red and brown,   130
Till human voices wake us, and we drown.

112 *attendant lord:* Like Polonius in Shakespeare's *Hamlet.*

ROBERT FROST (1874–1963)

Mending Wall   *1914*

To hear
"Mending Wall" read by
Robert Frost, visit
bedfordstmartins.com/
meyerlit/epages.

Something there is that doesn't love a wall,
That sends the frozen-ground-swell under it,
And spills the upper boulders in the sun;
And makes gaps even two can pass abreast.
The work of hunters is another thing: 5
I have come after them and made repair
Where they have left not one stone on a stone,
But they would have the rabbit out of hiding,
To please the yelping dogs. The gaps I mean,
No one has seen them made or heard them made,   10
But at spring mending-time we find them there.
I let my neighbor know beyond the hill;
And on a day we meet to walk the line
And set the wall between us once again.

We keep the wall between us as we go.   15
To each the boulders that have fallen to each.
And some are loaves and some so nearly balls
We have to use a spell to make them balance:
"Stay where you are until our backs are turned!"
We wear our fingers rough with handling them.   20
Oh, just another kind of outdoor game,
One on a side. It comes to little more:
There where it is we do not need the wall:
He is all pine and I am apple orchard.
My apple trees will never get across   25
And eat the cones under his pines, I tell him.
He only says, "Good fences make good neighbors."
Spring is the mischief in me, and I wonder
If I could put a notion in his head:
"*Why* do they make good neighbors? Isn't it   30
Where there are cows? But here there are no cows.
Before I built a wall I'd ask to know
What I was walling in or walling out,
And to whom I was like to give offense.
Something there is that doesn't love a wall,   35
That wants it down." I could say "Elves" to him,
But it's not elves exactly, and I'd rather
He said it for himself. I see him there
Bringing a stone grasped firmly by the top
In each hand, like an old-stone savage armed.   40
He moves in darkness as it seems to me,
Not of woods only and the shade of trees.
He will not go behind his father's saying,
And he likes having thought of it so well
He says again, "Good fences make good neighbors."   45

ROBERT FROST (1874–1963)

The Road Not Taken   *1916*

Two roads diverged in a yellow wood,
And sorry I could not travel both
And be one traveler, long I stood
And looked down one as far as I could
To where it bent in the undergrowth;   5

Then took the other, as just as fair,
And having perhaps the better claim,
Because it was grassy and wanted wear;

Though as for that the passing there
Had worn them really about the same,   10

And both that morning equally lay
In leaves no step had trodden black.
Oh, I kept the first for another day!
Yet knowing how way leads on to way,
I doubted if I should ever come back.   15

I shall be telling this with a sigh
Somewhere ages and ages hence:
Two roads diverged in a wood, and I—
I took the one less traveled by,
And that has made all the difference.   20

THOMAS HARDY (1840–1928)

Hap   *1866*

If but some vengeful god would call to me
From up the sky, and laugh: "Thou suffering thing,
Know that thy sorrow is my ecstasy,
That thy love's loss is my hate's profiting!"

Then would I bear it, clench myself, and die,   5
Steeled by the sense of ire unmerited;
Half-eased in that a Powerfuller than I
Had willed and meted me the tears I shed.

But not so. How arrives it joy lies slain,
And why unblooms the best hope ever sown?   10
—Crass Casualty obstructs the sun and rain,
And dicing Time for gladness casts a moan. . . .
These purblind Doomsters had as readily strown
Blisses about my pilgrimage as pain.

FRANCES E. W. HARPER (1825–1911)

Learning to Read   *1872*

Very soon the Yankee teachers
    Came down and set up school;
But oh! how the Rebs did hate it,—
    It was agin' their rule

Our masters always tried to hide   5
   Book learning from our eyes;
Knowledge did'nt agree with slavery —
   'Twould make us all too wise.

But some of us would try to steal
   A little from the book,   10
And put the words together,
   And learn by hook or crook.

I remember Uncle Caldwell,
   Who took pot-liquor fat
And greased the pages of his book,   15
   And hid it in his hat.

And had his master ever seen
   The leaves upon his head,
He'd have thought them greasy papers,
   But nothing to be read.   20

And there was Mr. Turner's Ben
   Who heard the children spell,
And picked the words right up by heart,
   And learned to read 'em well.

Well the Northern folks kept sending   25
   The Yankee teachers down
And they stood right up and helped us,
   Though Rebs did sneer and frown,

And, I longed to read my Bible,
   For precious words it said;   30
But when I begun to learn it,
   Folks just shook their heads,

And said there is no use trying,
   Oh! Chloe, you're too late;
But as I was rising sixty,   35
   I had no time to wait.

So I got a pair of glasses,
   And straight to work I went,
And never stopped till I could read
   The hymns and Testament.   40

Then I got a little cabin —
   A place to call my own —
And I felt as independent
   As the queen upon her throne.

GERARD MANLEY HOPKINS (1844–1889)

Pied Beauty   *1877*

Glory be to God for dappled things —
    For skies of couple-color as a brinded cow;
        For rose-moles all in stipple upon trout that swim;
Fresh-firecoal chestnut-falls;° finches' wings;   *fallen chestnut*
    Landscape plotted and pieced — fold, fallow, and plow;   5
        And all trades, their gear and tackle and trim.

All things counter, original, spare, strange;
    Whatever is fickle, freckled (who knows how?)
        With swift, slow; sweet, sour; adazzle, dim;
He fathers-forth whose beauty is past change: 10
        Praise him.

A. E. HOUSMAN (1859–1936)

To an Athlete Dying Young   *1896*

The time you won your town the race
We chaired° you through the marketplace;
Man and boy stood cheering by,
And home we brought you shoulder-high.

Today, the road all runners come,   5
Shoulder-high we bring you home,
And set you at your threshold down,
Townsman of a stiller town.

Smart lad, to slip betimes away
From fields where glory does not stay,   10
And early though the laurel° grows
It withers quicker than the rose.

Eyes the shady night has shut
Cannot see the record cut,
And silence sounds no worse than cheers   15
After earth has stopped the ears:

Now you will not swell the rout
Of lads that wore their honors out,
Runners whom renown outran
And the name died before the man.   20

2 *chaired:* Carried on the shoulders in triumphal parade.   11 *laurel:* Flowering shrub traditionally used to fashion wreaths of honor.

To set, before its echoes fade,
The fleet foot on the sill of shade,
And hold to the low lintel up
The still-defended challenge-cup.

And round that early-laureled head   25
Will flock to gaze the strengthless dead,
And find unwithered on its curls
The garland briefer than a girl's.

Julia Ward Howe (1819–1910)

Battle-Hymn of the Republic   1862

Mine eyes have seen the glory of the coming of the Lord:
He is trampling out the vintage where the grapes of wrath are stored:
He hath loosed the fateful lightning of his terrible swift sword:
        His truth is marching on.

I have seen Him in the watch-fires of a hundred circling camps;   5
They have builded Him an altar in the evening dews and damps;
I can read His righteous sentence by the dim and flaring lamps.
        His day is marching on.

I have read a fiery gospel, writ in burnished rows of steel:
"As ye deal with my contemners, so with you my grace shall deal;   10
Let the Hero, born of woman, crush the serpent with his heel,
        Since God is marching on."

He has sounded forth the trumpet that shall never call retreat;
He is sifting out the hearts of men before his judgment-seat:
Oh! be swift, my soul, to answer Him! be jubilant, my feet!   15
        Our God is marching on.

In the beauty of the lilies Christ was born across the sea,
With a glory in his bosom that transfigures you and me:
As he died to make men holy, let us die to make men free,
        While God is marching on.   20

Langston Hughes (1902–1967)

Harlem   1951

To hear "Harlem" read by Langston Hughes, visit bedfordstmartins.com/meyerlit/epages.

What happens to a dream deferred?

    Does it dry up
    like a raisin in the sun?
    Or fester like a sore —

And then run?   5
Does it stink like rotten meat?
Or crust and sugar over —
like a syrupy sweet?

Maybe it just sags
like a heavy load.   10

Or does it explode?

GEORGIA DOUGLAS JOHNSON (1877–1966)
Calling Dreams   *1920*

The right to make my dreams come true,
I ask, nay, I demand of life;
Nor shall fate's deadly contraband
Impede my steps, nor countermand;
Too long my heart against the ground
Has beat the dusty years around;
And now at length I rise! I wake!
And stride into the morning break!

BEN JONSON (1573–1637)
To Celia   *1616*

Drink to me only with thine eyes,
    And I will pledge with mine;
Or leave a kiss but in the cup,
    And I'll not ask for wine.
The thirst that from the soul doth rise   5
    Doth ask a drink divine;
But might I of Jove's nectar sup,
    I would not change for thine.

I sent thee late a rosy wreath,
    Not so much honoring thee   10
As giving it a hope that there
    It could not withered be.
But thou thereon didst only breathe,
    And sent'st it back to me;
Since when it grows, and smells, I swear,   15
    Not of itself but thee.

JOHN KEATS (1795–1821)

La Belle Dame sans Merci°

1819

To hear "La Belle Dame sans Merci" read by Sir Ralph Richardson, visit bedfordstmartins.com/meyerlit/epages.

O what can ail thee, knight-at-arms,
    Alone and palely loitering?
The sedge has withered from the lake,
    And no birds sing.

O what can ail thee, knight-at-arms,   5
    So haggard and so woe-begone?
The squirrel's granary is full,
    And the harvest's done.

I see a lily on thy brow,
    With anguish moist and fever dew,   10
And on thy cheeks a fading rose
    Fast withereth too.

I met a lady in the meads,
    Full beautiful — a faery's child,
Her hair was long, her foot was light,   15
    And her eyes were wild.

I made a garland for her head,
    And bracelets too, and fragrant zone;°   *belt*
She looked at me as she did love,
    And made sweet moan.   20

I set her on my pacing steed,
    And nothing else saw all day long,
For sidelong would she bend, and sing
    A faery's song.

She found me roots of relish sweet,   25
    And honey wild, and manna dew,
And sure in language strange she said,
    "I love thee true."

She took me to her elfin grot,
    And there she wept, and sighed full sore,   30
And there I shut her wild wild eyes
    With kisses four.

And there she lullèd me asleep,
    And there I dreamed — Ah! woe betide!

La Belle Dame sans Merci: This title is borrowed from a medieval poem and means "The Beautiful Lady without Mercy."

The latest° dream I ever dreamed   *last*   35
    On the cold hill side.

I saw pale kings and princes too,
    Pale warriors, death-pale were they all;
They cried — "La Belle Dame sans Merci
    Hath thee in thrall!"   40

I saw their starved lips in the gloam,
    With horrid warning gapèd wide,
And I awoke and found me here,
    On the cold hill's side.

And this is why I sojourn here,   45
    Alone and palely loitering,
Though the sedge has withered from the lake,
    And no birds sing.

JOHN KEATS (1795–1821)

Written in Disgust of Vulgar Superstition   *1816*

The church bells toll a melancholy round,
    Calling the people to some other prayers,
    Some other gloominess, more dreadful cares,
More hearkening to the sermon's horrid sound.
Surely the mind of man is closely bound   5
    In some black spell; seeing that each one tears
    Himself from fireside joys, and Lydian° airs,
And converse high of those with glory crown'd.
Still, still they toll, and I should feel a damp, —
    A chill as from a tomb, did I not know   10
That they are dying like an outburnt lamp;
    That 'tis their sighing, wailing ere they go
    Into oblivion; — that fresh flowers will grow,
And many glories of immortal stamp.

7 *Lydian:* Soft, sweet music.

EMMA LAZARUS (1849–1887)

The New Colossus   *1883*

Not like the brazen giant of Greek fame,
With conquering limbs astride from land to land;
Here at our sea-washed, sunset gates shall stand
A mighty woman with a torch, whose flame

Is the imprisoned lightning, and her name   5
Mother of Exiles. From her beacon-hand
Glows world-wide welcome; her mild eyes command
The air-bridged harbor that twin cities frame.
"Keep, ancient lands, your storied pomp!" cries she
With silent lips. "Give me your tired, your poor,   10
Your huddled masses yearning to breathe free,
The wretched refuse of your teeming shore.
Send these, the homeless, tempest-tost to me,
I lift my lamp beside the golden door!"

AMY LOWELL (1874–1925)

A Decade   1919

When you came, you were like red wine and honey,
And the taste of you burnt my mouth with its sweetness.
Now you are like morning bread,
Smooth and pleasant.
I hardly taste you at all for I know your savor;
But I am completely nourished.

JILL McDONOUGH (B. 1972)

Accident, Mass. Ave.   2008

> **WHEN I READ** "Read poems out loud! A, it's fun. 2, it helps you get over the impulse to freak out about things-with-line-breaks."
> —JILL McDONOUGH

I stopped at a red light on Mass. Ave.
in Boston, a couple blocks away
from the bridge, and a woman in a
        beat-up
old Buick backed into me. Like, cranked her wheel,
rammed right into my side. I drove a Chevy   5
pickup truck. It being Boston, I got out
of the car yelling, swearing at this woman,
a little woman, whose first language was not English.
But she lived and drove in Boston, too, so she knew,
we both knew, that the thing to do   10
is get out of the car, slam the door
as hard as you fucking can and yell things like *What the fuck*
were you thinking? You fucking blind? What the fuck
is going on? Jesus Christ! So we swore
at each other with perfect posture, unnaturally angled   15
chins. I threw my arms around, sudden
jerking motions with my whole arms, the backs
of my hands toward where she had hit my truck.

But she hadn't hit my truck. She hit
the tire; no damage done. Her car   20
was fine, too. We saw this while
we were yelling, and then we were struck.
The next line in our little drama should have been
Look at this fucking dent! I'm not paying for this
shit. I'm calling the cops, lady. Maybe we'd throw in a   25
You're in big trouble, sister, or *I just hope for your sake*
there's nothing wrong with my fucking suspension, that
sort of thing. But there was no fucking dent. There
was nothing else for us to do. So I
stopped yelling, and she looked at the tire she'd   30
backed into, her little eyebrows pursed
and worried. She was clearly in the wrong, I was enormous,
and I'd been acting as if I'd like to hit her. So I said
Well, there's nothing wrong with my car, nothing wrong
with your car . . . are you OK? She nodded, and started   35
to cry, so I put my arms around her and I held her, middle
of the street. Mass. Ave., Boston, a couple blocks from the bridge.
I hugged her, and I said *We were scared, weren't we?*
and she nodded and we laughed.

CLAUDE MCKAY (1889–1948)

The Lynching   *1920*

His spirit is smoke ascended to high heaven.
His father, by the cruelest way of pain,
Had bidden him to his bosom once again;
The awful sin remained still unforgiven.
All night a bright and solitary star   5
(Perchance the one that ever guided him,
Yet gave him up at last to Fate's wild whim)
Hung pitifully o'er the swinging char.
Day dawned, and soon the mixed crowds came to view
The ghastly body swaying in the sun.   10
The women thronged to look, but never a one
Showed sorrow in her eyes of steely blue.

And little lads, lynchers that were to be,
Danced round the dreadful thing in fiendish glee.

John Milton (1608–1674)

When I consider how my light is spent   c. 1655

When I consider how my light is spent,°
   Ere half my days in this dark world and wide,
   And that one talent° which is death to hide
Lodged with me useless, though my soul more bent
To serve therewith my Maker, and present   5
   My true account, lest He returning chide;
   "Doth God exact day-labor, light denied?"
I fondly° ask. But Patience, to prevent   *foolishly*
That murmur, soon replies, "God doth not need
   Either man's work or His own gifts. Who best   10
   Bear His mild yoke, they serve Him best. His state
Is kingly: thousands at His bidding speed,
   And post o'er land and ocean without rest;
   They also serve who only stand and wait."

1 *how my light is spent:* Milton had been totally blind since 1651.   3 *that one talent:*
Refers to Jesus's parable of the talents (units of money), in which a servant entrusted
with a talent buries it rather than invests it and is punished on his master's return
(Matt. 25:14–30).

Christina Georgina Rossetti (1830–1894)

Some Ladies Dress in Muslin Full and White   c. 1848

   Some ladies dress in muslin full and
      white,
Some gentlemen in cloth succinct and
    black;
Some patronise a dog-cart, some a hack,
   Some think a painted clarence only
     right.
   Youth is not always such a pleasing
     sight:
Witness a man with tassels on his back;
Or woman in a great-coat like a sack,
   Towering above her sex with horrid height.
If all the world were water fit to drown,
   There are some whom you would not teach to swim,   10

©Bettmann/CORBIS.

Rather enjoying if you saw them sink:
Certain old ladies dressed in girlish pink,
With roses and geraniums on their gown.
        Go to the basin, poke them o'er the rim—

WILLIAM SHAKESPEARE (1564–1616)

That time of year thou mayst in me behold   1609

That time of year thou mayst in me behold
When yellow leaves, or none, or few, do hang
Upon those boughs which shake against the cold,
Bare ruined choirs, where late the sweet birds sang.
In me thou see'st the twilight of such day   5
As after sunset fadeth in the west;
Which by and by black night doth take away,
Death's second self,° that seals up all in rest.   *sleep*
In me thou see'st the glowing of such fire,
That on the ashes of his youth doth lie,   10
As the deathbed whereon it must expire,
Consumed with that which it was nourished by.
        This thou perceiv'st, which makes thy love more strong,
        To love that well which thou must leave ere long.

WILLIAM SHAKESPEARE (1564–1616)

When, in disgrace with Fortune and men's eyes   1609

When, in disgrace with Fortune and men's eyes,
I all alone beweep my outcast state,
And trouble deaf heaven with my bootless cries,
And look upon myself and curse my fate,
Wishing me like to one more rich in hope,   5
Featured like him, like him with friends possessed,
Desiring this man's art, and that man's scope,
With what I most enjoy contented least,
Yet in these thoughts myself almost despising,
Haply I think on thee, and then my state,   10
Like to the lark at break of day arising
From sullen earth, sings hymns at heaven's gate;
        For thy sweet love remembered such wealth brings
        That then I scorn to change my state with kings.

PERCY BYSSHE SHELLEY (1792–1822)

Ozymandias°   *1818*

I met a traveler from an antique land
Who said: Two vast and trunkless legs of stone
Stand in the desert. . . . Near them, on the sand,
Half sunk, a shattered visage lies, whose frown,
And wrinkled lip, and sneer of cold command,   5
Tell that its sculptor well those passions read
Which yet survive, stamped on these lifeless things,
The hand that mocked them, and the heart that fed:
And on the pedestal these words appear:
"My name is Ozymandias, King of Kings: 10
Look on my works, ye Mighty, and despair!"
Nothing beside remains. Round the decay
Of that colossal wreck, boundless and bare
The lone and level sands stretch far away.

Ozymandias: Greek name for Ramses II, pharaoh of Egypt for sixty-seven years during the thirteenth century B.C. His colossal statue lies prostrate in the sands of Luxor. Napoleon's soldiers measured it (56 feet long, ear 3½ feet long, weight 1,000 tons). Its inscription, according to the Greek historian Diodorus Siculus, was "I am Ozymandias, King of Kings; if anyone wishes to know what I am and where I lie, let him surpass me in some of my exploits."

LYDIA HUNTLEY SIGOURNEY (1791–1865)

Indian Names   *1834*

*"How can the red men be forgotten, while so many of
our states and territories, bays, lakes and rivers, are
indelibly stamped by names of their giving?"*

Ye say they all have passed away
    That noble race and brave,
That their light canoes have vanished
    From off the crested wave;
That 'mid the forests where they roamed   5
    There rings no hunter shout,
But their name is on your waters,
    Ye may not wash it out.

'Tis where Ontario's billow
    Like Ocean's surge is curled,   10
Where strong Niagara's thunders wake
    The echo of the world.

Where red Missouri bringeth
　　Rich tribute from the west,
And Rappahannock sweetly sleeps   15
　　On green Virginia's breast.

Ye say their cone-like cabins,
　　That clustered o'er the vale,
Have fled away like withered leaves
　　Before the autumn gale,   20
But their memory liveth on your hills,
　　Their baptism on your shore,
Your everlasting rivers speak
　　Their dialect of yore.

Old Massachusetts wears it,   25
　　Within her lordly crown,
And broad Ohio bears it,
　　Amid his young renown;
Connecticut hath wreathed it
　　Where her quiet foliage waves,   30
And bold Kentucky breathed it hoarse
　　Through all her ancient caves.

Wachuset hides its lingering voice
　　Within his rocky heart,
And Alleghany graves its tone   35
　　Throughout his lofty chart;
Monadnock on his forehead hoar
　　Doth seal the sacred trust,
Your mountains build their monument,
　　Though ye destroy their dust.   40

Ye call these red-browed brethren
　　The insects of an hour,
Crushed like the noteless worm amid
　　The regions of their power;
Ye drive them from their father's lands,   45
　　Ye break of faith the seal,
But can ye from the court of Heaven
　　Exclude their last appeal?

Ye see their unresisting tribes,
　　With toilsome step and slow,   50
On through the trackless desert pass,
　　A caravan of woe;
Think ye the Eternal's ear is deaf?
　　His sleepless vision dim?
Think ye the *soul's blood* may not cry   55
　　From that far land to him?

ALFRED, LORD TENNYSON (1809–1892)

Ulysses°   *1833*

It little profits that an idle king,
By this still hearth, among these barren crags,
Matched with an agèd wife,° I mete and dole   *Penelope*
Unequal laws unto a savage race,
That hoard, and sleep, and feed, and know not me.   5
    I cannot rest from travel; I will drink
Life to the lees. All times I have enjoyed
Greatly, have suffered greatly, both with those
That loved me, and alone; on shore, and when
Through scudding drifts the rainy Hyades°   10
Vexed the dim sea. I am become a name;
For always roaming with a hungry heart
Much have I seen and known — cities of men
And manners, climates, councils, governments,
Myself not least, but honored of them all —   15
And drunk delight of battle with my peers,
Far on the ringing plains of windy Troy.
I am a part of all that I have met;
Yet all experience is an arch wherethrough
Gleams that untraveled world, whose margin fades   20
For ever and for ever when I move.
How dull it is to pause, to make an end,
To rust unburnished, not to shine in use!
As though to breathe were life. Life piled on life
Were all too little, and of one to me   25
Little remains; but every hour is saved
From that eternal silence, something more,
A bringer of new things; and vile it were
For some three suns to store and hoard myself,
And this gray spirit yearning in desire   30
To follow knowledge like a sinking star,
Beyond the utmost bound of human thought.

    This is my son, mine own Telemachus,
To whom I leave the scepter and the isle —
Well-loved of me, discerning to fulfill   35
This labor, by slow prudence to make mild
A rugged people, and through soft degrees

Ulysses: Ulysses, the hero of Homer's epic poem the *Odyssey*, is presented by Dante in *The Inferno*, XXVI, as restless after his return to Ithaca and eager for new adventures.
10 *Hyades:* Five stars in the constellation Taurus, supposed by the ancients to predict rain when they rose with the sun.

Subdue them to the useful and the good.
Most blameless is he, centered in the sphere
Of common duties, decent not to fail   40
In offices of tenderness, and pay
Meet adoration to my household gods,
When I am gone. He works his work, I mine.

    There lies the port; the vessel puffs her sail:
There gloom the dark, broad seas. My mariners,   45
Souls that have toiled, and wrought, and thought with me—
That ever with a frolic welcome took
The thunder and the sunshine, and opposed
Free hearts, free foreheads—you and I are old;
Old age hath yet his honor and his toil.   50
Death closes all; but something ere the end,
Some work of noble note, may yet be done,
Not unbecoming men that strove with Gods.
The lights begin to twinkle from the rocks;
The long day wanes; the slow moon climbs; the deep   55
Moans round with many voices. Come, my friends.
'Tis not too late to seek a newer world.
Push off, and sitting well in order smite
The sounding furrows; for my purpose holds
To sail beyond the sunset, and the baths   60
Of all the western stars, until I die.
It may be that the gulfs will wash us down;
It may be we shall touch the Happy Isles,°
And see the great Achilles,° whom we knew.
Though much is taken, much abides; and though   65
We are not now that strength which in old days
Moved earth and heaven, that which we are, we are:
One equal temper of heroic hearts,
Made weak by time and fate, but strong in will
To strive, to seek, to find, and not to yield.   70

63 *Happy Isles:* Elysium, the home after death of heroes and others favored by the
gods. It was thought by the ancients to lie beyond the sunset in the uncharted
Atlantic.   64 *Achilles:* The hero of Homer's Iliad.

WALT WHITMAN (1819–1892)
When I Heard the Learn'd Astronomer   *1865*

When I heard the learn'd astronomer,
When the proofs, the figures, were ranged in columns before me,
When I was shown the charts and diagrams, to add, divide, and
    measure them,

When I sitting heard the astronomer where he lectured with much
    applause in the lecture-room,
How soon unaccountable I became tired and sick,
Till rising and gliding out I wandered off by myself,
In the mystical moist night-air, and from time to time,
Looked up in perfect silence at the stars.

WILLIAM WORDSWORTH
(1770–1850)

The Solitary Reaper°   *1807*

By permission of Dove Cottage, the
Wordsworth Trust.

Behold her, single in the field,
Yon solitary Highland lass!
Reaping and singing by herself;
Stop here, or gently pass!
Alone she cuts and binds the grain,
And sings a melancholy strain;
O listen! for the vale profound
Is overflowing with the sound.

No nightingale did ever chaunt
More welcome notes to weary bands
Of travelers in some shady haunt
Among Arabian sands.
A voice so thrilling ne'er was heard
In springtime from the cuckoo-bird,
Breaking the silence of the seas   15
Among the farthest Hebrides.

Will no one tell me what she sings? —
Perhaps the plaintive numbers flow
For old, unhappy, far-off things,
And battles long ago.   20
Or is it some more humble lay,
Familiar matter of today?
Some natural sorrow, loss, or pain,
That has been, and may be again?

Whate'er the theme, the maiden sang   25
As if her song could have no ending;
I saw her singing at her work,

The Solitary Reaper: Dorothy Wordsworth (William's sister) wrote that the poem was
suggested by this sentence in Thomas Wilkinson's *Tour of Scotland:* "Passed a female
who was reaping alone; she sung in Erse, as she bended over her sickle; the sweetest
human voice I ever heard; her strains were tenderly melancholy, and felt delicious,
long after they were heard no more."

And o'er the sickle bending —
I listened, motionless and still;
And, as I mounted up the hill,   30
The music in my heart I bore
Long after it was heard no more.

WILLIAM WORDSWORTH (1770–1850)

Mutability   *1822*

From low to high doth dissolution climb,
And sink from high to low, along a scale
Of awful° notes, whose concord shall not fail;   *awe-filled*
A musical but melancholy chime,
Which they can hear who meddle not with crime,   5
Nor avarice, nor over-anxious care.
Truth fails not; but her outward forms that bear
The longest date do melt like frosty rime,
That in the morning whitened hill and plain
And is no more; drop like the tower sublime   10
Of yesterday, which royally did wear
His crown of weeds, but could not even sustain
Some casual shout that broke the silent air,
Or the unimaginable touch of Time.

WILLIAM BUTLER YEATS (1865–1939)

Leda and the Swan°   *1924*

A sudden blow: the great wings beating still
Above the staggering girl, her thighs
    caressed
By the dark webs, her nape caught in
    his bill,
He holds her helpless breast upon his
    breast.

How can those terrified vague fingers push
The feathered glory from her loosening
    thighs?

© Hulton-Deutsch Collection/CORBIS.

Leda and the Swan: In Greek myth, Zeus in the form of a swan seduced Leda and fathered Helen of Troy (whose abduction started the Trojan War) and Clytemnestra, Agamemnon's wife and murderer. Yeats thought of Zeus's appearance to Leda as a type of annunciation, like the angel appearing to Mary.

And how can body, laid in that white rush,
But feel the strange heart beating where it lies?

A shudder in the loins engenders there
The broken wall, the burning roof and tower   10
And Agamemnon dead.
                              Being so caught up,
So mastered by the brute blood of the air,
Did she put on his knowledge with his power
Before the indifferent beak could let her drop?   15

DRAMA

The Study
of Drama

24

Reading Drama

There are always angles in
every subject to find the
comedy in it.
— LARRY DAVID

READING DRAMA RESPONSIVELY

The publication of a short story, novel, or poem represents for most writers the final step in a long creative process that might have begun with an idea, issue, emotion, or question that demanded expression. *Playwrights* — writers who make plays — may begin a work in the same way as other writers, but rarely are they satisfied with only its publication, because most dramatic literature — what we call *plays* — is written to be performed by actors on a stage before an audience. Playwrights typically create a play keeping in mind not only readers but also actors, producers, directors, costumers, designers, technicians, and a theater full of other support staff who have a hand in presenting the play to a live audience.

Drama is literature equipped with arms, legs, tears, laughs, whispers, shouts, and gestures that are alive and immediate. Indeed, the word *drama* derives from the Greek word *dran,* meaning "to do" or "to perform." The text of many plays — the *script* — may come to life fully only when the written words are transformed into a performance. Although there are plays that do not invite production, they are relatively few. Such plays, written to be read rather than performed, are called *closet dramas.* In this kind of work (primarily associated with nineteenth-century

English literature), literary art outweighs all other considerations. The majority of playwrights, however, view the written word as the beginning of a larger creation and hope that a producer will deem their scripts worthy of production.

Given that most playwrights intend their works to be performed, it might be argued that reading a play is a poor substitute for seeing it acted on a stage — perhaps something like reading a recipe without having access to the ingredients and a kitchen. This analogy is tempting, but it overlooks the literary dimensions of a script; the words we hear on a stage were written first. Read from a page, these words can feed an imagination in ways that a recipe cannot satisfy a hungry cook. We can fill in a play's missing faces, voices, actions, and settings in much the same way that we imagine these elements in a short story or novel. Like any play director, we are free to include as many ingredients as we have an appetite for.

Trifles

In the following play, Susan Glaspell skillfully draws on many dramatic elements and creates an intense story that is as effective on the page as it is in the theater. Glaspell wrote *Trifles* in 1916 for the Provincetown Players on Cape Cod, in Massachusetts. Their performance of the work helped her develop a reputation as a writer sensitive to feminist issues. The year after *Trifles* was produced, Glaspell transformed the play into a short story titled "A Jury of Her Peers."

Glaspell's life in the Midwest provided her with the setting for *Trifles*. Born and raised in Davenport, Iowa, she graduated from Drake University in 1899 and then worked for a short time as a reporter on the *Des Moines News,* until her short stories were accepted in magazines such as *Harper's* and *Ladies' Home Journal.* Glaspell moved to the Northeast when she was in her early thirties to continue writing fiction and drama. She published some twenty plays, novels, and more than forty short stories. *Alison's House,* based on Emily Dickinson's life, earned her a Pulitzer Prize for drama in 1931. *Trifles* and "A Jury of Her Peers" remain, however, Glaspell's best-known works.

Glaspell wrote *Trifles* to complete a bill that was to feature several one-act plays by Eugene O'Neill. In *The Road to the Temple* (1926) she recalls how the play came to her as she sat in the theater looking at a bare stage. First, "the stage became a kitchen. . . . Then the door at the

© Nickolas Muray Photo Archives, LLC. Courtesy of the Sheaffer-O'Neill Collection, Connecticut College.

back opened, and people all bundled up came in—two or three men. I
wasn't sure which, but sure enough about the two women, who hung
back, reluctant to enter that kitchen. When I was a newspaper reporter
out in Iowa, I was sent downstate to do a murder trial, and I never forgot
going to the kitchen of a woman who had been locked up in town."

As you read the play, keep track of your responses
to the characters and note in the margin the moments
when Glaspell reveals how men and women respond
differently to the evidence before them. What do those
moments suggest about the kinds of assumptions these
men and women make about themselves and each other? How do their
assumptions compare with your own?

Explore
contexts for Susan
Glaspell and approaches
to this play at
bedfordstmartins.com/
meyerlit.

Susan Glaspell (1882–1948)

Trifles   1916

To hear *Trifles*
read aloud, visit
bedfordstmartins.com/
meyerlit/epages.

CHARACTERS

George Henderson, county attorney
Henry Peters, sheriff
Lewis Hale, a neighboring farmer
Mrs. Peters
Mrs. Hale

SCENE: The kitchen in the now abandoned farmhouse of John Wright, a
gloomy kitchen, and left without having been put in order—unwashed
pans under the sink, a loaf of bread outside the breadbox, a dish towel on
the table—other signs of incompleted work. At the rear the outer door
opens and the Sheriff comes in followed by the County Attorney and
Hale. The Sheriff and Hale are men in middle life, the County Attorney is
a young man; all are much bundled up and go at once to the stove. They
are followed by the two women—the Sheriff's wife first; she is a slight wiry
woman, a thin nervous face. Mrs. Hale is larger and would ordinarily be
called more comfortable looking, but she is disturbed now and looks fearfully about as she enters. The women have come in slowly, and stand close
together near the door.

County Attorney (*rubbing his hands*): This feels good. Come up to the fire,
    ladies.
Mrs. Peters (*after taking a step forward*): I'm not—cold.
Sheriff (*unbuttoning his overcoat and stepping away from the stove as if to mark
    the beginning of official business*): Now, Mr. Hale, before we move things
    about, you explain to Mr. Henderson just what you saw when you
    came here yesterday morning.

County Attorney: By the way, has anything been moved? Are things just as you left them yesterday?

Sheriff (looking about): It's just about the same. When it dropped below zero last night I thought I'd better send Frank out this morning to make a fire for us — no use getting pneumonia with a big case on, but I told him not to touch anything except the stove — and you know Frank.

County Attorney: Somebody should have been left here yesterday.

Sheriff: Oh — yesterday. When I had to send Frank to Morris Center for that man who went crazy — I want you to know I had my hands full yesterday. I knew you could get back from Omaha by today and as long as I went over everything here myself —

County Attorney: Well, Mr. Hale, tell just what happened when you came here yesterday morning.

Hale: Harry and I had started to town with a load of potatoes. We came along the road from my place and as I got here I said, "I'm going to see if I can't get John Wright to go in with me on a party telephone." I spoke to Wright about it once before and he put me off, saying folks talked too much anyway, and all he asked was peace and quiet — I guess you know about how much he talked himself; but I thought maybe if I went to the house and talked about it before his wife, though I said to Harry that I didn't know as what his wife wanted made much difference to John —

County Attorney: Let's talk about that later, Mr. Hale. I do want to talk about that, but tell now just what happened when you got to the house.

Hale: I didn't hear or see anything; I knocked at the door, and still it was all quiet inside. I knew they must be up, it was past eight o'clock. So I knocked again, and I thought I heard somebody say, "Come in." I wasn't sure, I'm not sure yet, but I opened the door — this door *(indicating the door by which the two women are still standing)* and there in that rocker — *(pointing to it)* sat Mrs. Wright. *(They all look at the rocker.)*

County Attorney: What — was she doing?

Hale: She was rockin' back and forth. She had her apron in her hand and was kind of — pleating it.

County Attorney: And how did she — look?

Hale: Well, she looked queer.

County Attorney: How do you mean — queer?

Hale: Well, as if she didn't know what she was going to do next. And kind of done up.

County Attorney: How did she seem to feel about your coming?

Hale: Why, I don't think she minded — one way or other. She didn't pay much attention. I said, "How do, Mrs. Wright, it's cold, ain't it?" And she said, "Is it?" — and went on kind of pleating at her apron. Well, I was surprised; she didn't ask me to come up to the stove, or

to set down, but just sat there, not even looking at me, so I said, "I
want to see John." And then she — laughed. I guess you would call it
a laugh. I thought of Harry and the team outside, so I said a little
sharp: "Can't I see John?" "No," she says, kind o'dull like. "Ain't he
home?" says I. "Yes," says she, "he's home." "Then why can't I see
him?" I asked her, out of patience. "'Cause he's dead," says she.
"Dead?" says I. She just nodded her head, not getting a bit excited,
but rockin' back and forth. "Why — where is he?" says I, not knowing what to say. She just pointed upstairs — like that *(himself pointing
to the room above)*. I started for the stairs, with the idea of going up
there. I walked from there to here — then I says, "Why, what did he
die of?" "He died of a rope round his neck," says she, and just went
on pleatin' at her apron. Well, I went out and called Harry. I thought
I might — need help. We went upstairs and there he was lyin' —

County Attorney: I think I'd rather have you go into that upstairs, where
you can point it all out. Just go on now with the rest of the story.

Hale: Well, my first thought was to get that rope off. It looked . . . *(stops;
his face twitches)* . . . but Harry, he went up to him, and he said, "No,
he's dead all right, and we'd better not touch anything." So we went
back downstairs. She was still sitting that same way. "Has anybody
been notified?" I asked. "No," says she, unconcerned. "Who did this,
Mrs. Wright?" said Harry. He said it businesslike — and she stopped
pleatin' of her apron. "I don't know," she says. "You don't *know*?" says
Harry. "No," says she. "Weren't you sleepin' in the bed with him?" says
Harry. "Yes," says she, "but I was on the inside." "Somebody slipped a
rope round his neck and strangled him and you didn't wake up?" says
Harry. "I didn't wake up," she said after him. We must 'a' looked as if
we didn't see how that could be, for after a minute she said, "I sleep
sound." Harry was going to ask her more questions but I said maybe
we ought to let her tell her story first to the coroner, or the sheriff, so
Harry went fast as he could to Rivers' place, where there's a telephone.

County Attorney: And what did Mrs. Wright do when she knew that you
had gone for the coroner?

Hale: She moved from the rocker to that chair over there *(pointing to
a small chair in the corner)* and just sat there with her hands held
together and looking down. I got a feeling that I ought to make some
conversation, so I said I had come in to see if John wanted to put in
a telephone, and at that she started to laugh, and then she stopped
and looked at me — scared. *(The County Attorney, who has had his notebook out, makes a note.)* I dunno, maybe it wasn't scared. I wouldn't
like to say it was. Soon Harry got back, and then Dr. Lloyd came and
you, Mr. Peters, and so I guess that's all I know that you don't.

County Attorney *(looking around)*: I guess we'll go upstairs first — and then
out to the barn and around there. *(To the Sheriff.)* You're convinced
that there was nothing important here — nothing that would point
to any motive?

Sheriff: Nothing here but kitchen things. *(The County Attorney, after again looking around the kitchen, opens the door of a cupboard closet. He gets up on a chair and looks on a shelf. Pulls his hand away, sticky.)*

County Attorney: Here's a nice mess. *(The women draw nearer.)*

Mrs. Peters (to the other woman): Oh, her fruit; it did freeze. *(To the Lawyer.)* She worried about that when it turned so cold. She said the fire'd go out and her jars would break.

Sheriff (rises): Well, can you beat the woman! Held for murder and worryin' about her preserves.

County Attorney: I guess before we're through she may have something more serious than preserves to worry about.

Hale: Well, women are used to worrying over trifles. *(The two women move a little closer together.)*

County Attorney (with the gallantry of a young politician): And yet, for all their worries, what would we do without the ladies? *(The women do not unbend. He goes to the sink, takes a dipperful of water from the pail, and pouring it into a basin, washes his hands. Starts to wipe them on the roller towel, turns it for a cleaner place.)* Dirty towels! *(Kicks his foot against the pans under the sink.)* Not much of a housekeeper, would you say, ladies?

Mrs. Hale (stiffly): There's a great deal of work to be done on a farm.

County Attorney: To be sure. And yet *(with a little bow to her)* I know there are some Dickson county farmhouses which do not have such roller towels. *(He gives it a pull to expose its full length again.)*

Mrs. Hale: Those towels get dirty awful quick. Men's hands aren't always as clean as they might be.

County Attorney: Ah, loyal to your sex, I see. But you and Mrs. Wright were neighbors. I suppose you were friends, too.

Mrs. Hale (shaking her head): I've not seen much of her of late years. I've not been in this house—it's more than a year.

County Attorney: And why was that? You didn't like her?

Mrs. Hale: I liked her all well enough. Farmers' wives have their hands full, Mr. Henderson. And then—

County Attorney: Yes—?

Mrs. Hale (looking about): It never seemed a very cheerful place.

County Attorney: No—it's not cheerful. I shouldn't say she had the home-making instinct.

Mrs. Hale: Well, I don't know as Wright had, either.

County Attorney: You mean that they didn't get on very well?

Mrs. Hale: No, I don't mean anything. But I don't think a place'd be any cheerfuller for John Wright's being in it.

County Attorney: I'd like to talk more of that a little later. I want to get the lay of things upstairs now. *(He goes to the left where three steps lead to a stair door.)*

Sheriff: I suppose anything Mrs. Peters does'll be all right. She was to take in some clothes for her, you know, and a few little things. We left in such a hurry yesterday.

County Attorney: Yes, but I would like to see what you take, Mrs. Peters, and keep an eye out for anything that might be of use to us.

Mrs. Peters: Yes, Mr. Henderson. *(The women listen to the men's steps on the stairs, then look about the kitchen.)*

Mrs. Hale: I'd hate to have men coming into my kitchen, snooping around and criticizing. *(She arranges the pans under sink which the lawyer had shoved out of place.)*

Mrs. Peters: Of course it's no more than their duty.

Mrs. Hale: Duty's all right, but I guess that deputy sheriff that came out to make the fire might have got a little of this on. *(Gives the roller towel a pull.)* Wish I'd thought of that sooner. Seems mean to talk about her for not having things slicked up when she had to come away in such a hurry.

Mrs. Peters (who has gone to a small table in the left rear corner of the room, and lifted one end of a towel that covers a pan): She had bread set. *(Stands still.)*

Mrs. Hale (eyes fixed on a loaf of bread beside the breadbox, which is on a low shelf at the other side of the room. Moves slowly toward it.): She was going to put this in there. *(Picks up loaf, then abruptly drops it. In a manner of returning to familiar things.)* It's a shame about her fruit. I wonder if it's all gone. *(Gets up on the chair and looks.)* I think there's some here that's all right, Mrs. Peters. Yes — here; *(holding it toward the window)* this is cherries, too. *(Looking again.)* I declare I believe that's the only one. *(Gets down, bottle in her hand. Goes to the sink and wipes it off on the outside.)* She'll feel awful bad after all her hard work in the hot weather. I remember the afternoon I put up my cherries last summer. *(She puts the bottle on the big kitchen table, center of the room. With a sigh, is about to sit down in the rocking-chair. Before she is seated realizes what chair it is; with a slow look at it, steps back. The chair which she has touched rocks back and forth.)*

Mrs. Peters: Well, I must get those things from the front room closet. *(She goes to the door at the right, but after looking into the other room, steps back.)* You coming with me, Mrs. Hale? You could help me carry them. *(They go in the other room; reappear, Mrs. Peters carrying a dress and skirt, Mrs. Hale following with a pair of shoes.)* My, it's cold in there. *(She puts the clothes on the big table, and hurries to the stove.)*

Mrs. Hale (examining the skirt): Wright was close. I think maybe that's why she kept so much to herself. She didn't even belong to the Ladies' Aid. I suppose she felt she couldn't do her part, and then you don't enjoy things when you feel shabby. I heard she used to wear pretty clothes and be lively, when she was Minnie Foster, one of the town girls singing in the choir. But that — oh, that was thirty years ago. This all you want to take in?

Mrs. Peters: She said she wanted an apron. Funny thing to want, for there isn't much to get you dirty in jail, goodness knows. But I suppose just to make her feel more natural. She said they was in the top drawer in this cupboard. Yes, here. And then her little shawl that always hung behind the door. *(Opens stair door and looks.)* Yes, here it is. *(Quickly shuts door leading upstairs.)*

Mrs. Hale (abruptly moving toward her): Mrs. Peters?

Mrs. Peters: Yes, Mrs. Hale?

Mrs. Hale: Do you think she did it?

Mrs. Peters (in a frightened voice): Oh, I don't know.

Mrs. Hale: Well, I don't think she did. Asking for an apron and her little shawl. Worrying about her fruit.

Mrs. Peters (starts to speak, glances up, where footsteps are heard in the room above. In a low voice): Mr. Peters says it looks bad for her. Mr. Henderson is awful sarcastic in a speech and he'll make fun of her sayin' she didn't wake up.

Mrs. Hale: Well, I guess John Wright didn't wake when they was slipping that rope under his neck.

Mrs. Peters: No, it's strange. It must have been done awful crafty and still. They say it was such a — funny way to kill a man, rigging it all up like that.

Mrs. Hale: That's just what Mr. Hale said. There was a gun in the house. He says that's what he can't understand.

Mrs. Peters: Mr. Henderson said coming out that what was needed for the case was a motive; something to show anger, or — sudden feeling.

Mrs. Hale (who is standing by the table): Well, I don't see any signs of anger around here. *(She puts her hand on the dish towel which lies on the table, stands looking down at table, one-half of which is clean, the other half messy.)* It's wiped to here. *(Makes a move as if to finish work, then turns and looks at loaf of bread outside the breadbox. Drops towel. In that voice of coming back to familiar things.)* Wonder how they are finding things upstairs. I hope she had it a little more red-up up there. You know, it seems kind of *sneaking.* Locking her up in town and then coming out here and trying to get her own house to turn against her!

Mrs. Peters: But, Mrs. Hale, the law is the law.

Mrs. Hale: I s'pose 'tis. *(Unbuttoning her coat.)* Better loosen up your things, Mrs. Peters. You won't feel them when you go out. *(Mrs. Peters takes off her fur tippet, goes to hang it on hook at back of room, stands looking at the under part of the small corner table.)*

Mrs. Peters: She was piecing a quilt. *(She brings the large sewing basket and they look at the bright pieces.)*

Mrs. Hale: It's a log cabin pattern. Pretty, isn't it? I wonder if she was goin' to quilt it or just knot it? *(Footsteps have been heard coming down the stairs. The Sheriff enters followed by Hale and the County Attorney.)*

Sheriff: They wonder if she was going to quilt it or just knot it! *(The men laugh, the women look abashed.)*

County Attorney (rubbing his hands over the stove): Frank's fire didn't do much up there, did it? Well, let's go out to the barn and get that cleared up. *(The men go outside.)*

Mrs. Hale (resentfully): I don't know as there's anything so strange, our takin' up our time with little things while we're waiting for them to get the evidence. *(She sits down at the big table smoothing out a block with decision.)* I don't see as it's anything to laugh about.

Mrs. Peters (apologetically): Of course they've got awful important things on their minds. *(Pulls up a chair and joins Mrs. Hale at the table.)*

Mrs. Hale (examining another block): Mrs. Peters, look at this one. Here, this is the one she was working on, and look at the sewing! All the rest of it has been so nice and even. And look at this! It's all over the place! Why, it looks as if she didn't know what she was about! *(After she has said this they look at each other, then start to glance back at the door. After an instant Mrs. Hale has pulled at a knot and ripped the sewing.)*

Mrs. Peters: Oh, what are you doing, Mrs. Hale?

Mrs. Hale (mildly): Just pulling out a stitch or two that's not sewed very good. *(Threading a needle.)* Bad sewing always made me fidgety.

Mrs. Peters (nervously): I don't think we ought to touch things.

Mrs. Hale: I'll just finish up this end. *(Suddenly stopping and leaning forward.)* Mrs. Peters?

Mrs. Peters: Yes, Mrs. Hale?

Mrs. Hale: What do you suppose she was so nervous about?

Mrs. Peters: Oh — I don't know. I don't know as she was nervous. I sometimes sew awful queer when I'm just tired. *(Mrs. Hale starts to say something, looks at Mrs. Peters, then goes on sewing.)* Well, I must get these things wrapped up. They may be through sooner than we think. *(Putting apron and other things together.)* I wonder where I can find a piece of paper, and string. *(Rises.)*

Mrs. Hale: In that cupboard, maybe.

Mrs. Peters (looking in cupboard): Why, here's a bird-cage. *(Holds it up.)* Did she have a bird, Mrs. Hale?

Mrs. Hale: Why, I don't know whether she did or not — I've not been here for so long. There was a man around last year selling canaries cheap, but I don't know as she took one; maybe she did. She used to sing real pretty herself.

Mrs. Peters (glancing around): Seems funny to think of a bird here. But she must have had one, or why would she have a cage? I wonder what happened to it?

Mrs. Hale: I s'pose maybe the cat got it.

Mrs. Peters: No, she didn't have a cat. She's got that feeling some people have about cats — being afraid of them. My cat got in her room and she was real upset and asked me to take it out.

Mrs. Hale: My sister Bessie was like that. Queer, ain't it?

Mrs. Peters (examining the cage): Why, look at this door. It's broke. One hinge is pulled apart.

Mrs. Hale (looking too): Looks as if someone must have been rough with it.

Mrs. Peters: Why, yes. *(She brings the cage forward and puts it on the table.)*

Mrs. Hale: I wish if they're going to find any evidence they'd be about it. I don't like this place.

Mrs. Peters: But I'm awful glad you came with me, Mrs. Hale. It would be lonesome for me sitting here alone.

Mrs. Hale: It would, wouldn't it? *(Dropping her sewing.)* But I tell you what I do wish, Mrs. Peters. I wish I had come over sometimes when *she* was here. I— *(looking around the room)* — wish I had.

Mrs. Peters: But of course you were awful busy, Mrs. Hale—your house and your children.

Mrs. Hale: I could've come. I stayed away because it weren't cheerful—and that's why I ought to have come. I—I've never liked this place. Maybe because it's down in a hollow and you don't see the road. I dunno what it is, but it's a lonesome place and always was. I wish I had come over to see Minnie Foster sometimes. I can see now—*(Shakes her head.)*

Mrs. Peters: Well, you mustn't reproach yourself, Mrs. Hale. Somehow we just don't see how it is with other folks until—something turns up.

Mrs. Hale: Not having children makes less work—but it makes a quiet house, and Wright out to work all day, and no company when he did come in. Did you know John Wright, Mrs. Peters?

Mrs. Peters: Not to know him; I've seen him in town. They say he was a good man.

Mrs. Hale: Yes—good; he didn't drink, and kept his word as well as most, I guess, and paid his debts. But he was a hard man, Mrs. Peters. Just to pass the time of day with him—*(Shivers.)* Like a raw wind that gets to the bone. *(Pauses, her eye falling on the cage.)* I should think she would 'a' wanted a bird. But what do you suppose went with it?

Mrs. Peters: I don't know, unless it got sick and died. *(She reaches over and swings the broken door, swings it again, both women watch it.)*

Mrs. Hale: You weren't raised round here, were you? *(Mrs. Peters shakes her head.)* You didn't know—her?

Mrs. Peters: Not till they brought her yesterday.

Mrs. Hale: She—come to think of it, she was kind of like a bird herself—real sweet and pretty, but kind of timid and—fluttery. How—she—did—change. *(Silence: then as if struck by a happy thought and relieved to get back to everyday things.)* Tell you what, Mrs. Peters, why don't you take the quilt in with you? It might take up her mind.

Mrs. Peters: Why, I think that's a real nice idea, Mrs. Hale. There couldn't possibly be any objection to it could there? Now, just what would I take? I wonder if her patches are in here—and her things. *(They look in the sewing basket.)*

Mrs. Hale: Here's some red. I expect this has got sewing things in it. *(Brings out a fancy box.)* What a pretty box. Looks like something somebody would give you. Maybe her scissors are in here. *(Opens box. Suddenly puts her hand to her nose.)* Why — *(Mrs. Peters bends nearer, then turns her face away.)* There's something wrapped up in this piece of silk.

Mrs. Peters: Why, this isn't her scissors.

Mrs. Hale (lifting the silk): Oh, Mrs. Peters — it's — *(Mrs. Peters bends closer.)*

Mrs. Peters: It's the bird.

Mrs. Hale (jumping up): But, Mrs. Peters — look at it! Its neck! Look at its neck! It's all — other side *to.*

Mrs. Peters: Somebody — wrung — its — neck. *(Their eyes meet. A look of growing comprehension, of horror. Steps are heard outside. Mrs. Hale slips box under quilt pieces, and sinks into her chair. Enter Sheriff and County Attorney. Mrs. Peters rises.)*

County Attorney (as one turning from serious things to little pleasantries): Well, ladies, have you decided whether she was going to quilt it or knot it?

Mrs. Peters: We think she was going to — knot it.

County Attorney: Well, that's interesting, I'm sure. *(Seeing the bird-cage.)* Has the bird flown?

Mrs. Hale (putting more quilt pieces over the box): We think the — cat got it.

County Attorney (preoccupied): Is there a cat? *(Mrs. Hale glances in a quick covert way at Mrs. Peters.)*

Mrs. Peters: Well, not *now.* They're superstitious, you know. They leave.

County Attorney (to Sheriff Peters, continuing an interrupted conversation): No sign at all of anyone having come from the outside. Their own rope. Now let's go up again and go over it piece by piece. *(They start upstairs.)* It would have to have been someone who knew just the — *(Mrs. Peters sits down. The two women sit there not looking at one another, but as if peering into something and at the same time holding back. When they talk now it is in the manner of feeling their way over strange ground, as if afraid of what they are saying, but as if they cannot help saying it.)*

Mrs. Hale: She liked the bird. She was going to bury it in that pretty box.

Mrs. Peters (in a whisper): When I was a girl — my kitten — there was a boy took a hatchet, and before my eyes — and before I could get there — *(Covers her face an instant.)* If they hadn't held me back I would have — *(catches herself, looks upstairs where steps are heard, falters weakly)* — hurt him.

Mrs. Hale (with a slow look around her): I wonder how it would seem never to have had any children around. *(Pause.)* No, Wright wouldn't like the bird — a thing that sang. She used to sing. He killed that, too.

Mrs. Peters (moving uneasily): We don't know who killed the bird.

Mrs. Hale: I knew John Wright.

Mrs. Peters: It was an awful thing was done in this house that night, Mrs. Hale. Killing a man while he slept, slipping a rope around his neck that choked the life out of him.

Mrs. Hale: His neck. Choked the life out of him. *(Her hand goes out and rests on the bird-cage.)*

Mrs. Peters (with rising voice): We don't know who killed him. We don't know.

Mrs. Hale (her own feeling not interrupted): If there'd been years and years of nothing, then a bird to sing to you, it would be awful—still, after the bird was still.

Mrs. Peters (something within her speaking): I know what stillness is. When we homesteaded in Dakota, and my first baby died—after he was two years old, and me with no other then—

Mrs. Hale (moving): How soon do you suppose they'll be through looking for the evidence?

Mrs. Peters: I know what stillness is. *(Pulling herself back.)* The law has got to punish crime, Mrs. Hale.

Mrs. Hale (not as if answering that): I wish you'd seen Minnie Foster when she wore a white dress with blue ribbons and stood up there in the choir and sang. *(A look around the room.)* Oh, I wish I'd come over here once in a while! That was a crime! That was a crime! Who's going to punish that?

Mrs. Peters (looking upstairs): We mustn't—take on.

Mrs. Hale: I might have known she needed help! I know how things can be—for women. I tell you, it's queer, Mrs. Peters. We live close together and we live far apart. We all go through the same things—it's all just a different kind of the same thing. *(Brushes her eyes, noticing the bottle of fruit, reaches out for it.)* If I was you I wouldn't tell her her fruit was gone. Tell her it *ain't*. Tell her it's all right. Take this in to prove it to her. She—she may never know whether it was broke or not.

Mrs. Peters (takes the bottle, looks about for something to wrap it in; takes petticoat from the clothes brought from the other room, very nervously begins winding this around the bottle. In a false voice): My, it's a good thing the men couldn't hear us. Wouldn't they just laugh! Getting all stirred up over a little thing like a—dead canary. As if that could have anything to do with—with—wouldn't they *laugh!* *(The men are heard coming down stairs.)*

Mrs. Hale (under her breath): Maybe they would—maybe they wouldn't.

County Attorney: No, Peters, it's all perfectly clear except a reason for doing it. But you know juries when it comes to women. If there was some definite thing. Something to show—something to make a story about—a thing that would connect up with this strange way of doing it—*(The women's eyes meet for an instant. Enter Hale from outer door.)*

Hale: Well, I've got the team around. Pretty cold out there.

County Attorney: I'm going to stay here a while by myself. *(To the Sheriff.)* You can send Frank out for me, can't you? I want to go over everything. I'm not satisfied that we can't do better.

Sheriff: Do you want to see what Mrs. Peters is going to take in? *(The Law-yer goes to the table, picks up the apron, laughs.)*

County Attorney: Oh, I guess they're not very dangerous things the ladies have picked out. *(Moves a few things about, disturbing the quilt pieces which cover the box. Steps back.)* No, Mrs. Peters doesn't need supervis-ing. For that matter a sheriff's wife is married to the law. Ever think of it that way, Mrs. Peters?

Mrs. Peters: Not—just that way.

Sheriff (chuckling): Married to the law. (Moves toward the other room.) I just want you to come in here a minute, George. We ought to take a look at these windows.

County Attorney (scoffingly): Oh, windows!

Sheriff: We'll be right out, Mr. Hale. *(Hale goes outside. The Sheriff follows the County Attorney into the other room. Then Mrs. Hale rises, hands tight together, looking intensely at Mrs. Peters, whose eyes make a slow turn, finally meeting Mrs. Hale's. A moment Mrs. Hale holds her, then her own eyes point the way to where the box is concealed. Suddenly Mrs. Peters throws back quilt pieces and tries to put the box in the bag she is wearing. It is too big. She opens box, starts to take bird out, cannot touch it, goes to pieces, stands there helpless. Sound of a knob turning in the other room. Mrs. Hale snatches the box and puts it in the pocket of her big coat. Enter County Attorney and Sheriff.)*

County Attorney (facetiously): Well, Henry, at least we found out that she was not going to quilt it. She was going to—what is it you call it, ladies?

Mrs. Hale (her hand against her pocket): We call it—knot it, Mr. Henderson.

Curtain

CONSIDERATIONS FOR CRITICAL THINKING AND WRITING

1. **FIRST RESPONSE.** Describe the setting of this play. What kind of atmo-sphere is established by the details in the opening scene? Does the atmosphere change through the course of the play?

2. Characterize John Wright. Why did his wife kill him?

3. Why do the men fail to see the clues that Mrs. Hale and Mrs. Peters discover?

4. How do the men's conversations and actions reveal their attitudes toward women?

5. What is the significance of the play's last line, spoken by Mrs. Hale: We call it—knot it, Mr. Henderson"? Explain what you think the tone of Mrs. Hale's voice is when she says this line. What is she feel-ing? What are you feeling?

6. **CONNECTION TO ANOTHER SELECTION.** Write an essay comparing the views of marriage in *Trifles* and in Kate Chopin's short story "The Story of an Hour" (p. 13). What similarities do you find in the themes of these two works? Are there any significant differences between the works?

A SAMPLE CLOSE READING

An Annotated Section of Susan Glaspell's Trifles

As you read a play for the first time, highlight lines, circle or underline words, and record your responses in the margins. These responses will allow you to retrieve initial reactions and questions that in subsequent readings you can pursue and resolve. Just as the play is likely to have layered meanings, so too will your own readings as you gradually piece together a variety of elements such as exposition, plot, and character that will lead you toward their thematic significance. The following annotations for an excerpt from *Trifles* offer an interpretation that was produced by several readings of the play. Of course, your annotations could be quite different, depending upon your own approach to the play.

The following excerpt appears four pages into this eleven-page play and is preceded by a significant amount of exposition that establishes the bleak Midwestern farm setting and some details about Mrs. Wright, who is the prime suspect in the murder of her husband. Prior to this dialogue, only the male characters speak as they try to discover a motive for the crime.

The Sheriff unknowingly announces a major conflict in the play that echoes the title: From a male point of view, there is nothing of any importance to be found in the kitchen — or in women's domestic lives. Mr. Hale confirms this by pronouncing such matters "trifles."

The County Attorney weighs in with his assessment of this "sticky" situation by calling it a "mess" from which he pulls away.

As the Attorney pulls away, the women move closer together (sides are slowly being drawn), and Mrs. Peters says more than she realizes when she observes, "Oh, her fruit; it did freeze." This anticipates our understanding of the cold, fruitless life that drove Mrs. Wright to murder.

The Sheriff's exasperation about women worrying about "preserves" will ironically help

County Attorney (looking around): I guess we'll go upstairs first — and then out to the barn and around there. *(To the Sheriff.)* You're convinced that there was nothing important here — nothing that would point to any motive?

Sheriff: Nothing here but kitchen things. *(The County Attorney, after again looking around the kitchen, opens the door of a cupboard closet. He gets up on a chair and looks on a shelf. Pulls his hand away, sticky.)*

County Attorney: Here's a nice mess. *(The women draw nearer.)*

Mrs. Peters (to the other woman): Oh, her fruit; it did freeze. *(To the Lawyer.)* She worried about that when it turned so cold. She said the fire'd go out and her jars would break.

Sheriff (rises): Well, can you beat the woman! Held for murder and worryin' about her preserves.

County Attorney: I guess before we're through she may have something more serious than preserves to worry about.

Hale: Well, women are used to worrying over trifles. *(The two women move a little closer together.)*

County Attorney (with the gallantry of a young politician): And yet, for all their worries, what would we do without the ladies? *(The women do not unbend. He goes to the sink, takes a dipperful of water from the pail, and pouring it into a basin, washes his hands. Starts to wipe them on the roller towel, turns it for a cleaner place.)* Dirty towels! *(Kicks his foot against the pans under the sink.)* Not much of a housekeeper, would you say, ladies?

Mrs. Hale (stiffly): There's a great deal of work to be done on a farm.

County Attorney: To be sure. And yet *(with a little bow to her)* I know there are some Dickson county farmhouses which do not have such roller towels. *(He gives it a pull to expose its full length again.)*

Mrs. Hale: Those towels get dirty awful quick. Men's hands aren't always as clean as they might be.

County Attorney: Ah, loyal to your sex, I see. But you and Mrs. Wright were neighbors. I suppose you were friends, too.

Mrs. Hale (shaking her head): I've not seen much of her of late years. I've not been in this house — it's more than a year.

County Attorney: And why was that? You didn't like her?

Mrs. Hale: I liked her all well enough. Farmers' wives have their hands full, Mr. Henderson. And then —

County Attorney: Yes — ?

Mrs. Hale (looking about): It never seemed a very cheerful place.

preserve the secret of Mrs. Wright—a woman who was beaten down by her husband but who cannot be beaten by these male authorities.

The Attorney has an eye for dirty towels but not for the real "dirt" embedded in the Wrights' domestic life.

The female characters are identified as "Mrs.," which emphasizes their roles as wives, while the men are autonomous and identified by their professions.

Mrs. Hale's comment begins a process of mitigating Mrs. Wright's murder of her husband. He—husbands, men—must share some of the guilt, too.

In contrast to men (a nice irony), farmers' wives' hands are full of responsibilities for which they receive little credit owing to the men's assumption that they fill their lives with trifles.

ELEMENTS OF DRAMA

Trifles is a **one-act play**; in other words, the entire play takes place in a single location and unfolds as one continuous action. As in a short story, the characters in a one-act play are presented economically, and the action is sharply focused. In contrast, full-length plays can include many characters as well as different settings in place and time. The main divisions of a full-length play are typically **acts**; their ends are indicated by lowering a curtain or turning up the houselights. Playwrights frequently employ acts to accommodate changes in time, setting, characters on stage, or mood. In many full-length plays, such as Shakespeare's *Hamlet*, acts are further divided into **scenes**; according to tradition, a scene changes when the location of the action changes or when a new character enters. Acts and scenes are **conventions** that are understood and accepted by audiences because they have come, through usage and time, to be recognized as familiar techniques. The major convention of a one-act play is that it typically consists of only a single scene; nevertheless, one-act plays contain many of the elements of drama that characterize their full-length counterparts.

Explore the literary elements in this chapter at bedfordstmartins.com/meyerlit.

One-act plays create their effects through compression. They especially lend themselves to modestly budgeted productions with limited stage facilities, such as those put on by little theater groups. However, the potential of a one-act play to move audiences and readers is not related to its length. As *Trifles* shows, one-acts represent a powerful form of dramatic literature.

The single location that composes the **setting** for *Trifles* is described at the very beginning of the play; it establishes an atmosphere that will later influence our judgment of Mrs. Wright. The "gloomy" kitchen is disordered, bare, and sparsely equipped with a stove, sink, rocker, cupboard, two tables, some chairs, three doors, and a window. These details are just enough to allow us to imagine the stark, uninviting place where Mrs. Wright spent most of her time. Moreover, "signs of incompleted work," coupled with the presence of the sheriff and county attorney, create an immediate tension by suggesting that something is terribly wrong. Before a single word is spoken, **suspense** is created as the characters enter. This suspenseful situation causes an anxious uncertainty about what will happen next.

The setting is further developed through the use of **exposition**, a device that provides the necessary background information about the characters and their circumstances. For example, we immediately learn through **dialogue**—the verbal exchanges between characters—that Mr. Henderson, the county attorney, is just back from Omaha. This establishes the setting as somewhere in the Midwest, where winters can be brutally cold and barren. We also find out that John Wright has been murdered and that his wife has been arrested for the crime.

Even more important, Glaspell deftly characterizes the Wrights through exposition alone. Mr. Hale's conversation with Mr. Henderson explains how Mr. Wright's body was discovered, but it also reveals that Wright was a noncommunicative man who refused to share a "party telephone" and did not consider "what his wife wanted." Later Mrs. Hale adds to this characterization when she tells Mrs. Peters that though Mr. Wright was an honest, good man who paid his bills and did not drink, he was a "hard man" and "Like a raw wind that gets to the bone." Mr. Hale's description of Mrs. Wright sitting in the kitchen dazed and disoriented gives us a picture of a shattered, exhausted woman. But it is Mrs. Hale who again offers further insights when she describes how Minnie Foster, a sweet, pretty, timid young woman who sang in the choir, was changed by her marriage to Mr. Wright and by her childless, isolated life on the farm.

This information about Mr. and Mrs. Wright is worked into the dialogue throughout the play in order to suggest the nature of the *conflict* or struggle between them, a motive, and, ultimately, a justification for the murder. In the hands of a skillful playwright, exposition is not merely a mechanical device; it can provide important information while simultaneously developing characterizations and moving the action forward.

The action is shaped by the *plot*, the author's arrangement of incidents in the play that gives the story a particular focus and emphasis. Plot involves more than simply what happens; it involves how and why things happen. Glaspell begins with a discussion of the murder. Why? She could have begun with the murder itself: the distraught Mrs. Wright looping the rope around her husband's neck. The moment would be dramatic and horribly vivid. We neither see the body nor hear very much about it. When Mr. Hale describes finding Mr. Wright's body, Glaspell has the county attorney cut him off by saying, "I think I'd rather have you go into that upstairs, where you can point it all out. Just go on now with the rest of the story." It is precisely the "rest of the story" that interests Glaspell. Her arrangement of incidents prevents us from sympathizing with Mr. Wright. We are, finally, invited to see Mrs. Wright instead of her husband as the victim.

Mr. Henderson's efforts to discover a motive for the murder appear initially to be the play's focus, but the real conflicts are explored in what seems to be a *subplot*, a secondary action that reinforces or contrasts with the main plot. The discussions between Mrs. Hale and Mrs. Peters and the tensions between the men and the women turn out to be the main plot because they address the issues that Glaspell chooses to explore. Those issues are not about murder but about marriage and how men and women relate to each other.

The *protagonist* of *Trifles*, the central character with whom we tend to identify, is Mrs. Hale. The *antagonist*, the character who is in some kind of opposition to the central character, is the county attorney, Mr. Henderson. These two characters embody the major conflicts presented in the play because each speaks for a different set of characters who represent disparate values. Mrs. Hale and Mr. Henderson are developed less individually than as representative types.

Mrs. Hale articulates a sensitivity to Mrs. Wright's miserable life as well as an awareness of how women are repressed in general by men; she also helps Mrs. Peters to arrive at a similar understanding. When Mrs. Hale defends Mrs. Wright's soiled towels from Mr. Henderson's criticism, Glaspell has her say more than the county attorney is capable of hearing. The *stage directions*, the playwright's instructions about how the actors are to move and behave, indicate that Mrs. Hale responds "stiffly" to Mr. Henderson's disparagements: "Men's hands aren't always as clean as they might be." Mrs. Hale eventually comes to see that the men are, in a sense, complicit because it was insensitivity like theirs that drove Mrs. Wright to murder.

Mr. Henderson, on the other hand, represents the law in a patriarchal, conventional society that blithely places a minimal value on the concerns of women. In his attempt to gather evidence against Mrs. Wright, he implicitly defends men's severe dominance over women. He also patronizes Mrs. Hale and Mrs. Peters. Like Sheriff Peters and Mr. Hale, he regards the women's world as nothing more than "kitchen things" and "trifles." Glaspell, however, patterns the plot so that the women see more about Mrs. Wright's motives than the men do and shows that the women have a deeper understanding of justice.

Many plays are plotted in what has come to be called a *pyramidal pattern*, because the plot is divided into three essential parts. Such plays begin with a *rising action*, in which complication creates conflict for the protagonist. The resulting tension builds to the second major division, known as the *climax*, when the action reaches a final *crisis*, a turning point that has a powerful effect on the protagonist. The third part consists of *falling action*; here the tensions are diminished in the *resolution* of the plot's conflicts and complications (the resolution is also referred to as the conclusion or *dénouement*, a French word meaning "unknotting"). These divisions may occur at different times. There are many variations to this pattern. The terms are helpful for identifying various moments and movements within a given plot, but they are less useful if seen as a means of reducing dramatic art to a formula.

Because *Trifles* is a one-act play, this pyramidal pattern is less elaborately worked out than it might be in a full-length play, but the basic elements of the pattern can still be discerned. The complication consists mostly of Mrs. Hale's refusal to assign moral or legal guilt to Mrs. Wright's murder of her husband. Mrs. Hale is able to discover the motive in the domestic details that are beneath the men's consideration. The men fail to see the significance of the fruit jars, messy kitchen, and badly sewn quilt.

At first Mrs. Peters seems to voice the attitudes associated with the men. Unlike Mrs. Hale, who is "more comfortable looking," Mrs. Peters is "a slight wiry woman" with "a thin nervous face" who sounds like her husband, the sheriff, when she insists, "the law is the law." She also defends the men's patronizing attitudes, because "they've got awful important things on their minds." But Mrs. Peters is a *foil* — a character whose behavior and values contrast with the protagonist's — only up to a point. When the most telling clue is discovered, Mrs. Peters suddenly understands, along with Mrs. Hale, the motive for the killing. Mrs. Wright's caged life was no longer tolerable to her after her husband had killed the bird (which was the one bright spot in her life and which represents her early life as the young

Minnie Foster). This revelation brings about the climax, when the two women must decide whether to tell the men what they have discovered. Both women empathize with Mrs. Wright as they confront this crisis, and their sense of common experience leads them to withhold the evidence.

This resolution ends the play's immediate conflicts and complications. Presumably, without a motive the county attorney will have difficulty prosecuting Mrs. Wright — at least to the fullest extent of the law. However, the larger issues related to the *theme*, the central idea or meaning of the play, are left unresolved. The men have both missed the clues and failed to perceive the suffering that acquits Mrs. Wright in the minds of the two women. The play ends with Mrs. Hale's ironic answer to Mr. Henderson's question about quilting. When she says "knot it," she gives him part of the evidence he needs to connect Mrs. Wright's quilting with the knot used to strangle her husband. Mrs. Hale knows — and we know — that Mr. Henderson will miss the clue she offers because he is blinded by his own self-importance and assumptions.

Though brief, *Trifles* is a masterful representation of dramatic elements working together to keep both audiences and readers absorbed in its characters and situations.

Quiet Torrential Sound

A successful playwright, screenwriter, journalist, and actress, Joan Ackermann is also cofounder and artistic director of the twenty-five-year-old Mixed Company Theater in Great Barrington, Massachusetts. She has published and produced more than a dozen of her plays around the country in such venues as the Guthrie Theater, Circle Rep, Cleveland Playhouse, Shakespeare & Company, and the Atlantic Theatre Company. Her plays include *Off the Map* (1994), which was adapted and released as a motion picture at the Sundance Film Festival in 2003; *The Batting Cage* (1996); *Marcus Is Walking* (1999); and *Ice Glen* (2005). Ackermann

Courtesy of Joan Ackermann.

was also a longtime writer and producer of the television series *Arli$$*. In addition to writing articles for *The Atlantic, Esquire,* and *Time,* she had a seven-year stint as a special contributor to *Sports Illustrated. Quiet Torrential Sound* is set in the Berkshires, where Ackermann resides and takes pleasure in being a part-time hiking guide and leading audiences on dramatic adventures.

JOAN ACKERMANN (B. 1951)

Quiet Torrential Sound   1995

CHARACTERS

Monica, late thirties
Claire, early thirties
Waiter

TIME & PLACE: The Present. Cafe table with two chairs.

> *Monica and Claire enter, dressed up, from a concert.*

Monica: Well, isn't this charming.

Claire: Mmm.

Monica: How about this cute little table right here? My. Aren't these flowers delightful.

Claire: Mmm.

Monica: A little past their prime but . . . such a precious little vase.

Claire: Mmmm.

Monica: *(Sighs.)* Beethoven. Beethoven. I feel so . . . renewed, don't you? That was the greatest classical experience of my life.

Claire: Mm-mm.

Monica: Claire, I believe I've expressed this to you before. I wish you would make more of an effort to expand your vocabulary. No one would ever think that you're a junior college graduate if all you do is go around hmmmming things. *(Beat.)* And another thing. I wouldn't tell you this if we weren't sisters and the best of friends, but quite frankly, that blouse does very little for you. Blue is your color, Claire. Keep away from the pastels. They tend to wash you out. You don't have very strong features so you need more vibrancy of color to perk you up. Do you feel a draft?

Claire: I like this blouse.

Monica: It's not a question of liking it or not. As far as blouses go that one is perfectly acceptable. It's just pointless to wear something that does absolutely nothing for you. Clothes should make us appear as attractive as possible. Like wrapping paper. *(Waiter enters.)* Would you rather receive a gift in a plain brown paper bag or in nice cheerful paper with a bright colorful bow?

Waiter: Hi, my name is Nathan. Can I help you?

Monica: Nathan. At long last. Where have you been? I would like a cup of decaf, please, Nathan. Your freshest pot. With some Sweet and Low.

Waiter: Right-y-o. Anything to eat?

Monica: We've just been to the outdoor concert at Tanglewood. Beethoven's Seventh Symphony. So lovely, sitting out on the lawn.

Waiter: That's nice. Do you want something to eat?

Monica: I'm only telling you because I'm sure we smell of Avon Skin So Soft. For the bugs. It's an excellent bug repellent. Not completely effective, but . . . can you smell it?

Waiter: I smell something.

Monica: Avon Skin So Soft. Do you ever go to Tanglewood, Nathan? To hear the classical concerts?

Waiter: No.

Monica: I thought not. Pardon me for asking, but is your decaf truly decaf?

Waiter: Yes, we brew our own.

Monica: I'm so glad. I have ordered decaf before and received real coffee instead. The effects are not pleasant. My digestive system; I won't go into detail. Is there a fan on in here?

Waiter: No.

Monica: Could you turn it off, please?

Waiter: Sure.

Claire: I'd like a Coke and a hot fudge sundae.

Monica: Claire, dear. Really. A Coke and a hot fudge sundae? We were only just moments ago discussing your figure in the car.

Claire: Oh. Well, make it Diet Coke.

Waiter: Right-y-o. *(Starts to leave.)*

Monica: You're sure now about that decaf?

Waiter: Yes, m'am.

Monica: Thank you so very much. I appreciate your courtesy. *(Waiter exits.)* What a charming waiter. Doesn't seem to have been to the dentist recently but I'm sure he has a heart of gold. My, we are having a splendid little vacation aren't we, Claire? I never dreamed that the Berkshires held so many cultural attractions. I am so looking forward to the Norman Rockwell Museum this afternoon, aren't you?

Claire: Mmm. *(Then quickly:)* Yes, I am. Monica. I am. Looking forward.

Monica: I really should get subscription tickets to the Boston Symphony. I've been telling myself that for years. When I get home I will, I will, I'm going to, I'm making myself a promise right now, you're a witness. There's something about classical music, especially live classical music . . . something so pure, so humane, so . . . *honest*. There's no such thing as dishonest classical music — Claire, please don't pick at your face — it simply doesn't exist. You can see why it takes a certain intellect, a certain upbringing to appreciate it. An uncultivated mind could never appreciate classical music. Couldn't. Our waiter, for instance, Nathan. Classical music would just wash right over Nathan. Like rain on a duck. So. Do you have any observations from this morning you'd care to share with me?

Claire: Oh. I enjoyed the concert.

Monica: Yes?

Claire: Huh-huh. Yes. I did.

Monica: And what about it did you enjoy in particular?

Claire: Uh . . .

Monica: Was it the lovely outdoor setting? The view of distant rolling hills? The harmonious marriage between the natural beauty and Beethoven's Seventh Symphony? Was it the thrilling final movement?

Claire: I thought the conductor was exceptional.

Monica: Exceptional? Interesting choice of words. You're picking at your face again. Perhaps if you used a different moisturizer it wouldn't break out so. I'll give you some of mine when we get back to the hotel. In what way exceptional?

Claire: In the way he conducted. *(Clears throat.)* His musicians.

Monica: Ah . . . how astute of you, Claire. You know I think your hair is due for a trim. You're looking rather mousey of late, though you do have a strange glow about you I can't quite figure. *(Waiter enters.)* Maybe after the museum we can find a beauty shop.

Waiter: Here you go. *(Serves both and exits.)*

Monica: Why thank you so much, Nathan. *(Eyeing Claire's sundae.)* Oh my. I'm not saying a word. *(Takes Sweet and Low, shakes it hard, pours and watches it settle.)* Ah, it is decaf, I can tell by the way the Sweet and Low penetrates. Real coffee offers more resistance.

Claire: Monica . . .

Monica: You know what I find hard to believe, Claire, what I'll never understand, is how it could be, how it could come to pass that a man like Beethoven, a man blessed with such extraordinary gifts, such a superhuman capacity to paint with sound, paint giant murals of sound, how such a genius could actually become deaf. Did you know he became deaf in later years? He did. Such a tragedy. My coffee tastes like Avon Skin So Soft.

(Claire is eating an enormous hot fudge sundae.)

Claire: Monica . . .

Monica: It's hard to imagine what it would be like to be deaf and be Beethoven. To only listen in your mind. Actually, you would be listening in your mind, *to* your mind, to what your mind remembered. Sound was. Just imagine being Beethoven, deaf; listening to all that quiet sound, that quiet torrential sound. Is that real whipped cream? No, honey, I'm counting calories. But you enjoy it. Funny that his ears — of all parts of Beethoven's body — his ears should be the ones to break down. You use a certain part of your body so much, you just plum wear it out. Like a painter going blind. Like Renoir, for instance, going blind. Or Matisse, or Manet, or Monet, or Van Gogh, or Jackson Pollock, or Leonardo da Vinci. Or any of the great impressionists. Going blind. From overuse. The opposite of vestigial. Classical music is so stimulating, isn't it? My brain is full of thoughts.

Claire: Monica . . .

Monica: What?

Claire: *(Eating her sundae.)* You know that workshop on "Human Intimacy" that you suggested I go to a couple months ago?

Monica: No.

Claire: Remember? You gave me this brochure with workshops . . . the Adult Education Center. You had several circled, with an eyebrow pencil?

Monica: Mmm.

Claire: Well, I took one.

Monica: Good for you. *(Wanting more coffee.)* Where is our waiter? Where is Mr. Right-y-o? Imagine, a grown man speaking like that.

Claire: Remember too how we once talked about orgasms and how neither of us had ever had one? *(Pause.)* Remember? That night we got a little tipsy on peach wine coolers at Rose's?

Monica: We are sisters, Claire. We've shared many secrets with each other over the years. Such confidences are quite natural.

Claire: Well, I learned a couple of things at that workshop that really . . . helped.

Monica: I'm so glad. I was thinking of taking a music appreciation class there over the winter session. It's given by a Harvard professor and it's supposed to be excellent.

Claire: Mmm. My teacher was excellent.

Monica: Was he from Harvard?

Claire: No.

Monica: Oh.

Claire: Have you ever heard of multiple orgasms?

Monica: I'm an educated woman, Claire, and an avid magazine reader. I've heard about just about everything under the sun from multiple orgasms to multiple sclerosis. Just because I have experienced neither does not mean I am poorly informed on either topic.

Claire: Well, I'm having them.

Monica: Right now?

Claire: No, not right now.

Monica: *(Pause.)* Truly?

Claire: *(Eating ice cream.)* Huh-huh.

Monica: Well. Bless your heart.

Claire: Lots of them.

Monica: I'm very happy for you, dear. Now. Would you care to hear about the Norman Rockwell Museum? This guide book has been most informative.

Claire: First I figured out how to have them by myself. In the bathtub? Then I started seeing this guy, Jim, I call him Jimbo, sometimes Jumbo, inside joke, he helped me with my tax returns, he works for H&R Block? Monica . . . I can't tell you how wonderful it's been.

Monica: Then don't. Listen to this. "The Corner House in Stockbridge has the largest collection of Rockwell originals in the world, over four hundred. The museum changes its exhibit twice a year with a few exceptional paintings remaining on permanent display (for example, 'Stockbridge at Christmas'). There are six galleries within this beautifully restored 18th-century house, and the tour is a delight. All sorts of colorful information is passed along (such as pointers about the portraits of Grandma Moses and Rockwell's family contained within one painting). Helpful hints are given about how to appreciate Rockwell's attention to detail: 'Notice the ring finger on the old woman's hand; it's been indented by many years of wear . . .'"

(While Monica reads, Claire speaks.)

Claire: I'm thirty-three years old, Monica, and I've finally gotten in touch with my own body.

(Monica continues reading.)

Claire: It's like I've been walking around all these years with this hidden sunken treasure. It was there the whole time! What a feeling, I am telling you. Woo!

(Monica reads louder.)

Claire: I could have died and never even known, Monica, I could have gone my whole life and never known. I mean, I could have been in a car accident last year, I could easily have died in a car accident without ever knowing. What a crying shame that would have been.

(Monica reads louder.)

Claire: And to share that feeling with someone else. Monica. There's just nothing like it. Nothing. Not distant rolling hills. Not Beethoven's Seventh Symphony. *(Monica stops.)* Not even the thrilling final movement. Talk about thrilling final movements!

Monica: SHUT UP!

(Pause.)

Claire: Jimbo likes this blouse, Monica. He likes what's inside it no matter how it's packaged. He thinks it's vibrant.

(Pause. Waiter enters.)

Waiter: Did you call? Did you need something?

Monica: Yes, I need something, I need you to know that I know that that was not decaffeinated coffee, young man, it was not decaffeinated coffee you gave me, there was caffeine in it you assured me there wouldn't be but there was. Caffeine. Am I right, am I? I am. Do you know how many times that happens to me, how many times waiters and waitresses love to intentionally do that to me, just love to intentionally give me straight black coffee all the while smirking inside, insisting oh yes it's decaffeinated? Smirking, do you know? And do you know that as a result I'll be awake all night tonight, I'll be awake with a splitting headache and severe stomach cramps, awake all by myself alone in my bed. Tell me, Nathan, is that a cheerful picture? Is that a cheerful Norman Rockwell Saturday Evening Post cover, a woman alone in bed with a splitting headache and stomach cramps? Jaws clenched?

(Pause.)

Waiter: I'm sorry. I didn't think you would notice.

Monica: You know, Nathan, if you were the sort of person who went to classical concerts, the sort of person who was capable of enjoying classical concerts, capable of sitting there, quietly listening, appreciating, you would not be so cruel. So cruel. It's because I'm a cultured woman, isn't it? That's why, because I'm cultured.

(Silence. He exits.)

Claire: I don't think you were very nice to Nathan.

Monica: Nathan who did not turn off that fan, did willfully not turn off that fan on purpose when I asked him, asked him very cordially, I'll most likely end up with an earache from the draft; lying alone tonight in my bed with an earache and stomach cramps and a headache while my baby sister lies in the next bed . . . glowing. *(Takes a breath.)* Are you ready to leave, Claire? I was planning to have a dish of frozen light yogurt after sitting here watching you eat that Mt. Vesuvius of a hot fudge sundae but quite frankly, the unexpected turn in our conversation has left a disagreeable note in the atmosphere.

Claire: I'm ready to go. *(Looks at bill, opens purse, puts down money.)*

Monica: *(Stands.)* They have tours at the museum every twenty minutes. I plan to buy several postcards and perhaps a poster, if they are reasonably priced. *(Takes another breath.)* I think, Claire, that Stockbridge will be one of the highlights of our trip.

Claire: Mmm.

Monica: And far be it from me to be the one to suggest that there is ample room for you to show a little more appreciation for the fact that I have organized this vacation, this entire vacation, entirely by myself and by a little more appreciation I mean any at all.

Claire: I do. Appreciate.

Monica: How anyone could fathom why you would feel moved to share that kind of information with me at this point in time, at the very peak of our vacation.

Claire: That's why. You were in such a good mood. You just had the greatest classical experience of your life. The information was pretty . . . upbeat. I thought.

Monica: Upbeat.

Claire: I thought it was perfect vacation information. To share with my only living sister.

Monica: *(Starts walking out, turns back.)* Claire?

Claire: Mmm?

Monica: I apologize for my choice of words just then.

Claire: When?

Monica: Back then.

Claire: You mean when you said shut up?

Monica: Mm.

Claire: It's okay.

Monica: It was inappropriate. Uncalled for. The caffeine . . .
Claire: It's all right. Really.
Monica: (Takes one step and turns back again.) Claire?
Claire: Yes, Monica.
Monica: If you received any pertinent literature in your workshop — books, pamphlets, diagrams, whatever — I'd venture to say that I'd be willing to peruse whatever material you had.
Claire: All right. *(Smiles.)*
Monica: All right. *(She goes back and puts a bill on the table.)*
Claire: Ten dollars? Geez Louise.
Monica: Claire, don't say "geez Louise." It doesn't become a woman of your age. *(Starts to exit.)*
Claire: Okay.
Monica: (Sarcastic.) Or breadth of experience.

(Claire follows Monica off.)

The end

CONSIDERATIONS FOR CRITICAL THINKING AND WRITING

1. FIRST RESPONSE. Analyze how Monica's opening conversation with Claire — before Nathan appears — serves to establish her character.

2. Discuss the significance of what the sisters order from Nathan in the café. What do their respective appetites reveal about them?

3. Describe the conflict that exists between Monica and Claire.

4. How is Monica's discussion of Beethoven relevant to the conflict in the play?

5. Comment on Ackermann's strategies for working humor and irony into the dialogue.

6. Consider the play's final scene. How would you characterize the tone of the ending and the sisters' future relationship?

DRAMA IN POPULAR FORMS

Audiences for live performances of plays have been thinned by high ticket prices but perhaps even more significantly by the impact of motion pictures and television. Motion pictures, the original threat to live theater, have in turn been superseded by television (along with DVDs and streaming video), now the most popular form of entertainment in America. Television audiences are measured in the millions. Probably more people have seen a single weekly episode of a top-rated prime-time program such as *Downton Abbey* in one evening than have viewed a live performance of *Hamlet* in nearly four hundred years.

Though most of us are seated more often before a television or computer screen than before live actors, our limited experience with the theater presents relatively few obstacles to appreciation because many of the basic elements of drama are similar whether the performance is on a screen or on a stage. Television has undoubtedly seduced audiences that otherwise might have been attracted to the theater, but television obviously satisfies some aspects of our desire for drama and can be seen as a potential introduction to live theater rather than as its irresistible rival.

Significant differences do, of course, exist between television and theater productions. Most obviously, television's special camera effects can capture phenomena such as earthquakes, raging fires, car chases, and space travel that cannot be realistically rendered on a live stage. The presentation of characters and the plotting of action are also handled differently owing to both the possibilities and limitations of television and the theater. Television's multiple camera angles and close-ups provide a degree of intimacy that cannot be duplicated by actors onstage, yet this intimacy does not achieve the immediacy that live actors create. On commercial television, the plot must accommodate itself to breaks in the action so that advertisements can be aired at regular intervals. Beyond these and many other differences, however, there are enough important similarities that the experience of watching television shows can enhance our understanding of a theater production.

Seinfeld

Seinfeld, which aired on NBC, was first produced during the summer of 1989. Although the series ended in the spring of 1998, it remains popular in syndicated reruns. No one expected the half-hour situation comedy that evolved from the pilot to draw some twenty-seven million viewers per week who avidly watched Jerry Seinfeld playing himself as a standup comic. Nominated for numerous Emmys, the show became one of the most popular programs of the 1990s. Although *Seinfeld* portrays a relatively narrow band of contemporary urban life—four thirty-something characters living in New York City's Upper West Side—its quirky humor and engaging characters have attracted vast numbers of devoted fans who have conferred on it a kind of cult status. If you haven't watched an episode on television, noticed the T-shirts and posters, or read *Seinlanguage* (a best-selling collection of Seinfeld's monologues), you can catch up on the Internet, where fans discuss the popularity and merits of the show.

The setting for *Seinfeld* is determined by its subject matter, which is everyday life in Manhattan. Most of the action alternates between two principal locations: Jerry's modest one-bedroom apartment on West 81st Street and the characters' favorite restaurant in the neighborhood. Viewers are often surprised to learn that the show was filmed on a soundstage before a live audience in Studio City, California, because the sights, sounds, and seemingly unmistakable texture of Manhattan appear in background shots so that the city functions almost as a major character in many episodes. If you ever find yourself on the corner of Broadway and 112th Street, you'll recognize the facade of Jerry's favorite restaurant; but don't bother to look for the building that matches the exterior shot of his apartment building because it is in Los Angeles, as are the scenes in which the characters actually appear on the street. The care with which the sets are created suggests how important the illusion of the New York City environment is to the show.

As the central character, Jerry begins and ends each episode with a standup comedy act delivered before a club audience. These monologues (played down in later episodes) are connected to the events in the episodes and demonstrate with humor and insight that ordinary experience — such as standing in line at a supermarket or getting something caught in your teeth — can be a source of genuine humor. For Jerry, life is filled with daily annoyances that he copes with by making sharp, humorous observations. Here's a brief instance from "The Pitch" (not reprinted in the excerpt on p. 628) in which Jerry is in the middle of a conversation with friends when he is interrupted by a phone call.

> *Jerry (into phone):* Hello?
>
> *Man (v[oice] o[ver]):* Hi, would you be interested in switching over to T.M.I. long distance service?
>
> *Jerry:* Oh gee, I can't talk right now, why don't you give me your home number and I'll call you later?
>
> *Man (v[oice] o[ver]):* Uh, well I'm sorry, we're not allowed to do that.
>
> *Jerry:* Oh, I guess you don't want people calling you at home.
>
> *Man (v[oice] o[ver]):* No.
>
> *Jerry:* Well now you know how I feel.
>
> *Hangs up.*

This combination of polite self-assertion and humor is Jerry's first line of defense in his ongoing skirmishes with the irritations of daily life. Unthreatening in his Nikes and neatly pressed jeans, Jerry nonetheless knows how to give it back when he is annoyed. Seinfeld has described his fictional character as a "nice, New York Jewish boy," but his character's bemused and pointed observations reveal a tough-mindedness that is often wittily on target.

Jerry's life and apartment are continually invaded by his three closest friends: George, Kramer, and Elaine. His refrigerator is the rallying point from which they feed each other lines over cardboard takeout cartons and containers of juice. Jerry's success as a standup comic is their cue to enjoy his groceries as well as his company, but they know their intrusions are welcome because the refrigerator is always restocked.

Jerry's closest friend is George Costanza (played by Jason Alexander), a frequently unemployed, balding, pudgy schlemiel. Any straightforward description of his behavior and sensibilities makes him sound starkly unappealing: He is hypochondriacal, usually upset and depressed, inept with women, embarrassingly stingy, and persistently demanding while simultaneously displaying a vain and cocky nature. As intolerable as he can be, he is nonetheless endearing. The pleasure of his character is in observing how he talks his way into trouble and then attempts to talk his way out of it to Jerry's amazement and amusement.

Across the hall from Jerry's apartment lives Kramer (played by Michael Richards), who is strategically located so as to be the mooch in Jerry's life. Known only as Kramer (until an episode later than "The Pitch" revealed his first name to be Cosmo), his slapstick twitching, tripping, and falling serve as a visual contrast to all the talking that goes on. His bizarre schemes and eccentric behavior have their physical counterpart in his vertical hair and his outrageous thrift-shop shirts from the 1960s.

Elaine Benes (played by Julia Louis-Dreyfus), on the other hand, is a sharp-tongued, smart, sexy woman who can hold her own and is very definitely a female member of this boy's club. As Jerry's ex-girlfriend, she provides some interesting romantic tension while serving as a sounding board for the relationship issues that George and Jerry obsess about. Employed at a book company at the time of the episode reprinted here, she, like George and Kramer, is also in the business of publishing her daily problems in Jerry's apartment.

The plots of most *Seinfeld* episodes are generated by the comical situations that Jerry and his friends encounter during the course of their daily lives. Minor irritations develop into huge conflicts that are offbeat, irreverent, or even absurd. The characters have plenty of time to create conflicts in their lives over such everyday situations as dealing with parents, finding an apartment, getting a date, riding the subway, ordering a meal, and losing a car in a mall parking garage. The show's screwball plots involve freewheeling misadventures that are played out in unremarkable but hilarious conversations.

The following scenes from *Seinfeld* are from a script titled "The Pitch" that concerns Jerry's and George's efforts to develop a television show for NBC. The script is loosely based on events that actually occurred when Jerry Seinfeld and his real-life friend Larry David (the author of "The Pitch" and the creator of HBO's *Curb Your Enthusiasm*, in which he plays himself) sat down to discuss ideas for the pilot NBC produced in 1989. As brief as these scenes are, they contain some of the dramatic elements found in a play.

LARRY DAVID (B. 1947)

Seinfeld   *1992*

"The Pitch"

[The following excerpted scenes do not appear one after the other in the original script but are interspersed through several subplots involving Kramer and Elaine.]

© Dan Winters.

ACT ONE

Scene A: *Int[erior] comedy club bar — night*

> *Jerry and George are talking. Suits enter, Stu and Jay.*

Stu: Excuse me, Jerry? I'm Stu Chermak. I'm with NBC.

Jerry: Hi.

Stu: Could we speak for a few moments?

Jerry: Sure, sure.

Jay: Hi, Jay Crespi.

Jerry: Hello.

George: C-R-E-S-P-I?

Jay: That's right.

George: I'm unbelievable at spelling last names. Give me a last name.

Jay: Mm, I'm not —

Jerry: George.

George (backing off): Huh? All right, fine.

Stu: First of all, that was a terrific show.

Jerry: Oh thank you very much.

Stu: And basically, I just wanted to let you know that we've been discussing you at some of our meetings and we'd be very interested in doing something.

Jerry: Really? Wow.

Stu: So, if you have an idea for like a TV show for yourself, well, we'd just love to talk about it.

Jerry: I'd be very interested in something like that.

Stu: Well, here, why don't you give us a call and maybe we can develop a series.

> *They start to exit.*

Jerry: Okay. Great. Thanks.

Stu: It was very nice meeting you.

Jerry: Thank you.

Jay: Nice meeting you.

Jerry: Nice meeting you.

> *George returns.*

George: What was that all about?

Jerry: They said they were interested in me.

George: For what?

Jerry: You know, a TV show.

George: Your own show?

Jerry: Yeah, I guess so.

George: They want you to do a TV show?

Jerry: Well, they want me to come up with an idea. I mean, I don't have any ideas.

George: Come on, how hard is that? Look at all the junk that's on TV. You want an idea? Here's an idea. You coach a gymnastics team in high school. And you're married. And your son's not interested in gymnastics and you're pushing him into gymnastics.

Jerry: Why should I care if my son's into gymnastics?

George: Because you're a gymnastics teacher. It's only natural.

Jerry: But gymnastics is not for everybody.

George: I know, but he's your son.

Jerry: So what?

George: All right, forget that idea, it's not for you. . . . Okay, okay, I got it, I got it. You run an antique store.

Jerry: Yeah and . . . ?

George: And people come in the store and you get involved in their lives.

Jerry: What person who runs an antique store gets involved in people's lives?

George: Why not?

Jerry: So someone comes in to buy an old lamp and all of a sudden I'm getting them out of a jam? I could see if I was a pharmacist because a pharmacist knows what's wrong with everybody that comes in.

George: I know, but antiques are very popular right now.

Jerry: No they're not, they used to be.

George: Oh yeah, like you know.

Jerry: Oh like you do.

> *Cut to:*

ACT ONE

SCENE B: *Int[erior] Jerry's apartment — day*

> *Jerry and Kramer.*

Kramer: . . . And you're the manager of the circus.

Jerry: A circus?

Kramer: Come on, this is a great idea. Look at the characters. You've got all these freaks on the show. A woman with a moustache? I mean, who wouldn't tune in to see a woman with a moustache? You've got the tallest man in the world; the guy who's just a head.

Jerry: I don't think so.

Kramer: Look Jerry, the show isn't about the circus, it's about watching freaks.

Jerry: I don't think the network will go for it.

Kramer: Why not?

Jerry: Look, I'm not pitching a show about freaks.

Kramer: Oh come on Jerry, you're wrong. People they want to watch freaks. This is a "can't miss."

ACT ONE

SCENE C: *Int[erior] coffee shop—lunchtime—day*

> *Jerry and George enter.*

George: So, what's happening with the TV show? You come up with anything?

Jerry: No, nothing.

George: Why don't they have salsa on the table?

Jerry: What do you need salsa for?

George: Salsa is now the number one condiment in America.

Jerry: You know why? Because people like to say "salsa." "Excuse me, do you have salsa?" "We need more salsa." "Where is the salsa? No salsa?"

George: You know it must be impossible for a Spanish person to order seltzer and not get salsa. *(Angry.)* "I wanted seltzer, not salsa."

Jerry: "Don't you know the difference between seltzer and salsa? You have the seltzer after the salsa!"

George: See, this should be the show. This is the show.

Jerry: What?

George: This. Just talking.

Jerry (dismissing): Yeah, right.

George: I'm really serious. I think that's a good idea.

Jerry: Just talking? What's the show about?

George: It's about nothing.

Jerry: No story?

George: No, forget the story.

Jerry: You've got to have a story.

George: Who says you gotta have a story? Remember when we were waiting for that table in that Chinese restaurant that time? That could be a TV show.

Jerry: And who is on the show? Who are the characters?

George: I could be a character.

Jerry: You?

George: You could base a character on me.

Jerry: So on the show there's a character named George Costanza?

George: Yeah. There's something wrong with that? I'm a character. People are always saying to me, "You know you're quite a character."

Jerry: And who else is on the show?

George: Elaine could be a character. Kramer.

Jerry: Now he's a character. . . . So, everyone I know is a character on the show.

George: Right.

Jerry: And it's about nothing?

George: Absolutely nothing.

Jerry: So you're saying, I go in to NBC and tell them I got this idea for a show about nothing.

George: We go into NBC.

Jerry: We? Since when are you a writer?

George: Writer. We're talking about a sit-com.

Jerry: You want to go with me to NBC?

George: Yeah, I think we really got something here.

Jerry: What do we got?

George: An idea.

Jerry: What idea?

George: An idea for the show.

Jerry: I still don't know what the idea is.

George: It's about nothing.

Jerry: Right.

George: Everybody's doing something, we'll do nothing.

Jerry: So we go into NBC, we tell them we've got an idea for a show about nothing.

George: Exactly.

Jerry: They say, "What's your show about?" I say, "Nothing."

George: There you go.

> *A beat.*

Jerry: I think you may have something there.

> *Cut to:*

ACT ONE

SCENE D: *Int[erior] Jerry's apartment — day*

> *Jerry and Kramer.*

Jerry: So it would be about my real life. And one of the characters would be based on you.

Kramer (thinks): No. I don't think so.

Jerry: What do you mean you don't think so?

Kramer: I don't like it.

Jerry: I don't understand. What don't you like about it?

Kramer: I don't like the idea of a character based on me.

Jerry: Why not?

Kramer: Doesn't sit well.

Jerry: You're my neighbor. There's got to be a character based on you.

Kramer: That's your problem, buddy.

Jerry: I don't understand what the big deal is.

Kramer: Hey I'll tell you what, you can do it on one condition.

Jerry: Whatever you want.

Kramer: I get to play Kramer.
Jerry: You can't play Kramer.
Kramer: I am Kramer.
Jerry: But you can't act.

ACT ONE

SCENE G: *Int[erior] NBC reception area—day*

   Jerry and George.

Jerry (to himself): Salsa, seltzer. Hey excuse me, you got any salsa? No not seltzer, salsa. *(George doesn't react.)* What's the matter?
George (nervous): Nothing.
Jerry: You sure? You look a little pale.
George: No, I'm fine. I'm good. I'm fine. I'm very good.
Jerry: What are you, nervous?
George: No, not nervous. I'm good, very good. *(A beat, then: explodes.)* I can't do this! Can't do this!
Jerry: What?
George: I can't do this! I can't do it. I have tried. I'm here. It's impossible.
Jerry: This was your idea.
George: What idea? I just said something. I didn't know you'd listen to me.
Jerry: Don't worry about it. They're just TV executives.
George: They're men with jobs, Jerry! They wear suits and ties. They're married, they have secretaries.
Jerry: I told you not to come.
George: I need some water. I gotta get some water.
Jerry: They'll give us water inside.
George: Really? That's pretty good. . . .

   Receptionist enters.

Receptionist: They're ready for you.
George: Okay, okay, look, you do all the talking, okay?
Jerry: Relax. Who are they?
George: Yeah, they're not better than me.
Jerry: Course not.
George: Who are they?
Jerry: They're nobody.
George: What about me?
Jerry: What about you?
George: Why them? Why not me?
Jerry: Why not you?

George: I'm as good as them.
Jerry: Better.
George: You really think so?
Jerry: No.

> *Door opens, Jerry and George P.O.V., the four execs stand up.*
>
> *Fade out.*

ACT TWO

SCENE G: *Int[erior] NBC president's office — day*

> *The mood is jovial. Stu Chermak is there — along with Susan Ross, Jay Crespi, and Russell Dalrymple, the head of the network.*

Stu (to Jerry): The bit, the bit I really liked was where the parakeet flew into the mirror. Now that's funny.
George: The parakeet in the mirror. That is a good one, Stu.
Jerry: Yeah, it's one of my favorites.
Russell: What about you George, have you written anything we might know?
George: Well, possibly. I wrote an off-Broadway show, "La Cocina." . . . Actually it was off-off-Broadway. It was a comedy about a Mexican chef.
Jerry: Oh it was very funny. There was one great scene with the chef — what was his name?
George: Pepe.
Jerry: Oh Pepe, yeah Pepe. And, uh, he was making tamales.
Susan: Oh, he actually cooked on the stage?
George: No, no, he mimed it. That's what was so funny about it.
Russell: So what have you two come up with?
Jerry: Well we've thought about this in a variety of ways. But the basic idea is I will play myself.
George (interrupting, to Jerry): May I?
Jerry: Go ahead.
George: I think I can sum up the show for you with one word. NOTHING.
Russell: Nothing?
George: Nothing.
Russell: What does that mean?
George: The show is about nothing.
Jerry (to George): Well, it's not about nothing.
George (to Jerry): No, it's about nothing.
Jerry: Well, maybe in philosophy. But even nothing is something.

> *Jerry and George glare at each other. Receptionist sticks her head in.*

Receptionist: Mr. Dalrymple, your niece is on the phone.

Russell: I'll call back.

George: D-A-L-R-I-M-P-E-L.

Russell: Not even close.

George: Is it with a "y"?

Russell: No.

Susan: What's the premise?

Jerry: . . . Well, as I was saying, I would play myself. And as a comedian, living in New York, and I have a friend and a neighbor and an ex-girlfriend, which is all true.

George: Yeah, but nothing happens on the show. You see, it's just like life. You know, you eat, you go shopping, you read. You eat, you read, you go shopping.

Russell: You read? You read on the show?

Jerry: Well I don't know about the reading. We didn't discuss the reading.

Russell: All right, tell me, tell me about the stories. What kind of stories?

George: Oh no, no stories.

Russell: No stories? So what is it?

George: What'd you do today?

Russell: I got up and came to work.

George: There's a show. That's a show.

Russell (confused): How is that a show?

Jerry: Well, uh, maybe something happens on the way to work.

George: No, no, no. Nothing happens.

Jerry: Well, something happens.

Russell: Well why am I watching it?

George: Because it's on TV.

Russell: Not yet.

George: Okay, uh, look, if you want to just keep on doing the same old thing, then maybe this idea is not for you. I for one will not compromise my artistic integrity. And I'll tell you something else. This is the show and we're not going to change it. *(To Jerry.)* Right?

Jerry: How about this? I manage a circus . . .

CONSIDERATIONS FOR CRITICAL THINKING AND WRITING

1. **FIRST RESPONSE.** What does George mean when he says the proposed show should be about "nothing"? Why is George's idea both a comic and a serious proposal?

2. How does the stage direction "Suits enter" serve to characterize Stu and Jay? Write a description of how you think they would look.

3. What is revealed about George's character when he spells Crespi's and Dalrymple's names?

4. Discuss Kramer's assertion that people "want to watch freaks." Do you think this line could be used to sum up accurately audience responses to *Seinfeld*?

5. Choose a scene, and explain how humor is worked into it. What other emotions are evoked in the scene?

6. View an episode of *Seinfeld*. How does reading a script compare with watching the show? Which do you prefer? Why?

Like those of many plays, the settings for these scenes are not detailed. Jerry's apartment and the coffee shop are, to cite only two examples, not described at all. We are told only that it is lunchtime in the coffee shop. Even without a set designer's version of these scenes, we readily create a mental picture of these places that provides a background for the characters. In the coffee shop scene we can assume that Jerry and George are having lunch, but we must supply the food, the plates and cutlery, the tables and chairs, and the other customers. For the television show, sets were used that replicated the details of a Manhattan coffee shop, right down to the menus and cash register. If the scene were presented on a stage, a set designer might use minimal sets and props to suggest the specific location. The director of such a production would rely on the viewers' imagination to create the details of the setting.

As brief as they are, these scenes include some exposition to provide the necessary background about the characters and their circumstances. We learn through dialogue, for example, that George is not a writer and that he doesn't think it takes very much talent to write a sitcom even though he's unemployed. These bits of information help to characterize George and allow an audience to place his attitudes and comments in a larger context that will be useful for understanding how other characters read them. Rather than dramatizing background information, the scriptwriter arranges incidents to create a particular focus and effect while working in the necessary exposition through dialogue.

The plot in these scenes shapes the conflicts to emphasize humor. As in any good play, incidents are carefully arranged to achieve a particular effect. In the first scene we learn that NBC executives are interested in having Jerry do his own television show. We also learn, through his habit of spelling people's last names when he meets them, that George is a potential embarrassment. The dialogue between Jerry and George quickly establishes the conflict. The NBC executives would like to produce a TV show with Jerry provided that he can come up with an idea for the series; Jerry, however, has no ideas (here's the complication of the pyramidal plot pattern discussed in Elements of Drama, p. 616). This complication sets up a conflict for Jerry because George assumes that he can help Jerry develop an idea for the show, which, after all, shouldn't be any more difficult than spelling a stranger's name. As George says, "How hard is that? Look at all the junk that's on TV."

All of a sudden everyone is an expert on scriptwriting. George's off-the-wall suggestions that the premise for the show be Jerry's running an antique shop or teaching gymnastics are complemented by Kramer's idea that Jerry be "the manager of the circus" because "people they want to watch freaks." As unhelpful as Kramer's suggestion is, there is some truth here as well as humor, given his own freakish behavior. However, it is George who comes through with the most intriguing suggestion. As a result of the exuberantly funny riff he and Jerry do on "the difference between seltzer and salsa," George suddenly realizes that the show should be "about nothing" — that it should consist of nothing more than Jerry talking and hanging out with his friends George, Elaine, and Kramer. Jerry's initial skepticism gives way as he seriously considers George's proposal and is intrigued enough to bring George with him to the NBC offices to make the pitch. His decision to bring George to the meeting can only, of course, complicate matters further.

Before the meeting with the NBC executives, George is stricken with one of his crises of confidence when he compares himself to the "men with jobs" who are married and have secretaries. Characteristically, George's temporary lack of confidence shifts to an equally ill-timed arrogance once the meeting begins. He usurps Jerry's role and makes the pitch himself: "Nothing happens on the show. You see, it's just like life. You know, you eat, you go shopping, you read. You eat, you read, you go shopping." The climax occurs when George refuses even to consider any of the reservations the executives have about "nothing" happening on the show. George's insistence that he not compromise his "artistic integrity" creates a crisis for Jerry, a turning point that makes him realize that George's ridiculous arrogance might cost him his opportunity to have a TV show. Jerry's final lines to the executives — "How about this? I manage a circus . . ." — work two ways: He resignedly acknowledges that something — not "nothing" — has just happened and that George is, indeed, something of a freak.

The falling action and resolution typical of a pyramidal plot are not present in "The Pitch" because the main plot is not resolved until a later episode. "The Pitch" also contains several subplots not included in the scenes excerpted in this book. Like the main plot, these subplots involving Elaine, Kramer, and a few minor characters are not resolved until later episodes. Self-contained series episodes are increasingly rare on television, as programmers attempt to hook viewers week after week by creating suspense once associated with serialized stories that appeared weekly or monthly in magazines.

The theme of "The Pitch" is especially interesting because it self-reflexively comments on the basic premise of *Seinfeld* scripts: They are all essentially about "nothing" in that they focus on the seemingly trivial details of the four main characters' lives. The unspoken irony of this theme is that such details are in fact significant because it is just such small, everyday activities that constitute most people's lives.

25

Sophocles
and Greek Drama

I depict men as they ought to be . . .
— SOPHOCLES

Not all things are to be discovered; many
are better concealed.
— SOPHOCLES

Sophocles lived a long, productive life (496?–406 B.C.) in Athens. During his life Athens became a dominant political and cultural power after the Persian Wars, but before he died Sophocles witnessed the decline of Athens as a result of the Peloponnesian Wars and the city's subsequent surrender to Sparta. He saw Athenian culture reach remarkable heights as well as collapse under enormous pressures.

Sophocles embodied much of the best of Athenian culture; he enjoyed success as a statesman, general, treasurer, priest, and, of course, prize-winning dramatist. Although surviving fragments indicate that he wrote over 120 plays, only a handful remain intact. Those that survive consist of the three plays he wrote about Oedipus and his children — *Oedipus the King, Oedipus at Colonus,* and *Antigone* — and four additional tragedies: *Philoctetes, Ajax, Maidens of Trachis,* and *Electra.*

His plays won numerous prizes at festival competitions because of his careful, subtle plotting and the sense of inevitability with which their action is charged. Moreover, his development of character is richly complex. Instead of relying on the extreme situations and exaggerated actions that earlier tragedians used, Sophocles created powerfully motivated characters who even today fascinate audiences with their psychological depth.

Explore contexts
for Sophocles at
bedfordstmartins.com/
meyerlit.

In addition to crafting sophisticated tragedies for the Greek theater, Sophocles introduced several important innovations to the stage. Most important, he broke the tradition of using only two actors; adding a third resulted in more complicated relationships and intricate dialogue among characters. As individual actors took center stage more often, Sophocles reduced the role of the chorus (discussed on p. 639). This shift placed even more emphasis on the actors, although the chorus remained important as a means of commenting on the action and establishing its tone. Sophocles was also the first dramatist to write plays with specific actors in mind, a development that many later playwrights, including Shakespeare, exploited usefully. But without question Sophocles' greatest contribution to drama was *Oedipus the King*, which, it has been argued, is the most influential drama ever written.

THEATRICAL CONVENTIONS OF GREEK DRAMA

More than twenty-four hundred years have passed since 430 B.C., when Sophocles' *Oedipus the King* was probably first produced on a Greek stage. We inhabit a vastly different planet than Sophocles' audience did, yet concerns about what it means to be human in a world that frequently runs counter to our desires and aspirations have remained relatively constant. The ancient Greeks continue to speak to us. But inexperienced readers or viewers may have some initial difficulty understanding the theatrical conventions used in classical Greek tragedies such as *Oedipus the King* and *Antigone*. If Sophocles were alive today, he would very likely need some sort of assistance with the conventions of an Arthur Miller play or a television production of *Seinfeld*.

Classical Greek drama developed from religious festivals that paid homage to Dionysus, the god of wine and fertility. Most of the details of these festivals have been lost, but we do know that the occasions included dancing and singing that celebrated legends about Dionysus. From these choral songs developed stories of both Dionysus and mortal culture-heroes. These heroes became the subject of playwrights whose works were produced in contests at the festivals. The Dionysian festivals took place over the course of more than five hundred years, but relatively few of their plays have survived. Among the works of the three great writers of tragedy, only seven plays each by Sophocles and Aeschylus (525?–456 B.C.) and nineteen plays by Euripides (480?–406 B.C.) survive.

Plays were such important events in Greek society that they were partially funded by the state. The Greeks associated drama with religious and community values as well as entertainment. In a sense, their plays celebrate their civilization; in approving the plays, audiences applauded their own culture. The enormous popularity of the plays is indicated by the size of surviving amphitheaters. Although information about these theaters is sketchy, we do know that most of them had a common form. They were built into hillsides with rising rows of seats accommodating more than fourteen thousand people. These seats partially encircled an *orchestra* or "dancing place," where the *chorus* of a dozen or so men chanted lines and danced.

Tradition credits the Greek poet Thespis with adding an actor who was separate from the choral singing and dancing of early performances. A second actor was subsequently included by Aeschylus and a third, as noted earlier, by Sophocles. These additions made possible the conflicts and complicated relationships that evolved into the dramatic art we know today. The two or three male actors who played all the roles appeared behind the orchestra in front of the skene, a stage building that served as dressing rooms. As Greek theater evolved, a wall of the skene came to be painted to suggest a palace or some other setting, and the roof was employed to indicate, for instance, a mountain location. Sometimes gods were lowered from the roof by mechanical devices to set matters right among the mortals below. This method of rescuing characters from complications beyond their abilities to resolve was known in Latin as *deus ex machina* ("god from the machine"), a term now used to describe any improbable means by which an author provides a too-easy resolution for a story.

Inevitably, the conventions of the Greek theaters affected how plays were presented. Few if any scene changes occurred because the amphitheater stage was set primarily for one location. If an important event happened somewhere else, it was reported by a minor character, such as a messenger. The chorus also provided necessary background information. In *Oedipus the King* and *Antigone,* the choruses, acting as townspeople, also assess the characters' strengths and weaknesses, praising them for their virtues, chiding them for their rashness, and giving them advice. The reactions of the chorus provide a connection between actors and audience because the chorus is at once a participant in and an observer of the action. In addition, the chorus helps structure the action by indicating changes in scene or mood. Thus the chorus could be used in a variety of ways to shape the audience's response to the play's action and characters.

Actors in classical Greek amphitheaters faced considerable challenges. An intimate relationship with the audience was impossible because many spectators would have been too far away to see a facial expression or subtle gesture. Indeed, some in the audience would have had difficulty even hearing the voices of individual actors. To compensate for these disadvantages, actors wore large masks that extravagantly expressed the major characters' emotions or identified the roles of minor characters. The masks also allowed the two or three actors in a

Classical Greek Theater. Based on scholarly sources, this drawing represents the features typical of a classical theater. (Drawing by Gerda Becker. From Kenneth Macgowan and William Melnitz, *The Living Stage*, © 1990 by Prentice Hall/A Division of Simon & Schuster.)

performance to play all the characters without confusing the audience. Each mask was fitted so that the mouthpiece amplified the actor's voice. The actors were further equipped with padded costumes and elevated shoes (***cothurni*** or ***buskins***) that made them appear larger than life.

As a result of these adaptive conventions, Greek plays tend to emphasize words — formal, impassioned speeches — more than physical action. We are invited to ponder actions and events rather than to see all of them enacted. Although the stark simplicity of Greek theater does not offer an audience realistic detail, the classical tragedies that have survived present characters in dramatic situations that transcend theatrical conventions. Tragedy, it seems, has always been compelling for human beings, regardless of the theatrical forms it has taken.

A Greek tragedy is typically divided into five parts: prologue, parodos, episodia, stasimon, and exodus. In some translations these terms appear as headings, but in more recent translations, as the one by Robert Fagles included here, the headings do not appear. Still, understanding these terms provides a sense of the overall rhythm of a Greek play. The opening speech or dialogue is known as the ***prologue*** and usually gives the exposition necessary to follow the subsequent action. In the ***parodos*** the chorus makes its first entrance and gives its perspective on what

TRAGEDY 641

the audience has learned in the prologue. Several *episodia*, or episodes, follow, in which characters engage in dialogue that frequently consists of heated debates dramatizing the play's conflicts. Following each episode is a choral ode, or *stasimon*, in which the chorus responds to and interprets the preceding dialogue. The *exodus*, or last scene, follows the final episode and stasimon; in it the resolution occurs and the characters leave the stage.

The effect of alternating dialogues and choral odes has sometimes been likened to that of opera. Greek tragedies were written in verse, and the stasima were chanted or sung as the chorus moved rhythmically, so the plays have a strong musical element that is not always apparent on the printed page. If we remember their musical qualities, we are less likely to forget that no matter how terrifying or horrific the conflicts they describe, these plays are stately, measured, and dignified works that reflect a classical Greek sense of order and proportion.

TRAGEDY

Newspapers are filled with daily reports of tragedies: A child is struck and crippled by a car; an airplane plunges into a suburban neighborhood; a volcano erupts and kills thousands. These unexpected instances of suffering are commonly and accurately described as tragic, but they are not tragedies in the literary sense of the term. A literary *tragedy* presents courageous individuals who confront powerful forces within or outside themselves with a dignity that reveals the breadth and depth of the human spirit in the face of failure, defeat, and even death.

Aristotle (384–322 B.C.), in his *Poetics,* defined *tragedy* on the basis of the plays contemporary to him. His definition has generated countless variations, qualifications, and interpretations, but we still derive our literary understanding of this term from Aristotle.

The protagonist of a Greek tragedy is someone regarded as extraordinary rather than typical: a great man or woman brought from happiness to agony. The character's stature is important because it makes his or her fall all the more terrifying. The protagonist also carries mythic significance for the audience. Oedipus and Antigone, for example, are not only human beings but legendary figures from a distant, revered past. Although the gods do not appear onstage in either *Oedipus the King* or *Antigone,* their power is ever present as the characters invoke their help or attempt to defy them. In addition, Greek tragedy tends to be public rather than private. The fate of the community—the state—is often linked with that of the protagonist, as when Thebes suffers a plague as a result of Oedipus's mistaken actions.

The protagonists of classical Greek tragedies (and of those of Shakespeare) are often rulers of noble birth who represent the monarchical values of their periods, but in modern tragedies the protagonists are more likely to reflect democratic values that make it possible for anyone to be a suitable subject. What is finally important is not so much the protagonist's social stature as a greatness of character that steadfastly confronts suffering, whether it comes from supernatural, social, or psychological forces. Although Greek tragic heroes were aristocrats, the nobility of their characters was more significant than their inherited titles and privileges.

The protagonist's eminence and determination to complete some task or goal make him or her admirable in Greek tragedy, but that does not free the protagonist from what Aristotle described as "some error or frailty" that brings about his or her misfortune. The term Aristotle used for this weakness is *hamartia*. This word has frequently been interpreted to mean that the protagonist's fall is the result of an internal *tragic flaw*, such as an excess of pride, ambition, passion, or some other character trait that leads directly to disaster.

Sometimes, however, misfortunes are not the result of a character flaw but of misunderstood events that overtake and thwart the protagonist's best intentions. Thus, virtue can lead to tragedy too. *Hamartia* has also been interpreted to mean "wrong act" — a mistake based not on a personal failure but on circumstances outside the protagonist's personality and control. Many readers find that a combination of these two interpretations sheds the most light on the causes of the tragic protagonist's fall. Both internal and external forces can lead to downfall because the protagonist's personality may determine crucial judgments that result in mistaken actions.

However the idea of tragic flaw is understood, it is best not to use it as a means of reducing the qualities of a complex character to an adjective or two that labels Oedipus as guilty of "overweening pride" (the Greek term for which is *hubris* or *hybris*) or Antigone as "fated." The protagonists of tragedies require more careful characterization than a simplistic label can provide.

Whatever the causes of the tragic protagonist's downfall, he or she accepts responsibility for it. Hence even in his or her encounter with failure (and possibly death) the tragic protagonist displays greatness of character. Perhaps it is the witnessing of this greatness, which seems both to accept and to transcend human limitations, that makes audiences feel relief rather than hopelessness at the end of a tragedy. Aristotle described this response as a *catharsis*, or purgation of the emotions of "pity and fear." We are faced with the protagonist's misfortune, which often seems out of proportion to his or her actions, and so we are likely to feel compassionate pity. Simultaneously, we may experience fear because the failure of the protagonist, who is so great in stature and power, is a frightening reminder of our own vulnerabilities. Ultimately, however, both these negative emotions are purged because the tragic protagonist's suffering is an affirmation of human values — even if they are not always triumphant — rather than a despairing denial of them.

Nevertheless, tragedies are disturbing. Instead of coming away with the reassurance of a happy ending, we must take solace in the insight produced by the hero's suffering. And just as our expectations are changed, so are the protagonist's. Aristotle described the moment in the plot when this change occurs as a *reversal* (*peripeteia*), the point when the hero's fortunes turn in an unexpected direction. He more specifically defined this term as meaning an action performed by a character that has the opposite of its intended effect. An example cited by Aristotle is the messenger's attempts to relieve Oedipus's anxieties about his relationship to his father and mother. Instead, the messenger reveals previously unknown information that eventually results in a *recognition* (*anagnorisis*); Oedipus discovers the terrible truth that he has killed his father and married his mother.

Tragedy is typically filled with ironies because there are so many moments in the plot when what seems to be turns out to be radically different from what actually is. Because of this, a particular form of irony called *dramatic irony* is also known as *tragic irony*. In dramatic irony, the meaning of a character's words or actions is understood by the audience but not by the character. Audiences of Greek tragedy shared with the playwrights a knowledge of the stories on which many tragic plots were based. Consequently, they frequently were aware of what was going to happen before the characters were. When Oedipus declares that he will seek out the person responsible for the plague that ravishes his city, the audience already knows that the person Oedipus pursues is himself.

Oedipus the King

A familiarity with the Oedipus legend allows modern readers to appreciate the series of ironies that unfolds in Sophocles' *Oedipus the King*. In the opening scene, Oedipus appears with a "telltale limp." As an infant, he had been abandoned by his parents, Laius and Jocasta, the king and queen of Thebes, because a prophecy warned that their son would kill his father and marry his mother. They instructed a servant to leave him on a mountain to die. The infant's feet were pierced and pinned together, but he was not left on the mountain; instead the servant, out of pity, gave him to a shepherd, who in turn presented him to the king and queen of Corinth. They named him Oedipus (for "swollen foot") and raised him as their own son.

On reaching manhood, Oedipus learned from an oracle that he would kill his father and marry his mother; to avoid this horrendous fate, he left Corinth forever. In his travels, Oedipus found his way blocked by a chariot at a crossroads; in a fit of anger, he killed the servants and their passenger. That passenger, unknown to Oedipus, was his real father. In Thebes, Oedipus successfully answered the riddle of the Sphinx, a winged lion with a woman's head. The reward for defeating this dreaded monster was both the crown and the dead king's wife. Oedipus and Jocasta had four children and prospered. But when the play begins, Oedipus's rule is troubled by a plague that threatens to destroy Thebes, and he is determined to find the cause of the plague in order to save the city again.

Oedipus the King is widely recognized as the greatest of the surviving Greek tragedies. Numerous translations are available; Robert Fagles's recent highly regarded translations of Antigone and Oedipus the King, the choice here, are especially accessible to modern readers. The play has absorbed readers for centuries because Oedipus's character—his intelligence, confidence, rashness, and suffering—represents powers and limitations that are both exhilarating and chastening. Although no reader or viewer is likely to identify with Oedipus's extreme circumstances, anyone can appreciate his heroic efforts to find the truth about himself. In that sense, he is one of us—at our best.

SOPHOCLES (496?–406 B.C.)

Oedipus the King   c. 430 B.C.

TRANSLATED BY ROBERT FAGLES

CHARACTERS

Oedipus, king of Thebes
A Priest of Zeus
Creon, brother of Jocasta
A Chorus of Theban citizens and their Leader
Tiresias, a blind prophet
Jocasta, the queen, wife of Oedipus
A Messenger from Corinth
A Shepherd
A Messenger from inside the palace
Antigone, Ismene, daughters of Oedipus and Jocasta
Guards and attendants
Priests of Thebes

TIME AND SCENE: The royal house of Thebes. Double doors dominate the facade; a stone altar stands at the center of the stage.

Many years have passed since Oedipus solved the riddle of the Sphinx and ascended the throne of Thebes, and now a plague has struck the city. A procession of priests enters; suppliants, broken and despondent, they carry branches wound in wool and lay them on the altar.

The doors open. Guards assemble. Oedipus comes forward, majestic but for a telltale limp, and slowly views the condition of his people.

Oedipus: Oh my children, the new blood of ancient Thebes,
    why are you here? Huddling at my altar,
    praying before me, your branches wound in wool.°
    Our city reeks with the smoke of burning incense,
    rings with cries for the Healer and wailing for the dead.   5
    I thought it wrong, my children, to hear the truth
    from others, messengers. Here I am myself—
    you all know me, the world knows my fame:
    I am Oedipus.

Helping a Priest to his feet.

                Speak up, old man. Your years,
    your dignity—you should speak for the others.   10
    Why here and kneeling, what preys upon you so?
    Some sudden fear? some strong desire?
    You can trust me; I am ready to help,
    I'll do anything. I would be blind to misery
    not to pity my people kneeling at my feet.   15
Priest: Oh Oedipus, king of the land, our greatest power!
    You see us before you, men of all ages
    clinging to your altars. Here are boys,
    still too weak to fly from the nest,
    and here the old, bowed down with the years,   20
    the holy ones—a priest of Zeus° myself—and here
    the picked, unmarried men, the young hope of Thebes.
    And all the rest, your great family gathers now,
    branches wreathed, massing in the squares,
    kneeling before the two temples of queen Athena°   25
    or the river-shrine where the embers glow and die
    and Apollo sees the future in the ashes.
                                    Our city—
    look around you, see with your own eyes—
    our ship pitches wildly, cannot lift her head
    from the depths, the red waves of death . . .   30
    Thebes is dying. A blight on the fresh crops
    and the rich pastures, cattle sicken and die,
    and the women die in labor, children stillborn,
    and the plague, the fiery god of fever hurls down

---

3 *wool:* Wool was used in offerings to Apollo, god of poetry, the sun, prophecy, and healing.   21 *Zeus:* The highest Olympian deity and father of Apollo.   25 *Athena:* Goddess of wisdom and protector of Greek cities.

on the city, his lightning slashing through us —   35
raging plague in all its vengeance, devastating
the house of Cadmus!° And Black Death luxuriates
in the raw, wailing miseries of Thebes.

Now we pray to you. You cannot equal the gods,
your children know that, bending at your altar.   40
But we do rate you first of men,
both in the common crises of our lives
and face-to-face encounters with the gods.
You freed us from the Sphinx; you came to Thebes
and cut us loose from the bloody tribute we had paid   45
that harsh, brutal singer. We taught you nothing,
no skill, no extra knowledge, still you triumphed.
A god was with you, so they say, and we believe it —
you lifted up our lives.
                          So now again,
Oedipus, king, we bend to you, your power —   50
we implore you, all of us on our knees:
find us strength, rescue! Perhaps you've heard
the voice of a god or something from other men,
Oedipus . . . what do you know?
The man of experience — you see it every day —   55
his plans will work in a crisis, his first of all.
Act now — we beg you, best of men, raise up our city!
Act, defend yourself, your former glory!
Your country calls you savior now
for your zeal, your action years ago.   60
Never let us remember of your reign:
you helped us stand, only to fall once more.
Oh raise up our city, set us on our feet.
The omens were good that day you brought us joy —
be the same man today!   65
Rule our land, you know you have the power,
but rule a land of the living, not a wasteland.
Ship and towered city are nothing, stripped of men
alive within it, living all as one.

Oedipus: My children,
I pity you. I see — how could I fail to see   70
what longings bring you here? Well I know
you are sick to death, all of you,
but sick as you are, not one is sick as I.
Your pain strikes each of you alone, each

---

37 *Cadmus:* The legendary founder of Thebes.

Oedipus the King: At center stage is Jocasta (Ching Valdes-Aran) in a scene from the 1993 production of *Oedipus the King* at Philadelphia's Wilma Theater, directed by Blanka Zizka and Jiri Zizka. © T. Charles Erikson.

in the confines of himself, no other. But my spirit   75
grieves for the city, for myself and all of you.
I wasn't asleep, dreaming. You haven't wakened me —
I've wept through the nights, you must know that,
groping, laboring over many paths of thought.
After a painful search I found one cure: 80
I acted at once. I sent Creon,
my wife's own brother, to Delphi° —
Apollo the Prophet's oracle — to learn
what I might do or say to save our city.

82 *Delphi:* The shrine where the oracle of Apollo held forth.

Today's the day. When I count the days gone by   85
it torments me . . . what is he doing?
Strange, he's late, he's gone too long.
But once he returns, then, then I'll be a traitor
if I do not do all the god makes clear.

Priest: Timely words. The men over there   90
are signaling — Creon's just arriving.

Oedipus:

Sighting Creon, then turning to the altar.

                                                    Lord Apollo,
let him come with a lucky word of rescue,
shining like his eyes!

Priest: Welcome news, I think — he's crowned, look,
and the laurel wreath is bright with berries.   95

Oedipus: We'll soon see. He's close enough to hear —

Enter Creon from the side; his face is shaded with a wreath.

Creon, prince, my kinsman, what do you bring us?
What message from the god?

Creon: Good news.
I tell you even the hardest things to bear,
if they should turn out well, all would be well.   100

Oedipus: Of course, but what were the god's *words*? There's no hope
and nothing to fear in what you've said so far.

Creon: If you want my report in the presence of these . . .

Pointing to the priests while drawing Oedipus toward the palace.

I'm ready now, or we might go inside.

Oedipus: Speak out,
speak to us all. I grieve for these, my people,   105
far more than I fear for my own life.

Creon: Very well,
I will tell you what I heard from the god.
Apollo commands us — he was quite clear —
"Drive the corruption from the land,
don't harbor it any longer, past all cure,   110
don't nurse it in your soil — root it out!"

Oedipus: How can we cleanse ourselves — what rites?
What's the source of the trouble?

Creon: Banish the man, or pay back blood with blood.
Murder sets the plague-storm on the city.

Oedipus: Whose murder?   115
Whose fate does Apollo bring to light?

Creon: Our leader,
my lord, was once a man named Laius,
before you came and put us straight on course.

Oedipus: I know —
   or so I've heard. I never saw the man myself.
Creon: Well, he was killed, and Apollo commands us now —   120
   he could not be more clear,
   "Pay the killers back — whoever is responsible."
Oedipus: Where on earth are they? Where to find it now,
   the trail of the ancient guilt so hard to trace?
Creon: "Here in Thebes," he said.   125
   Whatever is sought for can be caught, you know,
   whatever is neglected slips away.
Oedipus: But where,
   in the palace, the fields or foreign soil,
   where did Laius meet his bloody death?
Creon: He went to consult an oracle, he said,   130
   and he set out and never came home again.
Oedipus: No messenger, no fellow-traveler saw what happened?
   Someone to cross-examine?
Creon: No,
   they were all killed but one. He escaped,
   terrified, he could tell us nothing clearly,   135
   nothing of what he saw — just one thing.
Oedipus: What's that?
   One thing could hold the key to it all,
   a small beginning gives us grounds for hope.
Creon: He said thieves attacked them — a whole band,
   not single-handed, cut King Laius down.
Oedipus: A thief,   140
   so daring, wild, he'd kill a king? Impossible,
   unless conspirators paid him off in Thebes.
Creon: We suspected as much. But with Laius dead
   no leader appeared to help us in our troubles.
Oedipus: Trouble? Your *king* was murdered — royal blood!   145
   What stopped you from tracking down the killer
   then and there?
Creon: The singing, riddling Sphinx.
   She . . . persuaded us to let the mystery go
   and concentrate on what lay at our feet.
Oedipus: No,
   I'll start again — I'll bring it all to light myself!   150
   Apollo is right, and so are you, Creon,
   to turn our attention back to the murdered man.
   Now you have me to fight for you, you'll see:
   I am the land's avenger by all rights
   and Apollo's champion too.   155
   But not to assist some distant kinsman, no,
   for my own sake I'll rid us of this corruption.

Whoever killed the king may decide to kill me too,
with the same violent hand — by avenging Laius
I defend myself.

To the priests.

                          Quickly, my children.   160
Up from the steps, take up your branches now.

To the guards.

One of you summon the city here before us,
tell them I'll do everything. God help us,
we will see our triumph — or our fall.

Oedipus and Creon enter the palace, followed by the guards.

Priest: Rise, my sons. The kindness we came for   165
  Oedipus volunteers himself.
  Apollo has sent his word, his oracle —
  Come down, Apollo, save us, stop the plague.

The priests rise, remove their branches, and exit to the side. Enter a Chorus, the citizens of Thebes, who have not heard the news that Creon brings. They march around the altar, chanting.

Chorus: Zeus!
  Great welcome voice of Zeus, what do you bring?
  What word from the gold vaults of Delphi   170
  comes to brilliant Thebes? I'm racked with terror —
                     terror shakes my heart
  and I cry your wild cries, Apollo, Healer of Delos°
  I worship you in dread . . . what now, what is your price?
  some new sacrifice? some ancient rite from the past   175
  come round again each spring? —
               what will you bring to birth?
  Tell me, child of golden Hope
      warm voice that never dies!

  You are the first I call, daughter of Zeus   180
  deathless Athena — I call your sister Artemis,°
  heart of the market place enthroned in glory,
                guardian of our earth —
  I call Apollo astride the thunderheads of heaven —
  O triple shield against death, shine before me now!   185
  If ever, once in the past, you stopped some ruin
  launched against our walls
             you hurled the flame of pain

173 *Delos:* Apollo was born on this sacred island.   181 *Artemis:* Apollo's sister, goddess of hunting, the moon, and chastity.

far, far from Thebes — you gods
   come now, come down once more!
                                   No, no   190
the miseries numberless, grief on grief, no end —
too much to bear, we are all dying
O my people . . .
      Thebes like a great army dying
and there is no sword of thought to save us, no   195
and the fruits of our famous earth, they will not ripen
no and the women cannot scream their pangs to birth —
screams for the Healer, children dead in the womb
        and life on life goes down
               you can watch them go   200
   like seabirds winging west, outracing the day's fire
down the horizon, irresistibly
           streaking on to the shores of Evening
                           Death
so many deaths, numberless deaths on deaths, no end —
Thebes is dying, look, her children   205
stripped of pity . . .
      generations strewn on the ground
unburied, unwept, the dead spreading death
and the young wives and gray-haired mothers with them
cling to the altars, trailing in from all over the city —   210
Thebes, city of death, one long cortege
      and the suffering rises
           wails for mercy rise
  and the wild hymn for the Healer blazes out
clashing with our sobs our cries of mourning —   215
   O golden daughter of god, send rescue
   radiant as the kindness in your eyes!
Drive him back! — the fever, the god of death
           that raging god of war
not armored in bronze, not shielded now, he burns me,   220
battle cries in the onslaught burning on —
O rout him from our borders!
Sail him, blast him out to the Sea-queen's chamber
          the black Atlantic gulfs
   or the northern harbor, death to all   225
where the Thracian surf comes crashing.
Now what the night spares he comes by day and kills —
the god of death.

         O lord of the stormcloud,
you who twirl the lightning, Zeus, Father,
thunder Death to nothing!   230

Apollo, lord of the light, I beg you —
          whip your longbow's golden cord
showering arrows on our enemies — shafts of power
champions strong before us rushing on!

Artemis, Huntress,   235
torches flaring over the eastern ridges —
                    ride Death down in pain!

God of the headdress gleaming gold, I cry to you —
your name and ours are one, Dionysus° —
     come with your face aflame with wine   240
                    your raving women's cries°
     your army on the march! Come with the lightning
come with torches blazing, eyes ablaze with glory!
Burn that god of death that all gods hate!

*Oedipus enters from the palace to address the Chorus, as if addressing the
entire city of Thebes.*

Oedipus: You pray to the gods? Let me grant your prayers.   245
Come, listen to me — do what the plague demands:
you'll find relief and lift your head from the depths.

I will speak out now as a stranger to the story,
a stranger to the crime. If I'd been present then,
there would have been no mystery, no long hunt   250
without a clue in hand. So now, counted
a native Theban years after the murder,
to all of Thebes I make this proclamation:
if any one of you knows who murdered Laius,
the son of Labdacus, I order him to reveal   255
the whole truth to me. Nothing to fear,
even if he must denounce himself,
let him speak up
and so escape the brunt of the charge —
he will suffer no unbearable punishment,   260
nothing worse than exile, totally unharmed.

Oedipus pauses, waiting for a reply.

                              Next,
if anyone knows the murderer is a stranger,
a man from alien soil, come, speak up.
I will give him a handsome reward, and lay up
gratitude in my heart for him besides.   265

239 *Dionysus:* God of fertility and wine.   241 *your . . . cries:* Dionysus was attended
by female celebrants.

Silence again, no reply.

But if you keep silent, if anyone panicking,
trying to shield himself or friend or kin,
rejects my offer, then hear what I will do.
I order you, every citizen of the state
where I hold throne and power: banish this man—   270
whoever he may be—never shelter him, never
speak a word to him, never make him partner
to your prayers, your victims burned to the gods.
Never let the holy water touch his hands.
Drive him out, each of you, from every home.   275
He is the plague, the heart of our corruption,
as Apollo's oracle has revealed to me
just now. So I honor my obligations:
I fight for the god and for the murdered man.

Now my curse on the murderer. Whoever he is,   280
a lone man unknown in his crime
or one among many, let that man drag out
his life in agony, step by painful step—
I curse myself as well . . . if by any chance
he proves to be an intimate of our house,   285
here at my hearth, with my full knowledge,
may the curse I just called down on him strike me!

These are your orders: perform them to the last.
I command you, for my sake, for Apollo's, for this country
blasted root and branch by the angry heavens.   290
Even if god had never urged you on to act,
how could you leave the crime uncleansed so long?
A man so noble—your king, brought down in blood—
you should have searched. But I am the king now,
I hold the throne that he held then, possess his bed   295
and a wife who shares our seed . . . why, our seed
might be the same, children born of the same mother
might have created blood-bonds between us
if his hope of offspring hadn't met disaster—
but fate swooped at his head and cut him short.   300
So I will fight for him as if he were my father,
stop at nothing, search the world
to lay my hands on the man who shed his blood,
the son of Labdacus descended of Polydorus,
Cadmus of old and Agenor, founder of the line: 305
their power and mine are one.
                              Oh dear gods,
my curse on those who disobey these orders!

Let no crops grow out of the earth for them —
shrivel their women, kill their sons,
burn them to nothing in this plague   310
that hits us now, or something even worse.
But you, loyal men of Thebes who approve my actions,
may our champion, Justice, may all the gods
be with us, fight beside us to the end!

Leader: In the grip of your curse, my king, I swear   315
I'm not the murderer, cannot point him out.
As for the search, Apollo pressed it on us —
he should name the killer.

Oedipus: Quite right,
but to force the gods to act against their will —
no man has the power.

Leader: Then if I might mention   320
the next best thing . . .

Oedipus: The third best too —
don't hold back, say it.

Leader: I still believe . . .
Lord Tiresias sees with the eyes of Lord Apollo.
Anyone searching for the truth, my king,
might learn it from the prophet, clear as day.   325

Oedipus: I've not been slow with that. On Creon's cue
I sent the escorts, twice, within the hour.
I'm surprised he isn't here.

Leader: We need him —
without him we have nothing but old, useless rumors.

Oedipus: Which rumors? I'll search out every word.   330

Leader: Laius was killed, they say, by certain travelers.

Oedipus: I know — but no one can find the murderer.

Leader: If the man has a trace of fear in him
he won't stay silent long,
not with your curses ringing in his ears.   335

Oedipus: He didn't flinch at murder,
he'll never flinch at words.

*Enter Tiresias, the blind prophet, led by a boy with escorts in attendance.
He remains at a distance.*

Leader: Here is the one who will convict him, look,
they bring him on at last, the seer, the man of god.
The truth lives inside him, him alone.

Oedipus: O Tiresias,   340
master of all the mysteries of our life,
all you teach and all you dare not tell,
signs in the heavens, signs that walk the earth!
Blind as you are, you can feel all the more

what sickness haunts our city. You, my lord,   345
are the one shield, the one savior we can find.

We asked Apollo — perhaps the messengers
haven't told you — he sent his answer back:
"Relief from the plague can only come one way.
Uncover the murderers of Laius,   350
put them to death or drive them into exile."
So I beg you, grudge us nothing now, no voice,
no message plucked from the birds, the embers
or the other mantic ways within your grasp.
Rescue yourself, your city, rescue me —   355
rescue everything infected by the dead.
We are in your hands. For a man to help others
with all his gifts and native strength:
that is the noblest work.

Tiresias: How terrible — to see the truth
when the truth is only pain to him who sees!   360
I knew it well, but I put it from my mind,
else I never would have come.

Oedipus: What's this? Why so grim, so dire?

Tiresias: Just send me home. You bear your burdens,
I'll bear mine. It's better that way,   365
please believe me.

Oedipus: Strange response — unlawful,
unfriendly too to the state that bred and raised you;
you're withholding the word of god.

Tiresias: I fail to see
that your own words are so well-timed.
I'd rather not have the same thing said of me . . .   370

Oedipus: For the love of god, don't turn away,
not if you know something. We beg you,
all of us on our knees.

Tiresias: None of you knows —
and I will never reveal my dreadful secrets,
not to say your own.   375

Oedipus: What? You know and you won't tell?
You're bent on betraying us, destroying Thebes?

Tiresias: I'd rather not cause pain for you or me.
So why this . . . useless interrogation?
You'll get nothing from me.

Oedipus: Nothing! You,   380
you scum of the earth, you'd enrage a heart of stone!
You won't talk? Nothing moves you?
Out with it, once and for all!

Tiresias: You criticize my temper . . . unaware

of the one *you* live with, you revile me.   385
Oedipus: Who could restrain his anger hearing you?
    What outrage — you spurn the city!
Tiresias: What will come will come.
    Even if I shroud it all in silence.
Oedipus: What will come? You're bound to *tell* me that.   390
Tiresias: I'll say no more. Do as you like, build your anger
    to whatever pitch you please, rage your worst —
Oedipus: Oh I'll let loose, I have such fury in me —
    now I see it all. You helped hatch the plot,
    you did the work, yes, short of killing him   395
    with your own hands — and given eyes I'd say
    you did the killing single-handed!
Tiresias: Is that so!
    I charge you, then, submit to that decree
    you just laid down: from this day onward
    speak to no one, not these citizens, not myself.   400
    You are the curse, the corruption of the land!
Oedipus: You, shameless —
    aren't you appalled to start up such a story?
    You think you can get away with this?
Tiresias: I have already.
    The truth with all its power lives inside me.   405
Oedipus: Who primed you for this? Not your prophet's trade.
Tiresias: You did, you forced me, twisted it out of me.
Oedipus: What? Say it again — I'll understand it better.
Tiresias: Didn't you understand, just now?
    Or are you tempting me to talk?   410
Oedipus: No, I can't say I grasped your meaning.
    Out with it, again!
Tiresias: I say you are the murderer you hunt.
Oedipus: That obscenity, twice — by god, you'll pay.
Tiresias: Shall I say more, so you can really rage?   415
Oedipus: Much as you want. Your words are nothing — futile.
Tiresias: You cannot imagine . . . I tell you,
    you and your loved ones live together in infamy,
    you cannot see how far you've gone in guilt.
Oedipus: You think you can keep this up and never suffer?   420
Tiresias: Indeed, if the truth has any power.
Oedipus: It does
    but not for you, old man. You've lost your power,
    stone-blind, stone-deaf — senses, eyes blind as stone!
Tiresias: I pity you, flinging at me the very insults
    each man here will fling at you so soon.
Oedipus: Blind,   425
    lost in the night, endless night that nursed you!

You can't hurt me or anyone else who sees the light—
you can never touch me.
Tiresias: True, it is not your fate
    to fall at my hands. Apollo is quite enough,
    and he will take some pains to work this out.   430
Oedipus: Creon! Is this conspiracy his or yours?
Tiresias: Creon is not your downfall, no, you are your own.
Oedipus: O power—
    wealth and empire, skill outstripping skill
    in the heady rivalries of life,
    what envy lurks inside you! Just for this,   435
    the crown the city gave me—I never sought it,
    they laid it in my hands—for this alone, Creon,
    the soul of trust, my loyal friend from the start
    steals against me . . . so hungry to overthrow me
    he sets this wizard on me, this scheming quack,   440
    this fortune-teller peddling lies, eyes peeled
    for his own profit—seer blind in his craft!

    Come here, you pious fraud. Tell me,
    when did you ever prove yourself a prophet?
    When the Sphinx, that chanting Fury kept her deathwatch here, 445
    why silent then, not a word to set our people free?
    There was a riddle, not for some passer-by to solve—
    it cried out for a prophet. Where were you?
    Did you rise to the crisis? Not a word,
    you and your birds, your gods—nothing.   450
    No, but I came by, Oedipus the ignorant,
    I stopped the Sphinx! With no help from the birds,
    the flight of my own intelligence hit the mark.

    And this is the man you'd try to overthrow?
    You think you'll stand by Creon when he's king?   455
    You and the great mastermind—
    you'll pay in tears, I promise you, for this,
    this witch-hunt. If you didn't look so senile
    the lash would teach you what your scheming means!
Leader: I'd suggest his words were spoken in anger,   460
    Oedipus . . . yours too, and it isn't what we need.
    The best solution to the oracle, the riddle
    posed by god—we should look for that.
Tiresias: You are the king no doubt, but in one respect,
    at least, I am your equal: the right to reply.   465
    I claim that privilege too.
    I am not your slave. I serve Apollo.
    I don't need Creon to speak for me in public.

                                                So,
you mock my blindness? Let me tell you this.
You with your precious eyes,   470
you're blind to the corruption of your life,
to the house you live in, those you live with —
who *are* your parents? Do you know? All unknowing
you are the scourge of your own flesh and blood,
the dead below the earth and the living here above,   475
and the double lash of your mother and your father's curse
will whip you from this land one day, their footfall
treading you down in terror, darkness shrouding
your eyes that now can see the light!
                                    Soon, soon
you'll scream aloud — what haven won't reverberate?   480
What rock of Cithaeron° won't scream back in echo?
That day you learn the truth about your marriage,
the wedding-march that sang you into your halls,
the lusty voyage home to the fatal harbor!
And a load of other horrors you'd never dream   485
will level you with yourself and all your children.

There. Now smear us with insults — Creon, myself
and every word I've said. No man will ever
be rooted from the earth as brutally as you.
Oedipus: Enough! Such filth from him? Insufferable —   490
     what, still alive? Get out —
     faster, back where you came from — vanish!
Tiresias: I'd never have come if you hadn't called me here.
Oedipus: If I thought you'd blurt out such absurdities,
     you'd have died waiting before I'd had you summoned.   495
Tiresias: Absurd, am I? To you, not to your parents:
     the ones who bore you found me sane enough.
Oedipus: Parents — who? Wait . . . who is my father?
Tiresias: This day will bring your birth and your destruction.
Oedipus: Riddles — all you can say are riddles, murk and darkness. 500
Tiresias: Ah, but aren't you the best man alive at solving riddles?
Oedipus: Mock me for that, go on, and you'll reveal my greatness.
Tiresias: Your great good fortune, true, it was your ruin.
Oedipus: Not if I saved the city — what do I care?
Tiresias: Well then, I'll be going.

     To his attendant.

                         Take me home, boy.   505
Oedipus: Yes, take him away. You're a nuisance here.
     Out of the way, the irritation's gone.

481 *Cithaeron:* The mountains where Oedipus was abandoned as an infant.

Turning his back on Tiresias, moving toward the palace.

Tiresias: I will go,
    once I have said what I came here to say.
    I'll never shrink from the anger in your eyes—
    you can't destroy me. Listen to me closely: 510
    the man you've sought so long, proclaiming,
    cursing up and down, the murderer of Laius—
    he is here. A stranger,
    you may think, who lives among you,
    he soon will be revealed a native Theban   515
    but he will take no joy in the revelation.
    Blind who now has eyes, beggar who now is rich,
    he will grope his way toward a foreign soil,
    a stick tapping before him step by step.

Oedipus enters the palace.

    Revealed at last, brother and father both   520
    to the children he embraces, to his mother
    son and husband both—he sowed the loins
    his father sowed, he spilled his father's blood!

    Go in and reflect on that, solve that.
    And if you find I've lied   525
    from this day onward call the prophet blind.

Tiresias and the boy exit to the side.

Chorus: Who—
    who is the man the voice of god denounces
    resounding out of the rocky gorge of Delphi?
        The horror too dark to tell,
    whose ruthless bloody hands have done the work?   530
    His time has come to fly
        to outrace the stallions of the storm
                    his feet a streak of speed—
    Cased in armor, Apollo son of the Father
    lunges on him, lightning-bolts afire!   535
    And the grim unerring Furies°
            closing for the kill.
                        Look,
    the word of god has just come blazing
    flashing off Parnassus'° snowy heights!
        That man who left no trace—   540
    after him, hunt him down with all our strength!

---

536 *Furies:* Three spirits who avenged evildoers.   539 *Parnassus:* A mountain in
Greece associated with Apollo.

Now under bristling timber
   up through rocks and caves he stalks
                  like the wild mountain bull—
cut off from men, each step an agony, frenzied, racing blind   545
but he cannot outrace the dread voices of Delphi
ringing out of the heart of Earth,
      the dark wings beating around him shrieking doom
               the doom that never dies, the terror—

The skilled prophet scans the birds and shatters me with terror!   550
I can't accept him, can't deny him, don't know what to say,
I'm lost, and the wings of dark foreboding beating—
I cannot see what's come, what's still to come . . .
and what could breed a blood feud between
      Laius' house and the son of Polybus?°   555
I know of nothing, not in the past and not now,
no charge to bring against our king, no cause
to attack his fame that rings throughout Thebes—
      not without proof—not for the ghost of Laius,
      not to avenge a murder gone without a trace.   560

Zeus and Apollo know, they know, the great masters
            of all the dark and depth of human life.
But whether a mere man can know the truth,
whether a seer can fathom more than I—
there is no test, no certain proof   565
            though matching skill for skill
a man can outstrip a rival. No, not till I see
these charges proved will I side with his accusers.
We saw him then, when the she-hawk° swept against him,
saw with our own eyes his skill, his brilliant triumph—   570
      there was the test—he was the joy of Thebes!
      Never will I convict my king, never in my heart.

Enter Creon from the side.

Creon: My fellow-citizens, I hear King Oedipus
      levels terrible charges at me. I had to come.
      I resent it deeply. If, in the present crisis,   575
      he thinks he suffers any abuse from me,
      anything I've done or said that offers him
      the slightest injury, why, I've no desire
      to linger out this life, my reputation a shambles.
      The damage I'd face from such an accusation   580

---

555 *Polybus:* The King of Corinth, who is thought to be Oedipus's father.   569 *she-hawk:* The Sphinx.

is nothing simple. No, there's nothing worse:
branded a traitor in the city, a traitor
to all of you and my good friends.
Leader: True,
  but a slur might have been forced out of him,
  by anger perhaps, not any firm conviction.   585
Creon: The charge was made in public, wasn't it?
  I put the prophet up to spreading lies?
Leader: Such things were said . . .
  I don't know with what intent, if any.
Creon: Was his glance steady, his mind right   590
  when the charge was brought against me?
Leader: I really couldn't say. I never look
  to judge the ones in power.

  The doors open. Oedipus enters.

                                  Wait,
  here's Oedipus now.
Oedipus: You — here? You have the gall
  to show your face before the palace gates?   595
  You, plotting to kill me, kill the king —
  I see it all, the marauding thief himself
  scheming to steal my crown and power!
                                  Tell me,
  in god's name, what did you take me for,
  coward or fool, when you spun out your plot?   600
  Your treachery — you think I'd never detect it
  creeping against me in the dark? Or sensing it,
  not defend myself? Aren't you the fool,
  you and your high adventure. Lacking numbers,
  powerful friends, out for the big game of empire —   605
  you need riches, armies to bring that quarry down!
Creon: Are you quite finished? It's your turn to listen
  for just as long as you've . . . instructed me.
  Hear me out, then judge me on the facts.
Oedipus: You've a wicked way with words, Creon,   610
  but I'll be slow to learn — from you.
  I find you a menace, a great burden to me.
Creon: Just one thing, hear me out in this.
Oedipus: Just one thing,
  don't tell me you're not the enemy, the traitor.
Creon: Look, if you think crude, mindless stubbornness   615
  such a gift, you've lost your sense of balance.
Oedipus: If you think you can abuse a kinsman,
  then escape the penalty, you're insane.
Creon: Fair enough, I grant you. But this injury

you say I've done you, what is it?   620
Oedipus: Did you induce me, yes or no,
    to send for that sanctimonious prophet?
Creon: I did. And I'd do the same again.
Oedipus: All right then, tell me, how long is it now
    since Laius . . .
Creon: Laius — what did *he* do?
Oedipus: Vanished,   625
    swept from sight, murdered in his tracks.
Creon: The count of the years would run you far back . . .
Oedipus: And that far back, was the prophet at his trade?
Creon: Skilled as he is today, and just as honored.
Oedipus: Did he ever refer to me then, at that time?
Creon: No,   630
    never, at least, when I was in his presence.
Oedipus: But you did investigate the murder, didn't you?
Creon: We did our best, of course, discovered nothing.
Oedipus: But the great seer never accused me then — why not?
Creon: I don't know. And when I don't, *I* keep quiet.   635
Oedipus: You do know this, you'd tell it too —
    if you had a shred of decency.
Creon: What?
    If I know, I won't hold back.
Oedipus: Simply this:
    if the two of you had never put heads together,
    we'd never have heard about *my* killing Laius.   640
Creon: If that's what he says . . . well, you know best.
    But now I have a right to learn from you
    as you just learned from me.
Oedipus: Learn your fill,
    you never will convict me of the murder.
Creon: Tell me, you're married to my sister, aren't you?   645
Oedipus: A genuine discovery — there's no denying that.
Creon: And you rule the land with her, with equal power?
Oedipus: She receives from me whatever she desires.
Creon: And I am the third, all of us are equals?
Oedipus: Yes, and it's there you show your stripes —   650
    you betray a kinsman.
Creon: Not at all.
    Not if you see things calmly, rationally,
    as I do. Look at it this way first:
    who in his right mind would rather rule
    and live in anxiety than sleep in peace?   655
    Particularly if he enjoys the same authority.
    Not I, I'm not the man to yearn for kingship,
    not with a king's power in my hands. Who would?

No one with any sense of self-control.
Now, as it is, you offer me all I need,   660
not a fear in the world. But if I wore the crown . . .
there'd be many painful duties to perform,
hardly to my taste.
                              How could kingship
please me more than influence, power
without a qualm? I'm not that deluded yet,   665
to reach for anything but privilege outright,
profit free and clear.
Now all men sing my praises, all salute me,
now all who request your favors curry mine.
I'm their best hope: success rests in me.   670
Why give up that, I ask you, and borrow trouble?
A man of sense, someone who sees things clearly
would never resort to treason.
No, I've no lust for conspiracy in me,
nor could I ever suffer one who does.   675

Do you want proof? Go to Delphi yourself,
examine the oracle and see if I've reported
the message word-for-word. This too:
if you detect that I and the clairvoyant
have plotted anything in common, arrest me,   680
execute me. Not on the strength of one vote,
two in this case, mine as well as yours.
But don't convict me on sheer unverified surmise.

How wrong it is to take the good for bad,
purely at random, or take the bad for good.   685
But reject a friend, a kinsman? I would as soon
tear out the life within us, priceless life itself.
You'll learn this well, without fail, in time.
Time alone can bring the just man to light;
the criminal you can spot in one short day.
Leader: Good advice,   690
my lord, for anyone who wants to avoid disaster.
Those who jump to conclusions may be wrong.
Oedipus: When my enemy moves against me quickly,
plots in secret, I move quickly too, I must,
I plot and pay him back. Relax my guard a moment,   695
waiting his next move—he wins his objective,
I lose mine.
Creon: What do you want?
You want me banished?
Oedipus: No, I want you dead.

Creon: Just to show how ugly a grudge can . . .
Oedipus: So,
    still stubborn? you don't think I'm serious?   700
Creon: I think you're insane.
Oedipus: Quite sane — in my behalf.
Creon: Not just as much in mine?
Oedipus: You — my mortal enemy?
Creon: What if you're wholly wrong?
Oedipus: No matter — I must rule.
Creon: Not if you rule unjustly.
Oedipus: Hear him, Thebes, my city!
Creon: My city too, not yours alone!   705
Leader: Please, my lords.

    Enter Jocasta from the palace.

                  Look, Jocasta's coming,
    and just in time too. With her help
    you must put this fighting of yours to rest.
Jocasta: Have you no sense? Poor misguided men,
    such shouting — why this public outburst?   710
    Aren't you ashamed, with the land so sick,
    to stir up private quarrels?

    To Oedipus.

    Into the palace now. And Creon, you go home.
    Why make such a furor over nothing?
Creon: My sister, it's dreadful . . . Oedipus, your husband,   715
    he's bent on a choice of punishments for me,
    banishment from the fatherland or death.
Oedipus: Precisely. I caught him in the act, Jocasta,
    plotting, about to stab me in the back.
Creon: Never — curse me, let me die and be damned   720
    if I've done you any wrong you charge me with.
Jocasta: Oh god, believe it, Oedipus,
    honor the solemn oath he swears to heaven.
    Do it for me, for the sake of all your people.

    The Chorus begins to chant.

Chorus: Believe it, be sensible   725
    give way, my king, I beg you!
Oedipus: What do you want from me, concessions?
Chorus: Respect him — he's been no fool in the past
    and now he's strong with the oath he swears to god.
Oedipus: You know what you're asking?
Chorus: I do.
Oedipus: Then out with it!   730

Chorus: The man's your friend, your kin, he's under oath—
    don't cast him out, disgraced
    branded with guilt on the strength of hearsay only.
Oedipus: Know full well, if that's what you want
    you want me dead or banished from the land.
Chorus: Never—   735
    no, by the blazing Sun, first god of the heavens!
      Stripped of the gods, stripped of loved ones,
    let me die by inches if that ever crossed my mind.
    But the heart inside me sickens, dies as the land dies
    and now on top of the old griefs you pile this,   740
    your fury—both of you!
Oedipus: Then let him go,
    even if it does lead to my ruin, my death
    or my disgrace, driven from Thebes for life.
    It's you, not him I pity—your words move me.
    He, wherever he goes, my hate goes with him.   745
Creon: Look at you, sullen in yielding, brutal in your rage—
    you'll go too far. It's perfect justice:
    natures like yours are hardest on themselves.
Oedipus: Then leave me alone—get out!
Creon: I'm going.
    You're wrong, so wrong. These men know I'm right.   750

    Exit to the side. The Chorus turns to Jocasta.

Chorus: Why do you hesitate, my lady
        why not help him in?
Jocasta: Tell me what's happened first.
Chorus: Loose, ignorant talk started dark suspicions
    and a sense of injustice cut deeply too.   755
Jocasta: On both sides?
Chorus: Oh yes.
Jocasta: What did they say?
Chorus: Enough, please, enough! The land's so racked already
    or so it seems to me . . .
    End the trouble here, just where they left it.
Oedipus: You see what comes of your good intentions now?   760
    And all because you tried to blunt my anger.
Chorus: My king,
    I've said it once, I'll say it time and again—
      I'd be insane, you know it,
    senseless, ever to turn my back on you.
    You who set our beloved land—storm-tossed, shattered—   765
    straight on course. Now again, good helmsman,
    steer us through the storm!

The Chorus draws away, leaving Oedipus and Jocasta side by side.

Jocasta: For the love of god,
  Oedipus, tell me too, what is it?
  Why this rage? You're so unbending.
Oedipus: I will tell you. I respect you, Jocasta,   770
  much more than these . . .

  Glancing at the Chorus.

  Creon's to blame, Creon schemes against me.
Jocasta: Tell me clearly, how did the quarrel start?
Oedipus: He says I murdered Laius — I am guilty.
Jocasta: How does he know? Some secret knowledge   775
  or simple hearsay?
Oedipus: Oh, he sent his prophet in
  to do his dirty work. You know Creon,
  Creon keeps his own lips clean.
Jocasta: A prophet?
  Well then, free yourself of every charge!
  Listen to me and learn some peace of mind: 780
  no skill in the world,
  nothing human can penetrate the future.
  Here is proof, quick and to the point.
  An oracle came to Laius one fine day
  (I won't say from Apollo himself   785
  but his underlings, his priests) and it said
  that doom would strike him down at the hands of a son,
  our son, to be born of our own flesh and blood. But Laius,
  so the report goes at least, was killed by strangers,
  thieves, at a place where three roads meet . . . my son —   790
  he wasn't three days old and the boy's father
  fastened his ankles, had a henchman fling him away
  on a barren, trackless mountain.
                    There, you see?
  Apollo brought neither thing to pass. My baby
  no more murdered his father than Laius suffered —   795
  his wildest fear — death at his own son's hands.
  That's how the seers and their revelations
  mapped out the future. Brush them from your mind.
  Whatever the god needs and seeks
  he'll bring to light himself, with ease.
Oedipus: Strange,   800
  hearing you just now . . . my mind wandered,
  my thoughts racing back and forth.
Jocasta: What do you mean? Why so anxious, startled?
Oedipus: I thought I heard you say that Laius
  was cut down at a place where three roads meet.   805

Jocasta: That was the story. It hasn't died out yet.

Oedipus: Where did this thing happen? Be precise.

Jocasta: A place called Phocis, where two branching roads,
one from Daulia, one from Delphi,
come together—a crossroads. 810

Oedipus: When? How long ago?

Jocasta: The heralds no sooner reported Laius dead
than you appeared and they hailed you king of Thebes.

Oedipus: My god, my god—what have you planned to do to me?

Jocasta: What, Oedipus? What haunts you so?

Oedipus: Not yet. 815
Laius—how did he look? Describe him.
Had he reached his prime?

Jocasta: He was swarthy,
and the gray had just begun to streak his temples,
and his build . . . wasn't far from yours.

Oedipus: Oh no no,
I think I've just called down a dreadful curse 820
upon myself—I simply didn't know!

Jocasta: What are you saying? I shudder to look at you.

Oedipus: I have a terrible fear the blind seer can see.
I'll know in a moment. One thing more—

Jocasta: Anything,
afraid as I am—ask, I'll answer, all I can. 825

Oedipus: Did he go with a light or heavy escort,
several men-at-arms, like a lord, a king?

Jocasta: There were five in the party, a herald among them,
and a single wagon carrying Laius.

Oedipus: Ai—
now I can see it all, clear as day. 830
Who told you all this at the time, Jocasta?

Jocasta: A servant who reached home, the lone survivor.

Oedipus: So, could he still be in the palace—even now?

Jocasta: No indeed. Soon as he returned from the scene
and saw you on the throne with Laius dead and gone, 835
he knelt and clutched my hand, pleading with me
to send him into the hinterlands, to pasture,
far as possible, out of sight of Thebes.
I sent him away. Slave though he was,
he'd earned that favor—and much more. 840

Oedipus: Can we bring him back, quickly?

Jocasta: Easily. Why do you want him so?

Oedipus: I'm afraid,
Jocasta, I have said too much already.
That man—I've got to see him.

Jocasta: Then he'll come.

But even I have a right, I'd like to think,   845
to know what's torturing you, my lord.

Oedipus: And so you shall—I can hold nothing back from you,
now I've reached this pitch of dark foreboding.
Who means more to me than you? Tell me,
whom would I turn toward but you   850
as I go through all this?

My father was Polybus, king of Corinth.
My mother, a Dorian, Merope. And I was held
the prince of the realm among the people there,
till something struck me out of nowhere,   855
something strange . . . worth remarking perhaps,
hardly worth the anxiety I gave it.
Some man at a banquet who had drunk too much
shouted out—he was far gone, mind you—
that I am not my father's son. Fighting words!   860
I barely restrained myself that day
but early the next I went to mother and father,
questioned them closely, and they were enraged
at the accusation and the fool who let it fly.
So as for my parents I was satisfied,   865
but still this thing kept gnawing at me,
the slander spread—I had to make my move.

                                        And so,
unknown to mother and father I set out for Delphi,
and the god Apollo spurned me, sent me away
denied the facts I came for,   870
but first he flashed before my eyes a future
great with pain, terror, disaster—I can hear him cry,
"You are fated to couple with your mother, you will bring
a breed of children into the light no man can bear to see—
you will kill your father, the one who gave you life!"   875
I heard all that and ran. I abandoned Corinth,
from that day on I gauged its landfall only
by the stars, running, always running
toward some place where I would never see
the shame of all those oracles come true.   880
And as I fled I reached that very spot
where the great king, you say, met his death.
Now, Jocasta, I will tell you all.
Making my way toward this triple crossroad
I began to see a herald, then a brace of colts   885
drawing a wagon, and mounted on the bench . . . a man,
just as you've described him, coming face-to-face,
and the one in the lead and the old man himself
were about to thrust me off the road—brute force—

and the one shouldering me aside, the driver,   890
I strike him in anger! — and the old man, watching me
coming up along his wheels — he brings down
his prod, two prongs straight at my head!
I paid him back with interest!
Short work, by god — with one blow of the staff   895
in this right hand I knock him out of his high seat,
roll him out of the wagon, sprawling headlong —
I killed them all — every mother's son!

Oh, but if there is any blood-tie
between Laius and this stranger . . .   900
what man alive more miserable than I?
More hated by the gods? *I* am the man
no alien, no citizen welcomes to his house,
law forbids it — not a word to me in public,
driven out of every hearth and home.   905
And all these curses I — no one but I
brought down these piling curses on myself!
And you, his wife, I've touched your body with these,
the hands that killed your husband cover you with blood.

Wasn't I born for torment? Look me in the eyes!   910
I am abomination — heart and soul!
I must be exiled, and even in exile
never see my parents, never set foot
on native earth again. Else I'm doomed
to couple with my mother and cut my father down . . .   915
Polybus who reared me, gave me life.

                                But why, why?
Wouldn't a man of judgment say — and wouldn't he be right —
some savage power has brought this down upon my head?

Oh no, not that, you pure and awesome gods,
never let me see that day! Let me slip   920
from the world of men, vanish without a trace
before I see myself stained with such corruption,
stained to the heart.
Leader: My lord, you fill our hearts with fear.
But at least until you question the witness,   925
do take hope.
Oedipus: Exactly. He is my last hope —
I'm waiting for the shepherd. He is crucial.
Jocasta: And once he appears, what then? Why so urgent?
Oedipus: I'll tell you. If it turns out that his story
matches yours, I've escaped the worst.   930
Jocasta: What did I say? What struck you so?

Oedipus: You said *thieves* —
he told you a whole band of them murdered Laius.
So, if he still holds to the same number,
I cannot be the killer. One can't equal many.
But if he refers to one man, one alone,   935
clearly the scales come down on me:
I am guilty.

Jocasta: Impossible. Trust me,
I told you precisely what he said,
and he can't retract it now;
the whole city heard it, not just I.   940
And even if he should vary his first report
by one man more or less, still, my lord,
he could never make the murder of Laius
truly fit the prophecy. Apollo was explicit:
my son was doomed to kill my husband . . . my son,   945
poor defenseless thing, he never had a chance
to kill his father. They destroyed him first.

So much for prophecy. It's neither here nor there.
From this day on, I wouldn't look right or left.

Oedipus: True, true. Still, that shepherd,   950
someone fetch him — now!

Jocasta: I'll send at once. But do let's go inside.
I'd never displease you, least of all in this.

Oedipus and Jocasta enter the palace.

Chorus: Destiny guide me always
Destiny find me filled with reverence   955
                    pure in word and deed.
Great laws tower above us, reared on high
born for the brilliant vault of heaven —
          Olympian sky their only father,
nothing mortal, no man gave them birth,   960
their memory deathless, never lost in sleep:
within them lives a mighty god, the god does not grow old.

Pride breeds the tyrant
violent pride, gorging, crammed to bursting
          with all that is overripe and rich with ruin —   965
clawing up to the heights, headlong pride
crashes down the abyss — sheer doom!
          No footing helps, all foothold lost and gone,
But the healthy strife that makes the city strong —
I pray that god will never end that wrestling: 970
god, my champion, I will never let you go.

But if any man comes striding, high and mighty
    in all he says and does,
no fear of justice, no reverence
for the temples of the gods —   975
    let a rough doom tear him down,
repay his pride, breakneck, ruinous pride!
If he cannot reap his profits fairly
    cannot restrain himself from outrage —
mad, laying hands on the holy things untouchable!   980

    Can such a man, so desperate, still boast
    he can save his life from the flashing bolts of god?
      If all such violence goes with honor now
      why join the sacred dance?

Never again will I go reverent to Delphi,   985
    the inviolate heart of Earth
or Apollo's ancient oracle at Abae
or Olympia of the fires —
    unless these prophecies all come true
for all mankind to point toward in wonder.   990
King of kings, if you deserve your titles
    Zeus, remember, never forget!
You and your deathless, everlasting reign.

    They are dying, the old oracles sent to Laius,
    now our masters strike them off the rolls.   995
      Nowhere Apollo's golden glory now —
      the gods, the gods go down.

Enter Jocasta from the palace, carrying a suppliant's branch wound in wool.

Jocasta: Lords of the realm, it occurred to me,
just now, to visit the temples of the gods,
so I have my branch in hand and incense too.   1000
Oedipus is beside himself. Racked with anguish,
no longer a man of sense, he won't admit
the latest prophecies are hollow as the old —
he's at the mercy of every passing voice
if the voice tells of terror.   1005
I urge him gently, nothing seems to help,
so I turn to you, Apollo, you are nearest.

*Placing her branch on the altar, while an old herdsman enters from the side, not
the one just summoned by the king but an unexpected messenger from Corinth.*

I come with prayers and offerings . . . I beg you,
cleanse us, set us free of defilement!

Look at us, passengers in the grip of fear,   1010
watching the pilot of the vessel go to pieces.

Messenger:

Approaching Jocasta and the Chorus.

Strangers, please, I wonder if you could lead us
to the palace of the king . . . I think it's Oedipus.
Better, the man himself — you know where he is?

Leader: This is his palace, stranger. He's inside.   1015
But here is his queen, his wife and mother
of his children.

Messenger: Blessings on you, noble queen,
queen of Oedipus crowned with all your family —
blessings on you always!

Jocasta: And the same to you, stranger, you deserve it . . .   1020
such a greeting. But what have you come for?
Have you brought us news?

Messenger: Wonderful news —
for the house, my lady, for your husband too.

Jocasta: Really, what? Who sent you?

Messenger: Corinth.
I'll give you the message in a moment.   1025
You'll be glad of it — how could you help it? —
though it costs a little sorrow in the bargain.

Jocasta: What can it be, with such a double edge?

Messenger: The people there, they want to make your Oedipus
king of Corinth, so they're saying now.   1030

Jocasta: Why? Isn't old Polybus still in power?

Messenger: No more. Death has got him in the tomb.

Jocasta: What are you saying? Polybus, dead? — dead?

Messenger: If not,
if I'm not telling the truth, strike me dead too.

Jocasta:

To a servant.

Quickly, go to your master, tell him this!   1035

You prophecies of the gods, where are you now?
This is the man that Oedipus feared for years,
he fled him, not to kill him — and now he's dead,
quite by chance, a normal, natural death,
not murdered by his son.

Oedipus:

Emerging from the palace.

                    Dearest,   1040

what now? Why call me from the palace?

Jocasta:

Bringing the Messenger closer.

Listen to *him*, see for yourself what all
those awful prophecies of god have come to.

Oedipus: And who is he? What can he have for me?

Jocasta: He's from Corinth, he's come to tell you   1045
your father is no more — Polybus — he's dead!

Oedipus:

Wheeling on the Messenger.

What? Let me have it from your lips.

Messenger: Well,
if that's what you want first, then here it is:
make no mistake, Polybus is dead and gone.

Oedipus: How — murder? sickness? — what? what killed him?   1050

Messenger: A light tip of the scales can put old bones to rest.

Oedipus: Sickness then — poor man, it wore him down.

Messenger: That,
and the long count of years he'd measured out.

Oedipus: So!
Jocasta, why, why look to the Prophet's hearth,
the fires of the future? Why scan the birds   1055
that scream above our heads? They winged me on
to the murder of my father, did they? That was my doom?
Well look, he's dead and buried, hidden under the earth,
and here I am in Thebes, I never put hand to sword —
unless some longing for me wasted him away,   1060
then in a sense you'd say I caused his death.
But now, all those prophecies I feared — Polybus
packs them off to sleep with him in hell!
They're nothing, worthless.

Jocasta: There.
Didn't I tell you from the start?   1065

Oedipus: So you did. I was lost in fear.

Jocasta: No more, sweep it from your mind forever.

Oedipus: But my mother's bed, surely I must fear —

Jocasta: Fear?
What should a man fear? It's all chance,
chance rules our lives. Not a man on earth   1070
can see a day ahead, groping through the dark.
Better to live at random, best we can.
And as for this marriage with your mother —
have no fear. Many a man before you,
in his dreams, has shared his mother's bed.   1075
Take such things for shadows, nothing at all —

Live, Oedipus,
as if there's no tomorrow!

Oedipus: Brave words,
and you'd persuade me if mother weren't alive.
But mother lives, so for all your reassurances   1080
I live in fear, I must.

Jocasta: But your father's death,
that, at least, is a great blessing, joy to the eyes!

Oedipus: Great, I know . . . but I fear *her* — she's still alive.

Messenger: Wait, who is this woman, makes you so afraid?

Oedipus: Merope, old man. The wife of Polybus.   1085

Messenger: The queen? What's there to fear in her?

Oedipus: A dreadful prophecy, stranger, sent by the gods.

Messenger: Tell me, could you? Unless it's forbidden
other ears to hear.

Oedipus: Not at all.
Apollo told me once — it is my fate —   1090
I must make love with my own mother,
shed my father's blood with my own hands.
So for years I've given Corinth a wide berth,
and it's been my good fortune too. But still,
to see one's parents and look into their eyes   1095
is the greatest joy I know.

Messenger: You're afraid of that?
That kept you out of Corinth?

Oedipus: My *father*, old man —
so I wouldn't kill my father.

Messenger: So that's it.
Well then, seeing I came with such good will, my king,
why don't I rid you of that old worry now?   1100

Oedipus: What a rich reward you'd have for that.

Messenger: What do you think I came for, majesty?
So you'd come home and I'd be better off.

Oedipus: Never, I will never go near my parents.

Messenger: My boy, it's clear, you don't know what you're doing.   1105

Oedipus: What do you mean, old man? For god's sake, explain.

Messenger: If you ran from *them*, always dodging home . . .

Oedipus: Always, terrified Apollo's oracle might come true —

Messenger: And you'd be covered with guilt, from both your parents.

Oedipus: That's right, old man, that fear is always with me.   1110

Messenger: Don't you know? You've really nothing to fear.

Oedipus: But why? If I'm their son — Merope, Polybus?

Messenger: Polybus was nothing to you, that's why, not in blood.

Oedipus: What are you saying — Polybus was not my father?

Messenger: No more than I am. He and I are equals.

Oedipus: My father —   1115
    how can my father equal nothing? You're nothing to me!
Messenger: Neither was he, no more your father than I am.
Oedipus: Then why did he call me his son?
Messenger: You were a gift,
    years ago — know for a fact he took you
    from my hands.
Oedipus: No, from another's hands?   1120
    Then how could he love me so? He loved me, deeply . . .
Messenger: True, and his early years without a child
    made him love you all the more.
Oedipus: And you, did you . . .
    buy me? find me by accident?
Messenger: I stumbled on you,
    down the woody flanks of Mount Cithaeron.
Oedipus: So close,   1125
    what were you doing here, just passing through?
Messenger: Watching over my flocks, grazing them on the slopes.
Oedipus: A herdsman, were you? A vagabond, scraping for wages?
Messenger: Your savior too, my son, in your worst hour.
Oedipus: Oh —
    when you picked me up, was I in pain? What exactly?   1130
Messenger: Your ankles . . . they tell the story. Look at them.
Oedipus: Why remind me of that, that old affliction?
Messenger: Your ankles were pinned together; I set you free.
Oedipus: That dreadful mark — I've had it from the cradle.
Messenger: And you got your name from that misfortune too,   1135
    the name's still with you.
Oedipus: Dear god, who did it? —
    mother? father? Tell me.
Messenger: I don't know.
    The one who gave you to me, he'd know more.
Oedipus: What? You took me from someone else?
    You didn't find me yourself?
Messenger: No sir,   1140
    another shepherd passed you on to me.
Oedipus: Who? Do you know? Describe him.
Messenger: He called himself a servant of . . .
    if I remember rightly — Laius.

    Jocasta turns sharply.

Oedipus: The king of the land who ruled here long ago?   1145
Messenger: That's the one. That herdsman was *his* man.
Oedipus: Is he still alive? Can I see him?
Messenger: They'd know best, the people of these parts.

Oedipus and the Messenger turn to the Chorus.

Oedipus: Does anyone know that herdsman,
      the one he mentioned? Anyone seen him   1150
      in the fields, in town? Out with it!
      The time has come to reveal this once for all.
Leader: I think he's the very shepherd you wanted to see,
      a moment ago. But the queen, Jocasta,
      she's the one to say.
Oedipus: Jocasta,   1155
      you remember the man we just sent for?
      Is *that* the one he means?
Jocasta: That man . . .
      why ask? Old shepherd, talk, empty nonsense,
      don't give it another thought, don't even think —
Oedipus: What — give up now, with a clue like this?   1160
      Fail to solve the mystery of my birth?
      Not for all the world!
Jocasta: Stop — in the name of god,
      if you love your own life, call off this search!
      My suffering is enough.
Oedipus: Courage!
      Even if my mother turns out to be a slave,   1165
      and I a slave, three generations back,
      you would not seem common.
Jocasta: Oh no,
      listen to me, I beg you, don't do this.
Oedipus: Listen to you? No more. I must know it all,
      see the truth at last.
Jocasta: No, please —   1170
      for your sake — I want the best for you!
Oedipus: Your best is more than I can bear.
Jocasta: You're doomed —
      may you never fathom who you are!
Oedipus:

To a servant.

      Hurry, fetch me the herdsman, now!
      Leave her to glory in her royal birth.   1175
Jocasta: Aieeeeee —
                    man of agony —
      that is the only name I have for you,
      that, no other — ever, ever, ever!

Flinging (herself) through the palace doors. A long, tense silence follows.

Leader: Where's she gone, Oedipus?
      Rushing off, such wild grief . . .   1180

I'm afraid that from this silence
something monstrous may come bursting forth.
Oedipus: Let it burst! Whatever will, whatever must!
I must know my birth, no matter how common
it may be—must see my origins face-to-face.   1185
She perhaps, she with her woman's pride
may well be mortified by my birth,
but I, I count myself the son of Chance,
the great goddess, giver of all good things—
I'll never see myself disgraced. She is my mother!   1190
And the moons have marked me out, my blood-brothers,
one moon on the wane, the next moon great with power.
That is my blood, my nature—I will never betray it,
never fail to search and learn my birth!
Chorus: Yes—if I am a true prophet   1195
             if I can grasp the truth,
        by the boundless skies of Olympus,
at the full moon of tomorrow, Mount Cithaeron
you will know how Oedipus glories in you—
you, his birthplace, nurse, his mountain-mother!   1200
And we will sing you, dancing out your praise—
you lift our monarch's heart!
        Apollo, Apollo, god of the wild cry
                may our dancing please you!
                                                        Oedipus—
                son, dear child, who bore you?   1205
Who of the nymphs who seem to live forever
mated with Pan,° the mountain-striding Father?
Who was your mother? who, some bride of Apollo
the god who loves the pastures spreading toward the sun?
        Or was it Hermes, king of the lightning ridges?   1210
Or Dionysus, lord of frenzy, lord of the barren peaks—
did he seize you in his hands, dearest of all his lucky finds?—
        found by the nymphs, their warm eyes dancing, gift
to the lord who loves them dancing out his joy!

*Oedipus strains to see a figure coming from the distance. Attended by palace
guards, an old Shepherd enters slowly, reluctant to approach the king.*

Oedipus: I never met the man, my friends . . . still,   1215
        if I had to guess, I'd say that's the shepherd,
        the very one we've looked for all along.
        Brothers in old age, two of a kind,
        he and our guest here. At any rate

1207 *Pan:* God of shepherds, who was, like Hermes and Dionysus, associated with
the wilderness.

the ones who bring him in are my own men,   1220
I recognize them.

Turning to the Leader.

But you know more than I,
you should, you've seen the man before.

Leader: I know him, definitely. One of Laius' men,
a trusty shepherd, if there ever was one.

Oedipus: You, I ask you first, stranger,   1225
you from Corinth — is this the one you mean?

Messenger: You're looking at him. He's your man.

Oedipus:

To the Shepherd.

You, old man, come over here —
look at me. Answer all my questions.
Did you ever serve King Laius?

Shepherd: So I did . . .   1230
a slave, not bought on the block though,
born and reared in the palace.

Oedipus: Your duties, your kind of work?

Shepherd: Herding the flocks, the better part of my life.

Oedipus: Where, mostly? Where did you do your grazing?

Shepherd: Well,   1235
Cithaeron sometimes, or the foothills round about.

Oedipus: This man — you know him? ever see him there?

Shepherd:

Confused, glancing from the Messenger to the King.

Doing what — what man do you mean?

Oedipus:

Pointing to the Messenger.

This one here — ever have dealings with him?

Shepherd: Not so I could say, but give me a chance,   1240
my memory's bad . . .

Messenger: No wonder he doesn't know me, master.
But let me refresh his memory for him.
I'm sure he recalls old times we had
on the slopes of Mount Cithaeron;   1245
he and I, grazing our flocks, he with two
and I with one — we both struck up together,
three whole seasons, six months at a stretch
from spring to the rising of Arcturus° in the fall,
then with winter coming on I'd drive my herds   1250

1249 *Arcturus:* A star whose rising marked the end of summer.

to my own pens, and back he'd go with his
to Laius' folds.

To the Shepherd.

Now that's how it was,
wasn't it—yes or no?
Shepherd: Yes, I suppose . . .
   it's all so long ago.
Messenger: Come, tell me,
   you gave me a child back then, a boy, remember?   1255
   A little fellow to rear, my very own.
Shepherd: What? Why rake up that again?
Messenger: Look, here he is, my fine old friend—
   the same man who was just a baby then.
Shepherd: Damn you, shut your mouth—quiet!   1260
Oedipus: Don't lash out at him, old man—
   you need lashing more than he does.
Shepherd: Why,
   master, majesty—what have I done wrong?
Oedipus: You won't answer his question about the boy.
Shepherd: He's talking nonsense, wasting his breath.   1265
Oedipus: So, you won't talk willingly—
   then you'll talk with pain.

The guards seize the Shepherd.

Shepherd: No, dear god, don't torture an old man!
Oedipus: Twist his arms back, quickly!
Shepherd: God help us, why?—
   what more do you need to know?   1270
Oedipus: Did you give him that child? He's asking.
Shepherd: I did . . . I wish to god I'd died that day.
Oedipus: You've got your wish if you don't tell the truth.
Shepherd: The more I tell, the worse the death I'll die.
Oedipus: Our friend here wants to stretch things out, does he?   1275

Motioning to his men for torture.

Shepherd: No, no, I gave it to him—I just said so.
Oedipus: Where did you get it? Your house? Someone else's?
Shepherd: It wasn't mine, no, I got it from . . . someone.
Oedipus: Which one of them?

Looking at the citizens.

Whose house?
Shepherd: No—
   god's sake, master, no more questions!   1280
Oedipus: You're a dead man if I have to ask again.

Shepherd: Then — the child came from the house . . .
        of Laius.
Oedipus: A slave? or born of his own blood?
Shepherd: Oh no,
        I'm right at the edge, the horrible truth — I've got to say it!
Oedipus: And I'm at the edge of hearing horrors, yes, but I must hear!   1285
Shepherd: All right! His son, they said it was — his son!
        But the one inside, your wife,
        she'd tell it best.
Oedipus: My wife —
        she gave it to you?   1290
Shepherd: Yes, yes, my king.
Oedipus: Why, what for?
Shepherd: To kill it.
Oedipus: Her own child,
        how could she?   1295
Shepherd: She was afraid —
        frightening prophecies.
Oedipus: What?
Shepherd: They said —
        he'd kill his parents.   1300
Oedipus: But you gave him to this old man — why?
Shepherd: I pitied the little baby, master,
        hoped he'd take him off to his own country,
        far away, but he saved him for this, this fate.
        If you are the man he says you are, believe me,   1305
        you were born for pain.
Oedipus: O god —
        all come true, all burst to light!
        O light — now let me look my last on you!
        I stand revealed at last —
        cursed in my birth, cursed in marriage,   1310
        cursed in the lives I cut down with these hands!

*Rushing through the doors with a great cry. The Corinthian Messenger, the
Shepherd, and attendants exit slowly to the side.*

Chorus: O the generations of men
        the dying generations — adding the total
        of all your lives I find they come to nothing . . .
                does there exist, is there a man on earth   1315
        who seizes more joy than just a dream, a vision?
        And the vision no sooner dawns than dies
        blazing into oblivion.
        You are my great example, you, your life,
        your destiny, Oedipus, man of misery —   1320
        I count no man blest.

You outranged all men!
　　　Bending your bow to the breaking-point
you captured priceless glory, O dear god,
and the Sphinx came crashing down,
　　　　　　the virgin, claws hooked   1325
like a bird of omen singing, shrieking death —
like a fortress reared in the face of death
you rose and saved our land.

From that day on we called you king
we crowned you with honors, Oedipus, towering over all —   1330
mighty king of the seven gates of Thebes.

But now to hear your story — is there a man more agonized?
More wed to pain and frenzy? Not a man on earth,
the joy of your life ground down to nothing
O Oedipus, name for the ages —   1335
　　　one and the same wide harbor served you
　　　　　　　　　　son and father both
son and father came to rest in the same bridal chamber.
How, how could the furrows your father plowed
bear you, your agony, harrowing on   1340
in silence O so long?
　　　　　　　But now for all your power
Time, all-seeing Time has dragged you to the light,
judged your marriage monstrous from the start —
the son and the father tangling, both one —
O child of Laius, would to god   1345
　　　I'd never seen you, never never!
　　　　　Now I weep like a man who wails the dead
and the dirge comes pouring forth with all my heart!
I tell you the truth, you gave me life
my breath leapt up in you   1350
and now you bring down night upon my eyes.

Enter a Messenger from the palace.

Messenger: Men of Thebes, always the first in honor,
　　　what horrors you will hear, what you will see,
　　　what a heavy weight of sorrow you will shoulder . . .
　　　if you are true to your birth, if you still have   1355
　　　some feeling for the royal house of Thebes.
　　　I tell you neither the waters of the Danube
　　　nor the Nile can wash this palace clean.
　　　Such things it hides, it soon will bring to light —
　　　terrible things, and none done blindly now,   1360
　　　all done with a will. The pains

we inflict upon ourselves hurt most of all.
Leader: God knows we have pains enough already.
     What can you add to them?
Messenger: The queen is dead.
Leader: Poor lady—how?   1365
Messenger: By her own hand. But you are spared the worst,
     you never had to watch . . . I saw it all,
     and with all the memory that's in me
     you will learn what that poor woman suffered.

Once she'd broken in through the gates,   1370
dashing past us, frantic, whipped to fury,
ripping her hair out with both hands—
straight to her rooms she rushed, flinging herself
across the bridal-bed, doors slamming behind her—
once inside, she wailed for Laius, dead so long,   1375
remembering how she bore his child long ago,
the life that rose up to destroy him, leaving
its mother to mother living creatures
with the very son she'd borne.
Oh how she wept, mourning the marriage-bed   1380
where she let loose that double brood—monsters—
husband by her husband, children by her child.
                              And then—
but how she died is more than I can say. Suddenly
Oedipus burst in, screaming, he stunned us so
we couldn't watch her agony to the end,   1385
our eyes were fixed on him. Circling
like a maddened beast, stalking, here, there
crying out to us—
                              Give him a sword! His wife,
no wife, his mother, where can he find the mother earth
that cropped two crops at once, himself and all his children?   1390
He was raging—one of the dark powers pointing the way,
none of us mortals crowding around him, no,
with a great shattering cry—someone, something leading him on—
he hurled at the twin doors and bending the bolts back
out of their sockets, crashed through the chamber.   1395
And there we saw the woman hanging by the neck,
cradled high in a woven noose, spinning,
swinging back and forth. And when he saw her,
giving a low, wrenching sob that broke our hearts,
slipping the halter from her throat, he eased her down,   1400
in a slow embrace he laid her down, poor thing . . .
then, what came next, what horror we beheld!
He rips off her brooches, the long gold pins

holding her robes — and lifting them high,
looking straight up into the points,   1405
he digs them down the sockets of his eyes, crying, "You,
you'll see no more the pain I suffered, all the pain I caused!
Too long you looked on the ones you never should have seen,
blind to the ones you longed to see, to know! Blind
from this hour on! Blind in the darkness — blind!"   1410
His voice like a dirge, rising, over and over
raising the pins, raking them down his eyes.
And at each stroke blood spurts from the roots,
splashing his beard, a swirl of it, nerves and clots —
black hail of blood pulsing, gushing down.   1415

These are the griefs that burst upon them both,
coupling man and woman. The joy they had so lately,
the fortune of their old ancestral house
was deep joy indeed. Now, in this one day,
wailing, madness and doom, death, disgrace,   1420
all the griefs in the world that you can name,
all are theirs forever.

Leader: Oh poor man, the misery —
has he any rest from pain now?

A voice within, in torment.

Messenger: He's shouting,
"Loose the bolts, someone, show me to all of Thebes!
My father's murderer, my mother's —"   1425
No, I can't repeat it, it's unholy.
Now he'll tear himself from his native earth,
not linger, curse the house with his own curse.
But he needs strength, and a guide to lead him on.
This is sickness more than he can bear.

The palace doors open.

                                    Look,   1430
he'll show you himself. The great doors are opening —
you are about to see a sight, a horror
even his mortal enemy would pity.

*Enter Oedipus, blinded, led by a boy. He stands at the palace steps, as if
surveying his people once again.*

Chorus: O the terror —
the suffering, for all the world to see,
the worst terror that ever met my eyes.   1435
What madness swept over you? What god,
what dark power leapt beyond all bounds,

beyond belief, to crush your wretched life? —
godforsaken, cursed by the gods!
I pity you but I can't bear to look.   1440
I've much to ask, so much to learn,
so much fascinates my eyes,
but you . . . I shudder at the sight.

Oedipus: Oh, Ohhh —
the agony! I am agony —
where am I going? where on earth?   1445
            where does all this agony hurl me?
where's my voice? —
            winging, swept away on a dark tide —
My destiny, my dark power, what a leap you made!

Chorus: To the depths of terror, too dark to hear, to see.   1450

Oedipus: Dark, horror of darkness
my darkness, drowning, swirling around me
crashing wave on wave — unspeakable, irresistible
            headwind, fatal harbor! Oh again,
the misery, all at once, over and over   1455
the stabbing daggers, stab of memory
raking me insane.

Chorus: No wonder you suffer
twice over, the pain of your wounds,
the lasting grief of pain.

Oedipus: Dear friend, still here?
Standing by me, still with a care for me,   1460
the blind man? Such compassion,
            loyal to the last. Oh it's you,
I know you're here, dark as it is
I'd know you anywhere, your voice —
it's yours, clearly yours.

Chorus: Dreadful, what you've done . . .   1465
how could you bear it, gouging out your eyes?
What superhuman power drove you on?

Oedipus: Apollo, friends, Apollo —
he ordained my agonies — these, my pains on pains!
But the hand that struck my eyes was mine,   1470
mine alone — no one else —
            I did it all myself!
What good were eyes to me?
Nothing I could see could bring me joy.

Chorus: No, no, exactly as you say.

Oedipus: What can I ever see?   1475
            What love, what call of the heart
can touch my ears with joy? Nothing, friends.
            Take me away, far, far from Thebes,

quickly, cast me away, my friends —
   this great murderous ruin, this man cursed to heaven,   1480
      the man the deathless gods hate most of all!
Chorus: Pitiful, you suffer so, you understand so much . . .
   I wish you'd never known.
Oedipus: Die, die —
   whoever he was that day in the wilds
   who cut my ankles free of the ruthless pins,   1485
      he pulled me clear of death, he saved my life
      for this, this kindness —
            Curse him, kill him!
      If I'd died then, I'd never have dragged myself,
      my loved ones through such hell.   1490
Chorus: Oh if only . . . would to god.
Oedipus: I'd never have come to this,
      my father's murderer — never been branded
      mother's husband, all men see me now! Now,
         loathed by the gods, son of the mother I defiled
         coupling in my father's bed, spawning lives in the loins   1495
   that spawned my wretched life. What grief can crown this grief?
               It's mine alone, my destiny — I am Oedipus!
Chorus: How can I say you've chosen for the best?
   Better to die than be alive and blind.
Oedipus: What I did was best — don't lecture me,   1500
   no more advice. I, with *my* eyes,
   how could I look my father in the eyes
   when I go down to death? Or mother, so abused . . .
   I've done such things to the two of them,
   crimes too huge for hanging.
                  Worse yet,   1505
   the sight of my children, born as they were born,
   how could I long to look into their eyes?
   No, not with these eyes of mine, never.
   Not this city either, her high towers,
   the sacred glittering images of her gods —   1510
   I am misery! I, her best son, reared
   as no other son of Thebes was ever reared,
   I've stripped myself, I gave the command myself.
   All men must cast away the great blasphemer,
   the curse now brought to light by the gods,   1515
   the son of Laius — I, my father's son!

Now I've exposed my guilt, horrendous guilt,
   could I train a level glance on you, my countrymen?
   Impossible! No, if I could just block off my ears,
   the springs of hearing, I would stop at nothing —   1520

I'd wall up my loathsome body like a prison,
blind to the sound of life, not just the sight.
Oblivion — what a blessing . . .
for the mind to dwell a world away from pain.

O Cithaeron, why did you give me shelter?   1525
Why didn't you take me, crush my life out on the spot?
I'd never have revealed my birth to all mankind.

O Polybus, Corinth, the old house of my fathers,
so I believed — what a handsome prince you raised —
under the skin, what sickness to the core.   1530
Look at me! Born of outrage, outrage to the core.

O triple roads — it all comes back, the secret,
dark ravine, and the oaks closing in
where the three roads join . . .
You drank my father's blood, my own blood   1535
spilled by my own hands — you still remember me?
What things you saw me do? Then I came here
and did them all once more!
                            Marriages! O marriage,
you gave me birth, and once you brought me into the world
you brought my sperm rising back, springing to light   1540
fathers, brothers, sons — one deadly breed —
brides, wives, mothers. The blackest things
a man can do, I have done them all!
                                No more —
it's wrong to name what's wrong to do. Quickly,
for the love of god, hide me somewhere,   1545
kill me, hurl me into the sea
where you can never look on me again.

Beckoning to the Chorus as they shrink away.

                                Closer,
it's all right. Touch the man of sorrow.
Do. Don't be afraid. My troubles are mine
and I am the only man alive who can sustain them.   1550

Enter Creon from the palace, attended by palace guards.

Leader: Put your requests to Creon. Here he is,
just when we need him. He'll have a plan, he'll act.
Now that he's the sole defense of the country
in your place.
Oedipus: Oh no, what can I say to him?
How can I ever hope to win his trust?   1555

I wronged him so, just now, in every way.
You must see that—I was so wrong, so wrong.
Creon: I haven't come to mock you, Oedipus,
or to criticize your former failings.

Turning to the guards.

                         You there,
have you lost all respect for human feeling?   1560
At least revere the Sun, the holy fire
that keeps us all alive. Never expose a thing
of guilt and holy dread so great it appalls
the earth, the rain from heaven, the light of day!
Get him into the halls—quickly as you can.   1565
Piety demands no less. Kindred alone
should see a kinsman's shame. This is obscene.
Oedipus: Please, in god's name . . . you wipe my fears away,
coming so generously to me, the worst of men.
Do one thing more, for your sake, not mine.   1570
Creon: What do you want? Why so insistent?
Oedipus: Drive me out of the land at once, far from sight,
where I can never hear a human voice.
Creon: I'd have done that already, I promise you.
First I wanted the god to clarify my duties.   1575
Oedipus: The god? His command was clear, every word:
death for the father-killer, the curse—
he said destroy me!
Creon: So he did. Still, in such a crisis
it's better to ask precisely what to do.   1580
Oedipus: You'd ask the oracle about a man like me?
Creon: By all means. And this time, I assume,
even you will obey the god's decrees.
Oedipus: I will,
I will. And you, I command you—I beg you . . .
the woman inside, bury her as you see fit.   1585
It's the only decent thing,
to give your own the last rites. As for me,
never condemn the city of my fathers
to house my body, not while I'm alive, no,
let me live on the mountains, on Cithaeron,   1590
my favorite haunt, I have made it famous.
Mother and father marked out that rock
to be my everlasting tomb—buried alive.
Let me die there, where they tried to kill me.
Oh but this I know: no sickness can destroy me,   1595
nothing can. I would never have been saved
from death—I have been saved

for something great and terrible, something strange.
Well let my destiny come and take me on its way!

About my children, Creon, the boys at least,   1600
don't burden yourself. They're men;
wherever they go, they'll find the means to live.
But my two daughters, my poor helpless girls,
clustering at our table, never without me
hovering near them . . . whatever I touched,   1605
they always had their share. Take care of them,
I beg you. Wait, better — permit me, would you?
Just to touch them with my hands and take
our fill of tears. Please . . . my king.
Grant it, with all your noble heart.   1610
If I could hold them, just once, I'd think
I had them with me, like the early days
when I could see their eyes.

Antigone and Ismene, two small children, are led in from the palace by a
nurse.

                              What's that?
O god! Do I really hear you sobbing? —
my two children. Creon, you've pitied me?   1615
Sent me my darling girls, my own flesh and blood!
Am I right?
Creon: Yes, it's my doing.
I know the joy they gave you all these years,
the joy you must feel now.
Oedipus: Bless you, Creon!
May god watch over you for this kindness,   1620
better than he ever guarded me.
                              Children, where are you?
Here, come quickly —

Groping for Antigone and Ismene, who approach their father cautiously,
then embrace him.

                    Come to these hands of mine,
your brother's hands, your own father's hands
that served his once bright eyes so well —
that made them blind. Seeing nothing, children,   1625
knowing nothing, I became your father,
I fathered you in the soil that gave me life.

How I weep for you — I cannot see you now . . .
just thinking of all your days to come, the bitterness,
the life that rough mankind will thrust upon you.   1630

Where are the public gatherings you can join,
the banquets of the clans? Home you'll come,
in tears, cut off from the sight of it all,
the brilliant rites unfinished.
And when you reach perfection, ripe for marriage,   1635
who will he be, my dear ones? Risking all
to shoulder the curse that weighs down my parents,
yes and you too — that wounds us all together.
What more misery could you want?
Your father killed his father, sowed his mother,   1640
one, one and the selfsame womb sprang you —
he cropped the very roots of his existence.
Such disgrace, and you must bear it all!
Who will marry you then? Not a man on earth.
Your doom is clear: you'll wither away to nothing,   1645
single, without a child.

Turning to Creon.

                    Oh Creon,
you are the only father they have now . . .
we who brought them into the world
are gone, both gone at a stroke —
Don't let them go begging, abandoned,   1650
women without men. Your own flesh and blood!
Never bring them down to the level of my pains.
Pity them. Look at them, so young, so vulnerable,
shorn of everything — you're their only hope.
Promise me, noble Creon, touch my hand.   1655

Reaching toward Creon, who draws back.

You, little ones, if you were old enough
to understand, there is much I'd tell you.
Now, as it is, I'd have you say a prayer.
Pray for life, my children,
live where you are free to grow and season.   1660
Pray god you find a better life than mine,
the father who begot you.
Creon: Enough.
You've wept enough. Into the palace now.
Oedipus: I must, but I find it very hard.
Creon: Time is the great healer, you will see.   1665
Oedipus: I am going — you know on what condition?
Creon: Tell me. I'm listening.
Oedipus: Drive me out of Thebes, in exile.
Creon: Not I. Only the gods can give you that.
Oedipus: Surely the gods hate me so much —   1670

Creon: You'll get your wish at once.
Oedipus: You consent?
Creon: I try to say what I mean; it's my habit.
Oedipus: Then take me away. It's time.
Creon: Come along, let go of the children.
Oedipus: No—
don't take them away from me, not now! No no no!   1675

*Clutching his daughters as the guards wrench them loose and take them
through the palace doors.*

Creon: Still the king, the master of all things?
No more: here your power ends.
None of your power follows you through life.

*Exit Oedipus and Creon to the palace. The Chorus comes forward to address
the audience directly.*

Chorus: People of Thebes, my countrymen, look on Oedipus.
He solved the famous riddle with his brilliance,   1680
he rose to power, a man beyond all power.
Who could behold his greatness without envy?
Now what a black sea of terror has overwhelmed him.
Now as we keep our watch and wait the final day,
count no man happy till he dies, free of pain at last.   1685

Exit in procession.

CONSIDERATIONS FOR CRITICAL THINKING AND WRITING

1. **FIRST RESPONSE.** Is it possible for a twenty-first-century reader to
    identify with Oedipus's plight? What philosophic issues does he
    confront?

2. In the opening scene what does the priest's speech reveal about how
    Oedipus has been regarded as a ruler of Thebes?

3. What do Oedipus's confrontations with Tiresias and Creon indi-
    cate about his character?

4. Aristotle defined a tragic flaw as consisting of "error and frailties."
    What errors does Oedipus make? What are his frailties?

5. What causes Oedipus's downfall? Is he simply a pawn in a predeter-
    mined game played by the gods? Can he be regarded as responsible
    for the suffering and death in the play?

6. Locate instances of dramatic irony in the play. How do they serve as
    foreshadowings?

7. Describe the function of the Chorus. How does the Chorus's view
    of life and the gods differ from Jocasta's?

8. Trace the images of vision and blindness throughout the play. How
    are they related to the theme? Why does Oedipus blind himself
    instead of joining Jocasta in suicide?

9. What is your assessment of Oedipus at the end of the play? Was he foolish? Heroic? Fated? To what extent can your emotions concerning him be described as "pity and fear"?

10. **CONNECTION TO ANOTHER SELECTION.** Consider the endings of *Oedipus the King* and Shakespeare's *Othello* (p. 703). What feelings do you have about these endings? Are they irredeemably unhappy? Is there anything that suggests hope for the future at the ends of these plays?

26

William Shakespeare and Elizabethan Drama

© Bettmann/CORBIS.

Shakespeare — the nearest thing in incarnation to the eye of God.

— SIR LAURENCE OLIVIER

All the world's a stage,
And all the men and women
  merely players:
They have their exits and their
  entrances;
And one man in his time plays
  many parts . . .

— WILLIAM SHAKESPEARE

Although relatively little is known about William Shakespeare's life, his writings reveal him to have been an extraordinary man. His vitality, compassion, and insights are evident in his broad range of characters, who have fascinated generations of audiences, and his powerful use of the English language, which has been celebrated since his death nearly four centuries ago. Ben Jonson, his contemporary, rightly claimed that "he was not of an age, but for all time!" Shakespeare's plays have been produced so often and his writings read so widely that quotations from them have woven their way into our everyday conversations. If you have ever experienced "fear and trembling" because there was "something in the wind" or discovered that it was "a foregone conclusion" that you would "make a virtue of necessity," then it wouldn't be quite accurate for you to say that Shakespeare "was Greek to me" because these phrases come, respectively, from his plays *Much Ado about Nothing, Comedy of Errors, Othello, The Two Gentlemen of Verona,* and *Julius Caesar.* Many more examples could be cited, but it is enough to say that Shakespeare's art

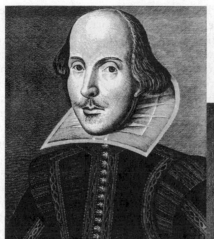

"First Folio" portrait (left). This image of William Shakespeare is a portrait included in the *First Folio,* a collected edition of Shakespeare's plays published seven years after his death. Reprinted by permission of the Folger Shakespeare Library.

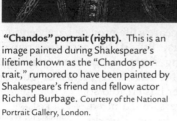

"Chandos" portrait (right). This is an image painted during Shakespeare's lifetime known as the "Chandos portrait," rumored to have been painted by Shakespeare's friend and fellow actor Richard Burbage. Courtesy of the National Portrait Gallery, London.

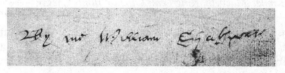

Shakespeare's signature. The signature shown here is one of the bard's six authenticated signatures in existence, and is from his last will and testament. Courtesy of the National Archives, United Kingdom.

endures. His words may give us only an oblique glimpse of his life, but they continue to give us back the experience of our own lives.

Shakespeare was born in Stratford-on-Avon on or about April 23, 1564. His father, an important citizen who held several town offices, married a woman from a prominent family; however, when their son was only a teenager, the family's financial situation became precarious. Shakespeare probably attended the Stratford grammar school, but no records of either his schooling or his early youth exist. As limited as his education was, it is clear that he was for his time a learned man. At the age of eighteen, he struck out on his own and married the twenty-six-year-old Anne Hathaway, who bore him a daughter in

1583 and twins, a boy and a girl, in 1585. Before he was twenty-one, Shakespeare had a wife and three children to support.

What his life was like for the next seven years is not known, but there is firm evidence that by 1592 he was in London enjoying some success as both an actor and a playwright. By 1594 he had also established himself as a poet with two lengthy poems, *Venus and Adonis* and *The Rape of Lucrece*. But it was in the theater that he made his living and his strongest reputation. He was well connected with a successful troupe first known as the Lord Chamberlain's Men; they built the famous Globe Theatre in 1599. Later this company, because of the patronage of King James, came to be known as the King's Men. Writing plays for this company throughout his career, Shakespeare also became one of its principal shareholders, an arrangement that allowed him to prosper in London as well as in his native Stratford, where in 1597 he bought a fine house called New Place. About 1611 he retired there with his family, although he continued writing plays. He died on April 23, 1616, and was buried at Holy Trinity Church in Stratford.

The documented details of Shakespeare's life provide barely enough information for a newspaper obituary. But if his activities remain largely unknown, his writings — among them thirty-seven plays and 154 sonnets — more than compensate for that loss. Plenty of authors have produced more work, but no writer has created so much literature that has been so universally admired. Within twenty-five years Shakespeare's dramatic works included *Hamlet, Macbeth, King Lear, Othello, Julius Caesar, Richard III, 1 Henry IV, Romeo and Juliet, Love's Labour's Lost, A Midsummer Night's Dream, The Tempest, Twelfth Night,* and *Measure for Measure*. These plays represent a broad range of characters and actions conveyed in poetic language that reveals human nature as well as the author's genius.

Explore contexts for William Shakespeare at bedfordstmartins.com/meyerlit.

SHAKESPEARE'S THEATER

Drama languished in Europe after the fall of Rome during the fifth and sixth centuries. From about A.D. 400 to 900 almost no record of dramatic productions exists except for those of minstrels and other entertainers, such as acrobats and jugglers, who traveled through the countryside. The Catholic church was instrumental in suppressing drama because the theater — represented by the excesses of Roman productions — was seen as subversive. No state-sponsored festivals brought people together in huge theaters the way they had in Greek and Roman times.

In the tenth century, however, the church helped revive theater by incorporating dialogues into the Mass as a means of dramatizing portions of the Gospels. These brief dialogues developed into more elaborate mystery plays, miracle plays, and morality plays, anonymous works that were created primarily to inculcate religious principles rather than to entertain. But these works also marked the reemergence of relatively large dramatic productions.

Mystery plays dramatize stories from the Bible, such as the Creation, the Fall of Adam and Eve, or the Crucifixion. The most highly regarded surviving example is *The Second Shepherd's Play* (c. 1400), which dramatizes Christ's nativity. *Miracle plays* are based on the lives of saints. An extant play of the late fifteenth century, for example, is titled *Saint Mary Magdalene*. *Morality plays* present allegorical stories in which virtues and vices are personified to teach humanity how to achieve salvation. *Everyman* (c. 1500), the most famous example, has as its central conflict every person's struggle to avoid the sins that lead to hell and practice the virtues that are rewarded in heaven.

The clergy who performed these plays gave way to trade guilds that presented them outside the church on stages featuring scenery and costumed characters. The plays' didactic content was gradually abandoned in favor of broad humor and worldly concerns. Thus by the sixteenth century religious drama had been replaced largely by secular drama.

Because theatrical productions were no longer sponsored and financed by the church or trade guilds during Shakespeare's lifetime, playwrights had to figure out ways to draw audiences willing to pay for entertainment. This necessitated some simple but important changes. Somehow, people had to be prevented from seeing a production unless they paid. Hence an enclosed space with controlled access was created. In addition, the plays had to change frequently enough to keep audiences returning, and this resulted in more experienced actors and playwrights sensitive to their audiences' tastes and interests. Plays compelling enough to attract audiences had to employ powerful writing brought to life by convincing actors in entertaining productions. Shakespeare always wrote his dramas for the stage — for audiences who would see and hear the characters. The conventions of the theater for which he wrote are important, then, for appreciating and understanding his plays. Detailed information about Elizabethan theater (theater during the reign of Elizabeth I, from 1558 to 1603) is less than abundant, but historians have pieced together a good sense of what theaters were like from sources such as drawings, building contracts, and stage directions.

Early performances of various kinds took place in the courtyards of inns and taverns. These secular entertainments attracted people of all classes. To the dismay of London officials, such gatherings were also settings for the illegal activities of brawlers, thieves, and prostitutes. To avoid licensing regulations, some theaters were constructed outside the city's limits. The Globe, for instance, built by the Lord Chamberlain's Company, with which Shakespeare was closely associated, was located on

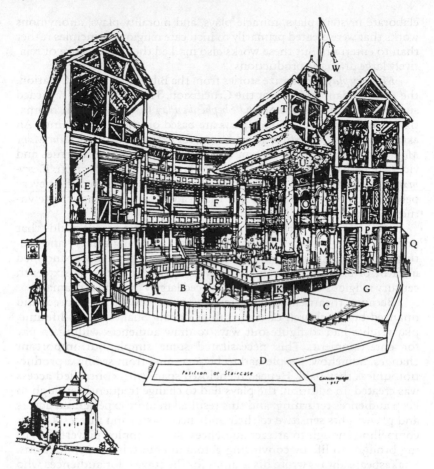

A   Main entrance
B   The yard
C   Entrances to lowest gallery
D   Position of entrances to staircase and upper galleries
E   Corridor serving the different sections of the middle gallery
F   Middle gallery ("Twopenny Rooms")
G   Position of "Gentlemen's Rooms" or "Lords' Rooms"
H   The stage
J   The hanging being put up round the stage
K   The "hell" under the stage
L   The stage trap leading down to the hell

M   Stage doors
N   Curtained "place behind the stage"
O   Gallery above the stage, used as required sometimes by musicians, sometimes by spectators, and often as part of the play
P   Backstage area (the tiring-house)
Q   Tiring-house door
R   Dressing-rooms
S   Wardrobe and storage
T   The hut housing the machine for lowering enthroned gods, etc., to the stage
U   The "heavens"
W   Hoisting the playhouse flag

A Conjectural Reconstruction of the Globe Theatre, 1599–1613. (Drawing by C. Walter Hodges from his *The Globe Restored*, published by Oxford University Press © 1968 C. Walter Hodges. Reprinted by permission of Oxford University Press.)

the south bank of the Thames River. Regardless of the play, an Elizabethan theatergoer was likely to have an exciting time. Playwrights understood the varied nature of their audiences, so the plays appealed to a broad range of sensibilities and tastes. Philosophy and poetry rubbed shoulders with violence and sexual jokes, and somehow all were made compatible.

Physically, Elizabethan theaters resembled the courtyards where they originated, but the theaters could accommodate more people — perhaps as many as twenty-five hundred. The exterior of a theater building was many-sided or round and enclosed a yard that was only partially roofed over, to take advantage of natural light. The interior walls consisted of three galleries of seats looking onto a platform stage that extended from the rear wall. These seats were sheltered from the weather and more comfortable than the area in front of the stage, which was known as the *pit.* Here "groundlings" paid a penny to stand and watch the performance. Despite the large number of spectators, the theater created an intimate atmosphere because the audience closely surrounded the stage on three sides.

This arrangement produced two theatrical conventions: asides and soliloquies. An *aside* is a speech directed only to the audience. It makes the audience privy to a character's thoughts, allowing them to perceive ironies and intrigues that other characters know nothing about. In a large performing space, such as a Greek amphitheater, asides would be unconvincing because they would have to be declaimed loudly to be heard, but they were well suited to Elizabethan theaters. A *soliloquy* is a speech delivered while an actor is alone on the stage; like an aside, it reveals a character's state of mind. Hamlet's "To be or not to be" speech is the most famous example of a soliloquy.

The Elizabethan platform stage was large enough — approximately twenty-five feet deep and forty feet wide — to allow a wide variety of actions, ranging from festive banquets to bloody battles. Sections of the floor could be opened or removed to create, for instance, the gravediggers' scene in *Hamlet* or to allow characters to exit through trapdoors. At the rear of the platform an inner stage was covered by curtains that could be drawn to reveal an interior setting, such as a bedroom or tomb. The curtains were also a natural location for a character to hide in order to overhear conversations. On each side of the curtains were doors through which characters entered and exited. An upper stage could be used as a watchtower, a castle wall, or a balcony. Although most of the action occurred on the main platform stage, there were opportunities for fluid movements from one acting area to another, providing a variety of settings.

These settings were not, however, elaborately indicated by scenery or props. A scene might change when one group of characters left the stage and another entered. A table and some chairs could be carried on quickly to suggest a tavern. But the action was not interrupted for set changes.

Instead, the characters' speeches often identify the location of a scene. (In modern editions of Shakespeare's plays, editors indicate in brackets the scene breaks, settings, and movements of actors not identified in the original manuscripts to help readers keep track of things.) Today's performances of the plays frequently use more elaborate settings and props. But Shakespeare's need to paint his scenery with words resulted in many poetic descriptions. Here is one of moonlight from *Merchant of Venice:*

> How sweet the moonlight sleeps upon this bank!
> Here will we sit and let the sounds of music
> Creep in our ears. Soft stillness and the night
> Become the touches of sweet harmony.

Although the settings were scant and the props mostly limited to what an actor carried onto the stage (a sword, a document, a shovel), Elizabethan costuming was an elaborate visual treat that identified the characters. Moreover, because women were not permitted to act in the theater, their roles were played by boys dressed in female costumes. In addition, elaborate sound effects were used to create atmosphere. A flourish of trumpets might accompany the entrance of a king; small cannons might be heard during a battle; thunder might punctuate a storm. In short, Elizabethan theater was alive with sights and sounds, but at the center of the stage was the playwright's language; that's where the magic began.

THE RANGE OF SHAKESPEARE'S DRAMA: HISTORY, COMEDY, AND TRAGEDY

Shakespeare's plays fall into three basic categories: histories, comedies, and tragedies. Broadly speaking, a history play is any drama based on historical materials. In this case, Shakespeare's *Antony and Cleopatra* and *Julius Caesar* would fit the definition, since they feature historical figures. More specifically, though, a history play is a British play based primarily on Raphael Holinshed's *Chronicles of England, Scotland, and Ireland* (1578). This account of British history was popular toward the end of the sixteenth century because of the patriotic pride that was produced by the British defeat of the Spanish Armada in 1588, and it was an important source for a series of plays Shakespeare wrote treating the reigns of British kings from Richard II to Henry VIII. The political subject matter of these plays both entertained audiences and instructed them in virtues and vices involved in England's past efforts to overcome civil war and disorder. Ambition, deception, and treason were of more than historical interest. Shakespeare's audiences saw these plays about the fifteenth century as ways of sorting through the meanings of both the calamities of the past and the uncertainties of the present.

Although Shakespeare used Holinshed's *Chronicles* as a source, he did not hesitate to make changes for dramatic purposes. In *1 Henry IV*, for example, he ages Henry IV to contrast him with the youthful Prince Hal, and he makes Hotspur younger than he actually was to have him serve as a foil to the prince. The serious theme of Hal's growth into the kind of man who would make an ideal king is counterweighted by Shakespeare's comic creation of Falstaff, that good-humored "huge hill of flesh" filled with delightful contradictions. Falstaff had historic antecedents, but the true source of his identity is the imagination of Shakespeare, a writer who was, after all, a dramatist first.

Comedy is a strong element in *1 Henry IV*, but the play's overall tone is serious. Falstaff's behavior ultimately gives way to the measured march of English history. While Shakespeare encourages us to laugh at some of the participants, we are not invited to laugh at the history of English monarchies. Comedy even appears in Shakespeare's tragedies, as in Hamlet's jests with the gravediggers or in Emilia's biting remarks in *Othello*. This use of comedy is called *comic relief*, a humorous scene or incident that alleviates tension in an otherwise serious work. In many instances these moments enhance the thematic significance of the story in addition to providing laughter. When Hamlet jokes with the gravediggers, we laugh, but something hauntingly serious about the humor also intensifies our more serious emotions.

A true comedy, however, lacks a tragedy's sense that some great disaster will finally descend on the protagonist. There are conflicts and obstacles that must be confronted, but in comedy the characters delight us by overcoming whatever initially thwarts them. We can laugh at their misfortunes because we are confident that everything will turn out fine in the end. Shakespearean comedy tends to follow this general principle; it begins with problems and ends with their resolution.

Shakespeare's comedies are called *romantic comedies* because they typically involve lovers whose hearts are set on each other but whose lives are complicated by disapproving parents, deceptions, jealousies, illusions, confused identities, disguises, or other misunderstandings. Conflicts are present, but they are more amusing than threatening. This lightness is apparent in some of the comedies' titles: The conflict in a play such as *A Midsummer Night's Dream* is, in a sense, *Much Ado about Nothing—As You Like It* in a comedy. Shakespeare orchestrates the problems and confusion that typify the initial plotting of a romantic comedy into harmonious wedding arrangements in the final scenes. In these comedies life is a celebration, a feast that always satisfies, because the generosity of the humor leaves us with a revived appetite for life's surprising possibilities. Discord and misunderstanding give way to concord and love. Marriage symbolizes a pledge that life itself is renewable, so we are left with a sense of new beginnings.

Although a celebration of life, comedy is also frequently used as a vehicle for criticizing human affairs. **Satire** casts a critical eye on vices and follies by holding them up to ridicule — usually to point out an absurdity so that it can be avoided or corrected. In *Twelfth Night* Malvolio is satirized for his priggishness and pomposity. He thinks himself better than almost everyone around him, but Shakespeare reveals him to be comic as well as pathetic. We come to understand what Malvolio will apparently never comprehend: that no one can take him as seriously as he takes himself. Polonius is subjected to a similar kind of scrutiny in *Hamlet*.

Malvolio's ambitious efforts to attract Olivia's affections are rendered absurd by Shakespeare's use of both high and low comedy. **High comedy** consists of verbal wit, while **low comedy** is generally associated with physical action and is less intellectual. Through puns and witty exchanges, Shakespeare's high comedy displays Malvolio's inconsistencies of character. His self-importance is deflated by low comedy. We are treated to a farce, a form of humor based on exaggerated, improbable incongruities, when the staid Malvolio is tricked into wearing bizarre clothing and behaving like a fool to win Olivia. Our laughter is Malvolio's pain, but though he has been "notoriously abus'd," vowing in the final scene to be "reveng'd on the whole pack" of laughing conspirators who have tricked him, the play ends on a light note. Indeed, it concludes with a song, the last line of which reminds us of the predominant tone of the play as well as the nature of comedy: "And we'll strive to please you every day."

Tragedy, in contrast, does not promise peace and contentment. The basic characteristics of tragedy have already been outlined in the context of Greek drama (see Chapter 25). Like Greek tragic heroes, Shakespeare's protagonists are exceptional human beings whose stature makes their misfortune all the more dramatic. These characters pay a high price for their actions. Oedipus's search for the killer of Laius, Hamlet's agonized conviction that "The time is out of joint," and Othello's willingness to doubt his wife's fidelity all lead to irreversible results. Comic plots are largely free of this sense of inevitability. Instead of the festive mood that prevails once the characters in a comedy recognize their true connection to each other, tragedy gives us dark reflections that emanate from suffering. The laughter of comedy is a shared experience, a recognition of human likeness, but suffering estranges tragic heroes from the world around them.

Some of the wrenching differences between comedy and tragedy can be experienced in *Othello*. Although this play is a tragedy, Shakespeare includes in its plot many of the ingredients associated with comedy. For a time it seems possible that Othello and Desdemona will overcome the complications of a disapproving father, along with the seemingly minor deceptions, awkward misperceptions, and tender illusions that hover around them. But in *Othello* marriage is not a sign of concord displacing discord; instead, love and marriage mark the beginning of the tragic action.

A NOTE ON READING SHAKESPEARE

Readers who have had no previous experience with Shakespeare's language may find it initially daunting. They might well ask whether people ever talked the way, for example, Hamlet does in his most famous soliloquy:

> To be, or not to be: that is the question:
> Whether 'tis nobler in the mind to suffer
> The slings and arrows of outrageous fortune,
> Or to take arms against a sea of troubles,
> And by opposing end them?

People did not talk like this in Elizabethan times. Hamlet speaks in poetry. Shakespeare might have had him say something like this: "The most important issue one must confront is whether the pain that life inevitably creates should be passively accepted or resisted." But Shakespeare chose poetry to reveal the depth and complexity of Hamlet's experience. This heightened language is used to clarify rather than obscure his characters' thoughts. Shakespeare has Hamlet, as well as many other characters, speak in prose too, but in general his plays are written in poetry. If you keep in mind that Shakespeare's dialogue is not typically intended to imitate everyday speech, it should be easier to understand that his language is more than simply a vehicle for expressing the action of the play.

Here are a few practical suggestions to enhance your understanding of and pleasure in reading Shakespeare's plays.

1. Keep track of the characters by referring to the *dramatis personae* (characters) listed and described at the beginning of each play.
2. Remember that poetic language deserves to be read slowly and carefully. A difficult passage can sometimes be better understood if it's read aloud. Don't worry if every line isn't absolutely clear to you.
3. Pay attention to the annotations, which explain unfamiliar words, phrases, and allusions in the text. These can be distracting, but they are sometimes necessary to determine the basic meaning of a passage.
4. As you read each scene, try to imagine how it would be played on a stage.
5. If you find the reading especially difficult, try listening to a recording of the play. (Most college libraries have recordings of Shakespeare's plays.) Allowing professional actors to do the reading aloud for you can enrich your imaginative reconstruction of the action and characters. Hearing a play can help you with subsequent readings of it.
6. After reading the play, view a film or DVD recording of a performance. It is important to view the performance *after* your reading, though, so that your own mental re-creation of the play is not short-circuited by a director's production.

And finally, to quote Hamlet, "Be not too tame . . . let your own discretion be your tutor." Read Shakespeare's work as best you can; it warrants such careful attention not because the language and characters are difficult to understand but because they offer so much to enjoy.

Othello, the Moor of Venice

Othello has compelled audiences since it was first produced in 1604. Its power is as simple and as complex as the elemental emotions it drama- tizes; the play ebbs and flows with the emotional energy derived from the characters' struggles with love and hatred, good and evil, trust and jeal- ousy, appearance and reality. These conflicts are played out on a domes- tic scale rather than on some metaphysical level. Anyone who has ever been in love will empathize with Othello and Desdemona. They embody a love story gone horribly — tragically — wrong.

Although the plot of *Othello* is filled with Iago's intrigues and a series of opaque mysteries for Othello, it moves swiftly and precisely to its cata- strophic ending as the tragedy relentlessly claims its victims. On one level the plot is simple. As the Moorish general of the Venetian army, Othello chooses Cassio to serve as his lieutenant, a selection Iago resents and decides to subvert. To discredit Cassio, Iago poisons Othello's faith in his wife, Desdemona, by falsely insinuating that she and Cassio are having an affair. Through a series of cleverly demonic manipulations, Iago succeeds in convincing Othello of his wife's infidelity and his lieutenant's betrayal. Believing these lies, Othello insists upon taking his revenge.

If the plot of *Othello* is relatively direct and simple in its focus on Iago's manipulation of events, the play's major characters are considerably more complex. Love and jealousy are central in *Othello*. The Moor's virtues of openness and trust cause him to experience betrayal as intensely as he does love. He is distinguished by his nobility, bravery, strength, and deep sense of honor, but he is also vulnerable to the doubts Iago raises owing to his race ("I am black") and marginal status in Venetian society.

Iago, whose motivations are much deeper and more mysterious than his maneuvering for a coveted lieutenancy, personifies a nearly inexplicable evil in the play. Just as Desdemona's nature seems to be all goodness, Iago's is malignant destruction. His profound villainy both horrifies and fascinates us: How can he be what he is? He thrives on ambition, envy, deception, jealousy, and doubt. Although he commands absolutely no respect, he holds our attention because of his cunning duplicity.

The play is finally, however, Othello's story. As we watch him be seduced by Iago's veiled hints and seeming confidences, we see how his trusting nature is inextricably related to his propensity to suspect Desde- mona. Iago plays on the complexity and paradox of Othello's character and manipulates those tensions to keep him off balance and blind to the truth of Desdemona's faithfulness. Ultimately, though, Othello must take responsibility for the destruction of his love, a responsibility that is both his tragedy and redemption.

William Shakespeare (1564–1616)
Othello, the Moor of Venice   *1604*

THE NAMES OF THE ACTORS

Othello, the Moor
Brabantio, [a Venetian senator,] father to Desdemona
Cassio, an honorable lieutenant [to Othello]
Iago, [Othello's ancient,] a villain
Roderigo, a gulled gentleman
Duke of Venice
Senators [of Venice]
Montano, governor of Cyprus
Lodovico and Gratiano, [kinsmen to Brabantio,] two noble Venetians
Sailors
Clowns
Desdemona, wife to Othello
Emilia, wife to Iago
Bianca, a courtesan
[Messenger, Herald, Officers, Venetian Gentlemen, Musicians, Attendants

SCENE: *Venice and Cyprus]*

To hear a scene
from *Othello* read by
Chicago's Shakespeare
Repertory, visit
bedfordstmartins.com/
meyerlit/epages.

ACT I

SCENE I: *A street in Venice.*

> *Enter Roderigo and Iago.*

Roderigo: Tush, never tell me! I take it much unkindly
> That thou, Iago, who hast had my purse
> As if the strings were thine, shouldst know of this.°
Iago: 'Sblood,° but you'll not hear me!
> If ever I did dream of such a matter,   5
> Abhor me.
Roderigo: Thou told'st me thou didst hold him in thy hate.
Iago: Despise me if I do not. Three great ones of the city,
> In personal suit to make me his lieutenant,
> Off-capped to him;° and, by the faith of man,   10
> I know my price; I am worth no worse a place.

Act I, Scene I.   3 *this:* i.e., Desdemona's elopement.   4 *'Sblood:* By God's blood.
10 *him:* i.e., Othello.

But he, as loving his own pride and
    purposes,
Evades them with a bombast
    circumstance.°
Horribly stuffed with epithets of war;
[And, in conclusion,]
Nonsuits° my mediators; for, "Certes,"
    says he,
"I have already chose my officer."
And what was he?
Forsooth, a great arithmetician,°
One Michael Cassio, a Florentine
(A fellow almost damned in a fair wife°)
That never set a squadron in the field,
Nor the division of a battle knows
More than a spinster; unless the bookish
    theoric,
Wherein the togèd consuls can propose

Othello: Irene Jacob and Laurence
Fishburne in the 1995 film *Othello,*
directed by Oliver Parker.
© Konow Rolf/CORBIS Sygma.

As masterly as he. Mere prattle without
    practice
Is all his soldiership. But he, sir, had th'
    election;
And I (of whom his eyes had seen the proof
At Rhodes, at Cyprus, and on other grounds
Christian and heathen) must be belee'd and calmed°   30
By debitor and creditor; this counter-caster,°
He, in good time, must his lieutenant be,
And I — God bless the mark! — his Moorship's ancient.°
Roderigo: By heaven, I rather would have been his hangman.
Iago: Why, there's no remedy; 'tis the curse of service.   35
Preferment goes by letter and affection,°
And not by old gradation, where each second
Stood heir to th' first. Now, sir, be judge yourself,
Whether I in any just term am affined°
To love the Moor.
Roderigo: I would not follow him then.   40
Iago: O, sir, content you;
I follow him to serve my turn upon him.
We cannot all be masters, nor all masters
Cannot be truly followed. You shall mark
Many a duteous and knee-crooking knave   45

---

13 *a bombast circumstance:* Pompous circumlocutions.   16 *Nonsuits:* Rejects.   19 *arithmetician:* Theoretician.   21 *almost . . . wife:* (An obscure allusion; Cassio is unmarried,
but see IV.i.114).   30 *belee'd and calmed:* Left in the lurch.   31 *counter-caster:* Book-
keeper.   33 *ancient:* Ensign.   36 *affection:* Favoritism.   39 *affined:* Obliged.

That, doting on his own obsequious bondage,
Wears out his time, much like his master's ass,
For naught but provender; and when he's old, cashiered.°
Whip me such honest knaves! Others there are
Who, trimmed° in forms and visages of duty,   50
Keep yet their hearts attending on themselves;
And, throwing but shows of service on their lords,
Do well thrive by them, and when they have lined their coats,
Do themselves homage. These fellows have some soul;
And such a one do I profess myself. For, sir,   55
It is as sure as you are Roderigo,
Were I the Moor, I would not be Iago.
In following him, I follow but myself;
Heaven is my judge, not I for love and duty,
But seeming so, for my peculiar end;   60
For when my outward action doth demonstrate
The native act and figure of my heart°
In compliment extern,° 'tis not long after
But I will wear my heart upon my sleeve
For daws to peck at; I am not what I am.   65
Roderigo: What a full fortune does the thick-lips° owe°
  If he can carry't thus!
Iago: Call up her father,
  Rouse him. Make after him, poison his delight,
  Proclaim him in the streets. Incense her kinsmen,
  And though he in a fertile climate dwell,   70
  Plague him with flies; though that his joy be joy,
  Yet throw such changes of vexation on't
  As it may lose some color.
Roderigo: Here is her father's house. I'll call aloud.
Iago: Do, with like timorous° accent and dire yell   75
  As when, by night and negligence, the fire
  Is spied in populous cities.
Roderigo: What, ho, Brabantio! Signior Brabantio, ho!
Iago: Awake! What, ho, Brabantio! Thieves! thieves! thieves!
  Look to your house, your daughter, and your bags!   80
  Thieves! thieves!

  Brabantio at a window.°

Brabantio (above): What is the reason of this terrible summons?
  What is the matter there?

---

48 *cashiered:* Turned off.   50 *trimmed:* Dressed up.   62 *The . . . heart:* What I really
believe and intend.   63 *compliment extern:* Outward appearance.   66 *thick-lips:*
An Elizabethan epithet for blacks, including Moors; *owe:* Own.   75 *timorous:*
Terrifying.   *Brabantio at a window:* (added from quarto).

Roderigo: Signior, is all your family within?
Iago: Are your doors locked?
Brabantio: Why, wherefore ask you this?   85
Iago: Zounds, sir, y' are robbed! For shame, put on your gown!
   Your heart is burst; you have lost half your soul.
   Even now, now, very now, an old black ram
   Is tupping your white ewe. Arise, arise!
   Awake the snorting° citizens with the bell.   90
   Or else the devil will make a grandsire of you.
   Arise, I say!
Brabantio: What, have you lost your wits?
Roderigo: Most reverend signior, do you know my voice?
Brabantio: Not I. What are you?   95
Roderigo: My name is Roderigo.
Brabantio: The worser welcome!
   I have charged thee not to haunt about my doors.
   In honest plainness thou hast heard me say
   My daughter is not for thee; and now, in madness,
   Being full of supper and distemp'ring draughts,   100
   Upon malicious knavery dost thou come
   To start my quiet.
Roderigo: Sir, sir, sir—
Brabantio: But thou must needs be sure
   My spirit and my place have in them power   105
   To make this bitter to thee.
Roderigo: Patience, good sir.
Brabantio: What tell'st thou me of robbing? This is Venice;
   My house is not a grange.°
Roderigo: Most grave Brabantio,
   In simple and pure soul I come to you.
Iago: Zounds, sir, you are one of those that will not serve God if the   110
   devil bid you. Because we come to do you service, and you think
   we are ruffians, you'll have your daughter covered with a Bar-
   bary horse; you'll have your nephews° neigh to you; you'll have
   coursers for cousins, and gennets for germans.°
Brabantio: What profane wretch art thou?   115
Iago: I am one, sir, that comes to tell you your daughter and the
   Moor are now making the beast with two backs.
Brabantio: Thou are a villain.
Iago: You are—a senator.
Brabantio: This thou shalt answer. I know thee, Roderigo.
Roderigo: Sir, I will answer anything. But I beseech you,   120

---

90 *snorting:* Snoring.   108 *grange:* Isolated farmhouse.   113 *nephews:* i.e., grandsons.
114 *gennets for germans:* Spanish horses for near kinsmen.

If 't be your pleasure and most wise consent,
As partly I find it is, that your fair daughter,
At this odd-even° and dull watch o' th' night,
Transported, with no worse nor better guard
But with a knave of common hire, a gondolier,   125
To the gross clasps of a lascivious Moor—
If this be known to you, and your allowance,°
We then have done you bold and saucy wrongs;
But if you know not this, my manners tell me
We have your wrong rebuke. Do not believe   130
That, from the sense° of all civility,
I thus would play and trifle with your reverence.
Your daughter, if you have not given her leave,
I say again, hath made a gross revolt,
Tying her duty, beauty, wit, and fortunes   135
In an extravagant and wheeling° stranger
Of here and everywhere. Straight satisfy yourself.
If she be in her chamber, or your house,
Let loose on me the justice of the state
For thus deluding you.

Brabantio: Strike on the tinder, ho!   140
Give me a taper! Call up all my people!
This accident° is not unlike my dream.
Belief of it oppresses me already.
Light, I say! light!   *Exit [above].*

Iago: Farewell, for I must leave you.
It seems not meet, nor wholesome to my place,   145
To be produced—as, if I stay, I shall—
Against the Moor. For I do know the state,
However this may gall him with some check,°
Cannot with safety cast° him; for he's embarked
With such loud reason to the Cyprus wars,   150
Which even now stand in act,° that for their souls
Another of his fathom° they have none
To lead their business; in which regard,
Though I do hate him as I do hell-pains,
Yet, for necessity of present life,   155
I must show out a flag and sign of love,
Which is indeed but sign. That you shall surely find him,
Lead to the Sagittary° the raisèd search;
And there will I be with him. So farewell.   *Exit.*

---

123 *odd-even:* Between night and morning.   127 *allowance:* Approval.   131 *from the sense:* In violation.   136 *extravagant and wheeling:* Expatriate and roving.   142 *accident:* Occurrence.   148 *check:* Reprimand.   149 *cast:* Discharge.   151 *stand in act:* Are going on.   152 *fathom:* Capacity.   158 *Sagittary:* An inn.

Enter [below] Brabantio in his nightgown,° and Servants with torches.

Brabantio: It is too true an evil. Gone she is;   160
 And what's to come of my despisèd time
 Is naught but bitterness. Now, Roderigo,
 Where didst thou see her? — O unhappy girl! —
 With the Moor, say'st thou? — Who would be a father? —
 How didst thou know 'twas she! — O, she deceives me   165
 Past thought! — What said she to you? — Get moe° tapers!
 Raise all my kindred! — Are they married, think you?
Roderigo: Truly I think they are.
Brabantio: O heaven! How got she out? O treason of the blood!
 Fathers, from hence trust not your daughters' minds   170
 By what you see them act. Is there not charms
 By which the property° of youth and maidhood
 May be abused? Have you not read, Roderigo,
 Of some such thing?
Roderigo: Yes, sir, I have indeed.
Brabantio: Call up my brother. — O, would you had had her! — 175
 Some one way, some another. — Do you know
 Where we may apprehend her and the Moor?
Roderigo: I think I can discover him, if you please
 To get good guard and go along with me.
Brabantio: I pray you lead on. At every house I'll call;   180
 I may command at most. — Get weapons, ho!
 And raise some special officers of night. —
 On, good Roderigo; I'll deserve° your pains.   *Exeunt.*

SCENE II: *Before the lodgings of Othello.*

Enter Othello, Iago, and Attendants with torches.

Iago: Though in the trade of war I have slain men,
 Yet do I hold it very stuff o' th' conscience
 To do no contrived murther. I lack iniquity
 Sometimes to do me service. Nine or ten times
 I had thought t' have yerked° him here under the ribs.   5
Othello: 'Tis better as it is.
Iago: Nay, but he prated,
 And spoke such scurvy and provoking terms
 Against your honor
 That with the little godliness I have
 I did full hard forbear him. But I pray you, sir,   10

---

nightgown: Dressing gown.   166 moe: More.   172 *property:* Nature.   183 *deserve:* Show
gratitude for.   **Scene II.**   5 *yerked:* Stabbed.

Are you fast° married? Be assured of this,
That the magnifico° is much beloved,
And hath in his effect a voice potential°
As double° as the Duke's. He will divorce you,
Or put upon you what restraint and grievance   15
The law, with all his might to enforce it on,
Will give him cable.

Othello: Let him do his spite.
My services which I have done the signiory°
Shall out-tongue his complaints. 'Tis yet to know° —
Which, when I know that boasting is an honor,   20
I shall promulgate — I fetch my life and being
From men of royal siege;° and my demerits°
May speak unbonneted to as proud a fortune
As this that I have reached.° For know, Iago,
But that I love the gentle Desdemona,   25
I would not my unhousèd° free condition
Put into circumscription and confine
For the sea's worth. But look what lights come yond?

Iago: Those are the raisèd father and his friends.
You were best go in.

Othello: Not I; I must be found.   30
My parts, my title, and my perfect soul°
Shall manifest me rightly. Is it they?

Iago: By Janus, I think no.

          Enter Cassio, with torches, Officers.

Othello: The servants of the Duke, and my lieutenant.
The goodness of the night upon you, friends!   35
What is the news?

Cassio: The Duke does greet you, general;
And he requires your haste-post-haste appearance
Even on the instant.

Othello: What's the matter, think you?

Cassio: Something from Cyprus, as I may divine.
It is a business of some heat. The galleys   40
Have sent a dozen sequent° messengers
This very night at one another's heels,
And many of the consuls, raised and met,
Are at the Duke's already. You have been hotly called for;

---

11 *fast:* Securely. 12 *magnifico:* Grandee (Brabantio). 13 *potential:* Powerful. 14 *double:* Doubly influential. 18 *signiory:* Venetian government. 19 *yet to know:* Still not generally known. 22 *siege:* Rank; *demerits:* Deserts. 23–4 *May speak . . . reached:* Are equal, I modestly assert, to those of Desdemona's family. 26 *unhousèd:* Unrestrained. 31 *perfect soul:* Stainless conscience. 41 *sequent:* Consecutive.

When, being not at your lodging to be found,   45
The Senate hath sent about three several quests
To search you out.
Othello: 'Tis well I am found by you.
I will but spend a word here in the house,
And go with you.   *[Exit]*
Cassio: Ancient, what makes he here?
Iago: Faith, he to-night hath boarded a land carack.°   50
If it prove lawful prize, he's made for ever.
Cassio: I do not understand.
Iago: He's married.
Cassio: To who?

    [Enter Othello.]

Iago: Marry, to — Come, captain, will you go?
Othello: Have with you.
Cassio: Here comes another troop to seek for you.

    Enter Brabantio, Roderigo, and others with lights and weapons.

Iago: It is Brabantio. General, be advised.   55
He comes to bad intent.
Othello: Holla! stand there!
Roderigo: Signior, it is the Moor.
Brabantio: Down with him, thief!

    [They draw on both sides.]

Iago: You, Roderigo! Come, sir, I am for you.
Othello: Keep up° your bright swords, for the dew will rust them.
Good signior, you shall more command with years   60
Than with your weapons.
Brabantio: O thou foul thief, where hast thou stowed my daughter?
Damned as thou art, thou hast enchanted her!
For I'll refer me to all things of sense,
If she in chains of magic were not bound,   65
Whether a maid so tender, fair, and happy,
So opposite to marriage that she shunned
The wealthy curlèd darlings of our nation,
Would ever have, t' incur a general mock,
Run from her guardage to the sooty bosom   70
Of such a thing as thou — to fear, not to delight.
Judge me the world if 'tis not gross in sense°
That thou hast practiced on her with foul charms,
Abused her delicate youth with drugs or minerals
That weaken motion.° I'll have't disputed on;   75

---

50 *carack:* Treasure ship.   59 *Keep up:* i.e., sheath.   72 *gross in sense:* Obvious.
75 *motion:* Perception.

'Tis probable, and palpable to thinking.
I therefore apprehend and do attach° thee
For an abuser of the world, a practicer
Of arts inhibited and out of warrant.
Lay hold upon him. If he do resist,   80
Subdue him at his peril.
Othello: Hold your hands,
Both you of my inclining and the rest.
Were it my cue to fight, I should have known it
Without a prompter. Where will you that I go
To answer this your charge?
Brabantio: To prison, till fit time   85
Of law and course of direct session°
Call thee to answer.
Othello: What if I do obey?
How may the Duke be therewith satisfied,
Whose messengers are here about my side
Upon some present business of the state   90
To bring me to him?
Officer: 'Tis true, most worthy signior.
The Duke's in council, and your noble self
I am sure is sent for.
Brabantio: How? The Duke in council?
In this time of the night? Bring him away.
Mine's not an idle° cause. The Duke himself,   95
Or any of my brothers of the state,
Cannot but feel this wrong as 'twere their own;
For if such actions may have passage free,
Bondslaves and pagans shall our statesmen be.   *Exeunt.*

SCENE III: *The Venetian Senate Chamber.*

Enter Duke and Senators, set at a table, with lights and Attendants.

Duke: There is no composition° in these news
That gives them credit.
1. Senator: Indeed they are disproportioned.
My letters say a hundred and seven galleys.
Duke: And mine a hundred forty.
2. Senator: And mine two hundred.
But though they jump° not on a just account —   5
As in these cases where the aim° reports
'Tis oft with difference — yet do they all confirm
A Turkish fleet, and bearing up to Cyprus.

77 *attach:* Arrest. 86 *direct session:* Regular trial. 95 *idle:* Trifling. **Scene III.**
1 *composition:* Consistency. 5 *jump:* Agree. 6 *aim:* Conjecture.

Duke: Nay, it is possible enough to judgment.
    I do not so secure me° in the error   10
    But the main article° I do approve°
    In fearful sense.
Sailor (within):   What, ho! what, ho! what, ho!
Officer: A messenger from the galleys.

    Enter Sailor.

Duke: Now, what's the business?
Sailor: The Turkish preparation makes for Rhodes.
    So was I bid report here to the state   15
    By Signior Angelo.
Duke: How say you by this change?
1. Senator: This cannot be
    By no assay° of reason. 'Tis a pageant
    To keep us in false gaze.° When we consider
    Th' importancy of Cyprus to the Turk,   20
    And let ourselves again but understand
    That, as it more concerns the Turk than Rhodes,
    So may he with more facile question bear° it,
    For that it stands not in such warlike brace,°
    But altogether lacks th' abilities   25
    That Rhodes is dressed in—if we make thought of this,
    We must not think the Turk is so unskillful
    To leave that latest which concerns him first,
    Neglecting an attempt of ease and gain
    To wake and wage° a danger profitless.   30
Duke: Nay, in all confidence, he's not for Rhodes.
Officer: Here is more news.

    Enter a Messenger.

Messenger: The Ottomites, reverend and gracious,
    Steering with due course toward the isle of Rhodes,
    Have there injointed them with an after fleet.   35
1. Senator: Ay, so I thought. How many, as you guess?
Messenger: Of thirty sail; and now they do restem°
    Their backward course, bearing with frank appearance
    Their purposes toward Cyprus, Signior Montano,
    Your trusty and most valiant servitor,   40
    With his free duty recommends you thus,
    And prays you to believe him.
Duke: 'Tis certain then for Cyprus.
    Marcus Luccicos,° is not he in town?

---

10 *so secure me:* Take such comfort.   11 *article:* Substance; *approve:* Accept.   18 *assay:* Test.   19 *in false gaze:* Looking the wrong way.   23 *with...bear:* More easily capture.   24 *brace:* Posture of defense.   30 *wake and wage:* Rouse and risk.   37 *restem:* Steer again.   44 *Marcus Luccicos:* (Presumably a Venetian envoy).

1. Senator: He's now in Florence.   45
Duke: Write from us to him; post, post-haste dispatch.
1. Senator: Here comes Brabantio and the valiant Moor.

> *Enter Brabantio, Othello, Cassio, Iago, Roderigo, and Officers.*

Duke: Valiant Othello, we must straight employ you
 Against the general enemy Ottoman.   *[To Brabantio.]*
 I did not see you. Welcome, gentle signior.   50
 We lacked your counsel and your help to-night.
Brabantio: So did I yours. Good your grace, pardon me.
 Neither my place, nor aught I heard of business,
 Hath raised me from my bed; nor doth the general care
 Take hold on me; for my particular grief   55
 Is of so floodgate° and o'erbearing nature
 That it engluts° and swallows other sorrows,
 And it is still itself.
Duke: Why, what's the matter?
Brabantio: My daughter! O, my daughter!
All: Dead?
Brabantio: Ay, to me.
 She is abused, stol'n from me, and corrupted   60
 By spells and medicines bought of mountebanks;
 For nature so prepost'rously to err,
 Being not deficient,° blind, or lame of sense,
 Sans witchcraft could not.
Duke: Whoe'er he be that in this foul proceeding   65
 Hath thus beguiled your daughter of herself,
 And you of her, the bloody book of law
 You shall yourself read in the bitter letter
 After your own sense; yea, though our proper° son
 Stood in your action.°
Brabantio: Humbly I thank your grace.   70
 Here is the man—this Moor, whom now, it seems,
 Your special mandate for the state affairs
 Hath hither brought.
All: We are very sorry for't.
Duke [to Othello]: What, in your own part, can you say to this?
Brabantio: Nothing, but this is so.   75
Othello: Most potent, grave, and reverend signiors,
 My very noble, and approved° good masters,
 That I have ta'en away this old man's daughter,
 It is most true; true I have married her.
 The very head and front of my offending   80

---

56 *floodgate:* Torrential.   57 *engluts:* Devours.   63 *deficient:* Feeble-minded.   69 *our proper:* My own.   70 *Stood in your action:* Were accused by you.   77 *approved:* Tested by experience.

Hath this extent, no more. Rude° am I in my speech,
And little blessed with the soft phrase of peace;
For since these arms of mine had seven years' pith°
Till now some nine moons wasted, they have used
Their dearest action in the tented field;   85
And little of this great world can I speak
More than pertains to feats of broil and battle;
And therefore little shall I grace my cause
In speaking for myself. Yet, by your gracious patience,
I will a round° unvarnished tale deliver   90
Of my whole course of love—what drugs, what charms,
What conjuration, and what mighty magic
(For such proceeding am I charged withal)
I won his daughter.
Brabantio: A maiden never bold;
Of spirit so still and quiet that her motion   95
Blushed° at herself; and she—in spite of nature,
Of years, of country, credit, everything—
To fall in love with what she feared to look on!
It is a judgment maimed and most imperfect
That will confess perfection so could err   100
Against all rules of nature, and must be driven
To find out practices° of cunning hell
Why this should be. I therefore vouch° again
That with some mixtures pow'rful o'er the blood,°
Or with some dram, conjured to this effect,   105
He wrought upon her.
Duke: To vouch this is no proof,
Without more certain and more overt test
Than these thin habits° and poor likelihoods
Of modern seeming° do prefer against him.
1. Senator: But, Othello, speak.   110
Did you by indirect and forcèd° courses
Subdue and poison this young maid's affections?
Or came it by request, and such fair question°
As soul to soul affordeth?
Othello: I do beseech you,
Send for the lady to the Sagittary   115
And let her speak of me before her father.
If you do find me foul in her report,
The trust, the office, I do hold of you

---

81 *Rude:* Unpolished. 83 *pith:* Strength. 90 *round:* Plain. 95–6 *her motion Blushed:* Her own emotions caused her to blush. 102 *practices:* Plots. 103 *vouch:* Assert. 104 *blood:* Passions. 108 *thin habits:* Slight appearances. 109 *modern seeming:* Everyday supposition. 111 *forcèd:* Violent. 113 *question:* Conversation.

Not only take away, but let your sentence
Even fall upon my life.
Duke: Fetch Desdemona hither.   120
Othello: Ancient, conduct them; you best know the place.
                    Exit [Iago, with] two or three [Attendants].
And till she come, as truly as to heaven
I do confess the vices of my blood,
So justly to your grave ears I'll present
How I did thrive in this fair lady's love,   125
And she in mine.
Duke: Say it, Othello.
Othello: Her father loved me, oft invited me;
Still° questioned me the story of my life
From year to year — the battles, sieges, fortunes   130
That I have passed.
I ran it through, even from my boyish days
To th' very moment that he bade me tell it.
Wherein I spoke of most disastrous chances,
Of moving accidents by flood and field;   135
Of hairbreadth scapes i' th' imminent deadly breach;
Of being taken by the insolent foe
And sold to slavery; of my redemption thence
And portance° in my travels' history;
Wherein of anters° vast and deserts idle,   140
Rough quarries, rocks, and hills whose heads touch heaven,
It was my hint° to speak — such was the process;
And of the Cannibals that each other eat,
The Anthropophagi,° and men whose heads
Do grow beneath their shoulders. This to hear   145
Would Desdemona seriously incline;
But still the house affairs would draw her thence;
Which ever as she could with haste dispatch,
She'ld come again, and with a greedy ear
Devour up my discourse. Which I observing,   150
Took once a pliant° hour, and found good means
To draw from her a prayer of earnest heart
That I would all my pilgrimage dilate,°
Whereof by parcels° she had something heard,
But not intentively.° I did consent,   155
And often did beguile her of her tears
When I did speak of some distressful stroke
That my youth suffered. My story being done,

---

129 *Still:* Continually.   139 *portance:* Behavior.   140 *anters:* Caves.   142 *hint:* Occasion.   144 *Anthropophagi:* Man-eaters.   151 *pliant:* Propitious.   153 *dilate:* Recount in full.   154 *parcels:* Portions.   155 *intentively:* With full attention.

She gave me for my pains a world of sighs.
She swore, i' faith, 'twas strange, 'twas passing strange;   160
'Twas pitiful, 'twas wondrous pitiful.
She wished she had not heard it; yet she wished
That heaven had made her such a man. She thanked me;
And bade me, if I had a friend that loved her,
I should but teach him how to tell my story,   165
And that would woo her. Upon this hint° I spake.
She loved me for the dangers I had passed,
And I loved her that she did pity them.
This only is the witchcraft I have used.
Here comes the lady. Let her witness it.   170

Enter Desdemona, Iago, Attendants.

Duke: I think this tale would win my daughter too.
    Good Brabantio,
    Take up this mangled matter at the best.
    Men do their broken weapons rather use
    Than their bare hands.
Brabantio: I pray you hear her speak.   175
    If she confess that she was half the wooer,
    Destruction on my head if my bad blame
    Light on the man! Come hither, gentle mistress.
    Do you perceive in all this noble company
    Where most you owe obedience?
Desdemona: My noble father,   180
    I do perceive here a divided duty.
    To you I am bound for life and education;°
    My life and education both do learn me
    How to respect you: you are the lord of duty;
    I am hitherto your daughter. But here's my husband;   185
    And so much duty as my mother showed
    To you, preferring you before her father,
    So much I challenge° that I may profess
    Due to the Moor my lord.
Brabantio: God be with you! I have done.
    Please it your grace, on to the state affairs.   190
    I had rather to adopt a child than get° it.
    Come hither, Moor.
    I here do give thee that with all my heart
    Which, but thou hast already, with all my heart
    I would keep from thee. For your sake,° jewel,   195

---

166 *hint:* Opportunity.   182 *education:* Upbringing.   188 *challenge:* Claim the right.
191 *get:* Beget.   195 *For your sake:* Because of you.

I am glad at soul I have no other child;
For thy escape° would teach me tyranny,
To hang clogs on them. I have done, my lord.

Duke: Let me speak like yourself° and lay a sentence°
Which, as a grise° or step, may help these lovers   200
[Into your favor.]
When remedies are past, the griefs are ended
By seeing the worst, which late on hopes depended.
To mourn a mischief that is past and gone
Is the next way to draw new mischief on.   205
What cannot be preserved when fortune takes,
Patience her injury a mock'ry makes.
The robbed that smiles steals something from the thief;
He robs himself that spends a bootless grief.

Brabantio: So let the Turk of Cyprus us beguile: 210
We lose it not so long as we can smile.
He bears the sentence well that nothing bears
But the free comfort which from thence he hears;
But he bears both the sentence and the sorrow
That to pay grief must of poor patience borrow.   215
These sentences, to sugar, or to gall,
Being strong on both sides, are equivocal.
But words are words. I never yet did hear
That the bruisèd heart was piercèd through the ear.
Beseech you, now to the affairs of state.   220

Duke: The Turk with a most mighty preparation makes for Cyprus.
Othello, the fortitude° of the place is best known to you; and
though we have there a substitute of most allowed° sufficiency,
yet opinion,° a more sovereign mistress of effects, throws a more
safer voice on you. You must therefore be content to slubber°   225
the gloss of your new fortunes with this more stubborn and
boist'rous expedition.

Othello: The tyrant custom, most grave senators,
Hath made the flinty and steel couch of war
My thrice-driven bed of down. I do agnize   230
A natural and prompt alacrity
I find in hardness;° and do undertake
These present wars against the Ottomites.
Most humbly, therefore, bending to your state,
I crave fit disposition for my wife,   235
Due reference of place, and exhibition,°

---

197 *escape:* Escapade. 199 *like yourself:* As you should; *sentence:* Maxim. 200 *grise:*
Step. 222 *fortitude:* Fortification. 223 *allowed:* Acknowledged. 224 *opinion:* Public
opinion. 225 *slubber:* Sully. 230–32 *agnize . . . hardness:* Recognize in myself a natural
and easy response to hardship. 236 *exhibition:* Allowance of money.

With such accommodation and besort°
As levels° with her breeding.
Duke: If you please,
Be't at her father's.
Brabantio: I will not have it so.
Othello: Nor I.
Desdemona: Nor I. I would not there reside,   240
To put my father in impatient thoughts
By being in his eye. Most gracious Duke,
To my unfolding lend your prosperous° ear,
And let me find a charter in your voice,
T' assist my simpleness.°   245
Duke: What would you, Desdemona?
Desdemona: That I did love the Moor to live with him,
My downright violence, and storm of fortunes,
May trumpet to the world. My heart's subdued
Even to the very quality of my lord.   250
I saw Othello's visage in his mind,
And to his honors and his valiant parts
Did I my soul and fortunes consecrate.
So that, dear lords, if I be left behind,
A moth of peace, and he go to the war,   255
The rites for which I love him are bereft me,
And I a heavy interim shall support
By his dear absence. Let me go with him.
Othello: Let her have your voice.
Vouch with me, heaven, I therefore beg it not   260
To please the palate of my appetite,
Not to comply with heat° — the young affects°
In me defunct — and proper satisfaction;
But to be free and bounteous to her mind;
And heaven defend your good souls that you think   265
I will your serious and great business scant
When she is with me. No, when light-winged toys
Of feathered Cupid seel° with wanton dullness
My speculative and officed instruments,°
That° my disports corrupt and taint my business,   270
Let housewives make a skillet of my helm,
And all indign° and base adversities
Make head against my estimation!°
Duke: Be it as you shall privately determine,

237 *besort:* Suitable company. 238 *levels:* Corresponds. 243 *prosperous:* Favorable.
245 *simpleness:* Lack of skill. 262 *heat:* Passions; *young affects:* Tendencies of youth.
268 *seel:* Blind. 269 *My . . . instruments:* My perceptive and responsible faculties.
270 *That:* So that. 272 *indign:* Unworthy. 273 *estimation:* Reputation.

Either for her stay or going. Th' affair cries haste,   275
And speed must answer it.

1. Senator: You must away to-night.

Othello: With all my heart.

Duke: At nine i' th' morning here we'll meet again.
     Othello, leave some officer behind,
     And he shall our commission bring to you,   280
     With such things else of quality and respect
     As doth import° you.

Othello: So please your grace, my ancient;
     A man he is of honesty and trust
     To his conveyance I assign my wife,
     With what else needful your good grace shall think   285
     To be sent after me.

Duke: Let it be so.
     Good night to every one.
          [*To Brabantio.*]   And, noble signior,
     If virtue no delighted° beauty lack,
     Your son-in-law is far more fair than black.

1. Senator: Adieu, brave Moor. Use Desdemona well.   290

Brabantio: Look to her, Moor, if thou hast eyes to see:
     She has deceived her father, and may thee.

                        Exeunt [Duke, Senators, Officers, &c.].

Othello: My life upon her faith! — Honest Iago,
     My Desdemona must I leave to thee.
     I prithee let thy wife attend on her,   295
     And bring them after in the best advantage.°
     Come, Desdemona. I have but an hour
     Of love, of worldly matters and direction,
     To spend with thee. We must obey the time.

                             Exit Moor and Desdemona.

Roderigo: Iago, —   300

Iago: What say'st thou, noble heart?

Roderigo: What will I do, think'st thou?

Iago: Why, go to bed and sleep.

Roderigo: I will incontinently° drown myself.

Iago: If thou dost, I shall never love thee after. Why, thou silly   305
     gentleman!

Roderigo: It is silliness to live when to live is torment; and then have
     we a prescription to die when death is our physician.

Iago: O villainous! I have looked upon the world for four times
     seven years; and since I could distinguish betwixt a benefit and 310

---

282 *import:* Concern.   288 *delighted:* Delightful.   296 *in the best advantage:* At the
best opportunity.   304 *incontinently:* Forthwith.

an injury, I never found man that knew how to love himself. Ere
I would say I would drown myself for the love of a guinea hen, I
would change my humanity with a baboon.

Roderigo: What should I do? I confess it is my shame to be so fond,
but it is not in my virtue to amend it.   315

Iago: Virtue? a fig! 'Tis in ourselves that we are thus or thus. Our
bodies are our gardens, to which our wills are gardeners; so that
if we will plant nettles or sow lettuce, set hyssop and weed up
thyme, supply it with one gender° of herbs or distract it with
many—either to have it sterile with idleness or manured with   320
industry—why, the power and corrigible authority° of this lies
in our wills. If the balance of our lives had not one scale of reason to poise° another of sensuality, the blood and baseness°
of our natures would conduct us to most preposterous conclusions. But we have reason to cool our raging motions,° our car-   325
nal strings, our unbitted° lusts; whereof I take this that you call
love to be a sect or scion.°

Roderigo: It cannot be.

Iago: It is merely a lust of the blood and a permission of the will.
Come, be a man! Drown thyself? Drown cats and blind pup-   330
pies! I have professed me thy friend, and I confess me knit to
thy deserving with cables of perdurable toughness. I could never
better stead thee than now. Put money in thy purse. Follow thou
the wars; defeat thy favor° with an usurped beard. I say, put
money in thy purse. It cannot be that Desdemona should long   335
continue her love to the Moor—put money in thy purse—nor
he his to her. It was a violent commencement in her, and thou
shalt see an answerable sequestration°—put but money in
thy purse. These Moors are changeable in their wills—fill thy
purse with money. The food that to him now is as luscious as   340
locusts shall be to him shortly as bitter as coloquintida.° She
must change for youth: when she is sated with his body, she will
find the error of her choice. [She must have change, she must.]
Therefore put money in thy purse. If thou wilt needs damn
thyself, do it a more delicate way than drowning. Make° all the   345
money thou canst. If sanctimony and a frail vow betwixt an err-
ing° barbarian and a supersubtle Venetian be not too hard for
my wits and all the tribe of hell, thou shalt enjoy her. Therefore
make money. A pox of drowning thyself! 'Tis clean out of the

---

319 *gender:* Species.   321 *corrigible authority:* Corrective power.   323 *poise:* Counter-
balance;   *blood and baseness:* Animal instincts.   325 *motions:* Appetites.   326 *unbitted:*
Uncontrolled.   327 *sect or scion:* Offshoot, cutting.   334 *defeat thy favor:* Spoil
thy appearance.   338 *sequestration:* Estrangement.   341 *coloquintida:* A medicine.
345 *Make:* Raise.   346–47 *erring:* Wandering.

way. Seek thou rather to be hanged in compassing thy joy than   350
to be drowned and go without her.
Roderigo: Wilt thou be fast to my hopes, if I depend on the issue?
Iago: Thou art sure of me. Go, make money. I have told thee often,
and I retell thee again and again, I hate the Moor. My cause is
hearted;° thine hath no less reason. Let us be conjunctive in our   355
revenge against him. If thou canst cuckold him, thou dost thy-
self a pleasure, me a sport. There are many events in the womb of
time, which will be delivered. Traverse,° go, provide thy money!
We will have more of this to-morrow. Adieu.
Roderigo: Where shall we meet i' th' morning?   360
Iago: At my lodging.
Roderigo: I'll be with thee betimes.
Iago: Go to, farewell — Do you hear, Roderigo?
[*Roderigo:* What say you?
Iago: No more of drowning, do you hear?   365
Roderigo: I am changed.
Iago: Go to, farewell. Put money enough in your purse.]
Roderigo: I'll sell all my land.   *Exit.*
Iago: Thus do I ever make my fool my purse;
  For I mine own gained knowledge should profane   370
  If I would time expend with such a snipe°
  But for my sport and profit. I hate the Moor;
  And it is thought abroad that 'twixt my sheets
  H'as done my office. I know not if't be true;
  But I, for mere suspicion in that kind,   375
  Will do as if for surety. He holds me well;°
  The better shall my purpose work on him.
  Cassio's a proper man. Let me see now:
  To get his place, and to plume up° my will
  In double knavery — How, how? — Let's see: —   380
  After some time, to abuse Othello's ears
  That he is too familiar with his wife.
  He hath a person and a smooth dispose°
  To be suspected — framed to make women false.
  The Moor is of a free° and open nature   385
  That thinks men honest that but seem to be so;
  And will as tenderly be led by th' nose
  As asses are.
  I have't! It is engend'red! Hell and night
  Must bring this monstrous birth to the world's light.   *Exit.* 390

354–55 *My cause is hearted:* My heart is in it.   358 *Traverse:* Forward march.   371
snipe: Fool.   376 *well:* In high regard.   379 *plume up:* Gratify.   383 *dispose:* Manner.
385 *free:* Frank.

ACT II

SCENE I: *An open place in Cyprus, near the harbor.*

Enter Montano and two Gentlemen.

Montano: What from the cape can you discern at sea?

1. Gentleman: Nothing at all: it is a high-wrought flood.
  I cannot 'twixt the heaven and the main
  Descry a sail.

Montano: Methinks the wind hath spoke aloud at land;   5
  A fuller blast ne'er shook our battlements.
  If it hath ruffianed so upon the sea,
  What ribs of oak, when mountains melt on them,
  Can hold the mortise?° What shall we hear of this?

2. Gentleman: A segregation° of the Turkish fleet.   10
  For do but stand upon the foaming shore,
  The chidden billow seems to pelt the clouds;
  The wind-shaked surge, with high and monstrous mane,
  Seems to cast water on the burning Bear
  And quench the Guards° of th' ever-fixèd pole.°   15
  I never did like molestation° view
  On the enchafèd flood.

Montano: If that the Turkish fleet
  Be not ensheltered and embayed, they are drowned;
  It is impossible to bear it out.

Enter a third Gentleman.

3. Gentleman: News, lads! Our wars are done.   20
  The desperate tempest hath so banged the Turks
  That their designment halts.° A noble ship of Venice
  Hath seen a grievous wrack and sufferance°
  On most part of their fleet.

Montano: How? Is this true?

3. Gentleman: The ship is here put in,   25
  A Veronesa;° Michael Cassio,
  Lieutenant to the warlike Moor Othello,
  Is come on shore; the Moor himself at sea,
  And is in full commission here for Cyprus.

Montano: I am glad on't. 'Tis a worthy governor.   30

3. Gentleman: But his same Cassio, though he speak of comfort
  Touching the Turkish loss, yet he looks sadly

Act II, Scene I. 9 *hold the mortise:* Hold their joints together. 10 *segregation:* Scattering. 15 *Guards:* Stars near the North Star; *pole:* Polestar. 16 *molestation:* Tumult. 22 *designment halts:* Plan is crippled. 23 *sufferance:* Disaster. 26 *Veronesa:* Ship furnished by Verona.

And prays the Moor be safe, for they were parted
With foul and violent tempest.
Montano: Pray heaven he be;
For I have served him, and the man commands   35
Like a full soldier. Let's to the seaside, ho!
As well to see the vessel that's come in
As to throw out our eyes for brave Othello,
Even till we make the main and th' aerial blue
An indistinct regard.°
3. Gentleman: Come, let's do so;   40
For every minute is expectancy
Of more arrivance.

    Enter Cassio.

Cassio: Thanks, you the valiant of this warlike isle,
That so approve the Moor! O, let the heavens
Give him defense against the elements,   45
For I have lost him on a dangerous sea!
Montano: Is he well shipped?
Cassio: His bark is stoutly timbered, and his pilot
Of very expert and approved allowance;
Therefore my hopes, not surfeited to death,°   50
Stand in bold cure.°
      (Within.)   A sail, a sail, a sail!   *Enter a messenger.*
Cassio: What noise?
Messenger: The town is empty; on the brow o' th' sea
Stand ranks of people, and they cry "A sail!"
Cassio: My hopes do shape him for the governor.   55

    A shot.

2. Gentleman: They do discharge their shot of courtesy:
Our friends at least.
Cassio: I pray you, sir, go forth
And give us truth who 'tis that is arrived.
2. Gentleman: I shall.   *Exit.*
Montano: But, good lieutenant, is your general wived?   60
Cassio: Most fortunately. He hath achieved a maid
That paragons° description and wild fame;
One that excels the quirks° of blazoning° pens,
And in th' essential vesture of creation
Does tire the ingener.°

    Enter Second Gentleman.

---

40 *An indistinct regard:* Indistinguishable.   50 *surfeited to death:* Overindulged.   51 *in bold cure:* A good chance of fulfillment.   62 *paragons:* Surpasses.   63 *quirks:* Ingenuities;   *blazoning:* Describing.   64–5 *And . . . ingener:* Merely to describe her as God made her exhausts her praiser.

How now? Who has put in?   65
2. Gentleman: 'Tis one Iago, ancient to the general.
Cassio: H'as had most favorable and happy speed:
   Tempests themselves, high seas, and howling winds,
   The guttered° rocks and congregated sands,
   Traitors ensteeped° to clog the guiltless keel,   70
   As having sense of beauty, do omit
   Their mortal° natures, letting go safely by
   The divine Desdemona.
Montano: What is she?
Cassio: She that I spake of, our great captain's captain,
   Left in the conduct of the bold Iago,   75
   Whose footing° here anticipates our thoughts
   A se'nnight's° speed. Great Jove, Othello guard,
   And swell his sail with thine own pow'rful breath,
   That he may bless this bay with his tall ship,
   Make love's quick pants in Desdemona's arms,   80
   Give renewed fire to our extinct spirits,
   [And bring all Cyprus comfort!]

   Enter Desdemona, Iago, Roderigo, and Emilia [with Attendants].

                        O, behold!
   The riches of the ship is come on shore!
   You men of Cyprus, let her have your knees.°
   Hail to thee, lady! and the grace of heaven,   85
   Before, behind thee, and on every hand,
   Enwheel thee round!
Desdemona: I thank you, valiant Cassio.
   What tidings can you tell me of my lord?
Cassio: He is not yet arrived; nor know I aught
   But that he's well and will be shortly here.   90
Desdemona: O but I fear! How lost you company?
Cassio: The great contention of the sea and skies
   Parted our fellowship.
      (Within.)   A sail, a sail! *[A shot.]*
                        But hark. A sail!
2. Gentleman: They give their greeting to the citadel;
   This likewise is a friend.
Cassio: See for the news.   95

                        [Exit Gentleman.]

   Good ancient, you are welcome.
      [To Emilia.]   Welcome, mistress. —
   Let it not gall your patience, good Iago,

---

69 *guttered:* Jagged.   70 *ensteeped:* Submerged.   72 *mortal:* Deadly.   76 *footing:*
Landing.   77 *se'nnight's:* Week's.   84 *knees:* i.e., kneeling.

That I extend my manners. 'Tis my breeding
That gives me this bold show of courtesy.
  [Kisses Emilia.°]

Iago: Sir, would she give you so much of her lips   100
  As of her tongue she oft bestows on me,
  You would have enough.
Desdemona: Alas, she has no speech!
Iago: In faith, too much.
  I find it still when I have list to sleep.
  Marry, before your ladyship, I grant,   105
  She puts her tongue a little in her heart
  And chides with thinking.
Emilia: You have little cause to say so.
Iago: Come on, come on! You are pictures out of doors,
  Bells in your parlors, wildcats in your kitchens,   110
  Saints in your injuries, devils being offended,
  Players in your housewifery,° and housewives° in your beds.
Desdemona: O, fie upon thee, slanderer!
Iago: Nay, it is true, or else I am a Turk:
  You rise to play, and go to bed to work.   115
Emilia: You shall not write my praise.
Iago: No, let me not.
Desdemona: What wouldst thou write of me, if thou shouldst
  praise me?
Iago: O gentle lady, do not put me to't,
  For I am nothing if not critical.
Desdemona: Come on, assay.° — There's one gone to the harbor?   120
Iago: Ay, madam.
Desdemona: I am not merry; but I do beguile
  The thing I am by seeming otherwise. —
  Come, how wouldst thou praise me?
Iago: I am about it; but indeed my invention   125
  Comes from my pate as birdlime° does from frieze° —
  It plucks out brains and all. But my Muse labors,
  And thus she is delivered:
  If she be fair and wise, fairness and wit —
  The one's for use, the other useth it.   130
Desdemona: Well praised! How if she be black° and witty?
Iago: If she be black, and thereto have a wit,
  She'll find a white that shall her blackness fit.
Desdemona: Worse and worse!
Emilia: How if fair and foolish?   135

Kisses Emilia: (Kissing was a common Elizabethan form of social courtesy).   112 *housewifery:* Housekeeping; *housewives:* Hussies.   120 *assay:* Try.   126 *birdlime:* A sticky
paste;   *frieze:* Rough cloth.   131 *black:* Brunette.

Iago: She never yet was foolish that was fair,
     For even her folly° helped her to an heir.
Desdemona: These are old fond° paradoxes to make fools laugh i’
     th’ alehouse. What miserable praise hast thou for her that’s
     foul° and foolish?   140
Iago: There’s none so foul, and foolish thereunto,
     But does foul pranks which fair and wise ones do.
Desdemona: O heavy ignorance! Thou praisest the worst best. But
     what praise couldst thou bestow on a deserving woman indeed —
     one that in the authority of her merit did justly put on the vouch°   145
     of very malice itself?
Iago: She that was ever fair, and never proud;
     Had tongue at will, and yet was never loud;
     Never lacked gold, and yet went never gay;
     Fled from her wish, and yet said “Now I may”;   150
     She that, being ang’red, her revenge being nigh,
     Bade her wrong stay, and her displeasure fly;
     She that in wisdom never was so frail
     To change the cod’s head for the salmon’s tail;°
     She that could think, and ne’er disclose her mind;   155
     See suitors following, and not look behind:
     She was a wight (if ever such wight were) —
Desdemona: To do what?
Iago: To suckle fools and chronicle small beer.°
Desdemona: O most lame and impotent conclusion! Do not learn of   160
     him, Emilia, though he be thy husband. How say you, Cassio? Is
     he not a most profane and liberal° counsellor?
Cassio: He speaks home,° madam. You may relish him more in the
     soldier than in the scholar.
Iago [aside]: He takes her by the palm. Ay, well said, whisper! With as   165
     little a web as this will I ensnare as great a fly as Cassio. Ay, smile
     upon her, do! I will gyve thee in thine own courtship.° — You
     say true; ’tis so, indeed! — If such tricks as these strip you out
     of your lieutenantry, it had been better you had not kissed your
     three fingers so oft — which now again you are most apt to play   170
     the sir° in. Very good! well kissed! an excellent courtesy! ’Tis
     so, indeed. Yet again your fingers to your lips? Would they were
     clyster pipes° for your sake! *(Trumpet within.)*
     The Moor! I know his trumpet.
Cassio: ’Tis truly so.   175

---

137 *folly:* Wantonness. 138 *fond:* Foolish. 140 *foul:* Ugly. 145 *put on the vouch:* Compel the approval. 154 *To . . . tail:* i.e., to exchange the good for the poor but expensive. 159 *chronicle small beer:* Keep petty household accounts. 162 *profane and liberal:* Worldly and licentious. 163 *home:* Bluntly. 167 *gyve . . . courtship:* Manacle you by means of your courtly manners. 171 *sir:* Courtly gentleman. 173 *clyster pipes:* Syringes.

Desdemona: Let's meet him and receive him.
Cassio: Lo, where he comes.

    Enter Othello and Attendants.

Othello: O my fair warrior!
Desdemona: My dear Othello!
Othello: It gives me wonder great as my content
    To see you here before me. O my soul's joy!   180
    If after every tempest come such calms,
    May the winds blow till they have wakened death!
    And let the laboring bark climb hills of seas
    Olympus-high, and duck again as low
    As hell's from heaven! If it were now to die,   185
    'Twere now to be most happy;° for I fear
    My soul hath her content so absolute
    That not another comfort like to this
    Succeeds in unknown fate.
Desdemona: The heavens forbid
    But that our loves and comforts should increase   190
    Even as our days do grow.
Othello: Amen to that, sweet powers!
    I cannot speak enough of this content;
    It stops me here; it is too much of joy.
    And this, and this, the greatest discords be

    They kiss.

    That e'er our hearts shall make!
Iago [aside]:   O, you are well tuned now!   195
    But I'll set down° the pegs that make this music,
    As honest as I am.
Othello: Come, let us to the castle.
    News, friends! Our wars are done; the Turks are drowned.
    How does my old acquaintance of this isle? —
    Honey, you shall be well desired° in Cyprus;   200
    I have found great love amongst them. O my sweet,
    I prattle out of fashion, and I dote
    In mine own comforts. I prithee, good Iago,
    Go to the bay and disembark my coffers.
    Bring thou the master° to the citadel;   205
    He is a good one, and his worthiness
    Does challenge° much respect. — Come, Desdemona,
    Once more well met at Cyprus.
                  Exit Othello [with all but Iago and Roderigo].

---

186 *happy:* Fortunate.   196 *set down:* Loosen.   200 *well desired:* Warmly welcomed.
205 *master:* Ship captain.   207 *challenge:* Deserve.

Iago [to an Attendant, who goes out]: Do thou meet me presently at the
harbor. *[To Roderigo.]* Come hither. If thou be'st valiant (as they   210
say base men being in love have then a nobility in their natures
more than is native to them), list me. The lieutenant to-night
watches on the court of guard.° First, I must tell thee this: Desdemona is directly in love with him.

Roderigo: With him? Why, 'tis not possible.   215

Iago: Lay thy finger thus,° and let thy soul be instructed. Mark me
with what violence she first loved the Moor, but for bragging
and telling her fantastical lies; and will she love him still for
prating? Let not thy discreet heart think it. Her eye must be fed;
and what delight shall she have to look on the devil? When the   220
blood is made dull with the act of sport, there should be, again
to inflame it and to give satiety a fresh appetite, loveliness in
favor, sympathy in years, manners, and beauties; all which the
Moor is defective in. Now for want of these required conveniences,° her delicate tenderness will find itself abused, begin   225
to heave the gorge,° disrelish and abhor the Moor. Very nature
will instruct her in it and compel her to some second choice.
Now, sir, this granted — as it is a most pregnant° and unforced
position — who stands so eminent in the degree of this fortune
as Cassio does? A knave very voluble; no further conscionable°   230
than in putting on the mere form of civil and humane° seeming
for the better compassing of his salt° and most hidden loose
affection? Why, none! why, none! A slipper° and subtle knave;
a finder-out of occasions; that has an eye can stamp and counterfeit advantages, though true advantage never present itself;   235
a devilish knave! Besides, the knave is handsome, young, and
hath all those requisites in him that folly and green minds look
after. A pestilent complete knave! and the woman hath found
him already.

Roderigo: I cannot believe that in her; she's full of most blessed   240
condition.°

Iago: Blessed fig's-end! The wine she drinks is made of grapes. If she
had been blessed, she would never have loved the Moor. Blessed
pudding! Didst thou not see her paddle with the palm of his
hand? Didst not mark that?   245

Roderigo: Yes, that I did; but that was but courtesy.

Iago: Lechery, by this hand! an index and obscure prologue to the
history of lust and foul thoughts. They met so near with their
lips that their breaths embraced together. Villainous thoughts,

---

213 *court of guard:* Headquarters.   216 *thus:* i.e., on your lips.   224–25 *conveniences:*
Compatibilities.   226 *heave the gorge:* Be nauseated.   228 *pregnant:* Evident.   230 *conscio-
nable:* Conscientious.   231 *humane:* Polite.   232 *salt:* Lecherous.   233 *slipper:* Slippery.   240
condition: Character.

Roderigo! When these mutualities° so marshal the way, hard   250
at hand comes the master and main exercise, th' incorporate°
conclusion. Pish! But, sir, be you ruled by me: I have brought
you from Venice. Watch you to-night; for the command, I'll lay't
upon you. Cassio knows you not. I'll not be far from you: do you
find some occasion to anger Cassio, either by speaking too loud,   255
or tainting° his discipline, or from what other course you please
which the time shall more favorably minister.

Roderigo: Well.

Iago: Sir, he's rash and very sudden in choler,° and haply with his
truncheon may strike at you. Provoke him that he may; for even   260
out of that will I cause these of Cyprus to mutiny; whose qualifi-
cation° shall come into no true taste° again but by the displant-
ing of Cassio. So shall you have a shorter journey to your desires
by the means I shall then have to prefer° them; and the impedi-
ment most profitably removed without the which there were no   265
expectation of our prosperity.

Roderigo: I will do this if you can bring it to any opportunity.

Iago: I warrant thee. Meet me by and by at the citadel; I must fetch
his necessaries ashore. Farewell.

Roderigo: Adieu.   *Exit.*   270

Iago: That Cassio loves her, I do well believe't;
That she loves him, 'tis apt° and of great credit.
The Moor, howbeit that I endure him not,
Is of a constant, loving, noble nature,
And I dare think he'll prove to Desdemona   275
A most dear husband. Now I do love her too;
Not out of absolute lust, though peradventure
I stand accountant° for as great a sin,
But partly led to diet° my revenge,
For that I do suspect the lusty Moor   280
Hath leaped into my seat; the thought whereof
Doth, like a poisonous mineral, gnaw my inwards;
And nothing can or shall content my soul
Till I am evened with him, wife for wife;
Or failing so, yet that I put the Moor   285
At least into a jealousy so strong
That judgment cannot cure. Which thing to do,
If this poor trash of Venice, whom I trash°

---

250 *mutualities:* Exchanges.   251 *incorporate:* Carnal.   256 *tainting:* Discrediting.
259 *sudden in choler:* Violent in anger.   261–62 *qualification:* Appeasement.   262 *true
taste:* Satisfactory state.   264 *prefer:* Advance.   272 *apt:* Probable.   278 *accountant:*
Accountable.   279 *diet:* Feed.   288 *I trash:* I weight down (in order to keep under
control).

For° his quick hunting, stand the putting on,°
I'll have our Michael Cassio on the hip,°   290
Abuse him to the Moor in the rank garb°
(For I fear Cassio with my nightcap too),
Make the Moor thank me, love me, and reward me
For making him egregiously an ass
And practicing upon° his peace and quiet   295
Even to madness. 'Tis here, but yet confused:
Knavery's plain face is never seen till used.   *Exit.*

SCENE II: *A street in Cyprus.*

Enter Othello's Herald, with a proclamation.

Herald: It is Othello's pleasure, our noble and valiant general, that,
    upon certain tidings now arrived, importing the mere perdi-
    tion° of the Turkish fleet, every man put himself into triumph;
    some to dance, some to make bonfires, each man to what sport
    and revels his addiction leads him. For, besides these beneficial   5
    news, it is the celebration of his nuptial. So much was his plea-
    sure should be proclaimed. All offices° are open, and there is
    full liberty of feasting from the present hour of five till the bell
    have told eleven. Heaven bless the isle of Cyprus and our noble
    general Othello!   *Exit.*   10

SCENE III: *The Cyprian Castle.*

Enter Othello, Desdemona, Cassio, and Attendants.

Othello: Good Michael, look you to the guard to-night.
    Let's teach ourselves that honorable stop,
    Not to outsport discretion.
Cassio: Iago hath direction what to do;
    But not withstanding, with my personal eye   5
    Will I look to't.
Othello: Iago is most honest.
    Michael, good night. To-morrow with your earliest
    Let me have speech with you.
        [To Desdemona.]   Come, my dear love.
    The purchase made, the fruits are to ensue;
    That profit's yet to come 'tween me and you. —   10
    Good night.

                Exit [Othello with Desdemona and Attendants].

289 *For:* In order to develop; *stand the putting on:* Responds to my inciting. 290 *on
the hip:* At my mercy. 291 *rank garb:* Gross manner. 295 *practicing upon:* Plotting
against. **Scene II.** 2–3 *mere perdition:* Complete destruction. 7 *offices:* Kitchens
and storerooms.

Enter Iago.

Cassio: Welcome, Iago. We must to the watch.

Iago: Not this hour, lieutenant; 'tis not yet ten o' th' clock. Our general cast° us thus early for the love of his Desdemona; who let us not therefore blame. He hath not yet made wanton the night   15
with her, and she is sport for Jove.

Cassio: She's a most exquisite lady.

Iago: And, I'll warrant her, full of game.

Cassio: Indeed, she's a most fresh and delicate creature.

Iago: What an eye she has! Methinks it sounds a parley to provocation.   20

Cassio: An inviting eye; and yet methinks right modest.

Iago: And when she speaks, is it not an alarum to love?

Cassio: She is indeed perfection.

Iago: Well, happiness to their sheets! Come, lieutenant, I have a stoup° of wine, and here without are a brace of Cyprus gallants   25
that would fain have a measure to the health of black Othello.

Cassio: Not to-night, good Iago. I have very poor and unhappy brains for drinking; I could well wish courtesy would invent some other custom of entertainment.

Iago: O, they are our friends. But one cup! I'll drink for you.   30

Cassio: I have drunk but one cup to-night, and that was craftily qualified° too; and behold what innovation° it makes here. I am unfortunate in the infirmity and dare not task my weakness with any more.

Iago: What, man! 'Tis a night of revels: the gallants desire it.   35

Cassio: Where are they?

Iago: Here at the door; I pray you call them in.

Cassio: I'll do't, but it dislikes me.   *Exit.*

Iago: If I can fasten but one cup upon him
With that which he hath drunk to-night already,   40
He'll be as full of quarrel and offense
As my young mistress' dog. Now my sick fool Roderigo,
Whom love hath turned almost the wrong side out,
To Desdemona hath to-night caroused
Potations pottle-deep;° and he's to watch.   45
Three lads of Cyprus — noble swelling spirits,
That hold their honors in a wary distance,°
The very elements° of this warlike isle —
Have I to-night flustered with flowing cups,
And they watch too. Now, 'mongst this flock of drunkards   50

Scene III.   14 *cast:* Dismissed.   25 *stoup:* Two-quart tankard.   32 *qualified:* Diluted; *innovation:* Disturbance.   45 *pottle-deep:* Bottoms up.   47 *That ... distance:* Very sensitive about their honor.   48 *very elements:* True representatives.

Am I to put our Cassio in some action
That may offend the isle.

Enter Cassio, Montano, and Gentlemen [; Servants following with wine].

But here they come.
If consequence do but approve my dream,
My boat sails freely, both with wind and stream.

Cassio: 'Fore God, they have given me a rouse° already.   55
Montano: Good faith, a little one; not past a pint, as I am a soldier.
Iago: Some wine, ho!
　　[Sings.]   And let me the canakin clink, clink;
　　　　　　And let me the canakin clink
　　　　　　　A soldier's a man;   60
　　　　　　　A life's but a span,
　　　　　　Why then, let a soldier drink.
　　Some wine, boys!
Cassio: 'Fore God, an excellent song!
Iago: I learned it in England, where indeed they are most potent   65
　　in potting. Your Dane, your German, and your swag-bellied
　　Hollander — Drink, ho! — are nothing to your English.
Cassio: Is your Englishman so expert in his drinking?
Iago: Why, he drinks you with facility your Dane dead drunk; he
　　sweats not to overthrow your Almain; he gives your Hollander a   70
　　vomit ere the next pottle can be filled.
Cassio: To the health of our general!
Montano: I am for it, lieutenant, and I'll do you justice.
Iago: O sweet England!
　　[Sings.]   King Stephen was a worthy peer;   75
　　　　　　　His breeches cost him but a crown;
　　　　　　　He held 'em sixpence all too dear,
　　　　　　　　With that he called the tailor lown.°
　　　　　　　He was a wight of high renown,
　　　　　　　　And thou art but of low degree.   80
　　　　　　　'Tis pride that pulls the country down;
　　　　　　　　Then take thine auld cloak about thee.
　　Some wine, ho!
Cassio: 'Fore God, this is a more exquisite song than the other.
Iago: Will you hear't again?   85
Cassio: No, for I hold him to be unworthy of his place that does
　　those things.° Well, God's above all; and there be souls must be
　　saved, and there be souls must not be saved.
Iago: It's true, good lieutenant.
Cassio: For mine own part — no offense to the general, nor any man   90
　　of quality — I hope to be saved.

---

55 *rouse:* Bumper.   78 *lown:* Rascal.   86-7 *does those things:* i.e., behaves in this
fashion.

Iago: And so do I too, lieutenant.

Cassio: Ay, but, by your leave, not before me. The lieutenant is to
be saved before the ancient. Let's have no more of this; let's to
our affairs. — God forgive us our sins! — Gentlemen, let's look   95
to our business. Do not think, gentlemen, I am drunk. This is
my ancient; this is my right hand, and this is my left. I am not
drunk now. I can stand well enough, and I speak well enough.

All: Excellent well!

Cassio: Why, very well then. You must not think then that I am   100
drunk.   *Exit.*

Montano: To th' platform, masters. Come, let's set the watch.

Iago: You see this fellow that is gone before.
          He's a soldier fit to stand by Caesar
          And give direction; and do but see his vice.   105
          'Tis to his virtue a just equinox,°
          The one as long as th' other. 'Tis pity of him.
          I fear the trust Othello puts him in,
          On some odd time of his infirmity,
          Will shake this island.

Montano: But is he often thus?   110

Iago: 'Tis evermore his prologue to his sleep:
          He'll watch the horologe a double set°
          If drink rock not his cradle.

Montano: It were well
          The general were put in mind of it.
          Perhaps he sees it not, or his good nature   115
          Prizes the virtue that appears in Cassio
          And looks not on his evils. Is not this true?

          Enter Roderigo.

Iago [*aside to him*]: How now, Roderigo?
          I pray you after the lieutenant, go!

                                        Exit Roderigo.

Montano: And 'tis great pity that the noble Moor   120
          Should hazard such a place as his own second
          With one of an ingraft° infirmity.
          It were an honest action to say
          So to the Moor.

Iago: Not I, for this fair island!
          I do love Cassio well and would do much   125
          To cure him of this evil.
                    (*Within.*) Help! help!
                              But hark! What noise?

---

106 *just equinox:* Exact equivalent.   112 *watch . . . set:* Stay awake twice around the
clock.   122 *ingraft:* i.e., ingrained.

Enter Cassio, driving in Roderigo.

Cassio: Zounds, you rogue! you rascal!
Montano: What's the matter, lieutenant?
Cassio: A knave to teach me my duty?
   I'll beat the knave into a twiggen° bottle.   130
Roderigo: Beat me?
Cassio: Dost thou prate, rogue? *[Strikes him.]*
Montano: Nay, good lieutenant!
                                    [Stays him.]
   I pray you, sir, hold your hand.
Cassio: Let me go, sir,
   Or I'll knock you o'er the mazzard.°
Montano: Come, come, you're drunk!
Cassio: Drunk?

   They fight.

Iago [aside to Roderigo]: Away, I say! Go out and cry a mutiny!   135
                                      Exit Roderigo.
   Nay, good lieutenant. God's will, gentlemen!
   Help, ho! — lieutenant — sir — Montano — sir —
   Help, masters! — Here's a goodly watch indeed!

   A bell rung.

   Who's that which rings the bell? Diablo, ho!
   The town will rise.° God's will, lieutenant, hold!   140
   You'll be shamed for ever.

   Enter Othello and Gentlemen with weapons.

Othello: What is the matter here?
Montano: Zounds, I bleed still. I am hurt to th' death.
   He dies!
Othello: Hold for your lives!
Iago: Hold, hold! Lieutenant — sir — Montano — gentlemen!   145
   Have you forgot all sense of place and duty?
   Hold! The general speaks to you. Hold, for shame!
Othello: Why, how now ho? From whence ariseth this?
   Are we turned Turks, and to ourselves do that
   Which heaven hath forbid the Ottomites?   150
   For Christian shame put by this barbarous brawl!
   He that stirs next to carve for° his own rage
   Holds his soul light; he dies upon his motion.
   Silence that dreadful bell! It frights the isle
   From her propriety.° What is the matter, masters?   155
   Honest Iago, that looks dead with grieving,

---

130 *twiggen:* Wicker-covered.   133 *mazzard:* Head.   140 *rise:* Grow riotous.   152 *carve
for:* Indulge.   155 *propriety:* Proper self.

        Speak. Who began this? On thy love, I charge thee.
Iago: I do not know. Friends all, but now, even now,
        In quarter,° and in terms like bride and groom
        Devesting them for bed; and then, but now—   160
        As if some planet had unwitted men—
        Swords out, and tilting one at other's breast
        In opposition bloody. I cannot speak
        Any beginning to this peevish odds,°
        And would in action glorious I had lost   165
        Those legs that brought me to a part of it!
Othello: How comes it, Michael, you are thus forgot?
Cassio: I pray you pardon me; I cannot speak.
Othello: Worthy Montano, you were wont to be civil;
        The gravity and stillness of your youth   170
        The world hath noted, and your name is great
        In months of wisest censure.° What's the matter
        That you unlace° your reputation thus
        And spend your rich opinion° for the name
        Of a night-brawler? Give me answer to it.   175
Montano: Worthy Othello, I am hurt to danger.
        Your officer, Iago, can inform you,
        While I spare speech, which something now offends° me,
        Of all that I do know; nor know I aught
        By me that's said or done amiss this night,   180
        Unless self-charity be sometimes a vice,
        And to defend ourselves it be a sin
        When violence assails us.
Othello: Now, by heaven,
        My blood° begins my safer guides to rule,
        And passion, having my best judgment collied,°   185
        Assays° to lead the way. If I once stir
        Or do but lift this arm, the best of you
        Shall sink in my rebuke. Give me to know
        How this foul rout began, who set it on;
        And he that is approved in° this offense,   190
        Though he had twinned with me, both at a birth,
        Shall lose me. What! in a town of war,
        Yet wild, the people's hearts brimful of fear,
        To manage° private and domestic quarrel?
        In night, and on the court and guard of safety?   195
        'Tis monstrous. Iago, who began't?

---

159 *quarter:* Friendliness.   164 *peevish odds:* Childish quarrel.   172 *censure:* Judgment.
173 *unlace:* Undo.   174 *rich opinion:* High reputation.   178 *offends:* Pains.   184 *blood:*
Passion.   185 *collied:* Darkened.   186 *Assays:* Tries.   190 *approved in:* Proved guilty
of.   194 *manage:* Carry on.

Montano: If partially affined, or leagued in office,°
    Thou dost deliver more or less than truth,
    Thou art no soldier.
Iago: Touch me not so near.
    I had rather have this tongue cut from my mouth   200
    Than it should do offense to Michael Cassio;
    Yet I persuade myself, to speak the truth
    Shall nothing wrong him. This it is, general.
    Montano and myself being in speech,
    There comes a fellow crying out for help,   205
    And Cassio following him with determined sword
    To execute° upon him. Sir, this gentleman
    Steps in to Cassio and entreats his pause.
    Myself the crying fellow did pursue,
    Lest by his clamor—as it so fell out—   210
    The town might fall in fright. He, swift of foot,
    Outran my purpose; and I returned then rather
    For that I heard the clink and fall of swords,
    And Cassio high in oath;° which till to-night
    I ne'er might say before. When I came back—   215
    For this was brief—I found them close together
    At blow and thrust, even as again they were
    When you yourself did part them.
    More of this matter cannot I report;
    But men are men; the best sometimes forget.   220
    Though Cassio did some little wrong to him,
    As men in rage strike those that wish them best,
    Yet surely Cassio I believe received
    From him that fled some strange indignity,
    Which patience could not pass.°
Othello: I know, Iago,   225
    Thy honesty and love doth mince this matter,
    Making it light to Cassio. Cassio, I love thee;
    But never more be officer of mine.

    Enter Desdemona, attended.

    Look if my gentle love be not raised up!
    I'll make thee an example.
Desdemona: What's the matter?   230
Othello: All's well now, sweeting; come away to bed.
    [To Montano.]
    Sir, for your hurts, myself will be your surgeon.
    Lead him off.

---

197 *partially . . . office:* Prejudiced by comradeship or official relations.   207 *execute:*
Work his will.   214 *high in oath:* Cursing.   225 *pass:* Pass over, ignore.

[Montano is led off.]

Iago, look with care about the town
And silence those whom this vile brawl distracted.°   235
Come, Desdemona; 'tis the soldiers' life
To have their balmy slumbers waked with strife.

                                      Exit [with all but Iago and Cassio].

Iago: What, are you hurt, lieutenant?

Cassio: Ay, past all surgery.

Iago: Marry, God forbid!   240

Cassio: Reputation, reputation, reputation! O, I have lost my reputation! I have lost the immortal part of myself, and what remains
is bestial. My reputation, Iago, my reputation!

Iago: As I am an honest man, I thought you had received some
bodily wound. There is more sense in that than in reputation.   245
Reputation is an idle and most false imposition; oft got without
merit and lost without deserving. You have lost no reputation at
all unless you repute yourself such a loser. What, man! there are
ways to recover° the general again. You are but now cast in his
mood° — a punishment more in policy than in malice, even so   250
as one would beat his offenseless dog to affright an imperious
lion. Sue to him again, and he's yours.

Cassio: I will rather sue to be despised than to deceive so good a commander with so slight, so drunken, and so indiscreet an officer.
Drunk! and speak parrot!° and squabble! swagger! swear! and   255
discourse fustian° with one's own shadow! O thou invisible
spirit of wine, if thou hast no name to be known by, let us call
thee devil!

Iago: What was he that you followed with your sword? What had he
done to you?   260

Cassio: I know not.

Iago: Is't possible?

Cassio: I remember a mass of things, but nothing distinctly; a
quarrel, but nothing wherefore. O God, that men should put
an enemy in their mouths to steal away their brains! that we   265
should with joy, pleasance, revel, and applause° transform ourselves into beasts!

Iago: Why, but you are now well enough. How came you thus
recovered?

Cassio: It hath pleased the devil drunkenness to give place to the   270
devil wrath. One unperfectness shows me another, to make me
frankly despise myself.

---

235 *distracted:* Excited. 249 *recover:* Regain favor with. 249–50 *in his mood:* Dismissed because of his anger. 255 *parrot:* Meaningless phrases. 256 *fustian:* Bombastic
nonsense. 266 *applause:* Desire to please.

Iago: Come, you are too severe a moraler. As the time, the place, and
the condition of this country stands, I could heartily wish this
had not so befall'n; but since it is as it is, mend it for your own   275
good.

Cassio: I will ask him for my place again: he shall tell me I am a
drunkard! Had I as many mouths as Hydra,° such an answer
would stop them all. To be now a sensible man, by and by a
fool, and presently a beast! O strange! Every inordinate cup is   280
unblest, and the ingredient° is a devil.

Iago: Come, come, good wine is a good familiar creature if it be well
used. Exclaim no more against it. And, good lieutenant, I think
you think I love you.

Cassio: I have well approved° it, sir. I drunk!   285

Iago: You or any man living may be drunk at some time, man. I'll
tell you what you shall do. Our general's wife is now the general.
I may say so in this respect, for that he hath devoted and given
up himself to the contemplation, mark, and denotement of her
parts and graces. Confess yourself freely to her; importune her   290
help to put you in your place again. She is of so free,° so kind,
so apt, so blessed a disposition she holds it a vice in her goodness not to do more than she is requested. This broken joint
between you and her husband entreat her to splinter;° and my
fortunes against any lay° worth naming, this crack of your love   295
shall grow stronger than it was before.

Cassio: You advise me well.

Iago: I protest, in the sincerity of love and honest kindness.

Cassio: I think it freely; and betimes in the morning will I beseech
the virtuous Desdemona to undertake for me. I am desperate of   300
my fortunes if they check me here.

Iago: You are in the right. Good night, lieutenant; I must to the watch.

Cassio: Good night, honest Iago.   *Exit Cassio.*

Iago: And what's he then that says I play the villain,
When this advice is free I give and honest,   305
Probal° to thinking, and indeed the course
To win the Moor again? For 'tis most easy
Th' inclining Desdemona to subdue°
In an honest suit; she's framed as fruitful
As the free elements. And then for her   310
To win the Moor—were't to renounce his baptism,
All seals and symbols of redeemèd sin—
His soul is so enfettered to her love
That she may make, unmake, do what she list,

---

278 *Hydra:* Monster with many heads.   281 *ingredient:* Contents.   285 *approved:*
Proved.   291 *free:* Bounteous.   294 *splinter:* Bind up with splints.   295 *lay:* Wager.
306 *Probal:* Probable.   308 *subdue:* Persuade.

Even as her appetite shall play the god   315
With his weak function. How am I then a villain
To counsel Cassio to this parallel° course,
Directly to his good? Divinity° of hell!
When devils will the blackest sins put on,°
They do suggest at first with heavenly shows,   320
As I do now. For whiles this honest fool
Plies Desdemona to repair his fortunes,
And she for him pleads strongly to the Moor,
I'll pour this pestilence into his ear,
That she repeals him° for her body's lust;   325
And by how much she strives to do him good,
She shall undo her credit with the Moor.
So will I turn her virtue into pitch,
And out of her own goodness make the net
That shall enmesh them all.

Enter Roderigo.

                    How, now, Roderigo?   330

Roderigo: I do follow here in the chase, not like a hound that hunts,
but one that fills up the cry.° My money is almost spent; I have
been to-night exceedingly well cudgelled; and I think the issue will
be—I shall have so much experience for my pains; and so, with no
money at all, and a little more wit, return again to Venice.   335

Iago: How poor are they that have not patience!
What wound did ever heal but by degrees?
Thou know'st we work by wit, and not by witchcraft;
And wit depends on dilatory time.
Does't not go well? Cassio hath beaten thee,   340
And thou by that small hurt hast cashiered Cassio.°
Though other things grow fair against the sun,
Yet fruits that blossom first will first be ripe.
Content thyself awhile. By the mass, 'tis morning!
Pleasure and action make the hours seem short.   345
Retire thee; go where thou art billeted.
Away, I say! Thou shalt know more hereafter.
Nay, get thee gone!   *Exit Roderigo.*
                    Two things are to be done:
My wife must move for Cassio to her mistress;
I'll set her on;   350
Myself the while to draw the Moor apart
And bring him jump° when he may Cassio find

---

317 *parallel:* Corresponding.   318 *Divinity:* Theology.   319 *put on:* Incite.   325 *repeals him:* Seeks his recall.   332 *cry:* Pack.   341 *cashiered Cassio:* Maneuvered Cassio's discharge.   352 *jump:* At the exact moment.

Soliciting his wife. Ay, that's the way!
Dull no device by coldness and delay.   *Exit.*

ACT III

SCENE I: *Before the chamber of Othello and Desdemona.*

Enter Cassio, with Musicians and the Clown.

Cassio: Masters, play here, I will content° your pains:
Something that's brief; and bid "Good morrow, general."

[They play.]

Clown: Why, masters, ha' your instruments been in Naples,° that
they speak i' th' nose thus?

Musician: How, sir, how?   5

Clown: Are these, I pray you, called wind instruments?

Musician: Ay, marry, are they, sir.

Clown: O, thereby hangs a tail.

Musician: Whereby hangs a tail, sir?

Clown: Marry, sir, by many a wind instrument that I know. But, mas-   10
ters, here's money for you; and the general so likes your music
that he desires you, for love's sake, to make no more noise with it.

Musician: Well, sir, we will not.

Clown: If you have any music that may not be heard, to't again: but,
as they say, to hear music the general does not greatly care.   15

Musician: We have none such, sir.

Clown: Then put up your pipes in your bag, for I'll away. Go, vanish
into air, away!   *Exit Musician [with his fellows].*

Cassio: Dost thou hear, my honest friend?

Clown: No, I hear not your honest friend. I hear you.   20

Cassio: Prithee keep up thy quillets.° There's a poor piece of gold
for thee. If the gentlewoman that attends the general's wife be
stirring, tell her there's one Cassio entreats her a little favor of
speech. Wilt thou do this?

Clown: She is stirring sir. If she will stir hither, I shall seem to notify   25
unto her.

Cassio: [Do, good my friend.]   *Exit Clown.*

Enter Iago.

                              In happy time,° Iago.

Iago: You have not been abed then?

Act III, Scene I.   1 *content:* Reward.   3 *Naples:* (Notorious for its association with
venereal disease).   21 *quillets:* Quips.   27 *In happy time:* Well met.

Cassio: Why, no; the day had broke
   Before we parted. I have made bold, Iago,   30
   To send in to your wife: my suit to her
   Is that she will to virtuous Desdemona
   Procure me some access.
Iago: I'll send her to you presently;
   And I'll devise a mean to draw the Moor
   Out of the way, that your converse and business   35
   May be more free.
Cassio: I humbly thank you for't.   *Exit [Iago].*
                                I never knew
   A Florentine° more kind and honest.

   Enter Emilia.

Emilia: Good morrow, good lieutenant. I am sorry
   For your displeasure: but all will sure be well.   40
   The general and his wife are talking of it,
   And she speaks for you stoutly. The Moor replied
   That he you hurt is of great fame in Cyprus
   And great affinity,° and that in wholesome wisdom
   He might not but refuse you; but he protests he loves you,   45
   And needs no other suitor but his likings
   [To take the safest occasion° by the front°]
   To bring you in again.
Cassio: Yet I beseech you,
   If you think fit, or that it may be done,
   Give me advantage of some brief discourse   50
   With Desdemona alone.
Emilia: Pray you come in.
   I will bestow you where you shall have time
   To speak your bosom° freely.
Cassio: I am much bound to you.   *Exeunt.*

Scene II: *The castle.*

   Enter Othello, Iago, and Gentlemen.

Othello: These letters give, Iago, to the pilot
   And by him do my duties to the Senate.
   That done, I will be walking on the works;°
   Repair there to me.
Iago: Well, my good lord, I'll do't.
Othello: This fortification, gentlemen, shall we see't?   5
Gentlemen: We'll wait upon your lordship.   *Exeunt.*

---

38 *Florentine:* i.e., even a Florentine (like Cassio; Iago was a Venetian).   44 *affinity:*
Family connections.   47 *occasion:* Opportunity;   *front:* Forelock.   53 *your bosom:*
Your inmost thoughts.   **Scene II.**   3 *works:* Fortifications.

SCENE III: *The castle grounds.*

Enter Desdemona, Cassio, and Emilia.

Desdemona: Be thou assured, good Cassio, I will do
    All my abilities in thy behalf.
Emilia: Good madam, do. I warrant it grieves my husband
    As if the cause were his.
Desdemona: O, that's an honest fellow. Do not doubt, Cassio,   5
    But I will have my lord and you again
    As friendly as you were.
Cassio: Bounteous madam,
    Whatever shall become of Michael Cassio,
    He's never anything but your true servant.
Desdemona: I know't; I thank you. You do love my lord;   10
    You have known him long; and be you well assured
    He shall in strangeness° stand no farther off
    Than in a politic distance.°
Cassio: Ay, but, lady,
    That policy may either last so long,
    Or feed upon such nice and waterish diet,°   15
    Or breed itself so out of circumstance,
    That, I being absent, and my place supplied,
    My general will forget my love and service.
Desdemona: Do not doubt° that; before Emilia here
    I give thee warrant of thy place. Assure thee,   20
    If I do vow a friendship, I'll perform it
    To the last article. My lord shall never rest;
    I'll watch him tame° and talk him out of patience;
    His bed shall seem a school, his board a shrift;°
    I'll intermingle everything he does   25
    With Cassio's suit. Therefore be merry, Cassio,
    For thy solicitor shall rather die
    Than give thy cause away.

Enter Othello and Iago [at a distance].

Emilia: Madam, here comes my lord.
Cassio: Madam, I'll take my leave.   30
Desdemona: Why, stay, and hear me speak.
Cassio: Madam, not now: I am very ill at ease,
    Unfit for mine own purposes.
Desdemona: Well, do your discretion.   *Exit Cassio.*
Iago: Ha! I like not that.
Othello: What dost thou say?   35

Scene III. 12 *strangeness:* Aloofness. 13 *Than . . . distance:* Than wise policy requires.
15 *Or . . . diet:* Or be continued for such slight reasons. 19 *doubt:* Fear. 23 *watch him tame:* Keep him awake until he gives in. 24 *shrift:* Confessional.

Iago: Nothing, my lord; or if—I know not what.
Othello: Was not that Cassio parted from my wife?
Iago: Cassio, my lord? No, sure, I cannot think it,
    That he would steal away so guilty-like,
    Seeing your coming.
Othello: I do believe 'twas he.   40
Desdemona: How now, my lord?
    I have been talking with a suitor here,
    A man that languishes in your displeasure.
Othello: What is't you mean?
Desdemona: Why, your lieutenant, Cassio. Good my lord,   45
    If I have any grace or power to move you,
    His present° reconciliation take;
    For if he be not one that truly loves you,
    That errs in ignorance, and not in cunning,
    I have no judgment in an honest face,   50
    I prithee call him back.
Othello: Went he hence now?
Desdemona: Yes, faith; so humbled
    That he hath left part of his grief with me
    To suffer with him. Good love, call him back.
Othello: Not now, sweet Desdemon; some other time.   55
Desdemona: But shall't be shortly?
Othello: The sooner, sweet, for you.
Desdemona: Shall't be to-night at supper?
Othello: No, not to-night.
Desdemona: To-morrow dinner then?
Othello: I shall not dine at home;
    I meet the captains at the citadel.
Desdemona: Why then, to-morrow night, or Tuesday morn,   60
    On Tuesday noon or night, or Wednesday morn.
    I prithee name the time, but let it not
    Exceed three days. I' faith, he's penitent;
    And yet his trespass, in our common reason
    (Save that, they say, the wars must make examples   65
    Out of their best), is not almost° a fault
    T' incur a private check.° When shall he come?
    Tell me, Othello. I wonder in my soul
    What you could ask me that I should deny
    Or stand so mamm'ring on.° What? Michael Cassio,   70
    That came a-wooing with you, and so many a time,
    When I have spoke of you dispraisingly,
    Hath ta'en your part—to have so much to do

---

47 *present:* Immediate.   66 *not almost:* Hardly.   67 *a private check:* Even a private reprimand.   70 *mamm'ring on:* Hesitating about.

To bring him in? By'r Lady, I could do much —
Othello: Prithee no more. Let him come when he will!   75
    I will deny thee nothing.
Desdemona: Why, this is not a boon;
    'Tis as I should entreat you wear your gloves,
    Or feed on nourishing dishes, or keep you warm,
    Or sue to you to do a peculiar profit
    To your own person. Nay, when I have a suit   80
    Wherein I mean to touch your love indeed,
    It shall be full of poise and difficult weight,
    And fearful° to be granted.
Othello: I will deny thee nothing!
    Whereon I do beseech thee grant me this,
    To leave me but a little to myself.   85
Desdemona: Shall I deny you? No. Farewell, my lord.
Othello: Farewell, my Desdemon: I'll come to thee straight.
Desdemona: Emilia, come. — Be as your fancies teach you;
    Whate'er you be, I am obedient.   *Exit [with Emilia].*
Othello: Excellent wretch!° Perdition catch my soul   90
    But I do love thee! and when I love thee not,
    Chaos is come again.
Iago: My noble lord —
Othello: What dost thou say, Iago?
Iago: Did Michael Cassio, when you wooed my lady,
    Know of your love?   95
Othello: He did, from first to last. Why dost thou ask?
Iago: But for a satisfaction of my thought;
    No further harm.
Othello: Why of thy thought, Iago?
Iago: I did not think he had been acquainted with her.
Othello: O, yes, and went between us° very oft.   100
Iago: Indeed?
Othello: Indeed? Ay, indeed! Discern'st thou aught in that?
    Is he not honest?
Iago: Honest, my lord?
Othello: Honest. Ay, honest.
Iago: My lord, for aught I know.
Othello: What dost thou think?
Iago: Think, my lord?
Othello: Think, my lord?   105
    By heaven, he echoes me,
    As if there were some monster in his thought
    Too hideous to be shown. Thou dost mean something:

83 *fearful:* Dangerous.   90 *wretch:* (A term of endearment).   100 *went between us:* (i.e.,
as messenger).

I heard thee say even now, thou lik'st not that,
When Cassio left my wife. What didst not like?   110
And when I told thee he was of my counsel
In my whole course of wooing, thou cried'st "Indeed?"
And didst contract and purse thy brow together,
As if thou then hadst shut up in thy brain
Some horrible conceit.° If thou dost love me,   115
Show me thy thought
Iago: My lord, you know I love you.
Othello: I think thou dost;
And, for I know thou'rt full of love and honesty
And weigh'st thy words before thou giv'st them breath,
Therefore these stops of thine fright me the more;   120
For such things in a false disloyal knave
Are tricks of custom; but in a man that's just
They are close dilations, working from the heart
That passion cannot rule.°
Iago: For Michael Cassio,
I dare be sworn I think that he is honest.   125
Othello: I think so too.
Iago: Men should be what they seem;
Or those that be not, would they might seem none!°
Othello: Certain, men should be what they seem.
Iago: Why then, I think Cassio's an honest man.
Othello: Nay, yet there's more in this.   130
I prithee speak to me as to thy thinkings,
As thou dost ruminate, and give thy worst of thoughts
The worst of words.
Iago: Good my lord, pardon me:
Though I am bound to every act of duty,
I am not bound to that all slaves are free to.°   135
Utter my thoughts? Why, say they are vile and false,
As where's that palace whereinto foul things
Sometimes intrude not? Who has a breast so pure
But some uncleanly apprehensions
Keep leets and law days,° and in Sessions sit   140
With meditations lawful?
Othello: Thou dost conspire against thy friend, Iago,
If thou but think'st him wronged, and mak'st his ear
A stranger to thy thoughts.
Iago: I do beseech you —

---

115 *conceit:* Fancy.   123–24 *close dilations . . . rule:* Secret emotions which well up in spite of restraint.   127 *seem none:* i.e., not pretend to be men when they are really monsters.   135 *bound . . . free to:* Bound to tell that which even slaves are allowed to keep to themselves.   140 *leets and law days:* Sittings of the courts.

Though I perchance am vicious in my guess   145
(As I confess it is my nature's plague
To spy into abuses, and oft my jealousy°
Shapes faults that are not), that your wisdom yet
From one that so imperfectly conjects°
Would take no notice, nor build yourself a trouble   150
Out of his scattering and unsure observance.
It were not for your quiet nor your good,
Nor for my manhood, honesty, and wisdom,
To let you know my thoughts.
Othello: What dost thou mean?
Iago: Good name in man and woman, dear my lord,   155
Is the immediate° jewel of their souls.
Who steals my purse steals trash; 'tis something, nothing;
'Twas mine, 'tis his, and has been slave to thousands;
But he that filches from me my good name
Robs me of that which not enriches him   160
And makes me poor indeed.
Othello: By heaven, I'll know thy thoughts!
Iago: You cannot, if my heart were in your hand;
Nor shall not whilst 'tis in my custody.
Othello: Ha!
Iago: O, beware, my lord, of jealousy!   165
It is the green-eyed monster, which doth mock°
The meat it feeds on. That cuckold lives in bliss
Who, certain of his fate, loves not his wronger;
But O, what damnèd minutes tells he o'er
Who dotes, yet doubts — suspects, yet strongly loves!   170
Othello: O misery!
Iago: Poor and content is rich, and rich enough;
But riches fineless° is as poor as winter
To him that ever fears he shall be poor.
Good God, the souls of all my tribe defend   175
From jealousy!
Othello: Why, why is this?
Think'st thou I'ld make a life of jealousy,
To follow still the changes of the moon
With fresh suspicions? No! To be once in doubt
Is once to be resolved. Exchange me for a goat   180
When I shall turn the business of my soul
To such exsufflicate and blown° surmises,
Matching this inference. 'Tis not to make me jealous

---

147 *jealousy:* Suspicion.   149 *conjects:* Conjectures.   156 *immediate:* Nearest the heart.
166 *mock:* Play with, like a cat with a mouse.   173 *fineless:* Unlimited.   182 *exsufflicate and blown:* Spat out and flyblown.

To say my wife is fair, feeds well, loves company,
Is free of speech, sings, plays, and dances;   185
Where virtue is, these are more virtuous.
Nor from mine own weak merits will I draw
The smallest fear or doubt of her revolt,°
For she had eyes, and chose me. No, Iago;
I'll see before I doubt; when I doubt, prove;   190
And on the proof there is no more but this —
Away at once with love or jealousy!
Iago: I am glad of this; for now I shall have reason
   To show the love and duty that I bear you
   With franker spirit. Therefore, as I am bound,   195
   Receive it from me. I speak not yet of proof.
   Look at your wife; observe her well with Cassio;
   Wear your eyes thus, not jealous nor secure:°
   I would not have your free and noble nature,
   Out of self-bounty,° be abused. Look to't.   200
   I know our country disposition well:
   In Venice they do let God see the pranks
   They dare not show their husbands; their best conscience
   Is not to leave't undone, but keep't unknown.
Othello: Dost thou say so?   205
Iago: She did deceive her father, marrying you;
   And when she seemed to shake and fear your looks,
   She loved them most.
Othello: And so she did.
Iago: Why, go to then!
   She that, so young, could give out such a seeming
   To seel° her father's eyes up close as oak° —   210
   He thought 'twas witchcraft — but I am much to blame.
   I humbly do beseech you of your pardon
   For too much loving you.
Othello: I am bound to thee for ever.
Iago: I see this hath a little dashed your spirits.
Othello: Not a jot, not a jot.
Iago: I' faith, I fear it has.   215
   I hope you will consider what is spoke
   Comes from my love. But I do see y' are moved.
   I am to pray you not to strain my speech
   To grosser issues° nor to larger reach
   Than to suspicion.   220
Othello: I will not.

---

188 *revolt:* Unfaithfulness.   198 *secure:* Overconfident.   200 *self-bounty:* Natural goodness.   210 *seel:* Close; *oak:* Oak grain.   219 *To grosser issues:* To mean something more
monstrous.

Iago: Should you do so, my lord,
   My speech should fall into such vile success°
   As my thoughts aim not at. Cassio's my worthy friend—
   My lord, I see y' are moved.
Othello: No, not much moved:
   I do not think but Desdemona's honest.°   225
Iago: Long live she so! and long live you to think so!
Othello: And yet, how nature erring from itself—
Iago: Ay, there's the point! as (to be bold with you)
   Not to affect many proposèd matches
   Of her own clime, complexion, and degree,   230
   Whereto we see in all things nature tends—
   Foh! one may smell in such a will most rank,
   Foul disproportions, thought unnatural—
   But pardon me—I do not in position°
   Distinctly speak of her; though I may fear   235
   Her will, recoiling° to her better judgment,
   May fall to match° you with her country forms,
   And happily° repent.
Othello: Farewell, farewell!
   If more thou dost perceive, let me know more.
   Set on thy wife to observe. Leave me, Iago.   240
Iago: My lord, I take my leave.   *[Going.]*
Othello: Why did I marry? This honest creature doubtless
   Sees and knows more, much more, than he unfolds.
Iago [returns]: My lord, I would I might entreat your honor
   To scan this thing no further: leave it to time.   245
   Although 'tis fit that Cassio have his place,
   For sure he fills it up with great ability,
   Yet, if you please to hold off a while,
   You shall by that perceive him and his means.
   Note if your lady strain his entertainment°   250
   With any strong or vehement importunity;
   Much will be seen in that. In the mean time
   Let me be thought too busy° in my fears
   (As worthy cause I have to fear I am)
   And hold her free,° I do beseech your honor.   255
Othello: Fear not my government.°
Iago: I once more take my leave.   *Exit.*
Othello: This fellow 's of exceeding honesty,

---

222 *vile success:* Evil outcome.   225 *honest:* Chaste.   234 *position:* Definite assertion.
236 *recoiling:* Reverting.   237 *fall to match:* Happen to compare.   238 *happily:*
Haply, perhaps.   250 *strain his entertainment:* Urge his recall.   253 *busy:* Meddle-
some.   255 *hold her free:* Consider her guiltless.   256 *government:* Self-control.

And knows all qualities,° with a learned spirit
Of° human dealings. If I do prove her haggard,°   260
Though that her jesses° were my dear heartstrings,
I'd whistle her off and let her down the wind
To prey at fortune.° Haply, for I am black
And have not those soft parts of conversation°
That chamberers° have, or for I am declined   265
Into the vale of years — yet that's not much —
She's gone. I am abused, and my relief
Must be to loathe her. O curse of marriage,
That we can call these delicate creatures ours,
And not their appetites! I had rather be a toad   270
And live upon the vapor of a dungeon
Than keep a corner in the thing I love
For others' uses. Yet 'tis the plague of great ones;°
Prerogatived° are they less than the base.
'Tis destiny unshunnable, like death.   275
Even then this forkèd plague° is fated to us
When we do quicken.° Look where she comes.

Enter Desdemona and Emilia.

If she be false, O, then heaven mocks itself!
I'll not believe't.
Desdemona: How now, my dear Othello?
Your dinner, and the generous° islanders   280
By you invited, do attend your presence.
Othello: I am to blame.
Desdemona: Why do you speak so faintly?
Are you not well?
Othello: I have a pain upon my forehead, here.
Desdemona: Faith, that's with watching;° 'twill away again.   285
Let me but bind it hard, within this hour
It will be well.
Othello: Your napkin° is too little;

[He pushes the handkerchief from him, and it falls unnoticed.]

Let it° alone. Come, I'll go in with you.
Desdemona: I am very sorry that you are not well.   *Exit [with Othello].*
Emilia: I am glad I have found this napkin;   290

---

259 *qualities:* Natures.   259–60 *learned spirit Of:* Mind informed about.   260 *haggard:* A wild hawk.   261 *jesses:* Thongs for controlling a hawk.   262–63 *whistle . . . fortune:* Turn her out and let her take care of herself.   264 *soft . . . conversation:* Ingratiating manners.   265 *chamberers:* Courtiers.   273 *great ones:* Prominent men.   274 *Prerogatived:* Privileged.   276 *forkèd plague:* i.e., horns of a cuckold.   277 *do quicken:* Are born.   280 *generous:* Noble.   285 *watching:* Working late.   287 *napkin:* Handkerchief.   288 *it:* i.e., his forehead.

This was her first remembrance from the Moor,
My wayward husband hath a hundred times
Wooed me to steal it; but she so loves the token
(For he conjured her she should ever keep it)
That she reserves it evermore about her   295
To kiss and talk to. I'll have the work ta'en out°
And give't Iago.
What he will do with it heaven knows, not I;
I nothing but to please his fantasy.°

Enter Iago.

Iago: How now? What do you here alone?   300
Emilia: Do not you chide; I have a thing for you.
Iago: A thing for me? It is a common thing—
Emilia: Ha?
Iago: To have a foolish wife.
Emilia: O, is that all? What will you give me now   305
For that same handkerchief?
Iago: What handkerchief?
Emilia: What handkerchief!
Why, that the Moor first gave to Desdemona;
That which so often you did bid me steal.
Iago: Hast stol'n it from her?   310
Emilia: No, faith; she let it drop by negligence,
And to th' advantage,° I, being here, took't up.
Look, here it is.
Iago: A good wench! Give it me.
Emilia: What will you do with't, that you have been so earnest
To have me filch it?
Iago: Why, what is that to you?   315

[Snatches it.]

Emilia: If it be not for some purpose of import,°
Give't me again. Poor lady, she'll run mad
When she shall lack it.
Iago: Be not acknown on't;° I have use for it.
Go, leave me.   *Exit Emilia.*   320
I will in Cassio's lodgings lose this napkin
And let him find it. Trifles light as air
Are to the jealous confirmations strong
As proofs of holy writ. This may do something.
The Moor already changes with my poison: 325
Dangerous conceits° are in their nature poisons,

296 *work ta'en out:* Pattern copied.   299 *fantasy:* Whim.   312 *to th' advantage:*
Opportunely.   316 *import:* Importance.   319 *Be . . . on't:* Do not acknowledge it.
326 *conceits:* Ideas.

Which at the first are scarce found to distaste,
But with a little act upon the blood
Burn like the mines of sulphur.

Enter Othello.

                              I did say so.
Look where he comes! Not poppy nor mandragora,°   330
Nor all the drowsy syrups of the world,
Shall ever med'cine thee to that sweet sleep
Which thou owedst yesterday.
Othello: Ha! ha! false to me?
Iago: Why, how now, general? No more of that!
Othello: Avaunt! be gone! Thou hast set me on the rack.   335
   I swear 'tis better to be much abused
   Than but to know't a little.
Iago: How now, my lord?
Othello: What sense had I of her stol'n hours of lust?
   I saw't not, thought it not, it harmed not me;
   I slept the next night well, fed well, was free° and merry;   340
   I found not Cassio's kisses on her lips
   He that is robbed, not wanting° what is stol'n,
   Let him not know't, and he's not robbed at all.
Iago: I am sorry to hear this.
Othello: I had been happy if the general camp,   345
   Pioneers° and all, had tasted her sweet body,
   So I had nothing known. O, now for ever
   Farewell the tranquil mind! farewell content!
   Farewell the plumèd troop, and the big° wars
   That make ambition virtue! O, farewell!   350
   Farewell the neighing steed and the shrill trump,
   The spirit-stirring drum, th' ear-piercing fife,
   The royal banner, and all quality,
   Pride, pomp, and circumstance° of glorious war!
   And O you mortal engines° whose rude throats   355
   Th' immortal Jove's dread clamors counterfeit,°
   Farewell! Othello's occupation's gone!
Iago: Is't possible, my lord?
Othello: Villain, be sure thou prove my love a whore!
   Be sure of it; give me the ocular proof;   360
   Or, by the worth of mine eternal soul,
   Thou hadst been better have been born a dog
   Than answer my waked wrath!

---

330 *mandragora:* A narcotic. 340 *free:* Carefree. 342 *wanting:* Missing. 346 *Pioneers:* Sappers, laborers. 349 *big:* Stately. 354 *circumstance:* Pageantry. 355 *mortal engines:* Deadly artillery. 356 *counterfeit:* Imitate.

Iago: Is't come to this?
Othello: Make me to see't; or at the least so prove it
    That the probation° bear no hinge nor loop   365
    To hang a doubt on — or woe upon thy life!
Iago: My noble lord —
Othello: If thou dost slander her and torture me,
    Never pray more; abandon all remorse;
    On horror's head horrors accumulate;   370
    Do deeds to make heaven weep, all earth amazed;
    For nothing canst thou to damnation add
    Greater than that.
Iago: O grace! O heaven forgive me!
    Are you a man? Have you a soul or sense? —
    God b' wi' you! take mine office. O wretched fool,   375
    That liv'st to make thine honesty a vice!
    O monstrous world! Take note, take note, O world,
    To be direct and honest is not safe.
    I thank you for this profit;° and from hence
    I'll love no friend, sith love breeds such offense.   380
Othello: Nay, stay. Thou shouldst be honest.
Iago: I should be wise; for honesty's a fool
    And loses that it works for.
Othello: By the world,
    I think my wife be honest, and think she is not;
    I think that thou art just, and think thou art not.   385
    I'll have some proof. Her name, that was as fresh
    As Dian's visage, is now begrimed and black
    As mine own face. If there be cords, or knives,
    Poison, or fire, or suffocating streams,
    I'll not endure it. Would I were satisfied!°   390
Iago: I see, sir, you are eaten up with passion:
    I do repent me that I put it to you.
    You would be satisfied?
Othello: Would? Nay, I will.
Iago: And may; but how? how satisfied, my lord?
    Would you, the supervisor,° grossly gape on?   395
    Behold her topped?
Othello: Death and damnation! O!
Iago: It were a tedious difficulty, I think,
    To bring them to that prospect. Damn them then,
    If ever mortal eyes do see them bolster°
    More than their own! What then? How then?   400
    What shall I say? Where's satisfaction?

365 *probation:* Proof.   379 *profit:* Profitable lesson.   390 *satisfied:* Completely
informed.   395 *supervisor:* Spectator.   399 *bolster:* Lie together.

It is impossible you should see this,
Were they as prime° as goats, as hot as monkeys,
As salt° as wolves in pride,° and fools as gross
As ignorance made drunk. But yet, I say,   405
If imputation and strong circumstances
Which lead directly to the door of truth
Will give you satisfaction, you may have't.
Othello: Give me a living reason she's disloyal.
Iago: I do not like the office.   410
    But sith I am ent'red in this cause so far,
    Pricked to't by foolish honesty and love,
    I will go on. I lay with Cassio lately,
    And being troubled with a raging tooth,
    I could not sleep.   415
    There are a kind of men so loose of soul
    That in their sleeps will mutter their affairs.
    One of this kind is Cassio.
    In sleep I heard him say, "Sweet Desdemona,
    Let us be wary, let us hide our loves!"   420
    And then, sir, would he gripe and wring my hand,
    Cry "O sweet creature!" and then kiss me hard,
    As if he plucked up kisses by the roots
    That grew upon my lips; then laid his leg
    Over my thigh, and sighed, and kissed, and then   425
    Cried "Cursèd fate that gave thee to the Moor!"
Othello: O monstrous! monstrous!
Iago: Nay, this was but his dream.
Othello: But this denoted a foregone conclusion;°
    'Tis a shrewd doubt,° though it be but a dream.
Iago: And this may help to thicken other proofs   430
    That do demonstrate thinly.
Othello: I'll tear her all to pieces!
Iago: Nay, but be wise. Yet we see nothing done;
    She may be honest yet. Tell me but this—
    Have you not sometimes seen a handkerchief
    Spotted with strawberries in your wife's hand?   435
Othello: I gave her such a one; 'twas my first gift.
Iago: I know not that; but such a handkerchief—
    I am sure it was your wife's—did I to-day
    See Cassio wipe his beard with.
Othello: If it be that—
Iago: If it be that, or any that was hers,   440
    It speaks against her with the other proofs.

---

403 *prime:* Lustful.   404 *salt:* Lecherous; *pride:* Heat.   428 *foregone conclusion:* Previous experience.   429 *a shrewd doubt:* Cursedly suspicious.

Othello: O, that the slave had forty thousand lives!
　　One is too poor, too weak for my revenge.
　　Now do I see 'tis true. Look here, Iago:
　　All my fond love thus do I blow to heaven.   445
　　'Tis gone.
　　Arise, black vengeance, from the hollow hell!
　　Yield up, O love, thy crown and hearted throne
　　To tyrannous hate! Swell, bosom, with thy fraught,°
　　For 'tis of aspics'° tongues!
Iago:　　　　　　　　　　　　Yet be content.   450
Othello: O, blood, blood, blood!
Iago: Patience, I say. Your mind perhaps may change.
Othello: Never, Iago. Like to the Pontic sea,°
　　Whose icy current and compulsive course
　　Ne'er feels retiring ebb, but keeps due on   455
　　To the Propontic and the Hellespont,
　　Even so my bloody thoughts, with violent pace,
　　Shall ne'er look back, ne'er ebb to humble love,
　　Till that a capable° and wide revenge
　　Swallow them up.
　　(He kneels.)　　　Now, by yond marble heaven,   460
　　In the due reverence of a sacred vow
　　I here engage my words.
Iago:　　　　　　　　　　Do not rise yet.
　　(Iago kneels.)
　　Witness, you ever-burning lights above,
　　You elements that clip° us round about,
　　Witness that here Iago doth give up   465
　　The execution° of his wit,° hands, heart
　　To wronged Othello's service! Let him command,
　　And to obey shall be in me remorse,°
　　What bloody business ever.

　　[They rise.]

Othello:　　　　　　　　　　I greet thy love,
　　Not with vain thanks but with acceptance bounteous,   470
　　And will upon the instant put thee to't.
　　Within these three days let me hear thee say
　　That Cassio's not alive.
Iago: My friend is dead; 'tis done at your request.
　　But let her live.   475
Othello: Damn her, lewd minx! O, damn her! damn her!
　　Come, go with me apart. I will withdraw

---

449 *fraught:* Burden.　450 *aspics:* Deadly poisonous snakes.　453 *Pontic sea:* Black
Sea.　459 *capable:* All-embracing.　464 *clip:* Encompass.　466 *execution:* Activities;
wit: Mind.　468 *remorse:* Pity.

    To furnish me with some swift means of death
    For the fair devil. Now art thou my lieutenant.
Iago: I am your own forever.   *Exeunt.* 480

SCENE IV: *The environs of the castle.*

    Enter Desdemona, Emilia, and Clown.

Desdemona: Do you know, sirrah, where Lieutenant Cassio lies?°
Clown: I dare not say he lies anywhere.
Desdemona: Why, man?
Clown: He's a soldier, and for me to say a soldier lies is stabbing.
Desdemona: Go to. Where lodges he?   5
Clown: To tell you where he lodges is to tell you where I lie.
Desdemona: Can anything be made of this?
Clown: I know not where he lodges; and for me to devise a lodging,
    and say he lies here or he lies there, were to lie in mine own throat.
Desdemona: Can you enquire him out, and be edified by report? 10
Clown: I will catechize the world for him; that is, make questions,
    and by them answer.
Desdemona: Seek him, bid him come hither. Tell him I have moved°
    my lord on his behalf and hope all will be well.
Clown: To do this is within the compass of man's wit, and therefore 15
    I'll attempt the doing of it.   *Exit.*
Desdemona: Where should I lose that handkerchief, Emilia?
Emilia: I know not, madam.
Desdemona: Believe me, I had rather have lost my purse
    Full of crusadoes;° and but my noble Moor   20
    Is true of mind, and made of no such baseness
    As jealous creatures are, it were enough
    To put him to ill thinking.
Emilia: Is he not jealous?
Desdemona: Who? he? I think the sun where he was born
    Drew all such humors° from him.

    Enter Othello.

Emilia: Look where he comes.   25
Desdemona: I will not leave him now till Cassio
    Be called to him — How is't with you, my lord?
Othello: Well, my good lady. *[Aside.]* O, hardness to dissemble! —
    How do you, Desdemona?
Desdemona: Well, my good lord.
Othello: Give me your hand. This hand is moist, my lady.   30

Scene IV. 1 *lies:* Lives, lodges. 13 *moved:* Made proposals to. 20 *crusadoes:* Portuguese gold coins. 25 *humors:* Inclinations.

Desdemona: It yet hath felt no age nor known no sorrow.
Othello: This argues fruitfulness and liberal heart.
    Hot, hot, and moist. This hand of yours requires
    A sequester° from liberty, fasting and prayer,
    Much castigation, exercise devout;   35
    For here's a young and sweating devil here
    That commonly rebels. 'Tis a good hand,
    A frank one.
Desdemona: You may, indeed, say so;
    For 'twas that hand that gave away my heart.   40
Othello: A liberal hand! The hearts of old gave hands;
    But our new heraldry° is hands, not hearts.
Desdemona: I cannot speak of this. Come now, your promise!
Othello: What promise, chuck?
Desdemona: I have sent to bid Cassio come speak with you.   45
Othello: I have a salt and sorry rheum° offends me.
    Lend me thy handkerchief.
Desdemona: Here, my lord.
Othello: That which I gave you.
Desdemona: I have it not about me.
Othello: Not?
Desdemona: No, faith, my lord.
Othello: That's a fault.
    That handkerchief   50
    Did an Egyptian° to my mother give.
    She was a charmer,° and could almost read
    The thoughts of people. She told her, while she kept it,
    'Twould make her amiable° and subdue my father
    Entirely to her love; but if she lost it   55
    Or made a gift of it, my father's eye
    Should hold her loathèd, and his spirits should hunt
    After new fancies. She, dying, gave it me,
    And bid me, when my fate would have me wive;
    To give it her. I did so; and take heed on't;   60
    Make it a darling like your precious eye.
    To lose't or give't away were such perdition°
    As nothing else could match.
Desdemona: Is't possible?
Othello: 'Tis true. There's magic in the web of it.
    A sibyl that had numb'red in the world   65
    The sun to course two hundred compasses,°
    In her prophetic fury sewed the work;

---

34 *sequester:* Removal.   42 *heraldry:* Heraldic symbolism.   46 *salt . . . rheum:* Distressing head cold.   51 *Egyptian:* Gypsy.   52 *charmer:* Sorceress.   54 *amiable:* Lovable.
62 *perdition:* Disaster.   66 *compasses:* Annual rounds.

The worms were hallowed that did breed the silk;
And it was dyed in mummy° which the skillful
Conserved of maidens' hearts.
Desdemona: I' faith? Is't true?   70
Othello: Most veritable. Therefore look to't well.
Desdemona: Then would to God that I had never seen't!
Othello: Ha! Wherefore?
Desdemona: Why do you speak so startingly and rash?
Othello: Is't lost? Is't gone? Speak, is it out o' th' way?   75
Desdemona: Heaven bless us!
Othello: Say you?
Desdemona: It is not lost. But what an if it were?
Othello: How?
Desdemona: I say it is not lost.
Othello: Fetch't, let me see't!   80
Desdemona: Why, so I can, sir; but I will not now.
  This is a trick to put° me from my suit:
  Pray you let Cassio be received again.
Othello: Fetch me the handkerchief! My mind misgives.
Desdemona: Come, come!   85
  You'll never meet a more sufficient man.
Othello: The handkerchief!
  [*Desdemona:*   I pray talk me of Cassio.
Othello: The handkerchief!]
Desdemona: A man that all his time°
  Hath founded his good fortunes on your love,
  Shared dangers with you —   90
Othello: The handkerchief!
Desdemona: I' faith, you are to blame.
Othello: Zounds!   *Exit Othello.*
Emilia: Is not this man jealous?
Desdemona: I ne'er saw this before.   95
  Sure there's some wonder in this handkerchief;
  I am most unhappy in the loss of it.
Emilia: 'Tis not a year or two shows us a man.
  They are all but stomachs, and we all but food;
  They eat us hungerly, and when they are full,   100
  They belch us.

    Enter Iago and Cassio.

                    Look you — Cassio and my husband!
Iago: There is no other way; 'tis she must do't.
  And lo the happiness!° Go and importune her.

---

69 *mummy:* A drug made from mummies.   82 *put:* Divert.   88 *all his time:* During
his whole career.   103 *happiness:* Good luck.

Desdemona: How now, good Cassio? What's the news with you?
Cassio: Madam, my former suit. I do beseech you   105
    That by your virtuous means I may again
    Exist, and be a member of his love
    Whom I with all the office of my heart
    Entirely honor. I would not be delayed.
    If my offense be of such mortal kind   110
    That neither service past, nor present sorrows,
    Nor purposed merit in futurity,
    Can ransom me into his love again,
    But to know so must be my benefit.
    So shall I clothe me in a forced content,   115
    And shut myself up in° some other course,
    To fortune's alms.
Desdemona: Alas, thrice-gentle Cassio!
    My advocation° is not now in tune.
    My lord is not my lord; nor should I know him,
    Were he in favor° as in humor altered.   120
    So help me every spirit sanctified
    As I have spoken for you all my best
    And stood within the blank° of his displeasure
    For my free speech! You must a while be patient.
    What I can do I will; and more I will   125
    Than for myself I dare. Let that suffice you.
Iago: Is my lord angry?
Emilia: He went hence but now,
    And certainly in strange unquietness.
Iago: Can he be angry? I have seen the cannon
    When it hath blown his ranks into the air   130
    And, like the devil, from his very arm
    Puffed his own brother—and is he angry?
    Something of moment then. I will go meet him.
    There's matter in't indeed if he be angry.
Desdemona: I prithee do so.   *Exit [Iago].*
            Something sure of state,°   135
    Either from Venice or some unhatched practice°
    Made demonstrable here in Cyprus to him,
    Hath puddled° his clear spirit; and in such cases
    Men's natures wrangle with inferior things,
    Though great ones are their object. 'Tis even so;   140
    For let our finger ache, and it endues°
    Our other, healthful members even to a sense

---

116 *shut myself up in:* Confine myself to.   118 *advocation:* Advocacy.   120 *favor:* Appearance.   123 *blank:* Bull's-eye of the target.   135 *state:* Public affairs.   136 *unhatched practice:* Budding plot.   138 *puddled:* Muddied.   141 *endues:* Brings.

Of pain. Nay, we must think men are not gods,
Nor of them look for such observancy
As fits the bridal. Beshrew me much, Emilia,   145
I was, unhandsome warrior° as I am,
Arraigning his unkindness with my soul;°
But now I find I had suborned the witness,
And he's indicted falsely.

Emilia: Pray heaven it be state matters, as you think,   150
And no conception nor no jealous toy°
Concerning you.

Desdemona: Alas the day! I never gave him cause.

Emilia: But jealous souls will not be answered so;
They are not ever jealous for the cause,   155
But jealous for they're jealous. 'Tis a monster
Begot upon itself,° born on itself.

Desdemona: Heaven keep that monster from Othello's mind!

Emilia: Lady, amen.

Desdemona: I will go seek him. Cassio, walk here about: 160
If I do find him fit, I'll move your suit
And seek to effect it to my uttermost.

Cassio: I humbly thank your ladyship.

Exeunt Desdemona and Emilia.

Enter Bianca.

Bianca: Save you, friend Cassio!

Cassio: What make you from home?
How is't with you, my most fair Bianca?   165
I' faith, sweet love, I was coming to your house.

Bianca: And I was going to your lodging, Cassio.
What, keep a week away? seven days and nights?
Eightscore eight hours? and lovers' absent hours,
More tedious than the dial° eightscore times?   170
O weary reck'ning!

Cassio: Pardon me, Bianca:
I have this while with leaden thoughts been pressed;
But I shall in a more continuate° time
Strike off this score of absence. Sweet Bianca,

[Gives her Desdemona's handkerchief.]

Take me this work out.°

Bianca: O Cassio, whence came this? 175
This is some token from a newer friend

---

146 *unhandsome warrior:* Inadequate soldier.   147 *Arraigning . . . soul:* Indicting his
unkindness before the bar of my soul.   151 *toy:* Fancy.   157 *Begot upon itself:* Self-
engendered.   170 *dial:* Clock.   173 *continuate:* Uninterrupted.   175 *Take . . . out:* Copy
this embroidery for me.

To the felt absence now I feel a cause.
Is't come to this? Well, well.
Cassio: Go to, woman!
  Throw your vile guesses in the devil's teeth,
  From whence you have them. You are jealous now   180
  That this is from some mistress, some remembrance.
  No, by my faith, Bianca.
Bianca: Why, whose is it?
Cassio: I know not, sweet; I found it in my chamber.
  I like the work° well; ere it be demanded,
  As like enough it will, I'd have it copied.   185
  Take it and do't, and leave me for this time.
Bianca: Leave you? Wherefore?
Cassio: I do attend here on the general
  And think it no addition, nor my wish,
  To have him see me womaned.
Bianca: Why, I pray you?   190
Cassio: Not that I love you not.
Bianca: But that you do not love me!
  I pray you bring me on the way a little,
  And say if I shall see you soon at night.
Cassio: 'Tis but a little way that I can bring you,
  For I attend here; but I'll see you soon.   195
Bianca: 'Tis very good. I must be circumstanced.°   *Exeunt.*

ACT IV

SCENE I: *The environs of the castle.*

  Enter Othello and Iago.

Iago: Will you think so?
Othello: Think so, Iago?
Iago: What,
  To kiss in private?
Othello: An unauthorized kiss.
Iago: Or to be naked with her friend in bed
  An hour or more, not meaning any harm?
Othello: Naked in bed, Iago, and not mean harm?   5
  It is hypocrisy against the devil.°
  They that mean virtuously, and yet do so,

---

184 *work:* Needlework. 196 *circumstanced:* Governed by circumstances. **Act IV, Scene I.** 6 *hypocrisy . . . devil:* i.e., feigned sin instead of feigned virtue.

The devil their virtue tempts, and they tempt heaven.
Iago: So they do nothing, 'tis a venial slip.
     But if I give my wife a handkerchief —   10
Othello: What then?
Iago: Why, then 'tis hers, my lord; and being hers,
     She may, I think, bestow't on any man.
Othello: She is protectress of her honor too;
     May she give that?   15
Iago: Her honor is an essence that's not seen;
     They have it very oft that have it not.
     But for the handkerchief —
Othello: By heaven, I would most gladly have forgot it!
     Thou said'st — O, it comes o'er my memory   20
     As doth the raven o'er the infected° house,
     Boding to all! — he had my handkerchief.
Iago: Ay, what of that?
Othello: That's not so good now.
Iago: What
     If I had said I had seen him do you wrong?
     Or heard him say — as knaves be such abroad   25
     Who having, by their own importunate suit,
     Or voluntary dotage of some mistress,
     Convincèd or supplied° them, cannot choose
     But they must blab —
Othello: Hath he said anything?
Iago: He hath, my lord; but be you well assured,   30
     No more than he'll unswear.
Othello: What hath he said?
Iago: Faith, that he did — I know not what he did.
Othello: What? what?
Iago: Lie —
Othello: With her?
Iago: With her, on her; what you will.   35
Othello: Lie with her? lie on her? — We say lie on her when they belie
     her. — Lie with her! Zounds, that's fulsome. — Handkerchief —
     confessions — handkerchief! — To confess, and be hanged for
     his labor — first to be hanged, and then to confess! I tremble
     at it. Nature would not invest herself in such shadowing pas-   40
     sion without some instruction.° It is not words that shakes me
     thus. — Pish! Noses, ears, and lips? Is't possible? — Confess? —
     Handkerchief? — O devil!

     (Falls in a trance.)

21 *infected:* Plague-stricken.   28 *Convincèd or supplied:* Overcome or gratified.
40–41 *Nature . . . instruction:* My natural faculties would not be so overcome by passion without reason.

Iago: Work on,
    My med'cine, work! Thus credulous fools are caught,   45
    And many worthy and chaste dames even thus
    All guiltless, meet reproach. — What, ho! my lord!
    My lord, I say! Othello!
    Enter Cassio.   How now, Cassio?
Cassio: What's the matter?
Iago: My lord is fall'n into an epilepsy.   50
    This is his second fit; he had one yesterday.
Cassio: Rub him about the temples.
Iago: No, forbear.
    The lethargy° must have his quiet course.
    If not, he foams at mouth, and by and by
    Breaks out to savage madness. Look, he stirs.   55
    Do you withdraw yourself a little while.
    He will recover straight. When he is gone,
    I would on great occasion speak with you.   *[Exit Cassio.]*
    How is it, general? Have you not hurt your head?
Othello: Dost thou mock me?
Iago: I mock you? No, by heaven.   60
    Would you would bear your fortune like a man!
Othello: A hornèd man's° a monster and a beast.
Iago: There's many a beast then in a populous city,
    And many a civil monster.
Othello: Did he confess it?
Iago: Good sir, be a man.   65
    Think every bearded fellow that's but yoked
    May draw with you. There's millions now alive
    That nightly lie in those unproper° beds
    Which they dare swear peculiar:° your case is better.
    O, 'tis the spite of hell, the fiend's arch-mock,   70
    To lip a wanton in a secure° couch,
    And to suppose her chaste! No, let me know;
    And knowing what I am, I know what she shall be.
Othello: O, thou art wise! 'Tis certain.
Iago: Stand you awhile apart;
    Confine yourself but in a patient list.°   75
    Whilst you were here, o'erwhelmèd with your grief —
    A passion most unsuiting such a man —
    Cassio came hither. I shifted him away
    And laid good 'scuse upon your ecstasy;°
    Bade him anon return, and here speak with me;   80

---

53 *lethargy:* Coma.   62 *hornèd man:* Cuckold.   68 *unproper:* Not exclusively their own.   69 *peculiar:* Exclusively their own.   71 *secure:* Free from fear of rivalry.   75 *in a patient list:* Within the limits of self-control.   79 *ecstasy:* Trance.

The which he promised. Do but encave° yourself
And mark the fleers, the gibes, and notable scorns
That dwell in every region of his face;
For I will make him tell the tale anew —
Where, how, how oft, how long ago, and when   85
He hath, and is again to cope° your wife.
I say, but mark his gesture. Marry, patience!
Or I shall say y'are all in all in spleen,°
And nothing of a man.

Othello: Dost thou hear, Iago?
I will be found most cunning in my patience;   90
But — dost thou hear? — most bloody.

Iago: That's not amiss:
But yet keep time in all. Will you withdraw?

                                    [Othello retires.]

Now will I question Cassio of Bianca,
A huswife° that by selling her desires
Buys herself bread and clothes. It is a creature   95
That dotes on Cassio, as 'tis the strumpet's plague
To beguile many and be beguiled by one.
He, when he hears of her, cannot refrain
From the excess of laughter. Here he comes.

Enter Cassio.

As he shall smile, Othello shall go mad;   100
And his unbookish° jealousy must conster°
Poor Cassio's smiles, gestures, and light behavior
Quite in the wrong. How do you now, lieutenant?

Cassio: The worser that you give me the addition°
Whose want even kills me.   105

Iago: Ply Desdemona well, and you are sure on't.
Now, if this suit lay in Bianca's power,
How quickly should you speed!

Cassio: Alas, poor caitiff!°

Othello: Look how he laughs already!

Iago: I never knew a woman love man so.   110

Cassio: Alas, poor rogue! I think, i' faith, she loves me.

Othello: Now he denies it faintly, and laughs it out.

Iago: Do you hear, Cassio?

Othello: Now he importunes him
To tell it o'er. Go to! Well said, well said!

Iago: She gives out that you shall marry her.   115

---

81 *encave:* Conceal. 86 *cope:* Meet. 88 *all in all in spleen:* Wholly overcome by
your passion. 94 *huswife:* Hussy. 101 *unbookish:* Uninstructed; *conster:* Construe,
interpret. 104 *addition:* Title. 108 *caitiff:* Wretch.

Do you intend it?

Cassio: Ha, ha, ha!

Othello: Do you triumph, Roman? Do you triumph?

Cassio: I marry her? What, a customer?° Prithee bear some charity
to my wit; do not think it so unwholesome. Ha, ha, ha!   120

Othello: So, so, so, so! They laugh that win!

Iago: Faith, the cry goes that you shall marry her.

Cassio: Prithee say true.

Iago: I am a very villain else.

Othello: Have you scored me?° Well.   125

Cassio: This is the monkey's own giving out. She is persuaded I will
marry her out of her own love and flattery, not out of my promise.

Othello: Iago beckons° me; now he begins the story.

Cassio: She was here even now; she haunts me in every place. I was
t' other day talking on the sea bank with certain Venetians, and   130
thither comes the bauble,° and, by this hand, she falls me thus
about my neck —

Othello: Crying "O dear Cassio!" as it were. His gesture imports it.

Cassio: So hangs, and lolls, and weeps upon me; so shakes and pulls
me! Ha, ha, ha!   135

Othello: Now he tells how she plucked him to my chamber. O, I see
that nose of yours, but not that dog I shall throw it to.

Cassio: Well, I must leave her company.

Enter Bianca.

Iago: Before me! Look where she comes.

Cassio: 'Tis such another fitchew!° marry, a perfumed one. What do   140
you mean by this haunting of me?

Bianca: Let the devil and his dam haunt you! What did you mean
by that same handkerchief you gave me even now? I was a fine
fool to take it. I must take out the whole work? A likely piece
of work that you should find it in your chamber and know not   145
who left it there! This is some minx's token, and I must take out
the work? There! Give it your hobby-horse.° Wheresoever you
had it, I'll take out no work on't.

Cassio: How now, my sweet Bianca? How now? how now?

Othello: By heaven, that should be my handkerchief!   150

Bianca: An you'll come to supper to-night, you may; an you will not,
come when you are next prepared for.   *Exit.*

Iago: After her, after her!

Cassio: Faith, I must; she'll rail in the street else.

Iago: Will you sup there?   155

---

119 *customer:* Prostitute. 125 *scored me:* Settled my account (?). 128 *beckons:*
Signals. 131 *bauble:* Plaything. 140 *fitchew:* Polecat (slang for *whore*). 147 *hobby-*
horse: Harlot.

Cassio: Yes, I intend so.

Iago: Well, I may chance to see you; for I would very fain speak with you.

Cassio: Prithee come. Will you?

Iago: Go to! say no more.   *Exit Cassio.*   160

Othello [comes forward]: How shall I murder him, Iago?

Iago: Did you perceive how he laughed at his vice?°

Othello: O Iago!

Iago: And did you see the handkerchief?

Othello: Was that mine?   165

Iago: Your, by this hand! And to see how he prizes° the foolish woman your wife! She gave it him, and he hath giv'n it his whore.

Othello: I would have him nine years a-killing—A fine woman! a fair woman! a sweet woman!   170

Iago: Nay, you must forget that.

Othello: Ay, let her rot, and perish, and be damned to-night; for she shall not live. No, my heart is turned to stone; I strike it, and it hurts my hand. O, the world hath not a sweeter creature! She might lie by an emperor's side and command him tasks.   175

Iago: Nay, that's not your way.

Othello: Hang her! I do but say what she is. So delicate with her needle! an admirable musician! O, she will sing the savageness out of a bear! Of so high and plenteous wit and invention° —

Iago: She's the worse for all this.   180

Othello: O, a thousand thousand times! And then, of so gentle a condition!°

Iago: Ay, too gentle.

Othello: Nay, that's certain. But yet the pity of it, Iago! O Iago, the pity of it, Iago!   185

Iago: If you are so fond over her iniquity, give her patent° to offend; for if it touch not you, it comes near nobody.

Othello: I will chop her into messes! Cuckold me!

Iago: O, 'tis foul in her.

Othello: With mine officer!   190

Iago: That's fouler.

Othello: Get me some poison, Iago, this night. I'll not expostulate with her, lest her body and beauty unprovide° my mind again. This night, Iago!

Iago: Do it not with poison. Strangle her in her bed, even the bed she   195
hath contaminated.

Othello: Good, good! The justice of it pleases. Very good!

---

162 *vice:* i.e., vicious conduct. 166 *prizes:* Values. 179 *invention:* Imagination.
182 *condition:* Disposition. 186 *patent:* License. 193 *unprovide:* Disarm.

Iago: And for Cassio, let me be his undertaker;° you shall hear more
 by midnight.
Othello: Excellent good!   200

  A trumpet.

  What trumpet is that same?
Iago: I warrant something from Venice.

  Enter Lodovico, Desdemona, and Attendants.

              'Tis Lodovico.
  This comes from the Duke; and see, your wife is with him.
Lodovico: God save you, worthy general!
Othello: With all my heart, sir.
Lodovico: The Duke and senators of Venice greet you.   205

  [Gives him a letter.]

Othello: I kiss the instrument of their pleasures.

  [Opens the letter and reads.]

Desdemona: And what's the news, good cousin Lodovico?
Iago: I am very glad to see you, signior.
  Welcome to Cyprus.
Lodovico: I thank you. How does Lieutenant Cassio?
Iago: Lives, sir.   210
Desdemona: Cousin, there's fall'n between him and my lord
  An unkind breach; but you shall make all well.
Othello: Are you sure of that?
Desdemona: My lord?
Othello [reads]: "This fail you not to do, as you will—"   215
Lodovico: He did not call; he's busy in the paper.
  Is there division 'twixt thy lord and Cassio?
Desdemona: A most unhappy one. I would do much
  T' atone° them, for the love I bear to Cassio.
Othello: Fire and brimstone!
Desdemona: My lord?
Othello: Are you wise?   220
Desdemona: What, is he angry?
Lodovico: May be the letter moved him;
  For, as I think, they do command him home,
  Deputing Cassio in his government.
Desdemona: By my troth, I am glad on't.
Othello: Indeed?
Desdemona: My lord?
Othello: I am glad to see you mad.°

---

198 *be his undertaker:* Undertake to deal with him. 219 *atone:* Reconcile. 225 *mad:*
i.e., waggish.

Desdemona: Why, sweet Othello —   225
Othello: Devil!

    [Strikes her.]

Desdemona: I have not deserved this.
Lodovico: My lord, this would not be believed in Venice,
    Though I should swear I saw't. 'Tis very much.
    Make her amends; she weeps.
Othello: O devil, devil!   230
    If that the earth could teem° with woman's tears,
    Each drop she falls would prove a crocodile.°
    Out of my sight!
Desdemona: I will not stay to offend you.   *[Going.]*
Lodovico: Truly, an obedient lady.
    I do beseech your lordship call her back.   235
Othello: Mistress!
Desdemona: My lord?
Othello: What would you with her, sir?
Lodovico: Who? I, my lord?
Othello: Ay! You did wish that I would make her turn.
    Sir, she can turn, and turn, and yet go on   240
    And turn again; and she can weep, sir, weep;
    And she's obedient; as you say, obedient,
    Very obedient. — Proceed you in your tears. —
    Concerning this, sir — O well-painted passion!° —
    I am commanded home. — Get you away;   245
    I'll send for you anon. — Sir, I obey the mandate
    And will return to Venice. — Hence, avaunt!

                     [Exit Desdemona.]

    Cassio shall have my place. And, sir, to-night
    I do entreat that we may sup together.
    You are welcome, sir, to Cyprus — Goats and monkeys!   *Exit.* 250
Lodovico: Is this the noble Moor whom our full Senate
    Call all in all sufficient? Is this the nature
    Whom passion could not shake? whose solid virtue
    The shot of accident nor dart of chance
    Could neither graze nor pierce?
Iago: He is much changed.   255
Lodovico: Are his wits safe? Is he not light of brain?
Iago: He's that he is; I may not breathe my censure.
    What he might be — if what he might he is not —
    I would to heaven he were!
Lodovico: What, strike his wife?

---

231 *teem:* Breed.   232 *crocodile:* (Crocodiles were supposed to shed hypocritical tears
to lure men to destruction).   244 *passion:* Grief.

Iago: Faith, that was not so well; yet would I knew   260
   That stroke would prove the worst!
Lodovico: Is it his use?°
   Or did the letters work upon his blood
   And new-create this fault?
Iago: Alas, alas!
   It is not honesty in me to speak
   What I have seen and known. You shall observe him,   265
   And his own courses will denote him so
   That I may save my speech. Do but go after
   And mark how he continues.
Lodovico: I am sorry that I am deceived in him.   *Exeunt.*

SCENE II: *Within the castle.*

   Enter Othello and Emilia.

Othello: You have seen nothing then?
Emilia: Nor ever heard, nor ever did suspect.
Othello: Yes, you have seen Cassio and she together.
Emilia: But then I saw no harm, and then I heard
   Each syllable that breath made up between them.   5
Othello: What, did they never whisper?
Emilia: Never, my lord.
Othello: Nor send you out o' th' way?
Emilia: Never.
Othello: To fetch her fan, her gloves, her mask, nor nothing?
Emilia: Never, my lord.   10
Othello: That's strange.
Emilia: I durst, my lord, to wager she is honest,
   Lay down my soul at stake. If you think other,
   Remove your thought; it doth abuse your bosom.°
   If any wretch have put this in your head,   15
   Let heaven requite it with the serpent's curse!°
   For if she be not honest, chaste, and true,
   There's no man happy; the purest of their wives
   Is foul as slander.
Othello: Bid her come hither. Go.   *Exit Emilia.*
   She says enough; yet she's a simple bawd   20
   That cannot say as much. This is a subtle whore,
   A closet lock and key of villainous secrets;
   And yet she'll kneel and pray; I have seen her do't.

   Enter Desdemona and Emilia.

---

261 *use:* Custom. **Scene II.** 14 *abuse your bosom:* Deceive your heart. 16 *serpent's curse:* (cf. Genesis 3: 14).

Desdemona: My lord, what is your will?
Othello: Pray, chuck, come hither.
Desdemona: What is your pleasure?
Othello: Let me see your eyes.   25
  Look in my face.
Desdemona: What horrible fancy's this?
Othello [to Emilia]: Some of your function, mistress.
  Leave procreants° alone and shut the door;
  Cough or cry hem if anybody come.
  Your mystery, your mystery!° Nay, dispatch!   30
                                              Exit Emilia.
Desdemona: Upon my knees, what doth your speech import?
  I understand a fury in your words,
  [But not the words.]
Othello: Why, what art thou?
Desdemona: Your wife, my lord; your true
  And loyal wife.
Othello: Come, swear it, damn thyself;   35
  Lest, being like one of heaven,° the devils themselves
  Should fear to seize thee. Therefore be double-damned —
  Swear thou art honest.°
Desdemona: Heaven doth truly know it.
Othello: Heaven truly knows that thou art false as hell.
Desdemona: To whom, my lord? With whom? How am I false?   40
Othello: Ah, Desdemona! away! away! away!
Desdemona: Alas the heavy day! Why do you weep?
  Am I the motive of these tears, my lord?
  If haply you my father do suspect
  An instrument° of this your calling back,   45
  Lay not your blame on me. If you have lost him,
  Why, I have lost him too.
Othello: Had it pleased heaven
  To try me with affliction, had they rained
  All kinds of sores and shames on my bare head,
  Steeped me in poverty to the very lips,   50
  Given to captivity me and my utmost hopes,
  I should have found in some place of my soul
  A drop of patience. But, alas, to make me
  A fixèd figure for the time of scorn°
  To point his slow unmoving finger at!   55
  Yet could I bear that too; well, very well.

---

28 *procreants:* Mating couples.   30 *mystery:* Trade, occupation.   36 *being . . . heaven:*
Looking like an angel.   38 *honest:* Chaste.   45 *An instrument:* To be the cause.
54 *time of scorn:* Scornful world.

But there where I have garnered up my heart,
Where either I must live or bear no life,
The fountain from the which my current runs
Or else dries up — to be discarded thence,   60
Or keep it as a cistern for foul toads
To knot and gender in — turn thy complexion there,°
Patience, thou young and rose-lipped cherubin!
Ay, there look grim as hell!
Desdemona: I hope my noble lord esteems me honest.   65
Othello: O, ay; as summer flies are in the shambles,°
That quicken° even with blowing. O thou weed,
Who art so lovely fair, and smell'st so sweet,
That the sense aches at thee, would thou hadst ne'er been born!
Desdemona: Alas, what ignorant sin have I committed?   70
Othello: Was this fair paper, this most goodly book,
Made to write "whore" upon? What committed?
Committed? O thou public commoner!°
I should make very forges of my cheeks
That would to cinders burn up modesty,   75
Did I but speak thy deeds. What committed?
Heaven stops the nose at it, and the moon winks;°
The bawdy wind, that kisses all it meets,
Is hushed within the hollow mine of earth
And will not hear it. What committed?   80
Impudent strumpet!
Desdemona: By heaven, you do me wrong!
Othello: Are not you a strumpet?
Desdemona: No, as I am a Christian!
If to preserve this vessel for my lord
From any other foul unlawful touch
Be not to be a strumpet, I am none.   85
Othello: What, not a whore?
Desdemona: No, as I shall be saved!
Othello: Is't possible?
Desdemona: O, heaven forgive us!
Othello: I cry you mercy° then.
I took you for that cunning whore of Venice
That married with Othello. — *[Calling.]* You, mistress,   90
That have the office opposite to Saint Peter
And keep the gate of hell!

Enter Emilia.

---

62 *turn thy complexion there:* Change thy color at that point.   66 *shambles:* Slaugh-
terhouse.   67 *quicken:* Come to life.   73 *commoner:* Harlot.   77 *winks:* Closes her
eyes.   88 *cry you mercy:* Beg your pardon.

         You, you, ay, you!
 We have done our course; there's money for your pains:
 I pray you turn the key, and keep our counsel.   *Exit.*
Emilia: Alas, what does this gentleman conceive?   95
 How do you, madam? How do you, my good lady?
Desdemona: Faith, half asleep.°
Emilia: Good madam, what's the matter with my lord?
Desdemona: With who?
Emilia: Why, with my lord, madam.   100
Desdemona: Who is thy lord?
Emilia: He that is yours, sweet lady.
Desdemona: I have none. Do not talk to me, Emilia.
 I cannot weep; nor answer have I none
 But what should go by water. Prithee to-night
 Lay on my bed my wedding sheets, remember;   105
 And call thy husband hither.
Emilia: Here's a change indeed!   *Exit.*
Desdemona: 'Tis meet I should be used so, very meet.
 How have I been behaved, that he might stick
 The small'st opinion° on my least misuse?°

 Enter Iago and Emilia.

Iago: What is your pleasure, madam? How is't with you?   110
Desdemona: I cannot tell. Those that do teach young babes
 Do it with gentle means and easy tasks:
 He might have chid me so; for, in good faith,
 I am a child to chiding.
Iago: What is the matter, lady?
Emilia: Alas, Iago, my lord hath so bewhored her,   115
 Thrown such despite and heavy terms upon her
 As true hearts cannot bear.
Desdemona: Am I that name, Iago?
Iago: What name, fair lady?
Desdemona: Such as she said my lord did say I was.
Emilia: He called her whore. A beggar in his drink   120
 Could not have laid such terms upon his callet.°
Iago: Why did he so?
Desdemona: I do not know; I am sure I am none such.
Iago: Do not weep, do not weep. Alas the day!
Emilia: Hath she forsook so many noble matches,   125
 Her father and her country, and her friends,
 To be called whore? Would it not make one weep?
Desdemona: It is my wretched fortune.

---

97 *half asleep:* i.e., stunned. 109 *small'st opinion:* Least suspicion; *least misuse:* Slightest misconduct. 122 *callet:* Whore.

Iago: Beshrew him for't!
    How comes this trick° upon him?
Desdemona: Nay, heaven doth know.
Emilia: I will be hanged if some eternal villain,   130
    Some busy and insinuating rogue,
    Some cogging, cozening° slave, to get some office,
    Have not devised this slander. I'll be hanged else.
Iago: Fie, there is no such man! It is impossible.
Desdemona: If any such there be, heaven pardon him!   135
Emilia: A halter pardon him! and hell gnaw his bones!
    Why should he call her whore? Who keeps her company?
    What place? what time? what form? what likelihood?
    The Moor's abused by some most villainous knave,
    Some base notorious knave, some scurvy fellow.   140
    O heaven, that such companions° thou 'dst unfold,°
    And put in every honest hand a whip
    To lash the rascals naked through the world
    Even from the east to th' west!
Iago: Speak within door.°
Emilia: O, fie upon them! Some such squire he was   145
    That turned your wit the seamy side without
    And made you to suspect me with the Moor.
Iago: You are a fool. Go to.
Desdemona: Alas, Iago,
    What shall I do to win my lord again?
    Good friend, go to him; for, by this light of heaven,   150
    I know not how I lost him. Here I kneel:
    If e'er my will did trespass 'gainst his love
    Either in discourse° of thought or actual deed,
    Or that mine eyes, mine ears, or any sense
    Delighted them in any other form,   155
    Or that I do not yet, and ever did,
    And ever will (though he do shake me off
    To beggarly divorcement) love him dearly,
    Comfort forswear° me! Unkindness may do much;
    And his unkindness may defeat° my life,   160
    But never taint my love. I cannot say "whore."
    It does abhor me now I speak the word;
    To do the act that might the addition earn
    Not the world's mass of vanity could make me.
Iago: I pray you be content. 'Tis but his humor.   165
    The business of the state does him offense,

---

129 *trick:* Freakish behavior.   132 *cogging, cozening:* Cheating, defrauding.   141 *companions:* Rogues; *unfold:* Expose.   144 *within door:* With restraint.   153 *discourse:* Course.   159 *Comfort forswear:* Happiness forsake.   160 *defeat:* Destroy.

[And he does chide with you.]
Desdemona: If 'twere no other —
Iago: 'Tis but so, I warrant.

[Trumpets within.]

Hark how these instruments summon you to supper.
The messengers of Venice stay the meat: 170
Go in, and weep not. All things shall be well.
                                        Exeunt Desdemona and Emilia.

Enter Roderigo.

How now, Roderigo?
Roderigo: I do not find that thou deal'st justly with me.
Iago: What in the contrary?
Roderigo: Every day thou daff'st me with some device,° Iago, and   175
    rather, as it seems to me now, keep'st from me all conveniency°
    than suppliest me with the least advantage of hope. I will indeed
    no longer endure it; nor am I yet persuaded to put up in peace
    what already I have foolishly suffered.
Iago: Will you hear me, Roderigo?   180
Roderigo: Faith, I have heard too much; for your words and perfor-
    mances are no kin together.
Iago: You charge me most unjustly.
Roderigo: With naught but truth. I have wasted myself out of my
    means. The jewels you have had from me to deliver to Desde-   185
    mona would half have corrupted a votarist.° You have told me
    she hath received them, and returned me expectations and com-
    forts of sudden respect° and acquaintance; but I find none.
Iago: Well, go to; very well.
Roderigo: Very well! go to! I cannot go to, man; nor 'tis not very   190
    well. By this hand, I say 'tis very scurvy, and begin to find myself
    fopped° in it.
Iago: Very well.
Roderigo: I tell you 'tis not very well. I will make myself known to
    Desdemona. If she will return me my jewels, I will give over my   195
    suit and repent my unlawful solicitation; if not, assure yourself I
    will seek satisfaction of you.
Iago: You have said now.
Roderigo: Ay, and said nothing but what I protest intendment of
    doing.   200
Iago: Why, now I see there's mettle in thee; and even from this instant
    do build on thee a better opinion than ever before. Give me thy

---

175 *thou . . . device:* You put me off with some trick.   176 *conveniency:* Favorable
opportunities.   186 *votarist:* Nun.   188 *sudden respect:* Immediate notice.   192 *fopped:*
Duped.

hand, Roderigo. Thou has taken against me a most just exception; but yet I protest I have dealt most directly° in thy affair.

Roderigo: It hath not appeared.   205

Iago: I grant indeed it hath not appeared, and your suspicion is not
without wit and judgment. But, Roderigo, if thou hast that in
thee indeed which I have greater reason to believe now than ever,
I mean purpose, courage, and valor, this night show it. If thou
the next night following enjoy not Desdemona, take me from   210
this world with treachery and devise engines for° my life.

Roderigo: Well, what is it? Is it within reason and compass?

Iago: Sir, there is especial commission come from Venice to depute
Cassio in Othello's place.

Roderigo: Is that true? Why, then Othello and Desdemona return   215
again to Venice.

Iago: O, no; he goes into Mauritania and takes away with him the
fair Desdemona, unless his abode be lingered here° by some
accident; wherein none can be so determinate° as the removing
of Cassio.   220

Roderigo: How do you mean removing of him?

Iago: Why, by making him uncapable of Othello's place — knocking
out his brains.

Roderigo: And that you would have me to do?

Iago: Ay, if you dare do yourself a profit and a right. He sups to-night   225
with a harlotry, and thither will I go to him. He knows not yet of
his honorable fortune. If you will watch his going thence, which
I will fashion to fall out between twelve and one, you may take
him at your pleasure. I will be near to second your attempt, and
he shall fall between us. Come, stand not amazed at it, but go   230
along with me. I will show you such a necessity in his death that
you shall think yourself bound to put it on him. It is now high
supper time, and the night grows to waste. About it!

Roderigo: I will hear further reason for this.

Iago: And you shall be satisfied.   *Exeunt.*   235

SCENE III: *Within the castle.*

Enter Othello, Lodovico, Desdemona, Emilia, and Attendants.

Lodovico: I do beseech you, sir, trouble yourself no further.

Othello: O, pardon me; 'twill do me good to walk.

Lodovico: Madam, good night. I humbly thank your ladyship.

Desdemona: Your honor is most welcome.

Othello: Will you walk, sir?
O, Desdemona —   5

---

204 *directly:* Straightforwardly.   211 *engines for:* Plots against.   218 *abode . . . here:*
Stay here be extended.   219 *determinate:* Effective.

Desdemona: My lord?

Othello: Get you to bed on th' instant; I will be returned forthwith.
   Dismiss your attendant there. Look't be done.

Desdemona: I will, my lord.

   Exit [Othello, with Lodovico and Attendants].

Emilia: How goes it now? He looks gentler than he did.   10

Desdemona: He says he will return incontinent.°
   He hath commanded me to go to bed,
   And bade me to dismiss you.

Emilia: Dismiss me?

Desdemona: It was his bidding; therefore, good Emilia,
   Give me my nightly wearing, and adieu.   15
   We must not now displease him.

Emilia: I would you had never seen him!

Desdemona: So would not I. My love doth so approve him
   That even his stubbornness,° his checks,° his frowns—
   Prithee unpin me—have grace and favor in them.   20

Emilia: I have laid those sheets you bade me on the bed.

Desdemona: All's one. Good faith, how foolish are our minds!
   If I do die before thee, prithee shroud me
   In one of those same sheets.

Emilia: Come, come! You talk.

Desdemona: My mother had a maid called Barbary.   25
   She was in love; and he she loved proved mad°
   And did forsake her. She had a song of "Willow";
   An old thing 'twas; but it expressed her fortune,
   And she died singing it. That song to-night
   Will not go from my mind; I have much to do   30
   But to go hang my head all at one side
   And sing it like poor Barbary. Prithee dispatch.

Emilia: Shall I go fetch your nightgown?°

Desdemona: No, unpin me here.
   This Lodovico is a proper man.

Emilia: A very handsome man.   35

Desdemona: He speaks well.

Emilia: I know a lady in Venice would have walked barefoot to
   Palestine for a touch of his nether lip.

Desdemona (sings): "The poor soul sat sighing by a sycamore tree
      Sing all a green willow;   40
   Her hand on her bosom, her head on her knee,
      Sing willow, willow, willow.
   The fresh streams ran by her and murmured her moans;

Scene III. 11 *incontinent:* At once.   19 *stubbornness:* Roughness;   *checks:* Rebukes.
26 *mad:* Wild, faithless.   33 *nightgown:* Dressing gown.

      Sing willow, willow, willow;
       Her salt tears fell from her, and soft'ned the stones" —   45
   Lay by these.
      "Sing willow, willow, willow" —
   Prithee hie thee;° he'll come anon.
      "Sing all a green willow must be my garland.
      Let nobody blame him; his scorn I approve" —   50
   Nay, that's not next. Hark! who is't that knocks?
Emilia: It's the wind.
Desdemona (sings): "I call my love false love; but what said he then?
      Sing willow, willow, willow:
      If I court moe women, you'll couch with moe men."   55
   So get thee gone; good night. Mine eyes do itch.
   Doth that bode weeping?
Emilia: 'Tis neither here nor there.
Desdemona: I have heard it said so. O, these men, these men!
   Dost thou in conscience think — tell me, Emilia —
   That there be women do abuse their husbands   60
   In such gross kind?
Emilia: There be some such, no question.
Desdemona: Wouldst thou do such a deed for all the world?
Emilia: Why, would not you?
Desdemona: No, by this heavenly light!
Emilia: Nor I neither by this heavenly light!
   I might do't as well i' th' dark.   65
Desdemona: Wouldst thou do such a deed for all the world?
Emilia: The world's a huge thing; it is a great price for a small vice.
Desdemona: In troth, I think thou wouldst not.
Emilia: In troth, I think I should; and undo't when I had done it.
   Marry, I would not do such a thing for a joint-ring,° nor for   70
   measures of lawn, nor for gowns, petticoats, nor caps, nor any
   petty exhibition;° but, for all the whole world — 'Ud's pity! who
   would not make her husband a cuckold to make him a mon-
   arch? I should venture purgatory for't.
Desdemona: Beshrew me if I would do such a wrong   75
   For the whole world.
Emilia: Why, the wrong is but a wrong i' th' world; and having the
   world for your labor, 'tis a wrong in your own world, and you
   might quickly make it right.
Desdemona: I do not think there is any such woman.   80
Emilia: Yes, a dozen; and as many to th' vantage° as
   would store° the world they played for.
   But I do think it is their husbands' faults

---

48 *hie thee:* Hurry. 70 *joint-ring:* Ring made in separable halves. 72 *exhibition:*
Gift. 81 *to th' vantage:* Besides. 82 *store:* Populate.

If wives do fall. Say that they slack their duties
And pour our treasures into foreign laps;   85
Or else break out in peevish° jealousies,
Throwing restraint upon us; or say they strike us,
Or scant our former having° in despite—
Why, we have galls;° and though we have some grace,
Yet have we some revenge. Let husbands know   90
Their wives have sense like them. They see, and smell,
And have their palates both for sweet and sour,
As husbands have. What is it that they do
When they change us for others? Is it sport?
I think it is. And doth affection breed it?   95
I think it doth. Is't frailty that thus errs?
It is so too. And have not we affections,
Desires for sport, and frailty, as men have?
Then let them use us well; else let them know,
The ills we do, their ills instruct us so.   100

Desdemona: Good night, good night. God me such usage° send,
    Not to pick bad from bad, but by bad mend!   *Exeunt.*

ACT V

SCENE I: *A street in Cyprus.*

    Enter Iago and Roderigo.

Iago: Here, stand behind this bulk;° straight will he come.
    Wear thy good rapier bare, and put it home.
    Quick, quick! Fear nothing; I'll be at thy elbow.
    It makes us, or it mars us—think on that,
    And fix most firm thy resolution.   5
Roderigo: Be near at hand; I may miscarry in't.
Iago: Here, at thy hand. Be bold, and take thy stand.

    [Stands aside.]

Roderigo: I have no great devotion to the deed,
    And yet he hath given me satisfying reasons.
    'Tis but a man gone. Forth my sword! He dies!   10
Iago: I have rubbed this young quat° almost to the sense,°
    And he grows angry. Now whether he kill Cassio,
    Or Cassio him, or each do kill the other,
    Every way makes my gain. Live Roderigo,

86 *peevish:* Senseless. 88 *having:* Allowance. 89 *galls:* Spirits to resent. 101 *usage:* Habits. **Act V, Scene I.** 1 *bulk:* Projecting shop-front. 11 *quat:* Pimple; *sense:* Quick.

He calls me to a restitution large   15
Of gold and jewels that I bobbed° from him
As gifts to Desdemona.
It must not be. If Cassio do remain,
He hath a daily beauty in his life
That makes me ugly; and besides, the Moor   20
May unfold me to him; there stand I in much peril.
No, he must die. Be't so! I hear him coming.

Enter Cassio.

Roderigo: I know his gait. 'Tis he. Villain, thou diest!

[Makes a pass at Cassio.]

Cassio: That thrust had been mine enemy indeed
But that my coat° is better than thou know'st.   25
I will make proof of thine.

[Draws, and wounds Roderigo.]

Roderigo: O, I am slain!

*[Iago darts from concealment behind Cassio, wounds him in the leg,
and exit.]*

Cassio: I am maimed for ever. Help, ho! Murder! murder!

[Falls.]
Enter Othello.

Othello: The voice of Cassio. Iago keeps his word.
Roderigo: O, villain that I am!
Othello: It is even so.
Cassio: O, help, ho! light! a surgeon!   30
Othello: 'Tis he. O brave Iago, honest and just,
That hast such noble sense of thy friend's wrong!
Thou teachest me. Minion,° your dear lies dead,
And your unblest fate hies.° Strumpet, I come.
Forth of my heart those charms, thine eyes, are blotted.   35
Thy bed, lust-stained, shall with lust's blood be spotted.

                                                        Exit Othello.

Enter Lodovico and Gratiano.

Cassio: What, ho? No watch? No passage?° Murder! murder!
Gratiano: 'Tis some mischance. The cry is very direful.
Cassio: O, help!
Lodovico: Hark!   40
Roderigo: O wretched villain!
Lodovico: Two or three groan. It is a heavy° night.

16 *bobbed:* Swindled.   25 *coat:* Undershirt of mail.   33 *Minion:* Mistress.   34 *hies:*
Hurries on.   37 *passage:* Passersby.   42 *heavy:* Cloudy, dark.

These may be counterfeits. Let's think't unsafe
To come in to the cry without more help.
Roderigo: Nobody come? Then shall I bleed to death.   45
Lodovico: Hark!

    Enter Iago, with a light.

Gratiano: Here's one comes in his shirt, with light and weapons.
Iago: Who's there? Whose noise is this that cries on° murder?
Lodovico: We do not know.
Iago: Did not you hear a cry?
Cassio: Here, here! For heaven's sake, help me!
Iago: What's the matter?   50
Gratiano: This is Othello's ancient, as I take it.
Lodovico: The same indeed, a very valiant fellow.
Iago: What are you here that cry so grievously?
Cassio: Iago? O, I am spoiled, undone by villains!
    Give me some help.   55
Iago: O me, lieutenant! What villains have done this?
Cassio: I think that one of them is hereabout
    And cannot make° away.
Iago: O treacherous villains!

    [To Lodovico and Gratiano.]

    What are you there? Come in, and give some help.
Roderigo: O, help me here!   60
Cassio: That's one of them.
Iago: O murd'rous slave! O villain!

    [Stabs Roderigo.]

Roderigo: O damned Iago! O inhuman dog!
Iago: Kill men i' th' dark? — Where be these bloody thieves? —
    How silent is this town! — Ho! murder! murder! —
    What may you be? Are you of good or evil?   65
Lodovico: As you shall prove us, praise us.
Iago: Signior Lodovico?
Lodovico: He, sir.
Iago: I cry you mercy. Here's Cassio hurt by villains.
Gratiano: Cassio?   70
Iago: How is't, brother?
Cassio: My leg is cut in two.
Iago: Marry,° heaven forbid!
    Light, gentlemen. I'll bind it with my shirt.

    Enter Bianca.

Bianca: What is the matter, ho? Who is't that cried?

---

48 *cries on:* Raises the cry of.   58 *make:* Get.   72 *Marry:* (From "By Mary").

Iago: Who is't that cried?   75
Bianca: O my dear Cassio! my sweet Cassio!
    O Cassio, Cassio, Cassio!
Iago: O notable strumpet! — Cassio, may you suspect
    Who they should be that have thus mangled you?
Cassio: No.   80
Gratiano: I am sorry to find you thus. I have been to seek you.
Iago: Lend me a garter. So. O for a chair°
    To bear him easily hence!
Bianca: Alas, he faints! O Cassio, Cassio, Cassio!
Iago: Gentlemen all, I do suspect this trash   85
    To be a party in this injury. —
    Patience a while, good Cassio. — Come, come!
    Lend me a light. Know we this face or no?
    Alas, my friend and my dear countryman
    Roderigo? No — Yes, sure. — O heaven, Roderigo!   90
Gratiano: What, of Venice?
Iago: Even he, sir. Did you know him?
Gratiano: Know him? Ay.
Iago: Signior Gratiano? I cry your gentle pardon.
    These bloody accidents must excuse my manners
    That so neglected you.
Gratiano: I am glad to see you.   95
Iago: How do you, Cassio? — O, a chair, a chair!
Gratiano: Roderigo?
Iago: He, he, 'tis he!

    [A chair brought in.]

    O, that's well said;° the chair.
    Some good man bear him carefully from hence.   100
    I'll fetch the general's surgeon. *[To Bianca.]* For you, mistress,
    Save you your labor. — He that lies slain here, Cassio,
    Was my dear friend. What malice was between you?
Cassio: None in the world; nor do I know the man.
Iago [to Bianca]: What, look you pale? — O, bear him out o' th' air.   105

        [Cassio and Roderigo are borne off.]

    Stay you, good gentlemen. — Look you pale, mistress? —
    Do you perceive the gastness° of her eye? —
    Nay, if you stare, we shall hear more anon.
    Behold her well; I pray you look upon her.
    Do you see, gentlemen? Nay, guiltiness will speak.   110
    Though tongues were out of use.

    Enter Emilia.

---

82 *chair:* Litter.   99 *well said:* Well done.   107 *gastness:* Terror.

Emilia: 'Las, what's the matter? What's the matter, husband?
Iago: Cassio hath here been set on in the dark
    By Roderigo, and fellows that are scaped.
    He's almost slain, and Roderigo dead.   115
Emilia: Alas, good gentlemen! alas, good Cassio!
Iago: This is the fruits of whoring. Prithee, Emilia,
    Go know of Cassio where he supped to-night.

    [*To Bianca.*]

    What, do you shake at that?
Bianca: He supped at my house; but I therefore shake not.   120
Iago: O, did he so? I charge you go with me.
Emilia: Fie, fie upon thee, strumpet!
Bianca: I am no strumpet, but of life as honest°
    As you that thus abuse me.
Emilia: As I? Foh! fie upon thee!
Iago: Kind gentlemen, let's go see poor Cassio dressed.   125

    [*To Bianca.*]

    Come, mistress, you must tell 's another tale.
    Emilia, run you to the citadel
    And tell my lord and lady what hath happed.
                                              [*Exit Emilia.*]
    Will you go on afore?   *Exeunt [all but Iago].*
                    This is the night
    That either makes me or fordoes° me quite.   [*Exit.*]   130

SCENE II: *A bedchamber in the castle.*

Desdemona [asleep] in her bed. Enter Othello with a light.

Othello: It is the cause, it is the cause,° my soul.
    Let me not name it to you, you chaste stars!
    It is the cause. Yet I'll not shed her blood,
    Nor scar that whiter skin of hers than snow,
    And smooth as monumental alabaster.   5
    Yet she must die, else she'll betray more men.
    Put out the light, and then put out the light.
    If I quench thee, thou flaming minister,°
    I can again thy former light restore,
    Should I repent me; but once put out thy light,   10
    Thou cunning'st pattern of excelling nature,
    I know not where is that Promethean heat°
    That can thy light relume.° When I have plucked the rose,

---

123 *honest:* Chaste.   130 *fordoes:* Destroys.   **Scene II.**   1 *cause:* Cause of justice.
8 *minister:* Servant.   12 *Promethean heat:* Divine fire.   13 *relume:* Relight.

I cannot give it vital growth again;
It needs must wither. I'll smell thee on the tree.   15

(He kisses her.)

O balmy breath, that dost almost persuade
Justice to break her sword! One more, one more!
Be thus when thou art dead, and I will kill thee,
And love thee after. One more, and that's the last!
So sweet was ne'er so fatal. I must weep,   20
But they are cruel tears. This sorrow's heavenly;
It strikes where it doth love. She wakes.
Desdemona: Who's there? Othello?
Othello: Ay, Desdemona.
Desdemona: Will you come to bed, my lord?
Othello: Have you prayed to-night, Desdemon?
Desdemona: Ay, my lord.   25
Othello: If you bethink yourself of any crime°
     Unreconciled as yet to heaven and grace,
     Solicit for it straight.
Desdemona: Alack, my lord, what may you mean by that?
Othello: Well, do it, and be brief; I will walk by.   30
     I would not kill thy unprepared spirit.
     No, heaven forfend!° I would not kill thy soul.
Desdemona: Talk you of killing?
Othello: Ay, I do.
Desdemona: Then heaven
     Have mercy on me!
Othello: Amen, with all my heart!
Desdemona: If you say so, I hope you will not kill me.   35
Othello: Hum!
Desdemona: And yet I fear you; for you're fatal then
     When your eyes roll so. Why I should fear I know not,
     Since guiltiness I know not; but yet I feel I fear.
Othello: Think on thy sins.
Desdemona: They are loves I bear to you.   40
Othello: Ay, and for that thou diest.
Desdemona: That death 's unnatural that kills for loving.
     Alas, why gnaw you so your nether lip?
     Some bloody passion shakes your very frame.
     These are portents,° but yet I hope, I hope,   45
     They do not point on me.
Othello: Peace and be still!
Desdemona: I will so. What's the matter?
Othello: That handkerchief which I so loved and gave thee

---

26 *crime:* Sin.   32 *forfend:* Forbid.   45 *portents:* Signs of impending violence.

Thou gav'st to Cassio.
Desdemona: No, by my life and soul!
    Send for the man and ask him.
Othello: Sweet soul, take heed,   50
    Take heed of perjury; thou art on thy deathbed.
Desdemona: Ay, but not yet to die.
Othello: Yes, presently.°
    Therefore confess thee freely of thy sin;
    For to deny each article with oath
    Cannot remove nor choke the strong conception°   55
    That I do groan withal. Thou art to die.
Desdemona: Then Lord have mercy on me!
Othello: I say amen.
Desdemona: And have you mercy too! I never did
    Offend° you in my life; never loved Cassio
    But with such general warranty of heaven   60
    As I might love. I never gave him token.
Othello: By heaven, I saw my handkerchief in's hand!
    O perjured woman! thou dost stone my heart,°
    And mak'st me call what I intend to do
    A murder, which I thought a sacrifice.   65
    I saw the handkerchief.
Desdemona: He found it then.
    I never gave it him. Send for him hither.
    Let him confess a truth.
Othello: He hath confessed.
Desdemona: What, my lord?
Othello: That he hath used thee.
Desdemona: How? Unlawfully?
Othello: Ay.   70
Desdemona: He will not say so.
Othello: No, his mouth is stopped.
    Honest Iago hath ta'en order° for't.
Desdemona: O, my fear interprets. What, is he dead?
Othello: Had all his hairs been lives, my great revenge
    Had stomach for them all.   75
Desdemona: Alas, he is betrayed, and I undone!
Othello: Out, strumpet! Weep'st thou for him to my face?
Desdemona: O, banish me, my lord, but kill me not!
Othello: Down, strumpet!
Desdemona: Kill me to-morrow; let me live to-night!   80
Othello: Nay, if you strive—
Desdemona: But half an hour!
Othello: Being done, there is no pause.

---

52 *presently:* At once.   55 *conception:* Belief.   59 *Offend:* Wrong.   63 *stone my heart:* Turn my heart to stone.   72 *ta'en order:* Taken measures.

Desdemona: But while I say one prayer!
Othello: It is too late.

   (Smothers her.)

[*Desdemona:* O Lord, Lord, Lord!]

   Emilia at the door.

Emilia (calls within): My lord, my lord! What, ho! my lord, my lord!   85
Othello: What noise is this? Not dead? not yet quite dead?
   I that am cruel am yet merciful;
   I would not have thee linger in thy pain.
   So, so.
Emilia (within): What, ho! my lord, my lord!
Othello: Who's there?   90
Emilia (within): O, good my lord, I would speak a word with you!
Othello: Yes, 'tis Emilia. — By and by.° — She's dead. —
   'Tis like she comes to speak of Cassio's death.
   The noise was here. Ha! no more moving?
   Still as the grave. — Shall she come in? Were't good! —   95
   I think she stirs again. No. — What's best to do?
   If she come in, she'll sure speak to my wife.
   My wife! my wife! what wife? I have no wife.
   O, insupportable! O heavy hour!
   Methinks it should be now a huge eclipse   100
   Of sun and moon, and that th' affrighted globe
   Should yawn° at alteration.
Emilia (within):   I do beseech you
   That I may speak with you, O good my lord!
Othello: I had forgot thee. O, come in, Emilia.
   Soft, by and by. — Let me the curtains draw. —   105

   [Closes the bed-curtains.]

   Where art thou?

   [Opens the door.]
   Enter Emilia.

                          What's the matter with thee now?
Emilia: O my good lord, yonder's foul murder done!
Othello: What? Now?
Emilia: But now, my lord.
Othello: It is the very error° of the moon.   110
   She comes more nearer earth than she was wont
   And makes men mad.
Emilia: Cassio, my lord, hath killed a young Venetian
   Called Roderigo.

---

92 *By and by:* Just a moment (addressed to Emilia).   102 *yawn:* Open, as in an earthquake.   110 *error:* Straying off course.

Othello: Roderigo killed?
   And Cassio killed?
Emilia: No, Cassio is not killed.   115
Othello: Not Cassio killed? Then murder's out of tune,
   And sweet revenge grows harsh.
Desdemona: O, falsely, falsely murdered?
Emilia: O, Lord! what cry is that?
Othello: That? What?
Emilia: Out and alas! that was my lady's voice.   120
   Help! help, ho! help! O lady, speak again!
   Sweet Desdemona! O sweet mistress, speak!
Desdemona: A guiltless death I die.
Emilia: O, who hath done this deed?
Desdemona: Nobody—I myself. Farewell.   125
   Commend° me to my kind lord. O, farewell!

   (She dies.)

Othello: Why, how should she be murd'red?
Emilia: Alas, who knows?
Othello: You heard her say herself, it was not I.
Emilia: She said so. I must needs report the truth.
Othello: She's like a liar gone to burning hell!   130
   'Twas I that killed her.
Emilia: O, the more angel she,
   And you the blacker devil!
Othello: She turned to folly, and she was a whore.
Emilia: Thou dost belie her, and thou art a devil.
Othello: She was false as water.°
Emilia: Thou art rash as fire to say   135
   That she was false. O, she was heavenly true!
Othello: Cassio did top her. Ask thy husband else.
   O, I were damned beneath all depth in hell
   But that I did proceed upon just grounds
   To this extremity. Thy husband knew it all.   140
Emilia: My husband?
Othello: Thy husband.
Emilia: That she was false to wedlock?
Othello: Ay, with Cassio. Nay, had she been true,
   If heaven would make me such another world   145
   Of one entire and perfect chrysolite,°
   I'ld not have sold her for it.
Emilia: My husband?
Othello: Ay 'twas he that told me first.

---

126 *Commend:* Remember.   135 *water:* (Which is yielding).   146 *chrysolite:* (Precious topaz).

An honest man he is, and hates the slime
That sticks on filthy deeds.
Emilia: My husband?   150
Othello: What needs this iterance,° woman? I say thy husband.
Emilia: O mistress, villainy hath made mocks with love!
My husband say that she was false?
Othello: He, woman.
I say, thy husband. Dost understand the word?
My friend, thy husband; honest, honest Iago.   155
Emilia: If he say so, may his pernicious soul
Rot half a grain a day! he lies to th' heart.
She was too fond of her most filthy bargain.
Othello: Ha!
Emilia: Do thy worst.   160
This deed of thine is no more worthy heaven
Than thou wast worthy her.
Othello: Peace, you were best.
Emilia: Thou hast not half the power to do me harm
As I have to be hurt.° O gull! O dolt!
As ignorant as dirt! thou hast done a deed—   165
I care not for thy sword; I'll make thee known,
Though I lost twenty lives. Help! help! Ho! help!
The Moor hath killed my mistress! Murder! murder!

Enter Montano, Gratiano, Iago, and others.

Montano: What is the matter? How now, general?
Emilia: O, are you come, Iago? You have done well,   170
That men must lay their murders on your neck.
Gratiano: What is the matter?
Emilia: Disprove this villain, if thou be'st a man.
He says thou told'st him that his wife was false.
I know thou didst not; thou'rt not such a villain.   175
Speak, for my heart is full.
Iago: I told him what I thought, and told no more
Than what he found himself was apt and true.
Emilia: But did you ever tell him she was false?
Iago: I did.   180
Emilia: You told a lie, an odious damnèd lie!
Upon my soul, a lie! a wicked lie!
She false with Cassio? Did you say with Cassio?
Iago: With Cassio, mistress. Go to, charm° your tongue.
Emilia: I will not charm my tongue; I am bound to speak: 185
My mistress here lies murdered in her bed—

---

151 *iterance:* Repetition. 164 *to be hurt:* To endure hurt. 184 *charm:* Cast a spell on.

All: O heavens forfend!

Emilia: And your reports have set the murder on.

Othello: Nay, stare not, masters. It is true indeed.

Gratiano: 'Tis a strange truth.   190

Montano: O monstrous act!

Emilia: Villainy, villainy, villainy!
    I think upon't — I think I smell't! — O villainy!
    I thought so then. — I'll kill myself for grief. —
    O villainy, villainy!

Iago: What, are you mad? I charge you get you home.   195

Emilia: Good gentlemen, let me have leave to speak.
    'Tis proper I obey him, but not now.
    Perchance, Iago, I will ne'er go home.

Othello: O! O! O!   *(Falls on the bed.)*

Emilia: Nay, lay thee down and roar!
    For thou hast killed the sweetest innocent   200
    That e'er did lift up eye.

Othello: O, she was foul!

    [Rises.]

    I scarce did know you, uncle. There lies your niece,
    Whose breath, indeed, these hands have newly stopped.
    I know this act shows° horrible and grim.

Gratiano: Poor Desdemon! I am glad thy father's dead.   205
    Thy match was mortal to him, and pure grief
    Shore his old thread in twain. Did he live now,
    This sight would make him do a desperate turn;°
    Yea, curse his better angel from his side,
    And fall to reprobation.°   210

Othello: 'Tis pitiful; but yet Iago knows
    That she with Cassio hath the act of shame
    A thousand times committed. Cassio confessed it;
    And she did gratify° his amorous works
    With that recognizance° and pledge of love   215
    Which I first gave her. I saw it in his hand.
    It was a handkerchief, an antique token
    My father gave my mother.

Emilia: O God! O heavenly God!

Iago: Zounds, hold your peace!

Emilia: 'Twill out, 'twill out! I peace?   220
    No, I will speak as liberal as the north,°
    Let heaven and men and devils, let them all,

---

204 *shows:* Appears.   208 *turn:* Act.   210 *reprobation:* Rejection by God, damnation.
214 *gratify:* Reward.   215 *recognizance:* Token.   221 *liberal as the north:* Unchecked as
the north wind blows.

All, all, cry shame against me, yet I'll speak.
Iago: Be wise, and get you home.
Emilia: I will not.

[*Iago draws and threatens Emilia.*]

Gratiano: Fie!
    Your sword upon a woman?   225
Emilia: O thou dull Moor, that handkerchief thou speak'st of
    I found by fortune, and did give my husband;
    For often with a solemn earnestness—
    More than indeed belonged to such a trifle—
    He begged of me to steal't.
Iago: Villainous whore!   230
Emilia: She give it Cassio? No, alas, I found it,
    And I did give't my husband.
Iago: Filth, thou liest!
Emilia: By heaven, I do not, I do not, gentlemen.
    O murd'rous coxcomb! what should such a fool
    Do with so good a wife?
Othello: Are there no stones° in heaven   235
    But what serves for the thunder? Precious villain!

The Moor runs at Iago [but is disarmed by Montano].
Iago kills his wife.

Gratiano: The woman falls. Sure he hath killed his wife.
Emilia: Ay, ay. O, lay me by my mistress' side.   *Exit Iago.*
Gratiano: He's gone, but his wife's killed.
Montano: 'Tis a notorious° villain. Take you this weapon,   240
    Which I have here recovered from the Moor.
    Come, guard the door without. Let him not pass,
    But kill him rather. I'll after that same villain,
    For 'tis a damnèd slave.

Exit [Montano, with all but Othello and Emilia].

Othello: I am not valiant neither;
    But every puny whipster° gets my sword.   245
    But why should honor outlive honesty?
    Let it go all.
Emilia: What did thy song bode, lady?
    Hark, canst thou hear me? I will play the swan,
    And die in music. [*Sings.*] "Willow, willow, willow."
    Moor, she was chaste. She loved thee, cruel Moor: 250
    So come my soul to bliss as I speak true.
    So speaking as I think, alas, I die.

---

235 *stones:* Bolts like those used for thunderbolts.   240 *notorious:* Notable.
245 *puny whipster:* Whippersnapper.

(She dies.)

Othello: I have another weapon in this chamber;
It is a sword of Spain, the ice brook's° temper.
O, here it is. — Uncle, I must come forth.   255
Gratiano (within): If thou attempt it, it will cost thee dear.
Thou hast no weapon, and perforce must suffer.
Othello: Look in upon me then and speak with me,
Or, naked° as I am, I will assault thee.

[Enter Gratiano.]

Gratiano: What is the matter?
Othello: Behold, I have a weapon;   260
A better never did itself sustain
Upon a soldier's thigh. I have seen the day
That with this little arm and this good sword
I have made my way through more impediments
Than twenty times your stop.° But O vain boast!   265
Who can control his fate? 'Tis not so now.
Be not afraid, though you do see me weaponed.
Here is my journey's end, here is my butt,°
And very seamark° of my utmost sail:
Do you go back dismayed? 'Tis a lost° fear.   270
Man but a rush° against Othello's breast,
And he retires. Where should Othello go?
Now, how dost thou look now? O ill-starred wench!
Pale as thy smock! When we shall meet at compt,°
This look of thine will hurl my soul from heaven,   275
And fiends will snatch at it. Cold, cold, my girl?
Even like thy chastity.
O cursèd, cursèd slave! Whip me, ye devils,
From the possession of this heavenly sight!
Blow me about in winds! roast me in sulphur!   280
Wash me in steep-down gulfs of liquid fire!
Oh Desdemon! dead Desdemon! dead! Oh! Oh!

Enter Lodovico, Montano, Iago [as prisoner], and Officers; Cassio in a chair.

Lodovico: Where is this rash and most unfortunate man?
Othello: That's he that was Othello. Here I am.
Lodovico: Where is that viper? Bring the villain forth.   285
Othello: I look down towards his feet° — but that's a fable.
If that thou be'st a devil, I cannot kill thee.

254 *ice brook:* i.e., a Spanish blade, tempered in cold running water.   259 *naked:*
Disarmed.   265 *stop:* Power to stop.   268 *butt:* Limit.   269 *seamark:* Beacon, desti-
nation.   270 *lost:* Wasted.   271 *Man but a rush:* Wield only a reed.   274 *compt:*
Final accounting, Last Judgment.   286 *I . . . feet:* i.e., to see if they are cloven, like the
Devil's.

[Wounds Iago.]

Lodovico: Wrench his sword from him.

    [Othello is disarmed.]

Iago: I bleed, sir, but not killed.

Othello: I am not sorry neither. I'ld have thee live;
    For in my sense, 'tis happiness to die.   290

Lodovico: O thou Othello that wert once so good,
    Fall'n in the practice° of a damnèd slave,
    What shall be said to thee?

Othello: Why, anything;
    An honorable murderer, if you will;
    For naught did I in hate, but all in honor.   295

Lodovico: This wretch hath part confessed his villainy.
    Did you and he consent in° Cassio's death?

Othello: Ay.

Cassio: Dear general, I never gave you cause.

Othello: I do believe it, and I ask your pardon.   300
    Will you, I pray, demand that demi-devil
    Why he hath thus ensnared my soul and body?

Iago: Demand me nothing. What you know, you know.
    From this time forth I never will speak word.

Lodovico: What, not to pray?

Gratiano: Torments will ope your lips.   305

Othello: Well, thou dost best.

Lodovico: Sir, you shall understand what hath befall'n,
    Which, as I think, you know not. Here is a letter
    Found in the pocket of the slain Roderigo;
    And here another. The one of them imports   310
    The death of Cassio to be undertook
    By Roderigo.

Othello: O villain!

Cassio: Most heathenish and most gross!

Lodovico: Now here's another discontented paper
    Found in the pocket too; and this, it seems,   315
    Roderigo meant t' have sent this damnèd villain;
    But that, belike, Iago in the nick°
    Came in and satisfied him.

Othello: O thou pernicious caitiff! —
    How came you, Cassio, by that handkerchief
    That was my wife's?

Cassio: I found it in my chamber;   320
    And he himself confessed but even now
    That there he dropped it for a special purpose

292 *practice:* Plot.   297 *consent in:* Agree upon.   317 *nick:* Nick of time.

Which wrought to his desire.

Othello: O fool! fool! fool!

Cassio: There is besides in Roderigo's letter,
How he upbraids Iago that he made him   325
Brave me upon the watch; whereon it came
That I was cast;° and even but now he spake,
After long seeming dead — Iago hurt him,
Iago set him on.

Lodovico: You must forsake this room and go with us.   330
Your power and your command is taken off,
And Cassio rules in Cyprus. For this slave,
If there be any cunning cruelty
That can torment him much and hold him long,
It shall be his. You shall close prisoner rest   335
Till that the nature of your fault be known
To the Venetian state. Come, bring away.

Othello: Soft you! a word or two before you go.
I have done the state some service, and they know't.
No more of that. I pray you, in your letters,   340
When you shall these unlucky° deeds relate,
Speak of me as I am. Nothing extenuate,
Nor set down aught in malice. Then must you speak
Of one that loved not wisely, but too well;
Of one not easily jealous, but, being wrought,   345
Perplexed° in the extreme; of one whose hand,
Like the base Judean,° threw a pearl away
Richer than all his tribe; of one whose subdued° eyes,
Albeit unusèd to the melting mood,
Drop tears as fast as the Arabian trees   350
Their med'cinable gum. Set you down this.
And say besides that in Aleppo once,
Where a malignant and a turbaned Turk
Beat a Venetian and traduced the state,
I took by th' throat the circumcisèd dog   355
And smote him — thus.

   (He stabs himself.)

Lodovico: O bloody period!°

Gratiano: All that's spoke is marred.

Othello: I kissed thee ere I killed thee. No way but this,
Killing myself, to die upon a kiss.

   (He [falls upon the bed and] dies.)

---

327 *cast:* Dismissed.   341 *unlucky:* Fatal.   346 *Perplexed:* Distracted.   347 *Judean:*
Judas Iscariot (?) (quarto reads "Indian").   348 *subdued:* i.e., conquered by grief.
357 *period:* Ending.

Cassio: This did I fear, but thought he had no weapon;   360
    For he was great of heart.
Lodovico [to Iago]:   O Spartan dog,
    More fell° than anguish, hunger, or the sea!
    Look on the tragic loading of this bed.
    This is thy work. The object poisons sight;
    Let it be hid.° Gratiano, keep the house,   365
    And seize upon° the fortunes of the Moor,
    For they succeed on you. To you, lord governor,
    Remains the censure° of this hellish villain,
    The time, the place, the torture. O, enforce it!
    Myself will straight aboard, and to the state   370
    This heavy act with heavy heart relate.

                                                Exeunt.

362 *fell:* Cruel.   365 *Let it be hid:* i.e., draw the bed curtains.   366 *seize upon:* Take
legal possession of.   368 *censure:* Judicial sentence.

CONSIDERATIONS FOR CRITICAL THINKING AND WRITING

1. **FIRST RESPONSE.** Characterize Othello. In what ways is he presented
   as having a jealous disposition as well as a noble one? Why is he so
   vulnerable to Iago's villainy?

2. Explain how Iago presents himself to the world. What is beneath the
   surface of his public identity? Why does he hate Othello so passionately? What makes Iago so effective at manipulating people? What
   do other characters, besides Othello, think of him?

3. Explain why you think Othello's racial background does or doesn't
   affect events in the play.

4. How does Othello change during the course of the play? Do you feel
   the same about him from beginning to end? Trace your response to
   his character as it develops, paying particular attention to Othello's
   final speech.

5. Consider how women — Desdemona, Emilia, and Bianca — are presented in the play. What characteristics do they have in common?
   How do they relate to the men in their lives?

6. Despite its grinding emotional impact and bleak ending, *Othello* does
   have its humorous moments. Locate a scene that includes humor
   and describe its tone and function in the play.

7. **CONNECTION TO ANOTHER SELECTION.** Here's a long reach but a potentially interesting one: Write an essay that considers Desdemona as
   a wife alongside Nora in Henrik Ibsen's *A Doll House* (p. 797). How
   responsible are they to themselves and to others? Can they be discussed in the same breath, or are they from such different worlds
   that nothing useful can be said about comparing them? Either way,
   explain your response.

27

Henrik Ibsen and Modern Drama

A play should give you something to think about. When I see a play and understand it the first time, then I know it can't be much good.

— T. S. ELIOT [1]

REALISM

Realism is a literary technique that attempts to create the appearance of life as it is actually experienced. Characters in modern realistic plays (written during and after the last quarter of the nineteenth century) speak dialogue that we might hear in our daily lives. These characters are not larger than life but representative of it; they seem to speak the way we do rather than in highly poetic language, formal declarations, asides, or soliloquies. It is impossible to imagine a heroic figure such as Oedipus inhabiting a comfortably furnished living room and chatting about his wife's household budget the way Torvald Helmer does in Henrik Ibsen's *A Doll House*. Realism brings into focus commonplace, everyday life rather than the extraordinary kinds of events that make up Sophocles' *Oedipus the King* or Shakespeare's *Othello*.

Realistic characters can certainly be heroic, but like Nora Helmer, they find that their strength and courage are tested in the context of

[1] Photograph reprinted by permission of the Houghton Library, Harvard University.

events ordinary people might experience. Work, love, marriage, children, and death are often the focus of realistic dramas. These subjects can also constitute much of the material in nonrealistic plays, but modern realistic dramas present such material in the realm of the probable. Conflicts in realistic plays are likely to reflect problems in our own lives. Hence, making ends meet takes precedence over saving a kingdom; middle-and lower-class individuals take center stage as primary characters in main plots rather than being secondary characters in subplots. Thus we can see why the nineteenth-century movement toward realism paralleled the rise of a middle class eagerly seeking representations of its concerns in the theater.

Before the end of the nineteenth century, however, few attempts were made in the theater to present life as it is actually lived. The chorus's role in Sophocles' *Oedipus the King*, the allegorical figures in morality plays, the remarkable mistaken identities in Shakespeare's comedies, or the rhymed couplets spoken in seventeenth-century plays such as Molière's *Tartuffe* represent theatrical conventions rather than life. Theatergoers have understood and appreciated these conventions for centuries — and still do — but in the nineteenth century social, political, and industrial revolutions helped create an atmosphere in which some playwrights found it necessary to create works that more directly reflected their audiences' lives.

Playwrights such as Henrik Ibsen and Anton Chekhov refused to join the ranks of their romantic contemporaries, who they felt falsely idealized life. The most popular plays immediately preceding the works of these realistic writers consisted primarily of love stories and action-packed plots. Such **melodramas** offer audiences thrills and chills as well as happy endings. They typically feature a virtuous individual struggling under the tyranny of a wicked oppressor, who is defeated only at the last moment. Suspense is reinforced by a series of pursuits, captures, and escapes that move the plot quickly and de-emphasize character or theme. These representations of extreme conflicts enjoyed wide popularity in the nineteenth century — indeed, they still do — because their formula was varied enough to be entertaining yet their outcomes were always comforting to the audience's sense of justice. From the realists' perspective, melodramas were merely escape fantasies that distorted life by refusing to examine the real world closely and objectively.

Realists attempted to open their audiences' eyes; to their minds, the only genuine comfort was in knowing the truth. Many of their plays concern controversial issues of the day and focus on people who fall prey to indifferent societal institutions. English dramatist John Galsworthy (1867-1933) examined social values in *Strife* (1909) and *Justice* (1910), two plays whose titles broadly suggest the nature of his concerns. British playwright George Bernard Shaw (1856-1950) often used comedy and irony as means of awakening his audiences to contemporary problems: *Arms and the Man* (1894) satirizes romantic attitudes toward war, and *Mrs. Warren's Profession* (1898) indicts a social and economic system that drives a woman to prostitution. Chekhov's major plays are populated by characters frustrated by their social situations and their own sensibilities; they are ordinary people who long for happiness but become entangled in everyday circumstances that limit their lives. Ibsen also took a close look at his characters' daily lives. His plays attack social conventions and challenge popular attitudes toward marriage; he stunned audiences by dramatizing the suffering of a man dying of syphilis.

With these kinds of materials, Ibsen and his contemporaries popularized the **problem play**, a drama that represents a social issue in order to awaken the audience to it. These plays usually reject romantic plots in favor of holding up a mirror that reflects not simply what audiences want to see but what the playwright sees in them. Nineteenth-century realistic theater was no refuge from the social, economic, and psychological problems that melodrama ignored or sentimentalized.

THEATRICAL CONVENTIONS OF MODERN DRAMA

The picture-frame stage that is often used for realistic plays typically reproduces the setting of a room in some detail. Within the stage, framed by a proscenium arch (from which the curtain hangs), scenery and props are used to create an illusion of reality. Whether the "small bookcase with richly bound books" described in the opening scene of Ibsen's *A Doll House* is only painted scenery or an actual case with books, it will probably look real to the audience. Removing the fourth wall of a room so that an audience can look in fosters the illusion that the actions onstage are real events happening before unseen spectators. The texture of Nora's life is communicated by the set as well as by what she says and does. That doesn't happen in a play like Sophocles' *Oedipus the King*. Technical effects can make us believe there is wood burning in a fireplace or snow falling outside a window. Outdoor settings are made similarly realistic by props and painted sets. In one of Chekhov's full-length plays, for example, the second act opens in a meadow with the faint outline of a city on the horizon.

In addition to lifelike sets, a particular method of acting is used to create a realistic atmosphere. Actors address each other instead of directing formal speeches toward the audience; they act within the setting, not merely before it. At the beginning of the twentieth century, Konstantin Stanislavsky (1863–1938), a Russian director, teacher, and actor, developed a system of acting that was an important influence in realistic theater. He trained actors to identify with the inner emotions of the characters they played. They were encouraged to recall from their own lives emotional responses similar to those they were portraying. The goal was to present a role truthfully by first feeling and then projecting the character's situation. Among Stanislavsky's early successes employing this method were the plays of Chekhov he directed.

There are, however, degrees of realism on the stage. Tennessee Williams's *The Glass Menagerie*, for example, is a partially realistic portrayal of characters whose fragile lives are founded on illusions. Williams's dialogue rings true, and individual scenes resemble the kind of real-life action we would imagine such vulnerable characters engaging in, but other elements of the play are nonrealistic. For instance, Williams uses Tom as a major character in the play as well as narrator and stage manager. Here is part of Williams's stage directions: "The narrator is an undisguised convention of the play. He takes whatever license with dramatic convention as is convenient to his purposes." Although this play can be accurately described as including realistic elements, Williams, like many other contemporary playwrights, does not attempt an absolute fidelity to reality. He uses *flashbacks* — as does Arthur Miller in *Death of a Salesman* — to present incidents that occurred before the opening scene because the past impinges so heavily on the present. Most playwrights don't attempt to duplicate reality, since that can now be done so well by motion pictures.

Realism needn't lock a playwright into a futile attempt to make everything appear as it is in life. There is no way to avoid theatrical conventions: Actors impersonate characters in a setting that is, after all, a stage. Indeed, even the dialogue in a realistic play is quite different from the pauses, sentence fragments, repetitions, silences, and incoherencies that characterize the way people usually speak. Realistic dialogue may seem like ordinary speech, but it, like Shakespeare's poetic language, is constructed. If we remember that realistic drama represents only the appearance of reality and that what we read on a page or see and hear onstage is the result of careful selecting, editing, and even distortion, then we are more likely to appreciate the playwright's art.

A Doll House

Henrik Ibsen was born in Skien, Norway, to wealthy parents, who lost their money while he was a young boy. His early experiences with small-town life and genteel poverty sensitized him to the problems that he subsequently dramatized in a number of his plays. At age sixteen he was apprenticed to a druggist; he later thought about studying medicine, but by his early twenties he was earning a living writing and directing plays in various Norwegian cities. By the time of his death he enjoyed an international reputation for his treatment of social issues related to middle-class life.

POPPERFOTO/Alamy.

Ibsen's earliest dramatic works were historical and romantic plays, some in verse. His first truly realistic work was *The Pillars of Society* (1877), whose title ironically hints at the corruption and hypocrisy exposed in it. The realistic social-problem plays for which he is best known followed. These dramas at once fascinated and shocked international audiences. Among his most produced and admired works are *A Doll House* (1879), *Ghosts* (1881), *An Enemy of the People* (1882), *The Wild Duck* (1884), and *Hedda Gabler* (1890). The common denominator in many of Ibsen's dramas is his interest in individuals struggling for an authentic identity in the face of tyrannical social conventions. This conflict often results in his characters' being divided between a sense of duty to themselves and their responsibility to others.

Ibsen used such external and internal conflicts to propel his plays' action. Like many of his contemporaries who wrote realistic plays, he adopted the form of the *well-made play*. A dramatic structure popularized in France by Eugène Scribe (1791–1861) and Victorien Sardou (1831–1908), the well-made play employs conventions including plenty of suspense created by meticulous plotting. Extensive exposition explains past events that ultimately lead to an inevitable climax. Tension is released when a secret that reverses the protagonist's fortunes is revealed. Ibsen, having directed a number of Scribe's plays in Norway, knew their cause-to-effect plot arrangements and used them for his own purposes in his problem plays.

A Doll House dramatizes the tensions of a nineteenth-century middle-class marriage in which a wife struggles to step beyond the limited identity imposed on her by her husband and society.

HENRIK IBSEN (1828–1906)

A Doll House   *1879*

TRANSLATED BY ROLF FJELDE

THE CHARACTERS

Torvald Helmer, a lawyer
Nora, his wife
Dr. Rank
Mrs. Linde
Nils Krogstad, a bank clerk
The Helmers' three small children
Anne-Marie, their nurse
Helene, a maid
A Delivery Boy

SCENE: The action takes place in Helmer's residence.

ACT I

A comfortable room, tastefully but not expensively furnished. A door to the right in the back wall leads to the entryway; another to the left leads to Helmer's study. Between these doors, a piano. Midway in the left-hand wall a door, and further back a window. Near the window a round table with an armchair and a small sofa. In the right-hand wall, toward the rear, a door, and nearer the foreground a porcelain stove with two armchairs and a rocking chair beside it. Between the stove and the side door, a small table. Engravings on the walls. An etagère with china figures and other small art objects; a small bookcase with richly bound books; the floor carpeted; a fire burning in the stove. It is a winter day.

A bell rings in the entryway; shortly after we hear the door being unlocked. Nora comes into the room, humming happily to herself; she is wearing street clothes and carries an armload of packages, which she puts down on the table to the right. She has left the hall door open; and through it a Delivery Boy is seen, holding a Christmas tree and a basket, which he gives to the Maid who let them in.

Nora: Hide the tree well, Helene. The children mustn't get a glimpse of it till this evening, after it's trimmed. (*To the Delivery Boy, taking out her purse.*) How much?

A Doll House: Owen Teale and Janet McTeer in the 1997 Bill Kenwright London production of *A Doll House* performed at New York's Belasco Theater—winner of the 1997 Tony Award for Best Revival of a Play.
© Joan Marcus.

Delivery Boy: Fifty, ma'am.

Nora: There's a crown. No, keep the change. *(The Boy thanks her and leaves. Nora shuts the door. She laughs softly to herself while taking off her street things. Drawing a bag of macaroons from her pocket, she eats a couple, then steals over and listens at her husband's study door.)* Yes, he's home. *(Hums again as she moves to the table right.)*

Helmer (from the study): Is that my little lark twittering out there?

Nora (busy opening some packages): Yes, it is.

Helmer: Is that my squirrel rummaging around?

Nora: Yes!

Helmer: When did my squirrel get in?

Nora: Just now. *(Putting the macaroon bag in her pocket and wiping her mouth.)* Do come in, Torvald, and see what I've bought.

Helmer: Can't be disturbed. *(After a moment he opens the door and peers in, pen in hand.)* Bought, you say? All that there? Has the little spend-thrift been out throwing money around again?

Nora: Oh, but Torvald, this year we really should let ourselves go a bit. It's the first Christmas we haven't had to economize.

Helmer: But you know we can't go squandering.

Nora: Oh yes, Torvald, we can squander a little now. Can't we? Just a tiny, wee bit. Now that you've got a big salary and are going to make piles and piles of money.

Helmer: Yes — starting New Year's. But then it's a full three months till the raise comes through.

Nora: Pooh! We can borrow that long.

Helmer: Nora! *(Goes over and playfully takes her by the ear.)* Are your scatter-brains off again? What if today I borrowed a thousand crowns, and you squandered them over Christmas week, and then on New Year's Eve a roof tile fell on my head and I lay there —

Nora (putting her hand on his mouth): Oh! Don't say such things!

Helmer: Yes, but what if it happened — then what?

Nora: If anything so awful happened, then it just wouldn't matter if I had debts or not.

Helmer: Well, but the people I'd borrowed from?

Nora: Them? Who cares about them! They're strangers.

Helmer: Nora, Nora, how like a woman! No, but seriously, Nora, you know what I think about that. No debts! Never borrow! Something of freedom's lost — and something of beauty, too — from a home that's founded on borrowing and debt. We've made a brave stand up to now, the two of us; and we'll go right on like that the little while we have to.

Nora (going toward the stove): Yes, whatever you say, Torvald.

Helmer (following her): Now, now, the little lark's wings mustn't droop. Come on, don't be a sulky squirrel. *(Taking out his wallet.)* Nora, guess what I have here.

Nora (turning quickly): Money!

Helmer: There, see. *(Hands her some notes.)* Good grief, I know how costs go up in a house at Christmastime.

Nora: Ten — twenty — thirty — forty. Oh, thank you, Torvald; I can manage no end on this.

Helmer: You really will have to.

Nora: Oh yes, I promise I will! But come here so I can show you everything I bought. And so cheap! Look, new clothes for Ivar here — and a sword. Here a horse and a trumpet for Bob. And a doll and a doll's bed here for Emmy; they're nothing much, but she'll tear them to bits in no time anyway. And here I have dress material and handkerchiefs for the maids. Old Anne-Marie really deserves something more.

Helmer: And what's in that package there?

Nora (with a cry): Torvald, no! You can't see that till tonight!

Helmer: I see. But tell me now, you little prodigal, what have you thought of for yourself?

Nora: For myself? Oh, I don't want anything at all.

Helmer: Of course you do. Tell me just what — within reason — you'd most like to have.

Nora: I honestly don't know. Oh, listen, Torvald —

Helmer: Well?

Nora (fumbling at his coat buttons, without looking at him): If you want to give me something, then maybe you could — you could —

Helmer: Come on, out with it.

Nora (hurriedly): You could give me money, Torvald. No more than you think you can spare; then one of these days I'll buy something with it.

Helmer: But Nora —

Nora: Oh please, Torvald darling, do that! I beg you, please. Then I could hang the bills in pretty gilt paper on the Christmas tree. Wouldn't that be fun?

Helmer: What are those little birds called that always fly through their fortunes?

Nora: Oh yes, spendthrifts: I know all that. But let's do as I say, Torvald; then I'll have time to decide what I really need most. That's very sensible, isn't it?

Helmer (smiling): Yes, very — that is, if you actually hung onto the money I give you, and you actually used it to buy yourself something. But it goes for the house and for all sorts of foolish things, and then I only have to lay out some more.

Nora: Oh, but Torvald —

Helmer: Don't deny it, my dear little Nora. *(Putting his arm around her waist.)* Spendthrifts are sweet, but they use up a frightful amount of money. It's incredible what it costs a man to feed such birds.

Nora: Oh, how can you say that! Really, I save everything I can.

Helmer (laughing): Yes, that's the truth. Everything you can. But that's nothing at all.

Nora (humming, with a smile of quiet satisfaction): Hm, if you only knew what expenses we larks and squirrels have, Torvald.

Helmer: You're an odd little one. Exactly the way your father was. You're never at a loss for scaring up money; but the moment you have it, it runs right out through your fingers; you never know what you've done with it. Well, one takes you as you are. It's deep in your blood. Yes, these things are hereditary, Nora.

Nora: Ah, I could wish I'd inherited many of Papa's qualities.

Helmer: And I couldn't wish you anything but just what you are, my sweet little lark. But wait; it seems to me you have a very—what should I call it?—a very suspicious look today—

Nora: I do?

Helmer: You certainly do. Look me straight in the eye.

Nora (looking at him): Well?

Helmer (shaking an admonitory finger): Surely my sweet tooth hasn't been running riot in town today, has she?

Nora: No. Why do you imagine that?

Helmer: My sweet tooth really didn't make a little detour through the confectioner's?

Nora: No, I assure you, Torvald—

Helmer: Hasn't nibbled some pastry?

Nora: No, not at all.

Helmer: Not even munched a macaroon or two?

Nora: No, Torvald, I assure you, really—

Helmer: There, there now. Of course I'm only joking.

Nora (going to the table, right): You know I could never think of going against you.

Helmer: No, I understand that; and you *have* given me your word. *(Going over to her.)* Well, you keep your little Christmas secrets to yourself, Nora darling. I expect they'll come to light this evening, when the tree is lit.

Nora: Did you remember to ask Dr. Rank?

Helmer: No. But there's no need for that: it's assumed he'll be dining with us. All the same, I'll ask him when he stops by here this morning. I've ordered some fine wine. Nora, you can't imagine how I'm looking forward to this evening.

Nora: So am I. And what fun for the children, Torvald!

Helmer: Ah, it's so gratifying to know that one's gotten a safe, secure job, and with a comfortable salary. It's a great satisfaction, isn't it?

Nora: Oh, it's wonderful!

Helmer: Remember last Christmas? Three whole weeks before, you shut yourself in every evening till long after midnight, making flowers for the Christmas tree, and all the other decorations to surprise us. Ugh, that was the dullest time I've ever lived through.

Nora: It wasn't at all dull for me.

Helmer (smiling): But the outcome *was* pretty sorry, Nora.

Nora: Oh, don't tease me with that again. How could I help it that the cat came in and tore everything to shreds.

Helmer: No, poor thing, you certainly couldn't. You wanted so much to please us all, and that's what counts. But it's just as well that the hard times are past.

Nora: Yes, it's really wonderful.

Helmer: Now I don't have to sit here alone, boring myself, and you don't have to tire your precious eyes and your fair little delicate hands —

Nora (clapping her hands): No, is it really true, Torvald, I don't have to? Oh, how wonderfully lovely to hear! *(Taking his arm.)* Now I'll tell you just how I've thought we should plan things. Right after Christmas — *(The doorbell rings.)* Oh, the bell. *(Straightening the room up a bit.)* Somebody would have to come. What a bore!

Helmer: I'm not home to visitors, don't forget.

Maid (from the hall doorway): Ma'am, a lady to see you —

Nora: All right, let her come in.

Maid (to Helmer): And the doctor's just come too.

Helmer: Did he go right to my study?

Maid: Yes, he did.

> *Helmer goes into his room. The Maid shows in Mrs. Linde, dressed in traveling clothes, and shuts the door after her.*

Mrs. Linde (in a dispirited and somewhat hesitant voice): Hello, Nora.

Nora (uncertain): Hello —

Mrs. Linde: You don't recognize me.

Nora: No, I don't know — but wait, I think — *(Exclaiming.)* What! Kristine! Is it really you?

Mrs. Linde: Yes, it's me.

Nora: Kristine! To think I didn't recognize you. But then, how could I? *(More quietly.)* How you've changed, Kristine!

Mrs. Linde: Yes, no doubt I have. In nine — ten long years.

Nora: Is it so long since we met? Yes, it's all of that. Oh, these last eight years have been a happy time, believe me. And so now you've come in to town, too. Made the long trip in the winter. That took courage.

Mrs. Linde: I just got here by ship this morning.

Nora: To enjoy yourself over Christmas, of course. Oh, how lovely! Yes, enjoy ourselves, we'll do that. But take your coat off. You're not still cold? *(Helping her.)* There now, let's get cozy here by the stove. No, the easy chair there! I'll take the rocker here. *(Seizing her hands.)* Yes, now you have your old look again; it was only in that first moment. You're a bit more pale, Kristine — and maybe a bit thinner.

Mrs. Linde: And much, much older, Nora.

Nora: Yes, perhaps a bit older: a tiny, tiny bit; not much at all. *(Stopping short; suddenly serious.)* Oh, but thoughtless me, to sit here, chattering away. Sweet, good Kristine, can you forgive me?

Mrs. Linde: What do you mean, Nora?

Nora (softly): Poor Kristine, you've become a widow.

Mrs. Linde: Yes, three years ago.

Nora: Oh, I knew it, of course: I read it in the papers. Oh, Kristine, you must believe me; I often thought of writing you then, but I kept postponing it, and something always interfered.

Mrs. Linde: Nora dear, I understand completely.

Nora: No, it was awful of me, Kristine. You poor thing, how much you must have gone through. And he left you nothing?

Mrs. Linde: No.

Nora: And no children?

Mrs. Linde: No.

Nora: Nothing at all, then?

Mrs. Linde: Not even a sense of loss to feed on.

Nora (looking incredulously at her): But Kristine, how could that be?

Mrs. Linde (smiling wearily and smoothing her hair): Oh, sometimes it happens, Nora.

Nora: So completely alone. How terribly hard that must be for you. I have three lovely children. You can't see them now; they're out with the maid. But now you must tell me everything—

Mrs. Linde: No, no, no, tell me about yourself.

Nora: No, you begin. Today I don't want to be selfish. I want to think only of you today. But there *is* something I must tell you. Did you hear of the wonderful luck we had recently?

Mrs. Linde: No, what's that?

Nora: My husband's been made manager in the bank, just think!

Mrs. Linde: Your husband? How marvelous!

Nora: Isn't it? Being a lawyer is such an uncertain living, you know, especially if one won't touch any cases that aren't clean and decent. And of course Torvald would never do that, and I'm with him completely there. Oh, we're simply delighted, believe me! He'll join the bank right after New Year's and start getting a huge salary and lots of commissions. From now on we can live quite differently—just as we want. Oh, Kristine, I feel so light and happy! Won't it be lovely to have stacks of money and not a care in the world?

Mrs. Linde: Well, anyway, it would be lovely to have enough for necessities.

Nora: No, not just for necessities, but stacks and stacks of money!

Mrs. Linde (smiling): Nora, Nora, aren't you sensible yet? Back in school you were such a free spender.

Nora (with a quiet laugh): Yes, that's what Torvald still says. *(Shaking her finger.)* But "Nora, Nora" isn't as silly as you all think. Really, we've been in no position for me to go squandering. We've had to work, both of us.

Mrs. Linde: You too?

Nora: Yes, at odd jobs—needlework, crocheting, embroidery, and such— *(Casually.)* and other things too. You remember that Torvald left the department when we were married? There was no chance of promotion in his office, and of course he needed to earn more money. But that first year he drove himself terribly. He took on all kinds of extra work that kept him going morning and night. It wore him down, and then he fell deathly ill. The doctors said it was essential for him to travel south.

Mrs. Linde: Yes, didn't you spend a whole year in Italy?

Nora: That's right. It wasn't easy to get away, you know. Ivar had just been born. But of course we had to go. Oh, that was a beautiful trip, and it saved Torvald's life. But it cost a frightful sum, Kristine.

Mrs. Linde: I can well imagine.

Nora: Four thousand, eight hundred crowns it cost. That's really a lot of money.

Mrs. Linde: But it's lucky you had it when you needed it.

Nora: Well, as it was, we got it from Papa.

Mrs. Linde: I see. It was just about the time your father died.

Nora: Yes, just about then. And, you know, I couldn't make that trip out to nurse him. I had to stay here, expecting Ivar any moment, and with my poor sick Torvald to care for. Dearest Papa, I never saw him again, Kristine. Oh, that was the worst time I've known in all my marriage.

Mrs. Linde: I know how you loved him. And then you went off to Italy?

Nora: Yes. We had the means now, and the doctors urged us. So we left a month after.

Mrs. Linde: And your husband came back completely cured?

Nora: Sound as a drum!

Mrs. Linde: But—the doctor?

Nora: Who?

Mrs. Linde: I thought the maid said he was a doctor, the man who came in with me.

Nora: Yes, that was Dr. Rank—but he's not making a sick call. He's our closest friend, and he stops by at least once a day. No, Torvald hasn't had a sick moment since, and the children are fit and strong, and I am, too. *(Jumping up and clapping her hands.)* Oh, dear God, Kristine, what a lovely thing to live and be happy! But how disgusting of me—I'm talking of nothing but my own affairs. *(Sits on a stool close by Kristine, arms resting across her knees.)* Oh, don't be angry with me! Tell me, is it really true that you weren't in love with your husband? Why did you marry him, then?

Mrs. Linde: My mother was still alive, but bedridden and helpless—and I had my two younger brothers to look after. In all conscience, I didn't think I could turn him down.

Nora: No, you were right there. But was he rich at the time?

Mrs. Linde: He was very well off, I'd say. But the business was shaky, Nora. When he died, it all fell apart, and nothing was left.

Nora: And then—?

Mrs. Linde: Yes, so I had to scrape up a living with a little shop and a little teaching and whatever else I could find. The last three years have been like one endless workday without a rest for me. Now it's over, Nora. My poor mother doesn't need me, for she's passed on. Nor the boys, either; they're working now and can take care of themselves.

Nora: How free you must feel—

Mrs. Linde: No—only unspeakably empty. Nothing to live for now. *(Standing up anxiously.)* That's why I couldn't take it any longer out in that desolate hole. Maybe here it'll be easier to find something to do and keep my mind occupied. If I could only be lucky enough to get a steady job, some office work—

Nora: Oh, but Kristine, that's so dreadfully tiring, and you already look so tired. It would be much better for you if you could go off to a bathing resort.

Mrs. Linde (going toward the window): I have no father to give me travel money, Nora.

Nora (rising): Oh, don't be angry with me.

Mrs. Linde (going to her): Nora dear, don't you be angry with me. The worst of my kind of situation is all the bitterness that's stored away. No one to work for, and yet you're always having to snap up your opportunities. You have to live; and so you grow selfish. When you told me the happy change in your lot, do you know I was delighted less for your sakes than for mine?

Nora: How so? Oh, I see. You think maybe Torvald could do something for you.

Mrs. Linde: Yes, that's what I thought.

Nora: And he will, Kristine! Just leave it to me; I'll bring it up so delicately—find something attractive to humor him with. Oh, I'm so eager to help you.

Mrs. Linde: How very kind of you, Nora, to be so concerned over me— doubly kind, considering you really know so little of life's burdens yourself.

Nora: I—? I know so little—?

Mrs. Linde (smiling): Well, my heavens—a little needlework and such— Nora, you're just a child.

Nora (tossing her head and pacing the floor): You don't have to act so superior.

Mrs. Linde: Oh?

Nora: You're just like the others. You all think I'm incapable of anything serious—

Mrs. Linde: Come now—

Nora: That I've never had to face the raw world.

Mrs. Linde: Nora dear, you've just been telling me all your troubles.

Nora: Hm! Trivia! *(Quietly.)* I haven't told you the big thing.

Mrs. Linde: Big thing? What do you mean?

Nora: You look down on me so, Kristine, but you shouldn't. You're proud that you worked so long and hard for your mother.

Mrs. Linde: I don't look down on a soul. But it *is* true: I'm proud — and happy, too — to think it was given to me to make my mother's last days almost free of care.

Nora: And you're also proud thinking of what you've done for your brothers.

Mrs. Linde: I feel I've a right to be.

Nora: I agree. But listen to this, Kristine — I've also got something to be proud and happy for.

Mrs. Linde: I don't doubt it. But whatever do you mean?

Nora: Not so loud. What if Torvald heard! He mustn't, not for anything in the world. Nobody must know, Kristine. No one but you.

Mrs. Linde: But what is it, then?

Nora: Come here. (*Drawing her down beside her on the sofa.*) It's true — I've also got something to be proud and happy for. I'm the one who saved Torvald's life.

Mrs. Linde: Saved — ? Saved how?

Nora: I told you about the trip to Italy. Torvald never would have lived if he hadn't gone south —

Mrs. Linde: Of course; your father gave you the means —

Nora (smiling): That's what Torvald and all the rest think, but —

Mrs. Linde: But — ?

Nora: Papa didn't give us a pin. I was the one who raised the money.

Mrs. Linde: You? That whole amount?

Nora: Four thousand, eight hundred crowns. What do you say to that?

Mrs. Linde: But Nora, how was it possible? Did you win the lottery?

Nora (disdainfully): The lottery? Pooh! No art to that.

Mrs. Linde: But where did you get it from then?

Nora (humming, with a mysterious smile): Hmm, tra-la-la-la.

Mrs. Linde: Because you couldn't have borrowed it.

Nora: No? Why not?

Mrs. Linde: A wife can't borrow without her husband's consent.

Nora (tossing her head): Oh, but a wife with a little business sense, a wife who knows how to manage —

Mrs. Linde: Nora, I simply don't understand —

Nora: You don't have to. Whoever said I *borrowed* the money? I could have gotten it other ways. (*Throwing herself back on the sofa.*) I could have gotten it from some admirer or other. After all, a girl with my ravishing appeal —

Mrs. Linde: You lunatic.

Nora: I'll bet you're eaten up with curiosity, Kristine.

Mrs. Linde: Now listen here, Nora — you haven't done something indiscreet?

Nora (sitting up again): Is it indiscreet to save your husband's life?

Mrs. Linde: I think it's indiscreet that without his knowledge you —

Nora: But that's the point: he mustn't know! My Lord, can't you understand? He mustn't ever know the close call he had. It was to *me* the doctors came to say his life was in danger—that nothing could save him but a stay in the south. Didn't I try strategy then! I began talking about how lovely it would be for me to travel abroad like other young wives; I begged and I cried; I told him please to remember my condition, to be kind and indulge me; and then I dropped a hint that he could easily take out a loan. But at that, Kristine, he nearly exploded. He said I was frivolous, and it was his duty as man of the house not to indulge me in whims and fancies—as I think he called them. Aha, I thought, now you'll just have to be saved—and that's when I saw my chance.

Mrs. Linde: And your father never told Torvald the money wasn't from him?

Nora: No, never. Papa died right about then. I'd considered bringing him into my secret and begging him never to tell. But he was too sick at the time—and then, sadly, it didn't matter.

Mrs. Linde: And you've never confided in your husband since?

Nora: For heaven's sake, no! Are you serious? He's so strict on that subject. Besides—Torvald, with all his masculine pride—how painfully humiliating for him if he ever found out he was in debt to me. That would just ruin our relationship. Our beautiful, happy home would never be the same.

Mrs. Linde: Won't you ever tell him?

Nora (thoughtfully, half smiling): Yes—maybe sometime, years from now, when I'm no longer so attractive. Don't laugh! I only mean when Torvald loves me less than now, when he stops enjoying my dancing and dressing up and reciting for him. Then it might be wise to have something in reserve—*(Breaking off.)* How ridiculous! That'll never happen—Well, Kristine, what do you think of my big secret? I'm capable of something too, hm? You can imagine, of course, how this thing hangs over me. It really hasn't been easy meeting the payments on time. In the business world there's what they call quarterly interest and what they call amortization, and these are always so terribly hard to manage. I've had to skimp a little here and there, wherever I could, you know. I could hardly spare anything from my house allowance, because Torvald has to live well. I couldn't let the children go poorly dressed; whatever I got for them, I felt I had to use up completely—the darlings!

Mrs. Linde: Poor Nora, so it had to come out of your own budget, then?

Nora: Yes, of course. But I was the one most responsible, too. Every time Torvald gave me money for new clothes and such, I never used more than half; always bought the simplest, cheapest outfits. It was a godsend that everything looks so well on me that Torvald never noticed. But it did weigh me down at times, Kristine. It *is* such a joy to wear fine things. You understand.

Mrs. Linde: Oh, of course.

Nora: And then I found other ways of making money. Last winter I was lucky enough to get a lot of copying to do. I locked myself in and sat writing every evening till late in the night. Ah, I was tired so often, dead tired. But still it was wonderful fun, sitting and working like that, earning money. It was almost like being a man.

Mrs. Linde: But how much have you paid off this way so far?

Nora: That's hard to say, exactly. These accounts, you know, aren't easy to figure. I only know that I've paid out all I could scrape together. Time and again I haven't known where to turn. *(Smiling.)* Then I'd sit here dreaming of a rich old gentleman who had fallen in love with me —

Mrs. Linde: What! Who is he?

Nora: Oh, really! And that he'd died, and when his will was opened, there in big letters it said, "All my fortune shall be paid over in cash, immediately, to that enchanting Mrs. Nora Helmer."

Mrs. Linde: But Nora dear — who *was* this gentleman?

Nora: Good grief, can't you understand? The old man never existed; that was only something I'd dream up time and again whenever I was at my wits' end for money. But it makes no difference now; the old fossil can go where he pleases for all I care; I don't need him or his will — because now I'm free. *(Jumping up.)* Oh, how lovely to think of that, Kristine! Carefree! To know you're carefree, utterly carefree; to be able to romp and play with the children, and to keep up a beautiful, charming home — everything just the way Torvald likes it! And think, spring is coming, with big blue skies. Maybe we can travel a little then. Maybe I'll see the ocean again. Oh yes, it *is* so marvelous to live and be happy!

The front doorbell rings.

Mrs. Linde (rising): There's the bell. It's probably best that I go.

Nora: No, stay. No one's expected. It must be for Torvald.

Maid (from the hall doorway): Excuse me, ma'am — there's a gentleman here to see Mr. Helmer, but I didn't know — since the doctor's with him —

Nora: Who is the gentleman?

Krogstad (from the doorway): It's me, Mrs. Helmer.

Mrs. Linde starts and turns away toward the window.

Nora (stepping toward him, tense, her voice a whisper): You? What is it? Why do you want to speak to my husband?

Krogstad: Bank business — after a fashion. I have a small job in the investment bank, and I hear now your husband is going to be our chief —

Nora: In other words, it's —

Krogstad: Just dry business, Mrs. Helmer. Nothing but that.

Nora: Yes, then please be good enough to step into the study. *(She nods indifferently as she sees him out by the hall door, then returns and begins stirring up the stove.)*

Mrs. Linde: Nora — who was that man?

Nora: That was a Mr. Krogstad — a lawyer.

Mrs. Linde: Then it really was him.

Nora: Do you know that person?

Mrs. Linde: I did once — many years ago. For a time he was a law clerk in our town.

Nora: Yes, he's been that.

Mrs. Linde: How he's changed.

Nora: I understand he had a very unhappy marriage.

Mrs. Linde: He's a widower now.

Nora: With a number of children. There now, it's burning. *(She closes the stove door and moves the rocker a bit to one side.)*

Mrs. Linde: They say he has a hand in all kinds of business.

Nora: Oh? That may be true; I wouldn't know. But let's not think about business. It's so dull.

> *Dr. Rank enters from Helmer's study.*

Rank (still in the doorway): No, no really — I don't want to intrude, I'd just as soon talk a little while with your wife. *(Shuts the door, then notices Mrs. Linde.)* Oh, beg pardon. I'm intruding here too.

Nora: No, not at all. *(Introducing him.)* Dr. Rank, Mrs. Linde.

Rank: Well now, that's a name much heard in this house. I believe I passed the lady on the stairs as I came.

Mrs. Linde: Yes, I take the stairs very slowly. They're rather hard on me.

Rank: Uh-hm, some touch of internal weakness?

Mrs. Linde: More overexertion, I'd say.

Rank: Nothing else? Then you're probably here in town to rest up in a round of parties?

Mrs. Linde: I'm here to look for work.

Rank: Is that the best cure for overexertion?

Mrs. Linde: One has to live, Doctor.

Rank: Yes, there's a common prejudice to that effect.

Nora: Oh, come on, Dr. Rank — you really do want to live yourself.

Rank: Yes, I really do. Wretched as I am, I'll gladly prolong my torment indefinitely. All my patients feel like that. And it's quite the same, too, with the morally sick. Right at this moment there's one of those moral invalids in there with Helmer —

Mrs. Linde (softly): Ah!

Nora: Who do you mean?

Rank: Oh, it's a lawyer, Krogstad, a type you wouldn't know. His character is rotten to the root — but even he began chattering all-importantly about how he had to *live.*

Nora: Oh? What did he want to talk to Torvald about?

Rank: I really don't know. I only heard something about the bank.

Nora: I didn't know that Krog — that this man Krogstad had anything to do with the bank.

Rank: Yes, he's gotten some kind of berth down there. *(To Mrs. Linde.)* I don't know if you also have, in your neck of the woods, a type of person who scuttles about breathlessly, sniffing out hints of moral corruption, and then maneuvers his victim into some sort of key position where he can keep an eye on him. It's the healthy these days that are out in the cold.

Mrs. Linde: All the same, it's the sick who most need to be taken in.

Rank (with a shrug): Yes, there we have it. That's the concept that's turning society into a sanatorium.

Nora, lost in her thoughts, breaks out into quiet laughter and claps her hands.

Rank: Why do you laugh at that? Do you have any real idea of what society is?

Nora: What do I care about dreary old society? I was laughing at something quite different — something terribly funny. Tell me, Doctor — is everyone who works in the bank dependent now on Torvald?

Rank: Is that what you find so terribly funny?

Nora (smiling and humming): Never mind, never mind! *(Pacing the floor.)* Yes, that's really immensely amusing: that we — that Torvald has so much power now over all those people. *(Taking the bag out of her pocket.)* Dr. Rank, a little macaroon on that?

Rank: See here, macaroons! I thought they were contraband here.

Nora: Yes, but these are some that Kristine gave me.

Mrs. Linde: What? I — ?

Nora: Now, now, don't be afraid. You couldn't possibly know that Torvald had forbidden them. You see, he's worried they'll ruin my teeth. But hmp! Just this once! Isn't that so, Dr. Rank? Help yourself! *(Puts a macaroon in his mouth.)* And you too, Kristine. And I'll also have one, only a little one — or two, at the most. *(Walking about again.)* Now I'm really tremendously happy. Now there's just one last thing in the world that I have an enormous desire to do.

Rank: Well! And what's that?

Nora: It's something I have such a consuming desire to say so Torvald could hear.

Rank: And why can't you say it?

Nora: I don't dare. It's quite shocking.

Mrs. Linde: Shocking?

Rank: Well, then it isn't advisable. But in front of us you certainly can. What do you have such a desire to say so Torvald could hear?

Nora: I have such a huge desire to say — to hell and be damned!

Rank: Are you crazy?

Mrs. Linde: My goodness, Nora!

Rank: Go on, say it. Here he is.

Nora (hiding the macaroon bag): Shh, shh, shh!

Helmer comes in from his study, hat in hand, overcoat over his arm.

Nora (going toward him): Well, Torvald dear, are you through with him?

Helmer: Yes, he just left.

Nora: Let me introduce you — this is Kristine, who's arrived here in town.

Helmer: Kristine — ? I'm sorry, but I don't know —

Nora: Mrs. Linde, Torvald dear. Mrs. Kristine Linde.

Helmer: Of course. A childhood friend of my wife's, no doubt?

Mrs. Linde: Yes, we knew each other in those days.

Nora: And just think, she made the long trip down here in order to talk with you.

Helmer: What's this?

Mrs. Linde: Well, not exactly —

Nora: You see, Kristine is remarkably clever in office work, and so she's terribly eager to come under a capable man's supervision and add more to what she already knows —

Helmer: Very wise, Mrs. Linde.

Nora: And then when she heard that you'd become a bank manager — the story was wired out to the papers — then she came in as fast as she could and — Really, Torvald, for my sake you can do a little something for Kristine, can't you?

Helmer: Yes, it's not at all impossible. Mrs. Linde, I suppose you're a widow?

Mrs. Linde: Yes.

Helmer: Any experience in office work?

Mrs. Linde: Yes, a good deal.

Helmer: Well, it's quite likely that I can make an opening for you —

Nora (clapping her hands): You see, you see!

Helmer: You've come at a lucky moment, Mrs. Linde.

Mrs. Linde: Oh, how can I thank you?

Helmer: Not necessary. *(Putting his overcoat on.)* But today you'll have to excuse me —

Rank: Wait, I'll go with you. *(He fetches his coat from the hall and warms it at the stove.)*

Nora: Don't stay out long, dear.

Helmer: An hour; no more.

Nora: Are you going too, Kristine?

Mrs. Linde (putting on her winter garments): Yes, I have to see about a room now.

Helmer: Then perhaps we can all walk together.

Nora (helping her): What a shame we're so cramped here, but it's quite impossible for us to —

Mrs. Linde: Oh, don't even think of it! Good-bye, Nora dear, and thanks for everything.

Nora: Good-bye for now. Of course you'll be back this evening. And you too, Dr. Rank. What? If you're well enough? Oh, you've got to be! Wrap up tight now.

In a ripple of small talk the company moves out into the hall; children's voices are heard outside on the steps.

Nora: There they are! There they are! *(She runs to open the door. The children come in with their nurse, Anne-Marie.)* Come in, come in! *(Bends down and kisses them.)* Oh, you darlings — ! Look at them, Kristine. Aren't they lovely!

Rank: No loitering in the draft here.

Helmer: Come, Mrs. Linde — this place is unbearable now for anyone but mothers.

Dr. Rank, Helmer, and Mrs. Linde go down the stairs. Anne-Marie goes into the living room with the children. Nora follows, after closing the hall door.

Nora: How fresh and strong you look. Oh, such red cheeks you have! Like apples and roses. *(The children interrupt her throughout the following.)* And it was so much fun? That's wonderful. Really? You pulled both Emmy and Bob on the sled? Imagine, all together! Yes, you're a clever boy, Ivar. Oh, let me hold her a bit, Anne-Marie. My sweet little doll baby! *(Takes the smallest from the nurse and dances with her.)* Yes, yes, Mama will dance with Bob as well. What? Did you throw snowballs? Oh, if I'd only been there! No, don't bother, Anne-Marie — I'll undress them myself. Oh yes, let me. It's such fun. Go in and rest; you look half frozen. There's hot coffee waiting for you on the stove. *(The nurse goes into the room to the left. Nora takes the children's winter things off, throwing them about, while the children talk to her all at once.)* Is that so? A big dog chased you? But it didn't bite? No, dogs never bite little, lovely doll babies. Don't peek in the packages, Ivar! What is it? Yes, wouldn't you like to know. No, no, it's an ugly something. Well? Shall we play? What shall we play? Hide-and-seek? Yes, let's play hide-and-seek. Bob must hide first. I must? Yes, let me hide first. *(Laughing and shouting, she and the children play in and out of the living room and the adjoining room to the right. At last Nora hides under the table. The children come storming in, search, but cannot find her, then hear her muffled laughter, dash over to the table, lift the cloth up and find her. Wild shouting. She creeps forward as if to scare them. More shouts. Meanwhile, a knock at the hall door; no one has noticed it. Now the door half opens, and Krogstad appears. He waits a moment; the game goes on.)*

Krogstad: Beg pardon, Mrs. Helmer —

Nora (with a strangled cry, turning and scrambling to her knees): Oh! What do you want?

Krogstad: Excuse me. The outer door was ajar; it must be someone forgot to shut it —

Nora (rising): My husband isn't home, Mr. Krogstad.

Krogstad: I know that.

Nora: Yes — then what do you want here?

Krogstad: A word with you.

Nora: With — ? *(To the children, quietly.)* Go in to Anne-Marie. What? No, the strange man won't hurt Mama. When he's gone, we'll play some more. *(She leads the children into the room to the left and shuts the door after them. Then, tense and nervous:)* You want to speak to me?

Krogstad: Yes, I want to.

Nora: Today? But it's not yet the first of the month —

Krogstad: No, it's Christmas Eve. It's going to be up to you how merry a Christmas you have.

Nora: What is it you want? Today I absolutely can't —

Krogstad: We won't talk about that till later. This is something else. You do have a moment to spare, I suppose?

Nora: Oh yes, of course — I do, except —

Krogstad: Good. I was sitting over at Olsen's Restaurant when I saw your husband go down the street —

Nora: Yes?

Krogstad: With a lady.

Nora: Yes. So?

Krogstad: If you'll pardon my asking: wasn't that lady a Mrs. Linde?

Nora: Yes.

Krogstad: Just now come into town?

Nora: Yes, today.

Krogstad: She's a good friend of yours?

Nora: Yes, she is. But I don't see —

Krogstad: I also knew her once.

Nora: I'm aware of that.

Krogstad: Oh? You know all about it. I thought so. Well, then let me ask you short and sweet: is Mrs. Linde getting a job in the bank?

Nora: What makes you think you can cross-examine me, Mr. Krogstad — you, one of my husband's employees? But since you ask, you might as well know — yes, Mrs. Linde's going to be taken on at the bank. And I'm the one who spoke for her, Mr. Krogstad. Now you know.

Krogstad: So I guessed right.

Nora (pacing up and down): Oh, one does have a tiny bit of influence, I should hope. Just because I am a woman, don't think it means that — When one has a subordinate position, Mr. Krogstad, one really ought to be careful about pushing somebody who — hm —

Krogstad: Who has influence?

Nora: That's right.

Krogstad (in a different tone): Mrs. Helmer, would you be good enough to use your influence on my behalf?

Nora: What? What do you mean?

Krogstad: Would you please make sure that I keep my subordinate position in the bank?

Nora: What does that mean? Who's thinking of taking away your position?

Krogstad: Oh, don't play the innocent with me. I'm quite aware that your friend would hardly relish the chance of running into me again; and I'm also aware now whom I can thank for being turned out.

Nora: But I promise you —

Krogstad: Yes, yes, yes, to the point: there's still time, and I'm advising you to use your influence to prevent it.

Nora: But Mr. Krogstad, I have absolutely no influence.

Krogstad: You haven't? I thought you were just saying—

Nora: You shouldn't take me so literally. I! How can you believe that I have any such influence over my husband?

Krogstad: Oh, I've known your husband from our student days. I don't think the great bank manager's more steadfast than any other married man.

Nora: You speak insolently about my husband, and I'll show you the door.

Krogstad: The lady has spirit.

Nora: I'm not afraid of you any longer. After New Year's, I'll soon be done with the whole business.

Krogstad (restraining himself): Now listen to me, Mrs. Helmer. If necessary, I'll fight for my little job in the bank as if it were life itself.

Nora: Yes, so it seems.

Krogstad: It's not just a matter of income; that's the least of it. It's something else—All right, out with it! Look, this is the thing. You know, just like all the others, of course, that once, a good many years ago, I did something rather rash.

Nora: I've heard rumors to that effect.

Krogstad: The case never got into court; but all the same, every door was closed in my face from then on. So I took up those various activities you know about. I had to grab hold somewhere; and I dare say I haven't been among the worst. But now I want to drop all that. My boys are growing up. For their sakes, I'll have to win back as much respect as possible here in town. That job in the bank was like the first rung in my ladder. And now your husband wants to kick me right back down in the mud again.

Nora: But for heaven's sake, Mr. Krogstad, it's simply not in my power to help you.

Krogstad: That's because you haven't the will to—but I have the means to make you.

Nora: You certainly won't tell my husband that I owe you money?

Krogstad: Hm—what if I told him that?

Nora: That would be shameful of you. *(Nearly in tears.)* This secret—my joy and my pride—that he should learn it in such a crude and disgusting way—learn it from you. You'd expose me to the most horrible unpleasantness—

Krogstad: Only unpleasantness?

Nora (vehemently): But go on and try. It'll turn out the worse for you, because then my husband will really see what a crook you are, and then you'll *never* be able to hold your job.

Krogstad: I asked if it was just domestic unpleasantness you were afraid of?

Nora: If my husband finds out, then of course he'll pay what I owe at once, and then we'd be through with you for good.

Krogstad (a step closer): Listen, Mrs. Helmer — you've either got a very bad memory, or else no head at all for business. I'd better put you a little more in touch with the facts.

Nora: What do you mean?

Krogstad: When your husband was sick, you came to me for a loan of four thousand, eight hundred crowns.

Nora: Where else could I go?

Krogstad: I promised to get you that sum —

Nora: And you got it.

Krogstad: I promised to get you that sum, on certain conditions. You were so involved in your husband's illness, and so eager to finance your trip, that I guess you didn't think out all the details. It might just be a good idea to remind you. I promised you the money on the strength of a note I drew up.

Nora: Yes, and that I signed.

Krogstad: Right. But at the bottom I added some lines for your father to guarantee the loan. He was supposed to sign down there.

Nora: Supposed to? He did sign.

Krogstad: I left the date blank. In other words, your father would have dated his signature himself. Do you remember that?

Nora: Yes, I think —

Krogstad: Then I gave you the note for you to mail to your father. Isn't that so?

Nora: Yes.

Krogstad: And naturally you sent it at once — because only some five, six days later you brought me the note, properly signed. And with that, the money was yours.

Nora: Well, then; I've made my payments regularly, haven't I?

Krogstad: More or less. But — getting back to the point — those were hard times for you then, Mrs. Helmer.

Nora: Yes, they were.

Krogstad: Your father was very ill, I believe.

Nora: He was near the end.

Krogstad: He died soon after?

Nora: Yes.

Krogstad: Tell me, Mrs. Helmer, do you happen to recall the date of your father's death? The day of the month, I mean.

Nora: Papa died the twenty-ninth of September.

Krogstad: That's quite correct; I've already looked into that. And now we come to a curious thing — *(Taking out a paper.)* which I simply cannot comprehend.

Nora: Curious thing? I don't know —

Krogstad: This is the curious thing: that your father co-signed the note for your loan three days after his death.

Nora: How — ? I don't understand.

Krogstad: Your father died the twenty-ninth of September. But look. Here your father dated his signature October second. Isn't that curious,

Mrs. Helmer? *(Nora is silent.)* Can you explain it to me? *(Nora remains silent.)* It's also remarkable that the words "October second" and the year aren't written in your father's hand, but rather in one that I think I know. Well, it's easy to understand. Your father forgot perhaps to date his signature, and then someone or other added it, a bit sloppily, before anyone knew of his death. There's nothing wrong in that. It all comes down to the signature. And there's no question about *that*, Mrs. Helmer. It really *was* your father who signed his own name here, wasn't it?

Nora (after a short silence, throwing her head back and looking squarely at him): No, it wasn't. *I* signed Papa's name.

Krogstad: Wait, now — are you fully aware that this is a dangerous confession?

Nora: Why? You'll soon get your money.

Krogstad: Let me ask you a question — why didn't you send the paper to your father?

Nora: That was impossible. Papa was so sick. If I'd asked him for his signature, I also would have had to tell him what the money was for. But I couldn't tell him, sick as he was, that my husband's life was in danger. That was just impossible.

Krogstad: Then it would have been better if you'd given up the trip abroad.

Nora: I couldn't possibly. The trip was to save my husband's life. I couldn't give that up.

Krogstad: But didn't you ever consider that this was a fraud against me?

Nora: I couldn't let myself be bothered by that. You weren't any concern of mine. I couldn't stand you, with all those cold complications you made, even though you knew how badly off my husband was.

Krogstad: Mrs. Helmer, obviously you haven't the vaguest idea of what you've involved yourself in. But I can tell you this: it was nothing more and nothing worse that I once did — and it wrecked my whole reputation.

Nora: You? Do you expect me to believe that you ever acted bravely to save your wife's life?

Krogstad: Laws don't inquire into motives.

Nora: Then they must be very poor laws.

Krogstad: Poor or not — if I introduce this paper in court, you'll be judged according to law.

Nora: This I refuse to believe. A daughter hasn't a right to protect her dying father from anxiety and care? A wife hasn't a right to save her husband's life? I don't know much about laws, but I'm sure that somewhere in the books these things are allowed. And you don't know anything about it — you who practice the law? You must be an awful lawyer, Mr. Krogstad.

Krogstad: Could be. But business — the kind of business we two are mixed up in — don't you think I know about that? All right. Do what you want now. But I'm telling you *this:* if I get shoved down a second time, you're going to keep me company. *(He bows and goes out through the hall.)*

Nora (pensive for a moment, then tossing her head): Oh, really! Trying to frighten me! I'm not so silly as all that. *(Begins gathering up the children's clothes, but soon stops.)* But—? No, but that's impossible! I did it out of love.

The Children (in the doorway, left): Mama, that strange man's gone out the door.

Nora: Yes, yes, I know it. But don't tell anyone about the strange man. Do you hear? Not even Papa!

The Children: No, Mama. But now will you play again?

Nora: No, not now.

The Children: Oh, but Mama, you promised.

Nora: Yes, but I can't now. Go inside; I have too much to do. Go in, go in, my sweet darlings. *(She herds them gently back in the room and shuts the door after them. Settling on the sofa, she takes up a piece of embroidery and makes some stitches, but soon stops abruptly.)* No! *(Throws the work aside, rises, goes to the hall door and calls out.)* Helene! Let me have the tree in here. *(Goes to the table, left, opens the table drawer, and stops again.)* No, but that's utterly impossible!

Maid (with the Christmas tree): Where should I put it, ma'am?

Nora: There. The middle of the floor.

Maid: Should I bring anything else?

Nora: No, thanks. I have what I need.

The Maid, who has set the tree down, goes out.

Nora (absorbed in trimming the tree): Candles here—and flowers here. That terrible creature! Talk, talk, talk! There's nothing to it at all. The tree's going to be lovely. I'll do anything to please you, Torvald. I'll sing for you, dance for you—

Helmer comes in from the hall, with a sheaf of papers under his arm.

Nora: Oh! You're back so soon?

Helmer: Yes. Has anyone been here?

Nora: Here? No.

Helmer: That's odd. I saw Krogstad leaving the front door.

Nora: So? Oh yes, that's true. Krogstad was here a moment.

Helmer: Nora, I can see by your face that he's been here, begging you to put in a good word for him.

Nora: Yes.

Helmer: And it was supposed to seem like your own idea? You were to hide it from me that he'd been here. He asked you that, too, didn't he?

Nora: Yes, Torvald, but—

Helmer: Nora, Nora, and you could fall for that? Talk with that sort of person and promise him anything? And then in the bargain, tell me an untruth.

Nora: An untruth—?

Helmer: Didn't you say that no one had been here? *(Wagging his finger.)* My little songbird must never do that again. A songbird needs a clean beak to warble with. No false notes. *(Putting his arm about her waist.)* That's the way it should be, isn't it? Yes, I'm sure of it. *(Releasing her.)* And so, enough of that. *(Sitting by the stove.)* Ah, how snug and cozy it is here. *(Leafing among his papers.)*

Nora (busy with the tree, after a short pause): Torvald!

Helmer: Yes.

Nora: I'm so much looking forward to the Stenborgs' costume party, day after tomorrow.

Helmer: And I can't wait to see what you'll surprise me with.

Nora: Oh, that stupid business!

Helmer: What?

Nora: I can't find anything that's right. Everything seems so ridiculous, so inane.

Helmer: So my little Nora's come to *that* recognition?

Nora (going behind his chair, her arms resting on its back): Are you very busy, Torvald?

Helmer: Oh—

Nora: What papers are those?

Helmer: Bank matters.

Nora: Already?

Helmer: I've gotten full authority from the retiring management to make all necessary changes in personnel and procedure. I'll need Christmas week for that. I want to have everything in order by New Year's.

Nora: So that was the reason this poor Krogstad—

Helmer: Hm.

Nora (still leaning on the chair and slowly stroking the nape of his neck): If you weren't so very busy, I would have asked you an enormous favor, Torvald.

Helmer: Let's hear. What is it?

Nora: You know, there isn't anyone who has your good taste—and I want so much to look well at the costume party. Torvald, couldn't you take over and decide what I should be and plan my costume?

Helmer: Ah, is my stubborn little creature calling for a lifeguard?

Nora: Yes, Torvald, I can't get anywhere without your help.

Helmer: All right—I'll think it over. We'll hit on something.

Nora: Oh, how sweet of you. *(Goes to the tree again. Pause.)* Aren't the red flowers pretty—? But tell me, was it really such a crime that this Krogstad committed?

Helmer: Forgery. Do you have any idea what that means?

Nora: Couldn't he have done it out of need?

Helmer: Yes, or thoughtlessness, like so many others. I'm not so heartless that I'd condemn a man categorically for just one mistake.

Nora: No, of course not, Torvald!

Helmer: Plenty of men have redeemed themselves by openly confessing their crimes and taking their punishment.

Nora: Punishment—?

Helmer: But now Krogstad didn't go that way. He got himself out by sharp practices, and that's the real cause of his moral breakdown.

Nora: Do you really think that would—?

Helmer: Just imagine how a man with that sort of guilt in him has to lie and cheat and deceive on all sides, has to wear a mask even with the nearest and dearest he has, even with his own wife and children. And with the children, Nora—that's where it's most horrible.

Nora: Why?

Helmer: Because that kind of atmosphere of lies infects the whole life of a home. Every breath the children take in is filled with the germs of something degenerate.

Nora (coming closer behind him): Are you sure of that?

Helmer: Oh, I've seen it often enough as a lawyer. Almost everyone who goes bad early in life has a mother who's a chronic liar.

Nora: Why just—the mother?

Helmer: It's usually the mother's influence that's dominant, but the father's works in the same way, of course. Every lawyer is quite familiar with it. And still this Krogstad's been going home year in, year out, poisoning his own children with lies and pretense; that's why I call him morally lost. *(Reaching his hands out toward her.)* So my sweet little Nora must promise me never to plead his cause. Your hand on it. Come, come, what's this? Give me your hand. There, now. All settled. I can tell you it'd be impossible for me to work alongside of him. I literally feel physically revolted when I'm anywhere near such a person.

Nora (withdraws her hand and goes to the other side of the Christmas tree): How hot it is here! And I've got so much to do.

Helmer (getting up and gathering his papers): Yes, and I have to think about getting some of these read through before dinner. I'll think about your costume, too. And something to hang on the tree in gilt paper, I may even see about that. *(Putting his hand on her head.)* Oh you, my darling little songbird. *(He goes into his study and closes the door after him.)*

Nora (softly, after a silence): Oh, really! It isn't so. It's impossible. It must be impossible.

Anne-Marie (in the doorway, left): The children are begging so hard to come in to Mama.

Nora: No, no, no, don't let them in to me! You stay with them, Anne-Marie.

Anne-Marie: Of course, ma'am. *(Closes the door.)*

Nora (pale with terror): Hurt my children—! Poison my home? *(A moment's pause; then she tosses her head.)* That's not true. Never. Never in all the world.

ACT II

Same room. Beside the piano the Christmas tree now stands stripped of ornament, burned-down candle stubs on its ragged branches. Nora's street clothes lie on the sofa. Nora, alone in the room, moves restlessly about; at last she stops at the sofa and picks up her coat.

Nora *(dropping the coat again):* Someone's coming! *(Goes toward the door, listens.)* No—there's no one. Of course—nobody's coming today, Christmas Day—or tomorrow, either. But maybe—*(Opens the door and looks out.)* No, nothing in the mailbox. Quite empty. *(Coming forward.)* What nonsense! He won't do anything serious. Nothing terrible could happen. It's impossible. Why, I have three small children.

Anne-Marie, with a large carton, comes in from the room to the left.

Anne-Marie: Well, at last I found the box with the masquerade clothes.
Nora: Thanks. Put it on the table.
Anne-Marie (does so): But they're all pretty much of a mess.
Nora: Ahh! I'd love to rip them in a million pieces!
Anne-Marie: Oh, mercy, they can be fixed right up. Just a little patience.
Nora: Yes, I'll go get Mrs. Linde to help me.
Anne-Marie: Out again now? In this nasty weather? Miss Nora will catch cold—get sick.
Nora: Oh, worse things could happen. How are the children?
Anne-Marie: The poor mites are playing with their Christmas presents, but—
Nora: Do they ask for me much?
Anne-Marie: They're so used to having Mama around, you know.
Nora: Yes, but Anne-Marie, I *can't* be together with them as much as I was.
Anne-Marie: Well, small children get used to anything.
Nora: You think so? Do you think they'd forget their mother if she was gone for good?
Anne-Marie: Oh, mercy—gone for good!
Nora: Wait, tell me, Anne-Marie—I've wondered so often—how could you ever have the heart to give your child over to strangers?
Anne-Marie: But I had to, you know, to become little Nora's nurse.
Nora: Yes, but how could you *do* it?
Anne-Marie: When I could get such a good place? A girl who's poor and who's gotten in trouble is glad enough for that. Because that slippery fish, he didn't do a thing for me, you know.
Nora: But your daughter's surely forgotten you.
Anne-Marie: Oh, she certainly has not. She's written to me, both when she was confirmed and when she was married.
Nora (clasping her about the neck): You old Anne-Marie, you were a good mother for me when I was little.

Anne-Marie: Poor little Nora, with no other mother but me.

Nora: And if the babies didn't have one, then I know that you'd — What silly talk! *(Opening the carton.)* Go in to them. Now I'll have to — Tomorrow you can see how lovely I'll look.

Anne-Marie: Oh, there won't be anyone at the party as lovely as Miss Nora. *(She goes off into the room, left.)*

Nora (begins unpacking the box, but soon throws it aside): Oh, if I dared to go out. If only nobody would come. If only nothing would happen here while I'm out. What craziness — nobody's coming. Just don't think. This muff — needs a brushing. Beautiful gloves, beautiful gloves. Let it go. Let it go! One, two, three, four, five, six — *(With a cry.)* Oh, there they are! *(Poises to move toward the door, but remains irresolutely standing. Mrs. Linde enters from the hall, where she has removed her street clothes.)*

Nora: Oh, it's you, Kristine. There's no one else out there? How good that you've come.

Mrs. Linde: I hear you were up asking for me.

Nora: Yes, I just stopped by. There's something you really can help me with. Let's get settled on the sofa. Look, there's going to be a costume party tomorrow evening at the Stenborgs' right above us, and now Torvald wants me to go as a Neapolitan peasant girl and dance the tarantella that I learned in Capri.

Mrs. Linde: Really, are you giving a whole performance?

Nora: Torvald says yes, I should. See, here's the dress. Torvald had it made for me down there; but now it's all so tattered that I just don't know —

Mrs. Linde: Oh, we'll fix that up in no time. It's nothing more than the trimmings — they're a bit loose here and there. Needle and thread? Good, now we have what we need.

Nora: Oh, how sweet of you!

Mrs. Linde (sewing): So you'll be in disguise tomorrow, Nora. You know what? I'll stop by then for a moment and have a look at you all dressed up. But listen, I've absolutely forgotten to thank you for that pleasant evening yesterday.

Nora (getting up and walking about): I don't think it was as pleasant as usual yesterday. You should have come to town a bit sooner, Kristine — Yes, Torvald really knows how to give a home elegance and charm.

Mrs. Linde: And you do, too, if you ask me. You're not your father's daughter for nothing. But tell me, is Dr. Rank always so down in the mouth as yesterday?

Nora: No, that was quite an exception. But he goes around critically ill all the time — tuberculosis of the spine, poor man. You know, his father was a disgusting thing who kept mistresses and so on — and that's why the son's been sickly from birth.

Mrs. Linde (lets her sewing fall to her lap): But my dearest Nora, how do you know about such things?

Nora (walking more jauntily): Hmp! When you've had three children, then you've had a few visits from — from women who know something of medicine, and they tell you this and that.

Mrs. Linde (resumes sewing; a short pause): Does Dr. Rank come here every day?

Nora: Every blessed day. He's Torvald's best friend from childhood, and *my* good friend, too. Dr. Rank almost belongs to this house.

Mrs. Linde: But tell me — is he quite sincere? I mean, doesn't he rather enjoy flattering people?

Nora: Just the opposite. Why do you think that?

Mrs. Linde: When you introduced us yesterday, he was proclaiming that he'd often heard my name in this house; but later I noticed that your husband hadn't the slightest idea who I really was. So how could Dr. Rank — ?

Nora: But it's all true, Kristine. You see, Torvald loves me beyond words, and, as he puts it, he'd like to keep me all to himself. For a long time he'd almost be jealous if I even mentioned any of my old friends back home. So of course I dropped that. But with Dr. Rank I talk a lot about such things, because he likes hearing about them.

Mrs. Linde: Now listen, Nora; in many ways you're still like a child. I'm a good deal older than you, with a little more experience. I'll tell you something: you ought to put an end to all this with Dr. Rank.

Nora: What should I put an end to?

Mrs. Linde: Both parts of it, I think. Yesterday you said something about a rich admirer who'd provide you with money —

Nora: Yes, one who doesn't exist — worse luck. So?

Mrs. Linde: Is Dr. Rank well off?

Nora: Yes, he is.

Mrs. Linde: With no dependents?

Nora: No, no one. But —

Mrs. Linde: And he's over here every day?

Nora: Yes, I told you that.

Mrs. Linde: How can a man of such refinement be so grasping?

Nora: I don't follow you at all.

Mrs. Linde: Now don't try to hide it, Nora. You think I can't guess who loaned you the forty-eight hundred crowns?

Nora: Are you out of your mind? How could you think such a thing! A friend of ours, who comes here every single day. What an intolerable situation that would have been!

Mrs. Linde: Then it really wasn't him.

Nora: No, absolutely not. It never even crossed my mind for a moment — And he had nothing to lend in those days; his inheritance came later.

Mrs. Linde: Well, I think that was a stroke of luck for you, Nora dear.

Nora: No, it never would have occurred to me to ask Dr. Rank — Still, I'm quite sure that if I had asked him —

Mrs. Linde: Which you won't, of course.

Nora: No, of course not. I can't see that I'd ever need to. But I'm quite positive that if I talked to Dr. Rank—

Mrs. Linde: Behind your husband's back?

Nora: I've got to clear up this other thing; *that's* also behind his back. I've *got* to clear it all up.

Mrs. Linde: Yes, I was saying that yesterday, but—

Nora (pacing up and down): A man handles these problems so much better than a woman—

Mrs. Linde: One's husband does, yes.

Nora: Nonsense. *(Stopping.)* When you pay everything you owe, then you get your note back, right?

Mrs. Linde: Yes, naturally.

Nora: And can rip it into a million pieces and burn it up—that filthy scrap of paper!

Mrs. Linde (looking hard at her, laying her sewing aside, and rising slowly): Nora, you're hiding something from me.

Nora: You can see it in my face?

Mrs. Linde: Something's happened to you since yesterday morning. Nora, what is it?

Nora (hurrying toward her): Kristine! *(Listening.)* Shh! Torvald's home. Look, go in with the children a while. Torvald can't bear all this snipping and stitching. Let Anne-Marie help you.

Mrs. Linde (gathering up some of the things): All right, but I'm not leaving here until we've talked this out. *(She disappears into the room, left, as Torvald enters from the hall.)*

Nora: Oh, how I've been waiting for you, Torvald dear.

Helmer: Was that the dressmaker?

Nora: No, that was Kristine. She's helping me fix up my costume. You know, it's going to be quite attractive.

Helmer: Yes, wasn't that a bright idea I had?

Nora: Brilliant! But then wasn't I good as well to give in to you?

Helmer: Good—because you give in to your husband's judgment? All right, you little goose, I know you didn't mean it like that. But I won't disturb you. You'll want to have a fitting, I suppose.

Nora: And you'll be working?

Helmer: Yes. *(Indicating a bundle of papers.)* See. I've been down to the bank. *(Starts toward his study.)*

Nora: Torvald.

Helmer (stops): Yes.

Nora: If your little squirrel begged you, with all her heart and soul, for something—?

Helmer: What's that?

Nora: Then would you do it?

Helmer: First, naturally, I'd have to know what it was.

Nora: Your squirrel would scamper about and do tricks, if you'd only be sweet and give in.

Helmer: Out with it.

Nora: Your lark would be singing high and low in every room —

Helmer: Come on, she does that anyway.

Nora: I'd be a wood nymph and dance for you in the moonlight.

Helmer: Nora — don't tell me it's that same business from this morning?

Nora (coming closer): Yes, Torvald, I beg you, please!

Helmer: And you actually have the nerve to drag that up again?

Nora: Yes, yes, you've got to give in to me; you *have* to let Krogstad keep his job in the bank.

Helmer: My dear Nora, I've slated his job for Mrs. Linde.

Nora: That's awfully kind of you. But you could just fire another clerk instead of Krogstad.

Helmer: This is the most incredible stubbornness! Because you go and give an impulsive promise to speak up for him, I'm expected to —

Nora: That's not the reason, Torvald. It's for your own sake. That man does writing for the worst papers; you said it yourself. He could do you any amount of harm. I'm scared to death of him —

Helmer: Ah, I understand. It's the old memories haunting you.

Nora: What do you mean by that?

Helmer: Of course, you're thinking about your father.

Nora: Yes, all right. Just remember how those nasty gossips wrote in the papers about Papa and slandered him so cruelly. I think they'd have had him dismissed if the department hadn't sent you up to investigate, and if you hadn't been so kind and open-minded toward him.

Helmer: My dear Nora, there's a notable difference between your father and me. Your father's official career was hardly above reproach. But mine is; and I hope it'll stay that way as long as I hold my position.

Nora: Oh, who can ever tell what vicious minds can invent? We could be so snug and happy now in our quiet, carefree home — you and I and the children, Torvald! That's why I'm pleading with you so —

Helmer: And just by pleading for him you make it impossible for me to keep him on. It's already known at the bank that I'm firing Krogstad. What if it's rumored around now that the new bank manager was vetoed by his wife —

Nora: Yes, what then —?

Helmer: Oh yes — as long as our little bundle of stubbornness gets her way —! I should go and make myself ridiculous in front of the whole office — give people the idea I can be swayed by all kinds of outside pressure. Oh, you can bet I'd feel the effects of that soon enough! Besides — there's something that rules Krogstad right out at the bank as long as I'm the manager.

Nora: What's that?

Helmer: His moral failings I could maybe overlook if I had to —

Nora: Yes, Torvald, why not?

Helmer: And I hear he's quite efficient on the job. But he was a crony of mine back in my teens — one of those rash friendships that crop up again and again to embarrass you later in life. Well, I might as well say it straight out: we're on a first-name basis. And that tactless fool makes no effort at all to hide it in front of others. Quite the contrary—he thinks that entitles him to take a familiar air around me, and so every other second he comes booming out with his "Yes, Torvald!" and "Sure thing, Torvald!" I tell you, it's been excruciating for me. He's out to make my place in the bank unbearable.

Nora: Torvald, you can't be serious about all this.

Helmer: Oh no? Why not?

Nora: Because these are such petty considerations.

Helmer: What are you saying? Petty? You think I'm petty!

Nora: No, just the opposite, Torvald dear. That's exactly why—

Helmer: Never mind. You call my motives petty; then I might as well be just that. Petty! All right! We'll put a stop to this for good. *(Goes to the hall door and calls.)* Helene!

Nora: What do you want?

Helmer (searching among his papers): A decision. *(The maid comes in.)* Look here; take this letter; go out with it at once. Get hold of a messenger and have him deliver it. Quick now. It's already addressed. Wait, here's some money.

Maid: Yes, sir. *(She leaves with the letter.)*

Helmer (straightening his papers): There, now, little Miss Willful.

Nora (breathlessly): Torvald, what was that letter?

Helmer: Krogstad's notice.

Nora: Call it back, Torvald! There's still time. Oh, Torvald, call it back! Do it for my sake—for your sake, for the children's sake! Do you hear, Torvald; do it! You don't know how this can harm us.

Helmer: Too late.

Nora: Yes, too late.

Helmer: Nora dear, I can forgive you this panic, even though basically you're insulting me. Yes, you are! Or isn't it an insult to think that *I* should be afraid of a courtroom hack's revenge? But I forgive you anyway, because this shows so beautifully how much you love me. *(Takes her in his arms.)* This is the way it should be, my darling Nora. Whatever comes, you'll see; when it really counts, I have strength and courage enough as a man to take on the whole weight myself.

Nora (terrified): What do you mean by that?

Helmer: The whole weight, I said.

Nora (resolutely): No, never in all the world.

Helmer: Good. So we'll share it, Nora, as man and wife. That's as it should be. *(Fondling her.)* Are you happy now? There, there, there—not these frightened dove's eyes. It's nothing at all but empty fantasies—Now you should run through your tarantella and practice your tambourine. I'll go to the inner office and shut both doors, so I won't hear a thing; you can make all the noise you like. *(Turning in the doorway.)* And when Rank comes, just tell him where he can find me. *(He nods to her and goes with his papers into the study, closing the door.)*

Nora (standing as though rooted, dazed with fright, in a whisper): He really could do it. He will do it. He'll do it in spite of everything. No, not that, never, never! Anything but that! Escape! A way out — *(The doorbell rings.)* Dr. Rank! Anything but that! *Anything,* whatever it is! *(Her hands pass over her face, smoothing it; she pulls herself together, goes over and opens the hall door. Dr. Rank stands outside, hanging his fur coat up. During the following scene, it begins getting dark.)*

Nora: Hello, Dr. Rank. I recognized your ring. But you mustn't go in to Torvald yet; I believe he's working.

Rank: And you?

Nora: For you, I always have an hour to spare — you know that. *(He has entered, and she shuts the door after him.)*

Rank: Many thanks. I'll make use of these hours while I can.

Nora: What do you mean by that? While you can?

Rank: Does that disturb you?

Nora: Well, it's such an odd phrase. Is anything going to happen?

Rank: What's going to happen is what I've been expecting so long — but I honestly didn't think it would come so soon.

Nora (gripping his arm): What is it you've found out? Dr. Rank, you have to tell me!

Rank (sitting by the stove): It's all over for me. There's nothing to be done about it.

Nora (breathing easier): Is it you — then — ?

Rank: Who else? There's no point in lying to one's self. I'm the most miserable of all my patients, Mrs. Helmer. These past few days I've been auditing my internal accounts. Bankrupt! Within a month I'll probably be laid out and rotting in the churchyard.

Nora: Oh, what a horrible thing to say.

Rank: The thing itself is horrible. But the worst of it is all the other horror before it's over. There's only one final examination left; when I'm finished with that, I'll know about when my disintegration will begin. There's something I want to say. Helmer with his sensitivity has such a sharp distaste for anything ugly. I don't want him near my sickroom.

Nora: Oh, but Dr. Rank —

Rank: I won't have him in there. Under no condition. I'll lock my door to him — As soon as I'm completely sure of the worst, I'll send you my calling card marked with a black cross, and you'll know then the wreck has started to come apart.

Nora: No, today you're completely unreasonable. And I wanted you so much to be in a really good humor.

Rank: With death up my sleeve? And then to suffer this way for somebody else's sins. Is there any justice in that? And in every single family, in some way or another, this inevitable retribution of nature goes on —

Nora (her hands pressed over her ears): Oh, stuff! Cheer up! Please — be gay!

Rank: Yes, I'd just as soon laugh at it all. My poor, innocent spine, serving time for my father's gay army days.

Nora (by the table, left): He was so infatuated with asparagus tips and pâté de foie gras, wasn't that it?

Rank: Yes—and with truffles.

Nora: Truffles, yes. And then with oysters, I suppose?

Rank: Yes, tons of oysters, naturally.

Nora: And then the port and champagne to go with it. It's so sad that all these delectable things have to strike at our bones.

Rank: Especially when they strike at the unhappy bones that never shared in the fun.

Nora: Ah, that's the saddest of all.

Rank (looks searchingly at her): Hm.

Nora (after a moment): Why did you smile?

Rank: No, it was you who laughed.

Nora: No, it was you who smiled, Dr. Rank!

Rank (getting up): You're even a bigger tease than I'd thought.

Nora: I'm full of wild ideas today.

Rank: That's obvious.

Nora (putting both hands on his shoulders): Dear, dear Dr. Rank, you'll never die for Torvald and me.

Rank: Oh, that loss you'll easily get over. Those who go away are soon forgotten.

Nora (looks fearfully at him): You believe that?

Rank: One makes new connections, and then—

Nora: Who makes new connections?

Rank: Both you and Torvald will when I'm gone. I'd say you're well under way already. What was that Mrs. Linde doing here last evening?

Nora: Oh, come—you can't be jealous of poor Kristine?

Rank: Oh yes, I am. She'll be my successor here in the house. When I'm down under, that woman will probably—

Nora: Shh! Not so loud. She's right in there.

Rank: Today as well. So you see.

Nora: Only to sew on my dress. Good gracious, how unreasonable you are. *(Sitting on the sofa.)* Be nice now, Dr. Rank. Tomorrow you'll see how beautifully I'll dance; and you can imagine then that I'm dancing only for you—yes, and of course for Torvald, too—that's understood. *(Takes various items out of the carton.)* Dr. Rank, sit over here and I'll show you something.

Rank (sitting): What's that?

Nora: Look here. Look.

Rank: Silk stockings.

Nora: Flesh-colored. Aren't they lovely? Now it's so dark here, but tomorrow—No, no, no, just look at the feet. Oh well, you might as well look at the rest.

Rank: Hm—

Nora: Why do you look so critical? Don't you believe they'll fit?

Rank: I've never had any chance to form an opinion on that.

Nora (glancing at him a moment): Shame on you. *(Hits him lightly on the ear with the stockings.)* That's for you. *(Puts them away again.)*

Rank: And what other splendors am I going to see now?

Nora: Not the least bit more, because you've been naughty. *(She hums a little and rummages among her things.)*

Rank (after a short silence): When I sit here together with you like this, completely easy and open, then I don't know—I simply can't imagine—whatever would have become of me if I'd never come into this house.

Nora (smiling): Yes, I really think you feel completely at ease with us.

Rank (more quietly, staring straight ahead): And then to have to go away from it all—

Nora: Nonsense, you're not going away.

Rank (his voice unchanged): —and not even be able to leave some poor show of gratitude behind, scarcely a fleeting regret—no more than a vacant place that anyone can fill.

Nora: And if I asked you now for—? No—

Rank: For what?

Nora: For a great proof of your friendship—

Rank: Yes, yes?

Nora: No, I mean—for an exceptionally big favor—

Rank: Would you really, for once, make me so happy?

Nora: Oh, you haven't the vaguest idea what it is.

Rank: All right, then tell me.

Nora: No, but I can't, Dr. Rank—it's all out of reason. It's advice and help, too—and a favor—

Rank: So much the better. I can't fathom what you're hinting at. Just speak out. Don't you trust me?

Nora: Of course. More than anyone else. You're my best and truest friend, I'm sure. That's why I want to talk to you. All right, then, Dr. Rank: there's something you can help me prevent. You know how deeply, how inexpressibly dearly Torvald loves me; he'd never hesitate a second to give up his life for me.

Rank (leaning close to her): Nora—do you think he's the only one—

Nora (with a slight start): Who—?

Rank: Who'd gladly give up his life for you.

Nora (heavily): I see.

Rank: I swore to myself you should know this before I'm gone. I'll never find a better chance. Yes, Nora, now you know. And also you know now that you can trust me beyond anyone else.

Nora (rising, natural and calm): Let me by.

Rank (making room for her, but still sitting): Nora—

Nora (in the hall doorway): Helene, bring the lamp in. *(Goes over to the stove.)* Ah, dear Dr. Rank, that was really mean of you.

Rank (getting up): That I've loved you just as deeply as somebody else? Was *that* mean?

Nora: No, but that you came out and told me. That was quite unnecessary—

Rank: What do you mean? Have you known—?

The Maid comes in with the lamp, sets it on the table, and goes out again.

Rank: Nora—Mrs. Helmer—I'm asking you: have you known about it?

Nora: Oh, how can I tell what I know or don't know? Really, I don't know what to say—Why did you have to be so clumsy, Dr. Rank! Everything was so good.

Rank: Well, in any case, you now have the knowledge that my body and soul are at your command. So won't you speak out?

Nora (looking at him): After that?

Rank: Please, just let me know what it is.

Nora: You can't know anything now.

Rank: I have to. You mustn't punish me like this. Give me the chance to do whatever is humanly possible for you.

Nora: Now there's nothing you can do for me. Besides, actually, I don't need any help. You'll see—it's only my fantasies. That's what it is. Of course! *(Sits in the rocker, looks at him, and smiles.)* What a nice one you are, Dr. Rank. Aren't you a little bit ashamed, now that the lamp is here?

Rank: No, not exactly. But perhaps I'd better go—for good?

Nora: No, you certainly can't do that. You must come here just as you always have. You know Torvald can't do without you.

Rank: Yes, but *you?*

Nora: You know how much I enjoy it when you're here.

Rank: That's precisely what threw me off. You're a mystery to me. So many times I've felt you'd almost rather be with me than with Helmer.

Nora: Yes—you see, there are some people that one loves most and other people that one would almost prefer being with.

Rank: Yes, there's something to that.

Nora: When I was back home, of course I loved Papa most. But I always thought it was so much fun when I could sneak down to the maids' quarters, because they never tried to improve me, and it was always so amusing, the way they talked to each other.

Rank: Aha, so it's *their* place that I've filled.

Nora (jumping up and going to him): Oh, dear, sweet Dr. Rank, that's not what I meant at all. But you can understand that with Torvald it's just the same as with Papa—

The Maid enters from the hall.

Maid: Ma'am—please! *(She whispers to Nora and hands her a calling card.)*

Nora (glancing at the card): Ah! *(Slips it into her pocket.)*

Rank: Anything wrong?

Nora: No, no, not at all. It's only some—it's my new dress—

Rank: Really? But—there's your dress.

Nora: Oh, that. But this is another one — I ordered it — Torvald mustn't know —

Rank: Ah, now we have the big secret.

Nora: That's right. Just go in with him — he's back in the inner study. Keep him there as long as —

Rank: Don't worry. He won't get away. *(Goes into the study.)*

Nora (to the Maid): And he's standing waiting in the kitchen?

Maid: Yes, he came up by the back stairs.

Nora: But didn't you tell him somebody was here?

Maid: Yes, but that didn't do any good.

Nora: He won't leave?

Maid: No, he won't go till he's talked with you, ma'am.

Nora: Let him come in, then — but quietly. Helene, don't breathe a word about this. It's a surprise for my husband.

Maid: Yes, yes, I understand — *(Goes out.)*

Nora: This horror — it's going to happen. No, no, no, it can't happen, it mustn't. *(She goes and bolts Helmer's door. The Maid opens the hall door for Krogstad and shuts it behind him. He is dressed for travel in a fur coat, boots, and a fur cap.)*

Nora (going toward him): Talk softly. My husband's home.

Krogstad: Well, good for him.

Nora: What do you want?

Krogstad: Some information.

Nora: Hurry up, then. What is it?

Krogstad: You know, of course, that I got my notice.

Nora: I couldn't prevent it, Mr. Krogstad. I fought for you to the bitter end, but nothing worked.

Krogstad: Does your husband's love for you run so thin? He knows everything I can expose you to, and all the same he dares to —

Nora: How can you imagine he knows anything about this?

Krogstad: Ah, no — I can't imagine it either, now. It's not at all like my fine Torvald Helmer to have so much guts —

Nora: Mr. Krogstad, I demand respect for my husband!

Krogstad: Why, of course — all due respect. But since the lady's keeping it so carefully hidden, may I presume to ask if you're also a bit better informed than yesterday about what you've actually done?

Nora: More than you could ever teach me.

Krogstad: Yes, I *am* such an awful lawyer.

Nora: What is it you want from me?

Krogstad: Just a glimpse of how you are, Mrs. Helmer. I've been thinking about you all day long. A cashier, a night-court scribbler, a — well, a type like me also has a little of what they call a heart, you know.

Nora: Then show it. Think of my children.

Krogstad: Did you or your husband ever think of mine? But never mind. I simply wanted to tell you that you don't need to take this thing too seriously. For the present, I'm not proceeding with any action.

Nora: Oh no, really! Well — I knew that.

Krogstad: Everything can be settled in a friendly spirit. It doesn't have to get around town at all; it can stay just among us three.

Nora: My husband must never know anything of this.

Krogstad: How can you manage that? Perhaps you can pay me the balance?

Nora: No, not right now.

Krogstad: Or you know some way of raising the money in a day or two?

Nora: No way that I'm willing to use.

Krogstad: Well, it wouldn't have done you any good, anyway. If you stood in front of me with a fistful of bills, you still couldn't buy your signature back.

Nora: Then tell me what you're going to do with it.

Krogstad: I'll just hold onto it — keep it on file. There's no outsider who'll even get wind of it. So if you've been thinking of taking some desperate step —

Nora: I have.

Krogstad: Been thinking of running away from home —

Nora: I have!

Krogstad: Or even of something worse —

Nora: How could you guess that?

Krogstad: You can drop those thoughts.

Nora: How could you guess I was thinking of *that*?

Krogstad: Most of us think about *that* at first. I thought about it too, but I discovered I hadn't the courage —

Nora (lifelessly): I don't either.

Krogstad (relieved): That's true, you haven't the courage? You too?

Nora: I don't have it — I don't have it.

Krogstad: It would be terribly stupid, anyway. After that first storm at home blows out, why, then — I have here in my pocket a letter for your husband —

Nora: Telling everything?

Krogstad: As charitably as possible.

Nora (quickly): He mustn't ever get that letter. Tear it up. I'll find some way to get money.

Krogstad: Beg pardon, Mrs. Helmer, but I think I just told you —

Nora: Oh, I don't mean the money I owe you. Let me know how much you want from my husband, and I'll manage it.

Krogstad: I don't want money from your husband.

Nora: What do you want, then?

Krogstad: I'll tell you what. I want to recoup, Mrs. Helmer; I want to get on in the world — and there's where your husband can help me. For a year and a half I've kept myself clean of anything disreputable — all that time struggling with the worst conditions; but I was satisfied, working my way up step by step. Now I've been written right off, and I'm just not in the mood to come crawling back. I tell you, I want to

move on. I want to get back in the bank — in a better position. Your
husband can set up a job for me —

Nora: He'll never do that!

Krogstad: He'll do it. I know him. He won't dare breathe a word of pro-
test. And once I'm in there together with him, you just wait and see!
Inside of a year, I'll be the manager's right-hand man. It'll be Nils
Krogstad, not Torvald Helmer, who runs the bank.

Nora: You'll never see the day!

Krogstad: Maybe you think you can —

Nora: I have the courage now — for *that.*

Krogstad: Oh, you don't scare me. A smart, spoiled lady like you —

Nora: You'll see; you'll see!

Krogstad: Under the ice, maybe? Down in the freezing coal-black water?
There, till you float up in the spring, ugly, unrecognizable, with your
hair falling out —

Nora: You don't frighten me.

Krogstad: Nor do you frighten me. One doesn't do these things, Mrs.
Helmer. Besides, what good would it be? I'd still have him safe in my
pocket.

Nora: Afterwards? When I'm no longer — ?

Krogstad: Are you forgetting that *I'll* be in control then over your final
reputation? *(Nora stands speechless, staring at him.)* Good; now I've
warned you. Don't do anything stupid. When Helmer's read my letter, I'll be waiting for his reply. And bear in mind that it's your husband himself who's forced me back to my old ways. I'll never forgive
him for that. Good-bye, Mrs. Helmer. *(He goes out through the hall.)*

Nora (goes to the hall door, opens it a crack, and listens): He's gone. Didn't
leave the letter. Oh no, no, that's impossible too! *(Opening the door
more and more.)* What's that? He's standing outside — not going
downstairs. He's thinking it over? Maybe he'll — ? *(A letter falls in
the mailbox; then Krogstad's footsteps are heard, dying away down a flight
of stairs. Nora gives a muffled cry and runs over toward the sofa table. A
short pause.)* In the mailbox. *(Slips warily over to the hall door.)* It's lying
there. Torvald, Torvald — now we're lost!

Mrs. Linde (entering with costume from the room, left): There now, I can't see
anything else to mend. Perhaps you'd like to try —

Nora (in a hoarse whisper): Kristine, come here.

Mrs. Linde (tossing the dress on the sofa): What's wrong? You look upset.

Nora: Come here. See that letter? *There!* Look — through the glass in the
mailbox.

Mrs. Linde: Yes, yes, I see it.

Nora: That letter's from Krogstad —

Mrs. Linde: Nora — it's Krogstad who loaned you the money!

Nora: Yes, and now Torvald will find out everything.

Mrs. Linde: Believe me, Nora, it's best for both of you.

Nora: There's more you don't know. I forged a name.

Mrs. Linde: But for heaven's sake—?

Nora: I only want to tell you that, Kristine, so that you can be my witness.

Mrs. Linde: Witness? Why should I—?

Nora: If I should go out of my mind—it could easily happen—

Mrs. Linde: Nora!

Nora: Or anything else occurred—so I couldn't be present here—

Mrs. Linde: Nora, Nora, you aren't yourself at all!

Nora: And someone should try to take on the whole weight, all of the guilt, you follow me—

Mrs. Linde: Yes, of course, but why do you think—?

Nora: Then you're the witness that it isn't true, Kristine. I'm very much myself; my mind right now is perfectly clear; and I'm telling you: nobody else has known about this; I alone did everything. Remember that.

Mrs. Linde: I will. But I don't understand all this.

Nora: Oh, how could you ever understand it? It's the miracle now that's going to take place.

Mrs. Linde: The miracle?

Nora: Yes, the miracle. But it's so awful, Kristine. It mustn't take place, not for anything in the world.

Mrs. Linde: I'm going right over and talk with Krogstad.

Nora: Don't go near him; he'll do you some terrible harm!

Mrs. Linde: There was a time once when he'd gladly have done anything for me.

Nora: He?

Mrs. Linde: Where does he live?

Nora: Oh, how do I know? Yes. *(Searches in her pocket.)* Here's his card. But the letter, the letter—!

Helmer (from the study, knocking on the door): Nora!

Nora (with a cry of fear): Oh! What is it? What do you want?

Helmer: Now, now, don't be so frightened. We're not coming in. You locked the door—are you trying on the dress?

Nora: Yes, I'm trying it. I'll look just beautiful, Torvald.

Mrs. Linde (who has read the card): He's living right around the corner.

Nora: Yes, but what's the use? We're lost. The letter's in the box.

Mrs. Linde: And your husband has the key?

Nora: Yes, always.

Mrs. Linde: Krogstad can ask for his letter back unread; he can find some excuse—

Nora: But it's just this time that Torvald usually—

Mrs. Linde: Stall him. Keep him in there. I'll be back as quick as I can. *(She hurries out through the hall entrance.)*

Nora (goes to Helmer's door, opens it, and peers in): Torvald!

Helmer (from the inner study): Well—does one dare set foot in one's own living room at last? Come on, Rank, now we'll get a look— *(In the doorway.)* But what's this?

Nora: What, Torvald dear?

Helmer: Rank had me expecting some grand masquerade.

Rank (in the doorway): That was my impression, but I must have been wrong.

Nora: No one can admire me in my splendor — not till tomorrow.

Helmer: But Nora dear, you look so exhausted. Have you practiced too hard?

Nora: No, I haven't practiced at all yet.

Helmer: You know, it's necessary —

Nora: Oh, it's absolutely necessary, Torvald. But I can't get anywhere without your help. I've forgotten the whole thing completely.

Helmer: Ah, we'll soon take care of that.

Nora: Yes, take care of me, Torvald, please! Promise me that? Oh, I'm so nervous. That big party — You must give up everything this evening for me. No business — don't even touch your pen. Yes? Dear Torvald, promise?

Helmer: It's a promise. Tonight I'm totally at your service — you little helpless thing. Hm — but first there's one thing I want to — *(Goes toward the hall door.)*

Nora: What are you looking for?

Helmer: Just to see if there's any mail.

Nora: No, no, don't do that, Torvald!

Helmer: Now what?

Nora: Torvald, please. There isn't any.

Helmer: Let me look, though. *(Starts out. Nora, at the piano, strikes the first notes of the tarantella. Helmer, at the door, stops.)* Aha!

Nora: I can't dance tomorrow if I don't practice with you.

Helmer (going over to her): Nora dear, are you really so frightened?

Nora: Yes, so terribly frightened. Let me practice right now; there's still time before dinner. Oh, sit down and play for me, Torvald. Direct me. Teach me, the way you always have.

Helmer: Gladly, if it's what you want. *(Sits at the piano.)*

Nora (snatches the tambourine up from the box, then a long, varicolored shawl, which she throws around herself, whereupon she springs forward and cries out): Play for me now! Now I'll dance!

Helmer plays and Nora dances. Rank stands behind Helmer at the piano and looks on.

Helmer (as he plays): Slower. Slow down.

Nora: Can't change it.

Helmer: Not so violent, Nora!

Nora: Has to be just like this.

Helmer (stopping): No, no, that won't do at all.

Nora (laughing and swinging her tambourine): Isn't that what I told you?

Rank: Let me play for her.

Helmer (getting up): Yes, go on. I can teach her more easily then.

*Rank sits at the piano and plays; Nora dances more and more wildly.
Helmer has stationed himself by the stove and repeatedly gives her directions;
she seems not to hear them; her hair loosens and falls over her shoulders;
she does not notice, but goes on dancing. Mrs. Linde enters.*

Mrs. Linde (standing dumbfounded at the door): Ah—!

Nora (still dancing): See what fun, Kristine!

Helmer: But Nora darling, you dance as if your life were at stake.

Nora: And it is.

Helmer: Rank, stop! This is pure madness. Stop it, I say!

Rank breaks off playing, and Nora halts abruptly.

Helmer (going over to her): I never would have believed it. You've forgotten everything I taught you.

Nora (throwing away the tambourine): You see for yourself.

Helmer: Well, there's certainly room for instruction here.

Nora: Yes, you see how important it is. You've got to teach me to the very last minute. Promise me that, Torvald?

Helmer: You can bet on it.

Nora: You mustn't, either today or tomorrow, think about anything else but me; you mustn't open any letters—or the mailbox—

Helmer: Ah, it's still the fear of that man—

Nora: Oh yes, yes, that too.

Helmer: Nora, it's written all over you—there's already a letter from him out there.

Nora: I don't know. I guess so. But you mustn't read such things now; there mustn't be anything ugly between us before it's all over.

Rank (quietly to Helmer): You shouldn't deny her.

Helmer (putting his arms around her): The child can have her way. But tomorrow night, after you've danced—

Nora: Then you'll be free.

Maid (in the doorway, right): Ma'am, dinner is served.

Nora: We'll be wanting champagne, Helene.

Maid: Very good, ma'am. (*Goes out.*)

Helmer: So—a regular banquet, hm?

Nora: Yes, a banquet—champagne till daybreak! (*Calling out.*) And some macaroons, Helene. Heaps of them—just this once.

Helmer (taking her hands): Now, now, now—no hysterics. Be my own little lark again.

Nora: Oh, I will soon enough. But go on in—and you, Dr. Rank. Kristine, help me put up my hair.

Rank (whispering, as they go): There's nothing wrong—really wrong, is there?

Helmer: Oh, of course not. It's nothing more than this childish anxiety I was telling you about. (*They go out, right.*)

Nora: Well?

Mrs. Linde: Left town.

Nora: I could see by your face.

Mrs. Linde: He'll be home tomorrow evening. I wrote him a note.

Nora: You shouldn't have. Don't try to stop anything now. After all, it's a wonderful joy, this waiting here for the miracle.

Mrs. Linde: What is it you're waiting for?

Nora: Oh, you can't understand that. Go in to them; I'll be along in a moment.

Mrs. Linde goes into the dining room. Nora stands a short while as if composing herself; then she looks at her watch.

Nora: Five. Seven hours to midnight. Twenty-four hours to the midnight after, and then the tarantella's done. Seven and twenty-four? Thirty-one hours to live.

Helmer (in the doorway, right): What's become of the little lark?

Nora (going toward him with open arms): Here's your lark!

ACT III

Same scene. The table, with chairs around it, has been moved to the center of the room. A lamp on the table is lit. The hall door stands open. Dance music drifts down from the floor above. Mrs. Linde sits at the table, absently paging through a book, trying to read, but apparently unable to focus her thoughts. Once or twice she pauses, tensely listening for a sound at the outer entrance.

Mrs. Linde (glancing at her watch): Not yet — and there's hardly any time left. If only he's not — *(Listening again.)* Ah, there he is. *(She goes out in the hall and cautiously opens the outer door. Quiet footsteps are heard on the stairs. She whispers:)* Come in. Nobody's here.

Krogstad (in the doorway): I found a note from you at home. What's back of all this?

Mrs. Linde: I just had to talk to you.

Krogstad: Oh? And it just had to be here in this house?

Mrs. Linde: At my place it was impossible; my room hasn't a private entrance. Come in; we're all alone. The maid's asleep, and the Helmers are at the dance upstairs.

Krogstad (entering the room): Well, well, the Helmers are dancing tonight? Really?

Mrs. Linde: Yes, why not?

Krogstad: How true — why not?

Mrs. Linde: All right, Krogstad, let's talk.

Krogstad: Do we two have anything more to talk about?

Mrs. Linde: We have a great deal to talk about.

Krogstad: I wouldn't have thought so.

Mrs. Linde: No, because you've never understood me, really.

Krogstad: Was there anything more to understand — except what's all too common in life? A calculating woman throws over a man the moment a better catch comes by.

Mrs. Linde: You think I'm so thoroughly calculating? You think I broke it off lightly?

Krogstad: Didn't you?

Mrs. Linde: Nils — is that what you really thought?

Krogstad: If you cared, then why did you write me the way you did?

Mrs. Linde: What else could I do? If I had to break off with you, then it was my job as well to root out everything you felt for me.

Krogstad (wringing his hands): So that was it. And this — all this, simply for money!

Mrs. Linde: Don't forget I had a helpless mother and two small brothers. We couldn't wait for you, Nils; you had such a long road ahead of you then.

Krogstad: That may be; but you still hadn't the right to abandon me for somebody else's sake.

Mrs. Linde: Yes — I don't know. So many, many times I've asked myself if I did have that right.

Krogstad (more softly): When I lost you, it was as if all the solid ground dissolved from under my feet. Look at me; I'm a half-drowned man now, hanging onto a wreck.

Mrs. Linde: Help may be near.

Krogstad: It was near — but then you came and blocked it off.

Mrs. Linde: Without my knowing it, Nils. Today for the first time I learned that it's you I'm replacing at the bank.

Krogstad: All right — I believe you. But now that you know, will you step aside?

Mrs. Linde: No, because that wouldn't benefit you in the slightest.

Krogstad: Not "benefit" me, hm! I'd step aside anyway.

Mrs. Linde: I've learned to be realistic. Life and hard, bitter necessity have taught me that.

Krogstad: And life's taught me never to trust fine phrases.

Mrs. Linde: Then life's taught you a very sound thing. But you do have to trust in actions, don't you?

Krogstad: What does that mean?

Mrs. Linde: You said you were hanging on like a half-drowned man to a wreck.

Krogstad: I've good reason to say that.

Mrs. Linde: I'm also like a half-drowned woman on a wreck. No one to suffer with; no one to care for.

Krogstad: You made your choice.

Mrs. Linde: There wasn't any choice then.

Krogstad: So — what of it?

Mrs. Linde: Nils, if only we two shipwrecked people could reach across to each other.

Krogstad: What are you saying?

Mrs. Linde: Two on one wreck are at least better off than each on his own.

Krogstad: Kristine!

Mrs. Linde: Why do you think I came into town?

Krogstad: Did you really have some thought of me?

Mrs. Linde: I have to work to go on living. All my born days, as long as I can remember, I've worked, and it's been my best and my only joy. But now I'm completely alone in the world; it frightens me to be so empty and lost. To work for yourself — there's no joy in that. Nils, give me something — someone to work for.

Krogstad: I don't believe all this. It's just some hysterical feminine urge to go out and make a noble sacrifice.

Mrs. Linde: Have you ever found me to be hysterical?

Krogstad: Can you honestly mean this? Tell me — do you know everything about my past?

Mrs. Linde: Yes.

Krogstad: And you know what they think I'm worth around here.

Mrs. Linde: From what you were saying before, it would seem that with me you could have been another person.

Krogstad: I'm positive of that.

Mrs. Linde: Couldn't it happen still?

Krogstad: Kristine — you're saying this in all seriousness? Yes, you are! I can see it in you. And do you really have the courage, then — ?

Mrs. Linde: I need to have someone to care for; and your children need a mother. We both need each other. Nils, I have faith that you're good at heart — I'll risk everything together with you.

Krogstad (gripping her hands): Kristine, thank you, thank you — Now I know I can win back a place in their eyes. Yes — but I forgot —

Mrs. Linde (listening): Shh! The tarantella. Go now! Go on!

Krogstad: Why? What is it?

Mrs. Linde: Hear the dance up there? When that's over, they'll be coming down.

Krogstad: Oh, then I'll go. But — it's all pointless. Of course, you don't know the move I made against the Helmers.

Mrs. Linde: Yes, Nils, I know.

Krogstad: And all the same, you have the courage to — ?

Mrs. Linde: I know how far despair can drive a man like you.

Krogstad: Oh, if I only could take it all back.

Mrs. Linde: You easily could — your letter's still lying in the mailbox.

Krogstad: Are you sure of that?

Mrs. Linde: Positive. But —

Krogstad (looks at her searchingly): Is that the meaning of it, then? You'll save your friend at any price. Tell me straight out. Is that it?

Mrs. Linde: Nils — anyone who's sold herself for somebody else once isn't going to do it again.

Krogstad: I'll demand my letter back.

Mrs. Linde: No, no.

Krogstad: Yes, of course. I'll stay here till Helmer comes down; I'll tell him to give me my letter again — that it only involves my dismissal — that he shouldn't read it —

Mrs. Linde: No, Nils, don't call the letter back.

Krogstad: But wasn't that exactly why you wrote me to come here?

Mrs. Linde: Yes, in that first panic. But it's been a whole day and night since then, and in that time I've seen such incredible things in this house. Helmer's got to learn everything; this dreadful secret has to be aired; those two have to come to a full understanding; all these lies and evasions can't go on.

Krogstad: Well, then, if you want to chance it. But at least there's one thing I can do, and do right away —

Mrs. Linde (listening): Go now, go quick! The dance is over. We're not safe another second.

Krogstad: I'll wait for you downstairs.

Mrs. Linde: Yes, please do; take me home.

Krogstad: I can't believe it; I've never been so happy. (*He leaves by way of the outer door; the door between the room and the hall stays open.*)

Mrs. Linde (straightening up a bit and getting together her street clothes): How different now! How different! Someone to work for, to live for — a home to build. Well, it is worth the try! Oh, if they'd only come! (*Listening.*) Ah, there they are. Bundle up. (*She picks up her hat and coat. Nora's and Helmer's voices can be heard outside; a key turns in the lock, and Helmer brings Nora into the hall almost by force. She is wearing the Italian costume with a large black shawl about her; he has on evening dress, with a black domino open over it.*)

Nora (struggling in the doorway): No, no, no, not inside! I'm going up again. I don't want to leave so soon.

Helmer: But Nora dear —

Nora: Oh, I beg you, please, Torvald. From the bottom of my heart, please — only an hour more!

Helmer: Not a single minute, Nora darling. You know our agreement. Come on, in we go; you'll catch cold out here. (*In spite of her resistance, he gently draws her into the room.*)

Mrs. Linde: Good evening.

Nora: Kristine!

Helmer: Why, Mrs. Linde — are you here so late?

Mrs. Linde: Yes, I'm sorry, but I did want to see Nora in costume.

Nora: Have you been sitting here, waiting for me?

Mrs. Linde: Yes. I didn't come early enough; you were all upstairs; and then I thought I really couldn't leave without seeing you.

Helmer (removing Nora's shawl): Yes, take a good look. She's worth looking at, I can tell you that, Mrs. Linde. Isn't she lovely?

Mrs. Linde: Yes, I should say —

Helmer: A dream of loveliness, isn't she? That's what everyone thought at the party, too. But she's horribly stubborn — this sweet little thing.

What's to be done with her? Can you imagine, I almost had to use force to pry her away.

Nora: Oh, Torvald, you're going to regret you didn't indulge me, even for just a half hour more.

Helmer: There, you see. She danced her tarantella and got a tumultuous hand—which was well earned, although the performance may have been a bit too naturalistic—I mean it rather overstepped the proprieties of art. But never mind—what's important is, she made a success, an overwhelming success. You think I could let her stay on after that and spoil the effect? Oh no; I took my lovely little Capri girl—my capricious little Capri girl, I should say—took her under my arm; one quick tour of the ballroom, a curtsy to every side, and then—as they say in novels—the beautiful vision disappeared. An exit should always be effective, Mrs. Linde, but that's what I can't get Nora to grasp. Phew, it's hot in here. *(Flings the domino on a chair and opens the door to his room.)* Why's it dark in here? Oh yes, of course. Excuse me. *(He goes in and lights a couple of candles.)*

Nora (in a sharp, breathless whisper): So?

Mrs. Linde (quietly): I talked with him.

Nora: And—?

Mrs. Linde: Nora—you must tell your husband everything.

Nora (dully): I knew it.

Mrs. Linde: You've got nothing to fear from Krogstad, but you have to speak out.

Nora: I won't tell.

Mrs. Linde: Then the letter will.

Nora: Thanks, Kristine. I know now what's to be done. Shh!

Helmer (reentering): Well, then, Mrs. Linde—have you admired her?

Mrs. Linde: Yes, and now I'll say good night.

Helmer: Oh, come, so soon? Is this yours, this knitting?

Mrs. Linde: Yes, thanks. I nearly forgot it.

Helmer: Do you knit, then?

Mrs. Linde: Oh yes.

Helmer: You know what? You should embroider instead.

Mrs. Linde: Really? Why?

Helmer: Yes, because it's a lot prettier. See here, one holds the embroidery so, in the left hand, and then one guides the needle with the right—so—in an easy, sweeping curve—right?

Mrs. Linde: Yes, I guess that's—

Helmer: But, on the other hand, knitting—it can never be anything but ugly. Look, see here, the arms tucked in, the knitting needles going up and down—there's something Chinese about it. Ah, that was really a glorious champagne they served.

Mrs. Linde: Yes, good night, Nora, and don't be stubborn anymore.

Helmer: Well put, Mrs. Linde!

Mrs. Linde: Good night, Mr. Helmer.

Helmer (accompanying her to the door): Good night, good night. I hope you
   get home all right. I'd be very happy to—but you don't have far to
   go. Good night, good night. *(She leaves. He shuts the door after her and
   returns.)* There, now, at last we got her out the door. She's a deadly
   bore, that creature.

Nora: Aren't you pretty tired, Torvald?

Helmer: No, not a bit.

Nora: You're not sleepy?

Helmer: Not at all. On the contrary, I'm feeling quite exhilarated. But
   you? Yes, you really look tired and sleepy.

Nora: Yes, I'm very tired. Soon now I'll sleep.

Helmer: See! You see! I was right all along that we shouldn't stay longer.

Nora: Whatever you do is always right.

Helmer (kissing her brow): Now my little lark talks sense. Say, did you
   notice what a time Rank was having tonight?

Nora: Oh, was he? I didn't get to speak with him.

Helmer: I scarcely did either, but it's a long time since I've seen him
   in such high spirits. *(Gazes at her a moment, then comes nearer her.)*
   Hm—it's marvelous, though, to be back home again—to be completely alone with you. Oh, you bewitchingly lovely young woman!

Nora: Torvald, don't look at me like that!

Helmer: Can't I look at my richest treasure? At all that beauty that's
   mine, mine alone—completely and utterly.

Nora (moving around to the other side of the table): You mustn't talk to me
   that way tonight.

Helmer (following her): The tarantella is still in your blood, I can see—and
   it makes you even more enticing. Listen. The guests are beginning to
   go. *(Dropping his voice.)* Nora—it'll soon be quiet through this whole
   house.

Nora: Yes, I hope so.

Helmer: You do, don't you, my love? Do you realize—when I'm out at
   a party like this with you—do you know why I talk to you so little,
   and keep such a distance away; just send you a stolen look now and
   then—you know why I do it? It's because I'm imagining then that
   you're my secret darling, my secret bride-to-be, and that no one suspects there's anything between us.

Nora: Yes, yes; oh, yes, I know you're always thinking of me.

Helmer: And then when we leave and I place the shawl over those fine
   young rounded shoulders—over that wonderful curving neck—then
   I pretend that you're my young bride, that we're just coming from the
   wedding, that for the first time I'm bringing you into my house—that
   for the first time I'm alone with you—completely alone with you,
   your trembling young beauty! All this evening I've longed for nothing but you. When I saw you turn and sway in the tarantella—my
   blood was pounding till I couldn't stand it—that's why I brought
   you down here so early—

Nora: Go away, Torvald! Leave me alone. I don't want all this.

Helmer: What do you mean? Nora, you're teasing me. You will, won't you? Aren't I your husband—?

A knock at the outside door.

Nora (startled): What's that?

Helmer (going toward the hall): Who is it?

Rank (outside): It's me. May I come in a moment?

Helmer (with quiet irritation): Oh, what does he want now? *(Aloud.)* Hold on. *(Goes and opens the door.)* Oh, how nice that you didn't just pass us by!

Rank: I thought I heard your voice, and then I wanted so badly to have a look in. *(Lightly glancing about.)* Ah, me, these old familiar haunts. You have it snug and cozy in here, you two.

Helmer: You seemed to be having it pretty cozy upstairs, too.

Rank: Absolutely. Why shouldn't I? Why not take in everything in life? As much as you can, anyway, and as long as you can. The wine was superb—

Helmer: The champagne especially.

Rank: You noticed that too? It's amazing how much I could guzzle down.

Nora: Torvald also drank a lot of champagne this evening.

Rank: Oh?

Nora: Yes, and that always makes him so entertaining.

Rank: Well, why shouldn't one have a pleasant evening after a well-spent day?

Helmer: Well spent? I'm afraid I can't claim that.

Rank (slapping him on the back): But I can, you see!

Nora: Dr. Rank, you must have done some scientific research today.

Rank: Quite so.

Helmer: Come now—little Nora talking about scientific research!

Nora: And can I congratulate you on the results?

Rank: Indeed you may.

Nora: Then they were good?

Rank: The best possible for both doctor and patient—certainty.

Nora (quickly and searchingly): Certainty?

Rank: Complete certainty. So don't I owe myself a gay evening afterwards?

Nora: Yes, you're right, Dr. Rank.

Helmer: I'm with you—just so long as you don't have to suffer for it in the morning.

Rank: Well, one never gets something for nothing in life.

Nora: Dr. Rank—are you very fond of masquerade parties?

Rank: Yes, if there's a good array of odd disguises—

Nora: Tell me, what should we two go as at the next masquerade?

Helmer: You little featherhead—already thinking of the next!

Rank: We two? I'll tell you what: you must go as Charmed Life—

Helmer: Yes, but find a costume for *that!*

Rank: Your wife can appear just as she looks every day.

Helmer: That was nicely put. But don't you know what you're going to be?

Rank: Yes, Helmer, I've made up my mind.

Helmer: Well?

Rank: At the next masquerade I'm going to be invisible.

Helmer: That's a funny idea.

Rank: They say there's a hat—black, huge—have you never heard of the hat that makes you invisible? You put it on, and then no one on earth can see you.

Helmer (suppressing a smile): Ah, of course.

Rank: But I'm quite forgetting what I came for. Helmer, give me a cigar, one of the dark Havanas.

Helmer: With the greatest pleasure. *(Holds out his case.)*

Rank: Thanks. *(Takes one and cuts off the tip.)*

Nora (striking a match): Let me give you a light.

Rank: Thank you. *(She holds the match for him; he lights the cigar.)* And now good-bye.

Helmer: Good-bye, good-bye, old friend.

Nora: Sleep well, Doctor.

Rank: Thanks for that wish.

Nora: Wish me the same.

Rank: You? All right, if you like—Sleep well. And thanks for the light. *(He nods to them both and leaves.)*

Helmer (his voice subdued): He's been drinking heavily.

Nora (absently): Could be. *(Helmer takes his keys from his pocket and goes out in the hall.)* Torvald—what are you after?

Helmer: Got to empty the mailbox; it's nearly full. There won't be room for the morning papers.

Nora: Are you working tonight?

Helmer: You know I'm not. Why—what's this? Someone's been at the lock.

Nora: At the lock—?

Helmer: Yes, I'm positive. What do you suppose—? I can't imagine one of the maids—? Here's a broken hairpin. Nora, it's yours—

Nora (quickly): Then it must be the children—

Helmer: You'd better break them of that. Hm, hm—well, opened it after all. *(Takes the contents out and calls into the kitchen.)* Helene! Helene, would you put out the lamp in the hall. *(He returns to the room shutting the hall door, then displays the handful of mail.)* Look how it's piled up. *(Sorting through them.)* Now what's this?

Nora (at the window): The letter! Oh, Torvald, no!

Helmer: Two calling cards—from Rank.

Nora: From Dr. Rank?

Helmer (examining them): "Dr. Rank, Consulting Physician." They were on top. He must have dropped them in as he left.

Nora: Is there anything on them?

Helmer: There's a black cross over the name. See? That's a gruesome notion. He could almost be announcing his own death.

Nora: That's just what he's doing.

Helmer: What! You've heard something? Something he's told you?

Nora: Yes. That when those cards came, he'd be taking his leave of us. He'll shut himself in now and die.

Helmer: Ah, my poor friend! Of course I knew he wouldn't be here much longer. But so soon — And then to hide himself away like a wounded animal.

Nora: If it has to happen, then it's best it happens in silence — don't you think so, Torvald?

Helmer (pacing up and down): He'd grown right into our lives. I simply can't imagine him gone. He with his suffering and loneliness — like a dark cloud setting off our sunlit happiness. Well, maybe it's best this way. For him, at least. *(Standing still.)* And maybe for us too, Nora. Now we're thrown back on each other, completely. *(Embracing her.)* Oh you, my darling wife, how can I hold you close enough? You know what, Nora — time and again I've wished you were in some terrible danger, just so I could stake my life and soul and everything, for your sake.

Nora (tearing herself away, her voice firm and decisive): Now you must read your mail, Torvald.

Helmer: No, no, not tonight. I want to stay with you, dearest.

Nora: With a dying friend on your mind?

Helmer: You're right. We've both had a shock. There's ugliness between us — these thoughts of death and corruption. We'll have to get free of them first. Until then — we'll stay apart.

Nora (clinging about his neck): Torvald — good night! Good night!

Helmer (kissing her on the cheek): Good night, little songbird. Sleep well, Nora. I'll be reading my mail now. *(He takes the letters into his room and shuts the door after him.)*

Nora (with bewildered glances, groping about, seizing Helmer's domino, throwing it around her, and speaking in short, hoarse, broken whispers): Never see him again. Never, never. *(Putting her shawl over her head.)* Never see the children either — them, too. Never, never. Oh, the freezing black water! The depths — down — Oh, I wish it were over — He has it now; he's reading it — now. Oh no, no, not yet. Torvald, good-bye, you and the children — *(She starts for the hall; as she does, Helmer throws open his door and stands with an open letter in his hand.)*

Helmer: Nora!

Nora (screams): Oh — !

Helmer: What is this? You know what's in this letter?

Nora: Yes, I know. Let me go! Let me out!

Helmer (holding her back): Where are you going?

Nora (struggling to break loose): You can't save me, Torvald!

Helmer (slumping back): True! Then it's true what he writes? How horrible! No, no, it's impossible—it can't be true.

Nora: It *is* true. I've loved you more than all this world.

Helmer: Ah, none of your slippery tricks.

Nora (taking one step toward him): Torvald—!

Helmer: What *is* this you've blundered into!

Nora: Just let me loose. You're not going to suffer for my sake. You're not going to take on my guilt.

Helmer: No more play-acting. *(Locks the hall door.)* You stay right here and give me a reckoning. You understand what you've done? Answer! You understand?

Nora (looking squarely at him, her face hardening): Yes. I'm beginning to understand everything now.

Helmer (striding about): Oh, what an awful awakening! In all these eight years—she who was my pride and joy—a hypocrite, a liar—worse, worse—a criminal! How infinitely disgusting it all is! The shame! *(Nora says nothing and goes on looking straight at him. He stops in front of her.)* I should have suspected something of the kind. I should have known. All your father's flimsy values—Be still! All your father's flimsy values have come out in you. No religion, no morals, no sense of duty—Oh, how I'm punished for letting him off! I did it for your sake, and you repay me like this.

Nora: Yes, like this.

Helmer: Now you've wrecked all my happiness—ruined my whole future. Oh, it's awful to think of. I'm in a cheap little grafter's hands; he can do anything he wants with me, ask for anything, play with me like a puppet—and I can't breathe a word. I'll be swept down miserably into the depths on account of a featherbrained woman.

Nora: When I'm gone from this world, you'll be free.

Helmer: Oh, quit posing. Your father had a mess of those speeches too. What good would that ever do me if you were gone from this world, as you say? Not the slightest. He can still make the whole thing known; and if he does, I could be falsely suspected as your accomplice. They might even think that I was behind it—that I put you up to it. And all that I can thank you for—you that I've coddled the whole of our marriage. Can you see now what you've done to me?

Nora (icily calm): Yes.

Helmer: It's so incredible, I just can't grasp it. But we'll have to patch up whatever we can. Take off the shawl. I said, take if off! I've got to appease him somehow or other. The thing has to be hushed up at any cost. And as for you and me, it's got to seem like everything between us is just as it was—to the outside world, that is. You'll go right on living in this house, of course. But you can't be allowed to bring up the children; I don't dare trust you with them—Oh, to have to say this to someone I've loved so much! Well, that's done with.

From now on happiness doesn't matter; all that matters is saving the bits and pieces, the appearance— *(The doorbell rings. Helmer starts.)* What's that? And so late. Maybe the worst—? You think he'd—? Hide, Nora! Say you're sick. *(Nora remains standing motionless. Helmer goes and opens the door.)*

Maid (half dressed, in the hall): A letter for Mrs. Helmer.

Helmer: I'll take it. *(Snatches the letter and shuts the door.)* Yes, it's from him. You don't get it; I'm reading it myself.

Nora: Then read it.

Helmer (by the lamp): I hardly dare. We may be ruined, you and I. But—I've got to know. *(Rips open the letter, skims through a few lines, glances at an enclosure, then cries out joyfully.)* Nora! *(Nora looks inquiringly at him.)* Nora! Wait—better check it again—Yes, yes, it's true. I'm saved. Nora, I'm saved!

Nora: And I?

Helmer: You too, of course. We're both saved, both of us. Look. He's sent back your note. He says he's sorry and ashamed—that a happy development in his life—oh, who cares what he says! Nora, we're saved! No one can hurt you. Oh, Nora, Nora—but first, this ugliness all has to go. Let me see—*(Takes a look at the note.)* No, I don't want to see it; I want the whole thing to fade like a dream. *(Tears the note and both letters to pieces, throws them into the stove and watches them burn.)* There—now there's nothing left—He wrote that since Christmas Eve you—Oh, they must have been three terrible days for you, Nora.

Nora: I fought a hard fight.

Helmer: And suffered pain and saw no escape but—No, we're not going to dwell on anything unpleasant. We'll just be grateful and keep on repeating: it's over now, it's over! You hear me, Nora? You don't seem to realize—it's over. What's it mean—that frozen look? Oh, poor little Nora, I understand. You can't believe I've forgiven you. But I have, Nora; I swear I have. I know that what you did, you did out of love for me.

Nora: That's true.

Helmer: You loved me the way a wife ought to love her husband. It's simply the means that you couldn't judge. But you think I love you any the less for not knowing how to handle your affairs? No, no—just lean on me; I'll guide you and teach you. I wouldn't be a man if this feminine helplessness didn't make you twice as attractive to me. You mustn't mind those sharp words I said—that was all in the first confusion of thinking my world had collapsed. I've forgiven you, Nora; I swear I've forgiven you.

Nora: My thanks for your forgiveness. *(She goes out through the door, right.)*

Helmer: No, wait—*(Peers in.)* What are you doing in there?

Nora (inside): Getting out of my costume.

Helmer (by the open door): Yes, do that. Try to calm yourself and collect your thoughts again, my frightened little songbird. You can rest easy now; I've got wide wings to shelter you with. *(Walking about close by the door.*) How snug and nice our home is, Nora. You're safe here; I'll keep you like a hunted dove I've rescued out of a hawk's claws. I'll bring peace to your poor, shuddering heart. Gradually it'll happen, Nora; you'll see. Tomorrow all this will look different to you; then everything will be as it was. I won't have to go on repeating I forgive you; you'll feel it for yourself. How can you imagine I'd ever conceivably want to disown you—or even blame you in any way? Ah, you don't know a man's heart, Nora. For a man there's something indescribably sweet and satisfying in knowing he's forgiven his wife—and forgiven her out of a full and open heart. It's as if she belongs to him in two ways now: in a sense he's given her fresh into the world again, and she's become his wife and his child as well. From now on that's what you'll be to me—you little, bewildered, helpless thing. Don't be afraid of anything, Nora; just open your heart to me, and I'll be conscience and will to you both—*(Nora enters in her regular clothes.)* What's this? Not in bed? You've changed your dress?

Nora: Yes, Torvald, I've changed my dress.

Helmer: But why now, so late?

Nora: Tonight I'm not sleeping.

Helmer: But Nora dear—

Nora (looking at her watch): It's still not so very late. Sit down, Torvald; we have a lot to talk over. *(She sits at one side of the table.)*

Helmer: Nora—what is this? That hard expression—

Nora: Sit down. This'll take some time. I have a lot to say.

Helmer (sitting at the table directly opposite her): You worry me, Nora. And I don't understand you.

Nora: No, that's exactly it. You don't understand me. And I've never understood you either—until tonight. No, don't interrupt. You can just listen to what I say. We're closing out accounts, Torvald.

Helmer: How do you mean that?

Nora (after a short pause): Doesn't anything strike you about our sitting here like this?

Helmer: What's that?

Nora: We've been married now eight years. Doesn't it occur to you that this is the first time we two, you and I, man and wife, have ever talked seriously together?

Helmer: What do you mean—seriously?

Nora: In eight whole years—longer even—right from our first acquaintance, we've never exchanged a serious word on any serious thing.

Helmer: You mean I should constantly go and involve you in problems you couldn't possibly help me with?

Nora: I'm not talking of problems. I'm saying that we've never sat down seriously together and tried to get to the bottom of anything.

Helmer: But dearest, what good would that ever do you?

Nora: That's the point right there: you've never understood me. I've been wronged greatly, Torvald—first by Papa, and then by you.

Helmer: What! By us — the two people who've loved you more than anyone else?

Nora (shaking her head): You never loved me. You've thought it fun to be
in love with me, that's all.

Helmer: Nora, what a thing to say!

Nora: Yes, it's true now, Torvald. When I lived at home with Papa, he told
me all his opinions, so I had the same ones too; or if they were different I hid them, since he wouldn't have cared for that. He used to call
me his doll-child, and he played with me the way I played with my
dolls. Then I came into your house —

Helmer: How can you speak of our marriage like that?

Nora (unperturbed): I mean, then I went from Papa's hands into yours.
You arranged everything to your own taste, and so I got the same
taste as you — or I pretended to; I can't remember. I guess a little of
both, first one, then the other. Now when I look back, it seems as if
I'd lived here like a beggar — just from hand to mouth. I've lived by
doing tricks for you, Torvald. But that's the way you wanted it. It's
a great sin what you and Papa did to me. You're to blame that nothing's become of me.

Helmer: Nora, how unfair and ungrateful you are! Haven't you been
happy here?

Nora: No, never. I thought so — but I never have.

Helmer: Not — not happy!

Nora: No, only lighthearted. And you've always been so kind to me. But
our home's been nothing but a playpen. I've been your doll-wife
here, just as at home I was Papa's doll-child. And in turn the children have been my dolls. I thought it was fun when you played with
me, just as they thought it fun when I played with them. That's been
our marriage, Torvald.

Helmer: There's some truth in what you're saying — under all the raving
exaggeration. But it'll all be different after this. Playtime's over; now
for the schooling.

Nora: Whose schooling — mine or the children's?

Helmer: Both yours and the children's, dearest.

Nora: Oh, Torvald, you're not the man to teach me to be a good wife to you.

Helmer: And you can say that?

Nora: And I — how am I equipped to bring up children?

Helmer: Nora!

Nora: Didn't you say a moment ago that that was no job to trust me
with?

Helmer: In a flare of temper! Why fasten on that?

Nora: Yes, but you were so very right. I'm not up to the job. There's
another job I have to do first. I have to try to educate myself. You
can't help me with that. I've got to do it alone. And that's why I'm
leaving you now.

Helmer (jumping up): What's that?

Nora: I have to stand completely alone, if I'm ever going to discover myself and the world out there. So I can't go on living with you.

Helmer: Nora, Nora!

Nora: I want to leave right away. Kristine should put me up for the night—

Helmer: You're insane! You've no right! I forbid you!

Nora: From here on, there's no use forbidding me anything. I'll take with me whatever is mine. I don't want a thing from you, either now or later.

Helmer: What kind of madness is this!

Nora: Tomorrow I'm going home—I mean, home where I came from. It'll be easier up there to find something to do.

Helmer: Oh, you blind, incompetent child!

Nora: I must learn to be competent, Torvald.

Helmer: Abandon your home, your husband, your children! And you're not even thinking what people will say.

Nora: I can't be concerned about that. I only know how essential this is.

Helmer: Oh, it's outrageous. So you'll run out like this on your most sacred vows.

Nora: What do you think are my most sacred vows?

Helmer: And I have to tell you that! Aren't they your duties to your husband and children?

Nora: I have other duties equally sacred.

Helmer: That isn't true. What duties are they?

Nora: Duties to myself.

Helmer: Before all else, you're a wife and mother.

Nora: I don't believe in that anymore. I believe that, before all else, I'm a human being, no less than you—or anyway, I ought to try to become one. I know the majority thinks you're right, Torvald, and plenty of books agree with you, too. But I can't go on believing what the majority says, or what's written in books. I have to think over these things myself and try to understand them.

Helmer: Why can't you understand your place in your own home? On a point like that, isn't there one everlasting guide you can turn to? Where's your religion?

Nora: Oh, Torvald, I'm really not sure what religion is.

Helmer: What—?

Nora: I only know what the minister said when I was confirmed. He told me religion was this thing and that. When I get clear and away by myself, I'll go into that problem too. I'll see if what the minister said was right, or, in any case, if it's right for me.

Helmer: A young woman your age shouldn't talk like that. If religion can't move you, I can try to rouse your conscience. You do have some moral feeling? Or, tell me—has that gone too?

Nora: It's not easy to answer that, Torvald. I simply don't know. I'm all confused about these things. I just know I see them so differently from you. I find out, for one thing, that the law's not at all what I'd thought—but I can't get it through my head that the law is fair. A woman hasn't a right to protect her dying father or save her husband's life! I can't believe that.

Helmer: You talk like a child. You don't know anything of the world you live in.

Nora: No, I don't. But now I'll begin to learn for myself. I'll try to discover who's right, the world or I.

Helmer: Nora, you're sick; you've got a fever. I almost think you're out of your head.

Nora: I've never felt more clearheaded and sure in my life.

Helmer: And—clearheaded and sure—you're leaving your husband and children?

Nora: Yes.

Helmer: Then there's only one possible reason.

Nora: What?

Helmer: You no longer love me.

Nora: No. That's exactly it.

Helmer: Nora! You can't be serious!

Nora: Oh, this is so hard, Torvald—you've been so kind to me always. But I can't help it. I don't love you anymore.

Helmer (struggling for composure): Are you also clearheaded and sure about that?

Nora: Yes, completely. That's why I can't go on staying here.

Helmer: Can you tell me what I did to lose your love?

Nora: Yes, I can tell you. It was this evening when the miraculous thing didn't come—then I knew you weren't the man I'd imagined.

Helmer: Be more explicit; I don't follow you.

Nora: I've waited now so patiently eight long years—for, my Lord, I know miracles don't come every day. Then this crisis broke over me, and such a certainty filled me: *now* the miraculous event would occur. While Krogstad's letter was lying out there, I never for an instant dreamed that you could give in to his terms. I was so utterly sure you'd say to him: go on, tell your tale to the whole wide world. And when he'd done that—

Helmer: Yes, what then? When I'd delivered my own wife into shame and disgrace—

Nora: When he'd done that, I was so utterly sure that you'd step forward, take the blame on yourself and say: I am the guilty one.

Helmer: Nora—!

Nora: You're thinking I'd never accept such a sacrifice from you? No, of course not. But what good would my protests be against you? That was the miracle I was waiting for, in terror and hope. And to stave that off, I would have taken my life.

Helmer: I'd gladly work for you day and night, Nora—and take on pain and deprivation. But there's no one who gives up honor for love.

Nora: Millions of women have done just that.

Helmer: Oh, you think and talk like a silly child.

Nora: Perhaps. But you neither think nor talk like the man I could join myself to. When your big fright was over — and it wasn't from any threat against me, only for what might damage you — when all the danger was past, for you it was just as if nothing had happened. I was exactly the same, your little lark, your doll, that you'd have to handle with double care now that I'd turned out so brittle and frail. *(Gets up.)* Torvald — in that instant it dawned on me that for eight years I've been living here with a stranger, and that I've even conceived three children — oh, I can't stand the thought of it! I could tear myself to bits.

Helmer (heavily): I see. There's a gulf that's opened between us — that's clear. Oh, but Nora, can't we bridge it somehow?

Nora: The way I am now, I'm no wife for you.

Helmer: I have the strength to make myself over.

Nora: Maybe — if your doll gets taken away.

Helmer: But to part! To part from you! No, Nora no — I can't imagine it.

Nora (going out, right): All the more reason why it has to be. *(She reenters with her coat and a small overnight bag, which she puts on a chair by the table.)*

Helmer: Nora, Nora, not now! Wait till tomorrow.

Nora: I can't spend the night in a strange man's room.

Helmer: But couldn't we live here like brother and sister —

Nora: You know very well how long that would last. *(Throws her shawl about her.)* Good-bye, Torvald. I won't look in on the children. I know they're in better hands than mine. The way I am now, I'm no use to them.

Helmer: But someday, Nora — someday — ?

Nora: How can I tell? I haven't the least idea what'll become of me.

Helmer: But you're my wife, now and wherever you go.

Nora: Listen, Torvald — I've heard that when a wife deserts her husband's house just as I'm doing, then the law frees him from all responsibility. In any case, I'm freeing you from being responsible. Don't feel yourself bound, any more than I will. There has to be absolute freedom for us both. Here, take your ring back. Give me mine.

Helmer: That too?

Nora: That too.

Helmer: There it is.

Nora: Good. Well, now it's all over. I'm putting the keys here. The maids know all about keeping up the house — better than I do. Tomorrow, after I've left town, Kristine will stop by to pack up everything that's mine from home. I'd like those things shipped up to me.

Helmer: Over! All over! Nora, won't you ever think about me?

Nora: I'm sure I'll think of you often, and about the children and the house here.

Helmer: May I write you?

Nora: No—never. You're not to do that.

Helmer: Oh, but let me send you—

Nora: Nothing. Nothing.

Helmer: Or help you if you need it.

Nora: No. I accept nothing from strangers.

Helmer: Nora—can I never be more than a stranger to you?

Nora (picking up her overnight bag): Ah, Torvald—it would take the greatest miracle of all—

Helmer: Tell me the greatest miracle!

Nora: You and I both would have to transform ourselves to the point that—Oh, Torvald, I've stopped believing in miracles.

Helmer: But I'll believe. Tell me! Transform ourselves to the point that—?

Nora: That our living together could be a true marriage. *(She goes out down the hall.)*

Helmer (sinks down on a chair by the door, face buried in his hands): Nora! Nora! *(Looking about and rising.)* Empty. She's gone. *(A sudden hope leaps in him.)* The greatest miracle—?

From below, the sound of a door slamming shut.

CONSIDERATIONS FOR CRITICAL THINKING AND WRITING

1. **FIRST RESPONSE.** What is the significance of the play's title?

2. Why is Nora "pale with terror" at the end of Act I? What is the significance of the description of the Christmas tree now "stripped of ornament, [with] burned-down candle stubs on its ragged branches" that opens Act II? What other symbols are used in the play?

3. What is Dr. Rank's purpose in the play?

4. How does the relationship between Krogstad and Mrs. Linde emphasize certain qualities in the Helmers' marriage?

5. Would you describe the ending as essentially happy or unhappy? Is the play more like a comedy or a tragedy?

6. Ibsen believed that a "dramatist's business is not to answer questions, but only to ask them." What questions are raised in the play? Does Ibsen propose any specific answers?

7. **CONNECTION TO ANOTHER SELECTION.** Explain how Torvald's attitude toward Nora is similar to the men's attitudes toward women in Susan Glaspell's *Trifles* (p. 601). Write an essay exploring how the assumptions the men make about women in both plays contribute to the plays' conflicts.

Plays for Further Reading

28

A Collection of
Short Plays

I've found that the more culturally specific
you are, the more universal the work is.
There's no conflict between wanting to
reach a large audience and being particular
and culturally accurate.

— DAVID HENRY HWANG

Naked Lunch

Born in Lancaster, Pennsylvania, Michael
Hollinger earned a B.A. in music at Oberlin
Conservatory and a master of arts degree
in theater from Villanova University, where
he now teaches theater. His comedies
and dramas have been widely produced
in the United States and abroad. Among
his plays are *An Empty Plate in the Café
Du Grand Boeuf* (1994), *Red Herring* (1996),
Hot Air (1997), *Tiny Island* (1998), *Eureka*
(1999), *Opus* (2006), and *Ghost Writer* (2011).
He has also written three short films and
coauthored *Philadelphia Diary* with Bruce
Graham and Sonia Sanchez for PBS.
His writing awards include the Roger L.

Courtesy of the Arden Theatre Company.

Stevens Award from the Kennedy Center's Fund for Outstanding New American Plays, the Barrymore Award for Outstanding New Play, and the Otto Haas Award for Emerging Theatre Artist. Hollinger's extensive music background strongly influences his work as a playwright. He has said about his own work, "Plays are music to me; characters are instruments, scenes are movements; tempo, rhythm and dynamics are critical; and melody and counterpoint are always set in relief by rests — beats, pauses, the spaces between." *Naked Lunch* (2003) is one of a group of sixteen plays written by various playwrights for *Trepidation Nation: A Phobic Anthology*, which was produced at the 2002–2003 Humana Festival by the Actor Theatre of Louisville.

> **WHEN I WRITE** "Conflict is the source of all drama, so I always return to the key questions when writing: Who wants what? What gets in the way? Why is it so important? Opposing forces engage our curiosity about outcome — a crucial element for an art from that requires such focused, sustained attention."   — MICHAEL HOLLINGER

MICHAEL HOLLINGER (B. 1962)

Naked Lunch   2003

Lights up on Vernon and Lucy sitting at a small dining-room table, eating. There's a small vase with too many flowers in it, or a large vase with too few. A bottle of wine has been opened. Vernon regales Lucy as he vigorously devours a steak. Lucy discreetly nibbles on her corn-on-the-cob.

Vernon: Larry thinks the whole show's a fake. He says the guy's just an actor and all the crocs are trained. I said, you can't train a crocodile! It's not like some poodle you can teach to ride a bike. It's got this reptile brain, a million years old. All it knows, or wants to know, is whether or not you're juicy. Anyway, this one show the guy's sneaking up on a mother protecting her nest. And she's huge — I mean, this thing could swallow a Buick. And the guy's really playing it up: *(Australian accent.)* "Amazing — look at the size of those teeth!" But just —

(He stops, looking at Lucy. Pause. She looks up from her corn.)

Lucy: What.
Vernon: What's the matter?
Lucy: I'm listening.
Vernon: You're not eating your steak.
Lucy: Oh. No.
Vernon: How come?
Lucy: I'll just eat the corn.

(She returns to nibbling.)

Vernon: What's wrong with the steak?

Lucy: Nothing.

Vernon: Then eat it. It's good.

Lucy: I'd . . . rather not.

Vernon: Why not?

   (Pause.)

Lucy: I'm vegetarian.

   (Beat.)

Vernon: What?

Lucy: I don't eat meat anymore.

Vernon: Since when?

Lucy: Since we, you know. Broke up.

   (Pause.)

Vernon: Just like that?

Lucy: Well —

Vernon: You break up with me and boom next day you start eating tofu?

Lucy: I'd been thinking about it for a while.

Vernon: First I ever heard of it.

Lucy: Well, I'd been thinking. *(Pause. Lucy picks up her corn again, guiding him back to the story:)* So anyway, the guy's sneaking up on the mother . . .

Vernon: Was it because of me?

Lucy: No . . .

Vernon: Something I said, or did . . .

Lucy: It's nothing like that.

Vernon: You were always fond of cataloguing the careless things I said and did . . .

Lucy: I just did some soul-searching, that's all.

   (Beat.)

Vernon: Soul-searching.

Lucy: About a lot of things.

Vernon: And your soul said to you "no more meat."

Lucy: You make it sound silly when you say it like that.

Vernon: Then what, what did your soul tell you?

   (Beat. Lucy exhales heavily and sets down her corn.)

Lucy: I decided I didn't want to eat anything with a face.

   (Beat.)

Vernon: A *face?*

   (He gets up, stands behind her and looks at her plate.)

Lucy: Vern . . .

Vernon: I don't see any face . . .

Lucy: This doesn't have to be a big deal . . .

Vernon: I don't see a face. Do you see a face?

(*He lifts the plate toward her face.*)

Lucy: There's other reasons.

Vernon: No face.

(*He sets the plate down again.*)

Lucy: I've been reading things.

Vernon: What things?

Lucy: You know, health reports . . .

Vernon: You can't believe that stuff.

Lucy: What do you mean?

Vernon: You can't! One day they say bran's good for you—"Want to live forever? Eat more bran."—the next day they find out bran can kill you.

Lucy: Whatever.

Vernon: Too much bran boom you're dead.

Lucy: There are diseases you can get from meat.

Vernon: Like what?

Lucy: Well, listeria . . .

Vernon: That's chicken. Chicken and turkey.

Lucy: Or Mad Cow.

Vernon: *Mad Cow?* Did you—That's not even—that's *English,* they have that in *England.* This isn't English meat, this is from, I don't know, Kansas, or . . . *Wyoming.*

Lucy: Even so,—

Vernon: No. Now you're making stuff up.

Lucy: I'm not; I saw an article—

Vernon: You're just being paranoid, this whole . . . You know what this is? Do you?

Lucy: What.

Vernon: Carnophobia.

Lucy: "Carnophobia"?

Vernon: It's a word, look it up.

Lucy: It's not like I'm scared of meat . . .

Vernon: How do you think this makes me feel?

Lucy: Look, let's just drop it.

Vernon: Huh?

Lucy: We were doing so well . . .

Vernon: I invite you over, cook a nice steak, set out flowers, napkins, the whole nine yards . . .

Lucy: I appreciate the napkins.

Vernon: . . . figure I'll open a bottle of wine, apologize . . . maybe we'll get naked, be like old times.

Lucy: So let's start over.

Vernon: Then you get *carnophobic* on me.
Lucy: Can we?
Vernon: Throw it in my face.
Lucy: Please?
Vernon: Start *cataloguing* what's wrong with everything . . .
Lucy: I never meant this to be a big deal. *(Beat. She puts her hand on his. He looks at her.)* I really didn't.

(Long pause.)

Vernon: Then eat it.

(Beat.)

Lucy: Vern . . . *(He picks up her fork, jams it into her steak, and cuts off a bite with his knife.)* Why do you always have to —

(He extends the piece of meat toward Lucy's mouth.)

Vernon: Eat the meat.
Lucy: I don't want to.
Vernon: Eat the meat.
Lucy: Vernon . . .
Vernon: I SAID EAT THE MEAT! *(They are locked in a struggle, he menacing, she terrified. Long pause. Finally, Lucy opens her mouth and takes the bite into it. Pause.)* Chew. *(She chews for fifteen or twenty seconds.)* Swallow. *(She swallows. Cheerfully, without malice:)* Good, isn't it. *(Lucy nods obediently.)* Nice and juicy. *(He stabs his fork into his own steak, cuts off a bite and lifts it.)* See, nothing to be afraid of.

(He pops it into his mouth and begins cutting another. After a moment, Lucy goes back to her corn. They eat in absolute silence. Lights fade.)

"Naked Lunch — *a frozen moment when everyone sees what is on the end of every fork.*" — William S. Burroughs.

Mistaken Identity

Sharon E. Cooper is an award-winning playwright and teacher whose five full-length plays and dozens of short plays have had workshops, staged readings, and productions across the United States, in Germany, and in India. Her full-length plays, including *Caught, Door of Hope,* and *Running,* cover a broad range of topics, and her short play

Courtesy of Sharon E. Cooper.

The Cooking King was produced in the Samuel French Off-Off Broadway Short Play Festival in 2009 and is published in *The Best Short Plays of 2010*. Cooper is a tutor, yoga instructor, member of the Dramatists Guild, and a Resident Playwright at The CRY HAVOC Company. *Mistaken Identity* starts the way a good many shaky blind dates begin but then takes an interesting turn.

> **WHEN I WRITE** "Don't be scared to write the truth as you know it and as you see it. Find like-minded, thoughtful people — people you can trust, who will listen and help you write the story you want to write. But if someone tries to rewrite or 'fix' your story, stop listening." —SHARON E. COOPER

SHARON E. COOPER (B. 1975)
Mistaken Identity   2004
(2008 Revised)

CHARACTERS

Kali Patel, 29. Single lesbian Hindu of Indian heritage; social worker who works as much as possible; lives in Leicester, England.
Steve Dodd, 32. Single straight guy, desperate to marry, raised Baptist but attends church only on Christmas and Easter; studying abroad for his final year as an undergraduate.

SETTING: The Castle, a pub in Kirby Muxloe in Leicester, England.

TIME: The present.

> *(Lights up on Steve and Kali in a busy pub on their first date. They are in the middle of dinner.)*

Steve: You must get tired of fish and chips all the time. Why do y'all call them "chips"? When they're french fries, I mean. And you ever notice when people swear, they say, "Excuse my French." Not me. Nope. I have nothing against the French.
Kali: Right, well, I'm not French, Steve, now am I?
Steve: I just didn't want you to think I was prejudiced against the French or *anyone else.* . . . They're like your neighbors, the French. And your neighbors are like my neighbors. And like a good neighbor, State Farm is there. Have you heard that commercial?
Kali: What? No. Steve —
Steve: It's for insurance. Y'all must not play it here. (*Pause.*) So I know that you all do the "arranged marriage thing." Rashid and I had a long talk about it. Of course, Rashid and I wanted you to approve, too, Kali.
Kali: How twenty-first century of you and my brother. Steve . . .
Kali: I'm gay. / *Steve:* Will you marry me?

Kali: Come again? / *Steve:* What?

Kali: How could you ask me to . . . / *Steve:* Well, I can't believe this.

Kali: Bloody hell, stop talking while I'm talking . . . / *Steve:* This is very strange.

Kali: So—what?

Steve: This new information is, well, new, and changes things, I guess.

Kali: You guess? What the hell is wrong with you? I'm sorry, Steve, you just happened to show up at the end of a very long line of a lot of very bad dates. You know, movies where the bloke negotiates holding your hand while you're just trying to eat popcorn; running across De Montfort University in the pouring rain; dropping a bowling ball on the bloke's pizza.

Steve: You had me until the bowling ball. Kali, this doesn't make sense. I invite you out on a lovely date. We eat fish and chips—when I would rather be eating a burger or lasagna—

Kali: Steve, I'm sorry.

Steve: I figured we would have a nice long traditional wedding with the colorful tents. All of my family would be there. We're more of the Christmas/Easter Christians, so we'd do your religion and I would wear—

Kali: *(Overlapping.)* You don't know anything about my people. What are you—

Steve: *(Overlapping.)* Ooohhh, yes, I do. I saw *Monsoon Wedding.* And the director's cut! And I saw *Slumdog Millionaire* like three times. Three times. Unbelievable!

Kali: Yes, this makes loads of sense at the end of the day. I am a lesbian who has to date every Hindu bloke in England until her brother gets so desperate that he sets her up with a cowboy—

Steve: I take offense to that.

Kali: *(Overlapping.)* But I should feel sorry for *you* because *you* watched *two,* count them, *two* movies about Indian people in your entire life and ordered fish when there are hamburgers on the menu! Forgive *me* for being so insensitive.

Steve: I ordered fish because I wanted you to like me. And I'm sure I've seen other Asian movies. Like all those fighting movies. You know, the ones where women are jumping through the air—

Kali: Aaahhh! Do you see how all of this is a moot point now?

Steve: I'm confused. Let's review.

Kali: Please, no, bloody hell, let's not review. Let's get the waiter. Haven't you had enough?

(She gets up. He follows.)

Steve: *(Overlapping.)* Why is your brother setting up his *lesbian* sister—

Kali: *(Overlapping.)* Will you please keep your voice down?

Steve: *(Overlapping.)* —up on dates for marriage and tricking well-meaning men—specifically me—into proposing to her? I'm here to finish my business degree, but I wasn't born yesterday. So I took a few years off and changed careers a few times, was a fireman —

Kali: *(Overlapping.)* What does that have to do with anything?

Steve: And I'm thirty-two years old, but that doesn't mean —

Kali: Mate, are you going to keep on and on?

Steve: Why did your brother put me through this? This isn't one of those new reality shows: "Little Brothers Set Up Their Lesbian Sisters." Is there a camera under the table? *(He looks.)* Let's talk about this. *(He sits back down.)* I'm a good listener. Go ahead. *(Pause.)* I'm listening. *(Pause.)* You have to say something if you want this to continue with what we call in America, a conversation.

Kali: Are you done?

Steve: Go ahead.

(She sits.)

Kali: I guess I was hoping you wouldn't tell Rashid.

Steve: He doesn't know?

Kali: You are finishing your bachelor's degree, is that right?

Steve: If you're so "bloody" smart, I'm wondering why you would tell me, a man that is friends with your brother and sits next to him twice a week in eight A.M. classes — why would you tell *me* you're a lesbian and *not* your brother?

Kali: Maybe for the same reason you would ask a woman you've never met before to marry you.

Steve: Your brother made it sound like it would be easy. I've been looking for that.

Kali: *(Overlapping.)* Look, you seem very nice, you do.

Steve: I am very nice.

Kali: And at the end of the day, I hope you find someone you like.

Steve: I like how you say "at the end of the day" and I like how you say "bloke" and "mate." It's so endearing. And you're beautiful and small and your hair falls on your back so.

Kali: Steve, being a lesbian is not negotiable. And don't start with how sexy it would be to be with me or to watch me and another woman —

Steve: *(Overlapping.)* Kali, I didn't say any of that.

Kali: You didn't have to. Up until a few minutes ago, you thought I was a quiet, subservient Asian toy for sale from her brother. Steve, go get a doll. She can travel with you to America whenever you want. In the meantime, I'll continue to be a loud, abrasive *(Whispering.)* lesbian while my brother sets me up with every bloke on the street — and they don't even have to be Hindu anymore! Do you have any idea what that's like? *(Pause.)* How would you know?

Steve: You're right. I wouldn't.

Kali: Steve, why did you want to be with me? I mean, before.

Steve: I figured that we would have visited my family in the winter when it's so cold here. I would have been willing to stay here when I'm done with school and we would get a nice little place by the —

Kali: Steve, we hadn't even shared dessert yet.

Steve: Don't blame me for all of this. Five minutes ago, we were on a date.

Kali: We're just two people in a pub.

Steve: Kali, do you remember the last time someone—man, woman, I don't care—had their hand down the small of your back or leaned into you like it didn't matter where you ended and they began?

Kali: Yes, I do remember that. And that was strangely poetic.

Steve: You don't have to sound so surprised. Anyway, I remember that feeling. Three years ago, at a Fourth of July celebration—you know, that's the holiday—

Kali: Yes, Steve, I know the holiday.

Steve: She was the only woman I ever really loved. I knew it was ending. Could taste it. I just held her as the fireworks went off and the dust got in our skin. Figured I would hold on, hoping that would keep me for a while. You know how they say babies will die if they're left alone too long. Always wondered if it's true for bigger people, too. Like how long would we last? . . . She left with her Pilates mat and Snoopy slippers a few days later. I bet it hasn't been three years for you.

Kali: No, it hasn't. But you wouldn't want to hear about that.

Steve: Why not?

Kali: Come on, Steve, I'm not here for your fantasies—

Steve: This thing where you assume you know what I'm thinking—it's gettin' old.

Kali: I'm . . . sorry. I do have a woman in my life, Michele—She's a teacher for people that are deaf. We've been together for eleven months. The longest we were away from each other was this one time for three weeks. She was at a retreat where they weren't allowed to talk—you know, total immersion. So she would call and I would say, "Is it beautiful there, love?" and she would hit a couple of buttons. Sometimes she would leave me messages: "beep, beep, beep beep beep beep." It didn't matter that she didn't say anything . . . But I can't take her home for Diwali.

Steve: What's that?

Kali: It's a festival of lights where—

Steve: You mean like Hanukkah.

Kali: No, like Diwali. It's a New Year's celebration where we remember ancestors, family, and friends. And reflect back and look to the future.

Steve: It sounds nice. You know, my mother has been asking me for grandchildren since I turned twenty-seven. Every year at Christmas, it's the same: "I can't wait to hang another stocking for my grandchildren, if I ever get to have them."

Kali: Now, imagine that same conversation, well, not about Christmas, and what if you could never give that to them—could never bring someone home for any holiday for the rest of your life?

Steve: Then why don't you just tell them the truth?

Kali: I can't say, Mum, Daddy, Rashid, I've chosen women over men — it's not a hamburger over fish. You just don't know how they'll react. I'd run the risk of not being allowed to see my nieces. I'm so exhausted from hiding, I can barely breathe.

Steve: So stop hiding.

Kali: Have you been listening to what I've been saying?

Steve: Have you?

Kali: Are you going to tell my brother?

Steve: Do you want me to?

Kali: I don't know.

Steve: I've never thought about that thing that you said.

Kali: Which thing would that be?

Steve: The one where maybe you can't see your nieces 'cause you're gay. That must suck.

Kali: Yes, well, thanks for trying to make me feel better.

Steve: Listen, you get to decide what you tell your family and when. As far as I'm concerned, I'll tell Rashid tomorrow that we're getting married. Or I can tell him you're a lesbian, and if he doesn't let you be with his kids anymore, I'll punch him in the face. That was me kidding.

Kali: You're funny. *(Pause.)* Maybe I told you because somewhere deep down, I do want him to know. But I don't know if I can take the risk.

Steve: You don't have to rush.

Kali: I just wish it could be more simple. Like, why can't what I want be part of the whole picket-fence thing? That's pretty ridiculous, huh?

Steve: We're all looking for that. My grandparents met before World War II, dated for seven days in a row, and my grandfather asked my grandmother to go with him to Louisiana, where he'd be stationed. She said, "Is that a proposal?" And he said, "Of course it is." And they've been together ever since. And I just want that, too. Huh — asking you to marry me on a first date! You must think I'm pretty desperate, huh?

Kali: Not any more than the rest of us . . . Oh, hell, do you want to have some dessert?

Steve: Oh, hell, sure. You know, we're going to share dessert.

Kali: Hey, mate, no one said anything about sharing.

Steve: I would go home with you for Diwali. I mean, as friends. If you ever wanted one around. You're a nice girl, Kali. I mean woman, mate, bloke. I mean —

Kali: Sssshhhh. Let's just get some dessert.

(Lights fade as they motion for the waiter. Blackout.)

What's the Meta?

Andrew Biss, a native of England and graduate of University of the Arts London, writes in the United States where many of his award-winning plays have been produced, including *The End of the World,* also published as a novel in 2011. In addition to *Schisms: A Psychological Thriller* (2011), he has published two short story collections, *The Impressionists* and *Strange Tales of the Curiously Uncommon*, in 2012. As brief as it is, *What's the Meta?* goes a long way in wittily articulating what constitutes a dramatic work of art.

> **WHEN I WRITE** "To misquote Shakespeare — this above all else: to thine own voice be true. Don't feel like you have to write in the style of someone else or mimic what's popular. Your influences will filter naturally into what becomes your own voice. Embrace it — it will be your best friend."   —ANDREW BISS

ANDREW BISS (B. 1962)
What's the Meta?   2004

CHARACTERS

Part 1, A written part in a script.
Part 2, A written part in a script.

SETTING: A stage.

TIME: The present.

NOTE: Both parts can be performed by any age, race, gender / orientation, etc., and in any combination thereof.

> *Two Parts on a stage in tableaux. After a moment, Part 1 emits a deep sigh. Part 2 turns and looks briefly at Part 1 before returning to his or her original pose. Soon after, Part 1 elicits another deep sigh.*

Part 2: (*Again, looking back at Part 1.*) Is something wrong?

(*Beat. Part 1 shrugs off the question dismissively.*)

Part 2: I asked you a question.
Part 1: I know.
Part 2: Well? What's the matter?
Part 1: You wouldn't understand. Don't worry about it.

(*Beat.*)

Part 2: All right, first of all you have but the most rudimentary knowledge of who I am — me — so to assume that I wouldn't understand is presumptuous to say the least, and more than a little condescending. And secondly, I have to worry about it because I'm alone out here with you and a show's about to begin, so if there is a problem, I freely and openly admit to harboring a desire to see it resolved as quickly as possible. OK?

(*Beat.*)

Part 1: Whatever.

Part 2: *(Enraged.)* What? How dare you — dare you! — you, as thoughtfully transcribed literature, utter that mindless catchall phrase that is the embodiment of total, unmitigated verbal and mental atrophy.

Part 1: It's not my fault. *(Beat.)* I'm a victim of circumstance.

Part 2: What circumstance? What's your problem? Stop whinging and just out with it.

(Beat.)

Part 1: I'm . . . I don't have . . . I lack motivation.

(Beat.)

Part 2: That's it?

Part 1: Yes.

Part 2: So what's the big deal? I don't have it either. Most people don't. We just have to force ourselves. Force ourselves to go on.

Part 1: I can't. There's nothing there.

Part 2: I know it feels that way sometimes, but you just have to buck up and press on.

Part 1: Oh yes, it's all right for you, isn't it?

Part 2: What do you mean?

Part 1: Because you're . . . fleshed out.

Part 2: No I'm not.

Part 1: Compared to me you are. You're multidimensional. I'm just a cipher. A convenient device thrown in by the writer to expound upon a certain point of view.

Part 2: But you're relevant. You have relevancy. You're integral to the story.

Part 1: Only in a narrative sense. I don't really belong.

Part 2: Don't be so self-pitying.

Part 1: I'm not, I'm just being honest.

Part 2: Look, a major and completely unexpected plot point hinges upon your sudden appearance in the proceedings. Without you the play wouldn't be turned on its head at the end of act one, leaving the audience breathless and gasping in anticipation — on a good night, at least.

Part 1: That's very kind of you, and I know you mean well, but I'm not so underwritten as to be painfully aware of the fact that I'm just a tool. And I can accept that — I can. But not happily.

Part 2: I think you're being a bit hard on yourself, don't you?

Part 1: *(Defensively.)* I'm not being hard on myself. It was all I was given.

Part 2: Then make the most of it.

Part 1: Oh, right! Says you. It's all right for you — it's all downhill for you. You get to reveal a multitude of levels and depths as you continue your ninety-minute journey from point A to point B. Your character's arc gradually draws the audience in and endears you to them in ways that initially they would never have dreamt possible, leaving them satisfied and intrigued. Much to their astonishment, this person that they found themselves initially repulsed by turns out to be a complex and all too human representation of someone that they can empathize and identify with. As they walk out of the main door into the night air, they feel buoyed from a sense of having spent an evening and some hard-earned money in a rewarding and enlightening manner . . . with you.

Part 2: What's wrong with that?

Part 1: Nothing at all. But it wasn't my journey they were taking, it was yours. I was just a plot point.

Part 2: A vital one.

Part 1: In your story.

Part 2: In the story.

Part 1: In your story. I am a catalyst—nothing more. I have no depth. I have no raison d'etre. I have no inner life. *(Beat.)* And I damned well want one and I don't care who knows it!

Part 2: I think you've already started to give yourself one, don't you, the way you're carrying on?

(Beat.)

Part 1: Perhaps. Perhaps it's a start. *(Beat.)* But I shouldn't have to fight for it, and that's my point.

Part 2: Why not? Anything in this life worth a damn is worth fighting for.

Part 1: Maybe so, but it's so much harder for me, don't you see, because I . . . I lack—

Part 2: (Impatiently.) Motivation—yes, yes, yes, I got that part.

Part 1: There's no need to be so testy. It's not my fault I was underwritten.

Part 2: No, but it's not mine either. I didn't ask to be written as a bigger part. I didn't ask to be more absorbing and relevant to the current state of the human condition. You're behaving as if it were some sort of competition.

Part 1: Oh, "absorbing" are we now?

Part 2: (Uncomfortably.) Well . . . I'm speaking theoretically, of course. I mean . . . that's the writer's intention, it's nothing to do with me. I'm not saying that I'm personally absorbing, I'm just reflecting the viewpoint of—

Part 1: Is this preshow, by the way?

Part 2: What?

Part 2: This.

Part 1: This? No.

Part 1: Then what is it?

Part 2: It's, uh . . . it's pre-preshow.

(Beat.)

Part 1: What's that?

Part 2: It's sort of like . . . Off-Off-Broadway.

Part 1: Meaning?

Part 2: Well, it's not there, but it's not quite there either . . . so it's sort of almost not quite there.

Part 1: Where's there?

Part 2: Somewhere else.

Part 1: Sounds very ephemeral.

Part 2: Yes it is — and that's the beauty of it. And by the way, you're sounding more dimensional by the minute.

Part 1: Oh, thank you. Against type, I might add.

Part 2: Indeed.

Part 1: Come to think of it, I meant to ask you about that earlier — are we characters?

Part 2: (*Astonished.*) Us?

Part 1: Yes.

Part 2: No, no, no, of course not. I'm happy to see you become a little more well rounded but don't get overinflated at the same time.

Part 1: Then what are we?

Part 2: Words! We're just words. Well, not just words. Words are the most important part. But after all, we mustn't get too far ahead of ourselves — we still only exist on paper.

Part 1: Then why are we here?

Part 2: I'm not here.

Part 1: You're not?

Part 2: Of course not.

Part 1: Am I?

Part 2: No.

(*Beat.*)

Part 1: (*Dispirited.*) But I . . . I thought I was a character. Or at the very least . . . struggling to become one out of what little I am.

Part 2: No, no, no, there you go again — you have it all wrong.

Part 1: Then what am I?

Part 2: (*Implicitly.*) Ink on paper.

(*Beat.*)

Part 1: That's all?

Part 2: "That's all"? You ingrate! Don't you have the slightest conception of what that means? You are the conception, you fool! You are the birth. Without you nothing happens. Without you there is no play. Without you there is no novel, no film, no poem, nor any of their bastard relations. You are the seed — the root of it all.

Part 1: (*Ingenuously.*) I don't feel like it.

Part 2: Not you in yourself, necessarily, but in what you represent. You are ink on paper. From quill to laser jet printer, you are and always will be the beginning. Others may mold you and shape you according to their will — for better or worse — but you will always be the font, in every sense of the word. It's what you are.

(*Pause.*)

Part 1: Gosh . . . I'd never thought about it like that. All of a sudden I . . . I don't feel so sketched out and plot-convenient. Thank you. Thank you very much.

Part 2: I'm glad. And don't thank me — they weren't my words.

(*Pause.*)

Part 1: So what's next?

Part 2: Preshow.

Part 1: And that is?

Part 2: When the others take over.

Part 1: Take over what?

Part 2: Us.

Part 1: Which, in strict definition, means?

Part 2: Strictly speaking I wouldn't like to say, but which includes — though is by no means limited to . . . makeup, gargling, vocal exercises, diarrhea, frantic last-minute line readings, focus, pace, sense memory recall, and stumbling around in the dark trying to find your spot, praying to God that you do before the lights come up and expose you as a co-conspirator in the enormous piece of artifice that you are attempting to lay before a potentially skeptical, though willingly complicit public.

(*Beat.*)

Part 1: Good heavens! (*Beat.*) I think I'll just sink back into the paper and relax for a while, if it's all the same to you.

Part 2: Trust me, I'm about to do the same thing.

(*Beat.*)

Part 1: (*Awkwardly.*) By the way . . . well . . . if you don't mind my asking . . . are you male or female?

Part 2: Didn't you read the play?

Part 1: (*Somewhat embarrassed.*) Yes, but . . . mostly my bits . . . skipped the rest. It was a quick read.

Part 2: (*Reprovingly.*) Then shame on you. As I told you before, big or small we are all part of a whole and our acknowledgment of that is the only way we can function properly — all working together. If you don't have the last little piece you'll never complete the puzzle.

Part 1: Sorry.

Part 2: Anyway, does it matter?

Part 1: What?

Part 2: My gender?

Part 1: Not to me.

Part 2: So why ask?

Part 1: Well . . . I was just wondering if you fancied going for a drink — with me.

Part 2: Now?

Part 1: Only if you want to. I'm not trying to . . . no strings . . . I just . . . well, I sort of like you . . . in a way, and . . . anyway . . .

Part 2: As a matter of fact, I would love to—I am, quite literally, dying for a drink. Let's leave them to do what they will—good, bad, or just plain incomprehensible.

Part 1: And perhaps afterwards I could show you a bit of my subtext I've been working on.

Part 2: Easy tiger, let's not get carried away. One step at a time.

Part 1: Sorry, I wasn't trying to . . . *(Gesturing.)* Anyway, after you.

Part 2: *(Gesturing.)* No, no, I insist—after you. *(Beat.)* Did you have somewhere in mind?

Part 1: *(Begins exiting.)* No, do you?

Part 2: *(Begins exiting.)* No, but I know a nice place on 46th and First.

Part 1: *(Upon exiting.)* Sounds like a good place to start.

Part 2: *(Upon exiting.)* And end.

(The light fades to black.)

End of play

Trying to Find Chinatown

Born in Los Angeles, David Henry Hwang is the son of immigrant Chinese American parents. Educated at Stanford University, from which he earned a B.A. in English in 1979, his marginal interest in a law career quickly gave way to his involvement in the engaging world of live theater. By his senior year, he had written and produced his first play, *FOB* (an acronym for "fresh off the boat"), which marked the beginning of a meteoric rise as a playwright.

Although Hwang was successful in having plays produced in the mid-1980s and won prestigious fellowships from the Guggenheim Foundation and the National Endowment for the Arts, it was not until 1988, when *M. Butterfly*— a complex treatment of social, political, racial, cultural, and sexual issues—was produced on Broadway, that he achieved astonishing commercial success as well as widespread acclaim. His awards for this play include the Outer Critics Circle Award for best Broadway play, the Drama Desk Award for best new play, the John Gassner Award for best American play, and the Tony Award for best play of the year. One of his most recent plays, *Chinglish,* is a humorous treatment of an American businessman in China. By the end of 1988, Hwang was regarded by many critics as the most talented

© Michal Daniel.

young playwright in the United States. *Trying to Find Chinatown* is a brief but complicated confrontation between two young men who argue about racial identity in unexpected ways. Hwang's strategy is to challenge the polemical stereotyping that often passes for discussions of ethnic and cultural heritage in the United States.

DAVID HENRY HWANG (B. 1957)

Trying to Find Chinatown   1996

CHARACTERS

Benjamin, Caucasian male, early twenties.
Ronnie, Asian-American male, mid-twenties.

TIME AND PLACE: A street corner on the Lower East Side, New York City. The present.

NOTE ON MUSIC: Obviously, it would be foolish to require that the actor portraying Ronnie perform the specified violin music live. The score of this play can be played on tape over the house speakers, and the actor can feign playing the violin using a bow treated with soap. However, in order to effect a convincing illusion, it is desirable that the actor possess some familiarity with the violin or another stringed instrument.

> *Darkness. Over the house speakers, sound fades in: Hendrix-like virtuoso rock 'n' roll riffs—heavy feedback, distortion, phase shifting, wah-wah—amplified over a tiny Fender pug-nose.*
>
> *Lights fade up to reveal that the music's being played over a solid-body electric violin by Ronnie, a Chinese-American male in his mid-twenties; he is dressed in retro-'60s clothing and has a few requisite '90s body mutilations. He's playing on a sidewalk for money, his violin case open before him; change and a few stray bills have been left by previous passersby.*
>
> *Benjamin enters; he's in his early twenties, blond, blue-eyed, a Midwestern tourist in the big city. He holds a scrap of paper in his hands, scanning street signs for an address. He pauses before Ronnie, listens for a while. With a truly bravura run, Ronnie concludes the number and falls to his knees, gasping. Benjamin applauds.*

Benjamin: Good. That was really great. (*Pause*) I didn't . . . I mean, a fiddle . . . I mean, I'd heard them at square dances, on country stations and all, but I never . . . wow, this must really be New York City!

> (*Benjamin applauds, starts to walk on. Still on his knees, Ronnie clears his throat loudly.*)

Oh, I . . . you're not just doing this for your health, right?

(Benjamin reaches in his pocket, pulls out a couple of coins. Ronnie clears his throat again.)

Look, I'm not a millionaire, I'm just . . .

(Benjamin pulls out his wallet, removes a dollar bill. Ronnie nods his head and gestures toward the violin case as he takes out a pack of cigarettes, lights one.)

Ronnie: And don't call it a "fiddle," OK?

Benjamin: Oh. Well, I didn't mean to —

Ronnie: You sound like a wuss. A hick. A dipshit.

Benjamin: It just slipped out. I didn't really —

Ronnie: If this was a fiddle, I'd be sitting here with a cob pipe, stomping my cowboy boots and kicking up hay. Then I'd go home and fuck my cousin.

Benjamin: Oh! Well, I don't really think —

Ronnie: Do you see a cob pipe? Am I fucking my cousin?

Benjamin: Well, no, not at the moment, but —

Ronnie: All right. Then this is a violin, now you give me your money, and I ignore the insult. Herein endeth the lesson.

(Pause.)

Benjamin: Look, a dollar's more than I've ever given to a . . . to someone asking for money.

Ronnie: Yeah, well, this is New York. Welcome to the cost of living.

Benjamin: What I mean is, maybe in exchange, you could help me —?

Ronnie: Jesus Christ! Do you see a sign around my neck reading "Big Apple Fucking Tourist Bureau"?

Benjamin: I'm just looking for an address, I don't think it's far from here, maybe you could . . . ?

(Benjamin holds out his scrap of paper, Ronnie snatches it away.)

Ronnie: You're lucky I'm such a goddamn softy. *(He looks at the paper)* Oh, fuck you. Just suck my dick, you and the cousin you rode in on.

Benjamin: I don't get it! What are you —?

Ronnie: Eat me. You know exactly what I —

Benjamin: I'm just asking for a little —

Ronnie: "13 Doyers Street"? Like you don't know where that is?

Benjamin: Of course I don't know! That's why I'm asking —

Ronnie: C'mon, you trailer-park refugee. You don't know that's Chinatown?

Benjamin: Sure I know that's Chinatown.

Ronnie: I know you know that's Chinatown.

Benjamin: So? That doesn't mean I know where Chinatown —

Ronnie: So why is it that you picked *me*, of all the street musicians in the city — to point you in the direction of Chinatown? Lemme guess — is

Trying to Find Chinatown: Richard Thompson as Benjamin and Zar Acayan as Ronnie in *Trying to Find Chinatown*, during the 20th Annual Humana Festival of New American Plays, at the Actors Theatre of Louisville, Kentucky, in 1996. Courtesy of the Actors Theatre of Louisville.

it the earring? No, I don't think so. The Hendrix riffs? Guess again, you fucking moron.

Benjamin: Now, wait a minute. I see what you're—

Ronnie: What are you gonna ask me next? Where you can find the best dim sum in the city? Whether I can direct you to a genuine opium den? Or do I happen to know how you can meet Miss Saigon for a night of nookie-nookie followed by a good old-fashioned ritual suicide? Now, get your white ass off my sidewalk. One dollar doesn't even begin to make up for all this aggravation. Why don't you go back home and race bullfrogs, or whatever it is you do for—?

Benjamin: Brother, I can absolutely relate to your anger. Righteous rage, I suppose, would be a more appropriate term. To be marginalized, as we are, by a white racist patriarchy, to the point where the accomplishments of our people are obliterated from the history books, this is cultural genocide of the first order, leading to the fact that you must do battle with all of Euro-America's emasculating and brutal stereotypes of Asians—the opium den, the sexual objectification of the Asian female, the exoticized image of a tourist's Chinatown which ignores the exploitation of workers, the failure to unionize, the high rate of mental illness and tuberculosis — against these, each day, you rage, no, not as a victim, but as a survivor, yes, brother, a glorious warrior survivor!

(Silence.)

Ronnie: Say what?
Benjamin: So, I hope you can see that my request is not —
Ronnie: Wait, wait.
Benjamin: — motivated by the sorts of racist assumptions —
Ronnie: But, but where . . . how did you learn all that?
Benjamin: All what?
Ronnie: All that — you know — oppression stuff — tuberculosis . . .
Benjamin: It's statistically irrefutable. TB occurs in the community at a rate —
Ronnie: Where did *you* learn it?
Benjamin: I took Asian-American studies. In college.
Ronnie: Where did you go to college?
Benjamin: University of Wisconsin. Madison.
Ronnie: Madison, Wisconsin?
Benjamin: That's not where the bridges are, by the way.
Ronnie: Huh? Oh, right . . .
Benjamin: You wouldn't believe the number of people who —
Ronnie: They have Asian-American studies in Madison, Wisconsin? Since when?
Benjamin: Since the last Third World Unity hunger strike. *(Pause)* Why do you look so surprised? We're down.
Ronnie: I dunno. It just never occurred to me, the idea of Asian students in the Midwest going on a hunger strike.
Benjamin: Well, a lot of them had midterms that week, so they fasted in shifts. *(Pause)* The administration never figured it out. The Asian students put that "They all look alike" stereotype to good use.
Ronnie: OK, so they got Asian-American studies. That still doesn't explain —
Benjamin: What?
Ronnie: Well . . . what *you* were doing taking it?
Benjamin: Just like everyone else. I wanted to explore my roots. And, you know, the history of oppression which is my legacy. After a lifetime of assimilation, I wanted to find out who I really am.

(Pause.)

Ronnie: And did you?
Benjamin: Sure. I learned to take pride in my ancestors who built the railroads, my Popo who would make me a hot bowl of jok with thousand-day-old eggs when the white kids chased me home yelling, "Gook! Chink! Slant-eyes!"

Ronnie: OK, OK, that's enough!

Benjamin: Painful to listen to, isn't it?

Ronnie: I don't know what kind of bullshit ethnic studies program they're running over in Wuss-consin, but did they bother to teach you that in order to find your Asian "roots," it's a good idea to first be Asian?

(Pause.)

Benjamin: Are you speaking metaphorically?

Ronnie: No! Literally! Look at your skin!

Benjamin: You know, it's very stereotypical to think that all Asian skin tones conform to a single hue.

Ronnie: You're white! Is this some kind of redneck joke or something? Am I the first person in the world to tell you this?

Benjamin: Oh! Oh! Oh!

Ronnie: I know real Asians are scarce in the Midwest, but . . . Jesus!

Benjamin: No, of course, I . . . I see where your misunderstanding arises.

Ronnie: Yeah. It's called, "You white."

Benjamin: It's just that—in my hometown of Tribune, Kansas, and then at school—see, everyone knows me—so this sort of thing never comes up. *(He offers his hand)* Benjamin Wong. I forget that a society wedded to racial constructs constantly forces me to explain my very existence.

Ronnie: Ronnie Chang. Otherwise known as "The Bow Man."

Benjamin: You see, I was adopted by Chinese-American parents at birth. So, clearly, I'm an Asian-American—

Ronnie: Even though you're blond and blue-eyed.

Benjamin: Well, you can't judge my race by my genetic heritage alone.

Ronnie: If genes don't determine race, what does?

Benjamin: Perhaps you'd prefer that I continue in denial, masquerading as a white man?

Ronnie: You can't just wake up and say, "Gee, I *feel* black today."

Benjamin: Brother, I'm just trying to find what you've already got.

Ronnie: What do I got?

Benjamin: A home. With your people. Picketing with the laundry workers. Taking refuge from the daily slights against your masculinity in the noble image of Gwan Gung.

Ronnie: Gwan who?

Benjamin: C'mon—the Chinese god of warriors and—what do you take me for? There're altars to him up all over the community.

Ronnie: I dunno what community you're talking about, but it's sure as hell not mine.

(Pause.)

Benjamin: What do you mean?

Ronnie: I mean, if you wanna call Chinatown *your* community, OK, knock yourself out, learn to use chopsticks, big deal. Go ahead, try and find your "roots" in some dim sum parlor with headless ducks hanging in the window. Those places don't tell you a thing about who *I* am.

Benjamin: Oh, I get it.

Ronnie: You get what?

Benjamin: You're one of those self-hating, *assimilated* Chinese-Americans, aren't you?

Ronnie: Oh, Jesus.

Benjamin: You probably call yourself "Oriental," huh? Look, maybe I can help you. I have some books I can—

Ronnie: Hey, I read all those Asian identity books when you were still slathering on industrial-strength sunblock. *(Pause)* Sure, I'm Chinese. But folks like you act like that means something. Like, all of a sudden, you know who I am. You think identity's that simple? That you can wrap it all up in a neat package and say, "I have ethnicity, therefore I am"? All you fucking ethnic fundamentalists. Always settling for easy answers. You say you're looking for identity, but you can't begin to face the real mysteries of the search. So instead, you go skin-deep, and call it a day. *(Pause. He turns away from Benjamin and starts to play his violin—slow and bluesy.)*

Benjamin: So what are you? "Just a human being"? That's like saying you *have* no identity. If you asked me to describe my dog, I'd say more than, "He's just a dog."

Ronnie: What—you think if I deny the importance of my race, I'm nobody? There're worlds out there, worlds you haven't even begun to understand. Open your eyes. Hear with your ears.

(Ronnie holds his violin at chest level, but does not attempt to play during the following monologue. As he speaks, rock and jazz violin tracks fade in and out over the house speakers, bringing to life the styles of music he describes.)

I concede—it was called a fiddle long ago—but that was even before the birth of jazz. When the hollering in the fields, the rank injustice of human bondage, the struggle of God's children against the plagues of the devil's white man, when all these boiled up into that bittersweet brew, called by later generations, the blues. That's when fiddlers like Son Sims held their chin rests at their chests, and sawed away like the hillbillies still do today. And with the coming of ragtime appeared the pioneer Stuff Smith, who sang as he stroked the catgut, with his raspy, Louis Armstrong–voice—gruff and sweet like the timber of horsehair riding south below the fingerboard—and who finally sailed for Europe to find ears that would hear. Europe—where Stephane Grappelli initiated a magical French violin, to be passed from generation to generation—first he, to Jean-Luc Ponty, then Ponty to Didier Lockwood. Listening to Grappelli play "A Nightingale Sang in Berkeley Square" is to understand not only the song of birds, but also how they learn to fly, fall in love on the wing, and finally falter one day, to wait for darkness beneath a

London street lamp. And Ponty — he showed how the modern violin man can accompany the shadow of his own lead lines, which cascade, one over another, into some nether world beyond the range of human hearing. Joe Venuti. Noel Pointer. Sven Asmussen. Even the Kronos Quartet, with their arrangement of "Purple Haze." Now, tell me, could any legacy be more rich, more crowded with mythology and heroes to inspire pride? What can I say if the banging of a gong or the clinking of a pickax on the Transcontinental Railroad fails to move me even as much as one note, played through a violin MIDI controller by Michael Urbaniak? *(He puts his violin to his chin, begins to play a jazz composition of his own invention)* Does it have to sound like Chinese opera before people like you decide I know who I am?

(Benjamin stands for a long moment, listening to Ronnie play. Then, he drops his dollar into the case, turns and exits right. Ronnie continues to play a long moment. Then Benjamin enters downstage left, illuminated in his own spotlight. He sits on the floor of the stage, his feet dangling off the lip. As he speaks, Ronnie continues playing his tune, which becomes underscoring for Benjamin's monologue. As the music continues, does it slowly begin to reflect the influence of Chinese music?)

Benjamin: When I finally found Doyers Street, I scanned the buildings for Number 13. Walking down an alley where the scent of freshly steamed char siu bao lingered in the air, I felt immediately that I had entered a world where all things were finally familiar. *(Pause)* An old woman bumped me with her shopping bag — screaming to her friend in Cantonese, though they walked no more than a few inches apart. Another man — shouting to a vendor in Sze-Yup. A youth, in white undershirt, perhaps a recent newcomer, bargaining with a grocer in Hokkien. I walked through this ocean of dialects, breathing in the richness with deep gulps, exhilarated by the energy this symphony brought to my step. And when I finally saw the number 13, I nearly wept at my good fortune. An old tenement, paint peeling, inside walls no doubt thick with a century of grease and broken dreams — and yet, to me, a temple — the house where my father was born. I suddenly saw it all: Gung Gung, coming home from his sixteen-hour days pressing shirts he could never afford to own, bringing with him candies for my father, each sweet wrapped in the hope of a better life. When my father left the ghetto, he swore he would never return. But he had, this day, in the thoughts and memories of his son, just six months after his death. And as I sat on the stoop, I pulled a hua-moi° from my pocket, sucked on it, and felt his spirit returning. To this place where his ghost, and the dutiful hearts of all his descendants, would always call home. *(He listens for a long moment)* And I felt an ache in my heart for all those lost souls, denied this most important of revelations: to know who they truly are.

hua-moi: A dry, sour plum that is a Cantonese specialty food.

(Benjamin sucks his salted plum and listens to the sounds around him. Ronnie continues to play. The two remain oblivious of one another. Lights fade slowly to black.)

End of play

The Blizzard

David Ives is perhaps best known for his evenings of one-act comedies collectively titled *All in the Timing* and *Time Flies* as well as for his drama *Venus in Fur*. Other plays include *New Jerusalem: The Interrogation of Baruch de Spinoza; The Liar* (adapted from Pierre Corneille's comedy); *The School for Lies* (adapted from Molière's *The Misanthrope*); *The Heir Apparent* (adapted from J-F. Regnard); and *Is He Dead?* (adapted from Mark Twain). Born in Chicago and educated at Northwestern University and the Yale School of Drama, Ives is a former Guggenheim Fellow in playwriting and lives in New York City. *The Blizzard* is a menacingly comic drama about a couple isolated by a storm in a country house.

© Peter Bellamy.

WHEN I WRITE "I have worked on writing schedules covering every hour of the day. All schedules are good. All rituals are good. All writing superstitions are good. The point is not to have a writing schedule; the point is to write." —DAVID IVES

DAVID IVES (B. 1950)

The Blizzard   2006

CHARACTERS

Jenny
Neil
Salim
Natasha

A country house, toward evening. Cold winter light in the windows. In the course of the play, the lights gradually dim around center stage to nighttime. At curtain, Jenny is onstage alone.

Jenny: *(Calls.)* Neil? — Neil! *(Neil enters from outside, stage right.)*
Neil: It's still coming down. Some of those drifts are three feet deep already. What's the matter?

Jenny: Nothing. I just wondered what happened to you.

Neil: Got scared, huh?

Jenny: No, I wasn't *scared.* The food's all ready. Do you really think they'll make it up here in this?

Neil: Joe's got those new chains on the car. The ones that Sandy made him fork out for? Just what you'd expect from Miss Rationality.

Jenny: Right. Mr. *List Maker.* Mr. My-Pencils-Have-to-Be-Laid-Out-in-the-Right-Order-on-My-Desk. No, you're not rational. Sandy is rational.

Neil: What about the TV?

Jenny: Nothing. Not a thing.

Neil: The electricity's on. You'd think with a satellite dish we'd pick up *some*thing.

Jenny: The telephone's still out.

Neil: They've probably been trying us since they left the city.

Jenny: There's no radio either.

Neil: No *radio?*

Jenny: Isn't it *great?* It's just like an Agatha Christie.

Neil: Thanks for that. I'm still not used to it. Being so remote. Nature's always scared the living crap out of me. Now I'm living in it. Or visiting it on weekends, anyway. You know I saw a bat flapping around out there? I didn't know there were bats in blizzards. No *radio?* The world could be ending out there, for Christ's sake. And we'd be the last ones to hear about it. No *radio . . .*

Jenny: Yes, we have no radio and a beautiful blizzard and a house and woods and a mountain that are all ours.

Neil: All ours in twenty-nine years and three months.

Jenny: I kind of wish they weren't coming up tonight. It's so cozy. I wouldn't mind curling up with a book.

Neil: I wish you hadn't said "Agatha Christie."

Jenny: You inflict *Torturama* One, Two and Three on people and I can't say "Agatha Christie"?

Neil: Those are movies, not a real house in the middle of the real country with the lines down. And *Torturama* paid for our little mansion on a hill, babe.

Jenny: You know what it is about murder mysteries? No, listen. I think the reason people like murder mysteries is that, in a murder mystery, everything is *significant.* The people in murder mysteries are living in a *significant world.* A world where everything is there for a reason. Even before the murder's happened, you know that one is going to happen and you know that everything is a *clue.* Or rather, you know that some things are clues and some things are just obfuscation, they're snow. And you know that everybody has a secret of some kind. A secret that's like a soul. Murder mysteries are religious, in a way. Don't laugh. They're life the way you feel it when you're in love. When everything's in a special light. Incandescent. They're a couple of hours of everything *meaning* something, for God's sake. And then they're over and you're back to your old life, to real life. To mortgages and pork loin and potatoes and making a cherry pie.

Neil: So real life doesn't feel like it means something to you these days?

Jenny: Sure it does. I'm just saying . . . Well, don't we all wish for that in real life? One of those moments when everything feels charged with meaning? When the air is electric?

Neil: Well here's your opportunity. Listen, we're probably going to be totally snowed in. Why don't we all do something different this weekend.

Jenny: Different, what does different mean?

Neil: I don't know. Something unusual. Something unexpected. Not you and Sandy holing yourself up in the kitchen and talking about whatever you talk about, not me and Joe sitting around talking about Mom and Dad and what happened in the third grade. Not the usual pour-a-glass-of-Jack-Daniel's, bullshit bullshit bullshit, what've you guys been doing, go in to dinner and break out the Margaux '01, have you seen any movies, did you catch that episode of blah blah blah. I don't know, something we've never done before, or let's talk about something we've never talked about before. Anything, instead of all the things we usually talk about.

Jenny: Okay. Something unusual. I love it.

Salim: (Offstage.) Hello —? Neil?

Neil: There they are. *(Salim and Natasha enter from the front door at stage left. Salim carries a black plastic valise.)*

Salim: Hello! Neil and Jenny, right? Sorry for the cold hand, I'm freezing. God, you're just like Joe and Sandy described you. I can't believe I'm finally meeting you, Neil. I am such a fan of *Torturama*. All of them. Natasha can't watch them herself. Natasha is squeamish.

Neil: I'm sorry, I don't understand . . .

Salim: Salim. And Natasha.

Natasha: Hello. I'm so happy to encounter you at last. And you, Jenny, you are just as beautiful as Sandy told me. You are exquisite.

Salim: And God, what a place up here! But so remote! Wow! We brought this for you. *(Holds up the black valise.)* A little house-warming gift.

Neil: Whoa, whoa, whoa. I'm sorry, maybe there's been a mistake . . .

Salim: I mean, this is the place, isn't it? You're Neil and Jenny? Oh, right, right. *Where are Joe and Sandy.* Middle of a snowstorm. Two strange people walk in. You're spooked. Totally natural. Natasha?

Natasha: Joe and Sandy couldn't make it, so they sent us instead.

Neil: They sent you instead. Wait a minute. They sent *you* instead . . .

Salim: They caught some kind of bug. God, Joe and Sandy have been telling us all about you two for I don't know how long.

Natasha: A long time.

Salim: A very long time.

Neil: I don't think Joe and Sandy ever mentioned knowing a . . . I'm sorry . . .

Salim: Salim.

Neil: A Salim and a Natasha.

Salim: You've been out of touch with your brother for too long, brother. They were really broken up they couldn't make it tonight. I'd say call them up and ask them but hey, are your cell phones as down as ours up here?

Jenny: How do you know Joe and Sandy?

Salim: (*The black valise.*) You know what's in here? Just for showing us your hospitality? It's this new tequila, a hundred bucks a bottle. Olé, right? Let's support those oppressed brothers churning this stuff out for ten pesos a day. Neil, you want to pour?

Jenny: You didn't answer me.

Natasha: How do we know Joe and Sandy.

Salim: How do we know Joe and Sandy. How do we know them, Natasha?

Natasha: Intimately.

Salim: Intimately. Good word. We know them intimately.

Jenny: Neil . . . Neil . . .

Neil: Look, I'm very sorry, but I'm going to have to ask you to leave.

Salim: To leave? But . . . okay, I get it, I get it, you want some kind of proof that we're not just what . . .

Natasha: Imposters.

Salim: Imposters. Ten points, Natasha. We're not imposters! We're the real thing! I'm sorry if I'm coming on kind of strong, it's my personality, you know what I mean? God, how do you prove that you know somebody? Let's see. Where do I start? Do I start with Joe or Sandy? You know she made him get these hotshot snow chains for the car. That is so Sandy. No imagination, but always thinking ahead. So *rational.* (*Pause.*) Listen. Listen, I'm sorry we barged in on you like this. Maybe we should leave, but . . . hey, are you really going to turn two freezing strangers back out into the storm? Neil, you're the guy who inflicted *Torturama* on the world, more killings per square frame than any movie in history. You're pouring blood in the aisles, man. Don't tell me you're scared. What are you scared of ? What am I, the wrong color? And what am I going to do to you, huh? If I was going to do something to you I'd've done it already, wouldn't I? (*Pause.*) So do we leave? Or do we stay? Aw, have a heart, Neil.

Neil: Well, we can't turn you out in this weather . . .

Jenny: Turn them out, Neil.

Neil: Honey, I . . .

Jenny: Turn them out.

Neil: It's a blizzard out there, honey.

Salim: Your wife is so sweet. Really. She is a doll.

Natasha: You know, with so much snow, it's like we're in a murder mystery here.

Salim: Natasha adores Agatha Christie. You know what I hate about murder mysteries? It's that everybody in them's got a secret. People

don't have secrets. People are open books. I don't know you personally, Neil, but just looking at you I'd say you're probably the kind of
guy who makes lists, for example. Lines his pencils up on the desk.
Likes things neat and tidy. Am I right? A Jack-Daniel's-before-dinner
kinda guy. You're not the kind of guy who, what, secretly worked for
the CIA once upon a time, you're not a guy with a secret history of
killing people, I mean *really* killing people, offscreen, you don't have
any real blood on your hands. You're in the entertainment industry.
You have nothing to hide.

Jenny: Send them away, Neil.

Salim: And Jenny, she probably made her usual dinner for tonight, let's
see what would it be, pork loin and some kind of special potato
recipe and a cherry-rhubarb pie for dessert. The perfect American
housewife. Nothing to conceal. I'm sorry, I'm sorry, there's that personality of mine again. I'm brash. I'm insensitive. I'm loud. Call me
American.

Neil: You know I have a gun in the house.

Salim: Oh, that's rich. What a liar! "I have a gun in the house." Right.
That's so cute. This isn't a movie, this is *real life*, Neil. And I'm your
brother for the night. I'm a stand-in for Joe. Remember me? Your
brother?

Jenny: Where are Joe and Sandy?

Salim: They're very sick in bed is where they are.

Jenny: What have you done with them?

Salim: They can't move is what they are. Aren't I your brother? Neil?
Come on. *(He puts his arm around Neil's waist.)* Am I your brother?

Neil: Sure . . .

Salim: Am I your brother? Am I your brother? Am I your brother?

Neil: You're my brother.

Salim: There you see? How hard was that? Now we can talk about all
those kids we used to beat up in third grade. Just like old times. Well,
brother, what do you say? We're here for the duration. You gonna
play the good host here or what? You want to show me around the
grounds?

Neil: Sure.

Salim: Sure what?

Neil: Sure, brother.

Salim: Attaboy! *(Salim follows Neil off through the back door. A pause.)*

Natasha: You know what I love about murder mysteries? Is that everything in them seems to mean something. The people in murder mysteries are living in a significant world. Everything holding its breath.
Waiting. The air is electric. And then, bang, it happens. The irrevo-
cable. Whatever that is. Changing everything. It's a kind of poetry.
To me, it's almost a religious feeling.

Jenny: I don't want any more fucking significance. I don't want it. I don't
want it.

Natasha: Poor Jenny. Afraid over nothing. Why? Why?
Jenny: You have the wrong people.
Natasha: You're the right people. Neil and Jenny. We're just here for din-
ner with you. And you have nothing to be afraid of. Really. Abso-
lutely nothing.
Jenny: (*Calls out.*) Neil . . .? *Neil* . . .?
Natasha: Absolutely nothing . . . (*The lights fade.*)

   End of play

Rodeo

Jane Martin is a pseudonym. The author's identity is known only
to a handful of administrators at the Actors Theatre of Louisville
who handle permissions for productions and reprints of the play.
Rodeo is one of eleven monologues in *Talking With.* . . . Martin has
also published other plays conveniently grouped in two volumes:
Jane Martin: Collected Plays 1980–1995 (1996) and *Jane Martin: Collected
Plays 1996–2001* (2001).
   Although only one character appears in *Rodeo*, the monologue is
surprisingly moving as she describes what the rodeo once was, how it
has changed, and what it means to her. At first glance the subject matter may not seem very promising for drama, but the character's energy,
forthrightness, and colorful language transform seemingly trivial details
into significant meanings.

JANE MARTIN

Rodeo   1981

> *A young woman in her late twenties sits working on a piece of tack.
> Beside her is a Lone Star beer in the can. As the lights come up we hear
> the last verse of a Tanya Tucker song or some other female country-
> western vocalist. She is wearing old worn jeans and boots plus a long-
> sleeved workshirt with the sleeves rolled up. She works until the song is
> over and then speaks.*

Big Eight: Shoot — Rodeo's just goin' to hell in a handbasket. Rodeo used
to be somethin'. I loved it. I did. Once Daddy an' a bunch of 'em was
foolin' around with some old bronc over to our place and this ol'
red nose named Cinch got bucked off and my Daddy hooted and
said he had him a nine-year-old girl, namely me, wouldn't have no
damn trouble cowboyin' that horse. Well, he put me on up there,
stuck that ridin' rein in my hand, gimme a kiss, and said, "Now
there's only one thing t' remember Honey Love, if ya fall off you
jest don't come home." Well I stayed up. You gotta stay on a bronc

eight seconds. Otherwise the ride don't count. So from that day on my daddy called me Big Eight. Heck! That's all the name I got anymore . . . Big Eight.

Used to be fer cowboys, the rodeo did. Do it in some open field, folks would pull their cars and pick-ups round it, sit on the hoods, some ranch hand'd bulldog him some rank steer and everybody'd wave their hats and call him by name. Ride us some buckin' stock, rope a few calves, git throwed off a bull, and then we'd jest git us to a bar and tell each other lies about how good we were.

Used to be a family thing. Wooly Billy Tilson and Tammy Lee had them five kids on the circuit. Three boys, two girls and Wooly and Tammy. Wasn't no two-beer rodeo in Oklahoma didn't have a Tilson entered. Used to call the oldest girl Tits. Tits Tilson. Never seen a girl that top-heavy could ride so well. Said she only fell off when the gravity got her. Cowboys used to say if she landed face down you could plant two young trees in the holes she'd leave. Ha! Tits Tilson.

Used to be people came to a rodeo had a horse of their own back home. Farm people, ranch people — lord, they *knew* what they were lookin' at. Knew a good ride from a bad ride, knew hard from easy. You broke some bones er spent the day eatin' dirt, at least ya got appreciated.

Now they bought the rodeo. Them. Coca-Cola, Pepsi Cola, Marlboro damn cigarettes. You know the ones I mean. Them. Hire some New York faggot t' sit on some ol' stuffed horse in front of a sagebrush photo n' smoke that junk. Hell, tobacco wasn't made to smoke, honey, it was made to chew. Lord wanted ya filled up with smoke he would've set ya on fire. Damn it gets me!

There's some guy in a banker's suit runs the rodeo now. Got him a pinky ring and a digital watch, honey. Told us we oughta have a watchamacallit, choriographus or somethin', some ol' ballbuster used to be with the Ice damn Capades. Wants us to ride around dressed up like Mickey Mouse, Pluto, crap like that. Told me I had to haul my butt through the barrel race done up like Minnie damn Mouse in a tu-tu. Huh uh, honey! Them people is so screwed-up they probably eat what they run over in the road.

Listen, they got the clowns wearin' Astronaut suits! I ain't lyin'. You know what a rodeo clown does! You go down, fall off whatever — the clown runs in front of the bull so's ya don't git stomped. Pin-stripes, he got 'em in space suits tellin' jokes on a microphone. First horse see 'em, done up like the Star Wars went crazy. Best buckin' horse on the circuit, name of Piss 'N' Vinegar, took one look at them clowns, had him a heart attack and died. Cowboy was ridin' him got hisself squashed. Twelve hundred pounds of coronary arrest jes fell right through 'em. Blam! Vio con dios. Crowd thought that was funnier than the astronauts. I swear it won't be

Rodeo: Margo Martindale
in *Rodeo,* during the Sixth
Annual Humana Festival
of New American Plays,
at the Actors Theatre of
Louisville, Kentucky, in
1982.
Katherine Wisniewski, photographer. Courtesy of the Actors
Theatre of Louisville.

long before they're strappin' ice-skates on the ponies. Big crowds
now. Ain't hardly no ranch people, no farm people, nobody I know.
Buncha disco babies and dee-vorce lawyers — designer jeans and day-
glo Stetsons. Hell, the whole bunch of 'em wears French perfume.
Oh it smells like money now! Got it on the cable T and V — hey, you
know what, when ya rodeo yer just bound to kick yerself up some
dust — well now, seems like that fogs up the ol' TV camera, so they
told us a while back that from now on we was gonna ride on some
new stuff called Astro-dirt. Dust free. Artificial damn dirt, honey.
Lord have mercy.

Banker Suit called me in the other day said "Lurlene ..." "Hold
it," I said, "Who's this Lurlene? Round here they call me Big Eight."
"Well, Big Eight," he said, "My name's Wallace." "Well that's a real
surprise t' me," I said, "Cause aroun' here everybody jes calls you
Dumb-ass." My, he laughed real big, slapped his big ol' desk, an'
then he said I wasn't suitable for the rodeo no more. Said they was
lookin' fer another type, somethin' a little more in the showgirl line,
like the Dallas Cowgirls maybe. Said the ridin' and ropin' wasn't the

thing no more. Talked on about floats, costumes, dancin' choreography. If I was a man I woulda pissed on his shoe. Said he'd give me a lifetime pass though. Said I could come to his rodeo any time I wanted.

Rodeo used to be people ridin' horses for the pleasure of people who rode horses—made you feel good about what you could do. Rodeo wasn't worth no money to nobody. Money didn't have nothing to do with it! Used to be seven Tilsons riding in the rodeo. Wouldn't none of 'em dress up like Donald damn Duck so they quit. That there's the law of gravity!

There's a bunch of assholes in this country sneak around until they see ya havin' fun and then they buy the fun and start in sellin' it. See, they figure if ya love it, they can sell it. Well you look out, honey! They want to make them a dollar out of what you love. Dress *you* up like Minnie Mouse. Sell your rodeo. Turn *yer* pleasure into Ice damn Capades. You hear what I'm sayin'? You're jus' merchandise to them, sweetie. You're jus' merchandise to them.

Blackout.

The Reprimand

Writer and director Jane Anderson started her career as an actor. She left college at the age of nineteen to pursue acting and was cast in the David Mamet hit play *Sexual Perversity in Chicago.* The experience familiarized Anderson with scriptwriting, and eventually she founded a writing group called New York Writers' Block. She later wrote and performed in a number of one-woman comedic plays, whose success afforded her the opportunity to write for the television sitcoms *The Facts of Life* and *The Wonder Years.*

Photo by permission of Jilly Wendell.

In 1986, Anderson wrote the play *Defying Gravity,* a composite of monologues about the space shuttle *Challenger* explosion. Her first screenplay, *The Positively True Adventures of the Alleged Texas Cheerleader-Murdering Mom,* was a satirical look at the true story of a Texas mother who tried to hire a contract killer to murder her daughter's rival (and her mother) for the junior high school cheerleading squad. The HBO movie starred Holly Hunter and gave Anderson instant notoriety as a screenwriter. She has written the screenplays for a number of movies since, including *The Baby Dance,* starring Jody Foster, and *When Billie Beat Bobby,* the story of tennis champion Billie Jean King beating an aging Bobby Riggs. In 2009 she was nominated for the Writer's Guild of

America Award for Best Dramatic Series for her writing on the second season of the television series *Mad Men*.

The Reprimand was one of five "phone plays" that premiered in February 2000 at the annual Humana Festival of New American Plays held at Actors Theatre in Louisville, Kentucky. The phone call is a traditional stage convention that consists of an actor providing one side of a conversation, but for the Humana Festival performances, the actors conversed offstage and the audience heard both sides of the three-minute conversations. In *The Reprimand,* the overheard conversation reveals a complicated power struggle between two women.

Jane Anderson (b. 1954)

The Reprimand   2000

CHARACTERS

Rhona
Mim

Rhona: . . . we need to talk about what you did in the meeting this morning.

Mim: My God, what?

Rhona: That reference you made about my weight.

Mim: What reference?

Rhona: When we came into the room and Jim was making the introductions, you said, "Oh Rhona, why don't you take the bigger chair."

Mim: But that was — I thought since this was your project that you should sit in the better chair.

Rhona: But you didn't say better, you said bigger.

Mim: I did? Honest to God, that isn't what I meant. I'm so sorry if it hurt your feelings.

Rhona: You didn't hurt my feelings. This has nothing to do with my feelings. What concerns me — and concerns Jim by the way — is how this could have undermined the project.

Mim: Jim said something about it?

Rhona: Yes.

Mim: What did he say?

Rhona: He thought your comment was inappropriate.

Mim: Really? How? I was talking about a chair.

Rhona: Mim, do you honestly think anyone in that room was really listening to what I had to say after you made that comment?

Mim: I thought they were very interested in what you had to say.

Rhona: Honey, there was a reason why Dick and Danny asked you all the follow-up questions.

Mim: But that's because I hadn't said anything up to that point. Look, I'm a little confused about Jim's reaction, because after the meeting he said he liked what I did with the follow-up.

Rhona: He should acknowledge what you do. And I know the reason why he's finally said something is because I've been telling him that you deserve more credit.

Mim: Oh, thank you. But I think Jim already respects what I do.

Rhona: He should respect you. But from what I've observed, I think — because you're an attractive woman — that he still uses you for window dressing. Especially when you're working with me. You know what I'm saying?

Mim: Well, if that's the case, Jim is a jerk.

Rhona: I know that. And I know you know that. But I think you still have a lot of anger about the situation and sometimes it really shows.

Mim: I don't mean it to show.

Rhona: I know that. Look, I consider you — regardless of what Jim thinks — I think you're really talented and I really love working with you.

Mim: And I enjoy working with you.

Rhona: Thank you. And that's why I want to keep things clear between us. Especially when we're working for men like Jim.

Mim: No, I agree, absolutely.

Rhona: *(To someone off-phone.)* Tell him I'll be right there. *(Back to Mim.)* Mim, sorry — I have Danny on the phone.

Mim: Oh — do you want to conference me in?

Rhona: I can handle it, but thank you. Mim, I'm so glad we had this talk.

Mim: Well, thank you for being so honest with me.

Rhona: And thank you for hearing me. I really appreciate it. Let's talk later?

Mim: Sure. *(Rhona hangs up. A beat.) (Mumbling.)* Fat pig. *(Hangs up.)*

CRITICAL THINKING AND WRITING

29

Reading and the Writing Process

© Mary Evans Picture
Library / Alamy.

> I can't write five words but that I change
> seven.
>
> —DOROTHY PARKER

THE PURPOSE AND VALUE
OF WRITING ABOUT LITERATURE

Introductory literature courses typically include three components—
reading, discussion, and writing. Students usually find the readings a
pleasure, the class discussions a revelation, and the writing assignments —
at least initially — a little intimidating. Writing an analysis of Melville's
use of walls in "Bartleby, the Scrivener" (p. 101), for example, may seem
considerably more daunting than making a case for animal rights or
analyzing a campus newspaper editorial that calls for grade reforms.
Like Bartleby, you might want to respond with "I would prefer not
to." Literary topics are not, however, all that different from the kinds
of papers assigned in English composition courses; many of the same
skills are required for both. Regardless of the type of paper, you must
develop a thesis and support it with evidence in language that is clear
and persuasive.

Whether the subject matter is a marketing survey, a political issue,
or a literary work, writing is a method of communicating information
and perceptions. Writing teaches. But before writing becomes an instrument for informing the reader, it serves as a means of learning for the
writer. An essay is a process of discovery as well as a record of what has

been discovered. One of the chief benefits of writing is that we frequently realize what we want to say only after trying out ideas on a page and seeing our thoughts take shape in language.

More specifically, writing about a literary work encourages us to be better readers because it requires a close examination of the elements of a short story, poem, or play. To determine how plot, character, setting, point of view, style, tone, irony, or any number of other literary elements function in a work, we must study them in relation to one another as well as separately. Speed-reading won't do. To read a text accurately and validly — neither ignoring nor distorting significant details — we must return to the work repeatedly to test our responses and interpretations. By paying attention to details and being sensitive to the author's use of language, we develop a clearer understanding of how the work conveys its effects and meanings.

READING THE WORK CLOSELY

Know the piece of literature you are writing about before you begin your essay. Think about how the work makes you feel and how it is put together. The more familiar you are with how the various elements of the text convey effects and meanings, the more confident you will be explaining whatever perspective on it you ultimately choose. Do not insist that everything make sense on a first reading. Relax and enjoy yourself; you can be attentive and still allow the author's words to work their magic on you. With subsequent readings, however, go more slowly and analytically as you try to establish relations between characters, actions, images, or whatever else seems important. Ask yourself why you respond as you do. Think as you read, and notice how the parts of a work contribute to its overall nature. Whether the work is a short story, poem, or play, you will read relevant portions of it over and over, and you will very likely find more to discuss in each review if the work is rich.

ANNOTATING THE TEXT AND JOURNAL NOTE TAKING

As you read, get in the habit of annotating your texts. Whether you write marginal notes, highlight, underline, or draw boxes and circles around important words and phrases, you'll eventually develop a system that allows you to retrieve significant ideas and elements from the text. Another way to record your impressions of a work — as with any other experience — is to keep a journal. By writing down your reactions to characters, images, language, actions, and other matters in a reading journal, you can often determine why you like or dislike a work or feel sympathetic or antagonistic to an author or discover paths into a work that might have eluded you if you hadn't preserved your impressions. Your journal notes and annotations may take whatever form you find useful; full sentences and grammatical correctness are not essential (unless they are to be handed in and your instructor requires that), though they might allow you to make better sense of your own reflections days later. The point is simply to put in writing thoughts that you can retrieve when you need them for class discussion or a writing assignment. Consider the following student annotation of the first twenty-four lines of Andrew Marvell's "To His Coy Mistress" (p. 382) and the journal entry that follows it:

Annotated Text

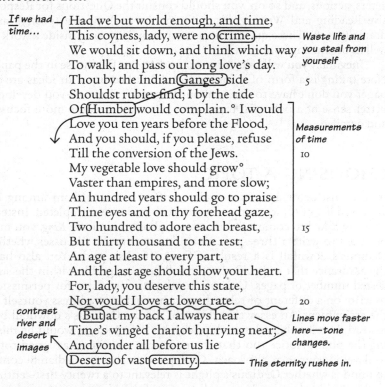

If we had time...

Had we but world enough, and time,
This coyness, lady, were no (crime.) —— *Waste life and you steal from yourself*
We would sit down, and think which way
To walk, and pass our long love's day.
Thou by the Indian (Ganges') side   5
Shouldst rubies find; I by the tide
Of (Humber) would complain.° I would
Love you ten years before the Flood,
And you should, if you please, refuse   *Measurements of time*
Till the conversion of the Jews.   10
My vegetable love should grow°
Vaster than empires, and more slow;
An hundred years should go to praise
Thine eyes and on thy forehead gaze,
Two hundred to adore each breast,   15
But thirty thousand to the rest:
An age at least to every part,
And the last age should show your heart.
For, lady, you deserve this state,
Nor would I love at lower rate.   20
contrast river and desert images (But) at my back I always hear   *Lines move faster here—tone changes.*
Time's wingèd chariot hurrying near;
And yonder all before us lie
(Deserts) of vast (eternity.) —— *This eternity rushes in.*

Journal Note

He'd be patient and wait for his "mistress" if they had the time—sing songs, praise her, adore her, etc. But they don't have that much time according to him. He *seems* to be patient but he actually begins by calling patience—her coyness—a "crime." Looks to me like he's got his mind made up from the beginning of the poem. Where's her response? I'm not sure about him.

This journal note responds to some of the effects noted in the annotations of the poem; it's an excellent beginning for making sense of the speaker's argument in the poem.

Taking notes will preserve your initial reactions to the work. Many times first impressions are the best. Your response to a peculiar character in a story, a striking phrase in a poem, or a subtle bit of stage business in a play might lead to larger perceptions. You should take detailed notes only after you've read through the work. If you write too many notes during the first reading, you're likely to disrupt your response. Moreover, until you have a sense of the entire work, it will be difficult to determine how connections can be made among its various elements. In addition to recording your first impressions and noting significant passages, characters, actions, and so on, you should consult the Questions for Responsive Reading and Writing about fiction (p. 905), poetry (p. 913), and drama (p. 928). These questions can assist you in getting inside a work as well as organizing your notes.

Inevitably you will take more notes than you finally use in the paper. Note taking is a form of thinking aloud, but because your ideas are on paper you don't have to worry about forgetting them. As you develop a better sense of a potential topic, your notes will become more focused and detailed.

CHOOSING A TOPIC

If your instructor assigns a topic or offers a choice from among an approved list of topics, some of your work is already completed. Instead of being asked to come up with a topic about *Oedipus the King,* you may be asked to write a three-page essay that specifically discusses whether Oedipus's downfall is a result of fate or foolish pride. You also have the assurance that a specified topic will be manageable within the suggested number of pages. Unless you ask your instructor for permission to write on a different or related topic, be certain to address yourself to the assignment. An essay that does not discuss Oedipus's downfall but instead describes his relationship with his wife, Jocasta, would be missing the point. Notice too that there is room even in an assigned topic to develop your own approach. One question that immediately comes to mind is whether Oedipus's plight is relevant to a twenty-first-century reader. Assigned topics do not relieve you of thinking about an aspect of a work, but they do focus your thinking.

At some point during the course, you may have to begin an essay from scratch. You might, for example, be asked to write about a short story that somehow impressed you or that seemed particularly well written or filled with insights. Before you start considering a topic, you should have a sense of how long the paper will be because the assigned length can help to determine the extent to which you should develop your topic. Ideally, the paper's length should be based on how much space you deem necessary to present your discussion clearly and convincingly, but if you have any doubts and no specific guidelines have been indicated, ask. The question is important; a topic that might be appropriate for a three-page paper could be too narrow for ten pages. Three pages would probably be adequate for a discussion of why Emily murders Homer in Faulkner's "A Rose for Emily." Conversely, it would be futile to try to summarize Faulkner's use of the South in his fiction in even ten pages; this would have to be narrowed to something like "Images of the South in 'A Rose for Emily.'" Be sure that the topic you choose can be adequately covered in the assigned number of pages.

DEVELOPING A THESIS

When you are satisfied that you have something interesting to say about a work and that your notes have led you to a focused topic, you can formulate a *thesis*, the central idea of the paper. Whereas the topic indicates what the paper focuses on (the setting in "A & P"), the thesis explains what you have to say about the topic (because the intolerant setting of "A & P" is the antagonist in the story, it is crucial to our understanding of Sammy's decision to quit his job). The thesis should be a complete sentence (though sometimes it may require more than one sentence) that establishes your argument in clear, unambiguous language. The thesis may be revised as you get further into the argument and discover what you want to say about it, but once the thesis is firmly established, it will serve as a guide for you and your reader because all the information and observations in your essay should be related to the thesis.

One student on an initial reading of Andrew Marvell's "To His Coy Mistress" saw that the male speaker of the poem urges a woman to love now before time runs out for them. This reading gave him the impression that the poem is a simple celebration of the pleasures of the flesh, but on subsequent readings he underlined or noted these images: "Time's wingèd chariot hurrying near"; "Deserts of vast eternity"; "marble vault"; "worms"; "dust"; "ashes"; and these two lines: "The grave's a fine and private place, / But none, I think, do there embrace."

By listing these images associated with time and death, he established an inventory that could be separated from the rest of his notes on point of view, character, sounds, and other subjects. Inventorying notes allows patterns to emerge that you might have only vaguely perceived otherwise. Once these images are grouped, they call attention to something darker and more complex in Marvell's poem than a first impression might suggest.

These images may create a different feeling about the poem, but they still don't explain very much. One simple way to generate a thesis about a literary work is to ask the question "why?" Why do these images appear in the poem? Why is Othello swayed by Iago's insinuations? Why does Hemingway choose the Midwest as the setting of "Soldier's Home"? Your responses to these kinds of questions can lead to a thesis.

Writers sometimes use freewriting to help themselves explore possible answers to such questions. It can be an effective way of generating ideas. Freewriting is exactly that: The technique calls for nonstop writing without concern for mechanics or editing of any kind. Freewriting for ten minutes or so on a question will result in fragments and repetitions, but it can also produce some ideas. Here's an example of a student's response to the question about the images in "To His Coy Mistress":

He wants her to make love. Love poem. There's little time. Her crime. He exaggerates.
Sincere? Sly? What's he want? She says nothing — he says it all. What about deserts,
ashes, graves, and worms? Some love poem. Sounds like an old Vincent Price movie. Full of
sweetness but death creeps in. Death — hurry hurry! Tear pleasures. What passion! Where's
death in this? How can a love poem be so ghoulish? She does nothing. Maybe frightened?
Convinced? Why death? Love and death — time — death.

This freewriting contains several ideas; it begins by alluding to the poem's plot and speaker, but the central idea seems to be death. A paper that merely pointed out the death images in "To His Coy Mistress" would not contain a thesis, but a paper that attempted to make a case for the death imagery as a grim reminder of how vulnerable flesh is would involve persuasion. In developing a thesis, remember that you are expected not merely to present information but to argue a point.

ARGUING ABOUT LITERATURE

An argumentative essay is designed to make persuasive your interpretation of a work. Arguing about literature doesn't mean that you're engaged in an angry, antagonistic dispute (though controversial topics do sometimes engender heated debates). Instead, argumentation requires that you present your interpretation of a work (or a portion of it) by supporting your discussion with clearly defined terms, ample evidence, and a detailed analysis of relevant portions of the text.

If you have a choice, it's generally best to write about a topic that you feel strongly about. If you're not fascinated by Bartleby the Scrivener's haunting presence in Melville's short story, then perhaps you'll find chilling Emily Grierson's behavior in Faulkner's "A Rose for Emily," or maybe you can explain why Bartleby's character is so excruciatingly boring to you. If your essay is to be interesting and convincing, what is important is that it be written from a strong point of view that persuasively argues your evaluation, analysis, and interpretation of a work.

It is not enough to say that you like or dislike a work; instead you must give your reader some ideas and evidence that can be accepted or rejected based on the quality of the answers to the questions you raise.

ORGANIZING A PAPER

After you have chosen a manageable topic and developed a thesis, a central idea about it, you can begin to organize your paper. Your thesis, even if it is still somewhat tentative, should help you decide what information will need to be included and provide you with a sense of direction.

Consider this sample thesis:

On the surface, "To His Coy Mistress" is a celebration of the pleasures of the flesh, but this witty seduction is tempered by a chilling recognition of the reality of death.

This thesis indicates that the paper can be divided into two parts — the pleasures of the flesh and the reality of death. It also indicates an order: Because the central point is to show that the poem is more than a simple celebration, the pleasures of the flesh should be discussed first so that another, more complex, reading of the poem can follow. If the paper began with the reality of death, its point would be anticlimactic.

Having established such a broad and informal outline, you can draw on your underlinings, margin notations, and notes for the subheadings and evidence required to explain the major sections of your paper. This next level of detail would look like the following:

1. Pleasures of the flesh

    Part of the traditional tone of love poetry
2. Recognition of death

    Ironic treatment of love

    Diction

    Images

    Figures of speech

    Symbols

    Tone

This list was initially a jumble of terms, but the student arranged the items so that each of the two major sections leads to a discussion of tone. (The student also found it necessary to drop some biographical information from his notes because it was irrelevant to the thesis.) The list indicates that the first part of the paper will establish the traditional tone of love poetry that celebrates the pleasures of the flesh, while the second part will present a more detailed discussion about the ironic recognition of death. The emphasis is on the latter because that is the point to be argued in the paper. Hence, the thesis has helped to organize the parts of the paper, establish an order, and indicate the paper's proper proportions.

The next step is to fill in the subheadings with information from your notes. Many experienced writers find that making lists of information to be included under each subheading is an efficient way to develop paragraphs. For a longer paper (perhaps a research paper), you should be able to develop a paragraph or more on each subheading. On the other hand, a shorter paper may require that you combine several subheadings in a paragraph. You may also discover that while an informal list is adequate for a brief paper, a ten-page assignment could require a more detailed outline. Use the method that is most productive for you.

WRITING A DRAFT

Be flexible. Your outline should smoothly conduct you from one point to the next, but do not permit it to railroad you. If a relevant and important idea occurs to you now, work it into the draft. By using the first draft as a means of thinking about what you want to say, you will very likely discover more than your notes originally suggested. Plenty of good writers don't use outlines at all but discover ordering principles as they write. Do not attempt to compose a perfectly correct draft the first time around. Grammar, punctuation, and spelling can wait until you revise. Concentrate on what you are saying. Good writing most often occurs when you are in hot pursuit of an idea rather than in a nervous search for errors.

Once you have a first draft on paper, you can delete material that is unrelated to your thesis and add material necessary to illustrate your points and make your paper convincing. The student who wrote "John Updike's 'A & P' as a State of Mind" (p. 909) wisely dropped a paragraph that questioned whether Sammy displays chauvinistic attitudes toward women. Although this is an interesting issue, it has nothing to do with the thesis, which explains how the setting influences Sammy's decision to quit his job. Instead of including that paragraph, she added one that described Lengel's crabbed response to the girls so that she could lead up to the A & P "policy" he enforces.

Remember that your initial draft is only that. You should go through the paper many times — and then again — working to substantiate and clarify your ideas. You may even end up with several entire versions of the paper. Rewrite. The sentences within each paragraph should be related to a single topic. Transitions should connect one paragraph to the next so that there are no abrupt or confusing shifts. Awkward or wordy phrasing or unclear sentences and paragraphs should be mercilessly poked and prodded into shape.

Writing the Introduction and Conclusion

After you have clearly and adequately developed the body of your paper, pay particular attention to the introductory and concluding paragraphs. It's probably best to write the introduction — at least the final version of it — last, after you know precisely what you are introducing. Because this paragraph is crucial for generating interest in the topic, it should engage the reader and provide a sense of what the paper is about. There is no formula for writing effective introductory paragraphs because each writing situation is different — depending on the audience, topic, and approach — but if you pay attention to the introductions of the essays you read, you will notice a variety of possibilities. The introductory paragraph to "John Updike's 'A & P' as a State of Mind," for example, is a straightforward explanation of why the story's setting is important for understanding Updike's treatment of the antagonist. The rest of the paper then offers evidence to support this point.

Concluding paragraphs demand equal attention because they leave the reader with a final impression. The conclusion should provide a sense of closure instead of starting a new topic or ending abruptly. In the final paragraph about the significance of the setting in "A & P," the student brings together the reasons Sammy quit his job by referring to his refusal to accept Lengel's store policies. At the same time she makes this point, she also explains the significance of Sammy ringing up the "No Sale" mentioned in her introductory paragraph. Thus, we are brought back to where we began, but we now have a greater understanding of why Sammy quits his job. Of course, the body of your paper is the most important part of your presentation, but do remember that first and last impressions have a powerful impact on readers.

Using Quotations

Quotations can be a valuable means of marshaling evidence to illustrate and support your ideas. A judicious use of quoted material will make your points clearer and more convincing. Here are some guidelines that should help you use quotations effectively.

Brief and lengthy quotations

Brief quotations (four lines or fewer of prose or three lines or fewer of poetry) should be carefully introduced and integrated into the text of your paper with quotation marks around them:

According to the narrator, Bertha "had a reputation for strictness." He tells us that she always "wore dark clothes, dressed her hair simply, and expected contrition and obedience from her pupils."

For brief poetry quotations, use a slash to indicate a division between lines:

The concluding lines of Blake's "The Tyger" pose a disturbing question: "What immortal hand or eye / Dare frame thy fearful symmetry?"

Lengthy quotations should be separated from the text of your paper. More than three lines of poetry should be double spaced and centered on the page. More than four lines of prose should be double spaced and indented ten spaces from the left margin, with the right margin the same as for the text. Do *not* use quotation marks for the passage; the indentation indicates that the passage is a quotation. Lengthy quotations should not be used in place of your own writing. Use them only if they are absolutely necessary.

Brackets and ellipses

If any words are added to a quotation, use brackets to distinguish your addition from the original source:

"He [Young Goodman Brown] is portrayed as self-righteous and disillusioned."

Any words inside quotation marks and not in brackets must be precisely those of the author. Brackets can also be used to change the grammatical structure of a quotation so that it fits into your sentence:

Smith argues that Chekhov "present[s] the narrator in an ambivalent light."

If you drop any words from the source, use ellipses to indicate the omission:

"Early to bed . . . makes a man healthy, wealthy, and wise."

Use ellipses following a period to indicate an omission at the end of a sentence:

"Early to bed and early to rise makes a man healthy. . . ."

Use a single line of spaced periods to indicate the omission of a line or more of poetry or more than one paragraph of prose:

Nothing would sleep in that cellar, dank as a ditch,
Bulbs broke out of boxes hunting for chinks in the dark,
. . . .
Nothing would give up life:
Even the dirt kept breathing a small breath.

Punctuation

You will be able to punctuate quoted material accurately and confidently if you observe these conventions.

Place commas and periods inside quotation marks:

"Even the dirt," Roethke insists, "kept breathing a small breath."

Even though a comma does not appear after "dirt" in the original quotation, it is placed inside the quotation mark. The exception to this rule occurs when a parenthetical reference to a source follows the quotation:

"Even the dirt," Roethke insists, "kept breathing a small breath" (11).

Punctuation marks other than commas or periods go outside the quotation marks unless they are part of the material quoted:

What does Roethke mean when he writes that "the dirt kept breathing a small breath"?

Yeats asked, "How can we know the dancer from the dance?"

REVISING AND EDITING

Put some distance—a day or so if you can—between yourself and each draft of your paper. The phrase that seemed just right on Wednesday may be revealed as all wrong on Friday. You'll have a better chance of detecting lumbering sentences and thin paragraphs if you plan ahead and give yourself the time to read your paper from a fresh perspective. Through the process of revision, you can transform a competent paper into an excellent one.

Begin by asking yourself if your approach to the topic requires any rethinking. Is the argument carefully thought out and logically presented? Are there any gaps in the presentation? How well is the paper organized? Do the paragraphs lead into one another? Does the body of the paper deliver what the thesis promises? Is the interpretation sound? Are any relevant and important elements of the work ignored or distorted to advance the thesis? Are the points supported with evidence? These large questions should be addressed before you focus on more detailed matters. If you uncover serious problems as a result of considering these questions, you'll probably have quite a lot of rewriting to do, but at least you will have the opportunity to correct the problems—even if doing so takes several drafts.

The following checklist offers questions to ask about your paper as you revise and edit it. Most of these questions will be familiar to you; however, if you need help with any of them, ask your instructor or review the appropriate section in a composition handbook.

Questions for Writing: A Revision Checklist

1. Is the topic manageable? Is it too narrow or too broad?
2. Is the thesis clear? Is it based on a careful reading of the work?
3. Is the paper logically organized? Does it have a firm sense of direction?

(continued)

4. Is your argument persuasive?

5. Should any material be deleted? Do any important points require further illustration or evidence?

6. Does the opening paragraph introduce the topic in an interesting manner?

7. Are the paragraphs developed, unified, and coherent? Are any too short or long?

8. Are there transitions linking the paragraphs?

9. Does the concluding paragraph provide a sense of closure?

10. Is the tone appropriate? Is it unduly flippant or pretentious?

11. Is the title engaging and suggestive?

12. Are the sentences clear, concise, and complete?

13. Are a mix of simple, complex, and compound sentences used for variety?

14. Have technical terms been used correctly? Are you certain of the meanings of all the words in the paper? Are they spelled correctly?

15. Have you documented any information borrowed from books, articles, or other sources? Have you quoted too much instead of summarizing or paraphrasing secondary material?

16. Have you used a standard format for citing sources (see p. 941)?

17. Have you followed your instructor's guidelines for the manuscript format of the final draft?

18. Have you carefully proofread the final draft?

When you proofread your final draft, you may find a few typographical errors that must be corrected but do not warrant reprinting an entire paper. Provided there are not more than a handful of such errors throughout the paper, they can be corrected as shown in the following passage. This example condenses a short paper's worth of errors; no single passage should be this shabby in your essay:

To add a letter or word, use a caret on the line where the addition is needed. To delete a

word draw a single line through through it. Run-on words are separated by a vertical line,

and inadvertent spaces are closed like this. Transposed letters are indicated this way.

New paragraphs are noted with the sign ¶ in front of where the next paragraph is to

begin. Unless you . . .

You can minimize these sorts of errors by proofreading on the screen and simply entering your corrections as you go along.

TYPES OF WRITING ASSIGNMENTS

The types of papers most frequently assigned in literature classes are *explication, analysis,* and *comparison and contrast.* Most writing about literature involves some combination of these skills. For genre-based assignments, see the following sample papers: for analysis (Chapter 30, "Writing about Fiction," p. 909), for explication (Chapter 31, "Writing about Poetry," p. 920), for comparison and contrast (Chapter 32, "Writing about Drama," p. 932). For a sample research paper that demonstrates a variety of strategies for documenting outside sources, see page 948.

30

Writing about Fiction

Courtesy of Jason Doiy.

Write every day. Even if it's just a paragraph, start writing! Then keep writing every day so that it becomes like eating or breathing, a part of your life that you can't live without.
— MAY-LEE CHAI

FROM READING TO WRITING

There's no question about it: Writing about fiction is a different experience than reading it. The novelist William Styron amply concedes that writing to him is not so much about pleasure as it is about work: "Let's face it, writing is hell." Although Styron's lament concerns his own feelings about writing prose fiction, he no doubt speaks for many other writers, including essayists. Writing is, of course, work, but it is also a pleasure when it goes well—when ideas feel solid and the writing is fluid. You can experience that pleasure as well if you approach writing as an intellectual and emotional opportunity rather than merely a vexing sentence.

Just as reading fiction requires an imaginative, conscious response, so does writing about fiction. Composing an essay is not just recording your interpretive response to a work because the act of writing can change your response as you explore, clarify, and discover relationships you hadn't previously considered or recognized. Most writers discover new ideas and connections as they move through the process of rereading and annotating the text, taking notes, generating ideas, developing a thesis, and organizing an argumentative essay (these matters are detailed in Chapter 29, "Reading and the Writing Process"). To become more conscious of the writing process, first study the following questions specifically aimed at sharpening your response to reading and writing about fiction. Then examine the student's analysis of John Updike's short story "A & P."

Questions for Responsive Reading and Writing

The following questions can help you consider important elements of fiction that reveal your responses to a story's effects and meanings. The questions are general, so they will not always be relevant to a particular story. Many of them, however, should prove useful for thinking, talking, and writing about a work of fiction.

PLOT

1. Does the plot conform to a formula? Is it like those of any other stories you have read? Did you find it predictable?

2. What is the source and nature of the conflict for the protagonist? Was your major interest in the story based on what happens next or on some other concern? What does the title reveal now that you've finished the story?

3. Is the story told chronologically? If not, in what order are its events told, and what is the effect of that order on your response to the action?

4. What does the exposition reveal? Are flashbacks used? Did you see any foreshadowings? Where is the climax?

5. Is the conflict resolved at the end? Would you characterize the ending as happy, unhappy, or somewhere in between?

6. Is the plot unified? Is each incident somehow related to some other element in the story?

CHARACTER

7. Do you identify with the protagonist? Who (or what) is the antagonist?

8. Did your response to any characters change as you read? What do you think caused the change? Do any characters change and develop in the course of the story? How?

9. Are round, flat, or stock characters used? Is their behavior motivated and plausible?

10. How does the author reveal characters? Are they directly described or indirectly presented? Are the characters' names used to convey something about them?

11. What is the purpose of the minor characters? Are they individualized, or do they primarily represent ideas or attitudes?

SETTING

12. Is the setting important in shaping your response? If it were changed, would your response to the story's action and meaning be significantly different?

(continued)

13. Is the setting used symbolically? Are the time, place, and atmosphere related to the theme?

14. Is the setting used as an antagonist?

POINT OF VIEW

15. Who tells the story? Is it a first-person or third-person narrator? Is it a major or minor character or one who does not participate in the action at all? How much does the narrator know? Does the point of view change at all in the course of the story?

16. Is the narrator reliable and objective? Does the narrator appear too innocent, emotional, or self-deluded to be trusted?

17. Does the author directly comment on the action?

18. If it were told from a different point of view, how would your response to the story change? Would anything be lost?

SYMBOLISM

19. Did you notice any symbols in the story? Are they actions, characters, settings, objects, or words?

20. How do the symbols contribute to your understanding of the story?

THEME

21. Did you find a theme? If so, what is it?

22. Is the theme stated directly, or is it developed implicitly through the plot, characters, or some other element?

23. Is the theme a confirmation of your values, or does it challenge them?

STYLE, TONE, AND IRONY

24. Do you think the style is consistent and appropriate throughout the story? Do all the characters use the same kind of language, or did you hear different voices?

25. Would you describe the level of diction as formal or informal? Are the sentences short and simple, long and complex, or some combination?

26. How does the author's use of language contribute to the tone of the story? Did it seem, for example, intense, relaxed, sentimental, nostalgic, humorous, angry, sad, or remote?

27. Do you think the story is worth reading more than once? Does the author's use of language bear close scrutiny so that you feel and experience more with each reading?

Analysis

An *analysis* usually examines only a single element—such as plot, character, point of view, symbol, tone, or irony—and relates it to the entire work. An analytic topic separates the work into parts and focuses on a specific one; you might, for example, consider "Point of View in 'A Rose for Emily.'" The specific element must be related to the work as a whole or it will appear irrelevant. Whether an analytic paper is just a few pages or many, it cannot attempt to discuss everything about the work it is considering. Only those elements that are relevant to the topic can be treated. This kind of focusing makes the topic manageable; this is why most papers that you write will probably be some form of analysis.

A SAMPLE STUDENT ANALYSIS

John Updike's "A & P" as a State of Mind

The following paper by Nancy Lager analyzes the setting in John Updike's "A & P" (the story appears on p. 157). The assignment simply asked for an essay of approximately 750 words on a short story written in the twentieth century. The approach was left to the student.

The idea for this essay began with Lager asking herself why Updike used "A & P" as the title. The initial answer to the question was that "the setting is important in this story." This answer was the rough beginning of a tentative thesis. What still had to be explained, though, was how the setting is important. To determine the significance of the setting, Lager jotted down some notes based on her underlinings and marginal notations:

A & P
"usual traffic"
lights and tile
"electric eye"
shoppers like "sheep," "houseslaves," "pigs"
"Alexandrov and Petrooshki"—Russia

New England Town	*Lengel*
typical: bank, church, etc.	"manager"
traditional	"doesn't miss that much"
conservative	(like lady shopper)
proper	Sunday school
near Salem—witch trials	"It's our policy"
puritanical	spokesman for A & P values
intolerant	

From these notes Lager saw that Lengel serves as the voice of the A & P. He is, in a sense, a personification of the intolerant atmosphere of the setting. This insight led to another version of her thesis statement: "The setting of 'A & P' is the antagonist of the story." That explained at least some of the setting's importance. By seeing Lengel as a spokesman for "A & P" policies, she could view him as a voice that articulates the morally smug atmosphere created by the setting. Finally, she considered why it is significant that the setting is the antagonist, and this generated her last thesis: "Because the intolerant setting of 'A & P' is the antagonist in the story, it is crucial to our understanding of Sammy's decision to quit his job." This thesis sentence does not appear precisely in these words in the essay, but it is the backbone of the introductory paragraph.

The remaining paragraphs consist of details that describe the A & P in the second paragraph, the New England town in the third, Lengel in the fourth, and Sammy's reasons for quitting in the concluding paragraph. Paragraphs 2, 3, and 4 are largely based on Lager's notes, which she used as an outline once her thesis was established. The essay is sharply focused, well organized, and generally well written. In addition, it suggests a number of useful guidelines for analytic papers:

1. Only the points related to the thesis are included. In another type of paper the role of the girls in the bathing suits, for example, might have been considerably more prominent.

2. The analysis keeps the setting in focus while at the same time indicating how it is significant in the major incident in the story — Sammy's quitting.

3. The title is a useful lead into the paper; it provides a sense of what the topic is. In addition, the title is drawn from a sentence (the final one of the first paragraph) that clearly explains its meaning.

4. The introductory paragraph is direct and clearly indicates the paper will argue that the setting serves as the antagonist of the story.

5. Brief quotations are deftly incorporated into the text of the paper to illustrate points. We are told what we need to know about the story as evidence is provided to support ideas. There is no unnecessary plot summary. Even though "A & P" is only a few pages in length, page numbers are included after quoted phrases. If the story were longer, page numbers would be especially helpful for the reader.

6. The paragraphs are well developed, unified, and coherent. They flow naturally from one to another. Notice, for example, the smooth transition worked into the final sentence of the third paragraph and the first sentence of the fourth paragraph.

7. Lager makes excellent use of her careful reading and notes by finding revealing connections among the details she has observed. The store's "electric eye," for instance, is related to the woman's and Lengel's watchfulness.

8. As events are described, the present tense is used. This avoids awkward tense shifts and lends an immediacy to the discussion.
9. The concluding paragraph establishes the significance of why the setting should be seen as the antagonist and provides a sense of closure by referring again to Sammy's "No Sale," which has been mentioned at the end of the first paragraph.
10. In short, Lager has demonstrated that she has read the work closely, has understood the relation of the setting to the major action, and has argued her thesis convincingly by using evidence from the story.

Lager 1

Nancy Lager
Professor Taylor
English 102-12
2 April 2013

John Updike's "A & P" as a State of Mind

The setting of John Updike's "A & P" is crucial to our understanding of Sammy's decision to quit his job. Although Sammy is the central character in the story and we learn that he is a principled, good-natured nineteen-year-old with a sense of humor, Updike seems to invest as much effort in describing the setting as he does in Sammy. The setting is the antagonist and plays a role that is as important as Sammy's. The title, after all, is not "Youthful Rebellion" or "Sammy Quits" but "A & P." Even though Sammy knows that his quitting will make life more difficult for him, he instinctively insists on rejecting what the A & P comes to represent in the story. When he rings up a "No Sale" and "saunter[s]" (Updike 162) out of the store, he leaves behind not only a job but the rigid state of mind associated with the A & P.

Sammy's descriptions of the A & P present a setting that is ugly, monotonous, and rigidly regulated. The fluorescent light is as blandly cool as the "checker-board green-and-cream rubber-tile floor" (159). We can see the uniformity Sammy describes because we have all been in chain stores. The "usual traffic" moves in one direction (except for the swimsuited girls, who move against it), and everything is neatly ordered and categorized in tidy aisles. The dehumanizing routine of this environment is suggested by Sammy's offhand references to the typical shoppers as "sheep" (159), "houseslaves" (159), and "pigs" (162). They seem to pace through the store in a stupor; as Sammy tells us, not even dynamite could move them.

Lager 2

The A & P is appropriately located "right in the middle" (159) of a proper, conservative, traditional New England town north of Boston. This location, coupled with the fact that the town is only five miles from Salem, the site of the famous seventeenth-century witch trials, suggests a narrow, intolerant social atmosphere in which there is no room for stepping beyond the boundaries of what is regarded as normal and proper. The importance of this setting can be appreciated even more if we imagine the action taking place in, say, a mellow suburb of southern California. In this prim New England setting, the girls in their bathing suits are bound to offend somebody's sense of propriety.

As soon as Lengel sees the girls, the inevitable conflict begins. He embodies the dull conformity represented by the A & P. As "manager" (160), he is both the guardian and enforcer of "policy" (161). When he gives the girls "that sad Sunday-school-superintendent stare" (161), we know we are in the presence of the A & P version of a dreary bureaucrat who "doesn't miss that much" (160). He is as unsympathetic and unpleasant as the woman "with rouge on her cheekbones and no eyebrows" (158) who pounces on Sammy for ringing up her "HiHo crackers" twice. Like the "electric eye" (162) in the doorway, her vigilant eyes allow nothing to escape their notice. For Sammy the logical extension of Lengel's "policy" is the half-serious notion that one day the A & P might be known as the "Great Alexandrov and Petrooshki Tea Company" (159). Sammy's connection between what he regards as mindless "policy" (161) and Soviet oppression is obviously an exaggeration, but the reader is invited to entertain the similarities anyway.

The reason Sammy quits his job has less to do with defending the girls than with his own sense of what it means to be a decent human being. His decision is not an easy one. He doesn't want to make trouble or disappoint his parents, and he knows his independence and self-reliance (the other side of New England tradition) will make life more complex for him. In spite of his own hesitations, he finds himself blurting out "Fiddle-de-doo" (162) to Lengel's policies and in doing so knows that his grandmother "would have been pleased" (162). Sammy's "No Sale" rejects the crabbed perspective on life that Lengel represents as manager of the A & P. This gesture is more than just a negative, however, for as he punches in that last entry on the cash register, "the machine whirs 'pee-pul'" (162). His decision to quit his job at the A & P is an expression of his refusal to regard policies as more important than people.

Lager 3

Work Cited

Updike, John. "A & P." *Literature to Go*. 2nd ed. Ed. Michael Meyer. Boston: Bedford/St. Martin's, 2014. 157-62. Print.

31

Writing about Poetry

© Derek Anderson.

> Many people, especially beginning writers, think that writing is mostly inspiration. The muse tosses down a lightning bolt and you write something good. I think writing is mostly perspiration. You go to your chair or desk, and you stay there.
>
> — MICHAEL CHITWOOD

FROM READING TO WRITING

Writing about poetry can be a rigorous means of testing the validity of your own reading of a poem. Anyone who has been asked to write several pages about a fourteen-line poem knows how intellectually challenging this exercise is, because it means paying close attention to language. Such scrutiny of words, however, sensitizes you not only to the poet's use of language but also to your own use of language. At first you may feel intimidated by having to compose a paper that is longer than the poem you're writing about, but a careful reading will reveal that there's plenty to write about what the poem says and how it says it. Keep in mind that your job is not to produce a definitive reading of the poem — even Carl Sandburg once confessed that "I've written some poetry I don't understand myself." It is enough to develop an interesting thesis and to present it clearly and persuasively.

An interesting thesis will come to you if you read and reread, take notes, annotate the text, and generate ideas (for a discussion of this process, see Chapter 29, "Reading and the Writing Process"). Although it requires energy to read closely and to write convincingly about the charged language found in poetry, there is nothing mysterious about such reading and writing. This chapter provides a set of questions designed to sharpen your reading and writing about poetry. Following these questions are two sample papers that offer explication of John Donne's "Death Be Not Proud" and Emily Dickinson's "There's a certain Slant of light."

Questions for Responsive Reading and Writing

The following questions can help you respond to important elements that reveal a poem's effects and meanings. The questions are general, so not all of them will necessarily be relevant to a particular poem. Many, however, should prove useful for thinking, talking, and writing about each poem in this collection.

Before addressing these questions, read the poem you are studying in its entirety. Don't worry about interpretation on a first reading; allow yourself the pleasure of enjoying whatever makes itself apparent to you. Then on subsequent readings, use the questions to understand and appreciate how the poem works.

1. Who is the speaker? Is it possible to determine the speaker's age, sex, sensibilities, level of awareness, and values?

2. Is the speaker addressing anyone in particular?

3. How do you respond to the speaker? Favorably? Negatively? What is the situation? Are there any special circumstances that inform what the speaker says?

4. Is there a specific setting of time and place?

5. Does reading the poem aloud help you to understand it?

6. Does a paraphrase reveal the basic purpose of the poem?

7. What does the title emphasize?

8. Is the theme presented directly or indirectly?

9. Do any allusions enrich the poem's meaning?

10. How does the diction reveal meaning? Are any words repeated? Do any carry evocative connotative meanings? Are there any puns or other forms of verbal wit?

11. Are figures of speech used? How does the figurative language contribute to the poem's vividness and meaning?

12. Do any objects, persons, places, events, or actions have allegorical or symbolic meanings? What other details in the poem support your interpretation?

13. Is irony used? Are there any examples of situational irony, verbal irony, or dramatic irony? Is understatement or paradox used?

14. What is the tone of the poem? Is the tone consistent?

15. Does the poem use onomatopoeia, assonance, consonance, or alliteration? How do these sounds affect you?

(continued)

16. What sounds are repeated? If there are rhymes, what is their effect? Do they seem forced or natural? Is there a rhyme scheme? Do the rhymes contribute to the poem's meaning?

17. Do the lines have a regular meter? What is the predominant meter? Are there significant variations? Does the rhythm seem appropriate for the poem's tone?

18. Does the poem's form — its overall structure — follow an established pattern? Do you think the form is a suitable vehicle for the poem's meaning and effects?

19. Is the language of the poem intense and concentrated? Do you think it warrants more than one or two close readings?

20. Did you enjoy the poem? What, specifically, pleased or displeased you about what was expressed and how it was expressed?

21. How might biographical information about the author help to determine the poem's central concerns?

22. How might historical information about the poem provide a useful context for interpretation?

23. To what extent do your own experiences, values, beliefs, and assumptions inform your interpretation?

24. What kinds of evidence from the poem are you focusing on to support your interpretation? Does your interpretation leave out any important elements that might undercut or qualify your interpretation?

EXPLICATION

The purpose of this approach to a literary work is to make the implicit explicit. *Explication* is a detailed explanation of a passage of poetry or prose. Because explication is an intensive examination of a text line by line, it is mostly used to interpret a short poem in its entirety or a brief passage from a long poem, short story, or play. Explication can be used in any kind of paper when you want to be specific about how a writer achieves a certain effect. An explication pays careful attention to language — the connotations of words, allusions, figurative language, irony, symbol, rhythm, sound, and so on. These elements are examined in relation to one another and to the overall effect and meaning of the work.

The simplest way to organize an explication is to move through the passage line by line, explaining whatever seems significant. It is wise to avoid, however, an assembly-line approach that begins each sentence with "In line one (two, three) . . ." Instead, organize your paper in whatever way best serves your thesis. You might find that the right place to start is with the final lines, working your way back to the beginning of the poem or passage. The sample explication on Dickinson's "There's a certain Slant of light," beginning on page 923 in this chapter, does just that. The student's opening paragraph refers to the final line of the poem in order to present her thesis. She explains that though the poem begins with an image of light, it is not a bright or cheery poem but one concerned with "the look of Death." Since the last line prompted her thesis, that is where she begins the explication.

You might also find it useful to structure a paper by discussing various elements of literature. The following sample explication on John Donne's "Death Be Not Proud" is organized in this manner. However your paper is organized, keep in mind that the aim of an explication is not simply to summarize the passage but to comment on the effects and meanings produced by the author's use of language in it. An effective explication (the Latin word *explicare* means "to unfold") displays a text to reveal how it works and what it signifies. Although writing an explication requires some patience and sensitivity, it is an excellent method for coming to understand and appreciate the elements and qualities that constitute literary art.

A SAMPLE PAPER-IN-PROGRESS

Mapping a Poem

When you write about a poem, you are, in some ways, providing a guide for a place that might otherwise seem unfamiliar and remote. Put simply, writing enables you to chart a work so that you can comfortably move around in it to discuss or write about what interests you. Your paper represents a record and a map of your intellectual journey through the poem, pointing out the things worth noting and your impressions about them. Your role as writer is to offer insights into the challenges, pleasures, and discoveries that the poem harbors. These insights are a kind of sightseeing as you navigate the various elements of the poem to make some overall point about it.

This section shows you how one student, Rose Bostwick, moves through the stages of writing about how a poem's elements combine for a final effect. Included here are Rose's first response, her informal outline, and the final draft of an explication of John Donne's "Death Be Not Proud." After reviewing the elements of poetry covered in Chapters 12 through 20, Rose read the poem (which follows) several times, paying careful attention to diction, figurative language, irony, symbol, rhythm, sound, and so on. Her final paper is more concerned with the overall effect of the combination of elements than with a line-by-line breakdown. As you read and reread "Death Be Not Proud," keep notes on how *you* think the elements of this poem work together and to what overall effect.

JOHN DONNE (1572–1631)

Death Be Not Proud   1611

Death be not proud, though some have
    callèd thee
Mighty and dreadful, for thou art not so;
For those whom thou think'st thou dost
    overthrow
Die not, poor Death, nor yet canst thou
    kill me.
From rest and sleep, which but thy
    pictures° be,   *images*
Much pleasure; then from thee much more
    must flow,
And soonest our best men with thee do go,
Rest of their bones, and soul's delivery.°   *deliverance*
Thou art slave to Fate, Chance, kings, and desperate men,
And dost with Poison, War, and Sickness dwell;   10
And poppy or charms can make us sleep as well,
And better than thy stroke; why swell'st° thou then?   *swell with pride*
One short sleep past, we wake eternally
And death shall be no more; Death, thou shalt die.

Courtesy of the National Portrait Gallery, London.

Asking Questions about the Elements

After reading a poem, use the Questions for Responsive Reading and Writing (pp. 913–14) to help you think, talk, and write about it. Before you do, though, be sure that you have read the poem several times without worrying actively about interpretation. With poetry, as with all literature, it's important to allow yourself the pleasure of enjoying whatever makes itself apparent to you. On subsequent readings, use the questions to understand and appreciate how the poem works; remember to keep in mind that not all questions will necessarily be relevant to a particular poem. A good starting point is to ask yourself what elements are exemplified in the parts of the poem that especially interest you. Then ask the Questions for Responsive Reading and Writing that relate to those elements. Finally, as you begin to get a sense of what elements are important to the poem and how those elements fit together, it often helps to put your impressions on paper.

A SAMPLE FIRST RESPONSE

First Response to John Donne's "Death Be Not Proud"

After Rose carefully read "Death Be Not Proud" and had a sense of how the elements work, she took the first step toward a formal explication by writing informally about the relevant elements and addressing the question *Why doesn't the speaker fear death? Explain why you find the argument convincing or not.* Note that at this point, she was not as concerned with textual evidence and detail as she would need to be in her final paper.

Bostwick 1

Rose Bostwick

English 101

Professor Hart

28 January 2013

First Response to John Donne's "Death Be Not Proud"

I've read the poem "Death Be Not Proud" by John Donne a few times now, and I have a sense of how it works. The poem is a sonnet, and each of the three quatrains presents a piece of the argument that Death should not be proud, because it is not really all-powerful, and may even be a source of pleasure. As a reader, I resist this seeming paradox at first, but I know it must be a trick, a riddle of some sort that the poem will proceed to untangle. I think one of the reasons the poem comes off as such a powerful statement is that Donne at first seems to be playful and paradoxical in his characterizations of Death. He's almost teasing Death. But beneath the teasing tone you feel the strong foundation of the real reason Death should not be proud—Donne's faith in the immortality of the soul. The poem begins to feel more solemn as it progresses, as the hints at the idea of immortality become more clearly articulated.

Donne utilizes two literary conventions to increase the effect of this poem: he uses the convention of personifying death, so that he can address it directly, and he uses the metaphor of death as a kind of sleep. These two things determine the tone and the progression from playful to solemn in the poem.

The last clause of the poem (line 14) plays with the paradoxical-seeming character of what he's been declaring. Ironically, it seems the only thing susceptible to death is death itself. Or, when death becomes powerless is when it only has power over itself.

Organizing Your Thoughts

Showing in a paper how different elements of a particular poem work together is often quite challenging. While you may have a clear intuitive sense of what elements are important to the poem and how they complement one another, it is important to organize your thoughts in such a way as to make the relationships clear to your audience. The simplest way is to go line by line, but that can quickly become rote for writer and reader. Because you will want to organize your paper in the way that best serves your thesis, it may help to write an informal outline that charts how you think the argument moves. You may find, for example, that the argument is not persuasive if you start with the final lines and go back to the beginning of the poem or passage. However you decide to organize your argument, keep in mind that a single idea, or thesis, will have to run throughout the entire paper.

A SAMPLE INFORMAL OUTLINE

Proposed Outline for Paper on John Donne's "Death Be Not Proud"

In her informal outline (following), Rose discovers that her argument works best if she begins at the beginning. Note that, though her later paper concerns itself with how several elements of poetry contribute to the poem's theme and message, her informal outline concerns itself much more with what that message is and how it develops as the poem progresses. She will fill in the details later.

Bostwick 1

Rose Bostwick

English 101

Professor Hart

6 February 2013

Proposed Outline for Paper on
John Donne's "Death Be Not Proud"

Thesis: From the very first word, addressing "Death" directly, Donne uses the literary conventions of personifying death and comparing it to sleep to begin an argument that Death should not be proud of its might or dreadfulness.

Bostwick 2

But these two elements of his argument come to be seen as the superficial points when the true reason for death's powerlessness becomes clear. The Christian belief in the immortality of the soul is the reason for death's powerlessness and likeness to sleep.

Body of essay: Show how argument proceeds by quatrains from playful address to Death, and statement that Death is much like sleep, its "picture," to statement that Death is "slave" to other forces (and so should not be proud of being the mightiest), to the couplet, which articulates clearly the idea of immortality and gives the final paradox, "Death, thou shalt die."

Conclusion: Donne's faith in the immortality of the soul enables him to "prove" in this argument that Death is truly like its metaphorical representation, sleep. Faith allows him to derive a source for this conventional trope, and it allows him to state his truth in paradoxes. He relies on the conventional idea that death is an end, and a conqueror, and the only all-powerful force, to make the paradoxes that lend his argument the force of mystery—the mystery of faith.

The Elements and Theme

As you create an informal outline, your understanding of the poem will grow, change, and finally, solidify. You will develop a much clearer sense of what the poem's elements combine to create, and you will have chosen a scheme for organizing your argument. The next step before drafting is to determine the paper's thesis, which will not only keep your paper focused but will also help you center your thoughts. For papers that discuss how the elements of poetry come together, the thesis is a single and concise statement of what the elements combine to create—the idea around which all the elements revolve. In Robert Herrick's "Delight in Disorder," for example, the two elements, rhythm and rhyme, work together to create the speaker's self-directed irony. To state this as a thesis, we might say that by making his own rhythm and rhyme "too precise," Herrick's speaker is making fun of himself while complimenting a certain type of woman. (You may ask yourself if he's doing a little flirting.)

Once you understand how all of the elements of a poem fit together and have articulated your understanding in the thesis statement, the next step is to flesh out your argument. By including quotations from the poem to illustrate the points you will be making, you will better explain exactly how each element relates to the others and, more specifically, to your thesis, and you will have created a finished paper that helps readers navigate the poem's geography.

FINAL PAPER: A SAMPLE EXPLICATION

The Use of Conventional Metaphors for Death in John Donne's "Death Be Not Proud"

In Rose's final draft, she focuses on the use of metaphor in "Death Be Not Proud." Her essay provides a coherent reading that relates each line of the poem to the speaker's intense awareness of death. Although the essay discusses each stanza in order, the introductory paragraph provides a brief overview explaining how the poem's metaphors and arguments contribute to its total meaning. In addition, Rose does not hesitate to discuss a line out of sequence when it can be usefully connected to another phrase. She also works quotations into her sentences to support her points. When she adds something to a quotation to clarify it, she encloses her words in brackets so that they will not be mistaken for the poet's, and she uses a slash to indicate line divisions: "soonest . . . with thee do go, / [for] Rest of their bones, and soul's delivery." Finally, Rose is sure to cite the line numbers for any direct quotations from the poem. As you read through her final draft, remember that the word *explication* comes from the Latin *explicare*, "to unfold." How successful do you think Rose is at unfolding this poem to reveal how its elements—here ranging from metaphor to structure, meter, personification, paradox, irony, and theme—contribute to its meaning?

Bostwick 1

Rose Bostwick

English 101

Professor Hart

24 February 2013

The Use of Conventional Metaphors for Death
in John Donne's "Death Be Not Proud"

In the sonnet that begins "Death be not proud . . ." John Donne argues that death is not "mighty and dreadful" but is more like its metaphorical representation, sleep. Death, Donne puts forth, is even a source of pleasure and

Bostwick 2

rest. The poet builds this argument on two foundations. One is made up of the metaphors and literary conventions for death: Death is compared with sleep and is often personified so that it can be addressed directly. The poem is an address to death that at first seems paradoxical and somewhat playful, but which then rises in all the emotion of faith as it reveals the second foundation of the argument—the Christian belief in the immortality of the soul. Seen against the backdrop of this belief, death loses its powerful threat and is seen as only a metaphorical sleep, or rest.

> Thesis providing interpretation of the poem's use of metaphor and how it contributes to the poem's central argument.

The poem is an ironic argument that proceeds according to the structure of the sonnet form. Each quatrain contains a new development or aspect of the argument, and the final couplet serves as a conclusion. The metrical scheme is mainly iambic pentameter, but in several places in the poem, the stress pattern is altered for emphasis. For example, the first foot of the poem is inverted, so that "Death," the first word, receives the stress. This announces to us right away that Death is being personified and addressed. This inversion also serves to begin the poem energetically and forcefully. The second line behaves in the same way. The first syllable of "Mighty" receives the stress, emphasizing the meaning of the word and its assumed relation to Death.

> Discussion of how form and meter contribute to the poem's central argument.

This first quatrain offers the first paradox and sets up the argument that death has been conventionally personified with the wrong attributes, might and dreadfulness. The poet tells death not to be proud, "though some have called thee / Mighty and dreadful," because, he says, death is "not so" (lines 1-2). Donne will turn this conventional characterization of death on its head with the paradox of the third and fourth lines: he says the people overthrown by death (as if by a conqueror) "Die not, poor Death, nor yet canst thou kill me." These lines establish the paradox of death not being able to cause death.

> Discussion of how personification contributes to the poem's central argument.

The next quatrain will not begin to answer the question of why this paradox is so, but will posit another slight paradox—the idea of death as pleasurable. In lines 5-8, Donne uses the literary convention of describing death as a metaphorical sleep, or rest, to construct the argument that death must give pleasure: "From rest and sleep, which but thy pictures be, / Much pleasure; then from thee much more must flow" (5-6). At this point, the argument seems almost playful, but is carefully hinting at the solemnity of

> Discussion of how metaphor of sleep and idea of immortality support the poem's central argument.

the deeper foundation of the belief in immortality. The metaphor of sleep for death includes the idea of waking; one doesn't sleep forever. The next two lines put forth the idea that death is pleasurable enough to be desired by "our best men" who "soonest . . . with thee do go, / [for] Rest of their bones, and soul's delivery" (7-8). This last line comes closer to announcing the true reason for death's powerlessness and pleasure: It is the way to the "soul's delivery" from the body and life on earth, and implicitly, into another, better realm.

A new reason for death's powerlessness arises in the next four lines. The poet says to death:

> Thou art slave to Fate, Chance, kings, and desperate men,
>
> And dost with Poison, War, and Sickness dwell;
>
> And poppy or charms can make us sleep as well,
>
> And better than thy stroke; why swell'st thou then? (9-12)

Discussion of how language and tone contribute to the poem's central argument.

Donne argues here that there are forces more powerful than death that actually control it. Fate and chance determine when death occurs, and to whom it comes. Kings, with the powers of law and war, can summon death and throw it on whom they wish. And desperate men, murderers or suicides, can also summon death with the strength of their emotions. In lines 11 and 12, Donne again uses the metaphor of death as a kind of sleep, but says that drugs or "charms" give one a better sleep than death. And he asks playfully why death should be so proud, after all these illustrations of its weakness have been given: "why swell'st thou then?" (12).

Discussion of function of religious faith in the poem and how word order and meter create emphasis.

Finally, with the last couplet, Donne reveals the true, deeper reason behind his argument that death should not be proud of its power. These lines also offer an explanation of the metaphor for death of sleep, or rest: "One short sleep past, we wake eternally / And death shall be no more; Death, thou shalt die" (13-14). After death, the soul lives on, according to Christian theology and belief. In the Christian heaven, where the soul is immortal, death will no longer exist, and so this last paradox, "Death, thou shalt die," becomes true. Again in this line, a significant inversion of metrical stress occurs. "Death," in the second clause, receives the stress, recalling the first line, emphasizing that it is an address and giving the clause a forceful sense of finality. His belief in the immortality of the soul enables Donne to "prove" in this argument that death is in actuality like its metaphorical representation, sleep. His faith allows him to derive a source for this conventional metaphor and to "disprove" the

Bostwick 4

metaphor of death as an all-powerful conqueror. His Christian beliefs also allow him to state his truth in paradoxes, the mysteries that are justified by the mystery of faith.

Conclusion supporting thesis in context of poet's beliefs.

Bostwick 5

Work Cited

Donne, John. "Death Be Not Proud." *Literature to Go*. 2nd ed. Ed. Michael Meyer. Boston: Bedford/St. Martin's, 2014. 916. Print.

A SAMPLE STUDENT EXPLICATION

A Reading of Emily Dickinson's "There's a certain Slant of light"

The sample paper by Bonnie Katz is the result of an assignment calling for an explication of about 750 words on any poem by Emily Dickinson. Katz selected "There's a certain Slant of light."

EMILY DICKINSON (1830–1886)

There's a certain Slant of light   *c. 1861*

There's a certain Slant of light,
Winter Afternoons —
That oppresses, like the Heft
Of Cathedral Tunes —

Heavenly Hurt, it gives us —   5
We can find no scar,
But internal difference,
Where the Meanings, are —

None may teach it — Any —
'Tis the Seal Despair —   10
An imperial affliction
Sent us of the Air —

When it comes, the Landscape listens —
Shadows — hold their breath —
When it goes, 'tis like the Distance   15
On the look of Death —

Bonnie Katz's essay comments on every line of the poem and provides a coherent reading that relates each line to the speaker's intense awareness of death. Although the essay discusses each stanza in the order that it appears, the introductory paragraph provides a brief overview explaining how the poem's images contribute to its total meaning. In addition, the student does not hesitate to discuss a line out of sequence when it can be usefully connected to another phrase. This is especially apparent in the third paragraph, in her discussion of stanzas 2 and 3. The final paragraph describes some of the formal elements of the poem. It might be argued that this discussion could have been integrated into the previous paragraphs rather than placed at the end, but the student does make a connection in her concluding sentence between the pattern of language and its meaning.

Several other matters are worth noticing. The student works quotations into her own sentences to support her points. She quotes exactly as the words appear in the poem, even Dickinson's irregular use of capital letters. When something is added to a quotation to clarify it, it is enclosed in brackets so that the essayist's words will not be mistaken for the poet's: "Seal [of] Despair." A slash is used to indicate line divisions as in "imperial affliction / Sent us of the Air."

Katz 1

Bonnie Katz
Professor Quiello
English 109–2
23 March 2013

A Reading of Emily Dickinson's
"There's a certain Slant of light"

Because Emily Dickinson did not provide titles for her poetry, editors follow the customary practice of using the first line of a poem as its title. However, a more appropriate title for "There's a certain Slant of light," one that

Thesis providing overview of explication.

Katz 2

suggests what the speaker in the poem is most concerned about, can be drawn from the poem's last line, which ends with "the look of Death" (Dickinson, line 16). Although the first line begins with an image of light, nothing bright, carefree, or cheerful appears in the poem. Instead, the predominant mood and images are darkened by a sense of despair resulting from the speaker's awareness of death.

In the first stanza, the "certain Slant of light" is associated with "Winter Afternoons" (2), a phrase that connotes the end of a day, a season, and even life itself. Such light is hardly warm or comforting. Not a ray or beam, this slanting light suggests something unusual or distorted and creates in the speaker a certain slant on life that is consistent with the cold, dark mood that winter afternoons can produce. Like the speaker, most of us have seen and felt this sort of light: it "oppresses" (3) and pervades our sense of things when we encounter it. Dickinson uses the senses of hearing and touch as well as sight to describe the overwhelming oppressiveness that the speaker experiences. The light is transformed into sound by a simile that tells us it is "like the Heft / Of Cathedral Tunes" (3-4). Moreover, the "Heft" of that sound—the slow, solemn measures of tolling church bells and organ music—weighs heavily on our spirits. Through the use of shifting imagery, Dickinson evokes a kind of spiritual numbness that we keenly feel and perceive through our senses.

By associating the winter light with "Cathedral Tunes," Dickinson lets us know that the speaker is concerned about more than the weather. Whatever it is that "oppresses" is related by connotation to faith, mortality, and God. The second and third stanzas offer several suggestions about this connection. The pain caused by the light is a "Heavenly Hurt" (5). This "imperial affliction / Sent us of the Air" (11-12) apparently comes from God above, and yet it seems to be part of the very nature of life. The oppressiveness we feel is in the air, and it can neither be specifically identified at this point in the poem nor be eliminated, for "None may teach it — Any" (9). All we know is that existence itself seems depressing under the weight of this "Seal [of] Despair" (10). The impression left by this "Seal" is stamped within the mind or soul rather than externally. "We can find no scar" (6), but once experienced this oppressiveness challenges our faith in life and its "Meanings" (8).

The final stanza does not explain what those "Meanings" are, but it does make clear that the speaker is acutely aware of death. As the winter

Line-by-line explication of first stanza, focusing on connotations of words and imagery, in relation to mood and meaning of poem as a whole; supported with references to the text.

Explication of second, third, and fourth stanzas, focusing on connotations of words and imagery in relation to mood and meaning of poem as a whole. Supported with references to the text.

daylight fades, Dickinson projects the speaker's anxiety onto the surrounding landscape and shadows, which will soon be engulfed by the darkness that follows this light: "the Landscape listens — / Shadows — hold their breath" (13-14). This image firmly aligns the winter light in the first stanza with darkness. Paradoxically, the light in this poem illuminates the nature of darkness. Tension is released when the light is completely gone, but what remains is the despair that the "imperial affliction" has imprinted on the speaker's sensibilities, for it is "like the Distance / On the look of Death — " (15-16). There can be no relief from what that "certain Slant of light" has revealed because what has been experienced is permanent — like the fixed stare in the eyes of someone who is dead.

The speaker's awareness of death is conveyed in a thoughtful, hushed tone. The lines are filled with fluid *l* and smooth *s* sounds that are appropriate for the quiet, meditative voice in the poem. The voice sounds tentative and uncertain — perhaps a little frightened. This seems to be reflected in the slightly irregular meter of the lines. The stanzas are trochaic with the second and fourth lines of each stanza having five syllables, but no stanza is identical because each works a slight variation on the first stanza's seven syllables in the first and third lines. The rhymes also combine exact patterns with variations. The first and third lines of each stanza are not exact rhymes, but the second and fourth lines are exact so that the paired words are more closely related: *Afternoons, Tunes; scar, are; Despair, Air;* and *breath, Death.* There is a pattern to the poem, but it is unobtrusively woven into the speaker's voice in much the same way that "the look of Death" (16) is subtly present in the images and language of the poem.

> **Explication of the elements of rhythm and sound throughout poem.**

> **Conclusion tying explication of rhythm and sound with explication of words and imagery in previous paragraphs.**

Work Cited

Dickinson, Emily. "There's a certain Slant of light." *Literature to Go.* 2nd ed. Ed. Michael Meyer. Boston: Bedford/St. Martin's, 2014. 923-24. Print.

32

Writing about Drama

When you create drama, you look for the best conflict.
—JANE ANDERSON

FROM READING TO WRITING

Because dramatic literature is written to be performed, writing about reading a play may seem twice removed from what playwrights intend the experience of drama to be: a live audience responding to live actors. Although reading a play creates distance between yourself and a performance of it, reading a play can actually bring you closer to understanding that what supports a stage production of any play is the literary dimension of a script. Writing about that script—examining carefully how the language of the stage directions, setting, exposition, dialogue, plot, and other dramatic elements serve to produce effects and meanings—can enhance an imaginative re-creation of a performance. In a sense, writing about a play gauges your own interpretative response as an audience member—the difference, of course, is that instead of applauding, you are typing.

"There's the rub," as Hamlet might say, because you're working with the precision of your fingertips rather than with the hearty response of your palms. Composing an essay about drama records more than your response to a play; writing also helps you explore, clarify, and discover dimensions of the play you may not have perceived by simply watching a performance of it. Writing is work, of course, but it's the kind of work that brings you closer to your own imagination as well as to the play. That process is more accessible if you read carefully, take notes, and annotate the text to generate ideas (for a discussion of this process see Chapter 29, "Reading and the Writing Process"). This chapter offers a set of questions to help you read and write about drama and includes a sample paper that compares and contrasts Henrik Ibsen's play *A Doll House* with James Joyce's short story "Eveline."

Questions for Responsive Reading and Writing

The questions below can help you consider important elements that reveal a play's effects and meanings. These questions are general and will not, therefore, always be relevant to a particular play. Many of them, however, should prove to be useful for thinking, talking, and writing about drama.

1. Did you enjoy the play? What, specifically, pleased or displeased you about what was expressed and how it was expressed?

2. What is the significance of the play's title? How does it suggest the author's overall emphasis?

3. What information do the stage directions provide about the characters, action, and setting? Are these directions primarily descriptive, or are they also interpretive?

4. How is the exposition presented? What does it reveal? How does the playwright's choice *not* to dramatize certain events on stage help to determine what the focus of the play is?

5. In what ways is the setting important? Would the play be altered significantly if the setting were changed?

6. Are foreshadowings used to suggest what is to come? Are flashbacks used to dramatize what has already happened?

7. What is the major conflict the protagonist faces? What complications constitute the rising action? Where is the climax? Is the conflict resolved?

8. Are one or more subplots used to qualify or complicate the main plot? Is the plot unified so that each incident somehow has a function that relates it to some other element in the play?

9. Does the author purposely avoid a pyramidal plot structure of rising action, climax, and falling action? Is the plot experimental? Is the plot logically and chronologically organized, or is it fantastical or absurd? What effects are produced by the plot? How does it reflect the author's view of life?

10. Who is the protagonist? Who (or what) is the antagonist?

11. By what means does the playwright reveal character? What do the characters' names, physical qualities, actions, and words convey about them? What do the characters reveal about each other?

12. What is the purpose of the minor characters? Are they individualized, or do they primarily represent ideas or attitudes? Are any character foils used?

13. Do the characters all use the same kind of language, or is their speech differentiated? Is it formal or informal? How do the characters' diction and manner of speaking serve to characterize them?

14. Does your response to the characters change in the course of the play? What causes the change?

15. Are words and images repeated in the play so that they take on special meanings? Which speeches seem particularly important? Why?

16. How does the playwright's use of language contribute to the tone of the play? Is the dialogue, for example, predominantly light, humorous, relaxed, sentimental, sad, angry, intense, or violent?

17. Are any symbols used in the play? Which actions, characters, settings, objects, or words convey more than their literal meanings?

18. Are any unfamiliar theatrical conventions used that present problems in understanding the play? How does knowing more about the nature of the theater from which the play originated help to resolve these problems?

19. Is the theme stated directly, or is it developed implicitly through the plot, characters, or some other element? Does the theme confirm or challenge most people's values?

20. How does the play reflect the values of the society in which it is set and in which it was written?

21. How does the play reflect or challenge your own values?

22. Is there a recording, film, or DVD of the play available in your library, media center, or online? How does this version compare with your own reading?

23. How would you produce the play on a stage? Consider scenery, costumes, casting, and characterizations. What would you emphasize most in your production?

24. How might biographical information about the author help the reader to grasp the central concerns of the play?

25. How might historical information about the play provide a useful context for interpretation?

26. To what extent do your own experiences, values, beliefs, and assumptions inform your interpretation?

27. What kinds of evidence from the play are you focusing on to support your interpretation? Does your interpretation leave out any important elements that might undercut or qualify your interpretation?

28. Given that there are a variety of ways to interpret the play, which one seems the most useful to you?

Comparison and Contrast

Essay assignments in literature courses often require you to write about similarities and differences between or within works. You might be asked to discuss "How Sounds Express Meanings in May Swenson's 'A Nosty Fright' and Lewis Carroll's 'Jabberwocky,'" or "Sammy's and Stokesie's Attitudes about Conformity in Updike's 'A & P.'" A *comparison* of either topic would emphasize their similarities, while a *contrast* would stress their differences. It is possible, of course, to include both perspectives in a paper if you find significant likenesses and differences. A comparison of Andrew Marvell's "To His Coy Mistress" and Ann Lauinger's "Marvell Noir" would, for example, yield similarities because each poem describes a man urging his lover to make the most of their precious time together; however, important differences also exist in the tone and theme of each poem that would constitute a contrast. (You should, incidentally, be aware that the term *comparison* is sometimes used inclusively to refer to both similarities and differences. If you are assigned a comparison of two works, be sure that you understand what your instructor's expectations are; you may be required to include both approaches in the essay.)

There is no single way to organize comparative papers since each topic is likely to have its own particular issues to resolve, but it is useful to be aware of two basic patterns that can be helpful with a comparison, a contrast, or a combination of both. One method that can be effective for relatively short papers consists of dividing the paper in half, first discussing one work and then the other. Here, for example, is a partial informal outline for a discussion of Sophocles' *Oedipus the King* and Shakespeare's *Othello*; the topic is a comparison and contrast: "Oedipus and Othello as Tragic Figures."

1. Oedipus
   a. The nature of the conflict
   b. Strengths and stature
   c. Weaknesses and mistakes
   d. What is learned
2. Othello
   a. The nature of the conflict
   b. Strengths and stature
   c. Weaknesses and mistakes
   d. What is learned

This organizational strategy can be effective provided that the second part of the paper combines the discussion of Othello with references to Oedipus so that the thesis is made clear and the paper unified without being repetitive. If the two characters were treated entirely separately, then the discussion would be merely parallel rather than integrated. In a lengthy paper, this organization probably would not work well because a reader would have difficulty remembering the points made in the first half as he or she reads on.

Thus, for a longer paper it is usually better to create a more integrated structure that discusses both works as you take up each item in your outline. Here is the second basic pattern using the elements in the partial outline just cited:

1. The nature of the conflict
   a. Oedipus
   b. Othello
2. Strengths and stature
   a. Oedipus
   b. Othello
3. Weaknesses and mistakes
   a. Oedipus
   b. Othello
4. What is learned
   a. Oedipus
   b. Othello

This pattern allows you to discuss any number of topics without requiring your reader to recall what you first said about the conflict Oedipus confronts before you discuss Othello's conflicts fifteen pages later. However you structure your comparison or contrast paper, make certain that a reader can follow its elements and keep track of its thesis.

A SAMPLE STUDENT COMPARISON

The Struggle for Women's Self-Definition in Henrik Ibsen's A Doll House and James Joyce's "Eveline"

The following paper was written in response to an assignment that required a comparison and contrast — about 750 words — of two works of literature. The student chose to write an analysis of how the women in each work respond to being defined by men.

Monica Casis

Professor Matthews

English 105-4

4 February 2013

The Struggle for Women's Self-Definition

in Henrik Ibsen's *A Doll House* and

James Joyce's "Eveline"

Although Henrik Ibsen's *A Doll House* (1879) and James Joyce's "Eveline"
(1914) were written more than thirty years apart and portray radically different
characters and circumstances, both works raise similar questions about the role of
women and how they are defined in their respective worlds. Each work presents
a woman who conforms to society's ideas of gender in an effort to be accepted
and loved. While both Ibsen's Nora Helmer and Joyce's Eveline are intelligent and
resourceful, Nora is able to break free of society's hold; Eveline cannot. Nevertheless,
these narratives show the emergence of each woman's identity—Nora's refusal to
be a submissive and belittled housewife and Eveline's awareness of the constraints
placed upon her by her father and community. From the beginning, these women are
more intelligent and self-aware than the people who oppress them; unfortunately,
that does not necessarily lead to complete autonomy.

In *A Doll House*, Nora is treated as her father's, then her husband's,
doll. She is called "squirrel," "spendthrift," and "lark" and is admonished for
such things as eating sweets or asking her husband to take her ideas into
consideration (799). Torvald's concept of the ideal woman is a showpiece who
can dress up, recite, and dance. As a mother, Nora only plays with her children;
it is Anne Marie who takes care of them. As a housewife, she has no control over
the household finances; her husband gives her an allowance.

Although Nora continually conforms to her husband's expectations, she has
the strength and courage to borrow money for a trip to Italy to save his life and
does odd jobs to pay the debt that she has committed forgery to secure. She is
proud of her sacrifice for her family. At the same time, she plays the role of a
frivolous, helpless, dependent woman in order to coax her husband into giving
her money and to keep him away from Krogstad's incriminating letter; she
lies in order to keep him happy. Though Nora appears to be a woman trapped
within her husband's expectations of her, she does have a will of her own. Once
she sees and understands Torvald's superficiality and selfishness—that he is
concerned only with what threatens him—Nora realizes she must abandon him

and the role he has defined for her. Eveline, who submits to her overbearing father for most of Joyce's story, ultimately sees the need for change — the need to break out of her current life. However, unlike Nora, Eveline does not imagine an independent life; she sees marriage to Frank as her only way out. It is marriage that she believes will bring respect, happiness, and a kind of freedom: "People would treat her with respect then. She would not be treated as her mother had been" (323).

The turning points in *A Doll House* and in "Eveline" occur when the women protagonists are faced with the choice of whether to leave the men in their lives. Nora is convinced that she will corrupt her children and home with the guilt she bears — for being with a man whom she no longer respects. When Torvald learns the truth from Krogstad, he regards her as liar, hypocrite, and criminal and therefore repudiates her. Once Nora realizes the selfishness of her husband, she knows she cannot stay with him. She must leave him and her children in order to search for her own identity.

Eveline's turning point, on the other hand, results in inaction. She cannot bring herself to leave her home or her father, however unpleasant her daily life. The reasons are not entirely clear, but we can assume that her reluctance stems from the fear of such overwhelming change. Leaving her home and the people she has known her entire life is understandably daunting, especially for such a young person. However, there is also the possibility that Eveline recognizes the problem with her plan. Relocating and marrying Frank will only substitute one dependence with another. Leaving would force her to, once again, rely on the male presence in her life. As a married woman she would never truly gain her own identity.

When Nora and Eveline come to terms with themselves, their situations are no less problematic than when they falsely fulfilled the expectations imposed on them by the men in their lives. Nora leaves to pursue what may seem to be selfish desires, yet this bold move is necessary to gain independence and self-reliance. Eveline, however, cannot free herself from her father's control or leave Dublin with Frank, because her fear and guilt entrap her "like a helpless animal" (325). She lacks Nora's strength and determination to embark on a new life of risky possibilities; instead, Eveline remains passive and unable to choose a different life for herself.

At the end of the work, both women face the struggles that will inform the rest of their lives, but whereas Nora's circumstances might be understood as potentially hopeful, Eveline's condition almost certainly must be considered as hopeless.

Casis 3

Works Cited

Ibsen, Henrik, *A Doll House*. *Literature to Go*. 2nd ed. Ed. Michael Meyer. Boston: Bedford/St. Martin's, 2014. 797-852. Print.

Joyce, James, "Eveline." *Literature to Go*. 2nd ed. Ed. Michael Meyer. Boston: Bedford/St. Martin's, 2014. 322-25. Print.

33

The Literary
Research Paper

Does anyone know a good poet who's a
vegetarian?
—DONALD HALL

© Nancy Crampton.

A close reading of a primary source such as a short story, poem, or play
can give insights into a work's themes and effects, but sometimes you
will want to know more. A published commentary by a critic who knows
the work well and is familiar with the author's life and times can provide
insights that otherwise may not be available. Such comments and interpretations — known as *secondary sources* — are, of course, not a substitute
for the work itself, but they often can take you into a work further than
if you made the journey by yourself.

After imagination, good sense, and energy, perhaps the next most
important quality for writing a research paper is the ability to organize
material. A research paper on a literary topic requires a writer to take
account of quite a lot at once: The text, ideas, sources, and documentation techniques all make demands on one's efforts to present a topic
clearly and convincingly.

The following list should give you a sense of what goes into creating
a research paper. Although some steps on the list can be folded into one
another, they offer an overview of the work that is required:

1. Choosing a topic
2. Finding sources
3. Evaluating sources
4. Taking notes
5. Developing a thesis
6. Organizing an outline

7. Writing drafts
8. Revising
9. Documenting sources
10. Preparing the final draft and proofreading

Even if you have never written a research paper, you most likely have already had experience choosing a topic, developing a thesis, organizing an outline, and writing a draft that you then revised, proofread, and handed in. Those skills represent six of the ten items on the list. This chapter briefly reviews some of these steps and focuses on the remaining tasks, unique to research paper assignments.

CHOOSING A TOPIC

Chapter 29 discussed the importance of reading a work closely and taking careful notes as a means of generating topics for writing about literature. If you know a work well and record your understanding of it in notes, you'll have impressions and ideas to choose from for potential topics.

The student author of the sample research paper "How William Faulkner's Narrator Cultivates a Rose for Emily" (p. 948) was asked to write a five-page paper that demonstrated some familiarity with published critical perspectives on a Faulkner story of his choice. Before looking into critical discussions of the story, he read "A Rose for Emily" several times, taking notes and making comments in the margin of his textbook on each reading.

What prompted his choice of "A Rose for Emily" was a class discussion in which many of his classmates found the story's title inappropriate or misleading because they could not understand how and why the story constituted a tribute to Emily given that she murdered a man and slept with his dead body over many years. The gruesome surprise ending revealing Emily as a murderer and necrophiliac hardly seemed to warrant a rose and a tribute for the central character. Why did Faulkner use such a title? Only after having thoroughly examined the story did the student go to the library to see what professional critics had to say about this question.

FINDING SOURCES

Whether your college library is large or small, its reference librarians can usually help you locate secondary sources about a particular work or author. Unless you choose a very recently published story, poem, play, or essay about which little or nothing has been written, you should be able to find out more about a literary work efficiently and quickly. Even if a work has been published recently, you can probably find relevant information on the Internet (see Electronic Sources, following).

Electronic Sources

Researchers can locate materials in a variety of sources, including library online catalogs, specialized encyclopedias, bibliographies, and indexes to periodicals. Libraries also provide online databases that you can access from home. This can be an efficient way to establish a bibliography on a specific topic. Consult a reference librarian about how to use your library's online resources and to determine how they will help you research your topic.

In addition to the many electronic databases ranging from your library's computerized holdings to the many specialized CD-ROMs available, such as *MLA International Bibliography* (a major source for articles and books on literary topics), the Internet also connects millions of sites with primary sources (the full texts of stories, poems, plays, and essays) and secondary sources (biography or criticism). If you have not had practice with research on the Web, it is a good idea to get guidance from your instructor or a librarian, and by using your library's home page as a starting point. Browsing on the Internet can be absorbing as well as informative, but unless you have plenty of time to spare, don't wait until the last minute to locate your electronic sources. You might find yourself trying to find reliable, professional sources among thousands of sites if you enter too-general search terms such as "Charles Dickens." Following are several especially useful electronic databases that will provide you with bibliographic information in literature studies. Your school's English Department home page may offer online support as well.

Internet Public Library Online Criticism. <ipl.org/div/litcrit>. Maintained by the University of Michigan, this site provides links to literary criticism by author, work, country, or period.

JSTOR. An index that also offers abstracts of journal articles on language and literature.

MLA International Bibliography. This is a standard resource for articles and books on literary subjects that allows topical and keyword searches.

Voice of the Shuttle. <vos.ucsb.edu>. Maintained by the University of California, this site is a wide-ranging resource for British and American literary studies.

Do remember that your own college library offers a broad range of electronic sources. If you're feeling uncertain or intimidated, your reference librarians are there to help you to get started.

EVALUATING SOURCES AND TAKING NOTES

Evaluate your sources for their reliability and the quality of their evidence. Check to see whether an article or book has been superseded by later studies; try to use up-to-date sources. A popular magazine article will probably not be as authoritative as an article in a scholarly journal. Sources that are well documented with primary and secondary materials usually indicate that the author has done his or her home-work. Books printed by university presses and established trade presses are preferable to books privately printed. But there are always excep-tions. If you are uncertain about how to assess a book, try to find out something about the author. Are there any other books listed in the online catalog that indicate the author's expertise? What do book reviews say about the work? Three valuable indexes to book reviews of literary studies are *Book Review Digest, Book Review Index,* and *Index to Book Reviews in the Humanities.* Your reference librarian can show you how to use these important tools for evaluating books. Reviews can be a quick means to gain a broad perspective on writers and their works because reviewers often survey previous approaches to the topic under discussion.

A cautionary note: Assessing online sources can be more problem-atic than evaluating print sources because anyone with a computer and online access can publish on the Internet. Be sure to determine the nature of your sources and their authority. Is the site the work of a pro-fessional or an amateur? Is the information likely to be reliable? Is it doc-umented? Before placing your trust in an Internet source, make sure that it warrants your confidence.

As you prepare a list of reliable sources relevant to your topic, record the necessary bibliographic information so that it will be available when you make up the list of works cited for your paper. For a book, include the author, complete title, place of publication, publisher, and date. For an article, include author, complete title, name of periodical, volume number, date of issue, and page numbers. For an Internet source, include the author, complete title, database title, periodical or site name, date of posting of the site (or last update), name of the institution or organiza-tion, and date when you accessed the source.

Once you have assembled a tentative bibliography, you will need to take notes on your readings. Be sure to keep track of where particular information comes from by noting the author's name and page number. If you use more than one work by the same author, include a brief title as well as the author's name.

DEVELOPING A THESIS AND ORGANIZING THE PAPER

As the notes on "A Rose for Emily" accumulated, the student sorted them into topics:

1.   Publication history of the story
2.   Faulkner on the title of "A Rose for Emily"
3.   Is Emily simply insane?

4.   The purpose of Emily's servant
5.   The narrator
6.   The townspeople's view of Emily
7.   The surprise ending
8.   Emily's admirable qualities
9.   Homer's character

The student quickly saw that items 1, 4, and 9 were not directly related to his topic concerning the significance of the story's title. The remaining numbers (2, 3, 5, 6, 7, 8) are the topics taken up in the paper. The student had begun his reading of secondary sources with a tentative thesis that stemmed from his question about the appropriateness of the title. That "why" shaped itself into the expectation that he would have a thesis something like this: "The title justifies Emily's murder of Homer because . . ."

The assumption was that he would find information that indicated some specific reason. But the more he read, the more he discovered that it was possible to speak only about how the narrator prevents the reader from making a premature judgment about Emily rather than justifying her actions. Hence, he wisely changed his tentative thesis to this final statement—"The narrator describes incidents and withholds information in such a way as to cause the reader to sympathize with Emily before her crime is revealed." This thesis helped the student explain why the title is accurate and useful rather than misleading.

Because the assignment was relatively brief, the student did not write up a formal outline but instead organized his notes and proceeded to write the first draft from them.

REVISING

After writing your first draft, you should review the advice and revision checklist on pages 901–02 so that you can read your paper with an objective eye. Two days after writing his next-to-last draft, the writer of "How William Faulkner's Narrator Cultivates a Rose for Emily" realized that he had allotted too much space for critical discussions of the narrator that were not directly related to his approach. He wanted to demonstrate a familiarity with these studies, but it was not essential that he summarize or discuss them. He corrected this by consolidating parenthetical references: "Though a number of studies discuss the story's narrator (see, for example, Curry; Kempton; Sullivan; and Watkins). . . ." His earlier draft had included summaries of these studies that were tangential to his argument. The point is that he saw this himself after he took some time to approach the paper from a fresh perspective.

DOCUMENTING SOURCES AND AVOIDING PLAGIARISM

You must acknowledge the use of a source when you (1) quote someone's exact words, (2) summarize or borrow someone's opinions or ideas, or (3) use information and facts that are not considered to be common knowledge. The purpose of this documentation is to acknowledge your sources, to demonstrate that you are familiar with what others have thought about the topic, and to provide your reader access to the same sources. If your paper is not adequately documented, it will be vulnerable to a charge of *plagiarism*—the presentation of someone else's work as your own. Conscious plagiarism is easy to avoid; honesty takes care of that for most people. However, there is a more problematic form of plagiarism that is often inadvertent. Whether inadequate documentation is conscious or not, plagiarism is a serious matter and must be avoided. Papers can be evaluated only by what is on the page, not by their writers' intentions.

Let's look more closely at what constitutes plagiarism. Consider the following passage quoted from John Gassner's introduction to *Four Great Plays by Henrik Ibsen* (New York: Bantam, 1959, p. viii):

> Today it seems incredible that *A Doll's House*° should have created the furor it did. In exploding Victorian ideals of feminine dependency the play seemed revolutionary in 1879. When its heroine Nora left her home in search of self-development it seemed as if the sanctity of marriage had been flouted by a playwright treading the stage with cloven-feet.

Now read this plagiarized version:

A Doll's House created a furor in 1879 by blowing up Victorian ideals about a woman's place in the world. Nora's search for self-fulfillment outside her home appeared to be an attack on the sanctity of marriage by a cloven-footed playwright.

Though the writer has shortened the passage and made some changes in the wording, this paragraph is basically the same as Gassner's. Indeed, several of his phrases are lifted almost intact. Even if a parenthetical reference had been included at the end of the passage and the source included in "Works Cited," the language of this passage would still be plagiarism because it is presented as the writer's own. Both language and ideas must be acknowledged.

Here is an adequately documented version of the passage:

John Gassner has observed how difficult it is for today's readers to comprehend the intense reaction against *A Doll's House* in 1879. When Victorian audiences watched Nora

°Rolf Fjelde, whose translation is included in Chapter 27, renders the title as *A Doll House* in order to emphasize that the whole household, including Torvald as well as Nora, lives an unreal, doll-like existence.

walk out of her stifling marriage, they assumed that Ibsen was expressing a devilish contempt for the "sanctity of marriage" (viii).

This passage makes absolutely clear that the observation is Gassner's, and it is written in the student's own language with the exception of one quoted phrase. Had Gassner not been named in the passage, the parenthetical reference would have included his name: (Gassner viii).

Some mention should be made of the notion of common knowledge before we turn to the standard format for documenting sources. Observations and facts that are widely known and routinely included in many of your sources do not require documentation. It is not necessary to cite a source for the fact that Alfred, Lord Tennyson was born in 1809 or that Ernest Hemingway loved to fish and hunt. Sometimes it will be difficult for you to determine what common knowledge is for a topic that you know little about. If you are in doubt, the best strategy is to supply a reference.

There are two basic ways to document sources. Traditionally, sources have been cited in footnotes at the bottom of each page or in endnotes grouped together at the end of the paper. Here is how a portion of the sample paper would look if footnotes were used instead of parenthetical documentation:

As Heller points out, before we learn of Emily's bizarre behavior we see her as a sympathetic — if antiquated — figure in a town whose life and concerns have passed her by; hence, "we are disposed to see Emily as victimized."[1]

[1]Terry Heller, "The Telltale Hair: A Critical Study of William Faulkner's 'A Rose for Emily,'" *Arizona Quarterly* 28.4 (1972): 306. Print.

Unlike endnotes, which are double spaced throughout under the title of "Notes" on separate pages at the end of the paper, footnotes appear four spaces below the text. They are single spaced with double spaces between notes.

No doubt you will have encountered these documentation methods in your reading. A different style is recommended, however, in the Modern Language Association's *MLA Handbook for Writers of Research Papers,* 7th ed. (New York: MLA, 2009). This style employs parenthetical references within the text of the paper; these are keyed to an alphabetical list of works cited at the end of the paper. This method is designed to be less distracting for the reader. Unless you are instructed to follow the footnote or endnote style for documentation, use the parenthetical method explained in the next section.

The List of Works Cited

Items in the list of works cited are arranged alphabetically according to the author's last name and indented a half inch after the first line. This allows the reader to locate quickly the complete bibliographic information for the author's name cited within the parenthetical reference in the text. The following are common entries for literature papers and should be used as models. If some of your sources are of a different nature, consult the *MLA Handbook for Writers of Research Papers,* 7th ed. (New York: MLA, 2009); or, for the latest updates, check MLA's Web site at <mlahandbook.org>.

The following entries include examples to follow when citing electronic sources. For electronic sources, include as many of the following elements as apply and as are available:

- Author's name
- Title of work (if it's a book, italicize the title; if it's a short work, such as an article or poem, use quotation marks)
- Title of the site (or of the publication, if you're citing an online periodical, for example), italicized
- Sponsor or publisher of the site (if not named as the author)
- Date of publication or last update
- Medium of publication
- Date you accessed the source

A book by one author

Hendrickson, Robert. *The Literary Life and Other Curiosities*. New York: Viking, 1981. Print.

An online book

Frost, Robert. *A Boy's Will*. New York: Holt, 1915. *Bartleby.com: Great Books Online*. Web. 11 May 2009.

Part of an online book

Frost, Robert. "Into My Own." *A Boy's Will*. New York: Holt, 1915. N. pag. *Bartleby.com: Great Books Online*. Web. 11 May 2009.

Notice that the author's name is in reverse order. This information, along with the full title, place of publication, publisher, and date, should be taken from the title and copyright pages of the book. The title is italicized and is also followed by a period. If the city of publication is well known, it is unnecessary to include the state. Use the publication date on the title page; if none appears there, use the copyright date (after ©) on the back of the title page. Include the medium of publication (print, Web).

A book by two authors

Horton, Rod W., and Herbert W. Edwards. *Backgrounds of American Literary Thought*. 3rd ed. Englewood Cliffs: Prentice, 1974. Print.

Only the first author's name is given in reverse order. The edition number appears after the title.

A book with more than three authors or editors

Gates, Henry Louis, Jr., et al., eds. *The Norton Anthology of African American Literature*. New York: Norton, 1997. Print.

(Note: The abbreviation *et al.* means "and others.")

A work in a collection by the same author

O'Connor, Flannery. "Greenleaf." *The Complete Stories*. By O'Connor. New York: Farrar, 1971. 311-34. Print.

Page numbers are given because the reference is to only a single story in the collection.

A work in a collection by a different writer

Frost, Robert. "Design." *Literature to Go*. 2nd ed. Ed. Michael Meyer. Boston: Bedford/St. Martin's, 2014. 365. Print.

Sophocles. *Oedipus the King*. *Literature to Go*. 2nd ed. Ed. Michael Meyer. Boston: Bedford/St. Martin's, 2014. 644-90. Print.

The titles of poems and short stories are enclosed in quotation marks; plays and novels are italicized.

Cross-reference to a collection

Frost, Robert. "Design." Meyer. 365.

Meyer, Michael, ed. *Literature to Go*. 2nd ed. Boston: Bedford/St. Martin's, 2014. Print.

O'Connor, Flannery. "A Good Man Is Hard to Find." Meyer. 249-61.

Sophocles. *Oedipus the King*. Meyer. 644-90.

When citing more than one work from the same collection, use a cross-reference to avoid repeating the same bibliographic information that appears in the main entry for the collection.

A translated book

Grass, Günter. *The Tin Drum*. Trans. Ralph Manheim. New York: Vintage-Random, 1962. Print.

An introduction, preface, foreword, or afterword

Johnson, Thomas H. Introduction. *Final Harvest: Emily Dickinson's Poems*. By Emily Dickinson. Boston: Little, Brown, 1961. vii-xiv. Print.

This cites the introduction by Johnson. Notice that a colon is used between the book's main title and subtitle. To cite a poem in this book, use this method:

Dickinson, Emily. "A Tooth upon Our Peace." *Final Harvest: Emily Dickinson's Poems.* Ed.

Thomas H. Johnson. Boston: Little, Brown, 1961. 110. Print.

An entry in an encyclopedia

"Wordsworth, William." *The New Encyclopedia Britannica.* 1984 ed. Print.

Because this encyclopedia is organized alphabetically, no page number or other information is given, only the edition number (if available) and date.

An article in a magazine

Morrow, Lance. "Scribble, Scribble, Eh, Mr. Toad." *Time* 24 Feb. 1986: 84. Print.

An article from an online magazine

Wasserman, Elizabeth. "The Byron Complex." *Atlantic Online.* The Atlantic Monthly Group,

22 Sept. 2002. Web. 4 Feb. 2004.

The citation for an unsigned article would begin with the title and be alphabetized by the first word of the title other than "a," "an," or "the."

An article in a scholarly journal with continuous pagination beyond a single issue

Mahar, William J. "Black English in Early Blackface Minstrelsy: A New Interpretation of the

Sources of Minstrel Show Dialect." *American Quarterly* 37.2 (1985): 260-85. Print.

Regardless of whether the journal uses continuous pagination or separate pagination for each issue, it is necessary to include the volume number and the issue number for every entry (for example, "11.5" indicates volume 11, issue 5). If a journal does not offer an issue number, use only the volume number, as in the next entry. If a journal uses *only* issue numbers, use that in place of the volume number.

An article in a scholarly journal with separate pagination for each issue

Updike, John. "The Cultural Situation of the American Writer." *American Studies*

International 15 (1977): 19-28. Print.

In the following citation, noting the winter issue helps a reader find the correct article among all of the articles published by the online journal in 2004.

An article from an online scholarly journal

Mamet, David. "Secret Names." *The Threepenny Review* 96 (Winter 2004): n. pag. Web.
    4 Feb. 2004.

The following citation indicates that the article appears on page 1 of section 7 and continues onto another page.

An article in a newspaper

Ziegler, Philip. "The Lure of Gossip, the Rules of History." *New York Times* 23 Feb. 1986:
    sec. 7: 1+. Print.

An article from an online newspaper

Brantley, Ben. "Souls Lost and Doomed Enliven London Stages." *New York Times.* New York
    Times, 4 Feb. 2004. Web. 5 Feb. 2004.

A lecture

Tilton, Robert. "The Beginnings of American Studies." English 270 class lecture. University
    of Connecticut, Storrs. 12 Mar. 2004. Lecture.

Letter, e-mail, or interview

Vellenga, Carolyn. Letter to the author. 9 Oct. 1997.

Harter, Stephen P. E-mail to the author. 28 Dec. 1997.

McConagha, Bill. Personal interview. 9 May 2009.

Following are additional examples for citing electronic sources.

Work from a subscription service

Libraries pay for access to databases such as *Lexis-Nexis, ProQuest Direct,* and *Expanded Academic ASAP.* When you retrieve an article or other work from a subscription database, cite your source based on this model:

Vendler, Helen Hennessey. "The Passion of Emily Dickinson." *New Republic* 3 Aug. 1992:
    34-8. *Expanded Academic ASAP.* Web. 4 Feb. 2004.

A document from a Web site

When citing sources from the Internet, include as much publication information as possible (see guidelines on p. 942). In some cases, as in the following example, a date of publication for the document "Dickens in America" is not available. The entry provides the author, title of document, title of site, sponsor of the site, medium, and access date:

Perdue, David. "Dickens in America." *David Perdue's Charles Dickens Page*. David A. Perdue,
1 Apr. 2009. Web. 13 Apr. 2009.

An entire Web site

Perdue, David. *David Perdue's Charles Dickens Page*. David A. Perdue, 1 Apr. 2009. Web.
13 Apr. 2009.

Treat a CD-ROM as you would any other source, but name the medium at the end of the entry.

A work from a CD-ROM

Aaron, Belèn V. "The Death of Theory." *Scholarly Book Reviews* 4.3 (1997): 146-47. CD-ROM.
ERIC. SilverPlatter. Dec. 1997.

An online posting

Shuck, John. "Hamlet." *PBS Discussions*. PBS, 16 May 2005. Web. 13 Apr. 2009.

Parenthetical References

A list of works cited is not an adequate indication of how you have used sources in your paper. You must also provide the precise location of quotations and other information by using parenthetical references within the text of the paper. You do this by citing the author's last name (or the source's title if the work is anonymous) and the page number:

Collins points out that "Nabokov was misunderstood by early reviewers of his work" (28).

or

Nabokov's first critics misinterpreted his stories (Collins 28).

Either way a reader will find the complete bibliographic entry in the list of works cited under Collins's name and know that the information cited in the paper appears on page 28. Notice that the end punctuation comes after the parentheses.

If you have listed more than one work by the same author, you would add a brief title to the parenthetical reference to distinguish between them. You could also include the full title in your text:

Nabokov's first critics misinterpreted his stories (Collins, "Early Reviews" 28).

or

Collins points out in "Early Reviews of Nabokov's Fiction" that Nabokov's early work was misinterpreted by reviewers (28).

For electronic sources, provide the author's name. Unless your online source is a stable, paginated document (such as a pdf file), do not include page numbers in your parenthetical references. The following example shows an in-text citation to William Faulkner's acceptance speech for the Nobel Prize in Literature, found at the Nobel Web site.

William Faulkner believed that it was his duty as a writer to "help man endure by lifting his heart" (Faulkner).

This reference would appear in the works cited list as follows:

Faulkner, William. "Banquet Speech: The Nobel Prize in Literature." *The Nobel E-Museum.*
     The Nobel Foundation, 10 Dec. 1950. Web. 4 Feb. 2009.

There can be many variations on what is included in a parenthetical reference, depending on the nature of the entry in the list of works cited. But the general principle is simple enough: Provide enough parenthetical information for a reader to find the work in "Works Cited." Examine the following sample research paper for more examples of works cited and strategies for including parenthetical references. If you are puzzled by a given situation, refer to the *MLA Handbook*.

A SAMPLE STUDENT RESEARCH PAPER

How William Faulkner's Narrator Cultivates a Rose for Emily

The following research paper by Tony Groulx follows the format described in the *MLA Handbook for Writers of Research Papers*, 7th ed. (2009). Though the sample paper is short, it illustrates many of the techniques and strategies useful for writing an essay that includes secondary sources. (Faulkner's "A Rose for Emily" is reprinted on p. 52.)

Groulx 1

Tony Groulx
Professor Hugo
English 109-3
4 February 2013

How William Faulkner's Narrator
Cultivates a Rose for Emily

William Faulkner's "A Rose for Emily" is an absorbing mystery story whose chilling ending contains a gruesome surprise. When we discover, along with the narrator and townspeople, what was left of Homer Barron's body, we may be surprised or not, depending on how carefully we have been reading the story and keeping track of details such as Emily Grierson's purchase of rat poison and Homer's disappearance. Probably most readers anticipate finding Homer's body at the end of the story because Faulkner carefully prepares the groundwork for the discovery as the townspeople force their way into that mysterious upstairs room where a "thin, acrid pall as of the tomb seemed to lie everywhere" (58). But very few readers, if any, are prepared for the story's final paragraph, when we realize that the strand of "iron-gray hair" (the last three words of the story) on the second pillow indicates that Emily has slept with Homer since she murdered him. This last paragraph produces the real horror in the story and an extraordinary revelation about Emily's character.

The final paragraph seems like the right place to begin a discussion of this story because the surprise ending not only creates a powerful emotional effect in us but also raises an important question about what we are to think of Emily. Is this isolated, eccentric woman simply mad? All the circumstantial evidence indicates that she is a murderer and necrophiliac, and yet Faulkner titles the story "A Rose for Emily," as if she is due some kind of tribute. The title somehow qualifies the gasp of horror that the story leads up to in the final paragraph. Why would anyone offer this woman a "rose"? What's behind the title?

Faulkner was once directly asked the meaning of the title and replied:

> Oh it's simply the poor woman had had no life at all. Her father had kept her more or less locked up and then she had a lover who was about to quit her, she had to murder him. It was just "A Rose for Emily"—that's all. (qtd. in Gwynn and Blotner 87-8)

This reply explains some of Emily's motivation for murdering Homer, but it doesn't actually address the purpose and meaning of the title. If Emily killed Homer out of a kind of emotional necessity—out of a fear of abandonment—

Reference to text of the story.

Reference to secondary source (Gwynn and Blotner).

Groulx 2

how does that explain the fact that the title seems to suggest that the story is a way of paying respect to Emily? The question remains.

Whatever respect the story creates for Emily cannot be the result of her actions. Surely there can be no convincing excuse made for murder and necrophilia; there is nothing to praise about what she does. Instead, the tribute comes in the form of how her story is told rather than what we are told about her. To do this Faulkner uses a narrator who tells Emily's story in such a way as to maximize our sympathy for her. The grim information about Emily's "iron-gray hair" on the pillow is withheld until the very end and not only to produce a surprise but to permit the reader to develop a sympathetic understanding of her before we are shocked and disgusted by her necrophilia.

Significantly, the narrator begins the story with Emily's death rather than Homer's. Though a number of studies discuss the story's narrator (see, for example, Curry; Kempton; Sullivan; and Watkins), Terry Heller's is one of the most comprehensive in its focus on the narrator's effects on the readers' response to Emily. As Heller points out, before we learn of Emily's bizarre behavior we see her as a sympathetic — if antiquated — figure in a town whose life and concerns have passed her by; hence, "we are disposed to see Emily as victimized" (306). Her refusal to pay her taxes is an index to her isolation and eccentricity, but this incident also suggests a degree of dignity and power lacking in the town officials who fail to collect her taxes. Her encounters with the officials of Jefferson — whether in the form of the sneaking aldermen who try to cover up the smell around her house or the druggist who unsuccessfully tries to get her to conform to the law when she buys arsenic — place her in an admirable light because her willfulness is based on her personal strength. Moreover, it is relatively easy to side with Emily when the townspeople are described as taking pleasure in her being reduced to poverty as a result of her father's death because "now she too would know the old thrill and the old despair of a penny more or less" (Faulkner 54). The narrator's account of their pettiness, jealousy, and inability to make sense of Emily causes the reader to sympathize with Emily's eccentricities before we must judge her murderous behavior. We admire her for taking life on her own terms, and the narrator makes sure this response is in place prior to our realization that she also takes life.

We don't really know much about Emily because the narrator arranges the details of her life so that it's difficult to know what she's been up to. We learn, for example, about the smell around the house before she buys the poison

> Reference to secondary sources (Curry; Kempton; Sullivan; Watkins) with signal phrase for Heller.

> Reference to secondary source (Heller) with signal phrase ("As Heller points out . . .").

> Reference to text of the story.

Groulx 3

and Homer disappears, so that the cause-and-effect relationship among these

events is a bit slippery (for a detailed reconstruction of the chronology, see
McGlynn and Nebecker's revision of McGlynn's work), but the effect is to suspend
judgment of Emily. By the time we realize what she has done, we are already
inclined to see her as outside community values almost out of necessity. That's
not to say that the murdering of Homer is justified by the narrator, but it is
to say that her life maintains its private — though no longer secret — dignity.
Despite the final revelation, Emily remains "dear, inescapable, impervious,
tranquil, and perverse" (Faulkner 58).

    The narrator's "rose" to Emily is his recognition that Emily is all these
things — including "perverse." She evokes "a sort of respectful affection for
a fallen monument" (Faulkner 52). She is, to be sure, "fallen," but she is also
somehow central — a "monument" — to the life of the community. Faulkner
does not offer a definitive reading of Emily, but he does have the narrator
pay tribute to her by attempting to provide a complex set of contexts for her
actions — contexts that include a repressive father, resistance to a changing
South and impinging North, the passage of time and its influence on the present,
and relations between men and women as well as relations between generations.
Robert Crosman discusses the narrator's efforts to understand Emily:

> The narrator is himself a "reader" of Emily's story, trying to put
> together from fragments a complete picture, trying to find the
> meaning of her life in its impact upon an audience, the citizens of
> Jefferson, of which he is a member. (212)

The narrator refuses to dismiss Emily as simply mad or to treat her life as merely
a grotesque, sensational horror story. Instead, his narrative method brings
us into her life before we too hastily reject her, and in doing so it offers us a
complex imaginative treatment of fierce determination and strength coupled
with illusions and shocking eccentricities. The narrator's rose for Emily is paying
her the tribute of placing that "long strand of iron-gray hair" in the context of
her entire life.

Works Cited

Crosman, Robert. "How Readers Make Meaning." *College Literature* 9.3 (1982): 207-15. Print.

Curry, Renee R. "Gender and Authorial Limitation in Faulkner's 'A Rose for Emily.'" *The Mississippi Quarterly* 47.3 (1994): 391-402. *Expanded Academic ASAP.* Web. 4 Feb. 2004.

Faulkner, William. "A Rose for Emily." *Literature to Go.* 2nd ed. Ed. Michael Meyer. Boston: Bedford/St. Martin's, 2014. 52-59. Print.

Gwynn, Frederick, and Joseph Blotner, eds. *Faulkner in the University: Class Conferences at the University of Virginia, 1957-58.* Charlottesville: U of Virginia P, 1959. Print.

Heller, Terry. "The Telltale Hair: A Critical Study of William Faulkner's 'A Rose for Emily.'" *Arizona Quarterly* 28.4 (1972): 301-18. Print.

Kempton, K. P. *The Short Story.* Cambridge: Harvard UP, 1954. 104-06. Print.

McGlynn, Paul D. "The Chronology of 'A Rose for Emily.'" *Studies in Short Fiction* 6.4 (1969): 461-62. Print.

Nebecker, Helen E. "Chronology Revised." *Studies in Short Fiction* 8.4 (1971): 471-73. Print.

Sullivan, Ruth. "The Narrator in 'A Rose for Emily.'" *Journal of Narrative Technique* 1.3 (1971): 159-78. Print.

Watkins, F. C. "The Structure of 'A Rose for Emily.'" *Modern Language Notes* 69.6 (1954): 508-10. Print.

Glossary of Literary Terms

Accent The emphasis, or stress, given a syllable in pronunciation. We say "*syl*lable" not "syl*lable*," "*em*phasis" not "em*pha*sis." Accents can also be used to emphasize a particular word in a sentence: *Is* she con*tent* with the *con*tents of the *yel*low *pack*age? See also METER.

Act A major division in the action of a play. The ends of acts are typically indicated by lowering the curtain or turning up the houselights. Playwrights frequently employ acts to accommodate changes in time, setting, characters onstage, or mood. In many full-length plays, acts are further divided into scenes, which often mark a point in the action when the location changes or when a new character enters. See also SCENE.

Allegory A narration or description usually restricted to a single meaning because its events, actions, characters, settings, and objects represent specific abstractions or ideas. Although the elements in an allegory may be interesting in themselves, the emphasis tends to be on what they ultimately mean. Characters may be given names such as Hope, Pride, Youth, and Charity; they have few if any personal qualities beyond their abstract meanings. These personifications are not symbols because, for instance, the meaning of a character named Charity is precisely that virtue. See also SYMBOL.

Alliteration The repetition of the same consonant sounds in a sequence of words, usually at the beginning of a word or stressed syllable: "*descend*ing *dew drops*"; "*luscious lemons*." Alliteration is based on the sounds of letters, rather than the spelling of words; for example, "*keen*" and "*car*" alliterate, but "*car*" and "*cite*" do not. Used sparingly, alliteration can intensify ideas by emphasizing key words, but when used too self-consciously, it can be distracting, even ridiculous, rather than effective. See also ASSONANCE, CONSONANCE.

Allusion A brief reference to a person, place, thing, event, or idea in history or literature. Allusions conjure up biblical authority, scenes from Shakespeare's plays, historic figures, wars, great love stories, and anything else that might enrich an author's work. Allusions imply reading and cultural experiences shared by the writer and reader, functioning as a kind of shorthand whereby the recalling of something outside the work supplies an emotional or intellectual context, such as a poem about current racial struggles calling up the memory of Abraham Lincoln.

Ambiguity Allows for two or more simultaneous interpretations of a word, phrase, action, or situation, all of which can be supported by the context of a work. Deliberate ambiguity can contribute to the effectiveness and richness of a work, for example, in Randall Jarrell's poem "The Death of the Ball Turret Gunner." However, unintentional ambiguity obscures meaning and can confuse readers.

Anagram A word or phrase made from the letters of another word or phrase, as "heart" is an anagram of "earth." Anagrams have often been considered merely an exercise of one's ingenuity, but sometimes writers use anagrams to conceal proper names or veiled messages, or to suggest important connections between words, as in "hated" and "death."

Anapestic meter See FOOT.

Antagonist The character, force, or collection of forces in fiction or drama that opposes the protagonist and gives rise to the conflict of the story; an opponent of the PROTAGONIST, such as Iago in Shakespeare's play *Othello*. See also CHARACTER, CONFLICT.

Apostrophe An address, either to someone who is absent and therefore cannot hear the speaker or to something nonhuman that cannot comprehend. Apostrophe often provides a speaker the opportunity to think aloud.

Approximate rhyme See RHYME.

Aside In drama, a speech directed to the audience that supposedly is not audible to the other characters onstage at the time. Iago's asides in *Othello*, for example, serve to reveal his sinister character. See also SOLILOQUY.

Assonance The repetition of internal vowel sounds in nearby words that do not end the same, for example, "asl*ee*p under a tr*ee*," or "*ea*ch *e*vening." Similar endings result in rhyme, as in "asl*eep* in the d*eep*." Assonance is a strong means of emphasizing important words in a line. See also ALLITERATION, CONSONANCE.

Ballad Traditionally, a ballad is a song, transmitted orally from generation to generation, that tells a story and that eventually is written down. As such, ballads usually cannot be traced to a particular author or group of authors. Typically, ballads are dramatic, condensed, and impersonal narratives. A **literary ballad** is a narrative poem that is written in deliberate imitation of the language, form, and spirit of the traditional ballad, such as Keats's "La Belle Dame sans Merci." See also STANZA, QUATRAIN.

Ballad stanza A four-line stanza, known as a QUATRAIN, consisting of alternating eight- and six-syllable lines. Usually only the second and fourth lines rhyme (an *abcb* pattern). Coleridge adopted the ballad stanza in "The Rime of the Ancient Mariner."

> All in a hot and copper sky
> The bloody Sun, at noon,
> Right up above the mast did stand,
> No bigger than the Moon.

See also BALLAD, QUATRAIN.

Blank verse Unrhymed iambic pentameter. Blank verse is the English verse form closest to the natural rhythms of English speech and therefore is the most common pattern found in traditional English narrative and dramatic poetry from Shakespeare to the early twentieth century. Shakespeare's plays use blank verse extensively. See also IAMBIC PENTAMETER.

Cacophony Language that is discordant and difficult to pronounce, such as this line from John Updike's "Player Piano": "never my numb plunker fumbles." Cacophony ("bad sound") may be unintentional in the writer's sense of music, or it may be used consciously for deliberate dramatic effect. See also EUPHONY.

Caesura A pause within a line of poetry that contributes to the rhythm of the line. A caesura can occur anywhere within a line and need not be indicated by punctuation. In scanning a line, caesuras are indicated by a double vertical line (||). See also METER, RHYTHM, SCANSION.

Canon Those works generally considered by scholars, critics, and teachers to be the most important to read and study, which collectively constitute the "masterpieces" of literature. Since the 1960s, the traditional English and American literary canon, consisting mostly of works by white male writers, has been rapidly expanding to include many female writers and writers of varying ethnic backgrounds.

Carpe diem The Latin phrase meaning "seize the day." This is a very common literary theme, especially in lyric poetry, which emphasizes that life is short, time is fleeting, and that one should make the most of present pleasures. Robert Herrick's poem "To the Virgins, to Make Much of Time" employs the *carpe diem* theme.

Catharsis Meaning "purgation," *catharsis* describes the release of the emotions of pity and fear by the audience at the end of a tragedy. In his *Poetics*, Aristotle discusses the importance of catharsis. The audience faces the misfortunes of the protagonist, which elicit pity and compassion. Simultaneously, the audience also confronts the failure of the protagonist, thus receiving a frightening reminder of human limitations and frailties. Ultimately, however, both these negative emotions are purged, because the tragic protagonist's suffering is an affirmation of human values rather than a despairing denial of them. See also TRAGEDY.

Character, characterization A character is a person presented in a dramatic or narrative work, and characterization is the process by which a writer makes that character seem real to the reader. A **hero** or **heroine**, often called the PROTAGONIST, is the central character who engages the reader's interest and empathy. The ANTAGONIST is the character, force, or collection of forces that stands directly opposed to the protagonist and gives rise to the conflict of the story. A **static character** does not change throughout the work, and the reader's knowledge of that character does not grow, whereas a **dynamic character** undergoes some kind of change because of the action in the plot. A **flat character** embodies one or two qualities, ideas, or traits that can be readily described in a brief summary. Flat characters are not psychologically complex characters and therefore are readily accessible to readers. Some flat characters are recognized as **stock characters**; they embody stereotypes such as the "dumb blonde" or the "mean stepfather." They become types rather than individuals. **Round characters** are more complex than flat or stock characters, and often display the inconsistencies and internal conflicts found in most real people. They are more fully developed, and therefore are harder to summarize. Authors have two major methods of presenting characters: **showing** and **telling**. **Showing** allows the author to present a character talking and acting, and lets the reader infer what kind of person the character is. In **telling**, the author intervenes to describe and sometimes evaluate the character for the reader. Characters can be convincing whether they are presented by showing or by telling, as long as their actions are motivated. **Motivated action** by the characters occurs when the reader or audience is offered reasons for how the characters behave, what they say, and the decisions they make. **Plausible action** is action by a character in a story that seems reasonable, given the motivations presented. See also PLOT.

Chorus In Greek tragedies (especially those of Aeschylus and Sophocles), a group of people who serve mainly as commentators on the characters and events. They add to the audience's understanding of the play by expressing traditional moral, religious, and social attitudes. The role of the chorus in dramatic works evolved through the sixteenth century, and the chorus occasionally is still used by modern playwrights such as T. S. Eliot in *Murder in the Cathedral*. See also DRAMA.

Cliché An idea or expression that has become tired and trite from overuse, its freshness and clarity having worn off. Clichés often anesthetize readers, and are usually a sign of weak writing. See also SENTIMENTALITY, STOCK RESPONSES.

Climax See PLOT.

Closet drama A play that is written to be read rather than performed on stage. In this kind of drama, literary art outweighs all other considerations. See also DRAMA.

Colloquial Refers to a type of informal diction that reflects casual, conversational language and often includes slang expressions. See also DICTION.

Comedy A work intended to interest, involve, and amuse the reader or audience, in which no terrible disaster occurs and that ends happily for the main characters. **High comedy** refers to verbal wit, such as a PUN, whereas **low comedy** is generally associated with physical action and is less intellectual. **Romantic comedy** involves a love affair that meets with various obstacles (like disapproving parents, mistaken identities, deceptions, or other sorts of misunderstandings) but overcomes them to end in a blissful union. Shakespeare's comedies, such as *A Midsummer Night's Dream*, are considered romantic comedies.

Comic relief A humorous scene or incident that alleviates tension in an otherwise serious work. In many instances these moments enhance the thematic significance of the story in addition to providing laughter. In

Othello, Desdemona's brief encounter with the clown reveals her gullible nature (III.i).

Conflict The struggle within the plot between opposing forces. The PRO-TAGONIST engages in the conflict with the ANTAGONIST, which may take the form of a character, society, nature, or an aspect of the protagonist's personality. See also CHARACTER, PLOT.

Connotation Associations and implications that go beyond the literal meaning of a word, which derive from how the word has been commonly used and the associations people make with it. For example, the word *eagle* connotes ideas of liberty and freedom that have little to do with the word's literal meaning. See also DENOTATION.

Consonance A common type of near rhyme that consists of identical consonant sounds preceded by different vowel sounds: *home, same; worth, breath.* See also ALLITERATION, ASSONANCE, RHYME.

Contextual symbol See SYMBOL.

Controlling metaphor See METAPHOR.

Convention A characteristic of a literary genre (often unrealistic) that is understood and accepted by audiences because it has come, through usage and time, to be recognized as a familiar technique. For example, the division of a play into acts and scenes is a dramatic convention, as are soliloquies and asides. FLASHBACKS and FORESHADOWING are examples of literary conventions.

Conventional symbol See SYMBOL.

Cosmic irony See IRONY.

Couplet Two consecutive lines of poetry that usually rhyme and have the same meter. A **heroic couplet** is a couplet written in rhymed iambic pentameter.

Crisis A turning point in the action of a story that has a powerful effect on the protagonist. Opposing forces come together decisively to lead to the climax of the plot. See also PLOT.

Dactylic meter See FOOT.

Denotation The dictionary meaning of a word. See also CONNOTATION.

Dénouement A French term meaning "unraveling" or "unknotting," used to describe the resolution of the plot following the climax. See also PLOT, RESOLUTION.

Dialect A type of informational diction. Dialects are spoken by definable groups of people from a particular geographic region, economic group, or social class. Writers use dialect to contrast and express differences in educational, class, social, and regional backgrounds of their characters. See also DICTION.

Dialogue The verbal exchanges between characters. Dialogue makes the characters seem real to the reader or audience by revealing firsthand their thoughts, responses, and emotional states. See also DICTION.

Diction A writer's choice of words, phrases, sentence structures, and figurative language, which combine to help create meaning and STYLE. **Formal diction** consists of a dignified, impersonal, and elevated use of language; it follows the rules of syntax exactly and is often characterized by complex words and lofty tone. **Middle diction** maintains correct language usage, but is less elevated than formal diction; it reflects the way most educated people speak. **Informal diction** represents the plain language of everyday use, and often includes idiomatic expressions, slang, contractions, and many simple, common words. **Poetic diction** refers to the way poets sometimes employ an elevated diction that deviates significantly from the common speech and writing of their time, choosing words for their supposedly inherent poetic qualities. Since the eighteenth century, however, poets have been incorporating all kinds of diction in their work and so there is no longer an automatic distinction between the language of a poet and the language of everyday speech. See also COLLOQUIAL, DIALECT, DIALOGUE.

Didactic poetry Poetry designed to teach an ethical, moral, or religious lesson. John Donne's poem "Death Be Not Proud" is an example of didactic poetry.

Doggerel A derogatory term used to describe poetry whose subject is trite and whose rhythm and sounds are monotonously heavy-handed.

Drama Derived from the Greek word *dram*, meaning "to do" or "to perform," the term *drama* may refer to a single play, a group of plays ("Jacobean drama"), or to all plays ("world drama"). Drama is designed for performance in a theater; actors take on the roles of characters, perform indicated actions, and speak the dialogue written in the script. **Play** is a general term for a work of dramatic literature, and a **playwright** is a writer who makes plays.

Dramatic irony See IRONY.

Dramatic monologue A type of lyric poem in which a character (the speaker) addresses a distinct but silent audience imagined to be present in the poem in such a way as to reveal a dramatic situation and, often unintentionally, some aspect of his or her temperament or personality. See also LYRIC.

Dynamic character See CHARACTER.

Editorial omniscience See NARRATOR.

Elegy A mournful, contemplative lyric poem written to commemorate someone who is dead, often ending in a consolation; see, for example, Ben Jonson's "On My First Son." *Elegy* may also refer to a serious meditative poem produced to express the speaker's melancholy thoughts. See also LYRIC.

End rhyme See RHYME.

End-stopped line A poetic line that has a pause at the end. End-stopped lines reflect normal speech patterns and are often marked by punctuation. The first line of Keats's "Endymion" is an example of an end-stopped line;

the natural pause coincides with the end of the line, and is marked by a period:

> A thing of beauty is a joy forever.

English sonnet See SONNET.

Enjambment In poetry, when one line ends without a pause and continues into the next line for its meaning. This is also called a **run-on line**. The transition between the first two lines of Wordsworth's poem "My Heart Leaps Up" demonstrates enjambment:

> My heart leaps up when I behold
> A rainbow in the sky:

Envoy See SESTINA.

Epigram A brief, pointed, and witty poem that usually makes a satiric or humorous point. Epigrams are most often written in couplets, but take no prescribed form.

Epiphany In fiction, when a character suddenly experiences a deep realization about himself or herself; a truth that is grasped in an ordinary rather than a melodramatic moment.

Escape literature See FORMULA FICTION.

Euphony *Euphony* ("good sound") refers to language that is smooth and musically pleasant to the ear. See also CACOPHONY.

Exact rhyme See RHYME.

Exposition A narrative device, often used at the beginning of a work, that provides necessary background information about the characters and their circumstances. Exposition explains what has gone on before, the relationships between characters, the development of a theme, and the introduction of a conflict. See also FLASHBACK.

Extended metaphor See METAPHOR.

Eye rhyme See RHYME.

Falling action See PLOT.

Falling meter See METER.

Feminine rhyme See RHYME.

Figures of speech Ways of using language that deviate from the literal, denotative meanings of words in order to suggest additional meanings or effects. Figures of speech say one thing in terms of something else, such as when an eager funeral director is described as a vulture. See also HYPERBOLE, METAPHOR, SIMILE, UNDERSTATEMENT.

First-person narrator See NARRATOR.

Fixed form A poem that may be categorized by the pattern of its lines, meter, rhythm, or stanzas. A sonnet is a fixed form of poetry because by definition it must have fourteen lines. Other fixed forms include LIMERICK, SESTINA, and VILLANELLE. However, poems written in a fixed form may not always fit into categories precisely, because writers sometimes vary traditional forms to create innovative effects. See also OPEN FORM.

Flashback A narrated scene that marks a break in the narrative in order to inform the reader or audience member about events that took place before the opening scene of a work. See also EXPOSITION.

Flat character See CHARACTER.

Foil A character in a work whose behavior and values contrast with those of another character in order to highlight the distinctive temperament of that character (usually the protagonist). In Hawthorne's "The Birthmark," the grossly physical Aminadab is a foil to the idealistic Aylmer.

Foot The metrical unit by which a line of poetry is measured. A foot usually consists of one stressed and one or two unstressed syllables. An *iambic foot,* which consists of one unstressed syllable followed by one stressed syllable ("away"), is the most common metrical foot in English poetry. A *trochaic foot* consists of one stressed syllable followed by an unstressed syllable ("lovely"). An *anapestic foot* is two unstressed syllables followed by one stressed one ("understand"). A *dactylic foot* is one stressed syllable followed by two unstressed ones ("desperate"). A *spondee* is a foot consisting of two stressed syllables ("dead set"), but is not a sustained metrical foot and is used mainly for variety or emphasis. See also IAMBIC PENTAMETER, LINE, METER.

Foreshadowing The introduction early in a story of verbal and dramatic hints that suggest what is to come later.

Form The overall structure or shape of a work, which frequently follows an established design. Forms may refer to a literary type (narrative form, short story form) or to patterns of meter, lines, and rhymes (stanza form, verse form). See also FIXED FORM, OPEN FORM.

Formal diction See DICTION.

Formula fiction Often characterized as "escape literature," formula fiction follows a pattern of conventional reader expectations. Romance novels, westerns, science fiction, and detective stories are all examples of formula fiction; while the details of individual stories vary, the basic ingredients of each kind of story are the same. Formula fiction offers happy endings (the hero "gets the girl," the detective cracks the case), entertains wide audiences, and sells tremendously well.

Found poem An unintentional poem discovered in a nonpoetic context, such as a conversation, news story, or advertisement. Found poems serve as reminders that everyday language often contains what can be considered poetry, or that poetry is definable as any text read as a poem.

Free verse Also called OPEN FORM poetry, *free verse* refers to poems characterized by their nonconformity to established patterns of meter, rhyme, and stanza. Free verse uses elements such as speech patterns, grammar, emphasis, and breath pauses to decide line breaks, and usually does not rhyme. See also OPEN FORM.

Genre A French word meaning kind or type. The major genres in literature are poetry, fiction, drama, and essays. Genre can also refer to more specific types of literature such as comedy, tragedy, epic poetry, or science fiction.

Haiku A style of lyric poetry borrowed from the Japanese that typically presents an intense emotion or vivid image of nature, which, traditionally, is designed to lead to a spiritual insight. Haiku is a fixed poetic form, consisting of seventeen syllables organized into three unrhymed lines of five, seven, and five syllables. Today, however, many poets vary the syllabic count in their haiku. See also FIXED FORM, LYRIC.

Hamartia A term coined by Aristotle to describe "some error or frailty" that brings about misfortune for a tragic hero. The concept of *hamartia* is closely related to that of the tragic flaw: Both lead to the downfall of the protagonist in a tragedy. *Hamartia* may be interpreted as an internal weakness in a character (like greed or passion or HUBRIS); however, it may also refer to a mistake that a character makes that is based not on a personal failure, but on circumstances outside the protagonist's personality and control. See also TRAGEDY.

Hero, heroine See CHARACTER.

Heroic couplet See COUPLET.

Hubris or Hybris Excessive pride or self-confidence that leads a protagonist to disregard a divine warning or to violate an important moral law. In tragedies, hubris is a very common form of *hamartia*. See also HAMARTIA, TRAGEDY.

Hyperbole A boldly exaggerated statement that adds emphasis without intending to be literally true, as in the statement "He ate everything in the house." Hyperbole (also called **overstatement**) may be used for serious, comic, or ironic effect. See also FIGURES OF SPEECH, UNDERSTATEMENT.

Iambic meter See FOOT.

Iambic pentameter A metrical pattern in poetry that consists of five iambic feet per line. (An iamb, or iambic foot, consists of one unstressed syllable followed by a stressed syllable.) See also BLANK VERSE, FOOT, METER.

Image A word, phrase, or figure of speech (especially a SIMILE or a METAPHOR) that addresses the senses, suggesting mental pictures of sights, sounds, smells, tastes, feelings, or actions. Images offer sensory impressions to the reader and also convey emotions and moods through their verbal pictures. See also FIGURES OF SPEECH.

Implied metaphor See METAPHOR.

In medias res See PLOT.

Informal diction See DICTION.

Internal rhyme See RHYME.

Irony A literary device that uses contradictory statements or situations to reveal a reality different from what appears to be true. It is ironic for a firehouse to burn down, or for a police station to be burglarized. **Verbal irony** is a figure of speech that occurs when a person says one thing but means the opposite. **Sarcasm** is a strong form of verbal irony that is calculated to hurt someone through, for example, false praise. **Dramatic irony** creates a discrepancy between what a character believes or says and what the reader or audience member knows to be true. **Tragic irony** is a form of dramatic irony found in tragedies such as *Oedipus the King*, in which Oedipus searches for the person responsible for the plague that ravishes his city and ironically ends up hunting himself. **Situational irony** exists when there is an incongruity between what is expected to happen and what actually happens due to forces beyond human comprehension or control. The suicide of the seemingly successful main character in Edwin Arlington Robinson's poem "Richard Cory" is an example of situational irony. **Cosmic irony** occurs when a writer uses God, destiny, or fate to dash the hopes and expectations of a character or of humankind in general. In cosmic irony, a discrepancy exists between what a character aspires to and what universal forces provide. Stephen Crane's poem "A Man Said to the Universe" is a good example of cosmic irony, because the universe acknowledges no obligation to the man's assertion of his own existence. See also HYPERBOLE, SATIRE, UNDERSTATEMENT.

Italian sonnet See SONNET.

Limerick A light, humorous style of fixed form poetry. Its usual form consists of five lines with the rhyme scheme *aabba*; lines 1, 2, and 5 contain three feet, while lines 3 and 4 usually contain two feet. Limericks range in subject matter from the silly to the obscene, and since Edward Lear popularized them in the nineteenth century, children and adults have enjoyed these comic poems. See also FIXED FORM.

Limited omniscient narrator See NARRATOR.

Line A sequence of words printed as a separate entity on the page. In poetry, lines are usually measured by the number of feet they contain. The names for various line lengths are as follows:

monometer: one foot	pentameter: five feet
dimeter: two feet	hexameter: six feet
trimeter: three feet	heptameter: seven feet
tetrameter: four feet	octameter: eight feet

The number of feet in a line, coupled with the name of the foot, describes the metrical qualities of that line. See also END-STOPPED LINE, ENJAMBMENT, FOOT, METER, SCANSION.

Literary ballad See BALLAD.

Literary symbol See SYMBOL.

Low comedy See COMEDY.

Lyric A type of brief poem that expresses the personal emotions and thoughts of a single speaker. It is important to realize, however, that although the lyric is uttered in the first person, the speaker is not necessarily the poet. There are many varieties of lyric poetry, including the DRAMATIC MONOLOGUE, ELEGY, HAIKU, ODE, and SONNET forms.

Masculine rhyme See RHYME.

Melodrama A term applied to any literary work that relies on implausible events and sensational action for its effect. The conflicts in melodramas typically arise out of plot rather than characterization; often a virtuous individual must somehow confront and overcome a wicked oppressor. Usually, a melodramatic story ends happily, with the protagonist defeating the antagonist at the last possible moment. Thus, melodramas entertain the reader or audience with exciting action while still conforming to a traditional sense of justice. See also SENTIMENTALITY.

Metafiction The literary term used to describe a work that explores the nature, structure, logic, status, and function of storytelling.

Metaphor A metaphor is a figure of speech that makes a comparison between two unlike things, without using the word *like* or *as*. Metaphors assert the identity of dissimilar things, as when Macbeth asserts that life *is* a "brief candle." Metaphors can be subtle and powerful, and can transform people, places, objects, and ideas into whatever the writer imagines them to be. An **implied metaphor** is a more subtle comparison; the terms being compared are not so specifically explained. For example, to describe a stubborn man unwilling to leave, one could say that he was "a mule standing his ground." This is a fairly explicit metaphor; the man is being compared to a mule. But to say that the man "brayed his refusal to leave" is to create an implied metaphor, because the subject (the man) is never overtly identified as a mule. Braying is associated with the mule, a notoriously stubborn creature, and so the comparison between the stubborn man and the mule is sustained. Implied metaphors can slip by inattentive readers who are not sensitive to such carefully chosen, highly concentrated language. An **extended metaphor** is a sustained comparison in which part or all of a poem consists of a series of related metaphors. Robert Francis's poem "Catch" relies on an extended metaphor that compares poetry to playing catch. **Synecdoche** is a kind of metaphor in which a part of something is used to signify the whole, as when a gossip is called a "wagging tongue," or when ten ships are called "ten sails." Sometimes synecdoche refers to the whole being used to signify the part, as in the phrase "Boston won the baseball game." Clearly, the entire city of Boston did not participate in the game; the whole of Boston is being used to signify the individuals who played and won the game. **Metonymy** is a type of metaphor in which something closely associated with a subject is substituted for it. In this way, we speak of the "silver screen" to mean motion pictures, "the crown" to stand for the king, "the White House" to stand for the activities of the president. See also FIGURES OF SPEECH, PERSONIFICATION, SIMILE.

Meter When a rhythmic pattern of stresses recurs in a poem, it is called *meter*. Metrical patterns are determined by the type and number of feet in a line of verse; combining the name of a line length with the name of a foot concisely describes the meter of the line. **Rising meter** refers to metrical feet which move from unstressed to stressed sounds, such as the iambic foot and the anapestic foot. **Falling meter** refers to metrical feet that move from stressed to unstressed sounds, such as the trochaic foot and the dactylic foot. See also ACCENT, CAESURA, FOOT, IAMBIC PENTAMETER, LINE, SCANSION.

Metonymy See METAPHOR.

Middle diction See DICTION.

Motivated action See CHARACTER.

Naive narrator See NARRATOR.

Narrative poem A poem that tells a story. A narrative poem may be short or long, and the story it relates may be simple or complex. See also BALLAD.

Narrator The voice of the person telling the story, not to be confused with the author's voice. With a **first-person narrator**, the *I* in the story presents the point of view of only one character. The reader is restricted to the perceptions, thoughts, and feelings of that single character. For example, in Melville's "Bartleby, the Scrivener," the lawyer is the first-person narrator of the story. First-person narrators can play either a major or a minor role in the story they are telling. An **unreliable narrator** reveals an interpretation of events that is somehow different from the author's own interpretation of those events. Often, the unreliable narrator's perception of plot, characters, and setting becomes the actual subject of the story, as in Melville's "Bartleby, the Scrivener." Narrators can be unreliable for a number of reasons: They might lack self-knowledge (like Melville's lawyer), they might be inexperienced, they might even be insane. A **naive narrator** is usually characterized by youthful innocence, such as Mark Twain's Huck Finn or J. D. Salinger's Holden Caulfield. An **omniscient narrator** is an all-knowing narrator who is not a character in the story and who can move from place to place and pass back and forth through time, slipping into and out of characters as no human being possibly could in real life. Omniscient narrators can report the thoughts and feelings of the characters, as well as their words and actions. The narrator of *The Scarlet Letter* is an omniscient narrator. **Editorial omniscience** refers to an intrusion by the narrator in order to evaluate a character for a reader, as when the narrator of *The Scarlet Letter* describes Hester's relationship to the Puritan community. Narration that allows the characters' actions and thoughts to speak for themselves is called **neutral omniscience**. Most modern writers use neutral omniscience so that readers can reach their own conclusions. **Limited omniscience** occurs when an author restricts a narrator to the single perspective of either a major or minor character. The way people, places, and events appear to that character is the way they appear to the reader. Sometimes a limited omniscient narrator can see into more than one character, particularly in a work that focuses on two characters alternately from one chapter to the next. Short stories, however, are frequently limited to a single character's point of view. See also PERSONA, POINT OF VIEW, STREAM-OF-CONSCIOUSNESS TECHNIQUE.

Near rhyme See RHYME.

Neutral omniscience See NARRATOR.

Objective point of view See POINT OF VIEW.

Octave A poetic stanza of eight lines, usually forming one part of a sonnet. See also SONNET, STANZA.

Ode A relatively lengthy lyric poem that often expresses lofty emotions in a dignified style. Odes are characterized by a serious topic, such as truth, art, freedom, justice, or the meaning of life; their tone tends to be formal. There is no prescribed pattern that defines an ode; some odes repeat the same pattern in each stanza, while others introduce a new pattern in each stanza. See also LYRIC.

Off rhyme See RHYME.

Omniscient narrator See NARRATOR.

One-act play A play that takes place in a single location and unfolds as one continuous action. The characters in a one-act play are presented economically and the action is sharply focused. See also DRAMA.

Onomatopoeia A term referring to the use of a word that resembles the sound it denotes. *Buzz, rattle, bang,* and *sizzle* all reflect onomatopoeia. Onomatopoeia can also consist of more than one word; writers sometimes create lines or whole passages in which the sound of the words helps to convey their meanings.

Open form Sometimes called **free verse**, open form poetry does not conform to established patterns of METER, RHYME, and STANZA. Such poetry derives its rhythmic qualities from the repetition of words, phrases, or grammatical structures, the arrangement of words on the printed page, or by some other means. The poet E. E. Cummings wrote open form poetry; his poems do not have measurable meters, but they do have rhythm. See also FIXED FORM, PICTURE POEM, PROSE POEM.

Organic form Refers to works whose formal characteristics are not rigidly predetermined but follow the movement of thought or emotion being expressed. Such works are said to grow like living organisms, following their own individual patterns rather than external fixed rules that govern, for example, the form of a SONNET.

Overstatement See HYPERBOLE.

Oxymoron A condensed form of PARADOX in which two contradictory words are used together, as in "sweet sorrow" or "original copy."

Paradox A statement that initially appears to be contradictory but then, on closer inspection, turns out to make sense. For example, John Donne ends his sonnet "Death Be Not Proud" with the paradoxical statement "Death, thou shalt die." To solve the paradox, it is necessary to discover the sense that underlies the statement. Paradox is useful in poetry because it arrests a reader's attention by its seemingly stubborn refusal to make sense.

Paraphrase A prose restatement of the central ideas of a poem, in your own language.

Parody A humorous imitation of another, usually serious, work. It can take any fixed or open form, because parodists imitate the tone, language, and shape of the original in order to deflate the subject matter, making the original work seem absurd. Parody may also be used as a form of literary criticism to expose the defects in a work. But sometimes parody becomes an affectionate acknowledgment that a well-known work has become both institutionalized in our culture and fair game for some fun. For example, Ann Lauinger's "Marvell Noir" gently mocks Andrew Marvell's "To His Coy Mistress." See also SATIRE.

Persona Literally, a *persona* is a mask. In literature, a *persona* is a speaker created by a writer to tell a story or to speak in a poem. A persona is not a character in a story or narrative, nor does a persona necessarily directly reflect the author's personal voice. A persona is a separate self, created by and distinct from the author, through which he or she speaks. See also NARRATOR.

Personification A form of metaphor in which human characteristics are attributed to nonhuman things. Personification offers the writer a way to give the world life and motion by assigning familiar human behaviors and emotions to animals, inanimate objects, and abstract ideas. For example, in Keats's "Ode on a Grecian Urn," the speaker refers to the urn as an "unravished bride of quietness." See also METAPHOR.

Petrarchan sonnet See SONNET.

Picture poem A type of open form poetry in which the poet arranges the lines of the poem so as to create a particular shape on the page. The shape of the poem embodies its subject; the poem becomes a picture of what the poem is describing. Michael McFee's "In Medias Res" is an example of a picture poem. See also OPEN FORM.

Plausible action See CHARACTER.

Play See DRAMA.

Playwright See DRAMA.

Plot An author's selection and arrangement of incidents in a story to shape the action and give the story a particular focus. Discussions of plot include not just what happens, but also how and why things happen the way they do. Stories that are written in a **pyramidal pattern** divide the plot into three essential parts. The first part is the **rising action**, in which complication creates some sort of conflict for the protagonist. The second part is the **climax**, the moment of greatest emotional tension in a narrative, usually marking a turning point in the plot at which the rising action reverses to become the falling action. The third part, the **falling action** (or RESOLUTION), is characterized by diminishing tensions and the resolution of the plot's conflicts and complications. *In medias res* is a term used to describe the common strategy of beginning a story in the middle of the action. In this type of plot, we enter the story on the verge of some important moment. See also CHARACTER, CRISIS, DÉNOUEMENT, RESOLUTION, REVERSAL, SUBPLOT.

Poetic diction See DICTION.

Point of view Refers to who tells us a story and how it is told. What we know and how we feel about the events in a work are shaped by the author's choice of point of view. The teller of the story, the narrator, inevitably affects our understanding of the characters' actions by filtering what is told through his or her own perspective. The various points of view that writers draw upon can be grouped into two broad categories: (1) The third-person narrator uses *he, she,* or *they* to tell the story and does not participate in the action; and (2) the first-person narrator uses *I* and is a major or minor participant in the action. In addition, a second-person narrator, *you,* is also possible, but is rarely used because of the awkwardness of thrusting the reader into the story, as in "You are minding your own business on a park bench when a drunk steps out and demands your lunch bag." An **objective point of view** employs a third-person narrator who does not see into the mind of any character. From this detached and impersonal perspective, the narrator reports action and dialogue without telling us directly what the characters think and feel. Since no analysis or interpretation is provided by the narrator, this point of view places a premium on dialogue, actions, and details to reveal character to the reader. See also NARRATOR, STREAM-OF-CONSCIOUSNESS TECHNIQUE.

Problem play Popularized by Henrik Ibsen, a problem play is a type of DRAMA that presents a social issue in order to awaken the audience to it. These plays usually reject romantic plots in favor of holding up a mirror that reflects not simply what the audience wants to see but what the playwright sees in them. Often a problem play will propose a solution to the problem that does not coincide with prevailing opinion. The term is also used to refer to certain Shakespeare plays that do not fit the categories of tragedy, comedy, or romance.

Prologue The opening speech or dialogue of a play, especially a classic Greek play, that usually gives the exposition necessary to follow the subsequent action. Today the term also refers to the introduction to any literary work. See also DRAMA, EXPOSITION.

Prose poem A kind of open form poetry that is printed as prose and represents the most clear opposite of fixed form poetry. Prose poems are densely compact and often make use of striking imagery and figures of speech. See also FIXED FORM, OPEN FORM.

Prosody The overall metrical structure of a poem. See also METER.

Protagonist The main character of a narrative; its central character who engages the reader's interest and empathy. See also CHARACTER.

Pun A play on words that relies on a word's having more than one meaning or sounding like another word. Shakespeare and other writers use puns extensively, for serious and comic purposes; in *Romeo and Juliet* (III.i.101), the dying Mercutio puns, "Ask for me tomorrow and you shall find me a grave man." Puns have serious literary uses, but since the eighteenth century, puns have been used almost purely for humorous effect. See also COMEDY.

Pyramidal pattern See PLOT.

Quatrain A four-line stanza. Quatrains are the most common stanzaic form in the English language; they can have various meters and rhyme schemes. See also METER, RHYME, STANZA.

Recognition The moment in a story when previously unknown or withheld information is revealed to the protagonist, resulting in the discovery of the truth of his or her situation and, usually, a decisive change in course for that character. In *Oedipus the King*, the moment of recognition comes when Oedipus finally realizes that he has killed his father and married his mother.

Resolution The conclusion of a plot's conflicts and complications. The resolution, also known as the **falling action**, follows the climax in the plot. See also DÉNOUEMENT, PLOT.

Reversal The point in a story when the protagonist's fortunes turn in an unexpected direction. See also PLOT.

Rhyme The repetition of identical or similar concluding syllables in different words, most often at the ends of lines. Rhyme is predominantly a function of sound rather than spelling; thus, words that end with the same vowel sounds rhyme, for instance, *day, prey, bouquet, weigh,* and words with the same consonant ending rhyme, for instance *vain, feign, rein, lane.* Words do not have to be spelled the same way or look alike to rhyme. In fact, words may look alike but not rhyme at all. This is called **eye rhyme**, as with *bough* and *cough,* or *brow* and *blow.* **End rhyme** is the most common form of rhyme in poetry; the rhyme comes at the end of the lines:

> It runs through the reeds
>   And away it proceeds,
> Through meadow and glade,
>   In sun and in shade.

The **rhyme scheme** of a poem describes the pattern of end rhymes. Rhyme schemes are mapped out by noting patterns of rhyme with small letters: The first rhyme sound is designated *a*, the second becomes *b*, the third *c*, and so on. Thus, the rhyme scheme of the stanza above is *aabb*. **Internal rhyme** places at least one of the rhymed words within the line, as in "Dividing and gliding and sliding" or "In mist or cloud, on mast or shroud." **Masculine rhyme** describes the rhyming of single-syllable words, such as *grade* or *shade*. Masculine rhyme also occurs with rhyming words of more than one syllable, when the same sound occurs in a final stressed syllable, as in *defend* and *contend, betray* and *away.* **Feminine rhyme** consists of a rhymed stressed syllable followed by one or more identical unstressed syllables, as in *butter, clutter; gratitude, attitude; quivering, shivering.* All the examples so far have illustrated **exact rhymes**, because they share the same stressed vowel sounds as well as sharing sounds that follow the vowel. In **near rhyme** (also called **off rhyme**, **slant rhyme**, and **approximate rhyme**), the sounds are almost but not exactly alike. A common form of near rhyme is CONSONANCE, which consists of identical consonant sounds preceded by different vowel sounds: *home, same; worth, breath.*

Rhyme scheme See RHYME.

Rhythm A term used to refer to the recurrence of stressed and unstressed sounds in poetry. Depending on how sounds are arranged, the rhythm of a poem may be fast or slow, choppy or smooth. Poets use rhythm to create pleasurable sound patterns and to reinforce meanings. Rhythm in prose arises from pattern repetitions of sounds and pauses that create looser rhythmic effects. See also METER.

Rising action See PLOT.

Rising meter See METER.

Romantic comedy See COMEDY.

Round character See CHARACTER.

Run-on line See ENJAMBMENT.

Sarcasm See IRONY.

Satire The literary art of ridiculing a folly or vice in order to expose or correct it. The object of satire is usually some human frailty; people, institutions, ideas, and things are all fair game for satirists. Satire evokes attitudes of amusement, contempt, scorn, or indignation toward its faulty subject in the hope of somehow improving it. See also IRONY, PARODY.

Scansion The process of measuring the stresses in a line of verse in order to determine the metrical pattern of the line. See ALSO CAESURA, LINE, METER.

Scene In DRAMA, a scene is a subdivision of an ACT. In modern plays, scenes usually consist of units of action in which there are no changes in the setting or breaks in the continuity of time. According to traditional conventions, a scene changes when the location of the action shifts or when a new character enters. See also ACT, CONVENTION.

Script The written text of a play, which includes the dialogue between characters, stage directions, and often other expository information. See also EXPOSITION, PROLOGUE, STAGE DIRECTIONS.

Sentimentality A pejorative term used to describe the effort by an author to induce emotional responses in the reader that exceed what the situation warrants. Sentimentality especially pertains to such emotions as pathos and sympathy; it cons readers into falling for the mass murderer who is devoted to stray cats, and it requires that readers do not examine such illogical responses. Clichés and stock responses are the key ingredients of sentimentality in literature. See also CLICHÉ, MELODRAMA, STOCK RESPONSES.

Sestet A stanza consisting of exactly six lines. See also STANZA.

Sestina A type of fixed form poetry consisting of thirty-six lines of any length divided into six sestets and a three-line concluding stanza called an **envoy**. The six words at the end of the first sestet's lines must also appear at the ends of the other five sestets, in varying order. These six words must also appear in the envoy, where they often resonate important themes. An example of this highly demanding form of poetry is Florence Cassen Meyers's "All-American Sestina." See also SESTET.

Setting The physical and social context in which the action of a story occurs. The major elements of setting are the time, the place, and the social environment that frames the characters. Setting can be used to evoke a mood or atmosphere that will prepare the reader for what is to come, as in Muriel Spark's short story "The First Year of My Life." Sometimes writers choose a particular setting because of traditional associations with that setting that are closely related to the action of a story. For example, stories filled with adventure or romance often take place in exotic locales.

Shakespearean sonnet See SONNET.

Showing See CHARACTER.

Simile A common figure of speech that makes an explicit comparison between two things by using words such as *like, as, than, appears,* and *seems:* "A sip of Mrs. Cook's coffee is like a punch in the stomach." The effectiveness of this simile is created by the differences between the two things compared. There would be no simile if the comparison were stated this way: "Mrs. Cook's coffee is as strong as the cafeteria's coffee." This is a literal translation because Mrs. Cook's coffee is compared with something like it—another kind of coffee. See also FIGURES OF SPEECH, METAPHOR.

Situational irony See IRONY.

Slant rhyme See RHYME.

Soliloquy A dramatic convention by means of which a character, alone onstage, utters his or her thoughts aloud. Playwrights use soliloquies as a convenient way to inform the audience about a character's motivations and state of mind. Shakespeare's Hamlet delivers perhaps the best known of all soliloquies, which begins: "To be or not to be." See also ASIDE, CONVENTION.

Sonnet A fixed form of lyric poetry that consists of fourteen lines, usually written in iambic pentameter. There are two basic types of sonnets, the Italian and the English. The **Italian sonnet**, also known as the **Petrarchan sonnet**, is divided into an octave, which typically rhymes *abbaabba,* and a sestet, which may have varying rhyme schemes. Common rhyme patterns in the sestet are *cdecde, cdcdcd,* and *cdccdc.* Very often the octave presents a situation, attitude, or problem that the sestet comments upon or resolves, as in John Keats's "On First Looking into Chapman's Homer." The **English sonnet**, also known as the **Shakespearean sonnet**, is organized into three quatrains and a couplet, which typically rhyme *abab cdcd efef gg*. This rhyme scheme is more suited to English poetry because English has fewer rhyming words than Italian. English sonnets, because of their four-part organization, also have more flexibility with respect to where thematic breaks can occur. Frequently, however, the most pronounced break or turn comes with the concluding couplet, as in Shakespeare's "Shall I compare thee to a summer's day?" See also COUPLET, IAMBIC PENTAMETER, LINE, OCTAVE, QUATRAIN, SESTET.

Speaker The voice used by an author to tell a story or speak a poem. The speaker is often a created identity, and should not automatically be equated with the author's self. See also NARRATOR, PERSONA, POINT OF VIEW.

Spondee See FOOT.

Stage directions A playwright's written instructions about how the actors are to move and behave in a play. They explain in which direction characters should move, what facial expressions they should assume, and so on. See also DRAMA, SCRIPT.

Stanza In poetry, *stanza* refers to a grouping of lines, set off by a space, that usually has a set pattern of meter and rhyme. See also LINE, METER, RHYME.

Static character See CHARACTER.

Stock character See CHARACTER.

Stock responses Predictable, conventional reactions to language, characters, symbols, or situations. The flag, motherhood, puppies, God, and peace are common objects used to elicit stock responses from unsophisticated audiences. See also CLICHÉ, SENTIMENTALITY.

Stream-of-consciousness technique The most intense use of a central consciousness in narration. The stream-of-consciousness technique takes a reader inside a character's mind to reveal perceptions, thoughts, and feelings on a conscious or unconscious level. This technique suggests the flow of thought as well as its content; hence, complete sentences may give way to fragments as the character's mind makes rapid associations free of conventional logic or transitions. James Joyce's novel *Ulysses* makes extensive use of this narrative technique. See also NARRATOR, POINT OF VIEW.

Stress The emphasis, or accent, given a syllable in pronunciation. See also ACCENT.

Style The distinctive and unique manner in which a writer arranges words to achieve particular effects. Style essentially combines the idea to be expressed with the individuality of the author. These arrangements include individual word choices as well as matters such as the length of sentences, their structure, tone, and use of irony. See also DICTION, IRONY, TONE.

GLOSSARY OF LITERARY TERMS

Subplot The secondary action of a story, complete and interesting in its own right, that reinforces or contrasts with the main plot. There may be more than one subplot, and sometimes as many as three, four, or even more, running through a piece of fiction. Subplots are generally either analogous to the main plot, thereby enhancing our understanding of it, or extraneous to the main plot, to provide relief from it. See also PLOT.

Suspense The anxious anticipation of a reader or an audience as to the outcome of a story, especially concerning the character or characters with whom sympathetic attachments are formed. Suspense helps to secure and sustain the interest of the reader or audience throughout a work.

Symbol A person, object, image, word, or event that evokes a range of additional meaning beyond and usually more abstract than its literal significance. Symbols are educational devices for evoking complex ideas without having to resort to painstaking explanations that would make a story more like an essay than an experience. **Conventional symbols** have meanings that are widely recognized by a society or culture. Some conventional symbols are the Christian cross, the Star of David, a swastika, or a nation's flag. Writers use conventional symbols to reinforce meanings. Kate Chopin, for example, emphasizes the spring setting in "The Story of an Hour" as a way of suggesting the renewed sense of life that Mrs. Mallard feels when she thinks herself free from her husband. A **literary** or **contextual symbol** can be a setting, character, action, object, name, or anything else in a work that maintains its literal significance while suggesting other meanings. Such symbols go beyond conventional symbols; they gain their symbolic meaning within the context of a specific story. For example, the white whale in Melville's *Moby-Dick* takes on multiple symbolic meanings in the work, but these meanings do not automatically carry over into other stories about whales. The meanings suggested by Melville's whale are specific to that text; therefore, it becomes a contextual symbol. See also ALLEGORY.

Synecdoche See METAPHOR.

Syntax The ordering of words into meaningful verbal patterns such as phrases, clauses, and sentences. Poets often manipulate syntax, changing conventional word order, to place certain emphasis on particular words. Emily Dickinson, for instance, writes about being surprised by a snake in her poem "A narrow Fellow in the Grass," and includes this line: "His notice sudden is." In addition to the alliterative hissing *s*-sounds here, Dickinson also effectively manipulates the line's syntax so that the verb *is* appears unexpectedly at the end, making the snake's hissing presence all the more "sudden."

Telling See CHARACTER.

Tercet A three-line stanza. See also STANZA, TRIPLET.

Terza rima An interlocking three-line rhyme scheme: *aba, bcb, cdc, ded,* and so on. Frost's "Acquainted with the Night" is written in *terza rima*. See also RHYME, TERCET.

Theme The central meaning or dominant idea in a literary work. A theme provides a unifying point around which the PLOT, CHARACTERS, SETTING, POINT OF VIEW, SYMBOLS, and other elements of a work are organized. It is important not to mistake the theme for the actual subject of the work; the theme refers to the abstract concept that is made concrete through the images, characterization, and action of the text. In nonfiction, however, the theme generally refers to the main topic of the discourse.

Thesis The central idea of an essay. The thesis is a complete sentence (although sometimes it may require more than one sentence) that establishes the topic of the essay in clear, unambiguous language.

Tone The author's implicit attitude toward the reader or the people, places, and events in a work as revealed by the elements of the author's style. Tone may be characterized as serious or ironic, sad or happy, private or public, angry or affectionate, bitter or nostalgic, or any other attitudes and feelings that human beings experience. See also STYLE.

Tragedy A story that presents courageous individuals who confront powerful forces within or outside themselves with a dignity that reveals the breadth and depth of the human spirit in the face of failure, defeat, and even death. Tragedies recount an individual's downfall; they usually begin high and end low. Shakespeare is known for his tragedies, including *Macbeth, King Lear, Othello,* and *Hamlet.* A **tragic flaw** is an error or defect in the tragic hero that leads to his downfall, such as greed, pride, or ambition. This flaw may be a result of bad character, bad judgment, an inherited weakness, or any other defect of character. **Tragic irony** is a form of **dramatic irony** found in tragedies such as *Oedipus the King*, in which Oedipus ironically ends up hunting himself. See also COMEDY, DRAMA, HAMARTIA.

Tragic flaw See TRAGEDY.

Tragic irony See irony, TRAGEDY.

Triplet A tercet in which all three lines rhyme. See also TERCET.

Trochaic meter See FOOT.

Understatement The opposite of hyperbole, understatement (or litotes) refers to a figure of speech that says less than is intended. Understatement usually has an ironic effect, and sometimes may be used for comic purposes, as in Mark Twain's statement, "The reports of my death are greatly exaggerated." See also HYPERBOLE, IRONY.

Unreliable narrator See NARRATOR.

Verbal irony See IRONY.

Verse A generic term used to describe poetic lines composed in a measured rhythmical pattern that are often, but not necessarily, rhymed. See also LINE, METER, RHYME, RHYTHM.

Villanelle A type of fixed form poetry consisting of nineteen lines of any length divided into six stanzas: five tercets and a concluding quatrain. The first and third lines of the initial tercet rhyme; these rhymes are repeated in each subsequent tercet (*aba*) and in the final two lines of the quatrain (*abaa*). Line 1 appears in its entirety as lines 6, 12, and 18, while line 3 reappears as lines 9, 15, and 19. Dylan Thomas's "Do Not Go Gentle into That Good Night" is a villanelle. See also FIXED FORM, QUATRAIN, RHYME, TERCET.

Well-made play A realistic style of play that employs conventions including plenty of suspense created by meticulous plotting. Well-made plays are tightly and logically constructed, and lead to a logical resolution that is favorable to the protagonist. This dramatic structure was popularized in France by Eugène Scribe (1791–1861) and Victorien Sardou (1831–1908) and was adopted by Henrik Ibsen. See also CHARACTER, PLOT.

POETRY

Paul Humphrey. "Blow" from *Light Year '86*. Reprinted with the permission of Eleanor Humphrey.

David Ignatow. "The Jobholder" from *At My Ease: Uncollected Poems of the Fifties and Sixties*. Copyright © 1998 by David Ignatow. Reprinted with the permission of The Permissions Company, Inc., on behalf of BOA Editions Ltd., www.boaeditions.org.

Colette Inez. "Back When All Was Continuous Chuckles." Reprinted by permission from *The Hudson Review* Vol. LVII, No. 3 (Autumn 2004). Copyright © 2004 by Colette Inez.

Mark Jarman. "Unholy Sonnet" from *Bone Fires: New and Selected Poems* by Mark Jarman. Copyright © 1997 by Mark Jarman. Reprinted with the permission of The Permissions Company, Inc., on behalf of Sarabande Books, www.sarabandebooks.org.

Randall Jarrell. "The Death of the Ball Turret Gunner" from *The Complete Poems* by Randall Jarrell. Copyright © 1969, renewed 1997 by Mary von S. Jarrell. Reprinted by permission of Farrar, Straus and Giroux, LLC.

Alice Jones. "The Foot" from *Anatomy* by Alice Jones (San Francisco: Bullnettle Press, 1997). Copyright © 1997 by Alice Jones. Reprinted by permission of the author.

Donald Justice. "Order in the Streets" from *Losers Weepers: Poems Found Practically Everywhere*, edited by George Hitchcock. Reprinted by permission of Jean Ross Justice.

Carolyn Kizer. "After Bashō" from *Cool, Calm & Collected: Poems 1960–2000*. Copyright © 2001 by Carolyn Kizer. Reprinted with the permission of The Permissions Company, Inc, on behalf of Copper Canyon Press, www.coppercanyonpress.org.

Philip Larkin. "A Study of Reading Habits" from *The Complete Poems of Philip Larkin* by Philip Larkin, edited by Archie Burnett. Copyright © 2012 by the Estate of Philip Larkin. Reprinted by permission of Farrar, Straus and Giroux, LLC. Also from *The Whitsun Weddings*. Copyright © 1964 by Philip Larkin. Reprinted by permission of Faber and Faber Ltd.

Ann Lauinger. "Marvell Noir." First appeared in *Parnassus: Poetry in Review* 28, no. 1 & 2 (2005). Copyright © 2005 by Ann Lauinger. Reprinted by permission of the author.

Tato Laviera. "AmeRícan" is reprinted with permission from the publisher of *AmeRícan* by Tato Laviera (© 1985 Arte Público Press–University of Houston).

J. Patrick Lewis. "The Unkindest Cut" from *Light Quarterly* (Spring 1993). Reprinted with permission of the author.

Diane Lockward. "Linguini" from *What Feeds Us* by Diane Lockward (Wind Publications, 2006). Copyright © 2006 by Diane Lockward. First appeared in *Poet Lore*. Reprinted by permission of the author.

Katharyn Howd Machan. "Hazel Tells LaVerne" from *Light Year '85*. Reprinted by permission of the author.

Elaine Magarrell. "The Joy of Cooking" from *Sometime the Cow Kick Your Head, Light Year 88/89*. Reprinted with the permission of the author.

John Maloney. "Good!" from *Proposal* by John Maloney. Zoland Books, 1999. Copyright © 1999 by John Maloney. Reprinted by permission of the author.

Julio Marzán. "Ethnic Poetry." Originally appeared in *Parnassus: Poetry in Review*. Reprinted by permission of the author. "The Translator at the Reception for Latin American Writers." Reprinted by permission of the author.

Florence Cassen Mayers. "All-American Sestina," © 1996 Florence Cassen Mayers, as first published in *The Atlantic Monthly*. Reprinted with permission of the author.

David McCord. "Epitaph on a Waiter" from *Odds Without Ends*, copyright © 1954 by David T. W. McCord. Reprinted by permission of the estate of David T. W. McCord.

Jill McDonough. "Accident, Mass. Ave." Copyright © 2008 by Jill McDonough. Reprinted with the permission of the author; first printed in the Spring 2008 issue of the *Threepenny Review*.

Michael McFee. "In Medias Res" from *Colander* by Michael McFee. Copyright © 1996 by Michael McFee. Reprinted by permission of Michael McFee.

Peter Meinke. "The ABC of Aerobics" from *Night Watch on the Chesapeake* by Peter Meinke. Copyright © 1987. Reprinted by permission of the University of Pittsburgh Press.

Elaine Mitchell. "Form" from *Light 9* (Spring 1994). Reprinted by permission of the author.

Janice Townley Moore. "To a Wasp" first appeared in *Light Year*, Bits Press. Reprinted by permission of the author.

Robert Morgan. "Mountain Graveyard" from *Sigodlin*. Copyright © 1990 by Robert Morgan. Reprinted by permission of Wesleyan University Press, www.wesleyan.edu/wespress.

Joan Murray, "We Old Dudes," copyright © 2006 by Joan Murray. First appeared in the July/August 2006 issue of *Poetry* magazine. Reprinted by permission of the author.

Marilyn Nelson. "How I Discovered Poetry" from *The Fields of Praise: New and Selected Poems* by Marilyn Nelson. Copyright © 1997 by Marilyn Nelson. Reprinted by permission of the author and Louisiana State University Press.

John Frederick Nims. "Love Poem" from *Selected Poems*. Copyright © 1982 by the University of Chicago. Reprinted by permission of the University of Chicago Press.

Alden Nowlan. "The Bull Moose" from *Alden Nowlan: Selected Poems* by Alden Nowlan. Copyright © 1967. Reprinted by permission of House of Anansi Press, Toronto.

Sharon Olds. "Last Night" from *The Wellspring* by Sharon Olds. Copyright © 1996 by Sharon Olds. Used by permission of Alfred A. Knopf, a division of Random House, Inc. Any third party use of this material, outside of this publication, is prohibited. Interested parties must apply directly to Random House, Inc., for permission.

Mary Oliver. "Oxygen" and "The Poet with His Face in His Hands" from *New and Selected Poems, Volume Two* by Mary Oliver. Published by Beacon Press, Boston. Copyright © 2005 by Mary Oliver. Reprinted by permission of the Charlotte Sheedy Literary Agency, Inc.

Lisa Parker. "Snapping Beans" from the collection *This Gone Place* by Lisa Parker. Originally appeared in *Parnassus* 23, no. 2 (1998). Reprinted by permission of the author.

Molly Peacock. "Desire" from *Cornucopia: New and Selected Poems* by Molly Peacock. Copyright © 2002 by Molly Peacock. Used by permission of W. W. Norton & Company, Inc.

Laurence Perrine. "The limerick's never averse." Copyright © Laurence Perrine. Reprinted by permission of Douglas Perrine.

Kevin Pierce. "Proof of Origin" from *Light* 50 (Autumn 2005). Copyright © 2005 by Kevin Pierce. Reprinted with the permission of the author.

Marge Piercy. "To be of use" from *Circles on the Water* by Marge Piercy. Copyright © 1982 by Middlemarsh, Inc. Used by permission of Alfred A. Knopf, a division of Random House, Inc. Any third party use of this material, outside of this publication, is prohibited. Interested parties must apply directly to Random House, Inc., for permission.

Alberto Ríos. "Seniors" from *Five Indiscretions*. Copyright © 1985 by Alberto Ríos. Reprinted by permission of the author.

Sonia Sanchez. "c'mon man hold me" from *Like the Singing Coming Off the Drums: Love Poems* by Sonia Sanchez. Copyright © 1998 by Sonia Sanchez. Reprinted by permission of Beacon Press, Boston, via Copyright Clearance Center.

David Shumate. "Shooting the Horse" from *High Water Mark: Prose Poems* by David Shumate. Copyright © 2004. Reprinted by permission of the University of Pittsburgh Press.

Anya Krugovoy Silver. "French Toast" from *The Ninety-Third Name of God* by Anya Krugovoy Silver. Copyright © 2010 by Anya Krugovoy Silver. Reprinted by permission of Louisiana State University Press.

Louis Simpson. "In the Suburbs" from *At the End of the Open Road* by Louis Simpson. Wesleyan UP, 1963.

David R. Slavitt. "Titanic" from *Change of Address: Poems New and Selected* by David R. Slavitt. Copyright © 2005 by David R. Slavitt. Reprinted by permission of Louisiana State University Press.

Ernest Slyman. "Lightning Bugs" from *Sometime the Cow Kick Your Head, Light Year 88/89*. Reprinted by permission of the author.

Gary Snyder. "How Poetry Comes to Me" from *No Nature* by Gary Snyder. Copyright © 1992 by Gary Snyder. Used by permission of Pantheon Books, a division of Random House, Inc. Any third party use of this material, outside of this publication, is prohibited. Interested parties must apply directly to Random House, Inc., for permission.

David Solway. "Windsurfing." Reprinted by permission of the author.

Bruce Springsteen. "Devils & Dust." Copyright © 2005 by Bruce Springsteen (ASCAP). Reprinted by permission. International copyright secured. All rights reserved.

Timothy Steele. "Waiting for the Storm" from *Sapphics and Uncertainties: Poems, 1970–1986*. Copyright © 1986, 1995 by Timothy Steele. Reprinted with the permission of The Permissions Company, Inc., on behalf of the University of Arkansas Press, www.uapress.com.

Jim Stevens. "Schizophrenia." Originally appeared in *Light: The Quarterly of Light Verse* (Spring 1992). Copyright © 1992 by Jim Stevens. Reprinted by permission.

Joyce Sutphen. "Guys Like That" from *The Writer's Almanac* online, January 7, 2007. Copyright © 2007 by Joyce Sutphen. Reprinted by permission of the author.

May Swenson. "A Nosty Fright," reprinted with the permission of the Literary Estate of May Swenson. All rights reserved.

Dylan Thomas. "Do not go gentle into that good night" from *The Poems of Dylan Thomas*. Copyright © 1952 by Dylan Thomas. "The Hand That Signed the Paper" from *The Poems of Dylan Thomas*. Copyright © 1939 by New Directions Publishing Corporation. Reprinted by permission of New Directions Publishing Corp.

Jim Tilley. "Boys" from *In Confidence* by Jim Tilley (Pasadena, CA: Red Hen Press, 2011). Copyright © 2011 by Jim Tilley. Reprinted by permission of Red Hen Press.

Natasha Trethewey. "On Captivity" from *Thrall: Poems* by Natasha Trethewey. Copyright © 2012 by Natasha Trethewey. Reprinted by permission of Houghton Mifflin Harcourt Publishing Company. All rights reserved.

William Trowbridge. "Drumming Behind You in the High School Band" from *Enter Dark Stranger*. Copyright © 1989 by William Trowbridge. Reprinted with the permission of The Permissions Company, Inc., on behalf of the University of Arkansas Press, www.uapress.com.

John Updike. "Dog's Death" from *Midpoint and Other Poems* by John Updike. Copyright © 1969 and renewed 1997 by John Updike. "Player Piano" from *Collected Poems, 1953–1993* by John Updike. Copyright © 1993 by John Updike. Used by permission of Alfred A. Knopf, a division of Random House, Inc. Any third party use of this material, outside of this publication, is prohibited. Interested parties must apply directly to Random House, Inc., for permission.

Richard Wakefield. "The Bell Rope" from *East of Early Winters: Poems* by Richard Wakefield (University of Evansville Press, 2006). Copyright © 2006 by Richard Wakefield. Reprinted with permission from the author.

William Carlos Williams. "Poem" and "The Red Wheelbarrow," copyright © 1938 by New Directions Publishing Corp. From *Collected Poems, Volume 1: 1909–1939*. Reprinted by permission of New Directions Publishing Corp.

William Butler Yeats. "Leda and the Swan." Reprinted with the permission of Scribner, a division of Simon & Schuster, Inc., from *The Collected Works of W. B. Yeats, Volume I: The Poems, Revised*, ed. Richard J. Finneran. Copyright © 1928 by the Macmillan Company. Copyright renewed © 1956 by Bertha Georgie Yeats. All rights reserved.

DRAMA

Joan Ackermann. *Quiet Torrential Sound* from *Ten-Minute Plays: Volume 3 from Actors Theatre Of Louisville*, ed. by Michael Bigelow Dixon and Michele Volansky (New York: Samuel French, 1995). Copyright © 1994 by Joan Ackermann. Reprinted by permission of Bret Adams Ltd.

Jane Anderson. *The Reprimand.* Copyright © 2000 by Jane Anderson. All rights reserved.

Andrew Biss. *What's the Meta?* Copyright © 2004. Published in Lawrence Harbison, ed., *2009: The Best 10-Minute Plays for 2 or More Actors.* Smith & Kraus, 2009. Reprinted by permission of the author.

Sharon E. Cooper. *Mistaken Identity.* Copyright © 2003, 2009 by Sharon E. Cooper. Originally published by Vintage Press in the anthology *Laugh Lines: Short Comic Plays*, ed. by Eric Lane and Nina Shengold. Reprinted by permission of the author. For inquiries regarding producing, please contact the author at secooper1@yahoo.com, or visit her Web site, www.SharonECooper.com.

Larry David. Episode entitled "The Pitch" from the television series *Seinfeld* © 1992 Castle Rock Entertainment, written by Larry David. All Rights Reserved. Reprinted by permission of Castle Rock Entertainment.

Michael Hollinger. *Naked Lunch* from *Humana Festival 2003*, ed. Tanya Palmer and Amy Wegener. Copyright © 2003 by Michael Hollinger. Reprinted by permission.

David Henry Hwang. *Trying to Find Chinatown* from *Trying to Find Chinatown: The Selected Plays of David Henry Hwang*. Copyright © 2000 by David Henry Hwang. Published by Theatre Communications Group. Used by permission of Theatre Communications Group.

Henrik Ibsen. *A Doll House* from *The Complete Major Prose Plays of Henrik Ibsen* by Henrik Ibsen, translated by Rolf Fjelde, copyright © 1965, 1970, 1978 by Rolf Fjelde. Used by permission of Dutton Signet, a division of Penguin Group (USA) Inc.

David Ives. *The Blizzard.* Copyright © 2008 by David Ives. Reprinted by permission of Abrams Artists Agency on behalf of David Ives. *The Blizzard* was created as part of the 24 Hour Plays series (Tina Fallon, Artistic Director). It was first presented at the American Airlines Theatre in New York City on October 23, 2006. It was directed by Bennett Miller. The cast was as follows: Anna Paquin (Jenny), Fisher Stevens (Neil), Aasif Mandvi (Salim), and Gaby Hoffmann (Natasha).

Jane Martin. *Rodeo.* Copyright © 1982 by Alexander Speer, as Trustee. Reprinted by permission. CAUTION: Professionals and amateurs are hereby warned that *Rodeo* is subject to a royalty. It is fully protected under the copyright laws of the United States of America, the British Commonwealth, including Canada, and all other countries of the Copyright Union. All rights, including professional, amateur, motion pictures, recitation, lecturing, public reading, radio broadcasting, television, and the rights of translation into foreign languages are strictly reserved. In its present form the play is dedicated to the reading public only. Particular emphasis is laid on the question of amateur or professional readings, permission and terms for which must be secured in writing from Samuel French, Inc., 45 West 25th Street, New York, NY 10010.

William Shakespeare. *Othello* (notes and commentary), edited by Gerald Eades Bentley. Copyright © 1958, 1970 by Penguin Books. Used by permission of Penguin, a division of Penguin Group (USA) Inc.

Sophocles. *Oedipus the King* from *Three Theban Plays* by Sophocles, translated by Robert Fagles. Copyright © 1982 by Robert Fagles. Used by permission of Viking Penguin, a division of Penguin Group (USA) Inc.

Index of First Lines

Index of Authors and Titles

Entries marked with this symbol are also available as streaming audio at
bedfordstmartins.com/meyerlit/epages

Index of Terms

Boldface numbers refer to the Glossary of Literary Terms

Inside the e-Pages for *Literature to Go*

Listening to Literature Aloud
Suggestions for Responsive Reading
Suggested Topics for Writing

FICTION

James Joyce, *Eveline* (read by Gabriel Byrne)
Jamaica Kincaid, *Girl* (read by Jamaica Kincaid)
Annie Proulx, *55 Miles to the Gas Pump* (read by Campbell Scott and Frances Fisher)
John Updike, *A & P* (read by John Updike)

POETRY

Regina Barreca, *Nighttime Fires* (read by Regina Barreca)
William Blake, *The Lamb* (read by Brian Murray)
Gwendolyn Brooks, *We Real Cool* (read by Gwendolyn Brooks)
Robert Browning, *My Last Duchess* (read by Richard Howard)
E. E. Cummings, *next to of course god america i* (read by E. E. Cummings)
Emily Dickinson, *I heard a Fly buzz — when I died —* (read by Robert Pinsky)
John Donne, *The Flea* (read by Richard Burton)
Robert Frost, *Acquainted with the Night* (read by Robert Frost)
Robert Frost, *Mending Wall* (read by Robert Frost)
Judy Page Heitzman, *The Schoolroom on the Second Floor of the Knitting Mill* (read by Judy
    Page Heitzman)
Langston Hughes, *Harlem* (read by Langston Hughes)
Randall Jarrell, *The Death of the Ball Turret Gunner* (read by Randall Jarrell)
John Keats, *La Belle Dame sans Merci* (read by Sir Ralph Richardson)
Katharyn Howd Machan, *Hazel Tells LaVerne* (read by Katharyn Howd Machan)
Andrew Marvell, *To His Coy Mistress* (read by Paul Muldoon)
John Milton, *When I consider how my light is spent* (read by Robert Speaight)
William Shakespeare, *My mistress' eyes are nothing like the sun* (read by Sir John Gielgud)
William Shakespeare, *Shall I compare thee to a summer's day?* (read by Sir John Gielgud)
Dylan Thomas, *Do Not Go Gentle into That Good Night* (read by Dylan Thomas)
Walt Whitman, From *"I Sing the Body Electric"* (read by Brian Murray)
William Carlos Williams, *The Red Wheelbarrow* (read by William Carlos Williams)
William Butler Yeats, *That the Night Come* (read by Samantha Eggar)

DRAMA

Susan Glaspell, A Scene from *Trifles* (read by L.A. Theatre Works)
William Shakespeare, A Scene from *Othello* (read by Chicago's Shakespeare Repertory)